Contemporary Authors®

A Bio-Bibliographical Guide to
Current Writers in Fiction, General Nonfiction,
Poetry, Journalism, Drama, Motion Pictures,
Television, and Other Fields

SUSAN M. TROSKY
Editor

NEW REVISION SERIES
volume 42

Gale Research Inc. • DETROIT • WASHINGTON, D.C. • LONDON

Susan M. Trosky, *Editor, New Revision Series*

Elizabeth A. Des Chenes, Kathleen J. Edgar, Marie Ellavich, David M. Galens, Denise E. Kasinec, Thomas F. McMahon, Mark F. Mikula, Terrie M. Rooney, Pamela L. Shelton, Kenneth R. Shepherd, Deborah A. Stanley, Polly A. Vedder, and Thomas Wiloch, *Associate Editors*

Pamela S. Dear, Margaret Mazurkiewicz, Mary L. Onorato, Scot Peacock, Geri J. Speace, Aarti D. Stephens, Linda Tidrick, Brandon Trenz, and Kathleen Wilson, *Assistant Editors*

Sharon Malinowski, *Contributing Editor*

Diane Andreassi, Anne Blankenbaker, Judith Farer, Valerie Grim, Elizabeth Henry, Elizabeth Judd, Charles Kemnitz, Charles F. Kennedy, Gordon Mayer, Lynda Morris, Megan Ratner, Susan M. Reicha, Lillian Roland, Carole Trautman, Carol Was, Denise Wiloch, and Michaela Swart Wilson, *Sketchwriters*

James G. Lesniak, *Senior Editor, Contemporary Authors*

Victoria B. Cariappa, *Research Manager*

Mary Rose Bonk, *Research Supervisor*

Reginald A. Carlton, Clare Collins, Andrew Guy Malonis, and Norma Sawaya, *Editorial Associates*

Laurel Sprague Bowden, Rachel A. Dixon, Eva Marie Felts, Shirley Gates, Doris Lewandowski, Sharon McGilvray, Dana R. Schleiffers, and Amy B. Wieczorek, *Editorial Assistants*

™ This book is printed on acid-free paper that meets the minimum requirements of American National Standard for Information Sciences-Permanence Paper for Printed Library Materials, ANSI Z39.48-1984.

Library of Congress Catalog Card Number 81-640179

ISBN 0-8103-1973-X
ISSN 0275-7176

Printed in the United States of America.
Published simultaneously in the United Kingdom
by Gale Research International Limited
(An affiliated company of Gale Research Inc.)

I(T)P™

The trademark **ITP** is used under license.

10 9 8 7 6 5 4 3 2 1

Contents

Indexing note: All *Contemporary Authors New Revision Series* entries are indexed in the *Contemporary Authors* cumulative index, which is published separately and distributed with even-numbered *Contemporary Authors* original volumes and odd-numbered *Contemporary Authors New Revison Series* volumes.

As always, the most recent *Contemporary Authors* cumulative index continues to be the user's guide to the location of an individual author's listing.

Preface

The *Contemporary Authors New Revision Series* (*CANR*) provides completely updated information on authors listed in earlier volumes of *Contemporary Authors* (*CA*). Entries for individual authors from *any* volume of *CA* may be included in a volume of the *New Revision Series*. *CANR* updates only those sketches requiring significant change.

Authors are included on the basis of specific criteria that indicate the need for significant revision. These criteria include bibliographical additions, changes in addresses or career, major awards, and personal information such as name changes or death dates. All listings in this volume have been revised or augmented in various ways. Some sketches have been extensively rewritten, and many include informative new sidelights. As always, a *CANR* listing entails no charge or obligation.

How to Get the Most out of *CA*: Use the Index

The key to locating an author's most recent entry is the *CA* cumulative index, which is published separately and distributed with even-numbered original volumes and odd-numbered revision volumes. It provides access to *all* entries in *CA* and *CANR*. Always consult the latest index to find an author's most recent entry.

For the convenience of users, the *CA* cumulative index also includes references to all entries in these Gale literary series: *Authors and Artists for Young Adults, Authors in the News, Bestsellers, Black Literature Criticism, Black Writers, Children's Literature Review, Concise Dictionary of American Literary Biography, Concise Dictionary of British Literary Biography, Contemporary Authors Autobiography Series, Contemporary Authors Bibliographical Series, Contemporary Literary Criticism, Dictionary of Literary Biography, DISCovering Authors, Drama Criticism, Hispanic Writers, Major Authors and Illustrators for Children and Young Adults, Major 20th-Century Writers, Poetry Criticism, Short Story Criticism, Something about the Author, Something about the Author Autobiography Series, Twentieth-Century Literary Criticism, World Literature Criticism,* and *Yesterday's Authors of Books for Children.*

A Sample Index Entry:

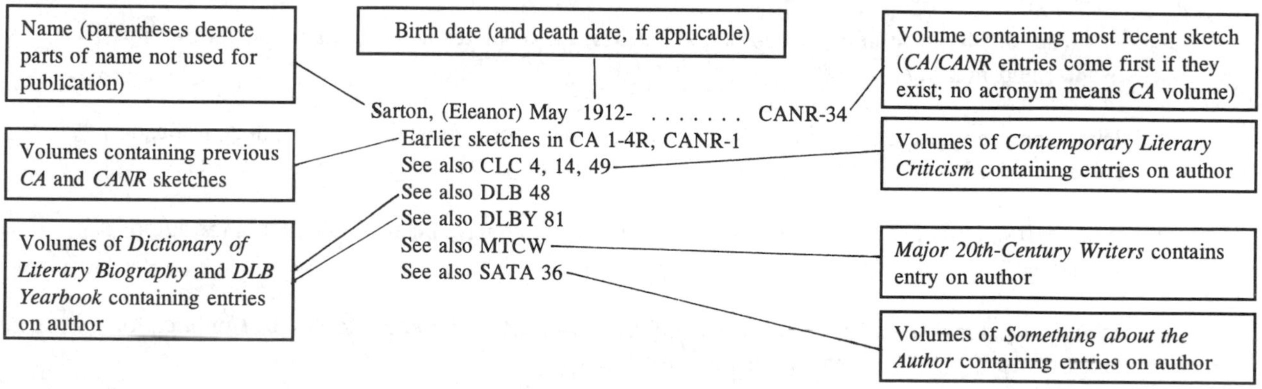

For the most recent *CA* information on Sarton, users should refer to Volume 34 of the *New Revision Series,* as designated by "CANR-34"; if that volume is unavailable, refer to CANR-1. And if CANR-1 is unavailable, refer to CA 1-4R, published in 1967, for Sarton's First Revision entry.

How Are Entries Compiled?

The editors make every effort to secure new information directly from the authors. Copies of all sketches in selected *CA* and *CANR* volumes previously published are routinely sent to listees at their last-known addresses, and returns from these authors are then assessed. For deceased writers, or those who fail to reply to requests for data, we consult other reliable biographical sources, such as those indexed in Gale's *Biography and Genealogy Master Index,* and bibliographical sources, such as *National Union Catalog, LC MARC,* and *British National Bibliography.* Further details come from published interviews, feature stories, and book reviews, and often the authors' publishers supply material.

** Indicates that a listing has been compiled from secondary sources believed to be reliable but has not been personally verified for this edition by the author sketched.*

What Kinds of Information Does an Entry Provide?

Sketches in *CANR* contain the following biographical and bibliographical information:

- **Entry heading:** the most complete form of author's name, plus any pseudonyms or name variations used for writing
- **Personal information:** author's date and place of birth, family data, educational background, political and religious affiliations, and hobbies and leisure interests
- **Addresses:** author's home, office, or agent's addresses as available
- **Career summary:** name of employer, position, and dates held for each career post; résumé of other vocational achievements; military service
- **Membership information:** professional, civic, and other association memberships and any official posts held
- **Awards and honors:** military and civic citations, major prizes and nominations, fellowships, grants, and honorary degrees
- **Writings:** a comprehensive, chronological list of titles, publishers, dates of original publication and revised editions, and production information for plays, television scripts, and screenplays
- **Adaptations:** a list of films, plays, and other media which have been adapted from the author's work
- **Work in progress:** current or planned projects, with dates of completion and/or publication, and expected publisher, when known
- **Sidelights:** a biographical portrait of the author's development; information about the critical reception of the author's works; revealing comments, often by the author, on personal interests, aspirations, motivations, and thoughts on writing
- **Biographical and critical sources:** a list of books and periodicals in which additional information on an author's life and/or writings appears

Related Titles in the *CA* Series

Contemporary Authors Autobiography Series complements *CA* original and revised volumes with specially commissioned autobiographical essays by important current authors, illustrated with personal photographs they provide. Common topics include their motivations for writing, the people and experiences that shaped their careers, the rewards they derive from their work, and their impressions of the current literary scene.

Contemporary Authors Bibliographical Series surveys writings by and about important American authors since World War II. Each volume concentrates on a specific genre and features approximately ten writers; entries list works written by and about the author and contain a bibliographical essay discussing the merits and deficiencies of major critical and scholarly studies in detail.

Suggestions Are Welcome

The editors welcome comments and suggestions from users on any aspects of the *CA* series. If readers would like to recommend authors whose entries should appear in future volumes of the series, they are cordially invited to write: The Editors, *Contemporary Authors,* 835 Penobscot Bldg., Detroit, MI 48226-4094; call toll-free at 1-800-347-GALE; or fax to 1-313-961-6599.

CA Numbering System and Volume Update Chart

Occasionally questions arise about the *CA* numbering system and which volumes, if any, can be discarded. Despite numbers like "29-32R," "97-100" and "141," the entire *CA* series consists of only 110 physical volumes with the publication of *CA New Revision Series* Volume 42. The following charts note changes in the numbering system and cover design, and indicate which volumes are essential for the most complete, up-to-date coverage.

CA First Revision

- 1-4R through 41-44R (11 books)
  Cover: Brown with black and gold trim.
  There will be no further First Revision volumes because revised entries are now being handled exclusively through the more efficient *New Revision Series* mentioned below.

CA Original Volumes

- 45-48 through 97-100 (14 books)
  Cover: Brown with black and gold trim.
- 101 through 141 (41 books)
  Cover: Blue and black with orange bands.
  The same as previous *CA* original volumes but with a new, simplified numbering system and new cover design.

CA Permanent Series

- *CAP*-1 and *CAP*-2 (2 books)
  Cover: Brown with red and gold trim.
  There will be no further *Permanent Series* volumes because revised entries are now being handled exclusively through the more efficient *New Revision Series* mentioned below.

CA New Revision Series

- *CANR*-1 through *CANR*-42 (42 books)
  Cover: Blue and black with green bands.
  Includes only sketches requiring extensive changes; **sketches are taken from any previously published *CA, CAP,* or *CANR* volume.**

If You Have:	You May Discard:
CA First Revision Volumes 1-4R through 41-44R **and** *CA Permanent Series* Volumes 1 and 2	*CA* Original Volumes 1, 2, 3, 4 Volumes 5-6 through 41-44
CA Original Volumes 45-48 through 97-100 **and** 101 through 141	**NONE:** These volumes will not be superseded by corresponding revised volumes. Individual entries from these and all other volumes appearing in the left column of this chart may be revised and included in the various volumes of the *New Revision Series*.
CA New Revision Series Volumes *CANR*-1 through *CANR*-42	**NONE:** The *New Revision Series* does not replace any single volume of *CA*. Instead, volumes of *CANR* include entries from many previous *CA* series volumes. All *New Revision Series* volumes must be retained for full coverage.

A Sampling of Authors and Media People Featured in This Volume

Maya Angelou
Well known for her autobiographies, including *I Know Why the Caged Bird Sings,* Angelou also wrote and recited the 1993 U.S. Presidential inaugural poem, *On the Pulse of Morning.*

Fernand Braudel
Prior to his death in 1985, Braudel was the foremost advocate of the "new history," which postulates that everyday life, not major political events, determines the course of history.

Rita Dove
Dove, who received the Pulitzer Prize in 1987 for her poetry collection *Thomas and Beulah,* was named Poet Laureate of the United States in 1993.

Dick Francis
A former British steeplechase jockey, Francis draws upon his racing background for his crime thrillers, including the Edgar Award-winning *Whip Hand* and, more recently, *Driving Force.*

William Gibson
Although Gibson has had more than fifteen plays produced, he remains most famous for his 1957 work *The Miracle Worker,* about the relationship between handicapped Helen Keller and her teacher Annie Sullivan.

Billy Graham
Described in *Time* magazine as "America's premier evangelist," Graham has written more than thirty books, including the best-seller *Angels: God's Secret Agents* and *Storm Warning: Deceptive Evil Looms on the Horizon.*

Joseph Heller
Heller's book *Catch-22* has earned a reputation as one of the great American novels of the twentieth century since its publication in 1961. More recently the author has published an autobiography, *No Laughing Matter,* and the novel *Picture This.*

Tony Hillerman
Hillerman depicts crime, Native American customs and values, and great Southwestern open spaces in novels such as *Dance Hall of the Dead, Coyote Waits,* and *Sacred Clowns.*

Spike Lee
An independent filmmaker, Lee is known for his controversial films that focus on black themes, including *She's Gotta Have It, Do the Right Thing,* and *Malcolm X.*

Eric Van Lustbader
Lustbader's works, such as *The Ninja* and *The Floating City,* are set in the Far East. Ranging in genre from science fiction/fantasy to international thrillers, they have become bestsellers all over the world.

Cormac McCarthy
A Southern writer in the tradition of William Faulkner, McCarthy is the author of the National Book Award winner *All the Pretty Horses.*

Gregory Mcdonald
Mcdonald is world renowned for his series about a conniving detective, first introduced in the eponymous novel *Fletch.* Fletch's antics have won Mcdonald the Edgar Award twice.

Toni Morrison
Morrison's work, including the Pulitzer Prize-winning novel *Beloved,* highlights the plight of African Americans struggling to survive in an America that the author depicts as alternately racist and indifferent. She was awarded a Nobel Prize in 1993.

Mario Puzo
Best known for his blockbuster 1969 novel *The Godfather* and its filmed sequels, Puzo published *The Fourth K* in 1991 and collaborated on the 1992 film *Christopher Columbus: The Discovery.*

David Toma
A former police officer whose exploits inspired the TV series *Toma* and *Baretta,* Toma now works with troubled teens and writes about the hazards of drug abuse among youths.

Mario Vargas Llosa
After confronting corruption on many levels in his novels *La ciudad y lost perros* and *La casa verde,* Vargas Llosa became a candidate for the office of president of Peru in 1989.

Joseph Wambaugh
In books such as *The Choirboys* and *Finnegan's Week,* Wambaugh portrays the moral stresses that affect police officers in modern America. He also wrote screen adaptations for several of his works.

August Wilson
Wilson's many credits include the Tony Award-nominated *Ma Rainey's Black Bottom* and the Pulitzer Prize-winners *Fences* and *The Piano Lesson.*

Contemporary Authors®

NEW REVISION SERIES

**Indicates that a listing has been compiled from secondary sources believed to be reliable but has not been personally verified for this edition by the author sketched.*

ADAMS, Bart
See BINGLEY, David Ernest

* * *

AGARD, H. E.
See EVANS, Hilary

* * *

AGUOLU, Christian Chukwunedu 1940-

PERSONAL: Born December 22, 1940, in Nimo, Nigeria; son of Samuel A. (a teacher) and Rosaline (Nwabude) Aguolu; married Ify Eunice (a librarian), December 4, 1976. *Education:* Attended University of Ibadan, 1961-65; University of London, B.A., 1965; University of Washington, Seattle, M.L.S., 1968; University of California, Berkeley, M.A., 1975, Ph.D., 1977. *Religion:* Christian.

Avocational Interests: Table tennis, reading, debate.

ADDRESSES: *Office*—Department of Library Science, University of Maiduguri, Maiduguri, Nigeria.

CAREER: Teacher and head of departments of French and Latin at Anglican grammar school in Oraukwu, Nigeria, 1965-66; University of California, Santa Barbara, reference librarian and bibliographer, 1968-72; writer; University of Maiduguri, Maiduguri, Nigeria, senior lecturer, 1977-79, associate professor and reader, 1979-82, professor of library science, 1982—, head of department of library science, 1978-92, dean of education, 1979-82, 1984-86, chairman of Senate Publications Committee and acting director of University of Maiduguri Press, 1988—.

MEMBER: Worldwide Academy of Scholars (fellow), International Platform Association, Intercontinental Biographical Association (fellow), Nigerian Library Association, Scholarly Publishers Association of Nigeria (vice-president, 1988—).

WRITINGS:

Ghana in the Humanities and Social Sciences, 1900-1971: A Bibliography, Scarecrow, 1973.

Nigerian Civil War, 1967-1970: An Annotated Bibliography, G. K. Hall, 1973.

Nigeria: A Comprehensive Bibliography in the Humanities and Social Sciences, 1900-1971, G. K. Hall, 1973.

Library Development in Borno State, Department of Library Science, University of Maiduguri, 1984.

Libraries, Knowledge, and National Development, University of Maiduguri Press, 1989.

Libraries and Information, University of Maiduguri Press, in press.

OTHER

Also author of *Selecting Materials for School Libraries in a Developing Society,* revised edition, Department of Library Science, University of Maiduguri, 1982, and *Libraries in Nigeria: Essays on Evolution, Development and Services.* Contributor to African studies, education, and library journals. Editor-in-chief, *Annals of Borno,* 1988—.

WORK IN PROGRESS: Booktrade in Borno State, Nigeria.

SIDELIGHTS: Christian Chukwunedu Aguolu commented to *CA*:: "My bibliographical interests are conditioned by the need to order and chart knowledge about Africa, making it readily available to those interested in African subjects."

ALCALDE, Miguel
See BURGESS, Michael (Roy)

* * *

ALEXANDER, L(ouis) G(eorge) 1932-

PERSONAL: Born January 15, 1932, in London, England; son of George (a doctor) and Mary (Manolas) Ftyaras-Alexandrou; married Athena Voyiatzis (a teacher), 1958 (deceased); married Julia Banner-Mendus (a teacher trainer), 1980; children: (first marriage) Mary-Anne, George. *Education:* Attended Aquinas College, Perth, Australia; University of London, B.A. (with honors).

ADDRESSES: *Home*—Garden House, Weydown Rd., Haslemere, Surrey, GU27 1DT, England.

CAREER: Protypon Lykeion Athinon, Athens, Greece, teacher and head of department of English, 1957-65; writer and consultant to Longman Group, 1966—. Member of threshold level committee, Council of Europe, 1973-79.

MEMBER: Society of Authors (chairman of educational writers group, 1975-77; member of committee of management, 1981-83), Society of Bookmen.

WRITINGS:

PUBLISHED BY LONGMANS, GREEN

Sixty Steps to Precis, 1962.
Poetry and Prose Appreciation, 1963.
A First Book in Comprehension, 1965.
Essay and Letter Writing, 1965.
Detectives from Scotland Yard, 1966.
The Carters of Greenwood, 1966.
April Fools Day, 1966.
Worth a Fortune, 1967.
First Things First, 1967.
Practice and Progress, 1967.
Developing Skills, 1967.
Fluency in English, 1967.
Question and Answer, 1967.
For and Against, 1968.
At the Zoo, 1968.
Look, Listen, and Learn, four volumes, 1968-71.
Reading and Writing English, 1969.
Car Thieves, 1969.
Professor Boffin's Robot, 1969.
Mr. Punch, 1969.

PUBLISHED BY LONGMAN

Operation Mastermind, 1971.
Guided Composition in ELT, 1971.
Marley Castle, 1971.
Professor Boffin's Umbrella, 1971.
Tell Us a Story, 1972.
(With Janet Tadman and Roy Kingsbury) *Target,* three volumes, 1972-74.
Mainline's Progress, Books A and B, 1973.
(With Catherine Wilson) *In Other Words,* 1974.
K's First Case, 1975.
Good Morning, Mexico, 1975.
(With Monica Vincent and Kingsbury) *Mainline Skills A,* 1975.
(With W. A. Allen, R. A. Close, and R. J. O'Neill) *English Grammatical Structure,* 1975.
(With Vincent) *Make Your Point,* 1975.
Operation Janus, 1976.
Clint Magee, 1976.
(With Kingsbury) *I Think, You Think,* 1976.
Dangerous Game, 1977.
(With Kingsbury) *Mainline Skills B,* 1977.
Mainline Beginners A, 1978.
(With Albert Evangelisti and others) *Way In,* 1978.
(With E. T. Cornelius) *Exercises in Comprehension and Composition,* 1978.
(With others) *Talk It Over,* 1978.
Mainline Beginners B, 1979.
(With Kingsbury) *Follow Me* (also see below), two volumes, 1980.
(With others) *Audiovisual English Course for Secondary Schools,* 1980.
(With Judith Clopeau and Madeleine Le Cunff-Renouard) *Survive in French,* 1980.
(With Timothy Holme and Bianca Holme) *Survive in Italian,* 1980.
(With Antony Peck and Ingeborg Peck) *Survive in German,* 1980.
(With Carolina Haro and Peter Vickers) *Survive in Spanish,* 1980.
(With Teresa de Souza) *Survive in Portuguese,* 1983.
(With others) *French Pocket Traveller,* 1983.
(With others) *German Pocket Traveller,* 1983.
(With others) *Italian Pocket Traveller,* 1983.
(With others) *Spanish Pocket Traveller,* 1983.
Adventure Story, 1983.
Foul Play, 1983.
Excel in English, 1985.
Plain English, 1987.
Longman English Grammar, 1988.
Longman English Grammar Practice, 1990.
Step by Step, three volumes, 1991.
Longman Advanced Grammar, 1993.
The Essential English Grammar, 1993.

OTHER

(With Evangelisti) *Language and Life,* Longman/Zanichelli, 1970.

(With Karl Preis, Franz Schimek, and Anton Prochazka) *Look, Listen, and Learn for Austria,* four volumes, Langenscheidt/Longman, 1974-78.

Some Methodological Implications of Waystage and Threshold Level, Council of Europe, 1977.

(With Jan van Ek and A. M. Fitzpatrick) *Waystage,* Council of Europe, 1977.

(Consultant) *Junior English for China,* Peoples Educational Press (Beijing), 1990.

Also author of foreign language instruction programs for Atari computers, 1980-81, and, with Guy Capelle and Kingsbury, of *Systeme, Methode de francais pour debutants.* Course designer, with Fitzpatrick, of television series *Follow Me,* broadcast on German television, 1979-80.

WORK IN PROGRESS: Right Word, Wrong Word.

SIDELIGHTS: L. G. Alexander told *CA:* "The mindless time filling that characterizes a great many language courses has prompted me throughout my professional life to attempt to develop simpler and more cost-effective systems for learning languages. Using English-as-a-foreign-language as a starting point, I have increasingly become concerned with creating blueprint course-designs which can be adapted to the learning of other languages either in the classroom or through self-study systems. Since 1981, I have been mainly involved in the study of English grammar from a non-native point of view. I am convinced that the main problem in the acquisition of English as a foreign language is mother tongue interference. For me writing is a habit, and I do not feel I have done any true work in a day unless I have written. It is all too easy for a writer who has achieved any success at all to be lured into talking about writing instead of writing. Inspiration, if it exists at all, in my view, is the by-product of habitual application."

* * *

ALEXANDER, Ric
See LONG, Richard A(lexander)

* * *

ALEXANDER, Roy 1928-

PERSONAL: Born February 3, 1928, in Asheville, NC; son of William Roy (a dairyman) and Ruth (a teacher; maiden name, Upshaw) Alexander. *Education:* Northwestern University, Ph.B., 1954.

ADDRESSES: Home and office—239 East 32nd St., New York, NY 10016. *Agent*—Connie Jason, 201 East 31st, New York, NY 10016.

CAREER: Food Retailing, Evanston, IL, associate editor, 1951-52; Mid-States Corp., Chicago, IL, director of public relations, 1952-53; Philip Lesly Co., New York City, account executive, 1956-58, vice-president, 1958-62; Alexander Co. (public relations), New York City, president, 1962-92. Member of faculty, New School for Social Research, 1971. President, Taggant & Alexander (financial council/service); manager of New York product publicity activities, Wurlitzer Co.; director of consumer education program, Youth for the Federal Union; director of public education program, Iron Mountain Stoneware; consultant to Lincoln Logs Ltd., Maleck Group, and Barter Advantage, Inc.; public relations council to Solar Additions, Inc., Hearthstone Homes, Flexmaster of Canada. Executive producer of film *The Greening of Augusta,* 1973. *Military service:* U.S. Army, 1946-49, feature editor of Armed Forces Press Service, 1948-49.

MEMBER: Northwestern University Alumni Association, Sons of the Revolution (NY chapter).

WRITINGS:

Direct Salesman's Handbook, Prentice-Hall, 1958.

Ricer's Guide to Work and Play in Durham, Medical Center, Duke University, 1975, revised with Jayne Leavy, 1992.

Mehdi: Nothing Is Impossible, Farnsworth Publishing, 1978.

(With James A. Newman) *Climbing the Corporate Matterhorn,* Wiley, 1985.

Power Speech: Your Guide to Personal and Business Success, AMACOM, 1986.

(With Philip W. Maggant) *Making Your Company Public,* AMACOM, 1991.

Commonsense Time Management, AMACOM, 1992.

Everything Is Possible (sequel to *Mehdi: Nothing Is Impossible*), Farnsworth Publishing, 1993.

(With Charles Roth) *Secrets of Closing Sales,* Prentice-Hall, 1993.

Editor of *Specialty Salesman,* 1953-56; *Mobile Homes,* 1953-54; *Marketing Times,* 1973-84; *Readout,* 1974-75; *Lowenbrau Letter;* and *Journal of Footwear Management.*

SIDELIGHTS: Roy Alexander once told *CA:* "I've been influenced considerably by the late Bergen Evans, a professor of English at Northwestern University, who (when asked how his teaching methods differed from other professors') said: 'I have tried to be interesting.' In business publications and business books, the reader can be entertained as well as informed—further, it's the writer's duty to do both. As to why writers write, I'm with H. L. Mencken: 'A writer must write for the same reason a hen must lay eggs.'

"In *Climbing the Corporate Matterhorn* (an advisory book for careerists), *Mehdi: Nothing Is Impossible* (a manual for insurance salesfolk), and *Power Speech* . . . I have followed this principle: advise, yes, but make it entertaining and informative in the process.

"I also specialize in 'as-told-to books' dually bylined by source and author (me). I do these books on contract to: 1. publishers, and with 2. companies and individuals. This naturally leads me to advice to financial management, counsel to career-climbers, case history inventories for salesfolk and for marketers. In all these areas, the use of speech as a tool is emphasized."

* * *

ALEXANDERSON, Gerald L(ee) 1933-

PERSONAL: Born November 13, 1933, in Caldwell, ID; son of Albert William and Alvina (Gertlar) Alexanderson. *Education:* University of Oregon, B.A. (with highest honors), 1955; Stanford University, M.S., 1958. *Politics:* Democrat.

ADDRESSES: Home—1133 Highland Ave., Santa Clara, CA 95050. *Office*—Department of Mathematics, Santa Clara University, Santa Clara, CA 95053.

CAREER: Santa Clara University, Santa Clara, CA, instructor, 1958-62, assistant professor, 1962-68, associate professor, 1968-72, professor of mathematics, 1972—, Michael and Elizabeth Valeriote Professor, 1979—, chairman of department, 1967—, trustee of university, 1979-86, director of Division of Mathematics and Natural Sciences, 1981-90, vice-chairman of board of trustees, 1984-86. Lecturer at Stanford University, summers, 1958-59; lecturer in Geneva, Switzerland, 1964-65. Associate Director of William Lowell Putnam Mathematical Competition, 1975—.

MEMBER: American Mathematical Society, Mathematical Association of America (chairman of northern California section, 1971-72; member of national board of governors, 1975-78, 1984—; first vice-president, 1984-86; secretary, 1990—), Fibonacci Association (president, 1980-84), Phi Beta Kappa (member of Senate, 1991—), Sigma Xi, Pi Mu Epsilon, Pi Delta Phi, Phi Eta Sigma.

WRITINGS:

(With Abraham P. Hillman) *Functional Trigonometry*, Allyn & Bacon, 1961, 3rd edition, 1971.

(With Hillman) *Algebra and Trigonometry*, Allyn & Bacon, 1963.

(With Hillman) *Algebra through Problem Solving*, Allyn & Bacon, 1966.

(With Hillman) *A First Undergraduate Course in Abstract Algebra*, Wadsworth, 1973, 5th edition, Prindle, Weber & Schmidt, in press.

(Editor with Donald J. Albers) *Mathematical People*, Birkauser Boston, 1985.

(With Hillman, L. F. Klosinski, and D. E. Logothetti) *The Santa Clara Silver Anniversary Contest Book*, Dale Seymour, 1985.

(With Klosinski and L. C. Larson) *The William Lowell Putnam Mathematical Competition*, Mathematical Association of America, 1986.

(With Hillman and Richard M. Grassl) *Discrete and Combinatorial Mathematics*, Dellen, 1986.

(With Albers and Constance Reid) *International Mathematical Congresses*, Springer, 1986.

(With George Polya) *Polya Picture Album*, Birkhauser Boston, 1987.

(With Albers and Reid) *More Mathematical People*, Harcourt Brace Jovanovich, 1990.

Contributor to mathematics journals. Associate editor of *College Math Journal*, 1979-83; associate editor of *American Mathematical Monthly*, 1983-86; editor of *Mathematics Magazine*, 1986-90.

WORK IN PROGRESS: A third volume of *Mathematical People*; a collection of work of R. P. Boas, Jr.; a biography of G. Polya.

SIDELIGHTS: Gerald L. Alexanderson's "Mathematical People" series is a collection of informal interviews with various mathematical experts. They represent an effort to dispel the sense of isolation that has increasingly surrounded twentieth-century mathematical scholars as their discipline has grown more abstract and complex and as communication, even with scientists and other mathematicians, has grown more difficult. The *Mathematical People* volumes reveal that mathematicians are not so alien and single-minded as they are stereotypically believed to be. Alexanderson writes in his preface that mathematicians are an "interesting bunch" who, in many ways, "share more traits with creative artists than with experimental scientists." *Mathematical People* has been widely praised by critics for presenting what Philip Morrison of *Scientific American* termed a "lighthearted" view of a subject that is too often presented only in its more intimidating aspects.

Alexanderson once told *CA:* "*Mathematical People* was inspired by the classic by E. T. Bell, *Men of Mathematics*, which, though it is not great history, is often cited by mathematicians as a significant factor in their choosing to do mathematics for a career. It also has influenced others to realize that mathematics is, like other liberal arts, a human endeavor. We hope that *Mathematical People* might make its own contribution to this effort."

BIOGRAPHICAL/CRITICAL SOURCES:

PERIODICALS

Byte, March, 1991.
New York Times, June 30, 1985.
San Francisco Chronicle, December 1, 1985.
Scientific American, October, 1985.

* * *

ALISKY, Marvin (Howard) 1923-

PERSONAL: Surname is accented on first syllable; born March 12, 1923, in Kansas City, MO; son of Joseph A. and Bess June (Capp) Alisky; married Beverly Kay, June 10, 1955; children: Sander Michael, Joseph Martin. *Education:* University of Texas, B.A., 1946, M.J., 1947, Ph.D., 1953; Instituto Tecnologico de Monterrey, Monterrey, Mexico, certificate, 1951.

ADDRESSES: Office—Department of Political Science, Arizona State University, Tempe, AZ 85287.

CAREER: Newscaster with Southwest and Midwest stations and in Latin America, National Broadcasting Co., 1947-50; Indiana University at Bloomington, assistant professor of journalism and government, 1953-57; *Christian Science Monitor,* Boston, MA, correspondent in Latin America, 1957-62; Arizona State University, Tempe, associate professor, 1957-60, professor of journalism and political science, 1960-72, professor of political science, 1972—, chair of department of mass communications, 1957-66, director of Center for Latin American Studies, 1966-72. Fulbright professor at Catholic University, Lima, Peru, 1958; first Smith-Mundt visiting professor in Central America, 1960; visiting fellow in politics at Princeton University, 1963; visiting professor at University of California, Irvine, summers, 1971 and 1972; United States Information Agency-State Department lecturer in Central and South America, summer, 1983. Researcher in Lima, Peru, National Science foundation, summer, 1984. U.S. delegate to UNESCO Conference on Communications, Quito, Ecuador, 1960; White House appointee, U.S. Board of Foreign Scholarships (public formulator, Fulbright Commission), 1984-87. Member of Governor's Arizona-Mexico Commission Board, 1975—. Former judge of broadcasting scripts for Grand Prix of Radio-Televizione Italiana de Rome; currently member of committee for Maria Moors Cabot Inter-American Journalism Awards. Guest commentator on Latin American topics, ABC-TV, 1982, PBS-TV, 1983, and CBS Radio, 1984. Hoover Institution fellow, 1978; Arizona Academy Town Hall fellow, 1981; World Media Association researcher, Soviet Union, 1989. Consultant to Syracuse University, 1980, University of Southern California, 1981, and European Center for Strategic Studies, London, 1985. *Military service:* U.S. Navy, 1944-45.

MEMBER: Inter-American Press Association, American Political Science Association, Hispanic Society of America, Western Political Science Association, Sigma Delta Chi (also known as Society of Professional Journalists; co-founder of Phoenix professional chapter and former president).

WRITINGS:

Latin American Journalism Bibliography, Fondo de P.I., 1958.

(With others) *Modern Journalism,* Pitman, 1962.

(With John C. Merrill and Carter Bryan) *The Foreign Press,* Louisiana State University Press, 1964, 2nd edition, 1970.

(Contributor) B. G. Burnett and K. F. Johnson, editors, *Political Forces in Latin America: Dimensions of the Quest for Stability,* Wadsworth, 1968, revised edition, 1970.

Who's Who in Mexican Government, Arizona State University, Center for Latin American Studies, 1969.

Uruguay: A Contemporary Survey, Praeger, 1970.

(Contributor) M. C. Needler, editor, *Political Systems of Latin America,* Van Nostrand, 1970.

Guide to the Mexican State of Sonora, Arizona State University, Center for Latin American Studies, 1971.

Government of the Mexican State of Nuevo Leon, Arizona State University, Center for Latin American Studies, 1971.

Peruvian Political Perspective, Arizona State University, Center for Latin American Studies, 1972.

Historical Dictionary of Peru, Scarecrow, 1979.

(Contributor) Dan Nimmo and Michael Mansfield, editors, *Government and the News Media,* Baylor University Press, 1980.

(Contributor) Edward H. Moseley, editor, *Yucatan: A World Apart,* University of Alabama Press, 1980.

Historical Dictionary of Mexico, Scarecrow, 1981.

Latin American Media: Guidance and Censorship, Iowa State University Press, 1981.

(Co-author) *Latin America Contemporary Record,* Holmes & Meier, 1982.

(Co-author) *Political Parties of the Americas,* Greenwood Press, 1982.

(Co-author) *Arms Production in Developing Countries,* Lexington Books, 1984.

(Co-author) *Global Journalism,* Longman, 1984.

(Co-author) *Biographical Dictionary of Latin American Political Leaders,* Greenwood Press, 1988.

International Handbook of Broadcasting Systems, Greenwood Press, 1988.

Mexico: A Country in Crisis, University of Texas-El Paso Press, 1989.

La Prensa of Monagha, Bevin Press of Mexico, 1990.
(Co-author) *Mass Media and the Caribbean,* Gordon & Breach, 1990.

Also author of radio scripts for National Broadcasting Company. Syndicated columnist on Latin America, P.R.S. Syndicate and U.S.I.C. Writers Syndicate, 1982—; occasional columnist on Latin America, *Wall Street Journal,* 1982—. Contributor of numerous articles to periodicals, including *Reporter, New Mexico Historical Review, Arizona Highways, Wall Street Journal,* and *Reader's Digest.* Editor of *Latin American Digest,* 1966-72; associate editor, *Intellect,* 1974—, and *USA Today* magazine, 1983—.

SIDELIGHTS: Marvin Alisky once told *CA:* "I write at the scholarly and at the popular level in order to reach not only those who teach about Latin America's public life but also the average citizens who need to understand the crises in neighboring nations. As for excursions into humor, quips and puns often teach as well as does academic verbiage. Some professors do not understand that one can be a serious scholar without being solemn. Those with insight will perceive life's paradoxes and laugh."

* * *

ALLABY, (John) Michael 1933-

PERSONAL: Born September 18, 1933, in Belper, Derbyshire, England; son of Albert (a chiropodist) and Jessie May (King) Allaby; married Ailsa Marthe McGregor, January 3, 1957; children: Vivien Gail, Robin Graham.

ADDRESSES: *Home*—Penquite, Fernleigh Rd., Wadebridge, Cornwall PL27 7B8, England.

CAREER: Variously employed as police cadet, 1949-51, and actor, 1954-64; Soil Association, Suffolk, England, member of editorial department, 1964-72, editor of *Span,* 1967-72; Ecosystems Ltd., Wadebridge, Cornwall, England, member of board of directors and editor of *Ecologist,* 1972-73; free-lance writer, 1973—. *Military service:* Royal Air Force, 1951-54, served as pilot; became pilot officer.

MEMBER: Royal Society of Arts (fellow), Society for the History of Natural History, Planetary Society, Society of Authors, New York Academy of Sciences.

WRITINGS:

The Eco-Activists, Knight & Co., 1971.
Who Will Eat? The World Food Problem, Stacey, 1972.
(With others) *A Blueprint for Survival,* Houghton, 1972.
(With Floyd Allen) *Robots behind the Plow,* Rodale Press, 1974.
Ecology, Hamlyn, 1975.
(With Marika Hanbury-Tenison, Hugh Sharman, and John Seymour) *The Survival Handbook: Self-Sufficiency for Everyone,* Macmillan (London), 1975.
Inventing Tomorrow: How to Live in a Changing World, Hodder & Stoughton, 1976.
(Editor) *A Dictionary of the Environment,* Macmillan, 1977, 2nd revised edition, New York University Press, 1984.
World Food Resources: Actual and Potential, Elsevier, 1977.
(With Colin Tudge) *Home Farm: Complete Food Self-Sufficiency,* Macmillan, 1977.
Animals That Hunt, Hamlyn, 1979.
Wildlife of North America, Hamlyn, 1979.
Making and Managing a Smallholding, David & Charles, 1980.
(With Peter Bunyard) *The Politics of Self-Sufficiency,* Oxford University Press, 1980.
A Year in the Life of a Field, David & Charles, 1981.
Le Foreste Tropicale, Instituto Geografico de Agostini, 1981.
Animal Artisans, Knopf, 1982.
(With Peter Crawford) *The Curious Cat,* M. Joseph, 1982, Merrimack Book Service, 1983.
The Changing Uplands, Countryside Commission, 1983.
(With James Lovelock) *The Great Extinction: The Solution to One of the Great Mysteries of Science, the Disappearance of the Dinosaurs,* Doubleday, 1983.
The Food Chain, Andre Deutsch, 1984.
(With Lovelock) *The Greening of Mars,* St. Martin's/Marek, 1984.
2040: Our World in the Future, Gollancz, 1985.
(Editor) *The Oxford Dictionary of Natural History,* Oxford University Press, 1985.
Your Child and the Computer, Methuen, 1985.
(With Jane Burton) *Your Cat's First Year,* Simon & Schuster, 1985.
The Woodland Trust Book of British Woodlands, David & Charles, 1986.
(With Burton) *A Dog's Life,* Howell Book, 1986.
Ecology Facts, Hamlyn, 1986, 2nd revised edition published as *Green Facts,* 1989.
(With Burton) *A Pony's Tale,* Ebury Press, 1987.
The Ordnance Survey Outdoor Handbook, Macmillan/Ordnance Survey, 1987.
Conservation at Home: A Practical Handbook, Unwin-Hyman, 1988.
A Guide to Gaia, Macdonald-Optima, 1989, Dutton, 1990.
(Editor) *Thinking Green: An Anthology of Essential Ecological Writing,* Barrie & Jenkins, 1989.
Living in the Greenhouse, Thorsons, 1990.
Into Harmony with the Planet, Bloomsbury Publishing, 1990.

(Editor, with Ailsa Allaby) *The Concise Oxford Dictionary of Earth Sciences,* Oxford University Press, 1990.
(Editor) *The Concise Oxford Dictionary of Zoology,* Oxford University Press, 1991.
(Editor) *The Concise Oxford Dictionary of Botany,* Oxford University Press, 1992.
Air: The Nature of Atmosphere and the Climate, Facts on File, 1992.
Water: Its Global Nature, Facts on File, 1992.
Earth: Our Planet and Its Resources, Facts on File, 1993.
Fire: The Vital Source of Energy, Facts on File, 1993.
(Editor) *The Concise Oxford Dictionary of Ecology,* Oxford University Press, 1993.

Contributor to books, including *The Environmental Handbook,* edited by John Barr, Ballantine, 1971; *Can Britain Survive?,* edited by Edward Goldsmith, Stacey, 1971; *Teach-In for Survival,* edited by Michael Schwab, Robinson & Watkins Books, 1972; *Ecology,* edited by Jonathan Benthall, Longmans, Green, 1973; *Nightwatch,* edited by Linda Gamlin, M. Joseph, 1983; and *Ecology 2000: The Changing Face of the Earth,* edited by Edmund Hillary, Beaufort Books, 1984. Also contributor to *Encyclopaedia Britannica,* and to magazines, journals, and newspapers.

A Dog's Life has been published in French, German, Italian, Norwegian, Swedish, and Finnish editions.

WORK IN PROGRESS: Research into the positive influence technology has made on the quality of human life.

SIDELIGHTS: Michael Allaby told *CA:* "In recent years I have become increasingly disturbed by the shift away from scientific, indeed rational, thought in popular culture. Fed by the exaggerated propaganda of the populist environmental movement and by wide, but uninformed concern over ethical issues raised by potential scientific or technological developments, the distrust of scientists and technologists has developed into a fear and rejection of the future itself. The evidence can be seen in the quest for spurious certainties by adherents of fundamentalist religions, the invention of new pseudo-religions that rely on magic to achieve control of the natural forces, and the sentimental yearning for a world in which plants and animals can live in cozy harmony with humans enjoying the supposedly simple life that our ancestors are alleged to have enjoyed in the distant past.

"I believe these views must be challenged in the strongest possible terms, lest their gloomy forebodings become self-fulfilling prophecies, and I am working to develop an argument that will achieve this. The resulting book will reassert the positive contribution to the quality of our lives that has been made in the past by scientific discoveries and technological development and will list some of the contributions that may be made in years to come."

BIOGRAPHICAL/CRITICAL SOURCES:

PERIODICALS

Christian Science Monitor, August 31, 1983.
New York Times Book Review, January 6, 1985.
Times (London), January 23, 1986.
Times Literary Supplement, July 29, 1986.

* * *

ALLDRITT, Keith 1935-

PERSONAL: Born December 10, 1935, in Wolverhampton, England; son of Alan James and Elsie (Tongue) Alldritt; married Judith Morse, 1960 (divorced); married Joan Hardwick, 1980, children: (first marriage) Mark; (second marriage) Miranda, Benjamin. *Education:* St. Catharine's College, Cambridge, B.A., 1957, M.A., 1960.

ADDRESSES: *Office*—Department of English, University of British Columbia, Vancouver, British Columbia, Canada.

CAREER: University of Vienna, Vienna, Austria, government scholar, 1958-59; University of Illinois, Urbana, assistant professor of English, 1959-63; University of British Columbia, Vancouver, associate professor, then professor of English, 1963—.

AWARDS, HONORS: Canada Council fellow, 1968-69, 1973-74, 1992-5.

WRITINGS:

The Making of George Orwell: An Essay in Literary History, St. Martin's, 1969.
The Visual Imagination of D. H. Lawrence, Northwestern University Press, 1971.
The Good Pit Man, St. Martin's, 1976.
The Lover Next Door, Deutsch, 1977, St. Martin's, 1978.
Eliot's "Four Quartets": Poetry as Chamber Music, Woburn Press, 1978.
Elgar on the Journey to Hanley: A Novel, St. Martin's, 1979.
Modernism in the Second World War, Peter Lang, 1989.
Churchill the Writer, Hutchinson, 1992.

WORK IN PROGRESS: *The Greatest of Friends: Winston Churchill and Franklin Delano Roosevelt,* publication by John Hale/St. Martin's, 1995.

BIOGRAPHICAL/CRITICAL SOURCES:

BOOKS

Dictionary of Literary Biography, Volume 14: *British Novelists since 1960,* Gale, 1983.

ANDERSON, Norman Dean 1928-

PERSONAL: Born January 29, 1928, in Dickens, IA; son of Eddie (a farmer) and Effie (Condra) Anderson; married Mary Martha Breuer, November 23, 1952 (separated); children: Brent, Beth, Jeffrey, Todd, Jonathan, Julie. *Education:* University of Iowa, B.A., 1951, M.A., 1956; Ohio State University, Ph.D., 1965. *Religion:* Presbyterian.

ADDRESSES: Home—2431 H Wesvill Ct., Raleigh, NC 27607. *Office*—Department of Science Education, 326 Poe Hall, North Carolina State University, Raleigh, NC 27695-7801.

CAREER: High school science teacher in Burlington, IA, 1952-57, 1958-59, and Bettendorf, IA, 1959-61; Ohio State University, Columbus, instructor in science education, 1961-63; North Carolina State University, Raleigh, assistant professor, 1963-66, associate professor, 1966-71, professor of science education, 1971—. Summer master teacher in science, Harvard University, 1964; visiting lecturer, Ohio State University, summers, 1967, 1968, 1969, University of Maryland, 1970, and East Carolina University, 1970; director of National Science Foundation summer institutes in earth science, 1966, 1967, 1968, and in marine environments, 1971. Trustee, Peace College, 1970-75. Chairman, North Carolina State Advisory Council on Elementary and Secondary Education, 1968-70. *Military service:* U.S. Army, Engineers, 1946-47.

MEMBER: American Association for the Advancement of Science (fellow), National Education Association (life member), National Science Teachers Association (life member), National Association for Research in Science Teaching, Association for Education of Teachers of Science, Phi Delta Kappa, Phi Kappa Phi, Sigma Xi.

AWARDS, HONORS: North Carolina State University Outstanding Teaching Awards, 1965, 1970, Alumni Distinguished Professor, 1971; Distinguished Service Award, North Carolina Science Teachers Association, 1989; Faculty Award, North Carolina State University, 1992.

WRITINGS:

(With J. Allen Hynek) *Challenge of the Universe,* Scholastic Book Services, 1962.

(Contributing editor in astronomy and astronautics) *Compton's Illustrated Science Dictionary,* David-Stewart, 1963.

Investigating Science Using Your Whole Body, McGraw, 1975.

Investigating Science in the Swimming Pool and Ocean, McGraw, 1978.

(With Ronald D. Simpson) *Science, Students, and Schools: A Guide for the Middle and Secondary School Teacher,* Wiley, 1981.

Ferris Wheels: An Illustrated History, Bowling Green State University Popular Press, 1992.

WITH WALTER R. BROWN

Life Science: A Search for Understanding, Lippincott, 1971, revised edition, 1977.

Physical Science: A Search for Understanding, Lippincott, 1972, revised edition, 1977.

Earth Science: A Search for Understanding, Lippincott, 1973, revised edition, 1977.

Famines, Addison-Wesley, 1976.

Fires, Addison-Wesley, 1976.

Snowstorms and Avalanches, Addison-Wesley, 1976.

Catastrophe, Addison-Wesley, 1979.

Halley's Comet, Dodd, Mead, 1981.

Sea Disasters, Addison-Wesley, 1981.

Ferris Wheels, Pantheon, 1983.

Fireworks!: Pyrotechnics on Display, Dodd, Mead, 1983.

Rescue!: True Stories of the Winners of the Young American Medal for Bravery, Walker, 1983.

Lemurs, Dodd, Mead, 1984.

Contributor to journals of science education.

SIDELIGHTS: Norman Dean Anderson once told *CA*: "As a former junior high school science teacher, as a father of six, and as a university professor of science education, my continuous contacts with young people and science provide more ideas than I can write about in a lifetime. And as I read and do research for a book, more ideas for writing projects are generated. There are many motivations for writing these books—to share the excitement of science with adolescents, to create new ways of presenting ideas and activities that can be performed as part of the learning process, and perhaps most important, to organize my own thoughts and to learn, myself, about the many fascinating aspects of science."

* * *

ANDERSON, Olive M(ary) 1915-

PERSONAL: Born May 2, 1915, in Dakota City, NE; daughter of Francis J. (a clergyman) and Olive Angeline (McKenzie) Aucock; married Fred N. Anderson (a clergyman), August 20, 1935; children: Mary Anderson Sarber, Francis Nels. *Education:* Nebraska Wesleyan University, A.B., 1937. *Religion:* Methodist.

Avocational Interests: Nature photography, nature study, hiking, camping, books.

ADDRESSES: Home—4037 Albright Lane, Rockford, IL 61102.

CAREER: Writer, 1941—.

MEMBER: Natural Land Institute, North Country Trail Association, Pecatonica Prairie Path (former member of board of directors), historical societies of Alger, Schoolcraft, and Marquette Counties in Michigan, Pecatonica Historical Society (Illinois), Family History Society of Sussex County, England.

WRITINGS:

A Wilderness of Wonder, Augsburg, 1971.
Seeker at Cassandra Marsh, Christian Herald Books, 1978.
Utopia in Upper Michigan: The Story of a Cooperative Village, Northern Michigan University Press, 1982.
Pictured Rocks Lakeshore Trail: A North Country Trail Guide, North Country Trail Association, 1983.
Pictured Rocks National Lakeshore: A Guide, Bayshore Press, 1988.
By the Shining Big-Sea-Water: The Story of Pictured Rocks, Alger County Historical Society, 1989.

Author of "Lizzie Hawkins Speaking," a column appearing in more than twenty weekly periodicals, 1955-71. Contributor of articles and stories to magazines.

WORK IN PROGRESS: A sequel to her first two books, "continuing her life and adventures in the north woods of Michigan, now that she and her husband are retired. The recurring theme is experiencing and accepting the changes that come with age."

SIDELIGHTS: Olive M. Anderson once told *CA:* "I began serious nature study after we built our family cabin in the unfamiliar setting of the north woods. The story of this is told in *A Wilderness of Wonder*. My insatiable curiosity about the natural world and my observation of it led to *Seeker at Cassandra Marsh,* where I lived close to the earth and its Creator. My current writing concerns man's relationship to the earth on which he lives."

She added: "Writing is an exciting occupation which has led me to many new adventures. I discovered the thrill of original research as I delved into the history of an 1890s cooperative village for *Utopia in Upper Michigan.* I did my first backpacking because it seemed necessary to have that experience to write a trail guide. Who knows what tomorrow may bring?"

She later added, "In answer to my own question: 'It brings more years.' The interruption of my current project by genealogical research in this country and England resulted in a story written for my family, about my father's first thirty years in England. It introduced me to him as a young man, and to relatives whom I did not know existed. It was a good interruption, for I am now back to my northwoods book with more perspective on the problems of aging, in myself and others."

ANDERSON, Roberta 1942-
(Fern Michaels, a joint pseudonym)

PERSONAL: Born August 22, 1942, in New Jersey; daughter of John P. (in electronics) and Sophie F. (a retailer; maiden name, Kwityn) Cuomo; married Alfred P. Anderson (a teacher and research chemist); children: Arlene Lorraine, David Alan.

ADDRESSES: *Home*—14 West Side Ave., Avenel, NJ, 07001.

CAREER: Writer. Worked in market research.

WRITINGS:

ROMANCES WITH MARY KUCZKIR UNDER JOINT PSEUDONYM FERN MICHAELS

Pride and Passion, Ballantine, 1975.
Vixen in Velvet, Ballantine, 1976.
Captive Passions, Ballantine, 1977.
Valentina, Ballantine, 1978.
Captive Embraces, Ballantine, 1979.
Captive Splendors, Ballantine, 1980.
Golden Lasso, Silhouette, 1980.
The Delta Ladies, Pocket Books, 1980.
Captive Innocence, Ballantine, 1981.
Sea Gypsy, Silhouette, 1981.
Whisper My Name, Silhouette, 1981.
Beyond Tomorrow, Silhouette, 1981.
Wild Honey, Pocket Books, 1982.
Nightstar, G. K. Hall, 1982.
Paint Me Rainbows, G. K. Hall, 1982.
All She Can Be, Ballantine, 1983.
Free Spirit, Ballantine, 1983.
Tender Warrior, Ballantine, 1983.
Cinders to Satin, Ballantine, 1984.
Texas Rich, Ballantine, 1985.
Texas Heat, Ballantine, 1986.
To Taste the Wine, Ballantine, 1987.
Texas Fury, Ballantine, 1989.

THRILLERS WITH MARY KUCZKIR UNDER JOINT PSEUDONYM FERN MICHAELS

Without Warning, Pocket Books, 1981.
Panda Bear Is Critical, Macmillan, 1982.

SIDELIGHTS: Under the joint pseudonym Fern Michaels, Roberta Anderson and her co-author Mary Kuczkir created several best-selling novels in the romance genre. Among their most successful publications are *Captive Embraces* and *The Delta Ladies.* Although most of their early books were historical romances, Anderson and Kuczkir have also written contemporary romances. In this category fall their short novels *All She Can Be* and *Free Spirit. All She Can Be* is the story of a middle-aged woman's attempt to define herself as an individual and a woman rather than as wife and mother, after her husband leaves her for another woman. *Free Spirit* also deals with the conflict explored in *All She Can Be,* but from a different angle. In this book, the heroine is a successful career woman who decides to give up her identity as a professional because of the pressures of traditional social values. In the end, she realizes that the decision to do so has been a betrayal of her self as a woman. Anderson continued writing with Kuczkir until 1989, when the collaboration came to an end. Kuczkir continued using the pseudonym Fern Michaels to write other books.

BIOGRAPHICAL/CRITICAL SOURCES:

BOOKS

Falk, Kathryn, *Love's Leading Ladies,* Pinnacle Books, 1982.

PERIODICALS

New York Times Book Review, July 8, 1979.
Us, June 27, 1978.
Writers' Digest, December, 1978.

* * *

ANDRESEN, Julie Tetel
See TETEL, Julie

* * *

ANDREWS, Raymond 1934-1991

PERSONAL: Born June 6, 1934, in Madison, GA; son of George Cleveland (a sharecropper) and Viola (Perryman) Andrews; married Adelheid Wenger (an airline sales agent), December 28, 1966 (divorced June 2, 1980); died November 26, 1991, in Athens, GA, from a self-inflicted gunshot wound. *Education:* Attended Michigan State University, 1956-57. *Politics:* None. *Religion:* None.

ADDRESSES: Home—2013 Morton Rd., Athens, GA 30605. *Agent*—Susan Ann Protter, 110 West 40th St., Suite 1408, New York, NY 10018.

CAREER: Writer. Worked variously as sharecropper, 1943-49, hospital orderly, 1949-51, bartender, busboy, dishwasher, and stockroom worker, 1951-52, postal mail sorter, 1956, and stockroom clerk, 1957; KLM Royal Dutch Airlines, New York City, airline employee, 1958-66; photograph librarian, 1967-72; Archer Courier, New York City, messenger, telephone operator, night dispatcher, and bookkeeper, 1972-84. *Military service:* U.S. Air Force, 1952-56.

AWARDS, HONORS: James Baldwin Prize for Fiction, 1978, for *Appalachee Red.*

WRITINGS:

FICTION

Appalachee Red (novel), illustrations by brother, Benny Andrews, Dial, 1978.
Rosiebelle Lee Wildcat Tennessee (novel), illustrations by B. Andrews, Dial, 1979.
Baby Sweet's (novel), illustrations by B. Andrews, Dial, 1983.
Jessie and Jesus [and] Cousin Claire (novellas), illustrations by B. Andrews, Peachtree, 1991.

MEMOIRS

The Last Radio Baby: A Memoir, Peachtree, 1990.

OTHER

(Illustrator) Lily Mathieu LaBraque, *Man from Mono,* LaBraque, 1991.

Contributor to *Sports Illustrated* and *Ataraxia.*

SIDELIGHTS: Raymond Andrews once commented: "As children, my brother and I drew, with him continuing on and becoming an artist, while I stopped drawing and became more interested in reading. To me, there was nothing better than a *good* story. But in the farming—sharecropping—community I came from, most people couldn't read. This, along with a poor school system, did not encourage budding authors. Yet in the back of my head a writer was what I wanted to be most of all, and I couldn't help but feel that someday, *somehow,* I would write.

"It wasn't until the day of my thirty-second birthday that I finally got around to doing something about this nagging in the back of my head which down through the years had absolutely refused to shut up. At the time I was working for an airline and was being given what I felt was an uncalled-for hard time over the telephone by a client. I told him to wait and put the call on hold. At precisely 12:36, after eight years, two months, two weeks, and three days, I walked out, never to return. I went home and had my telephone disconnected. The next morning upon rising at my usual early hour, I told myself, 'you *are* going to write.' And I've been at it ever since."

In his writing, Andrews draws upon his personal experience as a youth in a small sharecropping community in the South. He has set each of his novels in the town of Appalachee, the county seat of the fictional Muskhogean county in northern Georgia. The close connection between Andrews's stories and their setting is part of their appeal. "Andrews has a deep and intricate understanding of the small southern town," writes David Guy in the *Washington Post Book World,* "and displays this understanding not only in passages of exposition but also in the hearts of his narratives." The author's choice of a small southern town with its population of blacks and whites living in close proximity also allows him to examine, as Janet Boyarin Blundell notes in *Library Journal,* the "complex interracial relationships" that occur.

Andrews's first novel, *Appalachee Red,* won for its author the first James Baldwin Prize for Fiction. It is the story of a young black woman who, while her husband is in jail, has the child of one of the town's most influential white men. The child, Appalachee Red, is sent north to be raised. Years later he returns to take revenge upon his father and the town. Although *Best Sellers* contributor Russ Williams finds that "the thin line between sociological trauma and stark fiction is not drawn," he does admit, "Raymond Andrews has an especial gift and skill of narrative, one which enables him to compel the reader through even the most unlikely passages." A *Publishers Weekly* reviewer also comments upon the author's ability: "Andrews is an extremely gifted storyteller in the best Southern revivalist tradition." Concludes Blundell, "This is a pungent, witty, and powerful first novel, deserving winner of the first James Baldwin Prize for Fiction."

The title of the author's second novel, *Rosiebelle Lee Wildcat Tennessee,* is also the name of its main character, a part American Indian, part black woman who comes to Appalachee, goes to work for the town's richest man, becomes first the mistress of the man's son, and much later the matriarch to the town's black population. "Andrews has skillfully created a portrait of an aggressive, life-hungry black woman, her four children, and the surrounding community," comments Blundell. Once again, reviewers note the author's capacity to fashion a good tale. A reviewer for the *New Yorker* writes, "Mr. Andrews is well versed in the rights and duties of the traditional storyteller, and he knows just how far to stretch his audience's memory and credulity as he spins and weaves his colorful yarns." And a *Publishers Weekly* contributor adds, "Raymond Andrews is an extraordinary writer—a true and absolutely original American voice."

In *Baby Sweet's* "the characters are larger than life and often seem to represent phenomena as much as they do flesh and blood human beings," observes David Guy in the *Washington Post Book World.* Baby Sweet's is the name given to the brothel opened by the eccentric son of Appalachee's leading citizen to provide black prostitutes for the white population. Once again, Andrews examines how the intermingling of the races affects the entire community. Reviewers also note the folksy style evident in *Baby Sweet's.* "Andrews' writing stems from a black oral tradition and could effectively be read aloud," notes Guy. In the *New York Times Book Review* Frederick Busch writes that *Baby Sweet's* "is a novel chanted to achieve the feeling of blues . . . [and] it is the music of Mr. Andrews's narrative that makes this book a pleasure to read." Finally, Guy commends Andrews "for his raucous and robust humor, his really profound knowledge of the South, his ultimately accepting and benign vision . . . and most of all for the entertaining voice that tells the stories."

Andrews returns to his rural Georgia home of the '30s and '40s for *The Last Radio Baby: A Memoir,* which *People Magazine* calls "a cross between *Roots* and *'Prairie Home Companion.'* " In this memoir, Andrews remembers the special qualities of the radio—not only did it link rural America to the outside world, it was a cornerstone of family entertainment. He recalls, for example, hiking more than a mile to listen to the first Joe Louis and Billy Conn heavyweight fight at an uncle's house because the batteries in his own radio were dead. Noting that "fantastic" characters fill Andrews' work, a *Washington Post Book World* contributor points to Mrs. Hill, who was born into slavery and when she was in her nineties, ran around with a "set of fast girls in their sixties."

In Andrews' two novellas, *Jessie and Jesus [and] Cousin Claire,* he continues his style of telling a story as if his readers were personally nearby. Placing the action in fictional downstate Georgia's Muskhogean County, Andrews paints a pair of portraits that Al Young, in his *Washington Post Book World* review, says "reveals that both of these determined *femmes fatales* are as cunning as they are attractive. The flies in these powerful women's ointment take the form of male treachery and neglect." Both of these woman, rural Jesse and city-bred Claire, are dark-hearted ladies who in their own eccentric ways, Young believes, are "sisters under the skin, determined to keep their ointment flyless."

BIOGRAPHICAL/CRITICAL SOURCES:

PERIODICALS

Best Sellers, February, 1979.
Chicago Tribune Book World, February 8, 1981.
Ebony, September, 1980.
Essence, December, 1980.
New Yorker, August 11, 1980.
New York Times Book Review, August 17, 1980; July 24, 1983.
People Magazine, February 25, 1991.
Publishers Weekly, July 24, 1978; May 2, 1980; August 30, 1991.
Synergos, spring, 1981.
Washington Post Book World, July 31, 1983; February 3, 1991; February 16, 1992.

OBITUARIES:

PERIODICALS

Chicago Tribune, December 12, 1991.

ANGELOU, Maya 1928-

PERSONAL: Name originally Marguerita Johnson; surname is pronounced "*An*-ge-lo"; born April 4, 1928, in St. Louis, MO; daughter of Bailey (a naval dietician) and Vivian (Baxter) Johnson; married Tosh Angelou (divorced); married Paul Du Feu, December, 1973 (divorced); children: Guy. *Education:* Attended public schools in Arkansas and California; studied music privately; studied dance with Martha Graham, Pearl Primus, and Ann Halprin; studied drama with Frank Silvera and Gene Frankel.

ADDRESSES: *Home*—Sonoma, CA. *Office*—c/o Dave La Camera, Lordly and Dame, Inc., 51 Church St., Boston, MA 02116.

CAREER: Author, poet, playwright, professional stage and screen producer, director, performer, and singer. Appeared in *Porgy and Bess* on twenty-two-nation tour sponsored by the U.S. Department of State, 1954-55; appeared in Off-Broadway plays *Calypso Heatwave,* 1957, and *The Blacks,* 1960; produced and performed in *Cabaret for Freedom,* with Godfrey Cambridge, Off-Broadway, 1960; University of Ghana, Institute of African Studies, Legon-Accra, Ghana, assistant administrator of School of Music and Drama, 1963-66; appeared in *Mother Courage* at University of Ghana, 1964, and in *Medea* in Hollywood, 1966; made Broadway debut in *Look Away,* 1973; directed film *All Day Long,* 1974; directed her play *And Still I Rise* in California, 1976; appeared in film *Roots,* 1977; directed Errol John's *Moon on a Rainbow Shawl* in London, England, 1988; also appeared on numerous television programs. Television narrator, interviewer, and host for African American specials and theatre series, 1972. Modern Dance instructor at The Rome Opera House and Hambina Theatre, Tel Aviv, c. 1955; lecturer at University of California, Los Angeles, 1966; writer in residence at University of Kansas, 1970; distinguished visiting professor at Wake Forest University, 1974, Wichita State University, 1974, and California State University, Sacramento, 1974; first Reynolds professor of American Studies (lifetime appointment), Wake Forest University, 1981—. Northern coordinator of Martin Luther King, Jr.'s Southern Christian Leadership Conference, 1959-60; appointed member of American Revolution Bicentennial Council by President Gerald R. Ford, 1975-76; member of National Commission on the Observance of International Women's Year.

MEMBER: American Federation of Television and Radio Artists, American Film Institute (member of board of trustees, 1975—), Directors Guild, Harlem Writers Guild, Equity, Women's Prison Association (member of advisory board).

AWARDS, HONORS: Nominated for National Book Award, 1970, for *I Know Why the Caged Bird Sings;* Yale University fellowship, 1970; Pulitzer Prize nomination, 1972, for *Just Give Me a Cool Drink of Water 'fore I Diiie;* Antoinette Perry ("Tony") Award nomination, League of New York Theatres and Producers, 1973, for performance in *Look Away;* Rockefeller Foundation scholar in Italy, 1975; named Woman of the Year in Communications, 1976; Tony Award nomination for best supporting actress, 1977, for *Roots;* honorary degrees from Smith College, 1975, Mills College, 1975, and Lawrence University, 1976; named one of the Top 100 Most Influential Women by *Ladies' Home Journal,* 1983; Matrix award, 1983; North Carolina Award in Literature, 1987.

WRITINGS:

I Know Why the Caged Bird Sings (autobiography), Random House, 1970.

Just Give Me a Cool Drink of Water 'fore I Diiie (poetry), Random House, 1971.

Gather Together in My Name (autobiography), Random House, 1974.

Oh Pray My Wings Are Gonna Fit Me Well (poetry), Random House, 1975.

Singin' and Swingin' and Gettin' Merry Like Christmas (autobiography), Random House, 1976.

And Still I Rise (poetry), Random House, 1978.

The Heart of a Woman (autobiography), Random House, 1981.

Shaker, Why Don't You Sing? (poetry), Random House, 1983.

All God's Children Need Traveling Shoes (autobiography), Random House, 1986.

Mrs. Flowers: A Moment of Friendship (fiction), illustrations by Etienne Delessert, Redpath Press, 1986.

Poems: Maya Angelou, four volumes, Bantam, 1986.

Now Sheba Sings the Song, illustrations by Tom Feelings, Dial Books, 1987.

Selected from I Know Why the Caged Bird Sings and The Heart of A Woman, Literacy Volunteers of New York City, 1989.

I Shall Not Be Moved (poetry), Random House, 1990.

On the Pulse of Morning (inaugural poem), Random House, 1993.

Also author of *All Day Long* (short stories) and (with Abbey Lincoln) *The True Believers* (poetry). Contributor of poetry to film *Poetic Justice,* Columbia, 1993. Contributor and author of foreword, *Double Stitch: Black Women Write about Mothers and Daughters,* edited by Patricia Bell-Scott, Beacon Press, 1991; author of foreword, *Dust Tracks on the Road: An Autobiography,* Zora Neale Hurston, HarperCollins, 1991.

PLAYS

(With Godfrey Cambridge) *Cabaret for Freedom* (musical revue), first produced in New York at Village Gate Theatre, 1960.

The Least of These (two-act drama), first produced in Los Angeles, 1966.

(Adaptor) Sophocles, *Ajax* (two-act drama), first produced in Los Angeles at Mark Taper Forum, 1974.

And Still I Rise (one-act musical), first produced in Oakland, CA, at Ensemble Theatre, 1976.

Also author of two-act drama *The Clawing Within,* 1966, and of two-act musical *Adjoa Amissah,* 1967, both as yet unproduced.

SCREENPLAYS

Georgia, Georgia, Independent-Cinerama, 1972.

All Day Long, American Film Institute, 1974.

TELEVISION PLAYS

Blacks, Blues, Black (ten one-hour programs), National Educational Television (NET-TV), 1968.

(With Leonora Thuna and Ralph B. Woolsey) *I Know Why the Caged Bird Sings* (based on Angelou's book), Columbia Broadcasting System, Inc. (CBS-TV), 1979.

Sister, Sister (drama), National Broadcasting Co. (NBC-TV), 1982.

Also author of *Assignment America* series, 1975, and two Afro-American specials *The Legacy* and *The Inheritors,* 1976.

RECORDINGS

Miss Calypso (songs), Liberty Records, 1957.

The Poetry of Maya Angelou, GWP Records, 1969.

Women in Business, University of Wisconsin, 1981.

OTHER

Conversations with Maya Angelou, edited by Jeffrey M. Elliot, University Press of Mississippi, 1989.

Composer of songs, including two songs for movie *For Love of Ivy,* and composer of musical scores for both her screenplays. Contributor to Ghanaian Broadcasting Corp., 1963-65. Contributor of articles, short stories, and poems to periodicals, including *Harper's, Cosmopolitan, Ebony, Ghanaian Times, Mademoiselle, Essence, Redbook,* and *Black Scholar.* Associate editor, *Arab Observer* (English-language news weekly in Cairo, Egypt), 1961-62; feature editor, *African Review* (Accra, Ghana), 1964-66.

SIDELIGHTS: By the time she was in her early twenties, Maya Angelou had been a Creole cook, a streetcar conductor, a cocktail waitress, a dancer, a madam, and an unwed mother. The following decades saw her emerge as a successful singer, actress, and playwright, an editor for an English-language magazine in Egypt, a lecturer and civil rights activist, and a popular author of four collections of poetry and five autobiographies. Lynn Z. Bloom in *Dictionary of Literary Biography* wrote that Angelou "is forever impelled by the restlessness for change and new realms to conquer that is the essence of the creative artist, and of exemplary American lives, white and black."

Angelou is hailed as one of the great voices of contemporary black literature and as a remarkable Renaissance woman. She began producing books after some notable friends, including author James Baldwin, heard Angelou's stories of her childhood spent shuttling between rural, segregated Stamps, Arkansas, where her devout grandmother ran a general store, and St. Louis, Missouri, where her worldly, glamorous mother lived. *I Know Why the Caged Bird Sings,* a chronicle of her life up to age sixteen (and ending with the birth of her son, Guy) was published in 1970 with great critical and commercial success. Although many of the stories in the book are grim, as in the author's revelation that she was raped at age eight by her mother's boyfriend, the volume also recounts the self-awakening of the young Angelou. "Her genius as a writer is her ability to recapture the texture of the way of life in the texture of its idioms, its idiosyncratic vocabulary and especially in its process of image-making," reports Sidonie Ann Smith in *Southern Humanities Review.* "The imagery holds the reality, giving it immediacy. That [the author] chooses to recreate the past in its own sounds suggests to the reader that she accepts the past and recognizes its beauty and its ugliness, its assets and its liabilities, its strengths and its weaknesses. Here we witness a return to the final acceptance of the past in the return to and full acceptance of its language, the language a symbolic construct of a way of life. Ultimately Maya Angelou's style testifies to her reaffirmation of self-acceptance, [which] she achieves within the pattern of the autobiography."

Her next two volumes of autobiography, *Gather Together in My Name* and *Singin' and Swingin' and Gettin' Merry Like Christmas,* take Angelou from her late adolescence, when she flirted briefly with prostitution and drug addiction, to her early adulthood as she established a reputation as a performer among the avant-garde of the early 1950s. Not as commercially successful as *I Know Why the Caged Bird Sings,* the two books were guardedly praised by some critics. Lynn Sukenick, for example, remarks in *Village Voice* that *Gather Together in My Name* is "sculpted, concise, rich with flavor and surprises, exuding a natural confidence and command." Sukenick adds, however, that one fault lies "in the tone of the book. . . . [The author's] refusal to let her earlier self get off easy, and the self-mockery which is her means to honesty, finally becomes in itself a glossing over; although her laughter at herself is witty, intelligent, and a good preventative against maudlin confession, . . . it eventually becomes a tic and a substitute for a deeper look." Annie Gottlieb has another view of *Gather Together in My Name.* In her *New York Times Book Review* article, Gottlieb states that Angelou "writes like a song, and like the truth. The wisdom, rue and humor of her storytelling are borne on a lilting rhythm completely her own, the product of a born writer's senses nourished on black church singing and preaching, soft mother talk and salty street talk, and on literature."

The year 1981 brought the publication of *The Heart of a Woman,* a book that "covers one of the most exciting periods in recent African and Afro-American history," according to Adam David Miller in *Black Scholar.* Miller refers to the era of civil rights marches, the emergence of Martin Luther King, Jr., and Malcolm X, and the upheaval in Africa following the assassination of the Congolese statesman Patrice Lumumba. The 1960s see Angelou active in civil rights both in America and abroad; at the same time she enters into a romance with African activist Vusumzi Make, which dissolves when he cannot accept her independence or even promise fidelity. In a *Dictionary of Literary Biography* piece on Angelou, Lynn Z. Bloom considers *The Heart of a Woman* the author's best work since *I Know Why the Caged Bird Sings:* "Her enlarged focus and clear vision transcend the particulars and give this book a fascinating universality of perspective and psychological depth that almost matches the quality of [Angelou's first volume]. . . . Its motifs are commitment and betrayal."

Washington Post Book World critic David Levering Lewis also sees a universal message in *The Heart of a Woman.* "Angelou has rearranged, edited, and pointed up her coming of age and going abroad in the world with such just-rightness of timing and inner truthfulness that each of her books is a continuing autobiography of Afro-America. Her ability to shatter the opaque prisms of race and class between reader and subject is her special gift," he says. To Bloom, "it is clear from [this series of autobiographies] that Angelou is in the process of becoming a self-created Everywoman. In a literature and a culture where there are many fewer exemplary lives of women than of men, black or white, Angelou's autobiographical self, as it matures through successive volumes, is gradually assuming that exemplary stature."

In her fifth autobiographical work, *All God's Children Need Traveling Shoes,* Angelou describes her four-year stay in Ghana, "just as that African country had won its independence from European colonials," according to Barbara T. Christian in the *Chicago Tribune Book World.* Christian indicates that Angelou's "sojourn in Africa strengthens her bonds to her ancestral home even as she concretely experiences her distinctiveness as an Afro-American."

All God's Children Need Traveling Shoes has also received praise from reviewers. Wanda Coleman in the *Los Angeles Times Book Review* calls it "a thoroughly enjoyable segment from the life of a celebrity," while Christian describes it as "a thoughtful yet spirited account of one Afro-American woman's journey into the land of her ancestors." In Coleman's opinion, *All God's Children Need Traveling Shoes* is "an important document drawing more much needed attention to the hidden history of a people both African and American."

"As [Angelou] adds successive volumes to her life story," writes Bloom, "she is performing for contemporary black American women—and men, too—many of the same functions that escaped slave Frederick Douglass performed for his nineteenth-century peers through his autobiographical writings and lectures. Both became articulators of the nature and validity of a collective heritage as they interpret the particulars of a culture for a wide audience of whites as well as blacks. . . . As people who have lived varied and vigorous lives, they embody the quintessential experiences of their race and culture."

I Shall Not Be Moved is Angelou's fifth collection of poetry. The title is drawn from the poem "Our Grandmothers," in which an elderly woman refuses to be moved from her "heartfelt stand," as Jacqueline Gropman writes in the *School Library Journal.* Angelou "is able to command our ear," declares Gloria T. Hull in *Belles Lettres.* "As I listen, what I hear in her open, colloquial poems is racial wit and earthy wisdom, honest black female pain and strength, humor, passion, and rhetorical force." Other themes include "loss of love and youth, human oneness in diversity, the strength of blacks in the face of racism and adversity," notes a reviewer in *Publishers Weekly. Library Journal* contributor Lenard D. Moore judges the poems to be "highly controlled and yet powerful," using language that is "precise and filled with imagery." Gropman concludes that the poems in *I Shall Not Be Moved* "possess the drama of the storyteller and the imagery and soul of the poet."

BIOGRAPHICAL/CRITICAL SOURCES:

BOOKS

Angelou, Maya, *I Know Why the Caged Bird Sings,* Random House, 1970.

Angelou, Maya, *Gather Together in My Name,* Random House, 1974.

Angelou, Maya, *Singin' and Swingin' and Gettin' Merry Like Christmas,* Random House, 1976.

Angelou, Maya, *The Heart of a Woman,* Random House, 1981.

Angelou, Maya, *All God's Children Need Traveling Shoes,* Random House, 1986.
Contemporary Literary Criticism, Gale, Volume 12, 1980, Volume 35, 1985.
Dictionary of Literary Biography, Volume 38: *Afro-American Writers after 1955: Dramatists and Prose Writers,* Gale, 1985.

PERIODICALS

Belles Lettres, spring, 1991, pp. 2-4.
Black Scholar, summer, 1982.
Black World, July, 1975.
Chicago Tribune, November 1, 1981.
Chicago Tribune Book World, March 23, 1986.
Detroit Free Press, May 9, 1986.
Harper's, November, 1972.
Harvard Educational Review, November, 1970.
Ladies' Home Journal, May, 1976.
Library Journal, June 1, 1990, p. 132.
Los Angeles Times, May 29, 1983.
Los Angeles Times Book Review, April 13, 1986; August 9, 1987.
Ms., January, 1977.
New Republic, July 6, 1974.
New Statesman, September, 15, 1989, p. 37.
Newsweek, March 2, 1970.
New York Times, February 25, 1970.
New York Times Book Review, June 16, 1974.
Observer (London), April 1, 1984.
Parnassus: Poetry in Review, fall-winter, 1979.
Poetry, August, 1976.
Publishers Weekly, March 23, 1990, p. 69.
School Library Journal, September, 1990, p. 268.
Southern Humanities Review, fall, 1973.
Time, March 31, 1986.
Times (London), September 29, 1986.
Times Literary Supplement, February 17, 1974; June 14, 1985; January 24, 1986.
Village Voice, July 11, 1974, October 28, 1981.
Washington Post, October 13, 1981.
Washington Post Book World, October 4, 1981; June 26, 1983; May 11, 1986.*

* * *

ARIDAS, Chris 1947-

PERSONAL: Born November 12, 1947, in New York, NY; son of Christie and Katherine (Caputo) Aridas. *Education:* Attended St. Francis College, Brooklyn, NY; Cathedral College of the Immaculate Conception, B.A., 1969; Immaculate Conception Seminary, Huntington, NY, M.Div., 1973; additional study at Fordham University.

ADDRESSES: Home—40 Groves Pl., Babylon, NY 11702.

CAREER: Ordained Roman Catholic priest, 1973; Diocese of Rockville Centre, NY, priest, 1973—, director of Diocesan Office of the Charismatic Renewal, 1982—. President of Aslan Records, Inc., 1979—.

WRITINGS:

Discernment: Seeking God in Every Situation, Living Flame Press, 1981.
Your Catholic Wedding, Doubleday, 1982.
Soundings: A Thematic Guide for Daily Scripture Prayer, Doubleday, 1984.
Reconciliation: Celebrating God's Healing Forgiveness, Doubleday, 1987.
Bringing Prayer Meetings to Life, Dove, 1989.

WORK IN PROGRESS: The Elephant Who Stood on His Head, a children's book.

SIDELIGHTS: Chris Aridas told *CA:* "I never intended to write one book, much less five. However, when the opportunity came, I decided to try my hand at it. After all, it would help me proclaim the message in which I so strongly believe, without having to worry about how many people I was able to meet with each day.

"*Discernment: Seeking God in Every Situation* was written after I offered a series of retreats and workshops on the topic. *Your Catholic Wedding* arrived on the scene because I happened to be in the right place at the right time. *Soundings: A Thematic Guide for Daily Scripture Prayer* emerged as a result of a very understanding editor who saw a need 'to fill in a gap' existing within the Catholic book market. The book *Reconciliation: Celebrating God's Healing Forgiveness* sprung from my studies at Fordham, while my latest book, *Bringing Prayer Meetings to Life,* is a direct result of my work in the charismatic renewal movement.

"I must admit, my first love and desire would have been to continue working in the field of Christian music. To that end, I have already written and/or produced several albums under my privately owned record label, Aslan Records. I thought that this would be a place to spend my extra energy doing something useful and enjoyable. Some things, however, don't work out as planned. Although several of my songs were published in hymnals and although several albums were recorded, sales never allowed me the opportunity to continue working on this level. One door, therefore, was closed; but another, through the published word, was opened.

"Despite the heavy work load involved in my ministry of teaching and writing, I have managed to find a constant source of refreshment through a series of 'unusual' vacations: Grand Canyon mule trips, canoeing through the Everglades, and scuba diving. In fact, it was while struggling through a three-day storm in the Gulf of Mexico that I started to write the children's book I am still working on. Perhaps it began that way because I was feeling very much like a child throughout the storm—helpless, out of control, and just a little bit frightened!

"For the future, I hope to continue as best as I can in my main work, that of a Roman Catholic priest. It is here that I am most fulfilled and with God's help will continue. Writing will undoubtedly continue for as long as my publishers are willing to allow me. Since I never desired or sought out this area, however, it would not upset me if the well ran dry."

* * *

ARP, Hans
See ARP, Jean

* * *

ARP, Jean 1887-1966
(Hans Arp; Michel Seuphor, a pseudonym)

PERSONAL: Worked under names Jean Arp and Hans Arp; born September 16, 1887, in Strasbourg, Alsace, Germany (now France); died of heart failure, June 7, 1966, in Locarno, Switzerland; son of Pierre Guillaume (owner of a cigar and cigarette factory) and Josephine (Koeberle) Arp; married Sophie Henriette Gertrude Taeuber (an artist), 1921 (died in an accident, January 13, 1943); married Marguerite Hagenbach, 1959. *Education:* Studied art in Germany at Kunstakademie, 1905-07, and in France at Academie Julian, 1907-09. *Religion:* Roman Catholic.

CAREER: Sculptor, painter, author and poet. Associated with Der Moderner Bund (co-founder), Lucerne, Switzerland, 1911-12, Der Blaue Reiter, Munich, Germany, 1912, Der Sturm, Berlin, Germany, 1913, Dada (co-founder), Zurich, Switzerland, 1916-18, Dada, Cologne, Germany, 1919-20, Dada, Paris, France, 1920-24, Surrealism, Paris, 1924-31, Cercle et Carre, Paris, 1930, Abstraction-Creation, Paris, 1931, and with other art groups and movements. Member of committee, Salon des Realities Nouvelles, Paris, 1946-48, and Salon de la Jeune Sculpture, 1950-52. One-man exhibitions held at galleries and museums, including Buchholz Gallery, New York City, 1949, Galleria del Naviglio, Milan, 1957, Museum of Modern Art, New York City, 1958, Galerie Denise Rene, Paris, 1959, Musee d'Art Moderne, Paris, 1962, Guggenheim Museum, New York City, 1969, and Metropolitan Musuem of Art, New York City, 1972. Works represented in permanent collections of museums in Paris, New York, London, Zurich, Rome, San Francisco, Stockholm, and other cities.

AWARDS, HONORS: International Sculpture Prize, Venice Biennale, 1954; Chevalier de la Legion d'Honneur, 1960; Stephen Lochner Medal, City of Cologne, 1961; Officier de l'Ordre des Arts et Lettres, 1961; Grand Prix National des Arts, 1963; Carnegie Prize, 1964; Goethe Prize, University of Hamburg, 1965; Order of Merit with Star, German Republic, 1965; named honorary citizen of Locarno, Switzerland, 1965.

WRITINGS:

Der Vogel selbdritt (poems and woodcuts), [Berlin], 1920.
Die Wolkenpumpe (poems), [Hanover], 1920.
Der Pyramidenrock (poems), [Erlenbach], 1924.
(With El Lissitsky) *Die Kunstismer: The Isms of Art,* E. Rentsch, 1925, reprinted, Ayer, 1968.
Konfiguration, [Paris], 1930.
Weisst du Schwartz du (poems), with illustrations by Max Ernst, [Zurich], 1930.
Neue Franzosische Malerei, [Leipzig], 1931.
(With Vicente Huidobro) *Tres Novelas Ejemplares* (novel), [Santiago], 1935, [Berlin], 1963.
Des Taches dans le Vide (poems), [Paris], 1937.
Sciure de Gamme (poems), [Paris], 1938.
Muscheln und Schirme (poems), [Meudon], 1939.
(Editor with others) *Plastique, Nos. 1-5,* 1939.
Poemes sans prenoms (poems), [Grasse], 1941.
Rire de Coquille (poems), [Amsterdam], 1944.
1924-1925-1926-1943: Gedichte (poems), [Bern], 1944.
Le Blanc aux Pieds de Negre (prose poems), [Paris], 1945.
(Self-illustrated) *Le Siege de l'Air: Poemes, 1915-1945,* Vrille, 1946.
Monuments a lecher, [Paris], 1946.
On My Way: Poetry and Essays, 1912-1947, edited by Robert Motherwell, Wittenborn, Schultz, 1948.
Onze Peintres vus par Arp, [Zurich], 1949.
Souffle (poems), [Ales], 1950.
Auch das ist nur eine Wolke: Aus den Jahren, 1920-1950 (prose poems), [Basel], 1951, reprinted, Pfullingen, 1960.
Wegweiser—Jalons, [Meudon], 1951.
Die Engelsschrift (poems), [Tubingen], 1952.
Dreams and Projects, Curt Valentin, 1952.
Worttraeume und schwartze Sterne: Auswahl aus den Gedichten der Jahre, 1911-1952, [Wiesbaden], 1953.
Behaarte Herzen, 1923-1926: Koenige vor der Sintflut, 1952-1953 (poems), [Frankfurt], 1953.
Un jour—des annees—une vie, [Ales], 1955.
Auf einem Bein (poems), [Wiesbaden], 1955.
Arp Collages, [Paris], 1955.

Unsern Taeglichen Traum . . . : Erinnerungen, Dichtungen, und Betrachtungen aus den Jahren, 1914-1954, [Zurich], 1955.

Le Voilier dans la foret (poems), [Paris], 1957.

Worte mit und ohne Anker (poems), [Wiesbaden], 1957.

Notre petit continent, [Ales], 1958.

(With others) *Arp,* edited and with an introduction by James Thrall Soby, Doubleday, 1958, reprinted, Arno Press, 1980.

Mondsand (poems and illustrations), G. Neske, 1959.

Vers le blanc infini (poems and illustrations), La Rose des vents, 1960.

Zweiklang—Sophie Taeuber Arp—Hans Arp, edited by Ernst Sheidegger, [Zurich], 1960.

Fagel och Slips, [Malmo], 1961.

Sinnende Flammen, [Zurich], 1961.

Gesammelte Gedichte, three volumes, [Zurich], 1963-84.

Logbuch des Traumkapitans (poems), Verlag die Arche, 1965.

L'Ange et la rose (poems and designs), Robert Morel, 1965.

Le Soleil recerle (poems), [Paris], 1966.

Jours effeuilles: Poemes, essais, souvenirs, 1920-1965, edited by Marcel Jean, Gallimard, 1966, translation published as *Arp on Arp: Poems, Essays, Memories,* Viking, 1971, published as *Collected French Writings,* Calder & Boyars, 1974, published as *Arp: Collected French Writings,* Riverrun Press, 1985.

(With Paul Klee and Kurt Schwitters) *Three Painter-Poets: Arp, Schwitters, Klee,* Penguin, 1974.

Hans Arp: The Graphic Work, G. Arntz-Winter, 1980.

Ich bin in der Natur geboren: Ausgewaehlte Gedichte, edited by Hans Bolliger, Guido Magnaguagno and Harriett Watts, [Zurich], 1986.

Also author of *Chair de reve,* 1915, and *Auf verschleierten Schaukeln,* 1955.

OTHER

(Illustrator) Richard Huelsenbeck, *Phantastische Gebete* (poems; title means "Fantastic Prayers"), W. Heuberger (Zurich), 1916.

Also author of art catalog commentaries, sometimes under pseudonym Michel Seuphor. Also illustrator of books, including *Bhagavad-Gita,* 1914, Tristan Tzara's books *25 Poemes,* 1918, and *Cinema Calendrier du Coeur Abstrait,* 1920, and Camille Bryen's *Temps Troue,* 1951. Contributor of articles and poems to periodicals, including *Dada, Die Schammade, Merz, Dada W/3, Das Neue Magazin, XX siecle,* and *transition.*

SIDELIGHTS: One of the most prominent artists of the twentieth century, and a forerunner of abstract and concrete art, Jean Arp was a sculptor, painter and writer who emphasized the organic creation of art. Arp explained in the essay "Dadaland," printed in his collection *On My Way,* that he wanted to create art in the same manner as nature created objects. "Art is a fruit that grows in man, like a fruit on a plant, or a child in its mother's womb," Arp wrote. "But whereas the fruit of the plant, the fruit of the animal, the fruit in the mother's womb, assume autonomous and natural forms, art, the spiritual fruit of man, usually shows an absurd resemblance to the aspect of something else." As Alexandre Partens wrote in *Almanach Dada,* in his sculpture and paintings, Arp "wanted immediate and direct production, like a stone breaking away from a cliff, a bud bursting, an animal reproducing. He wanted objects impregnated with imagination and not museum pieces, he wanted animalesque objects with wild intensities and colors, he wanted a new body among us which would suffice unto itself." Arp was born in Alsace, a region which has often passed between France and Germany. Because he worked in both France and Germany at different stages in his career—and changing political conditions sometimes dictated a prudent subterfuge—the artist went by the French version of his name (Jean Arp) or the German version of his name (Hans Arp) at various times.

After dropping out of art school, which he thought irrelevant to his own concerns, Arp joined Der Moderner Bund, a group of modern artists in Lucerne, Switzerland, who shared his interest in abstract art. He participated in their first exhibition in 1911. The following year he joined the Blaue Reiter (Blue Rider) group of expressionist artists in Munich, a group which included the artist Kandinsky. At the outbreak of World War I, Arp found that his mixed French-German background made him a suspicious character to both countries; he moved to neutral Switzerland. (When German authorities tried to draft him as a soldier in 1915, Arp convinced the German Consulate in Zurich that he was mentally defective and thus avoided service.)

In Zurich, Arp met such other artists as Tristan Tzara, Hugo Ball, and Richard Huelsenbeck, all of whom were sitting out the war years in Switzerland. Their common interest in abstract art, combined with a general revulsion against the war and its causes, led these artists to form the avant-garde Dada group in February of 1916 at Zurich's Cabaret Voltaire. "Dada," Arp explained in his "Dadaland" essay, "aimed to destroy the reasonable deceptions of man and recover the natural and unreasonable order. Dada wanted to replace the logical nonsense of the men of today by the illogically senseless. . . . Dada is for the senseless, which does not mean nonsense. Dada is senseless like nature. Dada is for nature and against art. Dada is direct like nature. Dada is for infinite sense and definite means."

Under the common banner of experimental revolt against the rational thought which had led to the destruction of

World War I, the Dadaists explored a number of new techniques and approaches to art. Rejecting established traditions and forms—which they believed were aesthetic equivalents of the rational thought of society at large—the Dadaists took painting back to its origins as lines and colors, poetry to its beginnings as letters and sounds, and sculpture to its component elements of shape and size. From these basics they hoped to construct a new art capable of expressing humanity's true desires in a pure and natural form.

Beginning as a painter and sculptor of abstracts, under the influence of Dada Arp soon began to formulate a different approach to artistic creation. He experimented with paper collages formed by bits of colored paper dropped by chance onto a white canvas. He created works using an automatic drawing technique in which the conscious mind's direction was subverted. Writing in *On My Way,* Arp explained his use of chance: "The 'law of chance,' which embraces all laws and is unfathomable like the first cause from which all life arises, can only be experienced through complete devotion to the unconscious. I maintained that anyone who followed this law was creating pure life." Herbert Read saw a mystical quality in Arp's technique. Writing in *The Art of Jean Arp,* Read compared Arp's use of chance to the *I Ching,* the traditional Chinese divination tool, which is consulted by throwing coins or sticks and reading the pattern they form on the ground. "Arp assumed . . . ," Read wrote, "that a work of art could be made in exactly the same way. Tear up the paper and throw the pieces on the floor, and the position thay assume will have some occult significance." Hans Richter, writing in his *Dada: Art and Anti-Art,* admitted that Arp "became one of the most consistent exponents of the use of chance and finally made of it an almost religious presence."

In 1915, Arp was commissioned to decorate the interior walls of a theosophical institute in Paris. He cut large paper shapes in a variety of colors and covered the walls with these "lyrical abstractions," as Richter called them. In 1916, these paper shapes evolved into amoeba-like wood reliefs which Arp painted in various colors, cut rounded holes into, superimposed in several layers, and hung on walls. Although given names suggesting representational images, few of these sculptures were anything but abstract flights of fancy. Speaking of Arp's sculpture, Robert Melville wrote in *Arp* that many of Arp's works could "be described as the relief maps of a poetic cosmogony: they appear to relate to Arp's avowed interest in the Pre-Socratic philosophers, and in particular to their speculations upon the originative material of things and the coherence of the natural world." Thomas B. Hess, writing in *ARTNews,* found that Arp's sculpture exhibited a kind of mysticism set off by his "balancing force, wit. It combines with all his philosophies to set up an equilibrium and tension of form and content."

Over the years, Arp created sculpture in a variety of media, including stone, marble, bronze and wood. Some of these were reliefs while others were free-standing sculpture meant to be displayed in a natural setting. His work went through several evolutionary phases during his career as Arp experimented with different materials and approaches. His largest and perhaps best sculptures were executed in the 1950s: a series of wood reliefs of monumental size for Harvard University's Graduate Center in 1950; and in 1956, a metal-on-concrete relief for the library of the University of Caracas, Venezuela. Speaking of the Harvard reliefs in her book *Jean Arp,* Carola Giedion-Welcker found that they "brighten the surroundings with a penetrating lyrical accent. Like passing stars, clouds, birds and leaves, the forms move along the regularly veined wooden wall, broadening finally into 'constellations.' It is relaxed poetic interplay of motions, forms and surfaces." She described the Caracas library relief as a "fantastic being placed among plants, architecture, and various structures . . . in full harmony. . . . [They are] precisely cut and roundly undulant forms which describe their movement before great wall surfaces in a script-like manner. The hovering interplay of open and closed forms, perforated and continuous surfaces, is executed in the language of a fantastic geometry."

In addition to his work as an artist, Arp also wrote a significant body of poetry. His poems displayed an innocent quality in sharp contrast to the work of some of his fellow Dadaists. As Richter explained, "The fortissimo of Tzara and Huelsenbeck would largely have drowned the soft flute-tones of the Alsation painter, if he had not, by the magic of his strange personality and the childlike charm and wisdom of his poems, found himself a place during one of their pauses for breath." As Robert Motherwell wrote in the prefatory note to *On My Way,* Arp "writes true poetry, spontaneous and unforced, without desire to 'be' a poet." In his *Dada and Surrealist Art,* William S. Rubin found that "though many Dada and Surrealist artists were practicing poets, Arp is one of the very few whose poetry stands in both quality and quantity as an important contribution in its own right. . . . Arp's collages, reliefs, and sculpture share with his poetry an iconography—e.g., navels, mustaches, and clouds—a gentle whimsy, and a feeling of naturalness."

As in his artwork, Arp often created poems by using the law of chance. As Raoul Hausmann pointed out in *German Life and Letters,* "One of Arp's most important discoveries was his recognition of the role of chance—not a chance senselessly destroying order, but on the contrary, a chance that has its own meaning, and makes new sense." Fritz Usinger, writing in *Deutsche Rundschau,* noted that

Arp's poetry "raises the logical laws of consciousness into the alogical, into paradoxes, one might even say into a region where the paradox is no longer paradoxical but begins to be a matter of course. . . . The alogical becomes the normal, as it were, and all Arp's poetry is a sort of exploration of these realms of the alogical, which are being disclosed for the first time."

Beyond the alogical meanings of Arp's poetry is its value on a verbal level. Roger Shattuck in the *New York Review of Books* called attention to "the sound surfing and syllable sledding" to be found in Arp's poetry. In his work, Shattuck explained, Arp finds "verbal patterns in which sound and sense have approximately equal weight." In this way, the disparate images of Arp's poetry "constitute a unity of their own," as Armine Kotin wrote in *Papers on Language and Literature,* apart from their literal meanings. "It is the language-consciousness," Kotin explained, "the consistent exploitation of interrelationships on the linguistic level, that creates the sense of unity and coherence." This approach, Kotin believed, was a "prelude to the 'discovery' of concrete poetry, the importance of which as a modern poetry movement cannot be denied." "After Apollinaire (and, before Apollinaire, Mallarme)," Hausmann concluded, "Arp was incontestably one of the most important innovators in French poetry."

BIOGRAPHICAL/CRITICAL SOURCES:

BOOKS

Arp, Jean, *On My Way: Poetry and Essays, 1912-1947,* Wittenborn, Schultz, 1948.

Barr, Alfred H., Jr., *Fantastic Art, Dada, Surrealism,* [New York], 1937, Ayer, 1970.

Cathelin, Jean, *Jean Arp,* Grove, 1959.

Contemporary Literary Criticism, Volume 5, Gale, 1976.

Coutts-Smith, Kenneth, *Dada,* Dutton, 1970.

Dachy, March, *The Dada Movement,* Rizzoli International, 1990.

Fauchereau, Serge, *Hans Arp,* Rizzoli International, 1988.

Foster, Stephen C., and Rudolf E. Kuenzli, editors, *Dada Spectrum: The Dialectics of Revolt,* University of Iowa, 1979, pp. 175-205.

Foster, editor, *Dada/Dimensions,* UMI Research Press, 1985.

Giedion-Welcker, Carola, *Jean Arp,* Abrams, 1957.

Hancock, Jane, and Stefanie Poley, editors, *Arp: 1886-1966,* Cambridge University Press, 1986.

Krolow, Karl, *Aspekte zeitgenoessischer deutscher Lyrik,* Mohn (Guetersloh), 1961.

Last, Rex William, *Hans Arp: The Poet of Dadaism,* Dufour Editions, 1969.

Lemoine, Serge, *Dada,* Universe, 1987.

Lippard, Lucy R., editor, *Dadas on Art,* Prentice-Hall, 1971.

Modern Arts Criticism, Volume 1, Gale, 1991.

Motherwell, Robert, editor, *The Dada Painters and Poets: An Anthology,* Harvard University Press, 1989.

Poley, Stefanie, *Hans Arp: die Formensprache im plastischen Werk,* G. Hatje (Stuttgart), 1978.

Read, Herbert, *The Art of Jean Arp,* Abrams, 1968.

Richter, Hans, *Dada: Art and Anti-Art,* Abrams, 1965.

Rubin, William S., *Dada and Surrealist Art,* Abrams, 1968, pp. 75-81.

Rubin, William S., *Dada, Surrealism and Their Heritage,* Museum of Modern Art, 1968.

Soby, James Thrall, editor, *Arp,* Doubleday, 1958.

Soergel, Albert, *Dichtung und Dichter der Zeit,* Voigtlaender (Leipzig), 1925.

Wohl, Helmut, *Dada: Berlin, Cologne, Hannover,* ICA International, 1980.

PERIODICALS

Art Bulletin, March, 1983, pp. 122-137.

Art Digest, March 1, 1954; July 1, 1954.

Art in America, September, 1983, pp. 41-43.

Art International, May 20, 1969, pp. 17-20.

ARTNews, January, 1949, pp. 20-21; November, 1958.

Arts, November, 1958, pp. 48-51.

Books Abroad, 1962, p. 246; 1968, p. 261.

Bulletin of the Detroit Institute of Arts, Volume 61, number 4, 1984, pp. 14-21.

Choice, October, 1972.

Deutsche Rundschau, February, 1960, p. 150.

Forum, November, 1956.

German Life and Letters, 1967-68, pp. 63-64.

German Quarterly, March, 1963, pp. 152-163.

Horizon, October, 1946, pp. 232-239.

New Statesman, March 22, 1974, pp. 404-406.

New York Review of Books, May 18, 1972.

New York Times, March 7, 1954.

Papers on Language and Literature, spring, 1974.

Time, January 31, 1949, p. 37.

Times Literary Supplement, October 18, 1974; October 14, 1977.

Universitas, 1967, pp. 643-644.

OBITUARIES:

PERIODICALS

New York Times, June 8, 1966.*

—Sketch by Thomas Wiloch

* * *

ARTHUR, Kay L(ee) 1933-

PERSONAL: Born November 11, 1933, in Jackson, MI; daughter of John Edward (an Episcopal priest) and Leah

Winifred (a housewife) Lee; married Frank Thomas Goetz, Jr., July 10, 1954 (died, 1963); married Jack Arthur (president of Precept Ministries), December 17, 1965; children: (first marriage) Tom, Mark; (second marriage) David. *Education:* St. Luke's School of Nursing, R.N., 1954; attended Case Western Reserve University; Tennessee Temple Bible School, Th.G., 1965.

ADDRESSES: Home—7324 Noah Reid Rd., Chattanooga, TN 37421. *Office*—Precept Ministries, P.O. Box 23000, Chattanooga, TN 37422.

CAREER: Henry Ford Hospital, Detroit, MI, registered nurse, 1961-62; Johns Hopkins University, Baltimore, MD, registered nurse on research team, 1962-63; Diagnostic Hospital, Chattanooga, TN, registered nurse, 1964; missionary in Mexico, 1966-69; Precept Ministries, Chattanooga, co-founder and teacher, 1969—. Member of Advisory Board for Family Concerns; member of advisory board of Committee of Biblical Exposition and Southern Evangelical Seminary; member of board of directors of National Religious Broadcasters.

WRITINGS:

How Can I Live, Fleming Revell, 1981.
With An Everlasting Love, Precept Ministries, 1982.
Lord, Teach Me to Pray, Precept Ministries, 1983.
Teach Me How to Live, Fleming Revell, 1984.
Lord, I Want to Know You, Multnomah, 1984.
How Can I Be Blessed, Fleming Revell, 1985.
Lord, Heal My Hurts, Multnomah, 1988.
Lord, I Need Grace to Make It, Multnomah, 1989.
Lord, Where Are You When Bad Things Happen?, Multnomah, 1991.
Lord, Is It Warfare?: Teach Me to Stand, Multnomah, 1992.
(With others) *Spiritual Life: Questions Women Ask,* Multnomah, 1992.
The International Inductive Study Bible, Harvest House, 1992.

Also author of "Precept Upon Precept" series of Bible study courses and "In and Out" series of Bible study courses, all published by Precept Ministries. Author of "Line Upon Line" study courses for children.

SIDELIGHTS: Kay L. Arthur told *CA:* "There are two quotes found inside the cover of all of the Precept Bible studies produced at Precept Ministries. The first is from George McDonald, 'I believe that no teacher should strive to make men think as he thinks, but to lead them to the living truth, to the Master Himself, of whom alone they can learn anything, Who will make in themselves know what is true by the very seeing of it.' His quote is followed by one from me, 'This is why I have written this course.'

"George McDonald's quote expresses my motivation well. However, there is a background story that brought me to the point of taking pen in hand and beginning to write the studies that now number twenty-six

'Precept Upon Precept' courses, eighteen 'In and Out' series, and three 'Line Upon Line' courses for children.

"God moved my husband, Jack, and me to Chattanooga, Tennessee, from the mission field. It was only a little over a year before God took us to a thirty-two acre ranch which he gave us to house the ministry he had birthed after bringing us home from Mexico. Reach Out, Inc., which had begun in our living room, now had a permanent address.

"As the ministry God had entrusted to us expanded, a call from Atlanta asked us to come on a weekly basis to take over an existing Bible study where two hundred women met in the home of Grace Kinser. So, Reach Out literally began its reaching out in the fall of 1973. I had been teaching the Atlanta class for about two years when one day I began to think of the time that God might possibly lead me away from Atlanta: 'Lord, when you ask me to leave Atlanta, what will these people have besides what I've taught them? Will they be able to feed themselves from your Word? Will they be able to think for themselves . . . not as someone tells them to think? Will they be able to see truth for themselves?' As an answer to the cry of my heart on behalf of those whom I had grown to love dearly, the Lord directed me to write a Bible study using the same methods of observation, interpretation, and application I used in my study. 'Precept Upon Precept' Bible study courses were given to me as God's way of seeing that these people in Atlanta were established and that they could indeed know what was truth by the very seeing of it.

"The day did come to leave the class in Atlanta, which had grown to eighteen hundred, but left behind were the 'Precept Upon Precept' Bible study courses which were done by three thousand people the first year I left Atlanta! These courses are being used throughout the city still today—six years later! New direction came, too, as a result of leaving Atlanta. The continued writing and production of 'Precept Upon Precept' became the burden of the ministry. Reach Out became Precept Ministries. Teams began to travel throughout the United States and internationally, training people in the Precept method and teaching God's Word. Today over one hundred thousand people are students of Precept studies. The studies are currently being translated into several foreign languages.

"My deepest desire and the driving force behind the works I write is for people to be established in the Word of God and that in the establishing process of getting to know the Word, that they would get to know the God of the Word and develop a reverence for him which would be displayed in living a godly and holy life."

Arthur recently told *CA* that her "most recent vehicle to reach people and establish them in God's word is *The International Inductive Study Bible*. . . . This Bible is designed to teach anyone, anywhere, how to delve into God's word and to make the truth of it their own."

* * *

ARUEGO, Jose (Espiritu) 1932-

PERSONAL: Born August 9, 1932, in Manila, Philippines; son of Jose M. (a

lawyer) and Constancia (Espiritu) Aruego; married Ariane Dewey (an illustrator), January 27, 1961 (divorced, 1973); children: Juan. *Education:* University of the Philippines, B.A., 1953, LL.B., 1955; Parsons School of Design, Certificate in Graphic Arts and Advertising, 1959.

ADDRESSES: Home—New York, NY.

CAREER: Village Display Co., New York City, apprentice, 1959-60; Hayden Publishing Co., New York City, designer, 1960-62; Mervin & Jesse Levine (fashion advertising agency), New York City, mechanical boardman, 1963-64; Norman Associates (studio), New York City, mechanical boardman, 1964-65; Ashton B. Collins, Inc. (advertising agency), New York City, assistant art director, 1965-68; free-lance cartoonist; writer and illustrator of books for children.

AWARDS, HONORS: Outstanding picture book of the year awards from the *New York Times,* for *Juan and the Asuangs: A Tale of Philippine Ghosts and Spirits,* 1970, for *The Day They Parachuted Cats on Borneo: A Drama of Ecology,* 1971, and for *Look What I Can Do!,* 1972; *Whose Mouse Are You?,* 1970, *Milton the Early Riser,* 1972, *Mushroom in the Rain,* 1974, and *We Hide, You Seek,* 1979, were American Library Association Notable Book selections; *Look What I Can Do!,* 1972, *The Chick and the Duckling,* 1973, *A Crocodile's Tale,* 1973, and *Owliver,* 1974, were included in Children's Book Council Showcase; *A Crocodile's Tale,* 1972, *Marie Louise and Christophe,* 1974, and *Mushroom in the Rain,* 1974, were included in the American Institute of Graphic Arts' list of children's books of the year; Brooklyn Art Books for Children citations, 1973, for *Leo the Late Bloomer,* and 1974, for *Milton the Early Riser;* Horn Book honor award from *Boston Globe,* 1974, for *Herman the Helper;* Society of Illustrators citation, 1976, for *Milton the Early Riser;* Outstanding Filipino Abroad in Arts award, Philippine government, 1976; Gold Medal, Internationale Buchkunst-Ausstellung (Leipzig), 1977, for *Mushroom in the Rain.*

WRITINGS:

SELF-ILLUSTRATED CHILDREN'S BOOKS

The King and His Friends, Scribner, 1969.

Juan and the Asuangs: A Tale of Philippine Ghosts and Spirits, Scribner, 1970.

Symbiosis: A Book of Unusual Friendships, Scribner, 1970.

Pilyo the Piranha, Macmillan, 1971.

(With Ariane Aruego) *Look What I Can Do!,* Scribner, 1971.

(With A. Aruego) *A Crocodile's Tale,* Scribner, 1972.

(With Ariane Dewey) *We Hide, You Seek,* Greenwillow, 1979.

(With Dewey) *Rockabye Crocodile,* Greenwillow, 1988.

OTHER

Illustrator of numerous books, including Robert Kraus, *Whose Mouse Are You?,* Macmillan, 1970; Charlotte Pomerantz, *The Day They Parachuted Cats on Borneo: A Drama of Ecology* (play), Young Scott Books, 1971; Kraus, *Leo the Late Bloomer,* Windmill Books, 1971; Christina Rossetti, *What Is Pink?,* Macmillan, 1971; Elizabeth Coatsworth, *Good Night,* Macmillan, 1972; and Norma Farber, *Never Say Ugh to a Bug,* Greenwillow, 1979. Also illustrator of over thirty-five books with Ariane Dewey, including Natalie Savage Carlson, *Marie Louise and Christophe,* Scribner, 1974; Suteyev, *Mushroom in the Rain,* Macmillan, 1974; Kraus, *Herman the Helper,* Windmill Books, 1974; Kraus, *Owliver,* Windmill Books, 1974; David Kherdian, editor, *If Dragon Flies Made Honey: Poems,* Morrow, 1977; Mitchell Sharmat, *Gregory, the Terrible Eater,* Four Winds Press, 1980; Kraus, *Leo the Late Bloomer Takes a Bath,* Simon & Schuster, 1981; Pomerantz, *One Duck, Another Duck,* Greenwillow, 1984; Crescent Dragonwagon, *Alligator Arrived with Apples: A Potluck Alphabet Feast,* Macmillan, 1987; Raffi, *Five Little Ducks,* Crown, 1989; *Birthday Rhymes, Special Times,* selected by Bobbye S. Goldstein, Delacorte, 1991. Illustrator, with Dewey, of Windmill picture books "Puppet Pal" series, including *Milton the Early Riser Takes a Trip, Owliver the Actor Takes a Bow, Herman the Helper Lends a Hand,* and *Leo the Late Bloomer Bakes a Cake.*

Contributor of cartoons to *New Yorker, Look, Saturday Review,* and other periodicals.

SIDELIGHTS: Jose Aruego is an inventive illustrator and author whose colorful picture books have enduring appeal. Born in the Philippines, but a resident of New York City since the mid-1950s, Aruego combines humor and sensitivity in the pen-and-ink drawings of funny animals that have become his hallmark. The award-winning titles *Look What I Can Do!* and *We Hide, You Seek* are representative of his approach of presenting his stories in picture form, with little or no accompanying text. *Look What*

I Can Do! consists of twenty words, while *We Hide, You Seek* is told in three sentences. Both are co-authored by Aruego's former wife and frequent partner, Ariane Dewey, and both rely on the antics of comic-looking animals to expand and advance the simple text. Besides his own works, Aruego regularly illustrates folk tales and original stories for other authors. In all his text and illustrations, Aruego's "appeal lies in the universality of his themes, his deep understanding of human nature, and his positive outlook on life," as summarized by Ida J. Appel and Marion P. Turkish in *Language Arts.*

Aruego was born in Manila into a family of lawyers and politicians. His early interests ran not to matters of law, but to comic books and pet animals. At one time, his household included three horses; seven dogs and their puppies; half-a-dozen cats and their kittens; a yard full of chickens, roosters, and pigeons; a pond of frogs, tadpoles, and ducks; and three fat pigs. The happy times Aruego spent in the company of such animals is still apparent in his work. "One thing about my picture books," Aruego explained in the *Fourth Book of Junior Authors and Illustrators,* "they always have funny animals doing funny things. . . . Most of the characters in my books are animals. It seems no matter how I draw them they look funny." And Appel and Turkish pointed out in *Language Arts* that "Aruego creates unusual animals which have endeared themselves to children as well as adults. With a touch of magic and genius, he manages to change a commonplace theme into an object of irresistible charm."

Despite his lack of interest in legal matters, Aruego followed his father's example and earned a law degree from the University of the Philippines in 1955. Looking back on his career choice, Aruego expresses continued amazement. "I still cannot figure out why I took up law," he wrote in the *Fourth Book of Junior Authors and Illustrators.* "I guess it is because my father is a lawyer, my sister is a lawyer, and all my friends went to law school." It did not take long for Aruego to realize that he was not suited to the legal profession. He practiced law for only three months, handling one case—which he lost.

After abandoning his legal practice, Aruego moved to New York City to pursue his boyhood interest in humorous illustration. He enrolled at the Parsons School of Design, where he studied graphic arts and advertising and developed an interest in line drawing. His first job after graduating in 1959 was at a Greenwich Village studio, where he pasted feathers on angel wings of mannequins. He was laid off shortly after the Christmas season and for the next six years, he worked for advertising agencies, design studios, and magazines. But once he began selling his cartoons to magazines, such as the *Saturday Evening Post* and *Look,* he quit the world of advertising for a risky free-lance cartooning career. "Every Wednesday I would go to the cartoon editor with fifteen or sixteen drawings in hand, from which he might select one for publication," Aruego said in a biographical portrait released by Greenwillow Books. "The tension was terrible, because selling cartoons was how I made my living. But I learned a lot from the rejected work, so it wasn't wasted. The sink-or-swim experience of drawing cartoons was how I learned to make the most of a small amount of space."

By 1968 Aruego had turned most of his attention to writing and illustrating books for children. His first book, published the following year, was *The King and His Friends.* Illustrated with cartoon-like drawings in red, pink, gray and tan, *The King and His Friends* is a fantasy about a griffin and two dragons who entertain their friend King Doowah by styling themselves into decorative objects—such as a book stand, a throne, a bed. *School Library Journal* reviewer Elma Fesler dismissed the tale as "a nonstory that serves only to showcase the artistic dexterity of Mr. Aruego," but the book was successful enough to land him illustration work for other authors and to launch his own writing career.

Many of Aruego's most popular books are collaborations with his former wife Ariane Dewey. After divorcing in 1973, the couple continued their professional partnership, producing *We Hide, You Seek,* one of their enduring favorites, in 1979. Eight years in the making, the twenty-seven-word book uses the game of hide-and-seek to present a lesson in camouflage that both instructs and entertains. A clumsy rhino, joining his East African animal friends in a game of hide-and-seek, bumbles through the East African jungle, accidently flushing out the hiders by sneezing, stepping on their tails, or tripping over them. Through careful use of shape and color, Aruego and Dewey hide the animals in their natural settings in such a way that young children can still find them, and then show them clearly jumping out of hiding. "This is done in a series of double-page spreads," explained *New York Times Book Review* contributor William Cole. "First spread a scene full of animals blending with their habitation, second spread with clumsy rhino barging in and sending them fleeing." The story ends playfully with the rhino taking a turn at hiding—cleverly concealing himself in a herd of rhinos. Endpapers identify each species pictured.

The book, which has been continuously in print since 1979, has been widely praised. "It combines an invitation to develop one's powers of observation with the entertainment evolving from antic play," said a *Publishers Weekly* reviewer. "Even in scenes with the wildest unscrambling of creatures . . .the chaos is controlled," noted *Wilson Library Journal* critics Donnarae MacCann and Olga Richard, who concluded, "Aruego and Dewey have made an inspired and ingenious book."

Although he has written and illustrated more than fifty children's books, Aruego told his publisher that he is still learning his craft. "Each project teaches me something new and makes me a better artist," he stated in Greenwillow's biographical profile. "Each book brings me closer to children."

BIOGRAPHICAL/CRITICAL SOURCES:

BOOKS

Children's Literature Review, Volume 5, Gale, 1983, pp. 27-32.

Fourth Book of Junior Authors and Illustrators, H. W. Wilson, 1978, p. 15.

PERIODICALS

"Jose Aruego" (biographical profile), Greenwillow Books, c. 1986.

Junior Literary Guild, September, 1979.

Language Arts, May, 1977, pp. 585, 590.

New York Times Book Review, October 21, 1979, p. 52.

Publishers Weekly, September 17, 1979, p. 145.

School Library Journal, May, 1970, p. 57.

Wilson Library Bulletin, January, 1980, p. 325; February, 1988.*

* * *

ASHE, Arthur (Robert Jr.) 1943-1993

PERSONAL: Born July 10, 1943, in Richmond, VA; died of pneumonia, February 6, 1993, in Richmond, VA; son of Arthur Robert, Sr. (a park superintendent) and Mattie (Cunningham) Ashe; married Jeanne-Marie Moutoussamy (a photographer), February 20, 1977; children: Camera Elizabeth. *Education:* University of California, Los Angeles, B.S., 1966.

CAREER: Amateur tennis player, 1958-69; professional tennis player, 1969-80. U.S. Davis Cup Tennis Team, member, beginning 1963. Played in numerous tennis championships, including National Indoor Junior Tennis Championship, 1960 and 1961; U.S. Men's Hard Court Championship, 1963; U.S. intercollegiate championships, 1965; U.S. Men's Clay Court Championship, 1967; U.S. Amateur Title, 1968; U.S. Open Championship, 1968; Australian Open Championship, 1970; and Wimbledon Singles Championship, 1975. President of Players Enterprises, Inc., beginning in 1969; lecturer and writer. American Broadcasting Company (ABC) Sports and Home Box Office (HBO), correspondent; Le Coq Sportif, vice-president; Doral Resort and Country Club, Miami, FL, tennis director. National campaign chair, American Heart Association, 1981-82; member of board of directors, Aetna Life and Casualty; chair of advisory staff, Head Sports. *Military service:* U.S. Army, 1967-69; became first lieutenant.

AWARDS, HONORS: Named Player of the Year, Association of Tennis Profiles, 1975; inducted into the International Tennis Hall of Fame, 1985; Sportsman of the Year, *Sports Illustrated,* 1992; honorary doctorates from Princeton University, Dartmouth College, Le Moyne University, Virginia Commonwealth University, Bryant College, and Trinity University.

WRITINGS:

(With Clifford G. Gewecke, Jr.) *Advantage Ashe* (autobiography), Coward, 1967.

(With Frank Deford) *Arthur Ashe: Portrait in Motion* (autobiography), Houghton, 1975.

(With Louie Robinson, Jr.) *Getting Started in Tennis,* photographs by wife, Jeanne Moutoussamy, Atheneum, 1977.

Mastering Your Tennis Strokes, Macmillan, 1978.

(With Neil Amdur) *Off the Court* (autobiography), New American Library, 1981.

Arthur Ashe's Tennis Clinic, Simon & Schuster, 1981.

(With Kip Branch, Ocania Chalk, and Francis Harris) *A Hard Road to Glory: A History of the African-American Athlete,* 3 volumes, Warner, 1988.

(With Arnold Rampersad) *Days of Grace: A Memoir,* Knopf, 1993.

Contributor to newspapers and magazines, including the *New York Times, Tennis Magazine, Washington Post,* and *People.* Author, with Stan Smith and Vic Braden, of video "Tennis Our Way," 1986.

ADAPTATIONS: A Hard Road to Glory has been adapted for television.

SIDELIGHTS: "It's not merely because he is the only black male thus far to achieve superstardom in professional tennis that Arthur Ashe stands out from the crowd," says Jonathan Yardley in *Sports Illustrated.* "It's also because he is one of the few genuinely multidimensional individuals ever to achieve superstardom in any sport." Indeed, Ashe's life and career have provided material enough to fill a number of biographies and autobiographies. After working his way through the amateur and professional tennis circuits during the 1960s and 1970s, Ashe attained worldwide acclaim in his 1975 Wimbledon singles triumph over Jimmy Connors.

Tennis was Ashe's top priority from an early age. As the son of a playground superintendent in then-segregated Richmond, Virginia, Ashe showed promise in tennis by age seven. A few years later, he studied the game under the tutelage of Robert Walter Johnson, a black physician who dedicated himself to developing young black tennis players in an era when the sport was the bastion of upper-class whites.

In his writings, Ashe often mentioned the admiration he had for Johnson and discussed the racism black athletes encountered before the days of the civil rights movement. Although he was a top-ranked teenage player, for example, Ashe was barred from some tennis clubs when he toured. Later, as a member of the University of California, Los Angeles tennis team, Ashe alone was excluded from the team's invitation to compete at an exclusive country club tournament. But, far from openly retaliating, Ashe demonstrated a grace under pressure and a sense of self-control that he attributed to Johnson's training.

In 1979 Ashe was a member of the Davis Cup team and ranked as one of America's leading players when, after returning from a tournament, he began experiencing chest pains that culminated in a heart attack. He underwent quadruple bypass surgery and then endured a slow, but steady, recovery. While high blood pressure and heart disease run in Ashe's family, the athlete admitted that he thought himself immune to their effects. "Why should I have worried?" Ashe remarked in an interview with Judy Kessler and Allan Ripp of *People* magazine. "My blood pressure and cholesterol are low, I don't smoke or take drugs, and with all the tennis I play, I'm as physically fit as a 36-year-old man can be. People like me simply don't get heart attacks." As Ashe later explained to Richard K. Rein in *People,* "One thing I've learned is that it's not so much the heart attack that kills most people, though there are a few who die on the spot. Most people die because they deny it; they say it's indigestion or heartburn. A heart attack is not something that goes click, boom. A heart attack can occur in a few minutes or over a period of days. If we could just get people not to go through the denial stage, then we would save even more lives." The incident ended Ashe's professional tennis career, but he remained active in the sport, serving as captain of the Davis Cup team. Ashe also became campaign chairman of the American Heart Association. "There's a hell of a lot I can do," he told Kessler and Ripp in *People.* "I am a determined person. I expect to live a long time."

Ashe discovered writing as therapy after his second coronary bypass surgery in 1983, when he began *A Hard Road to Glory: A History of the African-American Athlete.* Spanning the years from 1619 to 1986, the three-volume history focuses on black athletes and their struggles to overcome prejudice as they excelled in their sport. Alex Ward in the *New York Times Book Review* relates that when Ashe began his research, "he was astounded to discover that there was only a single 'comprehensive' volume on the history of American black athletes. . . . So for the next five years [Ashe] worked to fill that void." Athletes featured include Joe Louis, Jack Johnson, Wilma Rudolph, Kenny Washington, Jackie Robinson, and Willie Mays. "The project," Ashe told the *Chicago Tribune,* "brought both sides of me, the bookish and the sports-minded, together." *A Hard Road to Glory* met with critical acclaim and earned Ashe a great number of honorary degrees from colleges and universities throughout the nation.

It is ironic that the very medical procedure that saved Ashe's life after his heart attack, a blood transfusion, would also cause his later demise. Well aware of the social stigma attached to contracting the Acquired Immune Deficiency Syndrome (AIDS) virus, Ashe kept his secret until a news reporter confronted him on April 7, 1992, for confirmation. Christopher Lehman-Haupt reports in the *New York Times* that Ashe argued vehemently for his right to privacy, but when he realized that the newspaper would not honor his request, he called a press conference to announce that he had contracted AIDS through a blood transfusion after heart surgery in 1983. Ashe was concerned about his reputation and wanted the public to know that he had contacted AIDS not through moral turpitude or irresponsible behavior but through a medical procedure. He explained in his autobiography *Days of Grace: A Memoir*: "Did I feel a sense of shame, however subdued, about having AIDS, although I was guilty of nothing in contracting it? Very little. I could not shake off completely that irrational sense of guilt . . . to recognize that it was based on nothing substantial." Ashe's reflections on his life include self-recriminations for not having done or said enough on the issues of race and racism, an examination of his shortcomings, and a reprimand to basketball superstar Earvin (Magic) Johnson for neglecting the importance of "religion and morality" in discussions on the prevention of AIDS. Equally important to Ashe during his last days were the quiet moments when he "centered down," a phrase taken from Howard Thurman, an admired theologian. During these times, Ashe cherished music, memories, contemplation on the Bible, and reading. Usually not prone to emotional exuberance, Ashe broke his usual pattern of restraint in the last chapter of his memoir, an open letter to his daughter, Camera.

Ashe, the first black man to win at Wimbledon and the first to be inducted into the International Tennis Hall of Fame, was a successful writer, lecturer, and a spokesperson for equality. Described as "the very personification of the educated gentleman-athlete" by *Contemporary Black Biography,* he was eulogized by Paul A. Witteman in *Time* as a gentle man, "a paradigm of understated reason and elegance" and "a man of fire and grace."

BIOGRAPHICAL/CRITICAL SOURCES:

BOOKS

Ashe, Arthur, and Clifford G. Gwecke, Jr., *Advantage Ashe,* Coward, 1967.
Ashe, Arthur, and Frank Deford, *Arthur Ashe: Portrait in Motion,* Houghton, 1975.
Ashe, Arthur, and Arnold Rampersad *Days of Grace: A Memoir,* Knopf, 1993.
Ashe, Arthur, and Neil Amdur, *Off the Court,* New American Library, 1981.
Contemporary Black Biography: Profiles from the International Black Community, Volume 1, Gale, 1992.
McPhee, John, *Levels of the Game,* Farrar, Straus, 1969.
Robinson, Louie, Jr., *Arthur Ashe: Tennis Champion,* Doubleday, 1970.

PERIODICALS

Chicago Tribune, November 28, 1988, p. 3.
Ebony, November, 1979.
Life, October 15, 1965.
Newsday, February 12, 1991.
Newsweek, September 7, 1964.
New Yorker, June 7, 1969; June 14, 1969; October 13, 1975.
New York Times, July, 1985.
New York Times Book Review, June 1, 1975; November 22, 1981; December 4, 1988, pp. 11, 46.
People, March 12, 1979; March 6, 1989.
Sports Illustrated, September 20, 1965; August 29, 1966.
Time, August 13, 1965; July 14, 1975.
Times Literary Supplement, July 1, 1977.
Village Voice, January 6, 1982.
Wichita Eagle, February 21, 1990.
World Tennis, December, 1980.

OBITUARIES:

PERIODICALS

New York Times, June 10, 1993, p. B2.
Time, February 15, 1993, p. 70.*

* * *

ATKINSON, Mary
See HARDWICK, Mollie

* * *

AVI
See WORTIS, Avi

AWOONOR, Kofi (Nyidevu) 1935-
(George Awoonor-Williams)

PERSONAL: Name originally George Awoonor-Williams; born March 13, 1935, in Wheta, Ghana; son of Atsu E. (a tailor) and Kosiwo (Nyidevu) Awoonor; married; children: three sons, one daughter, including Sika, Dunyo, Kalepe. *Education:* University College of Ghana, B.A., 1960; University College, London, M.A., 1970; State University of New York at Stony Brook, Ph.D., 1972. *Religion:* Ancestralist.

Avocational Interests: Politics, jazz, tennis, herbal medicine (African).

ADDRESSES: Home and office—Embassy of Ghana, SQS 111 Bloco B, Apt. 603, Brasilia, Brazil 70466. *Agent*—Harold Ober Associates, Inc., 40 East 49th St., New York, NY 10017.

CAREER: University of Ghana, Accra, lecturer and research fellow, 1960-64; Ghana Ministry of Information, Accra, director of films, 1964-67; State University of New York at Stony Brook, assistant professor of English, 1968-75; arrested for suspected subversion, charged with harboring a subversionist, served one year in prison in Ghana, 1975-76; University of Cape Coast, Cape Coast, Ghana, professor of English, beginning 1976; Ghana ambassador to Brazil in Brasilia, with accreditation to Argentina, Uruguay, Venezuela, Surinam, and Guyana, 1983—.

MEMBER: African Studies Association of America.

AWARDS, HONORS: Longmans fellow at University of London, 1967-68; Fairfield fellow; Gurrey Prize and National Book Council award, both 1979, for poetry.

WRITINGS:

(Under name George Awoonor-Williams) *Rediscovery, and Other Poems,* Northwestern University Press, 1964.
(Editor with G. Adali-Mortty) *Messages: Poems from Ghana,* Heinemann, 1970, Humanities, 1971.
Ancestral Power [and] *Lament* (plays), Heinemann, 1970.
This Earth, My Brother: An Allegorical Tale of Africa, Doubleday, 1971.
Night of My Blood (poetry), Doubleday, 1971.
Ride Me, Memory (poetry), Greenfield Review Press, 1973.
(Translator) *Guardians of the Sacred Word: Ewe Poetry,* NOK Publishers, 1974.
The Breast of the Earth: A Survey of the History, Culture, and Literature of Africa South of the Sahara, Doubleday, 1975.
The House by the Sea (poetry), Greenfield Review Press, 1978.

(Translator) *When Sorrow-Song Descends on You* (chapbook), edited by Stanley H. Barkan, Cross-Cultural Communications, 1981.

Fire in the Valley: Ewe Folktales, Nok Publishers, 1983.

The Ghana Revolution: Background Account from a Personal Perspective (essays), Oasis Publishers, 1984.

Until the Morning After: Selected Poems, 1963-1985, Greenfield Review Press, 1987.

Alien Corn (novel), Oasis Publishers, 1988.

Ghana: A Political History from Pre-European to Modern Times, Sedco Publishing, 1990.

Comes the Voyager at Last: A Tale of Return to Africa, Africa World Press, 1992.

Contributor to *Africa Report* and *Books Abroad.* Associate editor of *Transition,* 1967-68, *World View,* and *Okike.*

WORK IN PROGRESS: Notes from Prison, a personal account; *The Zambezi Flows Here,* a screenplay.

SIDELIGHTS: Noted African poet Kofi Awoonor is also an accomplished novelist, critic, and playwright, as well as Ghana's ambassador to Brazil. Interested in the language of his people, he incorporates the vernacular into much of his poetry. His first book, *Rediscovery,* was "very much an effort to move the oral poetry from which I learnt so much into perhaps a higher literary plane, even if it lost much in the process," explains Awoonor in *Contemporary Authors Autobiography Series* (*CAAS*). Jon M. Warner, writing in the *Library Journal,* notes that "his themes are soul-deep in African identity: his voice is gentle and painfully honest; and he perceives things we perhaps know but have never heard said so concisely."

Awoonor was born in the anteroom of his grandfather's hut in Wheta, Ghana, in 1935. "Childhood, as it must have been for many Africans of my generation and peasant background, was for me a time of general poverty and deprivation, even though it was relieved by the warmth of a doting extended family," writes Awoonor in an essay in *CAAS.* Raised with his mother's family, he remembers his maternal grandparents "most lovingly," and his grandmother appears in several pieces of poetry as a focus of childhood memories. As a baby, Awoonor was baptized a Presbyterian due to his father's beliefs, but was raised in traditional African towns with shrines to the thunder gods Yeve and So. He grew up hearing the native stories, war songs, and funeral dirges of his people in their own language, which later influenced his poetry. At the age of nine, Awoonor was sent away to school and boarded with a wealthy family for whom he worked as a domestic servant. The rest of his education followed a similar pattern, always boarding and learning away from home. Eventually, Awoonor's studies took him to England and the United States. "But it is Wheta, my natal village, which remains my spiritual hometown," declares Awoonor in *CAAS.*

In *This Earth, My Brother: An Allegorical Tale of Africa,* Awoonor explores the journey of one man from his native African roots into the contemporary Western world. "It is a journey not only across distances, but also across several hundred years," describes *New York Times Book Review* contributor Jan Carew. From school inspections and the King's Birthday parade to ritual circumcision and home-made gin, Awoonor's protagonist, a lawyer called Amamu, remembers growing up in West Africa. As an adult, Amamu returns to the continent and becomes disillusioned with what he sees around him. "The novel is part visionary, part realistic . . . [with] a strongly biographical element," comments a reviewer in *Choice.* The "sketches add up to a mysterious but not wholly opaque portrait of Amamu and an account of his disintegration," judges a critic in the *Times Literary Supplement.* Carew, however, writes: "The author seems intoxicated not only with life but with language. His words assault the senses and the intellect simultaneously. Images leap from the pages . . . and yet the book is serious and its message of new and positive forces emerging from the African chaos, unmistakable."

Awoonor takes a closer look at his African heritage in *The Breast of the Earth: A Survey of the History, Culture, and Literature of Africa South of the Sahara.* A collection of essays based on his lectures, *The Breast of the Earth* covers precolonial and colonial history as well as oral tradition and literature, and includes commentary on contemporary African writing. Several critics noted that Awoonor concentrates on literature—"a term which he interprets broadly and constantly relates to other concepts"—using history and culture as "backdrops," as R. Kent Rasmussen notes in the *Library Journal.* As a survey, *The Breast of the Earth* is "necessarily selective and subject to broad generalization," remarks a reviewer in *Choice,* noting that the critical commentary will please readers because of its "perceptive intelligence and wit." Writing in *Publishers Weekly,* Albert H. Johnson judges *The Breast of the Earth* to be "wide-ranging and sensitive," and Rasmussen comments that the book's "significance lies in [Awoonor's] broad, integrative approach."

Until the Morning After: Selected Poems, 1963-85, is a collection of Awoonor's poetry from his earliest published work, *Rediscovery,* through *The House by the Sea* and contains nine previously unpublished poems. He also includes a brief autobiographical appendix explaining his relationship with language and writing. *Until the Morning After* traces Awoonor's development as a poet, from his early lyrics about nature and heritage, through his "transitional" period formed by his experiences in a Ghanaian prison, to his more politically oriented, contemporary verse. The title of the volume is based on Awoonor's belief in the basic human need for freedom, and two of his later poems explain that freedom is so important that death will be postponed "until the morning after" it is finally achieved. "The selection is judicious," comments M. Tucker in *Choice,* judging that "this volume is a fine tribute to a significant . . . African poet." *World Literature Today* contributor Richard F. Bauerle concludes: "*Until the Morning After* should increase Awoonor's already large audience and further enhance his international stature."

Awoonor once wrote: "The written word came almost as if it had no forebears. So my poetry assays to restate the oral beginnings, to articulate the mysterious relation between the WORD and the magical dimensions of our cognitive world. I work with forces that are beyond me, ancestral and ritualized entities who dictate and determine all my literary endeavors. Simply put, my work takes off from the world of all our aboriginal instincts. It is for this reason that I have translated poetry from my own society, the Ewes, and sat at the feet of ancient poets whose medium is the voice and whose forum is the village square and the market place."

BIOGRAPHICAL/CRITICAL SOURCES:

BOOKS

Awoonor, Kofi, *Ghana: A Political History from Pre-European to Modern Times,* Sedco Publishing, 1990.

Contemporary Authors Autobiography Series, Volume 13, Gale, 1991.

PERIODICALS

Ariel, January, 1975.

Choice, July, 1971, p. 682; July/August, 1975, p. 690; April, 1988, p. 1253.

Library Journal, June 1, 1971, p. 1984; April 15, 1975, p. 763.

New York Times Book Review, April 2, 1972, p. 7.

Publishers Weekly, February 24, 1975, p. 110.

Times Literary Supplement, March 24, 1972, p. 325.

World Literature Today, autumn, 1988, p. 715.*

* * *

AWOONOR-WILLIAMS, George
See AWOONOR, Kofi (Nyidevu)

B

BAGG, Robert Ely 1935-

PERSONAL: Born September 21, 1935, in Orange, NJ; son of Theodore Ely (an insurance broker) and Elma Hague (an author; maiden name, White) Bagg; married Sarah Frances Robinson (a cellist and music teacher), August 24, 1957; children: Theodore Antibes Ariel, Christopher Augustus, Jonathan, Melissa, Robert Hazzard. *Education:* Amherst College, A.B., 1957; graduate study at American Academy, Rome, 1958-59, and Harvard University, 1960; University of Connecticut, M.A., 1961, Ph.D., 1965. *Politics:* Democrat. *Religion:* Atheist.

ADDRESSES: *Home*—Bagg Edge, Linseed Rd., West Hatfield, MA 01038. *Office*—Department of English, University of Massachusetts, Amherst, MA 01003.

CAREER: University of Washington, Seattle, instructor in English, 1963-65; University of Massachusetts, Amherst, assistant professor, 1965-70, associate professor, 1970-75, professor of English, 1975—, director of graduate studies in English, 1982-86, chairman of department, 1986-92. Lecturer at Smith College, 1967; National Translation Center, Austin, TX, fellow and translator in residence, 1969. Visiting associate professor, University of Texas, 1971; visiting writer, American Academy in Rome, 1980.

MEMBER: Modern Language Association of America, Phi Kappa Phi.

AWARDS, HONORS: Armstrong Poetry Prize, 1956, 1957; Glascock Poetry Prize, 1957; Simpson fellowship, 1957-58; Prix de Rome from American Academy of Arts and Letters, 1958-59; Ingram Merrill Foundation grant, 1960, 1974; National Endowment for the Arts creative writing grant, 1974; Guggenheim fellowship, 1979.

WRITINGS:

Poems, 1956-1957, Grosvenor House and Amherst Journal Record, 1957.
Madonna of the Cello (poems), Wesleyan University Press, 1961.
Liberations (three one-act plays), Spiritus Mundi Press, 1969.
(Translator) *Euripides' Hippolytos,* Oxford University Press, 1971, published as *Hippolytos,* 1992.
The Scrawny Sonnets and Other Narratives (poems), University of Illinois Press, 1973.
(Translator) Euripides, *The Bakkhai,* University of Massachusetts Press, 1978.
(Translator) Sophocles, *Oedipus the King,* University of Massachusetts Press, 1982.
The Worst Kiss (poems), Hollow Spring, 1985.
Special Occasions (poems), Hollow Spring, 1987.
Body Blows: Poems New and Selected, University of Massachusetts Press, 1988.
(Translator) Sophocles, *Women of Trachis,* produced at University of Massachusetts Rand Theater, 1993.

Also author of film *Siege of the Summer House,* 1962. Contributor to periodicals, including *Arion, Mosaic, Atlantic,* and *Boston Review.*

WORK IN PROGRESS: A novel about life in Paris, Southern France and Spain, c. 1957-58.

* * *

BAILEY, Pearl (Mae) 1918-1990

PERSONAL: Born March 29, 1918, in Newport News, VA; died of a heart attack after collapsing, August 17, 1990, in Philadelphia, PA; daughter of Joseph James (a minister) and Ella Mae Bailey; married John Randolph

Pinkett, Jr., August 31, 1948 (divorced, March, 1952); married Louis Bellson, Jr. (a jazz drummer), November 19, 1952; children: Tony Bellson, DeeDee Bellson. *Education:* Attended public schools in Philadelphia, PA; Georgetown University, bachelor's degree in theology, 1985.

CAREER: Singer, stage performer, and author, 1933-1990; vocalist with various popular bands, including Count Basie and Cootie Williams bands; made Broadway stage debut in *St. Louis Woman,* 1946, followed by *Arms in the Girl,* 1950, *Bless You All,* 1950, *House of Flowers,* 1954, and *Hello, Dolly,* 1967-69; motion pictures include *Variety Girl,* 1947, *Isn't It Romantic,* 1948, *Carmen Jones,* 1954, *That Certain Feeling,* 1955, *St. Louis Blues,* 1957, *Porgy and Bess,* 1959, *All the Fine Young Cannibals,* 1960, *The Landlord,* 1970, *Norman, Is That You?,* 1976, and *Lost Generation;* television work includes the *Pearl Bailey Show,* a musical variety program on American Broadcasting Co. (ABC-TV), 1970-71, *Pearl's Kitchen,* a cooking show, and guest appearances on several variety programs; night club entertainer in New York, Boston, Hollywood, Las Vegas, Chicago, and London; contract recording artist for Coral Records, Decca Records, and Columbia Records. Special representative, United States delegation to United Nations.

AWARDS, HONORS: Donaldson Award for most promising new performer, 1946, for *St. Louis Woman;* Entertainer of the Year Award, *Cue* magazine, and special Tony Award, both 1967, both for *Hello, Dolly;* March of Dimes Woman of the Year, 1968; U.S.O. Woman of the Year, 1969; citation from Mayor John Lindsay of New York City, 1969; Coretta Scott King Award, American Library Association, 1976, for *Duey's Tale;* honorary degree from Georgetown University, 1978; Medal of Freedom, 1988.

WRITINGS:

The Raw Pearl (autobiography), Harcourt, 1968.
Talking to Myself (autobiography), Harcourt, 1971.
Pearl's Kitchen: An Extraordinary Cookbook, Harcourt, 1973.
Duey's Tale (juvenile), Harcourt, 1975.
Hurry Up, America, and Spit, Harcourt, 1976.
Between You and Me: A Heartfelt Memoir on Learning, Loving and Living (autobiography), Doubleday, 1989.

SIDELIGHTS: Pearl Bailey's entertainment career began in 1933 when she won first prize in an amateur night contest at the Pearl Theatre in Philadelphia. She continued in vaudeville, then moved into cabarets, eventually appearing on the stage, in movies, on television, and as one of the most popular nightclub performers in the United States. Her starring role in the long-running Broadway musical *Hello, Dolly* earned her a special Tony Award and widespread critical acclaim. "For Miss Bailey this was a Broadway triumph for the history books," wrote Clive Barnes in the *New York Times.* "She took the whole musical in her hands and swung it around her neck as easily as if it were a feather boa. Her timing was exquisite, with asides tossed away as languidly as one might tap ash from a cigarette, and her singing had that deep throaty rumble that . . . is always so oddly stirring."

In 1968, Bailey published an autobiographical account of her life entitled *The Raw Pearl.* Although she expressed reservations about her skill with language in the book's foreword, writing that "this is all new to me. I don't always have the kind of words I want to express myself," many reviewers praised the book. "Pearl Bailey writes about her life the way she sings," observed a *Saturday Review* critic, "with gusto and warmth and honesty."

Following the success of *The Raw Pearl,* Bailey penned a second autobiographical account, *Talking to Myself.* According to *Publishers Weekly,* it offers "affectionate homilies laced with recollections of her life and travels during recent years." Jo Hudson acknowledged in *Black World* that the book "may be criticized from a literary standpoint as being very loosely constructed, a little off-beat, and repetitive in its message. However, if we accept Pearl as being distinctive and truly possessing a style of her own, we will accept *Talking to Myself* in like manner."

In 1978, upon accepting an honorary degree from Georgetown University in Washington, DC, Bailey surprised the audience by announcing she would enroll as a real student and work toward a college degree. After six years of attending classes, writing papers, and taking exams, the sixty-seven-year-old Bailey was awarded her bachelor's degree in theology. The event prompted the writing of her third autobiography, *Between You and Me: A Heartfelt Memoir on Learning, Loving and Living,* in which she encouraged senior citizens to pursue their lifelong dreams. She divided her book into three sections: the first describes her experiences as a college student; the second is a commentary on the breakdown of the American family; and the third recalls memorable people and experiences of her long and varied career. Praising Bailey's ability to "juggle professional and personal responsibilities," a *Publishers Weekly* reviewer commented favorably about the book and found it "buoyed by humor, compassion and a strong faith."

Bailey's fifty-seven-year musical career included volunteering her time and talents toward the goal of racial equality and harmony. She was also active in promoting research for a cure for AIDS. While in Philadelphia, visiting her two sisters and recuperating from recent knee replacement surgery, Bailey suffered a heart attack and died on August 17, 1990.

BIOGRAPHICAL/CRITICAL SOURCES:

BOOKS

Bailey, Pearl, *The Raw Pearl,* Harcourt, 1968.
Bailey, Pearl, *Talking to Myself,* Harcourt, 1971.

PERIODICALS

Black World, March, 1972.
Booklist, September 1, 1989.
Cue, January 6, 1968.
Ebony, January, 1968.
Kenyon Review, July 15, 1989.
Maclean's, August 27, 1990.
Newsweek, December 4, 1967.
New York Times, November 13, 1967; November 26, 1967.
People, September 3, 1990.
Publishers Weekly, August 23, 1971; July 28, 1989.
Saturday Review, February 22, 1969.
Time, November 24, 1967; August 27, 1990.*

* * *

BAILLIE, Allan (Stuart) 1943-

PERSONAL: Born January 29, 1943, in Prestwick, Scotland; son of Alistair (a teller) and Anne (a hotel manager; maiden name, Scott) Baillie; married Agnes Chow (a librarian), January 14, 1972; children: Lynne, Peter. *Education:* Attended University of Melbourne, 1962-63. *Politics:* Australian Labour Party. *Religion:* None.

ADDRESSES: Home—49 Prince Alfred Pde., Newport, New South Wales 2106, Australia.

CAREER: Full-time author, 1987—. *Sun-News Pictorial,* Melbourne, Australia, reporter and subeditor, 1961-64; *Middlesex Advertiser,* London, England, subeditor, 1966-67; Australian Associated Press, Sydney, Australia, subeditor, 1968-69; free-lance writer, Cambodia and Laos, 1969; *Sunday Telegraph*, Sydney, subeditor, 1970-73; *Daily Telegraph*, Sydney, subeditor, 1973-74; Australian Broadcasting Commission, Sydney, subeditor, 1974-78; *Women's Weekly*, Sydney, subeditor, 1978-80; *Sun* and *Sun-Herald*, Sydney, casual subeditor, 1980-87.

MEMBER: Australian Society of Authors.

AWARDS, HONORS: Captain Cook Literature Award, 1970, for the short story "Chuck's Town"; Warana Short Story Award, 1973, for "Empty House"; Kathleen Fidler Award, National Book League, 1982, for *Adrift*; Arts Council Special Purpose Grants, 1983, for *Riverman*, and 1984, for *Eagle Island*; Australian Children's Book Award, Book of the Year Highly Commended citation, for *Little Brother,* 1986; Arts Council Fellowship, 1988, for *China Coin;* International Board on Books for Young People Honour Diploma, 1988, for *Riverman*; CBCA Picture Book of the Year, 1989, for *Drac and Gremlin*; *Children's Literary Monthly,* Beijing, Peace and Friendship Prize for Children's Literature of the World, 1990, for "The Sorcerers"; Multicultural Children's Book Award, 1992, for *The China Coin.*

WRITINGS:

ADULT FICTION

Mask Maker, Macmillan, 1975.

CHILDREN'S FICTION

Adrift, Blackie & Son, 1983, Viking, 1992.
Little Brother, Blackie & Son, 1985, Viking, 1992.
Riverman, Blackie & Son, 1986.
Eagle Island, Blackie & Son, 1987.
Creature, Methuen, 1987.
Megan's Star, Nelson, 1988.
Drac and the Gremlin (illustrated by Jane Tanner), Viking Kestrel, 1988, Dial, 1989.
Mates, Omnibus, 1989.
Hero, Viking O'Neil, 1990.
(With Chun-Chan Yeh) *Bawshou Rescues the Sun: A Han Folktale* (illustrated by Michelle Power), Ashton, 1991, Scholastic, 1991.
The China Coin, Viking O'Neil, 1991.
Little Monster, Omnibus/Ashton, 1991.
The Boss, Ashton, 1992.
Magician, Viking O'Neil, 1993.
The Bad Guys, Omnibus, 1993.
Rebel!, Ashton, 1993.

Baillie has contributed many short stories to anthologies and magazines in Australia, Britain, the United States, and China.

A number of his books are available in Braille or on audio tape; some have also been published in Japan, South Africa, and several European countries.

WORK IN PROGRESS: Songman, a children's book.

SIDELIGHTS: Allan Baillie told *CA:* "A Cambodian refugee on the Thai border thirteen years ago got me into writing for young people and has kept me at it. I'd been to Cambodia in 1969, when life was slow and sweet, and went back in 1980 to write a novel about what Pol Pot had done to it. I figured I had to. But I couldn't. I ran around the refugee camps, asking bloody stupid questions of one-legged men, widows and kids with nightmares and came home. I tried to write a story about a holocaust that people would read, and failed. So I put it away and started to write *Adrift,* a lighter story about two children stuck on a crate in the ocean—and one of the refugee youths began to haunt me. . . .

"I had been introduced to Vethy in the camp of Khao-I-Dang by an American woman doctor a day after he had saved her life. She'd been attacked by a wounded Khmer Rouge soldier with a pair of scissors and Vethy had wrestled him to the ground. When I first saw him he was bandaging the Khmer Rouge soldier. 'Family?' he said later. 'Before or after? Before I have a father, a mother, four brothers and three sisters. Now I have a brother and a sister.' He told me how he worked in a starvation paddy, ran from an execution squad, hid in a loaded truck in Phnom Penh and crept toward the safety of Thailand.

"About half way through *Adrift* I realized that I could tell the tragedy of Cambodia through Vethy. Aim for a younger audience and there is no need to write of torture schools or kids learning games to kill kids. Build on Vethy's story, get it right and people just might read it. So *Little Brother* was written, *had* to be written. I've written several books since then, science fiction, adventure, humor, picture books, and many of them had me shoveling for that elusive kernel of truth. I've chased books in the Tasmanian wilderness, the Barrier Reef, Arnhem Land, Sulawesi and most of them have been fun to work on. Or *part* of the work has been fun.

"But until recently *Little Brother* has been the only book that absolutely demanded that it be written. Then I was researching a book in China in 1989, and I was in Beijing on the night of the Tiananmen Massacre. The book *China Coin* also *had* to be written."

* * *

BAKER, Houston A., Jr. 1943-

PERSONAL: Born March 22, 1943, in Louisville, KY; married Charlotte Pierce; children: Mark Frederick. *Education:* Howard University, B.A. (magna cum laude), 1965; University of California, Los Angeles, M.A., 1966, Ph.D., 1968; graduate study at University of Edinburgh, 1967-68.

ADDRESSES: Office—Department of English, University of Pennsylvania, Philadelphia, PA 19104.

CAREER: Howard University, Washington, DC, instructor in English, summer, 1966; Yale University, New Haven, CT, instructor, 1968-69, assistant professor of English, 1969-70; University of Virginia, Charlottesville, associate professor, 1970-73, professor of English, 1973-74, member of Center for Advanced Studies, 1970-73; University of Pennsylvania, Philadelphia, professor of English, 1974—, director of Afro-American Studies Program, 1974-77, Albert M. Greenfield Professor of Human Relations, 1982—. Distinguished visiting professor at Cornell University, 1977; visiting professor at Haverford College, 1983-85. Member of Fulbright-Hays literature screening committee, 1973-74; member of committee on scholarly worth, Howard University Press, 1973—.

MEMBER: Modern Language Association of America, College Language Association, Phi Beta Kappa, Kappa Delta Pi.

AWARDS, HONORS: Alfred Longueil Poetry Award from University of California, Los Angeles, 1966; National Phi Beta Kappa visiting scholar, 1975-76; Center for Advanced Study in the Behavioral Sciences fellow, 1977-78; Guggenheim fellow, 1978-79; National Humanities Center fellow, 1982-83; Rockefeller Minority Group fellow, 1982-83.

WRITINGS:

(Contributor) John Morton Blum, general editor, *Key Issues in the Afro-American Experience,* Harcourt, 1971.

(Editor) *Black Literature in America,* McGraw, 1971.

Long Black Song: Essays in Black American Literature and Culture, University Press of Virginia, 1972.

(Editor) *Twentieth-Century Interpretations of Native Son,* Prentice-Hall, 1972.

Singers of Daybreak: Studies in Black American Literature, Howard University Press, 1974.

A Many-Colored Coat of Dreams: The Poetry of Countee Cullen, Broadside Press, 1974.

(Contributor) *Contemporary Poets,* St. Martin's, 1975.

(Editor) *Reading Black: Essays in the Criticism of African, Caribbean, and Black American Literature,* Africana Studies and Research Center, Cornell University, 1976.

(Editor with wife, Charlotte Pierce-Baker) *Renewal: A Volume of Black Poems,* Afro-American Studies Program, University of Pennsylvania, 1977.

(Editor) *A Dark and Sudden Beauty: Two Essays in Black American Poetry by George Kent and Stephen Henderson,* Afro-American Studies Program, University of Pennsylvania, 1977.

No Matter Where You Travel, You Still Be Black (poems), Lotus Press, 1979.

The Journey Back: Issues in Black Literature and Criticism, University of Chicago Press, 1980.

Spirit Run, Lotus Press, 1981.

(Editor with Leslie Fiedler) *English Literature: Opening Up the Canon, Selected Papers from the English Institute, 1979,* English Institute, Johns Hopkins University, 1981.

(Editor) *Three American Literatures: Essays in Chicano, Native American, and Asian-American Literature for Teachers of "American" Literature,* Modern Language Association of America, 1982.

(Editor and author of introduction) *Narrative of the Life of Frederick Douglass, an American Slave, Written by Himself,* Penguin Books, 1982.
Blues, Ideology, and Afro-American Literature: A Vernacular Theory, University of Chicago Press, 1984.
Blues Journeys Home, Lotus, 1985.
(Editor with Joe Weixlmann) *Belief versus Theory in Black American Literary Criticism,* Penkevill, 1985.
Modernism and the Harlem Renaissance, University of Chicago Press, 1987.
Afro-American Poetics: Revisions of Harlem & the Black Aesthetic, University of Wisconsin Press, 1988.
(Editor with Patricia Redmond) *Afro-American Literary Study in the 1990s,* University of Chicago Press, 1989.
(With Redmond and Elizabeth Alexander) *Workings of the Spirit: The Poetics of Afro-American Women's Writing,* University of Chicago Press, 1990.

Also contributor of about twenty articles and reviews to literature and black studies journals, including *Victorian Poetry, Phylon, Black World, Callaloo, Obsidian, Poetics Today, Yale Review,* and *Journal of African-Afro-American Affairs.* Advisory editor of *Columbia Literary History of the United States,* Columbia University Press. Member of advisory boards of *Maji,* 1974-76, *Black American Literature Forum,* 1976—, and *Minority Voices,* 1977—.

BIOGRAPHICAL/CRITICAL SOURCES:

PERIODICALS

Journal of American History, June, 1991.
Los Angeles Times Book Review, December 16, 1984.
New York Times Book Review, May 11, 1986; March, 22, 1987; October 4, 1987; January 24, 1988; April 2, 1989.
Washington Post Book World, January 3, 1988; February 5, 1989.

* * *

BAKEWELL, K(enneth) G(raham) B(artlett) 1931-

PERSONAL: Born July 13, 1931, in Dudley, Worcestershire, England; son of James Arthur and Mabel (Bartlett) Bakewell; married Agnes Lawson (a librarian), June 9, 1956; children: Linda Carol, June Christine. *Education:* Queen's University of Belfast, Northern Ireland, M.A., 1972. *Religion:* Christian.

Avocational Interests: Information retrieval, management, theatre, cinema, travel (Scandinavia, Germany, Brazil, Chile, Peru).

ADDRESSES: Home—9 Greenacre Rd., Liverpool L25 0LD, England. *Office*—Liverpool Business School, Liverpool John Moorer University, 98 Mount Pleasant, Liverpool L3 5UZ, England.

CAREER: Worked in public and special libraries in England, 1947-66; Liverpool John Moorer University, Liverpool, England, lecturer, 1966-69, senior lecturer, 1969-78, principal lecturer in librarianship, 1978-91, professor of information and library management, 1991—. Chairman of British Standards Institution Committees on Indexing Alphabetical Arrangement and Documentation Terminology; vice-president of Librarians' Christian Fellowship.

MEMBER: International Society for Knowledge Organization, Institute of Management, Library Association (fellow), Society of Indexers (chairman, 1976-79; president, 1987-91), Institute of Information Scientists.

AWARDS, HONORS: Wheatley Medal, Library Association, 1979, for index to *Anglo-American Cataloguing Rules,* 2nd edition; Carey Award, Society of Indexers, 1991, for services to indexing and the Society.

WRITINGS:

How to Find Out: Management and Productivity, Pergamon, 1966, 2nd edition, 1970.
(Editor) *Classification for Information Retrieval,* Bingley, 1968.
(Editor) *Library and Information Services for Management,* Bingley, 1968.
Industrial Libraries throughout the World, Pergamon, 1969.
A Manual of Cataloguing Practice, Pergamon, 1972.
Management Principles and Practice: A Guide to Information Sources, Gale, 1977.
Classification and Indexing Practice, Bingley, 1978.
(With J. M. Bibby, E. J. Hunter, and V. de P. Roper) *A Study of Indexers' Reactions to the PRECIS Indexing System,* Department of Library and Information Studies, Liverpool Polytechnic, 1978.
(With Hunter) *Cataloguing,* Bingley, 1979, 3rd edition, 1991.
(With K. D. C. Vernon, V. Lang, and D. A. Cotton) *The London Classification of Business Studies,* 2nd edition, Aslib, 1979.
(With G. M. Dare) *The Manager's Guide to Getting the Answers,* Library Association, 1980.
How to Organise Information, Gower, 1984.
(With Roper) *Business Information Services in Public Libraries,* School of Librarianship and Information Studies, Liverpool Polytechnic, 1984.
Business Information and the Public Library, Gower, 1986.
Managing User-Centred Libraries and Information Services, Mansell Publishing, 1990.

Also author of index to 2nd edition of *Anglo-American Cataloguing Rules.* Editor, *Library Management.* Contributor to periodicals, including *Library Management, Catalogue and Index, Education Libraries Bulletin, Indexer, Journal of Documentation, Library Association Record,* and *Library Resources and Technical Services.*

WORK IN PROGRESS: Research into management methods in libraries, with particular reference to their impact on users; public library provision of business information services and their use.

SIDELIGHTS: K. G. B. Bakewell's reference books have received high praise from reviewers for their thoroughness and readability. A reviewer for *Teacher in Commerce* described *How to Organise Information* as "a very unusual and worthwhile reference book." He added, "And I don't suppose the Komityet Gosudarstvyennoy Byezopaznosti existed when the author's parents chose his initials." About *Business Information and the Public Library,* Malcolm Stacey observed in *Public Library Journal,* "The specialists will be grateful to Ken Bakewell for presenting their interests in such a satisfying way," while Lawrence Tagg noted in *Business Information Review* that "Bakewell has written with authority and obvious enthusiasm for the subject." John Blunden-Ellis stated in the *Library Association Record* that the merit of *Managing User-Centred Libraries and Information Services* "as a teaching aid and in exploring topics for research is substantial."

Bakewell told *CA:* "I began writing because of the problem of teaching with out-of-date or otherwise unsatisfactory textbooks. My original teaching interest was classification, cataloguing, and indexing, and I have been stimulated by the contributions of a number of writers and innovators including S. R. Ranganathan, H. E. Bliss, J. Mills, D. J. Foskett, C. D. Needham, Seymour Lubetzky, and Derek Austin. My main teaching area now is library management but I retain my interest in indexing. Writing and research are pleasurable pastimes for me, but I also enjoy reading purely for recreation—especially Graham Greene and Douglas Adams. I take my Christianity very seriously, being actively involved in my local church and vice-president of the Librarians' Christian Fellowship."

BIOGRAPHICAL/CRITICAL SOURCES:

PERIODICALS

Business Information Review, April, 1987.
Library Association Record, August, 1978; October, 1990.
Library Quarterly, January, 1973.
Personnel Psychology, summer, 1978.
Public Library Journal, July/August, 1987.
Teacher in Commerce, winter, 1985.
Times Literary Supplement, May 18, 1967.

BARDI, Pietro Maria 1900-

PERSONAL: Born February 21, 1900, in La Spezia, Italy; son of Pasquale (a merchant) and Elisa (Viggiani) Bardi; married Lina Bo (an architect). *Religion:* Roman Catholic.

ADDRESSES: *Home*—Rua General Moura 200, Morumby, Sao Paulo, Brazil. *Office*—Museu de Arte de Sao Paulo, Caixa Postal 6789, Sao Paulo, Brazil.

CAREER: Museu de Arte de Sao Paulo, Sao Paulo, Brazil, co-founder (with Assis Chateaubriand) and director, 1947-90, President of Honor, 1990—; Instituto Lina Bo e P. M. Bardi, Sao Paulo, co-founder with wife.

WRITINGS:

Carra e soffici, Galleria Bardi, 1930.
Emilio Gola, Istituto Nazionale l'Unione Cinematografica Educativa, 1930.
Rapporto sull architettura, Critica Fascista, 1931.
Un fascista nel pacsc dei soviet, Quadrante, 1933.
Belvedere dell architettura italiana, Quadrante, 1933.
Federico Faruffini, Istituto Nazionale l'Unione Cinematografica Educativa, 1934.
La Prima veto di So it dro Botticelli, Bompiani, 1948.
(Editor) *Ernesto de Fiori,* Hoepli, 1950.
Lasar Segail, 1891-1957, Museu de Arte de Sao Paulo, 1952.
The Arts in Brazil: A New Museum at Sao Paulo, Abrams, 1956.
Pequena Historia da Arte: Introducao ao estudo das Artes Plasticas, Edicoes Melhoramentos, 1958, 2nd edition, 1990.
(Editor) Marino Marini, *Graphic Work and Paintings,* Abrams, 1960.
A Colorslide Tour of the Museum of Art of Sao Paulo, Brazil, Abrams, 1961.
Museu de Arte de Sao Paulo (title means "Museum of Art of Sao Paulo"), Editora Codex, 1968.
Berco Udler: meninos, namorados, morte (title means "Berco Udler: Boys, Lovers, Death"), Kosmos, 1969.
L'opera completa di Velazquez (title means "Velazquez's Complete Works"), Rizzoli, 1969.
New Brazilian Art, Praeger, 1970, published in the Netherlands as *Profile of the New Brazilian Art,* Kosmos, 1970.
Museu de arte de Sao Paulo "Assis Chateaubriand" (title means "Museum of Art of Sao Paulo 'Assis Chateaubriand' "), Graficos Brunner, 1973.
Historia da arte brasileira: pintura, escultura, arquitetura, outras artes (title means "History of Brazilian Art: Painting, Sculpture, Architecture, and Other Types of Art"), Edicoes Melhoramentos, 1975.
Maria Auxiliadora da Silva, Giulio Bolaffi Editore, 1977.
O modernismo no Brasil, Sudameris, 1978.

Arte da prata no Brasil, Sudameris, 1979.
Arte da ceramica no Brasil, Sudameris, 1980.
Mestres, artifices, oficiais e aprendizes no Brasil, Sudameris, 1981.
Contribuicao dos italianos na arquitetura brasileira, Fiat do Brasil, 1981.
A madeira, do Pau-Brasil ate a celulose, Sudameris, 1982.
A cultura nacional e a presenca do Museu de Arte de Sao Paulo, Fiat do Brasil, 1982.
Sodalicio com Assis Chateaubriand, Museu de Arte de Sao Paulo, 1982.
Lembranca do tre deferro, Sudameris, 1983.
Comunicacao: noticias de cabral a informatica, Sudameris, 1984.
Lembranca de Le Corbusier, Atenas, Italia, Brasil, Sudameris, 1984.
Engenharia e arquitetura no construcao, Sudameris, 1985.
Excursao ao territorio do design, Sudameris, 1986.
40 anos de Museu de Arte de Sao Paulo, Crefisul, 1986.
Em torno da fotografia no Brasil, Sudameris, 1987.
O ouro no Brasil, Sudameris, 1988.
Em torno da escultura no Brasil, Sudameris, 1989.
Historia do Museu de Arte de Sao Paulo, Quadrante, 1992.

IN ENGLISH TRANSLATION

(Editor) *16 Dipinti di Giorgio Morandi,* Il Milione, 1957, translation published as *Sixteen Paintings of Giorgio Morandi,* Edizioni del Milione, 1957.
I giardini tropicali di Burle Marx, G. G. Goerlich, 1964, translation published as *The Tropical Gardens of Burle Marx,* Reinhold, 1964.
Viaggio nell architettura, Rizzoli, 1972, translation published as *Architecture: The World We Build,* F. Watts, 1972.

OTHER

Also author of *Quindici pittori inglesi,* Studio de'Arte Palma; also author of exhibition catalogues. Editor of *Belvedere,* 1928-30, *Quadrante,* 1931-33, *Habitat,* 1950-53, and *Mirante das Artes,* 1967-68.

WORK IN PROGRESS: Arte Brasileira: colorama.

SIDELIGHTS: Pietro Maria Bardi co-founded the Museu de Arte de Sao Paulo in 1947 and served as the museum's director until 1990, at which time he became President of Honor of the institution. The museum houses a collection of Brazilian and European art, including works of the Impressionists and the Italian, Spanish, and Flemish Schools. After his retirement Bardi and his wife co-founded the Instituto Lina Bo e P. M. Bardi, which was designed to promote and support projects in the Brazilian cultural field.

[Sketch reviewed by Eugenia Gorini Esmeraldo.]

BARR, Jene
See COHEN, Jene Barr

* * *

BEASLEY, Maurine 1936-

PERSONAL: Born January 28, 1936, in Sedalia, MO; daughter of Dimmitt H. (a judge) and Maurine (Hieronymus) Hoffman; married Henry R. Beasley (director of Office of International Relations, National Marine Fisheries Service), December 24, 1970; children: Susan Sook. *Education:* University of Missouri, B.J. and B.A., both 1958; Columbia University, M.S., 1963; George Washington University, Ph.D., 1974.

ADDRESSES: Home—4920 Flint Dr., Bethesda, MD 20816. *Office*—College of Journalism, University of Maryland, College Park, MD 20742.

CAREER: Kansas City Star, Kansas City, MO, reporter, 1959-62; *Washington Post,* Washington, DC, reporter, 1963-73; University of Maryland, College Park, assistant professor, 1975-80, associate professor, 1980-87, professor of journalism, 1987—.

MEMBER: Association for Education in Journalism and Mass Communication (president, 1993-94), American Journalism Historians Association, American Newswomen's Club, Women in Communications, Society of Professional Journalists, Phi Beta Kappa.

AWARDS, HONORS: Named outstanding teacher of reporting by Modern Media Institute, 1981; named outstanding woman of College Park campus of University of Maryland, 1983.

WRITINGS:

(With Sheila Gibbons) *Women in Media: A Documentary Source Book,* Women's Institute for Freedom of the Press, 1977.
(With Richard Harlow) *Voices of Change: Southern Pulitzer Winners,* University Press of America, 1979.
(Editor with Richard Lowitt) *One Third of a Nation: Lorena Hickok Reports on the Great Depression,* University of Illinois Press, 1981.
The White House Press Conferences of Eleanor Roosevelt, Garland Publishing, 1983.
Eleanor Roosevelt and the Media: A Public Quest for Self-Fulfillment, University of Illinois Press, 1987.
(With Kathryn Thesus) *The New Majority: A Look at What the Preponderance of Women in Journalism Education Means to the Schools and the Professions,* University Press of America, 1988.
(With Gibbons) *Taking Their Place: A Documentary History of Women and Journalism,* American University Press, 1993.

SIDELIGHTS: As investigator to Harry Hopkins (federal administrator of emergency relief under President Franklin Roosevelt), Lorena Hickok toured the United States from 1933 to 1935 to discover firsthand how Americans were faring during the Great Depression. *One Third of a Nation,* which Maurine Beasley co-edited, is a collection of Hickok's reports from that tour. "Hickok's U.S.A. is real and sad. Characters are individual people, not faceless statistics," observes Peter Kovler in the *Washington Post.* "Her work has profound meaning," he adds, for it offers the "needed reminder that there are real people who are 'ill-housed, ill-clad, ill-nourished.' "

Beasley recently told *CA:* "Society has discounted, misinterpreted and ignored the roles of women journalists in producing the reality of their times. They have not been taken seriously as elements in the communications process that has identified the American experience. Therefore, women in journalism/mass communications have no useable past. I want to dedicate myself to helping remedy this lack. Women journalists need to know their story. So does society at large. My work on Eleanor Roosevelt has shown me how vital it is for women to utilize the media to develop their own picture of the world around them."

BIOGRAPHICAL/CRITICAL SOURCES:

PERIODICALS

Washington Post, July 7, 1981; March 23, 1984.

* * *

BEHR, Edward (Samuel) 1926-

PERSONAL: Born May 7, 1926, in Paris, France; son of Felix and Eugenia (Kadinski) Behr; married Christiane Wagrez, April 1, 1967. *Education:* Magdalene College, Cambridge, B.A., 1951, M.A., 1953.

Avocational Interests: Travel, historical research, swimming.

ADDRESSES: Home—86 Rue de Monceau, Paris 75008, France. *Office*—*Newsweek,* 162 Faubourg St. Honore, Paris 75008, France.

CAREER: Reuters (news agency), correspondent in London, England, and Paris, France, 1950-54; European Coal and Steel Community, Luxembourg, information officer, 1955-56; Time Inc., correspondent in Paris, the Middle East, and India, 1957-63; *Saturday Evening Post,* contributing editor, 1963-65; French news-in-depth television program, *Cinq Colonnes a la Une,* reporter-director, 1963-65; *Newsweek,* Paris correspondent, 1965-66, Hong Kong bureau chief, 1966-68, Paris bureau chief, 1968-72, European editor, Paris, 1973-83, cultural editor, 1984-87, contributing editor, 1987—. Frequent contributor to the British Broadcasting Corporation (radio and television). *Military service:* Indian Army, Royal Garhwal Rifles, 1944-48; became acting major.

MEMBER: Oriental Club, Groucho Club (London), Royal Automobile Club.

AWARDS, HONORS: Gutenberg Prize, 1988; Emmy nomination, Academy of Television Arts and Sciences, 1992, for *The Rise and Fall of Ceausescu.*

WRITINGS:

The Algerian Problem, Norton, 1961, Greenwood Press, 1976.

(Translator, adapter, and editor with Sydney Liu) Lai Ying, *The Thirty-Sixth Way: A Personal Account of Imprisonment and Escape from Red China,* Doubleday, 1969.

Bearings: A Foreign Correspondent's Life behind the Lines, Viking, 1978 (published in England as *Anyone Here Been Raped and Speaks English?,* Hamish Hamilton, 1981).

Getting Even (novel), Harper, 1980.

(With Bob Swaim) *Half Moon Street* (screenplay; based on the novella *Doctor Slaughter* by Paul Theroux), Twentieth Century-Fox, 1986.

The Last Emperor (novelization of the film), Bantam, 1987.

Hirohito: Behind the Myth (biography), Random House, 1989.

The Complete Book of Les Miserables, Arcade Publishing, 1990.

(With Mark Steyn) *The Story of Miss Saigon,* Arcade Publishing, 1991.

Kiss the Hand You Cannot Bite: The Rise and Fall of the Ceausescus, Random House, 1991.

The Good Frenchman: The True Story of the Life and Times of Maurice Chevalier, Random House, 1993.

Also author of *Indonesia: A Voyage through the Archipelago,* 1990.

OTHER

(Correspondent) *The Rise and Fall of Ceausescu,* Public Broadcasting System, July 2, 1992.

The Last Emperor was translated into Japanese.

SIDELIGHTS: Edward Behr's career as a news correspondent for Reuters, *Time,* and *Newsweek* has carried him around the world, covering events—usually wars—in such locales as India, Algeria, Indonesia, China, and Vietnam. He has detailed some of his adventures and anecdotes in the collection *Bearings: A Foreign Correspondent's Life behind the Lines,* published in England under the curious title, *Anyone Here Been Raped and Speaks English?*

Behr recalls his memoirs in a conspiratorial tone, almost like gossip; by doing so, a reviewer for the *New Yorker* notes, Behr "plainly dissociates himself from his more pompous colleagues." Unfortunately, this also gives the book an air of cattiness; Tony Samstag explains in the London *Times:* "[Behr] displays an unattractive tendency to bear grudges and to pay off old scores wherever possible. . . . As one colleague after another is found wanting, each finely judged aside seems a little more tedious than the last." Most critics, however, consider *Anyone Here Been Raped and Speaks English?* to be a pleasant and amusing look at reporters and reporting; James Cameron, writing in *Spectator,* proclaims: "The one thing wrong with it is that its silly and vulgar title does no justice to one of the best journalistic books there has been as far as I can remember."

In 1988 Behr was given the opportunity to write the biographical tie-in to Bernardo Bertolucci's film *The Last Emperor.* Unlike novelizations, which are often simply prose-renderings of the screenplay, Behr's book is a well-documented biography of China's last emperor, Pu Yi, who ascended to his throne at the age of three. In order to write *The Last Emperor,* Behr was allowed to use the same materials compiled by the authors of the screenplay, as well as any research he conducted on his own. Reviewing the book for the *New York Times Book Review,* Malcolm Bosse admits *The Last Emperor* "is an acknowledged spinoff from the movie, yet it shows none of the haste and carelessness often associated with that kind of writing," pointing out how Behr "ranges knowledgeably among the intricacies of Pu Yi's life."

The success of *The Last Emperor* led Behr to compose *Hirohito: Behind the Myth.* In contrast to the tragic Pu Yi, Japan's Emperor Hirohito is depicted as a shrewd and ruthless manipulator—a very different picture than that of the benevolent, near-powerless monarch, as painted by Japanese and U.S. politicians in the years following World War II. *Los Angeles Times* reviewer Jonathan Kirsch tells how Behr's book "points out that history has been kind, perhaps too kind, to the Japanese emperor, and . . . suggests that Hirohito must bear some blame for Japanese militarism and expansionism in the 1930s and '40s." While Kirsch describes Behr as "an accomplished popular historian with a gift for telling a tale," he admits that much of his case against Hirohito is built on circumstantial evidence; this shortcoming is also identified by John W. Dower, who complains in the *New York Times Book Review:* "[Behr's] sources on the whole are thin and sometimes unreliable. His footnotes are casual to the point of being almost worthless. He exaggerates and makes mistakes of fact as well as of inference." This is not a fatal flaw, however, for Dower continues by saying "Mr. Behr . . . has the virtue of being an intelligent observer traveling across a landscape old to others but new to him, and seeing things with fresh eyes." Kirsch, too, concludes by saying: "Even if Behr's arguments must be regarded with caution, I came away from *Hirohito* with the sense that a curtain had been drawn aside, and an inner chamber of history had been revealed to our gaze."

BIOGRAPHICAL/CRITICAL SOURCES:

PERIODICALS

Business Week, December 25, 1978, p. 10.
Christian Science Monitor, March 12, 1979, p. 82; September 12, 1991, p. 13.
Economist, January 24, 1981, p. 107; July 24, 1982, p. 83; July 22, 1989, p. 77.
Globe and Mail (Toronto), July 6, 1991, p. C8.
Guardian Weekly, February 8, 1981, p. 20; March 31, 1991, p. 26.
Listener, January 1, 1981, p. 23; January 22, 1981, p. 117.
Los Angeles Times, November 19, 1978.
Los Angeles Times Book Review, July 14, 1991, p. 4.
Newsweek, January 5, 1981, p. 56.
New Yorker, January 8, 1979, p. 78.
New York Review of Books, February 18, 1988, p. 14; October 26, 1989, p. 31.
New York Times Book Review, January 18, 1981, p. 29; February 28, 1988, p. 22; October 8, 1989, p. 8; July 28, 1991, p. 24.
Observer, September 21, 1980, p. 29; January 25, 1981, p. 29; March 21, 1982, p. 30; April 30, 1989, p. 46; April 14, 1991, p. 62.
Spectator, November 28, 1981, p. 19; April 27, 1991, p. 27.
Times (London), January 29, 1981; May 4, 1991, p. 26.
Times Educational Supplement, June 30, 1989, p. 28; December 21, 1990, p. 18.
Times Literary Supplement, October 3, 1980, p. 1087; May 24, 1991, p. 13.
Virginia Quarterly Review, winter, 1991, p. 33.
Wall Street Journal, July 26, 1991, p. A7.
Washington Monthly, October, 1978, p. 59.

* * *

BEINER, Ronald 1953-

PERSONAL: Born May 22, 1953, in Montreal, Quebec, Canada; son of David (a dress cutter) and Sarah (Fisher) Beiner; married Ann Hodsdon, July 2, 1983 (separated); children: Zimra; stepchildren: Marcus, Mia. *Education:* McGill University, B.A., 1975; Balliol College, Oxford, D.Phil., 1980.

ADDRESSES: Home—262 Concord Ave., Toronto, Ontario, Canada M6H 2P5. *Office*—Department of Political

Science, University of Toronto, 100 St. George St., Toronto, Ontario, Canada M5S 1A1.

CAREER: University of Southampton, Southampton, England, lecturer in politics, 1978-83; Queen's University, Kingston, Ontario, assistant professor of philosophy and Webster Fellow in the Humanities, 1983-84; University of Toronto, Toronto, Ontario, assistant professor, 1984-85, associate professor, 1985-90, professor of political science, 1990—.

WRITINGS:

(Editor) Hannah Arendt, *Lectures on Kant's Political Philosophy,* University of Chicago Press, 1982.
Political Judgment, University of Chicago Press, 1983.
(Co-editor) *Democratic Theory and Technological Society,* M. E. Sharpe, 1988.
What's the Matter with Liberalism?, University of California Press, 1992.
(Co-editor) *The Starry Heavens and the Moral Law: Kant's Legacy for Political Philosophy,* Yale University Press, 1993.

Some of Beiner's work has been translated into German, Japanese, Italian, French, and Spanish.

SIDELIGHTS: In *Political Judgment* Ronald Beiner explores the concept of judgment and, on the basis of the conclusions he reaches, sketches the outline of a political philosophy. He challenges the modern trend to delegate judgments on the issues of political life to "experts and technocrats," seeking instead, according to *Times Literary Supplement* reviewer Jeremy Waldron, to instill confidence in "the competence of ordinary men and women" to make political judgments. In the process of exploring an alternate theory of political judgment, Beiner examines the philosophies of Aristotle and Kant and, asserts Waldron, "outlines clearly and precisely the contrasting ways in which this material has been digested by those modern writers whose approach to politics Beiner sees as most consonant with his own—Hannah Arendt, Hans-Georg Gadamer, and Juergen Habermas." Waldron criticizes the author's "attempt to formulate insights of his own" but praises *Political Judgment* for its "scholarly vigour."

New York Times Book Review contributor Michael J. Sandel notes Beiner's recommendation of "a synthesis of Kant and Aristotle" which would "include the best of both—detachment and commitment, universality and particularity." Sandel faults Beiner's lack of specific suggestions to "transform spectator-citizens into judging citizens," yet lauds *Political Judgment* for its "valuable critique of prevailing instrumental views of politics."

Ronald Beiner told *CA:* "In recent years I have devoted my energies to a critique of liberalism, understood as the 'official philosophy' of liberal society, a society defined primarily in terms of individual rights and liberties. This has involved criticism of influential liberal philosophers like John Rawls, Ronald Dworkin, and Bruce Ackerman, as well as moral and cultural criticism of the practices of contemporary liberal society. This has issued in a new book of mine, entitled *What's the Matter with Liberalism?,* published by the University of California Press."

BIOGRAPHICAL/CRITICAL SOURCES:

PERIODICALS

Globe & Mail (Toronto), October 24, 1992, p. C20.
New York Times Book Review, August 19, 1984, p. 16.
Times Literary Supplement, April 27, 1984.

* * *

BENNETT, Jay 1912-

PERSONAL: Born December 24, 1912, in New York, NY; son of Pincus Shapiro (a businessman) and Estelle Bennett; married Sally Stern, February 2, 1937; children: Steven Cullen, Randy Elliott. *Education:* Attended New York University.

ADDRESSES: Home—64 Greensward, Cherry Hill, NJ 08002.

CAREER: Writer, 1930—. Worked as a farmhand, factory worker, lifeguard, mailman, salesman, and other various occupations. Scriptwriter for radio and television dramas during 1940s and 1950s. *Wartime service:* U.S. Office of War Information, English features writer and editor, 1942-45.

MEMBER: Mystery Writers of America, Authors League of America, Writers Guild, Dramatists Guild (life member).

AWARDS, HONORS: Edgar Allan Poe Award for best juvenile mystery novel, Mystery Writers of America, 1974, for *The Long Black Coat,* and 1975, for *The Dangling Witness;* Variety Award for television script for *Monodrama Theatre;* Shakespeare Society award for television adaptation of *Hamlet.*

WRITINGS:

Catacombs, Abelard-Schuman, 1959.
Murder Money, Fawcett, 1963.
Death Is a Silent Room, Abelard-Schuman, 1965.
Shadows Offstage, Nelson, 1974.

YOUNG ADULT MYSTERIES

Deathman, Do Not Follow Me, Meredith Press, 1968.
The Deadly Gift, Meredith Press, 1969.
Masks: A Love Story, F. Watts, 1971.
The Killing Tree, F. Watts, 1972.

The Long Black Coat, Delacorte, 1973.
The Dangling Witness, Delacorte, 1974.
Say Hello to the Hit Man, Delacorte, 1976.
The Birthday Murderer, Delacorte, 1977.
The Pigeon, Methuen, 1980.
The Executioner, Avon, 1982.
Slowly, Slowly I Raise the Gun, Avon, 1983.
I Never Said I Loved You, Avon, 1984.
To Be a Killer, Scholastic, Inc., 1985.
The Skeleton Man, F. Watts, 1986.
The Haunted One, F. Watts, 1987.
The Dark Corridor, F. Watts, 1988.
Sing Me a Death Song, F. Watts, 1990.
Coverup, F. Watts, 1991.
Skinhead, F. Watts, 1991.
Hooded Man, Fawcett-Juniper, 1993.
Death Grip, Fawcett-Juniper, 1993.

PLAYS

No Hiding Place (three-act), produced in New York, 1949.
Lions after Slumber (three-act), produced in London, 1951.

OTHER

Also author of numerous radio scripts, including *Miracle before Christmas* and *The Wind and Stars Are Witness;* author of television scripts for *Alfred Hitchcock Presents, Harlem Detective, Crime Syndicated, Wide, Wide World, Cameo Theater,* and *Monodrama Theater.* Senior editor of encyclopedias for Grolier Education Corp., c. 1960.

ADAPTATIONS: One of Bennett's novels for adults was adapted as a film produced by Warner Brothers.

WORK IN PROGRESS: Another young adult suspense mystery.

SIDELIGHTS: Jay Bennett's suspense stories for young adults have sold over four million copies in some sixteen languages, and his work for young readers has twice been honored with the prestigious Edgar Allan Poe Award. Called the "master of short sentences" by a *School Library Journal* reviewer, Bennett writes about violent, life-threatening situations from the point of view of the potential victims. Readers suffer and triumph along with the author's lonely heroes who pit themselves against organized crime, deadly racists, and—especially—sinister adults who seem harmless on the surface. *New York Times Book Review* editor George A. Woods notes that in a Bennett mystery "victims have real blood, not catchup, and the screams aren't caused by the rocking chair coming down on the cat's tail."

"I speak to the loner in our society," Bennett explained in an essay in *Something about the Author Autobiography Series* (*SAAS*). "There are so many loners, especially among the young and I say to them in my novels, You cannot make it alone, you have to reach out and embrace another human being and human values. There is no other way, or you are lost." Bennett is compelled to write out of a fierce passion against life's injustices, a sense that young people are sometimes burdened with guilt or placed in great danger by the actions of their elders. His books go beyond the standard murder mystery in an exploration of crises of conscience, psychological traumas, and bitter confrontations between parents and children. In *Voice of Youth Advocates,* Mary K. Chelton calls the average Bennett book "a satisfying read on a complicated topic" and praises the author for his ability to evoke mood and plot "with an absolute minimum of description."

"All through my years I have been intensely interested in the young and their problems and hopes. Their dreams and despairs," Bennett notes in *SAAS.* "My wife still calls me a child who will never grow up and in one sense she's absolutely right. And that's why it's so easy for me to write my books for that readership. But there's more to it than that. I feel very strongly that it's up to the young to help turn things around. We can't go on much longer the way we are."

BIOGRAPHICAL/CRITICAL SOURCES:

BOOKS

Contemporary Literary Criticism, Volume 35, Gale, 1985, pp. 52-53.
Donelson, Kenneth L., and Aleen Pace Nilsen, *Literature for Today's Young Adults,* Scott, Foresman, 1980, pp. 228-257.
Something about the Author Autobiography Series, Volume 4, Gale, 1987, pp. 75-91.

PERIODICALS

Best Sellers, January, 1981, p. 349.
English Journal, February, 1969, pp. 295-296; April, 1970, p. 591.
Kirkus Reviews, April 1, 1973, p. 395.
New York Times Book Review, August 22, 1965; July 7, 1968, p. 16; November 10, 1974, pp. 8, 10; May 2, 1976, p. 38.
Publishers Weekly, May 7, 1973, p. 65; June 3, 1974, p. 157; August 12, 1974, p. 58; August 22, 1977, p. 66; July 1, 1983, p. 103; September 27, 1985, p. 97; October 28, 1988, p. 83.
School Library Journal, May, 1970, p. 92; May, 1974, p. 69; May, 1976, p. 77; May, 1980, p. 86; May, 1982, p. 84; December, 1983, p. 84; August, 1984, p. 80; October, 1986, pp. 185-186; November, 1987, p. 112; April, 1990, p. 139; May, 1991, p. 108; August, 1991, p. 195.
Times Literary Supplement, August 19, 1988.

Voice of Youth Advocates, August, 1982, p. 28; February, 1984, p. 337; August, 1984, p. 143.
Washington Post Book World, October 7, 1979, p. 15.

* * *

BERGREEN, Laurence R. 1950-

PERSONAL: Born February 4, 1950, in New York, NY; son of Morris H. (a lawyer) and Adele (a lawyer; maiden name, Gabel) Bergreen; married Elizabeth Freeman (a musician), June, 1975. *Education:* Harvard University, A.B., 1972.

ADDRESSES: *Office*—40 East 94th St., New York, NY 10128-0709. *Agent*—Wylie, Aitken and Stone, 250 West 57th St., Suite 2114, New York, NY 10107.

CAREER: Correspondent, *Newsweek* (international edition), 1973-74; Museum of Broadcasting, New York City, assistant to president, 1977-78; New School for Social Research, New York City, faculty member, 1981-82.

WRITINGS:

Look Now, Pay Later: The Rise of Network Broadcasting, Doubleday, 1980.
James Agee: A Life, Dutton, 1984.
As Thousands Cheer: The Life of Irving Berlin, Viking, 1990.
Capone, Simon & Schuster, 1994.

Also contributor to *Academic American Encyclopedia.*

SIDELIGHTS: Laurence R. Bergreen once told *CA:* "When writing my first book, a history of the American broadcasting industry, I found myself becoming more imaginatively engaged in the story of the rise of a business venture than I would have guessed possible at the outset. After a while it struck me that the networks served as a huge metaphor for the craggy face of American enterprise. It was a microcosm of society—at least as it looks to me here in New York—a fascinating, discordant combination of remarkable elements and people." *Look Now, Pay Later* contained sketches of major journalists and broadcasting executives, including Edward R. Murrow, Eric Sevareid, Edwin Armstrong, and Fred Silverman. Writing for the *Washington Journalism Review,* E. William Henry praised Bergreen for both his "highly readable, perceptive study of the broadcasting industry" and his "compelling portraits of the broadcast pioneers and their successors." Blaik Kirby of the Toronto *Globe and Mail* recommended *Look Now, Pay Later* for "anyone interested in broadcasting," declaring, "It is often an exciting tale and it is so thorough that I have complete faith in its accuracy and fairness."

Further exploring biographical writing, Bergreen wrote *James Agee: A Life,* chronicling the Pulitzer Prize-winning author's varied career and tumultuous personal life. Melvin Maddocks in *Time* pointed out that Bergreen "spent three years in research and interviews amassing the minute data of Agee's life," and asserted that the book is a "solid, unassuming biography." Jonathan Yardley stated in *Washington Post Book World,* "It is a terribly familiar story, and a terribly sad one, and it is told exceptionally well by Laurence Bergreen in what is, rather surprisingly, the first full Agee biography." Yardley also praised Bergreen for not "succumb[ing] to the literary biographer's temptation to overrate his subject's work."

Bergreen's next biography, *As Thousands Cheer: The Life of Irving Berlin,* traced the life of the songwriter known for such classics as "God Bless America," "White Christmas," "There's No Business Like Show Business," and "Puttin' on the Ritz." According to reviewer Alex Witchel of the *New York Times,* Berlin and his three daughters "refused to cooperate with Mr. Bergreen, who began his research when the songwriter was 97." Witchel added that Bergreen said he "did not feel that the family's lack of cooperation hurt his work." Gene Lees stressed in the *New York Times Book Review,* "In view of how hard Berlin tried to keep anyone from writing about him, Mr. Bergreen's vivid portrait is impressive indeed." In a Chicago *Tribune Books* review, Gerald Bordman called the work "a complete, carefully researched biography" and a "major accomplishment. It will probably stand as the definitive biography of a man whose fathomless well of unforgettable melody and rare gift for simple, homey, touching lyrics made his songs among the best that Tin Pan Alley, Broadway, and Hollywood had to offer." Witchel, however, noted that the book "has descriptions of a darker side of Mr. Berlin's character," and Lees described Berlin as "a mystery, and for the last three decades he was a crabby recluse, enveloped in a cocoon of memories, ingratitude, egotism and self-doubt." The *New York Times*'s Michiko Kakutani concluded, "The reader finishes this biography with the feeling that there is often no correlation between genius and sensitivity, talent and temperament. The man who wrote such wonderfully romantic songs as 'Cheek to Cheek,' 'Always,' and 'What'll I Do?' appears to have been an egotist and a boor."

"Writing has found me, rather than my rushing to embrace it," Bergreen once remarked to *CA.* "I first began to write in a more than scatterbrained fashion when living in London from 1972 to 1974. Though most nonfiction is too limited to inspire my deepest responses, the discipline of journalism has contributed a great deal to my fiction, and it is fiction that I regard as the ultimate challenge."

BIOGRAPHICAL/CRITICAL SOURCES:

PERIODICALS

Bestsellers, Volume 90, number 4, pp. 13-15.
Chicago Tribune, July 23, 1988; July 8, 1990, section 13, pp. 12-13.
Chicago Tribune Book World, July 29, 1984.
Detroit Free Press, July 1, 1990, p. 7Q.
Globe and Mail (Toronto), June 28, 1980; October 6, 1984; July 28, 1990.
Los Angeles Times, July 28, 1988.
Los Angeles Times Book Review, July 15, 1984, p. 2; July 1, 1990, pp. 6, 8.
New York Times, June 30, 1984; June 19, 1990; August 18, 1990.
New York Times Book Review, July 8, 1984, pp. 1, 31; July 1, 1990, pp. 1, 23.
Time, July 2, 1984, p. 85; July 23, 1990, pp. 74-75.
Times Literary Supplement, August 31, 1990.
Tribune Books (Chicago), July 8, 1990, pp. 1, 5.
Washington Journalism Review, July/August, 1980.
Washington Post Book World, June 10, 1984, pp. 3-4; June 24, 1990, p. 3.*

* * *

BESCHLOSS, Michael R(ichard) 1955-

PERSONAL: Born November 30, 1955, in Chicago, IL. *Education:* Attended Andover College; Williams College, B.A. (with highest honors), 1977; Harvard University, M.B.A., 1980.

Avocational Interests: Tennis, running, playing digital piano.

ADDRESSES: Home—Washington, DC. *Agent*—c/o Russell and Volkening, 50 West 29th St., New York, NY 10001.

CAREER: Smithsonian Institution, Washington, DC, historian, 1982-85, adjunct historian of American diplomacy and politics, 1985—; writer. Brookings Institution, guest scholar, 1985-86. Director, Annenberg Project on Television and American Foreign Policy; foreign affairs analyst, Cable News Network (CNN).

MEMBER: PEN/Faulkner Foundation (treasurer).

WRITINGS:

Kennedy and Roosevelt: The Uneasy Alliance, with foreword by James MacGregor Burns, Norton, 1980.
Mayday: Eisenhower, Khrushchev, and the U-2 Affair, Harper, 1986.
(Editor with Thomas E. Cronin) *Essays in Honor of James MacGregor Burns,* Prentice Hall, 1989.
Eisenhower: A Centennial Life, illustrated with photographs edited by Vincent Varga, HarperCollins, 1990.
The Crisis Years: Kennedy and Khrushchev, 1960-1963, Edward Burlingame Books, 1991.
(With Strobe Talbott) *At the Highest Levels: The Inside Story of the End of the Cold War,* Little, Brown, 1993.

Also contributor of book reviews and articles to newspapers and periodicals, including *Vanity Fair, New York Times Book Review, TV Guide, U.S. News and World Report,* and *Washington Monthly.*

SIDELIGHTS: Michael R. Beschloss has examined leadership styles, campaign politics, and international relations in his acclaimed works about U.S. presidents and their political foes and allies. Described by Adam Clymer of the *New York Times* as "one of the leading practitioners of the diminishing art of diplomatic history," Beschloss possesses a reputation as a meticulous researcher and perceptive analyst whose historical narratives blend information from once-classified documents with the public record. According to Chris Goodrich in *Publishers Weekly,* Beschloss "wants to synthesize, not debunk, previous understandings of the past, incorporating research of his own to form a coherent whole."

Beschloss's first book, *Kennedy and Roosevelt: The Uneasy Alliance,* is a study of the unlikely political alliance between Franklin D. Roosevelt and Joseph P. Kennedy. Although the first encounter between the two men was a stormy one, Kennedy became a staunch Roosevelt supporter during the 1932 election, his personal and financial backing helping Roosevelt win the Democratic nomination. In turn Kennedy expected, and received, prestigious political appointments: he was named the first chairman of the Securities and Exchange Commission and later ambassador to London. By the 1940 presidential election, however, Kennedy's public opposition to some of Roosevelt's war policies caused a permanent rift in their alliance. Despite this quarrel, Beschloss believes that the Kennedy-Roosevelt relationship benefited both men. In an interview with Jean M. White of the *Washington Post,* he said, "In the end Kennedy and Roosevelt were more effective [together] than they would have been on their own."

Kennedy and Roosevelt grew out of a senior thesis Beschloss wrote at Williams College. "A form of faint damning is to say that a book began as a thesis in pursuit of an academic degree," wrote Leonard Silk in the *New York Times.* "But this book is a real credit, not only to the author and his teacher, but also to the academic discipline. . . . Beschloss's thesis is that Franklin D. Roosevelt and Joseph P. Kennedy, the father of an assassinated President and a political dynasty that has not yet ended, were bound together in a love-hate relationship whose twists and turns and ultimate collapse reflected their powerful but opposing visions of the public good and how to achieve it." Robert Kirsch of the *Los Angeles Times* also admired Beschloss's account, calling it "a textbook, a case study in how political alliance works."

Beschloss turned his attention to post-World War II America and the escalating Soviet-American Cold War for his next book, *Mayday: Eisenhower, Khrushchev, and the U-2 Affair.* Deemed "part thriller and part political history" by Alexander Dallin in the *New York Times Book Review, Mayday* recounts the rise in tensions between the United States and the Soviet Union after the downing of an American U-2 reconnaissance plane over Russia on May 1, 1960. (This incident led to the collapse of a four-country superpower summit just weeks later.) The "U-2 affair" marked the low point in U.S.-Soviet relations during the presidency of Dwight D. Eisenhower; an attempted cover-up of the incident by Eisenhower and the State Department created problems domestically as well.

In addition to providing an account of the shoot-down, Beschloss traces the development of the U-2 program from its inception and profiles some of the key figures in the project's design. He also explores the political climate surrounding the failed summit, suggesting that the dashed peace initiatives of Eisenhower and Soviet leader Nikita Khrushchev resulted from foreign policy miscalculations by the two leaders. Reviewers were impressed with Beschloss's extensive research. The scope of the work prompted *Washington Post Book World* contributor James Bamford to call *Mayday* "the most comprehensive analysis of the U-2 incident to date," and Dallin judged that Beschloss "has done an excellent job of asking good questions, digging for answers wherever he could and making his way through the shoals of complexity and contradiction." Other reviewers commented on Beschloss's attention to political as well as scientific matters. John Ranelagh, writing in the *Times Literary Supplement,* noted that Beschloss "is as concerned with Eisenhower's search for detente as with the engineering and the intelligence role of the U-2."

Beschloss continued his study of the Cold War and Khrushchev's role in that history in *The Crisis Years: Kennedy and Khrushchev, 1960-1963.* Focusing on the often confrontational relationship between the Soviet premier and his American counterpart, President John F. Kennedy, *The Crisis Years* looks at several politico-military conflicts that erupted during the two leaders' administrations, including the ill-fated, American-backed Bay of Pigs invasion of Cuba and the construction of the Berlin Wall. The book concludes with the leaders' dramatic showdown over the Cuban Missile Crisis—a chain of events triggered by the installation of Soviet missiles on Cuba that led the world to the brink of nuclear war.

Aided by newly available information about these events, Beschloss offers a fresh perspective on the role that each leader played. The author reassesses Kennedy's actions in particular, arguing that the American president, through a series of threats and counterthreats, forced Khrushchev to take a hard-line approach to foreign policy issues. "Mr. Beschloss tells a richly textured story of how the American nuclear buildup and Khrushchev's blustering were mutually reinforcing," stated Michael Krepon in a critique of *Kennedy and Khrushchev* for the *New York Times Book Review.* "The more Kennedy and his lieutenants clarified the hollowness of Soviet boasting, the more they placed Khrushchev in an untenable position with his military and its supporters in the Kremlin." *Observer* critic Frederic Paul Smoler agreed with Beschloss that the two leaders shared responsibility for the hostilities that existed, stating, "Both [Kennedy and Khrushchev] believed that only their willingness to risk apocalyptic war kept the peace and alliances intact and ruling domestic coalitions in power."

Beschloss later collaborated with arms control analyst Strobe Talbott on *At the Highest Levels: The Inside Story of the End of the Cold War,* which documents the momentous changes in Soviet-American relations that took place during the tenures of Soviet president Mikhail Gorbachev and U.S. president George Bush. Under glasnost—Gorbachev's policy of openness—Beschloss and Talbott were granted unprecedented access to top-level Soviet and American officials, allowing the two authors to witness firsthand the obstacles that Gorbachev faced in his attempts at domestic reform. Mel Small, reviewing *At the Highest Levels* in the *Detroit Free Press,* found that Beschloss and Talbott "uncover a good deal of information about the conflicts a weak and often 'frazzled' Gorbachev had with his military on the right and emerging democrats like Boris Yeltsin on the left."

Through his narratives, Beschloss seeks to educate readers about both the famous and the not-so-famous figures who have played a part in history. Beschloss hopes that his work not only informs, but also entertains and enlightens. In an interview with Goodrich, Beschloss stated that he is "motivated to make history 'relevant' to current events. What I hope to do is not only tell a story in an interesting way, but also to explain why it happened that way, and to use it as guidance for people in the current age."

BIOGRAPHICAL/CRITICAL SOURCES:

PERIODICALS

Chicago Tribune Book World, April 27, 1986, p. 42.

Globe and Mail (Toronto), August 16, 1986; June 29, 1991, p. C8.

Los Angeles Times, May 14, 1980, p. 14.

Los Angeles Times Book Review, May 18, 1986, p. 10.

Maclean's, September 9, 1991, p. 46.
New Statesman, August 30, 1991, p. 46.
Newsweek, May 26, 1986, p. 69.
New Yorker, August 26, 1991, pp.77-79.
New York Review of Books, February 13, 1992, pp. 16-20.
New York Times, August 13, 1980; July 25, 1991.
New York Times Book Review, June 22, 1980, p. 15; May 4, 1986, p. 7; August 23, 1987, p. 28; June 16, 1991, p. 3.
Observer, August 25, 1991, p. 51.
Publishers Weekly, March 14, 1986, p. 91; April 19, 1991, p. 50; May 31, 1991, pp. 56-57.
Time, May 6, 1991, p. 17; June 17, 1991, pp. 77-78.
Tribune Books (Chicago), June 7, 1987, p. 4.
Washington Post, May 22, 1980, pp. C1, C9.
Washington Post Book World, May 4, 1980, p. 5; April 6, 1986, p. 1; July 26, 1987, p. 12.

* * *

BETTY, L(ewis) Stafford 1942-

PERSONAL: Born December 31, 1942, in Mobile, AL; son of Samuel Marks (a retired college professor) and Lillian (a homemaker; maiden name, Conover) Betty; married Christa Campbell, October 18, 1969 (divorced, 1976); married Lynette Doyle (a part-time college instructor) August 15, 1981; children: West, Sage, Southey, Louis, Sam. *Education:* Spring Hill College, B.S., 1964; University of Detroit, M.A., 1966; Fordham University, Ph.D., 1975. *Politics:* Democrat. *Religion:* "Mystic in the making (hopefully)."

ADDRESSES: Office—Department of Philosophy and Religious Studies, California State University, Bakersfield, CA 93311.

CAREER: California State University, Bakersfield, lecturer, 1972-75, assistant professor, 1975-77, associate professor, 1977-83, professor of religious studies, 1983—. Part-time instructor at Spring Hill College, 1984-85. *Military service:* U.S. Army, Corps of Engineers, 1966-68; served in Vietnam; became first lieutenant; received Bronze Star.

WRITINGS:

(Translator and commentator) *Vadiraja's Refutation of Sankara's Non-Dualism: Clearing the Way for Theism,* Motilal Banarsidass, 1978.
The Rich Man (novel), St. Martin's, 1984.
Sing Like the Whippoorwill (fiction), Twenty-Third Publications, 1987.
Sunlit Waters (fiction), Twenty-Third Publications, 1990.

Contributor to philosophy, psychology, parapsychology, and religious studies journals.

WORK IN PROGRESS: Two novels, *The Imprisoned Splendor* and *Thomas in India* (tentative titles).

SIDELIGHTS: L. Stafford Betty once told *CA:* "I don't look at man's place in the world as do most contemporary novelists and literary critics. They are on the whole a thoroughly secular lot. They navigate through life without an absolute to guide or sustain them, and they would have it no other way. I know that I need God and transcendent values to make sense of the world; without them, nothing that we do is of any ultimate importance. My fiction exists to drive this point home.

"*The Rich Man,* on the surface a historical novel about the rich young man of the Christian gospels who decided to follow Jesus, is on a deeper level a meditation on God and evil. My purpose in writing it was to show that evil is logically reconcilable with loving God.

"My novel in progress, *Thomas in India* is concerned with the adventures of Thomas the Apostle in India, the land he came to convert. But what most interests me is what Thomas came to represent: he is caught between two worlds, the Indian and the Judaeo-Christian. He responds not by scorning the Hindu or by chucking the whole religious enterprise, as modern men often do, but by constructing a synthesis out of what is best in both worlds. My third novel, tentatively titled *The Imprisoned Splendor,* tells the story of a modern unspiritual man who dies in a plane crash only to find himself surveying the shattered remains of his own corpse. Based on my years of research in parapsychology, I think it likely we survive bodily death. I think it is important that modern men and women believe in their own survival, and thus I have chosen to write this difficult novel about the afterlife to dramatize the infinite value of persons living in a universe loved by its creator."

"I've been working on both these novels for years," Betty later added. "*The Imprisoned Splendor* has taught me that it's safer to write about matters you have direct experience of. *Thomas in India,* a seven-hundred-page manuscript, has taught me that editors prefer shorter novels to longer, as a rule.

"Art does not exist merely to entertain. If that is all it does, then it is decadent. Great art must always inspire. It must make better persons of us. Nothing has changed since Plato, except that today there are more fools."

* * *

BICKERS, Richard (Leslie) Townshend 1917- (Mark Charles, Ricardo Cittafino, Philip Dukes, Richard Hall, Paul Kapusta, Burt Keene, Fritz Kirschner, Gui Lefevre, Richard Leslie,

Gerhardt Mueller, David Richards, Richard Townshend)

PERSONAL: Born July 5, 1917, in Shillong, Assam, India; son of Maurice Henry Townshend (an official of the British Government in India) and Gladwys Mary (Williams) Bickers; married Winifred Warne Richardson, November 21, 1938; children: Richard Paul Townshend, David Charles Townshend. *Education:* Attended Monkton Combe School and St. Paul's School, England. *Politics:* Conservative. *Religion:* Roman Catholic.

Avocational Interests: Small boat sailing, skiing, tennis, squash, and riding.

ADDRESSES: Home—Bridge Cottage, Appleshaw, Andover, Hants SP11 9BH, England. *Agent*—A. M. Heath & Co. Ltd., 40-42 William IV St., London WC2N 4DD, England.

CAREER: Royal Air Force, 1939-57, serving as regular officer in Fighter Command, Mediterranean Allied Air Forces, Far East Command, and Desert Air Force; Richard Bickers and Associates Ltd. (international marketing consultants), managing director.

MEMBER: Institute of Marketing, Institute of Export, Society of Authors.

WRITINGS:

Air Patrol: Biscay, Brown Watson, 1958.
Full Ahead—Both!, Brown Watson, 1958.
Italian Episode, Brown Watson, 1958.
(Under pseudonym Mark Charles) *Here Come the Marines!,* Brown Watson, 1958.
Jungle Pilot, Brown Watson, 1958.
(Under pseudonym Paul Kapusta) *Avenging Eagle,* Brown Watson, 1958.
(Under pseudonym Fritz Kirschner) *S.S.,* Brown Watson, 1958.
The Liberators, Brown Watson, 1958.
(Under pseudonym Gui Lefevre) *We Were Three,* Brown Watson, 1958.
Night Intruder, Brown Watson, 1958.
(Under pseudonym Ricardo Cittafino) *Conscript,* Brown Watson, 1958.
(Under pseudonym Philip Dukes) *Kidnap,* Brown Watson, 1958.
Ten Hundred Hours, Brown Watson, 1958.
(Under pseudonym Burt Keene) *Death but No Glory,* Brown Watson, 1958.
"*Scramble!,*" Brown Watson, 1958.
(Under pseudonym Gerhardt Mueller) *Luftwaffe,* Brown Watson, 1958.
Volunteers for Danger, Brown Watson, 1958.
The Guns Boom Far, Hutchinson, 1960.
The Savage Sky, R. Hale, 1961.
Ginger Lacey: Fighter Pilot: Battle of Britain Top Scorer (biography), R. Hale, 1962.
Jagger's Secret Challenge, illustrated by John Lawrence, Macdonald, 1964.
The Hellions, R. Hale, 1965.
Scent of Mayhem, R. Hale, 1965.
Maraskar Bound, R. Hale, 1968.
Hunt and Kill, R. Hale, 1969.
Marketing in Europe (nonfiction), Gower Press, 1971.
Summer of No Surrender, R. Hale, 1976.
My Enemy Came Nigh, R. Hale, 1978.
The Desert Falcons, R. Hale, 1978.
Their Flarepath the Moon, R. Hale, 1979.
The Beaufighters, R. Hale, 1979.
Air Strike, R. Hale, 1980.
Operation Fireball, R. Hale, 1980.
Sea Strike, R. Hale, 1980.
Operation Thunderflash, R. Hale, 1981.
Battle Climb, R. Hale, 1981.
Bombs Gone!, R. Hale, 1981.
Panther Squadron, R. Hale, 1982.
The Burning Blue, R. Hale, 1982.
Target Ahead, R. Hale, 1982.
Killing Zone, R. Hale, 1983.
Eagles, Crying Flames, R. Hale, 1983.
The Gifts of Jove, R. Hale, 1983.
A Time for Haste, R. Hale, 1984.
Too Late the Morrow, R. Hale, 1984.
The Sands of Truth, R. Hale, 1984.
The Sure Recompense, R. Hale, 1985.
Bomburst, R. Hale, 1985.
While Fates Permit, R. Hale, 1985.
Bombing Run, R. Hale, 1986.
The Mooncomers, R. Hale, 1986.
Fighters Up, R. Hale, 1986.
The Cauldron, R. Hale, 1987.
Torpedo Attack, R. Hale, 1987.
The First Great Air War, Hodder & Stoughton, 1988.
The Battle of Britain, Prentice-Hall, 1990.
The Desert Air War, 1939-1945, Shoe String, 1991.
Home Run: Great RAF Escapes of World War II, Shoe String, 1992.

UNDER PSEUDONYM RICHARD LESLIE

Dusk Patrol, R. Hale, 1980.
The Sky Aflame, R. Hale, 1981.
The Bloodied Hawks, R. Hale, 1981.
Sunset Flight, R. Hale, 1982.
Night Raiders, R. Hale, 1982.
The Fire's Breath, R. Hale, 1982.
No Wrath of Men, R. Hale, 1983.
The Fire of Spring, R. Hale, 1983.
Trouble in the Wind, R. Hale, 1984.
The Fateful Dawn, R. Hale, 1984.

Under a Shrieking Sky, R. Hale, 1984.
The Thundering Line, R. Hale, 1984.
Dawn Readiness, R. Hale, 1985.
The Raging Skies, R. Hale, 1985.
The Hunters, R. Hale, 1986.

UNDER PSEUDONYM RICHARD HALL

The Steel Fist, R. Hale, 1984.
Seize and Ravage, R. Hale, 1985.
Midnight Raid, R. Hale, 1985.
Patriots in Disguise: Women Warriors of the Civil War, Paragon House, 1993.

UNDER PSEUDONYM DAVID RICHARDS

Double Game, Brown Watson, 1958.
Hurricane Squadron, Brown Watson, 1958.
Four Men, Brown Watson, 1958.
Played Out: The Jean Seberg Story, Random House, 1981.

UNDER PSEUDONYM RICHARD TOWNSHEND

Angels Twenty-five, Edwin Self, 1955.
Malayan Episode, Edwin Self, 1956.
Japanese Encounter, Edwin Self, 1956.
Terror in Cyprus, Edwin Self, 1957.

OTHER

Also author with Berkely Mather of *The Pagoda Well,* a six-part serial for British Broadcasting Corporation (BBC) radio; author of *Hunt for Zalek* and *Zero Fuel,* for BBC radio. Author of numerous plays and scripts for television and radio, and of numerous short stories broadcast and published in various languages. Contributor to magazines and newspapers.

WORK IN PROGRESS: More novels about India and about the Royal Air Force at war.*

* * *

BINGLEY, D. E.
See BINGLEY, David Ernest

* * *

BINGLEY, David Ernest 1920-1985
(D. E. Bingley; pseudonyms: Bart Adams, Adam Bridger, Andrew Camber, Abe Canuck, Dave Carver, Larry Chatham, Henry Chesham, Will Coltman, Ed Coniston, Luke Dorman, George Fallon, David Horsley, Bat Jefford, Syd Kingston, Eric Lynch, James Martell, Colin North, Ben Plummer, Caleb Prescott, Mark Remington, John Roberts, Steve Romney, Frank Silvester, Henry Starr, Link Tucker, Christopher Wigan, Roger Yorke)

PERSONAL: Born April 16, 1920, in Leeds, Yorkshire, England; died October 9, 1985; son of Frank Silvester (an engineer) and Amy (Thornton) Bingley; married Vera Pilkington; children: Joan Elizabeth, Paul David, Peter Andrew. *Education:* Shenstone Teachers' Training College, Teacher's Certificate, 1948. *Politics:* Liberal. *Religion:* Non-conformist.

CAREER: W. D. Burlinson & Co., Incorporated Accountants, Dewsbury, England, auditor, 1938-39; Vickers-Armstrongs Ltd., Batrow-in-Furness, England, clerk, 1939 and 1946-47; Kirkby-Ireleth, the Burlington School, Lancashire, England, teacher, 1948-50; Horsley's Green School, High Wycombe, Buckinghamshire, England, housemaster, 1950-56; Spring Gardens County Primary, High Wycombe, Buckinghamshire, England, teacher, 1957-62; New Romney Church of England Primary School, Romney Marsh, Kent, England, teacher, 1966—. Member of committee, Writers Summer School, 1962-65. *Military service:* Royal Navy, 1939-45.

MEMBER: National Union of Teachers.

WRITINGS:

Malayan Adventure, Blackie & Son, 1962.
Famous Storybook Heroes, Odhams Press, 1964.
Gunsmoke at Nester Creek, R. Hale, 1964.
Elusive Witness, R. Hale, 1966.
Caribbean Crisis, R. Hale, 1967.
Bridges, Bodley Head, 1969.
Rustlers' Moon, R. Hale, 1972.
Hellions' Hideaway, R. Hale, 1974.
The Man from Abilene, R. Hale, 1975.
The Sword and the Trumpet, British Broadcasting Corp., 1985.

UNDER PSEUDONYM BART ADAMS

Owlhoot Raiders, Gresham, 1966.
Renegades' Rampage, Gresham, 1967.

UNDER PSEUDONYM DAVE CARVER

The Bar T Brand, R. Hale, 1964.
Gunsmoke Gambler, Foyle, 1966.
Renegade River, R. Hale, 1973.

UNDER PSEUDONYM HENRY CHESHAM

Naples, or Die!, R. Hale, 1965.
Skyborne Sapper, R. Hale, 1966.
The Place of the Chins, R. Hale, 1975.
A Surfeit of Soldiers, R. Hale, 1978.
The Angry Atoll, R. Hale, 1981.
A Tide of Chariots, R. Hale, 1983.
Saboteurs from the Sea, R. Hale, 1985.

Torpedo Tide, R. Hale, 1985.
Long Range Deserter, R. Hale, 1985.

UNDER PSEUDONYM WILL COLTMAN

The Torrington Trail, Gresham, 1966.
Killer's Creek, R. Hale, 1969.
Ghost Town Killer, Foyle, 1970.

UNDER PSEUDONYM ED CONISTON

Bar X Bandit, Gresham, 1965.

UNDER PSEUDONYM GEORGE FALLON

Rendezvous in Rio, R. Hale, 1966.

UNDER PSEUDONYM DAVID HORSLEY

Operation Pedestal, Brown, Watson, 1957.
Tinfish Running, Brown, Watson, 1958.
The Ocean, Their Grave, Brown, Watson, 1958.
Torpedoes in the Wake, Brown, Watson, 1958.
Vinegar Johnnie, Brown, Watson, 1958.
The Decoys, Brown, Watson, 1959.
Living Death, Brown, Watson, 1959.
Dive, Dive—Dive!, Brown, Watson, 1960.
The Time of the Locust: The Terrible Aftermath of the Fall of Singapore, Brown, Watson, 1960.
Johnny Pronto, R. Hale, 1964.
The Reluctant Renegade, R. Hale, 1965.
Flying Horseshoe Trail, R. Hale, 1966.
Sunset Showdown, R. Hale, 1977.
Brigand's Blade, R. Hale, 1978.
The Beauclerc Brand, R. Hale, 1979.
Troubleshooter on Trial, R. Hale, 1980.
Salt Creek Killing, R. Hale, 1981.
Badlands Bonanza, R. Hale, 1982.
The Long Siesta, R. Hale, 1983.
Stolen Star, R. Hale, 1984.
Wild Bunch Wanton, R. Hale, 1985.

UNDER PSEUDONYM BAT JEFFORD

Brigand's Bounty, R. Hale, 1969.
Silver Creek Trail, R. Hale, 1971.

UNDER PSEUDONYM SYD KINGSTON

Railtown Roundup, R. Hale, 1964.
The Necktie Trail, R. Hale, 1965.
The Kid from Cougar, R. Hale, 1972.
Alias Jake Dollar, R. Hale, 1974.
Hideaway Heist, R. Hale, 1975.
Boot Hill Bandit, R. Hale, 1982.
Renegade Preacher, R. Hale, 1985.

UNDER PSEUDONYM ERIC LYNCH

Renegade's Retreat, R. Hale, 1971.

UNDER PSEUDONYM CALEB PRESCOTT

Pecos River Posse, Gresham, 1968.

UNDER PSEUDONYM JOHN ROBERTS

Showdown at the Lazy T, R. Hale, 1964.
Colorado Gun Law, R. Hale, 1966.
Trailman's Truce, R. Hale, 1973.

UNDER PSEUDONYM LINK TUCKER

Renegade Valley, Gresham, 1965.

UNDER PSEUDONYM CHRISTOPHER WIGAN

Mossyhorn Trail, Mills & Boon, 1957.
The Man from Casagrande, R. Hale, 1964.
The Trail Blazer, R. Hale, 1964.
Buckboard Barber, R. Hale, 1981.
El Yanqui's Woman, R. Hale, 1983.

UNDER PSEUDONYM ROGER YORKE

The Iron Trail, Gresham, 1966.
Guadalupe Bandit, Gresham, 1967.

OTHER

Also author, under various pseudonyms, of numerous other published books, including *The Judge's Territory, Rogue's Remittance, Adam of Pendle Grange, Quarrel Island, Six Shooter Junction, Cowtown Kidnap, The Legionnaire, Showdown at Cedar Springs, Convoy Courageous, Mission to Corsica, The Gun, Secret Weapon, Don't Compel Me!, Perchance to Die, Trails of Destiny, The Restless Breed, Horse and Man, The Heroes, Gunsmokecounry, Short Triggervalley, Trail of Reckoning, Sons of the Diamond V, Trail of the Timber Wolves, Colorado Gunsmoke, Border Brigands, Railroad Renegades, Buckboard Bandit, Counterfeit Trail, Bullhead's Canyon, Hellion's Roost, The Reluctant Gunman, Little Pecos Trail, Renegade's Blade, Gunsmoke Lawyer, The Ruthless Renegades, Creek Town Killer, South Fork Showdown, The Rioting Renegades, Circle M Showdown, Elusive Renegade, Gunsmoke Gorge, Settler's Stampede, Silver Ciry Showdown, Trail of Tragedy, Renegade Trail, Buzzard's Breed, Sawbones City, Badman's Bounty, Murder Mesa, Salt Creek Showdown, Silvertown Trail, Hellions at Large, Boulder Creek Trial, Renegade Range, Palomino Kid, El Yanqui's Gold, Trailtown Trickster, Owlhoot Bandits, Coyote Kid, Red Rock Renegades, Showdown City, Hangtown Heiress, Red Bluff Renegades, Redman Range, Lopez' Loot, Hellions' Hostage, Remuda Renegades, Two Horse Trail, The Diamond Kid, Cowtown Killers, Lawman's Lament, Killer's Canyon, The Judge's Territory, Smith's Canyon, Tenderfoot Trail Boss, Banjo's Brand, Greenhorn Gorge,* and *Renegade Lady.*

Contributor of short stories and comic strips to magazines.

SIDELIGHTS: David Ernest Bingley's books have been published in Norway, Sweden, Holland, Brazil, and Germany.

[Sketch reviewed by widow, Mrs. Vera Bingley]

* * *

BLACKSTONE, Tessa Ann Vosper 1942-

PERSONAL: Born September 27, 1942, in London, England; daughter of Geoffrey Vaughan (a fire officer) and Joanna (a medical secretary; maiden name, Vosper) Blackstone; married Tom Evans, 1963 (divorced, 1975); children: Benedict, Liesel. *Education:* London School of Economics and Political Science, B.Sc., 1964, Ph.D., 1969.

ADDRESSES: Home—Birkbeck College, Malet Street, London WC1E 7HX, England.

CAREER: University of London, London School of Economics and Political Science, London, England, assistant lecturer, 1966-69, lecturer in social administration, 1969-75; Cabinet Office—Central Policy Review Staff, London, advisor, 1975-78; University of London, Institute of Education, professor of educational administration, 1978-83; Inner London Education Authority, London, deputy education officer, 1983-86, clerk to the Authority and Director of Education, 1986; Policy Studies Institute, London, Rowntree Special Research Fellow, 1986-87; Birkbeck College, London, master, 1987—. Fellow of Centre for Studies in Social Policy, 1972-74; member of educational advisory council of Independent Broadcasting Authority, 1973-79; member of Labour party's national executive committee on education, 1974-75, 1978-83; member of Hackney Community Health Council, 1976-78; chairman, General Advisory Council, BBC, 1987-91; director, Royal Opera House, 1987—; chairman, Ballet Board, Royal Opera House, 1991—; chairman, Board of Trustees, Institute for Public Policy Research, 1988—; member, Board of Trustees of British Museum (Natural History), 1992—.

MEMBER: House of Lords, Front Bench Spokesman on Education and Science (1990-92), Front Bench Spokesman on Foreign Affairs (1992—), Fabian Society (member of executive committee 1979-92; chairman, 1984-85), Royal Institute of International Affairs (1989-92).

WRITINGS:

(With Roger Hadley, Kathleen Gales, and Wyn Lewis) *Students in Conflict: LSE in Conflict,* Weidenfeld & Nicolson, 1970.

A Fair Start: The Provision of Pre-School Education, Allen Lane, London, 1971.

Education and Day Care for Young Children in Need: The American Experience, Bedford Square Press, 1973.

(With Garett Williams and David Metcalf) *The American Labour Market: Economic and Social Aspects of a Profession,* Elsevier, 1974.

Social Policy and Administration in Britain: Bibliography, Frances Pinter, 1975.

(With Paul Lodge) *Education Policy and Educational Inequality,* Martin Robertson, 1982.

How Many Teachers?, Bedford Way Paper, 1982.

(With Jo Mortimore) *Disadvantage and Education,* Heinemann, 1982.

(With Williams) *Response to Adversity,* S.R.H.E., 1983.

(With Caroline Gripps, Stephen Steadman, and Barry Stierer) *Testing Children,* Heinemann, 1983.

(With Ian McKay and Jenny Ozga) *Educational Policy Making,* Pergamon, 1985.

(With William Plowden) *Inside the Think Tank: Advising the Cabinet 1971-83,* Heinemann, 1988.

(Contributor) *CounterBlast No. 11, Prisons and Penal Reform,* Chatto & Windus, 1990.

SIDELIGHTS: Tessa Ann Vosper Blackstone once told *CA:* "I am interested in the relationship between educational policy and other areas of social policy, and how the two interact with respect to creating equality. I am in favor of extending educational provision so that a wider range of the population is able to benefit from the opportunities it offers. This includes preschool education at one end of the system and continuing education for adults at the other. Much of my writing explores ways in which this expansion could be achieved."

BIOGRAPHICAL/CRITICAL SOURCES:

PERIODICALS

Listener, July 16, 1970.

* * *

BLAMIRES, Harry 1916-

PERSONAL: Born November 6, 1916, in England; son of Tom (a food merchant) and Clara (Size) Blamires; married Nancy Bowles, December 26, 1940; children: Gabriel, Alcuin, Cyprian, Benedict, Fabian. *Education:* University College, Oxford, M.A., 1939. *Religion:* Anglican.

ADDRESSES: Home—Rough Close, Braithwaite, Keswick, Cumbria CA12 5RY, England.

CAREER: King Alfred's College, Winchester, Hampshire, England, principal lecturer in English, 1948-76. Visiting professor of English literature, Wheaton College, 1987.

WRITINGS:

Repair the Ruins: Reflections on Educational Matters from the Christian Point of View, Bles, 1950.

English in Education, Bles, 1951.

The Devil's Hunting-Grounds: A Fantasy, Longmans, Green, 1954.

Cold War in Hell (novel), Longmans, Green, 1955.

Blessing Unbounded: A Vision, Longmans, Green, 1955.

The Faith and Modern Error: An Essay on the Christian Message in the Twentieth Century, Macmillan, 1956, published as *The Secularist Heresy,* Servant Publications, 1980.

The Will and the Way: A Study of Divine Providence and Vocation, Macmillan, 1957, published as *A God Into Acts,* Servant Publications, 1981.

The Kirkbride Conversations: Six Dialogues of the Christian Faith, Morehouse, 1958.

Kirkbride and Company, S.P.C.K., 1959.

The Offering of Man, Church Literature Association, 1959, Morehouse, 1960.

The Christian Mind, Seabury, 1963.

The Tyranny of Time: A Defence of Dogmatism, Morehouse, 1965, published in England as *A Defence of Dogmatism,* S.P.C.K., 1965.

The Bloomsday Book: A Guide through Joyce's "Ulysses," Barnes & Noble, 1966, published in England as *The New Bloomsday Book,* Routledge & Kegan Paul, 1988.

Word Unheard: A Guide through Eliot's "Four Quartets," Methuen, 1969, Barnes & Noble, 1970.

Milton's Creation: A Guide through "Paradise Lost," Methuen, 1971.

A Short History of English Literature, Barnes & Noble, 1974, 2nd edition, Methuen, 1984.

Where Do We Stand?: An Examination of the Christian's Position in the Modern World, Servant Publications, 1980.

Twentieth Century English Literature, Macmillan, 1982, 2nd edition, 1986.

(Editor) *A Guide to Twentieth-Century Literature in English,* Methuen, 1982.

On Christian Truth, Servant Publications, 1983.

Words Made Flesh, Servant Publications, 1985.

Studying James Joyce, Longman, 1986.

Recovering the Christian Mind, IVP, 1988.

The Victorian Age of Literature, Longman, 1988.

The Age of Romantic Literature, Longman, 1990.

A History of Literary Criticism, Macmillan, 1991.

BIOGRAPHICAL/CRITICAL SOURCES:

PERIODICALS

Library Journal, May 15, 1970.

Times Literary Supplement, May 11, 1984.

BLASHFORD-SNELL, John (Nicholas) 1936-

PERSONAL: Born October 22, 1936, in Hereford, England; son of Leland John (a minister of Church of England) and Gwendolyn (Sadler) Blashford-Snell; married Judith Frances Sherman; children: Emma, Victoria. *Education:* Attended Victoria College; attended Royal Military Academy, Sandhurst, 1955-57. *Religion:* Church of England.

Avocational Interests: Jogging, fishing for giant perch, shooting, Scotch whiskey, wine, seafood, Peter Sellers films.

ADDRESSES: Home—c/o Lloyds Bank Ltd., 9 Broad St., St. Helier, Jersey, Channel Islands. *Office*—c/o The Scientific Exploration Society Expedition Base, Motcombe, North Shaftsbury, Dorset SP7 9PB, England.

CAREER: British Army, Royal Engineers, career officer, 1955-c.1990, instructor at Royal Military Academy, Sandhurst, and organizer of adventure training, beginning 1963; rank at retirement, colonel. Chairman, Discovery Expeditions Ltd; writer and lecturer.

MEMBER: Scientific Exploration Society (chairman, 1969—), The Royal Scottish Geographical Society (fellow), Explorers Club (fellow; chairman, British chapter, 1977—).

AWARDS, HONORS: Member of Order of the British Empire; named British Army man of the year, 1972; Gold Medal, Darien action committee, 1972, for exploration; Livingstone Medal, Royal Scottish Geographical Society, 1975; Segrave Trophy, Royal Automobile Club, 1975; Freeman award, city of Hereford, England, 1984; honorary Ph.D., Durham University, 1986.

WRITINGS:

(With G. R. Snailham) *The Expedition Organizer's Guide,* Daily Telegraph, 1969.

(With Tom Wintringham) *Weapons and Tactics,* Penguin, 1974.

Where the Trail Runs Out, Hutchinson, 1974.

In the Steps of Stanley, Hutchinson, 1975.

(With Alistair Ballantine) *Expeditions: The Experts' Way,* Faber, 1977.

A Taste for Adventure, Hutchinson, 1978.

(With Mike Cable) *The Official Books of Operation Drake,* W. H. Allen, Volume 1: *In the Wake of Drake,* 1980, Volume 2: *Operation Drake,* 1981.

Mysteries: Encounters with the Unexplained, Bodley Head, 1983.

The Official Books of Operation Raleigh, HarperCollins, Volume 1: *The Start of an Adventure,* 1986, (with Ann Tweedy) Volume 2: *Adventure Challenge,* 1987, (with Tweedy) Volume 3: *Adventure Unlimited,* 1989.

SIDELIGHTS: Colonel John Blashford-Snell's career with the British Army corps of Royal Engineers has taken him all over the world, and in his capacity as instructor at Royal Military Academy, Sandhurst, he launched his students in over sixty expeditions for the purpose of adventure training. Blashford-Snell has also provided the initiative for many projects involving both young people, many from Britain's inner cities, and older adults in the challenge and excitement experienced as members of an expeditionary force.

Blashford-Snell has served as the leader of many expeditions. In 1968, he and a team of joint civilian-military personnel made the first descent and exploration of the Blue Nile in the Great Abbai Expedition. Six years later, he led an international group of explorers, soldiers, and scientists in an attempt to follow the path of H. M. Stanley's historic expedition of a century before and navigate the Zaire River. Using a fleet of large inflatable craft, with jet boats and air support, the group started at the river's source and, after three-and-one-half months, navigated almost every rapid around which his predecessor had been forced to portage. The group finally reached the Atlantic Ocean in 1975. Blashford-Snell's Zaire River Expedition experienced many casualties but, fortunately, no deaths; boats were destroyed in cataracts and one was eaten by a hippopotamus.

Blashford-Snell travelled to Panama's Darien Gap in 1976 where, with the backing of the Explorers Club, he searched for the remains of the abandoned seventeenth-century Scots colony of New Caledonia. His team discovered the site and what seemed to be evidence of the lost Spanish city of Acla. While there, Blashford-Snell had the misfortune of being bitten by a vampire bat and had to undergo anti-rabies injections to avoid poisoning. By 1978, with the encouragement of Charles, Prince of Wales, he launched a mammoth expedition to inspire and challenge young people. Aboard the flagship *Eye of the Wind,* his group of soldiers, scientists, and young people set out from Plymouth, England on an around-the-world voyage of discovery. As director of operations for the venture, named *Operation Drake,* Blashford-Snell led the explorers through the Panama jungle, to the crater of Mount Soufriere shortly before it erupted, to Papua New Guinea, Africa, and the Mediterranean. The group confirmed the discovery of the lost city of Acla and achieved other scientific results during its two-year excursion.

In 1979, at the request of the Ethiopian government, Blashford-Snell headed the Dahlak Quest expedition to explore an archipelago of the Red Sea. Then, in 1984, following further encouragement by the Prince of Wales, he launched a new, even more ambitious expedition, which he later commemorated in *The Official Books of Operation Raleigh.* Involving over eight thousand young adults—as well as three thousand scientists, servicemen, and other experts—in expeditions, community service, and conservation projects worldwide, Operation Raleigh has commandeered a fleet of ships in its continuing circumnavigation of the globe. The expedition has achieved a success worthy of a commemoration of the anniversary of the founding of English-speaking America by Sir Walter Raleigh's colonists in 1584.

BIOGRAPHICAL/CRITICAL SOURCES:

PERIODICALS

Times Literary Supplement, June 22, 1984.

* * *

BOLTHO, Andrea 1939-

PERSONAL: Surname is pronounced *bol*-toe; born October 13, 1939, in Berlin, Germany; son of Alexander (a journalist) and Ellis (von Hedenstroem) Boltho von Hohenbach; married Maya Nandi, July 15, 1967; children: Fabrice, Alexei. *Education:* London School of Economics and Political Science, B.Sc., 1962; University of Paris, D.E.S., 1963; Nuffield College, Oxford, B.Litt., 1968. *Politics:* Progressive.

ADDRESSES: *Office*—Magdalen College, Oxford, OX1 4AU, England.

CAREER: Organization for Economic Co-operation and Development (OECD), Paris, France, administrator, 1966-71, head of division, 1971-77; Magdalen College, Oxford, England, economics fellow and tutor, 1977—. Visiting professor at International University of Japan, College d'Europe, Bruges, University of Venice, University of Turin, and University of Paris.

AWARDS, HONORS: Japan Foundation Fellowship, 1973-74.

WRITINGS:

Foreign Trade Criteria in Socialist Economics, Cambridge University Press, 1971.

Japan: An Economic Survey, Oxford University Press, 1975.

(Editor) *The European Economy,* Oxford University Press, 1982.

SIDELIGHTS: "I was born of Russian parents," Andrea Boltho told *CA,* "brought up in Italy, speaking five languages (plus some rudimentary Japanese). I am strongly interested in comparative economic work and drawn to international institutions."

BORNET, Vaughn Davis 1917-

PERSONAL: Born October 10, 1917, in Philadelphia, PA; son of Vaughn Taylor and Florence Davis (Scull) Bornet; married Mary Elizabeth Winchester, 1944; children: Barbara Lee, Stephen Folwell. *Education:* Emory University, B.A. (with honors), 1939, M.A., 1940; attended University of Georgia, 1940-41; Stanford University, Ph.D., 1951. *Politics:* Republican.

Avocational Interests: Fishing, golf, 35mm photography.

ADDRESSES: Home—365 Ridge Rd., Ashland, OR 97520.

CAREER: University of Miami, Coral Gables, FL, instructor in history, 1946-48; Stanford University, Institute of American History, Stanford, CA, research associate, 1951-53; Commonwealth Club of California, San Francisco, director of welfare research project, 1953-56; *Encyclopaedia Britannica,* Chicago, IL, associate editor, 1958; American Medical Association, Chicago, research associate, 1958-59; RAND Corp., Santa Monica, CA, staff member, 1959-63; Southern Oregon State College, Ashland, professor of history and social science, 1963-80, chairman of Division of Social Sciences, 1963-74, professor emeritus, 1980—; publisher, Bornet Books, 1992—. Visiting professor of history, World Campus Afloat, 1969. Has been on faculty of naval reserve officers' schools. Member of the U.S. Commission on Civil Rights, 1985—. Researcher for historians Edgar Eugene Robinson and T. A. Bailey during the 1950s. *Military service:* U.S. Naval Reserve, active duty, 1941- 45; retired as commander.

MEMBER: Sigma Chi, Pi Alpha Theta, Pi Sigma Alpha, Rogue Valley Symphony Association (president, 1973-74), Rogue Valley Yacht Club, Rotary.

AWARDS, HONORS: Ford Foundation fellow, 1951-52; Carson fellow; Ford fellow; Volker fellow; distinguished service medal from American Heart Association, 1967; meritorious service award from Oregon Heart Association, 1968; Lyndon Baines Johnson fellow, 1977; awards from Oregon Committee for the Humanities, 1978 and 1980, and Southern Oregon State College Alumni Association, 1985.

WRITINGS:

California Social Welfare, Legislation, Financing, Services, Statistics: A Research Study Commissioned by the Commonwealth Club of California, Prentice-Hall, 1956.

(Contributor) *Ideas In Conflict,* American Association for State and Local History, 1958.

(Editor) Herman Kahn, *On Thermonuclear War,* Princeton University Press, 1960.

Welfare in America, University of Oklahoma Press, 1960.

(Editor and contributor) *The Heart Future,* American Heart Association, 1961.

Labor Politics in a Democratic Republic, Spartan, 1964.

(With Edgar Eugene Robinson) *Herbert Hoover: President of the United States,* Hoover Institution Press, 1975.

(Contributor) *Herbert Hoover Reassessed,* U.S. Government Printing Office, 1981.

(Contributor) *The Quest for Security,* University of Iowa, 1982.

The Presidency of Lyndon B. Johnson, University Press of Kansas, 1983.

It's a Dog's Life and I Like It!, Bornet Books, 1992.

Also author of *Speaking Up for America,* 1974, and an autobiography, *Learning a Life: The Bornet Memoirs.* Author of "United States," *Encyclopaedia Britannica Yearbook,* 1956 and 1957. Contributor to *Encyclopaedia Britannica* and to various publications on historical, social welfare, and socioeconomic subjects.

SIDELIGHTS: Vaughn Davis Bornet told *CA:* "I have managed to write a number of serious books and to review many books. From this experience I have one particular point to make: authors too often fail to summarize at the outset exactly what their book is about, that is, what it covers, why it was written, and what it is supposed to achieve. One would think that the need for this would be obvious, but many scholars do not seem to think so. I suspect many reviewers would agree fully with me.

"Years ago, at *Encyclopaedia Britannica,* I learned that the obvious *must* be stated, if readers in Burma and Kiev are to really get the point. Scholars too often skip that, and, worse, sometimes ridicule those who routinely offer elementary information and generalization. Thus, something on 'the presidency' should state outright that it is the 'American' office being described. What is 'welfare'? Don't just use that common word. Why do people *give?* Don't assume that everybody knows why already. If one makes a detailed analysis of 1928, do say forthrightly *why* one did so, and *what* the final result means to later generations.

"Words are in print a long time. I rather think that they should be weighed carefully, in the respect I have indicated, as a first order of business.

"Concluding the foreword to my 400-page (unpublished) memoirs this year, I wrote, 'There was bound to be both pain, and rewards, in the remembering, both for him and for readers of his generation. For some, there might be pleasant remembrance—plus some jarring surprises. More distant readers in the next century, perhaps, would look back to the 20th century with some sense of adventure. Anyway, he was going to give birth to a narrative filled to the brim with thought he had once treasured, and many emotions he came to experience, during the jam-packed decades he lived while *learning a life.*' "

* * *

BRANDELL, (Erik) Gunnar 1916-

PERSONAL: Born October 1, 1916, in Soedertaelje, Sweden; son of Georg Albert and Frida Olavia (Franck) Brandell; married Kerstin K. V. Joenson (a teacher), 1937; children: Lars, Gerd, Inga, Eva (Mrs. Lars-Aake Brus). *Education:* University of Uppsala, Fil.mag., 1936; University of Stockholm, Fil.dr., 1950.

ADDRESSES: Home—Murklevaegen 1, Uppsala, Sweden 75646.

CAREER: High school teacher of Swedish language and literature in Storvik, Sweden, 1936-46; *Goeteborgs handelstidning,* Goeteborg, Sweden, Paris correspondent, 1946-48; *Svenska dagbladet,* Stockholm, Sweden, cultural editor, 1951-62; University of Uppsala, Uppsala, Sweden, professor of literary history, 1963-81, dean of faculty, 1977-80. Lecturer at about thirty universities in the United States and Europe. Organizer of international Strindberg symposia, 1973—. *Military service:* Swedish Army, 1938-40. Swedish Navy, 1941-43; became lieutenant.

MEMBER: International PEN, Swedish Psychoanalytical Society (honorary member), Academie septentrionale Paris, Strindberg Society (chairman, 1965-75), Royal Academy of Letters and History, Royal Scientific Society.

AWARDS, HONORS: Several prizes from Swedish Academy.

WRITINGS:

Strindbergs Infernokris, [Sweden], 1950, translation by Barry Jacobs published as *Strindberg in Inferno,* Harvard University Press, 1974.

Freud och sekelslutet, [Sweden], 1970, translation by Iain White published as *Freud: A Man of His Century,* Humanities, 1979.

IN SWEDISH

Bekaennare och uppfostrare (title means "Confessors and Educators"), Gebers, 1937.

Den europeiska nihilismen (title means "The European Nihilism"), Bonniers, 1943.

Paa Strindbergs vaegar genom Frankrike (title means "On Strindberg's Roads through France"), Wahlstroem & Widstrand, 1949.

Aattital och nittital (title means "The Eighties and the Nineties"), Natur och kultur, 1957.

Svensk litteratur, 1900-1950 (title means "Swedish Literature, 1900-1950"), Aldus, 1958, 3rd edition, 1974.

Vid seklets kaellor (title means "At the Sources of the Century"), Bonniers, 1961.

Konsten att citera (title means "The Art of Quoting"), Aldus, 1968.

Skolreform och universitetskris (title means "School Reform and University Crisis"), Aldus, 1969.

Drama i tre avsnitt (title means "Drama in Three Parts"), Wahlstroem & Widstrand, 1971.

Revolt i dikt (title means "Revolt in Literature"), Alba, 1977.

Strindberg-ett foerfattarliv (title means "Strindberg—A Writer's Life"), Alba, Volume 3: *Paris, till och fran* (title means "Paris—To and From"), 1983, Volume 2: *Borta och hemma* (title means "Away and at Home"), 1985, Volume 1: *Saoroaar och genombroff* (title means "Apprentice Years and Success"), 1987, Volume 4: *Hemkomsten—det mya aramat* (title means "Homecoming—The New Drama"), 1989.

WORK IN PROGRESS: A nordic drama.

SIDELIGHTS: Gunnar Brandell told *CA:* "My main interest has been the new problematic view of man which emerged in the late years of the nineteenth century (with Strindberg and Freud) and connected with it the question, 'What kind of a humanism is possible in the light of these and other experiences?' That is why I took great interest in French existential literature in the forties. I have also devoted myself to literary and other cooperation on an international scale, thereby following a tradition in Swedish literary history."

* * *

BRANDON, Joyce A(lmeta) 1938-

PERSONAL: Born November 17, 1938, in Farmersville, TX; daughter of Charlie (a machinist) and Alma (a housewife; maiden name, Parker) Miller; married Robert Harry Firestine, August 17, 1957 (divorced, 1964); married John C. Brandon, January 16, 1970; children: (first marriage) Robert Kevin, Suzanne Lonelle; (second marriage) John Lee (stepson), Kristina Wilson (foster child), Brian Mark (stepson), Darla Forrester Reta (foster child). *Education:* Attended Fresno City College, 1971. *Politics:* Democrat.

ADDRESSES: Home and office—1178 East Sierra, Fresno, CA 93710. *Agent*—Jane Jordan Browne, Multimedia Product Development, Inc., 410 S. Michigan, Suite 724, Chicago, IL 60605.

CAREER: County of Fresno, Fresno, CA, senior clerk in office of tax collector, 1966, principal account clerk in auditor-controller's office, 1966-70, assistant clerk to Board of Supervisors, 1970-75, acting clerk to Board, 1975-76, clerk to Board, 1976-79; Older Americans Organizations,

Fresno, deputy executive director, 1980-82; Washington National Life Insurance Co., Fresno, insurance agent, 1982-83; Security Mutual Life Insurance Co., Fresno, insurance agent, 1983—. Group insurance representative with Chargin Insurance Services, 1985. Member of Human Services Coalition, 1980-82; member of board of directors of Alpha House, Inc., 1981—; president of local chapter of California Women's Commission on Alcoholism, 1983-84; teacher of weekly creative writing class/critique group for writers, 1984—; founding president of Central Valley Chapter of Romance Writers of America (now Valley Writers Network), 1986-1987; Santa Barbara Writer's Conference, staff member and workshop leader, 1987—; Writer's Digest Novel Writing Workshop, editorial assistant, 1987-91; Division of Extended Education, California State University, Fresno, creative writing instructor, 1991—; director of Creative Writing in the Schools Project, 1991—; conference chair of annual WIN-WIN How to Get and Stay Published Writer's Conference.

MEMBER: Novelists Inc. (charter member), Writer's International Network/Writer's Inter-age Network, Inc. (founding president), WIN-WIN Auxiliary (charter member).

AWARDS, HONORS: Golden Medallion Finalist Award, Romance Writers of America, 1986, for *The Lady and the Outlaw; The Lady and the Outlaw* was chosen one of the best historical romances of 1985 by readers of *Affaire de Coeur* magazine, 1986; Lifetime Achievement Award as the Best New Western Romance Author, 1988, for *The Lady and the Lawman;* Silver Pen Award, *Affaire de Coeur,* 1988; Best Western Novel, Romantic Times Reviewers, 1988, for *After Eden;* Golden Certificate Award, *Affaire de Coeur,* 1989, for *After Eden;* Award of Merit, California Association of Teachers of English, 1993, for the WIN-WIN Creative Writing in the Schools Project.

WRITINGS:

The Lady and the Outlaw (historical fiction; also see below), Ballantine, 1985.

The Lady and the Lawman (historical fiction), Ballantine, 1987.

The Write to Sell Workbook & Tape Album, Preston House Books & Tapes, 1987.

After Eden (historical fiction), Ballantine, 1988.

Adobe Palace (historical fiction), Ballantine, 1993.

Also author of screenplay, "The Lady and the Outlaw," 1987.

WORK IN PROGRESS: The Lady and the Robber Baron, a historical romance novel, for Ballantine; *Amazing Grace, the Mystical Roots of One of America's Best-Loved Gospel Hymns;* "Salvation," a board game based on Eastern spiritual science.

SIDELIGHTS: Joyce A. Brandon told *CA:* "Teachers and schools take a lot of heat about the rising tide of illiteracy. Going into various classrooms as part of my volunteer work with the WIN-WIN Creative Writing in the Schools Project has been an eye-opening experience for me. I realized that classes are far too big, and teachers are carrying a heavy, heavy load. They need and deserve as much hands-on help as we can give them.

"The Creative Writing in the Schools Project started accidentally. I was invited to speak to a sixth-grade class at Mountain View Elementary School. After I had told them about being a writer, one of the students asked me to read from one of my books. I read a few paragraphs, then a boy asked if I'd like to read one of his stories. I told him I'd like that very much, but we were out of time. They moaned so loudly that I agreed to come back and tell them the basics of how to write a hero story. The next week I told them about the twelve guideposts for fiction based on Joseph Campbell's book *The Hero with a Thousand Faces.* Then I challenged the students to each write a hero story, and I told them if they did, I'd bring friends back, and we'd listen to their stories."

Brandon kept her promise, returning the next week with four other writers to read the children's stories, which were later collected in an anthology. "Kathy Thornburg, their teacher, said that we had turned a very ordinary roomful of fairly alienated eleven- and twelve-year-olds into an extraordinary group of writers on their way to becoming a close-knit family," Brandon remarked. "They bonded with each other and with their teacher. Their self-esteem went up phenomenally. They came in number two district-wide in the year-end writing sample. The kids wrote thank-you skits and sang and danced them for the volunteers the last week of school. We were again amazed at their creativity and ingenuity and deeply touched by their obvious gratitude and sincerity. Kathy nominated the project for the CATE Award of Merit, and we won it."

Brandon has since introduced the project in ten additional classrooms. In her CATE award acceptance speech, the author explained, "By going into different schools, we have learned that many of our children are in serious need and our teachers on the front lines are overwhelmed. I was appalled by the enormity of the problems facing both teachers and students. It is my belief that if we don't fix these kids now, we'll be tinkering with them the rest of their lives, in ever more expensive prisons and courtrooms." Brandon noted the value of creative writing in helping children to explore their fears and face problems more effectively. "In my own life, writing was my path to higher consciousness," she continued. "Each story I wrote (though I was not aware of it at the time) was later recognized as being reflective of a serious problem in my life. By writing the story I needed to write, I was able to resolve inner conflicts and heal old wounds. So it is no wonder that I would want to give this amazing gift of creative writing to every child in the world. And at no time in history have the world's children needed this gift more."

* * *

BRAUDEL, Fernand (Paul) 1902-1985

PERSONAL: Born August 24, 1902, in Luneville, Meuse, France; died November 28, 1985, in Paris, France; son of Charles (a school principal) and Louise (Falet) Braudel; married Paule Pradel, September 14, 1933; children: Marie-Pierre, Francoise. *Education:* University of Paris, Sorbonne, qualified as teacher, 1923, doctorate in literature, 1947.

ADDRESSES: Home—59 rue Brillat-Savarin, 75013 Paris, France. *Office*—Maison des Sciences de l'Homme, 54 boulevard Raspail, 75270 Paris, France.

CAREER: High school history teacher in Algiers, Algeria, 1924-32, and Paris, France, 1932-35; University of Sao Paulo, Brazil, professor of history of civilization, 1935-37; Ecole Pratique des Hautes Etudes, Paris, director of studies in fourth section, 1937-39, and in sixth section (economic and social sciences), beginning 1947, president of sixth section, beginning 1956; College de France, Paris, professor of modern history, 1949-72, honorary professor, beginning 1972; Maison des Sciences de l'Homme, Paris, chief administrator, beginning 1963. Visiting professor at University of Chicago, 1968. *Military service:* French Army, 1939-45; prisoner of war in Germany, 1940-45; became lieutenant.

MEMBER: Haut Comite de la Langue Francaise, Commission des Archives Diplomatiques, British Academy, American Philosophical Society, Polish Academy of Science, Academy of History (Spain), Academy of History (Argentina), Bavarian Academy of Sciences, Belgrade Academy of Science, Heidelberg Academy of Science.

AWARDS, HONORS: Officer de la Legion d'Honneur; Commandeur de l'Ordre National du Merite; the State University of New York at Binghamton established the Fernand Braudel Center for the Study of Economies, Historical Systems, and Civilizations in 1977; *Los Angeles Times* Book Prize, nominee, 1982, for *The Structures of Everyday Life,* winner, 1983, for *The Wheels of Commerce;* elected to Academie Francaise, 1984; honorary doctorates from institutions including Yale University, University of Chicago, Oxford University, Cambridge University, and universities in Canada, Scotland, Belgium, Germany, Switzerland, Spain, Italy, Poland, and Brazil.

WRITINGS:

IN ENGLISH TRANSLATION

The Mediterranean and the Mediterranean World in the Age of Philip II, translated by Sian Reynolds, Harper, Volume 1, 1972, Volume 2, 1974, second edition, 1976, revised second edition, 1977, abridged edition, 1992 (translation of revised edition of *La Mediterranee et le monde mediterraneen a l'epoque de Philippe II,* Colin, 1949, two-volume revised edition, 1966).

Capitalism and Material Life, 1400-1800, translated by Miriam Kochan, Harper, 1973 (originally published as *Civilisation materielle et capitalisme, XVe-XVIIIe siecle,* Colin, 1967; see translation of 1979 three-volume revised edition below).

Afterthoughts on Material Civilization and Capitalism, translation by Patricia M. Ranum of lectures delivered at 1976 Johns Hopkins Symposium in Comparative History, Johns Hopkins University Press, 1977 (published in French as *La dynamique du capitalisme,* Arthaud, 1985).

On History, University of Chicago Press, 1980 (originally published as *Ecrits sur l'histoire,* Flammarion, 1969).

Civilization and Capitalism, Fifteenth to Eighteenth Century, translation by Reynolds, Harper and Row, Volume 1: *The Structures of Everyday Life: The Limits of the Possible,* 1982, Volume 2: *The Wheels of Commerce,* 1983, Volume 3: *The Perspective of the World,* 1984 (originally published as *Civilisation materielle, economie et capitalisme, XVe-XVIIIe siecle,* three-volumes, revised edition, 1979, of *Civilisation materielle et capitalisme, XVe-XVIIIe siecle*).

The Identity of France, Volume 1: *History and Environment,* translated by Reynolds, Collins, Volume 2: *People and Production,* 1991 (originally published as *L'Identite de la France,* 3 volumes, Arthaud-Flammarion, 1986).

Out of Italy, 1450-1650, translated by Reynolds, Abbeville Press, 1991.

UNTRANSLATED WORKS

(With Ruggiero Romano) *Navires et marchandises a l'entree du port de Livourne, 1547-1611* (title means "Vessels and Merchandise Entering the Port of Leghorn, 1547-1611"), Colin, 1951.

(With Suzanne Baille and R. Philippe) *Le Monde actuel, histoire et civilisations* (high school text; title means "The Contemporary World: History and Civilizations") Eugene Belin, 1963 (also see below).

(Editor) A. Jara and others, *Temas de historia economica hispano-americana* (essays; title means "Themes in the Economic History of Spanish America"), Mouton, 1965.

(Editor, with Ernest Labrousse) *Histoire economique et sociale de la France,* (title means "Economic and Social History of France"), 8 volumes, Presses universitaires de France, 1970-82.

(Author of preface) *Conjoncture Economique, Structures Sociales: Hommage a Ernest Labrousse* (title means "Economic Conjuncture, Social Structures: Studies in Honor of Ernest Labrousse"), Mouton, 1974.

(Editor) *La Storia e le altre scienze sociali* (title means "History and the Other Social Sciences"), Laterza, 1974.

(With Pierre Gourou and others) *L'Europe* (title means "Europe"), Arts et metiers graphiques, 1982.

(Editor, with others) *Le Monde de Jacques Cartier: l'aventure au XVIe siecle* (title means "The World of Jacques Cartier: The Adventure of the Sixteenth Century"), Berger-Levrault, 1984.

(With Folco Quilici) *Venezia, immagine di una citta* (title means "Venice: images of a city"), Mulino, 1984.

I tempi della storia: economie, societa, civilta (title means "The Epochs of History: Economics, Society, Civilization"), Dedalo, 1986.

(Editor) *Prato, storia di una citta* (title means "Prato: The History of a City), Le Monnier, 1986.

La Grammaire des Civilisations (Braudel's contribution to 1963 high school text, *Le Monde actuel;* title means "The Grammar of Civilizations"), Arthaud-Flammarion, 1987.

Le modele italien (title means "The Italian Model"), Arthaud, 1989.

(With others) *Der Historiker als Menschenfresser: uber den Beruf des Geschichtsschreibers* (title means "The Historian as Cannibal: On the Profession of History-Writer"), Wagenbach, 1990.

Ecrits sur l'histoire, II (title means "Writings on History, II"), Arthaud, 1990.

Editor of *Annales,* 1956-68.

Works by Fernand Braudel have been translated into several languages.

SIDELIGHTS: One of the most influential historians of the twentieth century, Fernand Braudel was at his death the foremost representative of the "new history," a practice of historiography in which the physical, social, and cultural environment and the living conditions of everyday people are considered to be more important in determining the course of history than particular political events and the actions of "great men." "Marx was more than half wrong when he said that men make their own history," Braudel said in an interview quoted in *World Press Review* shortly before his death in 1985. "It is history that makes men; they merely endure it. The individual's capacity to shape history is an illusion." Also known as "*histoire totale*" or "global history," the new history combined knowledge and methods from such diverse fields as economics, geography, psychology, and folklore. It was developed by the *Annales* group, which took its name from the French interdisciplinary journal edited by Braudel from 1956 to 1968, and included French scholars Marc Bloch and Lucien Febvre, Braudel's mentor. In recording Braudel's death, *Time* commented that his approach to history "came to dominate French historiography, and substantially influenced scholars in Britain and the [United States] as well."

Braudel began his career in 1924 as a schoolteacher in Algiers. It was during this time that he began to work on his doctoral thesis, a project that would take him over twenty years to complete. Braudel chose as his topic the Mediterranean policy of Philip II of Spain, a sixteenth-century ruler whose reign saw military conflict with the Turkish empire for control of the Mediterranean Sea. In the course of his research, Braudel made use of the government archives at Simancas, Spain, where thousands of documents concerning fifteenth- and sixteenth-century life were stored. Scholars had long known of the archives, but the sheer mass of material available, all of it haphazardly organized, and the reluctance of authorities to allow outsiders to examine it, had prevented any extensive use of the archives for historical research. Braudel was the first to overcome this problem. He used an old movie camera to take still pictures of documents, pictures he could examine later with the aid of a film projector. He was soon taking two or three thousand pictures a day.

In his thesis Braudel broke with the tradition of academic histories in which a few great men were depicted as having determined the course of nations. Braudel stressed the need to examine the cultural, economic, and geographic forces at work in human history. The ideas of the French interdisciplinary journal *Annales* further influenced his outlook. *Annales* had been founded in 1929 by Lucien Febvre and Marc Bloch to express their impatience with traditional academic historiography and their demands for a new approach. History, they believed, was not the biography of a few influential individuals; nor was it a steady progress toward some sort of social or spiritual millennium. Rather, it was an endless struggle between human intentions and the limitations imposed by the environment and by human nature. The *Annales* group called for historians to make use of new technologies and the methods of other disciplines in their historical research, so that a deeper and more complete understanding of history might be gained. The study of climates and the use of aerial photography were just two innovations of the *Annales* group.

A disciple and then a close friend of Febvre, Braudel adopted the *Annales* approach in researching his thesis, widening the scope of his investigation as the years went by. He sifted through the records of fifteenth- and sixteenth-century shipping schedules, merchants' correspondence, diplomatic papers, crop records, and court documents, using every available bit of information to form as complete and accurate a picture of the time and place as possible. His aim was to present not the history of King Philip II's reign, but a history of how the nature of Spain and the Mediterranean region at that time influenced the policies Philip adopted. Accordingly, Braudel's thesis, wrote Naomi Blivenin in the *New Yorker,* "is about geography, economics, politics, and war; it is about the daily life—agricultural, urban, and maritime—of the rich and poor; it is gossip and description and anecdote; it is about endings—the ending of the Mediterranean world's domination of Western civilization—and it is about continuities and parallels."

When at last Braudel completed his research and prepared to write his thesis, World War II intervened. Called to serve as a lieutenant in the French Army, Braudel was captured by the Nazis and spent five years as a prisoner in Germany. During his incarceration, without a single note and relying entirely upon his formidable memory, Braudel wrote his thesis in a series of school copy books which, one by one, he mailed out to safety. "I had to believe that history, destiny, was written at a much more profound level," *Time* quotes Braudel as saying of this period. "So it was that I consciously set forth in search of a historical language in order to present unchanging, or at least very slowly changing, conditions which stubbornly assert themselves over and over again."

At war's end, Braudel returned to France and, in 1947, successfully defended his thesis to receive his doctoral degree from the Sorbonne. In 1949, his thesis was published in two volumes as *La Mediterranee et le monde mediterraneen a l'epoque de Philippe II.* In 1972, it was translated into English and published in the United States. The first volume was a geo-history of the entire Mediterranean area. "Braudel's book," wrote J.B. Plumb in the *New York Times Book Review,* "is geographically based—the huge Mediterranean basin with its mountains, deserts, alluvial plains, its forests and marshes, the problems of its boundaries, its routes and villages, its climates and weather are investigated and described in the historical context which Braudel has chosen—the age of Philip II." Braudel showed how geography and other factors gave rise to the embattled empires of Spain and Turkey. "Politics," he argued, "merely follows the outlines of an underlying reality. These two Mediterraneans, commanded by warring rulers, were physically, economically, and culturally different from each other." In the second volume, Braudel examined how the failure of agriculture to keep pace with a massive increase in the Mediterranean population, and the widening gulf between rich and poor, east and west, led the two empires inevitably into the political and military conflict in which Philip II played a prominent role.

The massive study received high praise from reviewers throughout the world. The *Economist* proclaimed it "one of the few great histories of our times." Writing in *Encounter,* John Bossy described the book as "a great work of historical art, indeed of art simply, a triumph of the constructive and concrete imagination, something to redeem the time." "This is evocative history at its best," wrote J. H. Elliot of the *New York Review of Books,* "pursued with such richness of detail and example over space and time that it dazzles as well as illuminates." Elliot termed the book "one of the crowning achievements of twentieth-century historical craftsmanship." In similar terms, Michael Ratcliffe of the London *Times* called the book "a masterpiece of French liberal humanism revitalized by the new technology of twentieth century scholarship." "Few other works of scholarship or the imagination," he added, "bring us so close to the living presence of our ancestors or reconstruct so brilliantly the resources and world view available to, and shared by, the heroes of both statesmanship and art."

In later works, Braudel continued to write minutely detailed histories using a multidisciplinary approach. *Capitalism and Material Life, 1400-1800* examined the period immediately preceding the era of capitalism. It showed how the population explosion that began in the sixteenth century outstripped the supply of food and other goods, leading in many parts of the world to the same sort of extreme disparity between the living standards of rich and poor that Braudel had already noted in *The Mediterranean and the Mediterranean World.* He went on to analyze staple diets, housing, and clothing throughout the world, then turned his attention to what he identified as the three major factors in the growth of the industrial revolution—the spread of technology, the development of sophisticated monetary and credit systems, and the rise of the city. Braudel concluded that the "capitalist spirit" of certain medieval towns in northern Europe gave birth to the era of "pre-capitalism, which is the source of all the economic creativeness in the world," as well as "all the most burdensome exploitation of man by man."

Hugh Trevor-Roper, in the *New York Times Book Review,* praised *Capitalism and Material Life* for its display of "the genial erudition, the profusion and variety of illustration, the stimulating (and sometimes paradoxical) suggestions, the delightfully unacademic vitality" that he found typical of Braudel's work. Keith Thomas, writing in the *New York Review of Books,* noted several weaknesses in the book, chief among them the author's "inability to take adequate account of ideas, religion, mental attitudes [and] cognitive structures." He nonetheless considered that "all criticisms of the achievement of Fernand Braudel are disarmed by the sheer status of the man, the brilliance of the writing, the range of the erudition, the largeness of the vision, the passionate interest in human life."

The same period covered in *Capitalism and Material Life* received an expanded treatment in the three-volume *Civilization and Capitalism,* published in France in 1979 and in the United States between 1982 and 1984. The enlarged study examined the economic and social evolution of medieval and modern Europe until the industrial revolution. Its three volumes dealt with three different aspects of the development of capitalism: the daily life of the people, the rise of market economies, and the creation of an international economic community.

Writing in the *Washington Post Book World,* Plumb described the first volume, *The Structures of Everyday Life: The Limits of the Possible,* as "the most remarkable picture of human life in the centuries before the human condition was radically changed by the growth of industry that has yet been presented." According to Richard Holmes of *Harper's,* the study had "no obvious compeer either in scope of reference or level of accessibility to the general reader." It presented, he said, "in vivid, ceaseless detail the daily condition of our ancestors' lives. . . . Their population numbers and their health; their diets and household budgets; their food, drink, clothes, and furniture; their transport, technologies, and inventions; their money and their banking systems; and above all their great cities."

Having defined the essential conditions of life in the period under discussion, Braudel moved in the second volume of *Civilization and Capitalism* to a discussion of how the technologies and knowledge of the time were put to use. In writing about the beginnings of capitalism, Braudel "tells in almost incredible detail," John Kenneth Galbraith stated in the *Washington Post Book World,* "who these merchants were, whence they came and where they operated, how much money they made, their place in the social and political hierarchy of the time, and of the world of peddlers, fairs, elementary retail shops, currency and stock exchanges, merchant companies and shipping routes in which they participated."

The Perspective of the World, the third volume in the study, focused on the rise of Europe to dominion over world trade. The role of city-states in the expansion of trade was one of Braudel's primary concerns. He traced how first one, then another European city came to dominate the economy of the region. Braudel's account of the rise and fall of Amsterdam as an economic power had "never been better told," commented Lawrence Stone in the *New Republic.* "The scope [of the book] is gigantic," Stone continued, "both in space and time, and it is full of recondite information." The reviewer for *Publishers Weekly* judged it "a dazzling economic history" and "a magisterial work."

Braudel's last great multivolume study was *The Identity of France,* intended, he said, "to look at the entire history of France in the light of the various social sciences in turn." Four volumes were planned, but Braudel was able to complete only three before his death in 1985 at the age of eighty-two. The first volume, published in the United States in 1988 as *History and Environment,* considered the role of geography and demographics, asking in particular how it happened that a region as diverse as France was nonetheless one of the first European countries to emerge as a unified nation. Richard Bernstein pointed out in the *New York Times* that although in this study Braudel focused for the first time on a single country, *The Identity of France,* no less than his earlier works, was "a tapestry woven out of numerous, diverse threads, from geological formations and patterns of early immigration to the study of place names as indexes of local character." Despite Braudel's stated goal of writing objectively, the book "positively glows with love, even personal touches of nostalgia," Bernstein observed.

The second and third volumes of Braudel's uncompleted final work were published in English in a single volume, entitled *Peoples and Production.*

A study of rural France and its role in French history, this volume received a mixed response. Roy Porter, in *New Statesman and Society,* praised Sian Reynolds's translation and described the book as "learned, provocative, and endlessly readable." Nonetheless, he decried what he termed Braudel's "flag-waving chauvinism" and his nostalgia for rural society. Porter also took exception to some of the underlying assumptions of Braudel's work and of *Annaliste* historical method in general, complaining that in privileging economic, geographic, and demographic factors the "new historical" approach undervalued the role of politics in shaping human history. Alan Forrester, however, writing in the *Times Literary Supplement,* described the book as "rich and thought-provoking," while Thomas, in the *Observer,* praised Braudel's ability to perceive interrelationships between seemingly insignificant bits of information. "Braudel looks at everything with an historical eye," Thomas observed, "and in the trivial experiences of daily life he sees the recurrence of larger patterns of human existence."

BIOGRAPHICAL/CRITICAL SOURCES:

PERIODICALS

American Journal of Sociology, May, 1982.

Chicago Tribune, March 15, 1989.
Economist, November 10, 1973.
Encounter, April, 1973.
Globe and Mail, July 22, 1989.
Harper's, May, 1982.
History, June, 1974; February, 1982.
History Today, April, 1974.
Journal of Economic History, November, 1950.
Journal of the History of Ideas, January, 1977.
Journal of Modern History, December, 1950; December, 1972.
Los Angeles Times Book Review, June 27, 1982; August 14, 1983.
Nation, February 16, 1974.
New Republic, October 1, 1984.
New Statesman, June 15, 1973; January 15, 1982; December 14, 1990, pp. 36-37.
Newsweek, March 3, 1980.
New Yorker, April 1, 1974; July 15, 1983.
New York Times, May 20, 1982; April 20, 1989.
New York Times Book Review, December 31, 1972; June 2, 1974; November 10, 1974; May 18, 1975; June 1, 1975; December 7, 1975; May 16, 1982; July 10, 1983.
Observer, November 11, 1973; December 16, 1990, p. 47.
Publishers Weekly, August 17, 1984.
Quill and Quire, July, 1983.
Saturday Review, February 27, 1973; February, 1982.
Time, May 23, 1977.
Times (London), January 22, 1981; June 21, 1984; December 17, 1988.
Times Higher Education Supplement, December 9, 1977.
Times Literary Supplement, February 15, 1968; January 21, 1983; March 29, 1991, p. 8.
Virginia Quarterly Review, spring, 1973.
Washington Post Book World, November 11, 1973; March 7, 1976; June 20, 1982; April 10, 1983.
World Press Review, March, 1985, pp. 30-32.

OBITUARIES:

BOOKS

Contemporary Authors, Volume 117, Gale, 1986.

PERIODICALS

New York Times, November 29, 1985.
Time, December 9, 1985.
Times (London), November 30, 1985.
Washington Post, November 29, 1985.*

* * *

BRIDGER, Adam
See BINGLEY, David Ernest

BROOKE, Christopher N(ugent) L(awrence) 1927-

PERSONAL: Born June 23, 1927, in Cambridge, England; son of Zachary Nugent (a university professor) and Rosa Grace (Stanton) Brooke; married Rosalind Beckford Clark (an author and historian), August 18, 1951; children: Francis Christopher, Philip David Beckford, Patrick Lawrence Harvey. *Education:* Attended Winchester College, 1940-45; Gonville and Caius College, Cambridge, B.A., 1948, M.A., 1952, Litt.D., 1973. *Religion:* Church of England.

ADDRESSES: Office—Gonville and Caius College, Cambridge CB2 1TA, England.

CAREER: Cambridge University, Cambridge, England, fellow of Gonville and Caius College, 1949-56, assistant lecturer, 1953-54, lecturer in history, 1954-56; University of Liverpool, Liverpool, England, professor of medieval history, 1956-67; University of London, Westfield College, London, England, professor of history, 1967-77; Cambridge University, Dixie Professor of Ecclesiastical History and fellow of Gonville and Caius College, 1977-94. Chair of British Academy's Medieval Episcopal Acta. *Military service:* British Army, 1948-50; became temporary captain.

MEMBER: Royal Historical Society (fellow; vice-president, 1971-74), British Academy (fellow), Society of Antiquaries of London (fellow; president, 1981-84), Cumberland and Westmorland Antiquarian and Archaeological Society (vice-president, 1985-89), Northamptonshire Record Society, Medieval Academy of America (corresponding fellow), Monumenta Germaniae Historica (corresponding member).

AWARDS, HONORS: Honorary docorate, University of York, 1984.

WRITINGS:

(Author of introduction) W. T. Mellows and P. I. King, *The Book of William Morton, Almoner of Peterborough Monastery, 1448-1467,* Northamptonshire Record Society, 1954.
(Author of introduction) W. J. Millor and H. E. Butler, editors, *The Letters of John of Salisbury,* Volume 1: *Early Letters,* Nelson, 1955.
The Dullness of the Past, Liverpool University Press, 1957.
(With others) *Studies in the Early British Church,* Cambridge University Press, 1958.
From Alfred to Henry III, Nelson, 1961.
The Saxon and Norman Kings, Batsford, 1963.
(With others) *Celt and Saxon,* Cambridge University Press, 1963.
Europe in the Central Middle Ages, Longmans, Green, 1964, 2nd edition, 1987.

(With Adrian Morey) *Gilbert Foliot and His Letters,* Cambridge University Press, 1965.
The Twelfth-Century Renaissance, Harcourt, 1971.
Medieval Church and Society, Sidgwick and Jackson, 1971.
The Structure of Medieval Society, Thames & Hudson, 1971.
(With David Knowles and V. C. M. London) *Heads of Religious Houses in England and Wales, 940-1216,* Cambridge University Press, 1972.
(With Wim Swaan) *The Monastic World,* Elek, 1974.
(With G. Keir) *London, 800-1216: The Shaping of a City,* Secker & Warburg, 1975.
Marriage in Christian History, Cambridge University Press, 1978.
(With wife, Rosalind Brooke) *Popular Religion in the Middle Ages: Western Europe, 1000-1300,* Thames & Hudson, 1984.
A History of Gonville and Caius College, Boydell & Brewer, 1985.
(And editor with David N. Dumville) *The Church and the Welsh Border in the Central Middle Ages,* Boydell and Brewer, 1986.
(With Roger Highfield and Swaan) *Oxford and Cambridge,* Cambridge University Press, 1988.
(With D. E. Luscombe) revised edition of David Knowles, *Evolution of Medieval Thought,* Longmans, 1988.
The Medieval Idea of Marriage, Oxford University Press, 1989.
(And editor of series) *A History of the University of Cambridge, IV: 1870-1990,* Cambridge University Press, 1993.

Also contributor to journals.

EDITOR

(With M. Postan) *Carte Nativorum: A Peterborough Abbey Cartulary of the Fourteenth Century,* Northamptonshire Record Society, 1960.
(With Morey) *The Letters and Charters of Gilbert Foliot, Bishop of Hereford and London, 1148-1187,* Cambridge University Press, 1967.
(With Luscombe, G. H. Martin, and D. M. Owen) *Church and Government in the Middle Ages: Essays presented to C. R. Cheney on his 70th Birthday,* Cambridge University Press, 1976.
(With Millor, and author of introduction) *The Letters of John of Salisbury,* Volume 2: *Later Letters,* Oxford Medieval Texts, 1979.
(With D. Whitelock and M. Brett) *Councils and Synods with Other Documents Relating to the English Church, 871-1204,* Oxford University Press, 1981.
(With B. H. I. H. Stewart, J. G. Pollard, and T. R. Volk) *Studies in Numismatic Method presented to Philip Grierson,* Cambridge University Press, 1983.
(With M. R. James and Sir Roger Mynors) Walter Map, *De nugis curialium,* Oxford Medieval Texts, 1983.
(With Brett and M. Winterbottom) revised edition of Hugh the Chanter, *The History of the Church of York, 1066-1127,* edited and translated by C. Johnson, Oxford Medieval Texts, 1990.
(And co-author, with Aelred Sillem, Luscombe, and Dr. Roger Lovatt) *David Knowles Remembered,* Cambridge University Press, 1991.

General editor of Oxford Medieval Texts series, 1959-87.

Many of Brooke's writings have been translated into French, Spanish, Portuguese, and Dutch.

SIDELIGHTS: Christopher N. L. Brooke described himself for *CA* as "a historian who has combined the attempt to reach a wide audience with fundamental work on medieval sources—hence 30 years of involvement in Oxford Medieval Texts series, and, more recently, Chair of the British Academy's Medieval Episcopal Acta. In the space between lay my study of medieval marriage, and of monastic remains, and Oxford and Cambridge in collaboration with the great American photographer Wim Swaan."

BIOGRAPHICAL/CRITICAL SOURCES:

BOOKS

Abulafia, David, Michael Franklin, and Miri Rubin, editors, *Church and City, 1000-1500: Essays in Honour of Christopher Brooke,* Cambridge University Press, 1992.

PERIODICALS

Times Literary Supplement, April 6, 1984.

* * *

BROOKS, Lester 1924-

PERSONAL: Born November 8, 1924, in Des Moines, IA; son of Lester James (a regional manager for Prudential Insurance) and Dorothy (Boldrick) Brooks; married Patricia Kersten (a writer), September 10, 1950; children: Lester James III, Jonathan, Christopher. *Education:* University of Iowa, A.B., 1948; Columbia University, A.M., 1949; further graduate study at University of London, 1949. *Politics:* Democrat.

ADDRESSES: *Home*—43 Marshall Ridge Rd., New Canaan, CT 06840.

CAREER: National Urban League, New York City, assistant public relations director, 1950-51, member of communication committee, 1954-74; U.S. Foreign Service, Manila, Philippines, information officer, 1951-53; Chase Manhattan Bank, New York City, community relations director, 1958-64; free-lance writer, 1965—. Director, Art Originals, Ltd.; vice-president, National Council on Philanthropy, 1964. *Military service:* U.S. Army, 1943-46; served in General Headquarters, Army Forces in the Pacific.

MEMBER: National Association for the Advancement of Colored People, National Urban League, Connecticut Civil Liberties Union, Caucus of Connecticut Democrats.

AWARDS, HONORS: Great Civilizations of Ancient Africa was a Library of Congress annual selection, American Library Association Booklist selection, and was listed by *School Library Journal* as one of the best books of 1971.

WRITINGS:

(Ghostwriter) Whitney M. Young, Jr., *To Be Equal,* McGraw, 1964.
Behind Japan's Surrender, McGraw, 1968.
(Ghostwriter) Henry Steeger, *You Can Remake America,* Doubleday, 1970.
Great Civilizations of Ancient Africa, Four Winds, 1971.
(With Guichard Parris) *Blacks in the City: A History of the Urban League,* Little, Brown, 1971.
Great American Autos (young adult), Scholastic, 1972.
African Achievements: Leaders, Civilizations and Cultures of Ancient Africa, De Gustibus Press, 1992.

WITH WIFE, PATRICIA BROOKS

How to Buy Property Abroad, Doubleday, 1974.
How to Buy a Condominium, Stein & Day, 1975, condensed edition, U.S. News & World Report, 1976.
Fisher Guide to Spain and Portugal, 1984, New American Library, 1983.
Fisher Guide to Europe, 1984, New American Library, 1983.
(Contributor) *Europe 1985* (Fisher Annotated Travel Guide Series), edited by Robert C. Fisher, Dutton, 1984.
Fisher Guide to Spain and Portugal, 1985 (Fisher Annotated Travel Guide Series), edited by Robert C. Fisher, Dutton, 1984.
Fisher Guide to Spain and Portugal, 1986 (Fisher Annotated Travel Guide Series), edited by Robert C. Fisher, Dutton, 1985.
Fisher Guide to Spain and Portugal, 1987 (Fisher Annotated Travel Guide Series), edited by Robert C. Fisher, Dutton, 1986.
(Contributor) *Fisher's World: Europe, 1988,* Fisher's World, Inc., 1988.
Fisher's World: Spain and Portugal, 1988, Fisher's World, Inc., 1988.
Crown Insider's Guide to Britain, edited by Robert C. Fisher, Crown, 1987.
Crown Insider's Guide to New York, edited by Robert C. Fisher, Crown, 1989.

BIOGRAPHICAL/CRITICAL SOURCES: periodicals

Village Voice, November 6, 1969.
Journal of Economic Literature, December, 1974.

* * *

BRUIN, John
See BRUTUS, Dennis

* * *

BRUTUS, Dennis 1924-
(John Bruin)

PERSONAL: Born November 28, 1924, in Salisbury, Southern Rhodesia (now Harare, Zimbabwe); came to the United States, 1971, granted political asylum, 1983; son of Francis Henry (a teacher) and Margaret Winifred (a teacher; maiden name, Bloemetjie) Brutus; married May Jaggers, May 14, 1950; children: Jacinta, Marc, Julian, Antony, Justina, Cornelia, Gregory, Paula. *Education:* Fort Hare University, B.A. (with distinction), 1947; University of the Witwatersrand, study of law, 1963-64.

ADDRESSES: Office—Department of Black Community Education Research and Development, University of Pittsburgh, Pittsburgh, PA 15260.

CAREER: Poet and political activist. High school teacher of English and Afrikaans in Port Elizabeth, South Africa, 1948-61; journalist in South Africa, 1960-61; imprisoned for anti-apartheid activities, Robben Island Prison, 1964-65; teacher and journalist in London, England, 1966-70; Northwestern University, Evanston, IL, professor of English, 1971-85; Swarthmore College, Swarthmore, PA, Cornell Professor of English Literature, 1985-86; University of Pittsburgh, Pittsburgh, PA, professor of black studies and English, chairman of department of black community education research and development, 1986—. Visiting professor, University of Denver, 1970, University of Texas at Austin, 1974-75, Amherst College, 1981-82, Dartmouth College, 1983, and Northeastern University, 1984. Founder of Troubadour Press. South African Sports Association (now South African Non-Racial Olympic Committee), founding secretary, 1958, president, 1963—; United Nations representative, International Defense and Aid Fund (London), 1966-71; chairman of International Campaign against Racism in Sport, 1972—; member of advisory board, ARENA: Institute for the Study of Sport and Social Analysis, 1975—; chairman, International Advisory Commission to End Apartheid in

Sport, 1975—; member of board of directors, Black Arts Celebration (Chicago), 1975—; member, Emergency Committee for World government, 1978—; member of Working Committee for Action against Apartheid (Evanston), 1978—; president of Third World Energy Resources Institute; director, World Campaign for Release of South African Political Prisoners (London).

MEMBER: International Poetry Society (fellow), International Platform Association, Union of Writers of the African People (Ghana; vice-president, 1974—), Modern Language Association, African Literature Association (founding chairman, 1975—; member of executive committee, 1979—), United Nations Association of Illinois and Greater Chicago (member of board of directors, 1978).

AWARDS, HONORS: Chancellor's prize, University of South Africa, 1947; Mbari Award, CCF, 1962, for *Sirens, Knuckles, Boots;* Freedom Writers Award, Society of Writers and Editors, 1975; Kenneth Kaunda Humanism Award, 1979; awarded key to city of Sumter, SC, 1979; Langston Hughes Award, City University of New York, 1987; Paul Robeson Award for excellence, political conscience, and integrity, 1989; honorary doctorates from institutions including Worcester State College and University of Massachusetts, 1984, and Northeastern University, 1990.

WRITINGS:

POETRY

Sirens, Knuckles, Boots, Mbari Publications, 1963.

Letters to Martha and Other Poems from a South African Prison, Heinemann, 1968.

Poems from Algiers, African and Afro-American Research Institute, University of Texas at Austin, 1970.

(Under pseudonym John Bruin) *Thoughts Abroad,* Troubadour Press, 1970.

A Simple Lust: Selected Poems Including "Sirens, Knuckles, Boots," "Letters to Martha," "Poems from Algiers," "Thoughts Abroad," Hill & Wang, 1973.

Strains, edited by Wayne Kamin and Chip Dameron, Troubadour Press, 1975, revised edition, 1982.

China Poems, translations by Ko Ching Po, African and Afro-American Studies and Research Center, University of Texas at Austin, 1975.

Stubborn Hope: New Poems and Selections from "China Poems" and "Strains," Three Continents Press, 1978.

Salutes and Censures, Fourth Dimension Publishers (Nigeria), 1984, Africa World Press, 1985.

Airs and Tributes, edited by Gil Ott, Whirlwind Press, 1989.

(Editor with Hal Wylie and Juris Silenieks) *African Literature, 1988: New Masks,* Three Continents/African Literature Association, 1990.

OTHER

The American-South African Connection (sound recording), Iowa State University of Science and Technology, 1975.

Informal Discussion in Third World Culture Class (sound recording), Media Resources Center, Iowa State University of Science and Technology, 1975.

Work represented in anthologies, including *Seven South African Poets,* edited by Cosmo Pieterse, Heinemann, 1966, Humanities, 1973; *From South Africa: New Writing, Photographs, and Art,* edited by David Bunn and Jane Taylor, University of Chicago Press, 1988; and *Words on the Page: The World in Your Hand,* edited by Catherine Lipkin and Virginia Solotaroff, Harper, 1989. Contributor to journals. Member of editorial board, *Africa Today,* 1976—, and *South and West.* Guest editor, *The Gar,* 1978.

WORK IN PROGRESS: Still the Sirens, a chapbook, for Pennywhistle Press.

SIDELIGHTS: Describing Dennis Brutus as a "soft-spoken man of acerbic views," Kevin Klose suggests in the *Washington Post* that "he is one of English-speaking Africa's best-known poets, and also happens to be one of the most successful foes of the apartheid regime in South Africa." Born in Southern Rhodesia of racially mixed parentage, Brutus spent most of his early life in South Africa.

Dismissed from his teaching post and forbidden to write by the South African government as a result of anti-apartheid activities, he was arrested in 1963 for attending a meeting in defiance of a ban on associating with any group. Seeking refuge in Swaziland following his release on bail, Brutus was apprehended in Mozambique by Portuguese secret police, who surrendered him to South African secret police.

Fearing that he would be killed in Johannesburg, where he was subsequently taken, he again tried to escape. Pursued by police, Brutus was shot in the back, tortured, and finally sentenced to eighteen months of hard labor at Robben Island Prison—"the escape-proof concentration camp for political prisoners off the South African coast," remarks Klose in another *Washington Post* article. The time Brutus spent there, says Klose, "included five months in solitary confinement, which brought him to attempt suicide, slashing at his wrists with sharp stones."

After Brutus's release from prison, he was placed under house arrest and was prohibited from either leaving his home or receiving visitors. He was permitted to leave South Africa, however, "on the condition that he not return, according to court records, and he took his family to England," states William C. Rempel in the *Los Angeles Times.* Granted a conditional British passport because of Rhodesia's former colonial status, Brutus journeyed to the

United States, where temporary visas allowed him to remain. Rempel notes, however, that Brutus's "passport became snarled in technical difficulties when Rhodesia's white supremacist government was overthrown and Zimbabwe was created." In the process of applying for a new passport, Brutus missed his application deadline for another visa; and the United States government began deportation proceedings immediately. Brutus was ultimately granted political asylum because a return to Zimbabwe, given its proximity to South Africa, would place his life in imminent danger. Klose indicates that Brutus's efforts to remain in the United States have been at the expense of his art, though: "He has written almost no poetry, which once sustained him through the years of repression and exile."

Suggesting that Brutus's "poetry draws its haunting strength from his own suffering and from the unequal struggle of 25 million blacks, 'coloreds,' Indians and Orientals to throw off the repressive rule by the 4.5 million South African whites," Klose remarks that "there is no doubt in Brutus' mind of the power and relevance of his poetry to the struggle." Brutus's works are officially banned in South Africa. When, for example, his *Thoughts Abroad,* a collection of poems concerned with exile and alienation, was published under the pseudonym of John Bruin, it was immediately successful and was even taught in South African colleges; but when the government discovered that Brutus was the author, all copies were confiscated. The effectiveness of the South African government's censorship policies is evidenced by the degree to which Brutus's writing is known there. Colin Gardner, who thinks that "it seems likely that many well-read South Africans, even some of those with a distinct interest in South African poetry, are wholly or largely unacquainted with his writing," declares in *Research in African Literatures* that "Brutus as a writer exists, as far as the Pretoria government is concerned, as a vacuum, an absence; in the firmament of South African literature, such as it is, Brutus could be described as a black hole. But it is necessary to find him and read him, to talk and write about him, to pick up the light which in fact he does emit, because he is at his best as important as any other South African who has written poetry in English."

Deeming Brutus's poetry "the reaction of one who is in mental agony whether he is at home or abroad," R. N. Egudu suggests in Christopher Heywood's *Aspects of South African Literature* that "this agony is partly caused by harassments, arrests, and imprisonment, and mainly by Brutus's concern for other suffering people." Brutus's first volume of poetry, *Sirens, Knuckles, Boots,* which earned him the Mbari Award, includes a variety of verse, including love poems as well as poems of protest against South Africa's racial policies. Much of his subsequent poetry concerns imprisonment and exile. For example, *Letters to Martha and Other Poems from a South African Prison* was written under the guise of letters—the writing of which, unlike poetry, was not prohibited—and is composed of poems about his experiences as a political prisoner. His *Simple Lust: Selected Poems Including "Sirens, Knuckles, Boots," "Letters to Martha," "Poems from Algiers," "Thoughts Abroad"* represents "a collection of all Brutus' poetry relating to his experience of jail and exile," notes Paul Kameen in *Best Sellers.* Similarly, *Stubborn Hope: New Poems and Selections from "China Poems" and "Strains"* "contains several poems which deal directly with the traumatic period of his life when he was imprisoned on the island," states Jane Grant in *Index on Censorship.* Discussing the "interaction between the personal and political" in Brutus's poetry, Gardner points out that "the poet is aware that he has comrades in his political campaigns and struggles, but under intense government pressure, there is no real sense of mass movement. The fight for liberation will be a long one, and a sensitive participant cannot but feel rather isolated. This isolation is an important aspect of the poet's mode and mood."

Chikwenye Okonjo Ogunyemi thinks that although Brutus's writing is inspired by his imprisonment, it is "artistic rather than overtly propagandistic"; the critic observes in *Ariel* that "he writes to connect his inner life with the outside world and those who love him. . . . That need to connect with posterity, a reason for the enduring, is a genuine artistic feeling." Perceiving an early "inner conflict between Brutus, the activist against *apartheid,* and Brutus, the highly literate writer of difficult, complex and lyrical poetry," Grant suggests that "the months in solitary confinement on Robben Island seem to have led him to a radical reassessment of his role as poet." Moving toward a less complex poetry, "the trend culminates in the extreme brevity and economy of the *China Poems* (the title refers both to where they were written and to the delicate nature of the poems)," says Grant. "They are seldom more than a few lines long, and are influenced by the Japanese *haiku* and its Chinese ancestor, the *chueh chu.*" These poems, according to Hans Zell's *New Reader's Guide to South African Literature,* evolved from Brutus's trip to the Republic of China and were composed "in celebration of the people and the values he met there." Calling him "learned, passionate, skeptical," Gessler Moses Nkondo says in *World Literature Today* that "Brutus is a remarkable poet, one of the most distinguished South Africa has produced." Nkondo explains that "the lucidity and precision which he is at pains to develop in his work are qualities he admires from artistic conviction, as a humanist opposed both to romantic haze and conventional trends. But they also testify to a profound cultivation of spirit, a certain wholeness and harmony of nature, as they do too to a fine independence of literary fashion."

Influenced by the seventeenth-century metaphysical poets, Brutus employs traditional poetic forms and rich language in his work; Nkondo proposes that what "Brutus fastens on is a composite sensibility made up of the passionate subtleties and the intellectual sensuousness of the metaphysical poets and the masculine, ironic force of [John] Donne." Noting that Brutus assumes the persona of a troubadour throughout his poetry, Tanure Ojaide writes in *Ariel* that while it serves to unify his work, the choice of "the persona of the troubadour to express himself is particularly significant as the moving and fighting roles of the medieval errant, though romantic, tally with his struggle for justice in South Africa, a land he loves dearly as the knight his mistress. The movement contrasts with the stasis of despair and enacts the stubborn hope that despite the suffering, there shall be freedom and justice for those *now* unfree." And Gardner believes that "Brutus's best poetry has a resonance which both articulates and generalizes his specific themes; he has found forms and formulations which dramatize an important part of the agony of South Africa and of contemporary humanity."

Brutus "has traveled widely and written and testified extensively against the Afrikaner-run government's policies," remarks Klose. "In the world of activism, where talk can easily outweigh results, his is a record of achievement." For instance, Klose states that Brutus's voice against apartheid is largely responsible for South Africa's segregated sports teams having been "barred from most international competitions, including the Olympics since 1964." Egudu observes that in Brutus's "intellectual protest without malice, in his mental agony over the apartheid situation in South Africa, in his concern for the sufferings of the others, and in his hope which has defied all despair—all of which he has portrayed through images and diction that are imbued with freshness and vision—Brutus proves himself a capable poet fully committed to his social responsibility." And according to Klose, Brutus maintains: "You have to make it a two-front fight. You have to struggle inside South Africa to unprop the regime, and struggle in the United States—to challenge the U.S. role, and if possible, inhibit it. Cut off the money, the flow of arms, the flow of political and military support. You have to educate the American people. And that is what I think I'm doing."

BIOGRAPHICAL/CRITICAL SOURCES:

BOOKS

Beier, Ulli, editor, *Introduction to African Literature,* Northwestern University Press, 1967.

Black Literature Criticism, Gale, 1992, pp. 307-20.

Contemporary Authors Autobiography Series, Volume 14, Gale, 1991, pp. 53-64.

Contemporary Literary Criticism, Volume 43, Gale, 1987.

Dictionary of Literary Biography, Volume 117: *Twentieth-Century Caribbean and Black African Writers,* Gale, 1992, pp. 98-106.

Heywood, Christopher, editor, *Aspects of South African Literature,* Africana Publishing, 1976.

A History of Africa, Horizon Press, 1971.

Legum, Colin, editor, *The Bitter Choice,* World Publishing, 1968.

Pieterse, Cosmo, and Dennis Duerden, editors, *African Writers Talking,* Africana Publishing, 1972.

Zell, Hans M., and others, *A New Reader's Guide to African Literature,* 2nd revised and expanded edition, Holmes & Meier, 1983.

PERIODICALS

Ariel, October, 1982; January, 1986.

Best Sellers, October 1, 1973.

Index on Censorship, July/August, 1979.

Los Angeles Times, September 7, 1983.

New York Times, January 29, 1986.

Research in African Literatures, fall, 1984.

Washington Post, August 13, 1983; September 7, 1983.

World Literature Today, spring, 1979; autumn, 1979; winter, 1981.*

* * *

BURGESS, Eric 1920-

PERSONAL: Born May 30, 1920, in Stockport, Cheshire, England; son of William (an engineer) and Lily Burgess; married Lilian Slater, August 9, 1947; children: Janis Marie, Stephen Roy, Howard John. *Education:* Attended College of Commerce, Manchester, England, 1934-40, College of Technology, Manchester, 1953-56, and University of California, Los Angeles, 1958-59.

ADDRESSES: Home and office—13361 Frati Lane, Sebastopol, CA 95472.

CAREER: Amson Associated Companies, Manchester, England, secretary-accountant, 1946-56; Telecomputing Corp., North Hollywood, CA, proposal-coordinator in Data Instruments Division, 1956-58, senior member of technical staff in Electronic Systems Division, 1958-60; Mellonics, Inc. (data systems consultants), Tucson, AZ, vice-president of technical services, 1960-62; Douglas Aircraft, Missiles and Space Systems Division, Santa Monica, CA, staff assistant in advance programs department, 1962-63; Informatics Inc., Sherman Oaks, CA, member of senior staff, 1963-65; Wolf Research and Development Corp., Encino, CA, deputy director of Los Angeles division, 1965-69; *Christian Science Monitor,* Boston, MA, staff correspondent, 1969-72; free-lance writer, 1972—.

Senior vice-president of Space Microwave Laboratories, Inc., 1982-85; president of American Only, Inc., 1984-89. Science advisor to the film *Moonraker,* 1978-79. Lecturer on space flight to technical groups and to lay audiences in Europe and the United States. *Military service:* Royal Air Force, Technical Training Command, 1940-46.

MEMBER: British Interplanetary Society (fellow; chairman, 1945-46), Royal Astronomical Society (fellow), American Institute of Aeronautics and Astronautics (associate fellow), Manchester Astronomical Society (honorary member; vice-president, 1952-56), American Astronautical Society (senior member; chairman, Los Angeles section, 1959-60), National Association of Science Writers.

AWARDS, HONORS: Royal Air Force Quarterly prize, 1945, for essay "Effects of Directed Missiles on Future Warfare and the Defense of the British Commonwealth"; Award of Excellence, Communications Art Magazine, 1979, for booklet, *Galileo to Jupiter.*

WRITINGS:

Rocket Propulsion, Chapman & Hall, 1952.
Frontier to Space, Chapman & Hall, 1955, Macmillan, 1956.
Rockets and Space Flight, Hodder & Stoughton, 1956.
Guided Weapons, Macmillan, 1956, Chapman & Hall, 1957.
Satellites and Space Flight, Chapman & Hall, 1957, Macmillan, 1958.
(With John Herrick) *Rocket Encyclopedia,* Aero, 1959.
(Editor with H. Jacobs) *Advances in the Astronautical Sciences,* Volume 6, Macmillan, 1960, Volume 7, Plenum, 1961, Volume 8, Plenum, 1962, (sole editor) Volumes 9 and 12, Western Periodicals, 1963.
Long Range Ballistic Missiles, Chapman & Hall, 1961, Macmillan, 1962.
(Editor) *On-Line Computing Systems,* American Data Processing, 1965.
Assault on the Moon, Hodder & Stoughton, 1967.
(Editor) *The Next Billion Years,* National Aeronautics and Space Administration, 1974.
(With R. O. Fimmel and W. Swindell) *Pioneer Odyssey: Encounter with a Giant,* National Aeronautics and Space Administration, 1974, revised edition, 1977.
(With Bruce Murray) *Flight to Mercury,* Columbia University Press, 1977.
(With James A. Dunne) *The Voyage of Mariner 10,* National Aeronautics and Space Administration, 1978.
To the Red Planet, Columbia University Press, 1978.
(With Fimmel and James Van Allen) *Pioneer: First to Jupiter, Saturn, and Beyond,* National Aeronautics and Space Administration, 1980.
Celestial Basic, Sybex, 1982, revised edition, 1985.
By Jupiter, Columbia University Press, 1982.
(With Howard J. Burgess) *Astronomy on Your Computer,* Sybex, 1983.
(With Fimmel and L. Colin) *Pioneer Venus,* National Aeronautics and Space Administration, 1983.
Venus, Columbia University Press, 1985.
Halley's Comet on Your Home Computer, American Only, Inc., 1985.
(With Douglass Torr) *Into the Thermosphere,* National Aeronautics and Space Administration, 1987.
Uranus and Neptune, Columbia University Press, 1988.
Return to the Red Planet, Columbia University Press, 1990.
Far Encounter: The Neptune System, Columbia University Press, 1991.
Outpost on Apollo's Moon, Columbia University Press, 1992.

Ghost writer for many NASA mission booklets and educational materials, including *Galileo to Jupiter.* Contributor to books, including *Space Encyclopedia,* Dutton, 1957; and *Space Weapons,* Praeger, 1959. General editor, "American Astronautical Society's Science and Technology" series, Volumes 1-6, Western Periodicals, 1965, and Volumes 7-12, American Astronautical Society, 1966. Contributor to aeronautical publications in the United States, England, Australia, and Switzerland.

WORK IN PROGRESS: Meteor Red, a novel; *From Hydrogen: With Love?,* a nonfiction work about cosmology.

SIDELIGHTS: Eric Burgess once told *CA:* "I have been privileged in my lifetime to witness and often gain an understanding of many wonderful aspects of the universe in which we live; of galaxies and stars, of people, and of molecules and atoms. My aim in all my writings is to convey the excitement of the universe and its exploration by the human mind in space and time, and particularly to encourage great optimism for the future prospects of our species and its developing and expanding consciousness."

BIOGRAPHICAL/CRITICAL SOURCES:

PERIODICALS

Los Angeles Citizen News, August 6, 1958.
Los Angeles Mirror News, August 6, 1958.
Mercury, October, 1976.

* * *

BURGESS, Jane K. 1928-
(Jane Burgess-Kohn)

PERSONAL: Born January 1, 1928, in Stevens Point, WI; daughter of Karl W. and Alice (Bruce) Menzel; married Samuel G. Burgess (died, 1964); married Willard K.

Kohn, November 20, 1974 (divorced, 1978); children: (first marriage) David Bruce, Elizabeth Burgess, Erven. *Education:* University of Wisconsin—Stevens Point, B.S., 1964; University of Wisconsin—Milwaukee, M.S., 1965; University of Illinois, Ph.D., 1972.

ADDRESSES: Home—Waukesha, WI. *Office*—Department of Sociology, University of Wisconsin Center—Waukesha County, Waukesha, WI 53188.

CAREER: University of Wisconsin Center—Waukesha County, Waukesha, assistant professor, 1967-71, associate professor, 1972-76, professor of sociology, 1979-90, professor emeritus. Lecturer to single adults and single parent groups, and to high school students and businesses.

MEMBER: Wisconsin Sociological Association (president, 1975-76), Wisconsin Council on Family Relations (president, 1981-82), Fay McBeath Council on Aging, National Forum for Death Education and Counseling, Midwest Human Relations Association, Midwest Society for Women Sociologists, Midwest Sociological Association, National Council on Family Relations.

AWARDS, HONORS: University of Oslo grant, 1970; University of Wisconsin travel grant, 1970.

WRITINGS:

(With Willard K. Kohn, under name Jane Burgess-Kohn) *The Widowers,* Beacon Press, 1978.

Straight Talk about Love and Sex for Teenagers, Beacon Press, 1979.

The Single-Again Man, Lexington Books, 1988.

Contributor to books, including *What Do I Do Now?,* edited by Charles Zastrow and Zae H. Chang, Spectrum, 1976; *Dimensions of Fathering: A Book of Readings,* edited by Frederick W. Bozett and Shirley Hanson, Auburn Publishers, 1984; *Family Strengths 6: Enhancement of Interaction,* edited by R. Williams, H. Lingren, et al., University of Nebraska Press, 1985. Also contributor of articles and reviews to periodicals, including *Parents' Magazine, Medical Aspects of Human Sexuality, Bulletin for Industrial Management, Family Coordinator,* and *Wisconsin Sociologist.*

WORK IN PROGRESS: The Stay at Home Professional Woman; Who Chooses to Remain Home with Her Young Children.

SIDELIGHTS: Jane K. Burgess told *CA:* "I feel that people need reliable, factual information written in a comfortable, easy-to-understand manner when they are coping with difficult emotional and social problems. Most of my recent articles and books are written with the desire to put information in the hands of the lay person rather than in a professional journal tucked away in some library. For example, my first attempt at writing a book was prompted by the realization that there was no literature to help a man cope with his pain when his wife dies.

"As for writing *Straight Talk about Love and Sex for Teenagers,* after ten years of speaking to high school students in an attempt to provide them with answers to their very personal, often delicate questions about their sexuality, I felt compelled to answer their questions in a book. My message to teenagers is that it is all right to say 'No.' It attempts to resolve the myths that young people have about sexual relations, which are [that] every girl expects a young man to proposition her for sex, and that every boy will be viewed as a 'square' if he doesn't. Young people need factual information about love, sex, intimacy, about the emotional aspects of a sexual relationship, about the consequences of irresponsible sexual behavior. It is curiosity and ignorance about these matters, not information, that is the root of so much of the tragedy related to venereal disease and premarital pregnancies."

Burgess added: "At this moment in time, with AIDS and chlamydia in epidemic proportions, it is even more important for children to receive accurate information."

* * *

BURGESS, M. R.
See BURGESS, Michael (Roy)

* * *

BURGESS, Michael (Roy) 1948-
(Miguel Alcalde, M. R. Burgess, Mike Burgess, Boden Clarke, C. Everett Cooper, Michael Demotes, G. Forbes Durand, Misha Grazhdanin, Andrew Kapel, Jacob Lawson, Peter Mauzy, Rex Miletus, Walt Mobley, Jack B. Nimble, Daniel Painter, R. R., Nero Rale, Reginald, R. Reginald, Robert Reginald, Lucretia Sharpe, Tertius Spartacus, Lucas Webb; Peter Harding, a house pseudonym)

PERSONAL: Born February 11, 1948, in Fukuoka, Japan; son of Roy Walter (an Air Force major) and Betty Jane (Kapel) Burgess; married Mary Alice Wickizer Rogers (co-publisher of Borgo Press), October 15, 1976; stepchildren: Richard Albert Rogers, (Mary) Louise Reynnells. *Education:* Gonzaga University, A.B. (with honors), 1969; University of Southern California, M.L.S., 1970. *Politics:* "Anarchist." *Religion:* "Basically anti-."

ADDRESSES: Home—P.O. Box 2845, San Bernardino, CA 92406. *Office*—California State University at San Bernardino, 5500 University Parkway, San Bernardino, CA 92407.

CAREER: California State University, San Bernardino, periodicals librarian, 1970-75, assistant librarian, 1975-78, senior assistant librarian, 1978-81, associate librarian, 1981-84, librarian (with rank of professor), 1984—, chief cataloger, 1980—; free-lance writer and editor, 1970—; Newcastle Publishing Co., Inc., North Hollywood, CA, editor, 1971-92; Arno Press, New York City, advisory editor, 1975-78; Borgo Press, San Bernardino, CA, co-founder, publisher and editor, 1975—; publisher and anonymous co-editor, *Science Fiction and Fantasy Book Review,* 1979-80. Member of state-wide Librarians Task Force and founding editor of *Librarians Task Force Newsletter,* 1987-89.

MEMBER: International PEN, International Association for the Fantastic in the Arts, International Genealogical Society, World Science Fiction Society, Science Fiction and Fantasy Writers of America, Inc., Science Fiction Research Association, Horror Writers of America, National Genealogical Society, Upper Cumberland Valley Genealogical Society, National Education Association, American Library Association, American Association of University Professors, California Teachers Association, California Faculty Association, California Library Association, William Morris Society and Kelmscott Fellowship, Kentucky Historical Society, Blue Earth County Historical Society, Grant County Historical Society, City of San Bernardino Historical and Pioneer Society, Muskingum County Historical Society, American Civil Liberties Union.

AWARDS, HONORS: Title II fellowship, University of Southern California, 1969-70; Hugo Award nomination, World Science Fiction Society, selection as an outstanding academic book, *Choice,* both 1980, both for *Science Fiction and Fantasy Literature;* bronze plaque, On-Line Computer Library Center, Inc. (OCLC), for inputting the ten-millionth entry into the OCLC data base, 1983; Meritorious Performance and Professional Promise Award, California State University, 1987; *Reference Guide to Science Fiction, Fantasy, and Horror* was selected as an outstanding academic book by *Choice* and was selected as an outstanding reference source by *American Libraries* and by *Booklist/Reference Books Bulletin,* all 1993; Lifetime Collectors Award, Barry R. Levin, 1993; Pilgrim Award, Science Fiction Research Association, 1993, for "his invaluable contribution to science fiction, fantasy, and horror literature;" Burgess named outstanding librarian for 1992-93 by California State University, San Bernardino.

WRITINGS:

(Published anonymously) *Stella Nova: The Contemporary Science Fiction Authors,* Unicorn & Son, 1970, revised edition published under pseudonym R. Reginald as *Contemporary Science Fiction Authors—First Edition,* Arno Press, 1975.

(Anonymous editor and rewriter) Robert A. Lee, *Alistair MacLean: The Key Is Fear,* Borgo, 1976.

(Anonymous editor and rewriter) Frank D. Campbell, Jr., *John D. MacDonald and the Colorful World of Travis McGee,* Borgo, 1977.

The House of the Burgesses, Borgo, 1983, second edition by Michael Burgess and Mary Wickizer, 1993.

(With wife, Mary A. Burgess) *The Wickizer Annals: Wickizer, Wickiser, Wickkiser, Wickkizer, Wickheiser,* Borgo, 1983.

A Guide to Science Fiction and Fantasy in the Library of Congress Classification Scheme, Borgo, 1984, 2nd edition, 1988.

(With Jeffrey M. Elliot) *The Work of R. Reginald: An Annotated Bibliography and Guide,* Borgo, 1985, revised edition by Michael Burgess published as *The Work of Robert Reginald: An Annotated Bibliography and Guide,* 1992.

Mystery and Detective Fiction in the Library of Congress Classification Scheme, Borgo, 1987.

(With Beverly A. Ryan) *Western Fiction in the Library of Congress Classification Scheme,* Borgo, 1988.

(Editor with M. A. Burgess) Burgess McK. Shumway, *California Ranchos: Patented Private Land Grants Listed by County,* Borgo, 1988.

(Author of introduction) Vere Langford Oliver, *The Monumental Inscriptions in the Churches and Churchyards of the Island of Barbados, British West Indies,* Borgo/Sidewinder, 1989.

(Editor with M. A. Burgess) William L. Clay, *To Kill or Not to Kill: Thoughts on Capital Punishment,* Borgo, 1990.

Reference Guide to Science Fiction, Fantasy, and Horror, Libraries Unlimited, 1992.

(With M. A. Burgess and Daryl F. Mallett) *The State and Province Vital Records Guide,* Borgo, 1993.

(Author of introduction) Oliver, *More Monumental Inscriptions: Tombstones of the British West Indies,* Sidewinder, 1993.

UNDER PSEUDONYM BODEN CLARKE

The Work of Jeffrey M. Elliot: An Annotated Bibliography and Guide, Borgo, 1984.

Lords Temporal and Lords Spiritual: A Chronological Checklist of the Popes, Patriarchs, Katholikoi, and Independent Archbishops and Metropolitans of the Autocephalous Monarchical Churches of the Christian East and West, Including the Roman Catholic Church and Its Eastern Dependencies, the Independent Eastern Orthodox Churches, the Armenian Churches, the Coptic Churches, the Jacobite Churches of Syria and

India, the Ethiopian Church, and the Church of the Sinai, Borgo, 1985, 2nd edition, 1993.
(With James Hopkins) *The Work of William F. Nolan: An Annotated Bibliography and Guide,* Borgo, 1988.
(Editor) Colin Stanley, *The Work of Colin Wilson: An Annotated Bibliography and Guide,* Borgo, 1989.
(Editor) Halbert W. Hall, *The Work of Chad Oliver: An Annotated Bibliography and Guide,* Borgo, 1989.
(Editor) Douglas Menville, *The Work of Ross Rocklynne: An Annotated Bibliography and Guide,* Borgo, 1989.
(Editor) Douglas A. Mackey, *The Work of Ian Watson: An Annotated Bibliography and Guide,* Borgo, 1989.
(Editor) Scott A. Burgess, *The Work of Reginald Bretnor: An Annotated Bibliography and Guide,* Borgo, 1989.
(Editor) Elliot, *The Work of Pamela Sargent: An Annotated Bibliography and Guide,* Borgo, 1990.
(Editor) S. A. Burgess, *The Work of Dean Ing: An Annotated Bibliography and Guide,* Borgo, 1990.
(Editor) Elliot, *The Work of Jack Dann: An Annotated Bibliography and Guide,* Borgo, 1990.
(Editor with Paul David Seldis) Sheikh R. Ali and Elliot, *The Trilemma of World Oil Politics,* Borgo, 1991.
(Editor) Hall, *The Work of Louis L'Amour: An Annotated Bibliography and Guide,* Borgo, 1991.
(Editor) Margaret Aldiss, *The Work of Brian W. Aldiss: An Annotated Bibliography and Guide,* Borgo, 1992.
(With M. A. Burgess) *The Work of Katherine Kurtz: An Annotated Bibliography and Guide,* Borgo, 1993.
(Editor) Mallet and Jerry Hewett, *The Work of Jack Vance: An Annotated Bibliography and Guide,* Borgo, Underwood/Miller, 1993.

UNDER PSEUDONYM C. EVERETT COOPER

Up Your Asteroid! A Science Fiction Farce, Borgo, 1977.

UNDER PSEUDONYM R. REGINALD

(Editor with Menville) *Ancestral Voices: An Anthology of Early Science Fiction,* Arno Press, 1975.
(Editor with Menville) *Phantasmagoria: An Original Anthology,* Arno Press, 1976.
(Editor with Menville) *Ancient Hauntings,* Arno Press, 1976.
(Editor with Menville) *R.I.P.: Five Stories of the Supernatural,* Arno Press, 1976.
(Editor with Menville) *The Spectre Bridegroom and Other Horrors,* Arno Press, 1976.
(With Menville) *Things to Come: An Illustrated History of the Science Fiction Film,* Times Books, 1977, Borgo, 1983.
(Editor with Menville) *King Solomon's Children: Some Parodies of H. Rider Haggard,* Arno Press, 1978.
(Editor with Menville) *Dreamers of Dreams: An Anthology of Fantasy,* Arno Press, 1978, revised edition, Starmont House, 1991.
(Editor with Menville) *They: Three Parodies of H. Rider Haggard's "She,"* Arno Press, 1978.
(Editor with Menville) *Worlds of Never: Three Fantastic Novels,* Arno Press, 1978.
(Editor with Neil Barron) *Science Fiction and Fantasy Book Review,* Borgo, 1980.
(With Kevin B. Hancer) *The Paperback Price Guide,* Overstreet Publications, 1980, 2nd edition, 1982, 3rd edition published as *Hancer's Price Guide to Paperback Books,* Wallace-Homestead, 1990.
(With Elliot) *If J.F.K. Had Lived: A Political Scenario,* Borgo, 1981.
Science Fiction and Fantasy Awards: A Comprehensive Guide to the Awards and Their Winners, Borgo, 1981, 2nd edition, 1991, 3rd edition by Robert Reginald and Mallett published as *Reginald's Science Fiction and Fantasy Awards,* 1993.
(Editor and author of introduction) Patricia and Lionel Fanthorpe, *The Holy Grail Revealed: The Real Secret of Rennes-Le-Chateau,* Newcastle, 1982, Borgo, 1989.
(Editor) Leszek Szymanski, *Candle for Poland: 469 Days of Solidarity,* Borgo, 1982.
(With Elliot) *Tempest in a Teapot: The Falkland Islands War,* Borgo, 1983.
(With Thaddeus Dikty) *The Work of Julian May: An Annotated Bibliography and Guide,* Borgo, 1985.
(With Menville and M. A. Burgess) *Futurevisions: The New Golden Age of the Science Fiction Film,* Newcastle, Borgo, 1985.
(Editor) *The Work of Bruce McAllister: An Annotated Bibliography and Guide,* Borgo, 1985, revised edition, 1986.
(With Elliot) *The Work of George Zebrowski: An Annotated Bibliography and Guide,* Borgo, 1986.
(Editor) Nolan, *The Work of Charles Beaumont: An Annotated Bibliography and Guide,* Borgo, 1986, 2nd edition published under pseudonym Boden Clarke, 1990.
(With Elliot) *The Arms Control, Disarmament, and Military Security Dictionary,* ABC-CLIO, 1989.

UNDER PSEUDONYM ROBERT REGINALD

Science Fiction and Fantasy Literature, Gale, Volume 1: *A Checklist, 1700-1974,* Volume 2: *Contemporary Science Fiction Authors II,* 1979.
(Contributor) Noelle Watson and Paul E. Schellinger, editors, *Twentieth-Century Science-Fiction Writers,* 3rd edition (Burgess not associated with earlier editions), St. James Press, 1991.
Science Fiction and Fantasy Literature, 1975-1991: A Bibliography of Science Fiction, Fantasy, and Horror Books and Nonfiction Monographs, Gale, 1992.
(Author of introduction) William Gandy, editor, *The Association Oath Rolls of the British Plantations (New*

York, Virginia, Etc.), A.D. 1696, Being a Contribution to Political History, Sidewinder, 1993.

(Editor) J. Kenneth Van Dover, *Polemical Popes: The Martin Beck Novels of Maj Sjowall and Peter Wahloo,* Brownstone, 1993.

Associate editor, *Science Fiction Research Association Review,* 1993—.

UNDER PSEUDONYMS R. REGINALD AND M. R. BURGESS

Cumulative Paperback Index, 1939-1959, Gale, 1973.

UNDER PSEUDONYM LUCAS WEBB

The Attempted Assassination of John F. Kennedy: A Political Fantasy, Borgo, 1976.

OTHER

Editor or co-editor of Borgo monographic series *Popular Writers of Today, Popular Music of Today, The Autocephalous Orthodox Churches, Bibliographies of Modern Authors, Black Literary Studies, Black Political Studies, Borgo Bioviews, Borgo Cataloging Guides, Borgo Ethnic Studies, Borgo Family Histories, Borgo Literary Guides, Borgo Political Scenarios, Borgo Reference Guides, Brownstone Mystery Guides, Classics of Fantastic Literature, Clipper Studies in the (American) Theater* (with Dr. William L. Slout), *Essays on Fantastic Literature, Great Issues of the Day, I.O. Evans Studies in the Philosophy and Criticism of Literature, Imaginary Wars and Battles, New Religious Movement Series, San Bernardino County Studies, Ship Registries of the United States, Sidewinder Reprints, St. Willibrord Studies in Philosophy and Religion, Stokvis Studies in Historical Chronology and Thought, Studies in Judaica and the Holocaust,* and *West Coast Studies.* Associate editor, *Forgotten Fantasy,* Nectar Press, 1970-71. Advisory editor, with Menville, of "Forgotten Fantasy Library" series, Newcastle, 1973-80, "Science Fiction" series, Arno Press, 1975, "Supernatural and Occult Fiction" series, Arno Press, 1976, and "Lost Race and Adult Fantasy" series, Arno Press, 1978.

Contributor under various pseudonyms of over 140 articles, reviews, and short stories to numerous periodicals.

SIDELIGHTS: Michael Burgess, better known to his readers and others in the publishing world as "R. Reginald," "Robert Reginald," or just "Reginald," first used his pseudonym in connection with an article he wrote for Gonzaga University's literary magazine. "I was rather shy and secretive as a kid," he explains, "and I rather relished the thought of publishing under an assumed name." Reginald expropriated the pseudonym from one of his favorite characters in the work of short story writer Saki (H. H. Munro), who had found *his* pseudonym in Edward FitzGerald's version of *The Rubaiyat of Omar Khayyam.* Continues the author: "At first, it was just 'R. Reginald,' but naturally I started getting questions about the 'R' part of it, so I adopted as my given name 'Robert'. . . . Once started, it's impossible to go back."

In the years since, Reginald has become a prolific author and editor of bibliographic and research books, primarily in the genres of science fiction and fantasy, but also dealing with politics and current affairs, religion, history, and genealogy. During the course of his career he has founded two publishing companies (Unicorn and Son, in 1970, and the Borgo Press, which he has operated with his wife, Mary Burgess, since 1975) and acquired nearly twenty more pseudonyms. "I suppose this is the price one pays for being prolific, and for having one's own press," he says in *The Work of R. Reginald.* "It's sometimes more convenient to run a particular book through Borgo. To avoid the appearance of going to the well once too often, I use other names; in this way, the books stand or fall on their own merits, as they should."

Reginald's career as a compiler of bibliographies began in 1968 when, inspired by a visit to a science fiction convention, he assembled a 'who's who' of science fiction writers entitled *Stella Nova.* Intended to be his senior Honor's project, *Stella Nova* served as a learning experience, exposing him to the many labors and responsibilities involved in publishing a book. In retrospect, he notes in *The Work of R. Reginald,* "I learned more from doing that book than I had from all the classes I had taken in my previous years of college."

Shortly after the completion of *Stella Nova,* Reginald queried several publishing companies as to their interest in producing a more detailed volume to be entitled *Science Fiction and Fantasy Literature, a Checklist.* Among those he queried was Gale Research, which offered him a contract for not one but two books: *Science Fiction and Fantasy Literature* and *Cumulative Paperback Index, 1939-1959.* Originally slated as a two-year project, *Science Fiction and Fantasy Literature* took five years to research, during which time Reginald read or skimmed through almost 20,000 books by more than 1,000 authors. He also added 350 entries from *Stella Nova,* bringing the total number of biographies to 1,443—most of them read and confirmed by the individual authors. Reginald spent another year typing the manuscript into a camera-ready form (a laborious task which Gale had offered him double royalty to complete himself). Six years and 1,200 pages later *Science Fiction and Fantasy Literature* was complete; its 1,500 page supplement, covering an additional 22,000 books printed between 1975 and 1991, was published by Gale in 1992.

As for his writing, Reginald told *CA* that "it's difficult to say much about oneself without seeming pompous or just plain silly. The mystique of the writer has been romanticized far beyond the bounds of reality or good sense; I sometimes wonder if any of us have contributed as much to society as one good licensed plumber. . . .

"But I love my work, I love the independence that goes with it, I love making things that would not have existed without me. Call it conceit or egoism or whatever you will, but I like seeing my name in print. The thought that some of my books might just survive this corporeal presence I call R. Reginald still manages to thrill me."

BIOGRAPHICAL/CRITICAL SOURCES:

BOOKS

Ash, Brian, *The Visual Encyclopedia of Science Fiction,* Harmony Books, 1977.

Barron, Neil, editor, *Anatomy of Wonder: A Critical Guide to Science Fiction,* Bowker, 1976, 3rd edition, 1987.

Burgess, Michael and Jeffrey M. Elliot, *The Work of R. Reginald: An Annotated Bibliography and Guide,* Borgo, 1985.

Burgess, Michael, *The Work of Robert Reginald: An Annotated Bibliography and Guide,* Borgo, 1992.

Harrison, Harry, and Brian W. Aldiss, editors, *Best SF: 1970,* Putnam, 1971.

Lerner, Frederick Andrew, *Modern Science Fiction and the American Literary Community,* Scarecrow, 1985.

Magill, Frank N., *Survey of Modern Fantasy Literature,* Salem Press, 1983, p. 2520.

Schlobin, Roger C., *The Literature of Fantasy,* Garland, 1979.

Tymn, Marshall B., *The Science Fiction Reference Book,* Starmont House, 1981.

PERIODICALS

American Political Science Review, September, 1983, pp. 794-795.

Bulletin of the Science Fiction Writers of America, winter, 1984, pp. 6-10.

Chicago Tribune Book World, December 28, 1980, p. 4.

Durham Morning Herald, October 2, 1983.

Fantasy Newsletter, January, 1980; March, 1980; January, 1981.

Fantasy Review, February, 1985, p. 29.

Foreign Affairs, winter, 1982/83, p. 475.

Gale Gazette, fall, 1987, pp. 27-29.

Los Angeles Times Book Review, January 27, 1980, p. 2; September 5, 1982, p. 4.

Magazine of Fantasy and Science Fiction, August, 1974, p. 58; May, 1978, p. 104; April, 1983, pp. 47-48.

OCLC Newsletter, November, 1983, p. 13.

Raleigh News and Observer, October 3, 1983.

Reference Services Review, winter, 1984.

San Bernardino Sun, July 17, 1977, p. C1; January 5, 1981, p. A5.

Science Fiction Review, May, 1978, p. 31.

Science Fiction and Fantasy Book Review, November, 1979, p. 140; February, 1980, p. 26; May, 1982, p. 13.

Texas Journal of Political Studies, spring/summer, 1984, pp. 77-78.

*   *   *

BURGESS, Mike
See BURGESS, Michael (Roy)

*   *   *

BURGESS-KOHN, Jane
See BURGESS, Jane K.

C

CAMBER, Andrew
See BINGLEY, David Ernest

* * *

CAMP, Candace (Pauline) 1949-
(Lisa Gregory, Kristin James)

PERSONAL: Born May 23, 1949, in Amarillo, TX; daughter of Grady W. (a newspaper business manager) and Lula Mae (Irons) Camp; married Pete Hopcus (a counselor), August 11, 1979. *Education:* Attended University of Texas, 1967-70; West Texas State University, B.A., 1971; University of North Carolina, J.D., 1977. *Politics:* Democrat. *Religion:* Roman Catholic.

Avocational Interests: Live theatre, travel.

ADDRESSES: Home and office—2714 Pecan Dr., Temple, TX 76501. *Agent*—Kathryne Walters, 1714 Church St., Rahway, NJ.

CAREER: Teacher at secondary public school in Eureka Springs, AR, 1972-73; Wachovia Bank, Winston-Salem, NC, administrative assistant in trust department, 1973-74; First City National Bank, Paris, TX, lawyer in trust department, 1977-78; private practice of law in Paris, 1979; writer, 1979—. Actress and director in amateur theatre. Member of the board of directors of Paris Community Theatre.

MEMBER: Texas Bar Association.

WRITINGS:

NOVELS

Light and Shadow, HarperCollins, 1991.
Rosewood, HarperCollins, 1991.
Bitterleaf, HarperCollins, 1992.
Crystal Heart, HarperCollins, 1992.
Heirloom, HarperCollins, 1992.

UNDER PSEUDONYM LISA GREGORY

Bonds of Love, Jove, 1978, published under name Candace Camp, HarperCollins, 1992.
The Rainbow Season, Jove, 1979.
Analise, Jove, 1981.
Solitaire, Warner Books, 1988.
The Rainbow Promise, Warner Books, 1989.
Seasons, Warner Books, 1990.

UNDER PSEUDONYM KRISTIN JAMES

Windswept, Richard Gallen, 1981.
The Letter of the Law, Silhouette Books, 1991.
A Very Special Favor, Silhouette Books, 1991.

SIDELIGHTS: Candace Camp once told *CA:* "Fantasy has been my mainstay since I was a child. I wrote my first book at age eleven, and the only time I did not write was when I taught school for a year. I wrote my first novel when I was in law school. My problem in writing was discipline, and I credit law school with giving me that. I then quit my law practice to write full time. I found that my practice did not allow enough time to write, and writing is my first love."*

* * *

CANNON, Frank
See MAYHAR, Ardath

* * *

CANUCK, Abe
See BINGLEY, David Ernest

CARL, Lillian Stewart 1949-

PERSONAL: Born June 22, 1949, in Columbia, MO; daughter of Robert E. (a professor) and Bonnie (a teacher and editor; maiden name, Nance) Stewart; married Harold Paul Carl (a geophysicist), December 12, 1971; children: Alan Stewart, Jared Sullivan. *Education:* University of Texas at Austin, B.S.Ed., 1971.

ADDRESSES: Home—3012 Glenhollow Circle, Carrollton, TX 75007. *Agent*—Donald Maass, 8P, 304 West 92nd, New York, NY 10025.

CAREER: Writer. Forney Engineering Co., Dallas, TX, engineering aide, 1972-74; Brookhaven College, Dallas, history teacher, 1978-81.

MEMBER: Authors Guild, Mystery Writers of America, Novelist, Inc., Sisters-in-Crime.

WRITINGS:

Sabazel (fantasy novel), Ace Books, 1985.
The Winter King (fantasy novel), Ace Books, 1986.
Shadow Dancers (fantasy novel), Ace Books, 1987.
Wings of Power (fantasy novel), Ace Books, 1989.
Ashes to Ashes (mystery novel), Diamond Books, 1990.
Dust to Dust (mystery novel), Diamond Books, 1991.
Garden of Thorns, (mystery novel), Diamond Books, 1992.

Contributor of stories to magazines, including *Isaac Asimov's Science Fiction, Amazing Science Fiction, Borderland, Amazons, Smithsonian, Mystery Scene,* and *Mostly Murder.*

WORK IN PROGRESS: A Time to Die, a mystery novel to be published in 1993; *Nothing Ventured, Nothing Dead,* a contemporary English country house mystery.

SIDELIGHTS: "I write because I love to read," Lillian Stewart Carl told *CA,* "I can't remember not being able to read, and I can't remember not writing. Since I enjoy history, mythology, archaeology, and travel/adventure nonfiction, I enjoy novels with interesting historical and geographical backgrounds and issues. And that's what I write.

"My fantasy novels are in a style I've christened 'gonzo mythology.' I juxtapose ancient societies and people who never met in reality, I leaven myth with science, I combine folktales from different traditions—all in the interest of exploring relationships between people and other people, between people and society, between people and themselves. For my mystery novels I focused on British history and myth and used a contemporary setting. I'm intrigued with the way the twentieth century is interleaved with the past. A human being's psyche is structured the same way 'today,' layered with memory. My plots involve old crimes uncovered and historical puzzles confronted. The characters' lives are interwoven not only with their own pasts, but with the pasts of others. Again, I write about relationships.

"I'm thrilled by the synchronicities that appear in my work. It's not unusual for a magazine to arrive in my mailbox with an article addressing exactly the issue I was writing about that day. I'll get halfway through a story and suddenly realize two disparate plot elements dovetail perfectly. Right after I finished *Ashes to Ashes,* concerning an American woman named Rebecca working at a replica of a Scottish castle, I visited the real castle only to find an American woman named Rebecca working there."

* * *

CARPENTER, (John) Allan 1917-

PERSONAL: Born May 11, 1917, in Waterloo, IA; son of John Alex Carpenter and Theodosia (Smith) Carpenter. *Education:* Iowa State Teachers College (now University of Northern Iowa), B.A., 1938. *Politics:* Independent. *Religion:* Presbyterian.

Avocational Interests: "Principal bassist of many nonprofessional symphony orchestras."

ADDRESSES: Home and office—175 East Delaware Place, Suite 4602, Chicago, IL 60611-1748.

CAREER: Des Moines Register, writer, mid-1930s; Des Moines public schools, Des Moines, IA, teacher, 1938-40; *Teacher's Digest,* Chicago, IL, founder, editor, and publisher, 1940-48; *Popular Mechanics,* Chicago, public relations director, 1943-62; Carpenter Publishing House, Chicago, founder, editor, and publisher, 1962—. Infordata International Inc., founder and chairman of board of directors, 1974-90; *Index to Reader's Digest,* founder and publisher, 1981; director of International Speakers Network Inc.; indexing consultant to major publishing houses. Founder and president of Music Council of Metropolitan Chicago, beginning 1954; Chicago Business Men's Orchestra, principal bassist, chairman of the board, 1942-65; clerk of session of the Second Presbyterian Church in Evanston, IL, 1954-77.

MEMBER: Arts Club of Chicago, East Bank Club.

AWARDS, HONORS: Achievement Award, University of Northern Iowa, 1988.

WRITINGS:

"ENCHANTMENT OF AMERICA" SERIES; FOR CHILDREN'S PRESS

Illinois, from Its Glorious Past to the Present, illustrations by Phil Austin, 1963, revised edition published as *Illinois,* 1979.

Ohio, from Its Glorious Past to the Present, illustrations by Austin, 1963, revised edition published as *Ohio,* 1978.

California, from Its Glorious Past to the Present, illustrations by Austin, 1964, revised edition published as *California,* 1978.

Iowa, from Its Glorious Past to the Present, illustrations by Tom Dunnington, 1964, revised edition, 1979.

Michigan, illustrations by Austin, 1964, revised edition, 1978.

Nevada, from Its Glorious Past to the Present, illustrations by Roger Herrington, 1964, revised edition published as *Nevada,* 1979.

Wisconsin, illustrations by Austin, 1964, revised edition, 1978.

Alaska, from Its Glorious Past to the Present, illustrations by Herrington, 1965, revised editon published as *Alaska,* 1978.

Florida, from Its Glorious Past to the Present, illustrations by Austin, 1965, revised edition published as *Florida,* 1978.

Kansas, from Its Glorious Past to the Present, illustrations by Herrington, 1965, revised edition published as *Kansas,* 1979.

Massachusetts, from Its Glorious Past to the Present, illustrations by Austin, 1965, revised editon published as *Massachusetts,* 1978.

New Jersey, illustrations by Herrington, 1965, revised edition, 1978.

North Carolina, from Its Glorious Past to the Present, illustrations by Herrington, 1965, revised edition published as *North Carolina,* 1979.

Oklahoma, from Its Glorious Past to the Present, illustrations by Austin, 1965, revised edition published as *Oklahoma,* 1979.

Oregon, from Its Glorious Past to the Present, illustrations by Austin, 1965, revised edition published as *Oregon,* 1978.

Texas, from Its Glorious Past to the Present, illustrations by Herrington, 1965, revised edition published as *Texas,* 1978.

Utah, from Its Glorious Past to the Present, illustrations by Herrington, 1965, revised edition published as *Utah,* 1979.

Arizona, from Its Glorious Past to the Present, illustrations by Herrington, 1966, revised edition, 1979.

Connecticut, illustrations by Austin, 1966, revised edition, 1979.

District of Columbia, from Its Glorious Past to the Present, illustrations by Dunnington, 1966, revised edition published as *District of Columbia,* 1979.

Far-flung America: Puerto Rico, Virgin Islands, Panama Canal Zone, Guam, American Samoa, Midway, Wake, Trust Territory, Ryukyus, Others, illustrations by Herrington, 1966, revised edition published as *Far-flung America,* 1979.

Hawaii, illustrations by Austin, 1966, revised edition, 1979.

Indiana, from Its Glorious Past to the Present, illustrations by Austin, 1966, revised editon published as *Indiana,* 1978.

Maine, illustrations by Austin, 1966, revised edition, 1979.

Maryland, illustrations by Herrington, 1966, revised edition, 1978.

Minnesota, illustrations by Herrington, 1966, revised edition, 1978.

Missouri, from Its Glorious Past to the Present, illustrations by Herrington, 1966, revised edition published as *Missouri,* 1978.

Pennsylvania, illustrations by Dunnington, 1966, revised edition, 1978.

South Dakota, illustrations by Herrington, 1966, revised edition, 1978.

Washington, from Its Glorious Past to the Present, illustrations by Austin, 1966, revised edition published as *Washington,* 1979.

Wyoming, from Its Glorious Past to the Present, illustrations by Herrington, 1966, revised edition published as *Wyoming,* 1979.

Arkansas, illustrations by Herrington, 1967, revised edition, 1978.

Colorado, illustrations by Austin, 1967, revised edition, 1978.

Delaware, illustrations by Herrington, 1967, revised edition, 1978.

Georgia, illustrations by Austin, 1967, revised edition, 1979.

Kentucky, illustrations by Darrell Wiskur, 1967, revised edition, 1979.

Louisiana, illustrations by Herrington, 1967, revised edition, 1978.

Nebraska, illustrations by Herrington, 1967, revised edition, 1978.

New Hampshire, illustrations by Dunnington, 1967, revised edition, 1979.

New Mexico, illustrations by Robert Glaubke, 1967, revised edition, 1978.

New York, illustrations by Dunnington, 1967, revised edition, 1978.

South Carolina, illustrations by Glaubke, 1967, revised edition, 1979.

Vermont, illustrations by Austin, 1967, revised edition, 1979.

Virginia, illustrations by Herrington, 1967, revised edition, 1978.

Alabama, illustrations by Richard Mlodock, 1968, revised edition, 1978.

Idaho, illustrations by Wiskur, 1968, revised edition, 1979.
Mississippi, illustrations by Dunnington, 1968, revised edition, 1978.
Montana, illustrations by Herrington, 1968, revised edition, 1979.
North Dakota, illustrations by Herrington, 1968, revised edition, 1979.
Rhode Island, illustrations by Herrington, 1968, revised edition, 1978.
Tennessee, illustrations by Dunnington, 1968, revised edition, 1978.
West Virginia, illustrations by Austin, 1968, revised edition, 1979.

"ENCHANTMENT OF SOUTH AMERICA" SERIES; FOR CHILDREN'S PRESS

Brazil, 1968.
Argentina, 1969.
Chile, 1969.
(With Jean Currens Lyon) *Colombia,* 1969.
(With Tom Balow) *Ecuador,* 1969.
(With Lyon) *Uruguay,* 1969.
(With Lyon) *Bolivia,* 1970.
French Guiana, 1970.
(With Balow) *Guyana,* 1970.
(With Balow) *Paraguay,* 1970.
Peru, 1970.
(With Lyon) *Surinam,* 1970.
(With Enno R. Haan) *Venezuela,* 1970.

"ENCHANTMENT OF CENTRAL AMERICA" SERIES; FOR CHILDREN'S PRESS

(With Balow) *British Honduras,* 1971.
Costa Rica, 1971.
(With Eloise Baker) *El Salvador,* 1971.
Guatemala, 1971.
(With Balow) *Honduras,* 1971.
(With Balow) *Nicaragua,* 1971.
Panama, 1971.

"ENCHANTMENT OF AFRICA" SERIES; FOR CHILDREN'S PRESS

Egypt (United Arab Republic), 1972.
(With Matthew Maginnis) *Malagasy Republic (Madagascar),* 1972.
(With Balow) *Botswana,* 1973.
(With Maginnis) *Burundi,* 1973.
(With Milan De Lany) *Kenya,* 1973.
(With Maginnis) *Rwanda,* 1973.
(With James Hughes) *Tanzania,* 1973.
(With Bechir Chourou) *Tunisia,* 1973.
(With James Hughes) *Uganda,* 1973.
(With Maginnis) *Zaire,* 1973.
(With Lynn Ragin) *Zambia,* 1973.
(With Harrison Owen) *Liberia,* 1974.
(With Hughes) *Rhodesia,* 1974.
(With Janice E. Baker) *Upper Volta,* 1974.
(With Susan L. Eckert) *Sierra Leone,* 1974.
(With Balow) *Lesotho,* 1975.
(With Mark LaPointe and Thomas O'Toole) *Mali,* 1975.
(With Janis Fortman) *Morocco,* 1975.
(With Maginnis) *Swaziland,* 1975.
(With Hughes) *Chad,* 1976.
(With Hughes) *Gabon,* 1976.
(With O'Toole) *Guinea,* 1976.
(With Baker) *Niger,* 1976.
(With O'Toole) *Senegal,* 1976.
(With Fortman) *Sudan,* 1976.
(With Hughes) *Cameroon,* 1977.
(With Baker) *Central African Republic,* 1977.
(With Hughes) *Congo,* 1977.
(With Hughes) *Ghana,* 1977.
(With Hughes) *Ivory Coast,* 1977.
(With Hughes) *Libya,* 1977.
(With De Lany) *Malawi,* 1977.
(With Hughes) *Mauritania,* 1977.
(With Loyd Kepferle and Susan Kepferle) *The Gambia,* 1977.
(With Fortman) *Togo,* 1977.
(With Balow) *Algeria,* 1978.
Benin (Dahomey), 1978.
Nigeria, 1978.

"MIGHTY WARRIORS" SERIES; FOR ROURKE PUBLICATIONS

Dwight David Eisenhower: The Warring Peacemaker, illustrations by Wesley Klug, 1987.
George Smith Patton, Jr.: The Lost Romantic, 1987.
Sam Houston: Champion of America, 1987.
Stonewall Jackson: The Eccentric Genius, 1987.

"REGIONAL ENCYCLOPEDIA OF THE U.S." SERIES; FOR FACTS ON FILE

The Encyclopedia of the Midwest, 1989.
The Encyclopedia of the Central West, 1990.
The Encyclopedia of the Far West, 1990.

OTHER

Between Two Rivers: Iowa Year by Year, 1846-1939, Klipto Loose Leaf Co., 1940.
(With mother, Theodosia Carpenter) *Hi, Neighbor!,* King, 1945.
(Editor with Norman Guess and others) *Primer for Home Builders,* illustrations by Alida Marsh, Windsor Press, 1947, published as *How to Plan, Build and Pay for Your Own Home: A Primer for Home Builders,* Popular Mechanics Press, 1950.
(Editor) *Your Guide to Successful Singing,* Windsor Press, 1950.
The Twelve (poetry), Farcroft, 1955.

(Editor) *Fix-It,* Popular Mechanics Press, 1958.

(Compiler and editor) *Home Handyman Encyclopedia and Guide,* sixteen volumes, Little & Ives, 1961, supplement, 1963.

(Compiler and editor) *Shop Projects,* Popular Mechanics, 1962.

Illinois, Land of Lincoln, Children's Press, 1968.

All about the U.S.A., Encyclopaedia Britannica Educational Corp., 1987.

Facts about the Cities, H. W. Wilson, 1992.

Contributor to *Compton's Encyclopedia,* 1946-48. *Issues in Education,* founding editor, 1973—; *Index to U.S. Government Periodicals,* editor, 1974-90. Contributor to periodicals, including *Reader's Digest, Science Digest,* and *Popular Mechanics.*

WORK IN PROGRESS: Twenty-six volumes on the provinces and independent municipalities of the People's Republic of China, for Foreign Language Press, Beijing.

SIDELIGHTS: Allan Carpenter told *CA:* "My writing career began while I was still in high school with a professional syndication of anecdotes on Iowa history. This nascent career continued with the publication of my first book at age 20, followed by my founding of a national magazine for teachers at age 21, and progressed to the publication of 225 volumes bearing my name, along with the founding of two publishing houses and other activities. This span of 59 years represents the course of a publishing career of variety and tenure that is possibly unequaled in publishing today."

BIOGRAPHICAL/CRITICAL SOURCES:

PERIODICALS

Journal of Youth Services in Libraries, winter, 1991, pp. 149-52.

* * *

CARROLL, Jim 1951-

PERSONAL: Born August 1, 1951; son of Thomas J. and Agnes (Coyle) Carroll; wife, Rosemary; children: Aaron, Cassandra. *Education:* Attended Wagner College and Columbia University. *Politics:* "Peace." *Religion:* "God."

ADDRESSES: *Agent*—c/o Viking Publicity, 375 Hudson, New York, NY 10014-3657.

CAREER: Poet, writer and musician. Critic, *Art News,* 1969; teacher at poetry workshops and poetry projects in New York City, 1968-71; has given poetry readings at New York area colleges and churches.

AWARDS, HONORS: Random House Young Writers Award, 1970, for excerpt from *The Basketball Diaries* published in *Paris Review.*

WRITINGS:

POETRY

Organic Trains, Penny Press, 1967.

Four Ups and One Down, Angel Hail Press, 1970.

Living at the Movies, Van Grossman, 1973, Penguin, 1980.

The Book of Nods, Penguin, 1986.

Contributor to anthologies, including *The World Anthology,* edited by Anne Waldman, Bobbs-Merrill, 1969; *Another World,* edited by Anne Waldman, Bobbs-Merrill, 1972; *The Young American Poets,* Volume II, edited by Paul Carroll, Random House, 1973; *Angel Vision,* edited by Jay Gaines, Huntington House, 1992. Also contributor to "The Authors and the Artists" series, 1977.

NONFICTION

The Basketball Diaries: Age Twelve to Fifteen, limited edition, Tombouctou, 1978, Bantam, 1980, Penguin, 1987.

Forced Entries: The Downtown Diaries, 1971-73, Penguin, 1987.

MUSICAL RECORDINGS

(With the Jim Carroll Band) *Catholic Boy,* ATCO, 1980.

Dry Dreams, ATCO, 1982.

I Write Your Name, Atlantic, 1983.

Praying Mantis (spoken word), Giant/Reprise, 1992.

WORK IN PROGRESS: A novel.

SIDELIGHTS: By the time he was eighteen years old, Jim Carroll had already gained a reputation as one of the most prominent poets in the New York-based beat community. His gritty urban poetry and earnest, near-formless prose was lauded by such giants of the genre as William S. Burroughs, Allen Ginsberg, and Jack Kerouac (in an oft-reprinted quotation, Kerouac once claimed: "At thirteen years of age, Jim Carroll writes better prose than eighty-nine percent of the novelists working today"). His writing is mostly autobiographical, describing his childhood in New York, his friends and acquaintances, and the heroin addiction that gradually eroded away his dreams of becoming a basketball star.

Though he had published two earlier poetry collections, *Organic Trains* and *Four Ups and One Down,* and had contributed numerous poems to magazines, Carroll did not receive widespread recognition until the 1973 publication of *Living at the Movies.* Gerald Malanga, writing in *Poetry,* called the book "a triumph. . . . There is not one awkward word or tacky locution disturbing the exquisite poise and flow." Carroll, pronounces Malanga, is "a genuine poet" who "has worked as only a man of inspiration is capable of working, and [whose] presence has added great dignity to the generation of poets of the seventies to which he belongs."

Throughout the late 60s and early 70s, as his reputation as a poet was growing, bits of Carroll's prose began dotting the New York literary landscape, appearing occasionally in journals and poetry magazines. These stories were allegedly written by Carroll between the ages of twelve and fifteen, and described in harsh detail the beginnings of his 10-year heroin addiction. As each story leaked out, it was invariably accompanied by rumors of the imminent publication of a complete collection.

That collection, published in limited edition in 1978 and then with widespread distribution in 1980, was *The Basketball Diaries: Age Twelve to Fifteen.* In it, the *Washington Post*'s Eve Zibart notes, Carroll depicts himself as "a sexually sophisticated, glue-sniffing, purse-snatching dopehead" whose "one untarnished vision is of himself as the basketball hero." What gives the book real power, though, are the descriptions of the city and its citizens. Zibart continues: "Jim Carroll's New York is a carnival crazy house, where the drunks and hustlers bobble out of dark doorways like phosphorescent skeletons. Reflected in its twisted mirrors is all the perversion, scum and inadvertent slapstick that flesh is heir to." Steven Simels, writing in *Stereo Review,* calls *The Basketball Diaries* "a scary, mordantly funny odyssey along the dark underbelly of the Sixties, a virtuoso performance that ought to be must reading for those who still tend to romanticize the counterculture."

The Basketball Diaries is, quite possibly, a unique work, because it views childhood in the present rather than in retrospect. "It is a portrait of the artist not just as a young man but as a child, written by the child, and thus free of the mature artist's complicated romantic love of himself in pain," observes Jamie James in the *American Book Review.* The power behind Carroll's narrative took many critics by surprise—particularly those who had been following the stories as they had leaked out, one by one, over the years. "It seemed to be the charming but trivial work of a precociously gifted young writer," explains James. "[However,] seeing it all together bears out one's ongoing suspicion that there's more here than the swaggering bravado of a smart kid grown up all wrong." While James labels *The Basketball Diaries* "a literary miracle," he later clarifies: "It is not literature, in the usual sense, at all. It is a great work of storytelling, in the most elemental sense . . . , the kind of storytelling that happens when two good friends on a cross-country drive find themselves on the interstate in the middle of the night, two hundred miles from nowhere."

Following the tremendous critical reception of *The Basketball Diaries,* Carroll was persuaded by an old girlfriend, Patti Smith, to try his hand at music; Smith had successfully made the transition from poetry to music a few years earlier. She offered Carroll the opportunity to play a few gigs with her in San Francisco and New York. "It was incredible fun," Carroll says in *New York,* "and it was so intense and beautiful at the same time. It was remarkable." After just two shows, The Jim Carroll Band was signed to a record deal, and in 1980 released its first album, *Catholic Boy.*

The songs on *Catholic Boy* address the same issues as Carroll's poetry: drugs, sex, religion, and, above all, New York City. "[It is] filled with imagery that is spiritual, sexual, and violent," writes Barbara Graustark in *Newsweek.* "His songs of a city morally gone to seed have a raw power." The album's single, "People Who Died," is a disturbing litany of Carroll's dead friends—victims of murder, suicide, and sheer overindulgence. Audiences were captivated by the dark energy of Carroll's lyrics, and within weeks "People Who Died" became a runaway hit. Graustark avers: "Not since Lou Reed wrote 'Walk on the Wild Side' has a rock singer so vividly evoked the casual brutality of New York City as has Jim Carroll. . . . ['People Who Died'] has propelled him from underground status [in literary circles] . . . to national attention as a contender for the title of rock's new poet laureate."

When the popularity of "People Who Died" began to dwindle, however, the critics quickly turned on Carroll. "The rest of the album has its share of lapses," writes Simels, and *New York*'s Chet Flippo says: "There can be little doubt that Carroll the poet is a far subtler and sharper persona than Carroll the rock-'n'-roll lyricist." Though The Jim Carroll Band released two more albums (*Dry Dreams,* in 1982, and *I Write Your Name,* in 1984), neither approached the initial popularity of *Catholic Boy.* Bob Pfeiffer, writing in the *Washington Post* in 1987, summarizes Carroll's musical career: "Lyrics, sure, but a good band, not simply a podium from which the poet can project, has eluded Carroll. A favorite rock critic put-down is to label him a 'second-rate Lou Reed.' "

His career as a musician apparently behind him, Carroll went back to writing poetry and prose. His first attempt to reenter the literary world was 1986's *The Book of Nods,* a collection of poems. A reviewer for *Publishers Weekly* found considerable room for improvement here; he calls the collection an example of "serious talent destroyed over the years by negligence and disregard for self-discipline," and further claims that Carroll's subject matter—addiction, desperation, and recovery—is "pretty much outworn."

Such reviews did not discourage Carroll from writing a second collection of memoirs entitled *Forced Entries: The Downtown Diaries, 1971-1973.* It picks up where *The Basketball Diaries* left off, with Carroll, now twenty, still hooked on heroin and associating with the "in" crowd that frequents Andy Warhol's Factory. "*Entries* is more introspective than *Diaries,* the upfront ingenuousness of the early years replaced by insight and irony," observes Pfeiffer, though the *New York Times*' Christopher Lehmann-Haupt insists: "The two diaries remain similar in their quest for extreme sensations and their eagerness to shock the reader." In *Forced Entries,* Carroll describes his attempt to kick heroin, his subsequent addiction to methadone, and his eventual flight to a California clinic. "When, ultimately, Carroll finds his redemption in California . . . , we sense the enormity of the underground experience, as lived, in ways a documentary history can only grope for," concludes *Los Angeles Times Book Review* writer William Hochswender.

Whether or not *Forced Entries* marks Carroll's successful return to literary circles is debatable: Mark Stevens, writing in the *New York Times Book Review,* labels Carroll's memoirs "plenty of diverting tinsel" whose writing "cannot sustain this more serious tone" of redemption. Still, writes Hochswender, Carroll's "junk-induced dreams and downtown adventures have inspired writings—beautiful ravings, actually—that are ornate and harrowingly stark," and Lehmann-Haupt proclaims: "Whether or not one believes Jim Carroll's redemption, his two diaries constitute a remarkable account of New York City's lower depths."

BIOGRAPHICAL/CRITICAL SOURCES:

BOOKS

Contemporary Literary Criticism, Volume 35, Gale, 1985.

PERIODICALS

American Book Review, February, 1980, p. 9.
Culture Hero, Volume 1, number 5.
Los Angeles Times Book Review, October 18, 1987, p. 10.
Newsweek, September 8, 1980, p. 80.
New York, January 26, 1981, pp. 32-35.
New York Times, July 9, 1987, p. C23; March 29, 1992, p. 34.
New York Times Book Review, August 2, 1987, p. 8.
Poetry, December, 1974, p. 164.
Publishers Weekly, April 4, 1986, p. 57.
Rolling Stone, winter, 1973.
Stereo Review, February, 1981, p. 40.
Washington Post, March 22, 1980; September 13, 1987.*

—Sketch by Brandon Trenz

CARTER, Martin (Wylde) 1927-

PERSONAL: Born June 7, 1927 in Georgetown, British Guiana (now Guyana). *Education:* Attended Queens College, Georgetown.

ADDRESSES: Office—c/o New Beacon Books, 76 Stroud Green Road, London N4 3EN, England.

CAREER: Secretary to superintendent of prisons, British Guiana Civil Service, until 1953; teacher, 1954-59; chief information officer, Booker Group of Companies, 1959-66; Republic of Guyana national government, Minister of Information, 1967-71, United Nations representative, 1966-67; lecturer, Essex University, England, 1975-76; University of Guyana, writer in residence, 1977-81, senior research fellow, 1981—.

WRITINGS:

POETRY

The Hill of Fire Glows Red, Miniature Poets, 1951.
To a Dead Slave, privately printed, 1951.
The Kind Eagle, privately printed, 1952.
The Hidden Man, privately printed, 1952.
Returning, privately printed, 1953.
Poems of Resistance from British Guiana, Lawrence and Gishart, 1954, republished as *Poems of Resistance,* University of Guyana Press, 1964, republished as *Poems of Resistance from Guyana,* Release, 1979.
Poems of Succession, New Beacon, 1977.
Poems of Affinity, 1978-1980, Release, 1980.
Selected Poems, Demerara, 1989.

Contributor to anthologies, including *Fifty Caribbean Writers,* Greenwood Press, 1986. Contributor to periodicals, including *Kyk-over-al* and *New World Fortnightly.*

OTHER

(Editor) *New World: Guyana Independence Issue,* New World Group Associates, Georgetown, 1966.
Man and Making—Victim and Vehicle (Edgar Mittelholzer Memorial Lecture), Guyanese National History and Art Council, 1971.
Creation: Works of Art, Cariana Press, 1977.

SIDELIGHTS: Writing that protests oppression is an important literary form in the developing world and Martin Carter is among the foremost practitioners of the art, particularly in the Caribbean. Born and educated in the colony of British Guiana, Carter was part of the struggles that transformed his country into an independent nation in the middle of the century. His writing, which is full of fury, righteous indignation, and the idealism of rebellion in the attempt to create a better world, reflects the birth of his country. Later in his writing career, Carter's poetry adopted a more philosophic tone, but he continues to be inspired by the problems of his society and its politics.

Carter was born in Georgetown, now the capital of Guyana, in Central America. In the early 1950s, he was a clerk in the civil service that Britain created to run its colony, serving as secretary to the superintendent of prisons. He was already involved in the politics of the day; Carter's early poetry traced the development of the revolution in Guyana. In his earliest work, *The Hill of Fire Glows Red* (1951), he wrote, in the poem "The Kind Eagle," as one who sees the colonial status of his country near an end: "I dance on the wall of prison!/It is not easy to be free and bold!"

When the British deposed the legitimately elected government of Cheddi Jagan in 1953, Carter's political involvement led to a three-month jail sentence. Although Carter had previously produced several privately published poetry collections, he was "jailed into poetic eminence," as *Release* critic Paul Singh said in a review of Carter's first work brought out by a publishing house, *Poems of Resistance from British Guiana.* The poems of that work are both darker and more inspired by the turbulence of the times than his earlier pieces. *Poems of Resistance* evokes not hope and idealism but the defiance and determination of a country in the midst of wresting power from a foreign government. The titles of the poems, "This Is the Dark Time My Love," "I Come from the Nigger Yard," "I Clench My Fist," and others, reflect the actual violence of rebelling against the British.

After the Guyanese triumphed over the British and went about constructing a new society, Carter retained his role of poetic interpreter of current events. Alongside his writing, he worked in private industry during the 1960s and later went on to serve in the government. Perhaps as a member of the government, or because the Guyanese political situation grew less and less clearcut in the 1960s and 1970s, critics found Carter's work less focused on the defiance and anger that energized his earlier work. He continued to work for the government, spent the only protracted stay abroad of his life lecturing in England for a year, and joined the faculty at the University of Guyana in Georgetown upon his return in 1977. He released two collections of poetry during this time.

By 1980, the year *Poems of Affinity* was published, Carter saw Guyanese political life differently. In part the book dealt with two murders: that of Catholic priest and activist Father Drake and that of Walter Rodney, a leader in the Working People's Party political party with which Carter was affiliated. Critic Bill Carr called the poems in the book "tragic lyric poetry" in *Release,* and Professor Selwyn Cudjoe, writing in *Dictionary of Literary Biography,* said Carter had become disillusioned: "Most of the images in this collection are those of defeat and despair," Cudjoe wrote. "Carter's terse structure and intensely painful lyrics reflect the sensibilities of a disillusioned person."

Carter's colleague, fellow Guyanese writer Edward Kamau Brathwaite, provides one possible reason for such disillusionment in an essay in *Contemporary Poets:* "Carter, poet of the revolution, has really only himself and the revolution and a hope for the future to sustain his vision." While former colonies like Guyana have in many cases failed to achieve all that their liberators hoped for them, it is perceived that Carter writes to preserve the hopes of their birth into freedom. Lines from his "I Come from the Nigger Yard" demonstrate this: "O it was the heart like this tiny star near to the sorrows/straining against the whole world and the long twilight/spark of man's dream conquering the night."

BIOGRAPHICAL/CRITICAL SOURCES:

BOOKS

Carter, Martin, *The Hill of Fire Glows Red,* Miniature Poets, 1951.

Carter, *Poems of Resistance from Guyana,* Release, 1979.

Contemporary Poets, 5th edition, St. James Press, 1991, pp. 138-139.

Cudjoe, Selwyn R., *Dictionary of Literary Biography,* Volume 117, *Twentieth-Century Caribbean and Black African Writers, First Series,* Gale, 1992, pp. 106-11.

Markham, E. A., editor, *Hinterland: Caribbean Poetry from the West Indies and Britain,* Bloodaxe Press, 1989, pp. 66-71.

Roopnaraine, Rupert, *Web of October: Rereading Martin Carter,* Peepal Tree, 1988.

PERIODICALS

Caliban, fall-winter, 1981, pp. 30-47.

Caribbean Contact, August, 1977, p. 7.

Caribbean Quarterly, June-September, 1977, pp. 7-23.

Jamaica Journal, June, 1972, pp. 40-45.

Journal of West Indian Literature, October, 1986, pp. 1-12.

Kyk-over-al, December, 1987, pp. 59-65; No. 39, December, 1988, pp. 76-81; December, 1989, pp. 80-83.

New Literature Review, number 7, 1979, pp. 66-72.

New Voices, August, 1981, pp. 50-61.

Release, number 1, first quarter, 1978, pp. 5-24; number 1, first quarter, 19, pp. 37-41.*

* * *

CARVER, Dave
See BINGLEY, David Ernest

CHAPMAN, Jennifer 1950-

PERSONAL: Born February 19, 1950, in Potters Bar, Hertfordshire, England; daughter of Peter Norman (an accountant) and Agnes Mabel (a nanny; maiden name, Taylor) Johnson; married Paul Robin Moncrieff Westoby, August, 1971 (divorced, 1980); married Geoffrey Richard Chapman (an electronics manufacturer), August, 1980; children: Frances, Anna, Quinta. *Education:* Attended girls' secondary school in St. Albans, England.

ADDRESSES: *Home*—The Mount, Sun Hill, Royston, Hertfordshire, England. *Office*—Multi Media, 6-8 Market Hill, Royston, Hertfordshire SG8 9JL, England. *Agent*—Caroline Dawnay, Peters, Fraser & Dunlop, 503/4 The Chambers, Chelsea Harbour, London SW10 OXF, England.

CAREER: Newspaper journalist, 1968-81; Multi Media (public relations consultants), Royston, England, principal, 1981—.

MEMBER: Society of Authors, PEN.

AWARDS, HONORS: Named Midlands Journalist of the Year by British Leyland Awards and Birmingham Press Club, 1974, for political story about Prime Minister Harold Wilson; Author's Foundation Grant, Society of Authors, 1989, for *The Last Bastion: The Case for and against Women Priests.*

WRITINGS:

The Geneva Touch (thriller), Arlington, 1982.
The Long Weekend (novel), Century, 1984.
Mysterious Ways (novel), Century, 1985.
Not Playing the Game (novel), Century, 1986.
Regretting It (novel), Century, 1987.
The Last Bastion: The Case for and against Women Priests, Methuen, 1989.
Victor Ludorum (novel), Hale, 1991.
Barnardo's Today, foreword by Her Royal Highness the Princess of Wales, Virgin Publishing, 1991.
Made in Heaven—the British Way of Marriage: Changing Attitudes towards and within Marriage during the 20th Century, Virgin Publishing, 1993.

WORK IN PROGRESS: A novel about mid-life crisis.

SIDELIGHTS: Jennifer Chapman told *CA:* "I have always been interested in writing only about life as it is, and I aim to capture the sort of thoughts and feelings that will strike a chord with my readers. I want them to think: 'Ah, that's just how I think and feel, but I didn't know other people felt the same.' In my novels, I like to explore how and why people become obsessive over matters such as religion and sport, although it is the being obsessive that interests me rather than the obsession itself. My books lean toward feminism in that I try to make all of my characters aware of the responsibility for their own destiny, regardless of friends, lovers, or spouses."

BIOGRAPHICAL/CRITICAL SOURCES:

PERIODICALS

Daily Telegraph, February 22, 1985.
Times (London), February 21, 1985.

* * *

CHAPMAN, Raymond 1924-
(Simon Nash)

PERSONAL: Born January 10, 1924, in Cardiff, Wales; son of Frederick William (a teacher) and Gladys (Evans) Chapman; married Patricia McCarthy, 1964; children: one son, one daughter. *Education:* Jesus College, Oxford, B.A., 1945, M.A., 1959; King's College, University of London, M.A., 1948, B.D., 1975, Ph.D., 1978. *Religion:* Anglican.

Avocational Interests: Theater, good food and wine, and talking to friends.

ADDRESSES: *Home*—6 Kitson Rd., Barnes, London SW13 9HJ, England.

CAREER: London School of Economics and Political Science, University of London, London, England, lecturer, 1948-81, professor of English studies, 1981-89, professor emeritus, 1989—. Warden of Passfield Hall of Residence, 1950-61.

MEMBER: Association of University Teachers, English Association (member of executive committee, 1977-89), Thomas Hardy Society, Gaskell Society, Prayer Book Society (member of executive council, 1990—), Anglican Society (member of executive committee, 1991—), Irish Literary Society (member of committee, 1993—).

AWARDS, HONORS: Sion College, fellow, 1984—; Bronze Medal, University of Helsinki, Finland, 1989.

WRITINGS:

A Short Way to Better English, G. Bell, 1956.
(Editor) *Religious Drama,* S.P.C.K., 1959.
The Ruined Tower, Bles, 1961.
The Loneliness of Man, S.C.M. Press, 1963.
Victorian Debate, Basic Books, 1968.
Faith and Revolt, Weidenfeld & Nicolson, 1970.
Linguistics and Literature, Edward Arnold, 1973.
(With Nora Gottlieb) *Letters to an Actress,* Allison & Busby, 1973.
The Language of English Literature, Edward Arnold, 1982.
The Treatment of Sounds in Language and Literature, Blackwell, 1984.

(Editor) *Essays and Studies,* Murray, 1984.

The Sense of the Past in Victorian Literature, St. Martin's, 1986.

The Language of Thomas Hardy, St. Martin's, 1990.

UNDER PSEUDONYM SIMON NASH

Dead of a Counterplot, Bles, 1962.

Killed by Scandal, Bles, 1962, Roy, 1964.

Death over Deep Water, Bles, 1963, Roy, 1965.

Dead Woman's Ditch, Bles, 1964.

Unhallowed Murder, Bles, 1966.

OTHER

Also editor of *Christian Drama,* 1959-62, and contributor of articles to scholarly journals, including *Modern Language Review, Review of English Studies, English, Poetica, Notes & Queries, Theology, Higher Education Journal, System, Oxford, Nineteenth-Century Literature, English Today, Thomas Hardy Society Journal,* and *Gaskell Society Newsletter.*

BIOGRAPHICAL/CRITICAL SOURCES:

PERIODICALS

Cambridge Review, January 29, 1971.

New Statesman, December 25, 1970.

Observer Review, July, 1968.

Times Literary Supplement, July 25, 1968; December 28, 1984, pp. 1491-1492; June 19, 1987, p. 652.

* * *

CHARLES, Mark
See BICKERS, Richard (Leslie) Townshend

* * *

CHATHAM, Larry
See BINGLEY, David Ernest

* * *

CHENG, Chu-yuan 1927-

PERSONAL: Born April 8, 1927, in Kwangtung Province, China; naturalized U.S. citizen; son of Kwan-san and Hsu-tsing Cheng; married Hua Liang, August 15, 1964; children: Anita, Andrew. *Education:* National Cheng Chih University, Nanking, China, B.A., 1957; Georgetown University, M.A., 1962, Ph.D., 1964.

ADDRESSES: Office—Department of Economics, Ball State University, Muncie, IN 47306.

CAREER: Seton Hall University, South Orange, NJ, research professor, 1960-64; University of Michigan, Ann Arbor, senior research economist, 1964-70; Lawrence University, Appleton, WI, associate professor of economics, 1970-71; Ball State University, Muncie, IN, associate professor, 1971-74, professor of economics and chairman of Asian Studies Committee, 1974—. Visiting research professor, George Washington University, 1963; president and member of board of directors, Dr. Sun Yat-sen Institute, 1987—. National Science Foundation, chief investigator, research project on scientific and engineering manpower in Communist China, 1959-63, evaluator of research proposals, 1965—.

MEMBER: Association of Chinese Social Scientists in North America (member of board of directors, 1988-90), American Economic Association, Association for Comparative Economic Studies, Association for Asian Studies, American Academy of Political and Social Sciences, American Business History Association, American Association for Chinese Studies (member of board of directors, 1990—), Chinese Academic and Professional Association in Mid-America (president, 1983-84), Chinese American Society (president, 1989-93), Indiana Academy of Social Sciences, Omicron Delta Epsilon.

AWARDS, HONORS: Outstanding Faculty Research Award, Ball State University, 1976; Outstanding Academic Achievement Award, Dr. Sun Yat-sen Institute, 1980; Chinese Cultural Award, Institute of Chinese Culture of New York, 1984; award from National Sun Yat-sen University, 1988, for contributions made in promoting Sun Yat-sen's doctrine in the U.S.; *Choice* outstanding academic book award, 1992, for *Behind the Tiananmen Massacre: Social, Political, and Economic Ferment in China.*

WRITINGS:

Income and Standard of Living in Mainland China, Union Research Institute (Hong Kong), two volumes, 1957, 2nd edition of Volume 1, 1958.

The People's Communes, Union Press, 1959.

Communist China's Economy, 1949-1962: Structural Changes and Crisis, Seton Hall University Press, 1963.

Economic Relations between Peking and Moscow, 1949-63, Praeger, 1964.

Scientific and Engineering Manpower in Communist China, 1949-1963, National Science Foundation, 1966.

The Machine-Building Industry in Communist China, Aldine, 1971.

Allocation of Fixed Capital Formation in China, Center for Chinese Studies, University of Michigan, 1974.

China's Petroleum Industry: Output Growth and Export Potential, Praeger, 1976.

China's Economic Development: Growth and Structural Change, Westview, 1981.

The Demand and Supply of Primary Energy in Mainland China, University of Washington Press, 1984.

Sun Yat-sen's Doctrine in the Modern World, Westview, 1989.

Behind the Tiananmen Massacre: Social, Political, and Economic Ferment in China, Westview, 1990.

IN ENGLISH TRANSLATION

Monetary Affairs of Communist China, Union Press, 1954, 3rd edition, 1959.

The Chinese Market under Communist Control, Union Press, 1955.

The Anshan Iron and Steel Industry in Communist China, Union Press, 1955, 2nd edition, 1956.

AVAILABLE ONLY IN CHINESE

The Forced Labor System of Communist China, Freedom Press (Hong Kong), 1952.

An Analysis of Financial and Economic Policies in Communist China, Freedom Press, 1952.

New Trends in Financial and Economic Politics in Communist China, two volumes, Freedom Press, 1953.

Financial and Economic Developments in Communist China during 1949-1954, New Cultural Institute (Hong Kong), 1954.

An Analysis of the First Five-Year Plan in Communist China, Freedom Press, 1955.

Communist China: Its Situation and Prospect, Freedom Press, 1959.

Selected Essays on Political and Economic Problems of China and the United States, Linking Press (Taiwan), 1976, enlarged edition, 1981.

An Anatomy of the Economy in Mainland China, Linking Press, 1980.

Economic Development in the Two-sides of Taiwan Strait, Linking Press, 1983.

Taiwan as a Model of China's Modernization, Linking Press, 1986.

Taiwan Developmental Experience and China's Reconstruction, Linking Press, 1989.

China: Dramatic Change and Future Prospects, Wu Nan, 1992.

Deng Xiaoping's Doctrine and Economic Development of Guangdong, Council for Mainland Affairs, 1993.

Economic Situation and Interactions Across the Taiwan Straits, Linking Press, 1993.

OTHER

Contributor to numerous books, including *Public Health in the People's Republic of China,* edited by Myron E. Wegman, Josiah Macy, Jr. Foundation, 1973; *American Opportunities for Doing Business in China in the 1970s,* edited by William W. Whitson, Praeger, 1974; *China's Four Modernizations: The New Technological Revolution,* edited by Richard Baum, Westview, 1980; *The China Question: Essays on Current Relations between Mainland China and Taiwan,* edited by Yu-san Wang, Praeger, 1985; *Changes and Continuities in Chinese Communism,* edited by Yu-Ming Shao, Westview, 1988; *Forces for Changes in Contemporary China,* edited by Bih-Jaw Lin and James T. Meyers, Institute for International Relations, 1992; and *Economic and Political Reforms in Asia,* edited by Thomas Chen, Young B. Choi, and Sung Lee, St. John's University Press, 1992.

Also contributor to *Encyclopaedia Britannica.* Contributor to Chinese, Japanese, and English periodicals, including *Chinese-American Society Quarterly, World Journal, Pei-Sheng, Hong Kong Times, United Daily News, Global View Monthly.*

WORK IN PROGRESS: Cultural Factor in the Economic Development of Four East Asian Countries; Toward a Greater Chinese Common Market; Sun Yat-sen's Doctrine and the Future of China; China's Road Toward Modernization.

SIDELIGHTS: Chu-yuan Cheng told *CA:* "Writing has been my lifelong hobby. I contributed my first essay to the local newspaper when I was twelve. At the age of sixteen, as a freshman in college, I won the grand prize of a national collegiate essay contest in China. Ever since, I have been a frequent contributor to national newspapers and periodicals including the most influential daily news in China, the Shanghai *Ta-Kung Pao.*

"When Communists took over the mainland in 1949, I took exile in Hong Kong and became a regular contributor to several leading Chinese and Japanese newspapers including the *Yomiuri Shimbun,* the *Tokyo Shimbun,* and the *Japan Times.* My first book on the Chinese economy was published in 1952 in Hong Kong and was well received in the Far East. Between 1952 and 1959, I published more than ten books and monographs on various aspects of Chinese social and economic development.

"In 1959, I came to the United States to pursue graduate studies. I attended classes at Georgetown University in the evenings while working full-time on a research project on Chinese scientific and engineering manpower sponsored by the National Science Foundation. I completed all of the requirements for the M.A. and Ph.D. degrees in four years and published three books during the same period.

"Although I became a full-time professor after 1971, my interest in research and writing has never subsided. I have typically worked fourteen hours a day, seven days a week during the past twenty-two years, publishing a total of twenty-two books and monographs: nine in English and thirteen in Chinese. Three of them have been translated into Japanese. I have also contributed two articles to the *Encyclopaedia Britannica* and two articles and four letters to the *New York Times.*

"In the summer of 1989 when millions of students and Beijing residents poured into the Tiananmen Square, I realized that a confrontation between the people and the government was inevitable. In a letter published by the *New York Times,* I offered my preliminary assessment of the emerging social and economic crisis. The letter prompted several local and overseas interviews which inspired me to conduct deeper research. The result was the book *Behind the Tiananmen Massacre: Social, Political, and Economic Ferment in China.*

"My lifelong goal, however, is to write a three-volume exposition of Chinese economic development analyzing the social and economic changes in China from the Opium War in 1840 to the end of this century. I hope the Chinese experience in the nineteenth and twentieth centuries may shed new light on the development of the Third World in the century ahead."

* * *

CHESHAM, Henry
See BINGLEY, David Ernest

* * *

CHOGYAM TRUNGPA 1939-1987
(Rinpoche)

PERSONAL: Born February, 1939, in Geje, Kham, Tibet; died of cardiac arrest and respiratory failure, April 4, 1987, in Halifax, Nova Scotia, Canada; son of Yeshe (a farmer) and Bo-chung Dargye. *Education:* Received the highest initiations of the Nyingma and Kaguy orders of Tibetan Buddhism; holds the Khenpo degree, the equivalent of a Doctor of Divinity degree; attended Oxford University, 1963-67. *Politics:* None.

CAREER: Known to his followers as Rinpoche, Chogyam Trungpa was the eleventh Trungpa Tulku, considered to be the tenth successive incarnation of a great Tibetan teacher; in 1959, forced to escape Tibet when the Chinese Communist government began a reign of terror against religious leaders, he fled to India where, by appointment of His Holiness the Dalai Lama, he served as spiritual advisor to the Young Lamas' Home School in Dalhousie; in 1967, he moved to Scotland and founded Samye Ling, a Buddhist meditation center; in 1970, he moved to the United States, where he served as president and founder of the Vajradhatu, a nationwide association of Tibetan Buddhist meditation communities and centers based in Boulder, CO; he also founded the Nalanda Foundation in Boulder, which includes Shambhala Training, the Naropa Institute, and the Mudra Theatre Group; in 1986, he moved his organization to Halifax, Nova Scotia, Canada.

AWARDS, HONORS: Spaulding fellow, Oxford University, 1963-67.

WRITINGS:

(As told to Esme Cramer Roberts) *Born in Tibet,* Allen & Unwin, 1966, Harcourt, 1968, revised edition, Great Eastern Book Co., 1968.

Meditation in Action, Shambhala, 1969.

Mudra, Shambhala, 1972.

Cutting through Spiritual Materialism, Shambhala, 1973.

Glimpses of Abhidharma, Prajna Press, 1975.

Visual Dharma: The Buddhist Art of Tibet, Shambhala, 1975.

(With Herbert Guenther) *The Dawn of Tantra,* Shambhala, 1975.

(Translator with Francesca Fremantle, and author of commentary) *The Tibetan Book of the Dead,* Shambhala, 1975.

The Myth of Freedom and the Way of Meditation, Shambhala, 1976.

Empowerment, Vajradhatu Publications, 1976.

(Translator and author of foreword) *The Rain of Wisdom,* Shambhala, 1980.

Journey without Goal: The Tantric Wisdom of the Buddha, Prajna Press, 1981.

(Contributor) Deborah E. Klimburg-Salter, editor, *The Silk Route and the Diamond Faith,* University of California, Los Angeles, Art Council, 1982.

(Translator and author of preface) *The Life of Marpa,* Prajna Press, 1982.

(Author of foreword) Osel Tendzin, *Buddha in the Palm of Your Hand,* Shambhala, 1982.

First Thought, Best Thought: One Hundred and Eight Poems, Shambhala, 1983.

Shambhala: The Sacred Path of the Warrior, Shambhala, 1984.

The Teachings of the Theravadin Tradition, Shambhala, 1984.

Exchanging Self for Others: The Mahayana Teachings of Compassion, Prajna Press, 1984.

Crazy Wisdom, Shambhala, 1991.

The Heart of the Buddha, Shambhala, 1991.

Orderly Chaos: The Mandala Principle, Shambhala, 1991.

The Lion's Roar: An Introduction to Tantra, edited by Sherab Chodzin, Shambhala, 1992.

Transcending Madness: The Experience of the Six Bardos, Shambhala, 1992.

Contributor to *Naropa Institute Journal of Psychology, Loka,* and *Loka 2* (journals of the Naropa Institute). Editor, with his students, of an occasional journal, *Garuda.*

SIDELIGHTS: At the age of one, Chogyam Trungpa was taken to a Buddhist monastery where he studied until the Chinese Communists invaded Tibet in 1949. When he was thirteen years old, he was enthroned as the supreme abbot of the Surmang group of monasteries. There he completed his scholastic and meditative training. In 1959, when a Tibetan revolt against the Chinese government failed, Chogyam Trungpa fled to India. After attending Oxford University, he founded the Samye Ling meditation center in Scotland before coming to the United States. He once explained that he felt an obligation to preserve the teachings he had received in his homeland. Settling in Boulder, Colorado, Chogyam Trungpa founded Vajradhatu, an association of Tibetan Buddhist meditation centers, and the Nalanda Foundation. The Naropa Institute, a branch of the Nalanda Foundation, is perhaps best known as the home of the Jack Kerouac School of Disembodied Poetics, headed by poet Allen Ginsberg. Chogyam Trungpa moved his organization to Halifax, Nova Scotia, in 1986.

OBITUARIES:

PERIODICALS

Chicago Tribune, April 8, 1987.
New York Times, April 8, 1987.*

* * *

CHRISTIE, Ian R(alph) 1919-

PERSONAL: Born May 11, 1919; son of John Reid and Gladys Lilian Christie. *Education:* Oxford University, B.A. and M.A., 1948.

ADDRESSES: Home—10 Green Lane, Croxley Green, Hertfordshire, England.

CAREER: University of London, University College, London, England, assistant lecturer, 1948-51, lecturer, 1951-60, reader, 1960-66, professor of modern British history, 1966-79, Astor Professor of British History, 1979-84, dean of arts, 1971-73, chairman of department, 1975-79. *Military service:* Royal Air Force, 1940-46; became acting flight lieutenant.

MEMBER: British Academy (fellow), Royal Historical Society, Historical Association.

WRITINGS:

The End of North's Ministry, 1780-1782, Macmillan (London), 1958.

Wilkes, Wyvill, and Reform, Macmillan (London), 1962.

Crisis of Empire: Great Britain and the American Colonies, 1754-1783, Norton, 1966.

(Editor) *Essays in Modern History Selected from the Transactions of the Royal Historical Society,* Royal Historical Society, 1968.

Myth and Reality in Late-Eighteenth Century British Politics and other Papers, Macmillan, 1970.

(Editor) *The Correspondence of Jeremy Bentham,* Volume 3, Athlone, 1971.

(With B. W. Labaree) *Empire or Independence, 1760-1776,* Norton, 1976.

(With Lucy M. Brown) *Bibliography of British History, 1789-1851,* Clarendon Press, 1977.

Wars and Revolutions: Britain, 1760-1815, Harvard University Press, 1982.

Stress and Stability in Late Eighteenth-Century Britain: Reflections on the British Avoidance of Revolution, Clarendon Press, 1984.

The Benthams in Russia, 1780-1790, Berg Publishers, 1993.

Contributor to numerous books, including *The Connoisseur Period Guide,* edited by Ralph Edwards and L. G. G. Ramsey, Crown, Volume 4: *Late Georgian, 1760-1810,* 1956, Volume 5: *Regency, 1810-1830,* 1958; *The History of Parliament: The House of Commons, 1754-1790,* three volumes, edited by Sir Lewis Namier and John Brooke, H.M.S.O., 1964; *William III and Louis XIV,* edited by Ragnhild Hatton and J. S. Bromley, Liverpool University Press, 1968; *Red, White, and True Blue: The Loyalists in the Revolution,* edited by Esmond Wright, AMS Press, 1976; *The French Revolution and British Popular Politics,* Cambridge University Press, 1991. Also contributor to *Handbook for History Teachers,* edited by W. H. Burston and C. W. Green, 1958.

Also contributor to history and archaeology journals. Member of editorial board, *The History of Parliament.*

SIDELIGHTS: Ian R. Christie is regarded as one of the most distinguished and prolific scholars of late eighteenth-century British history. Before retiring from his post as Astor Professor of British History at University College, London, he delivered the Ford Lectures at Oxford in 1983. Extended versions of these lectures were compiled and published as *Stress and Stability in Late Eighteenth-Century Britain: Reflections on the British Avoidance of Revolution.* According to *British Book News* contributor H. T. Dickinson, *Stress and Stability* attempts to explain why the majority of the British population neither revolted *en masse* nor supported radical reformers during an age of popular political revolution. Christie maintains that "British institutions took the strain of discontent pretty well, and . . . the ruling class defended those institutions with ability and humane good sense," as William Thomas summarized in a *Times Literary Supplement* review.

Thomas added, "This is a useful book, the modesty of which tends to veil the prodigious learning which it condenses." Though Dickinson believes that Christie's arguments can be strengthened by further discussion of conservative forces, he stated that Christie "has certainly succeeded in demonstrating once more those qualities for which he has become famous: prodigious research, an incisive mind, a cool appraisal of motives and achievements, and a brisk, clear style."

Christie recently described his professional focus to *CA* as a "commitment to the study and exposition of British constitutional and political history to the years of his military service in World War II, when the issue of overriding importance seemed to be the deference of Western democratic forms of government against the onslaught of tyrannous dictatorships born of European Fascism."

BIOGRAPHICAL/CRITICAL SOURCES:

PERIODICALS

British Book News, January, 1985.

New Statesman, August 21, 1970.

Spectator, August 8, 1970.

Times Educational Supplement, June 1, 1984.

Times Literary Supplement, July 9, 1970; August 6, 1976; September 24, 1982; April 19, 1985.

* * *

CHUKOVSKY, Kornei (Ivanovich) 1882-1969

PERSONAL: Born March 31, 1882, in St. Petersburg, Russia; died October 28, 1969; son of Ekatherina Ossipovna Korneichukova; married Maria Borisnova Goldfield; children: Nicholas, Lydia, Boris, Moora. *Education:* Self-taught.

CAREER: Children's writer and translator. Correspondent in Britain for Odessa newspaper, *Odesskije Novosti,* during the early 1900s; spent some months in jail, 1905-06; *Signal,* St. Petersburg, Russia, editor, 1905-08; editor and head of children's book department, "Parus" Publishing House, 1916-19; director, Anglo-American section, "Vsemirnaya Literatura" Publishing House, 1919-21. Ilchester Lecturer at Oxford University.

AWARDS, HONORS: Order of Lenin, 1957; Ph.D., Moscow University, 1957; D.Litt., Oxford University, 1962, for his services to British literature in the Soviet Union; Lenin Prize for Literary Activities, 1962; *Telephone* was named on the *Horn Book* honor list.

WRITINGS:

FOR YOUNG ADULTS; IN ENGLISH TRANSLATION

Crocodile, translated by Babette Deutsch, Lippincott, 1931, adapted by Richard Coe and illustrated by Alan Howard, Faber, 1964 (published in Russia as *Krokodil,* [St. Petersburg], 1916).

Wash-'em-Clean (also see below), translated by E. Felgenhauer, illustrated by A. Kanevsky, Foreign Languages Publishing (Moscow), 1962 (published in Russia as *Moidodyr,* 4th edition, 1924).

Ooki-Spooky, adapted by Mirra Ginsburg, illustrated by Emily McCully, Crown, 1979 (published in Russia as *Zakalaika,* c. 1925).

Telephone (adaptation of one of Hugh Lofting's "Doctor Dolittle" stories; also see below), translated by Padraic Breslin, Mezhdunarodnaja Kniga (Moscow), 1940, translated and adapted by Marguerite Rudolph, illustrated by Susan Perl, Bobbs-Merrill, 1971, adapted by William Jay Smith and Max Hayward, illustrated by Blair Lent, Delacorte, 1977 (published in Russia as *Telefon* [Moscow], 2nd edition, 1926).

Cock-the-Roach, translated by Tom Botting, illustrated by Olga Pushkaryova, Progress Publishers (Moscow), 1981 (published in Russia as *Tarakanishche,* [Leningrad], 1927).

Fairy Tales (includes *The Telephone, Doctor Powderpill, Wash-'em-Clean, The Stolen Sun,* and *The Muddle*), Raduga (Moscow), 1984 (published in Russia as *Skazki,* Academia, 1935).

Dr. Concocter (poem; adaptation of Lofting's *Doctor Dolittle*), adapted by Richard Coe, illustrated by William Papas, Oxford University Press, 1967 (published in Russia as *Doktor Aybolit,* [Moscow], 1936).

Chekhov, the Man, translated by Pauline Rose, Hutchinson, 1945.

The Stolen Sun, translated by Rottenberg, illustrated by Y. Vasnetsov, Progress Publishers (Moscow), c. 1965, translated by Richard Sadler as *The Day the Crocodile Stole the Sun: A Fairy Tale,* illustrated by Erich Guertzig, Salder & Brown, 1967 (published in Russia as *Kradenoe solntse,* Detzig [Moscow], 1958).

The Silver Crest: My Russian Boyhood, translated by Beatrice Stillman, Holt, 1976 (published in Russia as *Serebrianyi gerb,* [Moscow], 1961).

The Chick, translated by Felgenhauer, illustrated by Y. Charushin, Foreign Languages Publishing, c. 1962 (published in Russia as *Tsyplionok*).

The Wonder Tales, translated by Felgenhauer and Dorian Rottenberg, illustrated by Vladmir Konashevich, Progress Publishers, 1973 (published in Russia as *Kniga chudes*).

Doctor Powderpill, translated by Rottenberg, illustrated by Vladmir Suteyev, Raduga Publishers (Moscow), 1974, Central Books, 1980.

The Muddle, translated by Rottenberg, illustrated by Konashevich, Imported Publications, 1976.

Good Morning Chick, adapted by Mirra Ginsburg, illustrated by Byron Barton, Greenwillow Books, 1980.

The Art of Translation: Kornei Chukovsky's A High Art, translated and edited by Lauren G. Leighton, University of Tennessee Press, 1984.

IN RUSSIAN; FOR YOUNG ADULTS

Barmaley, illustrated by M. V. Dobuzbinskii, [Leningrad], 1924.

Domok (title means "Little Cabin"), [Leningrad], 1927.

Fedia-bredia (folktale), [Leningrad], 1927.

Ryzhii i krasnyi (folk verse; title means "Ginger and Red"), [Leningrad], 1927.

Skok-poskok (folktale), [Leningrad], 1927.

Cherepakha (title means "The Turtle"), [Leningrad], 1929.

Koshki v lukoshke (nonsense verse about cats), [Leningrad], 1929.

Novye zagadki (title means "New Riddles"), [Moscow], 1930.

Mukha-tsokotukha (title means "The Fly's Wedding"), [Leningrad], 1933.

Putanitsa (title means "The Mix-Up"), [Leningrad], 1934.

Limpopo (story of a hippo), [Leningrad], 1935.

Piat-desiat porosiat (folk songs; title means "Fifty Piglets"), [Leningrad], 1936.

Chtets-deklamator dlia detei (a reader-reciter for children), Detskaya Literatura (Moscow), 1941.

Detiam, Iskusstvo (Moscow), 1945.

Fedorino gore (title means "Fedora's Grief"), [Moscow], 1951.

Chudo-Derevo (title means "The Magic Tree"), [Moscow], 1956.

Tak ne tak (nonsense verse; title means "So and Not So"), [Moscow], 1959.

Toptygin i Lisa (verse; title means "Toptgin and the Fox"), Malysh (Moscow), 1965.

(Editor) *Isbrannye stikhotvoreniia dlia detei* (poetry), Detskaya Literatura, 1967.

Stikhi dlia detei (poetry), Detskaya Literatura, 1969.

Golovastiki (poetry), Detskaya Literatura, 1970.

Zagadki (title means "Riddles"), Detskaya Literatura, 1974.

Radost: stikhi i zagadki, Malysh, 1981.

Ilya Repin, Iskusstvo, 1983.

OTHER

Ot Chekhova do nashikh dnei (title means "From Chekhov to Our Days"), [St. Petersburg], 1907.

Aspects of Futurism, Prideaux Press, 1976 (published in Russia as *Ego-futuristy i kubo-futuristy,* [St. Petersburg], 1914).

The Poet and the Hangman: Nekrasov and Muraviov, translated by R. W. Rotsel, Ardis, 1977 (published in Russia as *Poet i palach,* 1922).

Alexander Blok as Man and Poet, translated by Burgin and O'Connor, Ardis, 1982 (published in Russia as *Aleksandr Blok kak chelovek i poet,* 1924).

From Two to Five, translated by Miriam Morton, University of California Press, 1963 (published in Russia as *Malen'kie deti,* 1928; also published as *Ot dvukh do piati,* [Leningrad]).

Gimnaziia (autobiography), Detskaya Literatura, 1938.

Sovetskiie pisateli; autobiografiia, [Moscow], 1959.

Also translator into Russian of William Shakespeare's *Love's Labour Lost,* William Wycherly's *Plain Dealer,* Rudyard Kipling's *Just So Stories,* John Millington Synge's *Playboy of the Western World,* G. K. Chesterton's *Manalive,* Mark Twain's *The Prince and the Pauper* and *Tom Sawyer,* O. Henry's *Cabbages and Kings,* and writings by Walt Whitman and others.

SIDELIGHTS: Considered the dean of Russian writers for children, Kornei Chukovsky was the author of fanciful tales that have been translated from Russian into English to the delight of many younger readers. Chukovsky especially excelled in creating stories for preschoolers and loved writing nonsense rhymes and riddles involving animal characters. His books sold more than 78 million copies in 800 editions and were required reading in many of the former Soviet Union's schools. Despite the disapproval of the Communist regime—who felt his work was detrimental to Soviet youth—Chukovsky continued to write nonsensical verse for children. His work was so popular with Russian children, who called him "Dedushka" (Grandfather) Chukovsky, that the Soviet authorities left him alone. The versatile author also translated English works by William Shakespeare, Walt Whitman, and others into Russian. When he died in 1969, he was known as the Soviet Union's best-loved children's author.

Chukovsky was born in St. Petersburg, Russia, in 1882. Sadly, his father abandoned the family, and Chukovsky's mother supported them by taking in washing. With hard work and a talent for economy, she managed to send the young author to a private school where she thought he would have a chance to succeed in life. Chukovsky liked school and seemed to be a good student. "I was considered the champion dictation taker in our class. I didn't understand it myself. From the age of seven, I could write the most complicated phrases without a mistake," he stated in his memoirs, *The Silver Crest: My Russian Boyhood.*

When the boy turned thirteen another sad event occurred. He was expelled from school with several other boys from poor families. His explanation was that it was because of his background, and not that he ever exhibited any bad behavior. "My mother owned nothing but her own two hands, rough to the point of bleeding from washing other people's dirty clothes," Chukovsky wrote in *The Silver Crest.* "That was the real reason for making sure I would never occupy a student's bench at the university."

Determined not to be a failure, Chukovsky began his own course of education. It consisted mainly of reading every book he could get his hands on—especially those written in English. Eventually, he was able to read in this language. Soon, he was reading British and American classics and falling in love with them. His progress surprised even himself. "In a word, I created an imaginary world of my own, a world of which I was the sole inhabitant," he related in *Soviet Literature.*

Along with his love of reading came the love of writing, and in a short time he was hired by the *Odessa News* to be a journalist. He also began to translate some classic American and English works into Russian. In 1915, Maxim Gorky hired him to head a children's book department of the publishing company, Parus. Chukovsky also married at this time, and soon after had a son. All these events were inspirations for him to write his own book for children. *Crocodile* was the result, a fanciful set of rhymes about that animal's adventures. Soon after came *Wash-'em-Clean,* an amusing tale of a boy who refuses to wash and how, consequently, household objects refuse to be near him.

Many of Chukovsky's other books were similar to these first efforts—fanciful works using nonsense rhymes. Despite criticism from adults for their lack of realism, Chukovsky persisted in writing these tales, believing that his style suited a preschooler's mindset. In his work, he tried to capture the total joy that he saw in very small children, a feeling that he would grasp onto at different times in his life. "From my youth I possessed—and it has survived to this day—one priceless quality: Despite all petty cares and minor mishaps, suddenly, from out of nowhere, without any apparent cause, one feels a most powerful surge of a crazy kind of happiness. In just those periods when one ought to be sniveling and whimpering, one springs suddenly out of bed with a feeling of mindless joy, like a five-year-old boy who has just been given a whistle," he related in *Horn Book.*

Much of Chukovsky's long life was spent trying to get this joy onto paper for young children to enjoy. For his efforts, he was richly rewarded with the adoration of young children. Chukovsky was fond of playing with children to experience their joy and was often looked down on by other adults for this. However, those in the literary community recognized him by giving him many coveted honors.

"It may well be asked: How are serious and joyless adults . . . to slip into the cloudless, sunny kingdom of children," Chukovsky mused in *Horn Book.* Realizing that falseness is the quickest thing children discover, Chukovsky concluded that " 'A writer for children must be happy without fail.' . . . It was just such a happy person I felt myself to be on those occasions I managed to write my tales in verse for children."

In addition to his writing, Chukovsky established and maintained a library of children's literature next door to his home in the town of Peredelkino. Most of the books were bought with his own money, although Russian and foreign authors contributed copies of their books as well. Twice a year, a children's book festival was held in Peredelkino and Chukovsky arranged a program of games and contests and read his poetry. During the Second World War, the author also established an organization to help Russian children and their parents locate each other in the aftermath of the Nazi invasion and occupation.

Speaking of Chukovsky's relationship with the Communist regime, Miriam Morton noted in *Horn Book:* "The question of propaganda and indoctrination is inevitably raised in connection with all Soviet writers. I have read most of this author's children's books and have found not one line that could remotely be considered political propaganda or indoctrination. The didactic implications in his tales are lightly and divertingly insinuated and treat of foibles of human behavior, the virtue of cleanliness, and, most of all, the need and possibility of courage. . . . These didactic elements express . . . the traditional, centuries-old conviction of Russian writers that it is their duty to help guide and enlighten their readers."

Chukovsky once told *CA:* "English and American literature has ever been a great source of joy to me. There was a time when I carried a volume of Edgar Poe with me wherever I went. I succumbed to the charm of Jane Austen, Henry James, Trollope, John Steinbeck, Sinclair Lewis. I consider the greatest boons of my life the fact that I can read *Pickwick Papers* and *Huckleberry Finn* in the tongue they were written in. And Robert Browning and Keats, and Thomas Hardy (his poetry), and Kipling and Dylan Thomas, and Robert Frost, and Ralph Waldo Emerson, and James Baldwin, and Bernard Malamud. Hemingway, Dos Passos, Singer, and Faulkner had much to tell me, too. (And my beloved H. L. Mencken!!!) Salinger's *Catcher in the Rye* and *Fanny and Zooey,* a landmark in artistic penetration into the inner world of modern soul. As regards the essayists and critics I would consider myself a poor creature indeed had I not had the opportunity to read them from Hazlitt to Max Beerbohm, to Edmund

Wilson, and [Hesketh] Pearson (although I am quite indifferent to his posthumous *The Marrying Americans*), and all writers of the *New Yorker* circle."

BIOGRAPHICAL/CRITICAL SOURCES:

BOOKS

Chukovskaya, Lydia, *To the Memory of Childhood,* translation by Eliza Kellogg Klose, Northwestern University Press, 1988.

Chukovsky, Kornei, *The Silver Crest: My Russian Boyhood,* translated by Beatrice Stillman, Holt, 1976.

PERIODICALS

Horn Book, October, 1962, pp. 458-468; June, 1972; October, 1974; December, 1970; February, 1971, pp. 28-39.

New York Times Book Review, January 30, 1966.

Publishers Weekly, June 17, 1988, p. 63.

Russian Review, January, 1972; January, 1974.

Soviet Literature, Number 8, 1956; Number 4, 1964; Number 4, 1978.

Times Literary Supplement, January 16, 1964; November 30, 1967.

Tri-Quarterly, winter, 1967.

OBITUARIES:

PERIODICALS

AB Bookman's Weekly, November 17, 1969.

Books Abroad, spring, 1970.

New York Times, October 29, 1969.*

* * *

CITTAFINO, Ricardo
See BICKERS, Richard (Leslie) Townshend

* * *

CLARKE, Boden
See BURGESS, Michael (Roy)

* * *

CLARKE, James W(eston) 1937-

PERSONAL: Born February 16, 1937, in Elizabeth, PA; son of Alonzo Peterson and Beatrice (Weston) Clarke; married Jeanne Nienaber; children: Julianne, Michael, James. *Education:* Washington & Jefferson College, B.A., 1962; Pennsylvania State University, M.A., 1964, PhD., 1968. *Politics:* Democrat.

ADDRESSES: *Home*—855 East Placita Leslie, Tucson, AZ 85718. *Office*—315 Social Sciences Building, University of Arizona, Tucson, AZ 85721. *Agent*—Gloria Stern Literary Agency, 1230 Park Avenue, New York, NY 10128.

CAREER: Florida State University, Tallahassee, assistant professor of political science, 1967-71; University of Arizona, professor of political science, 1971—. *Military service:* U.S. Marine Corps, 1955-58.

MEMBER: Authors Guild of America.

AWARDS, HONORS: *American Assassins* was named a Notable Book of the Year by the *New York Times Book Review,* 1982; American Book Award and Pulitzer Prize nominations in history, both 1982, both for *American Assassins;* Burlington Northern Foundation award for excellence in teaching, 1987; Golden Key, National Honor Society, 1989, for teaching; Pulitzer Prize nomination, 1990, for *On Being Mad or Merely Angry;* Social and Behavioral Sciences award for outstanding teaching, 1991; Udall fellow, 1993.

WRITINGS:

American Assassins: The Darker Side of Politics, Princeton University Press, 1982, revised edition with new preface, 1990.

Last Rampage: The Escape of Gary Tison, Houghton Mifflin, 1988.

On Being Mad or Merely Angry: John W. Hinckley Jr. and Other Dangerous People, Princeton University Press, 1990.

Contributor of articles to scholarly journals, including *American Journal of Political Science, American Political Science Review,* and *Political Psychology.*

WORK IN PROGRESS: A book about racial crime and punishment in America.

SIDELIGHTS: In *American Assassins: The Darker Side of Politics,* James W. Clarke profiles sixteen would-be and actual assassins, categorizes them according to motivation, and argues against the notion that all such killers are insane. Clarke places only three of the sixteen persons he examines in this study within the thoroughly irrational category: the remainder, he argues, exhibited differing degrees of rationality in coming to the decision to kill. Clarke also contends that the American insistence on "psychopathological" explanations for assassinations is a kind of political defense mechanism. The nation affirms the stability of "the system" by denying that any rational thought or political grievance might be behind these events.

Writing in the *Houston Post,* Charles Thobae praised *American Assassins,* declaring that Clarke's book "cuts through a tangle of myth and misconception surrounding a very perplexing issue." He judged the work "scholarly yet highly readable," adding that for some readers, including himself, "Clarke becomes a revisionist historian when John Wilkes Booth, for example, is revealed as a rational, successful actor, instead of a failure seeking notoriety through an insane act." Like Thobae, P. J. Parish deemed *American Assassins* "readable and thought-provoking." Although he observed in the *Times Literary Supplement* that "any such attempt to classify assassins into a few basic types must inevitably and quickly run into a whole minefield of difficulties," he added, "one can only express admiration for this bold attempt to provide a typology of assassination." Parish further noted: "Professor Clarke has written an absorbing and, in some respects, a pioneering book on a grimly fascinating subject. He may not always convince his readers, but he will surely provoke and intrigue them."

In *Journal of the American Medical Association,* psychiatrist Matthew Brody asserted that Clarke's "scholarly treatise . . . will undoubtedly find a well-deserved public acceptance." "Clarke is right," concluded Brody. "There are social and political reasons for the increase in violence." Carolyn See of the *Los Angeles Times Book Review* hailed Clarke's "diligent scholarship" and found *American Assassins* "disturbing, beyond its immediate interest and readability, because so many of these 'lone assassins' were not 'crazy' in the accepted sense and we cannot dismiss them as aberrations. The assassins too often mirror us." The reviewer praised Clarke's narrative approach, relating that "the complacent reader . . . is forced, by the point of view of the 'stories' themselves, to see the world as the assassin saw it: to see, then, that the killings fell almost rationally into their scheme of things." In the *New York Times Book Review,* Michael Kammen observed that "many other patterns appear in *American Assassins,* such as the idiosyncratic inconsistencies in the diverse laws of the states and of the District of Columbia . . . ." Kammen called *American Assassins* "a suggestive and rewarding book."

In his next book, *Last Rampage: The Escape of Gary Tison,* Clarke confronts similar issues of politics and violent crime as he relates the story of a daring prison escape and a series of killings. Gary Tison, who was serving a double life sentence for murder, simply walked out of Arizona State Prison in 1978 with his three sons and a fellow inmate, and while on the run, the "Tison Gang" murdered six people. T. J. English, in the *New York Times Book Review,* wrote that Clarke "uses the day-to-day minutiae of Tison's escape and the subsequent manhunt to illuminate a larger issue: the appalling corruption and incompetence that eventually led to seven senseless deaths."

"The killings alone," observed Kerry Luft in the *Chicago Tribune,* "are chilling enough to place this fascinating book alongside Joseph Wambaugh's *The Onion Field* or Joe McGinniss' *Fatal Vision,* but Clarke uncovered more—evidence of corruption permeating Arizona's government." According to Clarke, Tison was granted "preferred prisoner" status for having arranged the murder of another inmate who was about to reveal damaging information about the prison warden's political ally. Luft argued that while the details of corruption in Arizona are "absorbing, the story of Tison's psychological control over his three sons provides the most riveting reading." Clarke himself described the story to *CA* as playing out "like a moral drama of the Old West, while exposing political corruption and incompetence in Arizona."

On Being Mad or Merely Angry, Clarke's third book, is the story of John W. Hinckley Jr., who in 1981 shot then-President Ronald Reagan in what Hinckley described as a bid to attract the attention of actress Jodie Foster. Again, Clarke examines what characterizes the would-be assassin and here he recommends "a situational approach" that law enforcement might use to predict potential assassinations and thereby prevent them. For Lincoln Caplan, who reviewed *On Being Mad or Merely Angry* in the *Washington Post,* the most interesting part of the book is the portrait of Hinckley. Caplan observed, "Clarke provides a concise, fascinating and often one-sided account, focusing on his infamous deeds, and concludes that 'it is no longer useful to interpret these angry events as acts of madness, as the jury concluded . . . .' To Clarke, Hinckley was an angry, disturbed, fame-seeking sociopath who knew exactly what he was doing."

Clarke once told *CA:* "One cannot assume that acts of violence are necessarily the result of mental illness. There is an important difference between the person motivated by emotions we have all experienced—love, hate, jealousy, and loneliness, for example—and insanity. In my writing I have tried to explain such distinctions and how these differences have a direct bearing on our conceptions of criminal justice."

BIOGRAPHICAL/CRITICAL SOURCES:

PERIODICALS

Chicago Tribune, August 15, 1988.

Houston Post, October 10, 1982.

Journal of the American Medical Association, March 25, 1983.

Los Angeles Times Book Review, September 19, 1982; August 19, 1990, p. 10.

Nation, February 12, 1983.

New York Times Book Review, August 29, 1982; December 5, 1982; December 11, 1988, p. 38.

Times Literary Supplement, January 28, 1983.

Toronto Star, April 12, 1983.

Washington Post, May 24, 1990.

CLIFTON, (Thelma) Lucille 1936-

PERSONAL: Born June 27, 1936, in Depew, NY; daughter of Samuel Louis, Sr. (a laborer) and Thelma (a laborer; maiden name, Moore) Sayles; married Fred James Clifton (an educator, writer, and artist), May 10, 1958 (died November 10, 1984); children: Sidney, Fredrica, Channing, Gillian, Graham, Alexia. *Education:* Attended Howard University, 1953-55, and Fredonia State Teachers College (now State University of New York College at Fredonia), 1955.

ADDRESSES: Agent—Marilyn Marlow, Curtis Brown Ltd., 10 Astor Pl., New York, NY 10003.

CAREER: New York State Division of Employment, Buffalo, claims clerk, 1958-60; U.S. Office of Education, Washington, DC, literature assistant for CAREL (Central Atlantic Regional Educational Laboratory), 1969-71; Coppin State College, Baltimore, MD, poet in residence, 1971-74; writer. Visiting writer, Columbia University School of the Arts; Jerry Moore Visiting Writer, George Washington University, 1982-83; University of California, Santa Cruz, professor of literature and creative writing, 1985—. Trustee, Enoch Pratt Free Library, Baltimore.

MEMBER: International PEN, Authors Guild, Authors League of America.

AWARDS, HONORS: Discovery Award, New York YW-YMHA Poetry Center, 1969; *Good Times: Poems* was cited as one of the year's ten best books by the *New York Times,* 1969; National Endowment for the Arts awards, 1969, 1970, and 1972; Poet Laureate of the State of Maryland, 1979-82; Juniper Prize, 1980; Coretta Scott King Award, 1984, for *Everett Anderson's Goodbye;* honorary degrees from University of Maryland and Towson State University.

WRITINGS:

ADULT

Good Times: Poems, Random House, 1969.
Good News about the Earth: New Poems, Random House, 1972.
An Ordinary Woman (poetry), Random House, 1974.
Generations: A Memoir (prose), Random House, 1976.
Two-Headed Woman (poetry), University of Massachusetts Press, 1980.
Good Woman: Poems and a Memoir, 1969-1980, Boa Editions, 1987.
Next: New Poems, Boa Editions, 1987.
Ten Oxherding Pictures, Moving Parts Press, 1988.
Quilting: Poems 1987-1990, Boa Editions, 1991.
Book of Light, Copper Canyon Press, 1993.

JUVENILE

The Black BCs (alphabet poems), Dutton, 1970.
Good, Says Jerome, illustrations by Stephanie Douglas, Dutton, 1973.
All Us Come Cross the Water, pictures by John Steptoe, Holt, 1973.
Don't You Remember?, illustrations by Evaline Ness, Dutton, 1973.
The Boy Who Didn't Believe in Spring, pictures by Brinton Turkle, Dutton, 1973.
The Times They Used to Be, illustrations by Susan Jeschke, Holt, 1974.
My Brother Fine with Me, illustrations by Moneta Barnett, Holt, 1975.
Three Wishes, illustrations by Douglas, Viking, 1976.
Amifika, illustrations by Thomas DiGrazia, Dutton, 1977.
The Lucky Stone, illustrations by Dale Payson, Delacorte, 1979.
My Friend Jacob, illustrations by DiGrazia, Dutton, 1980.
Sonora Beautiful, illustrations by Michael Garland, Dutton, 1981.

"EVERETT ANDERSON" SERIES; JUVENILE

Some of the Days of Everett Anderson, Holt, 1970.
Everett Anderson's Christmas Coming, illustrations by Ness, Holt, 1971.
Everett Anderson's Year, illustrations by Ann Grifalconi, Holt, 1974.
Everett Anderson's Friend, illustrations by Grifalconi, Holt, 1976.
Everett Anderson's 1 2 3, illustrations by Grifalconi, Holt, 1977.
Everett Anderson's Nine Month Long, illustrations by Grifalconi, Holt, 1978.
Everett Anderson's Goodbye, illustrations by Grifalconi, Holt, 1983.

OTHER

(Contributor) Langston Hughes and Arna Bontemps, *Poetry of the Negro, 1746-1970,* Doubleday, 1970.
(Contributor) Marlo Thomas and others, *Free to Be . . . You and Me,* McGraw-Hill, 1974.

Also contributor to *Free to Be a Family,* 1987, *Norton Anthology of Literature by Women, Coming into the Light,* and *Stealing the Language.* Contributor of fiction to *Negro Digest, Redbook, House and Garden,* and *Atlantic.* Contributor of nonfiction to *Ms.* and *Essence.*

SIDELIGHTS: Lucille Clifton "began composing and writing stories at an early age and has been much encouraged by an ever-growing reading audience and a fine critical reputation," writes Wallace R. Peppers in a *Dictionary of Literary Biography* essay. "In many ways her themes are traditional: she writes of her family because she is greatly interested in making sense of their lives and relationships; she writes of adversity and success in the ghetto community; and she writes of her role as a poet." Clifton's work emphasizes endurance and strength through adversity. Ronald Baughman suggests in his *Dictionary of Literary Biography* essay that "Clifton's pride in being black and in being a woman helps her transform difficult circumstances into a qualified affirmation about the black urban world she portrays." Writing in Mari Evans's *Black Women Writers (1950-1980): A Critical Evaluation,* Haki Madhubuti (formerly Don L. Lee) states: "She is a writer of complexity, and she makes her readers work and think. Her poetry has a quiet force without being pushy or alien. Whether she is cutting through family relationships, surviving American racial attitudes, or just simply renewing love ties, she puts something heavy on your mind. The great majority of her published poetry is significant. At the base of her work is concern for the Black family, especially the destruction of its youth. Her eye is for the uniqueness of our people, always concentrating on the small strengths that have allowed us to survive the horrors of Western life."

Clifton's first volume of poetry, *Good Times: Poems,* which was cited by the *New York Times* as one of 1969's ten best books, is described by Peppers as a "varied collection of character sketches written with third person narrative voices." Baughman notes that "these poems attain power not only through their subject matter but also through their careful techniques; among Clifton's most successful poetic devices . . . are the precise evocative images that give substance to her rhetorical statements and a frequent duality of vision that lends complexity to her portraits of place and character." Calling the book's title "ironic," Baughman indicates, "Although the urban ghetto can, through its many hardships, create figures who are tough enough to survive and triumph, the overriding concern of this book is with the horrors of the location, with the human carnage that results from such problems as poverty, unemployment, substandard housing, and inadequate education." Baughman recognizes that although "these portraits of human devastation reflect the trying circumstances of life in the ghetto . . . the writer also records some joy in her world, however strained and limited that joy might be." Madhubuti thinks that although this is Clifton's first book of poetry, it "cannot be looked upon as simply a 'first effort.' The work is unusually compacted and memory-evoking." As Johari Amini (formerly Jewel C. Latimore) suggests in *Black World,* "The poetry is filled with the sensations of coming up black with the kind of love that keeps you from dying in desperation."

In Clifton's second volume of poetry, *Good News about the Earth: New Poems,* "the elusive good times seem more attainable," remarks Baughman, who summarizes the three sections into which the book is divided: the first section "focuses on the sterility and destruction of 'white ways,' newly perceived through the social upheavals of the early 1970s"; the second section "presents a series of homages to black leaders of the late 1960s and early 1970s"; and the third section "deals with biblical characters powerfully rendered in terms of the black experience." Harriet Jackson Scarupa notes in *Ms.* that after having read what Clifton says about blackness and black pride, some critics "have concluded that Clifton hates whites. [Clifton] considers this a misreading. When she equates whiteness with death, blackness with life, she says: 'What I'm talking about is a certain kind of white arrogance—and not all white people have it—that is not good. I think airs of superiority are very dangerous. I believe in justice. I try not to be about hatred.' " Writing in *Poetry,* Ralph J. Mills, Jr., says that Clifton's poetic scope transcends the black experience "to embrace the entire world, human and nonhuman, in the deep affirmation she makes in the teeth of negative evidence. She is a master of her style, with its spare, elliptical, idiomatic, rhythmical speech, and of prophetic warning in the same language." Angela Jackson, who thinks that it "is a book written in wisdom," concludes in *Black World* that "Clifton and *Good News about the Earth* will make you shake yo head. Ain't nothing else to say."

An Ordinary Woman, Clifton's third collection of poems, "abandons many of the broad racial issues examined in the two preceding books and focuses instead on the narrower but equally complex issues of the writer's roles as woman and poet," says Baughman. Peppers notes that "the poems take as their theme a historical, social, and spiritual assessment of the current generation in the genealogical line" of Clifton's great great-grandmother, who had been taken from her home in Dahomey, West Africa, and brought to America in slavery in 1830. Peppers notes that by taking an ordinary experience and personalizing it, "Clifton has elevated the experience into a public confession" which may be shared, and "it is this shared sense of situation, an easy identification between speaker and reader, that heightens the notion of ordinariness and gives . . . the collection an added dimension." Helen Vendler writes in the *New York Times Book Review* that "Clifton recalls for us those bare places we have all waited as 'ordinary women,' with no choices but yes or no, no art, no grace, no words, no reprieve." "Written in the same ironic, yet cautiously optimistic spirit as her earlier published work," observes Peppers, the book is "lively, full of vigor, passion, and an all-consuming honesty."

In *Generations: A Memoir,* "it is as if [Clifton] were showing us a cherished family album and telling us the story about each person which seemed to sum him or her up best," says a *New Yorker* contributor. Calling the book an "eloquent eulogy of [Clifton's] parents," Reynolds Price writes in the *New York Times Book Review* that, "as with most elegists, her purpose is perpetuation and celebration, not judgment. There is no attempt to see either parent whole; no attempt at the recovery of history not witnessed by or told to the author. There is no sustained chronological narrative. Instead, clusters of brief anecdotes gather round two poles, the deaths of father and mother." Price, however, believes that *Generations* stands "worthily" among the other modern elegies that assert that "we may survive, some lively few, if we've troubled to *be* alive and loved." However, a contributor to *Virginia Quarterly Review* thinks that the book is "more than an elegy or a personal memoir. It is an attempt on the part of one woman to retrieve and lyrically to celebrate, her Afro-American heritage."

"Clifton is a poet of a literary tradition which includes such varied poets as Walt Whitman, Emily Dickinson, and Gwendolyn Brooks, who have inspired and informed her work," writes Audrey T. McCluskey in Evans's *Black Women Writers (1950-1980).* McCluskey finds that "Clifton's belief in her ability (and ours) to make things better and her belief in the concept of personal responsibility pervade her work. These views are especially pronounced in her books for children." Clifton's books for children are characterized by a positive view of black heritage and an urban setting peopled by nontraditional families. Critics recognize that although her works speak directly to a specific audience, they reveal the concerns of all children. In a *Language Arts* interview with Rudine Sims, Clifton was asked where she gets her ideas for stories: "Well, I had six kids in seven years, and when you have a lot of children, you tend to attract children, and you see so many kids, you get ideas from that. And I have such a good memory from my own childhood, my own time. I have great respect for young people; I like them enormously."

Clifton's books for children are designed to help them understand their world. *My Friend Jacob,* for instance, is a story "in which a black child speaks with affection and patience of his friendship with a white adolescent neighbor . . . who is retarded," writes Zena Sutherland in *Bulletin of the Center for Children's Books.* "Jacob is Sam's 'very very best friend' and all of his best qualities are appreciated by Sam, just as all of his limitations are accepted. . . . It is strong in the simplicity and warmth with which a handicapped person is loved rather than pitied, enjoyed rather than tolerated." Critics find that Clifton's characters and their relationships are accurately and positively drawn. Ismat Abdal-Haqq notes in *Interracial Books for Children Bulletin* that "the two boys have a strong relationship filled with trust and affection. The author depicts this relationship and their everyday adventures in a way that is unmarred by the mawkish sentimentality that often characterizes tales of the mentally disabled." And a contributor to *Reading Teacher* states that "in a matter-of-fact, low-keyed style, we discover how [Sam and Jacob] help one another grow and understand the world."

Clifton's children's books also facilitate an understanding of black heritage specifically, which in turn fosters an important link with the past generally. *All Us Come Cross the Water,* for example, "in a very straight-forward way . . . shows the relationship of Africa to Blacks in the U.S. without getting into a heavy rap about 'Pan-Africanism,' " states Judy Richardson in the *Journal of Negro Education,* adding that Clifton "seems able to get inside a little boy's head, and knows how to represent that on paper." An awareness of one's origins figures also in *The Times They Used to Be.* Called a "short and impeccable vignette—laced with idiom and humor of rural Black folk," by Rosalind K. Goddard in *School Library Journal,* it is further described by Lee A. Daniels in the *Washington Post* as a "story in which a young girl catches her first glimpse of the new technological era in a hardware store window, and learns of death and life." "Most books that awaken adult nostalgia are not as appealing to young readers," says Sutherland in *Bulletin of the Center for Children's Books,* "but this brief story has enough warmth and vitality and humor for any reader."

In addition to quickening an awareness of black heritage, Clifton's books for children frequently include an element of fantasy as well. Writing about *Three Wishes,* in which a young girl finds a lucky penny on New Year's Day and makes three wishes upon it, Christopher Lehmann-Haupt in the *New York Times Book Review* calls it "an urbanized version of the traditional tale in which the first wish reveals the power of the magic object . . . the second wish is a mistake, and the third undoes the second." Lehmann-Haupt adds that "too few children's books for blacks justify their ethnicity, but this one is a winning blend of black English and bright illustration." And *The Lucky Stone,* in which a lucky stone provides good fortune for all of its owners, is described by Ruth K. MacDonald in *School Library Journal* as: "Four short stories about four generations of Black women and their dealings with a lucky stone. . . . Clifton uses as a frame device a grandmother telling the history of the stone to her granddaughter; by the end, the granddaughter has inherited the stone herself." A contributor to *Interracial Books for Children Bulletin* states that "the concept of past and present is usually hard for children to grasp but this book puts the passing of time in a perspective that children can understand. . . . This book contains information on various aspects of Black culture—slavery, religion and extended family—all conveyed in a way that is both positive and accurate." Michele Slung writes in the *Washington Post Book World* that the book "is at once talisman and anthology: over the years it has gathered unto it story after story, episodes indicating its power, both as a charm and as a unit of oral tradition. Clifton has a knack for projecting strong positive values without seeming too goody-goody; her poet's ear is one fact in this, her sense of humor another."

While Clifton's books for children emphasize an understanding of the past, they also focus on the present. Her series of books about Everett Anderson, for instance, explore the experiences of a young child's world in flux. Writing in *Language Arts* about *Everett Anderson's 1 2 3,* in which a young boy's mother considers remarriage, Ruth M. Stein notes that "previous books contained wistful references to Everett Anderson's absent daddy; the latest one tells how the worried little boy gradually became reconciled to the idea of a new father joining the family." And writing about *Everett Anderson's Nine Month Long,* which concerns the anticipated birth of the family's newest member, a contributor to *Interracial Books for Children Bulletin* considers that "this book, written in wonderful poetic style . . . projects a warm, loving, understanding and supportive family." Joan W. Blos, who feels that "the establishment of an active, effective, and supportive male figure is an important part of this story," adds in *School Library Journal,* "So is its tacit acknowledgement that, for the younger child, a mother's pregnancy means disturbing changes now as well as a sibling later." However, just as the birth of a sibling can cause upheaval in a child's world, so, too, can death. In *Everett Anderson's Goodbye,* Everett has difficulty coping with the death of his father; he "misses his Daddy, as he moves through the five stages of grief: denial, anger, bargaining, depression and acceptance," writes a *Washington Post Book World* contributor.

Barbara Walker writes in *Interracial Books for Children Bulletin* that "Clifton is a gifted poet with the greater gift of being able to write poetry for children." Clifton indicates to Sims that she doesn't think of it as poetry especially for children, though. "It seems to me that if you write poetry for children, you have to keep too many things in mind other than the poem. So I'm just writing a poem." *Some of the Days of Everett Anderson* is a book of nine poems, about which Marjorie Lewis observes in *School Library Journal,* "Some of the days of six-year-old 'ebony Everett Anderson' are happy; some lonely—but all of them are special, reflecting the author's own pride in being black." In the *New York Times Book Review,* Hoyt W. Fuller thinks that Clifton has "a profoundly simple way of saying all that is important to say, and we know that the struggle is worth it, that the all-important battle of image is being won, and that the future of all those beautiful black children out there need not be twisted and broken." *Everett Anderson's Christmas Coming* concerns Christmas preparations in which "each of the five days before Everett's Christmas is described by a verse," says Anita Silvey in *Horn Book,* observing that "the overall richness of Everett's experiences dominates the text." Jane O'Reilly suggests in the *New York Times Book Review* that "Everett Anderson, black and boyish, is glimpsed, rather than explained through poems about him." *Everett Anderson's Year* celebrates "a year in the life of a city child . . . in appealing verses," says Beryl Robinson in *Horn Book,* adding that "mischief, fun, gaiety, and poignancy are a part of his days as the year progresses. The portrayals of child and mother are lively and solid, executed with both strength and tenderness."

Language is important in Clifton's writing. In answer to Sim's question about the presence of both black and white children in her work, Clifton responds specifically about *Sonora Beautiful,* which is about the insecurities and dissatisfaction of an adolescent girl and which has only white characters: "In this book, I *heard* the characters as white. I have a tendency to *hear* the language of the characters, and then I know something about who the people are." However, regarding objections to the black vernacular she often uses, Clifton tells Sims: "I do not write out of weakness. That is to say, I do not write the language I write because I don't know any other. . . . But I have a certain integrity about my art, and in *my* art you have to be honest and you have to have people talking the way they really talk. So all of my books are not in the same language." Asked by Sims whether or not she feels any special pressures or special opportunities as a black author, Clifton responds: "I do feel a responsibility. . . . First, I'm going to write books that tend to celebrate life. I'm about that. And I wish to have children see people like themselves in books. . . . I also take seriously the responsibility of not lying. . . . I'm not going to say that life is wretched if circumstance is wretched, because that's not true. So I take that responsibility, but it's a responsibility to the truth, and to my art as much as anything. I owe everybody that. . . . It's the truth as I see it, and that's what my responsibility is."

"Browsing through a volume of Lucille Clifton's poems or reading one of her children's books to my son," says Scarupa, "always makes me feel good: good to be black, good to be a woman, good to be alive." "I am excited about her work because she reflects me; she tells my story in a way and with an eloquence that is beyond my ability," concurs Madhubuti, who concludes: "To be original, relevant, and revolutionary in the mouth of fire is the mark of a dangerous person. Lucille Clifton is a poet of *mean* talent who has not let her gifts separate her from the work at hand. She is a teacher and an example. To read her is to give birth to bright seasons." Clifton, herself, has commented on her role as a poet in *Black Women Writers (1950-1980):* "I am interested in trying to render big ideas in a simple way . . . in being understood not admired. I wish to celebrate and not be celebrated (though a little celebration is a lot of fun). I am a woman and I write from that experience. I am a Black woman and I write from that experience. I do not feel inhibited or bound by what I am." She adds: "Sometimes I think that the most anger comes from ones who were late in discovering that when the world said nigger it meant them too. I grew up knowing that the world meant me too but that was the world's insanity and not mine. I have been treated in publishing very much like other poets are treated, that is, not really very well. I continue to write since my life as a human only includes my life as a poet, it doesn't depend on it."

In Clifton's 1991 title, *Quilting: Poems 1987-1990,* the author uses a quilt as a poetic metaphor for life. Each poem is a story, bound together through the chronicles of history and figuratively sewn with the thread of experience. The result is, as Roger Mitchell in *American Book Review,* describes it, a quilt "made by and for people." Each section of the book is divided by a conventional quilt design name such as "Eight-Pointed Star" and "Tree of Life," which provides a framework within which Clifton crafts her poetic quilt. Clifton's main focus is on women's history; however, according to Mitchell her poetry has a far broader range: "Her heroes include nameless slaves buried on old plantations, Hector Peterson (the first child killed in the Soweto riot), Fannie Lou Hamer (founder of the Mississippi Peace and Freedom Party), Nelson and Winnie Mandela, W. E. B. DuBois, Huey P. Newton, and many other people who gave their lives to Black people from slavery and prejudice. Her confidence in the future wavers, however, because of the devastation now being wrought among Blacks by drugs."

Enthusiasts of *Quilting* include critic Bruce Bennett in the *New York Times Book Review,* who praises Clifton as a "passionate, mercurial writer, by turns angry, prophetic, compassionate, shrewd, sensuous, vulnerable and funny. . . . The movement and effect of the whole book communicate the sense of a journey" through which the poet achieves an understanding of "something new." Pat Monaghan in *Booklist* admires Clifton's "terse, uncomplicated" verse, and judges the poet "a fierce and original voice in American letters." Mitchell finds energy and hope in her poems, referring to them as "visionary." He concludes that they are "the poems of a strong woman, strong enough to . . . look the impending crises of our time in the eye, as well as our customary limitations, and go ahead and hope anyway."

BIOGRAPHICAL/CRITICAL SOURCES:

BOOKS

Beckles, Frances N., *20 Black Women,* Gateway Press, 1978.

Children's Literature Review, Volume 5, Gale, 1983.

Contemporary Literary Criticism, Volume 9, Gale, 1981.

Dictionary of Literary Biography, Gale, Volume 5: *American Poets since World War II,* 1980, Volume 41: *Afro-American Poets since 1955,* 1985.

Dreyer, Sharon Spredemann, *The Bookfinder: A Guide to Children's Literature about the Needs and Problems of Youth Aged 2-15,* Volume 1, American Guidance Service, 1977.

Evans, Mari, editor, *Black Women Writers (1950-1980): A Critical Evaluation,* Doubleday-Anchor, 1984.

PERIODICALS

America, May 1, 1976.

American Book Review, June, 1992, p. 21.

Black Scholar, March, 1981.

Black World, July, 1970; February, 1973.

Booklist, June 15, 1991, p. 1926.

Book World, March 8, 1970; November 8, 1970; November 11, 1973; November 10, 1974; December 8, 1974; December 11, 1977; September 14, 1980; July 20, 1986; May 10, 1987.

Bulletin of the Center for Children's Books, March, 1971; November, 1974; March, 1976; September, 1980.

Horn Book, December, 1971; August, 1973; February, 1975; December, 1975; October, 1977.

Interracial Books for Children Bulletin, Volume 5, numbers 7 and 8, 1975; Volume 7, number 1, 1976; Volume 8, number 1, 1977; Volume 10, number 5, 1979; Volume 11, numbers 1 and 2, 1980; Volume 12, number 2, 1981.

Journal of Negro Education, summer, 1974.

Journal of Reading, February, 1977; December, 1986.

Kirkus Reviews, April 15, 1970; October 1, 1970; December 15, 1974; April 15, 1976; February 15, 1982.

Language Arts, January, 1978; February 2, 1982.

Ms., October, 1976.

New Yorker, April 5, 1976.

New York Times, December 20, 1976.

New York Times Book Review, September 6, 1970; December 6, 1970; December 5, 1971; November 4, 1973; April 6, 1975; March 14, 1976; May 15, 1977; March 1, 1992; May 31, 1992, p. 28.

Poetry, May, 1973.

Reading Teacher, October, 1978; March, 1981.

Redbook, November, 1969.

Saturday Review, December 11, 1971; August 12, 1972; December 4, 1973.
School Library Journal, May, 1970; December, 1970; September, 1974; December, 1977; February, 1979; March, 1980.
Tribune Books, August 30, 1987.
Virginia Quarterly Review, fall, 1976.
Voice of Youth Advocates, April, 1982.
Washington Post, November 10, 1974; August 9, 1979.
Washington Post Book World, February 10, 1980.
Western Humanities Review, summer, 1970.*

* * *

COHEN, Arthur A(llen) 1928-1986

PERSONAL: Born June 25, 1928, in New York, NY; died of cancer, October 31, 1986, in New York, NY; son of Isidore M(eyer) and Bess (Junger) Cohen; married Elaine Firstenberg Lustig (a painter), October 14, 1956; children: Tamar Judith. *Education:* Attended Friends Seminary, New York, NY, 1941-44; University of Chicago, B.A., 1946, M.A., 1949, graduate study, 1949-51; additional studies at Union Theological Seminary, 1950, New School for Social Research, 1950, Columbia University, 1950, and Jewish Theological Seminary of America, 1950-52. *Politics:* "Liberal, if not left, Democrat." *Religion:* Jewish.

Avocational Interests: Horseback riding, traveling, learning languages.

CAREER: Noonday Press, New York City, co-founder and managing director, 1951-55; Meridian Books, Inc., New York City, founder and president, 1955-60; World Publishing Co., New York City, vice-president, 1960-61; Holt, Rinehart & Winston, Inc., New York City, director of religion department, 1961-64, editor-in-chief and vice-president of General Books Division, 1964-68; Viking Press, Inc., New York City, managing editor, 1968-75; Ex Libris (rare book dealer), New York City, founder and president, 1974-86. Visiting lecturer, Brown University, 1972, and Jewish Institute of Religion, 1977; Tisch Lecturer in Judaic Theology, Brown University, 1979. Consultant, Fund for the Republic "Religion and the Free Society" project, 1956-59; chairman of the board, YIVO Institute for Jewish Research; member of advisory board, Institute for Advanced Judaic Studies, Brandeis University; member of board, PEN American Center.

AWARDS, HONORS: Edgar Lewis Wallant Prize, 1973, for *In the Days of Simon Stern;* National Jewish Book Award in fiction, Jewish Book Council, 1984, for *An Admirable Woman;* William and Janice Epstein Award for a Book of Jewish Fiction, 1985, for *An Admirable Woman.*

WRITINGS:

Martin Buber, Hillary House, 1958.
The Natural and the Supernatural Jew: An Historical and Theological Introduction, Pantheon, 1963.
The Myth of the Judeo-Christian Tradition, Harper, 1970.
A People Apart: Hasidic Life in America, Dutton, 1970.
If Not Now, When? Conversations between Mordecai M. Kaplan and Arthur A. Cohen, Schocken, 1970.
Osip Emilevich Mandelstam: An Essay in Antiphon, Ardis, 1974.
Sonia Delaunay, Abrams, 1975.
The Tremendum: A Theological Interpretation of the Holocaust, Crossroad Publishing, 1981.
Herbert Bayer: The Complete Works, MIT Press, 1984.

NOVELS

The Carpenter Years, New American Library, 1967.
In the Days of Simon Stern, Random House, 1973.
A Hero in His Time, Random House, 1976.
Acts of Theft, Harcourt, 1980.
An Admirable Woman, David Godine, 1983.
Artists & Enemies: Three Novellas, David Godine, 1987.

EDITOR

The Anatomy of Faith: Theological Essays of Milton Steinberg, Harcourt, 1960.
Humanistic Education and Western Civilization: Essays in Honor of Robert Maynard Hutchins, Holt, 1964.
Arguments and Doctrines: A Reader of Jewish Thinking in the Aftermath of the Holocaust, Harper, 1970.
The New Art of Color: The Writings of Robert and Sonia Delaunay, Viking, 1978.
The Jew: Essays from Martin Buber's Journal "Der Jude," University of Alabama Press, 1980.
(With Paul Mendes-Flohr) *Contemporary Jewish Religious Thought: Original Essays on Critical Concepts, Movements, and Beliefs,* Scribner, 1987.

CONTRIBUTOR

Religion and the Free Society, Fund for the Republic, 1958.
American Catholics: A Protestant-Jewish View, Sheed, 1959.
Religion and Contemporary Society, Macmillan, 1963.
Christianity: Some Non-Christian Appraisals, McGraw, 1964.
What's Ahead for the Churches?, Sheed, 1964.
Varieties of Jewish Belief, Reconstructionist Press, 1966.
Confrontations with Judaism, Anthony Blond, 1966.
Negro and Jew, Macmillan, 1967.
McLuhan: Pro and Con, Funk, 1968.
Dada Spectrum, Coda Press, 1979.

OTHER

Contributor of articles and short stories to numerous publications, including *Commonweal, Partisan Review, Commentary, Harper's, Saturday Review,* and *New York Times Book Review.*

SIDELIGHTS: Publisher, editor, theologian, rare book dealer, art historian, and novelist Arthur A. Cohen wrote his first novel after spending more than twenty successful years writing and editing nonfiction. "I was terrified of writing fiction," he once told *CA,* "[and] for years put it off and, as a result, have no drawerful of partial manuscripts or shards from broken ideas. My training was in philosophy and theology, and my passion remains philosophy and theology. People, unfortunately, don't read philosophy and theology, certainly not Jewish theology." Despite his opinions on the unpopularity of the subjects, Cohen chose to draw heavily from Jewish philosophy and theology as a basis for his fiction. "Cohen has said that in his novels he seeks to give the reader 'a tale plus something else,' " noted Diane Cole in the *Dictionary of Literary Biography.* "He sees fiction as a 'smuggling device' which will allow him to follow the advice of philosopher Franz Rosenzweig 'to smuggle Jewish ideas into general culture.' " Cole concluded, "In presenting his vision of the world, Arthur A. Cohen helps clarify our own. His voice arouses his readers to thought, perplexity, the possibility of faith, and finally, the perception of art."

The Carpenter Years tells the story of a Jewish man who, perceiving himself as a failure, abandons his faith, his job, and his family and creates a new identity for himself as a successful and respected "WASP." Many reviewers praised the book for its theme while pointing out that Cohen lacked the skills of an accomplished novelist. "Mr. Cohen is not a novelist," observed a *Book World* critic. "Yet *The Carpenter Years* is a good novel. It is good because the man who made it, though not imaginatively gifted, has known how to take advantage of the possibilities of conventional fiction as a medium of discourse and as a tool of investigation. As philosophers use myth, as novelists have sometimes used theology, so Mr. Cohen, a theologian, uses fiction—for purposes foreign to its ends, but proper to his." Leonard Kriegel, in the *Nation,* faulted Cohen's characterizations but remarked that Cohen had been "daring in his choice of a theme." Richard Horchler in *Commonweal* observed, "Because Mr. Cohen is not a novelist—at least not yet a novelist—his interests, reflections and ideas are only hung on his characters and events, not embodied in them. It is hard to believe in any of the characters, in fact, and therefore hard to take very seriously the objectively very serious things that happen in the novel." Horchler concluded, "I am afraid that what [Cohen] was trying to convey . . . would have been clearer—and better realized—in one of his philosophic essays." Bernard Bergonzi, in the *New York Review of Books,* stated that Cohen's "seriousness exists only on the level of intention, not of imaginative enactment." On the other hand, *Christian Century* reviewer Mark Perlberg believed that the novel's characters were "vividly drawn and . . . observed at close range, as through a zoom lens. Hence the air of claustrophobic tension throughout. [*The Carpenter Years*] holds the reader's attention as it speeds to its climax." An *Illustrated London News* critic also took a favorable view of the novel, pronouncing it to be a "strong, simple narrative" that is "beautifully written, . . . well observed, and full of implicit wisdom."

In the Days of Simon Stern, perhaps Cohen's most well-known novel, is the story of a post-World War II messiah who uses his vast financial resources to set up a haven for victims of the Holocaust on New York's Lower East Side. Digressions, including a parable about the last Jew on Earth and discussions of Jewish holidays, widen the novel's scope. Doris Grumbach, in the *New Republic,* claimed that Cohen had "done better than any novelist of our time . . . with material that appears at first to be familiar, even shopworn. . . ." Cynthia Ozick, writing in the *New York Times Book Review,* said that "In its teeming particularity every vein of this book runs with a brilliance of Jewish insight and erudition to be found in no other novelist. . . . Arthur Cohen is the first writer of any American generation to compose a profoundly Jewish fiction on a profoundly Western theme." M. J. Bandler, a contributor to *Commonweal,* described *In the Days of Simon Stern* as "a jewel to be treasured; a majestic work of fiction that should stand world literature's test of time, to be read and reread in a search for new meanings and interpretations." Reviewers who dissented from this line of thought tended to be put off by the same sprawling, encyclopedic aspect of the work that delighted its partisans. A *Book World* critic wrote, "*In the Days of Simon Stern* is hollow. It blunders about in sociology, psychology, philosophy, all gracelessly, but never tells a convincing story. Instead, Arthur Cohen . . . overexplains every moment. . . . [His] fiction is not adequate to his sense of history." A *Books and Bookmen* reviewer referred to the novel as a "fictional labyrinth, with its theological meanderings, symbolical cobwebberies, stylistic obfuscations and anecdotal cul-de-sacs," and added, "I regret to say that I found [the novel] not so much 'deeply moving' as profoundly boring."

A Hero in His Time was greeted with less polarized reactions. It tells the story of an obscure Soviet Jewish poet who is chosen to attend a writers' conference in New York to read a special poem which, unknown to him, is really a coded message intended for a KGB agent. "Well-written and engaging in its ideas, this novel steers an uneven course between comedy and high seriousness," wrote

Ruth R. Wisse in a *Commentary* review. In an observation reminiscent of those made on Cohen's earlier works, Wisse noted that "some of his characters are mere occasions for aspects of social history, and even the hero, though witty and interesting, seems emotionally underdone, too flat for the fictional load he must carry." *Time*'s John Skow called the novel "a delightful minor-key farce. . . . [Cohen] uncannily manages to sound like a U.S.S.R. satirist writing riskily for *Samizdat* circulation. The New York section of the book is weaker; perhaps it should have been written by a Soviet." A *National Observer* reviewer described the book as "an acidly funny fable, but . . . a deeply human, moving fable as well." Valentine Cunningham in the *New Statesman* was impressed by Cohen's ability to "get inside the imaginative life of Russian Jews," and called the book an "amazing *tour de force*. . . . [S]olid, believable, and quite astonishing from an American, even a Jewish-American, writer."

Acts of Theft represented a departure for Cohen in that it did not deal specifically with Judaism. It tells the story of a European sculptor residing in Mexico who supplements his income by stealing pieces of pre-Colombian art from archeological sites in order to sell them to collectors. The tone of the book is philosophical, however: in the confrontation between the thief and the clever Mexican detective who tracks him down, the author's intellectual concerns come to the forefront. According to the *New York Times*'s John Leonard, *Acts of Theft* is an exploration of "the artist as God, art as theft, the ransom of the past, the ancient made modern, pride and sacrifice." Mark Shechner of the *New York Times Book Review* described it as a study of "the corruptions that attend worship of graven images." Shechner felt that *Acts of Theft* suffered as a work of fiction from the author's lofty intentions: "Mr. Cohen doesn't want the dramatics of pursuit and evasion to distract us from his ruminations on the morality of art. Hence he short-circuits his plot with flashbacks, asides, interior monologues, lectures, the works, for the sake of depth, weight, and moral tone." However, Shechner continued, "rather than challenging the reader, this strategy only exasperates him." The *Washington Post*'s Joseph McLellan, on the other hand, felt that Cohen did achieve a successful blend of philosophy and drama in *Acts of Theft* and remarked, "On one level, *Acts of Theft* is a very elaborate story of cops and robbers—but it aspires to much more and its aspirations are largely fulfilled. The parallels that spring to mind are *Crime and Punishment* or *Les Miserables,* and if it does not have quite the depth of the one or the sweeping scope of the other, it is certainly more than a routine novel. Its texture is rich. . . . Its central characters are deeply pondered."

Cohen continued to enlarge his creative scope with his fifth novel, *An Admirable Woman,* by writing in a female voice. The book is a fictional memoir of Erika Margaret Hertz, a character who, reports Anatole Broyard in the *New York Times,* Cohen said "was suggested to me by the remarkable personality and intellectual career of an old friend, Hannah Arendt." Arendt, a philosopher and political scientist, was considered one of the most important political thinkers of her time. Like Arendt, Erika Hertz came to New York's Upper West Side from Nazi Germany to become part of the community of "exiled German geniuses who transformed America's cultural landscape in the years after World War II," explained Jim Miller in *Newsweek.* "Mr. Cohen has not written a biography of Hannah Arendt," stated Earl Shorris in the *New York Times Book Review,* "nor has he intended a biography. Rather, he has used the novelist's imagination to explore fame in the intellectual world, to reveal life overwhelmed by ethics, to take the reader to a miraculous town. All through her memoir, Erika Hertz ponders the quality of admirableness, examines it in relation to each of her attributes. She is a doubter, a critic of herself. A measure of Mr. Cohen's accomplishment is that the reader wants to argue with her, often to insist that she *is* a 'wholly admirable' woman." Like Cohen's earlier novels, *An Admirable Woman* received some criticism for being too abstract, especially in its portrayal of the main character. Broyard noted that Erika's "career in New York City is more often summarized than dramatized. . . . [Cohen] has not given Erika the style, the intellectual texture, of a great woman." Miller remarked in a similar vein, "Unfortunately, Cohen's creation lacks Arendt's caustic wit and flair for philosophical fireworks." But Sharon Dirlam in the *Los Angeles Times Book Review* maintained that if Erika "is never more than a conduit for Cohen's philosophies of truth and meaning, this alone may justify her existence as a fictional character. . . . The book is a treasure."

Cohen's posthumously published trio of novellas, *Artists & Enemies,* shows him working in a vein of baroque fable marked by historical settings, ornate language, and stylized melodrama reminiscent of E. T. A. Hoffmann, Jorge Luis Borges, Heinrich von Kleist, and Isak Dinesen. "Arthur A. Cohen has created three novellas to be read in sequel to Dinesen's 'Seven Gothic Tales'; he has furthered the tradition by the originality of his imaginative concerns, through which he establishes his particular voice," said Morris Philipson in the *New York Times Book Review.* The novellas focus on three artists: a young German restorer of paintings, a French sculptor, and a Russian painter. "The themes the author plays upon are the prices paid in different coins for how each makes his way in the world," Philipson explained. Analyzing the book's title, Philipson found that the "enemies" of the artists are themselves, when "they misuse or take unfair advantage of other people, often by taking the path of least resistance." Reviewer Elaine Kendall, in the *Los Angeles Times,* commented, "These three novellas are so suffused with the sensibility of Europe between the wars that they seem to be the newly unearthed work of a forgotten emigre writer rather than brand-new fiction by a contemporary American. Cohen has not merely written 'historical novels,' he has become a historical person: living, thinking, and recording events in cadences and rhythms unheard for half a century."

Commenting on Cohen's career a few months after his death, Philipson wrote, "I suspect there is no one audience that shared all of Cohen's interests and, therefore, there is no common opinion remotely suggesting a consensus evaluation of his life and thought. . . . Perhaps we can expect further publications to throw more revealing light on the writings of this complex artist."

BIOGRAPHICAL/CRITICAL SOURCES:

BOOKS

Contemporary Literary Criticism, Gale, Volume 7, 1977, Volume 31, 1985.

Dictionary of Literary Biography, Volume 28: *Twentieth Century American-Jewish Fiction Writers,* Gale, 1984.

PERIODICALS

Books and Bookmen, July, 1967; March, 1976.
Book World, March 12, 1967; July 29, 1973.
Christian Century, March 1, 1967; March 10, 1971.
Christian Science Monitor, February 23, 1967.
Commentary, April, 1967; November, 1969; November, 1970; October, 1976.
Commonweal, September 8, 1967; September 28, 1973.
Illustrated London News, April 22, 1967.
Library Journal, October 1, 1966.
Los Angeles Times, April 17, 1987.
Los Angeles Times Book Review, November 20, 1983.
Nation, July 3, 1967.
National Observer, April 3, 1976.
New Republic, October 20, 1973.
New Statesman, February 27, 1976.
Newsweek, January 12, 1976; November 14, 1983.
New York Review of Books, June 1, 1967.
New York Times, January 27, 1968; February 12, 1980; February 22, 1980; November 17, 1983.
New York Times Book Review, June 3, 1973; March 9, 1980; November 20, 1983; April 12, 1987.
Observer, April 2, 1967.
Publishers Weekly, January 19, 1976.
Time, January 5, 1976.
Times Literary Supplement, April 27, 1967; November 9, 1967.
Washington Post, March 21, 1981.

OBITUARIES:

PERIODICALS

New York Times, November 1, 1986.
Publishers Weekly, November 11, 1986.*

* * *

COHEN, Jene Barr 1900-1985 (Jene Barr)

PERSONAL: Born July 28, 1900, in Kobrin, Russia; died April 5, 1985, in San Jose, CA; daughter of Joseph and Goldie (Barr) Cohen. *Education:* Chicago Normal School of Physical Education, graduate, 1920; attended University of Chicago, 1928-29, Chicago Teachers College, 1931, 1933, 1949-50, Art Institute of Chicago, 1932, Northwestern University, 1935-37. *Politics:* Independent. *Religion:* Jewish.

CAREER: Board of Education, Chicago, IL, physical education instructor, 1925-35, classroom teacher, 1935-50, teacher-librarian, 1950-64. Teacher of creative writing, Downtown YWCA, Chicago, 1953-56. Educational consultant in the social studies, Albert Whitman & Co.

MEMBER: National Federation of Press Women, Society of Midland Authors (chairman of library committee, beginning 1963), Children's Reading Round Table (program chairman, 1950; president, 1965-66), Illinois Woman's Press Association (second vice-president, 1957; chairman of student activities committee, beginning 1961; house chairman, 1961), Illinois Library Association, Chicago Teacher-Librarians's Club (recording secretary, 1962).

AWARDS, HONORS: Midwest Award, Children's Reading Round Table, 1959; National Federation of Press Women awards, including second prize, 1950, for *Little Circus Dog,* first prize, 1951, for *Mr. Mailman;* Mate Palmer Award, Illinois Woman's Press Association, 1950, for *Little Circus Dog,* 1951, for *Texas Pete, Little Cowboy,* 1955, for *Mr. Mailman,* and 1959, for *Baseball for Young Champions;* citation for meritorious service in the field of juvenile literature, Friends of American Writers.

WRITINGS:

UNDER NAME JENE BARR; CHILDREN'S BOOKS

Conrad the Clock, Wilcox & Follett, 1944.
Little Prairie Dog, Whitman, 1949.
Little Circus Dog, Whitman, 1949.
Surprise for Nancy, Whitman, 1950.
Texas Pete, Little Cowboy, Whitman, 1950.
Policeman Paul, Whitman, 1952.
Fireman Fred, Whitman, 1952.
Mike, the Milkman, Whitman, 1953.
Baker Bill, Whitman, 1953.

Mr. Mailman, Whitman, 1954.
Big Wheels! Little Wheels!, Whitman, 1955.
Ben's Busy Service Station, Whitman, 1956.
Fast Trains! Busy Trains!, Whitman, 1956.
Good Morning, Teacher, Whitman, 1957.
Dan the Weatherman, Whitman, 1958.
(With Catherine Bowers) *Here Is Chicago* (textbook), University Publishing Co., 1958, 4th edition, 1973.
This Is My Country, Whitman, 1959.
Miss Terry at the Library, Whitman, 1962.
(With others) *How Americans Produce and Obtain Goods and Services* (textbook), Education-Industry Service, 1962.
Mr. Zip and the U.S. Mail, Whitman, 1964.
Fire Snorkel Number 7, Whitman, 1965.
(With Cynthia Chapin) *What Will the Weather Be?,* Whitman, 1965.
What Can Money Do?, Whitman, 1967.
Busy Office, Busy People, Whitman, 1968.

UNDER NAME JENE BARR, WITH ROBERT J. ANTONACCI; "YOUNG CHAMPIONS" SERIES

Baseball for Young Champions, McGraw, 1956, 2nd edition, 1977.
Football for Young Champions, McGraw, 1958, 2nd edition, 1976.
Basketball for Young Champions, McGraw, 1960.
Physical Fitness for Young Champions, McGraw, 1962, 2nd edition, 1975.

OTHER

Contributor to *Illinois Libraries. Back of the Yards Journal,* editor of children's column, 1946-48, editor of women's column, 1947-48, 1952.

BIOGRAPHICAL/CRITICAL SOURCES:

PERIODICALS

Chicago Daily Tribune, November 14, 1954.
Chicago Schools Journal, May-June, 1951.

OBITUARIES:

PERIODICALS

Chicago Sun-Times, April 10, 1985.
Chicago Tribune, April 11, 1985.*

* * *

COHEN, William A(lan) 1937-

PERSONAL: Born June 25, 1937, in Baltimore, MD; son of Sidney Oliver (a U.S. Air Force officer) and Theresa (a teacher; maiden name, Bachman) Cohen; married Janice Stults, January 8, 1963 (divorced January 19, 1966); married Nurit Kovnator (a psychologist), May 28, 1967; children: William Alan II, Barak, Nimrod. *Education:* U.S. Military Academy, B.S., 1959; University of Chicago, M.B.A., 1967; Claremont Graduate School, M.A., 1978, Ph.D., 1979; Institute of the Armed Forces, distinguished graduate, 1989. *Politics:* Republican. *Religion:* Jewish.

Avocational Interests: Physical conditioning, applied psychology.

ADDRESSES: Home—1556 North Sierra Madre Villa, Pasadena, CA 91107. *Office*—Department of Marketing, California State University, 5151 State University Dr., Los Angeles, CA 90032.

CAREER: U.S. Air Force, pilot, navigator, and program manager, 1959-70, leaving service as major; Israel Aircraft Industries Ltd., Lod, deputy manager of human engineering department and project manager, 1970-73; Sierra Engineering Co., Sierra Madre, CA, manager of research and development, 1973-76; McDonnell-Douglas Astronautics Co., Huntington Beach, CA, advanced technology marketing manager, 1976-78; California State University, Los Angeles, professor of marketing, chairman of department of marketing, and director of Bureau of Business and Economic Research, 1979-83, director of Small Business Institute, 1979—. President of Global Associates (management consultants), 1973—; member of U.S. Senatorial Business Advisory Board and Association of Graduates of the U.S. Military Academy. *Military service:* Israeli Air Force, navigator, 1972-73, became major. U.S. Air Force Reserve, 1979—, currently brigadier-general.

MEMBER: Authors Guild, Air Force Association, Air Commando Association, Jewish War Veterans of the U.S.A., Association of the Industrial College of the Armed Forces, Reserve Officers Association, American Legion, Direct Marketing Club of Southern California (member of board of governors, 1979-88), West Point Society of Los Angeles (president, 1981-82; member of board of governors, 1980-84, 1986-88, 1988-90).

AWARDS, HONORS: Military—Pierce Currier Foster Memorial Award, U.S. Military Academy, 1959; Distinguished Flying Cross with three oak leaf clusters; Air Medal with eleven oak leaf clusters; Meritorious Service Medal; Commendation Medal with oak leaf cluster; Vietnamese Cross of Gallantry with palm and star. *Civilian*—Gold Medal, Daughters of the Confederacy, 1953; Gold Medal, *Chicago Tribune,* 1955, for academic achievement; outstanding service award, National Management Association, 1980; honor certificate, Freedoms Foundation at Valley Forge, 1984; George Washington Honor Medal for excellence in economic education, 1985; Commandant's Award for excellence in research, 1989; award for excellence in mobilization research, National Defense Preparedness Association.

WRITINGS:

Writer's Guide to Publication and Profit, Global Associates, 1975.
Writer's Guide to Professional Writers' Secrets, Global Associates, 1975.
Writer's Guide to Punctuation, Global Associates, 1975.
The Executive's Guide to Finding a Superior Job, American Management Association, 1978.
Principles of Technical Management, American Management Association, 1980.
How to Sell to the U.S. Government, Wiley, 1981.
(With Marshall E. Reddick) *Successful Marketing for Small Business,* American Management Association, 1981.
Building a Mail Order Business: A Complete Manual for Success, Wiley, 1982.
The Entrepreneur and Small Business Problem Solver: An Encyclopedia and Reference Guide, Wiley, 1983.
(With wife, Nurit Cohen) *Top Executive Performance: Eleven Keys to Success and Power,* Wiley, 1984.
Direct Response Marketing, Wiley, 1984.
How to Make It Big as a Consultant, American Management Association, 1985.
Winning on the Marketing Front, Wiley, 1986.
High Tech Management, Wiley, 1986.
The Student Guide to Finding a Superior Job, Avant Books, 1987.
Developing a Winning Marketing Plan, Wiley, 1987.
The Entrepreneur and Small Business Financial Problem Solver, Wiley, 1987.
The Practice of Marketing Management, Macmillan, 1988.
The Art of the Leader, Prentice-Hall, 1990.
The Entrepreneur and Small Business Marketing Problem Solver, Wiley, 1991.
How to Get a Great Job Fast, Global Associates, 1993.
The Pocket Job-Finding Guide, Global Associates, 1993.

Contributor of about two hundred articles to technical journalism periodicals in the United States and abroad.

WORK IN PROGRESS: Dr. Freud Looks at Business, for AMACOM.

SIDELIGHTS: William A. Cohen once told *CA:* "I am interested in writing books that show an individual how to become successful in business and in life. To write these books, I not only do conventional research, but rely on my own experience about the subject. For example, *The Executive's Guide to Finding a Superior Job* was based mainly on my own experiences as an executive recruiter. Similarly, I've been a technical manager, a small businessman, and so forth. These have all been topics of my books. I believe my contribution is to combine theory, research, and my experience and thinking about the subject.

"I have travelled in Europe, Asia, and the Middle East, including one year in Thailand and three years in Israel; I flew in the Yom Kippur War in 1973."

* * *

COLTMAN, Will
See BINGLEY, David Ernest

* * *

CONISTON, Ed
See BINGLEY, David Ernest

* * *

CONSTANTINO, Renato 1919-

PERSONAL: Born March 10, 1919, in Manila, Philippines; son of Amador (a lawyer) and Francisca (a housewife; maiden name, Reyes) Constantino; married Letizia Roxas (a teacher and writer), November 21, 1943; children: Renato Jr., Karina Constantino David. *Education:* University of the Philippines, B.Phil., 1946; graduate study at New York University, 1947.

ADDRESSES: Home—38 Panay Ave., Quezon City, Philippines. *Office*— Institute of Mass Communications Graduate Studies, University of the Philippines, Diliman, Quezon City 1103, Philippines.

CAREER: Journalist, 1945-46; Phillipines Mission to the United Nations, New York, NY, and Paris, France, executive secretary, 1946-49; counselor for Republic of the Philippines Department of Foreign Affairs, 1949-51; Far Eastern University, Manila, Philippines, professor of political science and history, 1951-54; Isabela Sugar Co., Binalbagan, Philippines, economist, 1954-60; director of Lopez Memorial Museum, 1960-72; chairman of Civil Liberties Union of the Philippines, 1972-75, 1984-85; PACES Industrial Corp., Manila, director, 1975-78; University of the Philippines, Quezon City, professorial lecturer in political science, 1978-81, professorial lecturer in social sciences, 1982—. Lecturer at Arellano University, 1946, 1949-51; professorial lecturer at Far Eastern University and Adamson University, 1949-51, and University of the Philippines, 1958-59, 1969-70, 1975-77; visiting lecturer at University of Lund, 1976, University of Tokyo and University of Hiroshima, 1978, Institute of Oriental Studies, Prague, Czechoslovakia, and Humboldt University, 1979; visiting professor at London School of Oriental and African Studies, London, 1976, and University of Stockholm, 1978; visiting scholar at International House of Japan, 1978, U.S.S.R. Academy of Science, 1980, and Vietnamese Committee on Social Sciences, 1980. News commentator for United Nations Radio, 1947-48; representative to International Educational Seminar of UNESCO, Garden City, NY, 1948; chairman of Foundation for National Studies, 1977—, and Civil Liberties Union, 1984-85; vice-chairman of Congress of Third World Economists, Havana, Cuba, 1981.

MEMBER: Association of Social Scientists of Asia and the Pacific (president of provisional executive committee, 1984).

AWARDS, HONORS: Grant from Louis M. Rabinowitz Foundation, 1976; Litt. D. (honoris causa), Polytechnic University of the Philippines, 1989; LL. D. (honoris causa), University of the Philippines, 1990; named Outstanding Filipino in the Field of History by the Philippines Jaycee Senate, 1992.

WRITINGS: *The United Nations,* Graphic House, 1950.

Early Philippine Imprints in the Lopez Memorial Museum, Manila, 1961.
Recto Reader, Recto Foundation, 1964.
The Filipinos in the Philippines, Philippine Signature, 1966.
The Making of a Filipino, Malaya Books, 1969.
Dissent and Counter-Consciousness, Malaya Books, 1970.
(Editor) J.R.M. Taylor, *The Philippine Insurrection against the United States,* five volumes, Lopez Foundation, 1971.
The Marcos Watch, Malaya Books, 1972.
(With wife, Letizia R. Constantino) *The Philippines: A Past Revisited,* Tala Publishing, 1975.
Insight and Foresight, Foundation for Nationalist Studies, 1977.
History of the Philippines, Monthly Review Press, 1977.
Neo-Colonial Identity and Counter-Consciousness, M. E. Sharpe, 1978.
(With L. R. Constantino) *The Philippines: The Continuing Past,* Foundation for Nationalist Studies, 1978.
The Nationalist Alternative, Foundation for Nationalist Studies, 1979, revised edition, 1984.
(Editor) *Soliongco Today,* Foundation for Nationalist Studies, 1981.
Synthetic Culture and Development, Foundation for Nationalist Studies, 1985.
(Editor) *Vintage Recto,* Foundation for Nationalist Studies, 1986.
The Aquino Watch, Karrel, Inc., 1987.
Civil Liberties, Human Rights: The Larger Focus, Karrel, Inc., 1988.
(With L. R. Constantino) *Distorted Priorities: The Politics of Food,* Foundation for Nationalist Studies, 1988.
Nationalism and Liberation, Karrel, Inc., 1988.
Demystifying Aquino, Karrel, Inc., 1989.
(Editor) *The Essential Tanada,* Karrel, Inc., 1989.
(Editor) *Claro M. Recto, 1890-1990: A Centenary Tribute of the Civil Liberties Union,* Karrel, Inc., 1990.
The Second Invasion, Karrel, Inc., 1990.
(With others) *A Filipino Vision of Development,* Foundation for Nationalist Studies, 1991.
(Editor) *Southeast Asian Perceptions of Japan,* Karrel, Inc., 1991.
History: Myths and Reality, Karrel, Inc., 1992.
The Sin of Some Fathers: Church-State Relations, Karrel, Inc., 1992.

Also editor of Filipiniana Reprint Series, Cacho Hermanos, Inc., 1985. Contributor to *The Far East and Australasia,* Europa, 1976-85. Columnist for *Evening Herald* (Manila), 1945-46, *Manila Chronicle,* 1970-72, *Daily Globe,* 1987-1992, *Manila Bulletin,* 1993—, and *Balita,* 1993—. Contributing editor of *Graphic,* 1967-72; member of editorial board of *Journal of Contemporary Asia.*

Several of Constantino's works have been translated into Japanese.

WORK IN PROGRESS: (Editor) *Memoirs of the Japanese Occupation; The Marcos-Aquino Years.*

SIDELIGHTS: Renato Constantino once told *CA:* "My writings are devoted to demythologizing Philippine history, which has been the transmission channel of colonial values. I have sought to expose the reality behind many myths Filipinos live by. As a social critic I have tried to bring out the consequences of colonial conditioning and have repeatedly stressed that we have yet to attain our independence and to rediscover our identity. Nationalism permeates all my writings. It is indeed gratifying to note that what were considered as my heresies three to four decades ago have become part of conventional wisdom today."

* * *

COOPER, C. Everett
See BURGESS, Michael (Roy)

* * *

COOPER, William 1910-
(H. S. Hoff)

PERSONAL: Born Harry Summerfield Hoff, August 4, 1910, in Crewe, England; son of Ernest (a teacher) and Edith Annie (a teacher; maiden name, Summerfield) Hoff; married Joyce Barbara Harris, 1951; children: Louisa,

Catherine. *Education:* Christ's College, Cambridge, M.A., 1933.

ADDRESSES: Home—22 Kenilworth Ct., Lower Richmond Rd., London SW1 1EW, England.

CAREER: School master in Leicester, England, 1933-40; assistant commissioner, Civil Service Commission, London, England, 1945-58; part-time personnel consultant, Atomic Energy Authority, London, 1958-71 and Central Electricity Generating Board, 1960-71, part-time assistant director, Civil Service Selection Board, 1971-75; member of board of Crown agents and personnel consultant, Millbank Technical Services, 1975-77; adjunct professor of English literature, Syracuse University, London Center, 1977-88. *Military service:* Royal Air Force, 1940-45, became squadron leader; assisted C. P. Snow in the organization of the supply of scientists.

MEMBER: International PEN (fellow), Royal Society of Literature (fellow), Savile Club.

WRITINGS:

AS H. S. HOFF

It Happened in PRK (novel), Coward, 1934, published in England as *Trina,* Heinemann, 1934.
Rhea (novel), Heinemann, 1935.
Lisa (novel), Heinemann, 1937.
Three Marriages (novel), Heinemann, 1946.

AS WILLIAM COOPER

The Struggles of Albert Woods, Doubleday, 1953.
The Ever-Interesting Topic, J. Cape, 1954.
Disquiet and Peace, Macmillan, 1956, Lippincott, 1957.
Young People, Macmillan, 1958.
Prince Genji (play), Evans Brothers, 1959.
Memoirs of a New Man, Macmillan, 1966.
Shall We Ever Know? The Trial of the Hosein Brothers for the Murder of Mrs. McKay (non-fiction), Hutchinson, 1971, published as *Brothers: The Trial of the Brothers Hosein for the Murder of Mrs. McKay,* Harper, 1972.
You Want the Right Frame of Reference, Macmillan, 1971.
Love on the Coast, Macmillan, 1973.
You're Not Alone, Macmillan, 1976.
Immortality at Any Price, Sinclair-Stephenson, 1991.

"SCENES FROM LIFE" SERIES; AS WILLIAM COOPER

Scenes from Provincial Life (first in the series; also see below), J. Cape, 1950.
Scenes from Married Life (third in the series; also see below), Macmillan (London), 1961.
Scenes from Life (contains *Scenes from Provincial Life* and *Scenes from Married Life*), Scribner, 1961.
Scenes from Metropolitan Life (second in the series; also see below), Macmillan (London), 1982.
Scenes from Later Life (fourth in the series; also see below), Macmillan (London), 1983.
Scenes from Provincial Life and Scenes from Metropolitan Life, Dutton, 1983.
Scenes from Married Life and Scenes from Later Life, Dutton, 1984.

OTHER

Author of pamphlet on C. P. Snow for British Council series, "Writers and Their Work."

WORK IN PROGRESS: Another novel, *Death and Life.*

SIDELIGHTS: William Cooper is one of the British writers who came of age after World War II. Though other members of that generation such as Kingsley Amis have been more celebrated, Cooper has been more prolific. In addition to several nonfiction works and one play, he has produced more than a dozen novels and a semi-autobiographical series which began with *Scenes from Provincial Life.* Cooper styled the anti-hero of the series, Joe Lunn, after himself, and used the significant people in his life as models for the other characters. For instance, Robert, Joe's civil service colleague and fellow writer in the *Scenes* novels, is supposedly modeled on C. P. Snow, Cooper's actual colleague and fellow novelist. The series follows Joe through the everyday scenes of matrimony in *Scenes from Married Life* and through old age in *Scenes from Later Life.*

Cooper's habit of styling the *Scenes* novels after real life led to a thirty-year delay in the publication of *Scenes from Metropolitan Life,* the second book in the series. Because the novel chronicles Joe's affair with Myrtle, a character supposedly modeled on Cooper's former young woman, the novel could not be published without threat of legal action until after the lady's death in 1981. Reviewer Alan Franks feels that the delay did no damage. "The simple truth," he writes in the London *Times,* "is that writing of this directness and economy does not date."

Critics concur that Cooper's novels rely on wit and humor rather than the "windiness and cant" of his early contemporaries, as Richard Eder puts it in the *Los Angeles Times Book Review.* "Cooper is a master of the sly comic aside, of the rueful rhetorical question, as he is at buttonholing the reader with sea-green candour. Such disarming comedy must deflect all but the sharpest critical arrows," J. K. L. Walker remarks in the *Times Literary Supplement.* Cooper once explained to *CA,* "I am a realistic novelist. My aim is to tell the truth, laughing." Commenting on a similar assertion made by Joe, Cooper's double in *Scenes from Metropolitan Life,* Walker estimates that "Cooper has followed the precept pretty well, both in this present highly entertaining and perceptive novel and subsequently."

BIOGRAPHICAL/CRITICAL SOURCES:

BOOKS

Allen, Walter, *Tradition and Dream,* Dent, 1964.

Karl, Frederick R., *The Contemporary English Novel,* Farrar, Straus, 1962.

Sinha, A. K., *William Cooper the Novelist,* Jnanda Prakashan (Patna), 1977.

PERIODICALS

Los Angeles Times Book Review, July 22, 1984.

Times (London), October 14, 1982; September 22, 1983.

Times Literary Supplement, October 22, 1982.

* * *

COSBY, Bill
See COSBY, William Henry, Jr.

* * *

COSBY, William Henry, Jr. 1937-
(Bill Cosby)

PERSONAL: Born July 12, 1937, in Philadelphia, PA; son of William Henry Cosby (a U.S. Navy mess steward) and Anna Cosby (a domestic worker); married Camille Hanks, January 25, 1964; children: Erika Ranee, Erinn Chalene, Ennis William, Ensa Camille, Evin Harrah. *Education:* Attended Temple University, 1961-62; University of Massachusetts, M.A., 1972, Ed. D., 1977.

ADDRESSES: *Agent*—The Brokaw Co., 9255 Sunset Blvd., Los Angeles, CA 90069.

CAREER: Comedian, actor, and recording artist. Performer in nightclubs, including The Cellar, Philadelphia, PA, Gaslight Cafe, New York City, Bitter End, New York City, and Hungry i, San Francisco, CA, 1962—; performer in television series including *I Spy,* National Broadcasting Co. (NBC-TV), 1965-68, *The Bill Cosby Show,* NBC-TV, 1969-71, *The New Bill Cosby Show,* Columbia Broadcasting System (CBS-TV), 1972-73, *Cos,* American Broadcasting Co. (ABC-TV), 1976, and *The Cosby Show,* NBC-TV, 1984-92; host of syndicated game show, *You Bet Your Life,* 1992-93; actor in motion pictures, including *Hickey and Boggs,* 1972, *Man and Boy,* 1972, *Uptown Saturday Night,* 1974, *Let's Do It Again,* 1975, *Mother, Jugs, and Speed,* 1976, *A Piece of the Action,* 1977, *California Suite,* 1978, *The Devil and Max Devlin,* 1981, *Bill Cosby Himself,* 1985, *Leonard Part VI,* 1987, and *Ghost Dad,* 1990; creator of animated children's programs *The Fat Albert Show* and *Fat Albert and the Cosby Kids,* CBS-TV, 1972-84. Performer on *The Bill Cosby Radio Program,* television specials *The First Bill Cosby Special* and *The Second Bill Cosby Special,* in animated feature *Aesop's Fables,* in *An Evening with Bill Cosby* at Radio City Music Hall, 1986, and in videocassette *Bill Cosby: 49,* sponsored by Kodak, 1987. Guest on Public Broadcasting Co. (PBS-TV) children's programs *Sesame Street* and *The Electric Company,* and NBC-TV's *Children's Theatre;* host of Picture Pages segment of CBS-TV's *Captain Kangaroo's Wake Up.* Commercial spokesman for Jell-O Pudding (General Foods Inc.), Coca-Cola Co., Ford Motor Co., Texas Instruments, E. F. Hutton, and Kodak Film.

President of Rhythm and Blues Hall of Fame, 1968. Member of Carnegie Commission for the Future of Public Broadcasting, board of directors of National Council on Crime and Delinquency, Mary Holmes College, and Ebony Showcase Theatre, board of trustees of Temple University, advisory board of Direction Sports, communications council at Howard University, and steering committee of American Sickle Cell foundation. *Military service:* U.S. Navy Medical Corps, 1956-60.

AWARDS, HONORS: Eight Grammy awards for best comedy album, National Society of Recording Arts and Sciences, including 1964, for *Bill Cosby Is a Very Funny Fellow . . . Right!,* 1965, for *I Started Out as a Child,* 1966, for *Why Is There Air?,* 1967, for *Revenge,* and 1969, for *To Russell, My Brother, Whom I Slept With;* Emmy Award for best actor in a dramatic series, Academy of Television Arts and Sciences, 1965-66, 1966-67, and 1967-68, for *I Spy;* named "most promising new male star" by *Fame* magazine, 1966; Emmy Award, 1969, for *The First Bill Cosby Special;* Seal of Excellence, Children's Theatre Association, 1973; Ohio State University award, 1975, for *Fat Albert and the Cosby Kids;* NAACP Image Award, 1976; named "Star Presenter of 1978" by *Advertising Age;* Gold Award for Outstanding Children's Program, International Film and Television Festival, 1981, for *Fat Albert and the Cosby Kids;* Emmy Award for best comedy series, 1985, for *The Cosby Show;* inducted to TV Hall of Fame, Academy of Television Arts and Sciences, 1992; Founder's Award, 19th International Emmy Awards, 1992; honorary degree, Brown University; Golden Globe Award, Hollywood Foreign Press Association; four People's Choice Awards; voted "most believable celebrity endorser" three times in surveys by Video Storyboard Tests Inc.

WRITINGS:

UNDER NAME BILL COSBY

The Wit and Wisdom of Fat Albert, Windmill Books, 1973.

Bill Cosby's Personal Guide to Tennis Power; or, Don't Lower the Lob, Raise the Net, Random House, 1975.

(Contributor) Charlie Shedd, editor, *You Are Somebody Special,* McGraw, 1978, 2nd edition, 1982.

Fatherhood, Doubleday, 1986.

Time Flies, Doubleday, 1987.

Love and Marriage, Doubleday, 1989.

Childhood, Putnam, 1991.

Also author of *Fat Albert's Survival Kit* and *Changes: Becoming the Best You Can Be.*

RECORDINGS

Bill Cosby Is a Very Funny Fellow . . . Right!, 1964, *I Started Out as a Child,* 1965, *Why Is There Air?,* 1966, *Wonderfulness,* 1967, *Revenge,* 1967, *To Russell, My Brother, Whom I Slept With,* 1969, *Bill Cosby Is Not Himself These Days, Rat Own, Rat Own, Rat Own,* 1976, *My Father Confused Me . . . What Must I Do? What Must I Do?,* 1977, *Disco Bill,* 1977, *Bill's Best Friend,* 1978, *It's True, It's True, Bill Cosby Himself, 200 MPH, Silverthroat, Hooray for the Salvation Army Band, 8:15, 12:15, For Adults Only, Bill Cosby Talks to Kids about Drugs,* and *Inside the Mind of Bill Cosby.*

SIDELIGHTS: "When I was a kid I always used to pay attention to things that other people didn't even think about," claims Bill Cosby. "I'd remember funny happenings, just little trivial things, and then tell stories about them later. I found I could make people laugh, and I enjoyed doing it because it gave me a sense of security. I thought that if people laughed at what you said, that meant they like you." As an adult, Bill Cosby has developed his childhood behavior into a comedic talent that earns him millions of dollars annually for his work in films, television, and commercials. In 1988, Cosby was ranked the second-highest-paid entertainer in the world. "Despite his wealth," Brian D. Johnson notes in *Maclean's,* "Cosby manages to pass himself off as a clownish Everyman, treating his life as a bottomless well of folk wisdom."

What Cosby calls his "storytelling knack" may have had its roots in his mother's nightly readings of Mark Twain and the Bible to her three sons. Their father, a Navy cook, was gone for long stretches of time, but Anna Cosby did her best to provide a strong moral foundation for the family she raised in Philadelphia's housing projects. Bill Cosby helped with the family's expenses by delivering groceries and shining shoes. His sixth-grade teacher described him as "an alert boy who would rather clown than study"; nevertheless, he was placed in a class for gifted students when he reached high school. His activities as captain of the track and football teams and member of the baseball and basketball teams continued to distract him from academics, however, and when his tenth-grade year ended, Cosby was told he'd have to repeat the grade. Instead of doing so, he quit school to join the Navy. It was a decision he soon came to regret, and during his four-year hitch in the Navy, Cosby earned his high school diploma through a correspondence course. He then won an athletic scholarship to Temple University in Philadelphia, where he entered as a physical education major in 1961.

Cosby had continued to amuse his schoolmates and shipmates with his tales. He first showcased his humor professionally while a student at Temple, in a five-dollar-a-night job telling jokes and tending bar at "The Cellar," a Philadelphia coffee-house. More engagements soon followed; before long Cosby's budding career as an entertainer was conflicting with his school schedule. Forced to choose between the two, Cosby dropped out of Temple, although the university eventually awarded him a bachelor's degree on the basis of "life experience." His reputation as a comic grew quickly as he worked in coffee-houses from San Francisco to New York City. Soon he was playing the biggest nightclubs in Las Vegas, and shortly after signing a recording contract in 1964, he became the best-selling comedian on records, with several of his recordings earning over one million dollars in sales.

His early performances consisted of about 35 percent racial jokes, but Cosby came to see this kind of humor as something that perpetuated racism rather than relieving tensions, and he dropped all such jokes from his act. "Rather than trying to bring the races together by talking about the differences, let's try to bring them together by talking about the similarities," he urges. Accordingly, he developed a universal brand of humor that revolved around everyday occurrences. A long-time jazz devotee, the comedian credits the musical improvisations of Miles Davis, Charles Mingus, and Charlie Parker with inspiring him to come up with continually fresh ways of restating a few basic themes. "The situations I talk about people can find themselves in . . . it makes them glad to know they're not the only ones who have fallen victims of life's little ironies," states Cosby.

The comedian first displayed his skill as an actor when he landed the co-starring lead in *I Spy,* a popular NBC-TV program of the late 1960s that featured suspense, action, and sometimes humor. Cosby portrayed Alexander Scott, a multilingual Rhodes scholar working as part of a spy team for the United States. Scott and his partner (played by Robert Culp) traveled undercover in the guises of a tennis pro and his trainer. The Alexander Scott role had not been created especially for a black actor, and Cosby's casting in the part was hailed as an important breakthrough for blacks in television.

The Bill Cosby Show followed *I Spy.* In this half-hour comedy, Cosby portrayed Chet Kincaid, a high-school gym teacher—a role closer to his real-life persona than that of Alexander Scott. In fact, at this time Cosby announced that he was considering quitting show business to become a teacher. Although he never followed through on that statement, Cosby did return to college and earned a doctorate in education in 1977. His doctoral thesis, "An Integration of the Visual Media via Fat Albert and the Cosby Kids into the Elementary School Curriculum as a Teaching Aid and Vehicle to Achieve Increased Learning," analyzed an animated Saturday-morning show that Cosby himself had created. *Fat Albert and the Cosby Kids* had its roots in the comedy routines about growing up in Philadelphia. It attempted to entertain children while encouraging them to confront moral and ethical issues, and it has been used as a teaching tool in schools.

During the 1970s, Cosby teamed with Sidney Poitier and several other black actors to make a highly successful series of comedies, including *Uptown Saturday Night, Let's Do It Again,* and *A Piece of the Action.* These comedies stood out in a time when most of the films for black audiences were oriented to violence. Critics are generous in their praise of Cosby's acting; Tom Allen notes his "freewheeling, jiving, put-down artistry," and Alvin H. Marritt writes that, in *Let's Do It Again,* Cosby "breezes through the outrageous antics."

Concern over his family's television viewing habits led Cosby to return to prime-time in 1984. "I got tired of seeing TV shows that consist of a car crash, a gunman and a hooker talking to a black pimp," the actor states in an article by Jane Hall in *People.* "It was cheaper to do a series than to throw out my family's six TV sets." But Cosby found that network executives were resistant to his idea for a family-oriented comedy. He was turned down by both CBS and ABC on the grounds that a family comedy—particularly one featuring a black family—could never succeed on modern television. NBC accepted his proposal and *The Cosby Show* very quickly became the top-rated show on television, drawing an estimated 60 million weekly viewers.

Like most of Bill Cosby's material, *The Cosby Show* revolves around everyday occurrences and interactions between siblings and parents. Cosby plays obstetrician Cliff Huxtable, who with his lawyer wife, Claire, has four daughters and one son—just as Cosby and wife Camille do in real life. Besides entertaining audiences, Cosby aims to project a positive image of a family whose members love and respect one another. The program is hailed by some as a giant step forward in the portrayal of blacks on television. Writes Lynn Norment in *Ebony,* "This show pointedly avoids the stereotypical Blacks often seen on TV. There are no ghetto maids or butlers wisecracking about Black life. Also, there are no fast cars and helicopter chase scenes, no jokes about sex and boobs and butts. And, most unusual, both parents are present in the home, employed and are Black."

The Cosby Show has not been unanimously acclaimed, however. As Norment explains, "Despite its success, the show is criticized by a few for not being 'Black enough,' for not dealing with more controversial issues, such as poverty and racism and interracial dating, for focusing on a Black middle-class family when the vast majority of Black people survive on incomes far below that of the Huxtables." Cosby finds this type of criticism racist in itself. "Does it mean only white people have a lock on living together in a home where the father is a doctor and the mother is a lawyer and the children are constantly being told to study by their parents?" Hall quotes Cosby in *People:* "This is a black American family. If anybody has difficulty with that, it's their problem, not ours."

The paternal image of Cliff Huxtable led a publisher to ask Cosby for a humorous book to be called *Fatherhood.* Cosby obliged, making notes for the project with shorthand and tape recorder between his entertainment commitments. The finished book sold a record 2.6 million hardcover copies and was quite well-received by critics. *Newsweek* book reviewer Cathleen McGuigan states that it "is like a prose version of a Cosby comedy performance—informal, commiserative anecdotes delivered in a sardonic style that's as likely to prompt a smile of recognition as a belly laugh. . . . [But] it's not all played for laughs. There's a tough passage in which he describes the only time he hit his son, and a reference to a drinking-and-driving incident involving a daughter and her friends that calls upon him to both punish and forgive. Cosby's big strength, though, is his eye and ear for the everyday event—sibling squabbles, children's excuses." Jonathan Yardley concurs in the *Washington Post Book World:* "Cosby has an extraordinarily keen ear for everyday speech and everyday event, and knows how to put just enough of a comic spin on it so that even as we laugh we know we are getting a glimpse of the truth."

Following the huge success of *Fatherhood,* Doubleday published *Time Flies,* in which Cosby treats the subject of aging in the same style as his earlier book. Toronto *Globe & Mail* reviewer Leo Simpson comments, "Decay and the drift into entropy wouldn't get everyone's vote as a lighthearted theme, yet *Time Flies* is just as illuminating, witty and elegantly hilarious as . . . *Fatherhood.*" The book sold over 1.7 million hardcover copies.

For his 1989 book, *Love and Marriage,* Cosby draws upon his own long marriage to wife Camille for an advice book on maintaining domestic tranquility. As Cosby explains to Johnson in *Maclean's,* "The book is to make people laugh, make them identify and have a good time." Some of the truths revealed by the author is that "the wife is in charge" and "even the deepest love doesn't stop a marriage from being a constant struggle for control." For any husband who believes himself to be the boss of his own house, Cosby advises that he buy some wallpaper and redecorate a room without consulting his wife first. Calling the book a "diverting but forgettable" work, Leah Rozen of *People* nonetheless finds *Love and Marriage* to be "gently amusing." Johnson finds the book "by turns tender, amusing and coy." The *New York Times Book Review* critic calls it "a scrapbook of the happier side of romance. . . . Cosby captures the give and take of happy marriages."

Cosby reminisces about his own youth in Philadelphia in 1991's *Childhood,* comparing that time in his life with the experiences of the present generation of children. His remembrances of childhood pranks, family advice, and schoolyard games form the bulk of the memoir. Dulcie Leimbach of the *New York Times Book Review* finds that Cosby presents a "rough-and-tumble (but never spoiled or weary) childhood." Because of his ability to reconstruct those times, she calls Cosby "a man trapped inside a child's mind."

Although Cosby complains in *Time Flies* that he is slowing down with age, his performing, directing, writing and devotion to charitable projects provide him with a very busy schedule. As he told the *Los Angeles Times,* "I think one of the most important things to understand is that my mother, as a domestic, worked 12 hours a day, and then she would do the laundry, and cook the meals and serve them and clean them up, and for this she got $7 a day. So 12 hours a day of whatever I do is as easy as eating a Jell-O Pudding Pop."

BIOGRAPHICAL/CRITICAL SOURCES:

BOOKS

Adams, Barbara Johnston, *The Picture Life of Bill Cosby,* F. Watts, 1986.
Johnson, Robert E., *Bill Cosby: In Words and Pictures,* Johnson Publishing (Chicago), 1987.
Smith, R. L., *Cosby,* St. Martin's, 1986.
Woods, H., *Bill Cosby, Making America Laugh and Learn,* Dillon, 1983.

PERIODICALS

Chicago Tribune, September 14, 1987.
Chicago Tribune Books, May 3, 1987.
Ebony, May, 1964; June, 1977; April, 1985; February, 1986; February, 1987.
Films in Review, November, 1975.
Globe & Mail (Toronto), July 5, 1986; October 24, 1987.
Good Housekeeping, February, 1991.
Jet, January 12, 1987; January 19, 1987; February 9, 1987; February 23, 1987; March 9, 1987.
Ladies Home Journal, June, 1985.
Los Angeles Times, September 25, 1987; December 20, 1987; January 24, 1988.
Los Angeles Times Book Review, June 15, 1986; June 18, 1989.
Maclean's, May 1, 1989.
National Observer, January 6, 1964.
Newsweek, November 5, 1984; September 2, 1985; May 19, 1986; September 14, 1987.
New York Post, February 23, 1964.
New York Times Book Review, September 20, 1987; May 14, 1989; October 27, 1991.
New York Times Magazine, March 14, 1965.
People, December 10, 1984; September 14, 1987; July 10, 1989.
Playboy, December, 1985.
Reader's Digest, November, 1986; November, 1987.
Saturday Evening Post, April, 1985; April, 1986.
Time, September 28, 1987.
Village Voice, November 3, 1975.
Washington Post, September 7, 1987.
Washington Post Book World, April 27, 1986.*

* * *

COTTERILL, Rodney M(ichael) J(ohn) 1933-

PERSONAL: Born September 27, 1933, in Bodmin, Cornwall, England; son of Harold Herbert and Aline (Le Cerf) Cotterill; married Vibeke Ejler Nielsen (a part-time teacher), February 7, 1959; children: Marianne, Jennifer. *Education:* University of London, B.Sc., 1957, D.Sc., 1973; Yale University, M.S., 1958; Cambridge University, Ph.D., 1962.

Avocational Interests: Sailing, choral singing, chess.

ADDRESSES: Home—Vibevangen 9, DK-3520 Farum, Denmark. *Office*—Department of Biophysics, Technical University of Denmark, Building 307, DK2800 Lyngby, Denmark.

CAREER: Argonne National Laboratory, Argonne, IL, assistant physicist, 1962-64, associate physicist in Materials Division, 1964-67; Technical University of Denmark, Lyngby, professor of materials science and chair of department of structural properties of materials, 1967-80, professor of biophysics and chair of department of biophysics, 1980—. Visiting professor at Tokyo University, 1978, 1985; consultant to United Kingdom Atomic Energy Authority and Danish Atomic Energy Commission. *Military Service:* Royal Air Force, 1952-54.

MEMBER: European Physical Society (chair of Metals Division, 1977-84), Danish Physical Society, Metallurgy Society, Danish Royal Academy of Sciences and Letters (fellow), Danish Academy of Technical Science (fellow), Danish Academy of Natural Science (fellow), English Physical Society, American Physical Society, Institute of Physics (fellow).

AWARDS, HONORS: Hermers Prize, Combined Danish Universities, 1978, for research on computer simulation in the physical and life sciences; Ridder of Dannebrog, 1979, for services to Danish science and education.

WRITINGS:

(Editor with Masao Doyama, James Jackson, and Masahiro Meshii) *Lattice Defects in Quenched Metals,* Academic Press, 1965.

Crystal Imperfections and Mechanical Properties of Materials, Compendium, 1972.

The Cambridge Guide to the Material World, Cambridge University Press, 1984, published as *The Material World,* Cambridge University Press, 1994.

(Editor) *Computer Simulation in Brain Science,* Cambridge University Press, 1988.

No Ghost in the Machine: Modern Science and the Brain, the Mind and the Soul, Heinemann, 1989.

(Editor) *Models of Brain Function,* Cambridge University Press, 1989.

Enchanted Looms: Neural Networks in Brains and Clever Computers, Penguin Books, 1994.

Contributor of numerous articles to scientific journals.

WORK IN PROGRESS: Research on the function of the brain.

SIDELIGHTS: Rodney M. Cotterill told *CA:* "I started my professional life as a physicist, and later spent a ten-year period in materials science, which led to my book, *The Cambridge Guide to the Material World.* It did very well in both hardback and paperback versions, and an updated version was published under my manuscript's original title, *The Material World.* A number of influences led to my switch to biophysics around 1980. My wife had worked as an assistant in the famous Medical Research Council department at Cambridge in the late 1950s, when Francis Crick, John Kendrew, and Max Perutz were all still there, and I saw that the grass on the other side of the fence really was greener. Considerable motivation to study the brain also derived from the fact that our youngest daughter, Jennifer, is autistic. But the greatest factor in the anti-religious tone of my next book, *No Ghost in the Machine: Modern Science and the Brain, the Mind and the Soul,* was probably the need to get the last of a repressively religious upbringing out of my system. The fact that this book was savaged by critics, as a consequence, left me with the desire to produce a strictly scientific book on the brain and consciousness. The result was *Enchanted Looms: Neural Networks in Brains and Clever Computers.* These activities have kindled interests in philosophy, and in other forms of writing, and I hope that other books will follow."

BIOGRAPHICAL/CRITICAL SOURCES:

PERIODICALS

Canberra Times, September 14, 1985.
Nature, April 25, 1985, p. 686.
New York Times Book Review, April 21, 1985, p. 38.
Physics in Canada, July, 1990, p. 84.
Scientific American, September, 1985, p. 35.
Times Educational Supplement, May 17, 1985, p. 50.
Washington Post Book World, December 8, 1985, p. 14.

* * *

CRABTREE, Judith 1928-

PERSONAL: Born September 23, 1928, in Melbourne, Australia; daughter of Frank Richard (a professor of economics) and Nora (a high school teacher; maiden name, Bowls) Mauldon; married Peter Crabtree (a teacher), December 12, 1954; children: Rowena Crabtree Cowan, Jonathan. *Education:* University of Western Australia, B.A., 1954; Associated Teachers' Training Institution, Certificate of Education, 1967.

ADDRESSES: *Home*—12 Bath Rd., Burwood, Victoria 3125, Australia.

CAREER: High school English and history teacher in Melbourne, Australia, 1965-79; Council of Adult Education, Melbourne, teacher of writing and illustrating children's books, 1979—; writer. Seven of her illustrations from *Song at the Gate* were included in a five-city Japanese exhibition of children's book illustrations, 1991. Participates in creative writing and illustration workshops and programs.

AWARDS, HONORS: Senior fellow, Australia Council Literature Board, 1981; mentioned in "Credici in Erba," Bologna Children's Book Festival, 1989, for *Song at the Gate.*

WRITINGS:

Skins and Shells and Peelings (young adult novel), Highland House, 1979.

JUVENILE

Emily Jean and the Grumphfs, Wren Publishing, 1975.
Carolyn Two, Wren Publishing, 1975.

(Self-illustrated) *Nicking Off,* Wren Publishing, 1975.
(Self-illustrated) *The High Rise Gang,* Wren Publishing, 1975.
(Self-illustrated) *Legs,* Penguin Australia, 1979.
(Self-illustrated) *The Sparrow's Story at the King's Command,* Oxford University Press, 1983.
(Self-illustrated) *Stolen Magic,* Oxford University Press, 1983.
(Self-illustrated) *Song at the Gate,* Oxford University Press, 1987.
(Self-illustrated) *Night of the Wild Geese,* Oxford University Press, 1990.
(Self-illustrated) *Skew-Whiff,* Omnibus Books, in press.

OTHER

Also author of short stories for educational publications.

ADAPTATIONS: The Sparrow's Story at the King's Command was adapted for video by Reva Lee Studios in 1985.

SIDELIGHTS: Judith Crabtree once told *CA:* "For the past few years I have worked with primary school children at writing and illustration workshops that are part of a government-funded Artists in the Community Program. I also give talks on my own working methods and the creative writing and illustration approach that I adopt when I am working with children.

"Many Australian primary schools have introduced the Donald Graves approach to writing. Because this is the natural way to write, it is very much a part of my workshop approach. However, I think I have gone beyond Graves by introducing creative visualization workshops in which children (and adults) create and become their characters.

"Since I began writing and illustrating fantasy stories, I have frequently been asked if I would ever consider writing for adults. My answer has always been the same. When all the universal human concerns can be woven into tales that are simple, yet endlessly varied, resonant and rich in dramatic imagery, what more could a writer-illustrator wish for?

"The best fairy tales are always allegorical. Like poetry, they are models of conciseness and address issues of the greatest importance in a form that gives clarity and vision. They are as timeless and as placeless as 'Once there was . . . ' can be, and they appeal to old and young and everybody in between.

"But for me the greatest beauty of these stories is in those omissions that give them their universality, those gaps through which the reader is drawn into inner spaces that give room to intuition and creative dreaming. When a story is complete in all its details, it leaves the reader still confined within the familiar and the commonplace self. In contrast, the gaps in an allegory are byways into the reader's creative self and beyond.

"In my last book and in the one I am working on now, I have left some incidents not fully explained and have used in my illustrations recurring images not mentioned in the text and not essential to the story line. I believe that both of these devices can give stories greater resonance, if not deeper meaning.

"When children write to ask for explanation of my stories, I hand on the ones given to me by children I have worked with. Many of their accounts are surprisingly close to my own, and even when they aren't, they are still useful because they make the story richer and more satisfying to those who give them. Some of these accounts express violence and anger, but these are feelings that the kindly fairy tale can comfortably encompass."

BIOGRAPHICAL/CRITICAL SOURCES:

PERIODICALS

Junior Bookshelf, August, 1983; April, 1992.
School Librarian, May, 1992, p. 55.
School Library Journal, March, 1984.

* * *

CRICK, Michael (Lawrence) 1958-

PERSONAL: Born May 21, 1958, in Northampton, England; son of John Fairhurst (a teacher) and Patricia (a teacher; maiden name, Wright) Crick; married Margaret Hounsell (a television journalist), July, 1985; children: Catherine. *Education:* New College, Oxford, B.A. (with first class honors), 1979. *Politics:* Labour. *Religion:* Atheist.

Avocational Interests: Stamp collecting, swimming, watching soccer, collecting soccer programs, railways.

ADDRESSES: Home—1 Sumburgh Rd., London SW12 8AJ, England; 2 Blue Row, Swerford, Chipping Norton, Oxon OX7 4BA, England. *Agent*—William Hamilton, A. M. Heath & Co., 79 St. Martin's Lane, London WC2N 4AA, England.

CAREER: Independent Television News, London, England, trainee journalist, 1980-82, producer, 1982-84, reporter for "Channel 4 News," 1984-90 (Washington correspondent, 1988-90); British Broadcasting Corporation (BBC), London, England, reporter for "Panorama," 1990-92, for "Newsnight," 1992—. Director of Oxford and Cambridge Careers Publications Ltd., 1979-81.

MEMBER: National Union of Journalists, Fabian Society (executive member, 1980-81; chairman of Young Fabians, 1980-81), Oxford Union (president, 1979).

AWARDS, HONORS: Royal Television Society award, 1989.

WRITINGS:

(With Michael Thompson and Eamonn Matthews) *The Oxford Handbook,* Oxford University Student Union, 1978.
(With Ian Paul) *The Oxbridge Careers Handbook,* Oxford University Student Union, 1979.
Militant, Faber, 1984.
Scargill and the Miners, Penguin, 1985, revised edition, 1985.
The March of Militant, Faber, 1986.
(With David Smith) *Manchester United: The Betrayal of a Legend,* Pelham, 1989, revised paperback edition, Pan, 1990.

Editor of Oxford University's newspaper, *Cherwell,* 1977.

WORK IN PROGRESS: A biography of British author and politician Jeffrey Archer.

SIDELIGHTS: Michael Crick once told *CA:* "My work as a BBC news reporter involves me mainly in British political and Labour affairs, and this was the subject of my first two books. At one time I intended to go into politics myself, but, for the time being, I find it easier to comment on it.

"*Militant* is the story of a Trotskyist group that began infiltrating the British Labour party in the 1950s and began to cause the party leadership considerable embarrassment in the 1970s. The book details the group's organization, policies, history, finances, and aims, and it chronicles the unsuccessful attempts by the party leadership to expel the group.

"*Scargill and the Miners* is a background book to the year-long British coal dispute that began in 1984. It shows how the Left within the National Union of Mineworkers gradually took control of the union in the 1960s and 1970s, turning it from one of Britain's most conservative unions to one of its most radical. In particular, the book covers the career of the miners' leader Arthur Scargill and examines his political background, beliefs, and goals.

Crick more recently added that "*Manchester United: The Betrayal of a Legend* examines the politics and finances of Britain's most popular football club."

BIOGRAPHICAL/CRITICAL SOURCES:

PERIODICALS

Times (London), February 9, 1985.
Times Literary Supplement, March 1, 1985.

CRONIN, Thomas E(dward) 1940-

PERSONAL: Born March 18, 1940, in Milton, MA; son of Joseph M. (in business; a lawyer) and Mary J. (Marr) Cronin; married Taniaz Zaroudny, 1966; children: Alexander. *Education:* Holy Cross College, A.B., 1961; Stanford University, M.A., 1962, Ph.D., 1968. *Politics:* Democrat. *Religion:* Roman Catholic.

ADDRESSES: Office—Whitman College, Walla Walla, WA 99362.

CAREER: U.S. Senate, Washington, DC, aide, 1963; White House, Washington, DC, aide, 1966-67; University of North Carolina, Chapel Hill, assistant professor of political science, 1967-70; Brookings Institution, Washington, DC, research political scientist, 1970-73; Center for the Study of Democratic Institutions, Washington, DC, research political scientist, 1972-74; University of Delaware, Newark, professor of political science, 1976-78; Colorado College, Colorado Springs, professor of political science, 1978-93, acting president, 1991; Whitman College, Walla Walla, WA, president, 1993—. Visiting professor at Brandeis University, 1975-77; lecturer at more than three hundred U.S. colleges and universities, and at twenty-five universities abroad, including those in the U.S.S.R., the People's Republic of China, Japan, Australia, Indonesia, Egypt, West Germany, and Spain. Member of board of directors of Center for the Study of the Presidency. President, CRC, Inc., 1980. Delegate, Democratic National Convention, 1980, 1984, 1988; Democratic candidate for U.S. Congress, 1982; former delegate, Democratic National Mid-Term Conference. Consultant to Cabinet Advisory Panels, 1967-69; consultant to Congressional committees.

MEMBER: American Political Science Association, American Society of Public Administration, Common Cause (member of national board of directors, 1977-82), National Civic League, American Leadership Forum (member of board of trustees, 1981-87), Presidency Research Group (president, 1981-82), Western Political Science Association (president, 1993-1994), Sierra Club.

AWARDS, HONORS: National Science Foundation fellowship, 1965; White House fellow, 1966; honorary LL.D, Marietta College, 1987, Franklin College, 1993.

WRITINGS:

(Editor and contributor) *The Presidential Advisory System,* Harper, 1969.
The State of the Presidency, Little, Brown, 1975, 2nd edition, 1980.
The Presidency Reappraised, Praeger, 1977.
America in the Seventies, Little, Brown, 1977.
Government by the People, Prentice-Hall, 1978.
State and Local Politics, Prentice-Hall, 1978.

U.S. versus Crime in the Streets, Indiana University Press, 1981.

Rethinking the Presidency, Little, Brown, 1982.

Direct Democracy: The Politics of Initiative, Referendum, and Recall, Harvard University Press, 1989.

(Co-author) *Colorado Politics and Government,* University of Nebraska Press, 1993.

The Write Stuff: Writing as a Political and Performing Art, Prentice-Hall, 1990, 2nd edition, 1993.

Contributor to newspapers, journals and magazines, including *Saturday Review, Politics, Today, Commonweal, Science, Society, Public Administration Review, Skeptic, New York Times Magazine, Christian Science Monitor,* and *Washington Monthly.*

SIDELIGHTS: In *The State of the Presidency,* originally published in 1975 and extensively revised for publication in 1980, Thomas E. Cronin draws from his experience as a White House aide and professor of political science to offer his insights into "how Presidents are chosen, what they do in their jobs, how the White House bureaucracy affects the federal bureaucracy, the uses of the Cabinet, and the executive's relations with the legislature," writes a contributor to the *New Yorker.* Cronin's approach, as Godfrey Hodgson points out in the *New York Times Book Review,* is to "concentrate on the ambiguities and the contradictions in what Americans want of the institution." One such contradiction, notes Hodgson, is that Americans "want a common man, but they expect an uncommon performance." The book also "explores the semi-mysticism surrounding the office," observes Louis Heren in the London *Times.* This study reveals that "the emotions, pressures, and checks and balances [the President] is subject to are fairly constant, and Mr Cronin knows them rather better than some other President watchers," writes Heren. Concludes Hodgson: "This is a fine book; rich in fact and insight; perhaps the best general textbook on the Presidency yet written."

Cronin once told *CA:* "My major interest is helping to clarify and explain American politics, our policy-making processes, and our leadership institutions. Experience in the White House, in Congress, in state and national politics has shaped and informed much of my research and writing."

BIOGRAPHICAL/CRITICAL SOURCES:

PERIODICALS

Los Angeles Times Book Review, May 18, 1980.

New Republic, April 28, 1982.

New Yorker, March 24, 1980.

New York Times Book Review, May 11, 1980; February 7, 1982.

Times (London), June 11, 1981.

CROUZET, Francois Marie-Joseph 1922-

PERSONAL: Born October 20, 1922, in Monts-sur-Guesnes, France; son of Maurice (a historian) and Henriette (Pactat) Crouzet; married Francoise Dabert, March 27, 1947; children: Marie-Anne, Denis, Joel. *Education:* Sorbonne, Universite de Paris, licence es-lettres, 1943, diplome d'etudes superieures, 1944, agregation d'histoire, 1945, doctorat-es-lettres, 1956; London School of Economics and Political Science, London, graduate study, 1946-49.

ADDRESSES: Home—6 rue Benjamin-Godard, 75116 Paris, France. *Office*—Universite de Paris-Sorbonne, 1 rue Victor-Cousin, 75005 Paris, France.

CAREER: Lycee de Beauvais, Beauvais, France, instructor, 1945; research fellow in Great Britain, 1945-46; Centre national de la recherche scientifique, France, research associate, 1947-49; Universite de Paris, Paris, France, assistant lecturer, 1949-53; instructor, Lycee Janson-de-Sailly, 1953-56; Universite de Bordeaux, Bordeaux, France, associate professor of history, 1956-58; Universite de Lille, Lille, France, professor of contemporary history, 1958-64; Universite de Paris, Nanterre, France, professor of economic and social history, 1964-69; Universite de Paris-Sorbonne, Paris, professor of northern European history, 1969-92, professor emeritus, 1992—, director of Centre de recherches sur la civilisation de l'Europe moderne, 1977-92. Visiting professor, Columbia University, spring, 1961, University of California, Berkeley, summer, 1964, University of Geneva, 1969-72, and Harvard University, winter, 1981-82; visiting fellow, University College, Cambridge University, autumn, 1969, and All Souls College, Oxford University, autumn, 1976, spring and summer, 1985. Chairman of committee for modern history, Centre national de la recherche scientifique, 1976-80.

MEMBER: Conseil superieur des corps universitaires (member of consulting committee, 1969-81), Academia Europaea, British Academy (corresponding fellow), Royal Historical Society (corresponding fellow), Association francaise des historiens economistes (president, 1974-77), Franco-British Council (French section).

AWARDS, HONORS: Bronze medal, Centre national de la recherche scientifique, 1957; Prix G. Maugin, Academie des sciences morales et politiques, 1959; honorary doctorate, University of Birmingham, 1977, University of Leicester, 1989, University of Kent at Canterbury, 1989, and University of Edinburgh, 1993; Grand Prix d'histoire de la Ville de Paris, 1987.

WRITINGS:

L'Economie du commonwealth, Presses universitaires de France, 1950.

L'Economie britannique et le blocus continental, 1806-1813, Presses universitaires de France, 1958, revised edition, Economica, 1987.

Le Conflit de Chypre, 1946-1959, E. Bruylant, 1973.

L'Economie de la Grand-Bretagne victorienne, S.E.D.E.S., 1978, translation published as *The Victorian Economy,* Methuen, 1982.

The First Industrialists: The Problem of Origins, Cambridge University Press, 1985.

De la superiorite de l'Angleterre sur la France, XVIIe-XXe siecle, Perrin, 1985, translation published as *Britain Ascendant,* Cambridge University Press, 1990.

EDITOR

(With Guy S. Metraux) *The Nineteenth-Century World: Readings from the History of Mankind,* New American Library, 1963.

(With Metraux) *The Evolution of Science: Readings from the History of Mankind,* New American Library, 1963.

(With Metraux) *The New Asia,* New American Library, 1965.

(With Metraux) *Religions and the Promise of the Twentieth Century,* New American Library, 1965.

(With Metraux) *Studies in the Cultural History of India,* Verry, 1965.

(With W. H. Chaloner and W. M. Stern) *Essays in European Economic History, 1789-1914,* Edward Arnold, 1969, St. Martin's, 1970.

(And author of introduction) *Capital Formation in the Industrial Revolution,* Barnes & Noble, 1972.

(With P. Leon) *L'Industrialisation en Europe au XIXe siecle,* Centre national de la recherche scientifique, 1972.

(And author of introduction) *Les Hommes d'etat celebres,* Volume 5, Mazenod, 1975.

(With F. Bedarida and D. Johnson) *De Guillaume le conquerant au Marche commun: Dix siecles d'histoire franco britannique,* Albin Michel, 1979.

Le negoie international, XIIIe-XXe siecle, Economica, 1989.

OTHER

Contributor of articles and book reviews to economic history journals. Member of editorial board, *Revue historique* and *Histoire, Economie et Societe.*

WORK IN PROGRESS: A book on money in France during the French Revolution; a short history of the European economy.

SIDELIGHTS: Francois Marie-Joseph Crouzet's main field of interest and research is the economic and social history of Britain and France in the late eighteenth and early nineteenth centuries, with a secondary interest in recent British history and Anglo-French relations.

* * *

CURTIS, Jackie
See HOLDER, John, Jr.

D

DANIEL, Colin
See WINDSOR, Patricia

* * *

DAVIDSON, Marshall B(owman) 1907-1989

PERSONAL: Born April 26, 1907, in New York, NY; died of pneumonia, August 8, 1989, in New York, NY; son of Henry Fletcher and Frances A. (Holt) Davidson; married Ruth Bradbury (an editor), August 20, 1935 (died 1979). *Education:* Princeton University, B.S., 1928.

ADDRESSES: Home—140 East 83rd St., New York, NY 10028. *Office*—American Heritage Publishing Co., 10 Rockefeller Plaza, New York, NY 10020.

CAREER: Metropolitan Museum of Art, New York City, assistant curator, 1935-41, associate curator, American wing, 1941-47, editor of publications, 1947-60; Horizon Books, New York City, editor, 1961-64, editor of *Horizon* (magazine), 1964-66, senior editor, beginning 1966.

AWARDS, HONORS: Carey-Thomas award for creative publishing, 1951, for *Life in America.*

WRITINGS:

Life in America, two volumes, Houghton, 1951.
(Editor in charge) *Horizon Book of Lost Worlds,* American Heritage, 1962.
(Author of introduction) James J. Audubon, *The Original Water-Color Paintings by James J. Audubon for the Birds of America,* two volumes, American Heritage, 1966.
American Heritage History of Colonial Antiques (also see below), American Heritage, 1967.
American Heritage History of American Antiques: 1784-1860 (also see below)American Heritage, 1968.
American Heritage History of Antiques: 1865-1917 (also see below), American Heritage, 1969.
American Heritage History of Notable American Houses, American Heritage, 1971.
Horizon Concise History of France, American Heritage, 1972.
American Heritage History of the Artists' America, American Heritage, 1973.
American Heritage History of the Writers' America, American Heritage, 1973.
Horizon Book of Great Historic Places of Europe, American Heritage, 1974.
Horizon History of the World in 1776, American Heritage, 1975.
Architecture in America: A Pictorial Survey, American Heritage, 1976.
Fifty Early American Tools, Olivetti Corp., 1976.
New York: A Pictorial History, Scribners, 1977.
Three Centuries of American Antiques, American Heritage, 1979 (3 volumes in one: *American Heritage History of Colonial Antiques, American Heritage History of American Antiques, American Heritage History of Antiques.*
The American Wing: A Guide, Metropolitan Museum of Art, 1980.
(Editor in charge) J. Christopher Herold, *Horizon Book of the Age of Napoleon,* American Heritage, 1983.
The Drawing of America: Eyewitnesses to History, Harry N. Abrams, 1983.
A History of Art: From 25,000 B.C. to the Present, Random House, 1984.
Treasures from the New York Public Library, Harry N. Abrams, 1985.
(With Elizabeth Stillinger) *The American Wing at the Metropolitan Museum of Art,* Metropolitan Museum/Knopf, 1985.

Contributor to books and to art, museum, and history journals.

OBITUARIES:

PERIODICALS

New York Times, August 11, 1989.*

* * *

DAVIES, (William) Robertson 1913-
(Samuel Marchbanks)

PERSONAL: Born August 28, 1913, in Thamesville, Ontario, Canada; son of William Rupert (a publisher and senator) and Florence Sheppard (MacKay) Davies; married Brenda Matthews (former stage manager for the Old Vic), February 2, 1940; children: Miranda, Jennifer (Mrs. C. T. Surridge), Rosamund (Mrs. John Cunnington). *Education:* Attended Upper Canada College, Toronto, and Queen's University, Kingston; Balliol College, Oxford, B.Litt., 1938.

ADDRESSES: Home—40 Oaklands Ave, Suite 303, Toronto, Ontario, Canada M4V 2E1. *Office*—Massey College, University of Toronto, 4 Devonshire Pl., Toronto, Ontario, Canada M5S 2E1. *Agent*—Curtis Brown Ltd., 10 Astor Pl., New York, NY 10003.

CAREER: Old Vic Company, London, England, teacher and actor, 1938-40; *Saturday Night,* Toronto, Ontario, literary editor, 1940-42; *Peterborough Examiner,* Peterborough, Ontario, editor and contributor under the name Samuel Marchbanks, 1942-58, then publisher, 1958-68; University of Toronto, visiting professor of English, 1960-62, then Master, Massey College, 1963, retired, 1981. Senator, Stratford Shakespeare Festival, Stratford, Ontario. Lecturer; has appeared on "Writers and Places," BBC-TV, 1984, and "The Magic Season of Robertson Davies," CBC-TV, 1990.

MEMBER: Royal Society of Canada (fellow), Playwright's Union of Canada, Royal Society of Literature (fellow), American Academy and Institute of Arts and Letters (honorary member), Authors Guild, Authors League of America, Writers' Union (Canada), PEN International.

AWARDS, HONORS: Best Canadian play award, Dominion Drama Festival, 1948, for *Eros,* and 1949, for *Fortune, My Foe;* Louis Jouvet Prize for directing, Dominion Drama Festival, 1949, for *The Taming of the Shrew;* Stephen Leacock Medal for humor, 1955, for *Leaven of Malice;* LL.D., University of Alberta, 1957, Queen's University, 1962, University of Manitoba, 1972, University of Calgary, 1975, University of Toronto, 1981, and University of Prince Edward Island, 1989; D.Litt., McMaster University, 1959, University of Windsor, 1971, York University, 1973, Mount Allison University, 1973, Memorial University of Newfoundland, 1974, University of Western Ontario, 1974, McGill University, 1974, Trent University, 1974, University of Lethbridge, 1981, University of Waterloo, 1981, University of British Columbia, 1983, University of Santa Clara, 1985, Trinity College, Dublin, 1990, and Oxford University, 1991; Lorne Pierce Medal, Royal Society of Canada, 1961; D.C.L., Bishop's University, 1967; Companion of the Order of Canada, 1972, Governor-General's Award for fiction, 1973, for *The Manticore;* D.Hum.Litt., University of Rochester, 1983, Dowling College, 1992; World Fantasy Convention Award, 1984, for *High Spirits;* Canadian Authors Association Literary Award, 1986, for *What's Bred in the Bone;* honorary fellowship, Balliol College, Oxford, 1986, Trinity College, University of Toronto, 1987; City of Toronto Book Award, Banff Centre School of Fine Arts Award, and Toronto Arts Lifetime Achievement Award, all 1986; Medal of Honor for Literature, National Arts Club, 1987; D.S.L., Thornloe College, University of Sudbury, Neil Gunn International Fellowship, Scottish Arts Council, Order of Ontario, Canadian Council Molson Prize in the Arts, and Diplome d'honneur, Canadian Conference of the Arts, all 1988; Author's Award, Foundation for the Advancement of Canadian Letters, and author of the year designation, Periodical Marketers of Canada, both 1990, both for *The Lyre of Orpheus.*

WRITINGS:

NOVELS; THE "SALTERTON TRILOGY"

Tempest-Tost, Clarke, Irwin, 1951, Rinehart, 1952.

Leaven of Malice (also see below), Clarke, Irwin, 1954, Scribner, 1955.

A Mixture of Frailties, Scribner, 1958.

The Salterton Trilogy (contains *Tempest-Tost, Leaven of Malice,* and *A Mixture of Frailties*), Penguin, 1986.

NOVELS; THE "DEPTFORD TRILOGY"

Fifth Business, Viking, 1970.

The Manticore, Viking, 1972.

World of Wonders, Macmillan (Toronto), 1975, Viking, 1976.

The Deptford Trilogy (contains *Fifth Business, The Manticore,* and *World of Wonders*), Penguin, 1983.

NOVELS; "THE CORNISH TRILOGY"

The Rebel Angels, Macmillan (Toronto), 1981, Viking, 1982.

What's Bred in the Bone, Viking, 1985.

The Lyre of Orpheus, Macmillan (Toronto), 1988, Viking, 1989.

The Cornish Trilogy (contains *The Rebel Angels, What's Bred in the Bone,* and *The Lyre of Orpheus*), Penguin, 1991.

FICTION

High Spirits; A Collection of Ghost Stories, Penguin (Toronto), 1982, Viking, 1983.

Murther & Walking Spirits, Viking, 1991.

Contributor of short fiction to periodicals including *City* (Toronto) and *Washington Post Book World.*

COLLECTIONS OF ESSAYS ORIGINALLY PUBLISHED UNDER THE NAME SAMUEL MARCHBANKS

The Diary of Samuel Marchbanks (originally published in the *Peterborough Examiner*), Clarke, Irwin, 1947.

The Table Talk of Samuel Marchbanks (originally published in the *Peterborough Examiner*), Clarke, Irwin, 1949.

Samuel Marchbanks' Almanack (originally published in the *Peterborough Examiner*), McClelland & Stewart, 1967.

The Papers of Samuel Marchbanks (contains excerpts from *The Diary of Samuel Marchbanks, The Table Talk of Samuel Marchbanks,* and *Samuel Marchbanks' Almanack*), Irwin Publishing, 1985.

NONFICTION; WITH SIR TYRONE GUTHRIE

(With Grant MacDonald) *Renown at Stratford: A Record of the Shakespearean Festival in Canada,* Clarke, Irwin, 1953, new edition, 1971.

Twice Have the Trumpets Sounded: A Record of the Stratford Shakespearean Festival in Canada, Clarke, Irwin, 1954.

(With Boyd Neal and Tanya Moiseiwitsch) *Thrice the Brinded Cat Hath Mew'd: A Record of the Stratford Shakespearean Festival in Canada,* Clarke, Irwin, 1955.

NONFICTION

Shakespeare's Boy Actors, Dent, 1939, Russell, 1964.

Shakespeare for Young Players: A Junior Course (textbook), Clarke, Irwin, 1942.

A Voice from the Attic: Essays on the Art of Reading, Knopf, 1960, published as *The Personal Art: Reading to Good Purpose,* Secker & Warburg, 1961, revised, Penguin, 1990.

Le Jeu de centenaire, Comission du Centenaire, c. 1967.

The Heart of a Merry Christmas, Macmillan (Toronto), 1970.

Stephen Leacock (literary criticism), McClelland & Stewart, 1970.

(Editor and author of introduction) *Feast of Stephen: An Anthology of Some of the Less Familiar Writings of Stephen Leacock,* McClelland & Stewart, 1970, published as *The Penguin Stephen Leacock,* Penguin, 1981.

(With Michael R. Booth, Richard Southern, Frederick Marker, and Lise-Lone Marker) *The Revels History of Drama in English,* Volume 6: *1750-1880,* Methuen, 1975.

One Half of Robertson Davies: Provocative Pronouncements on a Wide Range of Topics, Macmillan (Toronto), 1977, Viking, 1978.

The Enthusiasms of Robertson Davies, edited by Judith Skelton Grant, McClelland & Stewart, 1979, Viking, 1990.

Robertson Davies, The Well-Tempered Critic: One Man's View of Theatre and Letters in Canada, edited by Grant, McClelland & Stewart, 1981.

The Mirror of Nature (lectures), University of Toronto Press, 1983.

Conversations with Robertson Davies, edited by J. Madison Davis, University Press of Mississippi, 1989.

Reading and Writing (lectures), University of Utah Press, in press.

PLAYS

A Play of Our Lord's Nativity, produced in Peterborough, Ontario, 1946.

Fortune, My Foe (produced in Kingston, Ontario, 1948), Clarke, Irwin, 1948.

Eros at Breakfast, and Other Plays (one-act; contains "Eros at Breakfast" [produced in Montreal, Quebec], "Overlaid" [produced in Peterborough], "The Voice of the People" [produced in Montreal], "At the Gates of the Righteous" [produced in Peterborough], and "Hope Deferred" [produced in Montreal]), introduction by Sir Tyrone Guthrie, Clarke, Irwin, 1949, revised edition published as *Four Favourite Plays,* 1969.

At My Heart's Core (produced in Peterborough), Clarke, Irwin, 1952.

A Masque of Aesop (produced in Toronto, Ontario, 1952), Clarke, Irwin, 1952.

A Jig for the Gypsy (produced in Toronto, 1954), Clarke, Irwin, 1954.

Love and Libel (based on *Leaven of Malice;* produced in Toronto, then on Broadway, 1960), Studio Duplicating Service, 1960.

A Masque of Mr. Punch (for children: produced in Toronto, 1962), Oxford University Press, 1963.

(With others) *Centennial Play* (produced in Lindsay, Ontario, 1967), Centennial Commission, 1967.

The Voice of the People, Book Society of Canada, 1968.

Hunting Stuart, and Other Plays (contains "King Phoenix" [produced in Peterborough, 1950], "Hunting Stuart" [produced in Toronto, 1955], and "General Confession"), edited by Brian Parker, New Press, 1972.

Brothers in the Black Art (televised on the Canadian Broadcast Corporation [CBC], 1974), Alcuin Society, 1981.

Question Time (produced in Toronto, 1975), Macmillan, 1975.

Pontiac and the Green Man, produced in Toronto, 1977.

Also author of *Dr. Canon's Cure* (libretto; music by Derek Holman). Plays included in anthologies, including *Ten Canadian Short Plays,* edited by John Stevens, Dell, 1975; *Cues and Entrances,* compiled by Henry Beissel, Gage Educational Publishing, 1977; *Canada's Lost Plays,* edited by Anton Wagner, Canadian Theatre Review Publications, 1980; and *Major Plays of the Canadian Theatre, 1934-94,* edited by Richard Perkins, Irwin, 1984.

Davies' work has been translated into seventeen languages, including Czeck, Danish, Dutch, Estonian, Finnish, French, German, Greek, Hebrew, Hungarian, Italian, Japanese, Norwegian, Polish, Portuguese, Spanish, and Swedish.

A collection of Davies' manuscript is housed at The National Archives, Ottawa, Ontario.

ADAPTATIONS: What's Bred in the Bone is being adapted into a television mini-series produced jointly by the British Broadcasting Corporation (BBC-TV) and the Canadian Broadcasting Corporation (CBC-TV).

SIDELIGHTS: "In a Davies novel, life always imitates art," comments David Rollow in the *Spectator,* reviewing a novel by Canadian author Robertson Davies. Praised by critics as a masterful storyteller, Davies is a writer in possession of both a strong moral sense and a wealth of obscure facts that lay imbedded in his prose like treasured gems to be discovered by his many readers. The series of novels that combine to make up his "Deptford," "Salterton," and "Cornish" trilogies have brought Davies to international attention as one of his country's—indeed, North America's—leading men of letters. Along a path strewn with much success, in 1981 Davies became the first Canadian ever to become an Honorary Member of the American Academy and Institute of Arts and Letters. Claude Bissell writes in *Canadian Literature* that the novels in the "Deptford Trilogy" alone compose a "major piece of prose fiction in Canadian literature—in scope, in the constant interplay of wit and intelligence, in the persistent attempt to find a pattern in this 'life of marvels, cruel circumstances, obscenities, and commonplaces.' "

"Reading a Robertson Davies novel is oddly like going back to school, albeit a very special school with a very clever teacher," notes William French in the *Globe and Mail,* a reflection of the author's long academic career. Davies became first Master of Massey College, a graduate school of the University of Toronto, in 1962. As a specialist in English drama from the period 1660 to 1925, he both taught and supervised graduate students, all the while continuing to both write and lecture until his retirement from the university in 1981. "Davies cherishes language," Whitney Balliett of the *New Yorker* states, affirming the academic edge of Davies' prose. "He is apt to scatter in our path such words as 'whittoly' and 'sonsy' and 'chthonic.' But in the more elegant surroundings they are more like strange flowers than stumbling stones."

But to describe Davies as an academic in love with language and the accumulation of obscure bits and pieces of knowledge does scant justice to the entertaining quality of his prose. John Kenneth Galbraith praised his fellow Canadian in *The New York Times Book Review* as "a fine writer—deft, resourceful, diverse and . . . very funny." Davies himself credits his subtle sense of the absurd with his upbringing. "I was brought up in an atmosphere of ironic observation," he told Eva Seidner in an interview for *Maclean's.* "My family was a newspaper family, and in newspapers you know a lot about things that you simply couldn't print. You know what lies behind some apparently inoffensive happenings. Consequently, intelligent newspaper people . . . have a very wry attitude toward life and circumstances. They know that what you can write about is just the icing on a very rich, fruity, nutty and unwholesome cake."

The range of Davies' abilities is reflected not only in the variety of genres that he has explored—novels, plays, literary criticism, essays—but also in his ability to move "easily from the bawdiest humor to the loftiest abstraction, charging every character and idea with power and fascination," as Michael Mewshaw states in the *New York Times Book Review.* Calling Davies "a compelling inventive storyteller" who has garnered an "affectionate following," James Idema of the *Chicago Tribune Book World* explains that the appeal of Davies' fiction lies in "his way of placing ordinary humans in the midst of extraordinary events, of bringing innocent, resolutely straight characters into contact with bonafide exotics. The real world interests [Davies] only as a starting point. Enigma, myth, illusion and magic are the stuff of his elegant stories." "Davies is less interested in ideas than in myths," agrees Rollow. "What excites his imagination is the way things in the visible world connect with the unseen, the way myths lie buried under the lives of individuals or hidden under the surface structures of civilisation."

Davies' "Deptford Trilogy" traces the lives of three men raised in the fictitious Ontario town of Deptford whose lives are linked by a single tragic event. At the age of ten, Dunstan Ramsay and Percy "Boy" Staunton are throwing snowballs at one another. Staunton throws a snowball at Ramsay which contains a rock. Ramsay ducks; the snowball strikes a passerby, Mrs. Mary Dempster, in the head causing her to prematurely give birth to a son, Paul Dempster. As a result of the trauma, Mary Dempster has a mental breakdown that eventually culminates in permanent hospitalization. Each novel of the trilogy revolves around this incident and focuses in turn on each of the three men involved. *Fifth Business,* published in 1970, is the first-person account of Ramsay who has become a professor; his life intertwines with that of the other two men in unexpected ways. *The Manticore,* published two years later, revolves around the repercussions of the murder of Boy Staunton, who had risen from his affluent roots to become a successful politician. Davies concluded the trilogy in 1975 with *World of Wonders;* Paul Dempster travels the world building a career as a stage magician and becomes one of the most successful acts on the continent. "*Fifth Business* provides the brickwork," John Alwyne explains in the *New Statesman,* "the two later volumes, the lath and plaster. But what a magnificent building is the result. [The Deptford Trilogy] bears comparison with any fiction of the last decade."

Davies did not begin *Fifth Business* intending to write a trilogy. He initially envisioned his story idea as a novel but, as he told *Time* (Canada), "I found almost as soon as I had finished it that wasn't all I wanted to say." He was soon at work on *The Manticore* to tell more of his story. Even after the second novel was published, readers wrote, full of questions about Magnus Eisengrim, the magician who appeared in the two novels: "I thought 'Well, I know a lot about magicians' and I wrote the third book." Despite the unplanned development of the trilogy, it garnered extensive critical praise, both in North America and abroad. Sam Solecki notes in *Canadian Forum* that *Fifth Business* is "Davies' masterpiece and . . . among the handful of Canadian novels that count." Critical praise for the subsequent novels in the series was much the same. "The blend of masterly characterization, cunning plot, shifting point of view, and uncommon detail, all fixed in the clearest, most literate prose, is superbly achieved," notes Pat Barclay in his review of *The Manticore* in *Canadian Literature.*

In each of the "Deptford" novels the lead character undergoes a psychological transformation. Ramsay finds the key to himself in the study of saints and myth, David Staunton (the son of Boy Staunton) relies on Jungian psychoanalysis to help come to terms with his father's mysterious death, and Paul Dempster learns from his life in the theatre about reality and illusion. Peter Prescott writes in *Newsweek* that Davies "means to recharge the world with a wonder it has lost, to re-create through the intervention of saints and miracles, psychoanalysts and sleight-of-hand a proper sense of awe at life's mystery and a recognition of the price that must be paid for initiation into that discovery." The recurring theme of self-discovery follows patterns established by psychologist Carl Jung, although Davies' novels do not strictly adhere to Jungian psychology. In common with the Jungian belief in archetypal influence on the human mind, the author presents his readers with fictional characters who "discover the meaning of their lives," Roger Sale notes in the *New York Review of Books,* "by discovering the ways those lives conform to ancient patterns." Peter Baltensperger writes in *Canadian Literature* that this is a consistent theme in all of Davies' fiction and defines it as "the conquest of one's Self in the inner struggle and the knowledge of oneself as fully human."

"The theme which lies at the root of all my novels is the isolation of the human spirit," Davies once commented to *CA.* "I have not attempted to deal with it in a gloomy fashion but rather to demonstrate that what my characters do that might be called really significant is done on their own volition and usually contrary to what is expected of them. This theme is worked out in terms of characters who are trying to escape from early influences and find their own place in the world but who are reluctant to do so in a way that will bring pain and disappointment to others."

"Though his name is not a household word [in the U.S.], Davies has become something of a literary cult figure," Jean Strouse wrote in *Newsweek* in 1982. The "Deptford Trilogy" was indeed a success south of the Canadian border, and Davies had just published the first volume of what would become the "Cornish Trilogy." The first volume of this work, *The Rebel Angels* introduces an odd cast of characters: gypsies, homosexual defrocked monks, tycoons, college professors, and wealthy recluses. Within the closed academic society they inhabit at a Toronto university, all become entangled in a complex web of events leading to theft, and even murder. Reynolds Price, reviewing the work in the *Washington Post Book World,* finds the work complex. "What seems . . . the biggest difficulty of the novel is that it smacks strongly, from the beginning, of allegory," he comments. "The major characters are initially recognizable types . . . all intelligently and often elegantly displayed, [but] seem to acquire, for Davies, emblematic significances of the kind which his long-standing fascination with Jungian psychology has led his readers to expect." Price concludes that "confined as we are to the views of [the main characters], only an adept at both the systems of Jung and the prior novels of Davies could hope to extract the [novel's] full intention."

What's Bred in the Bone, published in 1985, continues the "Cornish Trilogy." It is a study of a character who appeared only briefly in *The Rebel Angels,* art collector Francis Cornish, who is saved from a lonely childhood in a small Canadian town by discovering his talent for painting. Calling the author's own approach to art "old-fashioned," reviewer Michiko Kakutani of the *New York*

Times likens Davies' structure—particularly the artifice of having the story narrated by two angels—to an old Frank Capra film. Amid this outward invention, Davies "performs a lot of energetic sleight of hand, twisting and turning a seemingly predictable plot into an altogether remarkable—and ornate—creation. There is an interlude at a German Castle with a Bavarian countess, a search for King Arthur in the back country of England, a complicated ruse to defraud the Nazis, and some art forgery that takes on metaphysical dimension."

Four years later *The Lyre of Orpheus* reunited characters of both *The Rebel Angels* and *What's Bred in the Bone* under the auspices of a foundation for promoting high-risk artistic endeavours. The first venture the board patronizes is the completion of an opera left unfinished by the nineteenth-century German composer E. T. A. Hoffmann. Linnea Lannon, reviewing the book for the *Detroit Free Press* states that the novel is "too much a vehicle for Davies' vivid imagination and interest in the mythological to be believable, but it is lively, even when Davies stretches credulity to its limits or succumbs to academia." Citing an instance in the novel wherein a gathering of academics argue over the meaning of an Old English word, Lannon comments: "The scene is, to a degree, a successful satire on the pedantry of professors, but for many readers it will come off as Davies showing us too well what he knows and we don't." However, Paul Gray praises the work in the *Times:* "The novel is crammed with funny renditions of wheezy professorial badinage and flamboyant dramatic monologues. But it is Davies' own voice that seems most memorable: confident, unhurried, interested and amused."

Gray maintains that in the third novel of the "Cornish Trilogy" Davies is "solicitous towards those who have been present and paying attention from the beginning; the plot and characters of *The Lyre of Orpheus* gain resonances from the earlier books that only initiates will hear." However, Phyllis Rose, writing in the *New York Times Book Review:* criticizes the book as not simply "gaining resonance" from the previous two volumes, but relying on them to fully understand the novel's characters. By the third volume of the trilogy, Davies is tying up loose ends, argues Rose; his characters have become distilled to their true archetypes, without the carapace of humanity that made their actions understandable in *The Rebel Angels* and *What's Bred in the Bone.* "Beyond conservative, this kind of novel writing is authoritarian," Rose declares. "There is no way to read this book except the allegorical way the author imposes on us."

In any work by Davies, the central character's questioning and search for knowledge ultimately lead to some sort of resolution. "For those seeking entertaining answers to perplexing questions, Davies is a godsend, if not the Holy Trinity itself," Janice Kulyk Keefer states in *Books in Canada.* Keefer praises the author for trying "not to exploit but to improve his times by offering his readers an imaginatively rendered schema whereby they may save or heal themselves as individuals in a destructive, not to say catastrophic, age." However, she questions whether the role of literature is indeed to provide the answers, as Davies so pointedly does: "*The Lyre of Orpheus* gives an unconvincing shape to what we most want—for the jumbled pieces of our lives to come beautifully and meaningfully together, for there to be a great and marvelous pattern to, and destination in, our lives."

In addition to his many novels, Davies has also written plays and a great deal of non-fiction. In 1986 he published *The Papers of Samuel Marchbanks,* a compilation of essays he once published under a pseudonym in the *Peterborough Examiner.* The fictitious Marchbanks is "the creation of the richest literary imagination in Canada," exclaims Stevenson Swanson of the *Chicago Tribune.* "But not to mention the fact would cheat Robertson Davies, fortunate possessor of that imagination, of well-earned credit for adding to the world's store of eccentrics, and Davies is decades late in garnering all the credit he deserves." After referring to fellow Canadians as "a nation of ash-choked grouches," Marchbanks goes on to verbally lambast everything from politicians to his home heating unit. The vociferations of this alter-ego are a counterpoint to *The Enthusiasms of Robertson Davies,* published in 1979. Praising the work as "a testimony to the depth of his thought and the breadth of his erudition," M. G. Lord compares *Enthusiasms* to *The Papers of Samuel Marchbanks* in the *Washington Post Book World:* "Writing in the voice of Marchbanks, his cranky alter-ego, Davies is whiny, provincial and off-putting. Writing in his own voice, however, he is endlessly beguiling and informative."

"I am a sort of outsider," Davies once told Barbara A. Bannon of *Publishers Weekly* in explanation of his position in the literary establishment of his own country. "My view of Canada is not that of any other Canadian writer. I cannot be ignored but I am thought by many people not to be a Canadian writer." Davies finds this difficult to understand—although he traveled abroad to attend Oxford University for several years, he has spent most of his life in Ontario. But it is easy to understand how Davies' vocal prodding of the Canadian intellect has resulted in some scarring over the years. His homeland has been a thread winding its way through the entire body of his work, with the result that Canadians have been the target of everything from the satirical bombasts of Samuel Marchbanks—disgruntled native of Skunk's Misery, Ontario—to Davies' cynical portraits of "provincial" life. But, whether in Marchbanks' diatribe or in a subtle aside from one of his other fictional characters, Canada has been portrayed with a frustration similar to that of a parent with a wayward child rather than with anger. As a character in his 1991 novel, *Murther & Walking Spirits*, states: "Canada isn't like a woman; it's like a family—various, often unsympathetic, sometimes detestable, frequently dumb as hell—but inescapable because you are part of it and can't ever, really, get away."

For a previously published interview, see entry in *Contemporary Authors New Revision*, Gale, Volume 17, 1986, pp. 94-97.

BIOGRAPHICAL/CRITICAL SOURCES:

BOOKS

Anthony, Geraldine, editor, *Stage Voices: 12 Canadian Playwrights Talk about Their Lives and Work*, Doubleday, 1978.

Buitenhuis, Elspeth, *Robertson Davies*, Forum House, 1972.

Cameron, Donald, *Conversations with Canadian Novelists*, Part 1, Macmillan, 1973.

Contemporary Dramatists, 4th edition, St. James, 1988, pp. 111-14.

Contemporary Novelists, 5th edition, St. James, 1991, pp. 227-30.

Contemporary Literary Criticism, Gale, Volume 2, 1974, Volume 7, 1977, Volume 13, 1980, Volume 25, 1983.

Davies, Robertson, *Murther & Walking Spirits*, Viking, 1991.

Grant, Judith Skelton, *Robertson Davies*, McClelland & Stewart, 1978.

Heath, Jeffrey M., editor, *Profiles in Canadian Literature #2*, Dundurn Press, 1980.

Jones, Joseph, and Johanna Jones, *Canadian Fiction*, Twayne, 1981.

Klinck, Carl F., editor, *Literary History of Canada*, 2nd edition, University of Toronto Press, 1976.

Lawrence, Robert G., and Samuel L. Macey, editors, *Studies in Robertson Davies' Deptford Trilogy*, English Literary Studies, University of Victoria, 1980.

Lecker, Robert, and Jack David, editors, *The Annotated Bibliography of Canada's Major Authors*, Volume 3, ECW Press, 1982.

Lecker, Robert, Jack David, and Ellen Luigley, editors, *Canadian Writers and Their Works*, Volume 6, ECW Press, 1985.

Monk, Patricia, *The Smaller Infinity: The Jungian Self in the Novels of Robertson Davies*, University of Toronto Press, 1982.

Moore, Mavor, *Four Canadian Playwrights*, Holt, 1973.

Morley, Patricia, *Robertson Davies*, Gage Educational Publishing, 1977.

New, William H., editor, *Dramatists in Canada: Selected Essays*, University of British Columbia Press, 1972.

Stone-Blackburn, Susan, *Robertson Davies, Playwright: A Search for the Self on the Canadian Stage*, University of British Columbia Press, 1985.

PERIODICALS

America, December 16, 1972.

Book Forum, Volume 4, number 1, 1978.

Book World, December 13, 1970.

Canadian Drama, Volume 7, number 2, 1981.

Canadian Forum, June, 1950; December, 1975; October, 1977; December-January, 1981-82.

Canadian Literature, spring, 1960; winter, 1961; spring, 1973; winter, 1974; winter, 1976.

Canadian Review, fall, 1976.

Chicago Tribune Book World, January 31, 1982.

Dalhousie Review, autumn, 1982.

Financial Post, January 19, 1963.

Globe & Mail (Toronto), March 5, 1977; January 7, 1984.

Journal of Canadian Fiction, winter, 1982.

Journal of Canadian Studies, February, 1977.

Library Quarterly, April, 1969.

Listener, April 15, 1971.

Los Angeles Times, January 29, 1982.

Maclean's, March 15, 1952; September, 1972.

Nation, April 24, 1982.

New Republic, March 13, 1976; April 15, 1978; March 10, 1982.

New Statesman, April 20, 1973; April 4, 1980.

Newsweek, January 18, 1971; March 22, 1976; February 8, 1982.

New York Review of Books, February 8, 1973.

New York Times, February 8, 1982; November 6, 1985.

New York Times Book Review, December 20, 1970; November 19, 1972; April 25, 1976; February 14, 1982.

Rolling Stone, December 1, 1977.

Saturday Night, April 26, 1947; December 13, 1947; February 14, 1953; November, 1967; October, 1985.

Saturday Review, December 26, 1970; April 3, 1976.

Spectator, August 21, 1982.

Tamarack Review, autumn, 1958.

Time, January 11, 1971; May 17, 1976.

Time (Canada), November 3, 1975.

Times Literary Supplement, March 26, 1982.

University of Toronto Quarterly, number 21, 1952.

Washington Post Book World, May 30, 1976; February 7, 1982; October 30, 1983.

—Sketch by Pamela L. Shelton

* * *

DAVIS, Frank Marshall 1905-1987

PERSONAL: Born December 31, 1905, in Arkansas City, KS; died July 26, 1987, in Honolulu, HI; married; children: Lynn, Beth, Jeanne, Jill, Mark. *Education:* Attended Friends University, 1923; attended Kansas State Agricultural College (now Kansas State University of Agricultural and Applied Science), 1924-27, 1929.

CAREER: Worked for various newspapers in Illinois, including the *Chicago Evening Bulletin, Whip,* and *Gary American,* 1927-29; *Atlanta Daily World,* Atlanta, GA, editor and co-founder, 1931-34; Associated Negro Press, Chicago, IL, executive editor, 1935-47; *Chicago Star,* Chicago, executive editor, 1946-48; owned wholesale paper business in Honolulu, HI, beginning c. 1948. Worked as a jazz radio disc jockey in the early 1940s. Toured black colleges as a lecturer, 1973.

MEMBER: League of American Writers, Allied Arts Guild, Southside Chicago Writers Group.

AWARDS, HONORS: Julius Rosenwald Foundation grant, 1937.

WRITINGS:

Black Man's Verse (poems; includes "Giles Johnson, Ph.D.," "Lynched [Symphonic Interlude for Twenty-One Selected Instruments]," "Mojo Mike's Beer Garden," "Cabaret," and "Ebony Under Granite"), Black Cat, 1935.

I Am the American Negro (poems; includes "I Am the American Negro," "Flowers of Darkness," "To One Who Would Leave Me," "Awakening," "Come to Me," "Modern Man—The Superman: A Song of Praise for Hearst, Hitler, Mussolini, and the Munitions Makers," "'Mancipation Day," "Onward Christian Soldiers," "Christ Is a Dixie Nigger," "Note Left by a Suicide," "Ebony Under Granite," and "Frank Marshall Davis: Writer"), Black Cat, 1937.

Through Sepia Eyes (poems; includes "Chicago Skyscrapers," "To Those Who Sing America," "Life Is a Woman," and "Coincidence"), Black Cat, 1938.

47th Street: Poems (includes "47th Street," "Pattern for Conquest," "Egotistic Runt," "Tenement Room," "Black Weariness," "Snapshots of the Cotton South," "Peace Quiz for America," "For All Common People," "War Zone," "Nothing Can Stop the People," "Peace Is a Fragile Cup," and "Self-Portrait"), Decker, 1948.

Awakening, and Other Poems, Black Cat, 1978.

Livin' the Blues: Memoirs of a Black Journalist and Poet, edited by John Edgar Tidwell, University of Wisconsin Press, 1993.

Also author of poem, "Chicago's Congo," and of a volume of poetry entitled *Jazz Interlude,* 1985; author of the unpublished manuscript, "That Incredible Waikiki Jungle." Poems published in anthologies, including *The Negro Caravan,* Dryden, 1942; *Kaleidoscope: Poems by American Negro Poets,* Harcourt, 1967; *Black Voices: An Anthology of Afro-American Literature,* New American Library, 1968; *The Poetry of the Negro, 1746-1970,* Anchor Books, 1970; *Black Insights,* Ginn, 1971; *Understanding the New Black Poetry,* Morrow, 1973; and *The New Negro Renaissance: An Anthology,* Holt, 1975. Contributor to periodicals, including *National, Light and Heebie Jeebies,* and *Voices.* Wrote weekly column for *Honolulu Record.*

SIDELIGHTS: Frank Marshall Davis's poetry "not only questioned social ills in his own time but also inspired blacks in the politically charged 1960s," according to John Edgar Tidwell in the *Dictionary of Literary Biography.* Sometimes likened to poets such as Walt Whitman and Carl Sandburg, Davis published his first volume, *Black Man's Verse,* in 1935. The book met with much applause from critics, including Harriet Monroe, who concluded in *Poetry* that its author was "a poet of authentic inspiration, who belongs not only among the best of his race, but who need not lean upon his race for recognition as an impassioned singer with something to say." Davis concerned himself with portraying black life, protesting racial inequalities, and promoting black pride. The poet described his work thus in the poem "Frank Marshall Davis: Writer" from his *I Am the American Negro:* "When I wrote/ I dipped my pen/ In the crazy heart/ Of mad America."

Davis grew up in Arkansas City, Kansas, surrounded by racism. Tidwell reported that when the poet was five years old he was nearly killed by some older white children who had heard stories of lynchings and wanted to try one for themselves. The result of this incident and others was that Davis hated whites in his youth. He gained some relief, according to Tidwell, when he left the prejudiced, small town atmosphere of Arkansas City in 1923 to attend Friends University in Wichita; he eventually transferred to Kansas State Agricultural College's school of journalism. There, because of a class assignment, Davis received his first introduction to writing free verse—his preferred poetic form. When he left Kansas State, he travelled to Chicago, where he wrote free-lance articles for magazines and worked for several black newspapers while continuing to produce poems. After a brief return to Kansas State, Davis moved to Atlanta, Georgia, to take an editing post on a semiweekly paper. With the help of his leadership, the periodical became the *Atlanta Daily World,* the first successful black daily newspaper in America. Meanwhile, one of Davis's published poems, "Chicago's Congo," which concerns the underlying similarities between the blacks of Chicago and those still living the tribal life of the African Congo, attracted the attention of bohemian intellectual Frances Norton Manning. When Davis returned to Chicago, Manning introduced him to Norman Forgue, whose Black Cat Press subsequently published Davis's *Black Man's Verse.*

A critical success, *Black Man's Verse* "is experimental, cacophonous, yet sometimes harmonious," according to Tidwell. The volume includes poems such as "Giles Johnson, Ph.D.," in which the title character starves to death in spite of his four college degrees and knowledge of Latin and Greek because he does not wish to teach and is incapable of doing the manual labor that made up the majority of work available to blacks. Other pieces in *Black Man's Verse*—"Lynched," "Mojo Mike's Beer Garden," and "Cabaret," for example—make use of Davis's expertise on the subject of jazz to combine "the spirit of protest in jazz and free verse with . . . objections to racial oppression, producing a poetry that loudly declaims against injustice," explained Tidwell. Another well-known part of the volume is entitled "Ebony Under Granite." Likened to author Edgar Lee Masters's *Spoon River Anthology,* this section discusses the lives of various black people buried in a cemetery. Characters include Reverend Joseph Williams, who used to have sex with most of the women in his congregation; Goldie Blackwell, a two-dollar prostitute; George Brown, who served life in prison for voting more than once, although in Mississippi he had seen white voters commit the same crime many times without punishment; and Roosevelt Smith, a black writer who was so frustrated by literary critics that he became a postman.

I Am the American Negro, Davis's second collection of poems, was published two years after his first. While drawing generally favorable reviews, it did not attract as much attention as *Black Man's Verse,* and some critics complained that it was too similar to the earlier book. For example, Tidwell quoted black critic Alain Locke's assertion that *I Am the American Negro* "has too many echoes of the author's first volume . . . it is not a crescendo in the light of the achievement of [*Black Man's Verse*]." One of the obvious similarities between the two collections is that Davis also included an "Ebony Under Granite" section in the second. Members of this cast are people like the two Greeley sisters—the first's earlier promiscuous lifestyle did not prevent her from marrying respectably, while the second's lack of sexual experience caused her husband to be unfaithful; Nicodemus Perry, killed by loiterers for accidentally bumping into a white woman while, ironically, lost in memories of the sexual abuse his female relatives suffered at the hands of white men; and Mrs. Clifton Townsend, prejudiced against the darker-skinned members of her own race, who dies after giving birth to a baby much blacker than herself. Other poems featured in *I Am the American Negro* are "Modern Man—The Superman," which laments the state of modern civilization and has mock musical notations in its margins such as "Eight airplane motors, each keyed to a different pitch, are turned on and off to furnish musical accompaniment within the range of an octave"; and the title poem, which is a diatribe against Southern laws treating blacks differently from whites. Davis also placed love poems such as "Flowers of Darkness" and "Come to Me" in this book.

"The culmination of Davis's thought and poetic development," is found in Davis's 1948 collection of poems, *47th Street,* according to Tidwell. Davis himself remarked on the time span between his first book, *I Am,* and his fourth book, *47th Street,* in a 1973 interview for *Black World:* "I was going through a number of changes during that particular time and I had to wait for these changes to settle and jell before I produced other work which I thought would be suitable to appear in a volume. And, of course, some critics naturally have thought that I would have been better off had I just continued to jell indefinitely." *47th Street* is composed of poems such as "Coincidence," which narrates the life stories of Donald Woods, a white man, and Booker Scott, a black man, who shared their dates of birth and death—by the poem's end the reader discovers that they also shared the same white biological father. The title poem, "unlike [Davis's] previous descriptions of Southside Chicago as exclusively black," noted Tidwell, "presents a 'rainbow race' of people." Indeed, Tidwell saw the whole of *47th Street* as having more universal concerns than his earlier works. When questioned about this issue Davis declared: "I am a Black poet, definitely a Black poet, and I think that my way of seeing things is the result of the impact [of] our civilization upon what I like to think of as a sensitive Black man. . . . But I do not think the Black poet should confine himself exclusively to Black readership. I think poetry, if it is going to be any good, should move members of all groups, and that is what I hope for."

In the same year that *47th Street* was published, Davis left Chicago for Honolulu, Hawaii. What began as a vacation turned into permanent residency. Except for a few poems that appeared in *Voices* in 1950, Davis virtually disappeared from the literary world until going on a college lecture tour in 1973. He later published another volume of poetry, and at the time of his death in 1987 had been working on a manuscript called "That Incredible Waikiki Jungle," about his Hawaiian experiences. When asked why he decided to remain in Hawaii, Davis cited the relative lack of racial problems and added, "I think one of the reasons why was that this [was] the first time that I began to be treated as a man instead of a Black curiosity. That was important to me, for my feeling of dignity and self-respect."

BIOGRAPHICAL/CRITICAL SOURCES:

BOOKS

Davis, Frank Marshall, *I Am the American Negro,* Black Cat, 1978.

Dictionary of Literary Biography, Volume 51: *Afro-American Writers from the Harlem Renaissance to 1940,* Gale, 1987.

PERIODICALS

Black World, January, 1974.
Poetry, August, 1936.

OBITUARIES:

PERIODICALS

Chicago Tribune, August 9, 1987.*

* * *

DEANE, Seamus (Francis) 1940-

PERSONAL: Born February 9, 1940, in Derry City, Northern Ireland; son of Frank (an electrician) and Winifred Deane; married Marion Frances Treacy (a teacher), August 19, 1963; children: Conor, Ciaran, Emer, Cormac. *Education:* Queen's University, Belfast, Northern Ireland, B.A., 1961, M.A., 1963; Cambridge University, Ph.D., 1966.

ADDRESSES: Home—33 Oakley Rd., Ranelagh, Dublin 6, Ireland. *Office*—Department of English, National University of Ireland, University College, Dublin 4, Ireland.

CAREER: Reed College, Portland, OR, assistant professor of English, 1966-67; University of California, Berkeley, assistant professor of English, 1967-68; National University of Ireland, University College, Dublin, lecturer, 1968-80, professor of English, 1980—. Visiting professor at University of Notre Dame and University of California, Berkeley, 1976-77; member of Field Day Theatre Company.

MEMBER: Royal Irish Academy, Aosdana (Irish Writers' Guild).

AWARDS, HONORS: A. E. Memorial Award for Literature, 1973, for *Gradual Wars;* America-Ireland Fund Award for Literature, 1988.

WRITINGS:

Gradual Wars (poems), Irish University Press, 1972.
(Editor) Thomas Holcroft, *The Adventures of Hugh Trevor,* Oxford University Press, 1973.
Sale Catalogues of Eminent Persons, Sotheby Parke-Bernet, 1973.
Rumours (poems), Dolmen Press, 1975.
History Lessons (poems), Gallery Press, 1985.
Celtic Revivals: Essays in Modern Irish Literature, Faber, 1985.
A Short History of Irish Literature, 1580-1980, Hutchinson, 1986.
Selected Poems, Gallery Press, 1988.
The French Enlightenment and Revolution in England 1789-1832, Harvard University Press, 1988.
The Field Day Anthology of Irish Writing, three volumes, Field Day, Derry, 1991.

Contributor to magazines and newspapers, including *Atlantis, Journal of the History of Ideas, Encounter, Cambridge Review, Sewanee Review, London Review of Books, Times Literary Supplement,* and *New York Times Book Review.*

SIDELIGHTS: Celtic Revivals: Essays in Modern Irish Literature is a collection of Seamus Deane's scholarly work on Irish writers including William Butler Yeats, James Joyce, and Sean O'Casey. Since the 1977 publication of his essay "The Literary Myths of the Revival," reprinted in *Celtic Revivals,* Deane has challenged the predominant Yeatsian vision of Irish people and Irish culture, arguing that Yeats "distorted history in the service of myth." Observed *Times Literary Supplement* critic Denis Donoghue, "Deane proposes that we abandon the Yeatsian myth . . . but he has not obeyed his own instruction." Donoghue suggested that "Deane, too, yearns for illusions and myths," that this one failing only shows "how disciplined one must be to live without a myth." Deane remains, judged Donoghue, "a fine descriptive critic."

Deane once told *CA:* "The dominant public experience of my career has been the political crisis in Northern Ireland. In scholarship, I have been influenced by the writings of the French Enlightenment, particularly those of Montesquieu, Diderot, and Irish political philosopher Edmund Burke; in modern letters, Theodor Adorno and Walter Benjamin; in poetry, the work of Yves Bonnefoy, W. S. Merwin, James Tate, and Rainer Maria Rilke."

BIOGRAPHICAL/CRITICAL SOURCES:

PERIODICALS

Times Literary Supplement, February 16, 1973; November 25, 1977; March 15, 1985; November 1, 1985.

* * *

de JONGE, Alex 1938-

PERSONAL: Born September 26, 1938, in London, England; son of Henry Robert Alexander and Alexandra (Skwarskaya) de Jonge; married Judith Twynam, August 20, 1962 (divorced, 1980); married Kathleen Russell Sharp, October, 1980; children: (first marriage) Edward, James. *Education:* New College, Oxford, B.A., 1962, M.A., 1966, Ph.D., 1969. *Religion:* Anglican.

Avocational Interests: Horse-racing, fishing, skiing, food and drink.

ADDRESSES: Office—Department of Russian, University of Arizona, Tucson, Arizona.

CAREER: Oxford University, New College, Oxford, England, tutorial fellow in French and Russian, 1964-86; University of Arizona, Tucson, professor of Russian and comparative literature, 1986—.

MEMBER: Piscatorial Society, Newbury Race Club.

WRITINGS:

Nightmare Culture, Lautreamont and les Chants de Maldoror (nonfiction), St. Martin's, 1973.

(Contributor) J. L. I. Fennell, editor, *Nineteenth Century Russian Literature: Studies of Ten Russian Writers,* University of California Press, 1973.

Dostoevsky and the Age of Intensity (nonfiction), St. Martin's, 1974.

Baudelaire: Prince of Clouds (biography), Paddington, 1976.

The Weimar Chronicle: Prelude to Hitler (nonfiction), Paddington, 1977.

(Translator from the French) *Napoleon's Last Will and Testament,* Paddington, 1977.

(Contributor) Peter Quennell, editor, *Vladimir Nabokov: A Tribute,* Weidenfeld & Nicolson, 1979.

Fire and Water: A Life of Peter the Great (biography), Coward, 1980.

The Life and Times of Grigorii Rasputin (biography), Coward, 1982.

Stalin and the Shaping of the Soviet Union, Morrow, 1986.

SIDELIGHTS: "Charles Baudelaire was a very good poet, whose life reads like that of a very bad poet," writes Anatole Broyard in a *New York Times* review of Alex de Jonge's *Baudelaire: Prince of Clouds.* Broyard continues: "The most irritating thing about [the book] is the author's habit of taking the poet at his own estimation of himself. Baudelaire's transparent bravado, his pathetic defensiveness, his delusions of grandeur, are rather like astonishingly naive rough drafts for his poetry." *Time* reviewer Melvin Maddocks observes: "The hand-tinted legend [of Baudelaire] has displaced the coruscating verse—a fault, says this terse, canny biography, of the poet himself. . . . It is hoped that Alex de Jonge's book will help dispel the poet's legend and resurrect his verse for a wider audience."

In *Fire and Water: A Life of Peter the Great,* his next biography, de Jonge turned to a heroic subject from his ancestral homeland, Russia. Peter the Great was a towering figure, and according to Richard Wortman in the *New York Times Book Review,* "For Mr. de Jonge, Peter is the almost mythical hero who embodies [the Russian] national spirit." Wortman praises the author's "chatty and effortless" style, which "draw[s] the reader into what seems less a biography than a cultivated conversation about Peter" and commends de Jonge's portrayal of Russian life, but found that the author "gives us a picture of how Peter looked and acted, but little sense of how Peter thought or felt. Most important, we do not understand the significance of his achievements—what made Peter great. . . . The result is to distort and even diminish Peter, despite the author's fascination with his subject."

De Jonge turned to another larger-than-life character from Russian history with *The Life and Times of Grigorii Rasputin.* Rasputin, a self-proclaimed monk and an "ex-horse thief . . . alcoholic and womanizer," according to *Time*'s Maddocks, acquired mesmeric power over Czar Nicholas and Czarina Alexandra after healing their son, the hemophiliac Prince Alexei. Rasputin's influence over the royal pair distressed the Russian people and played an integral role in the overthrow of the Romanov dynasty. He was killed in the early morning of December 17, 1916, after an epochal assassination attempt that included a failed cyanide poisoning, numerous bullet wounds, and, ultimately, drowning. Igor Vinogradoff, in the *Times Literary Supplement,* views de Jonge as an apologist for Rasputin, calling the biographer "anxious to believe in [Rasputin's] erstwhile simplicity, his true conversion, his sincerity and worthwhile policies," and adding, "De Jonge piles up damaging testimony yet is tireless in excuses, pitiless in rejecting hostile witnesses." "Biographers of Rasputin tend to take on the disorder of their subject," Maddocks remarks. "De Jonge is no exception, but he does the one essential thing—keeps his theories loose and rides the tiger where it takes him, in a deadly little circle."

De Jonge examined dictator Josef Stalin in his next book, *Stalin and the Shaping of the Soviet Union. Times Literary Supplement*'s John Keep notes that the author "does not try to assess the relative significance of Stalin's ideological appeal and his control of the Party apparatus, the sort of metaphysical question that academic historians like to puzzle over. Scorning such idle speculation, he explores . . . the mechanics of Stalin's personal secretariat and the so-called 'special sector,' his 'department of private intelligence and dirty tricks,' which developed into 'an extraordinary instrument for control . . . better by far than any more conspicuous Praetorian Guard.' " Keep calls the work "lively and authoritative," and concludes, "It does not radically change our picture of Stalin, but gains much from the use of dissidents' memoirs published in the West since his death." A negative assessment comes from Russian scholar Bruce Lincoln in the *Los Angeles Times,* who calls de Jonge's book "at best a superficial and unrevealing biography that draws mainly upon frequently studied and readily available sources. From de Jonge's account, we learn very little about Stalin's life and policies that has not already been told by others with greater accuracy and sensitivity." Peter Ackroyd, in the London *Times,* writes, "[T]his book has solid virtues, but, in the end, it cannot be said to be altogether satisfactory. De Jonge is the biographer as raconteur: this is not to say that he lacks scholarship but, rather, that he has decided to lend animation to otherwise familiar material by recounting journalistic 'stories' and repeating a few jokes. . . . De Jonge is an urbane and witty interpreter; but he is dealing here with a phenomenon that is neither civilized nor particularly amusing. So, on occasions, he hits a false note." The *New York Times Book Review*'s Anthony Austin finds *Stalin* a "sophisticated and chilling history."

BIOGRAPHICAL/CRITICAL SOURCES:

PERIODICALS

Choice, May, 1977.
Economist, October 9, 1976.
Los Angeles Times, March 25, 1986.
Los Angeles Times Book Review, July 16, 1989.
New York Times, February 18, 1977.
New York Times Book Review, June 29, 1980, p. 11; April 27, 1986, p. 23.
Time, February 14, 1977; May 24, 1982, p. 80.
Times (London), July 31, 1986.
Times Literary Supplement, October 24, 1980, p. 1182; January 14, 1983, p. 31.
Voice Literary Supplement, February, 1990.*

* * *

DEMOTES, Michael
See BURGESS, Michael (Roy)

* * *

DENDLE, Brian J(ohn) 1936-

PERSONAL: Born March 30, 1936, in Oxford, England; immigrated to United States, 1961, naturalized citizen, 1968; son of Frederick John and Alice Beatrice Dendle; divorced; children: Mark, Peter. *Education:* Oxford University, B.A., 1958, M.A., 1962; Princeton University, M.A., 1964, Ph.D., 1966.

Avocational Interests: Travel, reading, philosophy, regional history and literature of Murcia, Spain.

ADDRESSES: Office—Department of Spanish and Italian, University of Kentucky, Lexington, KY 40506.

CAREER: Kenyon College, Gambier, OH, instructor in French, 1961-63; Princeton University, Princeton, NJ, instructor in Spanish, 1966; University of Michigan, Ann Arbor, assistant professor of Spanish, 1966-69; University of Alabama, University, associate professor of Spanish, 1969-71; University of Kentucky, Lexington, associate professor, 1971-78, professor of Spanish, 1978—.

MEMBER: Asociacion Internacional de Galdosistas, International Institute of Spain, Modern Language Association of America, Academia Alfonso X el Sabio.

WRITINGS:

The Spanish Novel of Religious Thesis, 1876-1936, Castalia, 1968.
Galdos: The Mature Thought, University Press of Kentucky, 1980.
(Editor) Benito Perez Galdos, *Los articulos politicos en la Revista de Espana, 1871-1872* (title means "The Political Articles in the *Revista de Espana,* 1871-1872"), Dendle & Schraibman, 1982.
Galdos: The Early Historical Novels, University of Missouri Press, 1986.
Galdos y Murcia: Epistolario de Benito Perez Galdos y Alberto Seville Perez, Universidad de Murcia, 1987.
Galdos y "La Esfera," Universidad de Murcia, 1990.

Also author of annual critical bibliography of Spanish Romanticism in *The Romantic Movement,* 1966—. Contributor to journals, including *Studies in Romanticism, Hispanic Review, Anales Galdosianos,* and *Bulletin of Hispanic Studies.* Editor of *Romance Quarterly.*

WORK IN PROGRESS: Armando Palacio Valdes, Spain's Forgotten Novelist, publication expected in 1993.

SIDELIGHTS: Brian J. Dendle once told *CA* that his "research deals above all with interaction between history and fiction" and that his main field of research is Spain from 1800-1914.

* * *

DENZEL, Justin F(rancis) 1917-

PERSONAL: Born January 15, 1917, in Clifton, NJ; son of George and Alvina (Munzell) Denzel; married Josephine Ogazaly, 1947. *Education:* Attended College of Paterson, 1939; University of California, Los Angeles, 1940; and U.S. Army, Shrivenham, American University, England, 1945. *Politics:* Independent. *Religion:* Roman Catholic.

Avocational Interests: Natural history.

ADDRESSES: Home—73 Livingston St., Clifton, NJ 07013.

CAREER: Has worked as a field naturalist for American Museum of Natural History, New York City, sailed on oceanographic vessel, *Atlantis,* and collected marine life in

Alaska; also worked as scientific librarian with Hoffman La Roche in Nutley, NJ; full time writer. *Military service:* U.S. Army, 1941-45; became sergeant; received Purple Heart.

AWARDS, HONORS: New Jersey Institute of Technology Award, 1971, for *Genius with a Scalpel: Harvey Cushing,* 1973 and 1975, for *Jumbo: Giant Circus Elephant,* 1975, for *Black Kettle: King of the Wild Horses,* 1976, for *Wild Wing: Great Hunting Eagle,* 1977, for *Snowfoot: White Reindeer of the Arctic,* 1978, for *Scat: The Movie Cat,* and 1981, for *Sampson: Yankee Stallion;* New Jersey Association of Teachers of English award, 1972, for *Genius with a Scalpel: Harvey Cushing,* and 1973, for *Jumbo: Giant Circus Elephant; Wild Wing: Great Hunting Eagle* was chosen as a Children's Book of the Year by the Child Study Association of America, 1976; nominated for William Allen White award, 1990-91, for *Boy of the Painted Cave.*

WRITINGS:

JUVENILES, EXCEPT AS INDICATED

Adventure North (biography), Abelard, 1968.
Champion of Liberty (biography), Messner, 1969.
Genius with a Scalpel: Harvey Cushing (biography), Messner, 1971.
Jumbo: Giant Circus Elephant, illustrated by Richard Amundsen, Garrard, 1973.
Black Kettle: King of the Wild Horses, illustrated by Amundsen, Garrard, 1974.
Wild Wing: Great Hunting Eagle, illustrated by Herman B. Vestal, Garrard, 1975.
Snowfoot: White Reindeer of the Arctic, illustrated by Taylor Oughton, Garrard, 1976.
Scat: The Movie Cat, illustrated by Vestal, Garrard, 1977.
Sampson: Yankee Stallion, illustrated by William Hutchinson, Garrard, 1980.
Hiboy: Young Devil Horse, illustrated by Sam Savitt, Garrard, 1980.
Boy of the Painted Cave, Philomel Books, 1988.
Hunt for the Last Cat, Philomel Books, 1991.
Land of the Thundering Herds, Philomel Books, 1993.

OTHER

Contributor of more than one hundred short stories and articles to periodicals, including *Coronet, American Mercury, Frontiers, Twelve/Fifteen, Catholic Boy, Venture,* and *Snowy Egret.*

Boy of the Painted Cave has been translated into seven languages.

WORK IN PROGRESS: Land of the Sea Bear, a novel about the animals and birds of the Arctic.

SIDELIGHTS: Justin F. Denzel told *CA:* "As a boy I used to write long essays about nature, most of them imitations of William Beebe or some other popular naturalist of the day. Later, while living in Alaska, I began working on a little newspaper called the *Alaskan,* sponsored by the U.S. Forest Service. As a roving reporter, I toured the shores and back country writing stories about whales, bears, eagles and other wildlife, along with articles on Indians and Eskimos. Footloose and carefree, it was a life that any outdoor writer would envy.

"During World War II, I served in Europe as a tank gunner. At the same time I wrote combat stories for the 84th Infantry Division newspaper, the *Railsplitters,* occasionally landing in *Stars and Stripes.* I continued writing after the war. At that time there were dozens of denominational magazines aimed at teenagers, a wide open market for short stories. Plot was essential, with plenty of action. Sadly enough, most of those markets are gone now. But they served as an excellent training ground for young writers.

"Since then I have written everything from biographies to historicals and more recently a series of prehistoric adventure novels. The rewards of writing are many. There is great satisfaction and the joy of creation. But I think the best rewards of all are the hundreds of letters received from young readers, teachers and librarians, telling how much they liked the book, or how it helped them in their work and studies. And almost without exception they want to read a sequel. What more can a writer ask?"

* * *

Di CERTO, J(oseph) J(ohn) 1933-

PERSONAL: Born February 27, 1933, in New York, NY; son of Rocco (a barber) and Severina (Basile) Di Certo; married Josephine Valle, September 5, 1964; children: Lisa Ann, David, Jennifer Ann. *Education:* Hunter College of the City University of New York, B.A., 1968. *Politics:* Independent. *Religion:* Roman Catholic.

ADDRESSES: Home—1646 1st Ave., New York, NY 10028.

CAREER: Curtiss Wright Corp., Woodridge, NJ, senior technical writer, 1956-59; American Machine & Foundry, Greenwich, CT, technical writer and editor, 1959-62; Sperry Gyroscope, Great Neck, NY, publication engineer, 1962-66; Sylvania Electric Products, New York City, advertising supervisor, 1966-72; worked at Al Paul Lefton Co., Inc. (advertising agency), 1972-73; Marstella Advertising Agency, 1973-74; Sperry Rand Corp., New York City, manager of special projects, 1974-78; Columbia Broadcasting System, Inc., director of sales promotions,

CBS-TV stations, 1978-80, director of communications, CBS Cable, 1980-81, director of communications, CBS Broadcast International, 1981—. *Military service:* U.S. Air Force, 1952-56.

WRITINGS:

Planning and Preparing Data Flow Diagrams, Hayden, 1963.

Missile Base beneath the Sea, St. Martin's, 1967.

The Electric Wishing Well: The Energy Crisis, Macmillan, 1976.

From Earth to Infinity: A Guide to Space Travel, Messner, 1980.

Star Voyage, Messner, 1981.

Looking into T.V., Messner, 1983.

The Wall People (a novel), Atheneum, 1985.

The Pony Express: Hoofbeats in the Wilderness (for children), F. Watts, 1989.

Author of six audiovisual training programs published by Educational Activities; contributor to *Electronic Design.*

WORK IN PROGRESS: Mister, a suspense novel about the world of advanced computers; *The Dream and the Challenge,* an extensive volume on the era of the Pony Express.

* * *

DINTIMAN, George B(lough) 1936-

PERSONAL: Born October 4, 1936, in Hershey, PA; son of George B. (a businessman) and Gladys (Blough) Dintiman; married Elda Cabrera (president, International Translating Service), July 30, 1958; children: Brenda Jean, Lynne Rose, G. Brian. *Education:* Lock Haven State College, B.S., 1958; New York University, M.A., 1961; Columbia University, Ed.D., 1964.

ADDRESSES: Home—14150 Netherfield Dr., Midlothian, VA 23113. *Office*—Department of Physical Education, Virginia Commonwealth University, Richmond, VA 23284. *Agent*—Scott Meredith Literary Agency, Inc., 845 Third Ave., New York, NY 10022.

CAREER: South Williamsport High School, South Williamsport, PA, physical education teacher and coach, 1958-59; Inter-American University, San German, Puerto Rico, instructor, 1959-61, associate professor of physical education, 1961-65; Southern Connecticut State College, New Haven, associate professor of physical education, 1965-68; Virginia Commonwealth University, Richmond, professor of physical education, 1968-86, professor of health education, 1986—, chairman of department of physical education, 1985—. National Association of Speed and Explosion (NASE), NFL speed consultant, 1985—.

WRITINGS:

A Comprehensive Manual of Physical Education Activities for Men, Appleton-Century-Crofts, 1970.

Evaluation Manual in Health and Physical Education, Appleton-Century-Crofts, 1970.

Sprinting Speed: Its Improvement for Major Sports Competition, C. C. Thomas, 1971.

The Art and Science of Coaching, FI Productions, 1972.

What Research Tells the Coach about Sprinting, American Association for Health, Physical Education and Recreation, 1974.

How to Run Faster, Champion Athlete Publishing Co., 1979, published as *How to Run Faster: Step-by-Step Instructions on How to Improve Foot Speed,* Human Kinetics Publishers, 1984.

A Comprehensive Manual of Foundations and Activities for Men and Women, Burgess, 1979.

(With John Unitas) *Improving Health and Performance in the Athlete,* Prentice-Hall, 1979.

Health through Discovery, Addison-Wesley, 1980, 4th edition (with Jerrold S. Greenberg), Random House, 1989.

Teacher's Manual for Health through Discovery, Addison-Wesley, 1980.

Doctor Tennis: A Complete Book of Conditioning and Injury Prevention for Tennis, Champion Athlete Publishing Co., 1980.

(With Unitas) *The Athlete's Handbook,* Prentice-Hall, 1982.

Discovering Lifetime Fitness, West Publishing, 1984, 2nd edition, 1989.

Train America! Achieving Peak Performance and Fitness for Sports Competition, Kendall Hunt Publishing, 1988.

Sportspeed: The #1 Speed Improvement Book for All Athletes, Human Kinetics Publishers, 1988.

College Student Self-Care Diary, AAHPER, 1991.

Exploring Health: Expanding the Boundaries of Wellness, Prentice-Hall, 1992.

Exploring Fitness, Allyn & Bacon, 1994.

Also author, with Bob Ward and Larry Isaacs, of the videos *Speed and Explosion, Speed Improvement for Soccer,* and *Speed Improvement for Baseball.* Contributor of about one hundred articles on health, fitness, and prevention of heart disease to physical education journals.

* * *

DIVINE, Robert A(lexander) 1929-

PERSONAL: Born May 10, 1929, in Brooklyn, NY; son of Walter E. and Emily (Mable) Divine; married Barbara Christine Renick, August 6, 1955; children: John Douglas, Elisabeth Terry, Richard Lawrence, Kirk MacLennan. *Education:* Yale University, B.A., 1951, M.A., 1952, Ph.D., 1954. *Religion:* Methodist.

ADDRESSES: Home—2402 Rockingham Circle, Austin, TX 78704. *Office*—Department of History, University of Texas, Austin, TX 78712.

CAREER: University of Texas at Austin, instructor, 1954-57, assistant professor, 1957-61, associate professor, 1961-63, professor of history, 1963-81, George W. Littlefield Professor, 1981—, chair of department, 1963-68.

MEMBER: American Historical Association, Organization of American Historians, Society for Historians of American Foreign Relations.

AWARDS, HONORS: Center for Advanced Study in the Behavioral Sciences fellow in Stanford, CA, 1962-63.

WRITINGS:

American Immigration Policy, 1924-1952, Yale University Press, 1957.

(Editor) *American Foreign Policy,* Meridian, 1960.

The Illusion of Neutrality, University of Chicago Press, 1962.

The Reluctant Belligerent: American Entry into World War II, Wiley, 1965, 2nd edition, Random House, 1979.

Second Chance: The Triumph of Internationalism in America during World War II, Atheneum, 1967.

Roosevelt and World War II, Johns Hopkins Press, 1969.

(Editor and author of introduction) *The Cuban Missile Crisis,* Markus Wiener, 1970, 2nd edition, 1988.

Foreign Policy and U.S. Presidential Elections, two volumes, F. Watts, 1974.

Since 1945: Politics and Diplomacy in Recent American History, Wiley, 1975, 2nd edition published as *Since 1945: Politics and Foreign Policy in Recent American History,* Random House, 1979, 3rd edition, 1985.

Blowing on the Wind: The Nuclear Test Ban Debate, 1954-1960, Oxford University Press, 1978.

Eisenhower and the Cold War, Oxford University Press, 1981.

(Editor) *Exploring the Johnson Years,* University of Texas Press, 1981.

(Co-author) *America Past and Present,* Volume 1, Scott, Foresman, 1984, brief edition, 1985, 3rd edition, HarperCollins, 1991, Volume 2, Scott, Foresman, 1984, brief edition, 1985, 2nd edition, 1986.

The Johnson Years, Volume Two: Vietnam, the Environment, and Science, University Press of Kansas, 1987.

The Sputnik Challenge: Eisenhower's Response to the Soviet Satellite, Oxford University Press, 1993.

WORK IN PROGRESS: The Johnson Years, Volume Three: LBJ at Home and Abroad, for the University Press of Kansas.

SIDELIGHTS: Robert A. Divine, who *Times Literary Supplement* contributor D. C. Watt calls "one of the least 'schoolbound' of the American diplomatic historians," offers in *Eisenhower and the Cold War* a reassessment of the president long considered below average as a speaker, politician, and foreign policy executor. "Although it was often assumed that Ike was always out to lunch, or on the eighteenth tee, and let [Secretary of State John Foster] Dulles run the State Department as he pleased," writes Ronald Steel in the *New York Review of Books,* "Robert Divine in [this book] makes a good case for his argument that Eisenhower in fact used Dulles, and that the secretary of state served 'as the lightning rod, absorbing domestic criticism and warding off attacks from the right with his moralistic rhetoric.' "

Moreover, as Peter G. Boyle points out in the *Journal of American Studies,* "In this brief book of four chapters on aspects of Eisenhower's foreign policy, Divine not only portrays Eisenhower as fully in command, but portrays his foreign policy as for the most part as eminently successful as the world situation permitted." Ike was often criticized for his administration's handling of conflicts in Vietnam in 1954 and Lebanon in 1958, but notes Boyle: "Divine argues that Eisenhower astutely handled the crisis in these areas, skilfully and patiently consulting with adversaries in a manner which kept them slightly off guard and enabled Eisenhower to maintain peace and to protect America's interests."

Although he provides a revised, more positive image of the general who became president, as Watt observes, "Divine is no hagiographer seeking, as more illustrious American historians have sought, to rebuild his subject's reputation, in order to derive political advantage for some other cause in the here and now." The reviewer adds that despite some shortcomings "this is a fascinating and stimulating little book." *Best Sellers* reviewer James Doyle concurs, calling the book "informative, direct, organized, and comprehensible. It should become required reading in courses of Recent American History and Foreign Policy."

BIOGRAPHICAL/CRITICAL SOURCES:

PERIODICALS

Best Sellers, June, 1981.
Journal of American Studies, August, 1982.
New Republic, May 9, 1981.
New York Review of Books, September 24, 1981.
New York Times Book Review, June 28, 1981.
Times Literary Supplement, September 11, 1981.

DONKIN, Nance (Clare) 1915-

PERSONAL: Born in 1915 in West Maitland, New South Wales, Australia; daughter of Archie T. Pender and Clara Russell; married Victor Donkin, January 14, 1939; children: Nicola Williams, Richard Donkin.

ADDRESSES: Home—8/8 Mooltan Ave., Balaclava, Victoria 3183, Australia.

CAREER: Maitland Daily Mercury, Maitland, New South Wales, journalist, 1932-35; *Newcastle Morning Herald,* Newcastle, New South Wales, journalist, 1935-39; writer, 1946—. Broadcaster for Australian Broadcasting Commission (ABC) program, *Women's Session*; children's book reviewer for *Melbourne Herald,* 1970—; tutor for Council of Adult Education, c. 1975—. Children's Book Council, Victoria, president, 1968-75, vice-president, 1975-79.

MEMBER: Australian Society of Authors, Fellowship of Australian Writers, Women Writers Society, National Trust of Australian, Gallery Society of Victoria.

AWARDS, HONORS: Australian Arts Council travel grant, 1972, senior fellowship, 1980; A.M. (General Division of Order of Australia), 1986, for services to children's literature and adult education.

WRITINGS:

JUVENILE FICTION

Araluen Adventures, illustrated by Edith B. Bowden, Cheshire, 1946.
No Medals for Meg, Cheshire, 1947.
Julie Stands By, illustrated by Joan Turner, Cheshire, 1948.
Blue Ribbon Beth, Oxford University Press (Melbourne), 1948.
House by the Water, illustrated by Astra Lacis Dick, Angus & Robertson, 1969.
Johnny Neptune, Angus & Robertson, 1973.
A Friend for Petros, Hamish Hamilton, 1974.
Patchwork Grandmother, Hamish Hamilton, 1975, published as *Patchwork Mystery,* Beaver Books, 1978.
Green Christmas, Hamish Hamilton, 1976.
Yellowgum Gil, Hamish Hamilton, 1976.
The Maidens of Petka, Methuen, 1979.
Nini, Rigby Reading, 1979.
(Re-teller) Aeneas Gunn, *We of the Never Never,* Hutchinson, 1983.
Two at Sullivan Bay, Kangaroo Books, 1985.

OTHER

Sheep, illustrated by Jocelyn Jones, Oxford University Press, 1967.
Sugar, illustrated by Jones, Oxford University Press, 1967.
An Emancipist, illustrated by Jane Robinson, Oxford University Press, 1968.
A Currency Lass, illustrated by Jane Walker, Oxford University Press, 1969.
An Orphan, illustrated by Ann Culvenor, Oxford University Press, 1970.
(Contributor) *The Cool Man* (anthology), Angus & Robertson, 1973.
Margaret Catchpole, illustrated by Edwina Bell, Collins (Sydney), 1974.
(Contributor) *A Handful of Ghosts* (anthology), Hodder & Stoughton, 1976.
Best of the Bunch, Collins, 1978.
Stranger and Friend (adult), Dove Communications, 1983.
Blackout, Macmillan, 1987.
A Family Affair, illustrated by Lyn Sikiotis, Bookshelf, 1988.
The Women Were There, Collins Dove, 1988.
Always a Lady, Collins Dove, 1990.

SIDELIGHTS: Nance Donkin began her literary career as an adolescent when she contributed stories to her local newspaper. Her efforts led to jobs as women's editor for the *Maitland Daily Mercury* and, later, for the *Newcastle Morning Herald.*

After residing briefly in England, Donkin settled in Melbourne and worked as a freelancer for ABC (Australian Broadcasting Commission) in both radio and television. Her particular interest in Australian history and in migrant problems has provided themes for many books.

Donkin's *Green Christmas* concerns an English girl who takes time to adjust to a "hot picnicky Australian Christmas." *A Friend for Petros* and *Nini* are both concerned with Greek children in contemporary Australia, while *The Maidens of Petka* deals with an Australian family on a Greek island.

Stranger and Friend is an adult book which explores, according to Donkin, "the Greek-Australian experience." It was written after several long visits to Greece, including six months on the Island of Lesbos in 1980. Her *We of the Never Never* is a re-telling of the Australian classic of the same title by Aeneas Gunn, first published in 1908; this re-telling updates it for today's children. *Two at Sullivan Bay,* based on the first historical settlement in Victoria in 1803, shows the historical passion evident in her earlier books *Johnny Neptune, Margaret Catchpole,* and *Best of the Bunch.*

BIOGRAPHICAL/CRITICAL SOURCES:

PERIODICALS

Times Literary Supplement, April 16, 1970.

* * *

DORMAN, Luke
See BINGLEY, David Ernest

* * *

DORN, Edward (Merton) 1929-

PERSONAL: Born April 2, 1929, in Villa Grove, IL; son of William and Louise Abercrombie (Ponton) Dorn; married Jennifer Dunbar (a writer), 1969. *Education:* University of Illinois, Urbana, 1949-50; Black Mountain College, B.A., 1954.

ADDRESSES: Home—1035 Mapleton, Boulder, CO 80302. *Office*—Department of English, University of Colorado, Boulder, CO 80309.

CAREER: Idaho State University, Pocatello, lecturer, 1961-65; *Wild Dog,* Pocatello, co-editor, 1964-65; University of Essex, Colchester, England, Fulbright lecturer, 1965-67, visiting professor of English, 1967-68, 1974-75; University of Kansas, Lawrence, visiting professor, 1968-69; University of California, Riverside, regent's lecturer, 1973-74; University of California at San Diego, La Jolla, writer-in-residence, 1976; University of Colorado, Boulder, professor, 1977—.

AWARDS, HONORS: D. H. Lawrence fellow, 1969.

WRITINGS:

POETRY

The Newly Fallen, Totem Press, 1961.
Hands Up!, Totem Press, 1964.
From Gloucester Out, Matrix Press, 1964.
Idaho Out, Fulcrum Press, 1965.
Geography, Fulcrum Press, 1965.
The North Atlantic Turbine, Fulcrum Press, 1967.
Gunslinger, Black Sparrow Press, 1968.
Gunslinger: Book II, Black Sparrow Press, 1969.
The Midwest Is That Space Between the Buffalo Statler and the Lawrence Eldridge, T. Williams, 1969.
The Cosmology of Finding Your Spot, Cottonwood, 1969.
Twenty-four Love Songs, Frontier Press, 1969.
Gunslinger I & II, Fulcrum Press, 1970.
Songs: Set Two, a Short Count, Frontier Press, 1970.
Spectrum Breakdown: A Microbook, Athanor Books, 1971.
By the Sound, Frontier Press, 1971.
The Cycle, Frontier Press, 1971.
A Poem Called Alexander Hamilton, Tansy/Peg Leg Press, 1971.
The Hamadryas Baboon at the Lincoln Park Zoo, Wine Press, 1972.
Gunslinger, Book III: The Winterbook, Prologue to the Great Book IV Kornerstone, Frontier Press, 1972.
Recollections of Gran Apacheria, Turtle Island, 1974.
Slinger (contains *Gunslinger,* Books I-IV and *The Cycle*), Wingbow Press, 1975.
(With Jennifer Dunbar) *Manchester Square,* Permanent Press, 1975.
Collected Poems: 1956-1974, Four Seasons Foundation, 1975.
Hello, La Jolla, Wingbow Press, 1978.
Selected Poems, edited by Donald Allen, Grey Fox Press, 1978.
Abhorrences, Black Sparrow Press, 1989.

TRANSLATOR

(With Gordon Brotherston) *Our Word: Guerilla Poems From Latin America,* Grossman, 1968.
(With Brotherston) Jose Emilio Pacheco, *Tree Between Two Walls,* Black Sparrow Press, 1969.
Cesar Abraham Vallejo, *Selected Poems of Cesar Vallejo,* Penguin, 1976.

OTHER

What I See in the Maximum Poems, Migrant Press, 1960.
(With Michael Rumaker and Warren Tallman) *Prose 1,* Four Seasons Foundation, 1964.
The Rites of Passage: A Brief History, Frontier Press, 1965.
The Shoshoneans: The People of the Basin-Plateau, Morrow, 1966.
(Author of introduction) Daniel Drew, *The Book of Daniel Drew,* Frontier Press, 1969.
Some Business Recently Transacted in the White World (short stories), Frontier Press, 1971.

WORK IN PROGRESS: Way West: Essays.

SIDELIGHTS: Edward Dorn spent several years at Black Mountain College, a North Carolina school founded in 1933 as a liberal alternative for teachers and students seeking a creative educational environment. Breaking away from tradition, those affiliated with the school created art and literature that had a profound effect on American culture even after the college closed in 1956. Over the years numerous noteworthy artists and writers, including Dorn, Charles Olson, Robert Creeley, Allen Ginsberg, Denise Levertov, William Carlos Williams, and Gary Snyder, were associated with the college as teachers, students or contributors to Black Mountain publications.

Although poets who were involved with the college have often been grouped together as the "Black Mountain poets," Dorn told David Ossman in *The Sullen Art* that he has "been unable to find any similarity" among the writers associated with the school. Discussing his own inclusion in the group, Dorn added: "I think I'm rightly associated with the Black Mountain 'school,' not because of the way I write, but because I was there." Dorn once told *CA:* "I've always thought that the whole usage of 'Black Mountain Poets' only has an existence in the minds of the people who use it. I don't even know of such a thing myself . . . . I think Black Mountain as a school, irrespective of poets, denotes a certain value toward learning and the analysis of ideas. The perspective that I refer to as a school would refer to the whole school and its history and its conception and its principles and its various periods of authority and so forth—and not to poets, necessarily. I certainly believe that it was a school, in the old sense."

While at Black Mountain, Dorn was admittedly influenced by Charles Olson. Several critics have commented that Dorn's use of free verse and breath-determined rhythms is similar to Olson's: The *Virginia Quarterly Review* heralded him as "an experienced and accomplished poet who has absorbed Olson, Williams, and Pound and moved beyond them." Marjorie Perloff, however, suggested that other than some "thematic links, Dorn is really quite unlike Olson; he is, for that matter, quite unlike any poet writing today." Dorn explained: "The way I write is really in clots of phrase . . . . When the individual line ceases to have energy for me . . . I usually break the line there."

Dorn's most influential and highly acclaimed work was the four-volume epic poem, *Slinger,* which evolved from his earlier poem, "An Idle Visitation." Describing the first volume, *Gunslinger,* as "one of the fine poems of the decade," Charles Stein predicted that it was "the first part of what promises to be a major American narrative poem." Perloff later called the completed poem "one of the masterpieces of contemporary poetry."

Slinger is a fantasy about a demigod-cowboy, the poet-narrator, a madam of a saloon, and a talking horse named Claude Levi-Strauss, all of whom travel southwest America in search of Howard Hughes, a symbol of everything that can and has gone wrong with the modern world. Although Donald Wesling said that *Slinger* "tends to resist description," he observed that the poem "is 'about' how and why we spend money and words in this 'cosmological' place; about . . . surreal imagery, personifications, the texture of jokes, the paradoxical aspects of thinking . . . and about how a self or voice can be differentiated into a cluster of other selves."

In *Slinger,* Dorn cleverly mixes the jargon of junkies, Westerners, structuralists, and scientists to reflect the jumble of American speech. He intentionally frustrates the reader; syntax is ambiguous, punctuation is sparse, and puns, homonyms, and nonsense words become an integral part of conversation. Wesling declared that such frustration is "one of the pleasures of the poem when you finally discover the mechanism." Perloff pointed out that *Slinger's* collage of language "perfectly embodies Dorn's theme that nothing is what it seems to be."

This poem as well as many of Dorn's other writings are set in the western states. In fact, he has referred to himself as "a poet of the West—not by nativity but by orientation." William J. Lockwood speculated that "the southwestern landscape would seem to supply to his creative imagination those elements of brightness, clarity, and austerity that correspond to the forms of his own mind and appear as the distinctive qualities of the best of his early poems."

In some of Dorn's earlier poetry, critics have commented that his "prosy manner and chopped-up lines" detract from the ideas he presents. Martin Dodsworth noted that although Dorn tackles important themes in *The North Atlantic Turbine,* "I kept on getting the feeling that he could argue it all much better if he weren't trying to write poetry at the same time." A *Times Literary Supplement* critic echoed those sentiments in a review of *Geography,* suggesting that "Edward Dorn might do better to publish his fulminations against America . . . as prose."

Dorn's writing is almost always socially and politically oriented. From his earlier studies of Shoshoni Indians and the transients near Puget Sound to his reflections on the state of America in *Slinger,* Dorn's concern for his neighbors is evident in his work. Reviewer Peter Ackroyd argued, "Dorn has become the only plausible, political poet in America" because of "the quality of his response to public situations, not whether that response is 'right' or 'wrong.' " During the middle 1960s, Dorn moved to England and "his work for a time grew overtly political, that is, preachy," noted Bill Zavatsky in the *New York Time Book Review.* "His (perhaps temporary) need to slam his reader over the head with politics is unfortunate, for all of Dorn's work is inherently political, needing no soapbox."

When asked about his poetic critique of America for its imperialism, its carelessness with the environment, and its treatment of minorities, Dorn once remarked: "I take democracy very seriously, but on the other hand, it's a form of government that you have to change your mind about a lot because its form is protean, and its instinct, essentially, comes from a mob psychology. Unlike an adherent to a dogmatic position like Marxism, about which there is very little to change your mind, a democrat is liable to change his mind a lot. So none of these concerns and principles ever leave my mind much, but I vary my attitude according to the angles of perspective I'm able to get on them. Democracy literally has to be cracked on the head *all the time* to keep it in good condition. But all other forms are more or less sudden death."

A long-time teacher of writing, Dorn once told *CA* that rather than be taught to write, many students are able, instead, to be "provoked." "I wouldn't say someone *can't* be taught to write," Dorn explained, "although I'd be inclined to say it. So that's why I would prefer to say 'provoked,' because it doesn't involve that question. And I believe it completely. But of course that presupposes an intelligence that's provokable."

It is perhaps in the provocative union between poetry and political engagement that Dorn has most clearly made his mark. In Ackroyd's opinion, "Dorn's proper achievement has been to create single-handedly a language of public reference, and to have brought within the sphere of expressive language and poetic experience objects and feelings which had been, literally, *unimaginable* in those terms. It is in this context that he is one of the masters of our contemporary language."

For a previously published interview, see entry in *Contemporary Authors,* Volumes 93-96, Gale, 1980, pp. 128-29.

BIBLIOGRAPHICAL/CRITICAL SOURCES:

BOOKS

Allen, Donald, editor, *Interviews,* Four Seasons Foundation, 1979.
Allen, editor, *Views,* Four Seasons Foundation, 1980.
Duberman, Martin B., *Black Mountain: An Exploration in Community,* Doubleday, 1973.
Contemporary Literary Criticism, Volume 10, Gale, 1979.
Fredman, Steve, *Documents for New Poetry 1,* University of California, San Diego, 1978.
Ossman, David, *The Sullen Art,* Corinth Books, 1963.

PERIODICALS

Contemporary Literature, winter, 1978.
Hudson Review, winter, 1967-68.
Illustrated London News, May 6, 1967.
Listener, February 1, 1968.
Nation, May 12, 1969.
New Republic, April 24, 1976.
New Statesman, August 21, 1970.
New York Times Book Review, October 17, 1976.
Parnassus: Poetry in Review, spring-summer, 1977.
Poetry, March, 1969.
Spectator, January 10, 1975.
Times Literary Supplement, January 27, 1966.
Virginia Quarterly Review, summer, 1969; autumn, 1970.

DOUCET, Clive 1946-

PERSONAL: Born March 20, 1946, in London, England; Canadian citizen born abroad; son of Fernand Joseph (an economist) and Katherine Emma (a nurse; maiden name, Oliver) Doucet; married Patricia Steenberg, September 7, 1970; children: Julian, Emma. *Education:* University of Toronto, B.A., 1970; Universite de Montreal, M.Sc., 1971. *Politics:* "Voter." *Religion:* Quaker.

ADDRESSES: Home—38 Muriel St., Ottawa, Ontario, Canada K1S 4E1.

CAREER: Canadian Government, Ottawa, Ontario, senior information officer.

MEMBER: Playwrights Union of Canada, Ottawa Independent Writers (past president).

AWARDS, HONORS: First novel award nomination from *Books in Canada,* 1978, for *Disneyland, Please;* Canada Council B grant, 1979-80.

WRITINGS:

Hatching Eggs (two-act play), first produced in Ottawa, Ontario, at National Arts Centre, January 26, 1976.
A Very Desirable Residence (two-act play), first produced in Ottawa at Penguin Theatre, November 17, 1978.
Disneyland, Please (novel), Fitzhenry & Whiteside, 1978.
My Grandfather's Cape Breton (novel), McGraw-Hill Ryerson, 1980.
Before Star Wars (poetry), Black Moss Press, 1981.
May the Best Man Win (two-act play), first produced in Ottawa at Great Canadian Theatre Company, July 1, 1982.
John Coe's War (novel), McGraw-Hill Ryerson, 1983.
Ice Time (thirty-minute television drama), Canadian Broadcasting Corporation (CBC-TV), October, 1985.
The Gospel According to Mary Magdalene (novella), Black Moss Press, 1990.
The Priest's Boy (short stories), Black Moss Press, 1992.
The Debris of Planets (poems), Black Moss Press, 1993.

WORK IN PROGRESS: A trilogy composed of *See Alice Run, Notes for a Toast to the President of Mexico,* and *A Woman of the Hearth.*

SIDELIGHTS: Clive Doucet's novel *John Coe's War* tells of a young Toronto man whose life is irrevocably changed by his participation in World War II. A reticent youth ruled by his domineering mother, Coe matures into a well-liked, heroic officer whose combat fails to end with V-Day; for the next thirty-five years Doucet's protagonist struggles to define himself in a society where he doesn't quite fit. Reviewing the book for *Maclean's,* John Bemrose wrote that the novelist "has successfully created a complex and entertaining history of an innocent's war experiences and the effect of the conflict on the rest of his life," adding that Doucet "portrays [Coe's] confusion with refreshing candor." While the critic expressed major disappointment in the author's failure to exploit the "emotional potential" of some scenes, "gloss[ing] over them with his speedy, journalistic prose," Bemrose concluded: "Ultimately, in its colorful summary of a lifetime's events and in its evident passion for the struggle of an older generation, *John Coe's War* is a good book."

Doucet once told *CA:* "I write because it helps me make sense of the world." The author more recently added, "My writing career plods on as if God has hitched me to a plough and I must pull."

BIOGRAPHICAL/CRITICAL SOURCES:

PERIODICALS

Maclean's, August 29, 1983.

* * *

DOVE, Rita (Frances) 1952-

PERSONAL: Born August 28, 1952, in Akron, OH; daughter of Ray (a chemist) and Elvira (Hord) Dove; married Fred Viebahn (a writer); children: Aviva Chantal Tamu Dove-Viebahn. *Education:* Miami University, B.A. (summa cum laude), 1973; attended Universitaet Tuebingen, West Germany, 1974-75; University of Iowa, M.F.A., 1977.

ADDRESSES: Office—Department of English, University of Virginia, Charlottesville, VA, 22903.

CAREER: Arizona State University, Tempe, assistant professor, 1981-84, associate professor, 1984-87, professor of English, 1987-89; University of Virginia, Charlottesville, professor of English 1989—; United States Poet Laureate, 1993—. Writer-in-residence at Tuskegee Institute, 1982. National Endowment for the Arts, member of literature panel, 1984-86, chair of poetry grants panel, 1985. Commissioner, Schomburg Center for the Preservation of Black Culture, New York Public Library, 1987—.

MEMBER: PEN, Associated Writing Programs (member of board of directors, 1985-88; president, 1986-87), Academy of American Poets, Poetry Society of America, Poets and Writers, Phi Beta Kappa, Phi Kappa Phi.

AWARDS, HONORS: Fulbright fellow, 1974-75; grants from National Endowment for the Arts, 1978, and Ohio Arts Council, 1979; International Working Period for Authors fellow for West Germany, 1980; Portia Pittman fellow at Tuskegee Institute from National Endowment for the Humanities, 1982; John Simon Guggenheim fellow, 1983; Peter I. B. Lavan Younger Poets Award, Academy of American Poets, 1986; Pulitzer Prize in poetry, 1987, for *Thomas and Beulah;* General Electric Foundation Award for Younger Writers, 1987; Honorary Doctor of Letters, Miami University, 1988; Bellagio (Italy) residency, Rockefeller Foundation, 1988; Mellon fellow, National Humanities Center, North Carolina, 1988-89.

WRITINGS:

Ten Poems (chapbook), Penumbra Press, 1977.

The Only Dark Spot in the Sky (poetry chapbook), Porch Publications, 1980.

The Yellow House on the Corner (poems), Carnegie-Mellon University Press, 1980.

Mandolin (poetry chapbook), Ohio Review, 1982.

Museum (poems), Carnegie-Mellon University Press, 1983.

Fifth Sunday (short stories), Callaloo Fiction Series, 1985.

Thomas and Beulah (poems), Carnegie-Mellon University Press, 1986.

The Other Side of the House (poems), photographs by Tamarra Kaida, Pyracantha Press, 1988.

Grace Notes (poems), W. W. Norton & Company, Inc., 1989.

Through the Ivory Gate (novel), Pantheon Books, 1992.

Work represented in anthologies. Contributor of poems, stories, and essays to magazines, including *Agni Review, Antaeus, Georgia Review, Nation,* and *Poetry.* Member of editorial board, *National Forum,* 1984—; poetry editor, *Collaloo,* 1986—; advisory editor, *Gettysburg Review,* 1987—, and *TriQuarterly,* 1988—.

SIDELIGHTS: Black American writer Rita Dove has been described as a quiet leader, a poet who does not avoid race issues, but does not make them her central focus. As Dove herself explains in the *Washington Post:* "Obviously, as a black woman, I am concerned with race. . . . But certainly not every poem of mine mentions the fact of being black. They are poems about humanity, and sometimes humanity happens to be black. I cannot run from, I won't run from any kind of truth." As the first black poet laureate, Dove notes that, though it has less personal significance for her, "it is significant in terms of the message it sends about the diversity of our culture and our literature."

Dove is best known for her book of poems *Thomas and Beulah,* which garnered her the 1987 Pulitzer Prize in poetry. The poems in *Thomas and Beulah* are loosely based on the lives of Dove's maternal grandparents, and are arranged in two sequences: one devoted to Thomas, born in 1900 in Wartrace, Tennessee, and the other to Beulah, born in 1904 in Rockmart, Georgia. *Thomas and Beulah* is viewed as a departure from Dove's earlier works in both its accessibility and its chronological sequence that has, to use Dove's words, "the kind of sweep of a novel." On the book's cover is a snapshot of the author's grandparents, and *New York Review of Books* contributor Helen Vendler observes that "though the photograph, and the chronology of the lives of Thomas and Beulah appended to the sequence, might lead one to suspect that Dove is a poet of simple realism, this is far from the case. Dove has learned . . . how to make a biographical fact the buried base of an imagined edifice."

In the *Washington Post,* Dove describes the poems this way: "The poems are about industrialization, discrimination sometimes—and sometimes not—love and babies—everything. It's not a dramatic story—nothing absolutely tragic happened in my grandparents' life. . . . But I think these are the people who often are ignored and lost." Peter Stitt expresses a similar view in the *Georgia Review:* "The very absence of high drama may be what makes the poems so touching—these are ordinary people with ordinary struggles, successes, and failures." He concludes: "There is a powerful sense of community, residing both in a family and in a place, lying at the heart of this book, and it is this that provides a locus to the poems. Rita Dove has taken a significant step forward in each of her three books of poems; she must be recognized as among the best young poets in the country today."

The poems in *Grace Notes,* Dove's fourth book, are largely autobiographical. Alfred Corn remarks in *Poetry* that "glimpses offered in this collection of middle-class Black life have spark and freshness to them inasmuch as this social category hasn't had poetic coverage up to now." In *Parnassus,* Helen Vendler describes Dove's poems as "rarely without drama," adding, "I admire Dove's persistent probes into ordinary language of the black proletariat." Jan Clausen notes in *The Women's Review of Books* that Dove's "images are elegant mechanisms for capturing moods and moments which defy analysis or translation." In the *Washington Post Book World,* A. L. Nielsen finds that the poems "abound in the unforgettable details of family character" and adds that Dove "is one of those rare poets who approach common experience with the same sincerity with which the objectivist poets of an earlier generation approached the things of our world."

A later work, the novel *Through the Ivory Gate,* tells the story of Virginia King, a gifted young black woman who takes a position as artist in residence at an elementary school in her hometown of Akron, Ohio. The story alternates between past and present as Virginia's return stirs up strong, sometimes painful memories of her childhood. Barbara Hoffert observes in the *Library Journal* that the "images are indelible, the emotions always heartfelt and fresh," and in the *New York Times Book Review,* Geoff Ryman notes: "*Through the Ivory Gate* is mature in its telling of little stories—Virginia's recollections of life with a troupe of puppeteers, of visiting the rubber factory where her father worked, of neighborhood boys daubing a house so that it looked as if it had measles." He concludes: "The book aims to present the richness of a life and its connections to family and friends, culture, place, seasons, and self. In this it succeeds."

BIOGRAPHICAL/CRITICAL SOURCES:

PERIODICALS

American Book Review, July, 1985.
American Poetry Review, January, 1982.
Callaloo, winter, 1986.
Detroit Free Press, July 24, 1993, pp. 5A, 7A.
Georgia Review, summer, 1984; winter, 1986.
Library Journal, August, 1992.
New York Review of Books, October 23, 1986.
New York Times Book Review, October 11, 1992.
North American Review, March, 1986.
Parnassus: Poetry in Review, Volume 16, number 2, 1991.
Poetry, October, 1984; October, 1990.
Publishers Weekly, August 3, 1992.
Washington Post, April 17, 1987; May 19, 1993.
Washington Post Book World, April 8, 1990.
Women's Review of Books, July, 1990.*

* * *

DOWN, Michael (Graham) 1951-

PERSONAL: Born March 25, 1951, in Wimbledon, England; son of Frederick James (a civil servant) and Vera Emily (a homemaker; maiden name, Garnham) Down; married Margaret Elizabeth Grundy (a homemaker), October 18, 1975; children, James, Geoffrey. *Education:* Nottingham University, B.Sc., 1972, Ph.D., 1975.

ADDRESSES: *Home*—Southlands, Sandy Lane, Goostrey, Cheshire, CW4 8NT England. *Office*—National Nuclear Corp., Booths Hall, Knutsford, Cheshire, England.

CAREER: Nottingham University, Nottingham, England, research fellow in inorganic chemistry, 1975-77; Westinghouse Electric Corp., Pittsburgh, PA, manager of materials and plasma research, 1978-85; National Nuclear Corp., Knutsford, England, general manager of energy and environmental division, 1985—. Holder of six U. S. patents.

MEMBER: American Chemical Society, Cricket Society.

WRITINGS:

Archie: A Biography of A. C. MacLaren, Allen & Unwin, 1981.

Is It Cricket?: Power, Money, and Politics in Cricket Since 1945, Queen Anne Press, 1985.

(With Professor G. D. West) *Sketches at Lord's: The Cricket Lithographs of J. C. Anderson,* Collins, 1991.

(With G. A. Gooch) *For Essex and England: The Story of Graham Gooch's Century of Centuries,* Boundary Books, 1993.

Also author of more than thirty scientific papers.

SIDELIGHTS: Michael Down's *Archie: A Biography of A. C. MacLaren* presents the life of one of England's greatest cricketers. A player during cricket's "golden age" (surrounding the turn of the century), MacLaren also served as England's captain in the English-Australian test match series of 1902, considered one of the finest ever played. Reviewing the book for the *Times Literary Supplement,* John Lucas wrote that "Down, . . . MacLaren's first biographer, has done his homework well" on his "fascinating" subject. The critic also commended the author for including "some of the contradictions in [MacLaren's] character . . . usefully fill[ing] out the legend."

Down's second book, *Is It Cricket?: Power, Money, and Politics in Cricket Since 1945,* is a "social history of first-class cricket over the last forty years," wrote A. L. Le Quesne of the *Times Literary Supplement.* Down cites historical and societal factors as being responsible for the changes in the game of cricket, noted Le Quesne, who concluded that the book "successfully opens up new and very interesting territory, and can be strongly recommended."

Down told *CA:* "After university in England I was recruited by Westinghouse to manage their liquid metal and plasma research activities. After seven years I returned to England to live and work, and am now General Manager of NNC Ltd., a subsidiary of GEC. The study of cricket history is a spare time occupation that has now resulted in three successful volumes. I have also founded a cricket book publishing company, Boundary Books, which specialises in deluxe limited editions."

BIOGRAPHICAL/CRITICAL SOURCES:

PERIODICALS

Times Literary Supplement, June 26, 1981; November 15, 1985.

* * *

DRAKE, W. Anders
See ESHBACH, Lloyd Arthur

* * *

DRINKROW, John
See HARDWICK, (John) Michael (Drinkrow)

DUKES, Philip
See BICKERS, Richard (Leslie) Townshend

* * *

DUNNING, Robert William 1938-

PERSONAL: Born March 16, 1938, in East Coker, England; son of William T. H. (a farmer) and Constance Williams Dunning; married Anne Moyle, October 19, 1968; children: Jeremy P. S., Christianne L. *Education:* University of Bristol, B.A., 1959, Ph.D., 1962; University of Exeter, certificate in education, 1960. *Religion:* Anglican.

Avocational Interests: Travel (especially France and the United States).

ADDRESSES: Home—Musgrove Manor East, Barton Close, Taunton, Somerset TA1 4RU, England. *Office*—Somerset County Council, County Hall, Taunton, Somerset, England.

CAREER: History of Parliament Trust, London, England, researcher, 1962-64; Victoria County Histories, London, senior assistant to the general editor, 1964-67; *Victoria History of Somerset,* Taunton, England, county editor, 1967—.

MEMBER: Royal Historical Society, Ecclesiastical History Society, Society of Antiquaries (London), Somerset Archaeological Society, Somerset Record Society (honorary general editor, 1970—).

WRITINGS:

(Editor) *Hylle Cartulary,* Somerset Record Society, 1968.

(Editor with T. D. Tremlett and T. B. Dilks) *Bridgwater Borough Archives: 1468-1485,* Somerset Record Society, 1971.

Local Sources for the Young Historian, Muller, 1973, revised edition published as *Local History for Beginners,* Phillimore & Co., 1980.

(Editor) *Victoria History of Somerset,* Oxford University Press, Volume 3, 1974, Volume 4, 1978, Volume 5, 1985, Volume 6, 1992.

(Author of introduction) William Hale, editor, *A Series of Precedents and Proceedings in Criminal Causes,* Bratton, 1974.

(Editor and contributor) *Christianity in Somerset,* Somerset County Council, 1976.

(Editor with David Bromwich) *Victorian and Edwardian Somerset in Photographs,* Batsford, 1977.

A History of Somerset, Somerset County Council, 1978, 1987.

Somerset and Avon, Bartholomew, 1980, reprinted, Sutton, 1992.

(Author of introduction) C. Greenwood and J. Greenwood, *Somerset Delineated,* Sutton, 1980.

(Contributor) L. S. Winchester, editor, *Wens Cathedral,* Open Books, 1982.

A History of Somerset, Phillimore & Co., 1983.

The Monmouth Rebellion, Dovecote Press, 1984.

(Contributor) C. M. Barron and C. Harper-Bill, editors, *The Church in Pre-Reformation Society,* Boydell Press, 1985.

Somerset in Domesday, Somerset County Council, 1986.

Arthur, The King in the West, Sutton, 1988.

Some Somerset Country Houses, Dovecote Press, 1991.

(With John Bickersteth) *Clerks of the Closet in the Royal Household,* Sutton, 1991.

Bridgwater, History & Guide, Sutton, 1992.

Also editor, with J. B. Harley, of *Two Maps of Somerset, 1782 and 1822,* Somerset Record Society. Contributor to *Bulletin of the Institute for Historical Research, Proceedings of the Somerset Archaeological Society, Studies in Church History, Archives, Bulletin of the Board of Celtic Studies,* and *Transactions of the Ancient Monument Society.*

WORK IN PROGRESS: Editing *Victoria History of Somerset,* Volume 7. *Fifty Somerset Churches;* A history of the Reformation in southwest England.

SIDELIGHTS: Robert William Dunning once told *CA:* "Full-time research/writing Somerset's history is the serious, academic business. No less serious is interpreting the English countryside and its history for residents and visitors alike. The language has to be clear and simple, more of a challenge since the writer cannot retreat into technical and abstruse terms. And the information has to be accurate. People on the whole expect history to be dull and boring. How satisfactory when readers say they actually enjoy the work and only wish they had been taught history like that in school!"

* * *

DURAND, G. Forbes
See BURGESS, Michael (Roy)

E

ECKARDT, A(rthur) Roy 1918-

PERSONAL: Born August 8, 1918, in Brooklyn, NY; son of Frederick William (an electrician) and Anna (Fitts) Eckardt; married Alice Lyons (a writer and professor), September 2, 1944; children: Paula Jean Eckardt Strock, Stephen Robert. *Education:* Brooklyn College (now of the City University of New York), B.A., 1942; Yale University, M.Div., 1944; Columbia University, Ph.D., 1947. *Politics:* Democrat.

ADDRESSES: *Home*—6011 Beverly Hill Rd., Coopersburg, PA 18036. *Office*—Department of Religion Studies, Maginnes Hall, Lehigh University, Bethlehem, PA 18015.

CAREER: Clergyman of United Methodist Church; Hamline University, St. Paul, MN, assistant professor of philosophy and religion, 1946-47; Lawrence College, Appleton, WI, assistant professor of religion, 1947-50; Duke University, Durham, NC, assistant professor of religion, 1950-51; Lehigh University, Bethlehem, PA, associate professor, 1951-56, professor of religion, beginning 1956, head of department, 1951-80, professor emeritus, 1980—. City University of New York, visiting professor of Jewish studies, 1973; Oxford Centre for Post-Graduate Hebrew Studies, visiting scholar, 1982-88, Maxwell fellow, 1989-90, senior associate fellow, 1990—. Member of board of directors, National Committee on American Foreign Policy; member of international committee, Institute for Contemporary Jewry, Hebrew University of Jerusalem. Special advisor, United States Holocaust Memorial Commission.

MEMBER: American Academy of Religion (president, 1956), Phi Beta Kappa, Pi Gamma Mu.

AWARDS, HONORS: Ford Foundation fellow, Harvard University, 1955-56; Distinguished Alumnus Award, Brooklyn College, 1963; Lilly Foundation fellow, Cambridge University, 1963-64; National Foundation for Jewish Culture fellow, 1968-69; L.H.D., Hebrew Union College—Jewish Institute of Religion, 1969; (with wife, Alice L. Eckardt) Human Relations Award, American Jewish Committee of Philadelphia, 1971; (with A. L. Eckardt) Myrtle Wreath Achievement Award, Hadassah, Allentown, PA chapter, 1971, eastern Pennsylvania chapter, 1975, south New Jersey chapter, 1979; Rockefeller fellow, University of Tuebingen, 1975-76; Jabotinsky Centennial Medal, 1980.

WRITINGS:

Christianity and the Children of Israel, Kings Crown Press, 1948.

The Surge of Piety in America, Association Press, 1958.

Elder and Younger Brothers: The Encounter of Jews and Christians, Scribner, 1967.

(Editor) *The Theologian at Work,* Harper, 1968.

(With wife, Alice L. Eckardt) *Encounter with Israel: A Challenge to Conscience,* Association Press, 1970.

Your People, My People, Quadrangle, 1974.

(With A. L. Eckardt) *Long Night's Journey into Day: Life and Faith after the Holocaust,* Wayne State University Press, 1982, revised and enlarged edition published as *Long Night's Journey into Day: A Revised Retrospective on the Holocaust,* 1988.

Jews and Christians, Indiana University Press, 1986.

For Righteousness' Sake, Indiana University Press, 1987.

Black-Woman-Jew, Indiana University Press, 1989.

Reclaiming the Jesus of History: Christology Today, Fortress, 1992.

Sitting in the Earth and Laughing: A Handbook of Humor, Transaction Publishers, 1992.

Collecting Myself: A Writer's Retrospective, edited by A. L. Eckardt, Scholars Press, 1993.

OTHER

Also editor of *Christianity in Israel* (booklet), American Academic Association for Peace in the Middle East, 1971, and *Journal of the American Academy of Religion,* 1961-69. Contributor to *The Christian Century Reader,* edited by Harold E. Fey and Margaret Frakes, Association Press, 1962; *Ecumenical Theology Today,* edited by Gregory Baum, Paulist Press, 1964; *Jews and Christians,* edited by George A. F. Knight, Westminster, 1965; *Christian Mission in Theological Perspective,* edited by Gerald H. Anderson, Abingdon, 1967; *The Anatomy of Peace in the Middle East,* American Academic Association for Peace in the Middle East, 1969; *Jewish-Christian Relations in Today's World,* edited by James E. Wood, Jr., Baylor University Press, 1971; *Punishment,* edited by Harold Hart, Hart Publishing, 1972; *Confronting the Holocaust,* edited by Alvin H. Rosenfeld and Irving Greenberg, Indiana University Press, 1978; *The Future of Jewish-Christian Relations,* edited by Norma H. Thompson and Bruce K. Cole, Character Research, 1982; and *Christianity and Judaism,* edited by Richard W. Rousseau, Ridge Row Press, 1983. Also contributor with A. L. Eckardt to the *Annals of the American Academy of Political and Social Science,* 1981. Contributor to more than fifteen scholarly journals.

SIDELIGHTS: A. Roy Eckardt once told *CA:* "Reinhold Niebuhr has had a profound influence on my thought and theological viewpoint. He brought together an understanding of human nature in the individual and society with a keen perception of how political and social institutions must be devised to protect and foster both."

BIOGRAPHICAL/CRITICAL SOURCES:

BOOKS

Davies, Alan, *Anti-Semitism and the Christian Mind,* Herder & Herder, 1964.

Talmage, Frank E., *Disputation and Dialogue,* Ktav, 1975.

PERIODICALS

Christian Century, April 24, 1968; March 10, 1971.

Commentary, June, 1968.

New York Times Book Review, April 7, 1968.

Western Humanities Review, summer, 1968.

* * *

ECKARDT, Alice L(yons) 1923-

PERSONAL: Born April 27, 1923, in Brooklyn, NY; daughter of Henry Egmont (an executive) and Almira Blake (Palmer) Lyons; married A. Roy Eckardt (a professor and writer), September 2, 1944; children: Paula Jean Eckardt Strock, Stephen Robert. *Education:* Oberlin College, B.A., 1944; Lehigh University, M.A., 1966. *Politics:* Democrat. *Religion:* Protestant.

Avocational Interests: British history, English churches, brass rubbing, birds, wildflowers, gardening, photography.

ADDRESSES: Home—6011 Beverly Hill Rd., Coopersburg, PA 18036. *Office*—Department of Religion Studies, Maginnes Hall, Lehigh University, Bethlehem, PA 18015.

CAREER: Lehigh University, Department of Religion Studies, Bethlehem, PA, lecturer, 1972-75, assistant professor, 1976-85, associate professor, 1985-87, professor emerita, 1987—, Jewish Studies Program, co-founder and co-director, 1976-85, Berman Center for Jewish Studies, member of academic advisory board, 1985-89; City University of New York, visiting lecturer, 1973; Cedar Crest College, adjunct professor, 1982-83; Muhlenberg College, exchange professor, 1984, Institute for Jewish-Christian Understanding, member of board of directors, 1989—; Oxford Centre for Post-Graduate Hebrew Studies, visiting scholar, 1982, 1985, Maxwell fellow, 1989-90, senior associate fellow, 1990—. Special consultant, President Carter's Commission on the Holocaust, 1979; special advisor, United States Holocaust Memorial Council, 1981-86. Consultant to various projects dealing with Jewish studies and the Holocaust.

MEMBER: American Academy of Religion, American Professors for Peace in the Middle East, National Christian Leadership Conference for Israel (member of national board), Lehigh University Women's Club (president, 1960-61), Wednesday Club.

AWARDS, HONORS: (With husband, A. Roy Eckardt) Human Relations Award of American Jewish Committee of Philadelphia, 1971; (with A. R. Eckardt) Myrtle Wreath Achievement award, Hadassah, Allentown, PA chapter, 1971, eastern Pennsylvania chapter, 1975, south New Jersey chapter, 1979; Eternal Flame award, Anne Frank Institute, 1987; Righteous Person Award, Temple Beth El, 1987; Humanitarian Award, B'nai B'rith, Allentown, PA chapter, 1989.

WRITINGS:

(With husband, A. Roy Eckardt; and illustrator) *Encounter with Israel: A Challenge to Conscience,* Association Press, 1970.

(With A. R. Eckardt) *Long Night's Journey into Day: Life and Faith after the Holocaust,* Wayne State University Press, 1982, revised and enlarged edition published as *Long Night's Journey into Day: A Revised Retrospective on the Holocaust,* 1988.

(Editor and contributor) *Jerusalem: City of the Ages,* University Press of America, 1984.

(Editor) *Burning Memory: Times of Testing and Reckoning,* Pergamon, 1993.

(Editor) *Collecting Myself: A Writer's Retrospective,* by A. R. Eckardt, Scholars Press, 1993.

OTHER

Also author of foreword, *Too Young to Remember,* by Julie Heifetz, Wayne State University Press, 1989. Contributor to *Christians Confront the Holocaust,* edited by Donald McEvoy, National Conference of Christians and Jews, 1980; *Human Responses to the Holocaust,* edited by Michael A. Ryan, Edwin Mellen, 1981; *Issues in Teaching the Holocaust: A Guide,* Yeshiva University, 1981; *The Future of Jewish-Christian Relations,* edited by Norma H. Thompson and Bruce K. Cole, Character Research, 1982; *Toward the Understanding of Genocide,* edited by Israel Charney, Westview, 1984; *More Stepping Stones to Jewish-Christian Relations,* edited by Helga Croner, Paulist Press, 1985; *Liturgies on the Holocaust,* edited by Marcia Sachs Littell, Edwin Mellen, 1986; *Faith and Freedom,* edited by Richard Libowitz, Pergamon Press, 1987; (and member of editorial advisory board) *Remembering for the Future,* Pergamon Press, 1989; *Contemporary Responses to the Holocaust,* edited by Steven L. Jacobs, University of Alabama Press, 1990. Also contributor with A. R. Eckardt to the *Annals of the American Academy of Political and Social Science,* 1981. Contributor to *Christian Century, Midstream, Shoah, Judaism, Journal of the American Academy of Religion, Journal of Ecumenical Studies, Evangelische Theologie, Holocaust and Genocide Studies, Shofar,* and other periodicals.

SIDELIGHTS: Alice L. Eckardt once told *CA:* "Nothing is more true than the familiar observation that the most important aspect of writing is the application of the seat of the pants to the seat of the chair. But even once so situated, one can still engage in procrastination, for example, filling out forms for *Contemporary Authors.* Real engagement with a subject is the best antidote, and then one can lose track of time and other responsibilities totally. The next problem to overcome is an infatuation with the sound of one's own words and phrases in order to be able to delete, reorder, and otherwise revise for the ultimate good of the finished product."

BIOGRAPHICAL/CRITICAL SOURCES:

BOOKS

Talmage, Frank E., *Disputation and Dialogue,* Ktav, 1975.

PERIODICALS

Christian Century, March 10, 1971.

EKWENSI, C. O. D.

See EKWENSI, Cyprian (Odiatu Duaka)

* * *

EKWENSI, Cyprian (Odiatu Duaka) 1921-
(C. O. D. Ekwensi)

PERSONAL: Born September 26, 1921, in Minna, Nigeria; son of Ogbuefi David Duaka and Uso Agnes Ekwensi; married Eunice Anyiwo; children: five. *Education:* Attended Achimota College, Ghana, and Ibadan University; received B.A.; further study at Chelsea School of Pharmacy, London, and University of Iowa.

Avocational Interests: Hunting game, swimming, photography, motoring, weightlifting.

ADDRESSES: Home—12 Hillview, Independence Layout, P.O. Box 317, Enugu, Nigeria.

CAREER: Novelist and writer of short stories and stories for children. Igbodi College, Lagos, Nigeria, lecturer in biology, chemistry, and English, 1947-49; School of Pharmacy, Lagos, lecturer in pharmacognosy and pharmaceutics, 1949-56; pharmacist superintendent for Nigerian Medical Services, 1956-57; head of features, Nigerian Broadcasting Corporation, 1957-61; Federal Ministry of Information, Lagos, director of information, 1961-66; chairman of Bureau for External Publicity during Biafran secession, 1967-69, and director of an independent Biafran radio station; chemist for plastics firm in Enugu, Nigeria; managing director of Star Printing & Publishing Co. (publishers of *Daily Star*), 1975-79; managing director of Niger Eagle Publishing Company, 1980-81. Owner of East Niger Chemists and East Niger Trading Company. Chairman of East Central State Library Board, 1972-75. Newspaper consultant to *Weekly Trumpet* and *Daily News* of Anambra State and to *Weekly Eagle* of Imo State, 1980-83; consultant on information to the executive office of the president; consultant to Federal Ministry of Information; public relations consultant.

MEMBER: PEN, Society of Nigerian Authors, Pharmaceutical Society of Great Britain, Institute of Public Relations (London), Institute of Public Relations (Nigeria; fellow).

AWARDS, HONORS: Dag Hammarskjold International Prize for Literary Merit, 1969.

WRITINGS:

NOVELS

People of the City, Andrew Dakers, 1954, Northwestern University Press, 1967, revised edition, Fawcett, 1969.

Jagua Nana, Hutchinson, 1961.

Burning Grass, Heinemann, 1962.
Beautiful Feathers, Hutchinson, 1963.
Divided We Stand, Fourth Dimension Publishers, 1980.

JUVENILE

(Under name C. O. D. Ekwensi) *Ikolo the Wrestler and Other Ibo Tales,* Thomas Nelson, 1947.
(Under name C. O. D. Ekwensi) *The Leopard's Claw,* Thomas Nelson, 1950.
The Drummer Boy, Cambridge University Press, 1960.
The Passport of Mallam Ilia, Cambridge University Press, 1960.
An African Night's Entertainment (folklore), African Universities Press, 1962.
Yaba Roundabout Murder (short novel), Tortoise Series Books (Lagos, Nigeria), 1962.
The Great Elephant-Bird, Thomas Nelson, 1965.
Juju Rock, African Universities Press, 1966.
The Boa Suitor, Thomas Nelson, 1966.
Trouble in Form Six, Cambridge University Press, 1966.
Coal Camp Boy, Longman, 1971.
Samankwe in the Strange Forest, Longman, 1973.
The Rainbow Tinted Scarf and Other Stories (collection), Evans Africa Library, 1975.
Samankwe and the Highway Robbers, Evans Africa Library, 1975.
Masquerade Time, Heinemann Educational Books, 1992.
King Forever!, Heinemann Educational Books, 1992.

OTHER

(Under name C. O. D. Ekwensi) *When Love Whispers* (novella), Tabansi Bookshop (Onitsha, Nigeria), 1947.
The Rainmaker and Other Short Stories (short story collection), African Universities Press, 1965.
Lokotown and Other Stories (short story collection), Heinemann, 1966.
Iska, Hutchinson, 1966.
The Restless City and Christmas Gold, Heinemann, 1975.
Survive the Peace, Heinemann, 1976.
(Editor) *Festac Anthology of Nigerian Writing,* Festac, 1977.
Motherless Baby (novella), Fourth Dimension Publishers, 1980.
For a Roll of Parchment, Heinemann, 1987.
Jagua Nana's Daughter, Spectrum, 1987.

Also author of *Behind the Convent Wall,* 1987. Writer of plays and scripts for BBC radio and television, Radio Nigeria, and other communication outlets. Contributor of stories, articles, and reviews to magazines and newspapers in Nigeria and England, including *West African Review, London Times, Black Orpheus, Flamingo,* and *Sunday Post.* Several of Ekwensi's novels have been translated into other languages, including Russian, Italian, German, Serbo-Croatian, Danish, and French. His novellas have been used primarily in schools as supplementary readers.

SIDELIGHTS: "Cyprian Ekwensi is the earliest and most prolific of the socially realistic Nigerian novelists," according to Martin Tucker in his *Africa in Modern Literature: A Survey of Contemporary Writing in English.* "His first writings were mythological fragments and folk tales. From these African materials he turned to the city and its urban problems, which he now feels are the major issues confronting his people." Reviewing Cyprian Ekwensi's *Beautiful Feathers* in *Critique: Studies in Modern Fiction,* John F. Povey writes: "The very practice of writing, the developing professionalism of his work, makes us find in Ekwensi a new and perhaps important phenomenon in African writing. . . . Other Nigerian novelists have sought their material from the past, the history of missionaries and British administration as in Chinau Achebe's books, the schoolboy memoirs of Onuora Nzekwu, Ekwensi faces the difficult task of catching the present tone of Africa, changing at a speed that frighteningly destroys the old certainties. In describing this world, Ekwensi has gradually become a significant writer."

Ekwensi states that his life in government and quasi-government organizations like the Nigerian Broadcasting Corporation has prevented him from expressing any strong political opinions, but adds, "I am as much a nationalist as the heckler standing on the soap-box, with the added advantage of objectivity." During the late 1960s Biafran war, during which the eastern region of Biafra seceded temporarily from the rest of Nigeria, Ekwensi visited the United States more than once to help raise money for Biafra and to purchase radio equipment for the independent Biafran radio station of which he was director. He has also traveled in western Europe.

J. O. J. Nwachukwu-Agbada, in *World Literature Today,* describes Ekwensi as the "Nigerian Defoe:" "Ekwensi has been writing fiction since the 1940s. He is prolific and versatile, especially in the subject matter of his works, which can range from sex to science. . . . The 'new' work [*For a Roll of Parchment*] also reveals considerable artistic development, particularly in language and descriptive power."

In a later edition of *World Literature Today,* Nwachukwu-Agbada talks of "Cyprian Edkwensi's Rabelaisian jeu d'esprit whose obscene flavor sparked considerable outrage among Nigerian readers of the sixties [upon the release of *Jagua Nana* in 1961]. The new novel's [*Jagua Nana's Daughter*] bawdiness twenty-five years later has not attracted similar attention, probably due to the increased permissiveness and decreased influence of tradition in modern-day Nigeria."

BIOGRAPHICAL/CRITICAL SOURCES:

BOOKS

Contemporary Literary Criticism, Volume 4, Gale, 1975.

Emenyonu, Ernest N., *The Essential Ekwensi: A Literary Celebration of Cyprian Ekwensi's Sixty-Fifth Birthday,* Heinemann, 1987.

Tucker, Martin, *Africa in Modern Literature: A Survey of Contemporary Writing in English,* Ungar, 1967.

PERIODICALS

Books Abroad, autumn, 1967.

Critique: Studies in Modern Fiction, October, 1965.

Times Literary Supplement, June 4, 1964.

World Literature Today, autumn, 1988; winter, 1989.*

* * *

ELDRIDGE, Marian (Favel Clair) 1936-

PERSONAL: Born February 1, 1936, in Melbourne, Australia; daughter of Brian Arnold (a farmer) and Gwendoline May Favel (a housewife and farmer; maiden name, Stott) Stockfeld; married Kenneth George Eldridge (a forest geneticist), May 17, 1958; children: David, James, Elizabeth, Catherine. *Education:* University of Melbourne, B.A., 1957.

ADDRESSES: Home—Canberra, Australian Capital Territory 2605.

CAREER: High school history and English teacher in Traralgon, Australia, 1958-59; homemaker, 1960-73; high school substitute teacher in Canberra, Australia, 1973-79; Australian National University, Canberra, teacher of adult literature classes in department of continuing education, 1976—.

MEMBER: Australian Society of Authors, Fellowship of Australian Writers, Association for the Study of Australian Literature, Canberra Seven Writers.

AWARDS, HONORS: Bicentennial Grant, 1987, for writing of *Canberra Tales* (shared with other Canberra Seven Writers); Australia Council Literature Board Grant, 1992; ACT Arts Bureau Literary Fellowship, 1992.

WRITINGS:

Walking the Dog and Other Stories, University of Queensland Press, 1984.

The Woman at the Window (short stories), University of Queensland Press, 1989.

Springfield (novel), University of Queensland Press, 1992.

Also editor of *Amongst the Leaves: Poetry and Prose from Students' Workshops at Darwin High School,* DHS, 1989. Contributor to *Canberra Tales* (short stories), Penguin, 1988, and *Mirrors* (novellas), Women's Redress Press, 1989. Contributor of short stories to anthologies, journals, and newspapers in Australia and other countries, including *Australian Book Review* and *Canberra Times.*

WORK IN PROGRESS: The Greening of Alvie Skerritt (short stories); a psychological thriller set in France and Australia.

SIDELIGHTS: Marian Eldridge once told *CA:* "I write because I enjoy writing. It is what I have always wanted to do, and I am fortunate now in being able to write full time. I write about people. My stories are set in the Australian countryside, in the city, at the coast, and overseas. Whatever the setting, I am exploring the relationships between my characters.

"My aim is to both entertain the reader and to say something worth thinking about. I enjoy the constant challenge of using words, of developing a character and getting him or her from the opening of the story to its conclusion.

"My other interests include gardening, reading, going to concerts, plays, films, reviewing fiction, and teaching adult education. My aim as a teacher and as a writer too is to encourage discussion through the presentation of worthwhile and challenging ideas." "For example," Eldridge more recently added, "the major theme of my novel *Springfield* is the possibility of a healing process for two damaged people, one a Vietnam Veteran twenty years on, the other a woman formerly addicted to heroin. The novel is open-ended, leading to lively interpretation."

BIOGRAPHICAL/CRITICAL SOURCES:

PERIODICALS

New York Times Book Review, April 29, 1990, p. 26.

* * *

ENRIGHT, D(ennis) J(oseph) 1920-

PERSONAL: Born March 11, 1920, in Leamington, Warwickshire, England; son of George (a postman) and Grace (Cleaver) Enright; married Madeleine Harders, November 3, 1949; children: Dominique. *Education:* Downing College, Cambridge, B.A. (with honors), 1944, M.A., 1946; University of Alexandria, D. Litt., 1949.

ADDRESSES: Home—35A Viewfield Rd., London SW18 5JD, England. *Agent*—Watson, Little Ltd., 12 Egbert St., London NW1 8LJ, England.

CAREER: Poet, novelist, essayist, and editor. University of Alexandria, Alexandria, Egypt, assistant lecturer in English, 1947-50; University of Birmingham, Birmingham,

England, extramural lecturer, 1950-53; Koonan University, Kobe, Japan, visiting professor, 1953-56; Free University of Berlin, Berlin, Germany, visiting professor, 1956-57; Chulalongkorn University, Bangkok, Thailand, British Council Professor, 1957-59; University of Singapore, Singapore, professor of English, 1960-70; *Encounter* (magazine), London, England, co-editor, 1970-72; Chatto & Windus Ltd. (publishers), London, director, 1974-82. Honorary professor of English, Warwick University, 1975-80.

MEMBER: Royal Society of Literature (fellow).

AWARDS, HONORS: Cholmondeley Award for Poetry, British Society of Authors, 1974; Queen's Gold Medal for Poetry, 1981; D.Lett., University of Warwick, 1982; D.Univ., University of Surrey, 1985; Order of the British Empire, 1991.

WRITINGS:

POETRY

Season Ticket, Editions du Scarabee (Alexandria), 1948.
The Laughing Hyena and Other Poems, Routledge & Kegan Paul, 1953.
Bread Rather than Blossoms, Secker & Warburg, 1956.
The Year of the Monkey, Koonan University, 1956.
Some Men Are Brothers, Chatto & Windus, 1960.
Addictions, Chatto & Windus, 1962.
The Old Adam, Chatto & Windus, 1965.
Unlawful Assembly, Wesleyan University Press, 1968.
Selected Poems, Chatto & Windus, 1969.
The Typewriter Revolution and Other Poems, Library Press, 1971.
In the Basilica of the Annunciation, Poem-of-the-Month Club, 1971.
Daughters of Earth, Chatto & Windus, 1972.
Foreign Devils, Covent Garden Press, 1972.
The Terrible Shears: Scenes from a Twenties Childhood, Chatto & Windus, 1973, Wesleyan University Press, 1974.
Rhyme Times Rhyme (juvenile), Chatto & Windus, 1974.
Sad Ires, Chatto & Windus, 1975.
(Contributor) *Penguin Modern Poets 26: Dannie Abse, D. J. Enright, Michael Longley,* Penguin, 1975.
Paradise Illustrated, Chatto & Windus, 1978.
A Faust Book, Oxford University Press, 1979.
Collected Poems, Oxford University Press, 1981, revised and enlarged edition published as *Collected Poems, 1987,* 1987.
Instant Chronicles: A Life, Oxford University Press, 1985.
Selected Poems, 1990, Oxford University Press, 1990.
Under the Circumstances: Poems and Proses, Oxford University Press, 1991.
Old Men and Comets, Oxford University Press, 1993.

NOVELS

Academic Year, Secker & Warburg, 1955, Oxford University Press, 1985.
Heaven Knows Where, Secker & Warburg, 1957.
Insufficient Poppy, Chatto & Windus, 1960.
Figures of Speech, Heinemann, 1965.
The Joke Shop (juvenile), McKay, 1976.
Wild Ghost Chase (juvenile), Chatto & Windus, 1978.
Beyond Land's End (juvenile), Chatto & Windus, 1979.
The Way of the Cat, HarperCollins, 1992.

ESSAYS

Literature for Men's Sake, Kenkyusha Ltd. (Tokyo), 1955.
The Apothecary's Shop: Essays on Literature, Secker & Warburg, 1957, Dufour, 1959.
Conspirators and Poets, Dufour, 1966.
Man Is an Onion: Reviews and Essays, Chatto & Windus, 1972, Library Press, 1973.
A Mania for Sentences, Chatto & Windus, 1983, David Godine, 1985.
The Alluring Problem: An Essay on Irony, Oxford University Press, 1986.
Fields of Vision: Essays on Literature, Language, and Television, Oxford University Press, 1988.

EDITOR

(And author of introduction) *Poetry of the 1950s: An Anthology of New English Verse,* Kenkyusha Ltd. (Tokyo), 1955.
(With Takamichi Nimomiya) *The Poetry of Living Japan,* Grove, 1957.
(With Ernest de Chickera) *English Critical Texts: 16th Century to 20th Century,* Oxford University Press, 1962.
(And author of introduction) John Milton, *A Choice of Milton's Verse,* Faber, 1975.
(And author of introduction) Samuel Johnson, *The History of Rasselas, Prince of Abyssinia,* Penguin, 1976.
(And author of introduction) *The Oxford Book of Contemporary Verse, 1945-80,* Oxford University Press, 1980.
(And author of introduction) *The Oxford Book of Death,* Oxford University Press, 1983.
(And author of introduction), *Fair of Speech: The Uses of Euphemism,* Oxford University Press, 1985.
(And author of introduction) *The Faber Book of Fevers and Frets,* Faber, 1989, published as *Ill at Ease,* 1990.
(With David Rawlinson) *The Oxford Book of Friendship,* Oxford University Press, 1991.
Marcel Proust, *The Captive* [and] *The Fugitive* (revised edition), Modern Library, 1993.
Proust, *Time Regained,* Modern Library, 1993.
(And author of introduction) *The Oxford Book of the Supernatural,* Oxford University Press, 1994.

OTHER

A Commentary on Goethe's "Faust", New Directions Press, 1949.

The World of Dew: Aspects of Living Japan, Secker & Warburg, 1955, Dufour, 1959.

Robert Graves and the Decline of Modernism (text of lecture), Craftsman Press (Singapore), 1960.

Memoirs of a Mendicant Professor (autobiography), Chatto & Windus, 1969.

Shakespeare and the Students, Chatto & Windus, 1970.

Contributor to *Encounter, Scrutiny, Listener, New York Review of Books, Observer, London Review of Books,* and *Times Literary Supplement.*

SIDELIGHTS: D. J. Enright is known for his quiet, almost casual poetry. "Enright's form," M. L. Rosenthal observes in *The New Poets: American and British Poetry since World War II,* "is usually very flat and conversational, approaching in a way the 'minimal' style of Robert Creeley, and though actually the poetry is intellectually oriented the statement is kept as simple as possible." Speaking of the collection *The Terrible Shears: Scenes from a Twenties Childhood,* Dan Jacobson notes in the *New Statesman* that "many of the poems have the appearance of being as casual as they can be without lapsing into prose; they are given to unrhymed, conjunctional line-endings, broken rhythms, and a deliberate avoidance of sonority. Yet one does not feel for a moment that they have been easy to write. Candour is never easily come by." David Bromwich writes in the *Nation* that "the plainness of forms leads into a peculiarly stringent mode of vision, so that the most important notes are those struck most quietly."

A large number of Enright's poems are about the Far East, where he taught for a number of years, and often contain social commentary. "Many of [Enright's] Eastern poems," Douglas Dunn explains in the *New Statesman,* "conjure situations of the underdog beset by politicians." Enright's numerous poems about Japan, Philip Gardner remarks in *Contemporary Literature,* are not "testimonials to the Japan of the tourist brochures, the Japan of cherry blossom, Mount Fuji, Kyoto temple, Noh, Tea Ceremony, Flower Arrangement, and Zen. All these aspects appear, but as a background." Gardner emphasizes Enright's "concern for individuals rather than governments" and his depictions of "a Japan of overpopulation, poverty, landslides, suicides, [and] streetwalkers."

The collection *The Terrible Shears* concerns Enright's childhood in England. "Enright shows us vividly," a reviewer for the *Times Literary Supplement* states, "what it was like to grow up in a particular town in circumstances of poverty and an atmosphere of disease and death." Jacobson writes, "In the face of the large facts of death and poverty, the poems in this collection have the courage to speak repeatedly of the enduring littleness of a child's bewilderment and shame. Hence it is a measure of their painful exactness and truth that they should often be extremely funny. . . . But the funnier they are, the more poignant they are, too." A later collection, *Instant Chronicles: A Life,* deals largely with Enright's years as a self-described "mendicant professor" in Asia and elsewhere. Reviewing the book in the *New York Times Book Review,* John W. Aldridge writes, "At his best—as he clearly is here—Mr. Enright displays a remarkable gift for detecting the diabolical edge to the ordinary. . . . He is interested not in grandiose generalizations about the human condition, not in mankind but in men and women, not in grief but in griefs, particularly the suffering of those incurably exploited by an untouchable authority, human beings sentenced for life to the jails of the uncivilized."

Reviewing Enright's *Collected Poems, 1987* for the *New York Times,* John Gross observes that "critics have sometimes described Mr. Enright's poetry, rather sniffily, as light verse. Certainly he isn't a heavy poet; but he is a more serious poet than many of his more portentous colleagues, and the best way to approach him is to set distinctions between 'heavy' and 'light' to one side. If you do, you will find that his work yields innumerable pleasures and satisfactions." Enright's *Selected Poems, 1990* and Jacqueline Simms' *Life by Other Means: Essays on D. J. Enright* were published simultaneously to honor his seventieth birthday. In *Life by Other Means,* Simms collected numerous compositions written on Enright and his work. Many of the essayists in *Life by Other Means* remark repeatedly on the poet's use of irony and, in Douglas Dunn's words, his "grimly waggish" wit. In his essay, John Bayley praises Enright's fusion of "the literary and the domestically ordinary." In his review of both *Selected Poems* and *Life by Other Means,* Michael Walters writes in the *Times Literary Supplement* that he agrees with the view of essayist P. N. Furbank that Enright's "attitude toward writing and himself as a writer is both earnest and throwaway." Walters observes that Enright, at seventy, was still in his prime.

Throughout his career, Enright has supplemented verse with prose. All four of his novels are about British academics in foreign lands. According to Blake Morrison in the *Times Literary Supplement,* Enright's first novel, *Academic Year,* was greeted as "an Alexandrian *Lucky Jim*" by a *Daily Telegraph* reviewer when it first appeared in 1955. On its reissue a generation later as part of Oxford University Press's "Twentieth Century Classics" series, Morrison stated that *Academic Year* "is a novel which gives pleasure not at the level of its plot (which is less a sequence of events than a series of set-pieces taking us through the academic year), but the wry, ironic, authorial voice rumbling below."

Enright's nonfiction has brought him recognition as a witty critic of literature and television. *A Mania for Sentences* brings together many of his essays on literature. Reacting to Enright the essayist in the *New York Times Book Review,* Aldridge notes: "As a critic he is widely and deeply read and extremely eclectic in his tastes. . . . He represents, in short . . . the old-style practical critic and man of letters who knows and loves books and who can write about them with style, vigor and precision." "All in all," Aldridge summarizes, "D. J. Enright is a welcome reminder that poetry and criticism find their vitality not in theories but in the experiences of personal life and history." In the *Washington Post Book World,* Bob Halliday writes that Enright's *A Mania for Sentences* "straddles the divide between criticism and entertainment, and readers who follow his leads will discover the special virtues of books which may have been out of range for a more seriously didactic sensibility."

Enright has enlarged his public following by serving as editor for widely-read anthologies, including *The Oxford Book of Friendship* and *The Oxford Book of Death,* two compilations of quotations. Anthony Burgess, in the *Times Literary Supplement,* calls *The Oxford Book of Death* "mostly very heartening and sometimes even hilarious" in spite of its grim subject matter, and "one of the liveliest publications of the half-year." Anatole Broyard, in the *New York Times,* says, "[Enright's] editorial comments are among the best things in *The Oxford Book of Death,*" which includes quotations from Ludwig Wittgenstein, Sigmund Freud, Samuel Johnson, Virginia Woolf, and William James. Going from death to mere illness, Enright has edited *The Faber Book of Fevers and Frets,* which Roy Porter in the *Times Literary Supplement* terms "something altogether more ambitious than a rehash of drolleries about doctors: a superb book of embodiment, a documentation of our painful experience of the flesh—solid, sullied, sordid, absurd." Porter concludes that "reading, no less than writing, possesses a healing power."

BIOGRAPHICAL/CRITICAL SOURCES:

BOOKS

Contemporary Literary Criticism, Gale, Volume 4, 1975, Volume 8, 1978, Volume 31, 1985.

Dictionary of Literary Biography, Volume 27: *Poets of Great Britain and Ireland,* Gale, 1984.

Enright, D. J., *Memoirs of a Mendicant Professor,* Chatto & Windus, 1969.

O'Connor, William Van, *The New University Wits and the End of Modernism,* Southern Illinois University Press, 1963.

Rosenthal, M. L., *The New Poets: American and British Poetry since World War II,* Oxford University Press, 1967.

Simms, Jacqueline, editor, *Life by Other Means: Essays on D. J. Enright,* Oxford University Press, 1990.

Walsh, William, *D. J. Enright: Poet of Humanism,* Cambridge University Press, 1974.

PERIODICALS

Books and Bookmen, November, 1973; October, 1978.

Commonweal, December 1, 1967.

Contemporary Literature, winter, 1965, pp. 100-111; autumn, 1976.

Economist, January 18, 1969.

Globe & Mail (Toronto), August 29, 1987; May 19, 1990; May 11, 1991, p. 7.

Hudson Review, summer, 1969.

Listener, September 5, 1968; August 20, 1970; November 20, 1975.

Los Angeles Times Book Review, October 2, 1983, p. 2.

Nation, December 6, 1971, p. 599.

New Lugano Review, Volume 3, numbers 1-2, 1977.

New Republic, October 13, 1973.

New Statesman, June 18, 1965; September 28, 1973, p. 432; June 28, 1974, p. 927; May 19, 1978.

Newsweek, August 1, 1983, p. 69.

New York Review of Books, March 31, 1966.

New York Times, June 30, 1983; December 1, 1987, p. 25.

New York Times Book Review, February 13, 1972; April 6, 1975; June 19, 1983, p. 3; November 3, 1985, p. 28.

Observer, November 20, 1966.

Poetry, April, 1973; February, 1976.

Punch, April 7, 1965.

Saturday Review, March 15, 1969.

Spectator, August 25, 1973.

Times (London), February 27, 1964; June 2, 1983; August 18, 1983; August 17, 1985; October 9, 1986; February 5, 1990.

Times Educational Supplement, June 16, 1978.

Times Literary Supplement, March 18, 1965; July 29, 1965; June 9, 1972; June 8, 1973, p. 646; December 10, 1976; September 26, 1980, p. 1059; May 6, 1983, p. 499; September 9, 1983, p. 951; April 12, 1985, p. 399; June 7, 1985, p. 649; November 29, 1985, p. 1371; October 17, 1986, p. 1151; October 9, 1987, p. 1121; December 23, 1988, p. 1413; December 8, 1989, p. 1367; March 9, 1990, p. 248; May 3, 1991, p. 5; August 16, 1991, p. 24.

Washington Post Book World, September 23, 1973; July 10, 1983, p. 6; June 23, 1985, p. 3; January 26, 1986.

ESHBACH, Lloyd Arthur 1910-
(W. Anders Drake, Peter Gaunt, Judy Schuyler)

PERSONAL: Born in 1910 in Palm, PA; son of Oswin (a factory worker) and Kathryn (a homemaker; maiden name, Leeser) Eshbach; married Helen Margaret Richards, 1931 (died, 1978); children: Donald, Daniel. *Education:* Attended Charles Morris Price School of Advertising and Journalism. *Politics:* Republican. *Religion:* Protestant.

ADDRESSES: Home and office—220 South Railroad St., Myerstown, PA 17067. *Agent*—James Allen, 538 Harford St., Box 278, Milford, PA 18337.

CAREER: Worked in department stores as a window decorator, department manager, and buyer, 1925-41; Glidden Paint Co., Reading, PA, advertising copywriter, 1941-50; Fantasy Press, Reading, PA, publisher, 1950-58; Church Center Press, Myerstown, PA, manager, 1958-63; Moody Press, Chicago, IL, advertising manager, 1963-68, sales representative, 1968-75; pastor of three small churches in eastern Pennsylvania, 1975-79; writer, 1979—. Lapidary and silversmith, with work exhibited at Field Museum and Smithsonian Institution.

WRITINGS:

(Editor) *Of Worlds Beyond: The Science of Science Fiction Writing,* Fantasy Press, 1947.
The Tyrant of Time (stories), Fantasy Press, 1955.
(Editor and author of introduction) P. Schuyler Miller, *Alicia in Blunderland,* Oswald Train, 1983.
(Editor and author of introduction) E. E. "Doc" Smith, *Subspace Encounter,* Berkley Publishing, 1983.
Over My Shoulder: Reflections on a Science Fiction Era, Oswald Train, 1983.
The Land Beyond the Gate (novel), Ballantine, 1984.
The Armlet of the Gods (novel), Ballantine, 1986.
The Sorceress of Scath (novel), Ballantine, 1988.
The Scroll of Lucifer (novel), Ballantine, 1990.

Also coauthor of radio play series *The Crimson Phantom, The Bronze Buddha, Tales of the Crystal, Cupid's Capers, The Pennington Saga, The Doings of the Dinwiddies,* and *Tales of Tomorrow.* Work represented in anthologies, including *The History of Science Fiction Magazines,* edited by Ashley, 1974; *The Science Fiction Roll of Honor,* edited by Frederik Pohl, Random House, 1975; *Weird Tales Number Four,* 1983; and *Amazing Science Fiction Anthology, The Wonder Years 1926-1935,* edited by Martin H. Greenberg, TSR, Inc., 1987. Contributor of stories and novelettes to magazines (occasionally under pseudonyms W. Anders Drake, Peter Gaunt, and Judy Schuyler), including *Amazing Stories, Saint Detective, Startling Stories, Science Fiction, Wonder Stories,* and *Boys' Companion.*

WORK IN PROGRESS: The Spell of Amon-Ptah, for Ballantine.

SIDELIGHTS: Lloyd Arthur Eshbach once told *CA:* "At age seventy-six, my interests are somewhat circumscribed. I do some traveling, preach now and then, and speak to civic groups and students, but most of my time is given to writing. I enjoy writing, and I write what pleases me. I have five more novels in mind, with the actual writing begun on four of them.

"I find it difficult to believe, but my involvement in fantasy and science fiction spans more than sixty years. I began reading Edgar Rice Burroughs's Martian adventures and the science fantasy of Abraham Merritt and others of the era in 1919. I began writing science fiction in 1926 and sold my first story to *Amazing Stories* in 1929. In 1947 I began publishing science fiction through my own publishing company, Fantasy Press, initially as a sideline venture while I worked for Glidden Paint. The books I published, all clothbound, were largely the 'classics' of the period, the magazine serials that fans and collectors wanted in permanent form. A few of these, perhaps twenty percent, have survived in mass paperback form and are still in print today.

"As reader, writer, editor, and publisher I have seen science fiction come out of virtual nonexistence (except for H. G. Wells and Jules Verne), pass through the Hugo Gernsback era of gadget stories, through the John W. Campbell golden years, to when modern giants in the field—Robert A. Heinlein, Ray Bradbury, Isaac Asimov, Lester del Rey, Frederik Pohl, and Robert Silverberg—came into their own, into the present day when NASA invites science fiction writers to watch significant space events, and the writing of science fiction is taught on the university level. Incredible!

"Much that is good has developed throughout the last few decades: better writing, far greater emphasis on character development, some successful experiments in style, construction, contents, and so on. At the same time, in my opinion, some inexcusable offenses have been and continue to be made. The use of what were once called 'four letter words,' detailed descriptions of explicit sex, offensively bloody violence—in short, all that for some strange reason is called 'realism' in general fiction—has entered science fiction and fantasy, as though only the crude, coarse, and seamy side of life is real.

"One modern trend that annoys me as a reader is writers' attempts to tell a story as though it were written for readers of the future or the alien era or world in which the action takes place. Everybody knows what a 'squink' is, of course, so why describe a 'squink'? Obviously language will change, so stories are told with speech oddities, the almost unintelligible contractions and omissions, that the writer believes will exist in the world about which he writes. The result: I'm puzzled and have to try to figure out what the writer is trying to say. However, since I read for entertainment, I pass on to something else.

"Another annoying gimmick some writers employ is telling the story in the present tense. I've never been able to decide what this is supposed to accomplish. It certainly destroys realism. There is no way actions and conversations could be recorded as they happen. Then there's the real bellringer: the story told in the present tense and in second person. 'You hear the knock on the door and you answer. The man with the black attache case has a third eye in the middle of his forehead. You say, politely, "May I help you?," trying not to look at that staring third eye.' Some experiments are failures and as such should be abandoned.

"My own writing obviously reflects my rather upbeat philosophy of life. The tetralogy which now occupies my time takes place in Sheol, or Hell, and is part of the ages-old conflict between good and evil, God and Satan—hardly an original concept. My treatment, I think, is somewhat different. With the exception of the hero (I still believe in heroes), all the characters, including some of the 'gods' of mythology, have died and have been given new bodies by Lucifer. One reviewer of *The Land Beyond the Gate* referred to my 'strange theology;' and the view I present hardly matches the popular concept of Satan's domain, which after all is really a reflection of Dante rather than the Bible.

"In a totally different field, I am a skilled lapidary and silver-smith. Jewelry of my creation has won trophies and has been displayed at the Field Museum in Chicago, Illinois. Five stones of my cutting are in the Smithsonian. Unfortunately, writing precludes following my other hobby."

Eshbach more recently added, "During the last several years I have resumed cutting semi-precious gemstones. A creative silversmith on the West Coast buys all I produce. In my 80s I'm busier than ever. And I'm enjoying myself."

* * *

EVANS, Hilary 1929-
(H. E. Agard)

PERSONAL: Born March 6, 1929, in Shrewsbury, England; son of Eryk Agard and Winifred (Carter) Evans; married Caroline Mary Lander, 1956. *Education:* King's College, Cambridge, B.A.; University of Birmingham, M.A.

ADDRESSES: Home—11 Granville Park, London SE13 7DY, England.

CAREER: Writer, social historian, and librarian.

WRITINGS:

A World Fit for Grimsby, St. Martins, 1962.
The Land of Lost Control, Peter Dawnay, 1967.
(With Dik Evans) *Beyond the Gaslight: Science in Popular Fiction, 1885-1950,* Muller, 1976, Vanguard Press, 1977.
The Art of Picture Research: A Guide to Current Practice, Procedure, Techniques, and Resources, David & Charles, 1979.
Harlots, Whores and Hookers, Taplinger, 1979, published in England as *The Oldest Profession: An Illustrated History of Prostitution,* David & Charles, 1979.
UFOs: The Greatest Mystery, Albany, 1979.
Picture Librarianship, Clive Bingley, 1980.
Intrusions: Society and the Paranormal, Routledge & Kegan Paul, 1981.
The Evidence for Unidentified Flying Objects, Aquarian Press, 1983.
Visions, Apparitions, Alien Visitors: A Comparative Study of the Entity Enigma, Aquarian Press, 1984.
(Editor and co-author) *Frontiers of Reality,* Aquarian Press, 1990.

AUTHOR WITH MARY EVANS

Sources of Illustration: 1500-1900, Adams & Dart, 1971.
John Kay of Edinburgh, International Publications Service, 1973, 2nd revised edition published as *John Kay of Edinburgh: Barber, Miniaturist, and Social Commentator,* P. Harris, 1980.
The Victorians: At Home and at Work as Illustrated by Themselves, David & Charles, 1973.
(And Andra Nelki) *The Picture Researcher's Handbook: An International Guide to Picture Sources and How to Use Them,* David & Charles, 1975, 3rd edition, Van Nostrand Reinhold, 1986.
The Party That Lasted 100 Days: The Late Victorian Season, Beekman Publications, 1976.
Hero on a Stolen Horse: The Highwayman and His Brothers-in Arms, Muller, 1977.
The Man Who Drew the Drunkard's Daughter: The Life and Art of George Cruikshank, 1792-1878, Muller, 1978.
Alternate State of Consciousness, Aquarian Press, 1989.

UNDER PSEUDONYM H. E. AGARD

The Assassin, R. Hale, 1965.

F

FALK, Ze'ev W(ilhelm) 1923-

PERSONAL: Born May 11, 1923, in Breslau, Silesia (now Wroclaw, Poland); immigrated to Israel, 1939; son of Meyer (a physician) and Frieda (David) Falk; married Miriam Strauss, October 29, 1952; children: Hayim, Orah. *Education:* Attended Knesset Israel Rabbinical College, 1940-45; Israeli Government Law Classes, advocate, 1951; Hebrew University of Jerusalem, M.A., 1952, Ph.D., 1959. *Religion:* Jewish.

Avocational Interests: Writing Hebrew poetry, travel, books.

ADDRESSES: 10 Harav Berlin St., Jerusalem, 92503, Israel.

CAREER: Private law practice, 1952-55; Hebrew University of Jerusalem, Jerusalem, Israel, external teacher and fellow, 1959-67; Tel-Aviv University, Tel-Aviv, Israel, senior lecturer in Jewish law, 1965-70; Hebrew University of Jerusalem, Israel, Berman Professor of Family and Succession Law, 1970-89, Professor Emeritus, 1989—; Seminary of Judaic Studies, Jerusalem, Israel, professor of Jewish religions law, 1991—. Legal advisor to Israeli Ministry of Social Welfare, 1955-60, and Israeli Ministry of Interior, 1960-67. Visiting professor at Temple University, 1975-76, New York University, 1979-80, University of California, Berkeley, 1983-84, University of Sao Paulo, 1984, Jewish Theological Seminary, 1988-89, and Hebrew Union College.

MEMBER: International Society of Family Law (founder and honorary president, 1975—), Israel Interfaith Association (chairman).

AWARDS, HONORS: Israeli Fighters' Decoration.

WRITINGS:

Nisu'in Ve-gerushin, Hebrew University Faculty of Law, 1961, enlarged English edition published at *Jewish Matrimonial Law in the Middle Ages,* Oxford University Press, 1966.

Hebrew Law in Biblical Times, Wahrmann Books, 1964.

Current Bibliography of Hebrew Law, [Tel Aviv], 1966.

Halakhah u-ma'aseh bi-medinat Yisrael (title means "Halakhah and Reality in the State of Israel"), Wahrmann Books, 1967.

Mavo le-dine Yisrael, [Tel-Aviv], 2 volumes, 1969-71, translation published as *Introduction to Jewish Law of the Second Commonwealth,* E. J. Brill, Volume 1, 1972, Volume 2, 1978.

The Influence of Medical and Biological Progress on Private Law, Institute for Legislative Research and Comparative Law, Hebrew University of Jerusalem, 1970.

Yemalel gevurot: Me'et Ze'ev Falk, [Jerusalem], 1971.

Teviat gerushin mi-tsad ha-ishah be-dine Yisrael (title means "The Divorce Action by the Wife in Jewish Law"), [Jerusalem], 1973.

Erkhey Mishpat we Yahadut (title means "Legal Values and Judaism"), Jerusalem, 1980.

Law and Religion: The Jewish Experience, [Jerusalem], 1981.

Diney Nisu'in (title means "Law of Marriage"), [Jerusalem], 1983.

Dat ha Netsach we Tsorkhey Sha'ah (title means "Religious Law Between Eternity and Change"), [Jerusalem], 1986.

Direito Talmudico, [Sao Paulo], 1988.

Religous Law and Ethics: Studies in Biblical and Rabbinical Theonomy, [Jerusalem], 1991.

Also author of *Mekorot ba-mishpat ha-'ivre,* 1968, *Ketivat divre nevu'ah,* 1968, and *Tevi'at gerushin mi-tsad ha-ishah be-dine Yisrael,* 1973. Co-editor of *Dine Israel: Annual on*

Jewish and Israeli Family Law and editor of *Siach Mesharim: Quarterly of Jewish Law and State.* Contributor to encyclopedias and learned journals; author of booklets on Jewish law.

WORK IN PROGRESS: Commentary to the Pentateuch: Towards a Philosophy of Jewish Law.

SIDELIGHTS: Ze'ev Falk speaks Hebrew, English, German, and French.

* * *

FALLON, George
See BINGLEY, David Ernest

* * *

FARBER, Marvin 1901-1980

PERSONAL: Born December 14, 1901, in Buffalo, NY; died 1980; son of Simon (a businessman) and Matilda (Goldstein) Farber; married Lorraine F. Walle, December 26, 1930; children: Lawrence Alan, Roger Evan, Carol Louise. *Education:* Harvard University, S.B. (summa cum laude), 1922, Ph.D., 1925; postgraduate work at Heidelberg University, 1922-24, 1926-27.

ADDRESSES: Home—Williamsville, NY.

CAREER: Ohio State University, Columbus, OH, instructor, 1925-26; University of Buffalo, Buffalo, NY, instructor, 1927-28, assistant professor, 1928-30, professor of philosophy, 1930-54; distinguished professor of philosophy, 1954-61; University of Pennsylvania, Philadelphia, PA, professor of philosophy and chairman of department, 1961-64; State University of New York at Buffalo, NY, distinguished professor of philosophy and education, 1964-74; distinguished professor emeritus, 1974-80.

MEMBER: International Phenomenological Society (president, 1940), International Institute of Philosophy, American Philosophical Association (president, 1963-64), Symbolic Logic Association (member of executive committee, 1946-49), Phi Beta Kappa.

AWARDS, HONORS: Guggenheim fellow, 1944-45; Dr. honoris causa, University of Lille, 1955.

WRITINGS:

Phenomenology as a Method and as a Philosophical Discipline, University of Buffalo, 1928.

(Editor and contributor) *Philosophical Essays in Memory of Edmund Husserl,* Harvard University Press, 1940.

The Foundation of Phenomenology: Edmund Husserl and the Quest for a Rigorous Science of Philosophy, Harvard University Press, 1943, 3rd edition, State University of New York Press, 1967.

(Editor and contributor with R. W. Sellars and V. J. McGill) *Philosophy for the Future,* Macmillan, 1949.

(Editor and contributor) *Philosophic Thought in France and the United States,* University of Buffalo, 1950, 2nd edition, State University of New York Press, 1968.

Naturalism and Subjectivism, C. C. Thomas, 1959, 2nd edition, State University of New York Press, 1968.

The Aims of Phenomenology, Harper, 1966.

Phenomenology and Existence: Toward a Philosophy within Nature, Harper, 1967.

Basic Issues of Philosophy: Experience, Reality, and Human Values, Harper, 1968.

(Editor) *Philosophical Perspectives on Punishment,* C. C. Thomas, 1968.

(Contributor) A. Mercier and M. Svilar, editors, *Philosophers on Their Own Work,* Volume 1, Federation of International Philosophical Societies, 1975.

The Search for an Alternative: Philosophical Perspectives of Subjectivism and Marxism, University of Pennsylvania Press, 1984.

Also author of *L'activite philosophique contemporaine en France et aux Etats-Unis,* 1950; editor of *Philosophy and Phenomenological Research: An International Quarterly Journal,* 1940-80, *American Lectures in Philosophy,* 1951-80, and *Modern Concepts in Philosophy,* 1968-76; contributor of articles to academic journals of philosophy.

BIOGRAPHICAL/CRITICAL SOURCES:

BOOKS

Mathur, D. C., *Naturalistic Philosophies of Experience,* Warren Green, 1971.

Riepe, D. M., editor, *Phenomenology and Natural Existence: Essays in Honor of Marvin Farber,* State University of New York Press, 1973.

* * *

FEINBERG, Renee 1940-

PERSONAL: Given name is accented on first syllable; born April 10, 1940, in New York, NY; daughter of Boris and Sylvia (Schwartz) Feinberg; children: Sheelah A. *Education:* University of Chicago, B.A., 1961; Columbia University, M.A., 1966, M.L.S., 1968.

ADDRESSES: Office—Library, Brooklyn College of the City University of New York, 2900 Bedford Ave., Brooklyn, NY 11210-2889.

CAREER: Public schools in New York City, teacher, 1961-67; secondary school librarian, 1969-71; Brooklyn

College of the City University of New York, Brooklyn, NY, librarian, 1972—. Member of advisory committee, Office for Library Personnel Resources, 1984-85; member of executive committee, Brooklyn College Professional Staff Congress, 1993—; chair of Carroll Preston Baber Research Grant Awards Committee, 1993-94.

MEMBER: American Library Association (coordinator of Jewish Caucus, 1975-77), New York Library Association (coordinator of Roundtable on the Concerns of Women, 1976-78), Library Association of the City University of New York.

WRITINGS:

(Editor, with Carole Leita) *Sisters Have Resources Everywhere: A Directory of Feminist Libraries,* American Library Association Task Force on Women, 1975.

Women, Education and Employment: A Bibliography of Periodical Citations, Pamphlets, Newspapers, and Government Documents, 1970-1980, Shoe String, 1982.

The Equal Rights Amendment: An Annotated Bibliography of the Issues, 1976-1985, Greenwood, 1986.

(Compiler with Kathleen Knox) *The Feminization of Poverty in the United States: A Selected, Annotated Bibliography of the Issues, 1978-1989,* Garland, 1990.

Contributor of an article on David Shub to *Dictionary of American Biography,* Supplement Nine: *1971-1975,* Scribner. Contributor to *Reference Services Review, American Library Association Yearbook, Library Journal,* and other books and periodicals.

BIOGRAPHICAL/CRITICAL SOURCES:

PERIODICALS

American Reference Books Annual, 1988, p. 350; 1991, p. 363.

Booklist, May 15, 1987, p. 1426.

Choice, May, 1987, p. 1376; November, 1990, p. 454.

Reference & Research Book News, spring, 1987, p. 18; August, 1990, p. 34.

Reference Book Review, Volume 9, number 1, 1987, p. 22.

* * *

FINDLEY, Timothy 1930-

PERSONAL: Born October 30, 1930, in Toronto, Ontario, Canada; son of Allan Gilmore and Margaret (Bull) Findley. *Education:* Self-educated beyond the ninth grade after illness interrupted formal education.

ADDRESSES: Agent—The Turnbull Agency, P.O. Box 757, Dorset, VT 05251.

CAREER: Actor for fifteen years; was a charter member of Stratford (Ontario) Shakespeare Festival, 1953; went from Canada to England as protege of Alec Guinness; contracted with H. M. Tennant Productions, London, England, 1954-55, to appear in *The Prisoner* (with Alec Guinness), 1954, and *The Matchmaker* (with Ruth Gordon), 1955; toured with *The Matchmaker* in the United States, 1956-57; wrote advertising copy at a small radio station in Canada; presently full-time professional writer. Playwright-in-residence, National Arts Centre, Ottawa, Canada, 1974-75; writer-in-residence, University of Toronto, 1978-79.

MEMBER: International PEN (president, English-Canadian Centre, 1986-87), Authors Guild, Authors League of America, Writers' Union of Canada (chairman, 1977-78), Association of Canadian Television and Radio Artists.

AWARDS, HONORS: Canada Council Junior Arts Award, 1968; Major Armstrong Award, 1970, for radio drama, *The Journey;* Association of Canadian Television and Radio Artists award, 1975, for *The National Dream;* Governor General's Award for fiction in English, and City of Toronto Book Award, both 1977, both for *The Wars;* Canada Council Senior Arts Award, 1978; ANIK Award, 1980, for television documentary, *Dieppe: 1942;* D.Litt., Trent University, 1982, University of Guelph, 1984, York University, 1989; Canadian Authors Association Literary Award, 1985, for *Not Wanted on the Voyage,* and 1991, for *Inside Memory: Pages from a Writer's Workbook;* Officer of the Order of Canada, 1986; Order of Ontario, 1991.

WRITINGS:

NOVELS

The Last of the Crazy People, Meredith, 1967.

The Butterfly Plague, Viking, 1969.

The Wars (also see below), Clarke, Irwin, 1977.

Famous Last Words, Clarke, Irwin, 1981.

Not Wanted on the Voyage, Penguin, 1984.

The Telling of Lies: A Mystery, Penguin, 1986.

Headhunter, HarperCollins, 1993.

STORY COLLECTIONS

Dinner Along the Amazon, Penguin, 1984.

Stones, Penguin, 1988.

PLAYS

Can You See Me Yet? (first produced in Ottawa at the National Arts Centre, 1976), Talonbooks, 1977.

John A.—Himself, first produced by Theatre London, London, Ontario, 1979.

The Stillborn Lover (first produced by the Grand Theatre, London, and the National Arts Centre, 1993), Blizzard Publishers, 1993.

SCREENPLAYS

The Paper People, Canadian Broadcasting Corp. (CBC-TV), 1967.

Don't Let the Angels Fall, National Film Board of Canada-Columbia, 1969.

The Whiteoaks of Jalna (based on the novels by Mazo de la Roche), CBC-TV, 1971-72.

(With William Whitehead) *The National Dream,* CBC-TV, 1974.

(With Whitehead) *Dieppe: 1942,* CBC-TV, 1979.

The Wars (based on his novel of the same title), Nielsen-Ferns, National Film Board of Canada, 1983.

Also author of *Inside Memory: Pages from a Writer's Workbook.* Author of other television, radio, and film documentaries, including *The Journey* (radio drama), 1970. Author of novellas, including *Hello Cheeverland, Goodbye,* 1978, and *Lemonade,* 1981. Contributor of short stories to *Tamarack Review, New Orleans Review, Esquire, Cavalier,* and other periodicals; also contributor of critical reviews and essays to magazines and newspapers, including *Toronto Globe and Mail, Toronto Life,* and *Saturday Night.*

WORK IN PROGRESS: Pilgrim, a novel; *Other People's Children,* a play.

SIDELIGHTS: Timothy Findley is a Canadian actor-turned-novelist who started writing when he was in his teens. "At that time I had glandular fever," he told *Books.* "I was in bed for the whole of one winter and did little more than sleep, wake up, eat, and go back to sleep." When he wasn't sleeping, Findley wrote what he calls "a kind of modern day romance." His serious writing began almost a decade later when he wrote a story entitled "About Effie" to prove a point to actress Ruth Gordon with whom he was performing at the time.

"We had been to an exhibition of paintings in Manchester, all done by people under thirty years of age," he explained in an interview with Alison Summers in *Canadian Literature.* "I was in my twenties then. When we came out, Ruth asked me 'Why are you people so damned negative about everything? All those pictures were black, depressing, ugly. Can't you say *yes* to anything?' Aloud I said to her, 'I don't think we're negative, Ruth.' I had an argument, or rather a pleasant conversation, with her. Secretly I decided, 'I'll prove that we're not.' I went back to my digs and I wrote a story." As Findley told *Books,* it was " a very sad and negative story. But she loved it." Gordon lent him an old typewriter, showed his story to Thornton Wilder, and suggested to Findley that perhaps literature, not theatre, was his natural milieu.

Since that time, Findley has written seven novels and three novellas, as well as numerous short stories, plays, and films. An actor no longer, he still infuses his writing with the pageantry of the stage. "The importance of sound, spectacle, and style to a full appreciation of Findley's fictions, whether they be scripts intended to be *listened to* on the radio, scripts intended to be *seen* on television, the movie screen, or the theatre-stage, or whether they be the texts of short-stories and novels, cannot be overemphasized," John F. Hulcoop writes in *Canadian Literature.* "His work compels the critic to recover his senses (*see* more, *hear* more) by making direct appeals to the viewer-listener-reader through sight, sound and style: these are what force us to pay attention—to look and listen and mark his words."

In addition to stylistic similarities, Findley's fictions share some common themes. Fraught with violence, laced with images of fire, his books abound in symbolic details that reveal man's basic fears. "Everyone is so afraid of life itself that they would prefer to be locked up in an insane asylum," Findley commented in a 1981 CBC-TV interview. In several of his novels, including *The Last of the Crazy People* and *The Butterfly Plague,* Findley examines individuals who do insane things in order to clarify what, in his words, is "bright and good."

Peter Klovan believes that this idea receives its most powerful treatment in Findley's 1977 novel, *The Wars.* "Here," Klovan writes in *Canadian Literature,* the device of a story-within-a-story is used to illustrate how a personality transcends elemental forces even while being destroyed by them. . . . As Findley's narrator realizes, 'People can only be found in what they do.' His problem in *The Wars* is to understand the actions of Robert Ross, a young Canadian officer, who when caught up in a German offensive during the Great War, tries and fails to save one hundred and thirty horses from being killed. Robert's failure leaves him horribly burned, and in many ways is simply the inevitable outcome of the pattern of futility which characterized his brief life. . . . But, in the process, Robert's struggle is raised to mythological proportions as a metaphor of fate and man's place in the universe, so that an apparent defeat is turned into a triumph. Indeed, 'tragic' is not too strong a term to describe *The Wars.*"

In a later work, a curious mix of fantasy and Old Testament legend entitled *Not Wanted on the Voyage,* Findley retells the story of Noah and the Great Flood, portraying the ark's builder as a "sinister" individual, "given to brutal sacrifices and experiments," according to a *Publishers Weekly* reviewer. Findley's Noah sees God's plan to flood the earth as "the perfect opportunity to exclude, to condemn, to sacrifice the unwanted masses," writes Isabel Raphael of the *London Times,* and indeed, Noah dooms the Faeries by refusing to allow them on the ark, then sentences females and undesirable species to live below deck. Lucifer also appears—disguised as a mysterious geisha named Lucy—and schemes his way aboard, thus ensuring the presence of evil after the flood.

Not Wanted on the Voyage is enlivened with Findley's whimsical touches: he creates a talking cat and a shy unicorn, and describes how God's visit to Noah is heralded by a chorus of singing lambs. But the tone of the novel is pessimistic. To Raphael's thinking, *Not Wanted on the Voyage* "is a very angry book, indeed. It deals with exploitation and devastation on a mighty scale, all in the name of God that man has created in his own flawed image." William French, writing in the *Toronto Globe and Mail,* declared, "Timothy Findley clearly believes that . . . the world would have been a better place if its post-flood history hadn't owed its origin to a drastic act of vengeance."

Critical response to *Not Wanted on the Voyage* was positive. Douglas Hill of the *Toronto Globe and Mail* calls the work "an imaginative reinvention of the Biblical account of Noah and the Flood," and French states: "Findley's ark is freighted with a heavy cargo of symbolism, baggage that Noah didn't have to contend with. But he uses it effectively to get several messages across that have contemporary significance—equality for women, the need for conservation . . . the threat posed by fundamentalists and anti-evolutionists, the danger of obsessive beliefs and blind, unquestioning faith."

Findley's body of work has brought him both critical and popular acclaim. In the words of *Toronto Globe and Mail* reviewer Margaret Cannon, Findley is "one of [Canadian literature's] shiniest stars. His literary honors include the highest awards Canada offers. His literary concerns—memory, the burden of the past—are the hautest of concerns. His pages drip with symbolism . . . and his prose is supremely refined." And Neil Bissoondath, also writing in the *Toronto Globe and Mail,* opines, "[Findley] is a writer of prodigious talents who, through an uncalculated modesty, maintains the illusion that he is a simple spinner of tales. And yet it is through this modesty that he achieves a quiet grandeur."

BIOGRAPHICAL/CRITICAL SOURCES:

BOOKS

Atwood, Margaret, *Seconds Words,* Anansi Press, 1982.

PERIODICALS

Books, June, 1967.
Canadian Forum, June, 1968.
Canadian Literature, winter, 1981; autumn, 1982.
Chicago Tribune Book World, August 1, 1982.
Fiddlehead, summer, 1968.
Globe and Mail (Toronto), July 14, 1984; November 24, 1984; November 2, 1985; October 25, 1986; November 15, 1986; November 19, 1988.
Los Angeles Times, February 8, 1990.
Los Angeles Times Book Review, August 29, 1982.
New York Times, June 22, 1982.
New York Times Book Review, June 16, 1967; July 9, 1978; August 15, 1982; November 10, 1985, p. 14; October 9, 1988, p. 34; April 29, 1990, p. 38.
New Yorker, August 21, 1978; August 9, 1982.
Newsweek, July 19, 1982.
Profiles in Canadian Literature, number 51, 1982.
Publishers Weekly, June 28, 1985, pp. 62-63.
Time, August 2, 1982.
Times (London), October 31, 1985; March 19, 1987.
Times Literary Supplement, March 5, 1970; April 15, 1988, p. 421.
Saturday Night, May, 1967.
Washington Post Book World, July 18, 1982.

*　*　*

FLETCHER, Ronald 1921-1992

PERSONAL: Born August 11, 1921, in Hoyland, Yorkshire, England; died May 2, 1992; son of George William (a carpenter) and Winifred M. (Hatswell) Fletcher; married Clarice Roma Phipps, May 27, 1944; children: Paul, Adrian John. *Education:* University of Bristol, B.A. (first class honors), 1951; London School of Economics and Political Science, Ph.D., 1954. *Politics:* "Puzzled." *Religion:* "Puzzled."

Avocational Interests: "Interested in music (composition) and painting—but, alas, cannot find enough time."

ADDRESSES: Home and office—Engleholme, Three Marsh Lane, Reydon, Southwold, Suffolk IP18 6NP, England.

CAREER: University of London, London, England, lecturer in sociology at Bedford College and Birkbeck College, 1953-63; University of York, Heslington, England, professor of sociology and head of department, 1964-68; full-time researcher and writer, 1969-76; University of Reading, Reading, England, visiting lecturer, 1976-78, professor of sociology, 1979-82, professor emeritus, 1982—. Auguste Comte Memorial Trust Lecturer, London School of Economics and Political Science, University of London, 1966; visiting professor of sociology, University of Essex, Colchester, England, 1968-69; associate lecturer (consultancy), Thames Polytechnic; British Council lecturer in Denmark, Malta, and Rome. Course consultant, Open University. Consultant to the International Committee for Scientific and Cultural History of Mankind (UNESCO), 1980—.

MEMBER: Society of Authors, The Savage Club.

AWARDS, HONORS: Rockefeller Foundation fellow, 1962; Morris Ginsberg fellow, London School of Economics and Political Science, University of London, 1975-76; Marc Goldstein memorial fellow, Institute of Education, University of London, 1981-82.

WRITINGS:

Instinct in Man: In the Light of Recent Work in Comparative Psychology (revised and shortened version of doctoral thesis), International Universities Press, 1957, 2nd edition, Allen & Unwin, 1968.

Issues in Education, Ethical Union, 1960.

The Family and Marriage: An Analysis and Moral Assessment, Penguin, 1962, revised edition published as *The Marriage and Family in Britain: An Analysis and Moral Assessment,* 1966.

Human Needs and Social Order, M. Joseph, 1965, Schocken, 1966.

The Parkers at Saltram, 1769-89: Everyday Life in an Eighteenth-Century House (also see below), British Broadcasting Corp., 1970.

The Making of Sociology: A Study of Sociological Theory (core text), M. Joseph, Volume 1: *Beginnings and Foundations,* 1971, Volume 2: *Developments,* 1972.

(Editor and author of introduction) *John Stuart Mill: A Logical Critique of Sociology* (complementary volume to core text of *The Making of Sociology*), M. Joseph, 1971.

(Editor and author of introduction) *The Science of Society and the Unity of Mankind; A Memorial Volume for Morris Ginsberg,* Heinemann, 1974.

(Editor) Auguste Comte, *The Crisis of Industrial Civilization,* Heinemann, 1974.

The Akenham Burial Case, Wildwood House, 1974.

What's Wrong with Higher Education?, Methuen, 1975.

The Framework of Society, Open University Press, 1976.

(Editor and author of introduction) *The Biography of a Victorian Village: Richard Cobbold's Account of Wortham Suffolk, 1860,* Batsford, 1977.

In a Country Churchyard, Batsford, 1978.

The East Anglians, Stephens, 1980.

Sociology: Its Nature, Scope, and Elements, Batsford, 1980, Scribner, 1981.

Sociology: The Study of Social Systems, Scribner, 1981.

Education in Society: The Promethean Fire; A New Essay in the Sociology of Education, Penguin, 1984.

The Shaking of the Foundations: Family and Society, Routledge, 1988.

The Abolitionists: Family and Marriage under Attack (companion volume to *The Shaking of the Foundations: Family and Society*), Routledge, 1988.

Science, Ideology, and the Media: The Cyril Burt Scandal, Transaction, 1990.

Also author of *Old Pathways* (verse), 1979; *Margaret Catchpole: Two Worlds Apart* (opera libretto), 1980; and *Sheridan's First Edition: A Plan of Education,* 1987. General editor, *Making of Sociology* series, for M. Joseph. Also author of television scripts, including *The Artist in Society, Human Societies,* and *The Parkers at Saltram.* Contributor to sociology journals.

SIDELIGHTS: British sociologist Ronald Fletcher has explored various aspects of society and sociological thought in his writings. In *The Making of Sociology,* a proposed multi-volume work of which two have been published, he gives an overview of the science of sociology—its history and major contributors—focusing on British sociological theory. Critical analyses provide insight into the work of prominent sociologists, including Comte, Durkheim, and Hobhouse. "He appears to have two objects," writes Philip Abrams in the *Spectator,* "to demonstrate the underlying unity of sociology despite its apparent fragmentation . . . and to provide an encouraging guided tour through the mysteries of sociological theory." Abrams notes that Fletcher "is very comprehensive; no one who could possibly matter is ignored," but points out that "sociology has been made in terms of problems not men and Mr. Fletcher's procedure does not help us towards any clear sense of what is problematic about the problems." "Fletcher is often far too ready to present as evidence of a common perspective apparent similarities in the thought of the 'founders' which, on closer examination, prove to be superficial or artificial," comments John Goldthorpe in the *New Statesman. Times Literary Supplement* contributor Michael Joseph writes in his conclusion: "Mr. Fletcher has written at great length and with great sincerity and an immense desire to make the path plain to students who would otherwise go astray in mazes of 'fashionable' error . . . one must respect his integrity and unflagging determination to see the job through."

In *The Akenham Burial Case,* Fletcher presents a nineteenth-century scandal concerning burial rights between the Church of England and a nonconformist religious group called Dissenters. Assembled from contemporary newspaper clippings and court reports, the book pieces together the tale of the two-year-old son of a Baptist laborer who died unbaptized, due to the Dissenters' belief in adult baptism, in 1878. George Drury, the Anglican rector of the rural Suffolk town of Akenham, had the right at that time to prevent the Baptist minister, William Tozer, from officiating a burial ceremony. The case received much publicity, and thus aided in the ratifying of the Burial Laws Amendment Act of 1880 which ended the Anglican pastors' privilege. "*The Akenham Burial Case* is an ill-advised book," judged a critic in the *Time Literary Supplement,* remarking that "Mr. Fletcher's chief personal contribution is providing link-passages to whip up the reader's interest. . . . These fancies lie uneasily, in heavy type, alongside much untreated documentation." A reviewer in the *Spectator,* however, called *The Akenham Burial Case* an "intriguing tale." John Fowles, writing in the *New Statesman,* noted that "the documentation is valuable, if distinctly repetitive in places" in this "interesting little Victorian scandal."

BIOGRAPHICAL/CRITICAL SOURCES:

PERIODICALS

Listener, July 4, 1974, p. 29.
New Statesman, July 2, 1971, pp. 21-22; June 14, 1974, pp. 842-43.
Spectator, September 25, 1971, p. 443; June 15, 1974, p. 741.
Times Literary Supplement, July 30, 1971, pp. 901-02; August 30, 1974, p. 919.

[Date of death provided by wife, C. R. Fletcher]

* * *

FLETCHER, Winston 1937-

PERSONAL: Born July 15, 1937, in London, England; son of Albert (a shopkeeper) and Bessie (a housewife; maiden name, Miller) Fletcher; married Jean Brownston (a housewife); children: Amelia, Mathew. *Education:* Cambridge University, M.A. (with honors), 1958. *Politics:* Social Democrat. *Religion:* Agnostic.

ADDRESSES: *Home*—Chapman's Farm, Dunsden Green, Oxfordshire, England. *Office*—DFSD Bozell, 25 Wellington St., London W.C. 2, England. *Agent*—Peters, Fraser & Dunlop, 503 The Chambers, Chelsea Harbour, London SW10 0XF, England.

CAREER: Ogilvy & Mather (advertising agency), London, England, copywriter, 1958-59; Robert Sharp & Partners (advertising agency), London, began as account executive, promoted to board of directors, 1959-69; MCR Advertising, London, deputy chief executive, 1969-74; Fletcher, Shelton & Delaney (advertising agency) London, chairman, 1974-83; Ted Bates (advertising agency), London, chairman, 1983-85; Delaney, Fletcher & Delaney (advertising agency), London, chairman, 1985-90; DFSD Bozell (advertising agency), London, chairman, 1990—.

MEMBER: Royal Institution, Reform Club, Annabels Club, 30 Club.

WRITINGS:

The Admakers, M. Joseph, 1974.
Teach Yourself Advertising, Hodder & Stoughton, 1979.
Meetings, Meetings, M. Joseph, 1983, Morrow, 1984.
Commercial Breaks, Advertising Press, 1985.
Superefficiency, Sidgwick & Jackson, 1986.
Creative People, Hutchinson Business Books, 1988.
The Manipulators (novel), Macmillan, 1988.
A Glittering Haze, NTC Books, 1992.

Contributor to British business journals and newspapers.

SIDELIGHTS: Winston Fletcher once told *CA:* "I find writing about writing generally tedious, and prone to be portentous. I have no new insights on the subject that thousands of other, and better, writers have not had before me.

"I hold these truths to be self-evident: 1) Nobody particularly wants to read anything I write. They must be tempted into starting and persuaded to continue, from sentence to sentence. 2) The more you do it the better you get. 3) Almost no writers know anything about business, and almost no businessmen can write. (So I am exceptionally fortunate in that my experience and my talents to some small degree encompass both)."

* * *

FORMAN, James Douglas 1932-

PERSONAL: Born November 12, 1932, in Mineola, Long Island, NY; son of Leo Erwin (a lawyer) and Kathryn (Forman) Fonnan; married Marcia Fore, September 3, 1956; children: Karli Elizabeth. *Education:* Princeton University, A.B., 1954; Columbia University, LL.B., 1957.

Avocational Interests: Travel, photography, antique arms of the eighteenth century.

ADDRESSES: *Home*—2 Glen Rd., Sands Point, Port Washington, NY 11050. *Office*—290 Old Country Rd., Mineola, Long Island, NY. *Agent*—Theron Raines, Raines & Raines, 71 Fourth Ave., New York, NY 10016.

CAREER: Attorney, 1957—.

MEMBER: Lightning Fleet 142 (sailboats; past president).

AWARDS, HONORS: Children's Spring Book Festival award, *Book World,* 1969, for *My Enemy, My Brother;* best book award, American Library Association, 1979, for *A Ballad for Hogskin Hill.*

WRITINGS:

(With wife, Marcia Forman) *Islands of the Eastern Mediterranean* (booklet), Doubleday, 1960.
The Skies of Crete, Farrar, Straus, 1963.
Ring the Judas Bell, Farrar, Straus, 1965.
The Shield of Achilles, Farrar, Straus, 1966.
Horses of Attger, Farrar, Straus, 1967.
The Traitors, Farrar, Straus, 1968.
The Cow Neck Rebels, Farrar, Straus, 1969.

My Enemy, My Brother, Meredith, 1969.
Ceremony of Innocence, Hawthorn, 1970.
So Ends This Day, Farrar, Straus, 1970.
Song of Jubilee, Farrar, Straus, 1971.
Law and Disorder, Thomas Nelson, 1971.
Capitalism: Economic Individualism to Today's Welfare State, F. Watts, 1972.
Communism: From Marx's Manifesto to Twentieth-Century Reality, F. Watts, 1972, 2nd edition, 1979.
Socialism: Its Theoretical Roots and Present-Day Development, F. Watts, 1972.
People of the Dream, Farrar, Straus, 1972.
Code Name Valkyrie: Count Claus von Stauffenberg and the Plot to Kill Hitler, S. G. Phillips, 1973.
The Life and Death of Yellow Bird, Farrar, Straus, 1973.
Fascism: The Meaning and Experience of Reactionary Revolution, F. Watts, 1974.
Anarchism: Political Innocence or Social Violence?, F. Watts, 1975.
Follow the River, Farrar, Straus, 1975.
The Survivor, Farrar, Straus, 1976.
The White Crow, Farrar, Straus, 1976.
Inflation, F. Watts, 1977.
Nazism, F. Watts, 1978.
A Fine, Soft Day, Farrar, Straus, 1978.
Freedom's Blood, F. Watts, 1979.
A Ballad for Hogskin Hill, Farrar, Straus, 1979.
That Mad Game: War and the Chance for Peace, Scribner, 1980.
The Pumpkin Shell, Farrar, Straus, 1981.
Call Back Yesterday, Scribner, 1983.
Self-Determination: An Examination of the Question and Its Application to African-American People, Open Hand Publishing, 1984.
The Making of Black Revolutionaries, Open Hand Publishing, 1984.
Doomsday Plus Twelve, Scribner, 1984.
Sammy Younge, Jr.: The First Black College Student to Die in the Black Liberation Movement, Open Hand Publishing, 1986.
Cry Havoc, Scribner, 1988.
The Big Bang, Scribner, 1989.
Prince Charlie's Year, Scribner, 1991.
Becca's Story, Scribner, 1992.

Some of Forman's photographs appear in his works.

WORK IN PROGRESS: A pre-Civil War novel set on Long Island tentatively titled *North Shore;* a novel set in London, 1939-40.

SIDELIGHTS: James Douglas Forman told *CA:* "Of particular interest to me and my wife is *Becca's Story.* It derives from old family letters and diaries and tells of the Civil War romance of my great-grandfather and [great-grandmother]. The [book] jacket . . . was done by Marcia, so it is very much a family book. She also typed up the very difficult letters and diaries—a labor of love—without which I never would have undertaken the task." Forman added that there were about five hundred letters and eleven diaries that needed typing.

Forman is considering writing another book about his family, this one focusing on what his agent has termed "the four-generational house." The author explained: "This old family house where Marcia and I live also houses my mother and, until a few years ago, my father. For a time it also contained our daughter, her husband, and their first two kids. This was after Jim, our son-in-law, got out of the Air Force and while they were building their own home next door. So it remains a four-generational compound of sorts, and my agent is interested in the psychological dynamics of all the relationships involved. As I said, [the book is] only a gleam at the moment, but all parties seem interested and eager.

"How I began writing [involved] an early passion for photography and a friend at Doubleday who invited Marcia and me back in '59 to do one of a series of travel booklets in their 'Round the World' program. This was great fun and as the area done was islands of the Eastern Mediterranean, I got going at first with books set in Greece."

BIOGRAPHICAL/CRITICAL SOURCES:

BOOKS

Contemporary Literary Criticism, Volume 21, Gale, 1982.

PERIODICALS

New York Times Book Review, November 30, 1969.
Saturday Review, June 28, 1969.
Young Readers' Review, June, 1967; November, 1968.

* * *

FRANCIS, Dick 1920-

PERSONAL: Full name, Richard Stanley Francis; born October 31, 1920, in Tenby, Pembrokeshire, Wales; son of George Vincent (a professional steeplechase rider and stable manager) and Molly (Thomas) Francis; married Mary Brenchley (a teacher and assistant stage manager), June 21, 1947; children: Merrick, Felix. *Education:* Attended Maidenhead County School. *Religion:* Church of England.

Avocational Interests: Boating, fox hunting, tennis.

ADDRESSES: Home—P.O. Box 30866, S.M.B., Grand Cayman, British West Indies. *Agent*—Andrew Hewson, John Johnson Authors' Agent, 45/47 Clerkenwell Green,

London EC1R 0HT, England; Sterling Lord Literistic, Inc., 1 Madison Ave., New York, NY 10010.

CAREER: Novelist. Amateur steeplechase rider, 1946-48; professional steeplechase jockey, 1948-57; *Sunday Express,* London, England, racing correspondent, 1957-73. *Military service:* Royal Air Force, 1940-46; became flying officer (pilot).

MEMBER: Crime Writers Association (chair, 1973-74), Mystery Writers of America, Crime Writers of Canada, Detection Club.

AWARDS, HONORS: Steeplechase jockey championship, 1954; Silver Dagger Award, Crime Writers Association, 1965, for *For Kicks;* Edgar Allan Poe Award, Mystery Writers of America, 1969, for *Forfeit,* and 1980, for *Whip Hand;* Gold Dagger Award, Crime Writers Association, 1980, for *Whip Hand;* Order of the British Empire, 1984; Diamond Dagger award, 1990.

WRITINGS:

MYSTERY NOVELS

Dead Cert, Holt, 1962.
Nerve, Harper, 1964.
For Kicks, Harper, 1965.
Odds Against, M. Joseph, 1965, Harper, 1966.
Flying Finish, M. Joseph, 1966, Harper, 1967.
Blood Sport, Harper, 1967.
Forfeit, Harper, 1968.
Enquiry, Harper, 1969.
Rat Race, Harper, 1970.
Bonecrack, Harper, 1971.
Smokescreen, Harper, 1972.
Slay-ride, Harper, 1973.
Knockdown, Harper, 1974.
High Stakes, Harper, 1975.
In the Frame, Harper, 1976.
Risk, Harper, 1977.
Trial Run, Harper, 1978.
Whip Hand, Harper, 1979.
Reflex, M. Joseph, 1980, Putnam, 1981.
Twice Shy, M. Joseph, 1981, Putnam, 1982.
Banker, M. Joseph, 1982, Putnam, 1983.
The Danger, M. Joseph, 1983, Putnam, 1984.
Proof, M. Joseph, 1984, Putnam, 1985.
Break In, M. Joseph, 1985, Putnam, 1986.
Bolt, M. Joseph, 1986, Putnam, 1987.
Hot Money, M. Joseph, 1987, Putnam, 1988.
The Edge, M. Joseph, 1988, Putnam, 1989.
Straight, Putnam, 1989.
Longshot, Putnam, 1990.
Comeback, Putnam, 1991.
Driving Force, Putnam, 1992.
Decider, Putnam, 1993.

OTHER

The Sport of Queens (racing autobiography), M. Joseph, 1957.
(Editor with John Welcome) *Best Racing and Chasing Stories,* Faber, 1966.
(Editor with Welcome) *Best Racing and Chasing Stories II,* Faber, 1969.
The Racing Man's Bedside Book, Faber, 1969.
A Jockey's Life: The Biography of Lester Piggott, Putnam, 1986, published in England as *Lester, the Official Biography,* M. Joseph, 1986.
(Editor with Welcome) *The New Treasury of Great Racing Stories,* Norton, 1991.
(Editor with Welcome) *The Dick Francis Treasury of Great Racing Stories,* G. K. Hall, 1991.

Contributor to anthologies, including *Winter's Crimes 5,* edited by Virginia Whitaker, Macmillan, 1973; *Stories of Crime and Detection,* edited by Joan D. Berbrich, McGraw, 1974; *Ellery Queen's Crime Wave,* Putnam, 1976; and *Ellery Queen's Searches and Seizures,* Davis, 1977.

Francis's works have been translated into approximately thirty languages, including Japanese.

ADAPTATIONS: Dead Cert was filmed by United Artists in 1973; *Odds Against* was adapted for Yorkshire Television as *The Racing Game,* 1979, and also broadcast by the PBS-TV series "Mystery!," 1980-81; Francis's works adapted for television series "Dick Francis Mysteries" by Dick Francis Films Ltd., 1989. Many of Francis's books have been recorded on audiocassette.

SIDELIGHTS: When steeplejockey Dick Francis retired from horseracing at age thirty-six, he speculated in his autobiography that he would be remembered as "the man who didn't win the National," England's prestigious Grand National steeplechase. If he hadn't turned to fiction, his prediction might have been correct, but with the publication of his first novel, *Dead Cert,* in 1962, Francis launched a second career that was even more successful than his first: he became a mystery writer.

Since that time, Francis has produced a thriller a year, astounding critics with the fecundity of his imagination and garnering awards such as Britain's Silver Dagger (in 1965 for *For Kicks*) and two Edgars (for *Forfeit* in 1969 and *Whip Hand* in 1980). However, talking about his books and their success Francis says in *Sport of Queens,* his autobiography, that, "I still find the writing . . . grindingly hard, and I approach Chapter 1 each year with deeper foreboding." Gina MacDonald, writing in the *Dictionary of Literary Biography,* says that Francis's method of writing his books is very precise. He usually thinks of a plot by midsummer, and spends the rest of the year researching the book. He finally starts writing the following year and finishes the book by spring. Since most of his books concern horses, racing still figures in his life. His affinity for the racetrack actually enhances his prose, according to Julian Symons, who writes in the *New York Times Book Review* that "what comes most naturally to [Francis] is also what he does best—writing about the thrills, spills and chills of horse racing."

Before he began writing, Francis experienced one of racing's most publicized "spills" firsthand. In 1956, when he was already a veteran jockey, Francis had the privilege of riding Devon Loch—the Queen Mother's horse—in the annual Grand National. Fifty yards from the finish line, with the race virtually won, the horse inexplicably faltered. Later examination revealed no physical injury and no clue was ever found. "I still don't have the answer," Francis told Peter Axthelm of *Newsweek.* "Maybe he was shocked by the noise of 250,000 people screaming because the royal family's horse was winning. But the fact is that with nothing wrong with him, ten strides from the winning post he fell. The other fact is," he added, "if that mystery hadn't happened, I might never have written all these other ones."

Though each of his novels deals with what many consider a specialized subject, Francis's books have broad appeal. One explanation, offered by Judith Rascoe in the *Christian Science Monitor,* is that "you needn't know or care anything about racing to be his devoted reader." And, writing in the *New York Times,* book reviewer John Leonard agrees: "Not to read Dick Francis because you don't like horses is like not reading Dostoyevsky because you don't like God. . . . Race tracks and God are subcultures. A writer has to have a subculture to stand upon."

Francis's ability to make this subculture come alive for his reader—to create what Rascoe calls "a background of almost Dickensian realism for his stories"—is what sets him apart from other mystery writers. "In particular," observes Charles Champlin in the *Los Angeles Times,* "his rider's view of the strains and spills, disappointments and exultations of the steeplechase is breathtaking, a far cry from the languid armchair detecting of other crime solvers." Writing in the *London Magazine,* John Welcome expresses similar admiration, praising especially Francis's ability to infuse his races with a significance that extends beyond the Jockey Club milieu: "One can hear the smash of birch, the creak of leather and the rattle of whips. The sweat, the strain, the tears, tragedies and occasional triumphs of the racing game are all there, as well as its seductive beauty. In this—as in much else—no other racing novelist can touch him. He has made racing into a microcosm of the contemporary world."

While critics initially speculated that Francis's specialized knowledge would provide only limited fictional opportunities, most have since changed their minds. "It is fascinating to see how many completely fresh and unexpected plots he can concoct about horses," marvels Anthony Boucher in the *New York Times Book Review.* Philip Pelham takes this approbation one step further, writing in *London Magazine* that "Francis improves with every book as both a writer of brisk, lucid prose and as a concocter of ingenious and intricately worked-out plots." His racetrack thrillers deal with such varied storylines as crooks transporting horses by air (*Flying Finish*), stolen stallions (*Blood Sport*), and a jockey who has vanished in Norway (*Slay-ride*). To further preserve the freshness of his fiction, Francis creates a new protagonist for each novel and often develops subplots around fields unrelated to racing. "His books," notes Axthelm, "take him and his readers on global explorations as well as into crash courses in ventures like aviation, gold mining and, in *Reflex,* amateur photography."

Notwithstanding such variations in plot and theme, Francis is known as a formula writer whose novels, while well-written, are ultimately predictable. In all the Francis novels, writes Welcome, "the hard-done-by chap [is] blindly at grips with an unknown evil, the threads of which he gradually unravels. Frequently—perhaps too frequently—he is subjected to physical torture described in some detail. His heroes are hard men used to injury and pain and they learn to dish it out as once they had to learn to take it. Racing has made them stoics."

Barry Bauska, writing in the *Armchair Detective,* offers a more detailed version of the "typical" Francis thriller: "At the outset something has happened that looks wrong (a jockey is set down by a board of inquiry that seemed predetermined to find him guilty; a horse falls going over a final hurdle it had seemed to clear; horses perfectly ready to win consistently fail to do so). The narrator protagonist (usually not a detective, but always inherently curious) begins to poke around to try to discover what has occurred. In so doing he inevitably pokes too hard and strikes a hornets' nest. The rest of the novel then centers on a critical struggle between the searcher-after-truth and the mysterious agent of evil, whose villainy had upset things in the first place."

Despite the formulaic nature of his work, Francis deals with problems prevalent in modern society, says Marty Knepper in *Twelve Englishmen of Mystery.* He feels that Francis's works deal with social and moral issues "seriously and in some depth . . . including some topics generally considered unpleasant." For example, in *Blood Sport* the hero is struggling with his own suicidal urges. In Knepper's words, "To read *Blood Sport* . . . is to learn what it feels like to be lonely, paranoid and suicidal."

Character development also plays an important part in Francis's novels. Knepper says that biographical similarities between Francis's heroes may blind the reader to the important differences between them. For example, Francis's heroes have a wide variety of professions. This gives him a chance to examine professionalism, and the responsibilities that accompany it, in fields other than racing and detection. Each of Francis's heroes, according to Knepper, is "a unique person, but each hero . . . changes as a result of his adventures." In the end, characters learn from their experiences and have evolved.

While a number of Francis's books include a love story, a much more pressing theme, according to Axthelm, is that of pain. "Again and again," he writes in *Newsweek,* the author's "villains probe the most terrifying physical or psychic weakness in his heroes. A lifetime's most treasured mementos are destroyed by mindless hired thugs; an already crippled hand is brutally smashed until it must be amputated. The deaths in Francis novels usually occur 'off-camera.' The tortures are more intimate affairs, with the reader forced to watch at shudderingly close range."

The prevalence of such violence, coupled with Francis's tendency to paint the relationship between hero and villain as a confrontation between good and evil, makes some reviewers uneasy. In his *Times Literary Supplement* review of *Risk,* for example, Alex de Jong comments that "characterization is sometimes thin and stylized, especially the villains, out to inflict pain upon the accountant who has uncovered their villainy, crooked businessmen and trainers, all a little too well dressed, florid and unexpectedly brutal bullies, created with a faint hint of paranoia." Francis, however, justifies the punishment he metes out to his characters as something his fans have come to expect. "Somehow the readers like to read about it," he told Judy Klemesrud in the *New York Times Book Review.* "But I don't subject them to anything I wouldn't put up with myself. This old body has been knocked around quite a bit."

While the violence of his early novels is largely external, his later novels emphasize more internal stress, according to critics who believe that this shift has added a new dimension to Francis's work. Welcome, for instance, comments that in *Reflex* Francis's lessened emphasis on brutality has enabled him to "flesh out his characters. The portrait of Philip More, the mediocre jockey nearing the end of his career, is created with real insight; as is the interpretation of his relations with the horses he rides." MacDonald comments that Francis's later books "concentrate more specifically on psychological stress." In her opinion, his writing has gone beyond the "dramatic presentation of heroic action" to a deeper level, where the hero "is less a man who can endure torture than one who has the strength to face self-doubt, fear, and human inadequacy and still endure and thrive." And Bauska expresses a similar view when he says that Francis's later works, although not that different in the plot, focus on the protagonist. According to Bauska, Francis is increasingly "considering what goes into the making not so much of a 'hero' as of a good man." The focus of Francis's work is no longer the war outside, though the books are still action-packed, but on the struggle within the protagonist's mind and his attempts to conquer his own doubts and fears. Bauska attributes this shift in focus to Francis's own growing distance from his racing days. The result, he says, "is that Dick Francis is becoming less a writer of thrillers and more a creator of literature."

BIOGRAPHICAL/CRITICAL SOURCES:

BOOKS

Bargainnier, Earl F., editor, *Twelve Englishmen of Mystery,* Bowling Green University Popular Press, 1984, pp. 222-48.

Bestsellers 89, Issue 3, Gale, 1989.

Contemporary Literary Criticism, Gale, Volume 2, 1974, Volume 22, 1982, Volume 42, 1987.

Dictionary of Literary Biography, Gale, Volume 87, 1989.

Francis, Dick, *The Sport of Queens,* M. Joseph, 1957.

PERIODICALS

Armchair Detective, July, 1978.

Christian Science Monitor, July 17, 1969.

Family Circle, July, 1970.

Globe and Mail (Toronto), November 16, 1985; August 12, 1989.

London Magazine, February-March, 1975; March, 1980; February-March, 1981.

Los Angeles Times, March 27, 1981; April 9, 1982; September 12, 1984.

Newsweek, April 6, 1981.

New Yorker, March 15, 1969.

New York Times, March 6, 1969; April 7, 1971; March 20, 1981; December 18, 1989.

New York Times Book Review, March 21, 1965; March 10, 1968; March 16, 1969; June 8, 1969; July 26, 1970; May 21, 1972; July 27, 1975; September 28, 1975; June 13, 1976; July 10, 1977; May 20, 1979; June 1, 1980; March 29, 1981; April 25, 1982; February 12, 1989.

New York Times Magazine, March 25, 1984.

Time, March 11, 1974; July 14, 1975; May 31, 1976; July 7, 1978; May 11, 1981.

Times (London), December 18, 1986.

Times Literary Supplement, October 28, 1977; October 10, 1980; December 10, 1982.

U.S. News and World Report, March 28, 1988.

Washington Post, October 3, 1986.

Washington Post Book World, April 30, 1972; February 18, 1973; April 19, 1980; April 18, 1982; March 27, 1983; February 21, 1988; February 5, 1989.

* * *

FRENCH, R(oger) K(enneth) 1938-

PERSONAL: Born April 12, 1938, in Coventry, England; son of Kenneth David (a businessman) and Alice (Sadler) French; married Anne Goater (a schoolteacher), August 13, 1966; children: Anne, Edmund, Sally. *Education:* St. Catherine's College, Oxford, B.A., 1961, D.Phil., 1965.

ADDRESSES: Home—Checkley Brook, Checkley, Herefordshire, England. *Office*—Whipple Museum, Cambridge University, Free School Lane, Cambridge, England.

CAREER: University of Leicester, Leicester, England, research fellow, 1965-66, lecturer in history of science, 1966-67; University of Aberdeen, Aberdeen, Scotland, lecturer in history and philosophy of science, 1967-75; Cambridge University, Cambridge, England, lecturer in history of medicine and director of Wellcome Unit for the History of Medicine, 1975—; Fellow of Clare Hall, Cambridge, 1978—.

MEMBER: Fellow of Royal Society of Arts (FRSA), Athenaeum.

WRITINGS:

Robert Whytt, The Soul and Medicine, Wellcome Institute, 1969.

Anatomical Education in a Scottish University, 1620, Equipress, 1973.

The History of the Heart, Equipress, 1978.

The History and Virtues of Cyder, R. Hale, 1979.

(Editor and coauthor with Andrew Wear and Iain M. Lonie) *The Medical Renaissance of the Sixteenth Century,* Cambridge University Press, 1984.

(Editor and coauthor with Frank Greenaway) *Science in the Early Roman Empire,* [London], 1986.

(Editor and coauthor with Wear) *The Medical Revolution of the Seventeenth Century,* Cambridge University Press, 1989.

(Editor and coauthor with Andrew Cunningham) *The Medical Enlightenment of the Eighteenth Century,* Cambridge University Press, 1989.

(Editor with Wear) *British Medicine in an Age of Reform,* [London], 1991.

(Editor and coauthor with Garcia Ballester) *Practical Medicine from Salerno to the Black Death,* Cambridge University Press, 1993.

WORK IN PROGRESS: Research on the teaching of medieval medicine; natural history in antiquity.

SIDELIGHTS: R. K. French once told *CA:* "I have wanted to reproduce cider as it was made in seventeenth-century England, with the original machinery and techniques.

"Since buying a cottage with a cider mill deep in the countryside, I have been making cider using seventeenth-century machinery and techniques. The first step was to plant my own orchard and save the old varieties of apples from extinction. As the trees grew, I researched and wrote [*The History and Virtues of Cyder*], going through the practical operations of orcharding, grinding, and pressing as I wrote about them. Cider, or rather cyder, was a wine, laid down and matured in the corked bottle, with secondary fermentation. Sparkling wine was a seventeenth-century English, not French, invention; but up until now the process had been a forgotten technique, a lost literature. In place of cyder is modern 'cider': the descendant of watered 'ciderkin' with which the gentleman paid his laborers, reserving for himself the first runnings of his cyder press. The reconstruction of a forgotten technique and wine has all been worthwhile. The result is surprising, gratifying, and—I am happy to say—often toasted with a raised glass from a cellar full of ten year old Kingston Black.

"It would be idle to pretend that the links between William Harvey, the English physician and anatomist, and cyder are any stronger than the century they had in common (although Harvey certainly had his preferred recipe for the drink). My interest here has been to discover how Harvey came to such an—in the eyes of his contemporaries—absurd and (in practical terms) useless idea as the circulation of the blood. How did the 'circulators' (his followers, regarded as dangerous eccentrics) come to accept the doctrine? How were they proved right? What, in short, were the mechanisms of medical progress?"

* * *

FRIEDEN, Ken(neth) 1955-

PERSONAL: Born December 4, 1955, in New Rochelle, NY; son of Julian (a physician) and Nancy (a lawyer; maiden name, Mandelker) Frieden. *Education:* Yale University, B.A. (magna cum laude), 1977, M.Phil., 1983, Ph.D., 1984; University of Chicago, M.A., 1978; also attended University of Freiburg and University of Berlin, 1979-81, Hebrew University of Jerusalem, 1982 and 1985-86, Jewish Theological Seminary, 1984, and YIVO Institute for Jewish Research, summer, 1984 and 1985. *Religion:* Jewish.

ADDRESSES: Home—1163 Rosedale Drive, Atlanta, GA 30306. *Office*—Department of Near Eastern and Judaic Languages and Literatures, Emory University, Atlanta, GA 30322.

CAREER: Yale University, New Haven, CT, lecturer in English literature, 1984-85; Emory University, Atlanta, GA, assistant professor, 1985-90, associate professor of Judaic and comparative literature, 1990—.

MEMBER: Modern Language Association of America, Association for Jewish Studies.

AWARDS, HONORS: Goethe Institute grant for Freiburg, West Germany, 1978; German Academic Exchange grant for West Germany, 1979-81; Hillel Foundation grant for Israel, 1982; grants from American Council of Learned Societies and Memorial Foundation for Jewish Culture, 1985-86; fellow of Lady Davis Trust, 1985-86; grant from the Yad Hanadiv/Barecha Foundation, 1988-89.

WRITINGS:

Genius and Monologue, Cornell University Press, 1985.

Freud's Dream of Interpretation, State University of New York Press, 1990.

Contributor to *Prooftexts, Response,* and *Association for Jewish Studies Review.*

WORK IN PROGRESS: Research on Yiddish and Hebrew literature; Black-Jewish relations.

SIDELIGHTS: Ken Frieden told *CA:* "My new interest is Black and Jewish film and fiction."

* * *

FRISCH, Karl (Ritter) von 1886-1982

PERSONAL: Born November 20, 1886, in Vienna, Austria; died June 12, 1982, in Munich, Germany; son of Anton Ritter von (a surgeon and urologist) and Marie (Exner) Frisch; married Margarethe Mohr (an artist), July 20, 1917; children: Johanna (Mrs. Theo Schreiner), Maria, Helen (Mrs. E. Pflueger), Otto. *Education:* University of Munich and Venice, Ph.D., 1910.

CAREER: University of Munich, Munich, Germany, teacher and research assistant at zoological institute, 1911-19, assistant professor, 1919-21; University of Rostock, Rostock, Germany, professor of zoology, 1921-23; University of Breslau, Breslau, Germany, professor of zoology, 1923-25; University of Munich, director of zoological institute and professor of zoology, 1925-46; University of Graz, Oesterreich, Germany, professor of zoology, 1946-50; University of Munich, professor of zoology, 1950-58. *Military service:* Served in various medical capacities involving bacteriology during World War I.

MEMBER: American Entomological Society, American Physiological Society, Royal Society of London, Royal Entomological Society, Linnean Society, Academies of Science of Washington, Boston, Munich, Vienna, Goettingen, Uppsala, and Stockholm.

AWARDS, HONORS: Honorary degrees from numerous universities, including University of Bern, 1949, Technische Hochschule, Zurich, 1955, University of Graz, 1957, Harvard University, 1963, University of Tuebingen, 1964, and University of Rostock, 1969; Orden pour le merite fuer Wissenschaften und Kunste, 1952; Magellan Prize from American Philosophical Society, 1956; Kalinga Prize from United Nations Education, Scientific and Cultural Organization (UNESCO), 1959; Balzan Prize for biology, 1963; Nobel Prize, 1973, for contributions to sociobiology.

WRITINGS:

Aus dem Leben der Bienen, J. Springer, 1927, 9th edition, 1977, translation by Dora Ilse published as *The Dancing Bees: An Account of the Life and Senses of the Honey Bee,* Methuen, 1954, Harcourt, 1955.

Du und das Leben: Eine Moderne Biologie fuer Jedermann, Ullstein, 1936, 19th edition, 1974, translation by Elsa B. Lowenstein published as *About Biology,* Oliver & Boyd, 1962, published as *Man and the Living World,* Harcourt, 1963.

Zehn kleine Hausgenossen, E. Heimeran, 1940, published as *Zwoelf kleine Hausgenossen,* Rowohlt, 1976, translation by Margaret D. Senft published as *Twelve Little Housemates,* Pergamon, 1960, revised edition, 1978.

Bees: Their Vision, Chemical Senses and Language, Cornell University Press, 1950, revised edition, 1971.

Erinnerungen eines Biologen, J. Springer, 1962, 3rd edition, 1973, translation by Lisbeth Gombrich published as *A Biologist Remembers,* Pergamon, 1967.

Tanzsprache und Orientierung der Bienen, J. Springer, 1965, translation by Leigh E. Chadwick published as *The Dance Language and Orientation of Bees,* Harvard University Press, 1967.

Tiere als Baumeister, Ullstein, 1974, translation by Gombrich published as *Animal Architecture,* Helen and Kurt Wolf Books/Harcourt, 1974.

Fuenf Hauser am See, Springer-Verlag, 1980.

Experimental Behavioral Ecology and Sociobiology, Sinauer Associates, 1985.

SIDELIGHTS: Karl von Frisch was a pioneer in the study of insect communication systems. His research into the language of bees, a language dependent upon an intricate aerial dance for its expression, won him worldwide recognition. Further research proved that bees can use the sun as a compass, are able to remember locations in their environment, and possess a sense of color. In 1973, Frisch was awarded a Nobel Prize for his research.

As a boy, Frisch already showed signs of his deep interest in the natural world. He spent so much time studying nature, in fact, that he nearly failed to gain admittance into the University of Vienna. After graduation, he began research into the sensory capabilities of fish. In 1910, he discovered that fish possess a sense of color, going on to prove that they also possess an acute sense of hearing far in excess of that of man. This early research brought him immediate recognition among the world's biologists.

Beginning in 1919, Frisch began his study of bees. He soon found that the insects had a sense of color, eventually training them to associate food with a particular color. After placing the food on a different colored square, the bees would still return to the color they originally associated with the food. Frisch later used similar tests to prove that bees also possessed a sense of smell.

Frisch's study of bees also resulted in the observation that bees had a language which involved a kind of dance in the air. Circling meant that food was within 250 feet of the hive, while a wagging motion signified that food was a greater distance away. Further movements delineated directions to the food. Frisch also observed that the movements were particular to each subspecies and that bees from one subspecies could not interpret another subspecies' language.

Frisch's study of bee language was greatly accelerated during World War II. At that time, working as the director of the zoological institute of the University of Munich, Frisch was called upon by the Nazi government to work out a means of telling bees, in their own language, how to produce more honey. Though his efforts at communication were not successful, Frisch was able to devote time and resources to his project which led to yet further discoveries about the insects' language.

In 1949, Frisch announced that bees were able to use the sun as a compass when travelling. His announcement was met with general skepticism in the academic community. But professor William Homan Thorpe of Cambridge University was so intrigued with the idea that he visited Frisch to see the proof for himself. Carefully repeating Frisch's experiments, Thorpe confirmed Frisch's conclusions.

Even family members were at first skeptical of Frisch's research findings. His daughters refused to believe that their father could understand the language of bees. To test him, they hid food not far from the bees' hive and challenged their father to discover where it was. By reading the dancing movements of the bees as they spoke to each other, Frisch deciphered accurate directions to the nearby food. Speaking of Frisch's book *The Dance Language and Orientation of Bees* in the *New York Review of Books,* J. Z. Young observed: "This is a technical work, but it is beautifully produced, and anyone who wants a sound and simple account of von Frisch's extraordinary findings will get it best from von Frisch himself."

BIOGRAPHICAL/CRITICAL SOURCES:

BOOKS

Frisch, Karl von, *A Biologist Remembers,* Pergamon, 1967.

PERIODICALS

New York Review of Books, November 21, 1968.
New York Times, October 12, 1972.

OBITUARIES:

PERIODICALS

New Scientist, December 23-30, 1982.
Times (London), June 21, 1982.
Washington Post, June 19, 1982.*

* * *

FULLER, Jean (Violet) Overton 1915-

PERSONAL: Born March 7, 1915, in Iver Heath, Buckinghamshire, England; daughter of John Henry Middleton (a captain in the Indian Army) and Violet Overton (Smith) Fuller. *Education:* Attended Royal Academy of Dramatic Art, 1930-31; studied painting at Academie Julien, Paris; University of London, B.A. (with honors in English), 1945, University College, certificate in phonetics, 1950, studied astronomy at Goldsmiths' College, 1962-64. *Religion:* "Broadly Theosophical."

Avocational Interests: Painting.

ADDRESSES: Home—Steep House, 6 Church Lane, Wymington, Rushden, Northamptonshire NN10 9LW, England.

CAREER: Writer. Actress in England, 1932-34. Examiner in French and Italian, Postal Censorship Department, British Ministry of Information, 1941-45; lecturer in phonetics, Speech Fellowship, London, England, 1951-52; director of Fuller d'Arch Smith Ltd. (rare book dealers), 1968—.

MEMBER: Theosophical Society (past vice-president of Astrological Lodge), Society of Authors, Francis Bacon Society, Buddhist Society, Society for Physical Research.

AWARDS, HONORS: Co-winner of Manifold Chapman Competition, 1968, for *African Violets*; winner of Manifold Poems of the Decade Competition, 1970, for "Moonwalk."

WRITINGS:

Madeleine (biography), Gollancz, 1952, published as *Born for Sacrifice,* Pan Books, 1957, revised edition published as *Noor-un-Nisa Inayat Khan,* East-West Publications, 1971, 2nd revised edition published under original title, 1988.

The Starr Affair, Gollancz, 1954, published as *No. 13 Bob,* Little, Brown, 1955.

Double Webs, Putnam, 1958, published as *Double Agents,* Pan Books, 1961.

Horoscope for a Double Agent, Fowler, 1961.

Venus Protected, and Other Poems, Outposts Publications, 1964.

The Magical Dilemma of Victor Neuburg (biography), W. H. Allen, 1965, revised edition, Mandrake, 1990.

Carthage and the Midnight Sun (poetry), Villiers Publications, 1966.

Swinburne: A Critical Biography, Chatto & Windus, 1968.

Shelley: A Biography, J. Cape, 1968.

African Violets (poetry), Manifold, 1968.

Darun and Pitar (poetry), Fuller d'Arch Smith, 1970.

Tintagel (poetry), Sceptre Press, 1970.

Conversations with a Captor (poetry), Fuller d'Arch Smith, 1973.

The German Penetration of S.O.E., Kimber, 1975.

Shiva's Dance (poetry in translation), Fuller d'Arch Smith, 1979.

Sir Francis Bacon: A Biography, East-West Publications, 1981.

That the Gods May Remember (poetry in translation), Fuller d'Arch Smith, 1982.

The Comte de Saint-Germain, Last Scion of the House of Rakoczy, East-West Publications, 1986.

Blavatsky and her Teachers: An Investigative Biography, East-West Publications, 1988.

Dericourt, the Chequered Spy, Michael Russell, 1989.

Sickert and the Ripper Crimes, Mandrake, 1991.

(Self-illustrated) *Cats and Other Immortals,* Fuller d'Arch Smith, 1992.

The Court Lees Canings, Mandrake, 1993.

Contributor to *Essays in Criticism.* Contributor to *Sunday Referee, Comment, Aylesford Review,* and *Theosophical History.*

WORK IN PROGRESS: The Smoke and the Flame, "a big book on theosophical and similar (and dissimilar) movements from the death of Blavatsky to the death of Krishnamurti, 1891-1986. This will probably have to be split into two volumes."

SIDELIGHTS: Jean Overton Fuller's *Shelley: A Biography* received critical praise from Mary Gould in *Books and Bookmen,* "Fuller has done considerable service to Shelley's reputation by stressing not his oddities, . . . but his genuine and all-embracing goodness which was as unfashionable, misunderstood and unprofitable in his time as in any other." Gould continued, "Miss Fuller's biography reveals her fine scholarship linked to a deep understanding of the humanity of the people in her story, and she writes with a pleasant and fluent clarity."

About *Swinburne: A Critical Biography,* John A. Cuddon in *Books and Bookmen* observed that Fuller "is such an able sleuth, such an accomplished unfolder of a tale and writes such clear, unjargoned prose, that I found her researches continually interesting. At times her investigation has the suspense of a detective story." He assessed her research techniques as thorough and unbiased: "Her method, like that of any good scholar or detective, is not to overlook any evidence and at the same time to leave the mind free of any prejudice or the temptation to make a case." Cuddon concluded that "this is a major contribution to Swinburne studies."

Fuller's book, *Dericourt: The Chequered Spy,* detailed the escapades of British Special Operations double agent, Henri Dericourt. Godfrey Hodgson explained in the *Independent* that "this strange and compelling book is the story of a double agent who played along with the Gestapo to save his life while he continued to work for the French Resistance and the British Special Operations Executive. As it unpeels the intricate deceptions and moral ambiguities of the betrayers and the betrayed, layer by layer, it is a study, not in black and white, but in shades of grey. . . . This book is a satisfying account of the cruel and contradictory ethics which the Occupation inspired."

Fuller herself once saw literary and philosophical endeavors as her primary interest, despite an early fascination with World War II. Noor Inayat Khan, alias "Madeleine" in the World War II French resistance movement, was a pre-war friend of Fuller's. Fuller once told *CA* that "in making inquiries in France and Germany, of ex-Resistants, ex-Gestapo and prison officials, as to what had happened to her, I did the research which resulted in my first book, and uncovered the mysteries which were to absorb me for a decade and result in the two further books on Special Operations, *The Starr Affair* and *Double Webs.*"

Fuller recently told *CA:* "My lifestyle changed when in 1975 I sold my London flat and bought a house in the country (on the Bedfordshire-Northamptonshire border) taking with me my four cats, Tiutte, Bambina, Cynthia, and Cleo, whom I introduced to grass and to hens I bought, two of whom, Susan and Delia, became personal pets, who came into the house and ate with the cats. My book *Dericourt, the Chequered Spy* was (I hope) the last of those concerned with Special Operations in the last war. . . . Its publication left me free to write books of a different kind, my biographies of Sir Francis Bacon, the Comte de Saint-Germain and Mme. Blavatsky all having a more philosophical and spiritual slant. *Sickert and the Ripper Crimes* is an odd one out: I would never have written about the Ripper crimes but for the very odd circumstance that my mother, an artist, came to know another woman artist who had known the last of the Ripper's victims, so that I became the last receiver of a story containing primary information that would die with me unless I disclosed it. The most recent of my books, *Cats and Other Immortals,* is in a very different vein, one that is dear to my heart, being the story of my little family of cats (and hens), illustrated with seventy full colour reproductions of my oil paintings of them. Although principally a writer, I did study painting at the Academie Julien in Paris, and have exhibited at the Chelsea Arts and elsewhere. Some of my earlier books have had pictures by me in them, and I painted the portrait on the jacket of the recent new edition of my biography of Victor Neuburg, but this was the first chance to show the paintings extensively."

BIOGRAPHICAL/CRITICAL SOURCES:

PERIODICALS

Books and Bookmen, April, 1968; February, 1969.

Independent, May 26, 1989.

G

GAINES, Ernest J(ames) 1933-

PERSONAL: Born January 15, 1933, in Oscar, LA (some sources cite River Lake Plantation, near New Roads, Pointe Coupee Parish, LA); son of Manuel (a laborer) and Adrienne J. (Colar) Gaines. *Education:* Attended Vallejo Junior College; San Francisco State College (now University), B.A., 1957; graduate study at Stanford University, 1958-59.

ADDRESSES: *Office*—Department of English, University of Southwestern Louisiana, P.O. Box 44691, Lafayette, LA 70504. *Agent*—JCA Literary Agency, Inc., 242 West 27th St., New York, NY 10001.

CAREER: "Writing, five hours a day, five days a week." Denison University, Granville, OH, writer in residence, 1971; Stanford University, Stanford, CA, writer in residence, 1981; University of Southwestern Louisiana, Lafayette, professor of English and writer in residence, 1983—. Whittier College, visiting professor, 1983, and writer in residence, 1986. Subject of the film, *Louisiana Stories: Ernest Gaines,* which aired on WHMM-TV in 1993. *Military service:* U.S. Army, 1953-55.

AWARDS, HONORS: Wallace Stegner fellow, Stanford University, 1957; Joseph Henry Jackson Award from San Francisco Foundation, 1959, for "Comeback" (short story); award from National Endowment for the Arts, 1967; Rockefeller grant, 1970; Guggenheim fellow, 1971; award from Black Academy of Arts and Letters, 1972; fiction gold medal from Commonwealth Club of California, 1972, for *The Autobiography of Miss Jane Pittman,* and 1984, for *A Gathering of Old Men;* award from Louisiana Library Association, 1972; honorary doctorate of letters from Denison University, 1980, Brown University, 1985, Bard College, 1985, and Louisiana State University, 1987; award for excellence of achievement in literature from San Francisco Arts Commission, 1983; D.H.L. from Whittier College, 1986; literary award from American Academy and Institute of Arts and Letters, 1987; John D. and Catherine T. MacArthur Foundation fellowship, 1993.

WRITINGS:

FICTION

Catherine Carmier (novel), Atheneum, 1964.
Of Love and Dust (novel), Dial, 1967.
Bloodline (short stories; also see below), Dial, 1968.
A Long Day in November (story originally published in *Bloodline*), Dial, 1971.
The Autobiography of Miss Jane Pittman (novel), Dial, 1971.
In My Father's House (novel), Knopf, 1978.
A Gathering of Old Men (novel), Knopf, 1983.
A Lesson Before Dying (novel), Knopf, 1993.

Contributor of stories to anthologies and periodicals.

ADAPTATIONS: *The Autobiography of Miss Jane Pittman,* adapted from Gaines's novel, aired on the Columbia Broadcasting System (CBS-TV), January 31, 1974, starring Cicely Tyson in the title role; the special won nine Emmy Awards. "The Sky Is Gray," a short story originally published in *Bloodline,* was adapted for public television in 1980. *A Gathering of Old Men,* adapted from Gaines's novel, aired on CBS-TV, May 10, 1987, starring Lou Gossett, Jr., and Richard Widmark.

SIDELIGHTS: The fiction of Ernest J. Gaines, including his 1971 novel *The Autobiography of Miss Jane Pittman,* is deeply rooted in the black culture and storytelling traditions of rural Louisiana where the author was born and raised. His stories have been noted for their convincing characters and powerful themes presented within authentic—often folk-like—narratives that tap into the complex world of Southern rural life. Gaines depicts the strength and dignity of his black characters in the face of numerous struggles: the dehumanizing and destructive effects of racism; the breakdown in personal relationships as a result of social pressures; and the choice between secured traditions and the sometimes radical measures necessary to bring about social change. Although the issues presented in Gaines's fiction are serious and often disturbing, "this is not hot-and-breathless, burn-baby-burn writing," Melvin Maddocks points out in *Time;* rather, it is the work of "a patient artist, a patient man." Expounding on Gaines's rural heritage, Maddocks continues: "[Gaines] sets down a story as if he were planting, spreading the roots deep, wide and firm. His stories grow organically, at their own rhythm. When they ripen at last, they do so inevitably, arriving at a climax with the absolute rightness of a folk tale." Larry McMurtry in the *New York Times Book Review* adds that as "a swimmer cannot influence the flow of a river, . . . the characters of Ernest Gaines . . . are propelled by a prose that is serene, considered and unexcited." Jerry H. Bryant in the *Iowa Review* writes that Gaines's fiction "contains the austere dignity and simplicity of ancient epic, a concern with man's most powerful emotions and the actions that arise from those emotions, and an artistic intuition that carefully keeps such passions and behavior under fictive control. Gaines may be one of our most naturally gifted story-tellers."

Gaines's boyhood experiences growing up on a Louisiana plantation provide many of the impressions upon which his stories are based. Particularly important, he told Paul Desruisseaux in the *New York Times Book Review,* were "working in the fields, going fishing in the swamps with the older people, and, especially, listening to the people who came to my aunt's house, the aunt who raised me." Although Gaines moved to California at the age of fifteen and subsequently went to college there, his fiction has been based in an imaginary Louisiana plantation region named Bayonne, which a number of critics have compared to William Faulkner's Yoknapatawpha County. Gaines has acknowledged looking to Faulkner, in addition to Ernest Hemingway, for language, and to French writers such as Gustave Flaubert and Guy de Maupassant for style. A perhaps greater influence, however, has been the writings of nineteenth-century Russian authors. In a profile by Beverly Beyette for the *Los Angeles Times,* Gaines explains that reading the works of authors such as Nikolai Gogol, Ivan Turgenev, and Anton Chekhov helped unlock the significance of his rural past. "I found something that I had not truly found in American writers," he told Beyette. "They [the Russian writers] dealt with peasantry differently. . . . I did not particularly find what I was looking for in the Southern writers. When they came to describing my own people, they did not do it the way that I knew my people to be. The Russians were not talking about my people, but about a peasantry for which they seemed to show such feeling. Reading them, I could find a way to write about my own people." That Gaines knew a different South from the one he read about in books also provided an incentive to write. "If the book you want doesn't exist, you try to make it exist," he told Joseph McLellan in the *Washington Post.* Gaines later told Beyette: "That's the book that influenced me most. . . . I tried to put it there on that shelf, and I'm still trying to do that."

Gaines's first novel, *Catherine Carmier,* is "an apprentice work more interesting for what it anticipates than for its accomplishments," notes William E. Grant in the *Dictionary of Literary Biography.* The novel chronicles the story of a young black man, Jackson Bradley, who returns to Bayonne after completing his education in California. Jackson falls in love with Catherine, the daughter of a Creole sharecropper who refuses to let members of his family associate with anyone darker than themselves, believing Creoles racially and socially superior. The novel portrays numerous clashes of loyalty: Catherine torn between her love for Jackson and love for her father; Jackson caught between a bond to the community he grew up in and the experience and knowledge he has gained in the outside world. "Both Catherine and Jackson are immobilized by the pressures of [the] rural community," writes Keith E. Byermann in the *Dictionary of Literary Biography,* which produces "twin themes of isolation and paralysis [that] give the novel an existential quality. Characters must face an unfriendly world without guidance and must make crucial choices about their lives." The characters in *Catherine Carmier*—as in much of Gaines's fiction—are faced with struggles that test the conviction of personal beliefs. Winifred L. Stoelting in *CLA Journal* explains that Gaines is concerned more "with how they [his characters] handle their decisions than with the rightness of their decisions—more often than not predetermined by social changes over which the single individual has little control."

Gaines sets *Catherine Carmier* in the time of the Civil Rights movement, yet avoids making it a primary force in the novel. Grant comments on this aspect: "In divorcing his tale from contemporary events, Gaines declares his independence from the political and social purposes of much contemporary black writing. Instead, he elects to concentrate upon those fundamental human passions and conflicts which transcend the merely social level of human existence." Grant finds Gaines "admirable" for doing this, yet also believes Jackson's credibility marred because he remains aloof from contemporary events. For Grant, the novel "seems to float outside time and place rather than being solidly anchored in the real world of the modern South." Byerman concurs, stating that the novel "is not entirely successful in presenting its major characters and their motivations." Nonetheless, he points out that in *Catherine Carmier,* "Gaines does begin to create a sense of the black community and its perceptions of the world around it. Shared ways of speaking, thinking, and relating to the dominant white society are shown through a number of minor characters."

Gaines's next novel, *Of Love and Dust,* is also a story of forbidden romance, and, as in *Catherine Carmier,* a "new world of expanding human relationships erodes the old world of love for the land and the acceptance of social and economic stratification," writes Stoelting. *Of Love and Dust* is the story of Marcus Payne, a young black man bonded out of prison by a white landowner and placed under the supervision of a Cajun overseer, Sidney Bonbon. Possessed of a rebellious and hostile nature, Marcus is a threat to Bonbon, who in turn does all that he can to break the young man's spirit. In an effort to strike back, Marcus pays special attention to the overseer's wife; the two fall in love and plot to run away. The novel ends with a violent confrontation between the two men, in which Marcus is killed. After the killing, Bonbon claims that to spare Marcus would have meant his own death at the hands of other Cajuns. Grant notes a similarity between *Of Love and Dust* and *Catherine Carmier* in that the characters are "caught up in a decadent social and economic system that determines their every action and limits their possibilities." Similarly, the two novels are marked by a "social determinism [which] shapes the lives of all the characters, making them pawns in a mechanistic world order rather than free agents."

Of Love and Dust demonstrates Gaines's development as a novelist, offering a clearer view of the themes and characters that dominate his later work. Stoelting writes that "in a more contemporary setting, the novel . . . continues Gaines's search for human dignity, and when that is lacking, acknowledges the salvation of pride," adding that "the characters themselves grow into a deeper awareness than those of [his] first novel. More sharply drawn . . . [they] are more decisive in their actions." Byerman writes that the novel "more clearly condemns the economic, social, and racial system of the South for the problems faced by its characters." Likewise, the first-person narrator in the novel—a co-worker of Marcus—"both speaks in the idiom of the place and time and instinctively asserts the values of the black community."

Gaines turns to a first-person narrator again in his next novel, *The Autobiography of Miss Jane Pittman,* which many consider to be his masterwork. Miss Jane Pittman—well over one hundred years old—relates a personal history that spans the time from the Civil War and slavery up through the Civil Rights movement of the 1960s. "To travel with Miss Pittman from adolescence to old age is to embark upon a historic journey, one staked out in the format of the novel," writes Addison Gayle, Jr., in *The Way of the World: The Black Novel in America.* "Never mind that Miss Jane Pittman is fictitious, and that her 'autobiography,' offered up in the form of taped reminiscences, is artifice," adds Josh Greenfield in *Life,* "the effect is stunning." Gaines's gift for drawing convincing characters reaches a peak in *The Autobiography of Miss Jane Pittman.* "His is not . . . an 'art' narrative, but an authentic narrative by an authentic ex-slave, authentic even though both are Gaines's inventions," Bryant comments. "So successful is he in *becoming* Miss Jane Pittman, that when we talk about her story, we do not think of Gaines as her creator, but as her recording editor."

The character of Jane Pittman could be called an embodiment of the black experience in America. "Though Jane is the dominant personality of the narrative—observer and commentator upon history, as well as participant—in her odyssey is symbolized the odyssey of a race of people; through her eyes is revealed the grandeur of a people's journey through history," writes Gayle. "The central metaphor of the novel concerns this journey: Jane and her people, as they come together in the historic march toward dignity and freedom in Sampson, symbolize a people's march through history, breaking old patterns, though sometimes slowly, as they do." The important historical backdrop to Jane's narrative—slavery, Reconstruction, the Civil Rights movement, segregation—does not compromise, however, the detailed account of an individual. "Jane captures the experiences of those millions of illiterate blacks who never had a chance to tell their own stories," Byerman explains. "By focusing on the particular yet typical events of a small part of Louisiana, those lives are given a concreteness and specificity not possible in more general histories."

In his fourth novel, *In My Father's House,* Gaines focuses on a theme which appears in varying degrees throughout his fiction: the alienation between fathers and sons. As the author told Desruisseaux: "In my books there always seems to be fathers and sons searching for each other. That's a theme I've worked with since I started writing. Even when the father was not in the story, I've dealt with his absence and its effects on his children. And that is the theme of this book." *In My Father's House* tells of a prominent civil rights leader and reverend (Phillip Martin) who, at the peak of his career, is confronted with a troubled young man named Robert X. Although Robert's identity is initially a mystery, eventually he is revealed to be one of three offspring from a love affair the reverend had in an earlier, wilder life. Martin hasn't seen or attempted to locate his family for more than twenty years. Robert arrives to confront and kill the father whose neglect he sees as responsible for the family's disintegration: his sister has been raped, his brother imprisoned for the murder of her attacker, and his mother reduced to poverty, living alone. Although the son's intent to kill his father is never carried out, the reverend is forced "to undergo a long and painful odyssey through his own past and the labyrinthine streets of Baton Rouge to learn what really happened to his first family," writes William Burke in the *Dictionary of Literary Biography Yearbook.* McMurtry notes that as the book traces the lost family, "we have revealed to us an individual, a marriage, a community and a region, but with such an unobtrusive marshaling of detail that we never lose sight of the book's central thematic concern: the profoundly destructive consequences of the breakdown of parentage, of a father's abandonment of his children and the terrible and irrevocable consequences of such an abandonment."

Burke writes that *In My Father's House* presents the particular problem of manhood for the black male, which he notes as a recurring theme in Gaines's fiction: "Phillip Martin's failure to keep his first family whole, to honor his and [his companion's] love by marriage, and the dissipation of the first half of his adult life—these unfortunate events are clearly a consequence of Martin's fear of accepting the responsibilities of black manhood." Burke highlights the accumulated effects of racism on black males, and cites Gaines's comments to Desruisseaux: "You must understand that the blacks who were brought here as slaves were prevented from becoming the men that they could be. . . . A *man* can speak up, he can do things to protect himself, his home and his family, but the slaves could never do that. If the white said the slave was wrong, he was wrong. . . . So eventually the blacks started stepping over the line, [saying] 'Damn what *you* think I'm supposed to be—I will be what I ought to be. And if I must die to do it, I'll die'. . . . Quite a few of my characters step over that line."

A Gathering of Old Men, Gaines's fifth novel, presents a cast of aging Southern black men who, after a life of subordination and intimidation, make a defiant stand against injustice. Seventeen of them, together with the 30-year-old white heiress of a deteriorating Louisiana plantation, plead guilty to murdering a hostile member (Beau Boutan) of a violent Cajun clan. While a confounded sheriff and vengeful family wait to lynch the black they've decided is guilty, the group members—toting recently fired shotguns—surround the dead man and "confess" their motives. "Each man tells of the accumulated frustrations of his life—raped daughters, jailed sons, public insults, economic exploitation—that serve as sufficient motive for murder," writes Byerman. "Though Beau Boutan is seldom the immediate cause of their anger, he clearly represents the entire white world that has deprived them of their dignity and manhood. The confessions serve as ritual purgings of all the hostility and self-hatred built up over the years." Fifteen or so characters—white, black, and Cajun—advance the story through individual narrations, creating "thereby a range of social values as well as different perspectives on the action," notes Byerman. Reynolds Price writes in the *New York Times Book Review* that the black narrators "are nicely distinguished from one another in rhythm and idiom, in the nature of what they see and report, especially in their specific laments for past passivity in the face of suffering." The accumulated effect, observes Elaine Kendall in the *Los Angeles Times Book Review,* is that the "individual stories coalesce into a single powerful tale of subjugation, exploitation and humiliation at the hands of landowners." Price comments that although "some of them, especially at the beginning, are a little long-winded and repetitive, in the manner of country preachers[,] . . . a patient reader will sense the power of their stories through their dead-level voices, which speak not from the heart of a present fear but from lifetimes of humiliation and social impotence. They are choosing now to take a stand, on ground where they've yielded for centuries—ground that is valuable chiefly through their incessant labor."

Another theme of *A Gathering of Old Men,* according to Ben Forkner in *America,* is "the simple, natural dispossession of old age, of the traditional and well-loved values of the past, the old trades and the old manners, forced to give way to modern times." Sam Cornish writes in the *Christian Science Monitor* that the novel's "characters—both black and white—understand that, before the close of the novel, the new South must confront the old, and all will be irrevocably changed. Gaines portrays a society that will be altered by the deaths of its 'old men,' and so presents an allegory about the passing of the old and birth of the new."

A Lesson Before Dying, issued ten years after *A Gathering of Old Men,* continues the author's historical reflections on the Southern world captured in all of his novels to date. The setting remains relatively the same—a plantation near and a jail in Bayonne during a six-month span in 1948. The unlikely hero is Jefferson, a scarcely literate, twenty-one-year-old man-child who works the cane fields of the Pichot Plantation. Trouble finds the protagonist when he innocently hooks up with two men, who rob a liquor store and are killed in the process along with the shop's proprietor, leaving Jefferson as an accomplice. The young man's naivete in the crime is never recognized as he is brought to trial before a jury of twelve white men and sentenced to death. Jefferson's defense attorney ineffectively attempts to save his client by presenting him as a dumb animal, as "a thing that acts on command. A thing to hold the handle of a plow, a thing to load your bales of cotton." When Jefferson's godmother learns of this analogy, she determines that her nephew will face his execution as a man, not as an animal. Thus, she enlists the help of a young teacher named Grant Wiggins, who is initially resistant but works to help Jefferson achieve manhood in his final days.

According to Sandra D. Davis in the *Detroit Free Press,* "*A Lesson Before Dying* begins much like many other stories where racial tension brews in the background." Yet, as in Gaines's other works, the racial tension in this novel is more of a catalyst for his tribute to the perseverance of the victims of injustice. Unexpectantly, pride, honor, and manhood in a dehumanizing environment emerge as the themes of this novel. Through Wiggins, the young narrator and unwilling carrier of the "burden" of the community, and his interaction with the black community, as represented by Jefferson's godmother and the town's Reverend Ambrose, Gaines "creates a compelling, intense story about heroes and the human spirit," contends Davis. Ironically, Jefferson and Reverend Ambrose ultimately emerge as the real teachers, showing Wiggins that, as Davis asserts, "education encompasses more than the lessons taught in school." Wiggins is also forced to admit, according to Jonathan Yardley in *Washington Post Book World,* "his own complicity in the system of which Jefferson is a victim."

With *A Lesson Before Dying,* Gaines remains an objective realist, alluding to all of the horrors of Jim Crowism while creating complex relationships among white power brokers, such as plantation owner Henri Pichot, and Miss Emma and other members of the black and white communities. Paul, a white jailer first introduced in *Bloodline,* is, as Yardley states, "one of the most sympathetic characters" in the novel who "befriends Grant and quietly helps Jefferson." However, *Lesson* is neither a sentimental novel in which injustice is recognized nor in which the immediate social consequences of Jefferson's negation of the "myth" of black manhood are depicted. Conversely, "the drama of the novel's final pages is psychological," Yardley concludes, and "the questions involve how Jefferson will face his final hours and what the rest of the community, Grant most particularly, can learn from them." The novel, then, is not about a single lesson but various lessons "presented in the modest but forceful terms that we have come to expect from Ernest J. Gaines," asserts Yardley.

Of that community which yields the lessons of Gaines' fiction and his relation to it, Alice Walker writes in the *New York Times Book Review* that Gaines "claims and revels in the rich heritage of Southern Black people and their customs; the community he feels with them is unmistakable and goes deeper even than pride. . . . Gaines is mellow with historical reflection, supple with wit, relaxed and expansive because he does not equate his people with failure." Gaines has been criticized by some, however, who feel his writing does not more directly focus on problems facing blacks. Gaines responds to Desruisseaux that he feels "too many blacks have been writing to tell whites all about 'the problems,' instead of writing something that all people, including their own, could find interesting, could enjoy." Gaines has also remarked that more can be achieved than strictly writing novels of protest. In an interview for *San Francisco,* the author states: "So many of our writers have not read any farther back than [Richard Wright's] *Native Son.* So many of our novels deal only with the great city ghettos; that's all we write about, as if there's nothing else." Gaines continues: "We've only been living in these ghettos for 75 years or so, but the other 300 years—I think this is worth writing about."

BIOGRAPHICAL/CRITICAL SOURCES:

BOOKS

Authors in the News, Volume 1, Gale, 1976.

Babb, Valerie-Melissa, *Ernest Gaines,* Twayne, 1991.

Bruck, Peter, editor, *The Black American Short Story in the Twentieth Century: A Collection of Critical Essays,* B. R. Gruner (Amsterdam), 1977.

Concise Dictionary of American Literary Biography: Broadening Views, 1968-1988, Gale, 1989.

Contemporary Literary Criticism, Gale, Volume 3, 1975, Volume 11, 1979, Volume 18, 1981.

Dictionary of Literary Biography, Gale, Volume 2: *American Novelists since World War II,* 1978, Volume 33: *Afro-American Fiction Writers after 1955,* 1984.

Dictionary of Literary Biography Yearbook: 1980, Gale, 1981.

Gaudet, Marcia, and Carl Wooton, *Porch Talk with Ernest Gaines: Conversations on the Writer's Craft,* Louisiana State University Press, 1990.

Gayle, Addison, Jr., *The Way of the New World: The Black Novel in America,* Doubleday, 1975.

Hicks, Jack, *In the Singer's Temple: Prose Fictions of Barthelme, Gaines, Brautigan, Piercy, Kesey, and Kosinski,* University of North Carolina Press, 1981.

Hudson, Theodore R., *The History of Southern Literature,* Louisiana State University Press, 1985.

O'Brien, John, editor, *Interview with Black Writers,* Liveright, 1973.

PERIODICALS

America, June 2, 1984.

Black American Literature Forum, Volume 11, 1977; Volume 24, 1990.

Callaloo, Volume 7, 1984; Volume 11, 1988.

Chicago Tribune Book World, October 30, 1983.

Christian Science Monitor, December 2, 1983.

CLA Journal, March, 1971; December, 1975.

Detroit Free Press, June 6, 1993, p. 7J.

Essence, August, 1993, p. 52.

Griot, Volume 2, 1983; Volume 3, 1984.

Iowa Review, winter, 1972.

Life, April 30, 1971.

Los Angeles Times, March 2, 1983.
Los Angeles Times Book Review, January 1, 1984.
Meleus, Volume 11, 1984.
Nation, February 5, 1968; April 5, 1971; January 14, 1984.
Negro Digest, November, 1967; January, 1968; January, 1969.
New Orleans Review, Volume 1, 1969; Volume 3, 1972; Volume 14, 1987.
New Republic, December 26, 1983.
New Statesman, September 2, 1973; February 10, 1984.
Newsweek, June 16, 1969; May 3, 1971.
New Yorker, October 24, 1983.
New York Times, July 20, 1978.
New York Times Book Review, November 19, 1967; May 23, 1971; June 11, 1978; October 30, 1983.
Observer, February 5, 1984.
San Francisco, July, 1974.
Southern Review, Volume 10, 1974; Volume 21, 1985.
Studies in Short Fiction, summer, 1975.
Time, May 10, 1971; December 27, 1971.
Times Literary Supplement, February 10, 1966; March 16, 1973; April 6, 1984.
Village Voice Literary Supplement, October, 1983.
Washington Post, January 13, 1976.
Washington Post Book World, June 18, 1978; September 21, 1983; March 28, 1993, p. 3; May 23, 1993.
Washington Times, April 14, 1993, p. 3E.
Xavier Review, Volume 3, 1983.

* * *

GARRETT, George (Palmer) 1929-

PERSONAL: Born June 11, 1929, in Orlando, FL; son of George Palmer (a lawyer) and Rosalie (Toomer) Garrett; married Susan Parrish Jackson (a musician), June 14, 1952; children: William Palmer, George Gorham, Alice. *Education:* Attended Columbia University, 1948-49; Princeton University, B.A., 1952, M.A., 1956. *Politics:* Democrat. *Religion:* Episcopalian.

ADDRESSES: Home and office—1845 Wayside Place, Charlottesville, VA 22903.

CAREER: Wesleyan University, Middletown, CT, assistant professor, 1957-60; Rice University, Houston, TX, visiting assistant professor, 1961-62; University of Virginia, Charlottesville, associate professor, 1962-67; Princeton University, Princeton, NJ, writer-in-residence, 1964-65; Hollins College, Hollins College, VA, professor of English and director of graduate program, 1967-71; University of South Carolina, Columbia, professor and writer-in-residence, 1971-74; Florida International University, Miami, FL, visiting professor, 1974; Princeton University, Princeton, senior fellow of the Council of Humanities, 1975-77; Columbia University, New York, NY, adjunct professor, 1977-78; University of Michigan, Ann Arbor, writer-in-residence, 1979; Bennington College, Bennington, VT, visiting professor, 1979-80; Virginia Military Institute, Lexington, visiting professor, 1981; University of Michigan, Ann Arbor, professor of English, 1982-84; University of Virginia, Charlottesville, Hoyns Professor of English, 1984—. *Military service:* U.S. Army, field artillery, 1952-55.

MEMBER: Modern Language Association of America, Authors Guild, Writers Guild, Fellowship of Southern Writers (chancellor, 1993—), Poetry Society of America, Southern Historical Association, Florida Historical Society, Princeton Tower Club, Princeton Club of New York.

AWARDS, HONORS: *Sewanee Review* fellow, 1958; American Academy in Rome fellow, 1958-59; Ford Foundation grant, 1961, for drama; National Endowment for the Arts sabbatical fellow, 1966; *Contempora* writing award, 1971; Guggenheim fellow, 1974-75; American Academy and Institute of Arts and Letters award in literature, 1985; T. S. Eliot Award for creative writing, Ingersoll Foundation, 1989; PEN/Malamud Award for short fiction, 1991; Hollins College Medal, 1992.

WRITINGS:

POEMS

(Contributor) John Hall Wheelock, editor, *Poets of Today IV* (includes *The Reverend Ghost: Poems*), Scribner, 1957.
The Sleeping Gypsy and Other Poems, University of Texas Press, 1958.
Abraham's Knife and Other Poems, University of North Carolina Press, 1961.
For a Bitter Season: New and Selected Poems, University of Missouri Press, 1967.
Welcome to the Medicine Show: Postcards, Flashcards, Snapshots, Palaemon Press, 1978.
Luck's Shining Child: A Miscellany of Poems and Verses, Palaemon Press, 1981.
The Collected Poems of George Garrett, University of Arkansas Press, 1984.

STORY COLLECTIONS

King of the Mountain, Scribner, 1958.
In the Briar Patch, University of Texas Press, 1961.
Cold Ground Was My Bed Last Night, University of Missouri Press, 1964.
A Wreath for Garibaldi and Other Stories, Hart Davis, 1969.
The Magic Striptease, Doubleday, 1973.
To Recollect a Cloud of Ghosts: Christmas in England, Palaemon Press, 1979.

An Evening Performance: New and Selected Short Stories, Doubleday, 1985.

NOVELS

The Finished Man, Scribner, 1959.

Which Ones Are the Enemy?, Little, Brown, 1961.

Do, Lord, Remember Me, Doubleday, 1965.

Death of the Fox: A Novel about Ralegh, Doubleday, 1971, published as *Death of the Fox: A Novel of Elizabeth and Raleigh*, Harcourt, 1991.

The Succession: A Novel of Elizabeth and James, Doubleday, 1983.

Poison Pen, Wright, 1986.

Entered from the Sun, Doubleday, 1990, published as *Entered from the Sun: The Murder of Marlow*, Harcourt, 1991.

PLAYS

Sir Slob and the Princess: A Play for Children, Samuel French, 1962.

Garden Spot, U.S.A., produced in Houston, TX, at the Alley Theatre, April 25, 1962.

Enchanted Ground, Old Gaol Museum Press, 1981.

EDITOR

New Writing from Virginia, New Writing Associates, 1963.

The Girl in the Black Raincoat, Duell, 1966.

(With W. R. Robinson) *Man and the Movies*, Louisiana State University Press, 1967.

(With R. H. W. Dillard and John Moore) *The Sounder Few: Essays from 'The Hollins Critic,'* University of Georgia Press, 1971.

(With Jane R. Gelfman and O. B. Hardison, Jr.) *Film Scripts One* (contains *Henry V*, *The Big Sleep*, and *A Streetcar Named Desire*), Appleton, 1971.

(With Gelfman and Hardison) *Film Scripts Two* (contains *High Noon*, *Twelve Angry Men*, and *The Defiant Ones*), Appleton, 1971.

(With William Peden) *New Writing in South Carolina*, University of South Carolina, 1971.

(With John Graham) *Craft So Hard to Learn: Conversations with Poets and Novelists about the Teaching of Writing*, Morrow, 1972.

(With Gelfman and Hardison) *Film Scripts Three* (contains *The Apartment*, *The Misfits*, and *Charade*), Appleton, 1972.

(With Gelfman and Hardison) *Film Scripts Four* (contains *A Hard Day's Night*, *The Best Man*, and *Darling*), Appleton, 1972.

(With Graham) *The Writer's Voice: Conversations with Contemporary Writers*, Morrow, 1973.

(With Walton Beacham) *Intro 5*, University Press of Virginia, 1974.

(With Katherine Garrison Biddle) *The Botteghe Oscure Reader*, Wesleyan University Press, 1974.

Intro 6: Life as We Know It, Doubleday, 1974.

Intro 7: All of Us and None of You, Doubleday, 1975.

Intro 8: The Liar's Craft, Doubleday, 1977.

(With Michael Mewshaw) *Intro 9: Close to Home*, Hendel & Reinke, 1979.

(With Sheila McMillen) *Eric Clapton's Lover and Other Stories from the Virginia Quarterly Review*, University Press of Virginia, 1990.

(With Susan Stamberg) *The Wedding Cake in the Middle of the Road: 23 Variations on a Theme*, Norton, 1991.

(With Mary C. Flinn) *Elvis in Oz: New Stories and Poems from the Hollins Creative Writing Program*, University Press of Virginia, 1992.

(With Paul Ruffin) *That's What I Like about the South, and Other New Southern Stories for the Nineties*, University of South Carolina Press, 1993.

SCREENPLAYS

The Young Lovers, Metro-Goldwyn-Mayer, 1964.

The Playground (based on *My Brother Death* by Cyrus L. Sulzberger), Jerand Film Release, 1965.

(With others) *Frankenstein Meets the Space Monster*, Allied Artists, 1966, also released as *Mars Invades Puerto Rico*.

Also author of scripts for *Suspense* television series, CBS, 1958.

OTHER

James Jones, Harcourt, 1984.

Understanding Mary Lee Settle, University of South Carolina Press, 1988.

My Silk Purse and Yours: The Publishing Scene and American Literary Art, University of Missouri Press, 1992.

The Sorrows of Fat City: A Selection of Literary Essays and Reviews, University of South Carolina Press, 1992.

Whistling in the Dark: True Stories and Other Fables, Harcourt, 1992.

Editor, "Contemporary Poetry" series, University of North Carolina Press, 1962-68, and "Short Story" series, Louisiana State University Press, 1966-69. Contributor to *Dictionary of Literary Biography* series and *Dictionary of Literary Biography Yearbook* series, Gale. Contributor of stories to *Four Quarters*, *Approach*, *Transatlantic Review*, *New Mexico Quarterly*, *Texas Review*, *South Carolina Review*, and other periodicals. Poetry editor, *Transatlantic Review*, 1958-71; *Hollins Critic*, contributing editor, 1965-67, co-editor, 1967-71; contributing editor, *Contempora*, 1969-73; assistant editor, *Film Journal*, 1970-74; consulting editor, *Kudzu*, 1978—; co-editor, *Poultry: A Magazine of Voice*, 1979—; fiction editor, *Texas Review*,

1989—. Collections of Garrett's manuscripts are housed at Stuart Wright, Winston-Salem, NC.

SIDELIGHTS: George Garrett has had a varied writing career. He has published stories, poems, and criticism, edited anthologies, written screenplays, and taught at a number of universities across the United States. Garrett is best known, however, for his trilogy of historical novels—*Death of the Fox, The Succession,* and *Entered from the Sun.* These books have earned him critical praise for their authentic rendering of Elizabethan England and for their imaginative weaving of fact and speculation. Speaking of *Death of the Fox,* A. Z. Silver of *Saturday Review* finds the novel to be "a brilliant re-creation of Elizabethan and Jacobean England, a triumph of intellect and imagination." Writing of *The Succession,* Kendall Mitchell in the *Chicago Tribune Book World* concludes that "the book is a triumph of learning, imagination, wisdom and skill." Peter S. Prescott of *Newsweek* calls Garrett "an audacious writer," while the *Washington Post Book World*'s S. Schoenbaum calls him "a lucid, unromantic and unsentimental historical novelist."

In most of Garrett's writing there is a strong undercurrent of Christian faith. R. H. W. Dillard in the *Dictionary of Literary Biography Yearbook 1983* believes that Garrett's faith allows him to write successful historical fiction. "Aside from his talent and intelligence, both prodigious," Dillard explains, "what enabled George Garrett to write [*The Succession*] is what enabled Shakespeare or Tolstoy to write their work at the level they did: a religious belief that gives them an awareness of something larger than the passing moment, that gives them awareness of the presence of the eternal in the temporal, of the universal in the particular."

In all of his historical fiction, Garrett creates a richly textured world. "The time and times of *The Succession,*" Dillard remarks, "are fully imagined and realized, a world of complexity and duplicity, a world of masks and lies and players, a world in which reality and theatricality are inextricably confused, a world of sin and sinners in which the very existence of love seems in question." Speaking of the same novel, Mitchell finds that "in the end, the huge, beautiful tapestry covers the stone-cold walls of history with living people in taverns and palaces and all kinds of weather. . . . Garrett's use of the language is, in itself, remarkable—clear, rich, textured, somehow Elizabethan. . . . Everything looks absolutely right in Garrett's tapestry. . . . What Garrett—almost magically—recaptures is the Elizabethan outlook and tone." Julian Moynihan of the *New York Times Book Review,* in his review of *Death of the Fox,* states: "Garrett creates a labyrinthine world of speculation and inference filled out with a staggering amount of factual, literary, imaginative and sensuous detail."

Garrett began writing historical fiction by accident. As he explains to Dillard, his novel *Do Lord, Remember Me* had been accepted for publication by Duell, Sloan and Pearce. When Duell merged with Meredith Press, however, the new partners did not want the novel. Garrett was asked by Charles Duell if he had anything else available. "I had worked on a Ralegh biography back in the fifties—nothing came of it. . . . ," Garrett recounts. "I said what about Sir Walter Ralegh? I was still thinking about the biography. [Duell] said fine and hung up. Then I got a contract the next day in the mail for Sir Walter Ralegh. That's how I ended up writing historical novels." By the time Garrett finished *Death of the Fox,* Meredith was no longer publishing fiction and so the book was eventually published by Doubleday.

Death of the Fox received praise from the critics for its sweeping power and historical authenticity. As J. R. Frakes expresses it in the *Chicago Tribune Book World,* "Garrett illuminates the entire swarmy world of royalty and commoners, jewels and gutter-garbage, politic church and sharkfight state. All very rich, thick-textured, uncheating, nourishing. . . . *Death of the Fox* is a lovesong to England, a threnody to mutability, a work of committed art, informed with a rare fusion of guts and spirit." The critic for *Virginia Quarterly Review* notes that in Sir Walter Ralegh, "an astonishingly rich character emerges from the story, growing in our consciousness from a series of types into a profounder archetype: a superbly human creature, a genuine hero and maker of myths that we live by."

One of Garrett's primary purposes in his historical fiction is to show the process of time. In *Death of the Fox,* he delineates Sir Walter Ralegh "in a stream of time by use of reveries of telescoped events, told in magnificent, long, rapid sentences, curiously broken up yet continuous—suggesting the baroque prose of the early seventeenth century, without its obscurity or tedium," according to the *Virginia Quarterly Review* critic. In *The Succession,* Garrett presents a group of unrelated characters in the period between 1566 and 1626. Central to the era is the succession to the throne of King James I, although the story follows no particular character. The plot, Dillard notes, is guided by "the experiences and memories and imaginings of all [the] characters. The brilliance of the novel is not that it has so many characters and covers so much time, but that out of all this apparent disorder and disconnection such a coherent and orderly and meaningful whole takes shape." Maureen Quilligan of the *New York Times Book Review* explains that in the novel "chronological sequence is elided in favor of a subtle, complex meditation on the poetry of time. . . . The novel is a choral reflection on how our memories and imaginations shape time and history into polyphonic music."

In *Entered from the Sun,* Garrett creates two fictional characters who investigate the mysterious death of playwright Christopher Marlowe in 1593. Impartial and determined to learn the truth, the actor Joseph Hunnyman and the spy Captain William Barfoot dig through the possible motives and suspects in Marlowe's stabbing death. The critic for *Publishers Weekly* calls *Entered from the Sun* "a novel of rare literary quality, wondrously steeped in the world it artfully depicts," while Fred Shafer in *Tribune Books* finds it to be "a lively, absorbing book, rich in discoveries and insights. . . . The deep sympathy Garrett has for his characters is evident not only in the incidents and details of 'Entered from the Sun' but also in his remarkable narrative voice, which is by turns lyrical, boisterous, and reflective."

Garrett's short fiction has garnered critical praise for its willingness to honestly confront human emotions. Elaine Kendall in the *Los Angeles Times* explains that "Garrett's work is widely appealing, dealing in the most directly accessible way with a full range of human experience." Greg Johnson in the *New York Times Book Review* claims that Garrett's stories are "defiantly 'unfashionable' in style. In our age of pared-down realism, Mr. Garrett's flaws as a writer—a fondness for elaborate similes, an occasional straining after poetic effects and a general prolixity—are particularly noticeable." The collection *An Evening Performance,* Johnson finds, "displays a fitful but genuine power and shows Mr. Garrett as a master of this distinctive form." In her review of the book for the *Washington Post Book World,* Josephine Jacobsen judges the story "Noise of Strangers" to be "a contemporary classic. To describe it would be to injure it, but it deals, brilliantly, with the possibility of justice. . . . In it Garrett's strengths are at their height: atmosphere, characterization, dialogue, scope."

"I have been writing all my life and publishing and calling myself a 'professional' for more than 25 years," Garrett told *CA.* "And still I feel like a beginner. Which feeling is, I believe, accurate. Because one is always beginning, always challenged to learn newly. And what one learns is how you should have done the last book, the last story, the last poem. With that knowledge one commences the next and new ones with innocence rather than experience, with hope and faith and no security. Even habits, good or bad, aren't much help. This (to me) is the joy of the enterprise, always to be challenged, at hazard, working and living a quest without ending for as long as I may live. And for as long as I live I want to continue to try my all at doing it all—fiction, poetry, criticism, drama, films, etc. Treating each and every piece of work as first and last. 'Success' is mostly a matter of luck. But this joy, the joy of always beginning, making and doing, is a matter of faith and hope and love, given and received.

"Success and failure aside—and I guess now that I've known both sides of the coin, one is never quite as alone as I earlier implied. People, family and a few friends old and new, who have given love and support always, have made it more a shared and communal enterprise than I imagined. So, too, to those readers, old and new and yet to be, who ideally bring half the life of any poem or story to it. I am profoundly grateful to all my good readers and hope to be worthy of them."

BIOGRAPHICAL/CRITICAL SOURCES:

BOOKS

Carr, John, editor, *Kite Flying and Other Irrational Acts: Conversations with Twelve Southern Writers,* Louisiana State University, 1972, pp. 174-198.

Contemporary Authors Autobiography Series, Volume 5, Gale, 1987.

Contemporary Literary Criticism, Gale, Volume 3, 1975, Volume 11, 1979, Volume 51, 1989.

Dictionary of Literary Biography, Gale, Volume 2: *American Novelists since World War II,* 1978; Volume 5: *American Poets since World War II,* 1980.

Dictionary of Literary Biography Yearbook 1983, Gale, 1984.

Dillard, R. H. W., *Understanding George Garrett,* University of South Carolina Press, 1988.

Ruffin, Paul and Stuart Wright, editor, *To Come Up Grinning: A Tribute to George Garrett,* Texas Review Press, 1989.

Seven Princeton Poets, Princeton University Press, 1963.

Wheelock, John Hall, editor, *Poets of Today IV,* Scribner, 1957.

PERIODICALS

Americas, January, 1974.

Books and Bookmen, October, 1972, p. 75.

Bulletin of Bibliography, January-March, 1981.

Chicago Tribune Book World, October 24, 1971, p. 19; February 12, 1984.

Detroit News, December 19, 1990.

Fiction International, Number 2, 1984, pp. 135-141.

Hollins Critic, August, 1971, pp. 1-12.

Hudson Review, autumn, 1964, p. 474.

Life, September 24, 1971.

Lively Arts and Book Review, May 21, 1961, p. 27.

Los Angeles Times, September 2, 1984, p. 9; September 19, 1985.

Los Angeles Times Book Review, September 16, 1990, p. 8.

Michigan Quarterly Review, summer, 1984, pp. 446-451.

Mill Mountain Review, summer, 1971 (special George Garrett issue).

New Mexico Quarterly, autumn, 1959, pp. 379-380.

Newsweek, November 21, 1983; September 30, 1985, pp. 71-74.
New York Herald Tribune Book Review, April 6, 1958, p. 3; August 3, 1958, p. 4.
New York Times, December 15, 1983.
New York Times Book Review, March 2, 1958, p. 4; September 28, 1958, p. 40; October 11, 1959, p. 34; June 25, 1961, p. 24; June 14, 1964, p. 4; September 26, 1971, p. 52; December 16, 1973, p. 18; December 25, 1983, p. 6; September 30, 1984; October 6, 1985, p. 28; October 5, 1986, p. 25; October 13, 1991, p. 34.
Poetry, November, 1961, pp. 124-129; August, 1968, p. 340.
Princeton University Library Chronicle, autumn, 1963, pp. 26-32.
Publishers Weekly, December 2, 1983, pp. 90-91; July 6, 1990, p. 58.
Saturday Review, October 2, 1971, p. 48.
Sewanee Review, winter, 1963, pp. 120-121; winter, 1964; spring, 1969.
South Carolina Review, November, 1973, pp. 43-48; November, 1976, pp. 21-24.
Southern Review, winter, 1971, pp. 276-294.
Texas Review, summer, 1983.
Time, November 1, 1971.
Tribune Books (Chicago), October 14, 1990, p. 1.
Village Voice, July 29, 1986, p. 42.
Virginia Quarterly Review, winter, 1966, p. 8; winter, 1966, p. 15; spring, 1972; spring, 1985.
Washington Post Book World, December 2, 1983, p. D10; August 5, 1984, p. 12; September 15, 1985, p. 5; September 9, 1990.
Western Humanities Review, summer, 1985, pp. 155-164.
Western Review, autumn, 1958, pp. 83-89.
Writer's Digest, November, 1972.
Yale Review, autumn, 1959, pp. 126-127.

—Sketch by Thomas Wiloch

* * *

GAUNT, Peter
See ESHBACH, Lloyd Arthur

* * *

GEDULD, Harry M(aurice) 1931-

PERSONAL: Surname is accented on first syllable; born March 3, 1931, in London, England; son of Sol E. and Anne (Berliner) Geduld; married Carolyn Taft, December 24, 1963; children: Marcus Stephen, Daniel Joel. *Education:* University of Sheffield, B.A. (with first class honors), 1953, M.A., 1954; University of London, Ph.D., 1961.

ADDRESSES: Office—Comparative Literature Program, Indiana University at Bloomington, Bloomington, IN 47401.

CAREER: High school teacher in London, England, 1955-62; Indiana University at Bloomington, Bloomington, instructor, 1962-64, assistant professor, 1964-66, associate professor of English, 1966-70, professor of English and comparative literature, 1970-72; University of Maryland, Baltimore, professor of screen arts and English, 1972-73; Indiana University at Bloomington, professor of comparative literature, 1973—, professor of West European studies, 1989—, chairman of Comparative Literature Program, 1990—. Visiting faculty member, Queens College, 1965-66; visiting professor of film studies, University of California at Santa Barbara, 1979. Visiting scholar, University Center of Virginia, 1975.

MEMBER: Society for Cinema Studies.

AWARDS, HONORS: Fulbright scholar, 1959-60; Indiana University faculty fellowship, 1963; distinguished teaching award, Indiana University, 1979; Language Development Award, Indiana University, 1983.

WRITINGS:

(Editor, and author of introduction and notes) George Bernard Shaw, *The Rationalization of Russia,* Indiana University Press, 1964.
(Editor and author of introduction) *Film Makers on Film Making: Statements on Their Art by Thirty Directors,* Indiana University Press, 1967.
Prince of Publishers: A Study of the Life and Work of Jacob Tonson, Indiana University Press, 1969.
(Editor and contributor with Ronald Gottesman) *Sergei Eisenstein and Upton Sinclair: The Making and Unmaking of 'Que Viva Mexico!',* Indiana University Press, 1970, published in England as *The Making and Unmaking of 'Que Viva Mexico!' by Sergei Eisenstein and Upton Sinclair,* Thames & Hudson, 1970.
James Barrie: A Study, Twayne, 1971.
(Editor and author of introduction) *Focus on D. W. Griffith,* Prentice-Hall, 1971.
(Editor with Gottesman) *Guidebook to Film: An Eleven-in-One Reference,* Holt, 1972.
(Editor and author of introduction) *Authors on Film,* Indiana University Press, 1972.
(Editor with Gottesman) *An Illustrated Glossary of Film Terms,* Holt, 1973.
Filmguide to Henry V, Indiana University Press, 1973.
The Birth of the Talkies, Indiana University Press, 1975.
(Editor with Gottesman) *The Girl in the Hairy Paw,* Avon, 1976.
(Editor) *Robots, Robots, Robots,* New York Graphic Society, 1978.

The Definitive Jekyll and Hyde Companion, Garland Publishing, 1983.

(Editor) *The New York Times Film Encyclopedia,* thirteen volumes, Times Books, 1984.

(Editor) *Charlie Chaplin's Own Story,* Indiana University Press, 1985.

Chapliniana, Volume 1, Indiana University Press, 1985.

(Editor) *The Definitive Time Machine,* Indiana University Press, 1986.

German Requiem (play), produced at Fine Arts Auditorium, 1990.

Warsaw: Year Zero (docudrama), produced at Center for Jewish Culture and Creativity, 1991.

(Editor with David Y. Hughes) *Critical Edition of H. G. Wells's War of the Worlds,* Indiana University Press, 1993.

(Editor with Gottesman) *Critical Essays on Film,* Macmillan, 1993.

Also author of liner notes for Pelican record albums *My Man Godfrey, Tales for a Winter's Night, Flash Gordon's Trip to Mars, Sounds from the Silent Screen, The Rogue Song, The New Moon,* and *Garbo Soundtracks.* General editor, "Filmguides" series, Indiana University Press, "Visions" series, Indiana University Press, 1987—, "Film Focus" series, Prentice-Hall, and "The Literature of Mystery and Detection" series, Arno. Contributor of articles and book reviews to numerous journals, including *Denver Quarterly, Studies in Short Fiction, Quarterly Journal of Film Studies, Journal of Popular Culture, Quarterly Journal of Speech, Victorian Studies, Modern Drama, Radio Times,* and *Shaw Review.* Film reviewer for *Humanist,* 1967—.

SIDELIGHTS: In 1963, Harry M. Geduld established the first film study course at Indiana University. He once told *CA:* "Since then I have taught or proposed most of the basic courses in film. My writing and teaching have been intimately connected: The books I have published and the series I have edited have developed in response to practical pedagogical considerations. My introduction of courses on the study of television genres has followed the same lines as the film teaching. My writing and my teaching have always been expressions of passionate preoccupations. I constantly strive to break new ground, to teach new courses, to research and write about neglected or little-known subjects, and to create new interests for my students and readers. The reward is not only to succeed (at times), but also to have the pleasure of being among the first to see over the next hill."

BIOGRAPHICAL/CRITICAL SOURCES:

PERIODICALS

Hudson Review, summer, 1968.
Newsweek, August 10, 1970.
New York Times Book Review, December 17, 1967.
Times Literary Supplement, June 27, 1986.

* * *

GERTZ, Elmer 1906-

PERSONAL: Born September 14, 1906, in Chicago, IL; son of Morris (a merchant) and Grace (Grossman) Gertz; married Ceretta Samuels, August 16, 1931 (died, 1958); married Mamie Laitchin Friedman, June 21, 1959; children: (first marriage) Theodore Gerson, Margery Ann (Mrs. Henry R. Hechtman); (stepson) Jack M. Friedman. *Education:* University of Chicago, Ph.B., 1928, J.D., 1930. *Politics:* Independent Democrat. *Religion:* Jewish.

ADDRESSES: *Home*—6249 North Albany Ave., Chicago, IL 60659. *Office*—John Marshall Law School, 315 South Plymouth Ct., Chicago, IL 60604.

CAREER: Admitted to Illinois bar, 1930; McInerney, Epstein, & Arvey (law firm), Chicago, IL, associate, 1930-44; attorney in private practice in Chicago, 1941— (served as counsel to Sparling Commission investigating 1968 civil disorders in Chicago); Gertz & Giampietro (law firm), Chicago, partner, 1973-76. Illinois Police Association, director of public relations, 1934. John Marshall Law School, professor, 1970—. Active in civic affairs in Chicago for more than five decades, serving as president of Public Housing Association, 1943-49; member of law and order committee, Chicago Commission on Human Relations, 1945—; chairman of Veterans Housing Committee, 1945-47; member of Mayor's Emergency Housing Committee, 1946-48 (legal chairman, 1946-47), of Chicago Committee on Housing Action, 1947-49, and of Mayor's Housing Action Committee, 1949-51; member of advisory committee, Municipal Court of Chicago, 1950-51; president of Adult Education Council of Greater Chicago, 1965-69; elected delegate, Illinois Constitutional Convention, 1969-70 (chairman of Bill of Rights Committee of Convention); also served on executive committee of Illinois Commission on Equal Job Opportunity and as vice-president of the Illinois Freedom to Read Committee. Member of board of trustees, Bellefaire and City of Hope; member of board of directors, Jackson Park Hospital; executive vice-president, Blind Services Association, 1988—; member of Auditorium Theater Council.

MEMBER: American Bar Association (member of professors' committee on national security), American Judicature Society, Federal Bar Association, Illinois State Bar Association (chairman of civil rights committee, 1979-80, and council on individual rights and responsibilities), Chicago Bar Association (chairman of legal education committee, 1970-71, and civil rights committee, 1978-79),

First Amendment Lawyers Association (president, 1978-79, chairman, 1979-80), Appellate Lawyers Association of Illinois, Decalogue Society of Lawyers (president, 1954-55), Bar Association of the 7th Circuit, American Jewish Congress (president of Greater Chicago Council, 1959-63; member of national and Chicago advisory board commissions on law and social action), Public Housing Association (founder, counsel, president, 1943-49), Adult Education Council of Chicago (secretary, president), Blind Service Association (former president), Civil War Round Table of Chicago (a founder; president, 1952-53; honorary life member), Society of Midland Authors (secretary, 1976), Authors Guild, Friends of Literature, Shaw Society of Chicago (founder; president, 1956-61), Chicago Literary Club (vice-president, 1968-69, 1978-79, president, 1979-80), Cliff Dwellers (Chicago), City Club (Chicago), Caxton Club.

AWARDS, HONORS: Chicagoland Honor Roll, Chicago Council against Racial and Religious Discrimination, 1946, 1947; Award of Merit, Decalogue Society of Lawyers, 1949; citation for public service, University of Chicago Alumni Association, 1959; citations from Illinois Division of American Civil Liberties Union, 1963 and 1974; Golden Key Award, City of Hope, 1966; Prime Minister's Medal, State of Israel, 1972; Friends of Literature Award, for *To Life,* 1974; Educator of the Year award, 1975; Distinguished Service Award, Phi Beta Kappa Association of the Chicago area, 1993; named to the Senior Citizens Hall of Fame of the City of Chicago; Elmer Gertz Day proclaimed in Illinois and in Chicago; recipient of the first Bud Bergman Humanitarian Award, and of awards from many other organizations, including the American Jewish Congress, Jewish United Fund, Hadassah, Roosevelt University, Southern Illinois University, Society of Midland Authors, Civil War Round Table, Adult Education Council, Constitutional Rights Foundation of Chicago, Phi Alpha Delta Law Fraternity International, Hugo's Companions, Chicago Bar Association, Clarence Darrow Foundation, *Chicago Sun,* and Ethical Humanist Society.

WRITINGS:

(With A. I. Tobin) *Frank Harris: A Study in Black and White,* Mendelsohn, 1931, reprinted, Haskell, 1970.

The People vs. the Chicago Tribune, Union for Democratic Action, 1942.

American Ghettoes, American Jewish Congress, 1946.

(Contributor) *Henry Miller and the Critics,* Southern Illinois University Press, 1963.

A Handful of Clients, Follett, 1965.

Books and Their Right to Live, University of Kansas Library, 1965.

Moment of Madness: The People vs. Jack Ruby, Follett, 1968.

(Author of preface) Earl R. Hutchison, *"Tropic of Cancer" on Trial,* Grove, 1968.

(Contributor) David G. Clark and Hutchison, *Mass Media and the Law: Freedom and Restraint,* Wiley, 1970.

For the First Hours of Tomorrow: The New Illinois Bill of Rights, University of Illinois Press, 1972.

(Contributor) Alan S. Gratch and Virginia H. Ubik, *Ballots for Change: New Suffrage and Amending Articles for Illinois,* University of Illinois Press, 1974.

To Life (memoirs), McGraw, 1974, revised and enlarged edition published as *To Life: The Story of a Chicago Lawyer,* Southern Illinois University Press, 1990.

(Editor) *The Short Stories of Frank Harris,* Southern Illinois University Press, 1975.

(Editor with Felice F. Lewis) *Henry Miller: Years of Trial and Triumph, 1962-64: The Correspondence of Henry Miller and Elmer Gertz,* Southern Illinois University Press, 1978.

Odyssey of a Barbarian: The Biography of George Sylvester Viereck, Prometheus, 1979.

(With Joe Pisciotte) *Charter for a New Age: An Inside View of the Sixth Illinois Constitutional Convention,* University of Illinois Press, 1980.

(With son, Theodore G. Gertz, and Robert K. Garro) *A Guide to Estate Planning,* Southern Illinois University Press, 1983.

(With Edward Gilbreth) *Quest for a Constitution: A Man Who Wouldn't Quit,* University Press of America, 1984.

Gertz vs. Robert Welch, Inc.: The Story of a Landmark Libel Case, Southern Illinois University Press, 1992.

Also author of *Gertz Odyssey* (a collection of travel articles) and radio plays, including *Mrs. Bixby Gets a Letter,* 1942, and *Second Inaugural.* Author of *Joe Medill's War,* 1946. Contributor to *Encyclopaedia Britannica, Junior Britannica, Encyclopedia Judaica,* and *American People's Encyclopedia.* Contributor of articles to periodicals, including *Nation, Progressive, Public Opinion Quarterly, American Mercury, Journal of the Illinois State Historical Society, Chicago Tribune,* Chicago *Daily News,* and Chicago *Sun-Times.* Has also edited the *Decalogue Journal* and *The Paper.*

WORK IN PROGRESS: Books about the Paul Crump case (in collaboration with Donald S. Rothschild) and about capital punishment (with photographer Archie Lieberman).

SIDELIGHTS: Lawyer, law professor, and writer Elmer Gertz has participated, as he once told *CA,* in "some of the celebrated cases of the day: the freeing of Nathan Leopold, the setting aside of the death sentence of Jack Ruby, and many other capital cases; many censorship cases, including those involving [Henry Miller's novel] *Tropic of*

Cancer; cases involving basic aspects of the Illinois constitution; and a landmark libel case . . . that . . . caused the Supreme Court to modify the law in that basic area."

Writing of a 1981 trip on which he was sent by the National Conference on Soviet Jewry to meet with Soviet dissidents, Gertz called it "probably the most emotion-laden experience of my life."

Gertz's extensive travels around the world since 1984 have been the basis for over thirty articles published by the Chicago *Sun-Times* and for his book *Gertz Odyssey.*

BIOGRAPHICAL/CRITICAL SOURCES:

BOOKS

Gertz, Elmer, *To Life,* McGraw, 1974.

PERIODICALS

Chicago Tribune Book World, May 20, 1979.

* * *

GIBSON, William 1914-
(William Mass)

PERSONAL: Born November 13, 1914, in New York, NY; son of George Irving (a bank clerk) and Florence (Dore) Gibson; married first wife, c. 1935 (divorced); married Margaret Brenman (a psychoanalyst), September 6, 1940; children: Thomas, Daniel. *Education:* Attended College of City of New York (now City College of the City University of New York), 1930-32. *Politics:* Democrat. *Religion:* None.

ADDRESSES: Home—Stockbridge, MA. *Agent*—Flora Roberts, 157 West 57th St., New York, NY 10022.

CAREER: Author and playwright. Former piano teacher; president and co-founder of Berkshire Theatre Festival, Stockbridge, MA, 1966—.

MEMBER: PEN, Authors League of America, Dramatists Guild.

AWARDS, HONORS: Harriet Monroe Memorial Prize, 1945, for group of poems published in *Poetry;* Topeka Civic Theatre award, 1947, for *A Cry of Players;* Sylvania Award, 1957, for television play "The Miracle Worker."

WRITINGS:

PLAYS

I Lay in Zion (one-act; first produced in Topeka, KS, at Topeka Civic Theatre, Easter, 1943), Samuel French (acting edition), 1947.

(Under pseudonym William Mass) *The Ruby* (one-act lyrical drama based on Lord Dunsany's *A Night at an Inn*; music by Norman Dello Joio), Ricordi, 1955.

The Miracle Worker (three-act; based upon the teleplay by Gibson; first produced on Broadway at Playhouse Theatre, October 19, 1959; also see below), Knopf, 1957.

Dinny and the Witches [and] *The Miracle Worker* (the former first produced Off-Broadway at Cherry Lane Theatre, December 9, 1959; also see below), Atheneum, 1960.

Two for the Seesaw (three-act comedy; first produced on Broadway at Booth Theatre, January 16, 1958; also see below), Samuel French, 1960.

Dinny and the Witches: A Frolic on Grave Matters, Dramatists Play Service, 1961.

(With Clifford Odets) *Golden Boy* (musical adaptation of Odets' original drama, with lyrics by Lee Adams and music by Charles Strouse; first produced on Broadway at Majestic Theatre, October 20, 1964), Atheneum, 1965.

A Cry of Players (three-act; first produced in Topeka, KS, at Topeka Civic Theatre, February, 1948; produced on Broadway at the Vivian Beaumont Theatre, November 14, 1968), Atheneum, 1969, Dramatists Play Service, 1990.

John and Abigail (three-act drama; first produced in Stockbridge, MA, at Berkshire Theatre Festival, summer, 1969; produced in Washington, DC, at Ford's Theatre, January 9, 1970), published as *American Primitive: The Words of John and Abigail Adams Put into a Sequence for the Theater, with Addenda in Rhyme,* Atheneum, 1972.

The Body and the Wheel (first produced in Lenox, MA, at Pierce Chapel, April 5, 1974), Dramatists Play Service, 1975.

The Butterfingers Angel, Mary and Joseph, Herod the Nut, and the Slaughter of 12 Hit Carols in a Pear Tree (first produced in Lenox, MA, at Pierce Chapel, December, 1974), Dramatists Play Service, 1975.

Golda (first produced on Broadway at the Morosco Theatre, November 14, 1977; also see below), Samuel French, 1977.

Monday after the Miracle (sequel to *The Miracle Worker;* first produced in Charleston, SC, at the Dock Street Theatre, May, 1982; produced on Broadway at the Eugene O'Neill Theatre, December 14, 1982), Atheneum, 1983.

Raggedy Ann: The Musical Adventure, first produced in Albany, NY, December, 1985; produced on Broadway at Nederlander Theatre, October, 1986.

Goodly Creatures (first produced in Washington, DC, at the Round House Theatre, January, 1980), Dramatists Play Service, 1986.

Handy Dandy (first produced in Boston, MA, by Lyric Stage, October, 1984), Dramatists Play Service, 1986.

OTHER

Winter Crook (poems), Oxford University Press, 1948.

The Cobweb (novel; also see below), Knopf, 1954.

(With John Paxton) *The Cobweb* (screenplay; based on the novel by Gibson), Metro-Goldwyn-Mayer, 1957.

"The Miracle Worker" (based on the book *The Story of My Life* by Helen Keller), *Playhouse 90* (television series), Columbia Broadcasting System, February, 1957.

The Seesaw Log (a chronicle; includes the text of *Two for the Seesaw*), Knopf, 1959, published as *The Seesaw Log: A Chronicle of the Stage Production with the Text of Two for the Seesaw,* Limelight, 1984.

The Miracle Worker (screenplay; based on the play by Gibson), United Artists (UA), 1962.

A Mass for the Dead (chronicle and poems), Atheneum, 1968.

A Season in Heaven (chronicle), Atheneum, 1974.

Notes on How to Turn a Phoenix into Ashes: The Story of the Stage Production, with the Text of Golda, Atheneum, 1978.

Shakespeare's Game (criticism), Atheneum, 1978.

The Miracle Worker (television script; based on the play by Gibson), National Broadcasting Corporation, 1979.

The Miracle Worker (juvenile; based on the play by Gibson), Bantam, 1984.

Contributor to periodicals, including *Poetry.*

ADAPTATIONS: Two for the Seesaw was adapted for film and released by UA, 1962.

SIDELIGHTS: While William Gibson has published poetry, plays, fiction, and criticism, he is perhaps best known for his 1957 play *The Miracle Worker.* Originally written and performed as a television drama, it was later adapted for the stage, screen, and again for television in 1979; to this day, *The Miracle Worker* remains Gibson's most widely revived piece. Writing in the *Dictionary of Literary Biography,* Stephen C. Coy calls it "a classic American play—and television play, and film—the full stature of which has yet to be realized."

The story, which is based on real people and actual events, concerns the relationship between Helen Keller, a handicapped child who has been deaf and blind since infancy, and Annie Sullivan, the formerly blind teacher who has been called in to instruct her. When Annie arrives, she finds that Helen has been utterly spoiled by well-intentioned parents who, in their sympathy, allow her to terrorize the household. Annie's efforts to civilize Helen and Helen's resistance result in a fierce, and frequently physical, struggle that forms the central conflict of the play. The "miracle" occurs when, after months of frustration, Annie is finally able to reach the child. Coy explains: "Just as the struggle appears to be lost, Helen starts to work the pump in the Keller yard and the miracle—her mind learning to name things—happens before the audience as she feels the water and the wet ground. Annie and others realize what is happening as Helen, possessed, runs about touching things and learning names, finally, to their great joy, 'Mother' and 'Papa.' The frenzy slows as Helen realizes there is something she needs to know, gets Annie to spell it for her, spells it back, and goes to spell it for her mother. It is the one word which more than any other describes the subject of *The Miracle Worker:* 'Teacher.' "

Praising the play's "youthfulness and vigor," the *New York Times* reviewer Bosley Crowther described the tremendous concentration of energy apparent in the battle scenes between Helen and Annie: "The physical vitality and passion are absolutely intense as the nurse, played superbly by Anne Bancroft, moves in and takes on the job of 'reaching the soul' of the youngster played by Patty Duke. . . . When the child, who is supposed to be Helen Keller in her absolutely primitive childhood state, kicks and claws with the frenzy of a wild beast at the nurse who is supposed to be Annie Sullivan, the famous instructor of Miss Keller, it is a staggering attack. And when Annie hauls off and swats her or manhandles her into a chair and pushes food into her mouth to teach her habits, it is enough to make the viewer gasp and grunt."

The Broadway production of the play was so well-received that a film version with the same stars was made in 1962 and enjoyed similar success. Later revivals have not fared so well. When *The Miracle Worker* was filmed for television in 1979 (with Patty Duke Astin playing Annie Sullivan), Tom Shales commented in the *Washington Post* that "the only point in doing *The Miracle Worker* again was to give Patty Duke Astin a chance on the other side of the food." His objections range from what he calls "careless casting" to the inappropriateness (almost an insult, he calls it) of making a television movie from a screenplay written for live television. For the writing itself, however, Shales has nothing but praise. "William Gibson's play . . . remains, even when not perfectly done, a nearly perfect joy, one of the most assuredly affirmative dramatic works to come out of the optimistic '50s."

In 1982 Gibson returned to the characters of *The Miracle Worker* with the play *Monday after the Miracle.* Helen, now 21 years old, has entered college, with Annie Sullivan accompanying her as translator and tutor. There they meet John Macy, an idealistic student with whom Annie soon falls in love. Helen, in the meantime, is blossoming into womanhood—a transformation that brings with it a burning curiosity about the matters of love and sex. Theater critic Martin Hoyle of the London *Times* calls *Monday after the Miracle* "harsher and more complex [than its predecessor], spinning the threads of Annie's aching maternalism, John's frustrated professional pride and Helen's emotional curiosity into a sometimes abrasive texture." Though the performance he had seen was "rough-edged," Hoyle commends Gibson's uncompromisingly detailed accounting of Helen's physical and emotional struggle: "At the very least a well-made play," he says, "the work has passages that belong to the great American tradition . . . of laceratingly direct confrontation."

BIOGRAPHICAL/CRITICAL SOURCES:

BOOKS

Contemporary Literary Criticism, Volume 23, Gale, 1983.
Dictionary of Literary Biography, Volume 7: *Twentieth Century American Dramatists,* Gale, 1981.
Duprey, Richard A., *Just off the Aisle: The Ramblings of a Catholic Critic,* Newman Press, 1962.
Guernsey, Otis L., Jr., editor, *Broadway Song and Story: Playwrights/Lyricists/Composers Discuss Their Hits,* Dodd, 1986, pp. 301-319.

PERIODICALS

Boston Globe, July 6, 1969.
Cosmopolitan, August, 1958.
Dramatists Guild Quarterly, spring, 1981.
Los Angeles Times, October 19, 1982.
Nation, December 2, 1968.
New England Theatre, spring, 1970.
New Leader, December 16, 1968.
Newsweek, March 16, 1959; July 27, 1970.
New York, October 27, 1986, p. 139.
New Yorker, February 15, 1958; November 23, 1968; October 27, 1986, p. 116.
New York Post, November 4, 1959.
New York Times, March 7, 1954; January 27, 1958; October 18, 1959; October 26, 1959; May 24, 1962; May 27, 1962; June 3, 1962; May 31, 1964; October 21, 1964; May 23, 1965; March 27, 1966; June 18, 1967; December 10, 1967; April 6, 1968; November 15, 1968; November 24, 1968; April 15, 1977; November 16, 1977; December 9, 1980; May 26, 1982; December 15, 1982; October 23, 1990.
New York Times Book Review, April 14, 1968.
New York Times Magazine, March 15, 1959.
People, October 14, 1985.
Saturday Review, March 14, 1959; March 23, 1968.
Time, December 21, 1959.
Times (London), November 8, 1990.
Tulane Drama Review, May, 1960.
Variety, February 21, 1971; August 27, 1986, p. 100; October 22, 1986, p. 494; March 18, 1987, p. 90.
Village Voice, November 18, 1959.
Vogue, March, 1985.
Washington Post, October 13, 1979; January 20, 1980; January 26, 1980; November 27, 1981; December 3, 1981; October 3, 1982; October 14, 1982.

* * *

GOLDEN, Marita 1950-

PERSONAL: Born April 28, 1950, in Washington, DC; daughter of Francis Sherman (a taxi driver) and Beatrice (a landlord; maiden name, Reid) Golden; divorced; children: Michael Kayode. *Education:* American University, B.A., 1972; Columbia University, M.Sc., 1973.

ADDRESSES: Home—Boston, MA. *Agent*—Carol Mann, 168 Pacific Street, Brooklyn, NY 11201.

CAREER: WNET-Channel 13, New York City, associate producer, 1974-75; University of Lagos, Lagos, Nigeria, assistant professor of mass communications, 1975-79; Roxbury Community College, Roxbury, MA, assistant professor of English, 1979-81; Emerson College, Boston, MA, assistant professor of journalism, 1981-83; writer. Member of nominating committee for the George K. Polk Awards; executive director of the Institute for the Preservation and Study of African American Writing, 1986-87; consultant for the Washington DC Community Humanities Council, 1986-89.

MEMBER: Afro-American Writer's Guild (president, 1986—).

WRITINGS:

(Contributor) Beatrice Murphy, editor, *Today's Negro Voices,* Messner, 1970.
(Contributor) *Keeping the Faith: Writings by Contemporary Black American Women,* Fawcett, 1974.
Migrations of the Heart (autobiography), Doubleday, 1983.
A Woman's Place (novel), Doubleday, 1986.
Long Distance Life (novel), Doubleday, 1989.
And Do Remember Me (novel), Doubleday, 1992.

Contributor of poetry to several anthologies, and contributor to periodicals, including *Essence, Daily Times* (Nigeria), *National Observer, Black World,* and *Amsterdam News.*

SIDELIGHTS: Marita Golden began writing her autobiography, *Migrations of the Heart,* when she was only twenty-nine years old. When asked about her motivation for the book, Golden told *Washington Post* reporter Jacqueline Trescott that she "stumbled into" it, adding: "I wanted to meditate on what it meant to grow in the '60's, what it meant to go to Africa the first time, what it meant to be a modern black woman living in that milieu. I had to bring order to the chaos of memory. . . . What I wanted to do was write a book that would take my life and shape it into an artifact that could inform and possibly inspire."

The book met with generally favorable reviews and was described by Diane McWhorter in the *New York Times Book Review* as "interesting" and "told in a prose that often seems possessed by some perverse genius." Reviewer Elayne B. Byman Bass commended Golden in the *Washington Post Book World* for her account of how "the love of a girl for her father evolves through several migrations into a woman's love for her man, her child and finally herself," while in *Ms.* magazine, critic Carole Bovoso suggested that Golden has earned a place among those black women writers who share a "greater and greater commitment . . . to understand self, multiplied in terms of the community, the community multiplied in terms of the nation, and the nation multiplied in terms of the world."

Golden's novel *A Woman's Place*—a "truncated *herstory*" according to Wanda Coleman in the *Los Angeles Times Book Review*—follows the lives of three black women who meet and become friends at an elite Boston university. Each of them confronts problems facing women of color in today's society. One cannot adjust to the pressures her possessive Islamic husband puts on her, another suffers from guilt related to her love of a white man, and the third tries to lose herself working in a developing African nation. "By refusing to offer easy answers to the predicaments of women, and black women in particular," says *Washington Post Book World* contributor Susan Wood, "Golden makes us believe in her characters and care about them."

Long Distance Life, Golden's second novel, takes the reader into the black streets of Washington, D.C., where she was raised. Beginning in the 1920s, the story follows Naomi, a southern farmer's daughter, as she moves north in search of opportunity, marries, prospers, and loses part of her spirituality along the way. The tale then turns to the family's subsequent generations, their involvement in the civil rights movement, and one grandson's drug-related death. Laura Shapiro in *Newsweek* lauded *Long Distance Life,* commenting that "[Golden] writes about the city with understanding and a sense of commitment." The critic added that within these borders the author "traces a web of determination, suffering, and renewal."

Golden's third novel, *And Do Remember Me,* charts the lives of two black women, Jesse and Macon, whose search to better themselves leads to their involvement in the civil rights movement. Jesse leaves her poor, abusive home in the south and later finds fame as an actress. And Macon, a professor at a predominantly white college, tries to help her African American students contend with the racism that has become prevalent on campus. According to Ellen Douglas in the *Washington Post Book World,* the novel "addresses the political upheavals of the '60s and '70s and the personal difficulties and tragedies of these lives with a seriousness which one must respect." Lauding *And Do Remember Me,* Douglas concluded: "We need to be reminded that young people were murdered in Mississippi in 1964 for taking black people to register to vote. . . . And we need to be reminded that racism is again or still a deep national problem."

Golden remarked: "I was trained to be a journalist at Columbia's graduate school of journalism, but I was born, I feel, to simply write, using whatever medium best expresses my obsession at a particular time. I have written poetry and have been included in several anthologies and want in the future to write more. I use and need journalism to explore the external world, to make sense of it. I use and need fiction to give significance to and to come to terms with the internal world of my own particular fears, fantasies, and dreams, and to weave all of that into the texture of the outer, tangible world. I write essentially to complete myself and to give my vision a significance that the world generally seeks to deny."

BIOGRAPHICAL/CRITICAL SOURCES:

BOOKS

Migrations of the Heart, Doubleday, 1983.

PERIODICALS

Antioch Review, winter, 1984.
Los Angeles Times Book Review, April 17, 1983; September 7, 1986.
Ms., June, 1983; September, 1988.
Newsweek, November 20, 1989, p. 79.
New Yorker, February 21, 1983.
New York Times Book Review, May 1, 1983; September 14, 1986; December 27, 1987.
Publishers Weekly, June 20, 1986; September 1, 1989; April 27, 1992.
Village Voice Literary Supplement, May, 1990.
Voice Literary Supplement, June, 1983.
Washingtonian, October, 1990; November, 1990.
Washington Post, May 22, 1983; December 13, 1987.
Washington Post Book World, June 4, 1983; July 30, 1986; December 13, 1987; September 17, 1989; December 3, 1989; May 24, 1992, p. 12; June 21, 1992.*

*   *   *

GOSS, Clay(ton E.) 1946-

PERSONAL: Born May 26, 1946, in Philadelphia, PA; son of Douglas P. (a counselor) and Alfreda (a teacher;

maiden name, Ivey) Jackson; married Linda McNear (a teacher and performer), March 25, 1969; children: Aisha, Uhuru (daughters). *Education:* Howard University, B.F.A., 1972.

ADDRESSES: *Agent*—Dorothea Oppenheimer, 866 United Nations Plaza, New York, NY 10017.

CAREER: Department of Recreation, Washington, DC, drama specialist, 1969; Howard University, Washington, DC, playwright-in-residence in drama department, 1970-73, playwright-in-residence at Institute for the Arts and Humanities, 1973-75; poet, playwright, and writer. Instructor in poetry and development of Afro-American theater, Antioch College, Washington and Baltimore campuses, 1971-73.

MEMBER: Theatre Black, Kappa Alpha Psi.

WRITINGS:

JUVENILE

Bill Pickett: Black Bulldogger (novel), illustrated by Chico Hall, Hill and Wang, 1970.

(With wife, Linda Goss) *The Baby Leopard: An African Folktale,* illustrated by Suzanne Bailey-Jones and Michael R. Jones, Bantam Books, 1989.

(With L. Goss) *It's Kwanzaa Time!,* Philomel Books, 1993.

DRAMA

Hip Rumpelstiltskin, first produced in Washington, DC, by Department of Recreation, 1969.

Andrew (one-act), first produced in New York City at New York Shakespeare Festival Theatre, 1972.

Mars: Monument to the Last Black Eunuch, first produced in Washington, DC, at Howard University, 1972.

Oursides (one-act), first produced in New York City at New Federal Theatre, 1972.

Spaces in Time, produced in Washington, DC, by D. C. Black Repertory Company, 1973.

Of Being Hit, first produced in Brooklyn, NY, at Billie Holiday Theatre, 1973.

Homecookin': Five Plays, Howard University Press, 1974.

Ornette, first produced in Amherst, MA, at University of Massachusetts, 1974.

Also author of *Keys to the Kingdom.* Plays represented in anthologies, including *Transition,* Department of Afro-American Studies, Howard University, 1972; *Kuntu Drama,* edited by Paul Carter Harrison, Grove, 1974; and *The New Lafayette Theatre Presents: Six Black Playwrights,* edited by Ed Bullins, Anchor Press, 1974.

OTHER

Author of the television play *Billy McGhee,* for *The Place,* broadcast by WRC-TV (Washington, DC), 1974. Contributor to books, including *We Speak as Liberators: Young Black Poets,* edited by Orde Coombs, Dodd, 1970; *The Drama of Nommo,* edited by Paul Carter Harrison, Grove, 1972; and *The Sheet,* edited by Carol Kirkendall, Compared to What, Inc. (Washington, DC), 1974. Contributor of short fiction, articles, and reviews to periodicals, including *Liberator, Reflect, Black Books Bulletin, Blackstage,* and *Black World.*

SIDELIGHTS: Clay Goss once commented: "What we must first do is to make our goals become our models instead of models becoming our goals. Then build from there."

BIOGRAPHICAL/CRITICAL SOURCES:

PERIODICALS

Choice, January, 1976, p. 1444.

Grade Teacher, February, 1971, p. 147.

Kirkus Reviews, October 1, 1970, p. 1096.

Library Journal, March 15, 1971, p. 1114; June 15, 1975, p. 1236.*

* * *

GRAHAM, Billy
See GRAHAM, William Franklin

* * *

GRAHAM, William Franklin 1918-
(Billy Graham)

PERSONAL: Born November 7, 1918, in Charlotte, NC; son of William Franklin (a dairy farmer) and Morrow (Coffey) Graham; married Ruth McCue Bell, August 13, 1943; children: Virginia Leftwich (Mrs. Stephan Tchividjian), Ann Morrow (Mrs. Daniel Lotz), Ruth Bell (Mrs. Ted Dienert), William Franklin, Jr., Nelson Edman. *Education:* Florida Bible Institute (now Trinity College), Th.B., 1940; Wheaton College, Wheaton, IL, B.A., 1943.

Avocational Interests: Swimming and aerobic walking.

ADDRESSES: *Home*—Montreat, NC. *Office*—1300 Harmon Pl., Minneapolis, MN 55403.

CAREER: Ordained to Baptist ministry, 1940; pastor in Western Springs, IL, and radio personality, "Songs in the Night," on WCFL, Chicago, IL, 1943-45; began Crusades for Christ, 1946; Northwestern Schools (now Northwestern College), Minneapolis, MN, president, 1947-52; Billy Graham Evangelistic Association, Minneapolis, founder and president, 1950—. First vice-president, Youth for Christ International, 1945-48. Leader of weekly *Hour of*

Decision, television and radio program on American and Canadian broadcasting networks, and on worldwide short-wave hookups, 1950—. Founder of World Wide Pictures, Inc. (producers of religious films); president of Blue Ridge Broadcasting Corp. (operator of noncommercial radio station WFGW), Black Mountain, NC. Honorary chairman, Lausanne Congress on World Evangelization, 1974.

MEMBER: Royal Geographic Society (fellow), Royal Literary Society, Suburban Professional Men's Club (founder), 1943—.

AWARDS, HONORS: Voted one of ten most admired men in the world in Gallup Polls, 1951—; Bernard Baruch Award, 1955; Freedoms Foundation Awards, 1955, 1969; Clergyman Churchman of the Year, Washington Pilgrimage, 1956; Gold Medal, National Institute of Social Science, 1957; Humane Order of African Redemption, 1960; Ninth International Youth's Distinguished Service Citation, 1961; Gutenberg Award, Chicago Bible Society, 1962; Gold Medal, George Washington Carver Memorial Institute, 1963; Speaker of the Year Award, 1964; Horatio Alger Award, 1965; Golden Plate Award, American Academy of Achievement, 1965; National Citizenship Award, Military Chaplains Association of the United States, 1965; Wisdom Award of Honor, 1965; Big Brother of the Year Award at the White House, Washington, D.C., 1966; Silver Medallion, 1967 and International Brotherhood Award, 1971, both from the National Conference of Christians and Jews; Torch of Liberty Plaque, Anti-Defamation League of B'nai B'rith, 1969; George Washington Medal, Freedoms Foundation of Valley Forge, 1969, for sermon "The Violent Society," and 1974, for patriotism; Distinguished Service Award from the National Association of Broadcasters, 1972; Franciscan International Award, 1972; Sylvanus Thayer award, Association of Graduates of U.S. Military Academies, 1972; National Gold Medal, 1973; Heart Award, Variety Clubs International, 1974; Man of the South award, 1974; Liberty Bell award, 1975; Salesman of the Decade Award, Direct Selling Association, 1975; Philip Award, Association of United Methodist Evangelists, 1976; First National Interreligious Award, American Jewish Committee, 1977; Distinguished Communications Medal, Southern Baptist Radio and Television Commission, 1977; Jabotinsky Centennial Medal, Jabotinsky Foundation, 1980; named to Religious Broadcasting Hall of Fame, 1981; Templeton Prize for Progress in Religion, 1982; Presidential Medal of Freedom, 1983; National Religious Broadcasters Award of Merit, 1986; North Carolina Award in Public Service, 1986; Clergyman of the Year, National Pilgrim Society; Distinguished Service Medal, Salvation Army. D.D. from King's College, 1948, Wheaton College, Wheaton, Ill., and William Jewell College; D.Hum. from Bob Jones University, 1948; LL.D. from Houghton College, 1950, The Citadel, and Baylor University; honorary doctorate from Christian Academy of Theology, 1974.

WRITINGS:

UNDER NAME BILLY GRAHAM

Calling Youth to Christ, Zondervan, 1947.

(With others) *Revival in Our Time,* Van Kampen, 1950.

The Chance of a Lifetime: Helps for Servicemen, Zondervan, 1952.

The Work of an Evangelist: An Address, World's Evangelical Alliance (London), 1953.

Peace with God, Doubleday, 1953, reprinted, Pocket Books, 1976.

I Saw Your Sons at War: The Korean Diary of Billy Graham, Billy Graham Evangelistic Association (Minneapolis), 1953.

The Secret of Happiness: Jesus' Teaching on Happiness as Expressed in the Beatitudes, Doubleday, 1955 (published in England as *The Secret of Happiness: The Teaching of Jesus as Expressed in the Beatitudes,* World's Work, 1956), revised and enlarged edition, Word Books, 1985.

The Seven Deadly Sins, Zondervan, 1956.

Billy Graham Talks to Teenagers, Miracle Books, 1958, reprinted, Zondervan, 1976.

Hope for Tomorrow (bound with *Mass Public Education: The Tool of the Dictator,* by Hubert Eaton), Forest Lawn Memorial Park Association, 1958.

My Answer, Doubleday, 1960.

World Aflame (also see below), Doubleday, 1965.

The New Birth (excerpts from *World Aflame*), [Washington, D.C.], 1965.

The Quotable Billy Graham, compiled and edited by Cort R. Flint and the staff of *Quote,* Droke, 1966, reprinted as *Billy Graham Speaks! The Quotable Billy Graham,* Grosset & Dunlap, 1968.

The Wit and Wisdom of Billy Graham, edited and compiled by Bill Adler, Random House, 1967.

The Faith of Billy Graham, compiled and edited by T. S. Settel, Droke, 1968.

The Challenge: Sermons from Madison Square Garden, Doubleday, 1969.

The Jesus Generation, Zondervan, 1971.

Angels: God's Secret Agents, Doubleday, 1975, Random House, 1986, Word Books, 1991.

How to Be Born Again, Word Books, 1977.

Blow, Wind of God! Selected Writings of Billy Graham, edited by Donald E. Demaray, New American Library, 1977.

The Holy Spirit: Activating God's Power in Your Life, Word Books, 1978.

Till Armageddon: A Perspective on Suffering, Hodder & Stoughton, 1981.

Approaching Hoofbeats: The Four Horsemen of the Apocalypse, Word Books, 1983.

A Biblical Standard for Evangelists, World Wide Publications, 1984.

Unto the Hills: A Devotional Treasury of Billy Graham, Word Books, 1986.

You, His Witness, InterVarsity, 1991.

Hope for the Troubled Heart, Word Books, 1991.

Storm Warning: Deceptive Evil Looms on the Horizon, Word Books, 1992.

Author of syndicated daily newspaper column, "My Answer." Editor-in-chief, *Decision* (magazine).

CONTRIBUTOR

America's Hour of Decision (radio sermons), Van Kampen, 1951.

George Paul Butler, editor, *Best Sermons: 1955,* Crowell, 1955.

Oscar Handlin, editor, *American Principles and Issues: The National Purpose,* Holt, 1961.

Era Bell Thompson and Herbert Nipson, editors, *White on Black: The Views of Twenty-Two White Americans on the Negro,* Johnson Publishing Co., 1963.

Adler, compiler, *My Favorite Funny Story,* Four Winds, 1967.

Cliff Barrows, editor, *Crusade Hymn Stories,* Hope Publishing, 1967.

Charles M. Colson, editor, *Christ in Easter: A Family Celebration of Holy Week,* NewPress, 1990.

Charles Goodman, editor, *Church Humor Digest,* Castle Books, 1991.

Contributor to numerous periodicals, including *Saturday Evening Post, Christian Century, Good Housekeeping, Church Today, McCall's, Reader's Digest, Redbook, American Mercury,* and *Cosmopolitan.*

OTHER

(Author of introduction) James Edwin Orr, *Full Surrender,* Christian Literature Crusade, 1951.

(Author of speeches) Charles Thomas Cook, *The Billy Graham Story,* Van Kampen, 1954.

George Burnham, *To the Far Corners with Billy Graham in Asia* (includes excerpts from Graham's diary), Revell, 1956 (published in England, with an introduction by Graham, as *With Billy Graham in Asia,* Marshall, Morgan & Scott, 1956).

(Author of foreword and message) Robert O. Ferm, editor, *They Met God at the New York Crusade,* Billy Graham Evangelistic Association, 1957.

(Author of message) Ferm, *Persuaded to Live: Conversion Stories from the Billy Graham Crusades,* Revell, 1958.

(Author of foreword and keynote sermon) Sherwood Eliot Wirt, *Crusade at the Golden Gate,* Harper, 1959.

(Author of foreword) Warner Hutchinson and Cliff Wilson, *Let the People Rejoice,* Crusader Bookroom Society, Ltd. (Wellington, N.Z.), 1959.

(Author of preface) Curtis Mitchell, *Those Who Came Forward: Men and Women Who Responded to the Ministry of Billy Graham,* Chilton, 1966 (published in England as *Those Who Came Forward: An Account of Those Whose Lives Were Changed by the Ministry of Billy Graham,* World's Work, 1966).

(Author of introduction) Lewis F. Brabham, *A New Song in the South: The Story of the Billy Graham Greenville, SC Crusade,* Zondervan, 1966.

(Author of introduction) Andrew Walker, editor, *Betraying the Gospel,* Bristol House, 1988.

(Author of introduction) Charles R. Swindoll, *Growing Strong in the Seasons of Life: A Season of Reverence,* Walker & Co., 1989.

(Author of introduction) Fulton Oursler, *The Greatest Story Ever Told,* Doubleday, 1989.

(Author of foreword) Vance Havner, *In Tune with Heaven,* Baker Book, 1990.

(Author of foreword) Roger S. Greenway, editor, *Missions Now: This Generation,* Baker Book, 1991.

(Author of foreword) Arthur H. Matthews, *Standing Up, Standing Together: The Emergence of the National Association of Evangelicals,* National Association of Evangelicals, 1992.

(Author of foreword) Robert E. Coleman, *The Master Plan of Evangelism: Thirtieth Anniversary Edition,* Baker Book, 1993.

(Author of introduction) Hank Ketcham, *Dennis the Menace: Prayers and Graces,* Westminster/John Knox, 1993.

Several of Graham's works have been translated into Spanish.

SIDELIGHTS: Billy Graham, labeled "America's premier evangelist" by *Time,* has devoted the better part of his life to spreading the Christian message in his "Crusades" across the United States and around the world. A born-again Christian from the age of sixteen, Graham became a Baptist minister in 1940 and began writing books in 1947. He is currently the author of some three dozen volumes, often dismissed by critics as no more than transcripts of sermons but widely read by Graham's followers. The author acknowledges that his books sell well, everywhere in the United States except New York. One volume, *Angels: God's Secret Agents,* sold more than one million copies in its hardcover edition. When *How to Be Born Again* was released in 1977, its 800,000-copy first edition was said to be the largest initial printing to date in publishing history. Furthermore, Graham has had almost as many books written about him as he has written himself.

The minister has met with controversy during his long career. To some fundamentalist leaders, Graham is too liberal; others see his theological theories, stressing absolute good and evil, as too simplistic. Graham gained further notoriety through his association with Richard Nixon before and during the Watergate years. While the evangelist was a staunch Nixon supporter, he was reportedly shocked by the picture of the former president presented by the infamous White House transcripts.

Despite controversy, Graham continues to be a popular draw at his speaking engagements; his name often appears on the "most admired" lists in America. Of his success as an author, the minister says in a *New York Times* article: "I'm not an accomplished writer in any sense. I usually send my manuscripts off to the publishers to have them edited. I like to write, though, because I have many things in my heart to say before I get to Heaven."

BIOGRAPHICAL/CRITICAL SOURCES:

BOOKS

America's Hour of Decision, Van Kampen, 1951.

Babbage, Stuart Barton and Ian Siggins, *Light beneath the Cross,* Doubleday, 1960.

Bishop, M., *Billy Graham,* Grosset & Dunlap, 1978.

Brabham, Lewis F., *A New Song in the South: The Story of the Billy Graham Greenville, SC Crusade,* Zondervan, 1966.

Burnham, George, *Billy Graham: A Mission Accomplished,* Revell, 1955.

Burnham, George, *To the Far Corners with Billy Graham in Asia,* Revell, 1956.

Burnham, George and Lee Fisher, *Billy Graham and the New York Crusade,* Zondervan, 1957.

Chapple, Arthur R., *Billy Graham,* Marshall, Morgan & Scott, 1954.

Colquhoun, Frank, *Haringay Story,* Hodder & Stoughton, 1955.

Cook, Charles Thomas, *The Billy Graham Story,* Van Kampen, 1954.

Cook, Charles Thomas, *London Hears Billy Graham,* Grason Co., 1954.

England, Edward Oliver, *Afterwards: A Journalist Sets out to Discover What Happened to Some of Those Who Made a Decision for Christ during the Billy Graham Crusades in Britain in 1954 and 1955,* Elim, 1957.

Ferm, Robert O., *Cooperative Evangelism: Is Billy Graham Right or Wrong?,* Zondervan, 1958.

Ferm, Robert O., *Persuaded to Live: Conversion Stories from the Billy Graham Crusades,* Revell, 1958.

Fey, Harold E. and Margaret Frakes, editors, *The Christian Century Reader: Representative Articles, Editorials, and Poems Selected from More than Fifty Years of the Christian Century,* Association Press, 1962.

Frady, M., *Billy Graham: A Parable of American Righteousness,* Little, Brown, 1979.

Gillenson, Lewis W., *Billy Graham: The Man and His Message,* Fawcett, 1954.

High, Stanley, *Billy Graham: The Personal Story of the Man, His Message and His Mission,* McGraw, 1956.

Hutchinson, Warner and Cliff Wilson, *Let the People Rejoice,* Crusader Bookroom Society, 1959.

Kilgore, James E., *Billy Graham the Preacher,* Exposition, 1968.

Levy, Alan, *God Bless You Real Good: My Crusade with Billy Graham,* Essandess, 1969.

Martin, William, *A Prophet with Honor: The Billy Graham Story,* Morrow, 1991.

McLaughlin, William Gerald, *Billy Graham: Revivalist in a Secular Age,* Ronald, 1960.

Meet Billy Graham: A Pictorial Record of the Evangelist, His Family and His Team, Pitkin, 1966.

Mitchell, C. C., *Billy Graham: Saint or Sinner?,* Revell, 1979.

Mitchell, Curtis, *God in the Garden: The Story of the Billy Graham New York Crusade,* Doubleday, 1957.

Mitchell, Curtis, *Billy Graham: The Making of a Crusader,* Chilton, 1966.

Niebuhr, Reinhold, *Essays in Applied Christianity,* selected and edited by D. B. Robertson, Meridian Books, 1959.

Poling, D., *Why Billy Graham?,* Zondervan, 1977.

Pollock, John C., *Billy Graham: The Authorized Biography,* McGraw, 1966, reprinted, Harper, 1979.

Priestley, J. B., *Thoughts in the Wilderness,* Harper, 1957.

Stein, Maurice, Arthur J. Vidich, and David Manning White, editors, *Identity and Anxiety: Survival of the Person in Mass Society,* Free Press, 1960.

Streiker, Lowell D. and Gerald S. Strober, *Religion and the New Majority: Billy Graham, Middle America, and the Politics of the 70s,* [New York], 1972.

Strober, Gerald S., *Graham,* G. K. Hall, 1977.

Strober, Gerald S., *Billy Graham: His Life and Faith* (for juveniles), Word Books, 1977.

Wirt, Sherwood Eliot, *Crusade and the Golden Gate,* Harper, 1959.

PERIODICALS

Atlantic, June, 1957.

Christian Century, November 21, 1956.

Commonweal, June 21, 1957; July 25, 1969.

Holiday, March, 1958.

Library Journal, November 15, 1953; November 15, 1955; November 1, 1960; January 15, 1970.

Life, November 21, 1949; May 27, 1957; July 1, 1957; March 21, 1960; June 30, 1961; August 30, 1963.

Nation, April 7, 1956; May 11, 1957; February 8, 1958.

New Republic, August 22, 1955.

Newsweek, May 1, 1950; February 25, 1957; May 20, 1957; July 22, 1957; February 3, 1958; June 23, 1958; October 6, 1958; February 16, 1959; March 9, 1959; March 28, 1960; February 26, 1962; September 2, 1963; July 24, 1967; April 21, 1980.
New Yorker, June 8, 1957.
New York Times, December 6, 1953; December 11, 1955; May 5, 1969; June 24, 1978.
New York Times Book Review, April 3, 1977.
Time, March 20, 1950; July 15, 1966; July 21, 1967; February 7, 1969; June 27, 1969; July 25, 1977.
Times Literary Supplement, March 24, 1966.
Village Voice, July 19, 1969; January 5, 1976.

* * *

GRANT, Cynthia D. 1950-

PERSONAL: Born November 23, 1950, in Brockton, MA; daughter of Robert C. and Jacqueline (Ford) Grant; married Daniel Heatley (divorced); married Erik Neel, 1988; children: Morgan; (second marriage) Forest (son). *Education:* Attended high school in Palo Alto, Calif.

ADDRESSES: *Home*—Box 95, Cloverdale, CA 95425.

CAREER: Writer, 1974—.

AWARDS, HONORS: Annual book award from Woodward Park School, 1981, for *Joshua Fortune;* Best Book of the Year, Michigan Library Association's Young Adult Caucus, 1990, PEN/Norma Klein award, 1991, and Detroit Public Library Author Day Award, 1992, all for *Phoenix Rising.*

WRITINGS:

YOUNG ADULT NOVELS

Joshua Fortune, Atheneum, 1980.
Summer Home, Atheneum, 1981.
Big Time, Atheneum, 1982.
Hard Love, Atheneum, 1983.
Kumquat May, I'll Always Love You, Atheneum, 1986.
Phoenix Rising, Atheneum, 1989.
Keep Laughing, Atheneum, 1991.
Shadow Man, Atheneum, 1992.
Uncle Vampire, Atheneum, 1993.

WORK IN PROGRESS: *Mary Wolf,* a young adult novel.

SIDELIGHTS: Cynthia D. Grant commented to *CA:* "As a child, I was in love with the magic of words; their power to create worlds on paper. Childhood is a vivid time of intensely held emotions and experiences. Now I write what I feel strongly about. I believe that I am not alone, and will be speaking to, and for, people who don't have my gift for articulation, a gift I can't enjoy unless I share it.

"In *Phoenix Rising,* Helen says: 'I'd like to be able to make readers laugh and cry; to reach across the page and say, Hey, we're alive! I want to show the courage of fathers and mothers who bring forth babies who brave the maze of childhood; learning to crawl, standing up, oops, falling, starting over, getting up, going on, finding love, losing hope, enduring pain and disappointment; believing that happiness is just around the corner, if we don't give up, if we keep moving forward—There is so much I want to say.' She speaks for me."

* * *

GRAZHDANIN, Misha
See BURGESS, Michael (Roy)

* * *

GREEN, Elisabeth Sara 1940-
(Liz Tresilian)

PERSONAL: Born December 7, 1940, in Royal Leamington Spa, Warwickshire, England; daughter of Stewart and Elizabeth (Amis) Tresilian; married James Green (a solicitor), February 19, 1968; children: Crispin, Sophie. *Education:* Studied at West of England College of Art.

CAREER: Life and Countryside Publications Ltd., Aylesbury, England, staff of *Wilshire Life, Berkshire Life,* and *Buckinghamshire Life* (magazines), 1965-67; Woodrow Wyatt Group of Newspapers, women's editor and feature writer, 1966-67; Boogle-On-Design, London, partner, writer, illustrator, and designer, 1969-76; free-lance graphics and illustration, 1976—.

WRITINGS:

UNDER NAME LIZ TRESILIAN

The Dog Horoscope Book, self-illustrated, Arlington, 1967, Dutton, 1968.
The Cat Horoscope Book, self-illustrated, Arlington, 1967, Dutton, 1968.
Discovering Wiltshire: A Guide to Places of Interest, illustrated by David Uttley, Shire Publications, 1967.
Discovering Castle Combe, illustrated by David Uttley, Shire Publications, 1967.
The W. C. Companion: A Little Book of Meditations, self-illustrated, Arlington, 1968.
Mat's Surprise Parcel, self-illustrated, Benn, 1974.
Aldaniti, illustrated by Caroline Binch, Gollancz, 1984.

GREEN, Lawrence W(inter) 1940-

PERSONAL: Born September 16, 1940, in Bell, CA; son of Clifton Lawrence and Ora Elizabeth (Winter) Green; married Judith Ottoson (in adult education and health policy), May 1, 1982; children: Beth, Jennifer. *Education:* University of California, Berkeley, B.S., 1962, M.P.H., 1966, D.P.H., 1968.

ADDRESSES: *Home*—2545 West 2nd Avenue, Vancouver, BC V6K 1J7, Canada. *Office*—c/o Institute of Health Promotion Research, University of British Columbia, 6248 Biological Sciences Road, Vancouver, BC V6T 1Z4, Canada.

CAREER: Ford Foundation, Dacca, Bangladesh, training associate, 1963-65; University of California, Berkeley, lecturer in health education, 1968-70; Johns Hopkins University, Baltimore, MD, assistant professor, 1970-72, associate professor, 1972-77, professor of health education, 1977-81, assistant dean of School of Hygiene and Public Health, 1975-76; University of Texas Health Science Center at Houston, professor of community medicine and director of Center for Health Promotion Research and Development, 1981-88; Harvard University, Boston, MA, visiting lecturer, 1981-82; vice president, Kaiser Family Foundation, 1988-91; University of British Columbia, Vancouver, professor of health care and epidemiology, and director of Institute of Health Promotion Research, 1991—.

Founding member of Pregnancy Testing and Counseling Center and Family Planning Training Institute, Planned Parenthood Association of Maryland, 1972-74; member of expert panel on consumer health education, National Institute of Health, 1975-76; member of advisory committee on planning, National Center for Health Education, 1975. Consultant to World Health Organization, United Nations Fund for Population Activities, National Center for Health Services Research, National Heart, Lung, and Blood Institute, Arthur D. Little Co., Abt Associates, Medical Research Council of New Zealand, and the state health departments of California, District of Columbia, Hawaii, Kentucky, Louisiana, Ohio, Pennsylvania, Rhode Island, and Texas. *Military service:* U.S. Public Health Service, 1962-63.

MEMBER: International Union for Health Education, American Public Health Association (member of governing council, 1974-76), Society for Public Health Education (chairman of research and studies committee and monograph committee; president, 1983-84), Association for the Advancement of Health Education, American School Health Association, Society for Prospective Medicine, Society for Preventive Oncology, American Academy of Physical Education, American Academy of Behavioral Medicine Research, Society for Behavioral Medicine (trustee, 1985-87).

AWARDS, HONORS: Beryl J. Roberts Award for research in health education, Society for Public Health Education, 1972, for monograph *The Dacca Family Planning Experiment;* Distinguished Career Award, American Public Health Association, 1978; Presidential Citation, Association for the Advancement of Health Education, 1981; National Health Science Honorary Award, Eta Sigma Gamma, 1982; Distinguished Fellow, Society for Public Health Education, 1985; scholar award, 1986, and professional service award, 1989, both from Association for the Advancement of Health Education; Doyen Jacques Perisot Medal, International Union of Health Promotion and Education, 1991, for body of work.

WRITINGS:

Status Identity and Preventive Health Behavior, School of Public Health, University of California, Berkeley, 1970.

(With Harold C. Gustafson, William Griffiths, and David Yaukey) *The Dacca Family Planning Experiment: A Comparative Evaluation of Programs Directed at Males and at Females* (monograph), School of Public Health, University of California, Berkeley, 1972.

Community Health, Mosby, 1972, 6th edition, 1990.

(With Virginia Wang) *Not Forgotten but Still Poor,* University of Maryland Cooperative Extension, 1974.

(With Connie C. Kansler) *The Professional and Scientific Literature on Patient Education,* Gale, 1980.

Emerging Federal Perspectives on Health Promotion (monograph), Center for Health Promotion at Teachers College, Columbia University, 1981.

(With Rebecca Parkinson) *Managing Health Promotion in the Workplace: Guidelines for Implementation and Evaluation,* Mayfield, 1982.

(With Francis Marcus Lewis) *Measurement and Evaluation in Health Education and Health Promotion,* Mayfield, 1986.

(With Marshall Kreuter) *Health Promotion: An Educational and Environmental Approach,* Mayfield, 1991.

(With Dean Gerstein) *Preventing Drug Abuse: What Do We Know?,* National Academy Press, 1993.

WITH KAROL JOSEF KROTKI

Seven Years of Clinic Experience under the "Traditional Planned Parenthood Approach" in Karachi: A Baseline for Evaluating the Next Phase of Family Planning in Pakistan, Pakistan Institute of Development Economics, 1965.

Demographic Implications of the First Six Years of Family Planning in Karachi, 1958-1964, Pakistan Institute of Development Economics, 1966.

Also contributor to public health and other professional journals. Editor of *Health Education Monographs.* Member of editorial boards of *Health Education Quarterly, Journal of Public Health Policy, Journal of Community Health, Journal of Family and Community Health, American Journal of Health Promotion,* and *American Journal of Preventive Medicine.*

WORK IN PROGRESS: 7th edition of *Community Health* for Mosby.

SIDELIGHTS: Lawrence W. Green once told CA: "The field of health education has been given considerable attention and priority in recent health policy decisions and legislative actions of the federal government. The need for scientific literature on the effectiveness of health education in relation to life-style changes such as diet, exercise, accident prevention, and smoking has made work on evaluation of health education of interest to government planners, legislative analysts, hospital and health administrators, and others."

* * *

GREEN, Marc Edward 1943-

PERSONAL: Born March 11, 1943, in Cleveland, OH; son of Emery S. (an attorney) and Aileen (Goldman) Green; married Ellen Wilson (a librarian), June 29, 1969; children: Alec, Matthew. *Education:* Amherst College, B.A. (magna cum laude), 1965; Harvard University, M.A., 1966, doctoral study, 1965-71.

ADDRESSES: *Home*—Los Angeles, CA. *Agent*—Candace Lake Office.

CAREER: George Washington University, Washington, DC, instructor in American literature, 1971-74; free-lance writer, 1974-82; National Health Law Program, Los Angeles, CA, administrator, 1982-87. Screenwriter, 1970-93; story analyst for Melvin Simon Productions, 1978-81; senior editor, Grantsmanship Center, 1991—. Consultant to National Endowment for the Humanities.

AWARDS, HONORS: Woodrow Wilson fellow, 1965-66.

WRITINGS:

(With Stephen Farber) *Hollywood Dynasties,* Delilah, 1984.
Outrageous Conduct: Art, Ego and the "Twilight Zone" Case, Morrow, 1988.
Hollywood on the Couch, Morrow, 1993.

Film critic for *Books and Arts,* 1977-80. Contributor to magazines, including *New West, Film Comment, California,* and *Chronicle of Higher Education.*

SIDELIGHTS: Marc Edward Green once told *CA:* "I have a special interest in the social history of Hollywood, particularly as it relates to family life. *Hollywood Dynasties* explores the family dynamics of a number of major filmmaking clans—the correlations and discrepancies between their own private lives and the images of domesticity they have projected on screen."

BIOGRAPHICAL/CRITICAL SOURCES:

PERIODICALS

New York Times Book Review, August 19, 1984; August 11, 1985.
Washington Post Book World, August 12, 1984.

* * *

GREENHAUS, Thelma Nurenberg 1903-1984 (Thelma Nurenberg)

PERSONAL: Born December 25, 1903, in Warsaw, Poland; died of an apparent heart attack, August 8, 1984, in New York, NY; married Charles Greenhaus; children: Carla Lord. *Education:* Attended Columbia University, 1923-26, and Jewish Theological Seminary, 1925-27. *Religion:* Jewish.

Avocational Interests: International travel (England, Europe, Soviet Union, Israel).

ADDRESSES: *Home*—New York, NY.

CAREER: Journalist and author. Worked as a reporter for *Brooklyn Daily Eagle,* Brooklyn, NY, and *New York Evening Graphic,* New York City.

MEMBER: Authors Guild, Authors League of America.

AWARDS, HONORS: *The Time of Anger* was chosen as a Notable Children's Trade Book in the Field of Social Studies by the National Council for Social Studies and the Children's Book Council.

WRITINGS:

UNDER NAME THELMA NURENBERG

The New Red Freedom, Wadsworth, 1932.
My Cousin, the Arab, Abelard, 1965.
New York Colony (history), Crowell, 1969.
The Time of Anger (novel), Abelard, 1975.

Also author of teleplay *The Refugee Story,* 1958. Editor of *Woman Today,* 1936-38.

SIDELIGHTS: Following a stay in the Soviet Union during the 1920s, Thelma Nurenberg Greenhaus contributed articles about the details of her experiences to the *Brooklyn Daily Eagle* and the *New York Times.* In 1932 these articles were collected and published in book form as *The New Red Freedom.* She wrote her two books *My Cousin, the Arab* and *The Time of Anger* to encourage peaceful relations between Israel and its Arab neighbors.

BIOGRAPHICAL/CRITICAL SOURCES:

BOOKS

Authors of Books for Young People, Scarecrow, 1971.

OBITUARIES:

PERIODICALS

New York Times, August 24, 1984.*

* * *

GREGORICH, Barbara 1943-

PERSONAL: Born December 10, 1943, in Sharon, PA; daughter of Joseph and Mary (Detelich) Gregorich; married Philip Passen. *Education:* Kent State University, B.A., 1964; University of Wisconsin—Madison, M.A., 1965; also attended Harvard University, 1966-67.

ADDRESSES: Home—Chicago, IL. *Agent*—Jane Jordan Browne Multimedia Product Development, Inc., 410 South Michigan Ave., Suite 724, Chicago, IL 60605-1465.

CAREER: Kent State University, Kent, OH, instructor in English, 1965-66; Cleveland State University, Cleveland, OH, instructor in English, 1966; Cuyahoga Community College, Cleveland, instructor in English, 1967-71; *Boston Globe,* Boston, MA, typesetter, 1971-73; *Pot-Tribune,* Gary, IN, typesetter, 1973; *Chicago Tribune,* Chicago, IL, typesetter, 1973-76; U.S. Postal Service, Matton, IL, letter carrier, 1976-77; Society for Visual Education, Chicago, writer and producer, 1977-78; writer, 1978-83; School Zone Publishing Company, Grand Haven, MI, editor, 1983-91; writer, 1991—.

MEMBER: Mystery Writers of America, Sisters in Crime, Private Eye Writers of America, Author's Guild, Society for American Baseball Research, Children's Reading Round Table, Society of Children's Book Writers and Illustrators, Society of Midland Authors.

WRITINGS:

CHILDREN'S BOOKS

"HORIZONS II" SERIES, PUBLISHED BY SCHOOL ZONE PUBLISHING

Adjectives and Adverbs, 1980.
Apostrophe, Colon, Hyphen, 1980.
Capital Letters, 1980.
Comma, 1980.
Context Clues, 1980.
Dictionary Skills, 1980.
Figures of Speech, 1980.
Period, Question Mark, Exclamation Mark, 1980.
Prefixes, Bases, and Suffixes, 1980.
Prepositions and Conjunctions, 1980.

"AN I KNOW IT!" SERIES, PUBLISHED BY SCHOOL ZONE PUBLISHING

Blends, 1981.
Consonants, 1981.
Long Vowels, 1981.
Rhyming Families, 1981.
Short Vowels, 1981.
Word Problems: Grades 1-2, 1981.
Word Problems: Grades 3-4, 1981.

"GET READY!" SERIES, PUBLISHED BY SCHOOL ZONE PUBLISHING

Alphabet: Lowercase, 1983.
Alphabet: Uppercase, 1983.
Beginning Sounds, 1983.
Colors, 1983.
Connect the Dots, 1983.
Counting One to Ten, 1983.
Does It Belong? 1983.
Following Directions, 1983.
Hidden Pictures, 1983.
Mazes, 1983.
Rhyming Pictures, 1983.
Same or Different, 1983.
School Time Fun, 1983.
Shapes, 1983.
What's Missing, 1983.

"START TO READ" SERIES, PUBLISHED BY SCHOOL ZONE PUBLISHING

The Gum on the Drum, 1984.
My Friend Goes Left, 1984.
Up Went the Goat, 1984.
The Fox on the Box, 1984.
Jog, Frog, Jog, 1984.
Sue Likes Blue, 1984.
Say Good Night, 1984.
I Want a Pet, 1984.
Beep, Beep, 1984.
Nine Men Chase a Hen, 1984.
Jace, Mace, and the Big Race, 1985.
Elephant and Envelope, 1985.
Noise in the Night, 1991.

"BEGINNER GAMES" SERIES, PUBLISHED BY SCHOOL ZONE PUBLISHING

Alphabet Avalanche, 1986.
Counting Caterpillars, 1986.
Reading Railroad, 1986.
Word Wagon, 1986.

"READ AND THINK" SERIES, PUBLISHED BY SCHOOL ZONE PUBLISHING

The Great Ape Trick, 1987.
It's Magic, 1987.
Nicole Digs a Hole, 1987.
The Fox, the Goose, and the Corn, 1988.
Trouble Again: Reading Workbook, 1988.

OTHER BOOKS FOR CHILDREN

Vocabulary Vampire, Learning Works, 1982.
The Comprehension Adventure, Learning Works, 1984.
D'Nealian Handwriting Activity Book, Scott, Foresman, 1985.
Logical Logic, Learning Works, 1986.
"Lift Off Reproducible" series, eighteen books, School Zone Publishing, 1990.

Also author of *Dramatic Literature* and *Fables and Legends,* published by McDonald Publishing, and of *Easy Manners for Every Day, Words of a Feather,* and *World Geography Skills,* published by J. Weston Walch.

ADULT FICTION

She's on First, Contemporary Books, 1987.
Dirty Proof, Pageant Books, 1988.

ADULT NONFICTION

Writing for the Educational Market, J. Weston Walch, 1990.
Women at Play: The Story of Women in Baseball, Harcourt, 1993.

BIOGRAPHICAL/CRITICAL SOURCES:

PERIODICALS

New Directions for Women, July, 1987, p. 13.
USA Today, June 11, 1987, p. 2C.
Voice of Youth Advocates, June, 1991, p. 90.
West Coast Review of Books, Volume 14, number 2, 1988, p. 25.

* * *

GREGORY, Lisa
See CAMP, Candace (Pauline)

* * *

GRESHAM, Perry E(pler) 1907-

PERSONAL: Born December 19, 1907, in Covina, CA; son of George Edward and Mary Elizabeth (Epler) Gresham; married Elsie Stanbrough, December 9, 1926 (died, 1947); married Alice Fickling Cowan, May 5, 1953; children: (first marriage) Glen Edward; (second marriage) Nancy Cowan (Mrs. Robert E. Sandercox). *Education:* Texas Christian University, A.B. (summa cum laude), 1930, B.D., 1933, LL.D., 1949; additional study at University of Chicago, 1932-33, and Columbia University, 1931-41. *Politics:* Independent.

Avocational Interests: poetry, golf, travel.

ADDRESSES: Home—Highland Hearth, Bethany, WV 26032. *Office*—Bethany College, Bethany, WV 26032.

CAREER: Texas Christian University, Forth Worth, professor of philosophy, 1936-42; University of Washington, Seattle, professor of philosophy, 1942-47; University of Michigan, Ann Arbor, professor of philosophy, 1947-53; Bethany College, Bethany, WV, president, 1953-72, president emeritus, 1972—, distinguished professor of philosophy, 1973—, chairman of board of trustees, 1972-76. Public lecturer in philosophy, economics, politics, and religion. Minister of campus churches in Fort Worth, TX, 1933-42, Seattle, WA, 1942-45, and Detroit, MI, 1945-53. Member of study committee of Commission on Faith and Order, World Council of Churches, 1948-60, of clergy and industry commission, National Association of Manufacturers, 1957-65, and of commission on liberal education, Association of American Colleges, 1963-78. President of West Virginia Foundation of Independent Colleges, 1954-58; chairman of North Central Association of Colleges and Universities, 1964-66, examiner and consultant; board member, Foundation for Economic Education, Inc., 1960-86, chairman, 1966-68, president, 1983-84, Lawrence Institute of Technology, and John A. Hartford Foundation; trustee of Bethany College and International Convention of Christian Churches, president, 1960-61. President of Highland Broadcasting Co.; member of board of directors of several companies, including Chesapeake & Potomac Telephone Co. of West Virginia, Cooper Tire and Rubber Co., Wesbanco Corp., 1960-83, president, 1983, Wheeling Dollar Bank.

MEMBER: International Platform Association, International Federation of Robert Burns Societies (honorary life member), American Philosophical Society, Association for Higher Education, American Council on Education, Association of American Colleges, Disciples of Christ Historical Society (honorary life member), Mont Pelerin Society, West Virginia Historical Society and other state historical societies, Shriners, Rotary, Masons, Delta Tau Delta, Alpha Chi, Pi Delta Epsilon, Phi Delta Kappa, Authors' Club (London), Royal Scottish Automobile Club (Glasgow), University Club (New York), Duquesne Club (Pittsburg), Skytop Club (Pennsylvania), Wheeling Country Club, Pinehurst Country Club (North Carolina), Bermuda Run Country Club (NC), Piedmont Club (NC).

AWARDS, HONORS: Freedoms Foundation leadership award, for public service in education, 1963; West Virginia Speaker of the Year award, 1969; recipient of honorary degrees from more than sixteen universities, including Texas Christian University, Culver-Stockton College, Chapman College, Transylvania College, University of Cincinnati, Youngstown University, Findlay College, Concord College, West Virginia University, Rio Grande College, Lawrence Institute of Technology, and Alderson-Broaddus College; named honorary citizen of six states.

WRITINGS:

Incipient Gnosticism in the New Testament, Southwestern Society for Biblical Research, 1933.
Disciplines of the High Calling, Bethany Press, 1953.
(Compiler) *The Sage of Bethany,* Bethany Press, 1960, reprinted, College Press Publishing Co., 1988.
Answer to Conformity, Bethany Press, 1961.
Abiding Values, Simpson, 1972.
Campbell and the Colleges, Disciples of Christ Historical Society, 1973.
With Wings as Eagles, Anna, 1980, large-print version, J. Curley & Associates, 1980.

Also author of *Toasts—Plain, Spicy, and Wry,* 1986. Feature writer, *Detroit Free Press,* 1949-52. Has written songs and hymns, including West Virginia Inaugural song, "Mighty Mountain Land," with wife, Alice Gresham, 1969.

* * *

GRIFFITH, Benjamin Woodward, Jr. 1922-

PERSONAL: Born March 30, 1922, in Lanett, AL; son of Benjamin Woodward and Mary (Norman) Griffith; married Betty Irvine, 1948; children: Eugenia Griffith DuPell, Benjamin W. Griffith III. *Education:* Mercer University, A.B., 1944; Northwestern University, M.A., 1948, Ph.D., 1952. *Politics:* Democrat.

ADDRESSES: Home—330 Kramer St., Carrollton, GA 30117.

CAREER: Tift College, Forsyth, GA, professor of English and chairman of department, 1950-55; Mercer University, Macon, GA, associate professor, 1955-59, professor of English, 1959-60, Pollock Professor of English, 1964-70, chairman of department, 1961-70, director of freshman English, 1955-61; West Georgia College, Carrollton, GA, professor of English, 1970—, chairman of department, 1970-73, dean of Graduate School, 1973-87. Visiting scholar, Duke University, 1955; board member, Mercer University Press. Board member of Rotary Club of Carrollton, Carroll County Cultural Arts Alliance (and vice president and president elect), and Carrollton Country Club. Member of First Baptist Church board of deacons; commissioner of Carroll County Historical Preservation Commission. *Military service:* U.S. Navy, 1943-46, became lieutenant junior grade; received Atlantic, Pacific, China, Philippines, and Victory medals.

MEMBER: Modern Language Association of America, Keats Shelley Association, American Society of Composers, Authors, and Publishers, South Atlantic Modern Language Association, Rotary Club, Sunset Hills Country Club.

WRITINGS:

(Editor) John Dryden, *All for Love,* Barron's, 1961.
(Editor) John Gay, *The Beggar's Opera,* Barron's, 1962.
(Editor) Beaumont and Fletcher, *The Knight of the Burning Pestle,* Barron's, 1963.
A Simplified Approach to "Wuthering Heights," Barron's, 1966.
(Co-author) *A Simplified Approach to "Silas Marner,"* Barron's, 1967.
A Simplified Approach to Mark Twain's "Huckleberry Finn," Barron's, 1969.
(Co-author) *How to Prepare for the Graduate Examination in Literature,* Barron's, 1969, revised edition, 1974.
(Co-author) *Essentials of English,* Barron's, 1982, 4th edition, 1990.
(Co-author) *Essentials of Writing,* Barron's, 1983, 4th revised edition, 1991.
(Co-author) *A Pocket Guide to Correct Grammar,* Barron's, 1984.
A Pocket Guide to Literature and Language Terms, Barron's, 1986.
McIntosh and Weatherford, Creek Indian Leaders (biography), University of Alabama Press, 1988.
(Co-author) *A Pocket Guide to Grammar,* Barron's, 2nd edition, 1990.
Study Keys to English Literature, Barron's, 1991.
Who, What, When, Where and Why in the World of Art and Music, Barron's, 1991.

Also author of two-act play, *The Murder of Chief McIntosh,* produced in 1992. Contributor of over fifty essays and articles to periodicals, including *Hudson Review, Sewanee Review, Gettysburg Review, Atlanta Journal-Constitution,* and *Bookpage.*

WORK IN PROGRESS: "A novel about interactions between the Creek Indians and early settlers in frontier Alabama about 1810-1850; a musical comedy, set in medieval times, based on Chaucer's *Wife of Bath's Tale* and *Sir Gawain and the Green Knight.*"

SIDELIGHTS: Benjamin Woodward Griffith, Jr., told *CA:* "I have always loved reading, and I remember as a child awaking an hour or two before the rest of my family so that I could read until breakfast before beginning my day of outdoor sports and chores. My father used to boast that I read every book in our small-town library, but that was an exaggeration, I fear. My desire to write grew out of my love affair with the printed page. Only later did I learn of an even greater pleasure from writing, a kind of joyful massaging of the brain and the emotions as thoughts are transferred to paper and/or to my computer screen.

"Although I chose the career of professor of English, I never stopped writing and continued to write magazine articles along with academic and critical articles for academic journals as well as textbooks. When I retired in 1987, I turned to writing full-time and have published a biography, a play, a trivia book on music and art, more textbooks, and a number of articles and book reviews. I like to give my writing my most alert hours of the day, and I try to write every morning. My friend Flannery O'Connor once told me that she sat at the typewriter every work-day morning. 'If the muse whispers in my ear,' she said, 'I want to be ready to write it down.'

"I hope to be able to finish two creative projects I'm now absorbed in: [the first is] a novel about frontier life in Alabama during the early 19th century, with its Indian wars and the terrible process of Indian removal. I'm also trying to write a musical comedy based on two stories of medieval knighthood: Chaucer's 'The Wife of Bath's Tale' and *Sir Gawain and the Green Knight.* Chaucer was in his middle fifties when he wrote his Canterbury Tales; I think that's equivalent to seventy-plus years with today's medical technology."

* * *

GROB, Gerald N. 1931-

PERSONAL: Born April 25, 1931, in New York, NY; son of Sidney and Sylvia (Cohen) Grob; married Lila E. Kronick, 1954; children: Bradford Spencer, Evan David, Seth Adam. *Education:* City College of New York (now City College of the City University of New York), B.S., 1951; Columbia University, A.M., 1952; Northwestern University, Ph.D., 1958.

ADDRESSES: Home—821 Starview Way, Bridgewater, NJ 08807. *Office*—Institute of Health, Health Care Policy, and Aging Research, Rutgers University, New Brunswick, NJ 08903.

CAREER: New York Public Library, New York City, library technical assistant, 1945-52; Clark University, Worcester, MA, instructor, 1957-59, assistant professor, 1959-61, associate professor, 1961-66, professor of American history and chairman of department, 1966-69; Rutgers University, New Brunswick, NJ, professor of history, 1969—, Henry E. Sigerist Professor of the History of Medicine, 1990—. *Military service:* U.S. Army, 1955-57.

MEMBER: American Historical Association, Organization of American Historians, American Association for the History of Medicine, Phi Alpha Theta.

AWARDS, HONORS: National Institute for Mental Health and National Library of Medicine research grants, 1960-65, 1967-81, and 1984-92; National Endowment for the Humanities senior fellow, 1972-73; American Council of Learned Societies fellow, 1976-77, and 1989-90; Guggenheim fellow, 1981; William H. Welch Medal, American Association for the History of Medicine, 1986.

WRITINGS:

Workers in Utopia: A Study of Ideological Conflict in the American Labor Movement: 1856-1900, Northwestern University Press, 1961.

(Editor with Robert N. Beck) *American Ideas: Source Readings in the Intellectual History of the United States,* two volumes, Free Press, 1963.

The State and the Mentally Ill: A History of Worcester State Hospital in Massachusetts, 1830-1920, University of North Carolina Press, 1966.

(With G. A. Billias) *Interpretations of American History,* two volumes, Free Press, 1967, 6th edition, 1992.

(Editor) *Statesmen and Statescraft of the Modern West: Essays in Honor of Dwight E. Lee and H. Donaldson Jordon,* Barre-Westover, 1967.

(Compiler) *American Social History before 1860,* Appleton, 1970.

Insanity and Idiocy in Massachusetts: Report of the Commission on Lunacy, 1855, by Edward Jarvis, Harvard University Press, 1971.

Mental Institutions in America: Social Policy to 1875, Free Press, 1973.

Edward Jarvis and the Medical World of Nineteenth-Century America, University of Tennessee Press, 1978.

Mental Illness and American Society, 1875-1940, Princeton University Press, 1983.

The Inner World of American Psychiatry, 1890-1940, Rutgers University Press, 1985.

From Asylum to Community: Mental Health Policy in Modern America, Princeton University Press, 1991.

The Mad Among Us: A History of the Care of America's Mentally Ill, Free Press, 1994.

WORK IN PROGRESS: A history of the relationship between disease and environment in American history.

GROSSINGER, Richard (Selig) 1944-

PERSONAL: Born November 3, 1944, in New York, NY; son of Paul Leonard and Martha Washington (Rothkrug) Grossinger; married Lindy Downer Hough, June 21, 1966; children: Robin, Miranda. *Education:* Amherst College, B.A., 1966; University of Michigan, M.A., 1968, Ph.D., 1975.

ADDRESSES: Office—North Atlantic Books, 2741 8th St., Berkeley, CA 94710.

CAREER: University of Maine, Portland-Gorham, lecturer in anthropology and geography, 1970-72; Goddard College, Plainfield, VT, lecturer, 1972-75; North Atlantic Books, Richmond, CA, founder and publisher, 1974—. Visiting member of faculty at Kent State University, 1973; lecturer at Kent State University, University of California at Santa Cruz, Kansas University, and Pacific College of Naturopathic Medicine. Research associate at University of California, Berkeley, 1978-79. Independent publishing consultant. Member of board of Urban Ecology and the Fund for the Environment.

MEMBER: Society for the Study of Native Arts and Sciences.

AWARDS, HONORS: Grant from Vermont Council on the Arts, 1975; fellow of National Endowment for the Arts, 1976.

WRITINGS:

Solar Journal: Oecological Sections, Black Sparrow Press, 1970.
Spaces Wild and Tame, Mudra Books, 1971.
Book of the Earth and Sky, Black Sparrow Press, 1971.
Mars: A Science-Fiction Vision, North Atlantic Books, 1971.
The Continents, Black Sparrow Press, 1973.
Early Field Notes from the All-American Revival Church, North Atlantic Books, 1973.
Book of the Cranberry Islands, Harper, 1974.
The Long Body of the Dream, North Atlantic Books, 1974.
The Windy Passage from Nostalgia, North Atlantic Books, 1974.
The Book of Being Born Again into the World, North Atlantic Books, 1974.
The Slag of Creation, North Atlantic Books, 1974.
Martian Homecoming at the All-American Revival Church, North Atlantic Books, 1974.
The Provinces, North Atlantic Books, 1975.
The Unfinished Business of Dr. Hermes, North Atlantic Books, 1976.
(Editor with Kevin Kerrane) *Baseball, I Gave You All the Best Years of My Life,* North Atlantic Books, 1977, 3rd edition, 1979.
(Editor) *Ecology and Consciousness,* North Atlantic Books, 1978.
(Editor) *Alchemy: Pre-Egyptian Legacy, Millennial Promise,* North Atlantic Books, 1979.
Planet Medicine: From Stone Age Shamanism to Post-Industrial Healing, Doubleday, 1980.
(With Kerrane) *Baseball Diamonds,* Doubleday, 1980.
The Night Sky: The Science and Anthropology of the Stars and Planets, Sierra Club Books, 1981.
(Editor) *Nuclear Strategy and the Code of the Warrior,* North Atlantic Books, 1984.
Embryogenesis: From Cosmos to Creature; The Origins of Human Biology, Avon, 1984.
(Editor) *The Temple of Baseball,* North Atlantic Books, 1985.
(Editor) *Planetary Mysteries,* North Atlantic Books, 1986.
Waiting for the Martian Express, North Atlantic Books, 1989.
(With Kerrane) *Into the Temple of Baseball,* Celestial Arts, 1990.

Founder and editor of *Io,* 1965—.

WORK IN PROGRESS: The Dream Work.

SIDELIGHTS: Richard Grossinger once told *CA*: "I began writing autobiographical prose in high school. By the time I was a freshman in college, I was attempting fictional novels, much influenced by Faulkner and Lawrence. A faculty member there put me in touch with an editor at a New York publisher, and I worked with her for a year on an attempted novel called *The Moon* and another called *The Cloud*. About the middle of the time I was in college, I met the poet Robert Kelly, and he interested me in whole other genres of writing. I realized that the things I wanted to say were more apparent in the poetry tradition, so I wrote poetry for a year, but then ultimately went back to prose and began writing it in my own style and genre.

"Over the years, I produced some fourteen experimental prose books (basically from 1966 through 1974), published initially by Black Sparrow Press, Mudra Books, and Harper & Row, and then later by myself after starting North Atlantic Books, to maintain the integrity of the text. After completing this intense process, which involved work virtually every day and a continuous attention to subjective data, I stopped writing for a couple of years, doing only occasional fragments and reviews. When I began again, in 1977, I decided to deal with the objective elements, and I have since been at work on a series of books, beginning with *Planet Medicine: From Stone Age Shamanism to Post-Industrial Healing,* that deal with the origin and meaning of critical forms in our society and culture. The second, *The Night Sky,* is about the formation of an image of the creation in time and space. The third is about dreams, and the fourth will be about plants, animals, genetics, and life. These are prose narrative books, meant as literature (the same as novels in that sense), but without characters and without the standard fictional, or even nonfictional, sense of what constitutes a literary topic.

"Like many poets, I am primarily concerned with language, the source of meaning, and the complex interrelation of objective and subjective shapes. Like most prose writers, I am interested in narrative, exposition, and conventional use of sentences and paragraphs."

Grossinger recently added: "The trilogy of objective nonfiction books was completed with *Embryogenesis*; since then, I have gone back to simple narrative and have been writing autobiographically from my own life."

BIOGRAPHICAL/CRITICAL SOURCES:

PERIODICALS

New York Times Book Review, December 27, 1981.

*　*　*

GROSSKURTH, Phyllis 1924-

PERSONAL: Born March 16, 1924, in Toronto, Ontario, Canada; daughter of Milton Palmer (an actuary) and Winifred (Owen) Langstaff; married Robert A. Grosskurth (a naval commander; marriage ended); married Mavor Moore, May, 1968 (divorced February, 1980); married Robert McMullan, June, 1986; children: (first marriage) Christopher, Brian, Ann. *Education:* University of Toronto, B.A., 1946; University of Ottawa, M.A., 1960; University of London, Ph.D., 1962. *Religion:* Church of England.

ADDRESSES: Home—147 Spruce St., Toronto, Ontario, Canada M5A 26J. *Office*—Department of English, New College, University of Toronto, Toronto, Ontario, Canada M5S 1A8. *Agent*—David Higham Associates Ltd., 5-8 Lower John St., London W1R 4HA, England; Georges Borchardt, Inc., 136 East 57th Street, New York, NY 10022.

CAREER: Carleton University, Ottawa, Ontario, lecturer, 1964-65; University of Toronto, Toronto, Ontario, professor of English, 1965-87, member of faculty, humanities and psychoanalysis programme, 1987—. Honorary research fellow, University College, London.

MEMBER: PEN.

AWARDS, HONORS: Governor General's Literary Award for nonfiction and University of Columbia Medal for Biography, both for *John Addington Symonds: A Biography.*

WRITINGS:

John Addington Symonds: A Biography, Longmans, Green, 1964, published as *The Woeful Victorian,* Holt, 1965.

Notes on Browning's Works, [Toronto], 1967.

Leslie Stephen, Longmans, Green, for National Book League and British Council, 1968.

Gabrielle Roy, edited by William French, Forum House, 1969.

Havelock Ellis: A Biography, Knopf, 1980.

(Editor) *The Memoirs of John Addington Symonds,* Random House, 1984.

Melanie Klein: Her World and Her Work, Knopf, 1986.

Margaret Mead: A Life of Controversy, Penguin, 1988.

The Secret Ring: Freud's Inner Circle and the Politics of Psychoanalysis, Addison-Wesley, 1991.

Contributor to periodicals, including *New York Review of Books* and *Times Literary Supplement.* Literary editor of *Canadian Forum,* 1975-76.

SIDELIGHTS: Phyllis Grosskurth is recognized for her meticulously researched biographies on controversial figures of the late nineteenth and early twentieth centuries. In *Havelock Ellis: A Biography,* Grosskurth documents the life of this pioneer in the study of human sexuality, basing her biography on extensive research which included reading more than 20,000 letters written by Ellis himself. Stuart Hampshire reviews the book in the *Times Literary Supplement,* commenting on the amount of work done by Grosskurth: "The author's research and documentation are formidably complete . . . . Here one has the whole of Havelock Ellis, known and knowable." Robert Kirsch also notes the extent of Grosskurth's work, but writes in the *Los Angeles Times:* "Yet, for all the careful research, the massive detail which has gone into this work, there is, at times, a lack of sympathy for Ellis . . . which makes the portrait of [him] . . . seem cool and cerebral." Kirsch does, however, stress the significance of Grosskurth's biography in commenting that "Professor Grosskurth's biography is indispensable and . . . provides the reader with all the information necessary to make a private judgement" of Ellis.

With *Melanie Klein: Her World and Her Work,* Grosskurth tackles a controversial figure of modern psychoanalysis whose theories centered around children and the unconscious. Grosskurth's book is the first full-scale biography devoted to Klein and the first study of her unpublished papers and correspondence; it also includes interviews with Klein's now grown-up patients. Klein, a major presence in British psychoanalysis, pioneered play analysis, a variation on Freud's "talking cure." She spurred debate by basing many of her theories on the analysis of her own three children, and eventually broke with the traditional Freudians over disagreements with Anna Freud, who also established her reputation as an analyst of children.

In the *Times Literary Supplement,* David Ingleby praised Grosskurth for her handling of this much-debated figure: "Phyllis Grosskurth is by no means neutral when it comes to her importance as an analyst—indeed, she regards [Klein] as one of the great women of this century; but she has gone to great lengths to avoid either idealizing or caricaturing her subject. 'Melanie Klein was the stuff of which myths are made', she begins, and then sets out to demythologize her." In the *Nation,* Elisabeth Young-Bruehl writes, "The great merit of the biography is that the portrait of Klein is drawn with unflinching attention to the dark, tormented sides of her personality and behavior. Grosskurth writes admiringly of Klein's brilliance and her achievements, but she never white-washes her character."

Grosskurth's thorough scholarship is once again evident in *The Secret Ring: Freud's Inner Circle and the Politics of Psychoanalysis.* Here, Grosskurth depicts the rivalry and personal relationships of the psychoanalysts who made up Freud's inner circle: Karl Abraham, Sandor Ferenczi, Ernest Jones, Otto Rank, Hanns Sachs, and later, Max Eitingon. In the *New York Times Book Review,* Stuart Schneiderman comments, "The story of the creation of a cultural movement would have been engaging and compelling. Regrettably, Ms. Grosskurth . . . slides past the larger political and social questions to offer an account of the minutiae of the interpersonal relationships among the members of the Secret Committee. Thus a potentially edifying story quickly gets lost in tiresome details." Still, reviewers emphasize that with *The Secret Ring* Grosskurth has researched and written about the inner workings of one of the major intellectual revolutions of the twentieth century. "What emerges," comments Vivian Rakoff in the *Globe and Mail* (Toronto), "is akin to a Renaissance drama: the story of a group of courtiers manoeuvering for the affection and advancement of a king while developing their own careers. And the characters emerge with the clarity and idiosyncrasy of characters in a novel."

BIOGRAPHICAL/CRITICAL SOURCES:

PERIODICALS

Atlantic Monthly, January, 1992.
Chicago Tribune Book World, May 25, 1980.
Globe and Mail (Toronto), August 22, 1987; November 16, 1991.
London Times, July 17, 1980.
Los Angeles Times, May 12, 1980.
Los Angeles Times Book Review, March 10, 1985, p. 2; May 25, 1986, p. 6.
Nation, April 26, 1986.
New York Review of Books, April 8, 1965; May 8, 1986.
New York Times, May 8, 1980.
New York Times Book Review, May 16, 1965; June 22, 1980; May 18, 1986, p. 14; November 17, 1991.
Times Literary Supplement, November 28, 1980; July 20, 1984; May 1, 1987, p. 467; December 20, 1991.
Washington Post Book World, July 20, 1980; February 17, 1985, p. 6; June 8, 1986, p. 8.

* * *

GROSSMANN, Reinhardt S. 1931-

PERSONAL: Born January 10, 1931, in Berlin, Germany; came to the United States in 1955, naturalized citizen, 1963; son of Willy and Margarete (Neumann) Grossmann; children: Marcy, Martin. *Education:* Attended Paedagogische Hochschule, Berlin, Germany, 1950-54; University of Iowa, Ph.D., 1958.

ADDRESSES: Home—800 North Smith Rd., V7, Bloomington, IN 47408. *Office*—Department of Philosophy, Indiana University at Bloomington, Bloomington, IN 47405.

CAREER: University of Illinois at Urbana-Champaign, Urbana, instructor, 1958-61, assistant professor of philosophy, 1961-62; Indiana University at Bloomington, assistant professor, 1962-65, associate professor, 1965-70, professor of philosophy, 1970—.

MEMBER: American Philosophical Association.

WRITINGS:

(With Edwin B. Allaire and others) *Essays in Ontology,* Nijhoff, 1963.
The Structure of Mind, University of Wisconsin Press, 1965.
Reflections on Frege's Philosophy, Northwestern University Press, 1969.
Ontological Reduction, Indiana University Press, 1973.
Meinong, Routledge & Kegan Paul, 1974.
The Categorical Structure of the World, Indiana University Press, 1983.
Phenomenology and Existentialism: An Introduction, Routledge & Kegan Paul, 1984.
The Fourth Way: A Theory of Knowledge, Indiana University Press, 1990.
The Existence of the World: An Introduction to Ontology, Routledge & Kegan Paul, 1992.

* * *

GROSVENOR, Verta Mae 1938-

PERSONAL: Born April 4, 1938, in Fairfax, SC; married; children: Kali, Chandra. *Education:* Received high school education in Philadelphia, PA.

ADDRESSES: Office—c/o Penn Center, P. O. Box 126, Frogmore, SC 29920.

CAREER: Writer.

MEMBER: People United to Save Humanity (PUSH).

WRITINGS:

Vibration Cooking; or, The Traveling Notes of a Geechee Girl (autobiography), Doubleday, 1970.
Thursday and Every Other Sunday Off: A Domestic Rap, Doubleday, 1972.
Plain Brown Rapper (poems), Doubleday, 1975.
Black Atlantic Cooking, Prentice Hall, 1990.

Work represented in several anthologies, including *Visions of America by the Poets of Our Time.* Author of food column in *Amsterdam News* and of column in *Chicago Courier.* Contributor of articles and stories to magazines and newspapers.

BIOGRAPHICAL/CRITICAL SOURCES:

BOOKS

Vibration Cooking; or The Traveling Notes of a Geechee Girl, Doubleday, 1970.*

* * *

GRUMBACH, Doris (Isaac) 1918-

PERSONAL: Born July 12, 1918, in New York, NY; daughter of Leonard William and Helen Isaac; married Leonard Grumbach (a professor of physiology), October 15, 1941 (divorced, 1972); children: Barbara, Jane, Elizabeth, Kathryn. *Education:* Washington Square College, A.B., 1939; Cornell University, M.A., 1940. *Religion:* Episcopalian. *Politics:* Liberal.

ADDRESSES: Home—Sargentville, ME. *Agent*—Maxine Groffsky, 2 Fifth Ave., New York, NY 10011.

CAREER: Writer. Metro-Goldwyn-Mayer, New York City, title writer, 1940-41; *Mademoiselle,* New York City, proofreader and copy editor, 1941-42; Time Inc., associate editor of *Architectural Forum,* 1942-43; Albany Academy for Girls, Albany, NY, English teacher, 1952-55; College of Saint Rose, Albany, instructor, 1955-58, assistant professor, 1958-60, associate professor, 1960-69, professor of English, 1969-73; *New Republic,* Washington, DC, literary editor, 1973-75; American University, Washington, DC, professor of American literature, 1975-85. Visiting University fellow, Empire State College, 1972-73; adjunct professor of English, University of Maryland, 1974-75. Literary critic; *Morning Edition,* National Public Radio, book reviewer, beginning 1982. Board member for National Book Critics Circle and PEN/Faulkner Award; judge for writing contests. *Military Service:* U.S. Navy, Women Accepted for Volunteer Emergency Service, 1941-43.

MEMBER: American Association of University Professors, PEN, Phi Beta Kappa.

WRITINGS:

The Spoil of the Flowers, Doubleday, 1962.
The Short Throat, the Tender Mouth, Doubleday, 1964.
The Company She Kept (biography), Coward, 1967.
Chamber Music, Dutton, 1979.
The Missing Person, Putnam, 1981.
The Ladies, Dutton, 1984.
The Magician's Girl, Macmillan, 1987.
Coming into the Endzone: A Memoir, Norton, 1991.

Also author of introductions and forwards for books. Contributor to books, including *The Postconcilor Parish,* edited by James O'Gara, Kenedy, 1967, and *Book Reviewing,* edited by Silvia E. Kameran, Writer, Inc., 1978. Columnist for *Critic,* 1960-64, and *National Catholic Reporter,* 1968—; author of nonfiction column for *New York Times Book Review,* 1976—, column, "Fine Print," for *Saturday Review,* 1977-78, and fiction column, *Chronicle of Higher Education,* 1979—. Contributing editor, *New Republic,* 1971-73; book reviewer for *MacNeil-Leher Newshour,* Public Broadcasting Service. Contributor of reviews and criticism to periodicals, including *New York Times Book Review, Chicago Tribune, Commonweal, Los Angeles Times, Nation, Washington Post, Washington Star,* and *New Republic.* Grumbach's works have been translated into foreign languages.

WORK IN PROGRESS: A literary biography of Willa Cather.

SIDELIGHTS: Doris Grumbach, a biographer and respected literary critic, is the author of several novels with historical, biographical, and autobiographical elements. Early in her career, Grumbach worked as a title writer, copy and associate editor, literary editor, and an English teacher; her career as a novelist did not begin until her early forties. In an essay for *Contemporary Authors Autobiography Series (CAAS),* the author recalls the time when she sought to have her first book published: "The manuscript was in a typing-paper box, wrapped in a shopping bag from the A. & P., and taped shut with scotch tape. I left it with the receptionist, remembering too late that I had not put my name and address on the outside of the box. I expected, as one does with an unlabeled suitcase at the airport, never to see it again. Two weeks later I got a phone call from an editor at Doubleday telling me they wished to publish the novel. Two years later they published a second novel." These first two books, *The Spoil of the Flowers,* about student life in a boarding house, and

The Short Throat, the Tender Mouth, about life on a college campus three months before Hitler's march on Poland, "were by a beginner at a time in my life when I no longer should have been a beginner," Grumbach relates in *CAAS.* "There are some good things, I believe, in both novels: had I much time ahead of me now, I would rewrite them and resubmit them for publication."

Grumbach's third novel *The Company She Kept,* is a literary biography of the acerbic novelist Mary McCarthy. This book became the subject of a threatened lawsuit before its publication and of a volatile critical debate after its release. *The Company She Kept* parallels events and characters in McCarthy's novels with those in her life. "The fiction of Mary McCarthy is autobiographical to an extraordinary degree, in the widest sense of autobiography," Grumbach explains in the foreword to the book. "In the case of Mary McCarthy there is only a faint line between what really happened to her, the people she knew and knows, including herself, and the characters in her fictions." To prepare the biography, Grumbach spent a year reading McCarthy's work and criticism of it and interviewed the author extensively at her Paris home. Difficulties with McCarthy arose, Grumbach says, when McCarthy, who suggested she read the galleys of the book to catch any factual errors, protested against some of the information Grumbach had included in the manuscript.

In a *New York Times Book Review* article on her dispute with McCarthy, Grumbach reports that McCarthy voluntarily provided her with intimate biographical details in conversation and in a detailed memorandum. McCarthy's anger over their inclusion therefore came as a surprise, says Grumbach. "I was unprepared for the fury of her response when she saw the galleys . . . and realized that I had used the autobiographical details she had, as she said, given me," comments Grumbach. "She had said, once, that it felt strange to have a book written about one, 'a book that includes you as a person, not just a critical analysis of your writings.' Now she insisted that the *curriculum vitae* had been sent to be 'drawn upon,' not used, although just how this was to be done continues to be a mystery to me. . . . [McCarthy's] feeling was that the tapes and her letters to me had been intended solely for 'your own enlightenment.' "

For all the attendant publicity, however, *The Company She Kept* was not well received by the literary establishment. Writes Stephanie Harrington in *Commonweal:* "To anyone who has read *The Company She Kept,* . . . the newspaper stories that followed the book's publication must have seemed too preposterous to be anything but a desperate attempt by the publisher's publicity department to drum up business for a clinker." A *Times Literary Supplement* contributor, who describes *The Company She Kept* as "sparkily written and often critically sharp," feels that Grumbach falls short of her stated goal of "weaving one fabric of [the] diverse threads of McCarthy's biography and her fiction." Grumbach, says the reviewer, "never fully succeeds in dramatizing the complex interactions that go into such a process; [therefore, *The Company She Kept*] is likely to end up as required reading for gossips." Ellen Moers in the *New York Times Book Review* does not argue the validity of Grumbach's attempt to find the fact in Mary McCarthy's fiction—the process of "set[ting] out to name names," as Moers calls it—but instead claims that Grumbach misreads McCarthy and thus arrives at erroneous conclusions. To Grumbach's statement that "there is only a faint line" between fact and fiction for McCarthy, Moers responds: "This simply cannot be true. The husbands in McCarthy fiction . . . are such dreary mediocrities, her artist colonies and political oases are so bare of talent or distinction, her suites of college girls are so tediously third-rate—only a powerful imagination could have made such nonentities out of the very interesting company that Mary McCarthy actually kept."

Saturday Review critic Granville Hicks, however, does not find Grumbach's approach in *The Company She Kept* objectionable and approves of her straightforward manner in tackling it. "Although there is nothing novel about finding Miss McCarthy in her books, critics are usually cautious about identifying characters in fiction with real people, and I am grateful for Mrs. Grumbach's refusal to beat around that particular bush."

In the wake of the harsh reviews *The Company She Kept* received, Grumbach tried to deflect some of the criticism from herself by explaining the circumstances leading to her decision to write the McCarthy biography. Explaining in the *New York Times Book Review* that she was asked to write the book on McCarthy, rather than instigating the project herself, Grumbach states, "An editor asks, somewhere in the inner room of a dim New York restaurant, would you do a book on Her? And because you do not ordinarily eat and drink such sumptuous lunches in the proximate company of so many successful-looking people, and because you need the money, and because after all, She *is* a good writer (you've *always* thought this) and apparently a *fascinating* woman, you say yes, I will." Comments Harrington: "Mrs. Grumbach's apologia in the *Times* . . . [indicates] that it was foolhardy to expect a serious piece of work in the first place when she only decided to take on Mary McCarthy because an editor asked 'somewhere in the inner room of a dim New York restaurant, would you do a book on Her?' " Recognizing the shortcomings of *The Company She Kept,* Grumbach summarizes her difficulties with the book in the *New York Times Book Review:* "The value of the whole experience lies, for me," she says, "in the recognition of how difficult, even well-nigh impossible, it is to write a book that deals with a living person. It does not matter in the least that the living person is willing to assist the writer (beware the Greeks bearing . . .) in conversation or letter; the fact remains, the law being what it is, the subject can give with one hand, take back with the other, and in this process of literary Indian-giving the writer is virtually helpless."

Ten years after publishing *The Company She Kept* and fifteen years after writing her novels, *The Short Throat, the Tender Mouth* and *The Spoil of the Flowers,* Grumbach returned to fiction. Her first novel after the hiatus was *Chamber Music,* written as the memoirs of ninety year-old Caroline MacLaren, widow of a famous composer and founder of an artists' colony in his memory. Released with a 20,000 copy first printing and a $20,000 promotional campaign, *Chamber Music* won the popular and critical acclaim that eluded Grumbach's earlier books. Peter Davison in the *Atlantic Monthly* calls the book "artful, distinctive, provocative, [and] compassionate." *Chamber Music,* writes Victoria Glendinning in the *Washington Post Book World,* "is a book of originality and distinction." *Chamber Music* is the story of "the chamber of one heart," says Caroline MacLaren in the introduction to her memoirs.

The novel's plot revolves around the subjugation of Caroline to her husband Robert and to Robert's music. Their marriage is a cold and barren one and *Chamber Music* charts its course through Robert's incestuous relationship with his mother, his homosexual affair with a student, and, finally, to his agonizing death in the tertiary stage of syphilis. Especially noted for its sensitive handling of its delicate subject matter and for its characterizations, *Chamber Music* is called by the *New York Times*'s John Leonard, "one of those rare novels for adults who listen." The characters in *Chamber Music,* Leonard continues, "are all stringed instruments. The music we hear occurs in the chamber of Caroline's heart. It is quite beautiful." With her third novel, Grumbach "makes us hear the difficult music of grace," says Nicholas Delbanco in the *New Republic.*

Although *Chamber Music*'s "revelations of sexuality are meant to shatter," as one *Publishers Weekly* contributor comments, and the passage on Robert's illness gives "a clinical description so simply precise, so elegantly loathsome, that it would do nicely either in a medical text or in a book on style," as Edith Milton observes in *Yale Review,* it is the contrast between *Chamber Music*'s action and its language that gives the novel its impact. While much of the material in *Chamber Music* is meant to shock, the language is genteel and full of Victorian phrases. "What gives the main part of this book its polish and flavor is the contrast between matter and manner," says Glendinning. "Clarity and elegance of style account . . . for the distinction of *Chamber Music,*" writes Eleanor B. Wymard in *Commonweal,* and other critics have high praise for Grumbach's writing. A *Washington Post Book World* reviewer claims the book's language is "as direct and pure as a Hayden quartet," and Abigail McCarthy in *Commonweal* states that *Chamber Music* has "the classical form, clarity, and brilliance of a composition for strings." Because it is Caroline's story, the novel adopts her voice—a voice that is "slightly stilted, slightly vapid, of the genteel tradition," one *Atlantic* contributor observes. Asserts Milton: "The novel is wonderfully written in [Caroline's] voice to evoke a time gone by, an era vanished. . . . The prose, understated, beautiful in its economies, supports a story of almost uncanny bleakness."

In her short preface to *Chamber Music,* Grumbach states that the novel's characters "are based vaguely upon persons who were once alive" but stresses that the book is fiction. "*Chamber Music* is a thinly, and strangely, fictionalized variation on the life of Marian MacDowell, [composer] Edward MacDowell's widow, who . . . founded an artist's colony in New Hampshire. . . . The names are changed; though not by much considering what else changes with them," says Milton. Gail Godwin, writing in the *New York Times Book Review,* suspects that the parallels between the MacDowells and the MacLarens "handicap . . . [Grumbach's] own possibilites for creating a fictional hero who might have come to life more vividly." However, other critics, including Glendinning, find that "the illusion of authenticity is strengthened by the inclusion of real people." "Robert MacLaren himself is given a semihistorical glamour by the parallels between his career and that of . . . Edward MacDowell—the two share teachers, musical styles, even a Boston address, and MacDowell's widow did indeed found an artist's colony in his name," writes Katha Pollitt. "Such details give Caroline's memoirs the piquancy of a historical novel."

Franny Fuller, the protagonist of Grumbach's novel *The Missing Person,* is also patterned after an actual figure. Franny, a 1930s movie star and sex symbol, closely resembles actress Marilyn Monroe. Written as a series of vignettes interweaving the events of Franny's career with an ongoing commentary by a gossip columnist, *The Missing Person* traces the actress's life from her sad beginnings in Utica, New York, through her rise to stardom, and finally to her disappearance from both Hollywood and the public consciousness. "Here, with certain sympathetic changes, is quite visibly another tale about the sad life of Marilyn Monroe," observes the *New York Times*'s Herbert Mitgang. "Missing person," says Cynthia Propper Seton in the *Washington Post Book World,* refers to "this sense that one is all facade, that there is no self inside." Franny is supposed to serve as a prototype for all the "missing persons" who are, "above all, missing to themselves," claims Herbert Gold in the *New York Times Book Review.* "There seems evidence," Abigail McCarthy writes in *Commonweal,* "that Doris Grumbach may initially have thought of Franny Fuller's story as a feminist statement in that women like Franny whom America 'glorifies and elevates' are sex objects made larger than life. But if so, as often happens in the creative process, she has transcended the aim in the writing. The creatures of the Hollywood process she gives us, men as well as women, are all victims."

Grumbach, in a prefatory note to the novel, comments on the nature of the book. "This novel is a portrait, not of a single life but of many lives melded into one, typical of the women America often glorifies and elevates, and then leaves suspended in their lonely and destructive fame," she says. Still, comments Richard Combs in a *Times Literary Supplement,* "there is no prize for guessing that the novel's heroine is Marilyn Monroe." The close correlation between Marilyn Monroe's and Franny's lives is disturbing to many critics. "The question that poses itself about a book like this is, Why bother? If you must write about Marilyn Monroe then why not do so in fiction or otherwise?," asks James Campbell in the *New Statesman.* "Real names thinly disguised are a bore." Combs believes Grumbach's reliance on the facts of Marilyn Monroe's life hinders her ability to substantiate the point she makes in the preface. "The more the real Hollywood shows through [in the novel], the less satisfying the portrait becomes," Combs says. "The author's assumption . . . seems to be that since Hollywood put fantasy on an anonymous, mass-production basis, the results can be freely arranged by the inspired do-it-yourselfer. . . . But in refantasizing the fantasy factory, Mrs. Grumbach allows herself the license of fiction without taking on the responsibility . . . to find revised truth in the revised subject."

"It is hard for [Franny] to have a separate imaginary existence in the mind of the reader," states Abigail McCarthy. "But this flaw, if it is one, is more than compensated for by the writer's evocation of the scene against which Franny moves—tawdry, wonderful Hollywood at its peak." Indeed, Grumbach is praised for her fine writing and for "the adroit structure of the novel," as Gold calls it. "There is in this prose a certain leanness, a sparseness that separates most of the characters into a chapter each, surrounded by an implied emptiness. Instead of the usual crowded Hollywood narrative, [*The Missing Person*] has the melancholy air . . . of an underpopulated landscape," writes Combs. Seton comments on Grumbach's ability to capture the tone and feeling of old Hollywood films and newsreels in her writing. "Doris Grumbach's special gift lies in her ability to suit the style and structure of her novels to the world in which she writes," McCarthy says. "*The Missing Person* is itself like a motion picture—a pastiche of scenes centered on the star, complete with flashbacks, close-ups and fade-outs."

Grumbach switches her topic from the rise then demise of a 1930s starlet in *The Missing Person,* to the public ostracism then acceptance of two aristocratic lesbian lovers of the eighteenth century in her novel *The Ladies.* "Grumbach compellingly recreates the lives of two women who so defied convention and so baffled their contemporaries that they became celebrities," lauds Catharine R. Stimpson in the *New York Times Book Review.* The story relates Grumbach's concept of how Eleanor Butler and Sarah Ponsonby, two Irish aristocrats from the 1700s known as "the Ladies of Llangollen," shocked the community with their lesbian relationship but were eventually accepted and visited by such noteworthy individuals as Anna Seward, the Duke of Wellington, and Walter Scott. Stimpson notes the book "eloquently documents the existence of women who lived as they wished to, instead of as society expected them to."

As Grumbach relates, Lady Eleanor, feeling the lack of love from her parents because she wasn't a boy, becomes the boy in her behavior and dress. Always looking to fill her need for acceptance and love, Eleanor falls in love with the orphan, Sarah Ponsonby, who is being sexually harassed by her guardian. Eleanor attempts to rescue Sarah, but the two are caught before they get far. A second attempt prompts the families to allow the couple to leave together, but under the condition that Lady Eleanor is banned from Ireland forever. After a couple years of wandering, Eleanor and Sarah settle with a former servant and create their own haven in Wales. Eleanor and Sarah "seemed to each other to be divine survivors, well beyond the confines of social rules, two inhabitants of an ideal society. . . . They had uncovered a lost continent on which they could live, in harmony, quite alone and together," writes Grumbach in *The Ladies.* Eventually, visited by other aristocrats, they become more secure within the outer community, however, problems arise in their relationship as their greed and fame alters their lives.

The Ladies met with good reviews. Stimpson, while recognizing Grumbach's pattern of blurring biography and fiction, praises the book noting that "*The Ladies* is boldly imagined, [and] subtly crafted." Comparing Grumbach's work with the likes of Virginia Woolf and Charlotte Perkins Gillman, the *Washington Post Book World*'s Sandra Gilbert claims Grumbach has "recounted their story with grace and wit," and applauds "the sureness with which Grumbach accumulates small details about the lives of her protagonist and the tough but loving irony with which she portrays their idiosyncracies." She observes, though, that while the protagonists "road to reposeful Llangollen is strewn with obstacles for the runaway ladies. . . . All ends well once the weary travelers arrive in friendship's vale." Thus Gilbert maintains that "if there is anything problematic about *The Ladies,* it is that all seems to go almost too well" in the novel and "like Grumbach's earlier *Chamber Music,* seems here and there to flirt with the conventions of an increasingly popular new genre: The Happy Lesbian novel."

The title for Grumbach's next novel, the *The Magician's Girl,* is borrowed from Sylvia Plath's poem "The Bee Meeting." In this story Grumbach writes about three women who were college roommates and grew up during the twenties and thirties. In episodic fashion, the stories of Minna, Liz, and Maud are related from their childhood to their sixties, and from their hopes and dreams to their reality. Pretty, shy Minna marries a doctor, has a son, and becomes a history professor. After surviving years in a loveless marriage, at the age of sixty she finally develops a loving relationship with a young man in his twenties. Not long after they meet and she experiences this fullfillment, though, she is killed in a car accident. Maud, the overweight and unattractive daughter of a nurse and army sergeant, marries a handsome man whom she eventually rejects, has twins whom she neglects, and spends most of her time writing poetry. Her poetry is good but she destroys it all, except for the copies she sends to Minnie in her letters; she commits suicide before realizing the true success of her writings. Liz, the only survivor, lives with her partner in a lesbian relationship, achieving fame as a photographer, her subjects all freaks of one kind or another. Summarizing the book's theme, Anita Brookner in her review for the *Washington Post Book World,* states that the formulaic stories about these three women demonstrates "the way early beginnings mature into not very much, for despite the achievements that come with age, a sense of disillusion persits." Brookner asserts that Grumbach asks more questions about women's lives than she answers in her story, including the question, "Is that all?," and surmises that this may be more important than the answers. In conclusion, she praises *The Magician's Girl* as "a beautifully easy read, discreet and beguiling, and attractively low-key. It is an honorable addition to the annals of women's reading."

The reviews for *The Magician's Girl* were mixed. Several critics faulted Grumbach for too closely describing the lives of Sylvia Plath and Diane Arbus as the characters of Maud and Liz respectively. Other critics found her writing weak in definition and description. *Times Literary Supplement*'s Marianne Wiggins finds events "unlocated in time" and places "without a sense of period." She asserts that it is written "as if the text were a rehearsal for a talent contest," and considers this especially disconcerting since she regards Grumbach as the "master of the quick sketch" and points out that generally "when her narrative shifts to describing the specific, it soars." In contrast, Paula Deitz in the *New York Times Book Review* commends Grumbach's attention to detail in *The Magician's Girl.* She deems that the characters described "are all rich images, informed with the magic conveyed by the small details that reveal the forming of these lives." Deitz further maintains that "*The Magician's Girl* is most disturbing, and therfore at its best, in its acute awareness of the pains endured unflichingly by the young." *Christian Science Monitor*'s Merle Rubin summarizes: "What is most poignant about this novel is that its special aura of serenity tinged with sadness comes not from the pains and losses the characters endure, although there are many of these, but from the conviction it conveys that life, for all its sorrows, is so rich with possiblities as to make any one life—however long—much too short."

Grumbach shares feelings, events, and remembrances of the year she turned seventy in her 1991 autobiography, *Coming into the End Zone: A Memoir.* "What is most delightful about *Coming into the End Zone*—[is] the wry, spry, resilient, candid recording of present happenings and suddenly remembered past happenings which fill almost every page with anecdotes and reflections," exclaims *Washington Post Book World*'s Anthony Thwaite. Grumbach comments on a wide range of topics, including contemporary annoyances such as phrases like "the computer is down," the death of several friends from the complications of aquired immunodeficiency syndrome, her dislikes of travel, her move to rural Maine, her memories of being fired from the *New Republic,* and Mary McCarthy's last curt comment to her. "The best moments are the passages in which the author seems least to be writing for posterity, merely trying to capture herself on the page, moments when the need to maintain a public persona gives way to the vulnerability of the private person, sometimes even to the young girl still inside this old woman," declares Carol Anshaw in the Chicago *Tribune.* "The book that Ms. Grumbach intended as a confrontation with death winds up being a celebration of life," comments Noel Perrin in the *New York Times Book Review,* adding that "it is a deeply satisfying book." "Grumbach's reflections record—with honesty, fidelity, much important and unimportant detail, and with much grace and informal wit—her feelings of the time. I know no other book like it," hails Thwaite. He concludes, "This is a book to grow old with even before one is old. The best is yet to be."

BIOGRAPHICAL/CRITICAL SOURCES:

BOOKS

Contemporary Literary Criticism, Volume 22, Gale, 1980.
Grumbach, Doris, *The Company She Kept,* Coward, 1967.
Grumbach, *Chamber Music,* Dutton, 1979.
Grumbach, *The Missing Person,* Putnam, 1981.
Grumbach, in an interview with Jean W. Ross for *Contemporary Authors,* Volume 9, 1983.

Grumbach, in an essay for *Contemporary Authors Autobiography Series,* Volume 2, Gale, 1985.

PERIODICALS

America, June 2, 1979.
American Spectator, January, 1982.
Atlantic Monthly, March, 1979.
Christian Science Monitor, February 26, 1987, p. 22.
Commonweal, October 6, 1967; June 22, 1979; January 15, 1982.
Library Journal, March 1, 1979.
Listener, August 9, 1979.
Ms., April, 1979.
Nation, March 28, 1981, pp. 375-76.
National Review, June 8, 1979.
New Republic, March 10, 1979.
New Statesman, August 17, 1979; August 28, 1981.
Newsweek, March 19, 1979.
New Yorker, April 23, 1979.
New York Times, March 13, 1979; July 20, 1989.
New York Times Book Review, June 11, 1967; March 25, 1979; March 29, 1981, pp. 14-15; September 30, 1984, p. 12; February 1, 1987, p. 22; September 22, 1991.
Observer, August 12, 1979.
Publishers Weekly, January 15, 1979; Febuary 13, 1981.
Spectator, August 11, 1979.
Time, April 9, 1979.
Times Literary Supplement, December 7, 1967; November 30, 1979; September 11, 1981; July 12, 1985; June 19, 1987, p. 669.
Tribune (Chicago), September 29, 1991.
Washington Post Book World, March 18, 1979; February 10, 1980; April 5, 1981, pp. 9, 13; September 30, 1984, p. 7; January 4, 1987, pp. 3, 13; September 8, 1991.
Yale Review, autumn, 1979.*

* * *

GUEST, Ivor (Forbes) 1920-

PERSONAL: Born April 14, 1920, in Chislehurst, Kent, England; son of Cecil Marmaduke and Christian Forbes (Tweedie) Guest; married Ann Hutchinson, January 20, 1962. *Education:* Trinity College, Cambridge University, M.A., 1941.

ADDRESSES: Home—17 Holland Park, London W. 11, England. *Office*—Tweedie & Prideaux, 5 Lincoln's Inn Fields, London W.C. 2, England.

CAREER: Tweedie & Prideaux (formerly A. F. & R. W. Tweedie; solicitors), London, England, partner, 1951-85. Royal Academy of Dancing, London, chairman of executive committee, 1969-93, vice-president, 1993—; deputy chairman, Theatre Museum Advisory Committee. Organized books on Ballet Exhibition for National Book League, 1956-57; collaborated on Spotlight Exhibition, Victoria & Albert Museum, 1981. *Military service:* British Army, 1940-46.

MEMBER: Society for Theater Research, International Federation for Theatre Research, Societe d'Histoire du Theatre.

AWARDS, HONORS: Queen Elizabeth II Coronation Award, 1992, for services to ballet.

WRITINGS:

Napoleon III in England, B. T. & G. Press, 1952.
The Ballet of the Second Empire, 1858-1870, A. & C. Black, 1953, revised edition, Pitman, 1974.
The Romantic Ballet in England, Phoenix House, 1954, revised edition, Pitman, 1972.
The Ballet of the Second Empire, 1847-1858, A. & C. Black, 1955, revised edition, Pitman, 1974.
Fanny Cerrito, Phoenix House, 1956, revised edition, Dance Books, 1974.
Victorian Ballet Girl, A. & C. Black, 1957, revised edition, Da Capo Press, 1980.
Adeline Genee, A. & C. Black, 1958.
The Alhambra Ballet, Dance Perspectives, 1959.
The Dancer's Heritage, A. &. C. Black, 1960, 6th edition, Dancing Times, 1988.
La Fille mal gardee, Dancing Times, 1960.
The Empire Ballet, Society for Theatre Research, 1962.
A Gallery of Romantic Ballet, Mercury Trust, 1966.
The Romantic Ballet in Paris, Pitman, 1966, revised edition, Dance Books, 1980.
Dandies and Dancers, Dance Perspectives, 1969.
Carlotta Zambelli, Societe d'Histoire du Theatre, 1969.
Two Coppelias, Friends of Covent Garden, 1970.
The Pas de Quatre, London Dance Theatre Trust, 1970.
Fanny Elssler, A. & C. Black, 1970.
Le Ballet de l'Opera de Paris, Opera de Paris, 1976, revised edition, 1993.
The Divine Virginia, Marcel Dekker, 1977.
Lettres d'un maitre de ballet, Societe d'Histoire du Theatre, 1977, Dance Books, 1980.
Adeline Genee: A Pictorial Record, Royal Academy of Dancing, 1978.
(Contributor) *Designing for the Dancer,* Elron Press, 1981.
Adventures of a Ballet Historian, Dance Horizons, 1982.
Jules Perrot, Dance Books, 1985.
Gautier on Dance, Dance Books, 1986.
Dr. John Radcliffe and His Trust, Radcliffe Trust, 1991.
Ballet in Leicester Square, Dance Books, 1992.

Contributor to numerous magazines including, *Ballet, Dance and Dancers, Dancing Times, Opera-Ballet-Music-Hall, Paris-Comoedia, Theatre Research, About the House,* and *Theatre Notebook.* Writer of historical notes for Royal

Ballet programs. Consultant on dance, *Enciclopedia dello Spettacolo.* Associate editor, *Ballet Annual,* 1952-63; editorial adviser, *Dancing Times,* 1962—.

WORK IN PROGRESS: A history of the Paris Opera Ballet, 1770-1820.

SIDELIGHTS: The Royal Ballet made use of Ivor Guest's discovery of the original score of *La Fille mal gardee* in its production of this ballet in 1960; Guest found the original score of 1789 and Herold's score of 1828 while researching for his book, *La Fille mal gardee.*

* * *

GUNSTON, Bill
see GUNSTON, William Tudor

* * *

GUNSTON, William Tudor 1927-
(Bill Gunston)

PERSONAL: Born March 1, 1927, in London, England; son of William John (a professional soldier and linguist) and Stella Hazelwood (maiden name Cooper) Gunston; married Margaret Anne Jollif, October 10, 1964; children: Jeannette Christina, Stephanie Elaine Tracy. *Education:* University of Durham, Inter-B.Sc., 1946; attended Northampton College of Advanced Technology (now City University), London, 1948-51. *Politics:* Conservative. *Religion:* Church of England.

ADDRESSES: Home and office—High Beech, Kingsley Green, near Haslemere, Surrey GU27 3LL, England. *Agent*—Donald Copeman Ltd., Santa Monica, Felsted, Great Dunmow, Essex, England.

CAREER: Iliffe & Sons (publishers), London, England, member of editorial staff of *Flight International,* 1951-1954, technical editor, 1955-64, technology editor of *Science Journal,* 1964-70; freelance writer, 1970—. So Few Ltd., director. Sound and television broadcaster on thirty-two stations worldwide. *Military service:* Royal Air Force, flying instructor, 1945-48.

MEMBER: Association of British Science Writers, Circle of Aviation Writers (chairman, 1956, 1961), Fellow of Royal Aeronautical Society.

WRITINGS:

UNDER NAME BILL GUNSTON

Hydrofoils and Hovercraft, Doubleday, 1968.
Flight Handbook, Iliffe, 1968.
(With John W. R. Taylor, Kenneth Munson, and John W. Wood) *The Lore of Flight,* Time-Life, 1970.
The Jet Age, Arthur Barker, 1972.
Transport Problems and Prospects, Dutton, 1972.
Transport Technology, Crowell-Collier, 1972.
(With Frank Howard) *The Conquest of the Air,* Random House, 1973.
Bombers of the West, Scribner, 1973.
Attack Aircraft of the West, Scribner, 1974.
Philatelist's Companion, David & Charles, 1974.
Our World Encyclopedia, Volumes 6 and 7, Macmillan, 1975.
Transport, Macmillan, 1975.
F-4 Phantom, Scribner, 1975.
Supersonic Fighters of the West, Scribner, 1975.
Fighters 1914-1915, Hamlyn Publishing, 1975.
Aircraft, MacDonald & Co., 1975, revised edition, Macmillan, 1981.
Fabulous Facts in Transport, Theorem, 1975.
Submarines, Arcos, 1975.
Encyclopedia of Combat Aircraft, Salamander, 1975.
Fighters since 1945, Hamlyn Publishing, 1975.
Night Fighters, Patrick Stephens, 1976.
Helicopters 1900-1960, Hamlyn Publishing, 1976.
Helicopters since 1960, Hamlyn Publishing, 1976.
World Land Speed Record, Hamish Hamilton, 1976.
World Air Speed Record, Hamish Hamilton, 1976.
Finding out about Railways, Purnell, 1976.
(Co-author) *The Soviet War Machine,* Salamander, 1976.
Modern Military Aircraft, Salamander, 1976, Octopus Books, 1983.
(Co-author) *Coal: Technology for Britain's Future,* Macmillan, 1976.
The F-111, Ian Allan, 1977.
Combat Aircraft of World War II, Salamander, 1977.
(Co-author) *Hitler's Luftwaffe,* Salamander, 1977.
(Co-author) *Soviet Airpower,* Salamander, 1977.
Finding out about Aircraft, Purnell, 1978.
Bombers, Hamlyn Publishing, 1978.
Fighters, Hamlyn Publishing, 1978, Octopus Books, 1981.
By Jupiter (biography of Sir Roy Fedden), Royal Aeronautical Society, 1978.
Encyclopedia of Missiles and Rockets, Salamander, 1979.
Tornado, Ian Allan, 1980.
Aircraft of World War II, Octopus Books, 1980.
The Planemakers, New English Library, 1980.
Water, MacDonald Educational, 1980.
Jane's Aerospace Dictionary, Jane's Publishing Co., 1980.
Fighters of the 1950's, Patrick Stephens, 1980.
(Consulting editor) *The Colour Encyclopedia of Aviation,* Octopus Books, 1980.
Coal, F. Watts, 1981.
Airliners, Sundial Press, 1981.
Missiles, Granada Books, 1981.
Axis Fighters of World War II, Salamander, 1981.
Bombers of World War II, Salamander, 1981.

Ships and Boats, Macmillan, 1981.
Combat Aircraft of the African Nations, Defence Attache, 1981.
Modern Fighter and Attack Aircraft, Salamander, 1981.
Encyclopedia of American Aircraft, Orbis Books, 1982.
Military Helicopters, Salamander, 1982.
Guide to the U.S. Air Force, Salamander, 1982.
Encyclopedia of Aircraft and Missiles, Nomad Publishers, 1982.
British Fighters of World War II, Salamander, 1982.
(Consulting editor) *Aeroplanes, Rockets and Balloons,* Usborne West, 1982.
Modern Airliners, F. Watts, 1982.
Family Library of Aircraft, Octopus Books, 1982.
Aircraft of the Soviet Union, Osprey Books, 1983.
International Encyclopedia of Aviation, Octopus Books, 1983.
Soviet Air Forces, Salamander, 1983.
The Israeli Air Force, Salamander, 1983.
F-16 Fighting Falcon, Ian Allan, 1983.
Encyclopedia of Modern Warplanes, Salamander, 1983.
NATO Fighter and Attack Aircraft, Salamander, 1983.
(Co-author) *Rockets and Missiles of World War III,* Bison Books, 1983.
Motorcycles, Granada Books, 1984.
General Dynamics F-111, Salamander, 1984.
First Questions: Transport, Hodder & Stoughton, 1984.
(Co-author) *Encyclopedia of Modern Air Combat,* Salamander, 1984.
Big Book of Fighter Planes, Purnell, 1984.
Air-Launched Missiles, Salamander, 1984.
Not Much of an Engineer (autobiography of Sir Stanley Hooker), Airlife, 1984.
Modern Military Aircraft, St. Michael, 1984.
British Aerospace Carrier, Salamander, 1984.
R.A.F. Aircraft Today: No. 1, Phantom, Ian Allan, 1984.
Modern Civil Aircraft, Octopus Books, 1984.
Guide to Future Fighters and Attack Aircraft, Salamander, 1984.
Modern Fighting Aircraft, Salamander, 1985.
McDonnell Douglas F/A-18 Hornet, Ian Allan, 1985.
(Co-author) *Encyclopedia of Modern Weapons,* Salamander, 1985.
Combat Aircraft, Domino Books, 1985.
Commercial Aircraft, Domino Books, 1985.
Anatomy of Aircraft, Winchmore, 1985.
Combat Roles: Air Superiority, Ian Allan, 1985.
(Co-author) *Encyclopedia of Advanced Technology Warfare,* Salamander, 1985.
Warplanes of the Future, Salamander, 1985.
Grumman X-29, Linewrights, 1985.
World Encyclopedia of Aero Engines, Patrick Stephens, 1986.
Water Travel, MacDonald & Co., 1986.
Encyclopedia of Modern Fighting Helicopters, Salamander, 1986.
MiG-21, Osprey Books, 1986.
How It Works: Airbus, Grafton Books, 1986.
(Co-author) *Fighters and Bombers AS2000,* Bison, 1986.
Encyclopedia of American Military Aircraft, 1910-1990, Salamander, 1986.
MiG-23 Flogger, Bedford Editions, 1987.
AH-64 Apache, Bedford Editions, 1987.
EAP, Linewrights, 1987.
Harrier, Ian Allen, 1987.
Fighters, Yorkshire Post, 1987.
Guide to Modern Fighters, Salamander, 1987.
Encyclopedia of Aircraft Armament, Salamander, 1987.
Grumman: One of a Kind, TRH (London), 1987.
Grumman: 60 Years of Excellence, Orion (New York), 1987.
Firebombers, Osprey, 1987.
Farnborough International (programme), Pilot Press, 1988.
Guide to Modern Attack Aircraft, Salamander, 1988.
Railways, Wayland, 1988.
Jane's Aerospace Dictionary, Jane's Information Group, 1988.
Stealth Aircraft, Bedford Editions, 1988.
Bomber, Sigma Press, 1988.
American Military Aircraft, Image Bank/Gallery Books, 1988.
The Flier's Handbook, Marshall Editions, 1988.
International Encyclopedia of Aviation, Octopus Books, 1988.
(Co-author) *Encyclopedia of Fighter Missions,* Salamander, 1988.
Diamond Flight, Henry Melland, 1988.
Combat Arms: Fighters, Salamander, 1988.
Combat Arms: Modern Carriers, Salamander, 1988.
(Co-author) *Forces 89,* Marshall Cavendish, 1989.
Flight Filofax, Handmade Guides, 1989.
A Century of Flight, Brian Trodd, 1989.
Combat Arms: Attack Aircraft, Salamander, 1989.
Aerial Reconnaissance, Marshall Cavendish, 1990.
(Co-author) *. . . so few,* RAF Benevolent Fund, 1990.
Stingers: F/A-18, Octopus Books, 1990.
(Co-author) *Battle of Britain,* Salamander, 1990.
Aircraft Avionics, PSL, 1990.
P-51 Mustang, Salamander, 1990.
Combat Arms: Helicopters, Salamander, 1990.
Flights of Fantasy, Hamlyn/Octopus, 1990.
Rolls-Royce Aero Engines, PSL, 1990.
World Encyclopedia of Aero Engines, PSL, 1990.
Passenger Airliners, Bedford Editions, 1990.
Plane Speaking, PSL, 1991.
(Co-author) *Forces 91,* Pemberton Press, 1991.
Flight Without Formulae, Longman, 1991.

(Co-author) *Gulf Air War,* Salamander, 1991.
USAF Strike Aircraft, Osprey, 1991.
Giants of the Sky, PSL, 1992.
(Editor) *Chronicle of Aviation,* Chronicle, 1992.
Faster than Sound, PSL, 1992.
Visual Dictionary of Flight, Dorling-Kindersley, 1992.
Thrust for Flight, Longman, 1992.
How It Works: Flight, Hex, 1993.
Encyclopedia of Piston Aero Engines, PSL, 1993.
World Encyclopedia of Aircraft Manufacturers, PSL, 1993.
(Co-author) *Spirit in the Sky: F-4 Phantom,* Aerospace, 1993.

JUVENILE; UNDER NAME BILL GUNSTON

Your Book of Light, Faber, 1968.
Shaping Metals, MacDonald & Co., 1974.
Man and Materials, six volumes, Macmillan, 1975-76.
Minimacs, six volumes, Macmillan, 1976.
Aircraft, Usborne West, 1980.

OTHER

Also author of *Technology at Work,* Doubleday; consultant and contributor to *The Joy of Knowledge Encyclopedia.* Contributor to encyclopedias and other books, including *Aircraft versus Aircraft,* Macmillan, 1985; and *Basic Geography,* MacDonald & Co., 1985. Also contributor to magazines, juvenile periodicals, and newspapers all over the world, including *New Scientist, Aircraft* (Australia), *Speed and Power, Battle, Aeroplane Monthly, International Defence Review, Interavia, Melbourne Times-Herald, Herald Tribune,* and *Propliner.* Aviation editor, *Weapons and Warfare;* consulting editor, *The Illustrated International Encyclopedia of Aviation.* Member of the team which produces *Daily News* at each Paris and Farnborough airshow.

SIDELIGHTS: William Tudor Gunston, better known to his readers as Bill Gunston, once told *CA:* "I left my old firm in 1970 and cast around looking for a job (and the best offers were all outside the United Kingdom), but first I had to clear a vast backlog of free-lance work. I am still trying to clear it, but the pile is now twice as large. I have a golden rule for authors: if you are daunted at the size of the task, or the amount of research needed, just sit down and write the book. When it is finished you will wonder why you were worried.

"I am proud to have been one of the team of four who in 1990 created a beautiful book entitled . . . *so few.* Number one was given to Her Majesty the Queen (we went to Buckingham Palace) and the other 400 raised more money for the RAF Benevolent Fund than anything else ever! We now have a company, So Few Ltd., and are working on several companion volumes. The second will be about Bomber Command and will be entitled . . . *so many.*"

H

HALL, James Andrew 1935-

PERSONAL: Born September 15, 1935, in London, England; son of James Henry (a physician) and Monica (an actress; maiden name, MacDonald) Hall. *Education:* Attended private boys' secondary school in Rutland, England. *Religion:* Church of England.

ADDRESSES: Home—49 Richmond Park Ave., Bournemouth, Dorset, England. *Agent*—Cecily Ware, 19c John Spencer Sq., Canonbury, London N.1, England.

CAREER: Tatler, London, England, photographic editor, 1958-60; worked in Films Division of British Central Office of Information, London, England, 1963-65. *Military service:* British Army, 1956-58; became lieutenant.

MEMBER: Writers Guild of Great Britain, British Academy of Film and Television Arts.

WRITINGS:

Man in Aspic, Cassell, 1965.
Frost, Putnam, 1967.
Safe Behind Bars, Cassell, 1968.
Enemy at the Door, Weidenfeld & Nicolson, 1979.
Reasons to be Cheerful (play), Methuen, 1981.
Fowl Pest (children's novel), Bodley Head, 1994.

TELEVISION SCRIPTS; PRODUCED BY BBC-TV, EXCEPT AS NOTED

Kilvert's Diary, 1977.
The Mill on the Floss, 1978.
History of Mr. Polly, 1979.
Coming Out, 1979.
Great Expectations, 1981.
The Coral Island, produced by Thames Television, 1981.
Tales of the Unexpected, produced by Anglia Television, 1982.
Dombey and Son, 1982.
The Invisible Man, 1983.
Prisoner of Zenda, 1984.
My Brother Jonathan, 1984.
Brat Farrar, 1985.
David Copperfield, 1985.
Exploits at West Poley, produced by Children's Film Foundation, 1986.
The Franchise Affair, 1987.
Village by the Sea, 1992.

WORK IN PROGRESS: Good King Wenceslas, a two-hour original screenplay for the Family Channel, USA; *The Place of Lions,* an adaptation for Scottish TV; *Smokescreen,* a TV adaptation for Red Rooster Films, UK; *Goodbye Mr. Dickens,* an original play for BBC.

* * *

HALL, James B(yron) 1918-

PERSONAL: Born July 21, 1918, in Midland, OH; son of Harry and Florence (Moon) Hall; married Elizabeth Cushman, February 14, 1946; children: Elinor, Prudence, Kathryn, Millicent, James M. *Education:* Attended Miami University, Oxford, OH, 1938-39, and University of Hawaii, 1938-40; University of Iowa, B.A., 1947, M.A., 1948, Ph.D., 1953; graduate study, Kenyon College, summers, 1948-49. *Politics:* Democrat.

Avocational Interests: Computer applications.

ADDRESSES: Home—1670 East 27th Ave., Eugene, OR 97403. *Agent*—Gerard McCauley Agency, Inc., P.O. Box AE, Katona, NY 10536.

CAREER: Worked as a farm worker, merchant seaman, and soldier, 1936-45; Cornell University, Ithaca, NY, instructor, 1951-53; University of Oregon, Eugene, associate professor, 1953-60, professor of English, 1960-65; University of California, Irvine, professor of English, director of creative writing section, and chairman of creative writing committee, 1965-69; University of California, Santa Cruz, founding provost of College IV (arts college; now Porter College), 1969-77, professor of literature and writer-in-residence, 1978-84. Visiting writer-in-residence, Miami University, 1948-49, Women's College of the University of North Carolina (now University of North Carolina at Greensboro), 1954, University of British Columbia, 1955, University of Colorado, 1963, Kansas State University, 1978, and University of Missouri, 1981. University of Oregon Summer Academy of Contemporary Arts, founder, 1959, director, 1959-64, currently consultant; founding president, National Writers Union, 1981, West Coast grievance officer, 1986-87. Editorial consultant, Doubleday & Co., Inc., 1962-65; cultural specialist, U.S. Department of State, 1964. *Military service:* U.S. Army, Parachute Infantry, Anti-Aircraft, and military government in Germany, 1941-46; became chief warrant officer.

MEMBER: American Association of University Professors, Associated Writing Programs (president, 1975-76).

AWARDS, HONORS: Octave Thanet Prize, 1950; writer-in-residence, Yaddo, 1952; Rockefeller grant, 1955; Oregon State Poetry Prize, 1957, for *The Tortoise;* Emily Clark Balch Fiction Prize, 1967; Chapelbrook Award, 1967; the University of California dedicated the James B. Hall Gallery, 1984; finalist, Drue Heinze Prize, 1985; finalist, Oregon Institute of Literary Arts poetry award, 1992.

WRITINGS:

Not by the Door (novel), Random House, 1954.

TNT for Two (novel), Ace, 1956.

Racers to the Sun (novel), Obolensky, 1960.

Mayo Sergeant (novel), New American Library, 1967.

The Hunt Within (poems), Louisiana State University Press, 1973.

Bereavements (poems), Story Line Press, 1991.

Foxhandler (novel), in press.

SHORT STORIES

(With R. V. Cassill and Herbert Gold) *Fifteen by Three,* New Directions, 1957.

Us He Devours, New Directions, 1964.

The Short Hall: New and Selected Stories, Stonehenge Press, Castle Peak Editions, 1980.

I Like It Better Now, University of Arkansas Press, 1992.

EDITOR

(With Joseph Langland) *The Short Story,* Macmillan, 1956.

The Realm of Fiction: Sixty-One Short Stories, with instructor's manual, McGraw, 1965, 2nd edition published as *Realm of Fiction: Sixty-Five Short Stories,* 1970, 3rd edition (with wife, Elizabeth C. Hall) published as *The Realm of Fiction: Seventy-Four Short Stories,* 1977.

(With Barry Ulanov) *Modern Culture and the Arts,* with instructor's manual, McGraw, 1967, 2nd edition, 1972.

Jack London, *John Barleycorn: Alcoholic Memoirs,* Western Tanager Press, 1981.

(With Hotchkiss and Shears) *Perspectives on William Everson,* Castle Peak Editions, 1992.

OTHER

(Author of introduction) Alex Blackburn, editor, *Writers Forum,* Writers Forum, 1981.

(Author of introduction) Ellyn Bache, *The Value of Kindness: Stories,* Helicon Nine, 1993.

Also author of *Art and Craft of the Short Story,* 1993.

Work represented in anthologies, including *Best American Short Stories,* edited by Martha Foley, Houghton, 1949, 1952, 1953, and 1954; *Poems from the Iowa Poetry Workshop,* Prairie Press, 1951; *Prize Stories: The O. Henry Awards,* Doubleday, 1951 and 1954; *Oregon Signatures,* edited by R. D. Brown, Binfords, 1959; *Midland Anthology,* edited by Paul Engle, Random House, 1961; *A Country of the Mind,* edited by Ray B. West, Jr., Angel Island Publications, 1962; *Kenyon Review,* edited by Robie Macauley, Salem Press, 1966; *Pushcart Prose IV,* Pushcart, 1980; *Best of Omni Magazine,* Omni Publications, 1982; *Norton Anthology of Fiction,* and *New Directions Anthology.*

Contributor to *Collier's Encyclopedia.* Contributor of poems to journals, including *Sewanee Review, Poetry, Kayak,* and *New Letters;* also contributor of short stories and articles to *Esquire, Harper's Bazaar, Atlantic, Epoch, San Francisco Review, Los Angeles Times, Sewanee Review, Virginia Quarterly, Georgia Review,* and other magazines, newspapers, and literary reviews. *Northwest Review,* co-founder, faculty advisor, 1957-60, advisory editor, 1965-69. *Interim,* editorial advisory board, 1986—.

WORK IN PROGRESS: A fifth collection of short stories.

SIDELIGHTS: James B. Hall has built a reputation as a skillful writer of poetry, prose, and short fiction. His most popular novel to date, *Mayo Sergeant,* is set in a wealthy yachting community in Southern California. The narrator, Robert Glouster, tells of the arrival of Mayo Sergeant, described by Martin Levin in the *New York Times Book Review* as "a flint-hearted opportunist with a protean talent for reflecting his immediate habitat." Sergeant first marries his way into the community, then, following his wife's death, becomes a wealthy entrepreneur. All the while, the residents (including Glouster) stand idly by, unwilling to prevent the exploitation of their quiet little bay.

Though the conniving Sergeant exploits both Cutlass Bay and its natives, Levin claims that "this is less of a tragedy than the author means it to be. . . . Glouster is so much of an elegiac observer that there is little drama in his account of how Sergeant appropriates and corrupts the things the narrator holds dear." While a reviewer for *Best Sellers* also recognizes the novel's flaws, he proclaims *Mayo Sergeant* "a novel competently plotted and written that offers some interestingly ironic commentaries upon America past and present."

James B. Hall told *CA:* "I continue to write and to publish short fiction, poems, novels, and the odd review. In a literature's commercial age, the journeyman and literary artist alike too often are judged by profit, or the promise thereof. Being of and within this dispensation may make for conformist art, but such is my challenge: to be of, and yet 'above,' the (so-called) system."

BIOGRAPHICAL/CRITICAL SOURCES:

BOOKS

Contemporary Authors Autobiography Series, Volume 12, Gale, 1990.

PERIODICALS

Best Sellers, November 11, 1967.
Kenyon Review, June 1, 1968.
New York Times Book Review, October 15, 1967.
Virginia Quarterly Review, winter, 1968; summer, 1974, p. R84.

* * *

HALL, Richard
See BICKERS, Richard (Leslie) Townshend

* * *

HAMILTON, Charles V(ernon) 1929-

PERSONAL: Born October 19, 1929, in Muskogee, OK; son of Owen and Viola (Haynes) Hamilton; married Dona Louise Cooper, October 5, 1956; children: Carol, Valli. *Education:* Roosevelt University, B.A., 1951; Loyola University, Chicago, IL, J.D., 1954; University of Chicago, M.A., 1957, Ph.D., 1963.

ADDRESSES: *Office*—Department of Political Science, Columbia University, New York, NY 10027.

CAREER: Albany State College, Albany, GA, instructor in political science, 1957-58; Tuskegee Institute, Tuskegee, AL, assistant professor of political science, 1958-60; Rutgers University, New Brunswick, NJ, instructor in political science, 1963-64; Lincoln University, Lincoln University, PA, instructor in political science, 1964-67; Roosevelt University, Chicago, IL, professor of political science 1967-69; Columbia University, New York City, professor of political science, 1969—; Metropolitan Applied Research Center (MARC), New York City, head of organization, 1989—. *Military service:* U.S. Army, 1948-49.

MEMBER: National Association for the Advancement of Colored People (NAACP), American Political Science Association (vice-president, 1972-73 and 1989—), Twentieth Century Foundation (board of trustees, 1973—).

AWARDS, HONORS: John Hay Whitney fellowship, 1962; Lindback Distinguished Teaching award, Lincoln University, 1965; University of Chicago Alumni award and Roosevelt University Alumni award, both 1970; Phi Beta Kappa Visiting Lecturer scholar, 1972-73.

WRITINGS:

Minority Politics in Black Belt Alabama, McGraw, 1962.
(With Stokely Carmichael) *Black Power: The Politics of Liberation in America,* Vintage, 1967.
(With others) *Dialogue on Violence* (edited by George Vickers, from "The Dialogue" series), Bobbs-Merrill Co., 1968.
The Black Preacher In America, Morrow, 1972.
(Co-author) *The Social Scene,* Winthrop, 1972.
The Black Experience in American Politics, Putnam, 1973.
The Bench and the Ballot: Southern Federal Judges and Black Voters, Oxford University Press, 1973.
The Struggle for Political Equality (from "Black perspectives on the Bicentennial" series), National Urban League, 1976.
American Government, Scott, Foresman, 1982.
Adam Clayton Powell, Jr.: The Political Biography of an American Dilemma, Anteneum, 1991.

Also author of *The Fight for Racial Justice,* a public affairs pamphlet, 1974. Contributor to scholarly journals, including *Harvard Educational Review, Black Scholar, Wisconsin Law Review,* and *Urban Violence. Political Science Quarterly* (board of editors, 1975—).

SIDELIGHTS: As head of New York's Metropolitan Applied Research Center (MARC), Charles V. Hamilton is concerned with social problems related to community development. His writings focus on the social and political dilemmas faced by African Americans.

The Bench and the Ballot chronicles one aspect of the struggle for civil rights. A reviewer in *Choice* wrote that Hamilton "has done us a service with his detailed treatment of the handling of a sampling of voting rights cases by U.S. district judges in the South." In his book, Hamilton analyzes three judicial types: the justice-seeking judge who enforces the law; the racist judge who obstructs justice outright; and the racist judge who appears willing to be educated in order that justice might be dispensed. The reviewer goes on to call *The Bench and the Ballot* "a very readable lesson on the effectiveness of using the courts to administer the law."

A writer for *Saturday Review* reports that in *Black Power: The Politics of Liberation in America,* the authors "have set down the philosophy and concept of Black Power as it has painfully emerged out of the urban and rural black ghettos these last thirteen years." The reviewer contends that the book is an important document to have come forth from the whole black-white arena of public affairs and goes on to say that the work is "perhaps the most significant single piece of writing in this area since the 1954 Supreme Court decision declaring public school segregation unconstitutional. . . ."

Adam Clayton Powell, Jr.: The Political Biography of an American Dilemma examines the life of what *Nation* reviewer Peter Dailey described as "the flamboyant Congressman whose historic achievements were largely overshadowed by his controversial downfall." Hamilton's book explores the successes and foibles of Powell, from his early years as pastor of Abyssinian Baptist Church to his expulsion from the U.S. House of Representatives. The author also delves into a crucial, yet little covered period in civil rights history. According to Taylor Branch in the *New York Times Book Review* Hamilton "occasionally lapses into summary cliches, but his diligent scholarship has uncovered more than a good book's worth of Powell material."

BIOGRAPHICAL/CRITICAL SOURCES:

PERIODICALS

American Spectator, April, 1992, pp. 74-76.
Christian Science Monitor, November 18, 1967.
Choice, March, 1974.
Commonweal, April 26, 1974.
Nation, January 6, 1992, p. 24.
New York Times Book Review, October 20, 1991, p. 7.
Political Science Quarterly, March, 1974.
Saturday Review, November 11, 1967.*

* * *

HAMMETT, (Samuel) Dashiell 1894-1961

PERSONAL: Born May 27, 1894, in St. Mary's County, MD; died of lung cancer January 10, 1961; son of Richard Thomas (a farmer and politician) and Annie (Bond) Hammett; married Josephine Dolan, July 6, 1921 (separated, 1927; divorced, 1937); children: Mary Jane, Josephine. *Education:* Attended Baltimore Polytechnic Institute. *Politics:* Marxist.

ADDRESSES: Home—Katonah, NY; and New York, NY.

CAREER: Writer. Worked as freight clerk, stevedore, timekeeper, yardman, and railroad worker; private detective with Pinkerton National Detective Agency, c. 1914-18 and 1919-21; Albert S. Samuels Jewelers, San Francisco, CA, advertising copywriter, 1922-27; worked sporadically as screenwriter for various motion picture studios from 1930 until after World War II. Active in various left-wing organizations, beginning 1937; member of Civil Rights Congress, New York state president, 1946, national vice-chairman, 1948, New York state chairman, 1951; convicted and imprisoned for contempt of Congress, 1951. Jefferson School of Social Sciences, faculty member, 1946-47 and 1949-56, member of board of trustees, 1948. *Military service:* U.S. Army Ambulance Corps, 1918-19, became sergeant; U.S. Army Signal Corps, 1942-45, became sergeant.

WRITINGS:

NOVELS

Red Harvest (serialized in *Black Mask,* 1927), Knopf, 1929, J. Curley, 1983.
The Dain Curse (based on Hammett's short story "The Scorched Face"), Knopf, 1929, J. Curley, 1983.
The Maltese Falcon, Knopf, 1930, North Point Press, 1984.
The Glass Key, Knopf, 1931, Vintage Books, 1972.
The Thin Man, Knopf, 1934, Vintage Books, 1972.
Dashiell Hammett Omnibus: "Red Harvest," "The Dain Curse," "The Maltese Falcon," Knopf, 1935.
The Complete Dashiell Hammett (contains *The Thin Man, The Glass Key, The Maltese Falcon,* and *Red Harvest*), Knopf, 1942.
Novels (contains *Red Harvest, The Dain Curse, The Maltese Falcon, The Glass Key,* and *The Thin Man*), Knopf, 1965, published as *Dashiell Hammett: Five Complete Novels,* Outlet Book Co., 1991.

SHORT STORY COLLECTIONS

$106,000 Blood Money, Spivak, 1943, published as *Blood Money,* Dell, 1944, and as *The Big Knockover,* Jonathan Press, 1948.
The Adventures of Sam Spade, Spivak, 1944, published as *They Can Only Hang You Once,* Spivak, 1949.
The Continental Op, Spivak, 1945, Franklin Library, 1984.
A Man Called Spade, Dell, 1945.
The Return of the Continental Op, Spivak, 1945.

Hammett Homicides, Spivak, 1946.
Dead Yellow Women, Spivak, 1947.
Nightmare Town, Spivak, 1948.
Creeping Siamese, Spivak, 1950.
Woman in the Dark, Spivak, 1951, Random House, 1989.
A Man Named Thin, Ferman, 1962.
The Big Knockover, edited by Lillian Hellman, Random House, 1966 (published in England as *The Dashiell Hammett Story Omnibus,* Cassell, 1966).
The Continental Op: More Stories From "The Big Knockover," Dell, 1967.
The Continental Op (different from two collections above with same title), edited by Steven Marcus, Random House, 1974.
Dashiell Hammett's Secret Agent, Movie Publisher Services, 1990.

Works represented in numerous anthologies of detective fiction.

Contributor of stories and articles to more than thirty magazines, including *Black Mask, Smart Set, Brief Stories, True Detective Stories, Argosy All-Story Monthly, Saturday Review of Literature, Bookman, American Magazine, Collier's, Liberty, Redbook,* and *Ellery Queen's Mystery Magazine.*

OTHER

(Editor) *Creeps by Night* (short stories), John Day, 1931 (published in England as *Modern Tales of Horror,* Gollancz, 1932; selections published in England as *The Red Brain and Other Thrillers,* Belmont, 1961, and as *Breakdown and Other Thrillers,* New English Library, 1968).
Secret Agent X-9 (comic strip), McKay, 1934, International Polygonics, 1983.
Watch on the Rhine (screenplay; adapted from the play by Lillian Hellman), Warner Bros., 1943.
The Battle of the Aleutians (history), U.S. Army, 1944.

ADAPTATIONS: The Maltese Falcon, The Thin Man, Woman in the Dark, and *The Glass Key* were adapted for films in the 1930s and 1940s.

SIDELIGHTS: Dashiell Hammett is widely considered the father of hard-boiled detective fiction. Along with those of Caroll John Daley, Hammett's stories in *Black Mask* magazine helped to bring about a major movement in detective fiction away from the genteel detectives solving crimes perpetrated by masterminds, to rough, believable private eyes dealing with common crooks. In the words of Raymond Chandler, "Hammett took murder out of the Venetian vase and dropped it into the alley. . . . [He] gave murder back to the kind of people that commit it for reasons, not just to provide a corpse; and with the means at hand, not with hand-wrought duelling pistols, curare, and tropical fish."

Hammett's importance as a writer lies in his influence as an innovator, his impact as a stylist, and his skill in characterization. In 1948, Raymond Chandler wrote in a letter to fellow crime fiction writer Cleve F. Adams: "I did not invent the hard boiled murder story and I have never made any secret of my opinion that Hammett deserves most or all of the credit." Along with Chandler, Hammett is the most imitated writer of the genre. Erle Stanley Gardner declared: "I think of all the early pulp writers who contributed to the new format of the detective story, the word 'genius' was more nearly applicable to Hammett than to any of the rest. Unfortunately however, because Hammett's manner was so widely imitated it became the habit for the reviewers to refer to 'the Hammett School' as embracing the *type* of story as well as the *style.*"

Hammett was important as more than simply a genre writer. As Howard Haycraft observed, Hammett's novels "are also character studies of close to top rank in their own right, and are penetrating if often shocking as novels of manners as well. They established new standards for realism in the genre. Yet they are as sharply stylized and deliberately artificial as Restoration Comedy, and have been called an inverted form of romanticism."

In one sense Hammett's detectives are romantics. They dare to believe in and hold firmly to a strict code of behavior which is in opposition to that of the world in which they move. Realistic and resourceful enough to be able to operate effectively among thieves, murderers, kidnappers, and blackmailers, Hammett's Continental Op, Sam Spade, Ned Beaumont, and Nick Charles are incorruptible in their belief that criminals ought to pay for their acts. When the unnamed Continental Op is tempted with money and sex to let a Russian princess guilty of murder and theft go free, he explains: "You think I'm a man and you're a woman. That's wrong. I'm a manhunter and you're something that's been running in front of me. There's nothing human about it. You might just as well expect a hound to play tiddly-winks with the fox he's caught." That sentiment presages the famous farewell of Sam Spade to Brigid O'Shaughnessy, the murderess he loves but turns over to the police: "I'm going to send you over. The chances are you'll get off with life. That means you'll be out again in twenty years. You're an angel. I'll wait for you. . . . If they hang you I'll always remember you." Ellery Queen noticed the seeming paradox of Hammett's romanticism early on: "The skin of realism hides the inner body of romance. All you see at first glance is that tough outer skin. But inside—deep in the core of his plots and counterplots—Hammett is one of the purest and most uninhibited romantics of all."

But Hammett was most of all a realist, and he was successful because, unlike his predecessors, he knew the world about which he wrote. When he was an operative for the Pinkerton National Detective Agency, Hammett "rated at the very top." As a detective, Hammett searched for accused securities thief Nick Arnstein; he worked for the defense during Fatty Arbuckle's celebrated trial for rape and murder; and he once found $125,000 in stolen gold stuffed down the smoke stack of a ship about to embark for Australia. In 1921, tuberculosis contracted during World War I forced Hammett to give up detective work for a more sedate occupation. He apparently was determined to be a poet and sought to support himself by writing detective stories. In 1922, he began writing about the characters and the life he had been forced to abandon. Hammett remarked in 1929: "The 'op' I use . . . is the typical sort of private detective that exists in our country today. I've worked with half a dozen men who might be he with a few changes."

Black Mask magazine, begun by H. L. Mencken and George Jean Nathan, was the most important forum for writers of the hard-boiled school, and Hammett quickly became the most popular of the *Black Mask* writers with the magazine's readership. Between 1923 and 1927, thirty-two of his stories were published there. *Black Mask* editors took their work and their writers seriously; they demanded quality material and freely suggested new avenues for their writers' work. In 1926, Captain Joseph T. Shaw became editor of *Black Mask* and encouraged Hammett to write longer fiction. As a result, in November, 1927, the first installment of the four-part *Red Harvest,* Hammett's first novel, was published in *Black Mask.*

The opening lines of *Red Harvest* illustrate well the major elements of Hammett's style: "I first heard Personville called Poisonville by a red-haired mucker named Hickey Dewey in the Big Ship in Butte. He also called a shirt a shoit. I didn't think anything of what he had done to the city's name. Later I heard men who could manage their r's to give it the same pronunciation." Careful attention to vernacular speech, use of criminal argot, and a knowledgeable, objective point of view characterize Hammett's fiction.

In *Red Harvest* the unnamed Continental Op tells the story of one of his cases. Typically, he goes into Personville, a totally lawless community, and by manipulating one group of criminals against another causes them to kill each other off. William F. Nolan pointed out that by the end of the novel "more than thirty deaths are toted up, a total which includes twelve of the nineteen main characters." During the course of the novel, the op breaks some laws, tells some lies, betrays some confidences, but he does so in a criminal environment where, he is realist enough to know, an honest man wouldn't stand a chance.

Red Harvest was a critical success. Herbert Asbury in *Bookman* declared: "It is doubtful if even Ernest Hemingway has ever written more effective dialogue than may be found within the pages of this extraordinary tale of gunmen, gin and gangsters. The author displays a style of amazing clarity and compactness, devoid of literary frills and furbelows, and his characters, who race through the story with the rapidity and destructiveness of machine guns, speak the crisp hard-boiled language of the underworld." W. R. Brooks in *Outlook* echoed those remarks: "It is written by a man who plainly knows his underworld and can make it come alive for his readers."

Those comments are typical, and they forecast the success Hammett would achieve upon the publication in 1930 of his third novel, *The Maltese Falcon. The Dain Curse,* published in 1929, was not up to Hammett's standards. Though it received a share of reviewers' compliments, most contemporary readers might agree with William Nolan's description: "Lacking the cohesive element of a single locale, this story jumps from seacoast to city to country, while the reader is forced to cope with over thirty characters." Based on Hammett's short story "The Scorched Face," *The Dain Curse* is the story of a family curse caused by incest which links the op's client's daughter with her blackly religious captor. The story is of drugs and, most of all, murder in a gothic setting. Elizabeth Sanderson reported that Hammett himself considered *The Dain Curse* "a silly story."

If *The Dain Curse* was Hammett's least successful novel, *The Maltese Falcon* ranked with his very best. The novel brought Hammett instant fame and prosperity. Sam Spade, the novel's protagonist, has served as a standard of hard-boiled characterization. Tough, calloused, competent, and operating according to his own code of justice, Sam Spade is the epitome of the lone detective working without reward to make things right. When Spade was accused of murder by an incompetent district attorney, the private eye explained his position: "As far as I can see my best chance of clearing myself of the trouble you're trying to make for me is by bringing in the murderers—all tied up. And my only chance of ever catching them is by keeping away from you and the police, because neither of you show any signs of knowing what in hell it's all about." Spade perhaps best illustrates the emotional callousness characteristic of Hammett's detectives. Somerset Maugham complained that Spade was hardly distinguishable from the crooks he chased. That observation is critical to an understanding of Spade and his work. As Spade tells Brigid O'Shaughnessy: "Don't be too sure I'm as crooked as I'm supposed to be. That kind of reputation might be good business . . . making it easier to deal with the enemy." Good men can't deal with bad ones because being good, they obey a different set of rules. Spade deals with the enemy on his own terms.

In 1930, W. R. Brooks wrote in *Outlook* that *The Maltese Falcon* "is not only probably the best detective story we have ever read, it is an exceedingly well written novel." That opinion has worn well for more than half a century. *The Maltese Falcon* is widely considered a standard by which American mysteries are judged.

Hammett is said to have liked *The Glass Key* best among his novels. As Oliver Pilat has suggested, Ned Beaumont, the protagonist of *The Glass Key,* is "closer to the character of the author than some of Hammett's brassier detectives." Beaumont is tubercular, a gambler, a man with an intense sense of loyalty to his friend, yet a man who lives by a private code. Like Sam Spade, he is not impervious to human relationships, but he will not allow his personal feelings to blind him to the truth. When a U.S. senator, father of the woman Beaumont respects, if not loves, is proven to have murdered his son, he asks Beaumont for "the return of my revolver and five minutes—a minute—alone in this room" so that he may take the honorable way out. Beaumont's reply has the force of unrefined justice about it: "You'll take what's coming to you."

As Hammett's plots became less complex, his characters more realistic, his writing more mature, the heroes of his fiction continued to see that people got what they deserved. *The Glass Key* is a novel about justice, friendship, and priorities. Ned Beaumont's friend, Paul Madvig, is a political boss who very nearly lets his attraction to Senator Ralph B. Henry's daughter, Janet, ruin him. Beaumont serves his friend well by saving him, against Madvig's will, from a murder charge by exposing Senator Henry as his son's murderer and by saving Madvig from Janet Henry, who "hates him like poison." Madvig is unwilling to face the truth and Beaumont is too good a friend to allow him not to. Beaumont serves to make people accept reality—whether it be to take what's coming to them or to give up what they have no claim to having.

M. I. Cole, writing in *Spectator,* called *The Glass Key* "the work of a man who knows exactly what he means to do, and who knows, also, why the current tradition of English detective fiction cannot be translated into American. . . . His people are violent, grafty, and full of sex appeal and responsiveness thereto: he is a clever writer."

After *The Glass Key,* it was three years before Hammett's next and last novel, *The Thin Man,* was written. Five years earlier he had literally been a starving writer. In 1931, his income was estimated at over $50,000; it would soon double. He rode in a chauffeur-driven Rolls Royce (he was said to have refused to drive after he dumped an ambulance load of wounded soldiers during World War I) and tipped his barber with twenty-dollar bills. He had become a celebrity—and he had met perhaps the most influential woman in his life who was to be his companion until his death, Lillian Hellman.

While *The Maltese Falcon* was shocking to the readers of its day because it featured a homosexual villain, one line in *The Thin Man* which referred to a man's sexual arousal while wrestling with a young girl created such a furor that the publisher felt obliged to run an ad in the *New York Times Book Review* defending the book's popularity: "Twenty thousand people don't buy a book within three weeks to read a five-word question." The sex in Hammett's work is very mild by today's standards; what is more interesting about *The Thin Man* is the change of tone and the change in the character of the detective. Nick Charles hates his work. A former detective, he has married a rich woman and wants to enjoy liquor and leisure. In many ways Hammett was, in 1934, much like Nick Charles. He was wealthy, an alcoholic, and his interest in his work was waning. Curiously *The Thin Man,* a light mystery with a self-indulgent hero, was Hammett's best-selling and most lucrative book. The movie starring William Powell and Myrna Loy was so successful that five sequels were made. Hammett no longer had to write to survive.

Hammett wrote *The Thin Man* at a hotel run by writer Nathanael West. Lillian Hellman recalled the process: "I had known Dash when he was writing short stories, but I had never been around for a long piece of work. Life changed: the drinking stopped; the parties were over. The locking-in time had come and nothing was allowed to disturb it until the book was finished. I had never seen anyone work that way: the care for every word, the pride in the neatness of the typed page itself, the refusal for ten days or two weeks to go out even for a walk for fear something would be lost." Later, in a letter to Hellman, who served as the model for Nora Charles, Hammett wrote: "Maybe there are better writers in the world, but nobody ever invented a more insufferably smug pair of characters. They can't take that away from me, even for $40,000." The $40,000 referred to the money he made from one of the *Thin Man* sequels.

After 1934, movies played an important part in Hammett's life. F. Scott Fitzgerald called Hammett one of the good writers "ruined" by Hollywood. Raymond Chandler concurred: "He was one of the many guys who couldn't take Hollywood without trying to push God out of the high seat."

Whatever the reason, Hammett stopped writing after *The Thin Man.* All of the books that appeared under his name after 1934 are collections of stories written earlier. The extent of his literary activities appears to have been as a screenwriter—including the only screenplay for which he was credited, the adaptation of Lillian Hellman's *Watch on the Rhine*—a script doctor for stage plays, consultant for radio scripts, and occasional book reviewer. He did attempt a novel, but returned the advance he had accepted from Random House when it became clear that the novel would never be completed (the unfinished novel, *Tulip,* appears in *The Big Knockover*). William Nolan suggested that one clue to Hammett's silence lies in the words of Pop, *Tulip*'s Hammett-like narrator: "If you are tired you ought to rest, I think, and not try to fool yourself and your customers with colored bubbles."

Though Hammett's writing career effectively ended in 1934, he remained a nationally prominent man until his death. About 1937, Hammett apparently joined the Communist party and he figured in Communist party affairs for the next twenty years. At the height of the paranoia which accompanied McCarthyism, the FBI reported that Hammett was a sponsor, member, or supporter of over forty organizations sympathetic to communism; in 1948 he served as national vice-chairman of the Civil Rights Congress (CRC), declared by the U.S. Attorney General to be a subversive organization. Lillian Hellman faced squarely the subject of Hammett's politics: "I don't know if Hammett was a Communist Party member: most certainly he was a Marxist. But he was a very critical Marxist, often contemptuous of the Soviet Union in the same hick sense that many Americans are contemptuous of foreigners. He was often witty and bitingly sharp about the American Communist Party, but he was, in the end, loyal to them." On February 23, 1955, testifying before the joint legislative committee Investigation of Charitable and Philanthropic Agencies and Organizations at the Supreme Court-New York City, Hammett stated: "Communism to me is not a dirty word. When you are working for the advance of mankind it never occurs to you whether a guy is a Communist."

In 1951, Hammett was called to testify before the New York State Supreme Court as a trustee of the Bail Bond Committee of CRC in the wake of the violation of bail by eleven members of the Communist Party for whom the CRC had posted bond, four of whom could not be located. When Hammett refused to testify—even to identify his signature—he was sentenced to six months in federal prison for contempt of court. He served his term between July and December of 1951.

In April of 1953, Hammett was called to testify before the Senate Permanent Subcommittee on Investigations of the Committee on Government Operations, chaired by Joseph McCarthy. His testimony before that committee is often quoted. Asked by McCarthy if he would "purchase the works of some seventy-five Communist authors and distribute their works throughout the world," Hammett replied, "If I were fighting communism, I don't think I would do it by giving people any books at all."

Royalties from Hammett's work supported him well into the 1950s. Before he was jailed, Hammett still earned $1000 per week from royalties. But after his release, the Internal Revenue Service took an increasing interest in his affairs, resulting in February, 1957, in a $140,796 default judgment for tax deficiencies. Tubercular and physically exhausted, Hammett was unable to pay the judgment and his income was attached for the rest of his life. In 1957, he listed his income as less than $30. In November, 1960, he was found to have lung cancer. He died on January 10, 1961. At his funeral Lillian Hellman said of Dashiell Hammett: "He never lied, he never faked, he never stooped. He seemed to me a great man."

BIOGRAPHICAL/CRITICAL SOURCES:

BOOKS

Authors in the News, Volume 1, Gale, 1976.

Contemporary Literary Criticism, Gale, Volume 3, 1975, Volume 5, 1976, Volume 10, 1979, Volume 19, 1981, Volume 47, 1988.

Concise Dictionary of American Literary Biography: The Twenties, 1917-1929, Gale, 1989.

Dictionary of Literary Biography Documentary Series, Volume 6, Gale, 1989.

Gardiner, Dorothy, and Katherine Sorley Walker, editors, *Raymond Chandler Speaking,* Houghton, 1962.

Gores, Joe, *Hammett,* Putnam, 1975.

Hammett, Dashiell, *The Maltese Falcon,* Knopf, 1930.

Hammett, Dashiell, *The Glass Key,* Knopf, 1931.

Hammett, Dashiell, *The Continental Op,* Spivak, 1945.

Hammett, Dashiell, *They Can Only Hang You Once,* Spivak, 1949.

Haycraft, Howard, *Murder for Pleasure,* Appleton-Century, 1941.

Haycraft, Howard, editor, *The Art of the Mystery Story,* Simon & Schuster, 1946.

Hellman, Lillian, *An Unfinished Woman,* Little, Brown, 1969.

Hellman, Lillian, *Pentimento,* Little, Brown, 1973.

Hellman, Lillian, *Scoundrel Time,* Little, Brown, 1976.

Mundell, E. H., *A List of the Original Appearances of Dashiell Hammett's Magazine Work,* Kent State University Press, 1968.

Nolan, William F., *Dashiell Hammett: A Casebook,* McNally & Loftin, 1969.

PERIODICALS

Atlantic Monthly, December, 1944.

Baltimore News-American, August 19, 1973.

Bookman, March, 1929.

City of San Francisco, November 4, 1975.

Esquire, September, 1934.
Globe & Mail (Toronto), February 4, 1989.
Miami Herald, March 17, 1974.
New York Times, January 11, 1961; January 11, 1987; August 25, 1988.
Outlook, February 13, 1929; February 26, 1930.
Spectator, February 14, 1931.
Washington Post Book World, October 2, 1988.*

* * *

HARDING, Peter
See BURGESS, Michael (Roy)

* * *

HARDWICK, J. M. D.
See HARDWICK, (John) Michael (Drinkrow)

* * *

HARDWICK, (John) Michael (Drinkrow) 1924-1991
(John Drinkrow, J. M. D. Hardwick)

PERSONAL: Born September 10, 1924, in Leeds, England; died of cancer, March 4, 1991, in Canterbury, England; son of George Drinkrow (a civil servant) and Katherine A. (Townend) Hardwick; married Mollie Greenhalgh (an author and playwright), October 21, 1961; children: Julian Charles Drinkrow. *Education:* Attended Leeds Grammar School.

Avocational Interests: Collecting defunct bonds and stock certificates, watching good television, reading, watching cricket, classical music.

ADDRESSES: Home—2 Church St., Wye, Kent TN25 5BJ, England. *Agent*—London Management Ltd., 235 Regent St., London W1A 2JT, England.

CAREER: Writer. *Morley Observer,* Morley, Yorkshire, England, reporter, 1942-43; New Zealand National Film Unit, Wellington, writer and director, 1947-52; *Freedom* (newspaper), Wellington, feature writer and arts editor, 1952-54; British Broadcasting Corporation (BBC), London, England, drama script editor and director, 1955-63; free-lance author and playwright, 1963-91. Directed plays for television, stage, radio, and record albums. War correspondent from Korea, 1951. *Military service:* Indian Army, Grenadiers, 1943-47; served in Japan; became captain.

MEMBER: Society of Authors, Writers Guild of Great Britain, Royal Society of Arts (fellow), Sherlock Holmes Society of London, Dickens Fellowship.

WRITINGS:

(Under name J. M. D. Hardwick) *The Royal Visit to New Zealand: Her Majesty Queen Elizabeth II and His Royal Highness the Duke of Edinburgh, December 1953-January 1954,* A. H. & A. W. Reed, 1954.
Emigrant in Motley: The Journey of Charles and Ellen Kean in Quest of a Theatrical Fortune in Australia and America, as Told in Their Hitherto Unpublished Letters, Rockliff, 1954.
Seeing New Zealand, A. H. & A. W. Reed, 1955.
Opportunity in New Zealand, Rockliff, 1955, revised edition, Barrie & Rockliff, 1965.
(Editor and contributor with Baron Birkett) *The Verdict of the Court,* Jenkins, 1961.
Doctors on Trial, Jenkins, 1961.
The World's Greatest Air Mysteries, Odhams, 1970.
The Discovery of Japan, Hamlyn, 1970.
The Osprey Guide to Gilbert and Sullivan, Osprey, 1972, published as *The Drake Guide to Gilbert and Sullivan,* Drake, 1973.
The Drake Guide to Oscar Wilde, Drake, 1973 (published in England as *The Osprey Guide to Oscar Wilde,* Osprey, 1973).
A Guide to Jane Austen, Scribner, 1973 (published in England as *The Osprey Guide to Jane Austen,* Osprey, 1973).
(Under pseudonym John Drinkrow) *The Vintage Operetta Book,* Drake, 1973.
A Literary Atlas and Gazetteer of the British Isles, Gale, 1973.
A Guide to Anthony Trollope, Scribner, 1974 (published in England as *The Osprey Guide to Anthony Trollope,* Osprey, 1974).
(Under pseudonym John Drinkrow) *The Vintage Musical Comedy Book,* Osprey, 1974.
(Editor and author of introduction) Anthony Trollope, *The Pallisers,* Coward, 1974.
A Christmas Carol (dramatized version of Charles Dickens' book), Davis-Poynter, 1974.
The Inheritors, Mayflower, 1974.
The Four Musketeers: The Revenge of Milady (novelization of the film), Bantam, 1975.
The Man Who Would Be King (novelization of the film), Bantam, 1975.
The Cedar Tree: A Novel (first novel in trilogy), Corgi, 1976.
The Cedar Tree: Autumn of an Age (second novel in trilogy), Corgi, 1977.
The Cedar Tree: The Bough Breaks (third novel in trilogy), Corgi, 1978.
Prisoner of the Devil, Proteus, 1980.
The Chinese Detective (based on the television series), BBC, 1981.
Bergerac (based on the television series), BBC, 1981.

(Editor and author of introduction) Trollope, *The Barchester Chronicles,* Macdonald, 1982.

Last Tenko (based on the television series), BBC, 1984.

The Private Life of Dr. Watson, Dutton, 1983.

Sherlock Holmes: My Life and Crimes, Harvill, 1984, Holt, 1986.

The Complete Guide to Sherlock Holmes, Weidenfeld & Nicolson, 1986, St. Martin's, 1987.

The Revenge of the Hound, Weidenfeld & Nicolson, 1988, Windsor Publications, 1989.

Nightbone, Weidenfeld & Nicolson, 1989.

(With John Ball and Michael Harrison) *Studies in Scarlet,* Gasogene Press, 1989.

Contributor to magazines and newspapers, including *Sunday Telegraph, Kent Messenger,* and *Sussex Life.*

WITH WIFE, MOLLIE HARDWICK

The Jolly Toper, Jenkins, 1961, State Mutual Book, 1978.

The Sherlock Holmes Companion, Doubleday, 1962.

Sherlock Holmes Investigates, Lothrop, 1963.

The Man Who Was Sherlock Holmes, Doubleday, 1964.

Four Sherlock Holmes Plays (one-act plays), Samuel French, 1964.

The Charles Dickens Companion, Holt, 1965, revised edition, Murray, 1969.

The Plague and Fire of London, Parrish, 1966.

The World's Greatest Sea Mysteries, Odhams, 1967.

A Literary Journey, A.S. Barnes, 1968 (published in England as *Writers' Houses,* Dent, 1968).

Alfred Deller: A Singularity of Voice, Praeger, 1968, revised edition, Proteus, 1980.

Dickens's England, A. S. Barnes, 1970.

As They Saw Him . . . Charles Dickens: The Great Novelist as Seen through the Eyes of His Family, Friends and Contemporaries, Harrap, 1970.

Plays from Dickens, Samuel French, 1970.

The Game's Afoot: More Sherlock Holmes Plays, Samuel French, 1970.

The Private Life of Sherlock Holmes (adapted from the screenplay by Billy Wilder and I. A. L. Diamond), Bantam, 1970, Empire, 1993.

The Charles Dickens Encyclopedia, Scribner, 1973, Carol, 1993.

The Bernard Shaw Companion, St. Martin's, 1973.

Four More Sherlock Holmes Plays, Samuel French, 1973.

The Charles Dickens Quiz Book, Larousse, 1974.

The Gaslight Boy: A Novel Based on Yorkshire Television's Series Dickens of London, Weidenfeld & Nicolson, 1976.

The Hound of the Baskervilles and Other Sherlock Holmes Plays, John Murray, 1982.

UPSTAIRS, DOWNSTAIRS SERIES; BASED ON THE TELEVISION SERIES

Upstairs, Downstairs: Mr. Hudson's Diaries (also see below), Sphere Books, 1973.

Upstairs, Downstairs: Mr. Bellamy's Story (also see below), Sphere Books, 1974.

Upstairs, Downstairs: On With the Dance (also see below), Sphere Books, 1975.

Upstairs, Downstairs: Endings and Beginnings (also see below), Sphere Books, 1975.

(Editor and contributor with Mollie Hardwick) *The Upstairs, Downstairs Omnibus* (includes *Mr. Hudson's Diaries, Mr. Bellamy's Story, On With the Dance,* and *Endings and Beginnings*), Weidenfeld & Nicolson, 1975.

"REGENCY" SERIES

Regency Royal, Coward, 1979.

Regency Rake, M. Joseph, 1979.

Regency Revenge, M. Joseph, 1980.

Regency Revels, M. Joseph, 1982.

CONTRIBUTOR TO ANTHOLOGIES

John Canning, editor, *Fifty Great Ghost Stories,* Odhams, 1966.

Canning, editor, *Living History: 1914,* Odhams, 1967.

Canning, editor, *Fifty Great Horror Stories,* Souvenir Press, 1971.

Canning, editor, *Fifty True Tales of Terror,* Souvenir Press, 1972.

Canning, editor, *Great Europeans,* Souvenir Press, 1973.

SIDELIGHTS: A prolific author comfortable in a variety of media, Michael Hardwick spent much of his career writing companions to and interpretations of Sir Arthur Conan Doyle's Sherlock Holmes stories; among these are *The Man Who Was Sherlock Holmes, The Game's Afoot* (a collection of plays based on Holmes' adventures), and *The Return of the Hound,* a sequel to Doyle's *The Hound of the Baskervilles.* One of Hardwick's last books, *The Private Life of Dr. Watson,* describes the famous assistant's life before he met the great Sherlock Holmes, and ultimately reveals the doctor's well-kept secret: that his slow, dimwitted manner was, in fact, a clever act, designed to draw from Holmes his most profound observations.

Michael Hardwick told *CA:* "I am a compulsive writer, moving without break from one commission to the next—novel to play to article to book review to novel, and so ad infinitum. I find it a struggle to turn down any approach . . . unless the theme is distasteful or would bore me to work on. I do not take holidays, because I can not bear professional inactivity. . . . If I were to make a fortune tomorrow I should be back at work (hangover permitting) the day after."

Of his books co-authored with his wife, Mollie Hardwick, he said: "We share an almost identical writing style and so can write a book together (and argue later as to who wrote certain passages), or take over one another's commissions, when pressure is heavy . . . but often the collaboration is largely one of discussion, and only one of us writes the book or play. We have been told that this collaboration is unique, or virtually so. We work at our typewriters in a shared study and only interrupt one another 'by appointment.' "

BIOGRAPHICAL/CRITICAL SOURCES:

PERIODICALS

America, December 15, 1973, p. 467.
Antioch Review, fall, 1975, p. 248.
Christian Science Monitor, January 9, 1974, p. F7.
Drama, spring, 1970, p. 71.
Guardian Weekly, August 29, 1968, p. 14; June 6, 1970, p. 618; September 1, 1973, p. 23; September 4, 1988, p. 28.
Listener, December 9, 1976, p. 745.
Los Angeles Times Book Review, January 8, 1984, p. 2; November 1, 1987, p. 12; April 5, 1992, p. 10.
New Republic, January 25, 1975, p. 24.
New Statesman, November 6, 1970, p. 613.
New York Times Book Review, December 19, 1982, p. 30; January 1, 1984, p. 24.
Observer, July 4, 1965, p. 23; November 29, 1970, p. 31; March 11, 1973, p. 37; August 5, 1979, p. 36; March 10, 1985, p. 24.
Punch, March 13, 1983, p. 78; October 15, 1986, p. 40; June 24, 1988, p. 47.
Saturday Review, November 19, 1966, p. 52.
Sewanee Review, July, 1975, p. 493.
Time, December 24, 1973, p. 81; April 28, 1975, p. 93.
Times Educational Supplement, April 8, 1983, p. 23; January 11, 1991, p. 30.
Times Literary Supplement, July 8, 1965, p. 580; June 6, 1968, p. 604; July 11, 1968, p. 738; June 4, 1970, p. 618; December 11, 1970, p. 1461; December 22, 1972, p. 1550; March 2, 1973, p. 235; August 10, 1973, p. 937; October 26, 1973, p. 1325; January 18, 1974, p. 43; December 5, 1980, p. 1394.
Tribune Books (Chicago), December 13, 1987, p. 5.
Virginia Quarterly Review, spring, 1975, p. R66; winter, 1981, p. 18.
West Coast Review of Books, March, 1984, p. 32; Volume 13, number 5, 1988, p. 23.

OBITUARIES:

PERIODICALS

Times (London), March 14, 1991, p. 16.*

HARDWICK, Mollie (Mary Atkinson)

PERSONAL: Born in Manchester, England; daughter of Joseph (a manager of a textile factory) and Anne Frances (Atkinson) Greenhalgh; married Michael Hardwick (an author and playwright), October 21, 1961 (died, March 4, 1991); children: Julian Charles Drinkrow. *Education:* Attended Manchester High School for Girls.

Avocational Interests: Music, country life, light reading, television, animal welfare, cricket.

ADDRESSES: Home—2 Church St., Wye, Kent TN25 5BJ, England. *Agent*—London Management Ltd., 235 Regent St., London W1A 2JT, England.

CAREER: Writer. British Broadcasting Corporation (BBC), radio announcer in Manchester, England, 1940-45, drama script editor and director in London, England, 1946-63; free-lance author and playwright, 1963—.

MEMBER: Society of Authors, Writers Guild of Great Britain, Royal Society of Arts (fellow), Sherlock Holmes Society of London, Dickens Fellowship.

AWARDS, HONORS: Elizabeth Goudge Award for best historical novel, 1976, for *Beauty's Daughter.*

WRITINGS:

(Editor) *World of Prose: Stories from Dickens,* Edward Arnold, 1968.
Emma, Lady Hamilton: A Study (biography), Holt 1969.
Mrs. Dizzy: The Life of Mary Anne Disraeli, Viscountess Beaconsfield, St. Martin's, 1972.
Alice in Wonderland (dramatized version of Lewis Carroll's book), Davis-Poynter, 1974.
Beauty's Daughter: The Story of Lady Hamilton's "Lost" Child (novel), Methuen, 1976, Coward, 1977.
Charlie Is My Darling: A Novel, Coward, 1977.
Thomas and Sarah, Sphere Books, 1978.
The Atkinson Heritage (first novel in trilogy; also see below), Bantam, 1978.
Sisters in Love, (second novel in trilogy; also see below), Severn House, 1979.
Lovers Meeting: A Novel, St. Martin's, 1979.
Dove's Nest, (third novel in trilogy; also see below), Futura, 1980.
The Atkinson Century (contains *The Atkinson Heritage, Sisters in Love,* and *Dove's Nest*), Severn House, 1980.
Willowwood: A Novel, St. Martin's, 1980.
Juliet Bravo (based on the television series), Pan Books, 1980.
Juliet Bravo Two, Pan Books, 1980.
Calling Juliet Bravo: New Arrivals, BBC Publications, 1981.
Monday's Child, Macdonald, 1981.

I Remember Love, St. Martin's, 1982.
The Shakespeare Girl: A Novel, St. Martin's 1983.
By the Sword Divided (based on the television series), Sphere Books, 1983.
The Merrymaid: A Novel, St. Martin's, 1984.
Girl with a Crystal Dove, St. Martin's, 1985.
Blood Royal, Methuen, 1988, St. Martin's, 1989.
Uneaseful Death (mystery), Century, 1988.
Perish in July (mystery), Century, 1989, St. Martin's, 1990.

Also author of numerous plays for television, stage, radio, and record albums. Contributor to magazines and newspapers, including *Woman's Realm* and *Woman.*

WITH HUSBAND, MICHAEL HARDWICK

The Jolly Toper, Jenkins, 1961, State Mutual Book, 1978.
The Sherlock Holmes Companion, Doubleday, 1962.
Sherlock Holmes Investigates, Lothrop, 1963.
The Man Who Was Sherlock Holmes, Doubleday, 1964.
Four Sherlock Holmes Plays (one-act plays), Samuel French, 1964.
The Charles Dickens Companion, Holt, 1965, revised edition, Murray, 1969.
The Plague and Fire of London, Parrish, 1966.
The World's Greatest Sea Mysteries, Odhams, 1967.
A Literary Journey, A.S. Barnes, 1968 (published in England as *Writers' Houses,* Dent, 1968).
Alfred Deller: A Singularity of Voice, Praeger, 1968, revised edition, Proteus, 1980.
Dickens's England, A. S. Barnes, 1970.
As They Saw Him . . . Charles Dickens: The Great Novelist as Seen through the Eyes of His Family, Friends and Contemporaries, Harrap, 1970.
Plays from Dickens, Samuel French, 1970.
The Game's Afoot: More Sherlock Holmes Plays, Samuel French, 1970.
The Private Life of Sherlock Holmes (adapted from the screenplay by Billy Wilder and I. A. L. Diamond), Bantam, 1970, Empire, 1993.
The Charles Dickens Encyclopedia, Scribner, 1973, Carol, 1993.
The Bernard Shaw Companion, St. Martin's, 1973.
Four More Sherlock Holmes Plays, Samuel French, 1973.
The Charles Dickens Quiz Book, Larousse, 1974.
The Gaslight Boy: A Novel Based on Yorkshire Television's Series Dickens of London, Weidenfeld & Nicolson, 1976.
The Hound of the Baskervilles and Other Sherlock Holmes Plays, Murray, 1982.

UNDER PSEUDONYM MARY ATKINSON

The Junior School: Schemes of Work and Organization, Evans Brothers, 1961.
Junior School Community, Longmans, 1962.
The Thames-Side Book (with photography by Michael Hardwick), Osprey, 1973.
Maria Teresa (juvenile), Lollipop Power Books, 1979.

UPSTAIRS, DOWNSTAIRS SERIES; BASED ON THE TELEVISION SERIES

Upstairs, Downstairs: Sarah's Story (also see below), Sphere Books, 1973.
Upstairs, Downstairs: The Years of Change (also see below), Sphere Books, 1974.
Upstairs, Downstairs: Mrs. Bridges' Story (also see below), Sphere Books, 1975.
Upstairs, Downstairs: The War to End Wars (also see below), Sphere Books, 1975.
(Editor and contributor with Michael Hardwick) *The Upstairs, Downstairs Omnibus* (includes *Sarah's Story, The Years of Change, Mrs. Bridges' Story,* and *The War to End Wars*), Weidenfeld & Nicolson, 1975.
The World of Upstairs, Downstairs, Holt, 1976.

DUCHESS OF DUKE STREET SERIES; BASED ON THE TELEVISION SERIES

The Duchess of Duke Street: The Way Up (also see below), Hamish Hamilton, 1976.
The Duchess of Duke Street: The Golden Years (also see below), Hamish Hamilton, 1976.
The Duchess of Duke Street: The World Keeps Turning, Hamish Hamilton, 1977.
The Duchess of Duke Street (contains *The Way Up* and *The Golden Years*), Holt, 1977.

DETECTIVE NOVELS FEATURING DORAN FAIRWEATHER

Malice Domestic, St. Martin's, 1986.
Parson's Pleasure, Century, 1987, Fawcett, 1992.
The Bandersnatch, Century, 1989.
The Dreaming Damozel, Century, 1990, St. Martin's, 1991.

CONTRIBUTOR TO ANTHOLOGIES

John Canning, editor, *Fifty Great Ghost Stories,* Odhams, 1966.
Canning, editor, *Living History: 1914,* Odhams, 1967.
Canning, editor, *Fifty Great Horror Stories,* Souvenir Press, 1971.
Canning, editor, *Fifty True Tales of Terror,* Souvenir Press, 1972.
Canning, editor, *Great Europeans,* Souvenir Press, 1973.
Canning, editor, *One Hundred Great Adventures,* Souvenir Press, 1973.

WORK IN PROGRESS: A series of detective novels and a new historical novel set in Tudor times.

SIDELIGHTS: Many of Mollie Hardwick's most popular novels are period pieces set in Victorian England. These works include biography (such as *Emma, Lady Hamilton* and *Mrs. Dizzy*) as well as historical fiction based on real figures (as in *Charlie Is My Darling*, a fictional account of the loves of Charles Stuart, and the award-winning *Beauty's Daughter*). With this type of background, it was not surprising that she was asked to co-author (along with her husband, Michael Hardwick) the novelizations of the BBC series *Upstairs, Downstairs* and *The Duchess of Duke Street.* Hardwick told *CA:* "My novels are set in period because, though I enjoy the amenities of this century, I am irresistibly drawn to the past, and find research into it the most exciting and rewarding part of a literary life. If I describe myself as a 'romantic novelist,' it is because I prefer to write about beautiful/brave/amusing people in picturesque costume and settings; for which reason I am utterly bored by current trends in fiction and the theatre (which I have always loved and still do, when it sets out to entertain me)."

While Hardwick's historical romances remain her most acclaimed works among readers and critics alike, she has since dabbled in the genres of mystery and detective fiction. Although her first two attempts, *Uneaseful Death* and *Perish in July,* were panned by some critics, Hardwick scored with a series of detective novels featuring professional antique dealer-cum-amateur sleuth Doran Fairweather. Marilyn Stasio, writing in the *New York Times Book Review,* calls the 1990 Fairweather novel *The Dreaming Damozel* "gracefully written and full of interesting arcana about the antiques trade, both consistent virtues of this unusually pleasing series." Of her switch to mystery writing, Hardwick says, "[I] am much enjoying the change."

BIOGRAPHICAL/CRITICAL SOURCES

PERIODICALS

Christian Science Monitor, April 14, 1976, p. 27.
Listener, December 9, 1976, p. 745; April 7, 1988, p. 793.
New York Times Book Review, April 14, 1991, p. 25.
Observer, September 10, 1972, p. 33; August 14, 1977, p. 23; December 24, 1989, p. 41.
Punch, April 15, 1988, p. 43.
Time, April 28, 1975, p. 93.
Times Educational Supplement, June 20, 1980, p. 39.
Times Literary Supplement, November 24, 1966, p. 1094; November 6, 1969, p. 1275; August 25, 1972, p. 986; February 20, 1976, p. 187.*

* * *

HARPER, Karen 1945-

PERSONAL: Born April 6, 1945, in Toledo, OH; daughter of Robert A. (an engineer and draftsman) and Margaret (a teacher; maiden name, Mudge) Kurtz; married Don T. Harper, June 24, 1974. *Education:* Ohio University, B.A. (summa cum laude), 1967; Ohio State University, M.A., 1969.

ADDRESSES: *Home*—Columbus, OH. *Agent*—Jay Garon-Brooke Associates, Inc., 415 Central Park West, New York, NY 10025-4897.

CAREER: High school English teacher in Columbus, OH, 1969-74; Westerville Public Schools, Westerville, OH, high school English teacher, 1974-84; full-time writer, 1984—.

MEMBER: National Council of Teachers of English, Phi Beta Kappa.

WRITINGS:

HISTORICAL ROMANCE NOVELS

Island Fantasy, Zebra Books, 1982.
Passion's Reign, Zebra Books, 1983.
Sweet Passion's Pain, Zebra Books, 1984.
Rapture's Crown, Zebra Books, 1985.
Island Ecstasy, Zebra Books, 1986.
Almost Forever, Jove, 1991.
Circle of Gold, New American Library/Dutton, 1992.

Also author of *Love and Rage,* Zebra Books.

SIDELIGHTS: *Passion's Reign* fictionalizes the story of Mary Boleyn, sister of Anne, and her relationship with King Henry VIII of England. *Sweet Passion's Pain* presents a fourteenth-century love story about Joan of Kent and Edward, Prince of Wales, while *Rapture's Crown* takes place in the court of King Charles II.

Karen Harper once told *CA* that her "royal history" novels stem from her own love for England. She visits the country every other summer and spends much of her time studying historical maps, costumes, cosmetics, foods, and customs to provide her readers with realistic settings. She commented: "I feel I owe these heroines who lived in earlier eras, where the status of women often ranged from chattel at worse to pampered pets at best, the right to have their stories told honestly but entrancingly.

"To choose the historical central characters of my novels, I usually select an exciting period or even a monarch I find intriguing. Next I focus my reading on that era or person until I find a hero or heroine whose life really touched the times. Then much other reading occurs until I see if that life will fit the plot structure I desire (conflict, excitement, final victory or happiness over great odds—the character learns or grows in the process). I work entirely within the framework of what is known so that my novels are what Alex Haley termed 'faction'—fiction which has one foot in fact or biography.

"My love of history—history as people's lives unfolding in exciting times—and my love of travel first brought me to a writing career. Also, perhaps because I have taught British literature for years and because my father was an avid reader of Victorian novels, I have always felt a special love for British settings. My heritage is European with both Scottish and English strains, and I have always felt attuned to the lives my ancestors lived."*

* * *

HARRINGTON, William 1931-
(Megan Marklin)

PERSONAL: Born November 21, 1931, in Marietta, OH; son of William K. (an oil producer) and Virginia (Pickens) Harrington; married twice; divorced twice. *Education:* Marietta College, A.B., 1953; Duke University, M.A., 1955; Ohio State University, J.D., 1958.

ADDRESSES: Home—48 Gregory Rd., Cos Cob, CT 06807.

CAREER: Lawyer in private practice, Marietta, OH, 1958-62; Office of Ohio Secretary of State, Columbus, elections counsel, 1962-65; Ohio State Bar Association, Columbus, counsel, 1965-71; lawyer in private practice, Columbus, 1971-78; senior attorney, Mead Data Central, 1978-80; author, 1980—. Licensed pilot. Computer consultant.

MEMBER: PEN, American Civil Liberties Union, New York City Bar Association, Phi Beta Kappa.

AWARDS, HONORS: Ohioana Book Award, 1967, for *Yoshar the Soldier;* Litt.D., Marietta College, 1984.

WRITINGS:

Which the Justice, Which the Thief, Bobbs-Merrill, 1963.
The Power, Bobbs-Merrill, 1964.
Yoshar the Soldier, Dial, 1966, published as *One over One,* McKay, 1970.
The Gospel of Death, M. Joseph, 1966.
The Search for Elisabeth Brandt, McKay, 1969.
Trial, McKay, 1970.
The Jupiter Crisis, McKay, 1971.
Mister Target, Delacorte, 1971.
Scorpio 5, Coward, 1972.
Partners, Seaview, 1980.
The English Lady, Seaview, 1982.
Skin Deep, Putnam, 1983.
The Cromwell File, St. Martin's, 1986.
Oberst, Donald I. Fine, 1987.
The Lawyers Guide to Online Data Bases, Dow Jones-Irwin, 1987.
For the Defense, Donald I. Fine, 1988.
Virus, Morrow, 1991.
Endgame in Berlin, Donald I. Fine, 1991.
(Under pseudonym Megan Marklin) *The Summoned,* Pocket Books, 1993.

Also ghostwriter of fourteen books for celebrities; also author of seventeen books under several pseudonyms. Some of Harrington's work has been translated into Italian, Spanish, German, Hebrew, Turkish, Hungarian, and Japanese.

WORK IN PROGRESS: A novel based on a criminal trial; collaborating on the autobiography of a New York City homicide detective; developing new episodes for the *Columbo* television series.

SIDELIGHTS: William Harrington once told *CA:* "I remain convinced that writing is the art of communication. If a reader must read my sentence or paragraph twice to understand me, I have failed to communicate. Obscurity in writing is an affectation. No matter how complex an idea or how subtle an emotion, the writer's goal must be to communicate it to another—with clarity. I have no right to demand that my reader struggle to understand me. Why should he? It is my job to communicate to him, not his to extract my thoughts from my turgid prose."

He adds: "I work on two computers that I have programmed to work in tandem. My word processor uses WordPerfect 5.1. From time to time I read a review that says scornfully that such-and-so book (none of mine) seems to have been written on a word processor. I reserve my scorn for the technologically illiterate who peer down their noses at word processor work. It has often been said that the secret of good writing is rewriting. The word processor makes it practicable to rewrite endlessly—adding, deleting, substituting, moving words, sentences, and paragraphs—generating at the end a legible manuscript the editor can understand and the typesetter can set accurately.

"A single man after two marriages and divorces, my typical workday is nine to about six-thirty, taking time out for lunch and often a brief post-lunch nap—seven days a week. It is my privilege to earn my living doing the thing I most love in all the world."

BIOGRAPHICAL/CRITICAL SOURCES:

PERIODICALS

New Republic, October 16, 1971.
New York Times, April 3, 1972; April 3, 1982.
New York Times Book Review, February 26, 1969; April 12, 1970; December 19, 1971; May 30, 1982.
Observer Review, August 6, 1967.
Variety, December 17, 1969.

HAYTHORNTHWAITE, Philip John 1951-

PERSONAL: Born April 22, 1951, in Colne, England; son of John (a company director) and Joyce (a company director; maiden name, Duckworth) Haythornthwaite. *Education:* Attended University of Lancaster. *Religion:* Christian.

Avocational Interests: History, archaeology, antiques and antiquities, natural history and conservation, history and modern practice of the game of cricket.

ADDRESSES: Home—Park Hill, Parrock Rd., Barrowford, Nelson, Lancashire BB9 6QF, England.

CAREER: H. Gertard Ltd. (booksellers), Nelson, England, company director, 1970—.

WRITINGS:

Uniforms of the Napoleonic Wars, Hippocrene, 1973, 3rd edition, Blandford, 1985.
Uniforms of Waterloo, Hippocrene, 1975, 4th edition, Blandford, 1986.
Regiment of the Line: A History of the Duke of Wellington's Regiment, Halifax Antiquarian Society, 1975.
Uniforms of the Civil War, Macmillan, 1975, published in England as *Uniforms of the American Civil War,* Blandford, 1975, 3rd edition, 1985.
World Uniforms and Battles, 1815-50, Hippocrene, 1976.
Uniforms of the Retreat from Moscow, Hippocrene, 1976.
Uniforms of the Peninsular War, Sterling Publishing, 1978.
Weapons and Equipment of the Napoleonic Wars, Sterling Publishing, 1979.
Uniforms of the French Revolutionary Wars, 1789-1802, Sterling Publishing, 1981.
Uniforms of 1812: Napoleon's Retreat from Moscow, Sterling Publishing, 1982.
Napoleon's Line Infantry, Osprey Publishing, 1983.
Napoleon's Light Infantry, Osprey Publishing, 1983.
The English Civil War 1642-51: An Illustrated Military History, Blandford, 1983, 2nd edition, 1984.
Napoleon's Guard Infantry: The Old Guard, Osprey Publishing, 1984.
Napoleon's Guard Infantry: The Young Guard, Osprey Publishing, 1985.
Civil War Soldiers, Iceni Publications, 1985.
The Alamo and War of Texan Independence 1835-36, Osprey Publishing, 1986.
The Austrian Army of the Napoleonic Wars: Infantry, Osprey Publishing, 1986.
The Austrian Army of the Napoleonic Wars: Cavalry, Osprey Publishing, 1987.
Uniforms Illustrated: The Boer War, Arms & Armour Press, 1987.
The Russian Army of the Napoleonic Wars: Infantry, Osprey Publishing, 1987.
The Russian Army of the Napoleonic Wars: Cavalry, Osprey Publishing, 1987.
British Infantry of the Napoleonic Wars, Arms & Armour Press, 1987.
The Poster Book of the Civil War, New Orchard Editions, 1987.
Victorian Colonial Wars, Arms & Armour Press, 1988.
Napoleon's Military Machine, Spellmount, 1988.
Napoleon's Specialist Troops, Osprey Publishing, 1988.
Wellington's Specialist Troops, Osprey Publishing, 1988.
World War I: 1914, Arms & Armour Press, 1989.
Wellington's Military Machine, Spellmount, 1989.
World War I: 1915, Arms & Armour Press, 1989.
World War I: 1916, Arms & Armour Press, 1990.
Austrian Specialist Troops of the Napoleonic Wars, Osprey Publishing, 1990.
The Napoleonic Source Book, Facts on File, 1990.
World War I: 1917, Arms & Armour Press, 1990.
World War I: 1918, Arms & Armour Press, 1990.
Gallipoli 1915, Osprey Publishing, 1991.
Frederick the Great's Army: Cavalry, Osprey Publishing, 1991.
Frederick the Great's Army: Infantry, Osprey Publishing, 1991.
Invincible Generals, Indiana University Press, 1991.
Frederick the Great's Army: Specialist Troops, Osprey Publishing, 1992.
The World War I Source Book, Arms & Armour Press, 1992.
Napoleon's Campaigns in Italy, Osprey Publishing, 1993.
Nelson's Navy, Osprey Publishing, 1993.
British Cavalry of the Napoleonic Wars, Osprey Publishing, in press.

Contributor to periodicals, including *Art and Antiques Weekly, Lancashire Life,* and *Cumbria.*

WORK IN PROGRESS: Armies of Wellington and *Colonial Wars Source Book,* both for Arms & Armour Press; research on the social and military history of the British Volunteer Force of 1794-1814, the home guard formed to combat the threatened invasion by Napoleonic France.

* * *

HELLER, Joseph 1923-

PERSONAL: Born May 1, 1923, in Brooklyn, NY; son of Isaac (a truck driver) and Lena Heller; married Shirley Held, September 3, 1945 (divorced, 1984); married Valerie Humphries (a nurse), 1987; children: (first marriage) Erica Jill, Theodore Michael. *Education:* Attended University of Southern California; New York University,

B.A., 1948; Columbia University, M.A., 1949; graduate study, Oxford University, 1949-50.

ADDRESSES: Home—East Hampton, Long Island, New York. *Agent*—Donadio & Ashworth, 231 West 22nd St., New York, NY 10011.

CAREER: Novelist. Pennsylvania State University, University Park, instructor in English, 1950-52; *Time* magazine, New York City, advertising writer, 1952-56; *Look* magazine, New York City, advertising writer, 1956-58; *McCall's* magazine, New York City, promotion manager, 1958-61; former teacher of fiction and dramatic writing at Yale University and University of Pennsylvania; City College of the City University of New York, New York City, Distinguished Professor of English, until 1975; full-time writer, 1975—. Has worked in the theater, movies, and television. *Military service:* U.S. Army Air Forces, World War II; served as B-25 wing bombardier; flew sixty missions; became first lieutenant.

MEMBER: National Institute of Arts and Letters, Phi Beta Kappa.

AWARDS, HONORS: Fulbright scholar, 1949-50; National Institute of Arts and Letters grant in literature, 1963; Prix Interallie (France) and Prix Medicis Etranger (France), both 1985, both for *God Knows.*

WRITINGS:

(Contributor) *Nelson Algren's Own Book of Lonesome Monsters,* Lancer, 1960.

Catch-22 (novel; also see below; chapter one originally published in *New World Writing,* 1955; previously unreleased chapters published in *Playboy,* December, 1969, and December, 1987), Simon & Schuster, 1961, critical edition, edited by Robert M. Scotto, Dell, 1973.

Something Happened (novel; excerpt originally published in *Esquire,* September, 1966), Knopf, 1974.

Good as Gold (novel; Literary Guild selection), Simon & Schuster, 1979.

God Knows (novel), Knopf, 1984.

(With Speed Vogal) *No Laughing Matter* (autobiography), Putnam, 1986.

Picture This (novel), Putnam, 1988.

Contributor of short stories to periodicals, including *Atlantic Monthly, Esquire, Nation, Smart,* and *Cosmopolitan;* contributor of reviews to periodicals, including *New Republic.*

PLAYS

We Bombed in New Haven (two-act; first produced in New Haven, CN, at Yale School of Drama Repertory Theater, December 4, 1967, produced on Broadway at Ambassador Theater, October 16, 1968), Knopf, 1968.

Catch-22: A Dramatization (one-act play based on novel of same title; first produced in East Hampton, NY, at John Drew Theater, July 23, 1971), Samuel French, 1971.

Clevinger's Trial (based on chapter eight of novel *Catch-22;* produced in London, 1974), Samuel French, 1973.

SCREENPLAYS

(With David R. Schwartz) *Sex and the Single Girl* (based on book of same title by Helen Gurley Brown), Warner Brothers, 1964.

(Uncredited) *Casino Royale* (based on novel of same title by Ian Fleming), Columbia Pictures, 1967.

(With Tom Waldman and Frank Waldman) *Dirty Dingus Magee* (based on novel *The Ballad of Dingus Magee* by David Markson), Metro-Goldwyn-Mayer, 1970.

(Contributor) *Of Men and Women* (television drama), American Broadcasting Companies, 1972.

Also author of other television screenplays during the 1960s.

ADAPTATIONS: Catch-22 was produced as a motion picture by Paramount in 1970. The film was directed by Mike Nichols, adapted by Buck Henry, and starred Alan Arkin as Yossarian; *Good as Gold* has been adapted as a screenplay.

WORK IN PROGRESS: A "companion volume" to *Catch-22,* for Simon & Schuster.

SIDELIGHTS: "There was only one catch . . . and that was Catch-22," Doc Daneeka informs Yossarian. As Yossarian, the lead bombardier of Joseph Heller's phenomenal first novel, soon learns, this one catch is enough to keep him at war indefinitely. After pleading with Doc Daneeka that he is too crazy to fly any more missions, Yossarian is introduced to Catch-22, a rule which stipulates that anyone rational enough to want to be grounded could not possibly be insane and therefore must return to his perilous duties. The novel *Catch-22* is built around the multifarious attempts of Captain John Yossarian to survive the Second World War, and to escape the omnipresent logic of a regulation which somehow stays one step ahead of him.

At the time of its publication in 1961, Heller's antiwar novel met with modest sales and lukewarm reviews. John W. Aldridge, writing in the *New York Times Book Review,* recalls that criticism "ranged from the idiotically uncomprehending at the lowest end of the evaluative scale to the prophetically perceptive at the highest, and in between there were the reservedly appreciative, the puzzled but enthusiastic, the ambivalent and annoyed, and more than a few that were rigid with moral outrage." *Catch-22,* Aldrige explains, was totally foreign to reviewers, whose experience with war novels was limited to the "harshly documentary realism" of Norman Mailer and Irwin Shaw, or the "sweetly hygienic" works of Marion Hargrove and Thomas Heggen which "depicted military life—mostly well behind the combat zone—as being carried on with all the prankish exuberance of a fraternity house beer party. Coming into this context, *Catch-22* clearly seemed anomalous and more than a trifle ominous."

By mid-decade, however, the book began to sell in the American underground, becoming a favored text of the counter-culture. "[*Catch-22*] came when we still cherished nice notions about WW II," Eliot Fremont-Smith recalls in the *Village Voice.* "Demolishing these, it released an irreverence that had, until then, dared not speak its name." With more than ten million copies now in print, *Catch-22* is generally regarded as one of the most important novels of our time. It "is probably the finest novel published since World War II," Richard Locke declares in the *New York Times Book Review.* "*Catch-22* is the great representative document of our era, linking high and low culture." The title itself has become part of the language, and its "hero" Yossarian, according to Jack Schnedler of the *Newark Star-Ledger,* "has become the fictional talisman to an entire generation."

In the *New York Times Book Review,* Heller cites three reasons for the recent canonization of *Catch-22:* "First, it's a great book. I've come to accept the verdict of the majority. Second, a whole new generation of readers is being introduced to it. . . . Third, and most important: Vietnam. Because this is the war I had in mind; a war fought without military provocation, a war in which the real enemy is no longer the other side but someone allegedly on your side. The ridiculous war I felt lurking in the future when I wrote the book." "There seems no denying that though Heller's macabre farce was written about a rarefied part of the raging war of the forties during the silent fifties," Josh Greenfeld wrote in a 1968 *New York Times Book Review* article, "it has all but become the chapbook of the sixties." As Joseph Epstein summarizes in *Book World, Catch-22* "was a well-aimed bomb."

In his *Bright Book of Life,* Alfred Kazin finds that "the theme of *Catch-22* . . . is the total craziness of war . . . and the struggle to survive of one man, Yossarian, who knows the difference between his sanity and the insanity of the system." After his commanding officer repeatedly raises the number of bombing missions required for discharge, Yossarian decides to "live forever or die in the attempt." "Yossarian's logic becomes so pure that everyone thinks him mad," Robert Brustein writes in the *New Republic,* "for it is the logic of sheer survival, dedicated to keeping him alive in a world noisily clamoring for his annihilation." Brustein continues: "According to this logic, Yossarian is surrounded on all sides by hostile forces. . . . [He] feels a blind, electric rage against the Germans whenever they hurl flak at his easily penetrated plane; but he feels an equally profound hatred for those of his own countrymen who exercise an arbitrary power over his life."

"The urgent emotion in Heller's book is . . . every individual's sense of being directly in the line of fire," Kazin believes. In the *Dictionary of Literary Biography,* Inge Kutt views Pianosa, the fictional island in the Mediterranean Sea which is the setting of the novel, as a microcosm of "the postwar world which not only includes the Korean and Vietnam wars but also the modern mass society." "Heller's horrifying vision of service life in World War II is merely an illustration of the human condition itself," Jean E. Kennard asserts in *Mosaic.* "The world has no meaning but is simply there [and] man is a creature who seeks meaning. . . . Reason and language, man's tools for discovering the meaning of his existence and describing his world, are useless."

Language, as presented in *Catch-22,* is more than useless; it is dangerous, a weapon employed by the authorities to enslave individuals in a world of institutionalized absurdity, a world where pilots lose their lives because their commanding officer wants to see prettier bombing patterns. Language, in the form of Catch-22, is the mechanism which transforms military doublethink into concrete reality, into commands which profoundly affect human life and death. Catch-22, as the novel states, is the rule "which specified that a concern for one's safety in the face of dangers that were real and immediate was the process of a rational mind. Orr was crazy and could be grounded. All he had to do was ask; and as soon as he did, he would no longer be crazy and would have to fly more missions." As Jerry H. Bryant notes in his book *The Open Decision:* "Only the insane voluntarily continue to fly. This is an almost perfect catch because the law is in the definition of insanity. . . . The system is closed." In the *Arizona Quarterly,* Marcus K. Billson III examines Catch-22: "There is no way out of the tautological absurdity of [this] regulation. . . . The will of authority predominates by the force of language. Man is caught in an unrelenting cycle of oppression and brutality disguised in the convolutions of Catch-22." "Catch-22," Billson continues, "is law deriving its power from a universal faith in language as presence. The world of the novel projects the horrific, yet all too real, power of language to divest itself from any necessity of reference, to function as an independent, totally autonomous medium with its own perfect system and logic. That such a language pretends to mirror anything but itself is a commonplace delusion which Heller satirizes masterfully throughout the novel. Yet, civilization is informed by this very presence, and Heller shows how man is tragically and comically tricked and manipulated by such an absurdity."

The acquiescence of men to language in *Catch-22,* Carol Pearson observes, is rooted in their failure to find any "transcendental comfort to explain suffering and to make life meaningful. . . . People react to meaninglessness by renouncing their humanity, becoming cogs in the machine. With no logical explanation to make suffering and death meaningful and acceptable, people renounce their power to think and retreat to a simple-minded respect for law and accepted 'truth.'" Writing in the *CEA Critic,* Pearson cites one of the book's many illustrations of this moral retreat: "The M.P.s exemplify the overly law-abiding person who obeys law with no regard for humanity. They arrest Yossarian who is AWOL, but ignore the murdered girl on the street. By acting with pure rationality, like computers programmed only to enforce army regulations, they have become mechanical men." This incident, this "moment of epiphany," Raymond M. Olderman writes in *Beyond the Waste Land,* symbolizes "much of the entire novel's warning—that in place of the humane, . . . we find the thunder of the marching boot, the destruction of the human, arrested by the growth of the military-economic institution."

In the novel, the character Milo Minderbinder is the personification of this military-economic system. An enterprising mess officer, Minderbinder creates a one-man international syndicate whose slogan, "What's good for M & M Enterprises is good for the country," is used to justify a series of war-profiteering schemes. Minderbinder forms a private army of mercenaries (available to the highest bidder), corners the market on food and makes enormous profits selling it back to army mess halls, and convinces the U.S. government that it must buy up his overstock of chocolate-coated cotton balls in the interest of national security. Milo's empire soon stretches across Europe and North Africa. "His deals have made him mayor of every town in Sicily, Vice-Shah of Oran, Caliph of Baghdad, Imam of Damascus, and the Sheik of Araby," notes Brustein. Minderbinder's ambitions culminate in one final economic boom. As Olderman observes: "His wealth, influence, and sphere of action become enormous, until he and his profit-seeking are omnipotent and omnipresent. For business purposes he takes gas pellets from life jackets and morphine from first aid kits, leaving the drowning and the wounded without aid, but with the comforting message that 'what's good for M & M Enterprises is good for the country.' The ultimate inversion comes when Milo bombs and strafes his own camp for the Germans, who pay their bills more promptly than some, and kills many Americans at an enormous profit. In the face of criticism, he reveals the overwhelming virtue of his profit." In the *Canadian Review of American Studies,* Mike Franks concludes that "for Milo, contract, and the entire economic structure and ethical system it embodies and represents, is more sacred than human life."

"The military-economic institution rules, and the result is profit for some, but meaningless, inhuman parades for everyone else," Olderman writes. Confronted with this "totally irrelevant and bureaucratic power that either tosses man to his death or stamps out his spirit," Yossarian must make a moral decision. Olderman surveys Yossarian's alternatives: "He can be food for the cannon; he can make a deal with the system; or he can depart, deserting not the war with its implications of preserving political freedom, but abandoning a waste land, a dehumanized inverted, military-economic machine."

Yossarian, whose only wish is to stay alive, will not stand still for the cannon. Kennard recounts Yossarian's second alternative: "[He] is given the chance to save his own life if he lies about Colonels Cathcart and Korn to their superior officers. He will, in accepting the offer, probably act as an incentive to his fellow officers to fly more missions in which many of them may be killed. He is given a chance . . . to join forces with the pestilences. After accepting the offer he is stabbed by Nately's whore and realizes that by joining those who are willing to kill, he has given them the right to kill him." Nately's whore, who shadows Yossarian after his fellow pilot Lt. Nately is killed in action, "pops out of every bush and around every corner to attack him because of Nately's death," Olderman writes. "However guiltless Yossarian may be of that one death, he is not [completely] guiltless—he has suffered as a victim, but has also been a victimizer. So Nately's whore will follow him forever, a kind of universal principle reminding him that he will always be unjustly beset and will probably always deserve it." In the book, Yossarian sympathizes with his determined pursuer: "Someone had to do something. Every victim was a culprit, every culprit a victim, and somebody had to stand up and do something and break the lousy chain of inherited habit that was imperiling them all."

As Bryant notes, "The only way that the circular justification of Catch-22 can be dealt with is by breaking out of the circle." Yossarian's friend Orr had broken free by sailing off into the Mediterranean in a rowboat, bound for neutral Sweden. Guided by Orr's example and by the wisdom imparted by the death of a young gunner named Snowden, Yossarian reneges on his agreement with the colonels and decides to desert. "In the course of the narrative," Olderman says, "occasional references are made to Snowden, . . . whose insides are shot out as his plane flies over Italy and who dies in Yossarian's arms. The experience profoundly affects Yossarian. As the narrative advances, the reader is given longer and longer glimpses of the incident. But not until Yossarian decides to try another way of getting out of combat than to agree with Korn and Cathcart do we get Snowden's full story. As the boy whimpers, 'I'm cold,' Yossarian, horrified, sees his entrails slither to the floor. There is a message in those entrails that teaches Yossarian, finally, what he must do. The message reads: 'Man was matter, that was Snowden's secret. Drop him out of a window and he'll fall. Set fire to him and he'll burn. Bury him like other kinds of garbage and he'll rot. The spirit gone, man is garbage.' " Yossarian refuses to discard his spirit; he heads for Sweden, the only place left in the world, he believes, which is free of mob rule. The impossibility of reaching Scandinavia via rowboat does not deter him. What is important is the act, the attempt, not the destination, Ronald Wallace observes in *The Last Laugh.* As Frank concludes, "The Sweden he aims for is located, perhaps, not so much in the real world as in the geography of the moral imagination." And Yossarian "is still at large," Heller surmises in an interview in the *Newark Star-Ledger.* "He hasn't been caught."

In the *Partisan Review,* Morris Dickstein comments: "The insanity of the system . . . breeds a defensive counter-insanity. . . . [Yossarian is] a protagonist caught up in the madness, who eventually steps outside it in a slightly mad way." Heller remarks in *Pages* that much of the humor in his novel arises out of his characters' attempts to escape, manipulate, and circumvent the logic of Catch-22. Before deserting, Yossarian tries to outwit Catch-22 in order to survive; he employs "caution, cowardice, defiance, subterfuge, strategem, and subversion, through feigning illness, goofing off, and poisoning the company's food with laundry soap," Brustein writes. "He refuses to fly, goes naked, walks backward," adds Olderman. "Heller's comedy is his artistic response to his vision of transcendent evil, as if the escape route of laughter were the only recourse from a malignant world," Brustein states. "[He] is concerned with that thin boundary of the surreal, the borderline between hilarity and horror. . . . Heller often manages to heighten the macabre obscenity of war much more effectively through its gruesome comic aspects than if he had written realistic descriptions. And thus, the most delicate pressure is enough to send us over the line from farce to phantasmagoria."

"I never thought of *Catch-22* as a comic novel," Heller says in the *New York Times.* "[But] . . . I wanted the reader to be amused, and . . . I wanted him to be ashamed that he was amused. My literary bent . . . is more toward the morbid and the tragic. Great carnage is taking place and my idea was to use humor to make ridiculous the things that are irrational and very terrible." Dickstein cites the profiteering of Minderbinder as one example of the tragic underpinning of Heller's comedy: "[Milo's] amoral machinations, so hilarious at first, become increasingly sombre, ugly and deadly—like so much else in the book—that we readers become implicated in our own earlier laughter." "Below its hilarity, so wild that it hurts, *Catch-22* is the strongest repudiation of our civilization, in fiction, to come out of World War II," Nelson Algren states in *Nation.* As Brustein concludes, Heller is "at war with much larger forces than the army. . . . [He] has been nourishing his grudges for so long that they have expanded to include the post-war American world. Through the agency of grotesque comedy, Heller has found a way to confront the humbug, hypocrisy, cruelty, and sheer stupidity of our mass society. . . . Through some miracle of prestidigitation, Pianosa has become a satirical microcosm of the macrocosmic idiocies of our time."

In 1986, readers and critics alike celebrated the 25th anniversary of *Catch-22.* In honor of the book's silver anniversary, a symposium entitled "Yossarian at the Academy" was held—a birthday party thrown, ironically, by the U.S. Air Force at its academy in Colorado Springs, Colorado, where *Catch-22* has been added to the syllabi of several courses. "It's become a very popular book among Air Force officers," explains Major Thomas Coakley in the Chicago *Tribune Book World.* "It's a fun book to read, and at the same time it dramatizes the dehumanizing factors within our particular bureacracy that we can recognize as valid. We think we owe it to our cadets to make them aware of them." Heller attended the symposium, signing autographs and giving a brief lecture. "I understand the Air Force Academy has a Catch-22," the *New York Times* quotes the author's address to an Academy audience. "To repair a uniform it must be freshly cleaned. But the cleaning staff has orders not to clean any uniform needing repairs."

A number of reviewers took the silver anniversary as an opportunity to measure the impact of *Catch-22* on American literature and society. "It is only in recent years that we have begun to learn how to read this curious book," Aldridge contends, "[and] to understand how and why it got here and became what it is instead of what we may once have believed it to be." The most significant effect of Heller's novel, Aldridge continues, has been upon critics and the nature of literary criticism. "The complexity and originality of the work [Heller, Thomas Pynchon, John Barth] and other writers have produced imposed demands upon criticism that have forced it to grow in sophistication. . . . As evidence of this, we need only observe that most of the questions that perplexed or annoyed critics of [*Catch-22*] in the years immediately following its publication have now been answered, and as this has occurred, the size of Mr. Heller's achievement has been revealed to be far larger than it was first thought to be."

Heller, in contrast, often dismisses the greater "sophistication" of *Catch-22*'s more recent evaluations. "From reading the criticism, I've learned about many of the things I'd done in the book without being aware at all that I was doing them," he jokes in the *Washington Post.* "People keep finding buried messages in *Catch-22,* but they're not my buried messages." Heller later admits, in the *Los Angeles Times,* that in *Catch-22* he set out "primarily to write an impressive piece of fiction. I thought it would be significant as a novel. . . . Any author writing a novel hopes his book will have universal appeal." Heller continues: "It's astonishing to me still that people who were not even born [when *Catch-22* was published] are reading this book . . . and finding things of relevance. It does make me extremely proud."

If there is a down side to the universal appeal of *Catch-22,* it is only that it came so early in Heller's career, effectively eclipsing his four subsequent novels. "The very success of *Catch-22* has been Heller's burden," observes *Chicago Tribune* writer Ron Grossman. "Critics have been too quick to find each of his successive books unequal to that first one." Still, among the best received of these is Heller's second novel, *Something Happened,* published thirteen years after *Catch-22.* It is the story of Bob Slocum, a middle-level manager who describes himself as "one of those many people . . . who are without ambition already and have no hope."

"He is restless," Kurt Vonnegut, Jr., writes of Slocum in the *New York Times Book Review.* "He mourns the missed opportunities of his youth. He is itchy for raises and promotions, even though he despises his company and the jobs he does. He commits unsatisfying adulteries now and then at sales conferences in resort areas, during long lunch hours, or while pretending to work late at the office. He is exhausted," Vonnegut concludes. "He dreads old age." In the *New Republic,* William Kennedy analyzes Heller's restless protagonist: "Bob Slocum is no true friend of anybody's. He is a woefully lost figure with a profound emptiness, a sad, absurd, vicious, grasping, climbing, womanizing, cowardly, sadistic, groveling, loving, yearning, anxious, fearful victim of the indecipherable, indescribable malady of being born human." In the *Saturday Review/World,* Aldridge examines Slocum's plight: "His mental state is shaped by chronic feelings of loss divorced from an understanding of what precisely has been lost. . . . The elements that are most real in Slocum's life are precisely those that might be considered conducive to peace of mind: material affluence and comfort, abundant leisure time, professional success, satisfactory marital relations, and considerable extracurricular sex with a number of attractive women. Yet these are the primary sources of his suffering because he is forever searching them for meaning and can find none." Aldridge continues: "He is haunted by the sense that at some time in the past something happened to him, something that he cannot remember but that changed him from a person who had aspirations for the future, who believed in himself and his work, who trusted others and was able to love, into the person he has since unaccountably become, a man who aspires to nothing, believes in nothing and no one, least of all himself, who no longer knows if he loves or is loved."

Slocum's loss of meaning is symbolized by his search for a lost love, Virginia, and for the lost dreams of his youth. "As Yossarian kept flashing back to that primal, piteous scene in the B-25 where his mortally wounded comrade, Snowden, whimpered in his arms, so Slocum keeps thinking back, with impacted self-pity and regret, to the sweetly hot, teasing, slightly older girl in the insurance office where he worked after graduating from high school, whom he could never bring himself to 'go all the way' with," Edward Grossman writes in *Commentary.* "He blew it," D. Keith Mano remarks in the *National Review,* "and this piddling missed opportunity comes to stand for loss in general. He makes you accompany him again and again, and again and again to the back staircase for a quiet feel that never matures." As Mano notes, "Slocum becomes semi-obsessed: telephones the insurance company to ascertain if his . . . girlfriend is still employed there, if *he* is still employed there. And he isn't." Instead, Slocum finds that this haunting figure of a girl, like his own spirit, has committed suicide.

"What he wants now is to want something the way he once wanted Virginia," Kennedy declares. "Why can't some things other than stone remain always as they used to be, he wonders. Sad. . . . [Slocum] spends the whole book trying to recreate what was and what is, speculating endlessly on what caused the ruin of such glorious innocence, such exciting desire. He has no more desire, only a stale, processed lust."

Clearly, something happened to create such unhappiness. "Something happened indeed," Benjamin DeMott finds, "namely the death of the heart." In the novel, Slocum says he wants "to continue receiving my raise in salary each year, and a good cash bonus at Christmastime . . . to be allowed to take my place on the rostrum at the next company convention . . . and make my three minute report to the company of the work we have been doing in my department." In the *Atlantic Monthly,* DeMott attributes Slocum's pain to the fact that "caring at levels deeper than these is beyond him." Melvin Maddocks points out that "it is not what has happened, but what has not happened to Slocum that constitutes his main problem." In a *Time* review, Maddocks describes Slocum as "a weightless figure with no pull of gravity morally or emotionally" who can love only his nine-year-old son, and then only for "brief, affecting moments."

Slocum's life revolves around his office and home; in both of these worlds he folds, under the weight of external pressures and inner fears, into a helpless state of alienation. "Money and power and the corporation [are] for Bob Slocum what war and death and the Air Force had been for Yossarian," John Leonard notes in the *New York Times.* Just as Yossarian feared his own commanders and compatriots, so does Slocum, in the more secure confines of the business organization, live in fear of his associates. "He's afraid of closed doors and of accident reports. He's afraid of five people in his office," Jerome Klinkowitz observes. "At home Slocum fears and distrusts his family, although he loves them in his way," Aldridge adds. "Slocum's wife is attractive and intelligent but bored and without a sense of meaning in her life. She has begun to drink in the afternoon and to flirt at parties." The Slocums, as Kennedy details, are the parents of "an insecure and nasty sixteen-year-old daughter whose shins [Slocum] wants to kick, an idiot son he is sick of and would like to unload, another son, aged nine, who is the principal joy of his life and whom he ruins by allowing the company's values (get to the top, don't give your money away, compete, compete) smother the boy's wondrously selfless and noncompetitive good nature." "One cannot but recognize that many of the pressures on Slocum are generated by the nuclear family itself and by the establishments in which the family is trained," Elaine Glover writes in *Stand.* With the exception of Derek, the mentally retarded son, none of Slocum's family have names, Fremont-Smith points out. "All of them are unhappy in various ways, and Slocum knows it is largely his fault." "Slocum does his deadly best to persuade us, with his tap-tap-tapping of facts, that he is compelled to be as unhappy as he is, not because of . . . flaws in his own character, but because of the facts," Vonnegut states.

However much the "facts" may conspire against Slocum, the real pressure is exerted from within. As Heller comments in the *Newark Star-Ledger:* "All the threats to Bob Slocum are internal. His enemy is his own fear, his own anxiety." According to an *America* reviewer, "Heller has replaced the buzzing, booming world of an army at war with the claustrophobic universe of Bob Slocum's psyche, where all the complications, contradictions and absurdities are generated from within. . . . Like Yossarian, Slocum always feels trapped—by his wife, by his children, but mostly by himself." Slocum, who giggles inwardly at the thought of rape and glances over his shoulder for sodomists, confesses: "Things are going on inside me I cannot control and do not admire." "Within and without, his world is an unregenerate swamp of rack and ruin," Pearl K. Bell asserts in the *New Leader.* "Pathologically disassociated from himself, Slocum is a chameleon, taking on the gestures and vocabularies of whichever colleague he is with; even his handwriting is a forgery, borrowed from a boyhood friend." This disassociation is more than a middle-age malaise; it is symptomatic of a deeper affliction, a crippling of the spirit that leaves Slocum barely enough strength to lament, "I wish I knew what to wish."

As the novel draws to a close, Slocum finally and tragically expresses his love for his favorite son. As the boy lies bleeding after being struck by a car, someone yells, "Something happened!" Slocum rushes towards the child, horrified: "He is dying. A terror, a pallid, pathetic shock more dreadful than any I have been able to imagine, has leaped into his face. I can't stand it. He can't stand it. He hugs me. He looks beggingly at me for help. His screams are piercing. I can't bear to see him suffering such agony and fright. I have to do something. I hug his face deeper into the crook of my shoulder. I hug him tightly with both my arms. I squeeze. 'Death,' says the doctor, 'was due to asphyxiation. The boy was smothered. He had superficial lacerations of the scalp and face, a bruised face, a deep cut on his arm. That was all.' "

According to *Playboy, Something Happened* "unleashed a fusillade of violently mixed reviews. . . . Nearly three quarters of the critics viewed Heller's looping, memory-tape narrative as a dazzling, if depressing, literary tour de force." Fremont-Smith, for instance, calls *Something Happened* a "very fine, wrenchingly depressing" novel. "It gnaws at one, slowly and almost nuzzlingly at first, mercilessly toward the end. It hurts. It gives the willies." In his *New York Times Book Review* article, Vonnegut finds that the book is "splendidly put together and hypnotic to read. It is as clear and hard-edged as a cut diamond." Maddocks, however, labels Heller's second novel "a terrific letdown," while Grossman believes it is "a lump compared with *Catch-22.*" L. E. Sissman of the *New Yorker,* who calls *Something Happened* "a painful mistake," cites a frequent criticism of the novel: "[Heller] indulges in overkill. When we have seen Bob Slocum suffer a failure of nerve (or a failure of common humanity) in a dozen different situations, we do not need to see him fail a dozen times more." Mano asserts that "you can start *Something Happened* on page 359, read through to the end, and still pass a multiple choice test in plot, character, style. . . . [It] is overlong, a bit of an imposition."

Slocum's repetitive monologue has been criticized by certain reviewers, but, as George J. Searles points out in *Critique,* "Slocum, a businessman rather than a man of letters, is by necessity a limited narrator. Although articulate and aware of the fundamentals of language . . . , he is not a *writer.* His mode of speech—and the book has the feel of being spoken, rather than written—is flat, ordinary, and unexciting, and is an accurate reflection of his personality." Caroline Blackwood is uncomfortable with the narrative voice of the story for a different reason. In the *Times Literary Supplement,* she asks: "Is it possible [that such a man as Slocum] would be capable of viewing himself, his values, his work, and his relationship with his family, with the brutal and humorous introspection of Mr. Heller's central character? . . . Slocum asks for an enormous suspension of disbelief. Quite often he appears schizophrenic; the superior wit, insights, and sensibilities of his creator are superimposed so erratically and unsuitably on this commonplace and tiresome man." Schroth, however, finds Slocum a convincing narrator. He writes in *Commonweal:* "Who can read the paranoid utterances of Robert Slocum . . . and not recognize to some degree his own share in the competitive madness and chronic anxiety of American life? . . . [*Something Happened* is] a book which sums up the spiritual emptiness of the 1970s so excruciatingly that it may be another decade before many critics adequately appreciate it and most Americans can read it with sufficient detachment." This prediction has since been proven valid, for George J. Serles writes in a 1984 *Dictionary of Literary Biography:* "Although the book's gloominess and deadpan delivery alienated some reviewers, *Something Happened* is now gaining recognition as a major work. In at least one respect it is actually superior to *Catch-22.* Dependent on boisterous exaggeration, the earlier novel sometimes verges on self-parody. *Something Happened* is more sophisticated. Heller turned here from hyperbole to implication, and by opting for a less strident, less obvious approach, he produced a more mature work."

Heller's third novel "indicts a class of clerks," Leonard writes in the *New York Times. Good as Gold* is a fictional expose of the absurd workings of the machinery of government, of a politics reduced to public relations, of a President who spends most of his first year in office penning *My Year in the White House,* of an administrative aide who mouths such wisdom as "Just tell the truth . . . even if you have to lie" and "This President doesn't want yes-men. What we want are independent men of integrity who will agree with all our decisions after we make them." Into this world stumbles Bruce Gold, a professor of English who is called to public service after writing a favorable review of the Presidential book. Gold is rewarded for his kind words with a "spokesman" position but yearns for higher duty; specifically, he wants to be Secretary of State—more specifically, he wants to be the first *real* Jewish Secretary of State (Gold is convinced that Henry Kissinger, who prayed with Richard Nixon and "made war gladly," cannot possibly be Jewish). For his part, Gold chips in by coining such expressions as "You're boggling my mind" and "I don't know," phrases that enter the lexicon of the press conference and earn Gold the admiration of his superiors. As *Time*'s R. Z. Sheppard observes: "[Gold] is no stranger to double-think. A literary hustler whose interest in government is a sham, he does not even vote, a fact 'he could not publicly disclose without bringing blemish to the image he had constructed for himself as a radical moderate.' " Gold was schooled in absurdity during his tenure at a New York City university, where he devised a curriculum such that "it was now possible . . . for a student to graduate with an English major after spending all four years of academic study watching foreign movies in a darkened classroom." With this experience as a huckster of the academy, Gold, it would appear, is ready for Washington.

In the beginning, Gold flourishes in his new environment, where, according to Sheppard, "Catch-22 is now Potomac newspeak." He meets the Important People, elbows his way onto a Presidential Commission, and prepares to exchange his homey Jewish wife for the promiscuous daughter of a wealthy bigot in order to ease his advance to the upper echelons of the Administration. Along the way he is more than willing to endure the anti-Semitic prattle of his potential father-in-law and others, learning, as Leonard says, "to lick the boots that specialize in stepping on you."

Like *Something Happened, Good as Gold* is "another painful portrait of a bright but almost empty man watching his soul melt in his hands," writes Schroth. "The book is essentially about Jews, especially those like Gold, who wants to escape his identity while exploiting it, particularly by making a lot of money on a big book about Jews," Leonard Michaels comments in the *New York Times Book Review.* (Gold, despite his ignorance of his heritage, has received a substantial advance from a publisher for a book on "The Jewish Experience in America.") "It is one of the main themes of *Good as Gold* that Jews violate themselves in their relations with such unreal creatures of their own minds, especially when Jews yearn for tall blondes and jobs in Washington where successful Jews are slaves," Michaels continues. "Gold yearns to escape what he is so that he can become what he isn't, which is precisely what he hates. He nearly succeeds, nearly becomes a Washington non-Jewish Jew, a rich, powerful slave with a tall blonde wife." Gold, unlike other characters in the story, is very much aware of his moral degeneration; a passage from the book reads: "How much lower would he crawl to rise to the top? he asked himself with wretched self-reproval. Much, much lower, he answered in improving spirit, and felt purged of hypocrisy by the time he was ready for dinner." "Unlike Heller's earlier hero, Yossarian, Gold pants to embrace the insanity of our time," Peter S. Prescott observes in *Newsweek.* "His need for money and the chance to escape his suffocating family prick his ambition."

"He is totally out of sync with his family," Alex Taylor says in the *Detroit Free Press.* In the *Los Angeles Times Book Review,* Darryl Ponicsan explains: "He's got two sons away at college and he's not crazy about them. . . . He won't let them come home for a weekend. He's afraid of his daughter, who lives at home. He's bored with his wife, Belle. He has an older brother, Sid, who sets him up at every opportunity. . . . He has four older sisters and their mates harping about, an aged father who admits to having liked him briefly when he was a baby and a stepmother who suffers—if that's the word, and it isn't—insanity, ceaselessly knitting wool and talking just like a Joseph Heller character." Jack Beatty finds that "the scenes of the Golds at dinner belong to the heights of comedy. . . . These family dinners are torture for Gold. Yet underneath [all the eating] and the practiced taunts, the feverish intimacy of the Gold family, there are some abiding values at work which Heller wants us to recognize and, I think, celebrate." Beatty sees Gold's brother Sid as an example of such values: "Sid, a prosperous businessman, is no hero; he's just a good man. He hated his father, yet bailed the old man out of his last business, and still pays the bills for his Florida retirement. He resented his smarter kid brother but paid his way through Columbia nonetheless. Sid has done his duty." "The scenes with the family might at first seem disconnected from the Washington scenes," Ronald Hayman points out, "but the pivotal joke is that someone who can fly so high as Gold should be treated with such savage contempt by his family, should be so inept at defending himself, and so incapable of staying away."

In his *New York Times* article, Leonard elaborates on Gold's dilemma: "What is being proposed is that being brought up lower middle-class Jewish in this country means being humiliated by your own family; that you assimilate, by groveling, a vacuum and a lie; that you have masturbatory dreams of acquiring the power to exact revenge on the father who disdains you; that to acquire such power you will be willing to mortgage every morsel of your capacity for critical discrimination; that you lick the boots that specialize in stepping on you, and hate yourself in the morning." Leonard concludes: "Those critics who, over the years, have suggested that [Heller] be more Jewish in his fiction are going to be sorry they asked."

Indeed, Heller's treatment of "The Jewish Experience in America" has aroused criticism, including accusations that *Good as Gold* is anti-Semitic. According to Sheppard, the book "is a savage, intemperately funny satire on the assimilation of the Jewish tradition of liberalism into the American main chance. It is a delicate subject, off-limits to non-Jews fearful of being thought anti-Semitic and unsettling to successful Jewish intellectuals whose views may have drifted to the right in middle age. Heller, who is neither a Gentile nor a card-carrying intellectual, goes directly for the exposed nerve." Gene Lyons observes in *Nation* that "it was not so long ago . . . when a book dealing in such cultural stereotypes as Heller employs throughout would have been closely scrutinized by a self-appointed committee of rabbis and Jewish intellectuals to determine whether, on the balance, the portraits presented were 'good for the Jews' or 'bad for the Jews'. . . . Such stereotypes are nothing but peasant superstition and ought to be dismissed as such." In *Books and Bookmen,* Hayman points out that the Gentiles in Heller's satirical novel are "even more obnoxious" than the Jewish characters. "Both, fortunately, are extremely entertaining." But Fremont-Smith asserts in the *Village Voice* that *Good as Gold* is not "without offensiveness. It does bore. It is also anti-Semitic. If Heller believes (and I'm willing to think he thinks he does) that everything is rotten to the core, this goes double for the Jews. . . . The Jews in *Good as Gold* are uniformly portrayed as snivelling, deceitful, self-aggrandizing, and ambitious beyond their worth: *Much, much lower, he answered in improving spirit.*"

In the novel, Heller depicts Henry Kissinger as the epitome of the "non-Jewish Jew" and examines, as Schroth notes, "the germ of Kissingerism within each of us." "Gold's real tension comes from the fact that his own morality dangles barely a ledge above his enemy's. He knows the corrupting tendency within himself, in every intellectual and journalist to become corrupted by the mere smell of power, to become a Kissinger . . . and, worst of all," Schroth adds, "to forsake his heritage, to forget or deny he is a Jew." In the *New York Review of Books,* Thomas R. Edwards finds that Gold's political aspirations have "one distinct drawback. Gold hates everything connected with Henry Kissinger, sees him as a loathsomely pushy cartoon-Jew and a closet Nazi. . . . Whatever the merits of this view of Kissinger's character, Gold's assault on his good name . . . is exhilaratingly energetic and winning. Its single-mindedness serves the purposes not only of comedy and moral outrage but also gives the novel its structure." Similarly, Jack Beatty of the *New Republic* comments: "The risk Gold runs in trying to become the first real Jewish Secretary of State is that he will be forced to act like Henry Kissinger, and that would mean his moral destruction. . . . *Good as Gold* is a cultural event. A major novelist takes on our greatest celebrity with all the wit and language at his command, and . . . a central historical figure [has] been . . . intimately castigated by the Word. Score one for literature." Lyons, however, believes that the attack on Kissinger is only "occasionally funny, [and] often slides over into what seems like simple malice, and pretty much for its own sake. . . . Satirizing the man by presenting clippings from Anthony Lewis is not very funny or effective. They were much better the first time around." In the end, Gold is finally offered his alter ego's former cabinet position but, as Beatty observes, "is recalled to New York and to himself" by the death of his brother Sid. Like Yossarian, Gold decides to "desert" his absurd world; he refuses the coveted post, choosing instead to preside over the funeral of his brother, the grief of his family, and, finally, the restoration of his own integrity. "He is a man with a profound moral sense," William McPherson asserts in *Book World.* "Once in a while he is reminded of it, and reminds us."

The critical reaction to *Good as Gold* has been divided. Edwards remarks that "*Good as Gold,* if hardly a perfect novel, is continuously alive, very funny, and finally coherent. . . . Like Heller's other novels, [it] is a book that takes large risks: it is sometimes rambling, occasionally self-indulgent, not always sure of the difference between humor and silliness. But this time the risks pay off. . . . Heller is among the novelists of the last two decades who matter." The *Hudson Review* describes it as a "big, ugly book," and Aram Bakshian, Jr., of the *National Review* calls it "an embarrassing flop. . . . The best [Heller] has to offer us in his latest novel is fool's gold." Hayman finds the novel is flawed but says that "nothing is unforgivable when a book makes you laugh out loud so often," and McPherson concludes: "When I didn't hate it, I loved it. Joseph Heller, of all people, would understand that." Finally, Mel Brooks in *Book World* rates *Good as Gold* as "somewhere between *The Brothers Karamazov* and those dirty little books we used to read. . . . [Probably] closer to *Karamazov.*"

Five years after publishing *Good as Gold* Heller produced *God Knows,* a satiric novel whose tone has been likened to that of a stand-up comedy routine. The narrator of *God Knows* is the Old Testament's David—the killer of Goliath, poet and singer for Biblical royalty, king of Israel, and father of the wise ruler Solomon (who is portrayed in the book as an idiot). David relates the tale from his deathbed, explaining his relationship with God—an overbearing and occasionally petty entity with whom David is no longer on speaking terms (when asked, "Where is the sense" in his expectations for the Jews, God replies, "Whoever said I was going to make sense? . . . Show Me where it says I have to make sense"). Though *New York Times* writer Christopher Lehmann-Haupt accuses *God Knows* of lacking direction or serious intention, he admits that Heller "has a gift for spotting absurd situations, particularly when he can give them a bawdy twist. After a couple of hours with *God Knows,* you get in such a silly mood that it's even hard to go back to the King James version without laughing." "Under all the laughter, though, there is anger," warns the London *Times*'s Stuart Evans. "What for some will seem blasphemous must for many others go beyond bigotry or even faith to question the superstitions which justify pain and misery, let alone willful cruelty, in the name of supernatural justice. [*God Knows* is] a very funny, very serious, very *good* novel."

While working on *God Knows* during the early 1980s, Heller was stricken with a nerve disease, Guillain-Barre syndrome, that left him paralyzed for several months. Though the author became too weak to move and almost too weak to breathe on his own, he eventually regained his strength and recovered from the often fatal disorder. After completing *God Knows,* Heller began writing his first nonfiction book, *No Laughing Matter,* with Speed Vogel, an old friend who helped him considerably during his illness. *No Laughing Matter* tells the story of Heller's convalescence and his friendship with Vogel in sections that are written alternately by the two men. Noting that Vogel's observations "provide comic relief to Mr. Heller's medical self-absorption," Lehmann-Haupt praises the book as both serious and comic. "It was indeed no laughing matter," he observes. "And yet we do laugh, reading this account of his ordeal. We laugh because as well as being an astute observer of his suffering . . . Heller can be blackly funny about it." The reviewer adds that "most of all, we laugh at the way Mr. Heller and his friends relate to each other. . . . [Their] interaction is not only richly amusing, it is positively cheering."

Picture This, Heller's 1988 return to fiction, is a reflection on such figures in Western history as Dutch painter Rembrandt, Greek philosophers Socrates and Plato, and certain twentieth-century U.S. presidents. Similar in tone to *God Knows, Picture This* revels in anachronisms, mentioning the "freedom fighters" of the war between Athens and Sparta, for example, and of "police actions" in the fifth century B.C. Some reviewers, such as the *New York Times*'s Walter Goodman and the *Washington Post*'s Jonathan Yardley, have dismissed *Picture This* as an unstructured, overly researched and ultimately self-serving work; Yardley describes the novel as "devoid of energy, bite, wit, imagination—of just about everything save a dogged determination to plow through to the final page and fulfill the contract's demands," and Goodman warns: "You need a lot of interest in the opinions of Joseph Heller to get much of a kick out of *Picture This.*"

Such critical reaction came as no surprise to Heller. "I wanted to write a novel with no conflict," he told the London *Times*'s Richard Rayner, "no romance, no adventure, no storyline at all in the conventional sense. Critics have been saying, therefore, that it isn't a novel. . . . They have fixed rules about what a novel should and shouldn't be. I don't go along with that." Rayner observes certain themes in *Picture This:* "that power and intellect are incompatible, that politicians wage disastrous wars for no good reason, that genius tends to be given a hard time, and that humanity learns nothing from its mistakes." Heller pulls all of this off, Rayner contends, "for the simple reason that he is funny. . . . He refuses to take institutions seriously; or rather, . . . he takes them *so* seriously they become hilarious."

In 1987, Heller began work on an as-yet-untitled continuation of *Catch-22,* from which two excerpts have appeared in *Smart* and *Nation.* In this volume, which Heller describes as more of a companion than a sequel, some of the surviving characters from *Catch-22* reunite in New York City fifty years after the close of the first book. Around them the country is reeling from the effects of a long and incompetent Republican administration, featuring politicians reminiscent of George Bush and Dan Quayle. Among the returning characters is John Yossarian; as in *Catch-22,* he frequently attempts to isolate himself from his illogical surroundings by remaining in his hospital bed—despite the absence of any apparent illness. "The psychologist conferred with the chief of psychiatry . . . and they concluded with one voice that there was nothing psychosomatic about the excellent health [Yossarian] was enjoying."

Catch-22's companion will, like Heller's previous novels, undoubtably draw comparisons to its predecessor—and, as with his other novels, those comparisons will more than likely be unfavorable. Some critics have panned the very notion of a revisitation; Yardley writes in the *Washington Post:* "One can only cringe at the prospect of what the 'sequel' to *Catch-22* may bring." Rayner explains Heller's dilemma: "He will always be tagged as the man who wrote *that* book. . . . His novels [therefore] tend to be greeted as new cars rolling off a production line. They're all very well, it is said, but they lack somehow the zip and zing of that great early model." Still, Heller is not troubled by the fact that, thirty years after its publication, he continues to be billed as "the author of *Catch-22*". "It fills me with pleasure that 'Catch-22' has entered the language," Heller says in the London *Times.* "They say Catch-22 even in the Kremlin. . . . Both in English and Russian. I touched a nerve."

BIOGRAPHICAL/CRITICAL SOURCES:

BOOKS

A Dangerous Crossing, Southern Illinois University Press, 1973.

Aichinger, Peter, *The American Soldier in Fiction, 1880-1963,* Iowa State University Press, 1975.

American Novels of the Second World War, Mouton, 1969.

Authors in the News, Volume 1, Gale, 1976.

Bergonzi, Bernard, *The Situation of the Novel,* University of Pittsburgh Press, 1970.

Bier, Jesse, *The Rise and Fall of American Humor,* Holt, 1968.

Bruccoli, Matthew J. and C. E. Frazer Clark, Jr., editors, *Pages: The World of Books, Writers, and Writing,* Gale, 1976.

Bryant, Jerry H., *The Open Decision: The Contemporary American Novel and Its Intellectual Background,* Free Press, 1970.

Burgess, Anthony, *The Novel Now: A Guide to Contemporary Fiction,* Norton, 1967.

Colmer, John, editor, *Approaches to the Novel,* Rigby (Adelaide), 1967.

Contemporary Literary Criticism, Gale, Volume 1, 1973, Volume 3, 1975, Volume 5, 1976, Volume 8, 1978, Volume 11, 1979, Volume 36, 1986.

Dictionary of Literary Biography, Gale, Volume 2: *American Novelists since World War II,* 1978, *Yearbook: 1980,* 1981, Volume 28: *Twentieth-Century American Jewish Fiction Writers,* 1984.

Friedman, Bruce Jay, editor, *Black Humor,* Bantam, 1965.

Harris, Charles B., *Contemporary American Novelists of the Absurd,* College and University Press, 1971.

Harrison, Gilbert A., editor, *The Critic as Artist: Essays on Books, 1920-1970,* Liveright, 1972.

Hauck, Richard Boyd, *A Cheerful Nihilism: Confidence and the Absurd in American Humorous Fiction,* Indiana University Press, 1971.

Heller, Joseph, *Catch-22,* Simon & Schuster, 1961.

Heller, Joseph, *Something Happened,* Knopf, 1974.

Heller, Joseph, *Good as Gold,* Simon & Schuster, 1979.

Heller, Joseph, *God Knows,* Knopf, 1984.

Kazin, Alfred, *The Bright Book of Life: American Novelists and Storytellers from Hemingway to Mailer,* Little, Brown, 1973.

Kiley, Frederick and Walter McDonald, editors, *A Catch-22 Casebook,* Crowell, 1973.

Kostelanetz, Richard, editor, *On Contemporary Literature,* Avon, 1964.

Literary Horizons: A Quarter Century of American Fiction, New York University Press, 1970.

Littlejohn, David, *Interruptions,* Grossman, 1970.

Miller, James E., Jr., *Quests Surd and Absurd: Essays in American Literature,* University of Chicago Press, 1967.

Miller, Wayne Charles, *An Armed America, Its Face in Fiction: A History of the American Military Novel,* New York University Press, 1970.

Moore, Harry T., editor, *Contemporary American Novelists,* Southern Illinois University Press, 1964.

Moore, Harry T., editor, *American Dreams, American Nightmares,* Southern Illinois University Press, 1970.

Nagel, James, editor, *Critical Essays on Catch-22,* Dickenson, 1974.

Nelson, Gerald B., *Ten Versions of America,* Knopf, 1972.

New American Arts, Horizon Publishing, 1965.

Number and Nightmare: Forms of Fantasy in Contemporary Fiction, Archon, 1975.

Olderman, Raymond M., *Beyond the Waste Land: The American Novel in the Nineteen-Sixties,* Yale University Press, 1972.

Podhoretz, Norman, *Doings and Undoings: The Fifties and After in American Writing,* Farrar, Straus, 1964.

Richter, D. H., *Fable's End: Completeness and Closure in Rhetorical Fiction,* University of Chicago Press, 1974.

Scott, Nathan A., editor, *Adversity and Grace: Studies in Recent American Literature,* University of Chicago Press, 1968.

Scotto, Robert M., editor, *A Critical Edition of Catch-22,* Delta, 1973.

Tanner, Tony, *City of Words,* Harper, 1971.

Wallace, Ronald, *The Last Laugh,* University of Missouri Press, 1979.

Whitbread, Thomas B., editor, *Seven Contemporary Authors,* University of Texas Press, 1966.

PERIODICALS

America, October 26, 1974; May 19, 1979.

Arizona Quarterly, winter, 1980.

Atlantic Monthly, January, 1962; October, 1974; March, 1979.

Book Digest, May, 1976.

Books, October, 1967.

Books and Bookmen, June, 1979.

Book Week, February 6, 1966.

Book World, October 6, 1974; March 11, 1979; December 9, 1979.

Canadian Review of American Studies, spring, 1976.

CEA Critic, November, 1974.

Chicago Tribune, June 3, 1990.

Christian Science Monitor, October 9, 1974; March 28, 1979; April 9, 1979.

Commentary, November, 1974; June, 1979.

Commonweal, December 5, 1974; May 11, 1979.

Critique, Volume 5, number 2, 1962; Volume 7, number 2, 1964-65; Volume 9, number 2, 1967; Volume 22, number 2, 1970; Volume 17, number 1, 1975; Volume 18, number 3, 1977.

Detroit Free Press, March 18, 1979.

Globe and Mail (Toronto), October 6, 1984; March 8, 1986.

Harper's, March, 1979.

Hudson Review, winter, 1979-80.

Life, January 1, 1968.

Listener, October 24, 1974; May 10, 1979.

Los Angeles Times, October 15, 1984; October 6, 1986; August 16, 1987; January 13, 1988.

Los Angeles Times Book Review, March 25, 1979.

Mademoiselle, August, 1963.

Midwest Quarterly, winter, 1974.

Mosaic, fall, 1968; spring, 1971.

Motive, February, 1968.

Nation, November 4, 1961; October 19, 1974; June 16, 1979; June 4, 1990, p. 779.

National Review, November 22, 1974; July 20, 1979.

Newark Star-Ledger, October 6, 1974.

New Leader, October 28, 1974; March 26, 1979.

New Republic, November 13, 1961; October 19, 1974; March 10, 1979.

New Statesman, October 25, 1974.

Newsweek, March 18, 1974, p. 113; October 14, 1974; December 30, 1974; March 12, 1979; October 18, 1982, p. 68; September 17, 1984, p. 80; December 23, 1985, p. 81.

New York, September 30, 1974.

New Yorker, December 9, 1961; November 25, 1974; April 16, 1979.

New York Review of Books, October 17, 1974; April 5, 1979.

New York Times, October 23, 1961; December 3, 1967; December 7, 1967; June 19, 1970; October 1, 1974; March 5, 1979; September 19, 1984; September 24, 1984; November 26, 1985; February 13, 1986, p. C25; April 14, 1986; April 27, 1986; October 6, 1986; April 7, 1987; September 1, 1988; February 3, 1990.

New York Times Book Review, October 22, 1961; September 9, 1962; March 3, 1968; October 6, 1974; February 2, 1975; May 15, 1977; March 11, 1979; September 23, 1984, p. 1; February 16, 1986, p. 8; October 6, 1986, p. 3; February 1, 1987, p. 32.

New York Times Sunday Magazine, March 4, 1979; January 12, 1986.

Paris Review, winter, 1974.

Partisan Review, Volume 43, number 2, 1976.

People, April 27, 1987, p. 42.

Playboy, June, 1975.

Publishers Weekly, November 1, 1985.

Richmond Times-Dispatch, December 8, 1974.

Rolling Stone, April 16, 1981.

Saturday Review, October 14, 1961; August 31, 1968; February 6, 1971.

Saturday Review/World, October 19, 1974.

Spectator, June 15, 1962; October 26, 1974; May 5, 1979.

Stand, Volume 16, number 3, 1975.

Studies in the Novel, spring, 1971; spring, 1972.

Time, October 27, 1961; February 1, 1963; June 15, 1970; October 14, 1974; March 12, 1979; September 24, 1984, p. 74.

Times (London), November 9, 1984; November 29, 1984; November 19, 1985; October 19, 1988; October 20, 1988; Septemer 2, 1989.

Times Literary Supplement, October 25, 1974; November 14, 1986, p. 1266.

Tribune Books (Chicago), March 18, 1979; September 23, 1984, p. 27; February 23, 1986, p. 40; September 28, 1986, p. 1; August 28, 1988, p. 6.

Twentieth Century Literature, January, 1967; October, 1973.

U.S. News and World Report, April 9, 1979; October 13, 1986, pp. 67-68.
Village Voice, March 5, 1979.
Vogue, January 1, 1963.
Voice Literary Supplement, October, 1984, p. 6.
Washington Post, September 30, 1984, p. 1; October 8, 1984; October 6, 1986; April 9, 1987; August 31, 1988.
Washington Post Book World, February 23, 1986, p. 6.
Yale Review, summer, 1975.

—Sketch by Brandon Trenz

* * *

HERNADI, Paul 1936-

PERSONAL: Born November 9, 1936, in Budapest, Hungary; son of Lajos (a concert pianist) and Zsuzsanna (Fueredi) Hernadi; married Virginia Tucker (a computer programmer analyst), August 18, 1964; children: Charles, Christopher. *Education:* Attended University of Budapest, 1955-56; University of Vienna, Ph.D., 1963; Yale University, Ph.D. 1967.

ADDRESSES: Home—5537 Capellina Way, Santa Barbara, CA 93111. *Office*—Department of English, University of California, Santa Barbara, CA 93106.

CAREER: Drama critic and book reviewer for newspapers in Vienna, Austria, 1963; Colorado College, Colorado Springs, assistant professor of German, 1967-69; University of Rochester, Rochester, NY, associate professor of German and of comparative literature, 1969-75; University of Iowa, Iowa City, professor of English and comparative literature, 1975-84; University of California, Santa Barbara, professor of English, 1984—, director of Interdisciplinary Humanities Center, 1988-92.

MEMBER: Modern Language Association of America, American Comparative Literature Association, Midwest Modern Language Association.

WRITINGS:

Beyond Genre: New Directions in Literary Classification, Cornell University Press, 1972.
(Editor) *What is Literature?,* Indiana University Press, 1978.
(Editor) *What is Criticism?,* Indiana University Press, 1981.
(Editor) *The Horizon of Literature,* University of Nebraska Press, 1982. *Interpreting Events: Tragicomedies of History on the Modern Stage,* Cornell University Press, 1986.
(Editor) *The Rhetoric of Interpretation and the Interpretation of Rhetoric,* Duke University Press, 1989.

Contributor to journals in the United States and Europe.

WORK IN PROGRESS: Work on literary theory, on modern drama, and on Goethe's *Faust.*

BIOGRAPHICAL/CRITICAL SOURCES:

PERIODICALS

Times Literary Supplement, July 1, 1983.

* * *

HERRICK, Tracy Grant 1933-

PERSONAL: Born December 30, 1933, in Cleveland, OH; son of Stanford Avery and Elizabeth Grant (Smith) Herrick; married Maie Kaarsoo, October 12, 1963; children: Sylvi Anne, Alan Kalev. *Education:* Columbia University, B.A., 1956, M.A., 1958; graduate study at Yale University, 1956-57; Oxford University, M.A., 1960. *Politics:* Republican. *Religion:* Congregationalist.

ADDRESSES: Home—1150 University Ave., Palo Alto, CA 94301.

CAREER: Federal Reserve Bank, Cleveland, OH, economist, 1960-70; Stanford Research Institute (now SRI International), Menlo Park, CA, senior economist, 1970-73; Shuman, Agnew & Co., Inc., San Francisco, CA, vice-president and senior analyst, 1973-75; Bank of America, San Francisco, began as senior financial consultant, 1975, became vice-president; Tracy G. Herrick, Inc., president, 1981—. Lecturer at Stonier Graduate School of Banking, 1967-76. Member of board of directors of Jeffries Group, Inc., 1983—, Bank Valuation Inc., 1984—, Anderson Capital Management, 1988—, C.D. Anderson and Co., Inc., and Money Analyst, Inc.

MEMBER: National Association of Business Economists, San Francisco Business Economists Association, San Francisco Society of Security Analysts.

WRITINGS:

Bank Analyst's Handbook, Wiley, 1978.
Timing: How to Profitably Manage Money at Different Stages of Your Life, Argus Communications, 1981.
Power and Wealth, 1988.

Contributor to journals.

* * *

HERZOG, Chaim 1918-

PERSONAL: Born September 17, 1918, in Belfast, Northern Ireland; immigrated to Palestine, 1935; son of Isaac Halevy (first Chief Rabbi of Israel and formerly of Ireland) and Sarah (Hillman) Herzog; married Aura Ambache (a scientist and environmentalist), May 8, 1947; children: Joel, Michael, Isaac, Ronit (daughter). *Education:* Attended Wesley College, Government of Palestine Law School, Cambridge University, Royal Military College at Sandhurst; University of London, LL.B., 1941. *Religion:* Jewish.

Avocational Interests: Sailing, flying light aircraft, golf, reading.

ADDRESSES: *Home*—Israel. *Office*—Beit Amot Hamishpat, 8 King Saul Blvd., Tel-Aviv, Israel.

CAREER: President of Israel, 1983-93. G.U.S. Industries, Tel-Aviv, Israel, managing director, 1962-72; Herzog, Fox, & Neeman (law firm), Tel-Aviv, senior partner, 1972-83. President of World Organization for Rehabilitation through Training (ORT Israel), 1968-83; Israel's ambassador to the United Nations, 1975-78; member of Knesset (Israel's Parliament), 1981-83. Member of Board of Governors of Hebrew University of Jerusalem, Bar-Ilan University, and Weizmann Institute of Science. Member of board of directors, 1962-83: Israel Discount Bank, Industrial Development Bank of Israel, Israel Aircraft Industries, and Paz Oil Corp. Member of Leadership Bureau of Labour Party. Political and military commentator for Israel Broadcasting Authority; television and radio commentator in Israel and abroad. *Military service:* Jerusalem, 1936-38. British Army, 1940-46; served in Europe; became lieutenant colonel; received four service awards. Israel Defense Forces, 1948-62, director of military intelligence, 1948-50 and 1959-62, defense attache at Israel's embassy in Washington, D.C., 1950-53, and in Ottawa, 1953-54, commander of Jerusalem Brigade, 1954-57, Chief of Staff, southern command, 1957-59, retired, 1962; became major-general; military governor of the West Bank and Jerusalem, 1967; received six service awards.

MEMBER: Variety Club of Israel (president, 1968-70), Harmonie Club.

AWARDS, HONORS: Knight Commander of Order of the British Empire, 1969; honorary doctorates from numerous colleges and universities, including Yeshiva University, 1976, Jewish Theological Seminary, 1976, Bar-Ilan University, 1977, Hebrew University, 1984, Georgetown University, 1984, Haifa University, Weizmann Institute of Science, Buenos Aires University, University of Monrovia, Liberia; H. H. Wingate Prize, National Book League (Great Britain), 1984, for *The Arab-Israeli Wars: War and Peace in the Middle East;* honorary fellow, University College of London, 1986; Honorary Bencher, Lincoln's Inn.

WRITINGS:

Israel's Finest Hour, Maariv Book Guild, 1967.
Days of Awe, Weidenfeld & Nicolson, 1973.
(Editor) *Judaism, Law and Ethics,* Soncino, 1974.
The War of Atonement, Little, Brown, 1975.
Who Stands Accused? Israel Answers Its Critics, Random House, 1978.
(With Mordechai Gichon) *Battles of the Bible,* Random House, 1978.
The Arab-Israeli Wars: War and Peace in the Middle East, Arms and Armour Press, 1982, published as *The Arab-Israeli Wars: War and Peace in the Middle East, from the War of Independence through Lebanon,* Random House, 1983, revised and updated, Vintage Books, 1984.
Heroes of Israel: Profiles of Jewish Courage, Little, Brown, 1989.

Author of foreword, *Final Letters: From Victims of the Holocaust,* edited by Yehudit Kleiman, Paragon House, 1991.

SIDELIGHTS: Chaim Herzog, the former president of Israel, is a soldier-statesman who has served his country since its modern political inception just after World War II. His writings reflect his Jewish heritage and military and diplomatic experience. As Israel's chief delegate to the United Nations from 1975 to 1978, he had the opportunity to address such issues as the contemporary situation in the Middle East, the future of the West Bank and the Gaza strip, and the role of the Palestine Liberation Organization (PLO) in the area. A collection of his speeches before the U.N. have been published as *Who Stands Accused? Israel Answers Its Critics.* "Documents, admissions by the opposing parties, historical events, are all marshaled and presented effectively, if not uniformly convincingly," noted Jeff Greenfield in the *New York Times Book Review. Publishers Weekly* contributor Albert H. Johnston commented that Herzog's "is a readable and persuasive argument." "The speeches are masterly expositions of his views: lucid, comprehensible, meaty," judged Thomas Lask in the *New York Times.* "*Who Stands Accused?* is a partisan document. Nevertheless, even those who don't agree with him will find the material absorbing."

The War of Atonement, published in 1975, is Herzog's analysis of the 1973 war against Israel. On Yom Kippur, the Jewish Day of Atonement, Egyptian and Syrian forces joined together to attack the surprised country, creating two battle fronts. "There is no commentator closer to the Israeli military establishment, its dilemmas and its intrigues" than General Herzog, noted Martin Bell in the *Listener.* "The narrative of the Israeli war effort, gleaned from interviews with the soldiers themselves, is vivid." "Herzog is brutally frank in apportioning blame for events leading to the war, although somewhat heroic in describing it," commented *New York Times* contributor James Feron. Herzog argued that Israeli leaders knew about Syrian and Egyptian mobilizations, but overconfidence in their own mobilization abilities and the strength of the Israeli air force, combined with political concerns about first strike ramifications, prevented the Israeli government from mobilizing in time. Basil Collier, writing in *New York Times Book Review,* concluded: "In this detailed account of the Yom Kippur War [Herzog] is concerned with refuting the legend that Israel's armed forces fell short in 1973 of the standards they had set in 1967 and 1956, but he does not gloss over mistakes made both by military leaders and by the Government. This is certainly the best account of the war from the Israeli standpoint that has yet appeared or is likely to appear for some time to come."

Turning from modern warfare to ancient battles, Herzog published *Battles of the Bible* in 1978. Written with Mordechai Gichon, a military historian, the book covers the period from the Exodus (c. 13th century B.C.) through the final battle of the Maccabees (c. 160 B.C.). "The authors' analyses and historic descriptions are true" to both the Bible and history, as Moshe H. Spero remarked in the *Library Journal.* The Biblical battles are also placed in military context, being compared with similar situations in more contemporary battles, as in the Napoleonic Wars or one of the World Wars. The volume is illustrated with maps, diagrams, and photos, and archeological information is also used to reconstruct the events discussed. A critic in the *Kirkus Reviews* called *Battles of the Bible* "lavishly illustrated," and declared that Herzog and Gichon "handle their material reasonably and responsibly. The narrative is always clear . . . and generally free of jargon." Richard F. Shepard praised *Battles of the Bible* in the *New York Times,* saying that "It is a book that is fascinating not so much for its writing, which is clear and to the point but not especially dramatic, but for the wealth of detail and knowledge brought to bear on the subject."

Herzog's knowledge of contemporary warfare is displayed in *The Arab-Israeli Wars: War and Peace in the Middle East,* published in 1982. In this volume, he examines Israel's military conflicts with its Arab neighbors since 1948, including a chapter on the Israeli push into Lebanon in 1981. "*The Arab-Israeli Wars* is an accurate and well-written survey of almost thirty years of intermittent warfare, which gains in usefulness from Herzog's inside knowledge and personal expertise," commented Edward Luttwak in the *Times Literary Supplement.* "Herzog's analyses of what was important militarily are . . . both interesting and sound," declared H. D. S. Greenway in the *Washington Post Book World.* The critic also noted that "this is a book more for military buffs than for most general readers. The accounts of tactics and strategies are clear, well written, with just enough color and personal accounts to keep it from becoming a staff college lecture." Drew Middleton, writing in the *New York Times,* praised the objectivity of *The Arab-Israeli Wars,* and concluded: "Herzog has produced the best single volume history of the Arab-Israeli wars. It is a military story. But every page is alive with the exertions, the privations, the casualties of ordinary folk."

BIOGRAPHICAL/CRITICAL SOURCES:

PERIODICALS

Kirkus Reviews, May 1, 1978, p. 530; October 1, 1978, p. 1108.

Library Journal, October 15, 1978, p. 2112.

Listener, July 10, 1975, p. 60.

New Statesman, May 11, 1979, p. 686.

New York Times, November 15, 1975, p. 25; June 30, 1978, p. C24; December 22, 1978, p. C31; October 27, 1982, p. 23.

New York Times Book Review, October 5, 1975, p. 20; June 18, 1978, p. 18; February 12, 1984, p. 34.

Publishers Weekly, April 24, 1978, p. 73; September 4, 1978, p. 106.

Times Literary Supplement, November 19, 1982, p. 1262.

Washington Post Book World, December 19, 1982, p. 4.

* * *

HEZEL, Francis X(avier) 1939-

PERSONAL: Born January 29, 1939, in Buffalo, NY; son of Francis X. (a purchasing agent) and Patricia (a teacher; maiden name, Kolb) Hezel. *Education:* Fordham University, A.B., 1962, M.A., 1963; Woodstock College, M.Div., 1969, S.T.M., 1970.

Avocational Interests: Basketball, jogging.

ADDRESSES: *Home*—Kolonia, Pohnpei, Federated States of Micronesia. *Office*—Micronesian Seminar, P.O. Box 160, Pohnpei, Federated States of Micronesia 96941.

CAREER: Entered Society of Jesus (Jesuits; S.J.), 1956, ordained Roman Catholic priest, 1969; Xavier High School, Chuuk, Federated States of Micronesia, teacher, 1963-66, 1969-73, chair of social studies department, 1969-73, principal of school, 1973-75, director of school, 1976-82. Micronesian Seminar, curator of library, 1967—, director of seminar, 1972—; regional Jesuit superior, 1992—; associate of Micronesian Area Research Center, University of Guam. Conference and workshop organizer.

MEMBER: Association of Social Anthropologists in Oceania.

WRITINGS:

(With Charles Reafsnyder) *Micronesia: A Changing Society,* with teacher's guide, Trust Territory Education Department (Saipan, Mariana Islands), 1971.

(With Reafsnyder) *Micronesia Through the Years,* with teacher's guide, Trust Territory Education Department, 1972.

Foreign Ships in Micronesia: A Compendium of Ship Contacts With the Caroline and Marshall Islands, 1521-1885, Trust Territory Printing Office, 1979.

(With Mark Berg) *Micronesia: Winds of Change; A Book of Readings on the History of Micronesia,* Trust Territory Printing Office, 1980.

Reflections on Micronesia: Collected Papers of Father Francis X. Hezel, S.J., Pacific Islands Studies Center, University of Hawaii at Manoa, 1982.

The First Taint of Civilization: A History of the Caroline and Marshall Islands in Pre-Colonial Days, 1521-1885, University Press of Hawaii, 1983.

From Conquest to Colonization: Spain in the Mariana Islands, 1690-1740, Historic Preservation Office (Saipan, Mariana Islands), 1989.

The Catholic Church in Micronesia, Loyola University Press, 1991.

Correspondent for *Journal of Pacific History* and *Pacific Studies.* Contributor to magazines, including *Pacific* and *Guam Reporter.*

WORK IN PROGRESS: A history of Micronesia during its colonial period, publication by University of Hawaii Press expected in 1994.

SIDELIGHTS: Francis X. Hezel told *CA:* "I was educated to have a respect for, if not a love of, the antiquities since I majored in Latin and Greek in high school. During my years in the Jesuit seminary, my classical education continued right up until my assignment to foreign missions in the Caroline and Marshall Islands of the Pacific. There I found not the island paradise of romantic literature, but a future field of missionary activity with a strong appeal to my Teutonic soul. I returned to the Caroline and Marshall islands after my ordination to the priesthood in 1969, and I began to produce a stream of articles and books on my new island home. Social studies were among the first of these achievements. Soon my long exposure to the antiquities during my school days led to a fascination with local history, from which more articles and a handful of books followed. In the course of my work, I picked up enough German, Spanish, and French to struggle through foreign journals and papers, but always with a dictionary in one hand.

"Not content with my assigned task as an educator and my secondary avocation as an amateur historian, I became a self-appointed social critic for Micronesia during its boom days of development. Another torrent of articles flowed, largely because my celibate religious status precluded family life and my island location denied me any sort of real social life. Without television, there was not much to do in the evening other than write. Although my social life improved considerably when I learned Chukese in 1973, I continued to write just the same, more from habit than from anything else.

"My writing has been said to be unlike that of a historian, a comment that may represent the highest accolade yet received. My social criticism, while not especially incisive, is often controversial. When I am not writing, I am praying, playing basketball, or jogging. As David Nevin and other authors have attested, my sense of Nordic discipline often brings me into more than merely verbal conflict with others on my small island home, and I seem to have acquired a reputation for wrestling drunks to the ground. I now hold the island record for citizen's arrests."

* * *

HILL, Bob
See HILL, Robert C(ecil)

* * *

HILL, Robert C(ecil) 1929-
(Bob Hill)

PERSONAL: Born April 29, 1929, in St. Louis, MO; son of Lester S. (a manufacturer) and Pearl V. (a housewife; maiden name, Long) Hill; married Georgia Barr (an author), November 23, 1947; children: W. Terry, Sherry L. Hill Camp, Robert C. II, Ruston L. *Education:* Free Will Baptist College, B.A., 1957; Virginia Commonwealth University, M.A., 1967; graduate study at Austin Peay State University, 1963; Oxford Graduate School, Doctorate in Gerontology, 1992. *Politics:* Conservative.

ADDRESSES: *Home and office*—1100 N.W. Rutland Rd., Mount-Juliet, TN 37122.

CAREER: Ordained Baptist minister, 1957; pastor of Baptist church in Nashville, TN, 1957-67; *Christian Life,* Chicago, IL, managing editor, 1967-73; Cross Roads Publications, Atlanta, GA, president and chief executive officer, 1973-80; freelance writer, 1980—. Professor at Toccoa Falls College; vice president of Academic Affairs at Nashville Bible College.

WRITINGS:

UNDER NAME BOB HILL

Super Pro, Cross Roads, 1979.

The Evangelist, Cross Roads, 1980.

My Book, My Poem, My Song, Cross Reference, 1982.

Devotions from the Christians Secret of a Happy Life, Fleming Revell, 1983.

Friends with God, Thomas Nelson, 1984.

Obedience: The Key to Prosperity, Cross Reference, 1985.
How to Be Richer, Here's Life, 1986.
Why Do the Heathen Rage?, Cross Roads, 1987.
Maturity in Transition, Broadman, 1993.

SIDELIGHTS: Robert C. Hill once told *CA:* "All of my books were written with a religious theme—conservative Christianity—and are a result of Bible reading and its relationship to contemporary life."

* * *

HILLERMAN, Tony 1925-

PERSONAL: Born May 27, 1925; son of August Alfred (a farmer) and Lucy (Grove) Hillerman; married Mary Unzner, August 16, 1948; children: Anne, Janet, Anthony, Monica, Stephen, Daniel. *Education:* Attended Oklahoma State University, 1943; University of Oklahoma, B.A., 1946; University of New Mexico, M.A., 1966. *Politics:* Democrat. *Religion:* Roman Catholic.

ADDRESSES: *Home*—2729 Texas NE, Albuquerque, NM 87110.

CAREER: *Borger News Herald,* Borger, TX, reporter, 1948; *Morning Press-Constitution,* Lawton, OK, city editor, 1948-50; United Press International, Oklahoma City, OK, political reporter, 1950-52, Santa Fe, NM, bureau manager, 1952-54; *New Mexican,* Santa Fe, NM, political reporter and executive editor, 1954-63; University of New Mexico, Albuquerque, associate professor, 1965-66, professor, 1966-85, professor emeritus of journalism, 1985—, chairman of department, 1966-73, assistant to the president, 1975-80; writer. *Military service:* U. S. Army, 1943-45; received Silver Star, Bronze Star, and Purple Heart.

MEMBER: Albuquerque Press Club, Sigma Delta Chi, Phi Kappa Phi.

AWARDS, HONORS: Edgar Allan Poe Award, Mystery Writers of America, 1974, for *Dance Hall of the Dead.*

WRITINGS:

MYSTERY NOVELS

The Blessing Way, Harper, 1970.
The Fly on the Wall, Harper, 1971.
Dance Hall of the Dead, Harper, 1973.
Listening Woman, Harper, 1977.
The People of Darkness, Harper, 1978.
The Dark Wind, Harper, 1981.
Ghostway, Harper, 1984.
A Thief of Time, Harper, 1985.
Skinwalkers, Harper, 1986.
Talking God, Harper, 1989.
Coyote Waits, Harper, 1990.
Sacred Clowns, Harper, 1993.

COLLECTIONS

The Joe Leaphorn Mysteries, Harper, 1989.
The Jim Chee Mysteries, Harper, 1992.
Leaphorn and Chee: Three Classic Mysteries Featuring Lt. Joe Leaphorn and Officer Jim Chee, Harper, 1992.

OTHER

The Boy Who Made Dragonfly: A Zuni Myth (juvenile), Harper, 1972.
The Great Taos Bank Robbery and Other Indian Country Affairs, University of New Mexico Press, 1980.
(Editor) *The Spell of New Mexico,* University of New Mexico Press, 1984.
Indian Country: America's Sacred land, illustrated with photographs by Bela Kalman, Northland Press, 1987.
(Author of foreward) Erna Fergusson, *Dancing Gods: Indian Ceremonials of New Mexico and Arizona,* University of New Mexico Press, 1988.
Hillerman Country: A Journey through the Southwest with Tony Hillerman, illustrated with photographs by Barney Hillerman, Harper, 1991.
(With Ernie Bulow) *Talking Mysteries: A Conversation with Tony Hillerman,* University of New Mexico Press, 1991.
(Editor) *Best of the West: An Anthology of Classic Writing from the American West,* Harper, 1991.
(Author of foreward) Bulow, *Navajo Taboos,* Buffalo Medicine Books, 1991.
(Author of introduction) Howard Beyan, editor, *Robbers, Rogues, and Ruffians: True Tales of the Wild West,* Clear Light, 1991.
Mudhead Kiva: A Novel, Harper, 1992.
New Mexico, Rio Grande, and Other Essays, illustrated with photographs by David Muench and Robert Reynolds, Graphic Arts Center, 1992.

Also contributor to periodicals, including *New Mexico Quarterly, National Geographic,* and *Reader's Digest.* Many of Hillerman's mysteries have been recorded on audio cassette.

SIDELIGHTS: Tony Hillerman's interest in the American Southwest is evident in both his popular mystery series and nonfiction works that explore the natural wonders of the region. A student of Southwestern history and culture, Hillerman often draws his themes from the conflict between modern society and traditional Native American values and customs. The complex nature of this struggle is perhaps most evident in the author's works featuring Navajo Tribal Police officers Joe Leaphorn and Jim Chee, whose contrasting views about heritage and crime-fighting form an interesting backdrop to their criminal investigations. The intricate nature of Hillerman's plots, combined with detailed descriptions of people, places, and exotic rituals, has helped make novels like *Talking God* and *Coyote Waits* popular with readers and critics alike. Robin W. Winks, writing in *Washington Post Book World,* defined Hillerman's broad appeal by commenting: "I admire Tony Hillerman for his plots, the ease of his style, the quiet tension he draws between traditional and modern Navajo . . . but I admire even more the fact that he gets his Zuni rituals just right, that he knows Navajo land like the back of his hand, and that he can make the vast, sunny open spaces of the American Southwest as fully threatening . . . as the dark canyons of our corroding cities."

As Hillerman's main recurring characters, Leaphorn and Chee serve a dual function. On one level, the officers act as guides into a world of traditions and customs unfamiliar to most readers; on another level, Hillerman's depiction of Leaphorn and Chee's day-to-day struggles—with bureaucratic red tape, discrimination, and intimate relationships—helps readers understand the difficulty of living in what amounts to two worlds with different, and often contradictory, sets of rules. This culture clash is not always depicted in a negative light, however. In books such as *Listening Woman, The Ghostway,* and *Talking God,* Leaphorn and Chee use both standard police procedures and their special knowledge of tribal customs to solve a wide variety of baffling crimes. In *Listening Woman,* Leaphorn finds clues to a double murder in a group of ritual sand paintings. An oddly-performed death ceremony puts Chee on the trail of a missing girl and a killer in *The Ghostway.* Stolen pottery from a "lost" tribe becomes the focus of Leaphorn's investigation into artifact trafficking in *A Thief of Time,* while in *Talking God,* the two officers team up for an adventure that involves a religious mask housed at the Smithsonian National Museum of Natural History.

The adventures of Hillerman's rather unorthodox detectives have fared well with critics. A reviewer for the *Washington Post Book World* lauded *Listening Woman* for the author's "deft plotting and acute characterization." "Suspenseful" was the adjective given to *A Thief of Time* by Charles Solomon in a *Los Angeles Times Book Review* commentary. Charles Petersen of Chicago *Tribune Books* called *Skinwalkers* a "good introduction" to Hillerman's work, adding that "if you start the book . . . you won't stop reading until the end." And, in a review of *Coyote Waits* for the *New York Times Book Review,* Robert F. Gish remarked that "those who await Tony Hillerman's latest Navajo mystery novel are always rewarded. . . . In this book, the author continues to prove himself one of the nation's most convincing and authentic interpreters of Navajo culture, as well as one of our best and most innovative mystery writers."

Hillerman has also been commended for his nonfiction works that explore the natural beauty and unique history of the Southwest. In *New Mexico, Rio Grande, and Other Essays,* the author discusses a number of topics, including how geographical, political, and historical factors helped the Pueblo Indians thrive when many other tribes fell prey to conquering forces. In a review of Hillerman's pictorial narrative for the *New York Times Book Review,* Miriam Davidson termed the book a "lavish tribute" to the region. For *Hillerman Country,* the author and his brother travelled the sideroads of the desert country in search of interesting and atypical vistas. The result, concluded Georgia Jones-Davis of the *Los Angeles Times Book Review,* is "a pleasing coffee-table book" whose photography is "bold and sharp."

In *Talking Mysteries,* Hillerman provides readers with a unique glimpse into some of his working methods and story inspirations. The centerpiece of the book is an in-depth interview of the author by his close friend, Navajo trader and bookseller Ernie Bulow. Reviewing *Talking Mysteries* for the *Los Angeles Times Book Review,* Charles Champlin commented that Bulow's questions "evoke as good a picture of Hillerman's writing methods and philosophy as a full-dress biography might." In an interview with Patricia Holt for *Publishers Weekly,* Hillerman explained his ongoing fascination with Native American culture by noting that "it's always troubled me that the American people are so ignorant of these rich Indian cultures. For me, studying them has been absolutely fascinating, and I think it's important to show aspects of ancient Indian ways are still very much alive and are highly germane even to our ways."

BIOGRAPHICAL/CRITICAL SOURCES:

BOOKS

Bulow, Ernie, and Tony Hillerman, *Talking Mysteries: A Conversation with Tony Hillerman,* University of New Mexico Press, 1991.

PERIODICALS

Armchair Detective, fall, 1990, p. 426.

Los Angeles Times Book Review, January 21, 1990, p. 14; May 27, 1990, p. 10; December 16, 1990; November 17, 1991, p. 12; January 5, 1992, p. 9.

New York Times Book Review, December 23, 1990, p. 20; October 20, 1991, p. 36; February 2, 1992, p. 28; August 30, 1992, p. 14.

Publishers Weekly, October 24, 1980.

Tribune Books (Chicago), September 2, 1990.

Washington Post Book World, May 27, 1990, p. 12; July 26, 1992, p. 1.*

HIRSCH, Edward 1950-

PERSONAL: Born January 20, 1950, in Chicago, IL; son of Kurt and Irma (Ginsburg) Hirsch; married Janet Landay (an exhibition director), May 29, 1977; children: Gabriel. *Education:* Grinnell College, B.A., 1972; University of Pennsylvania, Ph.D., 1979.

ADDRESSES: Home—1528 Sul Ross, Houston, TX 77006. *Office*—Department of English, University of Houston, Houston, TX 77204.

CAREER: Wayne State University, Detroit, MI, assistant professor, 1979-82, associate professor of English, 1982-85; University of Houston, Houston, TX, associate professor, 1985-88, professor of English, 1988—.

MEMBER: Modern Language Association of America, Poetry Society of America, Authors League of America, Authors Guild, PEN, Phi Beta Kappa.

AWARDS, HONORS: Watson fellow, 1972-73; Academy of American Poets awards, 1975-77; Amy Lowell traveling fellow, 1978-79; Ingram Merrill Award, Ingram Merrill Foundation, 1978-79, for poetry; American Council of Learned Societies fellow, 1981; National Endowment for the Arts creative writing fellowship, 1982; National Book Critics Circle Award nomination, 1982, for *For the Sleepwalkers;* Peter I. B. Lavan Younger Poets Award, Academy of American Poets, 1983; Delmore Schwartz Memorial Poetry Award, New York University, 1985; Guggenheim poetry fellowship, 1985-86; National Book Critics Circle Award, 1987, for *Wild Gratitude;* Rome Prize, American Academy and Institute of Arts and Letters, American Academy in Rome, 1988; William Riley Parker Prize, Modern Language Association, 1992.

WRITINGS:

POETRY

For the Sleepwalkers, Knopf, 1981.
Wild Gratitude, Knopf, 1986.
The Night Parade, Knopf, 1989.
Earthly Measures, Knopf, 1994.

Contributor of articles, stories, poems, and reviews to periodicals, including *New Yorker, Poetry, American Poetry Review, Nation, New Republic, New York Times Book Review,* and *Paris Review.*

SIDELIGHTS: "I would like to speak in my poems with what the Romantic poets called 'the true voice of feeling,' " Edward Hirsch once told *CA.* "I believe, as Ezra Pound once said, that when it comes to poetry 'only emotion endures.' " Described by Peter Stitt in *Poetry* as "a poet of genuine talent and feeling," Hirsch has been highly acclaimed for his poetry collections, *For the Sleepwalkers* and *Wild Gratitude;* indeed, *For the Sleepwalkers* was nominated for the National Book Critics Circle Award in 1981 and *Wild Gratitude* won the award in 1987. The two books consist of vignettes of urban life and numerous homages to artists which, according to David Wojahn in the *New York Times Book Review,* "begin as troubled meditations on human suffering [but] end in celebration." *New Republic* contributor Jay Parini says that in *For the Sleepwalkers,* "Hirsch inhabits, poem by poem, dozens of other skins. He can become Rimbaud, Rilke, Paul Klee, or Matisse, in each case convincingly." "I admire Edward Hirsch," writes Phoebe Pettingell in the *New Leader,* "for his mystical vision, for the mastery he has . . . attained—and for his daring."

While many reviewers applaud Hirsch's poetry, saying that it goes beyond mere technique, and that it exhibits tenderness, intelligence, and musicality, they also recognize in his highly rhetorical style the propensity to "cross the borderline between effectiveness and excess," as Stitt asserts. For instance, Wojahn maintains that "Hirsch's tenderness [in *Wild Gratitude*] sometimes threatens to become merely ingratiating," and Hugh Seidman expresses in a *New York Times Book Review* article that Hirsch's first work, *For the Sleepwalkers,* is "a poetry of narcissistic invention employing exaggerated tone and metaphor," an excess that Seidman believes is typical of contemporary American poetry. Nevertheless, Parini insists that Hirsch's poems "easily fulfill Auden's request that poems be, above all else, 'memorable language,' " and Carolyn Kizer declares in the *Washington Post Book World* that Hirsch's "great strength lies in his descriptive powers." As Hirsch "learns to administer with lighter touch his considerable linguistic fertility," claims Stitt, "he will surely grow into one of the important writers of our age."

The poems in Hirsch's third book, *The Night Parade,* continue with the themes presented in his first two works, but stray from his stylistic and formal techniques, perhaps indicating a transitional period. Hirsch told *CA:* "Many of these poems are more meditative and narrative, linking the personal to the historical, contemplating the nature of family stories and expanding outward from there to consider the history and development of Chicago as a city." He added, "The passionate clarity of [my] style has not always met with critical approval." Indeed, in the *New York Times Book Review,* Stephen Dobyns remarks, "Despite several marvelous poems, *The Night Parade* doesn't seem as strong as his previous book. Too many poems become sentimental or seem willed rather than to come from the heart," but Pat Monaghan in *Booklist* praises Hirsch's "sure sense of the line between emotion and sentimentality." *New York Review of Books* critic Helen Vendler laments, "When Hirsch is not being historically stagy, he is being familially prosaic, as he recalls stories told by his parents," but also mentions Hirsch is "capable of quiet, believable poems," citing the poem "Infertility" from Hirsch's *The Night Parade* as the most believable poem of the book, and suggesting, "This poem, I suspect, will turn up in anthologies. It touches a particular connection between religious longing and secular pessimism that belongs both to the hope and desolation it commemorates and to the moment of scientific possibility and disappointment in which we live."

Hirsch told *CA:* "If I were to describe my new work, I would say that it is 'god hungry.' *Earthly Measures* is very much about what the soul does after hungering after God and He does not come. What does one do to fill the subsequent emptiness? The book begins in the dark wood with landscapes of ash and emptiness and hell. Throughout the book are elegies which point toward the loss of presence, power, and direction. The emptiness contains infertility but it is not defined by it. About halfway through the book it takes a turn—not toward celebration exactly, but a sort of agonized reconciliation. The tutelary figures are Simone Weil, Leopardi, and Hoffmansthal. The poems take the transformative and even redemptive powers of art seriously. Art stands against the emptiness. The book is about a soul-journey. It begins in 'Uncertainty' and concludes with an homage to the 17th century Dutch painters and their feeling for 'Earthly Light.' It is a pilgrim's progress struggling toward the light."

BIOGRAPHICAL/CRITICAL SOURCES:

BOOKS

Contemporary Literary Criticism, Gale, Volume 31, 1985, Volume 50, 1988.

Dictionary of Literary Biography, Volume 120: *American Poets since World War II, Third Series,* Gale, 1992.

PERIODICALS

Booklist, March 15, 1989, p. 1243.

Georgia Review, summer, 1982.

Nation, September 13, 1981, p. 14; September 27, 1986, p. 285.

New Leader, March 8, 1982.

New Republic, April 14, 1982, p. 37.

New York Review of Books, August 17, 1989, p. 26.

New York Times Book Review, September 13, 1981, p. 14; June 8, 1986, p. 38; January 28, 1990, p. 26.

Poetry, May, 1986.

Tribune Books, February 1, 1987, p. 2; August 6, 1989, p. 5.

Washington Post Book World, July 6, 1986, p. 8.

HIRSCHHORN, Howard H(arvey) 1931-

PERSONAL: Born April 26, 1931, in Baltimore, MD. *Education:* University of Miami, Coral Gables, FL, B.A., 1954; University of Florida, M.A., 1958; University of Heidelberg, certificates in basic medical sciences, 1959.

ADDRESSES: Home—6245 Maynada St., Coral Gables, FL 33146.

CAREER: U.S. Department of the Army, Office of the Surgeon-General, Washington, DC, civilian researcher in medical intelligence, 1960-61; Miami-Dade Community College, Miami, FL, instructor in English, German, and Spanish, 1961-66; senior medical writer for Norwich/Eaton, 1966-67; medical writer and editor for Hoffman-LaRoche, 1966-71; biomedical writer for Cordis Corp., 1972-73; independent technical writing consultant, 1973-80; Ciba-Geigy, Switzerland, head of medical communications, 1980-82; independent technical writing consultant, 1982-86. Part-time lecturer in scientific and technical English, University of Miami, 1975-84; Florida International University, 1986-90. Miami-Dade Community College, director of English as a Second Language writing laboratory, 1990—. *Military service:* U.S. Army, interpreter in military intelligence, 1954-57, criminalistics training officer in military police, 1964; became first lieutenant.

MEMBER: American Association of Physical Anthropologists.

WRITINGS:

Scientific and Technical German Reader, Odyssey, 1964.

Spanish-English Medical Interviewing Guide, Regents Publishing, 1968.

Technical and Scientific English for Spanish-Speaking Students, Regents Publishing, 1970.

A Jew Is . . . ("socio-psychological study of a Catholic Jew"), Christopher, 1972.

All about Rabbits, T. F. H. Publications, 1974.

All about Mice, T. F. H. Publications, 1974.

All about Rats, T. F. H. Publications, 1974.

All about Guard Dogs, T. F. H. Publications, 1976.

(With James E. Fulton) *Farewell to Pimples,* Acne Research Center, 1977.

Pain-Free Living, Parker, 1977.

The Moon Is a Heart, privately printed, 1977.

Health from the Sea, Parker, 1979.

(Translator from the German) Zimmerman, *Tropical Frogs,* T. F. H. Publications, 1979.

Writing for Science, Industry, and Technology, Van Nostrand, 1980.

Journal of the Herbalist of Erdendorf, Phoenix, 1980.

Miracle Health Secrets from the Old Country, Prentice-Hall, 1980.

The Home Herbal Doctor, Prentice-Hall, 1982.
(Self-illustrated) *In a Small Flemish Town,* privately printed, 1985.
Crocodilians of Florida and the Tropical Americas, Phoenix, 1986.
(Translator from the German) Kuehner, *Chinchillas,* T. F. H. Publications, 1987.
(Translator from the German) Untergasser, *Handbook of Fish Diseases,* T. F. H. Publications, 1989.
(Translator from the German) Aschenborn, *Finches and Their Care,* T. F. H. Publications, 1990.
Behind and Beyond Writing: Essays and Lectures on the Adventures of a "Technical Writer", Florida International University, 1990.
(Self-illustrated) *Little Pieces to Read Aloft, Afield, Afloat or Merely Adrift,* privately printed, 1991.
A Zoo Garden—Accounts and Events Told in Verse, privately printed, 1992.
(Translator from the German) Wischnath, *Atlas of Livebearers of the World,* T. F. H. Publications, 1993.

Contributor of book reviews and articles to periodicals, including *Dining Out, Current Anthropology, Journal of Ethnopharmacology, Sapporo Medical Journal, Human Biology,* and *American Journal of Physical Anthropology.*

SIDELIGHTS: Howard H. Hirschhorn told *CA:* "A patriotic letter—*I go so gladly*—to the Nashville *Tennessean* started my writing career during my freshman year in college. I've been writing ever since, through handfuls of wars, universities, wanderings, government and corporate affiliations. The stories behind and peripheral to many of the writings born of those experiences are often subjects for writing and reading themselves—although writers, surgeons, secret agents, cooks, bankers and lawyers scarcely dare to bare *all* their behind the scenes (mis)adventures.

"A bread-and-butter writer is often caught between speaking for others (yea, downright lying for hire) and speaking for himself, like John Alden. Nevertheless, a good writer climbs up out of it and eventually learns to state his own message, thanks to or despite the client world that molded or deformed him (or tried to do it). With energy, vision and daring (or impelling boredom, luck and foolhardiness), a writer can often do some molding of his own and inspire change in industry, government and scientific research, and perhaps in some lives here and there.

"Any writings of mine, both signed and anonymous, that still float about or rest in files or on shelves are an anthology of my own rebounds off of, and embraces with, that big, wide world out there just begging to be written up." Paraphrasing Pliny, "Don't let a day go by without writing or drawing a line."

BIOGRAPHICAL/CRITICAL SOURCES:

PERIODICALS

Current Anthropology, June, 1979.
Florida Anthropologist, June, 1982.

* * *

HOCHWAELDER, Fritz 1911-1986

PERSONAL: Born May 28, 1911, in Vienna, Austria; immigrated to Switzerland in 1938; died following a heart attack, October 20, 1986, in Zurich, Switzerland; son of Leonhard (an upholsterer) and Therese (Koenig) Hochwaelder; married Ursula Buchi, July 26, 1951 (divorced, 1957); married Susan Schreiner, July 20, 1960; children: (second marriage) Monique. *Education:* Attended school in Vienna, Austria.

ADDRESSES: *Home*—Am Oeschbrig 27, 8053 Zurich, Switzerland.

CAREER: Playwright. Served apprenticeship as an upholsterer in Vienna, Austria, where his first plays were performed in small theaters, 1932-36.

MEMBER: PEN (Austrian center), Societe des Auteurs (Paris), Schweizer Schriftsteller-Verein, Vereinigung Oesterreichischer Dramatiker.

AWARDS, HONORS: Literary Prize of City of Vienna, 1955; Grillparzer Prize of Austrian Academy of Sciences, 1956; Anton Wildgans Prize of Austrian Industry, 1963; Austrian State Prize for Literature, 1966; Oesterreichisches Ehrenkreuz fuer Kunst und Wissenschaft, 1971; Ehrenring der Stadt Wien, 1972.

WRITINGS:

PLAYS

Jehr, produced in Vienna at Kammerspiele, 1933.
Liebe in Florenz (comedy; title means "Love in Florence"), produced in Vienna at Theater, 1936.
Esther (five-act comedy; produced, 1940; also see below), Volksverlag Elgg, 1960.
Das heilige Experiment (five-act; produced, 1943, also produced in two acts as *Sur la Terre comme au Ciel* in Paris, and as *The Strong Are Lonely* in New York and London; also see below), Volksverlag Elgg (Zurich), 1947, translation of the French play by Eva le Gallienne published as *The Strong Are Lonely,* Samuel French, 1954, German version published in *Oesterreichisches Theater,* Buechergilde Gutenberg, 1964.
Hotel du commerce (comedy; produced, 1944; also see below), Volksverlag Elgg, 1954.

Der Fluechtling (title means "The Fugitive"; taken from a scenario by George Kaiser; produced, 1945; also see below), Volksverlag Elgg, 1955.

Meier Helmbrecht (produced, 1946; also see below), Volksverlag Elgg, 1956.

Der oeffentliche Anklaeger (three-act; produced in Stuttgart, Germany at Neues Theater, 1948; also see below), Paul Zsolnay, 1954, acting edition with translation by Kitty Black published as *The Public Prosecutor,* Samuel French, 1958; edition in German with introduction and notes by J. R. Foster in English published under original title, Methuen, 1962.

Virginia, produced in Hamburg, Germany, 1951.

Donadieu (three-act; based on the ballad "Die Fuesse im Feuer" by Conrad Ferdinand Meyer; produced at Burgtheater, 1953; also see below), Paul Zsolnay (Hamburg), 1953.

Die Herberge (three-act; title means "The Shelter;" produced at Burgtheater, 1957; also see below), Volksverlag Elgg, 1956.

Der Unschuldige (three-act comedy; title means "The Innocent One;" produced in Vienna at Burgtheater, 1958; also see below), privately printed in Zurich, 1949, Volksverlag Elgg, 1958.

Der Himbeerpfluecker (three-act comedy; produced in Zurich at Schauspielhaus, 1965; translation by Michael Bullock produced in London as *The Raspberry Picker,* 1967; also see below), Albert Langen/Georg Mueller, 1965.

Der Befehl (title means "The Command;" produced on British Broadcasting Corp. [BBC-TV], 1967; translation by Robin Hirsch published in *Modern International Drama,* Volume 3, number 2, 1970; also see below), Stiasny (Graz), 1967.

Lazaretti; oder, Der Saebeltiger (three-act; title means "Lazaretti; or, the Saber-toothed Tiger;" produced at Salzburg Festival, 1975; also see below), Verlag Styria, 1975.

Im Wechsel der Zeit: Autobiographische Skizzen und Essays, Verlag Styria, 1980.

Die Prinzessin von Chimay (three-act comedy; also see below), Verlag Styria, 1981.

Der verschwundene Mond (also see below), produced, 1982.

Die Buergschaft (also see below), first produced, 1984.

Also author of radio play *Der Reigen* based on the play *Weinsberger Ostern 1525* by Arthur Schnitzler; author of unproduced plays *Die verschleierte Frau* (title means "The Veiled Woman"), 1946, and *Schicksalskomoedie* (title means "A Comedy of Fate"), 1960.

PLAY COLLECTIONS

Dramen I (includes "Das heilige Experiment," "Die Herberge," and "Donnerstag;" "Donnerstag" produced in Salzburg at Landestheater, July 29, 1959), Albert Langen/Georg Mueller (Munich and Vienna), 1959.

Dramen II (includes "Der oeffentliche Anklaeger," "Der Unschuldige," and "1003;" "1003" first produced in Vienna at Theater in der Josefstadt, 1964), Albert Langen/Georg Mueller, 1964.

Dramen (includes "Das heilige Experiment," "Die Herberge," and "Der Himbeerpfluecker"), Albert Langen/Georg Mueller, 1968.

Stuecke (includes "Das heilige Experiment," "Die Herberge," "Der Unschuldige," and "Der Himbeerpfluecker"), [Berlin], 1968.

Dramen, Verlag Styria (Graz), Volume 1 (includes "Esther," "Das heilige Experiment," "Hotel du commerce," "Meier Helmbrecht," and "Der oeffentliche Anklaeger"), 1975, Volume 2 (includes "Donadieu," "Die Herberge," "Der Unschuldige," "Der Himbeerpfluecker," and "Der Befehl"), 1975, Volume 3 (includes "Die unziemliche Neugier," "Der Fluechtling," "Donnerstag," "1003," and "Lazaretti; oder, Der Saebeltiger"), 1979, Volume 4 (includes "Die Prinzessin von Chimay," "Der verschwundene Mond," and "Die Buergschaft"), 1985.

ENGLISH TRANSLATIONS

(Contributor) Martin Esslin, translator, *The New Theater of Europe* (includes "Das heilige Experiment," "Der oeffentliche Anklaeger," "Donadieu," "Die Herberge," and "Der Himbeerpfluecker"), Delta, 1970.

The Public Prosecutor and Other Plays, Ungar, 1979.

ADAPTATIONS: The Public Prosecutor was adapted for television and presented on the *US Steel Hour,* 1958.

SIDELIGHTS: Fritz Hochwaelder presented unusual twists of religious and moral themes in *Das heilige Experiment* and most of his later plays. According to Frederick Lumley, the Viennese-born playwright first attracted attention in 1952 when *Das heilige Experiment* was presented in Paris, where it "caused an immediate stir through the relationship of its theme with that of the worker-priest controversy then topical." Lumley mentioned Hochwaelder's constant experiment both in ideas and form; the play *1003,* for instance, has only two characters—the author and his imagination, with the author in the process of losing his creation, who seems more alive than himself. The development of Hochwaelder, Lumley said, "makes him not only an important dramatist for the German-speaking theater, but together with Duerrenmatt and Frisch, also living in Switzerland, and Peter Weiss, another 'exile' living in Sweden, it may be said that the most interesting living dramatists anywhere today are to be found in these [four] representatives of the German language." Three of Hochwaelder's plays have been published in Buenos Aires, and several in Paris.

BIOGRAPHICAL/CRITICAL SOURCES:

BOOKS

Contemporary Literary Criticism, Volume 36, Gale, 1986.
Demetz, Peter, *Post-War German Literature,* Western Publishing, 1970.
Feret, H. M., *"Sur la terre comme au ciel," le vrai drame de Hochwaelder,* Edition du Cerf, 1953.
Litteratur du vingtieme siecle, Volume 4, Casterman, 1960.
Lumley, Frederick, *New Trends in 20th Century Drama,* Oxford University Press, 1967.
McGraw-Hill Encyclopedia of World Drama, 2nd edition, McGraw, 1984.
Wellwarth, George, *The Theater of Protest and Paradox,* New York University Press, 1964.

OBITUARIES:

PERIODICALS

Times (London), October 24, 1986.*

* * *

HODGE, P. W.
See HODGE, Paul W(illiam)

* * *

HODGE, Paul W(illiam) 1934-
(P. W. Hodge)

PERSONAL: Born November 8, 1934, in Seattle, WA; son of Paul H. and Frances (Bakeman) Hodge; married Ann Uran, June 14, 1962; children: Paul Gordon, Erik Christopher, Sandra Ann. *Education:* Yale University, B.S., 1956; Harvard University, Ph.D., 1960.

ADDRESSES: Home—Seattle, WA. *Office*—Department of Astronomy, FM-20, University of Washington, Seattle, WA 98195.

CAREER: Harvard University, Cambridge, MA, teaching fellow, 1956-58, Agassiz Fellow, 1957-58, 1959-60, Margaret Weyerhauser Jewitt Fellow, 1958-59, Parker Fellow, 1959-60, lecturer in astronomy, 1960-61; California Institute of Technology, Pasadena, CA, research fellow, 1960-61; University of California, Berkeley, instructor, 1961-62, assistant professor of astronomy, 1962-65; University of Washington, Seattle, associate professor, 1965-69, professor of astronomy, 1969—, associate dean, 1971-73, 1978-79, chair of department, 1987—. Physicist, Smithsonian Astrophysical Observatory, 1966-69. Member of board of directors, Astronomical Society of the Pacific, 1968-74, vice-president, 1973-74; section chairman, American Association for the Advancement of Science, 1978-79, 1984-85.

MEMBER: International Astronomical Union (member of organizing committee), American Astronomical Society, American Association for the Advancement of Science (section chairman, 1978-79, 1984-85), American Geophysical Union, Astronomical Society of the Pacific (board of directors, 1968-74; vice-president, 1973-74), Committee on Space Research of International Council of Scientific Unions, Meteoritical Society.

AWARDS, HONORS: Beckwith Prize, 1956; National Science Foundation post-doctoral fellow, Mt. Wilson and Mt. Palomar Observatories, CA, 1960-61; National Science Foundation fellow, 1960-61; Bart J. Bok Prize, 1962; Professional and Scholarly Publishing Division award for Physical Science, Association of American Publishers, 1986, for *Galaxies.*

WRITINGS:

(With J. C. Brandt) *Solar System Astrophysics,* McGraw, 1963.
Galaxies and Cosmology, McGraw, 1966.
An Atlas and Catalog of HII Regions in Galaxies, University of Washington Press, 1966.
(With Frances W. Wright) *The Large Magellanic Cloud,* Smithsonian Press, 1967.
Concepts of the Universe, McGraw, 1969.
The Revolution in Astronomy, Holiday House, 1970.
(Reviser) Harlow Shapley, *Galaxies,* Harvard University Press, 1972.
Astronomy Study Guide, McGraw, 1973.
(Author of text) *Slides for Astronomy,* McGraw, 1973.
Concepts of Contemporary Astronomy, McGraw, 1974, 2nd edition, 1978.
(With Wright) *The Small Magellanic Cloud,* with supplement, University of Washington Press, 1977.
An Atlas of the Andromeda Galaxy, University of Washington Press, 1981.
(Under name P. W. Hodge) *Interplanetary Dust,* Gordon & Breach, 1981.
(Editor) *The Universe of Galaxies,* Freeman, 1984.
(Contributor) *Space and Mankind,* State Institute of Science Education (India), 1984.
(Contributor) S. van den Bergh and K. de Boer, editors, *Structure and Evolution of the Magellanic Clouds,* Reidel, 1984.
(Contributor) H. van Woerden and others, editors, *Milky Way Galaxy,* Reidel, 1985.
(Contributor) C. de Loore, A. Willis, and P. Laskarides, editors, *Luminous Stars and Associations in Galaxies,* Reidel, 1986.
Galaxies, Harvard University Press, 1986.

The Andromeda Galaxy, Kluwer Academic, 1992.

Contributor to *Encyclopedia of Science and Technology,* 6th edition, McGraw, 1984. Contributor of about three hundred papers to astronomy journals. Editor, *Astronomical Journal,* 1984—.

Concepts of the Universe was translated into Spanish.

*WORK IN PROGRESS: Meteorite Craters.**

* * *

HOFF, H. S.
See COOPER, William

* * *

HOLDER, John, Jr. 1947-1985 (Jackie Curtis)

PERSONAL: Professionally known as Jackie Curtis; born February 19, 1947, in Stony Creek, TN; died of a drug overdose, May 15, 1985, in New York, NY; son of John B. (a Veterans' Administration worker) and Jean (a certified public accountant; maiden name, Uglialoro) Holder; married Eric Emerson, July 21, 1969 (divorced June 6, 1970); married Artchie Dukeshire, October 28, 1970 (divorced April 17, 1971); married Hunter Robert Cayce, November 27, 1971 (divorced January 5, 1972); married Hiram Keller, February 14, 1972 (divorced March 1, 1973); married Lance Loud, June 9, 1973 (divorced August 7, 1975); married Peter Rufus Groby, December 24, 1976 (divorced May 14, 1978); married Kevin McPhee (a publicity manager), July 23, 1980. *Education:* Hunter College of the City University of New York, B.A., 1975; studied at Lee Strassberg's Actors' Studio, 1975-76. *Politics:* "Ever since I said I do, I don't." *Religion:* Roman Catholic-Free Will Baptist.

CAREER: Typist in New York City, 1964; cloak room attendant and elevator operator in Broadway theatres, 1965; Jackie Curtis Productions Unltd., New York City, president, 1979-85. Performer in stage plays, including *Scrooge,* 1965, *This Was Burlesque,* 1966, *The Life of Lady Godiva,* 1968-69, *Les Precieuses Ridicules,* 1972, and *A Modern Hamlet,* 1972; performer in all of his own plays and films; co-director with Roz Kelly of *Lucky Wonderful,* 1968, and director of *Vain Victory,* 1971.

AWARDS, HONORS: Three playwright honorarium awards from La Mama Experimental Theatre Club and other companies, 1971; Soho Arts Award nomination, 1980.

WRITINGS:

UNDER PSEUDONYM JACKIE CURTIS; PLAYS

Glamour, Glory and Gold: The Life and Legend of Nola Noonan, Goddess and Star, first produced in New York City, 1967.

Lucky Wonderful: Thirteen Musicals about Tommy Manville, first produced in New York City, 1968.

Heaven Grand in Amber Orbit, first produced in New York City, 1969.

Femme Fatale: The Three Faces of Gloria, first produced Off-Broadway at La Mama Experimental Theatre Club, 1970.

Vain Victory: The Vicissitudes of the Damned (first produced in New York City), published in *The Great American Family,* WNET-TV, 1972.

UNDER PSEUDONYM JACKIE CURTIS; SCREENPLAYS

Flesh, Andy Warhol Enterprises, 1967.

Big Badge: The Brigid Polk Detective Story, Andy Warhol Enterprises, 1970.

WR—Mysteries of the Organism, Cinema Five, 1971.

Tits, Larry Rivers Productions, 1971.

Women in Revolt, Andy Warhol Enterprises, 1971.

SIDELIGHTS: Jackie Curtis's plays deal with sex and social values in a bizarre and exaggerated manner. Often starring in his works, and assuming the female roles, Curtis's own gender was a matter of some speculation. He once explained: "[I'm] not a boy, not a girl, not a faggot, not a drag queen, not a transsexual—just me, Jackie. I have to laugh at those people who say they feel like a woman trapped in a man's body. What is a man? What is a woman?. . . . Those sex change operations—so 1950s. I am what I feel I am."

Curtis's first play, *Heaven Grand in Amber Orbit,* is a melange of lines from comic books, Shakespeare, television scripts and commercials, old movies, and various other media. Rosalyn Regelson of the *New York Times* said of the play: "There is a script, and the players' loud declamations and frenetic staging give the disorienting impression that there must be plot and dialogue that you could follow if you knew how." Throughout *Heaven Grand,* Curtis floods the stage with simultaneous activity. While the leading female character, Heaven Grand, is dying at center stage, a set of Siamese triplets cavorts lewdly about while other cast members lecture from a toilet seat.

Because of their deviance from theatrical norms, Curtis's plays have received mixed reviews. Regelson, commenting on Curtis's knack for mocking established social values, wrote: "For those in the audience who consider the old social values unfunctional, the actors are performing a satisfying rite of destruction. On the other hand, the bouyant nihilism of this theater, which communicates itself so directly to the audience, causes those viewers who resent the attack on the basic constructs of their existence to find the performances ugly, sordid, stupid and infantile."

Mel Gussow of the *New York Times* said of *Vain Victory:* "The jokes are abysmal, but the delivery is so ingenuous as to make almost the worst line excusable. A groan of recognition from the audience! For all the cornucopian theatricality, there is a lack of ostentation. One does not leave 'Vain Victory' humming the old nostalgia, but smiling at the energetic cavortings of this single-minded troupe."

Curtis once told *CA:* "Love is an astonishing thing, even in art. It can do what no amount of culture, criticism, or intellect can do, namely, connect the most widely divergent poles, bring together what is oldest and what is newest. It transcends time by relating everything to itself as a center. It alone gives certainty, it alone is right, because it has no interest in being right. Everything in the world can be imitated or forged, everything but love. Love can be neither stolen nor imitated; it lives only in the hearts that are able to give themselves wholly. It is the source of all art. To be loved is not happiness. Every man loves himself. To love: That is happiness."

BIOGRAPHICAL/CRITICAL SOURCES:

PERIODICALS

New York Herald, June 6, 1971.
New York Record, September, 1971.
New York Times, November 2, 1969; August 25, 1971.

OBITUARIES:

PERIODICALS

Chicago Tribune, May 19, 1985.
New York Times, May 17, 1985.*

* * *

HOOPES, David S. 1928-

PERSONAL: Born July 28, 1928, in Washington, DC; son of Roy H. (a lawyer) and Lydia (a writer; maiden name, Clawson) Hoopes; married Kathleen Rogers (an editor), July 10, 1952; children: Aaron Roy, Jennifer Ellen. *Education:* Attended University of Utah, 1946-48; George Washington University, B.A. (with honors), 1950; Harvard University, M.A., 1951, further graduate study, 1951-53.

ADDRESSES: Home—130 North Road, Vershire, VT 05079.

CAREER: Governmental Affairs Institute, Washington, DC, program officer, 1958-60; New England Book Service, Vershire, VT, proprietor, 1960-63; University of Pittsburgh, Pittsburgh, PA, assistant director of Office of Cultural and Educational Exchange, director of Pittsburgh International Seminars, and director of Intercultural Communications Workshop Program, 1964-68; Regional Council for International Education, Pittsburgh, vice-president, 1968-72, executive vice-president, 1972-73; Intercultural Communications Network, Pittsburgh, founder and executive director, 1970-80; Intercultural Press, Vershire, editor in chief and chairman of board of directors, 1980—. Director of Japan-U.S. Intercultural Communication Workshop Project, 1973-74; founder and executive secretary of Society for Intercultural Education, Training, and Research (SIETAR), 1974-78; co-director of Stanford University's Training Workshop for Intercultural Communication Facilitators and Programming Specialists, 1976; director of Project to Study the State of Intercultural Education, Training, and Research, 1976-77; president of Intercultural Network, Inc.; member of International Consultant's Foundation; consultant to Agency for International Development, U.S. Department of State, and Center for Human Resources Planning and Development. *Military service:* U.S. Army, Counter-Intelligence Corps, 1953-55.

WRITINGS:

(Editor with George Renwick and Paul Pedersen) *Overview of Intercultural Education, Training, and Research,* Society for Intercultural Education, Training, and Research, Volume I: *Theory,* 1977, Volume II: *Education and Training,* 1978, Volume III: *Special Research Areas,* 1978.

(Editor with Paul Ventura) *Intercultural Sourcebook: Cross-Cultural Training Methodologies,* Intercultural Press, 1979.

(Contributor) Margaret D. Pusch, editor, *Multicultural Education: The Cross-Cultural Training Approach,* Intercultural Press, 1979.

The Nature of Intercultural Education, Phi Delta Kappa, 1980.

Global Guide to International Business, Facts on File, 1983.

Global Guide to International Education, Facts on File, 1984.

(With Roy Hoopes) *The Making of a Mormon Apostle: The Story of Rudger Clawson,* Madison Books, 1990.

(With Kathleen R. Hoopes) *Guide to International Education in the United States,* Gale Research, 1991.

(With K. R. Hoopes) *Global Guide to International Education* (2nd edition), Gale Research, 1991.

Editor of series "Readings in International Communication," Intercultural Communication Network, 1970-76. Contributor of articles and stories to magazines, including *American Heritage, Seventeen,* and the *Bridge.* Editor of

Communique: Newsletter of Intercultural Communication, 1970-78.

SIDELIGHTS: David S. Hoopes once told *CA:* "I wished to be a writer from a very early age (when my eighth-grade teacher told me I already wrote better than Erle Stanley Gardner, whom I had praised inordinately in class). I had little success with the fiction I attempted, however, and so after graduate school, the army, and a few years on a hilltop in Vermont, I turned to other pursuits.

"I first became interested in intercultural communication when, from 1958 to 1960, I worked with foreign nationals visiting the United States as guests of the U.S. Government. Though I had been hired in part on the assumption that my training in the history of American civilization would enable me to communicate effectively about the United States with our visitors, I soon learned otherwise. The values and perspectives derived from my formal education were, I discovered, thoroughly ethnocentric, quite narrowly culture-bound, and more of a hindrance to communication than a help. Something else was needed.

"I did not fully understand what until I joined the international education staff at the University of Pittsburgh and began to have extensive contact with foreign students and faculty there. What I learned was that the process of intercultural communication (interaction between or among people with substantially different cultural backgrounds) is strongly influenced by culturally conditioned assumptions, values, perceptions, behaviors, and communication styles that are for the most part either unconsciously adhered to, taken as universal and therefore taken for granted, or assumed to be 'right' and thus superior. This disposition to make assumptions and attributions leads us astray in almost any kind of communication, but becomes more severe the greater the cultural difference between those attempting to communicate.

"Once I understood this process and its implications for the future of our 'global village,' I turned my attention as much as I could to fostering increased awareness of intercultural issues in the educational community and in the society at large. Thus came the establishment of the Intercultural Network, the founding of SIETAR, and the creation of the Intercultural Press—all of which, of course, were done with the support of others who were as convinced as I was of the significance of the subject.

"The results of our work can be seen in the development of new educational programs and approaches, the expansion of cross-cultural training in international businesses, and an increased awareness of intercultural issues among such people as international affairs specialists, technical advisers, health-care providers, officers of international volunteer agencies such as the Peace Corps, counselors and social workers, and missionaries. We have come a long way since 1965 when it was difficult simply to get people to understand what I was talking about. Now things are referred to as 'intercultural' and 'cross-cultural' in the daily newspapers, and 'culture shock' is a household phrase.

"Founding the Intercultural Press was particularly gratifying to me. I had many times in my life quipped that the only thing I resented about my father was that he didn't leave me a publishing house. It is curious that I should create my own. Also interesting was that I found—as I am sure many other writers have—that I enjoy editing almost as much as writing.

"I do continue to write, however, and am working on a series of novels with my son, Aaron R. Hoopes. The biography of my grandfather, Rudger Clawson, which I wrote with my brother, Roy Hoopes (also a writer and biographer), was especially enjoyable. Clawson was a member of the Mormon hierarchy, the Quorum of the Twelve Apostles, from 1898 to 1943 and at his death was in line to become its next president. In 1884 he became the first person to be convicted of polygamy under the Edmunds Act of 1883, a law which constituted the opening salvo in the federal government's final, and successful, attack on the practice of polygamy by the Mormons. The trial was marked by the dramatic capture and testimony of his second wife (who had gone underground and was pregnant) and by his stirring declamation to the court on freedom of religion—which earned him the harshest sentence the judge could mete out, four years in the penitentiary, of which he served slightly over three. He had earlier enjoyed a period of notoriety when, as a twenty-two year-old missionary in Georgia, he faced down a mob that had murdered his missionary companion, Joseph Standing, and was preparing to murder him as well."

* * *

HORNE, Donald (Richmond) 1921-

PERSONAL: Born December 26, 1921, in Sydney, Australia; son of David (a teacher) and Florence (Carpenter) Horne; married Myfanwy Jane Anna Gollan (a writer), March 22, 1960; children: Julia Jane, Nicholas Ross. *Education:* Attended University of Sydney, 1939-41, and Canberra University College (now Australian National University), 1944-45.

ADDRESSES: Home—53 Grosvenor St., Woollahra, Sydney, New South Wales 2025, Australia. *Office*—University of New South Wales, Sydney, New South Wales 2035, Australia.

CAREER: Diplomatic cadet, 1944-45; *Daily Telegraph,* Sydney, Australia, political correspondent, general reporter, and feature writer, 1946-49; free-lance writer, 1950-52; Associated Newspapers, London, England, foreign correspondent, 1952-53; Australian Consolidated Press, Sydney, foreign correspondent in London, 1953-54, managing editor of subsidiary publications in Sydney, 1954-62; Jackson Wain (advertising agency), Sydney, creative director, 1963-66; *Bulletin,* Sydney, editor, 1967-72; University of New South Wales, Kensington, research fellow at School of Political Science, 1973-75, senior lecturer, 1975-80, associate professor, 1980-84, professor, 1984-86, professor emeritus of political science, 1987—. Chancellor, University of Canberra, 1992—. Chairman of International Seminar on Literary Journals and Journals of Opinion, 1962, Copyright Agency Ltd., 1983-84, Australia Council, 1985-90, and Ideas for Australia Committee, 1991—. Member of Australian Institute of International Affairs; member of organizing committee of Quadrant Seminar on Development in South East Asia, Kuala Lumpur, 1966. New South Wales Cultural Grants Advisory Council, member, 1976-79, chairman of history, literature, broadcasting, and film committee; convener of National Conference for a Democratic Constitution, 1977, National "Change the Rules" Conference, 1980, and National Ideas Summit, 1990. Deputy chairman, Australian Republican Movement, 1991—. *Military service:* Australian Imperial Forces, 1942-44.

MEMBER: Australian Society of Authors (member of council, 1982—; president, 1984-85), Australian Studies Association, Australasian Political Studies Association, Australian Institute of International Affairs, Arts Action Australia.

AWARDS, HONORS: Order of Australia, 1982; D.Litt., University of New South Wales, 1986; D. Univ., Griffin University, 1991.

WRITINGS:

The Lucky Country, Penguin, 1964, 4th edition, 1971.
The Permit (novel), Sun Books, 1965.
The Education of Young Donald (autobiography), Angus & Robertson, 1967, Sun Books, 1968, revised edition, 1988.
(With David Beal) *Southern Exposure,* Collins, 1967.
God Is an Englishman, Penguin, 1969.
The Next Australia, Angus & Robertson, 1970.
But What If There Are No Pelicans? (novel), Angus & Robertson, 1971.
The Australian People, Angus & Robertson, 1972.
Death of the Lucky Country, Penguin, 1976.
Money Made Us, Penguin, 1976.
His Excellency's Pleasure, Thomas Nelson, 1977.
Power from the People, Victorian Fabian Society, 1977.
Right Way, Don't Go Back, Sun Books, 1978.
In Search of Billy Hughes, Macmillan, 1979.
Time of Hope: Australia, 1966-1972, Angus & Robertson, 1980.
Winner Take All?, Penguin, 1981.
(With E. Thompson) *Changing the System,* Australasian Political Studies Association, 1981.
The Great Museum: The Re-Presentation of History, Pluto Press, 1984.
Confessions of a New Boy, Viking, 1985.
The Story of the Australian People, Reader's Digest Association, 1985.
The Public Culture, Pluto Press, 1986.
The Lucky Country Revisited, Dent, 1987.
Portrait of an Optimist, Penguin, 1988.
Ideas for a Nation, Pan, 1989.
(Editor) *The Intelligent Tourist,* Margaret Gee, 1993.

Contributor to numerous books, including *Australian Civilization,* edited by Peter Coleman, F. W. Cheshire, 1962; *Introducing Australia,* edited by Hammond Innes, Deutsch, 1971; *The Pieces of Australian Politics,* edited by Richard Lucy, Macmillan, 1975; *Resource Development and the Future of Australian Society,* edited by S. Harris, Australian National University, 1982; *Australia: The Daedalus Symposium,* edited by R. Graubard, Angus & Robertson, 1985; and *Shooting the Pianist,* edited by Philip Parsons, Cunnenin Press, 1987.

Also contributor to *World Book Encyclopedia* and *Australian Encyclopedia.* Contributor to magazines and newspapers. Editor of Sydney periodicals, *Observer,* 1958-61, and *Bulletin,* 1961-62; co-editor of *Quadrant,* 1963-66; *Australian Encyclopedia,* advisory editor, 1973-86, chairman of advisory board, 1986-88; contributing editor of *Newsweek International,* 1973-76.

WORK IN PROGRESS: An autobiographical memoir.

SIDELIGHTS: Donald Horne told *CA:* "One of the results of my writing books has been the way it has changed me. I sit there and think, 'What could I possibly believe?' Later, when it is done, I think, 'Could I possibly believe that?' Too late.

"Although I do big sweeps of new reading, giving myself the chance for new perspectives, a lot of my developing has been inner-driven, not reactive, although done, of course, in a social context. For example, a big year of change for me—a definite program of change, observed and recorded in a diary—was 1972. That was the year of the eye operation that resulted in two-and-a-half months of recovery, mishaps, and the like that gave me a definite point of departure."

BIOGRAPHICAL/CRITICAL SOURCES:

PERIODICALS

British Book News, February, 1985.

Journal of Historical Geography, January, 1986.
New Statesman, November 26, 1965; March 1, 1968.
Times Literary Supplement, February 22, 1968; April 19, 1985.

* * *

HORSLEY, David
See BINGLEY, David Ernest

I-J

ISSAWI, Charles Philip 1916-

PERSONAL: Born March 15, 1916, in Cairo, Egypt; son of Elias (a civil servant) and Alexandra (Abouchar) Issawi; married Janina M. Haftke (a student adviser), July 20, 1946. *Education:* Oxford University, B.A., 1937, M.A., 1944. *Religion:* Greek Orthodox.

ADDRESSES: *Home*—97 Castle Howard Ct., Princeton, NJ 08540. *Office*—Department of Near Eastern Studies, Princeton University, Princeton, NJ 08544.

CAREER: Ministry of Finance, Cairo, Egypt, secretary, 1937-38; National Bank of Egypt, Cairo, chief of research, 1938-43; American University of Beirut, Beirut, Lebanon, assistant professor, 1943-47; United Nations, New York City, economic affairs officer, 1948-55; Columbia University, New York City, professor of economics, 1957-75, director of Middle East Institute, 1962-64; Princeton University, Princeton, NJ, professor of Near Eastern Studies, 1975-86; New York University, visiting professor, 1986-91. Consultant to United Nations and affiliated Food and Agricultural Organization, New York City and Rome, Italy, 1955, 1956, 1959-65.

MEMBER: Council on Foreign Relations, American Economic Association, Economic History Association, Middle East Studies Association (former president).

AWARDS, HONORS: Guggenheim fellow, 1961-62, 1968-69; Social Science Research Council fellow, 1962, 1969; LL.D., American University, Cairo, 1987.

WRITINGS:

Egypt: An Economic and Social Analysis, Royal Institute of International Affairs, 1947.

An Arab Philosophy of History, J. Murray, 1950.

Egypt at Mid-Century, Royal Institute of International Affairs, 1954.

Mushkilat qaumia, Dar al Hayat, 1958.

(With M. Yeganeh) *The Economics of Middle East Oil,* Praeger, 1962.

Egypt in Revolution, Royal Institute of International Affairs, 1963.

The Economic History of the Middle East, 1800-1914, University of Chicago Press, 1966.

The Economic History of Iran, 1800-1914, University of Chicago Press, 1971.

Issawi's Laws of Social Motion, Hawthorn, 1973, expanded edition, Darwin Press, 1991.

The Economic History of Turkey, 1800-1914, University of Chicago Press, 1980.

The Arab Legacy, Darwin Press, 1981.

An Economic History of the Middle East and North Africa, Columbia University Press, 1982.

The Fertile Crescent, 1800-1914, Oxford University Press, 1988.

Ta'amulat fi al-tarikh al'arabi, [Beirut], 1991.

(With Cyril E. Black and others) *Rebirth, A History of Europe since World War II,* Westview Press, 1992.

Contributor to symposia and to economic journals in the United States, Britain, Egypt, and Lebanon. Member of editorial board, *Middle East Journal* and *International Journal of Middle East Studies.*

WORK IN PROGRESS: A long-term project on the economic history of the fertile crescent.

SIDELIGHTS: Charles Philip Issawi told *CA:* "In addition to my main line of work, the economics and economic history of the Middle East, I have always been interested in such questions as: What are the causes of the economic and cultural retardation of the Middle East? When did this begin to manifest itself, and in what forms? What has been the effect of the impact of the West on the Middle East? In what ways has the region adapted itself to this challenge? I have sought to answer some of these questions in a variety of essays and articles published in symposia and journals. I am also very fond of poetry and, at various times, have tried my hand at translating Arabic and German poetry into English verse; some of this has been published in anthologies or articles."

BIOGRAPHICAL/CRITICAL SOURCES:

PERIODICALS

Times Literary Supplement, December 31, 1982.

* * *

JACOBY, Russell 1945-

PERSONAL: Born April 23, 1945, in New York, NY; married Naomi Glauberman (a writer); children: Sarah and Sam. *Education:* Attended University of Chicago, 1963-64; University of Wisconsin—Madison, B.A., 1967; University of Rochester, M.A., 1968, Ph.D., 1974; graduate study at Ecole Pratique des Hautes Etudes, 1969-70.

ADDRESSES: *Home*—32 Breeze Ave., Venice, CA 90291.

CAREER: Boston University, Boston, MA, lecturer in social science, 1974-75; Brandeis University, Waltham, MA, scholar-in-residence, 1975-76; University of California, Los Angeles, lecturer in history, 1976-79; University of California, Irvine, visiting assistant professor of history, 1979-80; Simon Fraser University, Vancouver, British Columbia, Canada, visiting associate professor of humanities, 1983-84; Lonergan University College/Liberal Arts College, Concordia University, Montreal, Quebec, Canada, visiting scholar/associate professor, 1985-86; University of California, San Diego, visiting senior lecturer, 1986-87; University of California, Riverside, visiting associate professor of history, 1988-90; University of California, Los Angeles, visiting associate professor of history, 1992—. Member of State of the Humanities Advisory Group, National Endowment for the Humanities, 1988.

MEMBER: International Pessimists Society (vice-president, 1975-78; chairman, credentials committee, 1983-84; executive secretary, 1985-90; life member, 1990—).

AWARDS, HONORS: Mellon postdoctoral fellowship, 1976-77; National Endowment for the Humanities fellowship, 1976; Guggenheim fellowship, 1980-81.

WRITINGS:

Social Amnesia: A Critique of Conformist Psychology from Adler to Laing, introduction by Christopher Lasch, Beacon Press, 1975.

Dialectic of Defeat: Contours of Western Marxism, Cambridge University Press, 1981.

The Repression of Psychoanalysis: Otto Fenichel and the Political Freudians, Basic Books, 1983.

The Last Intellectuals: American Culture in the Age of Academe, Basic Books, 1987.

Dogmatic Wisdom: How the Education and Culture Wars Have Misled America, Doubleday Anchor, in press.

Contributor of articles to anthologies, including *Critical Interruptions: New Left Perspectives on Herbert Marcuse,* edited by Paul Breines, Herder, 1970; *The Problem of Authority in America,* edited by John Diggins and M. Kann, Temple University Press, 1981; *Dictionary of Marxist Thought,* edited by T. Bottomore, Harvard University Press, 1983; *Free Associations,* edited by R. Young, Free Association Books, 1984; *Cultural Politics in Contemporary America,* edited by Ian Angus and Sut Jhally, Routledge, Chapman & Hall, 1989; *Encyclopedia of the American Left,* edited by Mari J. Buhle and others, Garland, 1990. Contributor of articles and reviews to periodicals, including *Nation, Los Angeles Times, Tikkun, Grand Street, Dissent, Telos, Voice Literary Supplement,* and *Canadian Journal of Political and Social Theory.* Member of editorial boards of *Telos; Theory, Culture and Society; and Free Associations.*

Social Amnesia: A Critique of Conformist Psychology from Adler to Laing has been translated into Portuguese, Danish, Spanish, German, Italian, Dutch, Serbo-Croatian, and Slovene; *The Repression of Psychoanalysis: Otto Fenichel and the Political Freudians* into German, French, Italian, Serbo-Croatian, and Danish; and *The Last Intellectuals: American Culture in the Age of Academe* into Portuguese.

SIDELIGHTS: Educator and cultural critic Russell Jacoby has produced several controversial studies focusing on the intellectual climate in the West in the twentieth century. His book *The Repression of Psychoanalysis: Otto Fenichel and the Political Freudians,* published in 1983, appeared at a time when orthodox psychoanalysis was already coming under attack, Walter Kendrick pointed out in a *Voice Literary Supplement* review. But by concentrating on injustices on the part of orthodox psychoanalysis against the analytic pioneer Otto Fenichel, Jacoby took a significantly different tack from other writers. Praising Jacoby for this approach, Kendrick wrote: "Alone among the newest crusaders [against psychoanalysis], Russell Jacoby has made the better effort: his *Repression of Psychoanalysis* isn't content with simple stories and easy outrage. He sees psychoanalysis not as the dastardly deed of a wicked individual, but as a discipline of thought developing through history, acted upon by many forces both good and evil. The pernicious sterility of contemporary psychoanalysis is due, for Jacoby, to a plot unfolding across three generations and employing scores of actors. The plot had no spinner, but it's no less tragic for that."

Many critics likened the impact of Jacoby's 1987 book, *The Last Intellectuals: American Culture in the Age of Academe,* to that of Allan Bloom's concurrent bestseller, *The Closing of the American Mind.* Both authors criticized American intellectual life in the age of academic specialization, Bloom from the right, and Jacoby from the left. "Mr. Jacoby's central thesis," stated Richard Bernstein in the *New York Times,* "is that the life of the American republic has been impoverished because there are so few intellectuals these days trying to explain the world to the general public. . . . [T]he younger generation of thinkers . . . lives in a straitjacket of professionalized academic jargon incomprehensible to nonspecialists." The high cost of living has forced the younger generation of intellectuals to seek academic careers, "and the university," Bernstein summarized, "imposes a dull conformity on the community of scholars." Jacoby argued that while the previous generation vaunted such "public intellectuals" as Edmund Wilson, Mary McCarthy, William F. Buckley, Jr., and Alfred Kazin, who wrote distinguished criticism for a relatively broad audience, in Jacoby's own generation there were very few intellectuals known to the public at large. Like several other reviewers, Bernstein noted Jacoby's personal bravery in writing a book that, by attacking the academic establishment, would make it harder for the author to obtain an academic position. Interviewed by Bernstein, Jacoby himself called his book "suicidal" and conceded, "It's clear that this was not a smart book to write if you're looking for the call from some university." More than one reviewer noted that Jacoby himself had moved from college to college several times during his teaching career without obtaining tenure.

While many critics took exception to various aspects of Jacoby's argument, the author won praise for raising timely and courageous questions. Writing in *Time,* Ezra Bowen suggested that Jacoby made "too narrow a case," concentrating on sociology, economics, and literary criticism at the expense of science, history, and law. He applauded Jacoby, however, for pointing out the hostility of university faculties toward professors who achieve popular success and the difficulty of earning a living as a free-lance critic. Reviewing the book for *Washington Post Book World,* Jonathan Yardley suggested that Jacoby focused too single-mindedly on the influence of academia, thus ignoring other factors—in particular, the impact of television and "the commercialization of the cultural and intellectual marketplace"—that would "bolster his overall argument." On the whole, however, Yardley found the book "both pertinent and welcome." Louis Menand, on the other hand, took Jacoby to task in the *New Republic* for seeming to view the word "intellectual" as synonymous with "radical," and suggested that the decline of the "new Left" intellectual movement of the 1960s might simply reflect the weakness of the movement's ideas.

Writing in the *New York Times,* Christopher Lehmann-Haupt criticized Jacoby for not placing the situation in contemporary America within a broader historical and cultural context. Thus, he claimed, the author had not demonstrated whether the perceived decline in America's intellectual life was a "unique" phenomenon or a cyclical one, whether it was, indeed, a decline, or merely a shift in the forms of discourse—from print to television, for instance. The *New York Times* reviewer, however, mentioned other aspects of Jacoby's book with approval, particularly such "interesting digressions" as the author's "scathing critiques of academic writing."

Reviewing the book in the *Nation,* Casey Blake called *The Last Intellectuals* "simultaneously too much and too little. Too much because Jacoby's style grows a bit wearisome after 200 pages," and "too little because the publication of a critical manifesto as a book promises a degree of historical analysis and comprehensiveness that Jacoby cannot deliver." Agreeing with Jacoby on the increasing "academicism of intellectual life," Blake decried the absence from Jacoby's argument of a discussion of minority, feminist, and religious intellectuals, as opposed to "radicals" and "Marxists." Blake also observed, "Jacoby is at his best when speaking in his own voice on recent trends in American culture. His discussions of the intellectual consequences of suburbanization and gentrification are superb, as are his original observations on the legendary—and to Jacoby's mind, overrated—'New York intellectuals.' " Despite the book's shortcomings, Blake felt that "it would be tragic if Jacoby's argument were ignored. . . . Those who don't mind his pitch and timbre would do well to listen—and then yell right back." Merle Rubin's *Christian Science Monitor* review also suggested that Jacoby's ideas were too important to overlook. "Written in the lively, pungent style that characterizes the best work of intellectuals intent on addressing a public audience, *The Last Intellectuals,*" Rubin concluded, "is a spirited, curiously invigorating investigation of a dispiriting phenomenon, a reminder of the critical spirit that is not only missing but also very much missed."

BIOGRAPHICAL/CRITICAL SOURCES:

BOOKS

Jacoby, Russell, *The Last Intellectuals: American Culture in the Age of Academe,* Basic Books, 1987.

Twentieth-Century Literary Criticism, Volume 30, Gale, 1989, pp. 182-187.

PERIODICALS

Christian Science Monitor, November 3, 1987.

Los Angeles Times Book Review, October 4, 1987, p. 15.
Nation, October 31, 1987, pp. 493-495.
New Republic, November 9, 1987, pp. 33-34, 36.
New York Times, October 5, 1987; December 28, 1987.
New York Times Book Review, October 25, 1987, p. 44.
Telos, summer, 1982.
Time, November 30, 1987, p. 70.
Voice Literary Supplement, June, 1984, p. 12; September, 1987, p. 13.
Washington Post Book World, October 11, 1987, p. 3.

* * *

JAMES, Kristin
See CAMP, Candace (Pauline)

* * *

JEFFORD, Bat
See BINGLEY, David Ernest

* * *

JENNINGS, Marianne Moody 1953-

PERSONAL: Born September 11, 1953, in Johnstown, PA; daughter of James L. (an accountant) and Jennie (a housewife; maiden name, Ure) Moody; married Terry H. Jennings (an attorney), November 5, 1976; children: Sarah, Claire, and Sam. *Education:* Brigham Young University, B.S., 1974, J.D., 1977. *Politics:* Republican. *Religion:* Church of Jesus Christ of Latter-Day Saints (Mormons).

ADDRESSES: Home—Mesa, AZ. *Office*—College of Business, Arizona State University, Tempe, AZ 85287.

CAREER: Federal Public Defender's Office—District of Nevada, Las Vegas, law clerk, 1975; U.S. Attorney's Office—District of Nevada, Las Vegas, law clerk, 1976; Udall, Shumway, Blackhurst, Allen, Bentley & Lyons (law firm), Mesa, AZ, law clerk, 1976-77; Arizona State University, Tempe, assistant professor, 1977-80, associate professor, 1980-83, professor of business law, 1983—. Pacific Southwest Academy of Legal Studies in Business, executive secretary, 1988—. Public speaker and workshop leader. Member of Arizona Corporation Commission, 1984-85; member of board of directors, Arizona Girls Ranch, 1979-80; board of directors (and second vice-president), Delta Dental, Inc., 1980-81; board of directors, Arizona Public Service, founding board member, Center for National Independence in Politics, 1989—.

MEMBER: Federal Bar Association, Academy of Legal Studies in Business, Pacific Southwest Academy of Legal Studies in Business, Arizona State Bar Association, Beta Gamma Sigma (president 1985-86).

AWARDS, HONORS: Outstanding Professor, College of Business, 1981 and 1985; Burlington Northern Teaching Excellence Award, 1986.

WRITINGS:

Student Study Guide for the Legal Environment of Business, West Publishing, 1983, revised edition, 1990.
(With Frank Shipper) *Business Strategy for the Public Arena,* Greenwood Press, 1984.
Real Estate Law, Kent Publishing, 1985, revised edition, 1992.
Law for Business, West Publishing, 1986, revised edition, 1992.
Legal, Political and Global Environment of Business, Wadsworth, 1993.

Columnist for the *Arizona Republic.* Contributor of about ninety articles to business and law journals, including *Marketing News, Business Horizons, Exceptional Parent, Business Lawyer, Arizona Attorney,* and newspapers. Member of board of contributing editors, *Legal News and Views,* 1979-85; editorial board, *Journal of Legal Studies Education;* board of advisors, *Real Estate Law Journal.*

SIDELIGHTS: Marianne Moody Jennings told *CA:* "After fourteen years of writing thirty-plus-page articles with an average readership rate of seven (eight if you count my husband's use of them as a sleeping aid) for no pay, something snapped. I headed into the world of 'I write, you reject, but occasionally accept and pay.' A nice change from the academic world of 'I write, you reject with a critique that would destroy Mick Jagger's ego and accept five percent of the time in exchange for more criticism.' "

* * *

JOHNSON, Charles (Richard) 1948-

PERSONAL: Born April 23, 1948, in Evanston, IL; son of Benjamin Lee and Ruby Elizabeth (Jackson) Johnson; married Joan New (an elementary school teacher), June, 1970; children: Malik, Elizabeth. *Education:* Southern Illinois University, B.A., 1971, M.A., 1973; post-graduate work at State University of New York at Stony Brook, 1973-76.

ADDRESSES: Office—Department of English, University of Washington, Seattle, WA 98105.

CAREER: Chicago Tribune, Chicago, IL, cartoonist and reporter, 1969-70; *St. Louis Proud,* St. Louis, MO, member of art staff, 1971-72; University of Washington, Seattle, assistant professor, 1976-79, associate professor, 1979-82, professor of English, 1982—, director of creative writing program. Writer and cartoonist. Fiction editor of *Seattle Review,* 1978—. Director of Associated Writing Programs Awards Series in Short Fiction, 1979-81, member of board of directors, 1983—.

AWARDS, HONORS: Named journalism alumnus of the year by Southern Illinois University, 1981; Governors Award for Literature from State of Washington, 1983, for *Oxherding Tale;* Callaloo Creative Writing Award, 1983, for short story "Popper's Disease"; citation in *Pushcart Prize*'s Outstanding Writers section, 1984, for story "China"; Writers Guild Award for best children's show, 1986, for "Booker"; nomination for the PEN/Faulkner Award from the PEN American Center, 1987, for *The Sorcerer's Apprentice;* National Book Award for *Middle Passage,* 1990.

WRITINGS:

NOVELS

Faith and the Good Thing, Viking, 1974.
Oxherding Tale, Indiana University Press, 1982.
Middle Passage, Atheneum, 1990.

CARTOON COLLECTIONS

Black Humor (self-illustrated), Johnson Publishing, 1970.
Half-Past Nation Time (self-illustrated), Aware Press, 1972.

Contributor of cartoons to periodicals, including *Ebony, Chicago Tribune, Jet, Black World,* and *Players.*

TELEVISION SCRIPTS

"Charlie's Pad" (fifty-two-part series on cartooning), PBS, 1970.
"Charlie Smith and the Fritter Tree," PBS "Visions" series, 1978.
(With John Alman) "Booker," PBS, 1983.

Contributor of scripts to numerous television series, including "Up and Coming," PBS, 1981, and "Y.E.S., Inc.," PBS, 1983.

OTHER

The Sorcerer's Apprentice: Tales and Conjurations (short stories), Atheneum, 1986.
(Contributor) Jeff Henderson, editor, *Thor's Hammer: Essays on John Gardner,* Arkansas Philological Association, 1986.
Being and Race: Black Writing since 1970, Indiana University Press, 1988.
All This and Moonlight, (play) Samuel French, 1990.
(With Ron Chernow) *In Search of a Voice,* Library of Congress, 1991.

Work represented in anthologies, including *Best American Short Stories, 1982,* edited by John Gardner and Shannon Ravenel, Houghton, 1982. Contributor of short stories and essays to periodicals, including *Mother Jones, Callaloo, Choice, Indiana Review, Nimrod, Intro 10, Obsidian, Playboy,* and *North American Review.*

SIDELIGHTS: "Charles Johnson has enriched contemporary American fiction as few young writers can," observed *Village Voice* critic Stanley Crouch, adding that "it is difficult to imagine that such a talented artist will forever miss the big time." A graduate of Southern Illinois University, Johnson studied with the late author John Gardner, under whose direction he wrote *Faith and the Good Thing.* Though Johnson had written six "apprentice" novels prior to his association with Gardner, *Faith* was the first to be accepted for publication. Johnson professes to "share Gardner's concern with 'moral fiction' " and believes in the "necessity of young (and old) writers working toward becoming technicians of language and literary form."

Faith and the Good Thing met with an enthusiastic response from critics such as Garrett Epps of *Washington Post Book World,* who judged it "a brilliant first novel" and commended its author as "one of this country's most interesting and inventive younger writers." Roger Sale, writing in the *Sewanee Review,* had similar praise for the novel. He commented: "Johnson, it is clear, is a writer, and if he works too hard at it at times, or if he seems a little too pleased with it at other times, he is twenty-six, and with prose and confidence like his, he can do anything."

The book is a complex, often humorous, folktale account of Faith Cross, a Southern black girl traveling to Chicago in search of life's "Good Thing," which she has learned of from her dying mother. In her quest, noted *Time*'s John Skrow, Faith "seeks guidance from a swamp witch, a withered and warty old necromancer with one green and one yellow eye," who nonetheless "spouts philosophy as if she were Hegel." Skrow deemed the work a "wry comment on the tension felt by a black intellectual," and Annie Gottlieb of *New York Times Book Review* called *Faith and the Good Thing* a "strange and often wonderful hybrid—an ebullient philosophical novel in the form of a folktale-cum-black-girl's odyssey." She noted that the novel's "magic falls flat" on occasion, "when the mix . . . is too thick with academic in-jokes and erudite references," but she added that "fortunately, such moments are overwhelmed by the poetry and wisdom of the book." In conclusion, Gottlieb found the novel "flawed yet still fabulous."

Johnson described his second novel, *Oxherding Tale,* as "a modern, comic, philosophical slave narrative—a kind of dramatization of the famous 'Ten Oxherding Pictures' of

Zen artist Kakuan-Shien," which represent the progressive search of a young herdsman for his rebellious ox, a symbol for himself. The author added that the novel's style "blends the eighteenth-century English novel with the Eastern parable."

Like his first novel, Johnson's *Oxherding Tale* received widespread critical acclaim. It details the coming of age of Andrew Hawkins, a young mulatto slave in the pre-Civil War South. Andrew is conceived when, after much drinking, plantation owner Jonathan Polkinghorne convinces his black servant, George Hawkins, to swap wives with him for the evening. Unaware that the man sharing her bed is not her husband, Anna Polkinghorne makes love with George and consequentially becomes pregnant with Andrew. After the child is born Anna rejects him as a constant reminder of her humiliation, and he is taken in by George's wife, Mattie. Though he is raised in slave quarters Andrew receives many privileges, including an education from an eccentric tutor who teaches him about Eastern mysticism, socialism, and the philosophies of Plato, Schopenhauer, and Hegel.

Writing in *Literature, Fiction, and the Arts Review,* Florella Orowan called Andrew "a man with no social place, caught between the slave world and free white society but, like the hapless hero Tom Jones, he gains from his ambiguous existence the timeless advantage of the Outsider's omniscience and chimerism: he can assume whatever identity is appropriate to the situation." *Oxherding Tale* accompanies its hero on a series of adventures that include an exotic sexual initiation, an encounter with the pleasures of opium, escape from the plantation, "passing" as white, and eluding a telepathic bounty hunter called the Soulcatcher. As Michael S. Weaver observed in *Gargoyle,* Andrew "lives his way to freedom through a succession of sudden enlightenments. . . . Each experience is another layer of insight into human nature" that has "a touch of Johnson's ripe capacity for laughter." The book's climax, noted Crouch, is "remarkable for its brutality and humble tenderness; Andrew must dive into the briar patch of his identity and risk destruction in order to express his humanity."

Weaver admitted that "at times *Oxherding Tale* reads like a philosophical tract, and may have been more adequately billed as Thus Spake Andrew Hawkins." But he concluded that the novel "is nonetheless an entertaining display of Johnson's working knowledge of the opportunities for wisdom afforded by the interplay between West and East, Black and White, man and woman, feeling and knowing—all of them seeming contradictions." According to Crouch, the novel is successful "because Johnson skillfully avoids melodramatic platitudes while creating suspense and comedy, pathos and nostalgia. In the process, he invents a fresh set of variations on questions about race, sex, and freedom."

The Sorcerer's Apprentice, Johnson's collection of short stories, met with highly favorable reviews and garnered him a nomination for the PEN/Faulkner Award for fiction. "These tales," reported Michael Ventura in the *New York Times Book Review,* "are realistic without strictly adhering to realism, fantastic without getting lost in fantasy." The title story concerns a young black man, Allan, who is the son of a former slave and wishes to become a sorcerer. He is taken under wing by Rubin, an African-born member of the Allmuseri, a tribe of wizards, and must accept his heritage before winning the ability to make true magic. The book also contains "Alethia," about a black professor, seemingly well-assimilated to academia, who must deal with his past in the slums of Chicago. "The Education of Mingo" again focuses attention on the Allmuseri, and "Popper's Disease" discusses the issues of assimilation and alienation through an encounter between a black doctor and the sick extraterrestrial he is called in to treat. "It is one of the achievements of these stories," lauded Michiko Kakutani of the *New York Times,* "that, while concerned at heart with questions of prejudice and cultural assimilation, they are never parochial and only rarely didactic. Rather, Mr. Johnson has used his generous storytelling gifts and his easy familiarity with a variety of literary genres to conjure up eight moral fables that limn the fabulous even as they remain grounded in the language and social idioms of black American communities." Kakutani did not, however, extend this praise to the volume's "Moving Pictures," calling it "a tired one-liner about escapism and the movies." Ventura concurred, lamenting that Johnson's "magic wears thin" in the case of "Moving Pictures," but he asserted that "there's no risk in predicting that 'The Education of Mingo,' . . . 'Alethia' and 'The Sorcerer's Apprentice' will be anthologized for a very long time."

Johnson's fiction reached a pinnacle of success with the awarding of the National Book Award for his novel, *Middle Passage.* Arend Flick, in the *Los Angeles Times Book Review* commented, "In his highly readable though densely philosophical fiction, Johnson gives us characters forced to chart a middle passage between competing ways of ordering reality: sensual or ascetic, Marxist or Freudian, Christian or pagan. They quest for a unity of being beyond all polarities, for what the heroine of his first novel calls 'the one thing all . . . things have in common.' And happily for them and for us, they usually find it." *New York Review of Books*'s Garry Wills stated, "In the novel as in his critical writing, Johnson resists the idea of expressing 'black experience' as opposed to a black's experience of his or her inevitably multicultural world."

Like his mentor, John Gardner, Johnson's belief is, according to Flick, "that all true art is moral, not the promulgating of doctrine (which inevitably distorts morality) but the exploration and testing of values," a formula consistent with *Middle Passage.* As Flick surmised, "It's informed by a remarkably generous thesis: that racism generally, and the institution of slavery in particular, might best be seen as having arisen from political or sociological or economic causes, not . . . from pigment envy, but from a deep fissure that characterizes Western thought in general, our tendency to split the world into competing categories: matter and spirit, subject and object, good and evil, black and white." Flick concluded, "What always saves the novel from the intellectual scheme that would otherwise kill it is the sheer beauty of its language. . . . Philosophy and art are not simply joined here. They are one."

Johnson commented: "As a writer I am committed to the development of what one might call a genuinely systematic philosophical black American literature, a body of work that explores classical problems and metaphysical questions against the background of black American life. Specifically, my philosophical style is phenomenology, the discipline of Edmund Husserl, but I also have a deep personal interest in the entire continuum of Asian philosophy from the Vedas to Zen, and this perspective inevitably colors my fiction to some degree.

"I have been a martial artist since the age of nineteen and a practicing Buddhist since about 1980. So one might also say that in fiction I attempt to interface Eastern and Western philosophical traditions, always with the hope that some new perception of experience—especially 'black experience'—will emerge from these meditations."

Johnson and two fellow writers, Frank Chin and Colleen McElroy, are the subjects of a documentary film profile titled "Spirit of Place." Written by filmmaker Jean Walkinshaw, the film was first broadcast by KCTS-TV in Seattle, Washington, and has been submitted for national broadcast by the Public Broadcasting Service.

BIOGRAPHICAL/CRITICAL SOURCES:

BOOKS

Contemporary Literary Criticism, Volume 7, Gale, 1977.
Dictionary of Literary Biography, Volume 33: *Afro-American Fiction Writers After 1955,* Gale, 1984.

PERIODICALS

Atlantic, April, 1986, p. 130.
Callaloo, October, 1978; summer, 1989.
CLA Journal, June, 1978.
Forbes, March 16, 1992.
Gargoyle, June, 1978.
Literature, Fiction, and the Arts Review, June 30, 1983.
Los Angeles Times Book Review, November 21, 1982; June 24, 1990, pp. 1, 7.
Nation, September 13, 1986.
New Statesman, April 22, 1988.
New Statesman and Society, June 14, 1991.
New Yorker, December 20, 1982.
New York Review of Books, January 17, 1991.
New York Times, February 5, 1986.
New York Times Book Review, January 12, 1975; January 9, 1983; March 30, 1986; July 1, 1990; November 3, 1991.
Sewanee Review, January, 1975.
Time, January 6, 1975.
Times Literary Supplement, January 6, 1984.
Tribune Books (Chicago), July 8, 1990.
Village Voice, July 19, 1983.
Washington Post Book World, December 15, 1982.*

* * *

JOHNSON, Ronald 1935-

PERSONAL: Born November 25, 1935, in Ashland, KS; son of A. T. and Helen (Mayse) Johnson. *Education:* Columbia University, B.A., 1960.

ADDRESSES: Home—73 Elgin Pk., San Francisco, CA 94103.

CAREER: Poet. Has worked at various occupations. Writer-in-residence at University of Kentucky, 1971; held Roethke Chair for Poetry, University of Washington, 1973; associated with Wallace Stegner Advanced Writing Workshop, Stanford University, 1991.

AWARDS, HONORS: Inez Boulton Award, *Poetry* magazine, 1965; National Endowment for the Arts Award, 1970, 1975; National Poetry Series, 1983; Tastemaker's Award, 1985, for *The American Table.*

WRITINGS:

POETRY

A Line of Poetry, A Row of Trees, Jargon Press, 1964.
Sports and Divertissements (contains poems written by Johnson from Eric Satie's notes, in French, to the piano pieces "Sports" and "Divertissements"), Wild Hawthorn Press, 1965.
Assorted Jungles: Rousseau, Auerhahn Press, 1966.
GORSE/GOOSE/ROSE, and Other Poems, Indiana University Fine Arts Department, 1966.
The Book of the Green Man, Norton, 1967.
Valley of the Many-Colored Grasses, Norton, 1969.
Balloons for Moonless Nights (limited edition), Finial Press, 1969.
The Spirit Walks, the Rocks Will Talk, Jargon Press, 1969.
Songs of the Earth, Grabhorn-Hoyem Press, 1970.

Maze/Mane/Wane, Pomegranate Press, 1973.
Eyes and Objects, Jargon Press, 1976.
RADIOS I-IV, Sand Dollar Press, 1977.
ARK: The Foundations, Northpoint Press, 1980.
The American Table, Morrow, 1983.
ARK 50, Dutton, 1984.

COOKBOOKS

The Aficionado's Southwestern Cooking, University of New Mexico Press, 1968.
Southwestern Cooking: New and Old, University of New Mexico Press, 1985.
Simple Fare, Simon & Schuster, 1989.
Company Fare, Simon & Schuster, 1991.

CONTRIBUTOR TO ANTHOLOGIES

An Anthology of Concrete Poetry, Something Else Press, 1967.
Young American Poets, Follett, 1968.
Holding Your Eight Hands, Doubleday, 1969.
Under 30, Indiana University Press, 1969.
Inside Outer Space, Doubleday Anchor, 1970.
The Voice That Is Great Within Us: American Poetry of the Twentieth Century, Bantam, 1970.
This Book Is a Movie, Delta, 1971.
Shake the Kaleidoscope, Pocket Books, 1973.

WORK IN PROGRESS: Collected shorter poems.

SIDELIGHTS: Ronald Johnson told *CA:* "I have spent the last twenty years writing a long poem titled *ARK,* which was completed in 1991. The work consists of three books, each of thirty-three sections: titled *The Foundations, The Spires,* and *The Ramparts.* Rather than being based on literary sources (as the early *The Book of the Green Man* was based on English seasonal poems) *ARK* was inspired by . . . architectures such as The Facteur Cheval's *Palais Idéal* in Hautrives, France, and Simon Rodia's Watts Towers in Los Angeles. . . . Having completed *ARK,* I am currently working on the completion of rewriting Milton's *Paradise Lost* by excision. The first four books of this were published as *RADIOS* in 1977. It uses an 1892 edition in which I omit most of the text to create a Blakeian visual page and a new Orphic text of my own."

Charles Philbrick of the *Saturday Review* finds *The Book of the Green Man* a "most unusual volume . . . which is both original and profoundly traditional. The reader becomes absorbed in the young Kansan as he tramps through the English countryside, discovering it with eyes that record the sights of a year's visit and that have also drawn into his brain the recorded lore of centuries. . . . Mr. Johnson has worked into his poem the writings of a multitude who knew 'the green man'—from Giraldus Cambrensis to Tolkien, and including Vaughan, Smart, Blake, and the Wordsworths. This book may be called literary mistletoe, since it is both symbiotic and magical." A *Beloit Poetry Journal* writer states that the book is "tightly written and beautifully planned—a tribute to Johnson's imagination and scholarship."

Valley of the Many-Colored Grasses was generally very well received. According to Dan Jaffe of the *Saturday Review,* the poems "are frankly romantic . . . they are verbal equivalents of the Rousseau paintings that Johnson celebrates, calculated expressions of the energy of the universe. These are symbolist poems in intention, but they are informed by the facts of art and flora. Writing in an often extremely elevated diction, hardly fashionable today, Johnson utilizes words most contemporary poets shun, words like ultimate, exquisite, chaos, fronds, gorgeous, and celestial. But Johnson is no purveyor of poesy. He counterpoints carefully."

Jerome Cushman writes in the *Library Journal* that in *Valley of the Many-Colored Grasses* "Johnson does not allow himself to get sidetracked into inconsequentials but ties his art to an objective world where seeing is as practical as a Kansas sunflower and as deep as Blake's visions. The sensuality of his language contrasts strangely with the ruggedness of a Kansas heritage."

BIOGRAPHICAL/CRITICAL SOURCES:

PERIODICALS

Beloit Poetry Journal, summer, 1967.
Booklist, September 15, 1969; May 1, 1977; December 15, 1977.
Library Journal, June 1, 1969.
Listener, October 19, 1967.
New York Times Book Review, June 8, 1969.
Poetry, February, 1968; October, 1969.
Saturday Review, June 3, 1967; September 6, 1969.

* * *

JONES, Michael (Christopher Emlyn) 1940-

PERSONAL: Born December 5, 1940, in Wrexham, Wales; son of Reginald Luther and Megan Bevan (Edwards) Jones; married Elizabeth Marjorie Smith (a teacher), July 9, 1966; children: Richard Luther Caradoc. *Education:* Attended University of Leicester, 1959-60; Trinity College, Oxford, B.A., 1963, D.Phil., 1966, M.A., 1967. *Religion:* Christian.

ADDRESSES: *Home*—3 Florence Boot Close, University Park, Nottingham NG7 2QF, England. *Office*—Department of History, University of Nottingham, Nottingham NG7 2RD, England.

CAREER: University of Exeter, Exeter, England, tutor in medieval history, 1966-67; University of Nottingham, Nottingham, England, assistant lecturer, 1967-69, lecturer in European history, 1969-80, senior lecturer in European history, 1980-91, reader in French history, 1984, professor of medieval French history, 1991—.

MEMBER: Royal Historical Society (fellow; literary director, 1990—), Society of Antiquaries (fellow), Marylebone Cricket Club.

WRITINGS:

Ducal Brittany, 1364-1399, Oxford University Press, 1970.

(Translator) Philippe de Commynes, *Memoirs, 1461-1483,* Penguin, 1972.

Recueil des actes de Jean IV, duc de Bretagne (title means "Collection of the Letters of John IV, Duke of Brittany"), Klincksieck, Volume 1: *1357-1382,* 1980, Volume 2: *1383-1399,* 1983.

(Translator) Philippe Contamine, *War in the Middle Ages,* Basil Blackwell, 1984.

(Editor) John Le Patourel, *Feudal Empires: Norman and Plantagenet,* Hambledon Press, 1984.

(Editor) *Gentry and Lesser Nobility in Late Medieval Europe,* Alan Sutton, 1986.

The Creation of Brittany: A Late Medieval State, Hambledon Press, 1988.

(Editor with Malcolm Vale) *England and Her Neighbours, 1066-1453,* Hambledon Press, 1989.

(With Patrick Galliow) *The Bretons,* Basil Blackwell, 1991.

(With Cewyn Meirion-Jones) *Aimer les Chateaux de Bretagne,* Ouest-France, 1991.

Contributor to history journals. Editor, *Nottingham Medieval Studies,* 1989—.

WORK IN PROGRESS: Editing letters of Charles de Blois and Jeanne de Penthievre, Duke and Duchess of Brittany, and *New Cambridge Medieval History,* Volume 6: *The Fourteenth Century*; *The Seignenrial Domestic Buildings of Brittany, 1000-1700.*

SIDELIGHTS: Michael Jones told *CA:* "My first experience of Brittany was a childhood holiday there shortly after World War II. Interest in its history was sparked by a desire not simply to do research in medieval history but particularly to study a region which formed both then and now part of another society, the development of which paralleled and contrasted with my own. I am still exploring these differences."

In a *Times Literary Supplement* review of John Le Patourel's *Feudal Empires: Norman and Plantagenet,* J. R. Maddicot praises the scholarship and editorial skills Jones brought to these essays: "All are informed by fine and consistent scholarship and are ably edited by Michael Jones, who also contributes a perceptive and affectionate preface. Both teachers and taught will be grateful to him for bringing together so useful a collection."

BIOGRAPHICAL/CRITICAL SOURCES:

PERIODICALS

French History, Volume 3, 1989, pp. 230-232.

Globe and Mail (Toronto), September 1, 1984.

Journal of Historical Geography, Volume 15, 1989, pp. 310-312.

Memoires de la societe d'histoire et d'archeologie de Bretagne, Volume LVI, 1979.

Times Literary Supplement, January 4, 1985.

* * *

JOSEY, E(lonnie) J(unius) 1924-

PERSONAL: Born January 20, 1924, in Norfolk, VA; son of Willie J. and Frances (Bailey) Josey; married Dorothy Johnson, September 11, 1954 (divorced); children: Elaine Jacqueline. *Education:* Howard University, A.B., 1949; Columbia University, M.A., 1950; State University of New York at Albany, M.S.L.S., 1953; Shaw University, L.H.D., 1973; University of Wisconsin-Milwaukee, D.P.S., 1987; North Carolina Central University, Ph.D., 1989. *Politics:* Democrat. *Religion:* Protestant.

ADDRESSES: Home—12C Old Hickory Dr., Albany, NY 12204. *Office*—School of Library & Information Science, University of Pittsburgh, Pittsburgh, PA 15260.

CAREER: Columbia University Libraries, New York City, desk assistant, 1950-52; New York Public Library, New York City, technical assistant, 1952; Free Library of Philadelphia, Philadelphia, PA, librarian, 1953-54; Savannah State College, Savannah, GA, instructor in social science, 1954-55; Delaware State College, Dover, librarian and assistant professor of library science, 1955-59; Savannah State College, librarian and associate professor of library science, 1959-66; New York State Education Department, Division of Library Development, Albany, associate in academic and research libraries, 1966-68; chief of Bureau of Academic and Research Libraries, 1968-76; chief of Bureau of Specialist Library Services, 1976-86; University of Pittsburgh, professional school of library & information science. Savannah Public Library, member of board of managers, 1962-66. *Military service:* U.S. Army, 1943-46.

MEMBER: American Library Association (member of council, 1970-74; chair of black caucus, 1970-71; member of board of directors), Association of college and Research Libraries (chair of committee on community use of academic libraries, 1965-69), Association for the Study of Afro-American Life and History, American Academy of Political and Social Science, National Association for the Advancement of Colored People (Georgia State youth adviser, 1960-66), American Civil Liberties Union, New York Library Association, Kappa Phi Kappa, Alpha Phi Omega.

AWARDS, HONORS: American Library Association John Cotton Dana Award, 1962, 1964; Savannah State College Chapter, National Association for the Advancement of Colored People (NAACP) Award, 1964; award from national office of NAACP, 1965, and from Georgia Conference, 1966, for service to youth; Savannah Chatham county merit Award for Work on Economic Opportunity Task Force, 1966; Savannah State College Award for distinguished service to librarianship, 1967; award from *Journal of Library History,* 1970, for best piece of historical research to appear in the *Journal* in 1969; L.H.D., Shaw University, 1973; ALA Black Caucus Award for Distinguished Service to Librarianship, 1979; New York Black Librarians Caucus Award for Excellence 1979; Distinguished Alumni Award for Contributions to Librarianship from School of Library & Information Science, State University of New York, 1981; Distinguished Service Award, Library Association of City University New York, 1982; DC Association of School Librarians Award, 1984; Africa Librarianship Award, Kenya Library Association, 1984; New York Library Association Award, 1985; Presidents Award, NAACP, 1986; Honorary Doctor of Humanities, North Carolina Central University, 1989; Equality Award, ALA, 1991.

WRITINGS:

(Editor) *The Black Librarian in America,* Scarecrow, 1970.

(Contributor) *Teaching for Better Use of Libraries,* edited by Charles Trinker, Shoe String, 1970.

(Editor) *What Black Librarians Are Saying,* Scarecrow, 1972.

(Editor) *New Dimensions for Academic Library Service,* Scarecrow, 1975. (Editor with Sidney L. Jackson and Eleanor B. Herling) *A Century of Service: Librarianship in the United States and Canada,* American Library Association, 1976.

(Editor with Kenneth E. Peoples) *Opportunities for Minorities in Librarianship,* Scarecrow, 1977.

(Editor with Ann Allen Shockley) *Handbook of Black Librarianship,* Libraries Unlimited Inc., 1977.

(Editor) *The Information Society: Issues and Answers,* Oryx Press, 1978.

(Editor) *Libraries in the Political Process,* Oryx Press, 1980.

(Editor with Marva L. DeLoach) *Ethnic Collections in Libraries,* Neal-Schuman, 1983.

(Editor) *Libraries, Coalitions, and the Public Good,* Neal-Schuman, 1987. (Editor with Kenneth D. Shearer) *Politics and the Support of Libraries,* Neal-Schuman, 1990.

Directory of Ethnic Professionals in LIS, edited by George C. Grant, Four G, 1991.

E. J. Josey: An Activist Librarian, edited by Ismail Abdullahi, Scarecrow Press, 1992.

Publications include library directories and surveys. Contributor of numerous articles and reviews to *Savannah Tribune, Savannah Herald,* and to library, history, and education journals.

SIDELIGHTS: E. J. Josey's writings focus on the special needs, problems, and circumstances surrounding libraries and librarians in both the academic and specialized categories. Strategies for funding, public relations, and other forms of support for libraries are all of concern to him, and he conveys information and ideas with what critics find to be sound, practical advice.

Special attention is paid to minority librarians and library needs in such works as *The Black Librarian in America,* a volume of 25 essays profiling two dozen black librarians. Their varying personal experiences provide an overview of differing opinions while concentrating on what Edsel Ford McCoy in *Library Journal* called "their shared collage of 'the black experience'." He concluded that *The Black Librarian in America* is "an indispensable volume for college, large public and high school libraries." Further observations by black librarians are presented in *What Black Librarians Are Saying.* Josey's co-edited volume *Handbook of Black Librarianship* presents 37 essays by 24 contributors speaking to topics such as resources for African and African American studies and the Black Caucus of American Library Association (ALA). A writer for *Booklist* called *Handbook of Black Librarianship* "a compilation of interesting, useful and valuable data on the distinguished history of black librarianship," and suggested that the statistical data revealed within would prove useful to a variety of persons from students and educators to writers and publishers.

Development of ethnic archives and library programs are covered in *Ethnic Collections in Libraries.* A variety of ethnic groups including Asian Americans, Native Americans, and African Americans are addressed. Another work centered on the special needs of minority groups is *Opportunities for Minorities in Librarianship.* As the title suggests, this 20-essay collection stimulates thought on the part of young minority group members seeking a career in librarianship.

Josey has also spent time focusing on the needs of libraries in the face of economic and political difficulties. *Politics and the Support of Libraries* is another collection of essays, this time addressing such topics as private fund raising, public relations, and local political issues that affect academic and special libraries. Another 27 essays appear in *Libraries in the Political Process.* Here, the discussion turns to the legislative histories of various regions of the United States and the role of the State Association and the State Library Agency. Critics find it a useful tool for private citizens who wish to support their libraries; featured in Josey's work is Miriam Bravermans's essay which states "to increase access to resources and services libraries' real strength and hope lie in the mobilization of local citizens concern for their own library."

Other volumes which critics reviewed are *Libraries, Coalitions, and the Public Good,* containing 16 papers originally presented at the ALA Annual Conference in 1985; *The Information Society: Issues and Answers;* and *New Dimensions for Academic Library Service.* All three volumes are concerned with the past, present, and future of libraries in the face of economic, political, and technological changes. Josey's work is library-specific, but numerous reviewers find the volumes well-researched and highly relevant to anyone interested in the history, preservation, and future of the library system in the United States.

BIOGRAPHICAL/CRITICAL SOURCES:

BOOKS

Josey, E. J., *Libraries in the Political Process,* Oryx Press, 1980.

PERIODICALS

Booklist, July 1, 1971, p. 879; May 15, 1973, p. 872; May 15, 1978, p. 1519; January 15, 1981, p. 669; April 1, 1988, p. 1310; April 1, 1991, p. 1542.

Library Journal, March 15, 1971, p. 937; December 15, 1975, p. 2308; October 1, 1977, p. 2017; January 1, 1979, p. 85; February 1, 1981, p. 315; July, 1983, p. 1345; July, 1987, p. 56.

Reference Quarterly, spring, 1978, pp. 263-64.

Wilson Library Bulletin, October, 1983, p. 142; May, 1991, p. 119-20.*

* * *

JOYCE, Julia

See TETEL, Julie

JULESBERG, Elizabeth Rider Montgomery 1902-1985 (Elizabeth Montgomery, Elizabeth Rider Montgomery)

PERSONAL: Born in Huaras, Peru; died after a long illness, February 19, 1985, in Seattle, WA; daughter of Charles Quantrell (a missionary) and Lula (Tralle) Rider; married Norman A. Montgomery, 1930 (divorced); married Arthur Julesberg, 1963; children: Janet Montgomery Small, Robin Athol. *Education:* Attended Washington State Normal School (now Western Washington University), 1924-25, and University of California, Los Angeles, 1927-28. *Religion:* Congregationalist.

Avocational Interests: Water color painting, braiding rugs, stamp collecting, theatre, music, and golf.

CAREER: Elementary school teacher, Los Angeles, CA, and Aberdeen, WA; Scott, Foresman & Co., Chicago, IL, staff writer, 1938-63; freelance writer, 1963-85.

MEMBER: National League of American Penwomen, Parents and Teachers Association (life member), Seattle Free Lance Writers, Friends of the Library, Alki Community Club.

AWARDS, HONORS: National Presswomen and Penwomen awards; honored at Matrix Table, 1953; several plays have won national prizes.

WRITINGS:

UNDER NAME ELIZABETH MONTGOMERY; CHILDREN'S FICTION

Sally Does It, Appleton, 1940.
Bonnie's Baby Brother, Lippincott, 1942.
Three Miles an Hour, Dodd, 1952.
Half-Pint Fisherman, Dodd, 1956.
Second-Fiddle-Sandra, Dodd, 1958.
Susan and the Storm, Thomas Nelson, 1960.
The Mystery of Edison Brown, Scott, Foresman, 1960.
Tide Treasure Camper, Washburn, 1963.
Two Kinds of Courage, Washburn, 1966.
Mystery of the Boy Next Door, Garrard, 1978.

UNDER NAME ELIZABETH MONTGOMERY; CHILDREN'S NONFICTION

The Story behind Great Inventions, Dodd, 1944.
The Story behind Great Medical Discoveries, Dodd, 1945.
The Story behind Great Books, Dodd, 1946.
Keys to Nature's Secrets, Dodd, 1946.
The Story behind Great Stories, Dodd, 1947.
The Story behind Modern Books, Dodd, 1949.
The Story behind Musical Instruments, Dodd, 1953.
The Story behind Popular Songs, Dodd, 1958.
Till Time Be Conquered, Alki Church, 1959.
Alexander Graham Bell, Garrard, 1963.

Hernando De Soto, Garrard, 1964.
Chief Seattle, Garrard, 1965.
Lewis and Clark, Garrard, 1965.
Toward Democracy, Washburn, 1967.
Old Ben Franklin's Philadelphia, Garrard, 1967.
Hans Christian Andersen, Garrard, 1968.
When a Ton of Gold Reached Seattle, Garrard, 1968.
William C. Handy: Father of the Blues, Garrard, 1968.
Chief Joseph, Garrard, 1969.
Henry Ford, Garrard, 1969.
When Pioneers Pushed West to Oregon, Garrard, 1969.
Will Rogers, Garrard, 1970.
Gandhi, Garrard, 1970.
Albert Schweitzer, Garrard, 1971.
Walt Disney, Garrard, 1971.
Duke Ellington, Garrard, 1972.
Three Jazz Greats, Garrard, 1973.
Dag Hammarskjold, Garrard, 1973.
Indian Patriots, Garrard, 1974.
Super Showmen, Garrard, 1974.
Founding Fathers, Garrard, 1975.
Trouble Is His Name, Garrard, 1976.
"Seeing" in the Dark, Garrard, 1979.
The Builder Also Grows, Ashley Books, 1979.

Also author of *Wonder Workers in Communication,* 1979.

UNDER NAME ELIZABETH MONTGOMERY; TEXTBOOKS

We Look and See, Scott, Foresman, 1940.
We Work and Play, Scott, Foresman, 1940.
We Come and Go, Scott, Foresman, 1940.
Good Times with Our Friends, Scott, Foresman, 1941.
Three Friends, Scott, Foresman, 1944.
Five in the Family, Scott, Foresman, 1946.
The Girl Next Door, Scott, Foresman, 1946.
You, Scott, Foresman, 1948.
Happy Days with Our Friends, Scott, Foresman, 1948.
Just Like Me, Scott, Foresman, 1957.
Being Six, Scott, Foresman, 1957.
Seven or So, Scott, Foresman, 1957.
Eight to Nine, Scott, Foresman, 1957.
Going on Ten, Scott, Foresman, 1958.
About Yourself, Scott, Foresman, 1959.
Health for All, six volumes, Scott, Foresman, 1965.

UNDER NAME ELIZABETH MONTGOMERY; PLAYS

All Kinds of People, Row Peterson, 1950.
Suburb of Heaven, produced by University of Washington, 1960.

Also author of juvenile plays, *Old Pipes and the Dryad,* 1948, and *Knights of the Silver Shield,* 1963, and of *Noah's Ark,* 1951, *Kla-How-Ya* (a symphonic drama of Pacific Northwest history), *Proxy Papa,* and *The Klep.*

OTHER

Contributor of stories and articles, sometimes under name Elizabeth Rider Montgomery, to juvenile magazines and newspapers.

ADAPTATIONS: Some of Juleberg's plays have been produced on radio and television; *Chief Joseph, Lewis and Clark, When Pioneers Pushed West to Oregon, Alexander Graham Bell, Will Rogers* and *Gandhi* have been recorded on cassette tape.

SIDELIGHTS: Best known for her children's textbooks featuring the characters Dick, Jane, Sally and Spot, Elizabeth Montgomery began her career as a first grade teacher in Los Angeles. She noticed at this time that there was a dearth of interesting material for children to read. In response to the shortage, Montgomery wrote *Look and See*—a grade school primer featuring the children Dick, Jane, and Sally, and their dog, Spot. "I wrote on a school typewriter an hour a day before school took up in the mornings," Montgomery once recalled. "I kept this up for three years." The book was eventually published by Scott, Foresman. *Look and See* was so successful that Scott, Foresman signed her on as a staff writer to continue the popular series.

Montgomery also wrote a successful series for young adults about the stories behind great inventions, events, and discoveries. In an article about her work for *Author and Journalist,* she explained: "Non-fiction for children is a fascinating field. It has a lot to recommend it. It has all the advantages of both book-length and magazine writing; the continuity of subject matter keeps you working until the book is finished, there is no period of waiting, when one article is completed, trying to decide—what to write about next. Yet each chapter is separate; you do not lose your train of thought when you stop at the end of an article."

Speaking of her writing habits, Montgomery once explained: "I usually keep two kinds of writing going at once; one acts as foil for the other. I do a great deal of notebook work before actual writing; much of this in connection with housework or with hobbies. I try to write a certain number of pages per week—writing three to five hours in the mornings. I revise a lot.

"Perhaps the chief satisfaction of writing is the joy of feeling that I'm doing what I was meant to do. In addition, there is the knowledge that I've had a part, however small and unrecognized, in the education and inspiration of countless children and young people. As long as my books are read, I'll keep on writing."

BIOGRAPHICAL/CRITICAL SOURCES:

PERIODICALS

Author and Journalist, October, 1945.
Baton, May, 1952.
Seattle Times, April 10, 1959; November 23, 1969.
West Seattle Herald, November 17, 1960; December 11, 1969.
Wilson Library Bulletin, May, 1952.
Young Wings, March, 1946.

OBITUARIES:

PERIODICALS

Chicago Sun-Times, February 21, 1985.
Detroit Free Press, February 22, 1985.
New London Day, February 21, 1985.
Washington Post, February 22, 1985.*

K

KAPEL, Andrew
See BURGESS, Michael (Roy)

* * *

KAPUSTA, Paul
See BICKERS, Richard (Leslie) Townshend

* * *

KATCHADOURIAN, Herant A(ram) 1933-

PERSONAL: Born January 23, 1933, in Alexandretta, Syria; came to the United States in 1958, naturalized citizen, 1973; son of Aram A. (in business) and Efronia (Nazarian) Katchadourian; married Stina Lindfors (a writer), August 30, 1964; children: Nina, Kai. *Education:* American University of Beirut, B.A. (cum laude), 1954, M.D. (cum laude), 1958.

ADDRESSES: Home—956 Mears Ct., Stanford, CA 94305. *Office*—Program in Human Biology, Stanford University, Stanford, CA 94305.

CAREER: American University of Beirut, Beirut, Lebanon, intern, 1957-58; University of Rochester, Rochester, NY, resident in psychiatry, 1958-61; National Institute of Mental Health, Bethesda, MD, visiting associate of U.S. Public Health Service, 1961-62; American University of Beirut, assistant professor of psychiatry, 1962-66; Stanford University, Stanford, CA, assistant professor, 1966-70, associate professor, 1970-75, professor of psychiatry, 1976—. Vice-provost and dean of undergraduate studies, 1977-82. Member of board of trustees of Haigazian College; director of Hewlett Foundation.

MEMBER: Alpha Omega Alpha.

AWARDS, HONORS: Richard C. Lyman Award, 1984; Association of Stanford Students Teaching Award, 1992; Dinkelspiel Award, 1993.

WRITINGS:

Fundamentals of Human Sexuality, Holt, 1972, 5th edition, 1989.

Human Sexuality: Sense and Nonsense, Stanford Alumni Association, 1972.

The Biology of Adolescence, W. H. Freeman, 1977.

(With D. T. Lunde and R. Trotter) *Human Sexuality,* brief edition, Holt, 1979.

(Editor) *Human Sexuality: A Comparative and Developmental Perspective,* University of California Press, 1979.

(Contributor) L. Carl Brown and Norman Itzkowitz, editors, *Psychological Dimensions of Near Eastern Studies,* Darwin Press, 1979.

(Contributor) P. B. Beeson, W. McDermott, and J. B. Wyngaarden, editors, *Cecil Textbook of Medicine,* 15th edition, W. B. Saunders, 1979, 17th edition, in press.

(Contributor) Lorna Brown, editor, *Sex Education in the 80s,* Plenum, 1981.

(With J. Boli) *Intellectualism and Careerism among College Students,* Jossey-Bass, 1985.

50: Midlife in Perspective, W. H. Freeman, 1987.

Also contributor to *Pediatric Clinics of North America,* Volume 27, edited by Iris Litt, 1980. Contributor of more than twenty articles to medicine and psychiatry journals, including *Social Psychiatry, Lebanese Medical Journal, British Journal of Psychiatry.*

SIDELIGHTS: Some of Herant A. Katchadourian's books have been translated into French, Spanish, and Portuguese.

KEANE, John B(rendan) 1928-

PERSONAL: Born July 21, 1928, in Listowel, County Kerry, Ireland; son of William B. (a teacher) and Hannah (Purtill) Keane; married Mary O'Connor, January 1, 1955; children: William Joseph, Conor Anthony, John Mary, Joanna Mary Colette. *Education:* St. Michael's College, Listowel, Ireland, graduate, 1946. *Politics:* Fine Gael. *Religion:* Roman Catholic.

ADDRESSES: Home—37 William St., Listowel, County Kerry, Ireland. *Agent*— William Keane, 37 William St., Listowel, County Kerry, Ireland.

CAREER: Writer, playwright, and free-lance journalist. Chemist's assistant in Ireland, 1946-51; pub owner and operator, Listowel, Ireland, 1955—.

MEMBER: Irish PEN Consultative Assembly (president, 1973-74).

AWARDS, HONORS: Honorary doctorate in literature, Trinity College, Dublin, 1977.

WRITINGS:

PLAYS

Sive (three-act; first produced in Cork, Ireland, by the Southern Theatre Group, 1959; produced in Dublin at Olympia Theatre, 1959; also see below), Progress House, 1959.

Sharon's Grave: A Folk Play (two-act; first produced in Cork, Ireland, by the Southern Theatre Group, 1960; produced in New York at Maidman Playhouse, November 8, 1961), Progress House, 1960, University of Minnesota Press, 1967.

The Highest House on the Mountain (three-act; first produced in Dun Laoghaire at Gas Company Theatre, September 14, 1960), Progress House, 1961.

Many Young Men of Twenty (first produced in Cork, Ireland, at Father Matthew Hall, July 5, 1960; produced in Dublin at Olympia Theatre, August 28, 1961), Progress House, 1961, University of Minnesota Press, 1967.

No More in Dust, first produced in Dun Laoghaire at Gas Company Theatre, September 12, 1961.

The Man from Clare (two-act; first produced in Cork, Ireland, by the Southern Theatre Group, July 1, 1962; produced in Dublin at Queen's Theatre, August 5, 1963), Mercier Press, 1962, Dufour, 1992, revised edition, 1993.

The Year of the Hiker (three-act; first produced in Cork, Ireland, by the Southern Theatre Group, July 17, 1962; produced in Dublin at Gate Theatre, August 18, 1964), Mercier Press, 1963, Dufour, 1991.

The Roses of Tralee, first produced in Cork, Ireland, at Opera House, November 29, 1965; produced in Dublin at Gaiety Theatre, April 12, 1966.

The Field (three-act; first produced in Dublin at the Olympia Theatre, November 1, 1965; produced in New York at Irish Rebel Theatre, 1976; also see below), Mercier Press, 1966, Dufour, 1991.

Hut 42 (first produced in Dublin at Queen's Theatre, November 12, 1962), Proscenium Press, 1968.

The Rain at the End of Summer (three-act; first produced in Dublin at Gaiety Theatre, June 19, 1967), Progress House, 1968.

Big Maggie (three-act; first produced in Cork, Ireland, at Opera House, January 20, 1969; produced in Dublin at Olympia Theatre, February 10, 1969; produced in South Orange, NJ, at Seton Hall University Irish-American Cultural Institute, May 24, 1979; also see below), Mercier Press, 1969.

Faoiseamh (one-act play; title means "Release"), first produced in Dublin at Damer Hall, October, 1970.

Moll (three-act; first produced in Killarney, Ireland, at Abbey Theatre, July 1, 1971; produced in Dublin at Olympia Theatre, October 4, 1971), Mercier Press, 1971, Dufour, 1991, revised edition, 1992.

The One-Way Ticket (one-act; first produced in Listowel, Ireland, at Plaza Theatre, March, 1972), Performance Publishing, 1972.

The Change in Mame Fadden (two-act; first produced in Cork, Ireland, at Opera House, May 10, 1971; produced in Dublin at Olympia Theatre, May 24, 1971), Dufour, 1973.

Values (one-act plays; contains *The Spraying of John O'Dorey, Backwater,* and *The Pure of Heart;* first produced in Cork, Ireland, by the Southern Theatre Group, April 25, 1973), Dufour, 1973.

The Crazy Wall (two-act; first produced in Waterford, Ireland, at Theatre Royal, June 27, 1973; produced in Dublin at Gaiety Theatre, May 6, 1974), Dufour, 1974.

The Matchmaker (based on the novel *Letters of a Matchmaker* by Keane; also see below), Mercier Press, 1975.

The Good Thing (first produced in Limerick, Ireland, at City Theatre, March 1, 1976; produced in Dublin at Eblana Theatre, April 19, 1976), Proscenium Press, 1976.

The Buds of Ballybunion (first produced in Clonmel, Ireland, at White Memorial Theatre, July 7, 1978; produced in Dublin at Olympia Theatre, July 24, 1978), Mercier Press, 1978, Dufour, 1979.

The Chastitute (two-act; based on the novel *Letters of a Love-Hungry Farmer* by Keane; first produced in Cork, Ireland, at Opera House, June 3, 1980; produced in Dublin at Olympia Theatre, June 16, 1980; also see below), Dufour, 1981.

Ben Barnes, editor, *Three Plays* (contains revised editions of *Sive, The Field,* and *Big Maggie*), Dufour, 1990.

Southern Theatre Group presented a season of Keane's plays in Killarney.

RADIO SCRIPTS

Barbara Shearing, Radio Telefis Eireann (RTE), 1959.
A Clutch of Duckeggs, RTE, 1970.
The War Crime, British Broadcasting Corp., 1976.
The Talk Specific, RTE, 1979.
The Battle of Ballybooley, RTE, 1980.

ESSAYS

The Gentle Art of Matchmaking and Other Important Things, Mercier Press, 1973, Dufour, 1988.
Strong Tea, Mercier Press, 1976.
Is the Holy Ghost Really a Kerryman?, and Other Topics of Interest, Mercier Press, 1976.
Unlawful Sex and Other Testy Matters, Mercier Press, 1978.
Stories from a Kerry Fireside, Mercier Press, 1980.
Unusual Irish Careers, Mercier Press, 1981.
Love Bites and Other Stories, Dufour, 1991.

"LETTERS" SERIES

Letters of a Successful T.D., Mercier Press, 1967, Dufour, 1990.
Letters of an Irish Parish Priest, Mercier Press, 1970, Dufour, 1972.
Letters of an Irish Publican, Mercier Press, 1974, Dufour, 1990.
Letters of a Love-Hungry Farmer, Mercier Press, 1974, Dufour, 1987.
Letters of a Matchmaker, Mercier Press, 1975, Dufour, 1990.
Letters of a Civic Guard, Mercier Press, 1976.
Letters of a Country Postman, Mercier Press, 1977.
Letters of an Irish Minister of State, Mercier Press, 1978.

OTHER

The Street and Other Poems, Progress House, 1961.
Self-Portrait (autobiography), Mercier Press, 1964.
(Contributor) Robert Hogan, editor, *Seven Irish Plays,* University of Minnesota Press, 1967.
Death Be Not Proud and Other Stories, Mercier Press, 1976.
More Irish Short Stories, Mercier Press, 1981, Dufour, 1991.
Man of the Triple Name, Brandon, 1984.
Owl Sandwiches, Brandon, 1985, revised edition, Irish Books & Media, 1993.
The Bodhran Makers, Brandon, 1986, Four Walls Eight Windows, 1992.
Irish Short Stories, Dufour, 1987.
The Power of the Word (humorous quotations), Brandon, 1989.
The Field (screenplay), Avenue Pictures, 1990.
The Celebrated Letters of John B. Keane, Dufour, 1991.
Durango (novel), Dufour, 1992.
(Author of foreword) John M. Freehan, *My Village—My World,* Dufour, 1993.
Letters to the Brain, Irish Books & Media, 1993.
The Ram of God and Other Stories, Dufour, 1993.

Weekly columnist for *Dublin Herald* and *Limerick Leader.*

SIDELIGHTS: James B. Keane has earned a place among Ireland's most successful playwrights. His plays, which are typically set in County Kerry, Ireland (where Keane makes his home), deal with the very traditional people of provincial Ireland as they cope with—or fall victim to—their country's changing social and moral landscape. Because they are typified by idiomatic and sometimes vulgar language, Keane's plays are occasionally mislabeled as "low" drama; Christopher Murray admits in the *Dictionary of Literary Biography* that "Keane's plays are noted for their entertainment value rather than for artistic merit." However, Murray points out that Keane "is a popular dramatist, in the purest sense of the word, authentically mirroring and articulating the passions and shortcomings of ordinary people. Because he deals with nonurban, non-technological man, in a style fundamentally realistic, Keane appears old-fashioned and unsophisticated; but his work possesses qualities of authenticity and honesty which entitle him to be regarded as the principal spokesman in the theater for Ireland's modern provincial society."

Keane was born in County Kerry in 1928. He was raised in an environment of poverty and hardship and, like many other Irishmen, he immigrated to England as a young man. There he worked in a variety of low-skill, low-paying jobs, writing poetry and fiction in his free time. He left England after just two years, returning to Kerry in 1954. In 1955 he married Mary O'Connor and purchased a local pub, which he operates to this day (in fact, many of the characters featured in Keane's plays are based upon those that frequent his pub). According to Murray, "some time in the late 1950s he saw the Listowel Drama Group's production of Joseph Tomelty's tragedy *All Soul's Night* . . . and felt inspired to write for the stage."

Keane's first play, *Sive,* made its debut in drama festivals in 1959; it was later produced in Cork and Dublin, and remains one of his most revived works. It tells the story of a young orphan girl named Sive, raised on a farm by her uncle Mike and his mean, barren wife, Mena. Keane heaps upon these characters layer after layer of misery and despair, culminating with Sive's suicide. While *Sive* is criticized as being heavy-handed and melodramatic, this does not detract from the play's power; such melodrama, says Keane in the *New York Times,* is essential to Irish theater, particularly in Kerry, "where life as we live it is slightly larger than elsewhere." "What is striking about [*Sive*]," Murray points out, ". . . is the impression it conveys of fierce poverty in its degrading, humanly destructive aspects."

Over the next six years Keane wrote seven two- and three-act plays, many of which were debuted by the Southern Theatre Group. In 1965 he composed what many consider to be his best play, *The Field.* Based loosely upon real events that occurred in 1958, *The Field* is the story of Thady "Bull" McCabe, a cattle owner who claims as his own a parcel of land he has rented for years; the land, however, is owned by a widow, who decides to sell it at public auction. Furious, McCabe vows to purchase the field, and through sheer intimidation dissuades the local residents from bidding against him. His only remaining challenger is a returned expatriate, William Dee, who is eager to use the widow's land to bring industry to Kerry. Unable to frighten him away, McCabe and his son Tadhg attack Dee during the night, beating him to death. The people of Kerry, though aware of the crime, remain silent, and McCabe, unopposed, purchases the field.

The Field was made into a film and released in America in 1990. While the play had enjoyed tremendous success on the Irish stage, the film was greeted coolly by American reviewers, many of whom were taken aback by Keane's overly-emotional characters. Said film critic Peter Rainer in the *Los Angeles Times:* "[*The Field*] is such an impassioned piece of blarney that you can't really laugh at it even when it's pulpy and ridiculous and wildly over the top" (though he eventually claims, "I intend this as both a detraction and a recommendation"). Such criticism of Keane's work is commonplace in American journals, for, as Pat Monaghan explains in *Booklist,* "some of his work doesn't travel well, being so deeply Irish and so broadly rural that the characters seem to American readers merely strange and quaint."

Keane's greatest financial success came in 1969 with the production of the play *Big Maggie.* The title character, Maggie Polpin, is a strong-willed widow who will not remarry, as her daughters wish, nor will she relinquish control of the family business to her son. The severe treatment she affords her children drives them out of the house one by one, so that by the end of the play she is alone. "The plot is slight," admits Murray, "allowing Keane to concentrate on the depiction of Big Maggie Polpin." The people of Ireland embraced the embittered widow, filling every theater at which *Big Maggie* was performed. Phyllis Ryan, as quoted in the *Dictionary of Literary Biography,* recalls: "No play I can remember in a life spent in theatre made such a powerful impact on the Irish playgoer. In terms of business, any previous records were broken all over the country. In terms of emotive response from audiences, it seemed they could not get enough of this play, and large numbers of people from every walk of life went four or five times to see it."

When *Big Maggie* came to America in 1979, it was well received; Marie Kean was awarded the State of New Jersey best actress honors for her portrayal of Maggie Polpin, a role she had originated on the Irish stage. Still, many critics were not yet ready to accept the over-the-top emotionalism of Keane's characters. Frank Rich, a reviewer for the *New York Times,* said of a 1983 performance: "The truth about *Big Maggie* is that it's a soap opera. Stripped of its Irish accents . . . this play would make an entertaining episode or two of *All My Children.*" It is impossible, however, to deny the play's popularity in Keane's homeland, for, as Desmond Rushe points out in the *New York Times, Big Maggie* "is credited with having notched up more aggregate performances than any other in modern Irish theater."

Since 1980 Keane has concentrated on writing essays, short fiction, and novels—many of which continue to tell the tales of real and fictional residents of County Kerry. One of his later works, the 1986 novel *The Bodhran Makers,* deals with the attempts of a rural priest to ban the celebration of an ancient pagan festival called the wrendance. Though touched with humor and sentimentality, *The Bodhran Makers* is a detailed account of the impoverished communities of rural Ireland as they struggle against the bonds of traditional Catholicism. Annabel Davis-Goff, writing in the *New York Times Book Review,* observed: "Denying these people the wrendance—a winter's night of pleasure and escape from care—is a foolish exercise of power, and the consequences leave most of them irrevocably changed."

Keane is seldom compared to such "serious" Irish authors and playwrights as William Trevor, Brendan Kennelly, and Sean O'Casey—probably because of his reputation as a popular writer. Still, as Davis-Goff contends, "Keane continues to provide, with the immediacy best conveyed in fiction, an accurate account of rural Irish life in the 1950's." She concludes by saying: "Mr. Keane, who represents a different, less literary role—that of chronicler—holds a necessary and valuable place in Irish literature."

BIOGRAPHICAL/CRITICAL SOURCES:

BOOKS

Dictionary of Literary Biography, Volume 13: *British Dramatists Since World War II,* Gale, 1982, pp. 263-272.

Feehan, John M., editor, *Fifty Years Young: A Tribute to John B. Keane,* Mercier Press, 1979.

Gaughan, J. Anthony, *Listowel and Its Vicinity,* Mercier Press, 1973, pp. 469-470.

Hogan, Robert, editor, *Seven Irish Plays,* University of Minnesota Press, 1967.

Hogan, *After the Irish Renaissance: A Critical History of the Irish Drama since 'The Plough and the Stars,'* Macmillan, 1968, pp. 208-220.

Hogan, editor, *Dictionary of Irish Literature,* Macmillan, 1980, pp. 345-348.

Keane, John B., *Self Portrait,* Mercier Press, 1963.

Smith, Gus, *Festival Glory in Athlone,* Aherlow Publishers, 1977, pp. 9-42.

PERIODICALS

Booklist, October 15, 1992, p. 402; November 15, 1992, p. 572.

Drama, summer, 1968.

Insight, September 3, 1990, p. 54.

Irish Times, June 19, 1976, p. 5.

Journal of Irish Literature, May, 1977, pp. 118-119.

Los Angeles Times, December 20, 1990.

National Catholic Reporter, January 11, 1991, p. 22.

New York Times, September 25, 1983; September 29, 1983.

New York Times Book Review, February 21, 1993, p. 17.

Publishers Weekly, August 17, 1992, p. 487.

Variety, October 19, 1992, p. 168.*

—Sketch by Brandon Trenz

* * *

KEENE, Burt
See BICKERS, Richard (Leslie) Townshend

* * *

KEITH-LUCAS, Alan 1910-

PERSONAL: Born February 5, 1910, in Cambridge, England; son of Keith (a physiologist) and Alys (Hubbard) Lucas; married Georgia Ruth Work, July 8, 1939 (died April 16, 1979); children: Susan, Timothy. *Education:* Cambridge University, B.A. (first class honors), 1931, M.A., 1935; Western Reserve University (now Case Western Reserve University), M.S.S.A., 1939; Duke University, Ph.D., 1955. *Religion:* Presbyterian.

Avocational Interests: "Building stone walls, cryptic crossword puzzles, and telling Uncle Remus stories."

ADDRESSES: Home—705 Greenwood Rd., Chapel Hill, NC 27514.

CAREER: Assistant master, Beclales Junior School, 1931-32; Hilden Oaks School, Tonbridge, England, principal, 1932-37; Cleveland Humane Society, Cleveland, OH, caseworker and supervisor, 1939-44; Louisiana State Department of Public Welfare, New Orleans, Shreveport, and Baton Rouge, child welfare consultant, became supervisor of children's services, 1944-50; University of North Carolina, School of Social Work, Chapel Hill, 1950-75, Alumni Distinguished Professor of Social Work, 1961-75, professor emeritus, 1975—, director of group child care project, 1956-69, associate dean, 1964-65, acting dean, 1951-52, 1965-66, 1971-72. Visiting professor, London School of Economics and Political Science, University of London, 1966; K. L. M. Pray Visiting Professor, University of Pennsylvania, 1969. Consultant to U.S. Children's Bureau, New Zealand Council for Church Social Service, and over one hundred children's homes. *Military service:* U.S. Army, 1943.

MEMBER: North American Association of Christians in Social Work, Child Welfare League of America, Council on Social Work Education, National Association of Social Workers, National Conference on Social Welfare, American Public Welfare Association, Phi Beta Kappa.

AWARDS, HONORS: Distinguished service awards, St. Francis Boys Homes, 1976 and National Association of Homes for Children, 1978; Friend of Children Award (renamed the Alan Keith-Lucas Friend of Children Award), North Carolina Child Care Association, 1978; first merit award, National Association of Christians in Social Work, 1979; John Park Lee Award, 1982; honorary doctor of letters, Campbell University, 1989.

WRITINGS:

Right Use of School Games, S.P.C.K., 1929.

Decisions about People in Need, University of North Carolina Press, 1957.

Some Casework Concepts for the Public Welfare Worker, University of North Carolina Press, 1957.

(Editor) *Readings for Houseparents in Children's Institutions,* Werkman's, 1958.

Your Neighbor as Yourself, Presbyterian Church, 1962.

The Church Children's Home in a Changing World, University of North Carolina Press, 1962.

The Church and Social Welfare, Westminster, 1963.

This Difficult Process of Helping, CLC Press, 1965.

Christian Education for Emotionally Disturbed Children, Council Press, 1967.

Giving and Taking Help, University of North Carolina Press, 1972.

(With Clifford W. Sanford) *Group Child Care as a Family Service,* University of North Carolina Press, 1977.

The Client's Religion and Your Own Belief in the Helping Process, University of North Carolina, Group Child Care Consultant Services, 1983.

So You Want to Be a Social Worker, North American Association of Christians in Social Work, 1986.

The Poor You Have with You Always, North American Association of Christians in Social Work, 1989.

Also author of twelve histories of childrens homes, and *Essays from More than Fifty Years in Social Work,* 1989. Contributor to numerous books, including *Growing up in an Anxious Age,* Association for Supervision and Curriculum Development, 1952; *Psychiatry and Responsibility,* edited by Helmut Shoeck and James W. Wiggins, Van Nostrand, 1962; *The Rights of Children,* edited by Albert E. Wilkerson, Temple University Press, 1973; *A Design for Social Work Practice,* edited by Felice Perlmutter, Columbia University Press, 1974; *The Field of Social Work,* edited by Arthur E. Fink, Jane H. Pfouts, and Andrew W. Dobelstein, 8th edition, Sage Publications, 1985. Contributor to professional journals.

Editor of monograph series for Group Child Care Consultant Services, 1979-83, and North American Association of Christians in Social Work, 1984—. Editor of *Chapel Hill Workshop Reports,* 1953-65, 1967-73, 1977-83, and *Programs and Problems in Child Welfare,* Volume 355, Annals of Academy of Political and Social Science, 1964. Book editor, *Residential Treatment of Children and Youth,* 1987—, and *Social Work and Christianity,* 1990—.

WORK IN PROGRESS: A history of the School Social Work at University of North Carolina; *South Georgia Methodist Home for Children and Youth;* second edition of *Giving and Taking Help.*

SIDELIGHTS: Alan Keith-Lucas told *CA:* "I was one of the early students of F. R. Leavis and I. A. Richards. This has helped me to write professional books in plain, accurate English and to eschew all forms of jargon. I hold, with Ezra Pound, that when the relationship between the word and the thing gets slushy and inexact, the whole order of civilization goes to pot. Professionally I am considered controversial, mainly because I love to upset sacred cows and believe very strongly in the rights of people to manage their own lives. Half of my writing has been since my retirement in 1975."

KILLDEER, John
See MAYHAR, Ardath

* * *

KINGSTON, Syd
See BINGLEY, David Ernest

* * *

KIRSCHNER, Fritz
See BICKERS, Richard (Leslie) Townshend

* * *

KNIGHT, George A(ngus) F(ulton) 1909-

PERSONAL: Born May 12, 1909, in Perth, Scotland; son of George Alexander Francis and Annie (Adamson) Knight; married Agnes Eadie, 1935; children: David Blair, Elizabeth Helen Ann. *Education:* University of Glasgow, M.A., 1930, M.A. (honors), 1932, B.D. (honors), 1935; Melbourne College of Divinity, D.D., 1962.

Avocational Interests: Gardening.

ADDRESSES: Home—3/20 Paunui St., Auckland 5, New Zealand.

CAREER: Church of Scotland School, Budapest, Hungary, director, 1935-41; minister in Glasgow, Scotland, 1941-46; Knox College, Dunedin, New Zealand, professor, 1947-58; St. Andrews University, St. Andrews, Scotland, professor, 1959-60; McCormick Theological Seminary, Chicago, IL, professor, 1960-65; Pacific Theological College, Suva, Fiji, president, 1965-72. Presbyterian Church of New Zealand, moderator, 1974-75. Chairman, National Council of Churches Study Commission on the church and the Jewish people. Radio preacher, broadcaster on religious topics in England, Scotland, and New Zealand.

MEMBER: International Society of Old Testament Scholars, British Society for Old Testament Study, American Society of Biblical Literature, Glasgow University Oriental Society.

AWARDS, HONORS: Knighted Officer of the Order of Orange Nassau by Queen Juliana of the Netherlands, 1959, for work among refugees in Europe and immigrants in New Zealand; honorary D.D. from Coe College, 1962, and University of Glasgow, 1964.

WRITINGS:

From Moses to Paul, Lutterworth, 1949.

A Biblical Approach to the Doctrine of the Trinity, Oliver & Boyd, 1953.
A History of the Hungarian Reformed Church, Hungarian Reformed Federation of America, 1954.
A Christian Theology of the Old Testament, John Knox and S.C.M. Press, 1959, revised, 1964.
Law and Grace, Westminster, 1962.
(Editor and contributor) *Jews and Christians—Preparation for Dialogue,* Westminster, 1965.
Exile and After: Studies in Isaiah, Allenson, 1966.
What Next? The Exciting Route Travelled by G. A. F. Knight, (autobiography), Saint Andrew Press, 1980.
Theology in Pictures: Commentary on Genesis, Handsel, 1981.
I Am . . . This is My Name: God of the Bible and the Religions of Man, Eerdmans, 1983.
Revelation of God, Eerdmans, 1988.

BIBLE COMMENTARIES

Ruth and Jonah, S.C.M. Press, 1951, revised edition, 1966.
Esther, Song of Songs, Lamentations, S.C.M. Press, 1955.
Hosea, S.C.M. Press, 1961.
Prophets of Israel: Isaiah, Abingdon, 1961.
Deutero-Isaiah, a Theological Commentary, Abingdon, 1965.
Theology as Narration: A Commentary on the Book of Exodus, Handsel, 1976; Eerdmans, 1977.
Leviticus, Westminster, 1981.
Psalms, Westminster, 1982.
Servant Theology: A Commentary on the Book of Isaiah 40-55, Handsel, 1984.
The New Israel: A Commentary on the Book of Isaiah 56-66, Handsel, 1985.

OTHER

Contributor of many articles to theological journals; coeditor with Frederick Holmgren of "International Theological Commentary" series, Eerdmans, 1984.*

* * *

KOHN, George C(hilds) 1940-

PERSONAL: Born May 27, 1940, in Hartford, CT; son of P. Corbin (a lawyer) and Elizabeth (Childs) Kohn; married Jutta Knechtsberger, August 27, 1966; children: Christina, Peter. *Education:* University of Pennsylvania, B.A., 1963; University of Hartford, M.Ed., 1968.

ADDRESSES: *Home*—104 Liberty St., Madison, CT 06443. *Office*—724 Boston Post Rd., Madison, CT 06443.

CAREER: *West Hartford News,* West Hartford, CT, advertising manager, 1964-67; high school English teacher in Deep River, CT, 1969-73; Laurence Urdang, Inc., Essex, CT, vice-president and editor, 1976-80; George C. Kohn/Research and Editorial Services, Madison, CT, principal, 1980—.

AWARDS, HONORS: New York Public Library selection as one of the "1986 Reference Books to Remember," Adult and Reference Sources, for *Dictionary of Wars,* and selection as one of the "Outstanding Reference Books of the Year, 1991," for *Dictionary of Historic Documents.*

WRITINGS:

Wentworth, Vantage, 1975.

REFERENCE BOOKS

(Senior editor) *Young Students Encyclopedia,* twenty-one volumes, Xerox Education Publications, revised edition, 1977, (sole editor) 2nd revised edition, 1982.
(Compiler with Walter C. Kidney) *Twentieth-Century American Nicknames,* H. W. Wilson, 1979.
(Managing editor) *Raintree Illustrated Science Encyclopedia,* twenty volumes, Macdonald-Raintree, 1979.
(Revision editor) *The Timetables of History,* Simon & Schuster, revised edition, 1979.
(Managing editor) *Nelson's Encyclopedia for Young Readers,* two volumes, Thomas Nelson, 1980.
(Managing editor) *The Timetables of American History,* Simon & Schuster, 1981.
(Editor with others) *Allusions—Cultural, Literary, Biblical, and Historical: A Thematic Dictionary,* Gale, 1982.
(Editor with others) *The World Almanac Dictionary of Dates,* World Almanac, 1982.
Dictionary of Culprits and Criminals, Scarecrow, 1986.
(And editor) *Dictionary of Wars,* Facts on File, 1986.
(And editor) *Encyclopedia of American Scandal,* Facts on File, 1989.
(And editor) *Dictionary of Historic Documents,* Facts on File, 1991.

OTHER

Contributor to *The Random House Encyclopedia,* Random House, 1977. Past contributor to *Human Events, New Guard, Adolescence, Law and Order, National Educator,* and *Christian Science Monitor.*

Dictionary of Wars has been published in Italian.

WORK IN PROGRESS: Researching, writing, and editing a new world encyclopedia.

KRAR, Stephen Frank 1924-

PERSONAL: Born July 20, 1924, in Mor, Hungary; son of John and Mary (Horack) Krar; married Elsie Helen Demko (a secretary), June 26, 1948; children: Judith Anne, Allan Michael. *Education:* Attended University of Toronto, 1954-55. *Religion:* Roman Catholic.

Avocational Interests: Golf, curling.

ADDRESSES: Home and office—420 Fitch St., Welland, Ontario, Canada L3C 4W8.

CAREER: Tool and die maker in Welland, Ontario, 1940-54; machine shop instructor in Niagara Falls, Ontario, 1955-56, and Guelph, Ontario, 1956-62; Eastdale Secondary School, Welland, technical director and machine shop instructor, 1962-74. Lecturer and head of teacher training department at University of Toronto, summers, 1961-71. President of Kostel Enterprises Ltd., 1971-84, Niagara Publishers, 1974-84, and Kelmar Associates, 1987—; associate director, GE Superabrasives Partnership for Manufacturing Productivity, 1987—. Member of Ontario Government Commission "Vision 2000," 1989.

MEMBER: American Technical Education Association (member of National Advisory Council on Technical Education, 1988—), Society of Manufacturing Engineers, Ontario Vocational Education Association (president, 1964), Ontario Machine Shop Roundtable (chairman, 1959-60), Ontario Technical Directors' Association, Niagara College Machine and Tool Trades Advisory Committee (chairman, 1990-93), Welland Curling Club (president, 1973-74).

WRITINGS:

(With J. E. St. Amand) *Machine Shop Training,* McGraw, 1962, 4th edition (with J. W. Oswald), 1986.

(With St. Amand and Oswald) *Machine Tools: Transparency Book No. 1,* McGraw, 1968.

(With St. Amand and Oswald) *Technology of Machine Tools,* McGraw, 1969, 4th edition (solely with Oswald), 1989.

(With E. Gudaitis) *Technical Drawing and Design: Transparency Book,* two volumes, Scott Graphics, 1969-70.

(With St. Amand and Oswald) *Measurement and Layout: Transparency Book No. 2,* McGraw, 1970.

(With Oswald) *Turning Technology,* Delmar, 1971.

(With St. Amand and Oswald) *Threads and Testing Instruments: Transparency Book No. 3,* McGraw, 1972.

(With Oswald) *Grinding Technology,* Delmar, 1973, 2nd edition, 1993.

(With St. Amand and Oswald) *Cutting Tools: Transparency Book No. 4,* McGraw, 1973.

(With St. Amand and Oswald) *Machine Shop Operations,* McGraw, 1974.

(With St. Amand, Oswald, and I. M. McGregor) *Metallurgy: Transparency Book No. 5,* McGraw, 1974.

(Co-author) *Your Car,* McGraw, 1976.

(With Oswald) *Drilling Technology,* Delmar, 1977.

Turning Technology: Engine & Turret Lathes, Van Nostrand, 1977.

(With St. Amand and Oswald) *Machine Tool Operations,* McGraw, 1983.

(With St. Amand and Oswald) *Machine Tool Operations Visutext,* McGraw, 1983.

(With St. Amand and Oswald) *Machine Tools Workbook,* McGraw, 1984.

(With Gill) *CNC Technology and Programming,* Glencoe-McGraw, 1989.

(With Gill) *CNC Technology and Programming Workbook,* Glencoe-McGraw, 1989.

(With Ratterman) *Superabrasive Grinding and Machining,* Glencoe-McGraw, 1989.

WITH OTHERS; "MATH MODULES" SERIES

Core Book, General Publishing, 1976.

Drafting Book, General Publishing, 1976.

Machine Shop Book, General Publishing, 1976.

Consumer Education, General Publishing, 1978.

WORK IN PROGRESS: A fifth edition of *Technology of Machine Tools,* to be published by Glencoe-McGraw in 1994; *Machining and Manufacturing Technology,* to be published by Delmar in 1995; *Numerical Control Machine Tools,* to be published by Delmar in 1996.

SIDELIGHTS: Stephen Frank Krar told *CA:* "The most rewarding part of writing technical texts has been the satisfaction it has given me. Knowing that I am somewhat responsible for passing on knowledge to anyone interested in learning has been especially satisfying. If through my writing I have helped to improve the standard of living of only one person, the time spent has been especially worthwhile. Naturally I am flattered that some of my books have been translated into other languages of the world [including French and Spanish].

"The research involved in keeping up-to-date with the latest technological developments in the machine tool industry has kept me busy and very excited. The dramatic effect of the computer and numerical control on manufacturing processes has made it possible to increase productivity, produce high quality goods, and reduce manufacturing costs. Those countries that incorporate new technology the quickest stand to gain an increasingly larger share of the world markets and improve their standard of living. Educators should look at this as an exciting period of history, learn the basics of all manufacturing technologies, and encourage their students to accept the challenge. The future belongs to those who recognize the tools of tomorrow and use them today."

KREISEL, Henry 1922-1991

PERSONAL: Born June 5, 1922, in Vienna, Austria; naturalized Canadian citizen; died April 22, 1991; son of David Leo (in sales) and Helen (Schreier) Kreisel; married Esther Lazerson (an archivist), June 22, 1947; children: Philip. *Education:* University of Toronto, B.A., 1946, M.A., 1947; University of London, Ph.D., 1954. *Religion:* Jewish.

Avocational Interests: Art collecting, music, travel.

ADDRESSES: Home—Alberta, Canada.

CAREER: University of Alberta, Edmonton, lecturer, 1947-50, assistant professor, 1950-55, associate professor, 1955-59, professor of English, 1959-87, professor emeritus, 1987-91, head of department, 1961-67, member of board of governors, 1966-69, senior associate dean of graduate studies, 1967-69, acting dean of graduate studies, 1969-70, academic vice-president, 1970-75, University Professor, 1975-91. Visiting professor of English, University of British Columbia, 1951; visiting fellow, Wolfson College, Cambridge University, 1975-76. Member, Advisory Committee on Fine Arts, Canadian Department of Transportation, 1959; chairman of English panel, postgraduate scholarship committee of Canada Council, 1963-65; member, Governor-General's Awards Jury for Literature, 1966-69, 1990; member of council, Edmonton Art Gallery, 1967-70; chairman, Canadian Studies Program, 1979-82; president, Edmonton Chamber Music Society, 1980-83. Advisor to Canadian Secretary of State (Multiculturalism), 1987.

MEMBER: Philosophical Society of University of Alberta (president, 1955-56), Association of Canadian University Teachers of English (president, 1962-63), Royal Society of Arts (fellow), International Institute of Arts and Letters (fellow), Association of Academic Staff of University of Alberta (vice-president, 1959-60; president, 1960-61), Humanities Association of Canada (national executive, 1964-66).

AWARDS, HONORS: President's medal for short story writing from University of Western Ontario, 1959, for "The Traveling Nude;" J. I. Segal Foundation Award for Literature, 1983; Rutherford Award for excellence in teaching, 1986; Sir Frederick Haultain Prize for Fine Arts, 1986; appointed Officer of the Order of Canada, 1987.

WRITINGS:

The Rich Man (novel; also see below), McClelland & Stewart, 1948.

(Editor and author of introduction) John Heath, *Aphrodite, and Other Poems,* Ryerson, 1959.

The Betrayal (novel; also see below), McClelland & Stewart, 1964.

The Almost Meeting, and Other Stories (includes "The Travelling Nude"), NeWest (Edmonton), 1981.

Another Country: Writings by and about Henry Kreisel, edited by Shirley Neuman, NeWest, 1985.

PLAYS

"He Who Sells His Shadow: A Fable for Radio" (radio play), *Wednesday Night,* Canadian Broadcasting Corp. (CBC), 1956.

"The Betrayal" (teleplay), *Bob Hope Theatre,* CBC, 1965.

The Broken Globe (adapted from a short story; first produced in Edmonton), CBC-TV, 1976.

Author of stage play adaptation of *The Rich Man,* 1987. Also author of radio and television plays in the 1950s for CBC, for programs including *Anthology* and *Stage.*

OTHER

Kreisel's work represented in anthologies, including *Modern Canadian Stories,* edited by Roberto Ruberto and Glose Rimanelli, Ryerson, 1962; *The Best American Short Stories,* edited by Martha Foley and David Burnett, Houghton, 1966; *A Book of Canadian Stories,* edited by Desmond Pacey, Ryerson, 1966; *Stories from Western Canada,* edited by Ruby Weibe, Macmillan, 1972. Contributor of articles and stories to literary journals, including *Literary Review, Canadian Forum, Canadian Literature, Tamarack Review, Queen's Quarterly, University of Toronto Quarterly,* and *Prism.*

Kreisel's papers are housed in the archives and special collections of the University of Manitoba Libraries.

SIDELIGHTS: Henry Kreisel, a noted Canadian author and academic, was perhaps best known for his portrayal of the immigrant experience in his novels and many of his short stories. Kreisel's works "document what he calls the 'double experience' of the immigrant struggling to bridge (or widen) the temporal, spiritual, and psychological gulfs between European background and Canadian foreground," describes Neil Besner in the *Dictionary of Literary Biography.* "To dissociate himself from either world, or to misperceive it, diminishes his humanity."

Kreisel based his writing on personal experience as an immigrant. Born in Venice, Austria, on June 5, 1922, Kreisel fled the Nazis in 1938 with his family, seeking shelter in England. He and his father, however, were interned as "enemy aliens" by the British government from May of 1940 to late in 1941. Sent to camps in Canada, Kreisel kept a journal recording his immediate, day-to-day impressions. Upon his release, he decided to remain in Canada and pursue his dream of becoming a writer.

Kreisel's first novel, *The Rich Man,* focuses on Jacob Grossman, an immigrant returning to his European roots. Creating a wealthy image to impress his family, Jacob poses as a successful clothes designer when he is actually a lowly clothes presser in a Toronto factory. On the eve of World War II and Hitler's invasion, he arrives to find a struggling city, anti-Semitism on the increase, and widespread unemployment. His own family is also in the midst of difficult times. It is only when he is asked for financial help that his deception is revealed. "The strength of the novel lies in Kreisel's sensitive and carefully controlled exploration of Jacob's failings," Besner comments. "With understated compassion he shows how Jacob, an immigrant Everyman, remolds his experience in the New World to fit his family's dreams, returning to present himself as a fifty-two-year-old prodigal, the incarnation of their hopes."

In *The Betrayal,* Kreisel brings a European to Canada to show the war experience from a different viewpoint. Mark Lerner, the narrator, is a young college professor lecturing students about the French Revolution. Through one of his students, Katherine Held, he meets Theodore Stappler, "the lone survivor of a group of Austrian refugees betrayed twelve years earlier by Joseph Held, Katherine's father," describes Besner. Held had been forced by the Nazis to choose between the safety of his own family or that of the refugees. Stappler is in Canada seeking revenge on Held, but he is hampered by feelings that he, too, may have betrayed the group through his own actions. Stappler confides in Lerner, and the professor is then forced to judge the two men's actions, looking at history in a personal, rather than detached, way. Finally, Stappler departs without his revenge, leaving Lerner to contemplate the meaning of Stappler's story. "*The Betrayal* is more ambitious, more complex, more technically accomplished, and more explicitly a literary novel than *The Rich Man,*" judges Besner.

Kreisel was also the author of several short stories, some of which have been collected in *The Almost Meeting, and Other Stories.* Within his short fiction, Besner explains, "Kreisel continues to explore the ruptures, discontinuities, and 'almost meetings' between Old and New World characters and visions." Of himself, Kreisel once commented: "I came to this country from Austria, via England, having escaped the Nazis in 1938. In my writings I have used the European as well as Canadian experience. This double experience, and its reflection in novels and stories, has been my major contribution to the literature of this country."

BIOGRAPHICAL/CRITICAL SOURCES:

BOOKS

Dictionary of Literary Biography, Volume 88: *Canadian Writers, 1920-1959, Second Series,* Gale, 1989.

PERIODICALS

Canadian Fiction, May, 1965, p. 45.
Quill & Quire, January, 1982, p. 31.*

* * *

KRISHNA, Gopi
See SHIVPURI, Gopi Krishna

* * *

KUCZKIR, Mary 1933-
(Fern Michaels, a joint pseudonym)

PERSONAL: Born April 9, 1933, in Hastings, PA; daughter of Albert and Lucy Kovac; married Michael Kuczkir (an engineer), October 3, 1952; children: Cynthia, Susy, Patty, Mike, Dave.

ADDRESSES: *Home*—9 David Ct., Edison, NJ 08820. *Agent*—c/o Ballantine, 201 E. 50th St., New York, NY 10022.

CAREER: Writer. Worked as market researcher.

WRITINGS:

ROMANCES WITH ROBERTA ANDERSON UNDER JOINT PSEUDONYM FERN MICHAELS

Pride and Passion, Ballantine, 1975.
Vixen in Velvet, Ballantine, 1976.
Captive Passions, Ballantine, 1977.
Valentina, Ballantine, 1978.
Captive Embraces, Ballantine, 1979.
Captive Splendors, Ballantine, 1980.
The Delta Ladies, Pocket Books, 1980.
The Golden Lasso, Silhouette, 1980.
Captive Innocence, Ballantine, 1981.
Sea Gypsy, Silhouette, 1981.
Whisper My Name, Silhouette, 1981.
Beyond Tomorrow, Silhouette, 1981.
Wild Honey, Pocket Books, 1982.
Nightstar, G. K. Hall, 1982.
Paint Me Rainbows, G. K. Hall, 1982.
All She Can Be, Ballantine, 1983.
Free Spirit, Ballantine, 1983.
Tender Warrior, Ballantine, 1983.
Cinders to Satin, Ballantine, 1984.
Texas Rich, Ballantine, 1985.
Texas Heat, Ballantine, 1986.

To Taste the Wine, Ballantine, 1987.
Texas Fury, Ballantine, 1989.

THRILLERS WITH ROBERTA ANDERSON UNDER JOINT PSEUDONYM FERN MICHAELS

Without Warning, Pocket Books, 1981.
Panda Bear Is Critical, Macmillan, 1982.

SOLE AUTHOR UNDER PSEUDONYM FERN MICHAELS

Sins of Omission, Ballantine, 1989.
Sins of the Flesh, Ballantine, 1990.
Captive Secrets, Ballantine, 1991.
For All Their Lives, Ballantine, 1991.
Texas Sunrise, Ballantine, 1993.

Also author of *My Dish Towel Flies at Half Mast* (collected columns), Ballantine, 1979 and "Merry Mary," a column in *Barnesboro Star.*

SIDELIGHTS: Under the joint pseudonym Fern Michaels, Mary Kuczkir has written numerous romance novels with collaborator Roberta Anderson. In 1989, she obtained full legal right to use the pseudonym herself. Among Kuczkir and Anderson's most popular works are *Captive Passions,* a story about a noblewoman who disguises herself as a pirate and plunders her husband's trading vessels, and *Valentina,* which relates the experiences of a handmaiden in the court of Richard the Lionheart. Other successful books include *Captive Embrace,* in which the heroine is deserted by her husband after the death of their child, and *The Delta Ladies,* about a man who returns to his hometown after having fled years earlier for seducing the town tycoon's daughter.

BIOGRAPHICAL/CRITICAL SOURCES:

BOOKS

Falk, Kathryn, *Love's Leading Ladies,* Pinnacle Books, 1982.

PERIODICALS

New York Times Book Review, July 8, 1979.
Us, June 27, 1978.
Writers' Digest, December, 1978.

* * *

KUNICZAK, W(ieslaw) S(tanislaw) 1930- (Amos Wallin)

PERSONAL: Born February 4, 1930, in Lwow, Poland; immigrated to United States in 1950, naturalized citizen, 1958; son of Stanislaw Bronislaw (a soldier) and Marie-Helene (a pianist; maiden name, de Georgeon) Kuniczak; married Barbara Bergstrom Carpenter, January, 1960 (divorced, May, 1961); married Kathryn Stein, March, 1962 (died, December, 1976); married Amy Wallin (a ballerina), May, 1979. *Education:* London School of Economics and Political Science, B.Sc., 1949; Alliance College, B.A., 1953; Columbia University, M.S., 1954. *Politics:* Independent Democrat. *Religion:* Roman Catholic.

ADDRESSES: c/o Mercyhurst College, Glenwood Hills, Erie, PA 16546.

CAREER: Auburn Citizen-Advertiser, Auburn, NY, reporter, feature writer, assistant telegraph editor, assistant city editor, and copy editor, 1954-55; *Cleveland Plain Dealer,* Cleveland, OH, reporter, feature writer, military editor, and columnist, 1957-60; staff writer for public relations firms and advertising agencies, including Edward Howard & Co., Griswold-Eschelman Co., and Standard Oil Co. of Ohio, all in Cleveland, and Ketchum McLeod & Grove and Burson-Marsteller, Inc., both in Pittsburgh, PA, 1960-68; *Pittsburgh Post-Gazette,* Pittsburgh, rewriter and feature writer, 1968-69; imprisoned in Greece, 1969-72; Allied Press Enterprises, Kyrenia, Cyprus, managing editor and feature columnist on Middle East affairs, 1972-74; ambulance driver in Israel during October War, 1973; free-lance writer, 1974—. Lecturer for adult education program in Chagrin Falls, OH, 1960-61; lecturer and director of Professional Workshop in the Novel, Denver Free University, Denver, CO, 1983; writer-in-residence and visiting professor, Alliance College, Cambridge, PA, 1983-85; writer-in-residence, Mercyhurst College, Erie, PA. *Military service:* U.S. Army, Infantry, 1955-58; served in Korea; became sergeant.

MEMBER: American Newspaper Guild, Authors Guild, Authors League of America, Dramatists' Guild, Polish Institute of Arts and Letters in America, Inc., Jozef Pilsudski Historical Institute (New York), Kosciuszko Foundation.

AWARDS, HONORS: Photojournalism Award, Associated Press, 1955; Pulitzer Prize nomination, 1956, for investigative reporting; Cleveland Newspaper Guild Award, 1957, for best feature; grant from National Translation Center, 1967, to complete translation of trilogy by Henryk Sienkiewicz; Gold Medal, Pittsburgh Advertising Club, 1968, for best print campaign; Silver Medal, Pittsburgh Advertising Club, 1968, for best radio campaign; Nobel Prize in Literature nomination, 1984, for his trilogy on the Polish experience in World War II, comprising *The Thousand Hour Day, The March,* and *Valedictory;* residency grant, Sendzimir Fund of the Kosciuszko Foundation, the Copernicus Society of America, and Dr. Walter M. Golaski of Philadelphia, 1983-86; grant, Copernicus Society of America and Polish Cultural Alliance, 1985-87, for special translations.

WRITINGS:

The Thousand Hour Day (novel; Book-of-the-Month Club selection), Dial, 1966. *The Sempinski Affair* (novel), Doubleday, 1969.

My Name Is Million: An Illustrated History of the Poles in America, Doubleday, 1978.

The March (novel), Doubleday, 1979.

Valedictory (novel), Doubleday, 1983.

(Editor) *The Glass Mountain: Twenty-Five-Twenty-Six Ancient Polish Folk Tales and Fables,* translated by Albert Juszczak, illustrated by Pat Bargielski, Hippocrene, 1992.

TRANSLATIONS OF NOVELS BY HENRYK SIENKIEWICZ

The Deluge (original title, *Potop;* second novel in trilogy), Hippocrene, 1991.

Fire in the Steppe (original title, *Pan Wolodyjowski;* third novel in trilogy), Hippocrene, 1992.

Quo Vadis, Macmillan, 1993.

With Fire and Sword (original title, *Ogniem i Mieczem;* first novel in trilogy), Collier, 1993.

Contributor of articles to magazines, including *American Heritage* and *Casa Geo* (Mexico City). Also author of *Journeys* (autobiographical novel), completed in 1984, and editor-translator of *The Pharoah,* by Boleslaw Prus, for the American Center for Polish Culture, completed in 1982, both unpublished. Former managing editor of *Tubular Steel Progress.*

WORK IN PROGRESS: States of Siege, a novel about contemporary Poland.

SIDELIGHTS: W. S. Kuniczak has written extensively about the Polish experience in American and European history. With the exception of one work of nonfiction, he has chosen the novel as the form in which to express his ideas. "A novel should be a piece of art," Kuniczak told Peter Gardner in *Publishers Weekly,* "something to last. It should say things that apply to everybody. . . . The great themes remain the same, but they have to be rephrased every so often. I regard novel writing as a great responsibility, almost a mission."

Kuniczak's World War II trilogy of meticulously researched and thoroughly documented novels—*The Thousand Hour Day, The March,* and *Valedictory*—evoked comparisons to Leo Tolstoy's *War and Peace* for their multitude of characters and to Ernest Hemingway's *For Whom the Bell Tolls* for their spare prose. The title of Kuniczak's first novel, *The Thousand Hour Day,* refers to the first thousand hours of World War II, which began with Germany's invasion of Poland in September of 1939. The author himself, along with his mother and sister, fled on foot from his native Poland in the wake of the invasion; he was reunited with his father in Great Britain more than a year later, having escaped via Rumania and France.

In addition to summoning his own recollections of the event, Kuniczak prepared to write his novel by interviewing more than seven hundred Polish, German, English, and French survivors. The result was generally considered to be a swiftly paced read that was not weighed down by the profusion of its facts and events. "His novel wears its vast scholarship lightly," Frederic Morton wrote in the *New York Times Book Review.* "The background of the story is a minutely textured, beautifully interlocked, fast-moving procession of details," Morton continued. "You can count the plaster cracks in the War Room of the Polish General Staff during the bombardments. You hear the teletype crackling out rivalries among German command posts. And you get a dreadfully good idea of how good Madeira tastes with the horse-steak that became inevitable in Warsaw besieged."

Kuniczak's highly detailed rendering of battlefield agonies and troop movements led some critics to complain about the lack of character development in his "massive and unremittingly gory novel," as a reviewer for *Time* described it. According to the *Spectator*'s Peter Vansittart, Kuniczak created "no unique personal world" in *The Thousand Hour Day,* which nonetheless represented "a remarkable feat of reconstruction of many levels of a short but particularly horrible war." Vansittart continued, "The impact sometimes stuns but the total effect, written out of conviction, knowledge, and narrative skill, should affect anyone who has not opted out of human decency."

By focusing on the overwhelming nature of historical events at the expense of fleshing out his characters, Kuniczak expressed his philosophy of a world without heroes as they have been conventionally understood. "When I conceived this trilogy," Kuniczak told Gardner, "I decided it would have no hero. History has neither heroes nor victims, by which I mean that people both suffer and inflict suffering. In the final analysis, no one's hands are entirely clean."

Despite the novel's unrelenting concentration on events, many critics were pleased with the overall effect of Kuniczak's method. "Without heroics," Peter Buitenhuis declared in *Harper's,* "Mr. Kuniczak splendidly creates the heroism of [the Polish] resistance. . . . This is a war novel, sometimes of the most horrifying kind, but it is more than that. It chronicles, psychologically, how a nation that is living by nineteenth-century values is crushed by a state that has adopted the technology and ideology of the twentieth."

Six years in the writing after four years of research, the second novel in Kuniczak's trilogy, *The March,* which depicts the wartime deportation to work camps in the Soviet

Union of more than two million Poles, elicited comparisons to Aleksander Solzhenitsyn and Boris Pasternak. Set partly in the author's native village of Lwow, the story ranges far and wide as Kuniczak describes such Russian atrocities as torture in the Lubyanka prison, the Katyn Forest massacre of Polish officers, and the less well-known White Sea drowning massacre. "[Kuniczak] depicts best such elemental things: the adventitious beauty of the autumn of Poland's humiliation; the death-dealing Russian winter; lamp-lit burrows of conspirators' quarters; the squalor of prison; life shorn, denied, or draining away; life on the edge," noted James Summerville in *Washington Post Book World.* Although Summerville found his depictions of intimacy somewhat lacking, Gardner described the book as "rich in thought as well as in passion and suffering."

The title of *The March,* Kuniczak told Gardner, "refers to a march that was both physical and spiritual. In the second sense it reflects the evolutionary history of the Polish people, particularly their tremendous capacity to survive." He added, "If there's a unifying thread running through the story, it's the redemptive power of love. And I chose a young woman [Catherine] as my main protagonist, incidentally, because so few people bother to think about what women go through in times of war."

The March's other main character, Abel, undergoes a prison ordeal based on Kuniczak's own incarceration in Greece from 1969 to 1972. The author told Gardner that his "cell became a sort of religious retreat," where he was able to draw upon his knowledge of Eastern mysticism and his experience of living in India with a yogi for six months in the late 1960s.

The final installment in the trilogy, *Valedictory,* concerns a contingent of Polish fighter pilots who are reunited in the 303rd (Polish) Squadron of the Royal Air Force, under whose auspices they fly missions against the Germans. In evaluating the novel for the *Los Angeles Times Book Review,* Paul Dean wrote, "Kuniczak presents brilliant thoughts ('affection, for lack of courage to use the stronger word, is too dangerous to attempt again,') that peel back three layers of emotion." Despite Dean's irritation with some of Kuniczak's "lesser" characterizations and with what Dean called the author's ignorance of flight, he concluded that "great portions of Kuniczak are stunning. His dialogue . . . forms automatic, graceful transitions with sufficient distinction to support each personality."

Kuniczak's other books include a gothic Cold War spy novel, *The Sempinski Affair,* and a work of nonfiction, *My Name Is Million: An Illustrated History of the Poles in America,* in which he contends that there is "no area of American life in which [the Poles] have not left an imprint of their own." Reviewing Kuniczak's "fascinating" anecdotal account of the Polish contributions to American theatre, finance, sports, education, business, and military science, Laurence Orzell wrote in *Best Sellers* that the few factual errors contained in the book "do not vitiate the work's overall objectivity."

Kuniczak's books have been published in seventeen languages and in twenty-two countries. He is fluent in Polish and understands French, Spanish, Russian, Greek, Serbian, and Arabic. Kuniczak is a world traveler who has lived in Mexico, Europe, the Middle East, and the United States.

BIOGRAPHICAL/CRITICAL SOURCES:

BOOKS

Kuniczak, W. S., *My Name Is Million: An Illustrated History of the Poles in America,* Doubleday, 1978.

Tynan, Daniel J., editor, *Biographical Dictionary of Contemporary Catholic American Writing,* Greenwood Press, 1989, pp. 155-158.

PERIODICALS

Best Sellers, June 15, 1967, p. 121; September 1, 1969, p. 198; December 1978, p. 278.

Book Week, May 7, 1967, p. 4.

Christian Science Monitor, August 17, 1967, p. 5.

Harper's, June 1967, pp. 106-107.

Los Angeles Times Book Review, November 6, 1983, p. 12.

New York Times Book Review, May 7, 1967, p. 5; November 9, 1969, p. 37.

Polish American Studies, spring, 1980, pp. 52-664.

Polish Review, autumn, 1967, pp. 78-83; spring, 1987, pp. 85-92.

Publishers Weekly, August 13, 1979, pp. 6-7.

Saturday Review, May 13, 1967, p. 40.

Spectator, September 8, 1967.

Time, June 30, 1967.

Times Literary Supplement, September 28, 1967, p. 870; April 9, 1970, p. 391.

Washington Post Book World, August 31, 1969, p. 8; October 13, 1979, p. B3; September 4, 1983, p. 8.*

—Sidelights by Cynthia Walker

* * *

KUPER, Adam (Jonathan) 1941-

PERSONAL: Born December 29, 1941, in Johannesburg, South Africa; son of Simon Meyer (a judge) and Gertrude (a teacher; maiden name, Hesselson) Kuper; married Jessica Cohen (a writer and publisher), December 15, 1966; children: Simon, Jeremy, Hannah. *Education:* University of the Witwatersrand, B.A., 1961; Cambridge University, Ph.D., 1966. *Religion:* Jewish.

ADDRESSES: Home—16 Muswell Rd., London N10 2BG, England. *Office*—Department of Human Sciences, Brunel University, Uxbridge UB8 3PH, England.

CAREER: Makerere University, Kampala, Uganda, lecturer in social anthropology, 1967-70; University of London, London, England, lecturer in anthropology, 1970-76; University of Leiden, Leiden, Netherlands, professor of African cultural anthropology, 1976-85; Brunel University, Uxbridge, England, professor of social anthropology and head of department of human sciences, 1985—. Fellow at Center for Advanced Study in the Behavioral Sciences, Palo Alto, CA, 1980-81.

MEMBER: Association of Social Anthropologists, Royal Anthropological Institute.

AWARDS, HONORS: Honorary doctorate from University of Gothenburg, 1978.

WRITINGS:

Kalahari Village Politics: An African Democracy, Cambridge University Press, 1970.

(Editor with A. I. Richards) *Councils in Action,* Cambridge University Press, 1971.

Anthropologists and Anthropology: The British School, 1922-1972, Universe Books, 1973, 2nd revised edition published as *Anthropology and Anthropologists: The Modern British School,* Routledge & Kegan Paul, 1983.

Changing Jamaica, Routledge & Kegan Paul, 1976.

(Editor) *The Social Anthropology of Radcliffe-Brown,* Routledge & Kegan Paul, 1977.

Wives for Cattle, Routledge & Kegan Paul, 1982.

(Editor with wife, Jessica Kuper) *The Social Science Encyclopedia,* Routledge & Kegan Paul, 1985.

South Africa and the Anthropologist, Routledge & Kegan Paul, 1987.

The Invention of Primitive Society, Routledge & Kegan Paul, 1988.

(Editor) *Conceptualizing Society,* Routledge & Kegan Paul, 1992.

WORK IN PROGRESS: Research on pre-conquest political systems in Southern Africa.

BIOGRAPHICAL/CRITICAL SOURCES:

PERIODICALS

Times Literary Supplement, July 2, 1982; May 9, 1986.

L

LANCASTER, F(rederick) Wilfrid 1933-

PERSONAL: Born September 4, 1933, in Durham, England; son of Frederick (a coal miner) and Violet (Blackburn) Lancaster; married Maria Cesaria Volpe, June 24, 1961; children: Miriam, Owen Frederick, Jude Joseph, Aaron Ralph. *Education:* Attended Newcastle-upon-Tyne School of Librarianship, 1950-54; Library Association of Great Britain, fellow (by thesis), 1969. *Religion:* Roman Catholic.

Avocational Interests: Music (especially opera—collects operas, operettas, and musicals on videotapes and videodiscs).

ADDRESSES: *Home*—1807 Cindy Lynn, Urbana, IL 61801. *Office*—Graduate School of Library and Information Science, University of Illinois, Urbana, IL 61801.

CAREER: Newcastle-upon-Tyne Public Libraries, Newcastle-upon-Tyne, England, senior assistant, 1953-57; Tube Investments Ltd., Birmingham, England, assistant information officer, 1957-59; Akron Public Library, Akron, OH, senior librarian, science technology, 1959-60; Babcock & Wilcox Co., Barberton, OH, technical librarian, 1960-62; ASLIB, London, England, senior research assistant, 1962; Herner & Co., Washington, DC, resident consultant and head of systems evaluation group, 1964-65; National Library of Medicine, Bethesda, MD, information systems specialist, 1965-68; Westat Research, Inc., Bethesda, director of information retrieval services, 1969-70; University of Illinois at Urbana-Champaign, Urbana, Graduate School of Library and Information Science, associate professor, 1970-72, professor of library science, 1972-92, professor emeritus, 1992—, director of program in biomedical librarianship, 1970-74.

Adjunct lecturer at School of Library and Information Services, University of Maryland, 1968-70; lecturer at NATO International Advanced Study Institutes, 1965, 1972, and 1975, at Graduate School, U.S. Department of Agriculture, 1967-69, at Defense Intelligence School, U.S. Department of Defense, 1970, and at universities in the United States, Europe, Australia, China, India, Brazil, and Taiwan, including University of Chicago, University of Texas, and University of Pittsburgh. Member of board of directors, Herner & Co., Washington, DC, 1992—; member of panel on information sciences technology of Federal Council for Science and Technology, 1966-67. Has participated in and presented papers at numerous conferences. Consultant to Association for Computing Machinery, 1969-70, Center for Applied Linguistics, 1970-71, National Institutes of Health, 1970-73, International Development Research Center, several United Nations organizations, and other government agencies, professional societies, and commercial organizations.

MEMBER: American Society for Information Science, American Library Association, Library Association (England), Phi Kappa Phi.

AWARDS, HONORS: American Society for Information Science, award for best paper of 1969, for "MEDLARS: Report on the Evaluation of Its Operating Efficiency," published in *American Documentation,* awards for best book on information science, 1970, for *Information Retrieval Systems,* 1975, for *Information Retrieval On-Line,* 1979, for *Toward Paperless Information Systems,* and 1992, for *Indexing and Abstracting in Theory and Practice,* and Award of Merit, 1988; Ralph Shaw Award, American Library Association, 1978, for *The Measurement and Evaluation of Library Services;* John Brubaker Memorial Award, *Catholic Library World,* 1980; Outstanding Information Science Teacher Award, American Society for Information Science, 1980; Fulbright teaching fellowship in Brazil, 1975, Denmark, 1985, and India, 1991; G. K. Hall

Award, American Library Association, 1989; University Scholar Award, University of Illinois, 1989-92.

WRITINGS:

Information Retrieval Systems: Characteristics, Testing, and Evaluation, Wiley, 1968.

Evaluation of the MEDLARS Demand Search Service, National Library of Medicine, 1968.

Vocabulary Control for Information Retrieval, Information Resources Press, 1972, 2nd edition, 1986.

(With Emily Gallup Fayen) *Information Retrieval On-Line,* Wiley, 1973.

(Editor with C. W. Cleverdon) *Evaluation and Scientific Management of Libraries and Information Centres,* Noordhoff, 1977.

The Measurement and Evaluation of Library Services, Information Resources Press, 1977, 2nd edition, 1991.

Toward Paperless Information Systems, Academic Press, 1978.

(With John Martyn) *Investigative Methods in Library and Information Science,* Information Resources Press, 1981.

Libraries and Librarians in an Age of Electronics, Information Resources Press, 1983.

If You Want to Evaluate Your Library . . . , Graduate School of Library and Information Science, University of Illinois, 1988.

Indexing and Abstracting in Theory and Practice, Graduate School of Library and Information Science, University of Illinois, 1991.

Also author of monographs and research reports. Also editor of books. Contributor of chapters to more than forty books. Contributor to *Encyclopedia of Library and Information Science* and *Annual Review of Information Science and Technology.* Editor, "Specialized Information Sources Guides" series, Herner & Co., 1970-73; editor of *Proceedings* of Annual Clinic on Library Applications of Data Processing, University of Illinois, 1971-75, 1978-79, 1983, 1987, and 1992. Contributor of more than one hundred articles and reviews to library and documentation journals and other periodicals, including *Journal of the American Medical Association, New Scientist,* and *National Forum.* Editor, *Library Trends,* 1986—; member of editorial board, *International Forum on Information and Documentation, Scientometrics, Infomediary, Revista AIBDA,* and *Libri.*

Information Retrieval Systems has been published in Japanese, Chinese, and Russian editions. Several other books have been translated into Japanese, Chinese, Spanish, Korean, Portuguese, and Arabic.

WORK IN PROGRESS: Working on a second edition of *If You Want to Evaluate Your Library . . . ;* editing a book on the future of the library for Haworth Press.

SIDELIGHTS: F. Wilfrid Lancaster once told *CA:* "I am writing books as quickly as possible in the firm belief that the book printed on paper has a limited life expectancy. The printed book will be replaced by new forms of communication/expression more suited to the age of electronics."

* * *

LANGDON, Robert Adrian 1924-

PERSONAL: Born September 3, 1924, in Adelaide, Australia; son of Arthur Louis (a carpenter) and Doris (a dressmaker; maiden name, McFarling) Langdon; married Iva Louise Layton, December 6, 1959 (died December 15, 1984); children: Louise. *Education:* Attended high school in Adelaide, Australia.

ADDRESSES: Home—15 Darambal St., Aranda, Australian Capital Territory 2614, Australia. *Office*—Pacific and Asian History Division, Research School of Pacific Studies, Australian National University, Canberra, Australian Capital Territory 2600, Australia.

CAREER: South Australian Public Service, Adelaide, clerk, 1941-42; worked as free-lance journalist, ship's fireman, dock laborer, and secretary in Australia and England, 1946-68; Grace & Co., La Paz, Bolivia, managerial secretary, 1948-51; Canadian National Railways, Toronto, Ontario, clerk, 1952; Advertiser Newspapers Ltd., Adelaide, journalist, 1953-61; Pacific Publications Pty. Ltd., Sydney, Australia, journalist 1962-63; assistant editor of *Pacific Islands Monthly,* 1964-68; Australian National University, Canberra, executive officer of Pacific Manuscripts Bureau, 1968-86; visiting fellow in Pacific and Asian History Division, Research School of Pacific Studies, 1986—. *Military service:* Royal Australian Navy, 1942-46.

MEMBER: Polynesian Society (New Zealand), Societe des Oceanistes (France), Societe d'Etudes Oceaniennes (Tahiti), Hakluyt Society (England).

AWARDS, HONORS: Australian National University research fellowship, 1977-79; Caballero de la Orden de Isabela la Catolica, 1980; M.A. (honoris causa), Australian National University, 1986.

WRITINGS:

Tahiti: Island of Love, Cassell, 1959, 5th edition, Pacific Publications, 1979.

The Lost Caravel, Pacific Publications, 1975.

(With Darrell Tryon) *The Language of Easter Island: Its Development and Eastern Polynesian Relationships,* Institute for Polynesian Studies, 1983.

The Lost Caravel Re-explored, Brolga Press, 1988.

EDITOR

Cumulative Index to "Pacific Islands Monthly," 1930-1945, Pacific Publications, 1968.

American Whalers and Traders in the Pacific: A Guide to Records on Microfilm, Pacific Manuscripts Bureau, 1978.

Thar She Went: An Interim Index to the Pacific Ports and Islands Visited by American Whalers and Traders in the Nineteenth Century, Pacific Manuscripts Bureau, 1984.

Cumulative Index to the "Pacific Islands Monthly," 1945-1955, Pacific Manuscripts Bureau, 1984.

The Catholic Church in the Western Pacific: A Guide to Records on Microfilm, Pacific Manuscripts Bureau, 1986.

An Index to "Quarterly Jottings from the New Hebrides", 1893-1966, Pacific Manuscripts Bureau, 1988.

The P.M.B. Book of Indexes, Pacific Manuscripts Bureau, 1988.

CONTRIBUTOR

Peter Hastings, editor, *Papua New Guinea: Prospero's Other Island,* Angus & Robertson, 1971.

Noel Rutherford, editor, *Friendly Islands: A History of Tonga,* Oxford University Press, 1977.

Niel Gunson, editor, *The Changing Pacific: Essays in Honour of H.E. Maude,* Oxford University Press, 1978.

Jukka Siikala, editor, *Oceanic Studies: Essays in Honour of Aarne A. Koskinen,* Finnish Anthropological Society, 1982.

Peter Stanbury and Lydia Bushell, editors, *South Pacific Islands,* Macleay Museum, 1984.

OTHER

Also contributor to *World Book Encyclopedia, World Book Year Book, Encyclopedia of Papua and New Guinea, Australian Dictionary of Biography,* and *Pacific Islands Year Book.* Contributor to many magazines, newspapers, and learned journals.

WORK IN PROGRESS: Every Goose a Swan, an autobiography; research into the prehistory of Polynesia, using data from oral traditions, linguistics, genetics, archaeology, ethnobotany, ethnozoology, etc.

SIDELIGHTS: Robert Adrian Langdon worked his way around the world from 1947 to 1953. He visited Fiji, New Guinea, Malaysia, India, England, the United States and Canada, Bolivia, Peru, Chile, Uruguay, Brazil, Spain, Morocco, Tahiti and New Zealand. Since 1962 he has made frequent visits to the Pacific islands from New Guinea eastward to Easter Island. In 1977, 1985, and 1989, Langdon's research interests took him on trips around the world.

Langdon told *CA:* "I decided before I was ten that I would be a historian when I grew up, and almost everything I did before I began writing professionally was with that end in view. I have always read omnivorously, but three writers have especially influenced me. George Borrow, the nineteenth-century English writer, aroused my interest in things Spanish with his book *The Bible in Spain.* Somerset Maugham turned my thoughts toward the South Seas and taught me the virtue of telling a story well. The sixteenth-century writer Francois Rabelais inspired me to adopt an encyclopedic approach to learning. Borrow and Rabelais also encouraged me to study languages, and all three moved me to travel widely, especially to the more exotic parts of the globe.

"I wrote my first book, a popular history of Tahiti, because that was the most fascinating place I visited during six years of wandering round the world, and because I found that no one had written such a book before.

"My research on Tahiti's history, combined with my knowledge of Spanish and things Spanish, made me uniquely qualified to write *The Lost Caravel,* which sets out to elucidate the fate of the crew of the Spanish caravel, *San Lesmes,* that disappeared on a voyage from the Strait of Magellan to the East Indies in 1526. The book puts forward the theory that the crew of the *San Lesmes* played an important but previously unsuspected role in the prehistory of a number of Polynesian islands from Eastern Island to New Zealand and that some aspects of Polynesian culture that had long been attributed to the genius of the Polynesians were, in fact, derived from Europe. *The Lost Caravel Re-explored* is a revised and expanded version of my original book, incorporating the fruits of 12 further years of research.

"Research on the fate of the *San Lesmes* and other Spanish ships lost in the Pacific Ocean in the sixteenth century has opened up so many new lines of inquiry that I see myself preoccupied with them for several years yet. In the process it seems to me that a good deal of the prehistory of Polynesia will have to be reinterpreted and that some interesting discoveries will be made of value to science."

* * *

LAPIERRE, Dominique 1931-

PERSONAL: Born July 30, 1931, in Chatelaillon, France; son of Jean (a diplomat) and Luce (Andreotti) Lapierre; married Aliette Spitzer, August 4, 1952; children: Alexandra. *Education:* Attended Institut des Sciences Politiques, Paris, 1951; Lafayette College, Easton, PA, B.A., 1952. *Religion:* Catholic.

Avocational Interests: Tennis, horseback riding.

ADDRESSES: Home and office—26 Avenue Kleber, 75116 Paris, France. *Agent*—Morton L. Janklow, 598 Madison Ave., New York, NY 10021.

CAREER: Paris Match (magazine), Paris, France, war correspondent in Korea, 1953, editor, 1954-67; author of books, 1967—.

AWARDS, HONORS: Grand prize, Foundation des bourses de Zellidja, 1949, for a study on Mexico and the United States; Christopher Award, 1986, for *The City of Joy.*

WRITINGS:

Un dollar les mille kilometres (title means "A Dollar for One Thousand Kilometers"), Grasset (Paris), 1949.

Lune de miel autour de la terre, preface by Andre Maurois, Grasset, 1954, translation by Helen Beauclerk published as *Honeymoon around the World,* Secker & Warburg, 1957.

En Liberte sur les routes d'U.R.S.S. (title means "Freely on Soviet Highways"), Grasset, 1957.

Russie portes ouvertes (title means "Open Doors to Soviet Russia"), Editions Vie (Lausanne, Switzerland), 1957.

Les Caids de New York (title means "The New York Bosses"), Julliard (Paris), 1958.

Chessman m'a dit (title means "Chessman Told Me"), Del Duca (Paris), 1960.

(With Stephane Groueff) *Les Ministres du crime* (title means "The Ministers of Crime"), Julliard, 1969.

The City of Joy, translated from the French by Kathryn Spink, Doubleday, 1985.

Beyond Love (Literary Guild selection), translated from the French by Spink, Warner, 1990.

WITH LARRY COLLINS

Paris brule-t-il?, Laffont (Paris), 1964, published as *Is Paris Burning?* (Literary Guild selection), Simon & Schuster, 1965.

Ou tu porteras mon deuil, Laffont, 1967, published as *Or I'll Dress You in Mourning* (Book-of-the-Month Club selection), Simon & Schuster, 1968.

O Jerusalem!, Laffont, 1971, published in English under same title (Literary Guild selection), Simon & Schuster, 1972.

Cette nuit la liberte, Laffont, 1975, published as *Freedom at Midnight* (Literary Guild selection), Simon & Schuster, 1975.

Le cinquieme Cavalier (novel), Laffont, 1980, published as *The Fifth Horseman* (Literary Guild selection), Simon & Schuster, 1980.

Mountbatten and the Partition of India, Vikas (New Delhi), 1982.

Mountbatten and Independent India, Vikas, 1983.

OTHER

Also author of filmscript adaptation of *O Jerusalem!*

ADAPTATIONS: Is Paris Burning? was adapted for film and released by Paramount, 1965; *The City of Joy* was adapted for film and released by Tri-Star, 1992; Paramount holds the film option for *The Fifth Horseman.*

WORK IN PROGRESS: A new book; a film on Mother Teresa of Calcutta.

SIDELIGHTS: Dominique Lapierre told *CA:* "My main professional interest is to bring back to life great moments of our contemporary history. I am interested in the great modern epics of humanity. History has the reputation to be dull: It's not dull if only you devote enough time and sweat to bring it back to life. I consider myself a historian using the modern technique of investigative journalism. My books are as thoroughly and seriously researched as the most serious history books, and in this sense can be of use to professional, or rather, to 'scholarly' historians. But because of the dramatic nature of their subjects and their kaleidoscopic treatment, they are also very popular with the general public."

Many of Lapierre's books have indeed been immensely popular with the general public, reaching best seller lists in Europe and the United States. The author is best known for his work with American writer Larry Collins; their collaborative titles include *Is Paris Burning?, O Jerusalem!,* and the novel *The Fifth Horseman. New York Times Book Review* correspondent Herbert Mitgang characterizes these and the other books by Lapierre and Collins as "international best sellers in fact-and-thriller documentary style." A journalist who turned exclusively to full-length book projects in 1967, Lapierre is perhaps one of the most critically acclaimed and commercially successful authors in the field of historical documentary nonfiction.

In 1981, subsequent to the publication of *The Fifth Horseman,* Lapierre and his wife travelled to Calcutta, India, to visit a home they had sponsored for children of leprosy victims. During their stay in the city, Mother Teresa took the Lapierres to one of the world's worst slums, an area of Calcutta the name of which translates as "The City of Joy." Lapierre later told the *New York Times Book Review* that though the hordes of people living in the City of Joy subsisted on less than ten cents a day, he witnessed "more joy, more compassion, more God-loving" than anywhere in his previous wide travels as a writer. He decided to chronicle life in the slum from the points of view of three people: a Bengali peasant struggling to earn a living there, a Polish priest devoting his life to the poor, and an American doctor generously battling the area's many deadly diseases. Lapierre's book *The City of Joy* was published in 1985, a year later received the prestigious Christopher

Award, and has sold more than seven million copies in 31 languages and editions, including five editions in Braille.

As Rumer Godden notes in the *New York Times Book Review, The City of Joy* "is about suffering, sorrow, cruelty and deprivation; about practices so hideous as almost to suspend belief, though they are shockingly true. It is about filth, rags, wounds, disease, even leprosy." Yet, writes Godden, "the book is about other words that wonderfully leaven the whole: loyalty, kindness, tolerance, generosity, patience, endurance, acceptance, faith, even holiness. And it is about such love that we cannot pass by on the other side. In any case, it is too fascinating to let us do that." Godden also feels that the book is, in a sense, "too overwhelming. It tells so much that the mind becomes numbed, as happens in a famine or cyclone . . . when compassion ceases simply because the heart can take no more." In a *Washington Post Book World* review of *The City of Joy,* Elisabeth Bumiller expresses the opinion that Lapierre "has actually managed to describe the poor from their own point of view. This is a remarkable feat." Though Bumiller feels that the author "sometimes overromanticizes the struggle of the poor . . . , diminishing their real pain and integrity," she nonetheless concludes: "*The City of Joy* is full of basic truths. Some of its moments may stay with a reader forever. . . . This book contains great lessons of resilience and dignity, and of what is really important when life is pared down to its essence. *The City of Joy* will make anyone a little richer for having read it."

Lapierre recently added that he supports five homes for five hundred children of lepers in Calcutta, "along with a whole humanitarian action including dispenseries, schools, rehabilitation centers for lepers, irrigation programs, etc., funded with my royalties from *The City of Joy* and donations from my readers."

BIOGRAPHICAL/CRITICAL SOURCES:

PERIODICALS

Atlantic, October, 1980.
Best Sellers, July 1, 1968.
Book World, June 2, 1968.
Chicago Tribune Book World, September 21, 1980.
Detroit News, November 13, 1966; May 7, 1972.
Harper's, August, 1968.
Life, June 4, 1965; June 7, 1968; July 14, 1972.
Los Angeles Times Book Review, August 31, 1980.
Nation, December 20, 1980.
National Observer, July 1, 1968.
Newsweek, November 24, 1975; September 8, 1980.
New York, September 1, 1980.
New York Review of Books, December 11, 1975; November 6, 1980.
New York Times, June 4, 1965; April 6, 1968; May 31, 1968; June 13, 1972; November 8, 1975; September 4, 1980.
New York Times Book Review, June 13, 1965; June 9, 1968; May 14, 1972; October 26, 1975; August 17, 1980; September 28, 1980; November 3, 1985.
Publishers Weekly, August 1, 1980.
Saturday Review, July 3, 1965; June 8, 1968; June 10, 1972; October 18, 1975.
Spectator, May 22, 1982.
Time, June 4, 1965; July 26, 1968; October 27, 1975.
Times Literary Supplement, September 30, 1965; May 8, 1969; October 13, 1972; October 3, 1980; August 6, 1982.
Village Voice, November 10, 1975.
Washington Post, June 8, 1968.
Washington Post Book World, August 10, 1980; February 6, 1983; October 27, 1985.

* * *

LASSNER, Jacob 1935-

PERSONAL: Born March 15, 1935; son of Kalman (a furrier) and Ruth (Friedman) Lassner. *Education:* University of Michigan, A.B., 1955; Brandeis University, M.A., 1957; Yale University, Ph.D., 1963.

ADDRESSES: Office—Department of History, Northwestern University, Evanston, IL 60201.

CAREER: Wayne State University, Detroit, MI, assistant professor, 1963-67, associate professor, 1967-71, professor, 1971-90, distinguished professor of Near Eastern languages and literatures, 1990-93, chairman of department, 1967, 1969-90, director of Center for Judaic Studies, 1986-93; Northwestern University, Evanston, IL, professor of history and religion and Phillip M. and Ethel Klutznick Professor of Jewish civilization, 1993—. Visiting research faculty member, Princeton University, 1979-80; visiting professor, University of California, Berkeley, 1984, University of Michigan, 1987, and Tel Aviv University, 1992; visiting research scholar, Center for Jewish Studies, Harvard University, 1987; visiting scholar, Oxford Postgraduate Center for Hebrew Studies, 1989, 1991. Member of Institute for Advanced Study, 1979-80.

MEMBER: American Oriental Society, American Historical Association.

AWARDS, HONORS: Archaeological fellow at Hebrew Union College—Jewish Institute of Religion, Biblical and Archaeological School, Jerusalem, 1968-69; Social Science Research Council grant, 1968-69, 1977, 1981; Guggenheim fellowship, 1972-73; National Endowment for the Humanities fellowship, 1979-80, 1987-88; Rockefeller Institute (Bellagio) fellowship, 1988.

WRITINGS:

The Topography of Baghdad in the Early Middle Ages: Text and Studies, Wayne State University Press, 1970.

The Shaping of Abbasid Rule, Princeton University Press, 1980.

Demonizing the Queen of Sheba, University of Chicago Press, 1983.

Islamic Revolution and Historical Memory, American Oriental Series, 1986.

(Editor and author of annotated translation with P. Fields) *The History of al-Tabari,* Volume 37: *The End of the Zanj Revolt,* State University of New York Press, 1986.

Also contributor to *Encyclopedia of Islam* and to journals.

WORK IN PROGRESS: Time and the Formation of Historical Consciousness in Judaism and Islam.

BIOGRAPHICAL/CRITICAL SOURCES:

PERIODICALS

Times Literary Supplement, September 19, 1980.

* * *

LAWSON, Jacob
See BURGESS, Michael (Roy)

* * *

Le CAIN, Errol (John) 1941-1989

PERSONAL: Surname is pronounced "lee cane;" born March 5, 1941, in Singapore; emigrated to England; died after a long illness, January 3, 1989; son of John (a policeman) and Muriel (Kronenburgh) Le Cain; married Dean Alison Thomson, December, 1976; children: Alfi. *Education:* Attended St. Joseph's Institution, Singapore. *Politics:* Liberal. *Religion:* "A totally committed member of Nichiren Shoshu United Kingdom, an organization that provides a central focus in the United Kingdom for Buddhist practice, study, and cultural activities."

Avocational Interests: Filmmaking, myths and legends of the Far East and the "exotic West."

ADDRESSES: Home—London, England.

CAREER: Pearl & Dean, London, animator, 1960-65; Richard Williams Studios, London, designer and animator, 1965-69; free lance designer, 1969-89. Set designer and animator for cartoon *Victoria's Rocking Horse,* c. 1963, and for British Broadcasting Corporation (BBC-TV) productions *The Snow Queen,* 1976, *The Light Princess,* 1978, *The Mystery of the Disappearing Schoolgirls,* 1980, and *The Ghost Downstairs,* 1982; art director on feature cartoon *The Thief Who Never Gave Up,* c. 1984. Producer of animation sequences for television commercials and motion pictures, including *The Apple Trees, The Spy with a Cold Nose, Gawain and the Green Knights, Casino Royale, Prudence and the Pill, The Charge of the Light Brigade,* and *The Last Valley.* Writer and illustrator of children's books.

AWARDS, HONORS: Top Ten Best award, *Amateur Cine World,* 1963, for *Victoria's Rocking Horse;* special mention for the most outstanding graphics in a drama, Designers and Art Directors Association, 1983 for *The Ghost Downstairs;* Kate Greenaway Medal, British Library Association, 1985, for *Hiawatha's Childhood.*

WRITINGS:

SELF-ILLUSTRATED CHILDREN'S BOOKS

King Arthur's Sword, Faber, 1968.

The Cabbage Princess, Faber, 1969.

The White Cat, Faber, 1973.

ILLUSTRATOR

Sir Orfeo: A Legend from England, retold by Anthea Davies, Faber, 1970, Bradbury, 1973.

Rhymes and Verses of Walter de la Mare, Faber, 1970.

The Faber Book of Children's Songs, selected and arranged by Donald Mitchell and Roderick Biss, Faber, 1970.

The Rhyme of the Ancient Mariner (adaptation of Samuel Taylor Coleridge's poem "The Rime of the Ancient Mariner"), Arcadia Press, 1971.

Daphne du Maurier, *The House on the Strand,* Heron Books, 1971.

Du Maurier, *My Cousin Rachel,* Heron Books, 1971.

Let's Find Out about Halloween, F. Watts, 1971.

Rosemary Harris, *The Child in the Bamboo Grove,* S. G. Phillips, 1971.

Helen Cresswell, *The Beachcombers,* Faber, 1971.

Charles Perrault, *Cinderella; or, The Little Glass Slipper,* Faber, 1972, Bradbury, 1973.

Herman Wouk, *The Caine Mutiny,* Heron Books, 1972.

W. Norman Pittenger, *Early Britain: The Celts, Romans and Anglo-Saxons,* F. Watts, 1973.

Thomas P. Lewis, *The Dragon Kite,* Holt, 1973.

Harris, *The King's White Elephant,* Faber, 1973.

Kathleen Abell, *King Orville and the Bullfrogs,* Little, Brown, 1974.

John Keats, *The Eve of St. Agnes,* Arcadia Press, 1974.

Elaine Andrews, *Judge Poo and the Mystery of the Dream,* Macmillan, 1974.

Harris, *The Lotus and the Grail: Legends from East to West,* Faber, 1974.

William Goldman, *Wigger,* Harcourt, 1974.

Harris, *The Flying Ship,* Faber, 1975.

Brothers Grimm, *Thorn Rose,* Faber, 1975, Bradbury, 1977.

The Rat, the Ox, and the Zodiac: A Chinese Legend, adapted by Dorothy Van Woerkom, Crown, 1976.

Harris, *The Little Dog of Fo,* Faber, 1976.

Brian Patten, *The Sly Cormorant and the Fishes: New Adaptations into Poetry of the Aesop Fables,* Kestrel Books, 1977.

Apuleius Madaurensis, *Cupid and Psyche,* adapted by Walter Pater, Faber, 1977.

(With Richard Williams) Idries Shah, *The Pleasantries of the Incredible Mulla Nasrudin,* Octagon, 1977.

Brothers Grimm, *The Twelve Dancing Princesses,* Viking, 1978.

Beauty and the Beast, retold by Harris, Doubleday, 1979.

Hans Christian Andersen, *The Snow Queen,* adapted by Naomi Lewis, Viking, 1979.

James Riordan, *The Three Magic Gifts,* Oxford University Press, 1980.

Sara Corrin and Stephen Corrin, *Mrs. Fox's Wedding,* Doubleday, 1980.

Aladdin and the Wonderful Lamp, retold by Andrew Lang, Viking, 1981.

Molly Whuppie, retold by Walter de la Mare, Farrar, Straus, 1983.

Hiawatha's Childhood (adapted from Henry Wadsworth Longfellow's poem "Song of Hiawatha"), Farrar, Straus, 1984.

Leslie Bricusse, *Christmas 1993; or, Santa's Last Ride,* Faber, 1987.

Matthew Price, *The Christmas Stockings,* Barron's, 1987.

T. S. Eliot, *Growltiger's Last Stand and Other Poems* (adaptation of three poems from *Old Possum's Book of Practical Cats*), Farrar, Straus, 1987.

Antonia Barber, *The Enchanter's Daughter,* J. Cape, 1987, Farrar, Straus, 1988.

Sally Miles, *Alfi and the Dark,* Chronicle Books, 1988.

The Pied Piper of Hamelin, retold by Sara Corrin and Stephen Corrin, Harcourt, 1989.

Eliot, *Mr. Mistoffelees with Mungojerrie and Rumpelteazer,* Harcourt, 1991.

Price, *Have You Seen My Sister?,* Gulliver, 1991.

SIDELIGHTS: A successful designer and animator of television commercials and motion pictures, Errol Le Cain also lent his artistic and writing talents to children's literature. During his twenty-five year career, he created the artwork for more than forty stories, composing the text for two of the projects himself. Among the famous fairy tales he helped reillustrate are Charles Perrault's *Cinderella,* Jakob and Wilhelm Grimm's *Thorn Rose* and *Twelve Dancing Princesses,* and Hans Christian Anderson's *Snow Queen.* Le Cain's venture into film animation produced sequences for movies like *Casino Royale, The Charge of the Light Brigade,* and *Prudence and the Pill.* He also designed the award-winning set for the British Broadcasting Corporation's television production of *The Ghost Downstairs.*

Born in Singapore in 1941, Le Cain spent his childhood and youth in the Far East, including five years in India. He visited many places such as Japan, Hong Kong, and Vietnam, becoming intrigued with the area's folklore. He began to study in earnest the myths and legends of the various peoples of the Orient and West. His fascination led to his involvement on projects like *King Arthur's Sword* and *The Cabbage Princess,* while his familiarity with the Orient become evident in his artistic style, especially on books such as Antonia Barber's *Enchanter's Daughter.*

During Le Cain's teenage years, he also developed an interest in filmmaking. Curious about animation, the illustrator made some experimental films when he was fourteen and fifteen years old. In his twenties he worked in England for Richard Williams Studios as a designer and animator. His employment at the agency lasted some five years before Le Cain turned to free-lancing. His work as an independent artist brought him a variety of assignments, including television animation projects like *The Light Princess* and illustration opportunities for novels such as Daphne du Maurier's *Cousin Rachel* and Herman Wouk's *Caine Mutiny.* He also completed the text for two self-illustrated children's books, although he once told *Something about the Author* that writing was very difficult for him.

Overall, Le Cain's work was frequently praised by reviewers of children's books as "colorful," "imaginative," and "elaborate." In a review of *Hiawatha's Childhood* for *School Library Journal,* Patricia Dooley noted, "Le Cain creates a natural world richly painted, patterned and peopled with the spirits of earth, air, water and fire." She explained that one of the poem's themes—that of understanding the true meaning of nature—"is reflected in the stylization and rhythmic ordering of Le Cain's vision." Betsy Hearne in the *Bulletin of the Center for Children's Books* asserts that some of Le Cain's best work was featured in *The Enchanter's Daughter.* Hearne surmised that his illustrations for the Antonia Barber book are "softened by a nuance of color and shape sometimes reminiscent of [twentieth-century British artist Edmund] Dulac." She concluded that while his paintings are very detailed, Le Cain's "orientally flavored compositions are . . . never out of control."

BIOGRAPHICAL/CRITICAL SOURCES:

BOOKS

Something About the Author, Volume 6, 1974.

PERIODICALS

Booklist, April 1, 1989.
Bulletin of the Center for Children's Books, November 4, 1988.
Christian Science Monitor, November 4, 1988.
Graphis, Volume 27, 1971-72.
Grow Point, May, 1989.
School Library Journal, January, 1985; December, 1988.
She, October, 1972.
Times Literary Supplement, April 16, 1970; September 29, 1973; July 24, 1981.

OBITUARIES:

PERIODICALS

Times (London), January 6, 1989.*

* * *

LEE, Shelton Jackson 1957- (Spike Lee)

PERSONAL: Born March 20, 1957, in Atlanta, GA; son of William (a musician and composer) and Jacqueline (a teacher; maiden name, Shelton) Lee. *Education:* Morehouse College, B.A., 1979; graduate study at New York University, 1982.

ADDRESSES: *Home*—Brooklyn, NY. *Office*—Forty Acres and a Mule Filmworks, 124 DeKalb Ave., Brooklyn, NY, 11217.

CAREER: Screenwriter, actor, and director and producer of motion pictures and music videos. Founder and director, Forty Acres and a Mule Filmworks, Brooklyn, NY, 1986—.

MEMBER: Screen Actors Guild.

AWARDS, HONORS: Student Director's Award from Academy of Motion Picture Arts and Sciences, 1982, for "Joe's Bed-Stuy Barber Shop: We Cut Heads"; Prix de Jeunesse from Cannes Film Festival and New Generation Award from the Los Angeles Film Critics, both 1986, for "She's Gotta Have It."

WRITINGS:

Spike Lee's "Gotta Have It": Inside Guerilla Filmmaking (includes interviews and a journal), illustrated with photographs by brother, David Lee, foreword by Nelson George, Simon & Schuster, 1987.
(With Lisa Jones) *Uplift the Race: The Construction of "School Daze,"* Simon & Schuster, 1988.
(With Jones) *"Do the Right Thing": The New Spike Lee Joint,* Fireside Press, 1989.
(With Jones) *"Mo' Better Blues,"* Simon & Schuster, 1990.
(With Ralph Wiley) *By Any Means Necessary: The Trials and Tribulations of the Making of "Malcolm X,"* Hyperion Adult, 1992.

SCREENPLAYS; AND DIRECTOR

"She's Gotta Have It," Island, 1986.
"School Daze," Columbia, 1988.
"Do the Right Thing," Universal Studios, 1989.
"Mo' Better Blues," Forty Acres and a Mule Filmworks, 1991.
"Jungle Fever," Forty Acres and a Mule Filmworks, 1991.
"Malcolm X," Forty Acres and a Mule Filmworks, 1992.

Also writer and director of short films, including "The Answer," 1980; "Sarah," 1981; and "Joe's Bed-Stuy Barbershop: We Cut Heads," 1982. Contributor of short films to *Saturday Night Live* and to the Music Television network (MTV).

SIDELIGHTS: The son of a musician, Spike Lee has become the equivalent of a composer, conductor, lead cellist and symphony T-shirt salesman in the industry of filmmaking. Since "She's Gotta Have It" was released in 1986 on a small budget, Lee has proven himself as a screenwriter, director/producer, actor, and merchandiser of films. "I truly believe I was put here to make films, it's as simple as that," Lee wrote in his book *Spike Lee's "Gotta Have It": Inside Guerilla Filmmaking.* "I'm doin' what I'm 'posed to be doin'. It's not for me to say whether ['She's Gotta Have It'] is a landmark film (I make 'em, that's all) but I do want people to be inspired by it, in particular, black people. Now there is a present example of how we can produce. We can do the things we want to do, there are no mo' excuses. We're tired of that alibi, 'White man this, white man that.' . . . It's on us. So let's all do the work that needs to be done by us *all.* And to y'all who aren't down for the cause, move out of the way, step aside."

Lee was born in Atlanta, Georgia, where he earned his nickname, Spike. "A lot of people think it's made up—one of those stage names," he explained in *Spike Lee's "Gotta Have It."* "My mother . . . said I was a very tough baby. . . . I was like three or four months old when I got the nickname." Lee's father, a jazz musician, Bill Lee, soon moved his family to the jazz mecca, Chicago. "Then there was an exodus of jazz musicians from Chicago to New York," Lee related, "and my father went with that. I think we came to New York in '59, '60." During his youth Lee's leadership ability began to emerge. For neighborhood sports, he said, he "was always the captain of the team, the spark plug. Not the best athlete, though."

A jazz purist, Lee's father placed strains on the family by adhering to his artistic principles. As Lee reported in

Spike Lee's "Gotta Have It": "In the early sixties [my father] was the top folk/jazz bassist. If you look on the albums of Peter, Paul and Mary, Bob Dylan, Judy Collins, Odetta, Theodore Bikel, Leon Bibbs and Josh White, you'll see that my father was playing with all of them. He also played with Simon and Garfunkel. He got tired of playing that music, though, and then the electric bass became popular and he refused to play it. To this day, he's never played Fender bass. With that kind of stance, you don't work. . . . I got some of my stubbornness from him, if the word is stubbornness. . . . [It's] nonconformist, to a degree."

Following a long family tradition, Lee went to college at Morehouse, an all-black college in Atlanta. "I'm a third-generation Morehouse graduate," he said. "My father and grandfather went to Morehouse. . . . The Lee family has always been like that." Majoring in mass communications, he decided by his sophomore year to become a filmmaker—though he still did a bit of everything else, including hosting his own radio show on jazz station WCLK and writing for the school newspaper. More importantly, he began making films. Of the first film he wrote, "Black College: The Talented Tenth," Lee said: "I do not like that film at all. . . . It's a corny love story at a black campus. Real corny. . . . I'm glad there's only one copy in existence."

After graduation from Morehouse, Lee enrolled at the New York University (NYU) Film School. "There's no way I could have made the films I made if I lived in [Los Angeles] 'cause I didn't know anybody," he explained in his book. "I couldn't have called people for locations. Also you had to have an astronomical score on the [Graduate Record Exams] to get in. Plus at USC and UCLA [University of Southern California and University of California, Los Angeles], not everybody makes a film. The teachers assign by committee who gets to make a film."

Filmed in his senior year, "Joe's Bed-Stuy Barbershop" earned Lee a student academy award. Monty Ross starred in the film about a local barber who gets caught up in the numbers racket and organized crime. "That summer before my final year in school I was in Atlanta writing a script," he wrote. "I let Monty read it and he suggested that he act in it. I never thought of Monty . . . coming up to New York, dropping what he was doing, to act in it. But he did. I think Monty gave a very fine performance. What people don't realize is that Monty—a very unselfish person—was not only acting in the film, he was driving the van, he was crewing, he was doing a lot of other things that no doubt affected his performance. But we got the film made."

Winning the student academy award didn't really surprise Lee. "Because I know that NYU is one of the best film schools, and I saw a lot of films that came out of the school. I know that this was as good or better than anything that was in USC or UCLA . . . I never went to NYU expecting teachers to teach me. I just wanted equipment, so I could make films, and learn filmmaking by making films. . . . That's the only way to learn. People call me now wanting to know what the secret to successful filmmaking is. I get so mad. There *is* no secret formula let's say, for the success of 'She's Gotta Have It.' I'm not gonna tell them anything that will help them. We just killed ourselves to get it made. That's how we did it."

After he won the student academy award, some of the larger talent agencies approached Lee and, although they represented him for a year-and-a-half, nothing much materialized, as he reported in his book. "I had the first draft of what is now 'School Daze,' but then it was called 'Homecoming.' The script was a lot different but I had the third draft of it. It was an all-black film. They said nah. Forget it. Nothing. Not even an 'Afterschool Special.' And there were a lot of my classmates who didn't even win Academy Awards who did get 'Afterschool Specials.' " Since then, Lee hasn't had an agent. "You've got to make your own personal choice," he asserted. "I will not have an agent, though I have a good lawyer and a good accountant. . . . That's all I need . . . you still have to find a job like everybody else."

Lee's first post-NYU production, "The Messenger," was a failed venture by a businessman's yardstick. Started in 1984, "The Messenger" was about a Brooklyn bike messenger and his family. After spending forty thousand dollars, Lee decided to terminate the project. "It just never really came together with all the money and stuff," he said in a *Film Comment* article. One of the project's obstacles that Lee was not able to hurdle was the Screen Actors Guild (SAG). Lee applied for experimental film rates so that he would be able to afford an actor like Larry Fishburne (later of "What's Love Got To Do With It"). The Guild refused Lee's application for waiver of the standard rates. "There are too many black actors out of work for them to nix it," he wrote in *Spike Lee's "Gotta Have It."* But "they said no. So I had to recast the entire picture in four days with non-SAG people. And it never came together so we were all devastated. I got a list of ten films that had been given a waiver within the [previous] year. All of them were done by white independent filmmakers. All of them worked with a whole lot more money than I had. Yet they said my film was too commercial. . . . That was a definite case of racism."

By the next year, 1985, Lee was immersed in his next project, "She's Gotta Have It." The screenplay, written by Lee, explores black female sexuality through its main character, Nola Darling, played by Tracy Camilla Johns. Nola dates three different men, Jamie Overstreet, Greer

Childs and Mars Blackmon (played by Lee). One offers stability; another, physical attraction; the third, humor. "Everybody's character was reflected in how they perceived Nola. That's the whole film, how everybody perceives Nola," Lee wrote in *Spike Lee's "Gotta Have It."* Eventually Nola leaves all three of her suitors. "It's about control," she explains in the film. "My body. My mind. Whose gonna own it, them or me?"

With the failure of "The Messenger," the American Film Institute withdrew the twenty thousand dollars it had granted Lee. "There were times when I didn't know where the next nickel was coming from," Lee related in his book, "but it would come. Sure enough, the money came whenever we needed it." With eighteen thousand dollars from the New York arts council as his most-sizable funding, Lee assembled a small cast and crew that included family members and directed "She's Gotta Have It" in only twelve days.

The release of "She's Gotta Have It" in 1986 made Spike Lee an international celebrity. The film was a financial success, grossing more than eight million dollars, and critically it was an even bigger success. *Washington Post* reviewer Paul Attanasio deemed it an "impressive first feature" and added that it was "discursive, jazzy, vibrant with sex and funny as heck." Michael Wilmington wrote in the *Los Angeles Times* that Lee's film was "a joyfully idiosyncratic little jazz-burst of a film, full of sensuous melody, witty chops and hot licks." Wilmington was particularly impressed with the film's non-stereotypical perspective and characters, declaring that it "gives you as non-standard a peek at black American life as you'll get: engaging, seductive and happily off-kilter. . . . These characters aren't the radiant winners or sad victims you usually see, and there's not a normal citizen . . . in the bunch." The film's appeal was evident at the Cannes Film Festival. When the power failed during the film's screening, the audience refused to leave until they saw the ending.

That success led to Lee securing approximately six million dollars from Columbia Pictures to film "School Daze," a musical comedy about rival factions at a black college. Lee discussed his subject in *Spike Lee's "Gotta Have It":* "I'm not going to say there are not a lot of ills on black college campuses. We [hoped] to address some of those things in the film 'School Daze.' But I still love Morehouse, regardless. The thing that amazed me about being there was how some guys couldn't get no play from women, but the minute they pledged to a fraternity the women were all over them. It was amazing."

Much of the humor in "School Daze" derives from the antics of Lee's character. Here he plays Half Pint, a Gamma Phi Gamma hopeful preoccupied with losing his virginity. The factional conflicts at the college are underscored by Half Pint, a Wannabee (as in want-to-be-white), and his relationship with his cousin, Dap, a dark-skinned Jigaboo (a member of the black underclass) and the key figure in a campus campaign to force the university divestiture from South Africa. Dap's rival is Julian, leader of the Gamma Phi Gammas. The characters' conflicts allow Lee to explore bigotry as well as elitism.

The major obstacle placed in Lee's path in filming "School Daze" was reluctance from his alma mater, Morehouse, as well as other Atlanta black colleges (Spelman College, Clark College, Morris Brown College and Atlanta University) to allow the use of their facilities. "There were so many rumors circulating around the [Atlanta University Center] about the movie," he wrote in his second book, *Uplift the Race: The Construction of "School Daze."* "The students were influenced by the propaganda being pushed out by the administrations. When I was at Morehouse the atmosphere was different. The student body was more vocal and certainly more political. We didn't take what the administration told us at face value. I think we would have been really upset if a young Black filmmaker came to our campus to shoot a film and got kicked off by the school. But there wasn't a whimper from any of the students at Morehouse, Spelman, Clark or Morris Brown." As it turned out, after three weeks of shooting, Lee was forced to use just Atlanta University's facilities and reshoot all of the footage shot on other campuses.

"School Daze" earned commendations from many critics, but it also brought Lee notoriety as a provocateur within the African American community. Prominent African Americans protested that Lee had produced an unfavorable depiction of their race and others, while conceding that he offered a valid perspective, nonetheless argued that his perception of black college campus life was one best withheld from a white society. In his third book, *"Do the Right Thing": The New Spike Lee Joint,* Lee wrote that he "did an interview with Bryant Gumbel on the 'Today' show" in which they discussed the film. "Bryant Gumbel jumped all over me, but I kept my composure. He disapproved of 'School Daze' because I aired Black folks' dirty laundry."

After the release of "School Daze," Lee shifted from internal prejudice to external when he began work on "Do the Right Thing." Occurring on the hottest day of the year, "Do the Right Thing" takes place in Bedford-Stuyvesant, a largely black neighborhood of New York City. It evokes real interracial incidents, like one he mentioned in his book *"Do the Right Thing":* "I heard a radio newscast that two Black youths had been beaten up by a gang of white youths," Lee wrote. "The two Black kids were hospitalized. They were collecting bottles and cans when they got jumped. This happened on Christmas night. . . . Can you imagine if [this incident] had taken place in the summer, on the hottest day of the year? I'd be a fool not to work the subject of racism into 'Do the Right Thing.' "

"Do the Right Thing" centers on a pizzeria owned and run by Italians and headed by Sal, ostensibly a non-racist who is comfortable with his black clientele and employees. Trouble begins when Buggin' Out, a black patron, asks Sal to add some black people to his pizzeria's "Wall of Fame," which consists of only Italian-Americans. Sal refuses, and as tempers rise, a racial slur triggers violence. The climax occurs when the police wind up choking one of the blacks to death in front of the whole neighborhood. Sal's delivery boy, Mookie (played by Lee), then incites a riot by throwing a garbage can through the pizzeria window. In a sequence preceding the fight, Lee had stopped the story to have his characters spout racial slurs into the camera. It "was meant to rouse emotions," Lee explained in *"Do the Right Thing."* "It's funny the way people react to it. They laugh at every slur except the one directed at their ethnic group." The honesty with which Lee treated his subject earned "Do the Right Thing" substantial praise from some critics and many laughs of self-recognition from audiences. David Chute, reviewing Lee's book about the film in the *Los Angeles Times Book Review,* called "Do the Right Thing" Lee's "most controlled and effective picture" to date and noted that his vision is that of an artist, not a journalist. "A personal frame of reference like this would not seem startling in an Italian-American or WASP director," Chute noted, "but to the great discredit of the American film biz the black version is still a novelty. Not for long."

Lee's next venture, "Mo' Better Blues," paired him for the first time with Denzel Washington, who would later star in another Lee film, "Malcolm X." "Mo' Better Blues" also brought Lee back to his father's work—music—a profession that Spike Lee had avoided. "Being the first born, not becoming a musician was a part of my rebelliousness," he wrote in *Spike Lee's "Gotta Have It."* But jazz was still close to his heart, and when filmmakers such as Clint Eastwood and Woody Allen started making films about it, Lee felt he had to get involved himself. As he said in his book about the making of "Mo' Better Blues": "I couldn't let Woody Allen do a jazz film before I did. I was on a mission." "Mo' Better Blues" follows the life of a modern-day trumpeter and shows the conflicts he faces between his music and his love life.

"Mo' Better Blues" was the first film produced by Lee's own company, Forty Acres and a Mule, named for what every black person in America had been promised at the end of slavery. He commented on his intention to make films in his own way in *Spike Lee's "Gotta Have It"*: "You really carry a burden as a black filmmaker. There are so few black films that when you do one it has to represent every black person in the world. If you're white, you're not going to protest in front of a theater because the film is about this or that because it is one of two hundred white Hollywood films that might have been released that year."

Lee's next release, "Jungle Fever," was his fifth film in six years. "I know for sure I cannot keep up this pace," he said in a 1991 book about his career, *Five for Five: The Films of Spike Lee.* "It could kill me. . . . Historically, black filmmakers have found it extremely hard to go from film to film. I didn't want a long layoff between films. When things are clicking, ya gotta stay with it."

Critics characterized "Jungle Fever" variously as a film about interracial sex, a cry from the heart about the tragedies of the drug culture, and a collection of vignettes on a wide range of current issues. The film features a married black architect named Flipper and his Italian-American secretary, Angie, who have an affair. The repercussions from their liaison ripple through their relationships with a host of others, including Flipper's crack-addicted brother and Angie's racist family. Calling "Jungle Fever" Lee's "best movie" in his *Newsweek* review of the film, Jack Kroll commented on how the filmmaker "uses the theme of interracial sex to explore the mythology of race, sex and class in an America where both blacks and whites are reassessing the legacy of integration and the concept of separatism from every point on the political spectrum." Lee's treatment of the issue of skin color, which is sometimes a point of contention even among blacks, was of particular interest to *Times Literary Supplement* writer Gerald Early, who noted that Lee shows both dark-skinned Flipper and his lighter-complexioned wife as being "obsessed with the insults they endured as children about their colour. What is racial identity if someone can be attacked from outside a group for pretensions of purity, and from inside because of a 'mongrelized' appearance?" Other critics pointed to the powerful drug theme that grows in importance as the film progresses. In his *Time* article on black filmmaking, Richard Corliss summed up "Jungle Fever" as an "assured" film about "the ghetto epidemic of drugs. . . . Who is sleeping with whom matters less here, as it should anywhere, than the people who die and the things that kill them."

The fall of 1992 saw the release of Lee's biggest film, "Malcolm X." Nearly three and a half hours long, it cost more than thirty million dollars and grossed nearly two and a half million the day it was released. The film chronicles the life of the controversial and multifaceted black leader who in a single lifetime was a street hustler, black-separatist preacher, and eloquent humanist. A number of reviewers acknowledged the challenge of portraying such a complex life on film, of pleasing the various factions in black society that each focused on their favorite aspects of the man. Lee himself felt that many blacks have "a very limited view of Malcolm" and fail to understand that "the man evolved, was constantly evolving, even at the time of [his] assassination," he said in a *Time* interview with Janice C. Simpson.

Lee embarked on the film amid a storm of controversy. Black cultural figures such as poet Amiri Baraka, a vocal critic of Lee's movies, warned the filmmaker not to "trash" Malcolm's legacy. Some worried that he would overemphasize certain aspects of Malcolm's life, like his street years or his split from the militant, separatist Black Muslim organization, which some say prompted Malcolm's assassination. Lee caused a stir of his own before winning the opportunity to make the film, when he questioned why a white director—Norman Jewison—had been selected to film a black story. He also wrestled with the Warner Brothers film studio over the movie's length and cost. When he exceeded his budget, financial—but not creative—control of the project was taken from Lee's hands.

Upon its release, late in 1992, Lee's treatment of Malcolm's life earned a mixed critical response. Assessing the film in the *New Yorker,* Terrence Rafferty acknowledged the dedication Lee showed in the making of the film but regretted what he saw as its impersonal feel. Still, Rafferty felt that "viewers who know nothing about Malcolm, or who know him only by his formidable reputation as a black-pride firebrand, might find everything in the film fascinating, revelatory." Opining that of all Lee's films it is "the least Spikey," *Time*'s Corliss judged it "the movie equivalent of an authorized biography." Several critics questioned the necessity of the film's length, a concern Lee addressed in his *Time* interview. "There was so much to tell," he asserted. "This was not going to be an abbreviated, abridged version of Malcolm X." Vincent Canby, writing for the *New York Times,* largely applauded Lee's efforts, calling the movie "an ambitious, tough, seriously considered biographical film that, with honor, eludes easy characterization." He did not find it entirely successful, but as he put it, Lee had "attempted the impossible and almost brought it off." One measure of "Malcolm X"'s impact was that soon after the film's release, the book upon which it was partly based, *The Autobiography of Malcolm X,* reached the top of the *New York Times* nonfiction best-seller list—nearly thirty years after its original 1965 publication.

BIOGRAPHICAL/CRITICAL SOURCES:

BOOKS

Authors and Artists for Children and Young Adults, Volume 4, Gale, 1990, pp. 165-79.

Five for Five: The Films of Spike Lee, Stewart, Tabori, 1991.

Lee, Spike, *Spike Lee's "Gotta Have It": Inside Guerilla Filmmaking,* Simon and Schuster, 1987.

Lee, Spike, and Lisa Jones, *Uplift the Race: The Construction of "School Daze,"* Simon & Schuster, 1988.

Lee, Spike, and Lisa Jones, *"Do the Right Thing": The New Spike Lee Joint,* Fireside Press, 1989.

PERIODICALS

American Film, September, 1986; January-February, 1988; July-August, 1989.

Chicago Tribune, August 13, 1986; August 20, 1986; October 5, 1986; February 25, 1988; March 3, 1988.

Ebony, January, 1987; September, 1987.

Essence, September, 1986; February, 1988; July 1988.

Film Comment, October, 1986.

Film Quarterly, winter, 1986-87.

Jet, November 10, 1986; February 2, 1988; May 2, 1988.

Los Angeles Times, August 21, 1986; February 11, 1988; February 12, 1988.

Los Angeles Times Book Review, June 30, 1989, p. 6.

Ms., September-October, 1991, p. 78.

Newsweek, September 8, 1986, p. 65; February 15, 1988, p. 62; July 3, 1989, pp. 64-66; October 2, 1989, p. 37; August 6, 1990, p. 62; June 10, 1991, pp. 44-47; August 26, 1991, pp. 52-54; November 16, 1992, pp. 66, 71, 74.

New Yorker, October 6, 1986, pp. 128-30; July 24, 1989, pp. 78-81; August 13, 1990, pp. 82-84; June 17, 1991, p. 99; November 30, 1992, pp. 160-62.

New York Review of Books, September 28, 1989, p. 37.

New York Times, March 27, 1983; August 8, 1986; April 10, 1986; September 7, 1986; November 14, 1986; August 9, 1987; February 12, 1988; February 20, 1989; October 29, 1992, p. C22; November 15, 1992, p. H1, H23; November 18, 1992, pp. C19, C23; November 19, 1992, p. B4.

New York Times Book Review, December 13, 1987, p. 14.

New York Times Magazine, August 9, 1987, pp. 26, 29, 39, 41.

People, October 13, 1986, p. 67; July 10, 1989, p. 67; March 5, 1990, pp. 97, 99.

Rolling Stone, December 1980; April 21, 1988, p. 32; June 30, 1988, p. 21; December 1, 1988, p. 31; June 29, 1989, p. 27; July 13, 1989, pp. 104, 107, 109, 174; June 27, 1991, p. 75; July 11, 1991, p. 63.

Time, October 6, 1986, p. 94; July 3, 1989, p. 62; July 17, 1989, p. 92; August 20, 1990, p. 62; June 17, 1991, pp. 64-66, 68; March 16, 1992, p. 71; November 23, 1992, pp. 64-65; November 30, 1992.

Times Literary Supplement, September, 6, 1991, p. 18.

Village Voice, February 16, 1988; March 22, 1988.

Wall Street Journal, November 16, 1992.

Washington Post, August 22, 1986; August 24, 1986; August 29, 1986; March 20, 1987; February 19, 1988.*

LEE, Spike
See LEE, Shelton Jackson

* * *

LEE, William R(owland) 1911-

PERSONAL: Born April 3, 1911, in Uxbridge, Middlesex, England; son of William Arthur (a headmaster) and Edith Bridget (Knight) Lee; married Zdena Marie Emilie Pausarova, July 9, 1948; children: Miriam Rosalie Zdena, Monica Caroline Janet. *Education:* University of London, Teacher's Diploma, 1934, M.A. (linguistics), 1954; University of Prague, Ph.D., 1950.

Avocational Interests: Music, conservation, travel, the fine arts, scientific developments, world affairs.

ADDRESSES: Home—16 Alexandra Gardens, Hounslow, Middlesex, TW3 4HU, England.

CAREER: Caroline University, Prague, Czechoslovakia, lecturer in English, 1946-51; University of London, Institute of Education, London, England, research fellow and lecturer, 1952-57, 1959-62; free-lance writer, consultant, teacher trainer, examiner, and lecturer in English as a foreign or second language, 1963—. Conductor of teacher-training courses in Ceylon, India, the Middle East, Czechoslovakia, Iceland, Greece, Bulgaria, Cyprus, Yugoslavia, Colombia, and other countries, and of three "English by Radio" series for British Broadcasting Corp., 1960. Member of standing committee, University of London Convocation, 1959-85; university representative governor, Haverstock Comprehensive School, 1961-70. British Council, language-teaching adviser, 1958-59, member of school inspection panel, 1963-73 and 1981-89, member of English studies advisory committee, 1964-77. Member of the language panel of the Professional and Linguistics Attainments Board of the General Medical Council, 1976-89. Consultancies or lecture tours to numerous countries for the British Council and UNESCO. *Military service:* British Army, Intelligence Corps, 1940-45.

MEMBER: International Phonetic Association, International Society of Phonetic Sciences, International Association of Teachers of English as a Foreign Language (founder, 1967; chairman, 1967-84; founder-chairman, 1984—), Federation Internationale des Professeurs de Langues Vivantes (member of executive committee, 1968-84), World Wildlife Fund, World Wide Fund for Nature, British Association of Applied Linguists, English-Speaking Union (member of English language committee, 1980—), Teaching of English to Speakers of Other Languages, Royal Commonwealth Trust, Royal Conservation Society, Royal Society for the Protection of Birds, Society of Authors, Woodland Trust, Music Club of London.

AWARDS, HONORS: Named honorary fellow, Trinity College, 1972; awarded Order of the British Empire, 1979; Medal Honour, University of Poznan, Poland, 1986.

WRITINGS:

English Intonation: A New Approach, North-Holland Publishing, 1958.

(With wife, Zdena Lee) *Teach Yourself Czech,* English Universities Press, 1959, 2nd edition, 1964.

Spelling Irregularity and Reading Progress, National Foundation for Educational Research in England and Wales, 1960.

An English Intonation Reader, Macmillan, 1960.

(With M. Dodderidge) *Time for a Song,* Longman, 1963.

(With Helen Coppen) *Simple Audio-Visual Aids to Foreign-Language Teaching,* Oxford University Press, 1964, 2nd edition, 1968.

Language-Teaching Games and Contests, Oxford University Press, 1965, revised and expanded edition, 1986.

(With Leonidas Koullis) *The Argonauts' English Course for Greek-Speaking Children,* Oxford University Press, Book 1, 1965, Book 2, 1966, Book 3, 1968, Book 4, 1973.

English at Home, Oxford University Press, 1966.

(Editor) *English Language Teaching Selections 1 and 2: Articles from the Journal "English Language Teaching,"* Oxford University Press, 1967.

The Dolphin English Course, Oxford University Press, 1970-73.

First Songs in English, Oxford University Press, 1970.

More Songs in English, Oxford University Press, 1973.

(With V. Maddock) *Getting through Trinity College English,* Pergamon, 1981.

A Study Dictionary of Social English, Prentice-Hall, 1984.

(With B. Haycraft) *It Depends How You Say It,* Pergamon, 1984.

(Editor) I. Poldauf, *English Word Stress,* Prentice-Hall, 1987.

TRANSLATOR

(With V. Fried) Vaclav Chaloupecky, *The Caroline University of Prague: Its Foundation, Character and Development in the Fourteenth Century,* Caroline University (Prague), 1948.

(Adapter with Z. Lee of additional chapters to 1919 edition) Tomas Garrigue Masaryk, *The Spirit of Russia,* 2nd edition, Allen & Unwin, 1955.

OTHER

Also author, with A. W. J. Barron, of "Phonetic Wall Charts," Oxford University Press, 1966. Contributor to numerous books, including *In Honour of Daniel Jones,* Longmans, Green, 1964; *Teachers of English as a Second Language: Their Training and Preparation,* edited by G.

E. Perren, Cambridge University Press, 1968; *Focus '80,* edited by Freudenstein, Oxford University Press, 1972; *The Context of Foreign Language Learning,* Van Gorcum, 1975; *The Melody of Language: Intonation and Prosody,* edited by Linda R. Waugh and C. H. van Schooneveld, University Park Press, 1980; *Linguistics across Historical and Geographical Boundaries,* edited by R. Freudenstein, De Gruyter, 1986; *Error in Foreign Languages: Analysis and Treatment,* Marburg University, 1989; and *Languages in Contact and Contrast,* edited by Ivic and Kalogjera, De Gruyter, 1991.

Also contributor to *Proceedings of the Eighth Annual Congress of Phonetic Sciences,* [Prague], 1967; *Papers from the International Symposium on Applied Contrastive Linguistics,* [Stuttgart], 1971; *Papers of the Yugoslav-Serbo-Croatian-English Contrastive Project,* [Zagreb], 1972; *Proceedings of the Third Congress of the Association Internationale de Linguistique Appliquee,* Volume 1, [Heidelberg], 1974; and to Georgetown University monograph series on language and linguistics. Contributor to journals and newspapers, including *Yearbook of Education, Lingua, Maitre Phonetique, Praxis, International Review for Applied Linguistics, Journal of the International Phonetic Association, Journal of Applied Linguistics, Phonetica, ELT Journal, Scuola e Lingue Moderne,* and *Times Educational Supplement.* Editor, *English Language Teaching Journal,* 1961-81, *World Language English,* 1982-84, and *English: A World Language,* 1990-92.

WORK IN PROGRESS: With C. V. James, *An Elementary Technical and Scientific Dictionary,* for Cassell; *Children Learning a Foreign Language: Options and Opportunities,* for Heinemann.

SIDELIGHTS: William R. Lee told *CA:* "I was trained at the University of London (as a grammar-school teacher of English) in the mid-thirties, during the great economic recession. Teaching practice with 'real' classes was included in the training, and one day an inspector turned up to see how I was getting on. He was not displeased, but was critical of my pronunciation of French. 'There's Daniel Jones's Department of Phonetics at University College,' he suggested, 'Why not go there?' I did, and attended evening classes, first in French phonetics and then in English. That was the beginning, in essence, of my professional career. I am deeply indebted to that inspector, although I cannot now remember his name.

"In my earliest jobs I taught at least eight different subjects, most of which I had not been trained to teach and knew little about, as a 'supply' teacher (filling in for absentee staff in a variety of schools; and undoubtedly learned a great deal from the learners. I enjoyed teaching in particular music and physical music and physical training, as it was then called, to primary school children.

"After World War II, I was delighted to be able to go to Prague, Czechoslovakia as a lecturer at the famous Caroline University. I remained there for about five years, teaching also in several embassies and at a big institute open to most adults studying languages. In Czechoslovakia I began to see English as an international rather than a 'native' language, an orientation extended and enhanced by teacher-training experience at the University of London Institute of Education on my return to Britain, and also by a British Council appointment as a language-teaching adviser and further study of linguistics (with J. R. Firth) at the School of Oriental Studies.

"Subsequently the process of transition from my predominantly nationalist viewpoints to, I hope, a much more international outlook has been strengthened by participation in numerous international conferences, by inspection of English as a foreign language schools in the United Kingdom, by lecture and advisory visits, and by planning and conducting teacher-training courses in many parts of the world, above all in Cyprus, Iceland, the Near and Middle East, South America, and the United States.

"Books and articles have on the whole emerged from my teaching and teacher-training work, and editorial experience from 1961 to 1992 has been associated chiefly with development of *ELT Journal* and two other (rather short-lived) journals.

"Some eighteen years of my life were taken up with the establishment and running, as elected chairman, of the International Association of Teachers of English as a Foreign Language, which is still developing vigorously and of which I am now founder-chairman.

"I am particularly interested in the teaching of international languages to children (roughly, the under-twelves) and in the contributions language teachers can make to everyday international co-operation and friendship in support of a less quarrelsome, much happier, and more genuinely civilized world. (But I have strong sympathy too with minorities trying to preserve their own local languages). Nowadays, also, I try to persuade language teachers to interest themselves in broader educational issues and to adopt a less passive and more forward-looking role in helping to shape the future—and to pursue the implications of democracy in helping to develop 'communicative' and mutually helpful methods of learning and teaching."

BIOGRAPHICAL/CRITICAL SOURCES:

BOOKS

A. van Essen and E. I. Burkart, editors, *Homage to W. R. Lee: Essays in English as a Foreign or Second Language,* De Gruyter, 1992.

LEFEVRE, Gui
See BICKERS, Richard (Leslie) Townshend

* * *

LEISER, Burton M. 1930-

PERSONAL: Surname is pronounced "*lee*-sur;" born December 12, 1930, in Denver, CO; son of Nathan (in retail furniture business) and Eva Mae (Newman) Leiser; married Miriam Waid (a teacher), August 10, 1954 (divorced); married C. Barbara Hurowitz Tabor, June 9, 1967 (divorced); married Janet A. Johnson (a law school dean), August 12, 1984; children: Shoshana Yafah, Illana Devorah, Phillip B.; stepchildren: Ellen Beth Tabor, David Lawrence Tabor, Susan Ruth Tabor, Sheri Taylor Johnson. *Education:* University of Chicago, B.A., 1951; graduate study at University of Colorado, 1951-52, and New York University, 1955-57; Yeshiva University, M.Heb.Lit., 1956; Brown University, Ph.D., 1968; Drake University, J.D., 1981. *Politics:* Republican. *Religion:* Jewish.

ADDRESSES: Home—11 Meadow Pl., Briarcliff Manor, NY 10510. *Office*—Pace University, 41 Park Row, New York, NY 10038.

CAREER: Admitted to the Bar of Iowa, 1982, New York state, 1985, U.S. District Court (southern district) New York, 1986, and U.S. Supreme Court, 1986. Teacher and principal at Hebrew schools in Rhode Island and Massachusetts, 1957-64; University of Denver, Denver, CO, instructor in philosophy, 1962-63; Fort Lewis College, Durango, CO, instructor in philosophy, 1963-65; State University of New York at Buffalo, assistant professor, 1965-68, associate professor of philosophy, 1968-70; Sir George Williams University, Montreal, Quebec, visiting associate professor, 1969-70, associate professor of Judaic studies, 1970-72; Drake University, Des Moines, Iowa, professor of philosophy and chairman of department, 1972-83; Pace University, New York City, Edward J. Mortola Professor of Philosophy and adjunct professor of law, 1983-88, distinguished professor of philosophy, 1988—. Chairman of the board of directors, Congress Bet Am Shalom, White Plains, NY, 1990-92.

MEMBER: International Society of Legal and Social Philosophy, American Philosophical Association, American Society for Value Inquiry (president, 1978-80), Society for Political and Legal Philosophy, Society for Philosophy and Public Policy, American Association of University Professors, American Professors for Peace in the Middle East (national secretary, 1983-91; delegate to United Nations, 1988-91; member of national executive committee), Authors Guild, Authors League of America.

AWARDS, HONORS: Fellowships, New York University, 1955-57, and Brown University, 1959-62; research grants from State University of New York Research Foundation and Memorial Foundation for Jewish Culture, 1966-68, 1970-71, Exxon Education Foundation, 1975-77, Drake University, 1975, 1981, and National Endowment for the Humanities, 1979; Drake University, Liberal Arts Honor Teacher award, 1978, and Centennial Scholar award, 1982.

WRITINGS:

Custom, Law, and Morality: Conflict and Continuity in Social Behavior, Doubleday, 1969.

Liberty, Justice, and Morals: Contemporary Value Conflicts, Macmillan, 1973, third edition, 1986.

(Compiler) *Values in Conflict: Life, Liberty, and the Rule of Law,* Macmillan, 1981.

Contributor to anthologies, including *Ethics, Free Enterprise, and Public Policy,* edited by Richard T. De George and Joseph A. Pichler, Oxford University Press, 1985; *Terrorism: How the West Can Win,* edited by Benjamin Netanyahu, Farrar, Strauss, 1986; *Ethical Theory and Business,* edited by Tom L. Beauchamp and Norman Bowie, Prentice-Hall, 1987; and *Ethics: Theory and Practice,* edited by Manuel Velasquez and Cynthia Rostenkowski, Prentice-Hall, 1987. Contributor to philosophy, religion, and law journals.

SIDELIGHTS: Burton M. Leiser once told *CA:* "Philosophers in the English-speaking world have lately written at length about ordinary language in the most obscure jargon. In attempting to impress their colleagues with their humility, they adopt such absurd mannerisms as qualifying substantive assertions with, 'It seems to me that it is the case that. . . .' And to demonstrate their technical competence, they riddle their articles with special symbols and letters in upper and lower case, in roman and italic type, and in Greek. They have impressed, bored, and bewildered one another. They have also cut themselves off from intelligent users of ordinary language who might have been interested in what they had to say, if only they could have made sense of it.

"When philosophers, from Plato to Sartre and Russell, have written lucidly about real issues, they have found an eager audience. The dogmatic assertion that a philosopher can achieve popularity only by sacrificing philosophical integrity is simply false. Every author who is eager to have his work published should remember that publishers are just as eager to find works from which readers will derive pleasure and enlightenment. Once one finds those delightful combinations of words that are aesthetically pleasing and intellectually edifying, the rest is easy."

LESLIE, Richard
See BICKERS, Richard (Leslie) Townshend

* * *

LEVINE, George 1931-

PERSONAL: Born August 27, 1931, in New York, NY; son of H. J. (a doctor) and Dorothy (Podolsky) Levine; married Margaret Bloom, August 19, 1956; children: David, Rachel. *Education:* New York University, B.A., 1952; University of Minnesota, M.A., 1953, Ph.D., 1959.

ADDRESSES: Home—419 Lincoln Ave., Highland Park, NJ 08904. *Office*—Department of English, Rutgers University, New Brunswick, NJ 08903.

CAREER: Indiana University, Bloomington, instructor, 1959-62, assistant professor, 1962-65, associate professor of English, 1965-68; Rutgers University, New Brunswick, NJ, professor of English literature, 1968-86, Kenneth Burke Professor of English, 1986—. Visiting professor, Stanford University, 1974-75; Helen Cam visiting fellow, Girton College, Cambridge University, 1983. *Military service:* U.S. Army, 1953-55; became sergeant.

MEMBER: Modern Language Association of America.

AWARDS, HONORS: American Council of Learned Societies grant, 1964; Guggenheim Foundation fellowship, 1971; National Endowment for the Humanities fellowships, 1978; Rockefeller Foundation fellowship, 1983.

WRITINGS:

(Editor) *The Emergence of Victorian Consciousness,* Free Press, 1967.
(Editor with William A. Madden) *The Art of Victorian Prose,* Oxford University Press, 1967.
The Boundaries of Fiction: Carlyle, Macaulay, Newman, Princeton University Press, 1968.
(Editor with David Leverenz) *Mindful Pleasures: Essays on Thomas Pynchon,* Little, Brown, 1976.
(Editor with U. C. Knoepflmacher) *The Endurance of Frankenstein: Essays on Mary Shelley's Novel,* University of California Press, 1979.
The Realistic Imagination: English Fiction from Frankenstein to Lady Chatterley, University of Chicago Press, 1981.
Darwin and the Novelists: Patterns of Science in Nineteenth-Century Fiction, Harvard University Press, 1988.
(Editor) *Constructions of the Self,* Rutgers University Press, 1992.

Also editor of *Realism and Representation,* University of Wisconsin Press, and co-editor of *Victorian Studies,* 1959-68.

SIDELIGHTS: In *The Realistic Imagination: English Fiction from Frankenstein to Lady Chatterley,* George Levine asserts that the realists were writers who consciously resisted the literary conventions they had inherited as novelists. Not satisfied to present "preestablished realities" in fiction, the realists, according to Levine, used language to explore a non-verbal reality that existed "out there," beyond their verbal descriptions. Levine's definition of realism sets it within a time frame that Denis Donoghue, writing in the *New York Review of Books,* finds too restricted; even so, Donoghue calls the study "an exceptionally interesting and far-reaching book." James R. Kincaid, a *New York Times Book Review* contributor, points out that realists have been accused of "operating under the preposterous illusion that words could reproduce or mirror a fixed reality," and that Levine's analyses show that the novelists were not so naive. Therefore, Kincaid concludes, "*The Realistic Imagination* is a masterly and compelling work that will alter significantly the study of the nineteenth-century novel."

BIOGRAPHICAL/CRITICAL SOURCES:

BOOKS

Levine, George, *The Realistic Imagination: English Fiction from Frankenstein to Lady Chatterley,* University of Chicago Press, 1981.

PERIODICALS

New Republic, August 15, 1981.
New York Review of Books, November 19, 1981.
New York Times Book Review, January 24, 1982.
Time, July 23, 1979.
Times Literary Supplement, August 22, 1968; November 13, 1981.
Washington Post Book World, September 2, 1979.

* * *

LINK, Mark J(oseph) 1924-

PERSONAL: Born April 21, 1924, in Coldwater, OH; son of Alois P. and Caroline (Antony) Link. *Education:* University of Cincinnati, B.S., 1950; West Baden College, licentiate in philosophy and theology, 1960; Lumen Vitae, Brussels, Belgium, advanced study in catechetics, 1961-62.

ADDRESSES: Home and office—Canisius House, 201 Dempster St., Evanston, IL 60201.

CAREER: Entered Society of Jesus (Jesuits), 1950, ordained Roman Catholic priest, 1960. St. Ignatius High School, Chicago, IL, instructor in religion, 1963-79; Loyola University, Chicago, religion editor of Loyola University Press, 1963-72, instructor in religion, 1964-72, instructor in theology, 1980-83; St. Elizabeth Seton Catholic Church, Plano, TX, author in residence, 1983—. *Military service:* U.S. Army Air Force, 1943-46; received Asiatic-Pacific Theater Ribbon with three Bronze Stars.

WRITINGS:

Christ Teaches Us Today, Loyola University Press, 1964.
(Editor) *Faith and Commitment,* Loyola University Press, 1964.
We Live in Christ, Loyola University Press, 1965.
(Editor) *Teaching the Sacraments and Morality,* Loyola University Press, 1965.
We Are God's People, Loyola University Press, 1966.
Man in the Modern World: Perspectives, Problems, Profiles, Loyola University Press, 1967.
Youth in the Modern World: Literature, Friends, Christ, Action, Loyola University Press, 1969.
Life in the Modern World: Home, Parish, Neighborhood, School, Loyola University Press, 1970.
He Is the Stillpoint of the Turning World, Argus Communications, 1971.
In the Stillness Is the Dancing, Argus Communications, 1972.
Take off Your Shoes, Argus Communications, 1972.
The Merriest Christmas Book, Argus Communications, 1974.
The Mustard Seed: A Prayer Guide to Mark's Gospel, Argus Communications, 1974.
These Stones Will Shout: A New Voice for the Old Testament, Argus Communications, 1975, revised edition, 1980.
You: Prayer for Beginners and Those Who Have Forgotten How, Argus Communications, 1976.
The Seventh Trumpet: The Good News Proclaimed, Argus Communications, 1978.
Breakaway: Twenty-Eight Steps to a More Reflective Life, Argus Communications, 1980.
Lord, Who Are You?: Acts, Letters, and Revelation, Argus Communications, 1981.
Experiencing Jesus, Argus Communications, 1985.
Experiencing Prayer, Argus Communications, 1985.
Path through Scripture, Tabor, 1986.
Illustrated Daily Homilies, Tabor, 1986-88.
Illustrated Sunday Homilies, Tabor, 1986-91.
Path through Scripture, Tabor, 1987.
Challenge, Tabor, 1988.
Decision, Tabor, 1988.
Journey, Tabor, 1988.
The Psalms for Today, Tabor, 1988.
The Catholic Vision, Tabor, 1989.
Prayer Paths, Tabor, 1990.
Path through Catholicism, Tabor, 1991.
Vision/2000, Tabor, 1992.
Mission/2000, Tabor, 1993.
Challenge/2000, Tabor, 1993.
Action/2000, Tabor, 1994.

Also scriptwriter for filmstrip, "Behold This Heart."

* * *

LITTLE, (Flora) Jean 1932-

PERSONAL: Born January 2, 1932, in T'ai-nan, Formosa (now Taiwan); daughter of John Llewellyn (a physician and surgeon) and Flora (a physician; maiden name, Gauld) Little. *Education:* University of Toronto, B.A., 1955; attended Institute of Special Education; received teaching certificate from University of Utah. *Religion:* Christian.

Avocational Interests: Designing and hooking rugs.

ADDRESSES: Home—198 Glasgow St. N., Guelph, Ontario, Canada N1H 4X2.

CAREER: Teacher of children with motor handicaps, Canada; specialist teacher at Beechwood School for Crippled Children, Guelph, Ontario; writer. Visiting instructor at Institute of Special Education and Florida University; summer camp director and leader of church youth groups.

MEMBER: Canadian Authors Association, Writers' Union of Canada, Authors League of America, Council for Exceptional Children, United Church Women.

AWARDS, HONORS: Canadian Children's Book Award, joint award of American and Canadian branches of Little, Brown, 1961, for *Mine for Keeps;* Vicky Metcalf Award, Canadian Authors Association, 1974, for body of work inspirational to Canadian boys and girls; Governor General's Literary Award for Children's Literature, Canada Council, 1977, for *Listen for the Singing;* Children's Book Award, Canada Council, 1979; Children's Book of the Year Award, Canadian Library Association, and Ruth Schwartz Award, both 1985, for *Mama's Going to Buy You a Mockingbird; Boston Globe-Horn Book* Honor Award, 1988, for *Little by Little: A Writer's Education;* numerous Junior Literary Guild awards.

WRITINGS:

It's a Wonderful World (poems), privately printed, 1947.
Mine for Keeps, illustrated by Lewis Parker, Little, Brown, 1962.
Home from Far, illustrated by Jerry Lazare, Little, Brown, 1965.
Spring Begins in March, illustrated by Parker, Little, Brown, 1966.
When the Pie Was Opened (poems), Little, Brown, 1968.
Take Wing, illustrated by Lazare, Little, Brown, 1968.

One to Grow On, illustrated by Lazare, Little, Brown, 1969.

Look through My Window, illustrated by Joan Sandin, Harper, 1970.

Kate, Harper, 1971.

From Anna, illustrated by Sandin, Harper, 1972.

Stand in the Wind, illustrated by Emily Arnold McCully, Harper, 1975.

Listen for the Singing, Dutton, 1977.

Mama's Going to Buy You a Mockingbird, Viking, 1984.

Lost and Found, illustrated by Leoung O'Young, Viking, 1985.

Different Dragons, Viking, 1986.

Hey World, Here I Am!, illustrated by Barbara DiLella, Kids Can Press, 1986, illustrated by Sue Truesdell, Harper, 1989.

Little by Little: A Writer's Education (autobiography), Viking, 1987.

Stars Come Out Within (autobiography), Penguin, 1990.

(With Maggie de Vries) *Once upon a Golden Apple,* illustrated by Phoebe Gilman, Viking, 1991.

Jess Was the Brave One, illustrated by Janet Wilson, Viking, 1992.

Revenge of the Small Small, illustrated by Wilson, Viking Children's Books, 1993.

Also author of novel *Let Me Be Gentle.* Contributor to periodicals, including *Horn Book, Canadian Library Journal,* and *Canadian Author and Bookman.*

Little's works have been translated into Dutch, German, Danish, Japanese, and Russian.

ADAPTATIONS: Hey World, Here I Am and *Little by Little: A Writer's Education* are available on audiocassette; *Mama's Going to Buy You a Mockingbird* was adapted as a television movie.

SIDELIGHTS: Jean Little is recognized throughout Canada and the United States for her candid and unsentimental portrayals of adolescent life. A teacher of handicapped children, Little herself is only partially sighted, and she uses much of her real-life experience as the basis for her books. Her characters often deal with physical disabilities, including cerebral palsy or blindness, or confront psychological difficulties involving fear or grief. However, none of her characters find magical cures for their problems. Instead they learn to cope with and survive the challenges they face, and thus they are led to greater self-understanding. "Ultimately," explained Meguido Zola in *Language Arts,* "that is the real thrust of Jean Little's novels—recognizing and mastering the enemy within rather than tilting at the one without." For her writings, Little has won numerous awards, including the Canadian Children's Book Award and the Vicky Metcalf Award.

Little was born in 1932 in Formosa, or Taiwan. Soon afterward, doctors detected scars over both her corneas, the "windows" that cover the eyes. Though she could see—she responded to light as an infant—her eyesight was significantly impaired, and she was diagnosed as legally blind. Her pupils were also off-center, so she had trouble focusing on one object for more than a brief moment. Later, schoolchildren would taunt her by calling her "cross-eyed."

Fortunately, Little's family was very supportive. Her parents read to her frequently, and as she gained limited vision, they taught her to read on her own. "Reading became my greatest joy," she wrote in her first autobiography, *Little by Little: A Writer's Education.* By 1939 Little's family had moved to Toronto, Canada. There she first attended a class for students with vision problems. By fourth grade, however, she transferred into a regular class and no longer received specialized treatment—large-print books, for example, or oversized lettering on the chalkboard. As a result, she struggled with many everyday tasks. "If I wanted to read what was written on the board," she recalled in *Little by Little,* "I would have to stand up so that my face was only inches away from the writing. Then I would have to walk back and forth, following the words not only with my eyes but with my entire body."

As Little progressed through school, she discovered that she enjoyed writing. Seeing her obvious talent, her father encouraged her and often edited her work. "From the first my Dad was my greatest critic and supporter," she once commented. "He plagued me to rewrite." When Little was fifteen, her father collected and printed her first booklet of poems, *It's a Wonderful World.* And a few years later, when the magazine *Saturday Night* published two of her verses, her father proudly read them aloud. "I listened," she remembered in *Little by Little,* "and [when] his voice broke, I knew why I wanted to be a writer."

Deciding to pursue a degree in English, Little entered Victoria College's English language and literature program. Just before classes began, though, her father suffered a severe heart attack. Throughout the following weeks and months his health improved just slightly, yet his enthusiasm for his daughter's schoolwork never diminished. "When I got to college [my father] did research on every essay topic I had," she recalled, "and insisted on tearing apart everything I wrote. He drove me crazy. Not until he died did I come to appreciate his unflagging zeal on my behalf."

Following her freshman year Little completed her first novel, *Let Me Be Gentle,* about a large family with a mentally retarded six-year-old girl. "When I carefully typed 'The End,' " she wrote in *Little by Little,* "I gazed at that stack of typed pages with intense satisfaction. . . . I was convinced that the entire world would be as fond of my characters as I was. After all, I had written a practically perfect book." Nevertheless, her manuscript was soon returned by publisher Jack McClelland, who pointed out its choppiness and lack of focus. Little was hardly discouraged, though—McClelland also told her she had talent.

In 1955 Little graduated with her bachelor's degree in English, and although she primarily wanted to write, she applied for a position teaching handicapped children. With her experience—she had spent three summers working with children with motor handicaps—and with additional training, she was hired. For the next six years she worked with handicapped children in camps, at special schools, and in their homes. She also taught at the Institute of Special Education in Salt Lake City, Utah, and at Florida University. These years helped inspire her to write for children. "Remembering how I had never found a cross-eyed heroine in a book," she remarked in *Little by Little,* "I decided to search for books about children with motor handicaps. I did not for one moment intend to limit my students to reading about crippled kids. I knew that . . . they actually became [fictional animal characters] Bambi, Piglet and Wilbur. I did not think they needed a book to help them adjust. I did believe, however, that crippled children had a right to find themselves represented in fiction."

As Little explained to Zola in *Language Arts,* the few books of the late 1950s and early 1960s that did portray handicapped children presented inaccurate views of them. Full of self-pity, the children were usually shown brooding over their limitations while dreaming of becoming more like their "normal" friends. And typically, by each story's end, they would undergo miraculous recoveries. "How my [students] laughed at all this silliness," Little told Zola. "And yet how cheated they felt. And so my first book—for them."

Mine for Keeps turns on Sally Copeland, a young girl with cerebral palsy, a disability frequently resulting from brain damage during birth. In the novel, Sally returns home after years of seclusion in a residential treatment center, then she learns to adjust to classes at a regular school. Her family and friends, too, must adapt to her special needs. *Mine for Keeps* "was different from *Let Me Be Gentle,*" Little recalled in *Little by Little,* "because I had intended the first for my family and friends and only afterwards wondered if it were publishable. This one I had written purposely for strangers to read. I had worked much harder and longer on it." Not knowing exactly how to proceed after her manuscript was finished, Little took the advice of a librarian and submitted the story to the Little, Brown Canadian Children's Book Award committee. And in May of 1961—in a letter signed by the same Jack McClelland who had rejected *Let Me Be Gentle* years earlier—she found out her book had won.

Little dedicated *Mine for Keeps* to her father, and since its publication in 1962 she has gone on to write almost twenty additional books. Among these are *Look through My Window* and *Kate,* a pair of stories that revolve around both Emily, a withdrawn, only child, and Kate, a young girl of both Jewish and Protestant descent. In *Look through My Window* Emily deals with her family's sudden move to the country and with the prolonged visit of her four boisterous cousins. She also begins to recognize the value of her newfound friendship with Kate. In *Kate* the title character struggles to understand not only her religion but also herself and her family's roots. She too learns to treasure her friendship with Emily. "*Kate* is a beautiful tribute to the power of love," concluded John W. Conner in the *English Journal.*

Little addresses the subject of blindness in *From Anna* and *Listen for the Singing,* which won the Governor General's Literary Award for Children's Literature in 1977. In the first story, Anna, a shy and awkward young girl, moves with her family from Germany to Canada just before the start of World War II. The move is painful for her since she not only dreads living in a strange land, she also fears her new teachers—who will undoubtedly criticize her inability to read. When Anna is found to have impaired vision, however, she is placed in a special class, and there she begins to overcome her insecurities. *Listen for the Singing,* which opens the day England declared war on Germany, follows Anna as she begins her first year in a public high school. Because of her nationality, she faces hostility and prejudice, yet she also finds friends who are willing to defend her. In addition she comes to accept her disability and is then able to help her brother survive the shock of a tragic accident. "This is a story of courage, then, in one of its more unspectacular guises," declared Susan Jackel in the *World of Children's Books:* "the courage of a young person who anticipates almost certain humiliation and nonetheless wins through to a number of small victories."

In 1985 Little won the Canadian Children's Book of the Year Award for *Mama's Going to Buy You a Mockingbird.* As the narrative unfolds, twelve-year-old Jeremy learns that his father, Adrian, is dying of cancer. To ease Jeremy's sorrow, Adrian introduces him to Tess, a strong, compassionate young girl who has withstood several tragedies of her own. Through Tess Jeremy discovers the strength to survive his father's death, and he also finds the courage to comfort his grieving mother and sister. "The story has depth and insight," noted a reviewer for the *Bulletin of the Center for Children's Books,* "and it ends on a convincingly positive note."

In 1987, Little chronicled her childhood in an autobiography entitled *Little by Little: A Writer's Education,* which concludes with the announcement that *Mine for Keeps* had been accepted for publication. Three years later, in 1990, Little completed her second autobiographical installment, *Stars Come Out Within.* Beginning each chapter with a fitting quote from American poet Emily Dickinson—in whose writings Little finds solace and encouragement—the author details in the work her depression over the subsequent loss of her left eye from glaucoma, and her frustration in dealing with the deteriorating vision in her remaining eye. She also recounts her experiences learning to work with Zephyr, her guide dog, and her struggles to compose her books by using a talking computer invented for blind writers. Eliciting praise from reviewers, *Stars Come Out Within* was deemed an uplifting memoir. Phyllis G. Sidorsky in *School Library Journal* decided that "Little's refusal to let her disability dominate her life . . . makes this a memorable account," while a *Horn Book* commentator found that in *Stars Come Out Within* "one not only marches with [Little] through the marshes of despair but ultimately ascends with her the mount of triumph."

When not writing Little keeps abreast of her audience by working with young people in the church, schools, and community. She also closely monitors the field of children's literature. "Children's books are chiefly what she reads," observed Zola in *Language Arts.* "She reads them because, for the most part, they are among the few books that still rejoice in life, still pulse with awe and wonder at its miracle, and still communicate a sense of growth and hope and love. It is in this spirit that she writes, to celebrate life."

BIOGRAPHICAL/CRITICAL SOURCES:

BOOKS

Children's Literature Review, Volume 4, Gale, 1982.

Little, Jean, *Little by Little: A Writer's Education,* Viking, 1987.

The Republic of Childhood: A Critical Guide to Canadian Children's Literature in English, Oxford University Press, 1975.

Something about the Author, Volume 2, Gale, 1971, pp. 178-179.

PERIODICALS

Books for Young People, April, 1987; December, 1987; autumn/winter, 1991, p. 24.

Bulletin of the Center for Children's Books, September, 1962; January, 1973; June, 1985, p. 189; October, 1986.

Canadian Children's Literature: A Journal of Criticism and Review, Numbers 5 and 6, 1976; Number 12, 1978.

CM, January, 1986.

English Journal, March, 1972, pp. 434-435.

Horn Book, September, 1988; September, 1989; January/February, 1992, p. 93.

In Review: Canadian Books for Children, autumn, 1970.

Kirkus Reviews, May 1, 1992, p. 613.

Language Arts, January, 1981, pp. 86-92.

Lion and the Unicorn, fall, 1977.

Publishers Weekly, April 6, 1992, p. 63.

Quill and Quire, November, 1990.

School Library Journal, October, 1985; October, 1986; June, 1988; July, 1989; January, 1992, p. 129; July, 1992, p. 60.

Times Literary Supplement, June 7, 1985.

World of Children's Books, spring, 1978, pp. 81-83.*

* * *

LOEWE, Raphael J(ames) 1919-

PERSONAL: Surname is pronounced *Loe*-wy; born April 16, 1919, in Calcutta, India; son of Herbert (a university teacher) and Ethel (Hyamson) Loewe; married Chloe Klatzkin, 1952; children: Elisabeth, Camilla N. *Education:* Cambridge University, M.A., 1948. *Religion:* Jewish.

ADDRESSES: Home—50 Gurney Dr., London N2 0DE, England.

CAREER: University of Leeds, Leeds, England, instructor in Hebrew, 1949-54; Cambridge University, Cambridge, England, Bye research fellow of Gonville & Caius College, 1954-57; taught at Carmel College, 1957-60; Leo Baeck College, London, England, lecturer in Hebrew, 1960-63; Brown University, Providence, RI, visiting professor of Jewish studies, 1963-64; University of London, London, England, lecturer, 1964-72, reader, 1972-80, professor, 1980-82, Goldsmid Professor of Hebrew, 1982-84. *Military service:* British army, 1940-45; served in North Africa and Italy; received Military Cross.

MEMBER: Jewish Historical Society of England (past president), Society for Old Testament Study (past president), Society of Antiquaries (fellow), Royal Asiatic Society (fellow).

AWARDS, HONORS: Tel Aviv Municipal Prize, 1982, for Hebrew translation of Omar Khayyam.

WRITINGS:

(Editor and contributor) *Studies in Rationalism, Judaism, and Universalism,* Humanities Press, 1969.

(Editor with Siegfried Stein, and contributor) *Studies in Jewish Religious and Intellectual History,* University of Alabama Press, 1979.

Gilguley Merubba'im, Magnes Press (Jerusalem), 1982.

The Rylands Haggadah, Harry N. Abrams, 1988.

Ibn Gabirol, Peter Halban Publishers, 1989, Grove Weidenfeld, 1990.

Also translator of Isaac Ibn Sahula's book of 13th century animal fables, *Meshal ha-qadmoni.* Contributor to *Encyclopaedia Judaica.* Contributor to learned journals.

WORK IN PROGRESS: Research on medieval Hebrew poetry and Jewish biblical exegesis.

SIDELIGHTS: Raphael J. Loewe told *CA:* "My scholarly interest in Jewish literature and history is derived from family tradition over three previous generations. In my case it has been permeated by the effects of a university training in Greek and Latin classics and by an abiding love of them and respect for the intellectual self-discipline which is a major legacy of Greece and Rome. I have been challenged by the achievements of Christian theology and religious culture in late antiquity and especially in the Middle Ages to seek out their parallels, rebuttals, and so forth within Judaism and make them more easily available and better understood—hence the attention I have given to translating medieval Hebrew poetry into English poetic forms. I do not set out hoping to prove anything by research, but I do hope to be able to accept my findings however emotionally disturbing they may be, if they have been checked and cannot be refuted. I hope that my personal views and values do not intrude into my scholarly writing. If, despite my best endeavors, they have done so, they are likely to be acceptance of Jewish monotheism as the authority for ethical living and institutional religious practice, skepticism in regard to conventional opinion entrenched by the backing of the establishment, and a mistrust and distaste for enthusiasm of any kind. Perhaps it was this combination which led me to translate Omar Khayyam into medieval Hebrew verse form, as against the numerous modern Hebrew versions already published, and to translate Ibn Gabriol's metaphysical Hebrew poetry into 16th-17th century English verse forms."

* * *

LOGUE, Christopher 1926-

PERSONAL: Born November 23, 1926, in Portsmouth, Hampshire, England; son of John and Molly (Chapman) Logue; married Rosemary Hill, 1985. *Education:* Prior Park College, Bath.

ADDRESSES: *Home*—41 Camberwell Grove, London SE5 8JA, England. *Agent*—Susan Bergholz, 340 West 72nd Street, New York, NY 10023.

CAREER: Poet. Acted in plays and films, including *The Devils,* 1970, and *Hamlet,* 1980; acted in television production of *The Gadfly,* 1977. *Military service:* British Army, 1944-48.

WRITINGS:

POETRY

Wand and Quadrant, [Paris], 1953.

Devil, Maggot and Son, Shots (Amsterdam), 1954.

The Weekdream Sonnets, Jack Straw (Paris), 1955.

The Man Who Told His Love: 20 Poems Based on P. Neruda's "Los Cantos d'amores," Scorpion Press, 1958, 2nd edition, 1959.

A Song for Kathleen (pamphlet), Villiers, 1958.

Songs, Hutchinson, 1959, McDowell, Obolensky, 1960.

Songs from "The Lily-White Boys," Scorpion Press, 1960.

(Adapter) Homer, *Patrocleia: Book 16 of Homer's Iliad Freely Adapted into English,* Scorpion Press, 1962, published as *Patrocleia of Homer: A New Version by Christopher Logue,* University of Michigan Press, 1963.

The Establishment Songs, Poet & Printer, 1966.

(Adapter) Homer, *Pax, from Book XIX of the Iliad,* Turret Books, 1967, published as *Pax,* Rapp & Carroll, 1967.

Gone Ladies (pamphlet; contemporary poetry set to music), music by Wallace Southam, arrangement by Patrick Gower, Turret Books, 1968.

The Girls, Turret Books, 1969.

New Numbers, J. Cape, 1969, Knopf, 1970.

Abecedary, illustrated by Bert Kitchen, J. Cape, 1977.

Ode to the Dodo, J. Cape, 1981.

War Music: An Account of Books 16 to 19 of Homer's Iliad, Penguin, 1981.

Fluff, incidental music by Stanley Meyers, Bernard Stone, 1984.

Kings: An Account of Books 1 and 2 of Homer's Iliad, Farrar, Straus, 1991, revised, Faber & Faber, 1992.

JUVENILE

Ratsmagic, illustrated by Wayne Anderson, J. Cape, 1977, Pantheon Books, 1979.

(Reteller) *Puss in Boots,* Greenwillow, 1977.

The Magic Circus, illustrated by Anderson, J. Cape, 1979.

Also adapter of *The Crocodile,* illustrated by Binette Schroeder, [London], 1976.

EDITOR

Count Palmiro Vicarion's Book of Limericks, Olympia Press (Paris), 1959.

The Children's Book of Comic Verse, Batsford, 1979.

London in Verse, Penguin, 1982.

Sweet & Sour: An Anthology of Comic Verse, Batsford, 1983.

The Children's Book of Children's Rhymes, Batsford, 1986.

PLAYS

(With Harry Cookson) *The Lily-White Boys,* produced in London, 1959.
The Trial of Cob and Leach, produced in London, 1959.
Antigone, produced in London, 1961.
Savage Messiah (screenplay), Metro-Goldwyn-Mayer, 1972.
War Music, produced in London, 1978.
Kings, produced in London, 1993.

Author of script and songs for *The End of Arthur's Marriage,* British Broadcasting Corporation, 1968.

OTHER

Lust, by Count Palmiro Vicarion, Olympia Press, 1955.
The Arrival of the Poet in the City: A Treatment for a Film, Mandarin Books, 1964.
True Stories, Four Square Books, 1966.
The Bumper Book of True Stories, Private Eye, 1980.

Also author of twenty-six illustrated verse posters; contributor to *Private Eye* and *The Times* (London). Translator of *Baal* by Berthold Brecht, 1985; *Seven Deadly Sins* by Brecht, 1988; and "Friday" by Hugo Claus.

ADAPTATIONS: Logue's poems have been recorded on disk as *Red Bird* and *Poets Reading,* both 1961, *The Death of Patroclus,* 1962, and *Loguerhythms,* 1967.

SIDELIGHTS: A poet who has made a wide range of subjects and genres available to new audiences, Christopher Logue has won recognition and praise from critics for his free adaptation of Homer's *Iliad* in four separate books: *Patrocleia, Pax, War Music,* and *Kings.* In the *Times Literary Supplement,* Jasper Griffen commented: "Christopher Logue, who knows no Greek, has been working on the *Iliad,* on and off, since 1959, using older published versions and consulting scholars at need; and his work is unmistakably of this age. That he should want to produce it is powerful evidence of the appeal of Homer." Of *War Music, New York Times'* reviewer John Gross observed: "The most modern thing about it is the cinematic fluidity of the narrative; but its key images remain broadly Homeric—the very last thing we see, as Achilles's chariot races away, is a spear that has been left stuck in the sand. Often, indeed, it seems more archaic and more barbaric than Homer, or at any rate than most previous English versions of Homer."

Griffen, who described Logue's departures from the *Iliad* as having a "splendid independence and assurance," noted that Logue makes *Kings* his own by creating a new episode in which the princes of Troy debate the war and by making explicit some undercurrents in Homer's original. In *Tribune Books,* David R. Slavitt reached a similar conclusion: "The undertaking would be a bold one, even rash, except that Logue's achievement is so impressive, at first disarming and then persuasive and satisfying. What he has produced is an original poem . . . . Logue's is no Byzantine exercise but an intense, personal encounter."

At the same time, George Steiner, writing in the London *Times,* described *Kings* as "frequently slow and out of breath." This judgement is in contrast to the praise he heaped on Logue's earlier work, *War Music,* which, he declared, verged on genius. Of *War Music,* Steiner wrote, "It is a poet's formidably penetrating *reading* of key moments, of crucial motions, of implicit nodes of supreme intensity and signification in the late books of Homer's songs of war. It is the inspired transcription of Logue's listening." Steiner argued that Logue's juxtapositions of present time on the epic tale do not mesh well with the original in *Kings.*

Edward Larrissy, reviewing Logue's selected poems, *Ode to the Dodo,* in the *Times Literary Supplement,* praised Logue's adaptations of Homer, but found his oeuvre—taken as a whole—uneven. Describing the author's early poems as "taut, plangent lyrics, with a hint of magical strangeness," Larrissy called the selected poems "at best . . . bright, at worst brittle and bleakly propositional."

In addition to his poems and his adaptations of Homer, Logue has demonstrated his versatility by retelling children's classics—like *Puss in Boots*—translating some of the love songs of Pablo Neruda, and writing and acting in several plays and films. Beginning in 1958 with "To My Fellow Artists," Logue made many of his poems into posters. When once asked by Davina Lloyd if his "prime motive in making posters [is] to get poems out," Logue answered: "One doesn't always know one's own motives. A poster seems two things: both a means to an end and an end in itself. The Iliad would go marvelously on a poster except that it would be a [very] large poster."

BIOGRAPHICAL/CRITICAL SOURCES:

PERIODICALS

Books and Bookmen, May, 1967.
Book World, November 15, 1970, p. 6.
Commonweal, November 11, 1977, p. 730.
Listener, November 8, 1979, p. 646.
London Magazine, August 1968; October 1969.
New Statesman, June 27, 1969, p. 914; August 7, 1981, p. 19; April 13, 1984, p. 23.
New York Review of Books, April 23, 1992.
New York Times, May 8, 1987, p. 25.
Observer, July 13, 1969, p. 25; December 9, 1973, p. 35; August 9, 1981, p. 23; December 5, 1982, p. 34; February 4, 1984, p. 52; April 28, 1991, p. 58.
Partisan Review, number 3, 1988, p. 484.
Saturday Review, November 27, 1976, p. 36.

Spectator, April 14, 1979, p. 20; July 4, 1981, p. 18; December 18, 1982, p. 38; December 17, 1983, p. 36; March 16, 1991, p. 32.

Times (London), March 30, 1991, p. 20. *Times Educational Supplement,* November 23, 1979, p. 31; May 22, 1981, p. 22; October 19, 1984, p. 48.

Times Literary Supplement, October 5, 1967, p. 937; August 28, 1981, p. 988; July 4, 1986, p. 746; March 29, 1991, p. 20; August 28, 1991.

Tribune Books, December 29, 1991, p. 5.

Virginia Quarterly Review, autumn 1987, p. 137.

Washington Post Book World, August 14, 1977.

* * *

LONG, Richard A(lexander) 1927-
(Ric Alexander)

PERSONAL: Born February 9, 1927, in Philadelphia, PA; son of Thaddeus B. and Leila (Washington) Long. *Education:* Temple University, A.B., 1947, M.A., 1948; further study at University of Pennsylvania and University of Paris; University of Poitiers, D.es L., 1965.

ADDRESSES: Office—Graduate Institute of the Liberal Arts, Emory University, Atlanta, GA 30322.

CAREER: West Virginia State College, Institute, WV, instructor in English, 1949-50; Morgan State College (now University), Baltimore, MD, assistant professor, 1951-64, associate professor of English, 1964-66; Hampton Institute, Hampton, VA, professor of English and French, 1966-68; Atlanta University, Atlanta, GA, professor of English and Afro-American studies, 1968-87; currently faculty member of Graduate Institute of the Liberal Arts, Emory University, Atlanta. Visiting lecturer in Afro-American Studies, Harvard University, 1970-72. *Military service:* U.S. Army, 1944-45.

MEMBER: American Dialect Society, American Studies Association, South Atlantic Modern Language Association, Modern Language Association of America, College Language Association (president, 1971-72), Modern Humanities Research Association, Linguistics Society of America, Southeastern Conference on Linguistics.

AWARDS, HONORS: Fulbright scholar, University of Paris, 1957-58.

WRITINGS:

(Editor with Albert H. Berrian) *Negritude: Essays and Studies,* Hampton Institute Press, 1967, revised edition, 1987.

(Editor with Eugenia W. Collier) *Afro-American Writing: An Anthology of Prose and Poetry,* two volumes, Pennsylvania State University Press, 1972, enlarged edition, 1985, 2nd enlarged edition, 1990.

Ascending and Other Poems, Du Sable Museum, 1975.

Black Americana, Chartwell, 1985.

Black Writers and the American Civil War, Blue and Gray Press, 1988.

The Black Tradition in American Dance, Rizzoli, 1989.

Black Americans: A Portrait, Crescent, 1993.

DRAMATIC WORKS UNDER NAME RIC ALEXANDER

The Pilgrim's Pride (sketches), 1963.

Stairway to Heaven (gospel opera), 1964.

Joan of Arc (folk opera), 1964.

Reasons of State (play), 1966.

Black Is Many Hues (play), 1969.

OTHER

Contributor to anthologies of essays, including *The Harlem Renaissance Re-Examined,* edited by Victor A. Kramer, AMS, 1987, and *Swords upon This Hill: Preserving the Literary Tradition of Black Colleges and Universities,* edited by Burney J. Hollis, Morgan State University Press, 1984. Former member of editorial board of *Black Books Bulletin.*

BIOGRAPHICAL/CRITICAL SOURCES:

PERIODICALS

American Visions, April, 1990.

Booklist, January 1, 1990.

Book World, December 3, 1989.

Choice, September, 1990.

Dance Magazine, March, 1991.

Ebony, March, 1990.

Essence, March, 1990.

Journal of American Studies, April, 1987.

Library Journal, February 1, 1973; January, 1990.

Reference & Research Book News, February, 1990.

* * *

LORRIMER, Claire 1921-
(Patricia Robins)

PERSONAL: Born February 1, 1921, in Hove, Sussex, England; daughter of Arthur and Denise (a writer; maiden name, Klein) Robins; married D. C. Clark, 1948 (divorced); children: two sons, one daughter.

ADDRESSES: Home—Chiswell Barn, Christmas Mill Lane, Marsh Green, Edenbridge, Kent TN8 5PR, England. *Agent*—Anthea Morton-Saner, Curtis Brown, 162-168 Regent St., London W1R 5TB, England.

CAREER: Writer. *Military service:* Women's Auxiliary Air Force, 1940-45; became flight officer.

WRITINGS:

NOVELS

A Voice in the Dark, Souvenir Press, 1967, Avon, 1968.
The Shadow Falls, Avon, 1974.
Relentless Storm, Avon, 1975.
The Secret of Quarry House, Avon, 1976.
Mavreen, Arlington, 1976, Bantam, 1977.
Tamarisk, Arlington, 1978, Bantam, 1979.
The Garden, Arlington, 1980.
Chantal, Arlington, 1980, Bantam, 1981.
The Chatelaine, Arlington, 1981.
The Wilderling, Arlington, 1982.
Last Year's Nightingale, Century, 1984.
Frost in the Sun, Century, 1986.
Ortolans, Bantam, 1990.
The Spinning Wheel, Bantam, 1991.
The Silver Link, Bantam, 1993.
Fool's Curtain, Bantam, in press.

UNDER PSEUDONYM PATRICIA ROBINS

To the Stars, Hutchinson, 1944.
See No Evil, Hutchinson, 1945.
Statues of Snow, Hutchinson, 1947.
Three Loves, Hutchinson, 1949.
Awake My Heart, Hutchinson, 1950.
Beneath the Moon, Hutchinson, 1951.
Leave My Heart Alone, Hutchinson, 1951.
The Fair Deal, Hutchinson, 1952.
Heart's Desire, Hutchinson, 1953.
So This Is Love, Hutchinson, 1953.
Heaven in Our Hearts, Hutchinson, 1954.
One Who Cares, Hutchinson, 1954.
Love Cannot Die, Hutchinson, 1955.
The Foolish Heart, Hutchinson, 1956.
Give All to Love, Hutchinson, 1956.
Where Duty Lies, Hutchinson, 1957.
He Is Mine, Hurst & Blackett, 1957.
Love Must Wait, Hurst & Blackett, 1958.
Lonely Quest, Hurst & Blackett, 1959.
Lady Chatterly's Daughter, Ace, 1961.
The Last Chance, Hurst & Blackett, 1961.
The Long Wait, Hurst & Blackett, 1962.
The Runaways, Hurst & Blackett, 1962.
Seven Loves, Consul, 1962.
With All My Love, Hurst & Blackett, 1963.
The Constant Heart, Hurst & Blackett, 1964.
Second Love, Hurst & Blackett, 1964.
The Night Is Thine, Consul, 1964.
There Is But One, Hurst & Blackett, 1965.
No More Loving, Consul, 1965.
Topaz Island, Hurst & Blackett, 1965.
Love Me Tomorrow, Hurst & Blackett, 1966.
The Uncertain Joy, Hurst & Blackett, 1966.
Forbidden, Mayflower, 1967.
Return to Love, Hurst & Blackett, 1968.
Sapphire in the Sand, Arrow, 1968.
Laugh on Friday, Hurst & Blackett, 1969.
No Stone Unturned, Hurst & Blackett, 1969.
Cinnabar House, Hurst & Blackett, 1970.
Under the Sky, Hurst & Blackett, 1970.
The Crimson Tapestry, Hurst & Blackett, 1972.
Play Fair with Love, Hurst & Blackett, 1972.
None But He, Hurst & Blackett, 1973.
Forever, Severn House, 1991.
Fulfilment, Severn House, 1993.
Forsaken, Severn House, 1993.

JUVENILES; UNDER PSEUDONYM PATRICIA ROBINS

The Adventures of Three Baby Bunnies, Nicholson & Watson, 1934.
Tree Fairies, Hutchinson, 1945.
Sea Magic, Hutchinson, 1946.
The Heart of a Rose, Hutchinson, 1947.
The 100-Pounds Reward, Wheaton, 1966.

OTHER

(Under pseudonym Patricia Robins) *Seven Days Leave* (poetry), Hutchinson, 1943.
(As Claire Lorrimer) *House of Tomorrow* (biography), Century, 1987.
(As Claire Lorrimer) *Variations* (short stories), Bantam, 1991.

BIOGRAPHICAL/CRITICAL SOURCES:

PERIODICALS

Best Sellers, August 15, 1970.
Books and Bookmen, February, 1968.
West Coast Review of Books, May, 1977.

* * *

LUCAS, J(ames) R(aymond) 1950-

PERSONAL: Born March 9, 1950, in St. Louis, MO; son of James Earl (a craftsman) and Anna Laverne (Ryan) Lucas; married Pamela Kay Petersen, June 10, 1972; children: Laura Christine, Peter Barrett, David Christopher, Bethany Gayle. *Education:* University of Missouri-Rolla, B.S., 1972; University of Missouri-Columbia, additional study, 1975. *Religion:* "Bible-believing Christian."

ADDRESSES: *Home*—P.O. Box 2566, Shawnee Mission, KS 66201. *Office*—Luman Consulting Co., P.O. Box 2566, Shawnee Mission, KS 66201.

CAREER: H. D. Lee Co. (clothing firm), Kansas City, MO, analyst, 1971-73; Black & Veatch (consulting engineers), Kansas City, planning engineer, 1973-79; Hallmark Cards, Kansas City, director in Crown Center Redevelopment Corp., 1979-81; Pritchard Corp. (engineering and construction firm), Kansas City, project manager, 1981-83; Luman Consulting Co. (management consultants), Prairie Village, KN, president, 1983—; Epic Manufacturing Co., Kansas City, president, 1984-87; PSM Co. (manufacturing firm), Kansas City, operations manager, 1987-91; Hermes Co. (design and construction firm), Leneya, KS, vice-president of administration, 1991—. President, Relationship Development Center, 1992—. Registered professional engineer in Missouri; licensed professional engineer in Kansas.

MEMBER: Society of Manufacturing Engineers (senior member).

WRITINGS:

And Then, Resurrection (three-act play), produced in Overland Park, KN, 1983.
Weeping in Ramah (novel), Crossway Books, 1985.
The Parenting of Champions: Raising Godly Children in an Evil Age (nonfiction), Wolgemuth & Hyatt, 1989.
Noah: Voyage to a New Earth (fiction), Wolgemuth & Hyatt, 1991.
Proactive Parenting: The Only Approach that Really Works, Harvest House, 1993.

WORK IN PROGRESS: A Marriage for All Seasons, "a biblical approach to marriage, beginning with singleness and correct decision-making and moving to making a marriage one that can be successful for a lifetime"; *Liberty's Lost Crescendo.*

SIDELIGHTS: J. R. Lucas told *CA:* "The driving force behind *Weeping in Ramah* was my desire to take current moral, philosophical, and social trends to their logical conclusions, to let people see the end from the beginning, as Orwell did in the novel *1984.* As Harriet Beecher Stowe was able to do in *Uncle Tom's Cabin,* I wanted to make things personal for the reader, rather than just intellectual. Although the book is predictive in nature (if current directions continue unaltered), the primary motivation behind the book is a desire to provide a warning to Americans, and others, so that the heartless society depicted in the book can be avoided or at least restrained. This book is more social fiction than science fiction; it is not so much an imaginary tour of some future world, in an allegorical or exaggerated form, as it is an extrapolation into the near future of the world we already have around us. I tried to accomplish the same point with *Noah: Voyage to a New Earth,* historical fiction that lets the reader see our culture through the eyes and life of a man who lived thousands of years ago. I used the literary device of making him a 'modern' man in an old but very modern culture.

"My belief that we are witnessing the rapid decline of Western civilization, even in the midst of astounding affluence, is also the driving force behind my work in progress, especially *Liberty's Last Crescendo.* I believe that America must be awakened or it will lose its rich cultural and moral heritage, perhaps forever. Even as the bookstores are being filled with books trumpeting even more peace and affluence—except for an occasional foray into something like nuclear war—I am convinced that the truth lies somewhere else, that a strong body cannot be built on a decaying skeleton, regardless of the number who disagree.

"I took this same orientation toward analyzing problems deeply and proposing strong solutions into my two published non-fiction books, both on the subject of parenting—the parenting of champions and proactive parenting. My goal was to give parents a vision for the powerful impact a parent can have on his or her children through effective communication and being a living example of integrity. The troubled condition of marriages has led me to begin work on *Marriage for All Seasons,* in which I intend to prepare unmarried people to ask the right questions and face all of the critical issues before they get married. By giving a strong but realistic and achievable vision of marriage, I hope to prevent some bad marriages from occurring, and to strengthen existing marriages to survive the storms and prosper.

"I firmly believe that this nation and culture can be restored to a morally powerful condition. I have dedicated my writing career to making this come to pass, through the application of timeless and godly values in drama, fiction, and non-fiction works."

* * *

LUDWIG, Charles Shelton 1918-

PERSONAL: Born January 8, 1918, in Macomb, IL; son of John Shelton and Twyla Innes (Ogle) Ludwig (both missionaries); married Mary Puchek, 1939; children: Charles II, Brenda M. *Education:* Anderson College and Theological Seminary (now Anderson College), Anderson, IN, B.S., 1945.

ADDRESSES: Home—7217 East 30th St., Tucson, AZ 85710.

CAREER: Minister of Church of God; pastor of churches in Palmerton, PA, 1940-41, Indiana, PA, 1942, Chicago, IL, 1972-73, Olympia, WA, Boise, ID, and Tucson, AZ.

MEMBER: Southwestern Writers (Tucson).

AWARDS, HONORS: National Religious Book Award for outstanding religious book, 1979, for *Michael Faraday, Father of Electronics;* honorary D.D., West Coast Bible College, 1973.

WRITINGS:

Thirteen Sermons on the Twenty-third Psalm: Wonderful Jesus, Gospel Trumpet, 1942.
The Adventures of Juma, Warner Press, 1944.
Witch Doctor's Holiday, Warner Press, 1945.
Christ at the Door, Warner Press, 1946.
Leopard Glue, Warner Press, 1946.
Sankey Still Sings, Warner Press, 1947.
Cannibal Country, Warner Press, 1948.
Rogue Elephant: A Missionary Adventure Story for Boys and Girls, Scripture Press, 1954.
Brenda Morgan at Uranium Valley, Zondervan, 1956.
At the Cross, Warner Press, 1961, reprinted, 1989.
General without a Gun: The Life of William Booth, Founder of the Salvation Army, for Teens, Zondervan, 1961.
The Lady General, Baker Book, 1962.
On Target: Illustrations for Christian Messages, Warner Press, 1963.
Mama Was a Missionary, Warner Press, 1963.
Nancy Hanks, Mother of Lincoln, Baker Book, 1965.
Their Finest Hour, David Cook, 1974.
Levi Coffin and the Underground Railroad, Herald Press, 1975.
Cities in New Testament Times, Accent Books, 1976.
Rulers of New Testament Times, Accent Books, 1976.
He Freed Britain's Slaves, Herald Press, 1977.
Michael Faraday, Father of Electronics, Herald Press, 1978.
Francis Asbury: God's Circuit Rider, Mott Media, 1984.
Susanna, Mother of John and Charles Wesley, Mott Media, 1984.
Ludwig's Handbook of New Testament Rulers and Cities, Accent Press, 1984.
Ludwig's Handbook of Old Testament Rulers and Cities, Accent Press, 1985.
They Gave Us Wings: The Wright Brothers, Mott Media, 1986.
God's Composer: George Friderick Handel, Mott Media, 1986.
Katie Luther: Queen of the Reformation, Bethany House, 1986.
Catherine Booth: Mother of an Army, Bethany House, 1987.
Spinning Shoes, Warner Press, 1988.
Defender of the Faith, Bethany House, 1988.
Stonewall Jackson: Loved in the South, Admired in the North, Mott Media, 1989.
At the Tomb, Warner Press, 1991.
At Pentecost, Warner Press, 1991.
Jason Lee: Winner of the Northwest, Mott Media, 1992.
A Foot in Two Cultures (autobiography), Warner Press, 1992.

"RADIO PALS" SERIES

Radio Pals Marooned, Van Kampen, 1952.
Radio Pals Fight the Flood, Van Kampen, 1953.
Radio Pals on Bar T Ranch, Van Kampen, 1953.
Radio Pals in the Hands of the Mau Mau, Van Kampen, 1955.
Radio Pals in the Flaming Forest, Zondervan, 1955.

"A MISSIONARY ADVENTURE STORY" SERIES

Man-Eaters and Masai Spears, Scripture Press, 1953.
Man-Eaters Don't Knock, Scripture Press, 1953.
Man-Eaters Don't Laugh, Scripture Press, 1955.
Man-Eater's Clauw, Scripture Press, 1957.

A MISSIONARY ADVENTURE STORY FOR GIRLS

Chuma, Scripture Press, 1954.
Chuma Finds a Baby, Scripture Press, 1956.

OTHER

Contributor of over two thousand articles, mostly nonfiction, to magazines.

ADAPTATIONS: Mama Was a Missionary was read on World-Wide Radio: *Michael Faraday, Father of Electronics* and *Levi Coffin and the Underground Railroad* were both dramatized on the Moody Network.

SIDELIGHTS: Charles Shelton Ludwig grew up in Kenya and received his education there, from age nine to nineteen. His work has appeared in fourteen languages. Ludwig told *CA:* "I write books for a purpose. The purpose is to teach—and especially to inspire. My basic hope is that one of my books will help a reader through a difficult place and that it will motivate some to make their lives count."

* * *

LUSTBADER, Eric Van 1946-

PERSONAL: Born December 24, 1946, in New York, NY; son of Melvin Harry (a state social security bureau director) and Ruth (Aaronson) Lustbader; married; wife's name, Victoria. *Education:* Columbia University, B.A., 1968.

Avocational Interests: Japanese and Mayan history, history of prewar Shanghai, music, landscaping, Japanese pruning, ballet.

ADDRESSES: Office—c/o Pocket Books, 1230 Avenue of the Americas, New York, NY 10022. *Agent*—Henry Morrison, Inc., Box 235, Bedford Hills, NY 10507.

CAREER: Writer, 1978—. CIS-TRANS Productions (music producers), New York City, owner, 1963-67; elementary school teacher in New York City, 1968-70; *Cashbox* (music trade journal), New York City, associate editor, 1970-72; Elektra Records, New York City, director of international artists and repertory and assistant to the president, 1972-73; Dick James Music, New York City, director of publicity and creative services, 1974-75; Sweet Dream Productions, New York City, owner, 1975-76; NBC-TV, New York City, writer and field producer of news film on Elton John, 1976; CBS Records, New York City, designer of publicity and album covers and manager of media services, 1976-78.

MEMBER: Nature Conservancy, Save the Manatee Club, Historical Preservation Society, Cousteau Society, World Wildlife Fund, Smithsonian Institution, Metropolitan Museum of Art, Museum of Modern Art, South Street Seaport Museum.

WRITINGS:

NOVELS

Sirens, M. Evans, 1981.
Black Heart, M. Evans, 1982.
Jian, Random House, 1985.
Shan (sequel to *Jian*), Fawcett, 1987.
Zero, Random House, 1988.
French Kiss, Fawcett, 1988.
Angel Eyes, Fawcett, 1991.
Black Blade, Fawcett, 1993.
Batman: The Last Angel, DC/Warner, 1994.

THE "SUNSET WARRIOR" CYCLE

The Sunset Warrior, Doubleday, 1977.
Shallows of Night, Doubleday, 1978.
Dai-San, Doubleday, 1978.
Beneath an Opal Moon, Doubleday, 1980.

THE "NINJA" SERIES

The Ninja, M. Evans, 1980.
The Miko, Villard Books, 1984.
White Ninja, Fawcett, 1989.
The Keishe, Pocket, 1993.
The Floating City, Pocket, 1994.

Contributor to popular music magazines, including *Crawdaddy, Good Times,* and *Rock.*

The Ninja has been translated into twenty-three languages.

SIDELIGHTS: The novels of Eric Van Lustbader are steeped in the culture and traditions of Japan. Though he first translated his fascination with the Far East into a series of science-fiction/fantasy books known as the "Sunset Warrior" cycle, he attained international success with his 1980 novel *The Ninja,* the first of what would become a long string of bestsellers interweaving sex, intrigue, murder and, of course, the traditions of the Far East. Lustbader's subject matter has divided reviewers into two very distinct groups: those who view his novels as too violent and often cliched, and those who praise their well-researched and intricately wrought plots, as well as the heart-pounding suspense which Lustbader evokes.

As a young man, Lustbader decided to pursue a career in the music industry. He began, while still a student at Columbia University, by producing several local acts. Not long after attaining his B.A. he took a position as an associate editor for the music magazine *Cashbox,* and from there steadily climbed the ladder to publicist and media-service manager for Elektra and CBS Records. Though his job enabled him to hobnob with such artists as Pink Floyd and Elton John, Lustbader became increasingly disillusioned with the industry. "It was no longer what it was when I first came in," he recalls in *Publishers Weekly.* "People who knew nothing about music were handling the money end, and the business was mired in the elephantine tracks of big conglomerates. . . . I was at a dead end." He had, over the previous few years, completed a trilogy of fantasy books, writing mostly on weekends, and in 1978 he sold the trilogy to Doubleday, thus beginning his career as a writer.

The trilogy, comprised of *The Sunset Warrior, Shallows of Night,* and *Dai-San,* served two important functions for its author. First, it gave him the freedom to leave the music industry forever. Second, it allowed him to explore a subject that had fascinated him since he was a teenager: the Samurai of ancient Japan. This fascination had been sparked by the artwork of 19th century artist Ando Hiroshige. Lustbader described in *Publishers Weekly* his introduction to Hiroshige's art: "Falling in love is not even the term for it. . . . I looked at Hiroshige's work, and I was there. His prints speak to me more of the Japanese sensibility—of honor, friendship and the code of the samurai—than any photography ever could."

Using this vision of sensibility and honor as a framework, Lustbader's "Sunset Warrior" trilogy chronicles the adventures of the Bladesman Ronin in a future world rich in Eastern tradition. To this backdrop, the author adds the fast-paced action associated with martial arts, giving a new look to the fantasy-adventure story. The trilogy did very well, and Lustbader was commissioned by Doubleday to write a fourth book, *Beneath an Opal Moon.*

Despite the success of the "Sunset Warrior" cycle, Lustbader abandoned the fantasy genre for his next novel in favor of a suspense-thriller entitled *The Ninja. The Ninja* was rejected by a number of publishers before being picked up by M. Evans and Company. Recognizing the novel's immense potential, the editors at M. Evans set into motion an ambitious—and expensive—publicity campaign. They stirred interest in the book by quickly selling the paperback and film rights; this impressed such booksellers as Waldenbooks and Barnes & Noble, whose advance-copy orders funded even more publicity. By the time *The Ninja*'s "official" release date arrived it had already spent three weeks on the best seller list, marking M. Evans's first best seller ever and making Lustbader a millionaire almost overnight.

The Ninja introduces Nicholas Linnear, a half-English, half-Asian businessman who, as a young man in Japan, was trained in the semi-mystical ways of ninjutsu. Linnear, now a player in New York City's world of high finance, becomes enmeshed in a series of martial arts-style murders. Recognizing the killing style as that of a ninja, Linnear surreptitiously investigates the murders, discovering ultimately that the killer is a boyhood rival with whom he had trained. By that time, though, Linnear has been marked as the assassin's next target. "Somewhere inside this sprawling novel . . . there is an exciting thriller trying to break out," complains a *Publishers Weekly* reviewer, who calls the plot "implausible." *Los Angeles Times Book Review* writer Don G. Campbell also found the story too fast-paced at times, occasionally leaving the reader behind; however, he ultimately pronounces Lustbader "a fluid storyteller," claiming that "few can match him in creating a mood that something terrible is just about to happen." The immense popularity of *The Ninja* eventually sparked two more novels featuring Nicholas Linnear: 1984's *The Miko,* and 1990's *White Ninja.*

"In the fall of 1993," Lustbader told *CA,* "I began a three book sequence involving Nicholas Linnear, beginning with *The Keishe* and *The Floating City.* Although all three novels are entirely separate, their overall theme is the exploration of Nicholas's father's role in the creation of the new post-war Japan and Linnear's role in tomorrow's Japan."

Lustbader's novels continue to receive wildly varying reviews: his 1988 novel *Zero,* for example, is described by a writer for *West Coast Review of Books* as an "action-paced, contemporary adventure" that will "undoubtably please readers," while the *New York Times Book Review*'s William J. Harding labels *Zero* "ponderous," "unimaginative," and "bloated." Critics such as Harding often point to the graphic sex and violence that pervade Lustbader's writing. "I suppose that's all true," the author responds in *Publishers Weekly.* "But my novels are about the most uncalculatedly written books possible. I never know what's going to happen in them from day to day. The whole excitement about writing . . . is not knowing what's going to happen." And his main concern, of course, is for his readers—not his critics. "I'm not out to get good reviews," he says in the *New York Times Book Review.* "I'm out to sell books and entertain people."

Despite the abundance of violence in his novels, Lustbader is consistently praised by critics for his engrossing and well-researched depictions of Japanese culture and honor. For all his fascination with its history and values, however, Lustbader did not actually visit Japan until October, 1992. He told *CA:* "I spent two weeks in the countryside steeping myself in the history and religions at Buddhist temples, retreats, and Shinto shrines."

BIOGRAPHICAL/CRITICAL SOURCES:

BOOKS

Bestsellers, Volume 2, Gale, 1990.

PERIODICALS

Booklist, July 15, 1980, p. 1658.

Los Angeles Times Book Review, June 22, 1980; April 10, 1983, p. 2; February 2, 1986, p. 6; May 15, 1988, p. 12; January 22, 1989; February 10, 1991, p. 6.

New York Times Book Review, May 18, 1980, p. 44; June 7, 1981, p. 15; April 10, 1983, p. 29; September 23, 1984; February 1, 1987; June 26, 1988; February 12, 1989; February 25, 1990, p. 35.

People, October 29, 1984, p. 117.

Publishers Weekly, April 11, 1980, p. 71; August 17, 1984, p. 70; December 15, 1989, p. 58.

Tribune Books (Chicago), January 22, 1989, p. 7.

Washington Post Book World, September 1, 1985, p. 8.

West Coast Review of Books, June, 1983, p. 29; Volume 12, number 5, 1987, p. 32; Volume 15, number 5, 1990, p. 36; Volume 16, number 2, 1991, p. 30.

—Sketch by Brandon Trenz

* * *

LYNCH, Eric
See BINGLEY, David Ernest

M

MANGIONE, Gerlando 1909-
(Jerre Mangione)

PERSONAL: Born March 20, 1909, in Rochester, NY; son of Gaspare (a pastry cook and paperhanger) and Giuseppina (Polizzi) Mangione; married Patricia Anthony (an artist), February 18, 1957. *Education:* Syracuse University, B.A., 1931.

ADDRESSES: *Home*—3300 Darby Road, No. 7315, Haverford, PA 19041-1075. *Office*—Department of English, University of Pennsylvania, Philadelphia, PA 19014.

CAREER: *Time,* New York City, staff writer, 1931; New York *Herald Tribune,* New York City, book reviewer, 1931-35; *New Republic,* New York City, book reviewer, 1931-37; Robert M. McBride & Co. (publishers), New York City, book editor, 1934-37; Federal Writers' Project, Washington, DC, national coordinating editor, 1937-39; public relations specialist, Census Bureau, U.S. Department of Commerce, 1939; U.S. Department of Justice, information specialist, 1940, member of public relations staff, 1941-42; U.S. Immigration and Naturalization Service, Washington, DC, and Philadelphia, PA, special assistant to commissioner, 1942-48, editor-in-chief of *Monthly Review* (official publication), 1945-47; writer for advertising and public relations firms, including N.W. Ayer & Sons, Inc. and Columbia Broadcasting System (CBS), New York City, and Philadelphia, 1948-61; University of Pennsylvania, Philadelphia, director of freshman composition, 1961-63, associate professor, 1963-68, professor of English and director of writing program, 1968-78, founding director of Italian Studies Center, 1978-80, professor emeritus of American literature, 1978—.

Visiting lecturer, Bryn Mawr College, 1966-67; visiting professor, Trinity College, Rome, Italy, summer, 1973, and Queens College, City University of New York, 1980. Lecturer at colleges and universities, including Smith College, Le Moyne College, La Salle College, Ursinus College, Haverford College, Pennsylvania State University, Moore College of Art, Queens College of the City University of New York, Barnard College, University of Delaware, University of Toronto, University of Wisconsin, University of Illinois, Columbia University, University of Rhode Island, University of Messina, Utica College, University of Massachusetts, and Harvard University. Editor-in-chief, *WFLN Philadelphia Guide,* 1959-61; advisory editor, *Humanist,* 1979. Judge, National Book Award in fiction, 1969. Member of board, Institute of Contemporary Art, University of Pennsylvania, 1964-77.

MEMBER: Authors Guild, Authors League of America, American Association of University Professors, Society of American Historians (fellow), American Friends of Danilo Dolci (president, 1969-72), American-Italian Historical Association (member of Executive Council, 1980), America-Italy Society (member of board, 1982-84), American Institute of Italian Studies (member of board, 1975-82), Philadelphia Art Alliance (chairman of literary arts committee, 1963-65), Library Associates of Haverford College (member of executive council, 1991—).

AWARDS, HONORS: Yaddo creative writing fellowships, 1939, 1944, 1946, 1962, 1965, 1972; Fulbright fellowship, 1945; Guggenheim fellowship, 1946; MacDowell Colony creative writing fellowships, 1957, 1958, 1959, 1960, 1964, 1967, 1971, 1974; received key to city of Rochester, NY, 1963; Fulbright research fellowship in Sicily, 1965; Friends of the Rochester Public Library award, 1966, for *Night Search;* Rockefeller foundation research grant, 1968-69; Commendatore decoration from Italian Republic, 1971; M.A., University of Pennsylvania, 1971; American Philosophical Society research grant, 1971; honorary M.A., 1971, and Litt.D., 1980, University of

Pennsylvania; Athenaeum literary award, 1972, and National Book Award in history nomination, both for *The Dream and the Deal;* Philadelphia Athenaeum award, 1973; fellow, Society of American Historians, 1974; American Institute for Italian Culture award, 1979; National Endowment for the Humanities research grant, 1980, 1983; American-Italian Historical Association special award, 1983; Premio Nazionale Empedocle, 1984, for *Mount Allegro;* Legion of Honor medallion, Chapel of the Four Chaplains, 1984; honorary D.H.L., State University of New York, Brockport, 1987; Pennsylvania Governor's Award for Excellence in the Humanities, 1989; Leonardo Da Vinci award, 1989; International Arts Award from Columbus Countdown 1992 Association, 1990.

WRITINGS:

ALL AS JERRE MANGIONE

Mount Allegro (memoir), illustrated by Peggy Bacon, Houghton, 1943, 2nd edition with introduction by Dorothy Canfield Fisher, Knopf, 1952, 4th edition with introduction by Maria Cimino, Crown, 1972, 5th edition with a new concluding chapter by the author and introduction by Herbert J. Gans published as *Mount Olive: A Memoir of Italian American Life,* Columbia University Press, 1981.

The Ship and the Flame, Wyn-Current, 1948.

Reunion in Sicily, Houghton, 1950, 2nd edition with introduction by Deirdre Gair, Columbia University Press, 1984.

Night Search, Crown, 1965, published as *To Walk the Night,* Muller, 1967.

Life Sentences for Everybody (satiric fables), Abelard, 1966.

A Passion for Sicilians: The World around Danilo Dolci, Morrow, 1968, 2nd edition with introduction by Alfred M. Hung Lee published as *The World around Danilo Dolci: A Passion for Sicilians,* Harper, 1972, 3rd edition with a new concluding chapter by the author published under original title, Transaction Books, 1985.

America is Also Italian, Putnam, 1969.

The Dream and the Deal: The Federal Writers' Project, 1936-1943, Little, Brown, 1972, 2nd edition, Avon, 1974, 3rd edition, University of Pennsylvania Press, 1983.

Mussolini's March on Rome (for children), F. Watts, 1975.

An Ethnic at Large: A Memoir of America in the Thirties and Forties, Putnam, 1978, 2nd edition with an introduction by Bernard Weisberger, University of Pennsylvania Press, 1983.

(With Ben Morreale) *La Storia: Five Centuries of the Italian American Experience,* HarperCollins, 1992.

Also author of *By Reason of Birth of Residence. . .* (pamphlet), Free Library of Philadelphia, 1982.

Mount Allegro has been translated into Spanish and Italian.

CONTRIBUTOR

Oscar Handlin, editor, *Children of the Uprooted,* Braziller, 1966.

Allan Angoff and Betty Shapin, editors, *Psi Factors in Creativity,* Parapsychology Foundation, 1969.

Peter I. Rose, editor, *Nation of Nations: The Ethnic Experience and the Racial Crisis,* Random House, 1971.

Francesco Cordasco, editor, *Studies in Italian American Social History,* Rowman & Littlefield, 1975.

Michael C. Jaye and Ann Chalmers Watt, editors, *Literature and the Urban Experience,* Rutgers University Press, 1981.

Alfredo Rizzardi, editor, *Italy and Italians in America,* Piovan Editore, 1985.

Anthony Tamburro, Paolo A. Giordano, and Fred L. Gardaphe, editors, *From the Margin: Writings in Italian Americano,* Purdue University Press, 1991.

Contributor to *Dictionary of American Biography,* Scribners; contributor of articles and short stories to magazines, including *Esquire, Harper's Bazaar, Holiday, Mademoiselle, Massachusetts Review, New Republic,* and *Saturday Review;* contributor of book reviews to the London *Spectator, New York Times Book Review, Pennsylvania Traveler, Philadelphia Evening Bulletin, Philadelphia Inquirer,* and *Washington Post Book Review.*

Author's manuscripts are included in the Jerre Mangione Archive, Department of Rare Books and Special Collections, University of Rochester Library, Rochester, NY.

SIDELIGHTS: Jerre Mangione was raised in a large family of Sicilian immigrants, and the bulk of his writings reflects his second-generation American consciousness. *Mount Allegro,* a memoir he first published in 1943, describes the author's experiences growing up in Rochester, New York, a community with strong Sicilian roots during the early part of this century. The book was well-received by readers of Italian-American descent as well as by the general public. A reviewer for the *New York Times Book Review* proclaimed *Mount Allegro* "a classic of our ethnic literature."

Mangione's memoir has had wide appeal—in fact, it has been marketed as fiction, nonfiction, sociology, biography, humor, as well as a book for young adults. "The book was written as a nonfiction memoir and accepted as such by Houghton Mifflin," Mangione told Edwin McDowell in the *New York Times,* "but a month or so before publication, they insisted on publishing it as fiction because their sales department decided it would sell better." Mangione objected, but his publisher held sway. The author changed the names of the friends and relatives about whom he had written and added the light-hearted disclaimer 'The characters in this book are fictitious and have fictitious names. Anyone who thinks he recognizes himself in it is kindly asked to bear that in mind.'

An Ethnic at Large: A Memoir of America in the Thirties and Forties is a continuation of Mangione's life story, an examination of the conflict between the author's love and respect for his Sicilian heritage and his desire to be more fully integrated into the American mainstream. As Bernard Weisberger commented on *An Ethnic at Large* in a review for the *Washington Post Book World,* "As Mangione's Uncle Stefano once wrote him . . . 'The most important language of all is the language of the heart.' Mangione knows it fluently, and it is a pleasure to hear him speak it."

Mangione is the author of several other books that deal in subjects of particular interest to people of Italian descent. *A Passion for Sicilians* is the story of Danilo Dolci, an Italian sometimes known as the "Ghandi of Sicily" because of his long, non-violent crusade against the misery, violence, and poverty that has prevailed in that country. *La Storia: Five Centuries of the Italian American Experience,* which Mangione coauthored with Ben Morreale, provides a dramatic history of the Italians who emigrated to the United States to escape the repressive and impoverished conditions of their homeland in the late nineteenth- and early twentieth-centuries. According to reviewer Joseph B. Scelsa of the *New York Times Book Review,* "it is a book that should be read by all Americans interested in what binds us together, despite our different backgrounds and histories."

"I write to please myself," Mangione once told *CA.* "For this reason, I prefer writing books to articles, and shun magazine editors as much as possible. Whether it be a book of fiction or nonfiction, I write each one as though it were going to be my last."

BIOGRAPHICAL/CRITICAL SOURCES:

BOOKS

Boelhower, William, *Immigrant Autobiography in the United States,* Essedue edizione, 1982.

Contemporary Novelists, St. James Press, 1991, pp. 595-97.

Green, Rose Basile, *The Italian-American Novel,* Farleigh Dickinson University Press, 1974.

Peragallo, Olga, *Italian-American Life,* Columbia University Press, 1981.

PERIODICALS

Nation, December 2, 1968.

New York Times, July 28, 1978; September 4, 1981.

New York Times Book Review, January 28, 1973; August 6, 1978; September 27, 1992, p. 12.

Philadelphia Evening Bulletin, May 25, 1965; September 4, 1972.

Philadelphia Inquirer, May 16, 1966; October 26, 1990, p. 3D.

Saturday Review, July 1, 1950.

Washington Post Book World, July 30, 1978.

* * *

MANGIONE, Jerre
See MANGIONE, Gerlando

* * *

MANSER, Martin H(ugh) 1952-

PERSONAL: Born January 11, 1952, in Bromley, England; son of N. R. (a banker) and M. (a hospital social worker; maiden name, Rubinstein) Manser; married Yusandra Tun, August 3, 1979; children: Hannah Louise, Benjamin Alex. *Education:* Attended University of Regensburg, 1971-72; University of York, B.A. (with honors), 1974. *Religion:* Christian.

ADDRESSES: Home and office—102 Northern Rd., Aylesbury, Buckinghamshire HP19 3QY, England.

CAREER: Polytechnic Wolverhampton, Wolverhampton, England, research assistant, 1974-77; Laurence Urdang Associates (now Market House Books), Aylesbury, England, editor, 1977-79; free-lance reference book editor, 1980—. Part-time research associate at University of Birmingham, Birmingham, England, 1981-83; managing editor of Bible Today Ltd., 1983—.

MEMBER: European Association for Lexicography, National Union of Journalists.

AWARDS, HONORS: M.Phil. from Council for National Academic Awards, 1977.

WRITINGS:

(Content editor) *Dictionary of the English Language,* Collins, 1979.

(With Laurence Urdang) *Dictionary of Synonyms and Antonyms,* David & Charles, 1980.

(Editor) *Concise Book of Bible Quotations,* Lion, 1982.

A Dictionary of Contemporary Idioms, Pan Books, 1983.

A Dictionary of Everyday Idioms, Macmillan, 1983.

(Editor) *Harper's Portable Book of Bible Selections with Complete Psalms,* Harper, 1983.

(Assistant editor) *The Macmillan Encyclopaedia,* Macmillan, 1983.

Listening to God: Eight Weeks with Luke, Bible Today, 1984.

Listening to God: Four Weeks with Romans, Bible Today, 1984.

(With Derck J. Tidball) *Listening to God: Four Weeks with Galatians,* Bible Today, 1984.

Pocket Thesaurus of English Words, George Newnes, 1984.

(General editor) *Macmillan Student's Dictionary,* Macmillan, 1984.

(With Nigel D. Turton) *Student's Dictionary of Phrasal Verbs,* Macmillan, 1985.

Children's Dictionary, Deans, 1985.

(With Isabel McCaig) *Learner's Dictionary of Idioms,* Oxford University Press, 1986.

(With Turton) *Penguin Companion Dictionary to the English Language,* Penguin, 1986.

Pan Dictionary of English Spelling, Pan, 1987.

(Compiler) *The Chambers Book of Business Quotations,* Chambers, 1987.

(Compiler) *A Closer Walk with God: Daily Readings from Matthew Henry,* Marshall Pickering, 1987.

(Editor with Jean-Claude Corbeil) *Visual Dictionary,* Facts on File, 1988.

(Editor) *Good Word Guide,* Bloomsbury, 1988, 3rd edition, 1994.

Dictionary of Publishing and Printing Terms, Chambers, 1988.

(Compiler) *Dictionary of Eponyms,* Sphere, 1988, published as *Melba Toast, Bowie's Knife and Caesar's Wife: A Dictionary of Eponyms,* Avon, 1990.

Guinness Book of Words, Guinness, 1988, 2nd edition, 1991.

Dictionary of Marketing Terms, Chambers, 1988.

(Compiler) *Daily Guidance,* Marshall Pickering, 1988.

(Editor) *Times Good Word Guide,* Federal Publications, 1988.

Promises of the Bible, Marshall Pickering, 1989.

(Lexicographer) *Advanced Learner's Dictionary,* Oxford University Press, 1989.

(Editor) *Chambers Dictionary of Synonyms and Antonyms,* Chambers, 1989.

(Compiler) *Pan/Chambers Book of Business Quotations,* Pan, 1989.

(Editor with Jeffrey McQuain) *World Almanac Guide to Good Word Usage,* Pharos, 1989.

Dictionary of Word and Phrase Origins, Sphere, 1990.

(Editor with Jean-Claude Corbeil and Ariane Archambault) *Junior Visual Dictionary,* Facts on File, 1990.

The Amazing Book of Bible Facts, Marshall Pickering, 1990.

(Editor with Kamal Abu-Deeb) *Al Bayan: English-Arabic Dictionary,* Macmillan, 1990.

(Compiler) *Oxford Learner's Pocket Dictionary,* 2nd edition, Oxford University Press, 1991.

(Compiler) *Oxford Learner's Pocket Dictionary with Illustrations,* Oxford University Press, 1992.

Get to the Roots: A Dictionary of Word and Phrase Origins, Avon 1992.

(Compiler) *The Lion Book of Bible Quotations,* Lion, 1992.

Editor of "Listening to God" series, Bible Today, 1984—.

SIDELIGHTS: Martin H. Manser once told *CA:* "I believe in presenting reference material in a popular, concise form. Interesting material that is accessible only to academics seems pointless to me. As a committed Christian, I also believe in presenting the Christian Gospel in an attractive and contemporary way."

* * *

MARCHBANKS, Samuel
See DAVIES, (William) Robertson

* * *

MARK, Jan(et Marjorie) 1943-

PERSONAL: Born June 22, 1943, in Welwyn, Hertfordshire, England; daughter of Colin Denis and Marjorie Brisland; married Neil Mark (a computer operator), March 1, 1969 (divorced, 1989); children: Isobel, Alexander. *Education:* Canterbury College of Art, N.D.D., 1965. *Politics:* Labour. *Religion:* None.

ADDRESSES: Home—98 Howard Street, Oxford OX4 3BG, England. *Agent*—Murray Pollinger, 222 Old Brompton Rd., London SW5 0B2, England.

CAREER: Writer. Southfields School, Gravesend, Kent, England, teacher of art and English, 1965-71; Oxford Polytechnic, Arts Council Writer Fellow, 1982-84.

AWARDS, HONORS: Penguin/*Guardian* Award, 1975, Carnegie Medal, Library Association, 1976, *Guardian* commendation, 1977, and American Library Association Notable Book citation, all for *Thunder and Lightnings;* Notable Children's Trade Book citation in the field of social studies, National Council for Social Studies and Children's Book Council, 1978, for *The Ennead;* Carnegie Medal runner-up, 1981, for *Nothing to Be Afraid Of;* (cowinner) Young *Observer*/Rank Teenage Fiction Prize, 1982, for *Aquarius;* Carnegie Medal, 1983, for *Handles;* Angel Literary Award for fiction, 1983, for *Feet,* and 1988, for *Zeno Was Here;* British nominee for Hans Christian Andersen Medal, 1984; *Guardian* Award runner-up for Children's Fiction, 1986, for *Trouble Halfway.*

WRITINGS:

JUVENILE NOVELS

Thunder and Lightnings, illustrated by Jim Russell, Kestrel, 1976, Crowell, 1979.

Under the Autumn Garden, illustrated by Colin Twinn, Kestrel, 1977, illustrated by Judith Gwyn Brown, Crowell, 1979.

The Ennead, Crowell, 1978.

Divide and Rule, Kestrel, 1979, Crowell, 1980.

The Short Voyage of the Albert Ross, illustrated by Gavin Rowe, Granada, 1980.

The Dead Letter Box, illustrated by Mary Rayner, Antelope Books, 1982.

Aquarius, Kestrel, 1982, Atheneum, 1984.

Handles, illustrated by David Parkins, Kestrel, 1983, Atheneum, 1985.

Trouble Halfway, illustrated by David Parkins, Viking Kestrel, 1985, published as *Trouble Half-Way,* Atheneum, 1986.

At the Sign of the Dog and Rocket (also see below), Longman, 1985.

Dream House, illustrated by Jon Riley, Viking Kestrel, 1987.

The Twig Thing, illustrated by Sally Holmes, Viking Kestrel, 1988.

Presents from Gran, Walker, 1988.

Man in Motion, illustrated by Jeff Cummins, Viking Kestrel, 1989.

Finders, Losers, Orchard Books, 1990.

The Hillingdon Fox, Turton & Chambers, 1991.

Great Frog and Mighty Moose (travel), Walker, 1992.

The Snow Maze, Walker, 1992.

All the King and Queens, Heinemann, 1993.

JUVENILE STORY COLLECTIONS

Nothing to Be Afraid Of (includes "William's Version"), illustrated by David Parkins, Kestrel, 1980, Harper, 1981.

Hairs in the Palm of the Hand, (contains "Time and the Hour" and "Chutzpah"), illustrated by Jan Ormerod, Kestrel, 1981, published as *Bold as Brass,* Hutchinson, 1984.

Feet and Other Stories (includes "Posts and Telecommunications," "Enough Is Too Much Already" [also see below], and "A Little Misunderstanding"), illustrated by Bert Kitchen, Viking Kestrel, 1983.

Frankie's Hat (includes "It Wasn't Me"), illustrated by Quentin Blake, Viking Kestrel, 1986.

Enough Is Too Much Already and Other Stories, Bodley Head, 1988.

(Editor) *School Stories,* Kingfisher, 1989.

A Can of Worms, Bodley Head, 1990.

In Black and White (ghost stories), illustrated by Neil Reed, Viking, 1991, new edition, Penguin, 1992.

(Editor) *A Book of Song and Dance,* Viking, 1992.

(Editor) *The Oxford Book of Children's Stories,* Oxford University Press, 1993.

PICTURE BOOKS

The Long Distance Poet, illustrated by Steve Smallman, Dinosaur, 1982.

Out of the Oven, illustrated by Antony Maitland, Viking Kestrel, 1986.

Fur, illustrated by Charlotte Voake, Walker, 1986.

Fun, illustrated by Michael Foreman, Gollancz, 1987.

Strat and Chatto, illustrated by David Hughes, Walker, 1989.

Carrot Tops and Cotton Tails, illustrated by Tony Ross, Andersen Press, 1993.

Fun with Mrs. Thumb, illustrated by Nicola Bayley, Walker, 1993.

This Bond of Earth, illustrated by Gay Shepard, Walker, 1993.

PLAYS

Izzy (three-act), Longman, 1985.

(Adaptor) *The Weathermonger* (based on a novel by Peter Dickinson), Longman, 1985.

Interference (three-act), Longman, 1987.

(With Stephen Cockett) *Captain Courage and the Rose Street Gang* (two-act), Collins, 1987.

Time and the Hour; and, Nothing to Be Afraid Of, Longman, 1990.

OTHER

Zeno Was Here (adult novel), Cape, 1987, Farrar, Straus, 1988.

Two Stories (adult story collection; contains "Childermas" and "Mr. and Mrs. Johnson"), illustrated by Clive King, Inky Parrot Press (Oxford), 1984.

Adaptor of *At the Sign of the Dog and Rocket* for radio. Also author of television plays and radio dramas. Contributor of stories to anthologies and periodicals. Also contributor of articles for adults to magazines.

ADAPTATIONS: Works have been adapted for television, including *Izzy,* 1983, *Interference,* 1986, and *Handles,* 1989; *The Dead Letter Box* was adapted as an audiocassette, Puffin/Cover to Cover, 1987; *Frankie's Hat, Hairs on the Palm of the Hand,* and *Nothing to Be Afraid Of* were adapted as audiocassettes, Chivers Press, 1987, 1988, and 1989, respectively.

SIDELIGHTS: Carnegie Award-winner Jan Mark writes for various ages, including picture books for preschoolers, stories for elementary and junior high students, and novels for adults. Her most prominent and prolific works are written for children and young adults, although Mark once told *CA:* "If I write stories about children they are normally read by children —I do not otherwise aim at any particular audience. I write about people." Mark's stories are characterized by narrations which focus on the relationships of the individual to society, institutions, and other individuals. She is consistently praised for her well developed characters, credited with a keen sense of detail in relating commonplace, daily events, and commended for her use of rich words, dialogue, and wit to present the bittersweet realism of life's unfairness. Mark's realistic style elicits both praise and criticism: praise because her writing does not condescend to children, and criticism because of the frequently depressing tone of her books.

Although Mark's work is often described as oppressive, gloomy, somber, bleak, and despairing, she is at the same time noted for her use of humor. Some critics question the appropriateness of her depressing tales and anti-authoritarian stance in children's books. Mark, writing in *English in Education,* defends her works: "If I find the human race a depressing spectacle, must I disguise the fact when I write, or must I stop writing? I should like to make use of all the virtues if I found them readily observable, but the smiling villain is always with us, and a more stimulating subject than the sober saint." Supporting Mark's style in *Painted Desert, Green Shade: Essays on Contemporary Writers of Fiction for Children and Young Adults,* David Rees comments, "Scarcely anyone writing today presents youth with a more somber picture of life than does Jan Mark. Sometimes the reader may feel that her novels go to an extreme beyond which it is not possible to venture in books for children and teenagers. This doesn't matter: the harsh truths of her vision of the world are infinitely preferable to the cozy pap that is sometimes served up for the young."

Mark's first novel, Carnegie award-winner *Thunder and Lightnings,* is one of her best known and most popular books. In this story she illustrates the developing friendship of two young English boys, Andrew Mitchell and Victor Skelton, both loners but from different social classes. Victor is from a working-class family—his parents are rigid and uncommunicative, his household is spotless, and his parents are often unfair in their treatment of him. Andrew is from a middle-class home—his parents are supportive and witty, his household looks lived in, and although Andrew does not always appreciate it, his parents are sympathetic and caring. As the boys' relationship develops, Andrew witnesses Mr. and Mrs. Skelton's judgmental and harsh behavior toward Victor, and discusses the unfairness of this treatment with his mother. "Nothing's fair," his Mum tells him. "There's no such thing as fairness. It's a word made up to keep children quiet. When you discover it's a fraud then you're starting to grow up. The difference between you and Victor is that you're still finding out and he knows perfectly well already." Although Victor's home situation never improves, he demonstrates in the end that he will not give in to the critical judgement of his parents. *Thunder and Lightnings* fared well with both the public and the critics. Writing in *Children's Book Review,* Valerie Alderson praises Mark for her "unerring eye" in illustrating the behavior of the working and middle-classes and her sensitive depiction of the friendship between the main characters. Robbie March-Penny notes in *Children's Literature in Education* that *Thunder and Lightnings* "sparkles with humour—sometimes gentle and sometimes irreverent, frequently at the expense of adults." Even Rees, who sees *Thunder and Lightnings* as lacking direction at times, acknowledges the book's merit, asserting that "the development of the slightly uneasy friendship between the two central characters, Andrew and Victor, is beautifully done—the joyous surface of the book masks the underlying tensions and complexities."

Subsequent children's books, including *The Dead Letter Box, Man in Motion, Finders, Losers,* and *Hillingdon Fox* are credited with the same straightforward style, wit, insight, and detail that won Mark acclaim in her first novel. Neil Philip reports in the *Times Educational Supplement*: "What is so refreshing about her writing both about and for children . . . is the accuracy with which she reflects the real concerns of childhood; an accuracy born of careful observation." As Mark describes in an interview for *Books for Keeps,* she is a writer "working from life." Elaborating on her theory about writing children's stories, she continues: "You owe it to the audience to provide a story. Children are not experienced in the way that adults are. They haven't got the equipment so you have to give them something more concrete to work on. There has to be something there other than hints, clues, allusions which you can expect a more experienced reader to pick up."

In addition to writing novels, Mark is also well known for her short stories; in fact, some critics consider them her best writing. Her titles include *Nothing to Be Afraid Of, Frankie's Hat,* and *In Black and White.* Writing in *Horn Book,* Aidan Chambers emphasizes that *Nothing to Be Afraid Of* "indicated just how appropriate the [short story] form is for [Mark's] talents. The collection is funny, uncomfortably accurate in its dialogue and in the persuasiveness of its narrative situations, and written throughout with the combination of an unflinchingly sharp eye for human foible and a detached sympathy for the underdog . . . that makes fiction . . . more potent than real life for the observing reader." Echoing these feelings, Lance Salway, writing in *Signal Review 2: A Selective Guide to Children's Books 1983,* maintains that the short story is the best medium for Mark's humor and detail, noting it takes "full advantage" of her style. Discussing her enjoyment of writing short stories in a *Horn Book* article, Mark expounds: "I much prefer writing short stories. I have to explain this to schoolchildren. They think I like writing short stories because short stories are quickly done and therefore easy. . . . In fact, writing short stories is harder than writing novels. You can't get away with anything in a short story. . . . It is said that in a novel every chapter must count; in a short story every sentence must count."

Mark departs from her typical realistic settings for children in her trio of science fiction novels, *The Ennead, Divide and Rule,* and *Aquarius.* Geared for older readers, junior high to adult, these novels are commonly cited as her most despairing works. The books explore issues such as manipulative relationships, the power of religion, life's unfairness, and the fate of those who are unwilling to conform to the rules of society. In each of these books the protagonists are defeated by institutions in spite of their own personal goodness. Mark once remarked to *CA* that "in novels for older readers I prefer to place a character in an unfamiliar environment and watch him struggle (or in one case disintegrate) in the best traditions of tragedy, through his own shortcomings. They tend to be studies in failure." Elaborating on what she is specifically exploring in *The Ennead, Divide and Rule,* and *Aquarius,* Mark tells Philip: "The idea of manipulation is what I'm working on in all three books. Not only why we do it, but why do we allow it? How much capital do you think you can make out of allowing yourselves to be used? Some people can, some can't. Some people need to be the used half in a relationship, or feel that in fact in a subliminal way they are the controlling force."

The Ennead, the first novel in the loose trilogy, takes place on the planet Erato in a far away galaxy. It is a planet ruled by the values of self-interest; people who lose their jobs are sent to another planet where survival is questionable. The three main characters, Moshe, Isaac, and Eleanor, heroically resist conforming to the self-absorbing values of their society and in the end risk self-destruction rather than submit to the unwholesome mores of their culture. Even though the novel is described as being generally gloomy, Rees maintains that "*The Ennead* is not a bleak novel in emphasizing the fact that without the capacity to love, to be unselfish, to have courage to continue to make our own moral decisions, we cease to be viable human beings, and that when Authority will not allow us to be viable human beings, we are better off dead." M. Crouch asserts in the *Junior Bookshelf* that "it is some indication of the power of her writing that . . . Mark leaves us exhilarated rather than depressed."

Divide and Rule continues Mark's "bleak" story telling tradition. The main character, non-believer and nonconformist Hanno, is chosen to spend a year in the religious temple. During his stay Hanno discovers that the religious book is consistently rewritten to fit current events. Hanno determines to expose this fraud, but finds even this has been added to the religious book. He leaves the temple at the end of the year lacking both credibility and sanity. Again critics hail Mark's skill in relating detail, but generally find the story steeped in too much despair. After commending Mark's use of words, symbols, and wit in a review for *School Library Journal,* Patricia Dooley finds the use of sarcasm and humor in *Divide and Rule* unable to "lighten the oppressive gloom." *Times Educational Supplement* contributor Neil Philip believes the novel "has much to offer" through its well developed characters and "intensity of purpose," but admits it is a "bleak, unhappy, difficult book."

The final novel in this group, *Aquarius,* portrays how Viner, the protagonist, manipulates others to achieve and maintain social status. Viner is a water-diviner but finds his skill of little use to the rain soaked village in which he resides. When he leaves he locates a town where water is desperately needed and achieves a position of power with his skills. He uses this power to manipulate the people he cares for the most, just to gain greater power, and in the end destroys the beauty of the relationships. Lisa Lane in the *Christian Science Monitor* praises *Aquarius* because "it does not condescend to its reader." Len Hatfield, however, faults the book in *Fantasy Review* for "dry" reading and underdeveloped minor characters. Philip concedes that although the language sometimes "clogs" and the style is "cumbersome," Mark "often attains a chilling beauty; her ability to communicate the subtle ebb and flow of obedience and command in unequal and unstable relationships." In a review of *Aquarius* for *Growing Point,* Margery Fisher observes that Mark has acquired the "gift to compel through words." Rees, seeing the similarities in *The Ennead, Divide and Rule,* and *Aquarius,* points out: "Adulthood, Jan Mark seems to be saying in all her books, is at best messy, at worst brutish and nasty; the growing up processes involve coming to terms with these facts and making of them what you will—but if you totally reject the demands of authority, however worthy and fine your motives may be, you won't be able to escape punishment."

Mark's emphasis on relationships continues through her first adult novel, *Zeno Was Here,* which concerns a school teacher plagued by his past actions through a book being written by an old, forgotten friend. The school teacher, McEvoy, becomes preoccupied with other's perceptions of him and begins evaluating and analyzing his own behavior until he is overcome with self-doubt. Deborah Kirk in the *New York Times Book Review* judges this novel as a good first attempt but faults it for underdeveloped characters and an unsatisfactory exploration of plot. Admiring Mark's success at this "unusual transition" from author of children stories to author of adult fiction, Gregory Feeley, on the other hand, describes *Zeno Was Here* in the *Washington Post Book World* as "an impressive and moving work, erudite and sexy by turns." He goes on to conclude: "So assured is Mark's performance that it survives even a last minute dive into tragedy, a beginner's mistake whose risks Mark doubtless weighed but does not, I think, avoid. Skating the edge of too-cleverness, Mark has cut an intricate design with considerable skill, and produced a novel of unusual capability and distinction."

Mark acknowledges the enjoyment she receives from writing, but also admits to very pragmatic feelings about her career. She once related to *CA:* "My prime motive in becoming a professional writer was the need to earn a living. Although writing gives me more pleasure than does anything else, I do not write for pleasure: I write for money. I am singularly fortunate in getting both." Whatever her motives, Mark is the recipient of much acclaim for her skill. Reviewer M. Crouch deems her a "writer of great resource and greater potential." John Rowe Townsend, writing in the *Times Educational Supplement,* proclaims her a "formidable" talent, noting: "She has a deft hand with a story line and a fine ear for dialogue. She can catch the likeness of a character, either in full-length portrait or rapid sketch. She plays on the English language like the infinitely subtle instrument it is. She can be marvellously funny, too. But her true originality, I think, lies less in these gifts than in her perceptions: she sees people and events freshly, through a highly individual eye."

BIOGRAPHICAL/CRITICAL SOURCES:

BOOKS

Chambers, Nancy, editor, *The Signal Review 2: A Selective Guide to Children's Books 1983,* Thimble Press, 1984, p. 41.

Children's Literature Review, Volume 11, Gale, 1986.

Mark, Jan, *Thunder and Lightnings,* Crowell, 1979.

Rees, David, *Painted Desert, Green Shade: Essays on Contemporary Writers of Fiction for Children and Young Adults,* Horn Book, 1984, pp. 62-74.

PERIODICALS

Books for Keeps, March, 1984, pp. 12-13.

Children's Book Review, October, 1976, p. 39.

Children's Literature in Education, spring, 1979, pp. 18-24.

Christian Science Monitor, February 1, 1985, p. B5.

English in Education, spring, 1981, pp. 8-10.

Fantasy Review, June, 1985, p. 23.

Growing Point, November, 1978, pp. 3413-14; July, 1982, pp. 3914-15.

Horn Book, September/October, 1984, pp. 665-70; January/February, 1988, pp. 42-45.

Junior Bookshelf, February, 1979, pp. 56-57.

New York Times Book Review, July 17, 1988, pp. 20-21.

Publishers Weekly, April 15, 1988.

School Library Journal, August, 1980, pp. 77-78.

Times Educational Supplement, November 30, 1979, p. 25; June 11, 1982, p. 41; June 3, 1983, pp. 37, 43.

Times Literary Supplement, July 23, 1982; November 24, 1989, p. 1311; March 30, 1990, p. 357; July 12, 1991, p. 20; November 22, 1991, p. 24.

Washington Post, November 12, 1978, pp. E1-E2.

Washington Post Book World, August 7, 1988, p. 11.

—Sketch by Pamela S. Dear

* * *

MARKLIN, Megan
See HARRINGTON, William

* * *

MARKS, Peter
See SMITH, Robert Kimmel

* * *

MARTELL, James
See BINGLEY, David Ernest

* * *

MASS, William
See GIBSON, William

* * *

MASSEY, Ellen Gray 1921-

PERSONAL: Born November 14, 1921, in Nevada, MO; daughter of Chester Harold (a trade association executive) and Pearl (a homemaker; maiden name, Welch) Gray; married David Lane Massey (a farmer), September 26, 1947 (died September 24, 1959); children: David Gray, Ruth Ellen, Frances Lane. *Education:* University of Maryland at College Park, B.A. (English and history), 1943; attended University of Mexico, summer, 1942; University of Missouri—Columbia, B.S. (home economics), 1945; Drury College, A.B. (education), 1960.

ADDRESSES: Home—126 Maple Dr., Lebanon, MO 65536.

CAREER: University of Missouri—Columbia, home agent with Agricultural Extension Service in Farmington and Lebanon, 1945-47; farmer in Conway, MO, 1947-63; elementary schoolteacher in Conway, 1957-60; high school teacher of home economics and Spanish and guidance counselor in Hartville, MO, 1960-63; Lebanon Schools, Lebanon, MO, high school English teacher, 1963-86, head of language arts department, 1968-78; Drury College, Springfield, MO, adjunct faculty, 1986—; speaker for Missouri Humanities Council, 1991—.

MEMBER: Missouri State Teachers Association, Missouri Folklore Society, Western Writers Association, Ozark Writers League, Delta Kappa Gamma.

AWARDS, HONORS: Heritage Award from Museum of the Ozarks, and Award of Merit from National Association of State and Local History, both 1980, both for developing the student publication *Bittersweet: The Ozark Quarterly;* Best Book, Missouri Writers' Guild, 1992, for *Moon Silver.*

WRITINGS:

(Editor) *Bittersweet Country,* Doubleday, 1978.
(Editor) *Bittersweet Earth,* University of Oklahoma Press, 1985.
Moon Silver, Avalon, 1991.
Too Many Secrets, Avalon, 1992.
The Bequest, Avalon, 1993.

Editor in chief of *Bittersweet: The Ozark Quarterly,* 1973-83; editor of *Briarwood,* 1988-90. Contributor to education journals and local magazines, including *Ozarks Mountaineer* and *Ozarks Watch.*

SIDELIGHTS: Ellen Gray Massey told *CA:* "My main interests are in writing, education, and the Ozarks, and all of my writings have been related to these subjects. Teaching in the Ozarks for thirty-six years has made me want to give my students a sense of their own heritage and a real experience in writing. That is why I created and became the faculty adviser for the quarterly journal *Bittersweet,* published by the students of Lebanon High School beginning in 1973, and why I am still teaching about the Ozarks to graduate education students.

"I feel strongly that the past can guide us today. The rather isolated Ozark region for many years retained the values of pioneer days. By studying that culture people may be able to live better. For that reason, and because the Ozarks are so colorful and interesting, I have dealt with the subject in most of my writings, whether they are biographical, historical, or fictional. Much of my writing is based on my own experiences in living on an Ozark farm and teaching in rural and smalltown schools."

MAUZY, Peter
See BURGESS, Michael (Roy)

See BURGESS, Michael (Roy)

* * *

MAYHAR, Ardath 1930-
(Frank Cannon, John Killdeer)

PERSONAL: Born February 20, 1930, in Timpson, TX; daughter of Bert Aaron (a farmer) and Ardath (a farmer; maiden name, Ellington) Hurst; married Joe Mayhar (a bookstore owner), June 7, 1958; children: Frank Edward, James Anthony; (stepsons) Robert William, William Earl. *Politics:* Independent. *Religion:* Independent.

ADDRESSES: Home—Route 1, Box 146, Chireno, TX 75937. *Agent*—Donald Maass, Apt. 8P, 304 West 92nd St., New York, NY 10025.

CAREER: Full-time writer, 1982—. Partner in a dairy farm in Nacogdoches County, TX, 1942-57; owner and manager of East Texas Bookstore, Nacogdoches, TX, 1957-62; proofreader in Salem, OR, 1968-75, and Nacogdoches, 1979-80; chicken farmer in Nacogdoches County, 1976-78; part-owner and operator of View from Orbit bookstore, Nacogdoches, 1984—. Instructor, Writer's Digest School, 1984—.

MEMBER: Science Fiction Writers of America.

WRITINGS:

SCIENCE FICTION AND FANTASY NOVELS

How the Gods Wove in Kyrannon, Doubleday, 1979.
The Seekers of Shar-Nuhn, Doubleday, 1980.
Soul-Singer of Tyrnos, Atheneum, 1981.
Warlock's Gift, Doubleday, 1982.
Golden Dream: A Fuzzy Odyssey, Ace Books, 1982.
Runes of the Lyre, Atheneum, 1982.
Lords of the Triple Moons, Atheneum, 1983.
Khi to Freedom, Ace Books, 1983.
Exile on Vlahil, Doubleday, 1984.
The World Ends in Hickory Hollow, Doubleday, 1985.
The Saga of Grittel Sundotha, Atheneum, 1985.
(With Ron Fortier) *Trail of the Seahawks,* TSR, 1987.
BattleTech: The Sword and the Dagger, FASA, 1987.
A Place of Silver Silence, Walker, 1988.
(With Fortier) *Monkey Station,* TSR, 1989.

"AMERINDIAN PREHISTORY" SERIES

People of the Mesa, Berkley, 1992.
Island in the Swamp, Berkley, 1993.

UNDER PSEUDONYM FRANK CANNON; WESTERN NOVELS

Feud at Sweetwater Creek, Zebra, 1987.
Bloody Texas Trail, Zebra, 1988.
Texas Gunsmoke, Zebra, 1988.

UNDER PSEUDONYM JOHN KILLDEER; "MOUNTAIN MAJESTY" NOVELS

Wild Country, Bantam, 1992.
The Untamed, Bantam, 1992.
Wilderness Rendezvous, Bantam, 1992.
Blood Kin, Bantam, 1993.

OTHER

Journey to an Ending (poetry chapbook), South and West, 1965.
(With Marylois Dunn) *The Absolutely Perfect Horse,* Harper, 1983.
Medicine Walk, Atheneum, 1985.
Carrots and Miggle, Atheneum, 1986.
Makra Choria, Atheneum, 1987.
The Wall, Space and Time Books, 1987.

Work represented in anthologies including *Stories to Be Read with the Lights On, Swords Against Darkness, Mummy!, Magic in Ithkar, Shadows, CatFantastic I, II,* and *III, Razored Saddles, Dark at Heart,* and *Masques.* Author of "View from Orbit," a column, 1980. Contributor of stories and poems to magazines, including *Fiction, Gothic, Weirdbook, Amazing, Fantasy and Science Fiction, Isaac Asimov's Science Fiction Magazine, Twilight Zone,* and *Dark Fantasy.*

WORK IN PROGRESS: Volumes 3 and 4 in the "Amerindian Prehistory" series; a fifth volume in the "Mountain Majesty" series; 1 mystery, 1 western, and 1 science fiction novel.

SIDELIGHTS: Ardath Mayhar told *CA:* "I have spent most of my adult life shoveling manure, writing poetry, and looking up at the stars. At the age of forty-three, I 'reformed' and stopped writing poetry, took up yoga and writing fantasy novels, and haven't looked back in the years since. I have been influenced, to a greater or lesser extent by Dickens, Shakespeare, Ayn Rand, Andre Norton, William Faulkner, and all the 'old heads' in the science fiction field.

"I earnestly believe that being upside down (yoga) directly stimulated my bursting forth into fantasy novels, short stories, and even a regular newspaper column.

"From the ages seventeen to twenty-seven, I ran my father's dairy. Not as some sort of lordly supervisor, but hand-to-hand (sometimes face-to-hoof) with the cows, the cruddy milking machines, the manure, the hay, the weather. In that time, I also studied Latin, Greek, German, French, Spanish, and Italian. At one time *I* read most of them with some ease, but I haven't kept my hand in. As I get older, time seems to telescope inward. In that time, I also mastered several forms of poetry. I was a very good poet, having work in many magazines (such as *Mark Twain Quarterly).* However, I finally realized that English teachers have destroyed any love of poetry that might remain in the English-speaking race.

"I escaped from the dairy into a bookstore. There I met my husband, for he worked just around the corner, and snared him infallibly with books. In the next few years we achieved two sons (he already had two), moved to Houston (which I will insist be deducted from any time in Hell, when and if) and Oregon. There I met mountains, yoga, and proofreading, all of which were seminal influences. We moved back to Texas in 1975, glad to have gone but gladder still to get back home to individualist country.

"Now we live in the mutilated edge of the Big Thicket, near Sam Rayburn Lake. We are so poor that church mice look affluent beside us, but we grow fine gardens and hear the wolves howl at night. Occasionally we see a bobcat. There are bear and deer and cougar in the woods around us. My husband and I work six days a week in our used book shop, located in Nacogdoches, Texas, and I write in the back office there. Since beginning novel-writing in 1972, I have completed fifty-three novels and am constantly working on several more. I don't even count short stories any more. If I ever quit writing, the U.S. Postal Service will go broke, for I buy enough stamps to keep them in business.

"I believe that hard work and early lack of success probably fitted me, more than anything else, to achieve what I wanted to: a control of my material which, whether it seems so or not, is deliberate. I have written some of my best poetry-stuff that won prizes while shoveling manure. Many writers, I note, would be far better craftsmen for a closer acquaintance with actual, rather than metaphysical, manure. The combination of physical labor and wild imagination works extremely well for me.

"I go to science fiction conventions, at times. I also love to speak to groups of intelligent people, so I do a bit of that. Because of the success of my children's novels, I spend quite a lot of time speaking to schools. In addition, I often conduct workshops at writers' conferences, and I instruct a short story course, via correspondence, for Writer's Digest School. I am a hard-core independent. Worse yet, I am objective and logical. Sacred cows, I find, make excellent steak."

BIOGRAPHICAL/CRITICAL SOURCES:

PERIODICALS

Beaumont Enterprise-Journal, October 5, 1980.
Nacogdoches Daily Sentinel, October 10, 1979; July 10, 1980.
Starlog, October, 1990.

McCARTHY, Charles, Jr. 1933-
(Cormac McCarthy)

PERSONAL: Nickname "Cormac" is Gaelicized version of Charles; born July 20, 1933, in Providence, RI; son of Charles Joseph and Gladys (McGrail) McCarthy; married Lee Holleman, 1961 (divorced); married Anne de Lisle, 1967 (divorced); children: (first marriage) Cullen. *Education:* Attended University of Tennessee, four years.

ADDRESSES: *Home*—El Paso, TX. *Agent*—Amanda Urban, International Creative Management, 40 West 57th St., New York, NY 10019.

CAREER: Writer. *Military service:* U.S. Air Force, 1953-56.

AWARDS, HONORS: Ingram-Merrill Foundation grant for creative writing, 1960; American Academy of Arts and Letters traveling fellowship to Europe, 1965-66; William Faulkner Foundation award, 1965, for *The Orchard Keeper;* Rockefeller Foundation grant, 1966; Guggenheim fellowship, 1976; MacArthur Foundation Grant, 1981; National Book Award for fiction, 1992, for *All the Pretty Horses;* Lyndhurst Foundation grant; Institute of Arts and Letters award.

WRITINGS:

UNDER NAME CORMAC McCARTHY

The Orchard Keeper, Random House, 1965, Vintage Books, 1993.

Outer Dark, Random House, 1968.

Child of God, Random House, 1974.

Suttree, Random House, 1979.

Blood Meridian, or The Evening Redness in the West, Random House, 1985, Vintage Books, 1993.

All the Pretty Horses, Random House, 1992.

Also author of *The Gardener's Son,* a teleplay produced for *Visions* series, Public Broadcasting System, 1977. Contributor to *Yale Review* and *Sewanee Review.*

WORK IN PROGRESS: Two novels in the "Border Trilogy."

SIDELIGHTS: Cormac McCarthy, whose novels are often set in eastern Tennessee, is frequently compared with such Southern-based writers as William Faulkner, Carson McCullers, and Flannery O'Connor. In a *Dictionary of Literary Biography* article, Dianne L. Cox states that McCarthy's work has in common with that of the others "a rustic and sometimes dark humor, intense characters, and violent plots; [he] shares as well their development of universal themes within a highly particularized fictional world, their seriousness of vision, and their vigorous exploration of the English language." "His characters are often outcasts—destitutes or criminals, or both," writes Richard B. Woodward in the *New York Times.* "Death, which announces itself often, reaches down from the open sky, abruptly, with a slashed throat or a bullet in the face. The abyss opens up at any misstep."

McCarthy has often been singled out for his individual prose style—beautifully lyrical yet spare, eschewing commas and totally stripped of quotation marks. This style has been a source of complaint for some reviewers; in a *New York Times* review of McCarthy's *All the Pretty Horses,* for example, Herbert Mitgang laments: "This reader was put off at first by the author's all too writerly writing. His joined words, without hyphenation, and his unpunctuated, breathless sentences, call too much attention to themselves." Kurt Tidmore of the *Washington Post Book World,* however, contends that "the reader is never confused. Sentences punctuate themselves by the natural rhythm of their words. Everything is perfectly clear. The poetic never overwhelms the realistic." In addition, writes Madison Smartt Bell of the *New York Times Book Review,* McCarthy's "elaborate and elevated" prose is "used effectively to frame realistic dialogue, for which his ear is deadly accurate." Bell continues: "Difficult as [McCarthy's writing] may sometimes be, it is also overwhelmingly seductive."

Throughout his career, McCarthy has actively avoided public attention, refusing to participate in lecture tours and seldom granting interviews. "Of all the subjects I'm interested in [talking about]," the author says in the *New York Times,* ". . . writing is way, *way* down at the bottom of the list." "Until very recently," observes Bell, "he shunned publicity so effectively that he wasn't even famous for it." Instead, he has concentrated upon crafting his unique and powerful fictions, unaffected by the critical acclaim that is heaped upon him with each new book. McCarthy has been described by Woodward as "a cult figure with a reputation as a writer's writer" who is, perhaps, "the best unknown novelist in America."

McCarthy's first novel, *The Orchard Keeper,* deals with three people—a young man who is coming of age in the Tennessee mountains, a bootlegger, and an aged orchard keeper—whose lives are intertwined, even though they never meet until the end of the story. "Through these characters," writes Cox, "the novel explores the relationship between individual integrity and independence achievable in the remote natural world of the mountains and the social obligations and strictures imposed by the community of men." J. G. Murray, reviewing *The Orchard Keeper* in *America,* feels that the book is interesting "because it does not seem to be autobiographical and [it] rejects the influence, more bad than good, of the Southern mystique." Murray finds McCarthy's view of adulthood "even more precise and sympathetic than his treatment of youth. And, as everyone knows, it is quite exceptional for young writers to be so objective." Writing in *Harper's,* K.

G. Jackson calls *The Orchard Keeper* "a complicated and evocative exposition of the transiency of life, well worth the concentration it demands."

Outer Dark, McCarthy's next novel, is "so centered on guilt and retribution that it is largely structured around scenes of judgment," according to Cox. *Outer Dark* tells the story of Culla and Rinthy, brother and sister who suffer the consequences of their incest in very different ways. Many critics, such as Guy Davenport, compare McCarthy's style in this book to that of William Faulkner. In a *New York Times Book Review* article, Davenport writes that *Outer Dark* "pays its homage to Faulkner"—but the reviewer believes that McCarthy's personal writing style "compels admiration, [being] compounded of Appalachian phrases as plain and as functional as an ax. In elegant counterpoint to this bare-bones English is a second diction taken from that rich store of English which is there in the dictionary to be used by those who can." A *Time* reviewer finds that the author's command of local dialect "is surpassed by his poetic descriptions of the land and its people. His is an Irish singing voice imbued with Southern Biblical intonations. The result is am antiphony of speech and verse played against a landscape of penance."

Lester Ballard, the title character of McCarthy's *Child of God,* is a demented backwoodsman, a murderer and necrophiliac. In this novel, the author depicts the spiritual demise of Ballard and at the same time makes him a sympathetic figure. But Richard P. Brickner, writing in the *New York Times Book Review,* describes *Child of God* as "an essentially sentimental novel that no matter how sternly it strives to be tragic is never more than morose." Similarly, in a *Commonweal* article, Robert Leiter calls the book "thinner [and] less full-bodied than either *The Orchard Keeper* or *Outer Dark* . . . *Child of God* is a swift exciting read, but we are left with only incisive images strung along a thin plot line, the why and wherefore unexplained." Leiter surmises that the book "will perhaps be looked upon as a bad novel written by a good writer" and concludes that "this would be regrettable, for *Child of God* marks a progression in McCarthy's career. He has learned restraint. The 'old themes' live on in him, but his South is not rendered with the precision of a realist. He has taken realism to the province of folk myth."

Child of God is "a reading experience so impressive, so 'new,' so clearly made well that it seems almost to defy the easy esthetic categories and at the same time cause me to thrash about for some help with the necessary description of my enthusiasm," states Doris Grumbach in *New Republic,* adding, "Cormac McCarthy is a Southerner, a born storyteller, . . . a writer of natural, impeccable dialogue, a literary child of Faulkner." Grumbach goes on to say that in McCarthy's style, "the journey from death-in-life to death-in-death, from the hunted to the discovery of the hunting . . . is accomplished in rare, spare, precise yet poetic prose." The reviewer feels the author "has allowed us direct communion with his special kind of chaos; every sentence he writes illuminates, if only for a moment, the great dark of madness and violence and inevitable death that surrounds us all."

In a *New Yorker* review of *Child of God,* Robert Coles compares McCarthy to ancient Greek dramatists, saying that he "simply writes novels that tell us we cannot comprehend the riddles of human idiosyncracy, the influence of the merely contingent or incidental upon our lives. He is a novelist of religious feeling who appears to subscribe to no creed but who cannot stop wondering in the most passionate and honest way what gives life meaning. . . . From the isolated highlands of Tennessee he sends us original stories that show how mysterious or confusing the world is. Moreover, his mordant wit, his stubborn refusal to bend his writing to the literary and intellectual demands of our era, conspire at times to make him seem mysterious and confusing—a writer whose fate is to be relatively unknown and often misinterpreted. But both Greek playwrights and Christian theologians have been aware that such may be the fate of anyone, of even the most talented and sensitive of human beings."

McCarthy's fourth novel, *Suttree,* again focuses on a misfit character, Cornelius Suttree, and the undesirable society he inhabits. In this book, the author describes Suttree as a man who has spent years in "the company of thieves, derelicts, miscreants, pariahs, poltroons, spalpeens, curmudgeons, clotpolls, murderers, gamblers, bawds, whores, trulls, brigands, topers, tosspots, sots and archsots, lobcocks, smellsmocks, runagates, rakes, and other assorted and felonious debauchees." Reviewing the book in *Spectator,* Frank Rudman calls McCarthy "a magnificent writer with a resonant style that moves easily and naturally into a grand register without losing truthfulness. His ear for dialogue is as funny and authentic as that of Mark Twain." Guy Davenport points out possible autobiographical elements in the novel and wonders if McCarthy "had asked what part of himself bears the imprint of the world in which he was raised, and answered himself by witnessing what these traits look like exemplified by a gallery of characters ranging from near-idiotic to noble." Writing in *National Review,* Davenport says that the reader is "won over . . . to Cormac McCarthy's radically original way with tone and his sense of the aloneness of people in their individuality. At the heart of *Suttree* there is a strange sense of transformation and rebirth in which the protagonist wanders in a forest, sees visions, and emerges as a stranger to all that was before familiar. This is a scene no one else could have written."

Anatole Broyard says of the author in a *New York Times* review of *Suttree:* "His people are so vivid that they seem exotic, but this is just another way of saying that we tend to forget the range of human differences. Mr. McCarthy's hyperbole is not Southern rhetoric, but flesh and blood. Every tale is tall, if you look at it closely enough." In the *Washington Post,* Edward Rothstein writes: "It is a measure . . . of McCarthy's skills that the reader becomes engaged with those of [Suttree's] world, even intoxicated by the miasmatic language. For every image that is tiresomely weighty, there is one which illuminates dark crevices. For every horror, there is a sensitive observation. For every violent dislocation, there is a subtly touching dialogue or gesture." Nelson Algren compares *Suttree* with McCarthy's earlier work, noting in the *Chicago Tribune Book World:* "There were no telephones, indoor plumbing, electricity, or TV in [his] previous novels. . . . The language of his people was closer to the time of Shakespeare than to our own time. Here he has brought them all to town and into today—without losing the sense of old, old America. And without losing the freshness and the magic of the old wilderness. Although his new wilderness is an industrial wasteland, the magic remains."

In his next novel, 1985's *Blood Meridian, or The Evening Redness in the West,* McCarthy leaves his home territory of Tennessee for the dusty plains of the Old West. (This change may be the result of McCarthy's own relocation to El Paso, Texas, in 1974.) It is by far his bloodiest novel to date, detailing the adventures of a fourteen-year-old boy referred to only as "the kid" as he travels with a band of bounty hunters, paid by a Mexican governor to collect Indian scalps. The hunters, however, are not picky about their victims, leaving a long, bloody trail behind them as they go. "*Blood Meridian* comes at the reader like a slap in the face," writes Caryn James in the *New York Times Book Review.* "While [it] is hard to get through, it is harder to ignore."

Though *Blood Meridian* is based loosely upon actual events of the 1840s and 1850s, it bears little resemblance to the historical westerns written by Louis L'Amour and others; instead, Woodward points out, it "has distinct echoes of *Moby Dick,* McCarthy's favorite book," for it concentrates on the barren, hellish landscape and near-surreal characters that make up the band of mercenaries. Most prominent among them is a huge, hairless man named Judge Holden. Though he is not the group's leader, the Judge commands the respect of the others as he pontificates by the fire each night. It is against the background of Judge Holden that "the kid" is placed, allowing the reader to evaluate for himself the morality of each character. "*Blood Meridian* stands the world of Louis L'Amour on its head (indeed, heaps hot coals upon it)," claims *Los Angeles Times Book Review*'s Tom Nolan, while Tom Pilkington, writing in the *World & I,* labels it "perhaps the bloodiest book ever penned by an American author."

In defense of the meticulously-detailed gore that pervades his novels, McCarthy told Woodward: "There's no such thing as life without bloodshed. . . . I think the notion that the species can be improved in some way, that everyone could live in harmony, is a really dangerous idea. Those who are afflicted with this notion are the first ones to give up their souls, their freedom. Your desire that it be that way will enslave you and make your life vacuous." Most importantly, though, the brutality depicted in McCarthy's writing has not reduced its power; rather, says James, he "has asked us to witness evil not in order to understand it but to affirm its inexplicable reality; his elaborate language invents a world hinged between the real and surreal, jolting us out of complacency."

"By comparison with the sonority and carnage of *Blood Meridian,*" writes Woodward, "the world of *All the Pretty Horses* [McCarthy's 1992 novel for which he won the National Book Award] is less risky—repressed but sane." Set in 1949, *Horses* is the first installment in a three-book epic entitled "The Border Trilogy." It tells the story of John Grady Cole, a sixteen-year-old Texan who, along with his friend, Lacey Rawlins, sets off on horseback for Mexico. It becomes a classic coming-of-age tale, with Cole learning the skills of survival, facing adversity, and finding romance, all against the backdrop of a land that has not lost the magic of the old West. "In the hands of some other writer," notes Bell, "this material might make for a combination of *Lonesome Dove* and *Huckleberry Finn,* but Mr. McCarthy's vision is deeper than Larry McMurtry's and, in its own way, darker than Mark Twain's." "What he has given us is a book of remarkable beauty and strength," writes Tidmore, "the work of a master in perfect command of his medium."

While *All the Pretty Horses* is almost universally considered McCarthy's most accessible novel so far, it did not receive universally favorable reviews. This is due, in part, to the popularity of the novel, which opened it to criticism by reviewers previously unfamiliar with McCarthy's work. While Richard Eder of the *Los Angeles Times Book Review* admits that "McCarthy's elevated prose does wonders for deserts, mountains, freezing winds, night landscapes and the tangibility of food, a bath and clean clothes," he warns that "loftiness gusts like a capsizing high wind, and the writing can choke on its own ornateness." Still, the strength of *All the Pretty Horses* seems to lie in the integrity of its central character, John Grady Cole, who is described by Bruce Allen in the *World & I* as "both a credible and admirable character; he is a perfect vehicle for the expression of the novel's themes." Watching Cole adhere to his values in the face of near-insurmountable adversity gives *All the Pretty Horses* "a sustained innocence and a lucidity new in McCarthy's work," according to Woodward.

There is no guarantee, however, that the success of *All the Pretty Horses* will gain McCarthy the wide audience that many reviewers feel he deserves. "He may simply be too strong for many readers," explains Tidmore. "In an age of TV, he is its antithesis." Not that McCarthy is seeking recognition. He is, as Woodward writes, "a radical conservative who still believes that the novel can, in his words, 'encompass all the various disciplines and interests of humanity.' " Summarizing his work, Cox stresses: "McCarthy is in no way a commercial writer. He is a novelist by profession, and he has not supplemented his income by turning his hand to more lucrative kinds of work such as Hollywood screenwriting. . . . His most perceptive reviewers have consistently predicted more of the same solid work from McCarthy, and he has fulfilled these predictions. He deserves, now, serious attention from students of literature." Woodward concludes, simply, by declaring: "There isn't anyone remotely like him in contemporary American literature."

BIOGRAPHICAL/CRITICAL SOURCES:

BOOKS

Bell, Vereen, *The Achievement of Cormac McCarthy,* Louisiana State University Press, 1988.
Contemporary Literary Criticism, Gale, Volume 4, 1975, Volume 57, 1990.
Dictionary of Literary Biography, Volume 6: *American Novelists since World War II,* Gale, 1980.
McCarthy, Cormac, *Suttree,* Random House, 1979.

PERIODICALS

America, June 12, 1965.
Boston Globe, January 3, 1991, p. CAL6; May 3, 1992, p. B41; July 5, 1992, p. A28; November 19, 1992, p. 65.
Chicago Tribune, November 19, 1992, sec. 1, p. 22; December 6, 1992, sec. 14, p. 1.
Chicago Tribune Book World, January 28, 1979.
Christian Science Monitor, June 11, 1992, p. 13.
Commonweal, March 29, 1974; September 25, 1992, p. 1412.
Esquire, March 27, 1979.
Los Angeles Times Book Review, June 9 1985, p. 2; May 17, 1992, p. 3.
National Review, March 16, 1979; March 8, 1985, p. 44.
New Republic, February 9, 1974; March 10, 1979; May 6, 1985, p. 37.
New Statesman, May 2, 1980, p. 682.
Newsweek, January 7, 1974; May 18, 1992, p. 68.
New York, May 18, 1992, p. 68.
New Yorker, August 26, 1974; August 10. 1992, p. 79.
New York Times, January 20, 1979; May 27, 1992, p. C18; November 19, 1992, p. C18.
New York Times Book Review, September 29, 1968; January 13, 1974; February 18, 1979; September 23, 1984, p. 46; April 28, 1985, p. 31; December 21, 1986, p. 24; May 17, 1992, p. 9; May 31, 1992, p. 23; August 30, 1992, p. 24.
New York Times Magazine, April 19, 1992, sec. 6, p. 28.
Saturday Review, June 12, 1965.
Sewanee Review, October, 1985, p. 649.
Southern Review, autumn, 1992, p. 920.
Spectator, May 24, 1980, p. 21.
Time, September 17, 1968; January 4, 1993, p. 64.
Times Literary Supplement, May 2, 1980, p. 500; April 21, 1989, p. 436.
Tribune Books (Chicago), May 10, 1992, p. 5.
Village Voice, July 15, 1986, p. 48; May 19, 1992, p. 64.
Virginia Quarterly Review, autumn, 1986, p. 746; autumn, 1992, p. 128.
Washington Post, November 2, 1990, p. WW16; November 19, 1992, p. D1.
Washington Post Book World, January 13, 1974; March 19, 1979; May 3, 1992, p. 1; June 28, 1992, p. 12.
World & I, September, 1992, pp. 339-383.*

—Sketch by Brandon Trenz

* * *

McCARTHY, Cormac
See McCARTHY, Charles, Jr.

* * *

McCOLLOUGH, Charles R(andolph) 1934-

PERSONAL: Born July 22, 1934, in Dallas, TX; son of George W. (in business) and Ruth L. (a teacher; maiden name, Sprott) McCollough; married Carol Keeney (a college administrator), June 2, 1959; children: Colin, Wendy, Timothy. *Education:* University of Texas at Austin, B.A., 1957; Southern Methodist University, B.D., 1960; Drew University, Ph.D., 1965. *Politics:* Democrat. *Religion:* Protestant.

ADDRESSES: *Home and office*—165 Hopewell-Wertsville Rd., Hopewell, NJ 08525.

CAREER: Ordained minister of United Church of Christ, 1964; teaching minister in Barrington, RI, 1964-69; United Church Board for Homeland Ministries, New York City, secretary for adult education, 1969-85; United Church Office of Church in Society, 1986—; writer, lecturer, and sculptor in bronze and clay.

WRITINGS:

Morality of Power, Pilgrim Press, 1977.
(With wife, Carol McCollough) *Lifestyles of Faithfulness,* Bethany Press, 1983.
Heads of Heaven, Feet of Clay, Pilgrim Press, 1984.

To Love the Earth, Christian Board of Publication, 1987.
Resolving Conflict with Justice and Peace, Pilgrim Press, 1990.

WORK IN PROGRESS: "A book of poetry and photographs of my sculpture."

* * *

MCDONALD, Gregory (Christopher) 1937-

PERSONAL: Born February 15, 1937, in Shrewsbury, MA; son of Irving Thomas (an author) and Mae (a painter; maiden name, Haggarty) Mcdonald; married Susan Aiken, January 13, 1963; divorced, 1990; children: Christopher Gregory, Douglas Gregory. *Education:* Harvard University, B.A., 1958.

ADDRESSES: Home—Tennessee. *Office*—c/o Arthur Greene, Esq., 101 Park Ave., New York, NY 10178. *Agent*—Goldman-Schneider, 250 West 57th St., New York, NY 10107.

CAREER: Novelist, 1973—. Former captain of sailing vessels; marine insurance underwriter, 1959-61; Peace Corps volunteer, 1962; teacher, 1963-64; *Boston Globe,* Boston, MA, critic-at-large columnist and editor of arts and humanities, 1964-73. Member of visiting committee, Boston Museum of Fine Arts, 1970-73, 1985—; board of directors, Camaldon Corporation, Third National Bank, Pulaski, TN, 1988-91.

MEMBER: Mystery Writers of America (former president), Authors Guild, Writers Guild, Dramatists Guild, Giles Countians United, Harvard Club of Boston, Winthrop House Senior Commons, Hillcrest Country Club (Pulaski, TN).

AWARDS, HONORS: Edgar Allan Poe Award, Mystery Writers of America, 1975, for *Fletch,* and 1977, for *Confess, Fletch;* Humanitarian of the Year award, Tennessee Association of Federal Executives, 1989; Citizen of the Year award, National Association of Social Workers, 1990; Roger Williams Strauss award, National Conference of Christians and Jews, 1990; Alex Haley Award (first annual), 1992

WRITINGS:

Running Scared, Obolensky, 1964.
Love among the Mashed Potatoes, Dutton, 1978.
Who Took Toby Rinaldi?, Putnam, 1980.
The Education of Gregory Mcdonald (nonfiction), Warner, 1985.
(Editor and contributor) *The Last Laughs: The Mystery Writers of America Anthology, 1986,* Mysterious Press, 1986.
Safekeeping, Penzler Press, 1985.
The Brave, Barricade Books, 1991.

Also author of *Bull's Eye* (drama), 1987. Contributor to *The Year's Ten Best Mystery and Suspense Stories,* edited by Edward D. Hoch, Walker Books, 1985, and to *A Wedding Cake in the Middle of the Road,* edited by Susan Stamberg and George Gannett, Norton, 1991.

THE "FLETCH" SERIES

Fletch (also see below), Bobbs-Merrill, 1974.
Confess, Fletch (also see below), Avon, 1976.
Fletch's Fortune (also see below), Avon, 1978.
Fletch Forever (contains *Fletch, Confess, Fletch,* and *Fletch's Fortune*), Avon, 1978.
Fletch and the Widow Bradley (also see below), Avon, 1981.
Fletch's Moxie (also see below), Warner, 1982.
Carioca Fletch (also see below), Warner, 1982.
Fletch and the Man Who (also see below), Warner, 1983.
Fletch Won (also see below), Warner, 1986.
Fletch, Too (also see below), Warner, 1987.
The Fletch Chronicles, Volume One (contains *Fletch Won, Fletch, Too,* and *Fletch and the Widow Bradley*), *Volume Two* (contains *Fletch, Carioca Fletch,* and *Confess, Fletch,*), *Volume Three* (contains *Fletch's Fortune, Fletch's Moxie,* and *Fletch and the Man Who*), Hill, 1988.
Son of Fletch, Putnam-Berkley, 1993.

THE "FLYNN" SERIES

Flynn, Avon, 1977.
The Buck Passes Flynn, Ballantine, 1981.
Flynn's In, Mysterious Press, 1984.

THE "TIME SQUARED" SERIES

A World Too Wide, Hill, 1987.
Exits and Entrances, Hill, 1988.
Merely Players, Hill, 1988.

Manuscript collection is held at Mugar Memorial Library, Boston University.

ADAPTATIONS: Running Scared was adapted for the screen by David Hemmings and Clive Exton and released by Paramount in 1972; *Fletch* was adapted for the screen by Andrew Bergman and released by Universal in 1985; *Fletch Lives,* based on the character "Fletch", was released by Universal in 1990. Many of Mcdonald's books have been released on audio tape.

SIDELIGHTS: Gregory Mcdonald is considered to be the clown prince of the mystery genre. He is described by Jean M. White of the *Washington Post Book World* as "a consummate farceur. No one writes sharper, wittier repartee. . . . He is the master of orchestrating riotous comic scenes." His liberal use of offbeat humor has made his series of "Fletch" books one of the most popular detective series ever written. Mcdonald is not simply a humorist, however, for behind each book's comic face lies a complex mystery—a twisty plot, often intertwining two or more seemingly independent storylines, whose solution is seldom anticipated by the reader, yet always brilliantly deduced by the protagonist. An incorrigible iconoclast, Mcdonald often sprinkles into the recipe a fair amount of social commentary, prompting H. R. F. Keating of the London *Times* to compare him to the great Dashiell Hammett. Looking back at the steady stream of witty, tightly woven and eminently readable mysteries Mcdonald has produced, the *New York Times Book Review*'s Newgate Callendar proclaims: "He can write circles around most of his competitors."

Though it is within the genre of mystery novels that Mcdonald has earned his reputation, he began his writing career with a dark novel entitled *Running Scared.* Written while Mcdonald was at Harvard, *Running Scared* deals with a college student who stands idly by as a friend contemplates—and ultimately commits—suicide. Mcdonald describes the novel to *Publishers Weekly* as "a loud complaint about how people are turned into computer punch cards." Though called "believable and readable despite the extremity and relative simplicity of characterization" by a *Washington Post Book World* reviewer, this bleak story of rationalized suicide caused some controversy; publishers labeled Mcdonald a "high-risk" author, and were reluctant to publish his manuscripts. Blacklisted, Mcdonald would wait ten years before selling another book.

In the meantime, Mcdonald worked as a reporter for the *Boston Globe.* While there, he recalls in the *Washington Post,* he began constructing a character, a reporter, based on the "myths and legends of the newsroom when [reporters] sit back at 3 a.m. and tell stories." Mcdonald quit his job at the *Globe* and devoted his time to writing a detective story featuring this character—a snide, smug, insightful investigative reporter named Irwin M. Fletcher, who would become well-known to readers simply as "Fletch."

In his first adventure, 1974's *Fletch,* the young journalist is wandering the beaches of southern California, mingling undercover with the junkies and small-time dope dealers in an attempt to break a story on big-time drugs. He is approached by a well-dressed businessman, Alan Stanwyk, who, mistaking Fletch for a drifter, makes an unusual proposition: three million dollars to kill a man. That man, it turns out, is Stanwyk himself; he is suffering from a terminal disease whose agony-filled later stages he would rather not endure. Suicide would invalidate his substantial insurance policy, leaving his wife with nothing; murder, however, would not. Fletch accepts the offer, and in the few days before the murder is to take place he investigates Stanwyk—his health, his business connections, and his wife—all the while continuing his report on the California beach drug community. The two plots ultimately merge, allowing Fletch to reveal the solutions to two mysteries at once. In the final chapter we find Fletch on the shores of Rio de Janeiro with three million untraceable dollars of Stanwyk's money.

White hails Mcdonald's first detective novel as "a top-rate thriller told in stripped-down language," attributing its success in no small part to the character of I. M. Fletcher, "an engaging, unconventional young man" who does not quite fit into the mold of a detective hero. Though he is intuitive, he seemingly has no set investigative technique, stumbling upon his clues and solutions more through sheer luck than deduction. Fletch is also a bit of an opportunist who cannot always be counted upon to do the "right" thing—particularly when it jeopardizes his own welfare. Even these traits are not absolute, though, for Fletch's actions often surprise even Mcdonald's most devoted readers—and not always pleasantly. "Fletch is not as sympathetic a character as he and his creator believe him to be," contends T. J. Binyon of the *Times Literary Supplement,* "but there is a brio and zip about the proceedings . . . which more than make up for this."

Fletch earned Mcdonald widespread popularity, critical praise, and an Edgar award for best first mystery novel. However, its success carried with it a disturbing situation: readers were clamoring for another Fletch novel, but Mcdonald had not prepared the reporter—or himself—for a sequel. "I had no idea it was going to turn into a series when I wrote the first book," he tells White. "If I had known, I wouldn't have left Fletch with $3 million in Rio." Somehow, he had to find a way to lure the roguish ex-reporter off the beach and into another mystery. "I sat under a tree and talked to the dog . . . [until] I finally worked it out," he recalls in the *Washington Post.* "If Fletch didn't care about money when he didn't have it, then he wouldn't care about it when he did have it."

With his stolen money to back him, Fletch now has the freedom to work only when he wants to and in a variety of capacities including art collector, political advisor, and, occasionally, journalist. His ill-gotten fortune allows him, as well, to remain unemployed for long stretches in between, time spent hobnobbing with starlets and visiting tropical locales. During the course of eight more novels, Mcdonald uses his irrepressible beach bum cum socialite sleuth to infiltrate the once-restricted inner circles of society, dragging the skeletons out of their not-so-tightly locked closets. Along the way, Fletch (and Mcdonald) passes up no chance to thumb his nose at the Establishment: in *Fletch and the Man Who,* for example, Fletch is hired as an advisor to a presidential candidate, giving the reader a peek behind the scenes of a political campaign and casting its players in a rather uncomplimentary light. Mcdonald affords similar treatment to actors (in *Fletch's Moxie*), lawyers (in *Fletch Won*), and journalists (in *Fletch's Fortune*). Robin W. Winks of the *New Republic* observes: "Mcdonald has quite a bit to say [in the Fletch novels], most of it terse."

Mcdonald published his last Fletch story, *Fletch, Too,* in 1986. It is a prequel, set before the events of the first novel. In *Fletch, Too,* the young aspiring reporter is informed that his presumed-dead father (whose name is also Fletch, thus the title) is alive in Africa. He and his new bride travel across the ocean to find the elder Fletch, during which time they become involved in a murder mystery. Though Don G. Campbell of the *Los Angeles Times* admits that the author's "tongue-in-cheek treatment" of Fletch is "as deft as ever" in *Fletch, Too,* he continues: "Mcdonald . . . may be doing a wise thing in quitting while he's ahead of the game." Still, many readers are not ready to say farewell to I. M. Fletcher. Recalling how Arthur Conan Doyle was forced by public outcry to revive Sherlock Holmes, White writes: "We can only hope that we haven't seen the last of Fletch."

After a six-year hiatus, Mcdonald responded to the pleas of his readers with 1993's *Son of Fletch,* possibly just the first in a series of new mysteries entitled, "Fletch—The Next Generation." In this novel, Fletch, older now and perhaps a bit wiser, is visited by a young man claiming to be his son. Fletch is typically dubious, particularly since the youth has arrived at his door in prison garb. Though the advanced reviews of *Son of Fletch* were quite positive—Peter Lovesey dubbed it "the wittiest, wisest, twistiest story I've read this year," and Peter Straub described it as "witty the way a Purdy shotgun would be witty"—Mcdonald himself does not consider "The Next Generation" to be a part of the grand "Fletch Saga" of the first nine novels.

Looking back at the tremendous success of the Fletch series, many critics have attempted to ascertain just what attracts readers to Mcdonald's mysteries. Callendar points out that Fletch appealed to younger readers: "[He] was young, smart, irreverent, honest and very mod. . . . He refused to kowtow to authority," and "saw through things his more complacent or cynical colleagues shrugged their shoulders at." When this character was coupled with Mcdonald's fast-paced and witty style, Callendar continues, Fletch's adventures "always were a pleasure to read." Campbell agrees: "The joy of any Fletch novel . . . isn't really the plot," but rather "in the wonderfully bizarre situations in which the personable Fletch finds himself on his way to the solution of the crime."

In considering the nine books that make up Mcdonald's Fletch Saga, it is important to observe the staggered chronology in which Fletch's adventures are presented: through a series of sequels, prequels, pre-prequels, and "post-quels", we are allowed to see first *how* Fletch is, and, much later *why.* While it is possible to arrange the novels into chronological order (*Fletch Won, Fletch, Too, Fletch and the Widow Bradley, Fletch, Carioca Fletch, Confess, Fletch, Fletch's Fortune, Fletch's Moxie,* and *Fletch and the Man Who*), Dr. John McAleer warns in the *Armchair Detective* that this would be a mistake: "To the reader who wants to partake of Fletch's own integrity . . . the [non-chronological] approach is the only allowable one. To read the novels in the sequence written is to listen to the tumblers of an intricate lock falling into place, one by one, till the last one attains its alignment, the door swinging open, and the contents within are visible to us at last." When read in its proper order, the saga culminates with *Fletch, Too,* in which Fletch confronts his estranged father. "He has found the origin of, and confirmed, the pattern of conduct he has worked out on his own," McAleer explains. "He has attained self-justification [and] has vindicated his iconoclasm. The rest of his life [as chronicled in the previous novels] will involve acting on the principles he has forged on his own yet found exemplified in [his father]."

In any literary genre, an author is fortunate to create just one character as memorable and enduring as Fletch. Mcdonald has created two. The character of Francis Xavier Flynn—described as "one of the smartest, gentlest, most sarcastic cops you will ever meet" by Callendar—first appeared in *Confess, Fletch,* as the tenacious Boston Police Department inspector who dogged Fletch for a murder confession. "Flynn stole the show" in *Confess, Fletch,* according to Callendar, "a commanding, droll figure . . . who deserved to be around again." So warmly was this character received that Mcdonald took a hiatus from his Fletch books in 1977 to write *Flynn.* In this novel, federal authorities are investigating the explosion of an airliner shortly after takeoff from Logan Airport, and the Boston Police Department has been instructed to deliver whatever assistance is necessary. Flynn, however, conducts his own investigation, much to the dismay of the by-the-book F.B.I. men, as well as his own inept partner (whom Flynn addresses as "Grover", though that is not the man's name). We soon discover that Flynn is actually an operant for a secret international agency called No-Name; he is sort of an older James Bond who, lying low in Boston, now uses his wits more than his gun. His experience with international espionage, it turns out, has come in handy in Boston more than once, though only the Chief of the Boston Police Department suspects that Flynn is more than he seems. Joseph McLellan of the *Washington Post Book World* writes that in *Flynn* Mcdonald "demonstrates that he can handle more than one kind of story, more than one kind of hero," and while Callendar warns that Francis Xavier Flynn is, at times, "too good to be true . . . , Mcdonald is so good a writer that his fantasies are transmitted with a good deal of charm." In the end, Callendar proclaims, *Flynn* is "more civilized and infinitely more enjoyable than most books of its kind."

The Flynn trilogy—*Flynn, The Buck Passes Flynn,* and *Flynn's In*—are considered by critics to be darker and more serious than the Fletch novels. *The Buck Passes Flynn,* in which very large sums of money are literally dropped from the sky into the hands of unsuspecting citizens and greedy government officials, is labeled "a parable of the economic woes of America" by Callendar, illustrating how money can corrupt just about everyone. Mcdonald explains in *Publishers Weekly: "The Buck Passes Flynn* is something unusual for a mystery. It's about the anxieties we all have over inflation and about the relationships between people and currency." *Flynn's In* details Flynn's investigation of a series of murders in the ultra-exclusive Rod and Gun Club, whose members are the "loathsomely rich, ridiculous and powerful holders of old names and money," according to a *Time* reviewer. He goes on to call the novel "shameless Establishment bashing," noting further that, while Flynn ultimately ferrets out the killer, "the murders themselves seem just and appropriate."

In 1986, having established both reputation and financial security, Mcdonald turned his efforts toward the publishing of a novel entitled *Safekeeping.* It is the story of young Robert Burnes, the son of an English Duke, whose parents are killed during the blitz on London. Just eight years old, the once-pampered boy is suddenly forced to live on his own. He takes a ship to New York City, where he lives in the dirty underground world of scavengers and thieves before happening, quite accidentally, upon a home for runaways in Harlem. Because of its dark subject matter, Mcdonald had trouble finding a publisher for *Safekeeping;* it sat on a shelf, completed, for almost twelve years. The novel was finally picked up by Penzler Press, who paid Mcdonald an advance of ten dollars (nine dollars after his agent's commission). "I would have published it for nothing," the author confesses in the *New York Times.* "I don't know if it's admirable to persist as I did, or thickheaded or stupid. . . . But I was so eager to have the book enjoyed by others that even at the risk of perpetually embarrassing myself I said, 'No, I'm going to try again.' "

That persistence has paid off, for *Safekeeping* garnered much critical acclaim. Laced with Mcdonald's trademark wit, a reviewer for *Time* writes, it allows the author to "mix sociology and satire, goofy narrative and authentic horror." Perry Glassner of the *New York Times Book Review* observes how "the naive point of view of a boy allows more space for an author's voice to comment about journalism, the treatment of children or the violence inherent in American society." Glassner concludes: "If Charles Dickens and Nathanael West had collaborated on *Oliver Twist,* they might have produced as wise and entertaining a book as *Safekeeping.* . . . Readers who know [Mcdonald] only by reputation are advised to take this opportunity to read a writer with considerable talent."

In more recent years, Mcdonald has been producing volumes for his "Time Squared" quartet, which he has described as "the heart and center of his life's work." The first novel, *A World Too Wide,* introduces a group of characters, old friends, who are passing steadily into their middle years. "Mcdonald is fascinated by the metaphysical baggage from our youth that we carry into middle age," notes an impressed Digby Diehl in the *Los Angeles Times Book Review.* "*A World Too Wide* is a dexterous delight of deceptive ease. . . . [It is] a sophisticated literary work filled with levels of meaning, symbolism and provocative philosophical subtleties. This is the kind of novel that forces you to set it down periodically as you are reading it and think about your own life." The other novels in the "Time Squared" series, *Exits and Entrances* and *Merely Players,* go back in time to explore the beginnings of the characters' relationships.

It is unclear whether Mcdonald will return to the world of mystery and detective fiction. "I think giving readers entertainment, and a laugh, is a nice thing to do," he tells White. "The mystery novel is a framework on which I can hang stories I want to tell and comment about life and people." He continues, however, with a warning: "A genre is a horse. . . . Either it rides you or you ride it. It's more exciting if the author is riding the horse. I want to try new things." He concludes in *Publishers Weekly:* "A novel, to be a novel, has to have something novel about it. . . . If it comes to a time when I can't do something novel, I hope I'll have the wisdom to stop."

BIOGRAPHICAL/CRITICAL SOURCES:

BOOKS

Carr, John C., *The Craft of Crime: Conversations with Crime Writers,* Houghton, 1983.

PERIODICALS

Armchair Detective, winter, 1988, pp. 17-35.
Christian Science Monitor, October 23, 1985, p. 22.
Listener, May 13, 1976, p. 621; April 2, 1987, p. 24.
Los Angeles Times Book Review, November 7, 1982, p. 8; July 24, 1983, p. 6; May 27, 1984, p. 7; August 11, 1985, p. 4; December 22, 1985, p. 6; October 19, 1986, p. 10; December 13, 1987, p. 6.
New Republic, March 4, 1978, p. 40; November 4, 1978, p. 53; March 14, 1983, p. 39; June 13, 1983, p. 36.
New Yorker, October 16, 1978, p. 197.
New York Times, February 10, 1986, p. C13.
New York Times Book Review, February 16, 1975, p. 13; December 19, 1976, p. 24; October 16, 1977, p. 32;

July 30, 1978, p. 34; August 3, 1980, p. 12; January 31, 1982, p. 22; December 19, 1982, p. 30; September 25, 1983, p. 20; October 27, 1985, p. 24; December 29, 1985, p. 18; November 9, 1986, p. 25; November 22, 1987, p. 32; December 18, 1988, p. 20; July 26, 1992, p. 25.

Observer, February 15, 1976, p. 27; February 6, 1977, p. 31; June 26, 1977, p. 29; September 18, 1977, p. 25; March 26, 1978, p. 24; January 14, 1979, p. 35; May 1, 1983, p. 29; October 16, 1983, p. 32; February 17, 1985, p. 26.

Publishers Weekly, December 18, 1981, pp. 14-16.

Spectator, October 29, 1977, p. 23.

Time, July 9, 1984, p. 84; November 4, 1985, p. 83.

Times (London), March 24, 1983.

Times Literary Supplement, April 23, 1976, p. 498; December 23, 1977, p. 1513.

Tribune Books (Chicago), November 2, 1986, p. 4; January 11, 1987, p. 6; September 20, 1987, p. 4.

Village Voice, September 18, 1978, p. 134.

Washington Post, October 11, 1980.

Washington Post Book World, April 27, 1975, p. 4; April 4, 1976, p. 4; February 20, 1977, p. 4; November 6, 1977, p. 6; January 15, 1978, p. 5; September 21, 1980, p. 6; October 20, 1985, p. 8; November 16, 1986, p. 8.

West Coast Review of Books, November, 1983, p. 49; September, 1984, p. 43; July, 1985, p. 27.

—Sketch by Brandon Trenz

* * *

MEACHAM, Margaret 1952-

PERSONAL: Born February 15, 1952, in Pittsburgh, PA; daughter of James Grier (a lawyer) and Rachel (Reed) Marks; married John B. Meacham (a stockbroker), June 14, 1973; children: Peter Campbell, Jennifer Reed, Katharine Margaret. *Education:* Trinity College, Hartford, CN, B.A., 1975; University of Maryland at College Park, M.L.S., 1976. *Politics:* Independent. *Religion:* Episcopal.

ADDRESSES: Home and office—P.O. Box 402, Brooklandville, MD 21002.

CAREER: Writer. Adult services librarian at Baltimore County Public Library, 1976-80, coordinator of Ready-to-Know Program, 1980-81; teacher at Catonsville Community College; teacher at Goucher College, 1987—.

MEMBER: Society of Children's Book Writers, National Writers Union, Baltimore Children's Writers Group.

AWARDS, HONORS: Fiction award, 1984, for "Rabbit's New Neighbor," and humorous fiction award, 1985, for "It All Started With the Ant," both from *Highlights for Children.*

WRITINGS:

Love in Focus (young adult novel), Berkley Publishing, 1983.

Vacation Blues (young adult novel), Berkley Publishing, 1985.

Secret of Heron Creek, Tidewater Publishers, 1991.

The Boy on the Beach, 1992.

Editor, *Goucher College Quarterly,* 1986-90. Contributor to magazines, including *Sesame Street* and *Children's Playmate.*

WORK IN PROGRESS: A novel for 8-12 year-olds.

SIDELIGHTS: Margaret Meacham once told *CA:* "I write for the child I once was and the adult I am now. My own children often suggest ideas for my stories. I try to express my values and my personal view of the world in the characters I create."

* * *

MELHEM, D(iana) H(elen)

PERSONAL: Surname rhymes with "vellum"; born in Brooklyn, NY; daughter of Nicholas (a textile executive) and Georgette (Deyratani) Melhem; children: Dana Marie Vogel, Gregory Melhem Vogel. *Education:* New York University, B.A. (cum laude), 1949; City College of the City University of New York, M.A., 1971; City University of New York, Ph.D., 1976.

ADDRESSES: Home—250 West 94th St., New York, NY 10025.

CAREER: Poet and writer. City College of the City University of New York, New York City, lecturer, 1971, assistant professor, 1981-82; College of Staten Island, Staten Island, NY, assistant professor of literature, 1978; New School for Social Research, New York City, faculty member, 1979 and 1982-85; Long Island University, Long Island, NY, associate professor of literature, 1981-83; Union for Experimenting Colleges and Universities, professor, 1985—. Active in community life of West Side New York City; International Women's Writing Guild (IWWG), director of regional writing workshops, 1977-80; conductor of IWWG workshops in cities, including Malibu, CA, Glen Cove, NY, and New York City; Southampton College, distinguished visiting artist, 1978. Has read (and sometimes sung) her poems on television and radio, at schools, libraries, theaters, coffee houses, and feminist and political gatherings.

MEMBER: Modern Language Association of America, Academy of American Poets, Poetry Society of America, PEN, Publishers and Writers, Phi Beta Kappa, Sigma

Delta Omicron, City College of the City University of New York Alumni Association, City University of New York Ph.D. Alumni Association.

AWARDS, HONORS: Calliope Poetry Award, 1974; Woodrow Wilson Foundation fellowship in women's studies nominee, 1975; honorable mention, Alice and Edith Hamilton Award competition, 1979, for *Gwendolyn Brooks: Prophecy and Poetic Process;* special commendation, New York Heart Association Media Award, 1979, for article in the *New York Times;* National Endowment for the Humanities fellowship, 1980-81; Marie T. Unger Award, Shelley Society—New York, 1984.

WRITINGS:

Notes on 94th Street (poetry), Poet's Press, 1972, second edition, Dovetail Press, 1979.

Rest in Love, Dovetail Press, 1975, second edition, 1978.

Children of the House Afire: More Notes on 94th Street (poetry), Dovetail Press, 1976.

(Author of introduction) Ree Dragonette, *This Is the Way We Wash Our Hands,* Calliope, 1977.

Reaching Exercises: The IWWG Workshop Book, Dovetail Press, 1981.

(Author of introduction) Martin Tucker, *Homes of Locks and Mysteries,* Dovetail Press, 1982.

Gwendolyn Brooks: Poetry and the Heroic Voice (criticism), University Press of Kentucky, 1987.

Heroism in the New Black Poetry: Introductions and Interviews (criticism), University Press of Kentucky, 1990.

(Author of afterword) George E. Kent, *A Life of Gwendolyn Brooks,* University Press of Kentucky, 1990.

Work represented in anthologies, including *Group 74: Poems from the New York Poets' Cooperative,* edited by Edward Butscher, Roberta Gould, and Donald Lev, New York Poets' Cooperative, 1974; *For Neruda, for Chile: An International Anthology,* edited by Walter Lowenfels, Beacon Press, 1975; *Womansong,* edited by Shirley Powell, Poet's Press, 1976; *Science of the Times 3,* Arno, 1980. Contributor to *Language and Style, Nation, Studies in Black Literature, VORT, For Now, Confrontation, Bitterroot, Croton Review, Gnosis, Sun Dog, Steppingstones, Gargoyle, Western Journal of Black Studies, Greenfield Review,* and *New York Times Magazine.*

SIDELIGHTS: D. H. Melhem's poetry has been praised by numerous poets, scholars, and critics. In *Newsart,* Robert Reinhold comments that Melhem "is one of our finest practitioners of verse." And in the introduction to her volume *Notes on 94th Street,* Donald Phelps commends Melhem for her poetic exploration of life on the New York City street. He concludes that she "is bringing poetry back to a vigorous, beauteous, and too-long-in-these-quarters discarded function: a tool of inquiry and correspondence and clear, true-functioning response." Ann Grace Mojtabai, writing in the *Library Journal,* notes a direct quality to Melhem's poems in *Notes on 94th Street,* describing that collection as "a packet of messages—telegrams, actually—in the cause of sanity and social conscience." Carolyn Jabs of *Wisdoms Child* adds that Melhem's vision of the city "wipes away the smog of insensitivity, the pollution of apathy and offers us a clear and vibrant view of our supermarkets, our park benches, our river."

In addition to being recognized as a poet, Melhem is also known for her critical studies of black literature. In *Gwendolyn Brooks: Poetry and the Heroic Voice,* Melhem, according to Clara Claiborne Park of *The Nation,* provides a "comprehensive, poem-by-poem survey" of Brooks's works that should inspire readers "to discover, or rediscover, Brooks's humorous, humane and unexpected ways with our common language, and something of 'the gist of black humanity' which is [Brooks's] subject."

A successive work by Melhem, *Heroism in the New Black Poetry,* was described by one reviewer in *Publishers Weekly* as a "rich anthology of six distinguished black poets." The volume includes biographical and critical data on Gwendolyn Brooks, Amiri Baraka, Jayne Cortez, Haki R. Madhubuti, Dudley Randall, and Sonia Sanchez. Also highlighted in the book are interviews with the poets, who are notable for their roles as leaders of social change. Complimenting Melhem's work on *Heroism in the New Black Poetry,* L. J. Parascandola, writing in *Choice,* maintains that "there is a candid quality to [the interviews], sometimes perhaps startingly so."

BIOGRAPHICAL/CRITICAL SOURCES:

BOOKS

Melhem, D. H., *Notes on 94th Street,* second edition, Dovetail Press, 1979.

Who's Who in Writers, Editors, and Poets, 1989-90, December Press, 1989.

PERIODICALS

Belles Lettres, March/April, 1988, p. 12.

Choice, November, 1990, p. 487.

Independent Press, March 9, 1977.

Library Journal, January 15, 1979, p. 170.

The Nation, September 26, 1987.

Newsart, August, 1979.

Poets Fortnightly, December 8, 1972.

Publishers Weekly, November 24, 1989, p. 65.

Westsider, October 26, 1972.

Wisdoms Child, January 22, 1973.*

MICHAELS, Fern
See ANDERSON, Roberta and KUCZKIR, Mary

* * *

MILETUS, Rex
See BURGESS, Michael (Roy)

* * *

MOBLEY, Walt
See BURGESS, Michael (Roy)

* * *

MOLNAR, Thomas 1921-

PERSONAL: Born June 26, 1921, in Budapest, Hungary; son of Alexander and Aurelie (Blon) Molnar. *Education:* Universite de Bruxelles, M.A. (French literature), 1948, M.A. (philosophy), 1948; Columbia University, Ph.D., 1952.

ADDRESSES: Home—238 Heights Rd., Ridgewood, NJ 07450.

CAREER: Brooklyn College of the City University of New York, Brooklyn, NY, professor of French and world literature, beginning 1957; University of Budapest, Budapest, Hungary, professor of philosophy of religion, 1991—. Visiting professor of political theory, Potchefstroom University, South Africa, 1969; visiting professor of philosophy, Hillsdale College, 1973-74; visiting professor, Yale University, 1983, and Catholic University of Santiago, 1986.

AWARDS, HONORS: Relm Foundation grant, 1963-64, for travel and study in French-speaking Africa, 1966, for travel in South America, 1967, for *Sartre: Ideologue of Our Time,* and 1987, for *Twin Powers: Politics and the Sacred.*

WRITINGS:

Bernanos: His Political Thought and Prophecy, Sheed & Ward, 1960.
The Future of Education, Fleet, 1961, revised edition, 1970.
The Decline of the Intellectual, Meridian Books, 1962.
The Two Faces of American Foreign Policy, Bobbs-Merrill, 1962.
L'Afrique du Sud, Nouvelles Editions Latines, 1964.
Africa: A Political Travelogue, Fleet, 1965.
South West Africa: The Last Pioneer Country, Fleet, 1967.
Utopia: The Perennial Heresy, Sheed & Ward, 1967.
Sartre: Ideologue of Our Time, Funk, 1968.
Ecumenism or New Reformation?, Funk, 1968, published as *Dialogues and Ideologues,* Franciscan Herald, 1977.
The Counter-Revolution, Funk, 1970.
La Gauche vue d'en face, Editions du Seuil, 1970.
The American Dilemma: A Consideration of United States Leadership in World Affairs, Centre for International Politics, Potchefstroom University for Christian Higher Education, 1971.
God and the Knowledge of Reality, Basic Books, 1973, new edition, Transaction Books.
L'Animal politique, Editions de la Table Ronde, 1974.
Le Socialisme sans visage: L'Avenement du tiers modele, Presses Universitaires de France, 1976.
Authority and Its Enemies, Arlington House, 1976, 2nd edition, Transaction Books.
Le modele defigure: L'Amerique de Tocqueville a Carter, Presses Universitaires de France, 1978.
Christian Humanism: A Critique of "The Secular City" and Its Ideology, Franciscan Herald, 1978.
Theists and Atheists: A Typology of Non-Belief, Mouton, 1980.
Le Tiers-Monde: Ideologie, Realite, Presses Universitaires de France, 1982.
Le Dieu immanent: La Grande Tentation de la pensee allemande, Editions du Cedre, 1982.
Twin Powers: Politics and the Sacred, Eerdmans, 1987.
The Pagan Temptation, Fordham University Press, 1988.

Also author of *The European Dilemma,* 1974, *The Catholic Concept of Politics and State,* 1981, *L'Eclipse du sacre,* 1986, *L'Americanologie: Triomphe d'un modele planetaire?,* 1990, *L'Europe entre parentheses,* 1991, *The Church: Pilgrim of Centuries,* 1991, *Philosophical Grounds,* 1991, and *L'Hegemonie liberale,* 1992.

Molnar's work has been translated into French, German, Italian, Spanish, Portuguese, and Hungarian.

BIOGRAPHICAL/CRITICAL SOURCES:

PERIODICALS

America, May 20, 1967.
Book World, October 27, 1968; June 7, 1970.
Catholic World, August, 1967.
Christian Century, February 20, 1974.
Commonweal, October 13, 1967.
Esquire, July, 1965; August, 1973.
Modern Age, summer, 1974; spring, 1978.
Nation, December 26, 1966.
National Review, March 7, 1967; August 22, 1967; February 10, 1970; March 28, 1975; October 15, 1976.
Negro Digest, August, 1965.
New York Review of Books, July 1, 1965.

New York Times Book Review, July 18, 1965; December 14, 1969.
Saturday Review, October 26, 1968.

* * *

MONTGOMERY, Elizabeth
See JULESBERG, Elizabeth Rider Montgomery

* * *

MONTGOMERY, Elizabeth Rider
See JULESBERG, Elizabeth Rider Montgomery

* * *

MOORE, Brian 1921-

PERSONAL: Born August 25, 1921, in Belfast, Northern Ireland; emigrated to Canada, 1948; Canadian citizen; son of James Brian (a surgeon) and Eileen (McFadden) Moore; married Jean Denney, October, 1967; children: Michael. *Education:* Graduated from St. Malachy's College, 1939.

ADDRESSES: *Home*—33958 Pacific Coast Hwy., Malibu, CA 90265. *Agent*—Perry Knowlton, Curtis Brown Ltd., 10 Astor Place, New York, N.Y. 10003.

CAREER: *Montreal Gazette,* Montreal, Quebec, proofreader, reporter, and rewrite man, 1948-52; writer, 1952—. *Military service:* Served with British Ministry of War Transport in North Africa, Italy, and France during World War II.

AWARDS, HONORS: Author's Club first novel award, 1956; Quebec Literary Prize, 1958; Guggenheim fellowship, 1959; Governor General's Award for Fiction, 1960, for *The Luck of Ginger Coffey,* and 1975, for *The Great Victorian Collection;* U.S. National Institute of Arts and Letters fiction grant, 1961; Canada Council fellowship for travel in Europe, 1962 and 1976; W. H. Smith Prize, 1972, for *Catholics;* James Tait Black Memorial Award, 1975, for *The Great Victorian Collection;* Booker Prize shortlist, 1976, for *The Doctor's Wife;* Neill Gunn International Fellowship from the Scottish Arts Council, 1983; "ten best books of 1983" citation from *Newsweek,* 1983, for *Cold Heaven;* Heinemann Award from the Royal Society of Literature, 1986, for *Black Robe;* Booker Prize shortlist citation, 1987, and *Sunday Express* Book of the Year Prize, 1988, both for *The Color of Blood;* Hon.D.Litt., Queens University Belfast, 1989; Booker Prize shortlist, 1990, for *Lies of Silence;* Hon.D.Litt., National University of Ireland, Dublin, 1991; Fellow of the Royal Society of Literature.

WRITINGS:

NOVELS

Judith Hearne, A. Deutsch, 1955, published as *The Lonely Passion of Judith Hearne,* Little, Brown, 1956.
The Feast of Lupercal, Little, Brown, 1957.
The Luck of Ginger Coffey (also see below), Little, Brown, 1960.
An Answer from Limbo, Little, Brown, 1962.
The Emperor of Ice-Cream, Viking, 1965.
I Am Mary Dunne, Viking, 1968.
Fergus, Holt, 1970.
The Revolution Script, Holt, 1971.
Catholics (also see below), J. Cape, 1972, Harcourt, 1973.
The Great Victorian Collection, Farrar, Straus, 1975.
The Doctor's Wife, Farrar, Straus, 1976.
The Mangan Inheritance, Farrar, Straus, 1979.
Two Stories, Santa Susana Press, 1979.
The Temptation of Eileen Hughes, Farrar, Straus, 1981.
Cold Heaven, Holt, 1983.
Black Robe (also see below), Dutton, 1985.
The Color of Blood, Dutton, 1987.
Lies of Silence, Doubleday, 1990.
No Other Life, Doubleday, 1993.

OTHER

(With others) *Canada* (travel book), Time-Life, 1963.
The Luck of Ginger Coffey (screenplay; based on his novel of same title), Continental, 1964.
Torn Curtain (screenplay), Universal, 1966.
Catholics (television script; based on his novel of same title), Columbia Broadcasting System, 1973.
Black Robe (screenplay; based on his novel of same title), Alliance Communications, 1987.

Also author of screenplays *The Slave,* 1967, *The Blood of Others,* 1984, *Brainwash,* 1985, and *Gabrielle Chanel,* 1988. Contributor of articles and short stories to *Spectator, Holiday, Atlantic,* and other periodicals. *The Lonely Passion of Judith Hearne, Lies of Silence, Color of Blood,* and *Cold Heaven* have been recorded on audio cassette.

ADAPTATIONS: *The Lonely Passion of Judith Hearne* was produced as a feature film by Island Pictures in 1988; *The Temptation of Eileen Hughes* was produced for television by the British Broadcasting Corporation in 1988; *Cold Heaven* was produced as a feature film in 1991.

SIDELIGHTS: Brian Moore is a Canadian citizen of Irish origin currently living in the United States. He is also a novelist who "has gradually won the recognition his stubborn artistry deserves," to quote Walter Clemons in *Newsweek.* For more than thirty years Moore has been publishing fiction that reflects his multinational wanderings, his fascination with Catholicism's influence on modern life, and his insight into strained interpersonal relationships. "Book by book," writes Bruce Cook in *New Republic,* "Brian Moore has been building a body of work that is, in its quietly impressive way, about as good as that of any novelist writing today in English." Cook adds: "If Moore lacks the fame he deserves, he nevertheless has an excellent reputation. He is a writer's writer. His special virtues—his deft presentation of his characters, whether they be Irish, Canadian, or American, and the limpid simplicity of his style—are those that other writers most admire."

Many of Moore's plots are conventional in their inception, but typically the author brings additional depth of characterization to his stories so that they transcend genre classifications. As Joyce Carol Oates observes in the *New York Times Book Review,* Moore has written "a number of novels prized for their storytelling qualities and for a wonderfully graceful synthesis of the funny, the sardonic, and the near tragic; his reputation as a supremely entertaining 'serious' writer is secure." In *Saturday Night,* Christina Newman notes that Moore has a growing readership which has come to expect "what he unfailingly delivers: lucidity, great craftsmanship, and perceptions that evoke our fears, dreams, and shameful absurdities." *New York Times Book Review* contributor Julian Moynahan calls Moore "one of the most intelligent and accessible novelists now working. . . . He seems to have no crochets to hook or axes to grind and is adept at reworking his personal experience for the fiction public on both sides of the Atlantic." Oates feels that the author's works "succeed most compellingly on an immediate level: rich with convincing detail, communicating the admixture of drollery and sorrow that characterizes 'real' life, populated with individuals who speak and act and dream and breathe as if altogether innocent of the fact that they are mere fictitious characters."

In the *Spectator,* Francis King explains how Moore constructs his stories: "His sentences are unelaborate and his vocabulary narrow. . . . But, mysteriously, beneath this surface flatness, strange creatures thresh, slither and collide with each other. Many sentences may seem bare, some may even seem banal; but the cumulative impression left by a sequence of them is one of complexity and originality." *Village Voice* reviewer Alan Hislop similarly contends that Moore's prose "is disarming and seductive: you are led, nay drawn, into alarming stories . . . so polite that you never suspect there might be a trap door in the scrupulously polished floor." Beneath that "trap door" is a view of the dark side of human events; temptation, guilt, disillusionment, and dissatisfaction often play primary roles in Moore's characters' lives. In the *Washington Post Book World,* Alan Ryan states that it is this skillful exploration of human failings that makes Moore's work such thoughtful entertainment. "In most of Brian Moore's writing," the critic concludes, "one is always aware of larger, and darker, worlds lurking just out of view."

"Brian Moore comes from the middle-class sector of the submerged and currently beleaguered Catholic minority of Belfast in Ulster," writes Moynahan. "Like many Irish writers before him, he has followed the path of voluntary exile in managing a successful career as a novelist and is the only writer I know of who has lived and worked, and collected a number of impressive literary prizes, in no less than four English-speaking countries—Ireland, England, Canada and the United States." Moore left his native land and rejected his Catholic upbringing at an early age. Shortly after completing war-time service he emigrated to Canada, and from there he began to write about the Belfast he knew as a youth. According to Christopher Hawtree in the *Spectator,* this transatlantic stance "has yielded some sharp views both of his native Ireland and of Canada and America." *Time* contributor Patricia Blake feels that Moore's expatriation has produced "a special talent for pungent portraiture of those Irish men and women who are, as James Joyce put it, 'outcast from life's feast': desperate spinsters, failed priests, drunken poets." Other critics note that the very process of moving from place to place fuels Moore's fiction. In *Critique: Studies in Modern Fiction,* John Wilson Foster contends that Moore's novels as a group "trace the growing fortunes in a new continent of one hypothetical immigrant who has escaped Belfast's lower middle-class tedium." London *Times* correspondent Chris Petit also concludes that absence is important to Moore's writing. "The stories have an air of cosmopolitan restlessness, often cross borders, and can be summarized as a series of departures," Petit states.

Eventually Moore moved to the United States—first to New York and then to Malibu, California. As Kerry McSweeney notes in *Critical Quarterly,* while the author retains Canadian citizenship, and Canada "was the halfway house which mediated his passage from the old world to the new, it has not stimulated his imagination in the way that America has done." Paul Binding elaborates in *Books and Bookmen:* "It is America, with its vigorous non-realistic, especially Gothic literary tradition, which would seem to have supplied Brian Moore with the fictional forms that he needed, that can express—with their violent epiphanies and their distortions and eruptions of the irrational—the anguishes of the uprooted and spiritually homeless, and the baffling diversities of Western society which can contain both puritan, taboo-ridden, pleasure-fearing Belfast and hedonistic, lost, restless California." In *Nation,* Jack Ludwig writes: "Moore is, like Joyce, essentially a city writer and, again like Joyce, someone who reacts to the city with lyric double awareness—the ugliness is there, but also the vigor. . . . The paralysis, hopelessness, colorlessness of Moore's first two novels is, I think, a dramatic equivalent of his Belfast. And it is not Europe which stands opposed to Belfast. It is New York."

Moore's early novels, *The Lonely Passion of Judith Hearne, The Feast of Lupercal, The Luck of Ginger Coffey,* and *The Emperor of Ice-Cream,* are character studies in which the protagonists rebel—sometimes unsuccessfully—against the essentially closed society of Northern Ireland. McSweeney suggests that the works "are studies of losers, whose fates are determined by the claustrophobic gentility of Belfast and the suffocating weight of Irish Catholicism. [They] illustrate one of the quintessential *donnees* of Moore's fiction: that (in his own words) 'failure is a more interesting condition than success. Success changes people: it makes them something they were not and dehumanizes them in a way, whereas failure leaves you with a more intense distillation of that self you are.' " In *Critique,* Hallvard Dahlie examines Moore's predilection for characters mired in hopelessness: "Moore [chooses] for his central figures people in their late thirties or early forties who [are] failures of one sort or another, and [have] been failures for some time. In his first four novels, Moore exploited the constituents of failure so skillfully and sensitively that the characters achieve much more stature than many triumphant heroes of less gifted writers. But with none of these earlier characters do we sense the likelihood of any lasting triumph over their limitations or obstacles." *Chicago Tribune Book World* reviewer Eugene Kennedy finds these novels "a look beneath the aspects of Irish culture that, with a terrible mixture of repression and misuse of its religious heritage, can create pitiable monsters fated to groan eternally beneath the facades of their hypocritical adjustments."

The Lonely Passion of Judith Hearne, Moore's first and best-known novel, is, to quote *Los Angeles Times* reviewer Leonard Klady, "an acclaimed work about an aging woman's struggle to find her identity as the secure elements in her life start to disintegrate." Set in Belfast, the story—which has never been out of print since 1955—revolves around Judith Hearne's desperate and futile attempts to gain the affection of a paunchy and unscrupulous suitor. *New York Times Book Review* contributor Frances Taliaferro notes that the Irish setting gives "a special poignancy to this portrait of a sad middle class spinster resolutely slipping into emotional destitution." In *Commonweal,* William Clancy observes that in the novel, Moore "has taken an Irish city and laid bare its most secret soul through characters who could not have been born elsewhere. . . . In its relentless pursuit of this woman's sorrow, in its refusal to sentimentalize or easily alleviate her plight, the book achieves a kind of vision, and it is a tragic vision. As she accepts, finally, the end of all her hopes, Judith Hearne attains . . . a certain grandeur." *Saturday Review* essayist Granville Hicks is among the critics who have praised *The Lonely Passion of Judith Hearne.* "As a book by a young man about a middle-aged woman," Hicks writes, "it [is] a remarkable tour de force, but it [is] more than that, for in it one [feels] the terrible pathos of life as it is often led."

A fascination with Catholicism is central to much of Moore's work. He told the *Los Angeles Times:* "I am not a religious person, but I come from a very religious background. Always in the back of my mind, I've wondered what if all this stuff was true and you didn't want it to be true and it was happening in the worst possible way?" According to Paul Gray in *Time,* a refrain common to all of Moore's novels is this: "When beliefs can no longer comfort, they turn destructive." Such is the case in a variety of Moore's works, from *The Lonely Passion of Judith Hearne* to the more recent *Cold Heaven, Black Robe, Catholics,* and *The Color of Blood.* Craig writes: "Someone who is heading for the moment of apostasy . . . is almost statutory in a Moore novel. . . . A frightening emptiness takes the place of whatever ideology had kept the character going." The opposite may also apply in some of Moore's tales; occasionally non-believing characters are forced to pay heed to the deity through extreme means. "Mr. Moore's later novels show the vestigial religious conscience straining to give depth to North American life," observes a *Times Literary Supplement* reviewer. "Faith itself is unacceptable, making unreasonable demands on the behaviour of anyone who is sporadically forced to be honest with himself. Yet bourbon, bedrooms and success do not content the soul: in this, at least, the priests were always right." Craig concludes that Moore is "an author who in the past has used the emblems of Catholicism with conspicuous success. . . . No one has examined with greater acuity the moral deficiencies inherent in a Belfast Catholic upbringing."

Several of Moore's novels—*Fergus, The Great Victorian Collection,* and *Cold Heaven*—make use of miracles and the supernatural to advance the stories. In *The Great Victorian Collection,* for instance, a college professor finds his vivid dream about an exhibit of Victorian memorabilia transformed into reality in a hotel parking lot. Binding suggests that in these works Moore "has tried to explore the complexities of American/Californian life while coming to further terms with the ghosts of his Irish past." These miracles and ghostly visitations do not comfort or sustain; Moore's vision of the supernatural "is terrifying: a brutal energy that mocks our pretensions and transcends our ideas of good and evil," to quote Mark Abley in *Books in Canada.* Peter S. Prescott likewise notes in *Newsweek* that Moore is "concerned with a secular sensibility confronting the more alien aspects of Roman Catholic tradition. . . . He warns us of the ambiguities of miracles in a world that is darker, more dangerous and above all more portentous than we think." Such plot devices can strain verisimilitude, but according to David MacFarlane in *Maclean's,* the author's strength "is his ability to make tangible the unbelievable and the miraculous." MacFarlane adds: "His consistently fine prose and the precision of his narrative create a reality in which characters and readers alike are forced to believe the improbable. Moore inhabits a world which is partly that of a religious visionary and partly that of a thriller writer."

"Mr. Moore is not only the laureate of Irish drabness but also a psychological writer with some interest in the quirkier aspects of profane love," writes Taliaferro. "Throughout his career, one has been able to rely on Mr. Moore for narrative competence and psychological interest." Through novels such as *I Am Mary Dunne, The Doctor's Wife,* and *The Temptation of Eileen Hughes,* Moore has attained a reputation for uncovering the pitfalls in modern emotional entanglements, especially from the female point of view. In *Nation,* Richard B. Sale comments that the author "has never avoided the silliness, selfishness and sexuality that constitute most people's waking and dreaming thoughts. . . . He can extend the embarrassing scene beyond the point where the ordinary naturalistic novelist would lower the curtain." *Times Literary Supplement* reviewer Paul Bailey notes that it is "typical of Brian Moore's honesty that he should acknowledge that, superficially at least, there are certain liaisons which bear a shocking resemblance to those described in the pages of women's magazines: life, unfortunately, has a nasty habit of imitating pulp fiction." However, *Spectator* correspondent Paul Ableman points out that Moore's characters "are not formula figures, whose responses to any situation are predictable, but rather fictional beings that behave like people in the world, generally consistent or revealing a thread of continuity, but always quirky, volatile and sometimes irrational." Bailey also admits that it is "a hallmark of Brian Moore's art that it respects and acknowledges a state of unhappiness as raw and as ugly as an open wound."

Prescott characterizes Moore as a novelist who "enjoys playing with his readers' expectations. Aha, he seems to say, you thought I was writing about this; now don't you feel a little foolish to discover that I was really up to something else—something more innocent and yet more terrible—all along?" Moore himself echoes this sentiment in the *Los Angeles Times:* "I find it interesting to lull the reader into a sense that he's reading a certain kind of book and then jolt the reader about halfway through to make him realize that it's a different kind of book. That is not a recipe for best sellerdom; it's the opposite." Even the thriller format in such works as *Black Robe* and *The Color of Blood* becomes "a vehicle to explore serious political and theological issues," to quote Anne-Marie Conway in the *Times Literary Supplement.* It is this willingness to explore and experiment that contributes to Moore's novelistic originality, according to critics. McSweeney writes: "One of the most impressive features of Moore's canon has been his ability to keep from repeating himself. Over and over again he has found fresh inventions which have developed his novelistic skills and enabled him to explore his obsessive themes and preoccupations in ways that have made for an increasingly complex continuity between old and new." Moreover, while the author's critical reputation is high, he is not particularly well-known to American readers—a state of affairs he welcomes. "I have never had to deal with the problem of a public persona becoming more important than the fiction," he said in the *Los Angeles Times.* "I've had a life where I've been able to write without having had some enormous success that I have to live up to."

Moore's success may not be enormous, but it is substantial in Canada and Great Britain. Cook claims that the author's retiring personality affects the tenor of his work for the better. "In a way," Cook concludes in *Commonweal,* "the sort of writer [Moore] is—private, devoted to writing as an end in itself—is the only sort who could write the intensely felt, personal, and close novels he has. The style, once again, is the man." Bailey writes: "It isn't fashionable to praise novelists for their tact, but it is that very quality in Brian Moore's writing that deserves to be saluted. It is a measure of his intelligence and his humanity that he refuses to sit in judgment on his characters. It is, as far as I am concerned, an honourable and a considerable measure." Perhaps the best summation of Moore's authorial talents comes from *Washington Post Book World* reviewer Jack Beatty, who says of the writer: "Pick him up expecting high talent in the service of a small design, go to him anticipating economy of style, characterization and description, as well as the pleasure of a plot that keeps you reading until the last page, and I can assure that your expectations will get along splendidly with his abilities."

BIOGRAPHICAL/CRITICAL SOURCES:

BOOKS

Contemporary Literary Criticism, Gale, Volume 1, 1973, Volume 3, 1975, Volume 5, 1976, Volume 7, 1977, Volume 8, 1978, Volume 19, 1981, Volume 32, 1985.

Dahlie, Hallvard, *Brian Moore,* Copp, 1969.

Flood, Jeanne, *Brian Moore,* Bucknell University Press, 1974.

O'Donoghue, Jo, *Brian Moore, A Critical Study,* McGill, Queens, 1991.

Raban, Jonathan, *The Techniques of Modern Fiction,* Edward Arnold, 1968.

PERIODICALS

Books & Bookmen, December, 1968; February, 1980.

Books in Canada, October, 1979; November, 1983.

Chicago Tribune, November 2, 1987.

Chicago Tribune Book World, July 12, 1981; October 30, 1983; May 19, 1985.

Commonweal, August 3, 1956; July 12, 1957; September 27, 1968; August 23, 1974.

Critical Quarterly, summer, 1976.

Critique: Studies in Modern Fiction, Volume 9, number 1, 1966; Volume 13, number 1, 1971.

Detroit News, October 14, 1979; May 19, 1985.

Globe & Mail (Toronto), March 30, 1985; September 5, 1987.

Harper's, October, 1965.

Life, June 18, 1968; December 3, 1972.

Los Angeles Times, September 14, 1983; July 2, 1987; September 15, 1987; December 23, 1987; January 1, 1988; April 10, 1988.

Los Angeles Times Book Review, September 11, 1983; April 7, 1985.

Maclean's, September 17, 1979; September 5, 1983.

Nation, March 15, 1965; June 24, 1968; October 12, 1970.

New Republic, August 17, 1968; June 9, 1973; October 24, 1983.

New Statesman, February 18, 1966; October 17, 1975; November 25, 1983.

Newsweek, June 2, 1975; September 20, 1976; October 15, 1979; July 20, 1981; September 5, 1983; March 18, 1985.

New Yorker, May 11, 1957; August 4, 1975; October 3, 1983; July 8, 1985.

New York Times, October 1, 1976; September 12, 1979; July 3, 1981; September 14, 1983; January 15, 1984; March 25, 1985; September 1, 1987; December 23, 1987; December 25, 1987.

New York Times Book Review, October 24, 1965; December 5, 1965; June 23, 1968; September 27, 1970; November 28, 1971; March 18, 1973; June 29, 1975; September 26, 1976; September 9, 1979; August 2, 1981; September 18, 1983; March 31, 1985; September 27, 1987.

People, October 12, 1987.

Saturday Night, September, 1968; November, 1970; July-August, 1975; October, 1976.

Saturday Review, October 13, 1962; September 18, 1965; June 15, 1968; February 12, 1972; July 26, 1975; September 18, 1976.

Spectator, November 1, 1975; November 10, 1979; October 10, 1981; November 12, 1983; July 13, 1985.

Time, June 18, 1956; June 21, 1968; October 12, 1970; July 14, 1975; September 6, 1976; September 19, 1983; March 18, 1985.

Times (London), October 1, 1981; November 3, 1983; June 13, 1985; September 24, 1987.

Times Literary Supplement, February 3, 1966; October 24, 1966; April 9, 1971; January 21, 1972; November 10, 1972; October 17, 1975; November 23, 1979; October 9, 1981; October 28, 1983; June 7, 1985; October 2, 1987.

Village Voice, June 30, 1957; October 22, 1979.

Washington Post, January 22, 1988.

Washington Post Book World, April 8, 1973; June 1, 1975; October 17, 1976; September 23, 1979; December 9, 1979; June 21, 1981; September 11, 1983; March 31, 1985; September 6, 1987; February 14, 1988.*

* * *

MORGAN, Robert 1921-

PERSONAL: Born April 17, 1921, in Wales; son of William Henry and Else Jane Morgan; married Jean Elizabeth Florence; children: Allison Mary, Marion Lesley. *Education:* Attended Fircroft College, 1949-51; Bognor Regis College of Education, 1951-53; Southampton University, 1969-71.

ADDRESSES: *Home*—72 Anmore Rd., Denmead, Hampshire P07 6NT, England.

CAREER: Coal miner, 1936-47; teacher in primary schools, 1951-64, and head of remedial department at secondary school in Cowplain, England, 1964-74; Gosport Education Authority, Gosport, England, advisory teacher for special education, 1974-80. His paintings have appeared in seventeen one-man shows in Wales, London, Southampton, Gosport Museum, and Winchester Museum and Art Gallery.

MEMBER: Welsh Academy, Guild of Anglo-Welsh Writers.

WRITINGS:

The Night's Prison (poems and verse play), Hart-Davis, 1967.

Rainbow Valley (verse play), first broadcast by BBC-Radio, August 4, 1967.

Poems and Extracts, Exeter University, 1968.

The Storm (poems and drawings), Christopher Davies, 1974.

The Master Miner (verse play), first broadcast by BBC Radio, June 16, 1974.

On the Banks of the Cynon (poems and drawings), A.R.C. Publications, 1976.
Voices in the Dark (verse play), A.R.C. Publications, 1976.
The Pass (poems), Indigo Publications, 1976.
My Lamp Still Burns (autobiography), Gomer Press, 1980.
Poems and Drawings, Indigo Publications, 1984.
The Miner and Other Stories, People's Publications, 1985.
Memoir (poems), Indigo Publications, 1988.
Landmarks (poems), Indigo Publications, 1989.
Saints on Islands (poems), Indigo Publications, 1991.
September Journey (poems), Indigo Publications, 1991.
Attic Poetry (poems), Indigo Publications, 1991.
Reminders (poems), Indigo Publications, 1992.
The Chosen (poems), Indigo Publications, 1992.
Fragments of a Dream (verse play), Indigo Publications, 1992.
The Master Miners (verse play), Indigo Publications, 1993.
Selected Poems, 1967-1977, Indigo Publications, 1993.
Selected Poems, 1978-1988, Indigo Publications, 1993.
Selected Poems, 1988-1993, Indigo Publications, 1993.

WORK IN PROGRESS: A verse play, *Voices in the Dark,* to be published by Indigo Publications in 1994.

SIDELIGHTS: Robert Morgan once told *CA:* "Most of my work is devoted to coal mining and miners and the landscape of mining Wales. In my work I have never offered a message or a remedy, but simply exposed a raw, parallel world that had seldom been seen in any light. I was a coal miner for more than eleven years. The experience was traumatic and writing creatively about it no doubt exorcised the effects of the trauma. The same can be said of my visual work in the form of painting.

"I began creative writing and published short stories when I was still a miner. I left mining and entered college after prodigious study as I had had little education before becoming a miner at a very young age. I did not return to creative writing until I had completed my studies in the second college. I began writing again at the age of thirty-one. Painting had been my special subject at the second college and later I practiced both art forms with reasonable success. I retired early to devote myself entirely to creative work."

Morgan more recently added, "I have written four unpublished novels, *The Shadow Valley, Moon and Stars, Dark Encounter,* and *Indigo Land.* All four novels are connected with miners, mines and landscape in South Wales mining communities. I also have three collections of short stories unpublished.

"At the moment I am preparing for a one-man show of my paintings and drawings at the National Library of Wales. The National Library has taken all my papers and they are now in the archives there."

BIOGRAPHICAL/CRITICAL SOURCES:

BOOKS

Contemporary Poets, St. James Press, 1987.
Writers on Tour, Welsh Arts Council, 1979.

* * *

MORRISON, Toni 1931-

PERSONAL: Born Chloe Anthony Wofford, February 18, 1931, in Lorain, OH; daughter of George and Ramah (Willis) Wofford; married Harold Morrison, 1958 (divorced, 1964); children: Harold Ford, Slade Kevin. *Education:* Howard University, B.A., 1953; Cornell University, M.A., 1955.

ADDRESSES: Office—Department of Creative Writing, Princeton University, Princeton, NJ 08544-1099. *Agent*—Amanda Urban, International Creative Management, 40 West 57th St., New York, NY 10019.

CAREER: Texas Southern University, Houston, instructor in English, 1955-57; Howard University, Washington, DC, instructor in English, 1957-64; Random House, New York, NY, senior editor, 1965-85; State University of New York at Purchase, associate professor of English, 1971-72; State University of New York at Albany, Albert Schweitzer Chair in the Humanities, 1984-89; Princeton University, Princeton, NJ, Robert F. Goheen Professor in the Council of the Humanities, 1989—. Visiting lecturer, Yale University, 1976-77, and Bard College, 1986-88; Clark Lecturer at Trinity College, Cambridge, and Massey Lecturer at Harvard University, both 1990. Trustee of the National Humanities Center; co-chair of the Schomburg Commission for the Preservation of Black Culture.

MEMBER: American Academy and Institute of Arts and Letters, American Academy of Arts and Sciences, National Council on the Arts, Authors Guild (member of council), Authors League of America.

AWARDS, HONORS: National Book Award nomination and Ohioana Book Award, both 1975, for *Sula;* National Book Critics Circle Award and American Academy and Institute of Arts and Letters Award, both 1977, for *Song of Solomon;* New York State Governor's Arts Award, 1986; first recipient of the Washington College Literary award, 1987; National Book Award nomination and National Book Critics Circle Award nomination, both 1987, and Pulitzer Prize for fiction and Robert F. Kennedy Award, both 1988, all for *Beloved;* Nobel Prize for literature, 1993; Elizabeth Cady Stanton Award from National Organization for Women.

WRITINGS:

The Bluest Eye (novel), Holt, 1969.

Sula (novel), Knopf, 1973.

(Editor) *The Black Book* (anthology), Random House, 1974.

Song of Solomon (novel; Book-of-the-Month Club selection), Knopf, 1977.

Tar Baby (novel), Knopf, 1981.

Dreaming Emmett (play), first produced in Albany, NY, 1986.

Beloved (novel), Knopf, 1987.

Jazz (novel), Knopf, 1992.

Playing in the Dark: Whiteness and the Literary Imagination (lectures), Harvard University Press, 1992.

(Editor) *Race-ing Justice, En-Gendering Power: Essays on Anita Hill, Clarence Thomas, and the Construction of Social Reality,* Pantheon, 1992.

Author of lyrics for "Honey and Rue," commissioned by Carnegie Hall for Kathleen Battle, with music by Andre Previn, 1992. Contributor of essays and reviews to numerous periodicals, including *New York Times Magazine.*

WORK IN PROGRESS: A journal; a revision of *The Bluest Eye;* a novel tentatively titled *Paradise,* third in a series chronicling the African American experience.

SIDELIGHTS: Through novels such as *The Bluest Eye, Song of Solomon, Beloved,* and *Jazz,* Toni Morrison has earned a reputation as a gifted storyteller whose troubled characters seek to find themselves and their cultural riches in a society that warps or impedes such essential growth. According to Charles Larson in the *Chicago Tribune Book World,* each of Morrison's novels "is as original as anything that has appeared in our literature in the last 20 years. The contemporaneity that unites them—the troubling persistence of racism in America—is infused with an urgency that only a black writer can have about our society."

Morrison's artistry has attracted critical acclaim as well as commercial success; *Dictionary of Literary Biography* contributor Susan L. Blake calls the author "an anomaly in two respects" because "she is a black writer who has achieved national prominence and popularity, and she is a popular writer who is taken seriously." Indeed, Morrison has won two of modern literature's most prestigious citations, the 1977 National Book Critics Circle Award for *Song of Solomon* and the 1988 Pulitzer Prize for *Beloved. Atlantic* correspondent Wilfrid Sheed notes: "Most black writers are privy, like the rest of us, to bits and pieces of the secret, the dark side of their group experience, but Toni Morrison uniquely seems to have all the keys on her chain, like a house detective. . . . She [uses] the run of the whole place, from ghetto to small town to ramshackle farmhouse, to bring back a panorama of black myth and reality that [dazzles] the senses." *Newsweek* contributor Jean Strouse observes: "Like all the best stories, [Morrison's] are driven by an abiding moral vision. Implicit in all her characters' grapplings with who they are is a large sense of human nature and love—and a reach for understanding of something larger than the moment."

"It seems somehow both constricting and inadequate to describe Toni Morrison as the country's preeminent black novelist, since in both gifts and accomplishments she transcends categorization," writes Jonathan Yardley in the *Washington Post Book World,* "yet the characterization is inescapable not merely because it is true but because the very nature of Morrison's work dictates it. Not merely has black American life been the central preoccupation of her . . . novels . . . but as she has matured she has concentrated on distilling all of black experience into her books; quite purposefully, it seems, she is striving not for the particular but for the universal." In her work Morrison strives to lay bare the injustice inherent in the black condition and blacks' efforts, individually and collectively, to transcend society's unjust boundaries. Blake notes that Morrison's novels explore "the difference between black humanity and white cultural values. This opposition produces the negative theme of the seduction and betrayal of black people by white culture . . . and the positive theme of the quest for cultural identity."

Quest for self is a motivating and organizing device in Morrison's writing, as is the role of family and community in nurturing or challenging the individual. In the *Times Literary Supplement,* Jennifer Uglow suggests that Morrison's novels "explore in particular the process of growing up black, female and poor. Avoiding generalities, Toni Morrison concentrates on the relation between the pressures of the community, patterns established within families, . . . and the developing sense of self." According to Dorothy H. Lee in *Black Women Writers (1950-1980): A Critical Evaluation,* Morrison is preoccupied "with the effect of the community on the individual's achievement and retention of an integrated, acceptable self. In treating this subject, she draws recurrently on myth and legend for story pattern and characters, returning repeatedly to the theory of *quest.* . . . The goals her characters seek to achieve are similar in their deepest implications, and yet the degree to which they attain them varies radically because each novel is cast in unique human terms." In Morrison's books, blacks must confront the notion that all understanding is accompanied by pain, just as all comprehension of national history must include the humiliations of slavery. She tempers this hard lesson by preserving "the richness of communal life against an outer world that denies its value" and by turning to "a heritage of folklore, not only to disclose patterns of living but also to close wounds," in the words of *Nation* contributor Brina Caplan.

Although Morrison herself told the *Chicago Tribune* that there is "epiphany and triumph" in every book she writes, some critics find her work nihilistic and her vision bleak. "The picture given by . . . Morrison of the plight of the decent, aspiring individual in the black family and community is more painful than the gloomiest impressions encouraged by either stereotype or sociology," observes Diane Johnson in the *New York Review of Books.* Johnson continues, "Undoubtedly white society is the ultimate oppressor, and not just of blacks; but, as Morrison [shows,] . . . the black person must first deal with the oppressor in the next room, or in the same bed, or no farther away than across the street." Morrison is a pioneer in the depiction of the hurt inflicted by blacks on blacks; for instance, her characters rarely achieve harmonious heterosexual relationships but are instead divided by futurelessness and the anguish of stifled existence. Uglow writes: "We have become attuned to novels . . . which locate oppression in the conflicts of blacks (usually men) trying to make it in a white world. By concentrating on the sense of violation experienced within black neighborhoods, even within families, Toni Morrison deprives us of stock responses and creates a more demanding and uncomfortable literature." *Village Voice* correspondent Vivian Gornick contends that the world Morrison creates "is thick with an atmosphere through which her characters move slowly, in pain, ignorance, and hunger. And to a very large degree Morrison has the compelling ability to make one believe that all of us (Morrison, the characters, the reader) are penetrating that dark and hurtful terrain—the feel of a human life—simultaneously." Uglow concludes that even the laughter of Morrison's characters "disguises pain, deprivation and violation. It is laughter at a series of bad, cruel jokes. . . . Nothing is what it seems; no appearance, no relationship can be trusted to endure."

Other critics detect a deeper undercurrent to Morrison's work that contains just the sort of epiphany for which she strives. "From book to book, Morrison's larger project grows clear," declares Ann Snitow in the *Voice Literary Supplement.* "First, she insists that every character bear the weight of responsibility for his or her own life. After she's measured out each one's private pain, she adds on to that the shared burden of what the whites did. Then, at last, she tries to find the place where her stories can lighten her readers' load, lift them up from their own and others' guilt, carry them to glory. . . . Her characters suffer—from their own limitations and the world's—but their inner life miraculously expands beyond the narrow law of cause and effect." *Harvard Advocate* essayist Faith Davis writes that despite the mundane boundaries of Morrison's characters' lives, the author "illuminates the complexity of their attitudes toward life. Having reached a quiet and extensive understanding of their situation, they can endure life's calamities. . . . Morrison never allows us to become indifferent to these people. . . . Her citizens . . . jump up from the pages vital and strong because she has made us care about the pain in their lives." In *Ms.,* Margo Jefferson concludes that Morrison's books "are filled with loss—lost friendship, lost love, lost customs, lost possibilities. And yet there is so much life in the smallest acts and gestures . . . that they are as much celebrations as elegies."

Morrison sees language as an expression of black experience, and her novels are characterized by vivid narration and dialogue. She acknowledges the powerful influences of her community and family on how she writes. In a PBS interview with Charlie Rose, Morrison said: "I'm completely informed by that community, by my extended family, the language particularly. Not just the survival, but the way they spoke, you know. The language of average, of poor African-Americans is always discredited as though it was impossible for them to speak, or they were stupid. But there was this incredible merging of new language and Biblical language and sermonic language and street language and standard that created a third thing for me. . . . A third kind of way of expressing myself. They pulled from all the places, and that's what I tried to incorporate in my books."

Village Voice essayist Susan Lydon observes that the author "works her magic charm above all with a love of language. Her soaring . . . style carries you like a river, sweeping doubt and disbelief away, and it is only gradually that one realizes her deadly serious intent." In the *Spectator,* Caroline Moorehead likewise notes that Morrison "writes energetically and richly, using words in a way very much her own. The effect is one of exoticism, an exciting curiousness in the language, a balanced sense of the possible that stops, always, short of the absurd." Although Morrison does not like to be called a poetic writer, critics often comment on the lyrical quality of her prose. "Morrison's style has always moved fluidly between tough-minded realism and lyric descriptiveness," notes Margo Jefferson in *Newsweek.* "Vivid dialogue, capturing the drama and extravagance of black speech, gives way to an impressionistic evocation of physical pain or an ironic, essay-like analysis of the varieties of religious hypocrisy." Uglow writes: "The word 'elegant' is often applied to Toni Morrison's writing; it employs sophisticated narrative devices, shifting perspectives and resonant images and displays an obvious delight in the potential of language." *Nation* contributor Earl Frederick concludes that Morrison, "with an ear as sharp as glass . . . has listened to the music of black talk and deftly uses it as the palette knife to create black lives and to provide some of the best fictional dialogue around today."

According to Jean Strouse, Morrison "comes from a long line of people who did what they had to do to survive. It is their stories she tells in her novels—tales of the suffering and richness, the eloquence and tragedies of the black American experience." Morrison was born Chloe Anthony Wofford in Lorain, Ohio, a small town near the shores of Lake Erie. *New York Review of Books* correspondent Darryl Pinckney describes her particular community as "close enough to the Ohio River for the people who lived [there] to feel the torpor of the South, the nostalgia for its folkways, to sense the old Underground Railroad underfoot like a hidden stream." While never explicitly autobiographical, Morrison's fictions draw upon her youthful experiences in Ohio. In an essay for *Black Women Writers at Work* she claims: "I am from the Midwest so I have a special affection for it. My beginnings are always there. . . . No matter what I write, I begin there. . . . It's the matrix for me. . . . Ohio also offers an escape from stereotyped black settings. It is neither plantation nor ghetto."

Two important aspects of Chloe Wofford's childhood—community spirit and the supernatural—inform Toni Morrison's mature writing. In a *Publishers Weekly* interview, Morrison suggests ways in which her community influenced her. "There is this town which is both a support system and a hammer at the same time," she notes. "Approval was not the acquisition of things; approval was given for the maturity and the dignity with which one handled oneself. Most black people in particular were, and still are, very fastidious about manners, very careful about behavior and the rules that operate within the community. The sense of organized activity, what I thought at that time was burdensome, turns out now to have within it a gift—which is, I never had to be taught how to hold a job, how to make it work, how to handle my time."

On several levels a unique and sometimes eccentric individual figures in Morrison's fictional reconstruction of black community life. "There is always an elder there," she notes of her work in *Black Women Writers: A Critical Evaluation.* "And these ancestors are not just parents, they are sort of timeless people whose relationships to the characters are benevolent, instructive, and protective, and they provide a certain kind of wisdom." Sometimes this figure imparts his or her wisdom from beyond the grave; from an early age Morrison absorbed the folklore and beliefs of a culture for which the supernatural holds power and portent. Strouse notes that Morrison's world, both within and outside her fiction, is "filled with signs, visitations, ways of knowing that [reach] beyond the five senses."

Morrison's birthplace of Lorain, Ohio, is in fact the setting of *The Bluest Eye,* published in 1969. Morrison's first novel portrays "in poignant terms the tragic condition of blacks in a racist America," to quote Chikwenye Okonjo Ogunyemi in *Critique: Studies in Modern Fiction.* In *The Bluest Eye,* Morrison depicts the onset of black self-hatred as occasioned by white American ideals such as "Dick and Jane" primers and Shirley Temple movies. The principal character, Pecola Breedlove, is literally maddened by the disparity between her existence and the pictures of beauty and gentility disseminated by the dominant white culture. As Phyllis R. Klotman notes in the *Black American Literature Forum,* Morrison "uses the contrast between Shirley Temple and Pecola . . . to underscore the irony of black experience. Whether one learns acceptability from the formal educational experience or from cultural symbols, the effect is the same: self-hatred." Darwin T. Turner discusses the novel's intentions in *Black Women Writers: A Critical Evaluation.* Morrison's fictional milieu, writes Turner, is "a world of grotesques—individuals whose psyches have been deformed by their efforts to assume false identities, their failures to achieve meaningful identities, or simply their inability to retain and communicate love."

Morrison elaborated on the theme of self-esteem in *The Bluest Eye* during the PBS interview. "I was really writing a book I wanted to read. . . . I hadn't seen a book in which black girls were center stage. . . . And I had a major, major question in my mind at that time, which was, How does a child learn self-loathing, for racial purposes? Who enables it? How is it infectious? And what might be the consequences?" Self-loathing can be learned, she says, from a society that lies about what is attractive. "It's interior death. You never have an opportunity to develop what's really valuable, which is grace, balance, health, virtue—all those good things that each of us can be."

Blake characterizes *The Bluest Eye* as a novel of initiation, exploring that common theme in American literature from a minority viewpoint. Ogunyemi likewise contends that, in essence, Morrison presents "old problems in a fresh language and with a fresh perspective. A central force of the work derives from her power to draw vignettes and her ability to portray emotions, seeing the world through the eyes of adolescent girls." Klotman, who calls the book "a novel of growing up, of growing up young and black and female in America," concludes her review with the comment that the "rite of passage, initiating the young into womanhood at first tenuous and uncertain, is sensitively depicted. . . . *The Bluest Eye* is an extraordinarily passionate yet gentle work, the language lyrical yet precise—it is a novel for all seasons."

In *Sula,* Morrison's 1973 novel, the author once again presents a pair of black women who must come to terms with their lives. Set in a Midwestern black community called The Bottom, the story follows two friends, Sula and Nel, from childhood to old age and death. Snitow claims that through Sula, Morrison has discovered "a way to offer her people an insight and sense of recovered self so dignified and glowing that no worldly pain could dull the final light." Indeed, *Sula* is a tale of rebel and conformist in which the conformity is dictated by the solid inhabitants of The Bottom and even the rebellion gains strength from the community's disapproval. *New York Times Book Review* contributor Sara Blackburn contends, however, that the book is "too vital and rich" to be consigned to the category of allegory. Morrison's "extravagantly beautiful, doomed characters are locked in a world where hope for the future is a foreign commodity, yet they are enormously, achingly alive," writes Blackburn. "And this book about them—and about how their beauty is drained back and frozen—is a howl of love and rage, playful and funny as well as hard and bitter." In the words of *American Literature* essayist Jane S. Bakerman, Morrison "uses the maturation story of Sula and Nel as the core of a host of other stories, but it is the chief unification device for the novel and achieves its own unity, again, through the clever manipulation of the themes of sex, race, and love. Morrison has undertaken a . . . difficult task in *Sula.* Unquestionably, she has succeeded."

Other critics have echoed Bakerman's sentiments about *Sula.* Yardley declares: "What gives this terse, imaginative novel its genuine distinction is the quality of Toni Morrison's prose. *Sula* is admirable enough as a study of its title character, . . . but its real strength lies in Morrison's writing, which at times has the resonance of poetry and is precise, vivid and controlled throughout." Turner also claims that in *Sula* "Morrison evokes her verbal magic occasionally by lyric descriptions that carry the reader deep into the soul of the character. . . . Equally effective, however, is her art of narrating action in a lean prose that uses adjectives cautiously while creating memorable vivid images." In her review, Davis concludes that a "beautiful and haunting atmosphere emerges out of the wreck of these folks' lives, a quality that is absolutely convincing and absolutely precise." *Sula* was nominated for a National Book Award in 1974.

From the insular lives she depicted in her first two novels, Morrison moved, in *Song of Solomon,* to a national and historical perspective on black American life. During the PBS interview, she explained how she made this happen. "*Song of Solomon* was about this sort of political problem that young adults have, which is trying to combine upward mobility—middle-class, bourgeois, upward mobility—with some kind of respect and reverence for their ancestors. There's always this conflict, as though if you go to college, you can't go back to Lorain, Ohio; or if you stay in Lorain, Ohio, you have to despise everybody who went on. Not quite that simple, but you understand what that tension is. So I was trying to figure out how somebody who's in his late 20s or 30s got educated . . . and what would help inform him to learn how to be a complete human being, without these conflicts, without these self-destructive impulses for material things. . . . I try to figure out what kinds of people can manifest that for me . . . and set that up. Then I have to fully realize the characters and sort of love them, without approving of them necessarily, but really love them, and my ernest desire is whomever they are . . . to do them justice."

"Here the depths of the younger work are still evident," contends Reynolds Price in the *New York Times Book Review,* "but now they thrust outward, into wider fields, for longer intervals, encompassing many more lives. The result is a long prose tale that surveys nearly a century of American history as it impinges upon a single family." With an intermixture of the fantastic and the realistic, *Song of Solomon* relates the journey of a character named Milkman Dead into an understanding of his family heritage and hence, himself. Lee writes: "Figuratively, [Milkman] travels from innocence to awareness, i.e., from ignorance of origins, heritage, identity, and communal responsibility to knowledge and acceptance. He moves from selfish and materialistic dilettantism to an understanding of brotherhood. With his release of personal ego, he is able to find a place in the whole. There is, then, a universal—indeed mythic—pattern here. He journeys from spiritual death to rebirth, a direction symbolized by his discovery of the secret power of flight. Mythically, liberation and transcendence follow the discovery of self." Blake suggests that the connection Milkman discovers with his family's past helps him to connect meaningfully with his contemporaries; *Song of Solomon,* Blake notes, "dramatizes dialectical approaches to the challenges of black life." According to Anne Z. Mickelson in *Reaching Out: Sensitivity and Order in Recent American Fiction by Women,* history itself "becomes a choral symphony to Milkman, in which each individual voice has a chance to speak and contribute to his growing sense of well-being."

Mickelson also observes that *Song of Solomon* represents for blacks "a break out of the confining life into the realm of possibility." Charles Larson comments on this theme in a *Washington Post Book World* review. The novel's subject matter, Larson explains, is "the origins of black consciousness in America, and the individual's relationship to that heritage." However, Larson adds, "skilled writer that she is, Morrison has transcended this theme so that the reader rarely feels that this is simply another novel about ethnic identity. So marvelously orchestrated is Morrison's narrative that it not only excels on all of its respective levels, not only works for all of its interlocking components, but also—in the end—says something about life (and death) for all of us. Milkman's epic journey . . . is a profound examination of the individual's understanding of, and, perhaps, even transcendence of the inevitable fate of his life." Gornick concludes: "There are so many individual moments of power and beauty in *Song of Solomon* that, ultimately, one closes the book warmed through by the richness of its sympathy, and by its breathtaking feel for the nature of sexual sorrow."

Song of Solomon won the National Book Critics Circle Award in 1977. It was also the first novel by a black writer to become a Book-of-the-Month Club selection since Richard Wright's *Native Son* was published in 1940. *World Literature Today* reviewer Richard K. Barksdale calls the work "a book that will not only withstand the test of time but endure a second and third reading by those conscientious readers who love a well-wrought piece of fiction." Describing the novel as "a stunningly beautiful book" in her *Washington Post Book World* piece, Anne Tyler adds: "I would call the book poetry, but that would seem to be denying its considerable power as a story. Whatever name you give it, it's full of magnificent people, each of them complex and multilayered, even the narrowest of them narrow in extravagant ways." Price deems *Song of Solomon* "a long story, . . . and better than good. Toni Morrison has earned attention and praise. Few Americans know, and can say, more than she has in this wise and spacious novel."

Morrison's 1981 book, *Tar Baby,* remained on best-seller lists for four months. A novel of ideas, the work dramatizes the fact that complexion is a far more subtle issue than the simple polarization of black and white. Set on a lush Caribbean Island, *Tar Baby* explores the passionate love affair of Jadine, a Sorbonne-educated black model, and Son, a handsome knockabout with a strong aversion to white culture. According to Caplan, Morrison's concerns "are race, class, culture and the effects of late capitalism—heavy freight for any narrative. . . . She is attempting to stabilize complex visions of society—that is, to examine competitive ideas. . . . Because the primary function of Morrison's characters is to voice representative opinions, they arrive on stage vocal and highly conscious, their histories symbolically indicated or merely sketched. Her brief sketches, however, are clearly the work of an artist who can, when she chooses, model the mind in depth and detail." In a *Dictionary of Literary Biography Yearbook* essay, Elizabeth B. House outlines *Tar Baby*'s major themes; namely, "the difficulty of settling conflicting claims between one's past and present and the destruction which abuse of power can bring. As Morrison examines these problems in *Tar Baby,* she suggests no easy way to understand what one's link to a heritage should be, nor does she offer infallible methods for dealing with power. Rather, with an astonishing insight and grace, she demonstrates the pervasiveness of such dilemmas and the degree to which they affect human beings, both black and white."

Tar Baby uncovers racial and sexual conflicts without offering solutions, but most critics agree that Morrison indicts all of her characters—black and white—for their thoughtless devaluations of others. *New York Times Book Review* correspondent John Irving claims: "What's so powerful, and subtle, about Miss Morrison's presentation of the tension between blacks and whites is that she conveys it almost entirely through the suspicions and prejudices of her black characters. . . . Miss Morrison uncovers all the stereotypical racial fears felt by whites and blacks alike. Like any ambitious writer, she's unafraid to employ these stereotypes—she embraces the representative qualities of her characters without embarrassment, then proceeds to make them individuals too." *New Yorker* essayist Susan Lardner praises Morrison for her "power to be absolutely persuasive against her own preferences, suspicions, and convictions, implied or plainly expressed," and Strouse likewise contends that the author "has produced that rare commodity, a truly public novel about the condition of society, examining the relations between blacks and whites, men and women, civilization and nature. . . . It wraps its messages in a highly potent love story." Irving suggests that Morrison's greatest accomplishment "is that she has raised her novel above the social realism that too many black novels and women's novels are trapped in. She has succeeded in writing about race and women symbolically."

Reviewers have praised *Tar Baby* for its provocative themes and for its evocative narration. *Los Angeles Times* contributor Elaine Kendall calls the book "an intricate and sophisticated novel, moving from a realistic and orderly beginning to a mystical and ambiguous end. Morrison has taken classically simple story elements and realigned them so artfully that we perceive the old pattern in a startlingly different way. Although this territory has been explored by dozens of novelists, Morrison depicts it with such vitality that it seems newly discovered." In the *Washington Post Book World,* Webster Schott claims: "There is so much that is good, sometimes dazzling, about *Tar Baby*—poetic language, . . . arresting images, fierce intelligence—that . . . one becomes entranced by Toni Morrison's story. The settings are so vivid the characters must be alive. The emotions they feel are so intense they must be real people." Maureen Howard states in *New Republic* that the work "is as carefully patterned as a well-written poem. . . . *Tar Baby* is a good American novel in which we can discern a new lightness and brilliance in Toni Morrison's enchantment with language and in her curiously polyphonic stories that echo life." Schott concludes: "One of fiction's pleasures is to have your mind scratched and your intellectual habits challenged. While *Tar Baby* has shortcomings, lack of provocation isn't one of them. Morrison owns a powerful intelligence. It's run by courage. She calls to account conventional wisdom and accepted attitude at nearly every turn."

In addition to her own writing, Morrison has served as an editor at Random House and has helped to publish the work of other noted black Americans, including Toni Cade Bambara, Gayle Jones, Angela Davis, and Muhammad Ali. Discussing her aims as an editor in a quotation printed in the *Dictionary of Literary Biography,* Morrison said: "I look very hard for black fiction because I want to participate in developing a canon of black work. We've had the first rush of black entertainment, where blacks were writing for whites, and whites were encouraging this kind of self-flagellation. Now we can get down to the craft of writing, where black people are talking to black people." One of Morrison's important projects for Random House was *The Black Book,* an anthology of items that illustrate the history of black Americans. *Ms.* magazine correspondent Dorothy Eugenia Robinson describes the work: "*The Black Book* is the pain and pride of rediscovering the collective black experience. It is finding the essence of ourselves and holding on. *The Black Book* is a kind of scrapbook of patiently assembled samplings of black history and culture. What has evolved is a pictorial folk journey of black people, places, events, handcrafts, inventions, songs, and folklore. . . . *The Black Book* informs, disturbs, maybe even shocks. It unsettles complacency and demands confrontation with raw reality. It is by no means an easy book to experience, but it's a necessary one."

While preparing *The Black Book* for publication, Morrison uncovered the true and shocking story of a runaway slave who, at the point of recapture, murdered her infant child so it would not be doomed to a lifetime of slavery. For Morrison the story encapsulated the fierce psychic cruelty of an institutionalized system that sought to destroy the basic emotional bonds between men and women, and worse, between parent and child. "I certainly thought I knew as much about slavery as anybody," Morrison told the *Los Angeles Times.* "But it was the interior life I needed to find out about." It is this "interior life" in the throes of slavery that constitutes the theme of Morrison's Pulitzer Prize-winning novel, *Beloved.* Set in Reconstruction-era Cincinnati, the book centers on characters who struggle fruitlessly to keep their painful recollections of the past at bay. They are haunted, both physically and spiritually, by the legacies slavery has bequeathed to them. The question in this novel, Morrison told PBS host Charlie Rose, was "Who is the beloved? Who is the person who lives inside us that is the one you can trust, who is the best thing you are. And in that instant, for that segment, because I had planned books around that theme, it was the effort of a woman to love her children, to raise her children, to be responsible for her children. And the fact that it was during slavery made all those things impossible for her."

According to Snitow, *Beloved* "staggers under the terror of its material—as so much holocaust writing does and must." In *People* magazine, V. R. Peterson describes *Beloved* as "a brutally powerful, mesmerizing story about the inescapable, excruciating legacy of slavery. Behind each new event and each new character lies another event and another story until finally the reader meets a community of proud, daring people, inextricably bound by culture and experience." Through the lives of ex-slaves Sethe and her would-be lover Paul D., readers "experience American slavery as it was lived by those who were its objects of exchange, both at its best—which wasn't very good—and at its worst, which was as bad as can be imagined," writes Margaret Atwood in the *New York Times Book Review.* "Above all, it is seen as one of the most viciously anti-family institutions human beings have ever devised. The slaves are motherless, fatherless, deprived of their mates, their children, their kin. It is a world in which people suddenly vanish and are never seen again, not through accident or covert operation or terrorism, but as a matter of everyday legal policy." *New York Times* columnist Michiko Kakutani contends that *Beloved* "possesses the heightened power and resonance of myth—its characters, like those in opera or Greek drama, seem larger than life and their actions, too, tend to strike us as enactments of ancient rituals and passions. To describe 'Beloved' only in these terms, however, is to diminish its immediacy, for the novel also remains precisely grounded in American reality—the reality of Black history as experienced in the wake of the Civil War."

Acclaim for *Beloved* has come from both sides of the Atlantic. In his *Chicago Tribune* piece, Larson claims that the work "is the context out of which all of Morrison's earlier novels were written. In her darkest and most probing novel, Toni Morrison has demonstrated once again the stunning powers that place her in the first ranks of our living novelists." *Los Angeles Times Book Review* contributor John Leonard likewise expresses the opinion that the novel "belongs on the highest shelf of American literature, even if half a dozen canonized white boys have to be elbowed off. . . . Without *Beloved* our imagination of the nation's self has a hole in it big enough to die from." Atwood states: "Ms. Morrison's versatility and technical and emotional range appear to know no bounds. If there were any doubts about her stature as a pre-eminent American novelist, of her own or any other generation, *Beloved* will put them to rest." London *Times* reviewer Nicholas Shakespeare concludes that *Beloved* "is a novel propelled by the cadences of . . . songs—the first singing of a people hardened by their suffering, people who have been hanged and whipped and mortgaged at the hands of white people—the men without skin. From Toni Morrison's pen it is a sound that breaks the back of words, making *Beloved* a great novel."

Jazz, the second in Morrison's suite of novels about black life from the 1800s to the present, continues many themes set out in *Beloved:* the individual's struggle to establish and sustain a personal identity, the clash between individual interests and community interests, and which takes priority. "Here," says Andrea Stuart, "the desire for individuation and rebirth collides with another of the author's favourite themes: the futility, even the danger, of jettisoning one's history." As Morrison noted in her PBS interview, the question, Who is the beloved? also repeats itself. The answer in *Jazz* has to do with "real passion," Morrison said, "the sort of thing where you say, 'I can't live without you,' and you really mean it." The inspiration came from a photo of a young girl in a coffin by the Harlem Renaissance photographer James VanderZee. Her boyfriend had shot her, and she kept his identity secret so that he could escape. Morrison explained, "And I thought, now if that isn't the most romantic teenage passion! And to put it right in the jazz age, which is full of passion, romance, music, license—you know, black people in the city, empowered now. . . . I wanted the book to really be about the people who didn't know they were living in an era."

Jazz is about a middle-aged couple—Joe Trace, waiter and door-to-door cosmetics salesman, and his wife, Violet, a home hairdresser—who migrated to Harlem from the rural South in the early 1900s. As background, Morrison offers some scenes of the brutal Virginia country life blacks endured as sharecroppers at the end of the nineteenth century. By contrast, Joe and Violet are initially dazzled by the prospect of life in New York. But novelist Edna O'Brien's critique in the *New York Times Book Review* describes the main characters as "people enthralled, then deceived by 'the music the world makes.' " Reality sets in.

Despite Joe's attachment to Violet, he falls in love with Dorcas, who is a teenager, then kills her when she tries to leave him. No one wants to turn Joe in. At the funeral parlor, Violet attempts to slash Dorcas's face but is thrown out, running home and freeing her treasured birds. Later she establishes a relationship with Dorcas's mother. Critic Richard Eder of the *Los Angeles Times Book Review* notes the grief and humor of the story, writing that *Jazz* "could have been either a tragedy or a melodrama with appropriate climactic endings. But Morrison has written a book that ruminates and discourses, . . . that follows its riffs through pain and celebration, . . . that is, in her word, jazz." In Chicago *Tribune Books,* acclaimed author Michael Dorris calls it a "brilliant, daring new novel" and observes that *Jazz* "is much more than 'story.' . . . It is the blues song of people who understand suffering and survival."

In another 1992 book, the nonfiction work *Playing in the Dark: Whiteness and the Literary Imagination,* Morrison examines how black people, often portrayed in stereotypical ways or ignored by white writers, nonetheless shaped white literature. It is a "revolutionary little monograph," in the opinion of *Los Angeles Times Book Review* contributor Diane Middlebrook, "a major work by a major American author." Morrison examines the writings of literary masters such as Saul Bellow, Willa Cather, Ernest Hemingway, Herman Melville, Edgar Allan Poe, and Mark Twain, exploring how their characters and symbolism reflected the African presence. Writing in the *New York Times Book Review,* Wendy Steiner relates how in literature blacks and blackness have been used variously to ward off whites' fears of powerlessness and to explore sexuality, for instance. But Morrison also explores a more positive side of stories of slavery, that of illuminating human nature. Morrison's study, the critic suggests, "is meant to teach a black author about white motivation. It should also teach whites about how they have constructed not only black but white identity, and how they have contemplated their own humanity by observing the dehumanization of others." Through her subtle and perceptive analysis, asserts Chicago *Tribune Books* contributor Michael Eric Dyson, Morrison shows that "an Africanist presence was essential in forming and extending an American national literature."

Morrison has no objection to being called a black woman writer. As she told the *New York Times:* "I really think the range of emotions and perceptions I have had access to as a black person and a female person are greater than those of people who are neither. . . . My world did not shrink because I was a black female writer. It just got bigger." Nor does she strive for that much-vaunted universality that purports to be a hallmark of fine fiction. "I never asked Tolstoy to write for me, a little colored girl in Lorain, Ohio," she told the *New Republic.* "I never asked [James] Joyce not to mention Catholicism or the world of Dublin. Never. And I don't know why I should be asked to explain your life to you. We have splendid writers to do that, but I am not one of them. It is that business of being universal, a word hopelessly stripped of meaning for me. [William] Faulkner wrote what I suppose could be called regional literature and had it published all over the world. That's what I wish to do. If I tried to write a universal novel, it would be water. Behind this question is the suggestion that to write for black people is somehow to diminish the writing. From my perspective there are only black people. When I say 'people,' that's what I mean."

Black woman writer or simply American novelist, Toni Morrison is a prominent and respected figure in modern letters. In the *Detroit News,* Larson suggests that hers has been "among the most exciting literary careers of the last decade" and that each of her books "has made a quantum jump forward." Ironically, Elizabeth House commends Morrison for the universal nature of her work. "Unquestionably," House writes, "Toni Morrison is an important novelist who continues to develop her talent. Part of her appeal, of course, lies in her extraordinary ability to create beautiful language and striking characters. However, Morrison's most important gift, the one which gives her a major author's universality, is the insight with which she writes of problems all humans face. . . . At the core of all her novels is a penetrating view of the unyielding, heartbreaking dilemmas which torment people of all races." Snitow notes that the author "wants to tend the imagination, search for an expansion of the possible, nurture a spiritual richness in the black tradition even after 300 years in the white desert." Dorothy Lee concludes of Morrison's accomplishments: "Though there are unifying aspects in her novels, there is not a dully repetitive sameness. Each casts the problems in specific, imaginative terms, and the exquisite, poetic language awakens our senses as she communicates an often ironic vision with moving imagery. Each novel reveals the acuity of her perception of psychological motivation of the female especially, of the Black particularly, and of the human generally."

"The problem I face as a writer is to make my stories mean something," Morrison states in *Black Women Writers at Work.* "You can have wonderful, interesting people, a fascinating story, but it's not about anything. It has no real substance. I want my books to always be about something that is important to me, and the subjects that are important in the world are the same ones that have always been important." In *Black Women Writers: A Critical Evaluation,* she elaborates on this idea. Fiction, she writes, "should be beautiful, and powerful, but it should also work. It should have something in it that enlightens; something in it that opens the door and points the way. Something in it that suggests what the conflicts are, what the problems are. But it need not solve those problems because it is not a case study, it is not a recipe." The author who has said that writing "is discovery; it's talking deep within myself" told the *New York Times Book Review* that the essential theme in her growing body of fiction is "how and why we learn to live this life intensely and well."

BIOGRAPHICAL/CRITICAL SOURCES:

BOOKS

Authors and Artists for Young Adults, Volume 1, Gale, 1989.

Bell, Roseann P., editor, *Sturdy Black Bridges: Visions of Black Women in Literature,* Doubleday, 1979.

Black Literature Criticism, Gale, 1992.

Christian, Barbara, *Black Women Novelists: The Development of a Tradition, 1892-1976,* Greenwood Press, 1980.

Concise Dictionary of American Literary Biography: Broadening Views, 1968-1988, Gale, 1989.

Contemporary Literary Criticism, Gale, Volume 4, 1975, Volume 10, 1979, Volume 22, 1982, Volume 55, 1989.

Cooper-Clark, Diana, *Interviews with Contemporary Novelists,* St. Martin's, 1986.

Dictionary of Literary Biography, Gale, Volume 6: *American Novelists since World War II,* 1980, Volume 33: *Afro-American Fiction Writers after 1955,* 1984.

Dictionary of Literary Biography Yearbook: 1981, Gale, 1982.

Evans, Mari, editor, *Black Women Writers (1950-1980): A Critical Evaluation,* Doubleday, 1984.

Mekkawi, Mod, *Toni Morrison: A Bibliography,* Howard University Library, 1986.

Mickelson, Anne Z., *Reaching Out: Sensitivity and Order in Recent American Fiction by Women,* Scarecrow Press, 1979.

Ruas, Charles, *Conversations with American Writers,* Knopf, 1985.

Tate, Claudia, editor, *Black Women Writers at Work,* Continuum, 1986.

PERIODICALS

American Literature, January, 1981.

Atlantic, April, 1981.

Black American Literature Forum, summer, 1978; winter, 1979.

Black Scholar, March, 1978.

Black World, June, 1974.

Callaloo, October-February, 1981.

Chicago Tribune, October 27, 1987.

Chicago Tribune Book World, March 8, 1981.

CLA Journal, June, 1979; June, 1981.

Commentary, August, 1981.

Contemporary Literature, winter, 1983.

Critique: Studies in Modern Fiction, Volume 19, number 1, 1977.

Detroit News, March 29, 1981.

Essence, July, 1981; June, 1983; October, 1987.

First World, winter, 1977.

Harper's Bazaar, March, 1983.

Harvard Advocate, Volume 107, number 4, 1974.

Hudson Review, spring, 1978.

Kirkus Reviews, September 1, 1992.

Los Angeles Times, March 31, 1981; October 14, 1987.

Los Angeles Times Book Review, August 30, 1987; April 19, 1992, pp. 3, 5; May 24, 1992, pp. 2, 7.

Massachusetts Review, autumn, 1977.
MELUS, fall, 1980.
Ms., June, 1974; December, 1974; August, 1987.
Nation, July 6, 1974; November 19, 1977; May 2, 1981.
New Republic, December 3, 1977; March 21, 1981.
New Statesman, May 1, 1992, p. 39.
Newsweek, November 30, 1970; January 7, 1974; September 12, 1977; March 30, 1981; April 27, 1992, p. 66.
New York, April 13, 1981.
New Yorker, November 7, 1977; June 15, 1981.
New York Post, January 26, 1974.
New York Review of Books, November 10, 1977; April 30, 1981.
New York Times, November 13, 1970; September 6, 1977; March 21, 1981; August 26, 1987; September 2, 1987.
New York Times Book Review, November 1, 1970; December 30, 1973; June 2, 1974; September 11, 1977; March 29, 1981; September 13, 1987; April 5, 1992, pp. 1, 25, 29.
New York Times Magazine, August 22, 1971; August 11, 1974; July 4, 1976; May 20, 1979.
Obsidian, spring/summer, 1979.
People, July 29, 1974; November 30, 1987.
Philadelphia Inquirer, April 1, 1988.
Publishers Weekly, August 21, 1987; August 17, 1992.
Saturday Review, September 17, 1977.
Spectator, December 9, 1978; February 2, 1980; December 19, 1981.
Studies in Black Literature, Volume 6, 1976.
Time, September 12, 1977; March 16, 1981; September 21, 1987; April 27, 1992, p. 70.
Times (London), October 15, 1987.
Times Literary Supplement, October 4, 1974; November 24, 1978; February 8, 1980; December 19, 1980; October 30, 1981; October 16-22, 1987; May 8, 1992, p. 21.
Tribune Books (Chicago), August 30, 1988; April 19, 1992, pp. 1, 5; May 3, 1992, pp. 7, 11.
U.S. News and World Report, October 19, 1987.
Village Voice, August 29, 1977; July 1-7, 1981.
Vogue, April, 1981; January, 1986.
Voice Literary Supplement, September, 1987.
Washington Post, February 3, 1974; March 6, 1974; September 30, 1977; April 8, 1981; February 9, 1983; October 5, 1987.
Washington Post Book World, February 3, 1974; September 4, 1977; December 4, 1977; March 22, 1981; September 6, 1987; April 19, 1992, pp. 1-2.
World Literature Today, summer, 1978.

OTHER

Interview on *Charlie Rose,* PBS, May 7, 1993.*

MOWAT, Farley (McGill) 1921-

PERSONAL: Born May 12, 1921, in Belleville, Ontario, Canada; son of Angus McGill (a librarian) and Helen Elizabeth (Thomson) Mowat; married Frances Thornhill, December 21, 1947 (marriage ended, 1959); married Claire Angel Wheeler (a writer), March, 1964; children: (first marriage) Robert Alexander, David Peter. *Education:* University of Toronto, B.A., 1949.

ADDRESSES: *Home*—Port Hope, Ontario, and Cape Breton, Nova Scotia. *Office*—c/o Key Porter Books Ltd., 70 The Esplanade, Toronto, Ontario M5E 1R2, Canada.

CAREER: Author. *Military service:* Canadian Army Infantry, 1939-45; became captain.

AWARDS, HONORS: President's Medal for best short story, University of Western Ontario, 1952, for "Eskimo Spring"; Anisfield-Wolfe Award for contribution to interracial relations, 1954, for *People of the Deer;* Governor General's Medal, 1957, and Book of the Year Award, Canadian Association of Children's Librarians, both for *Lost in the Barrens;* Canadian Women's Clubs Award, 1958, for *The Dog Who Wouldn't Be;* Hans Christian Andersen International Award, 1958; Boys' Clubs of America Junior Book Award, 1962, for *Owls in the Family;* National Association of Independent Schools Award, 1963, for juvenile books; Hans Christian Andersen Honours List, 1965, for juvenile books; Canadian Centennial Medal, 1967; Stephen Leacock Medal for humor, 1970, and L'Etoile de la Mer Honours List, 1972, both for *The Boat Who Wouldn't Float;* D.Lit., Laurentian University, 1970; Vicky Metcalf Award, 1970; Mark Twain Award, 1971; Doctor of Law from Lethbridge University, 1973, University of Toronto, 1973, and University of Prince Edward Island, 1979; Curran Award, 1977, for "contributions to understanding wolves"; Queen Elizabeth II Jubilee Medal, 1978; Knight of Mark Twain, 1980; Officer, Order of Canada, 1981; Doctor of Literature, University of Victoria, 1982, and Lakehead University, 1986; Author's Award, Foundation for the Advancement of Canadian Letters, 1985, for *Sea of Slaughter;* Book of the Year designation, Foundation for the Advancement of Canadian Letters, and named Author of the Year, Canadian Booksellers Association, both 1988, both for *Virunga;* Gemini Award for best documentary script, 1989, for *The New North;* Take Back the Nation Award, Council of Canadians, 1991.

WRITINGS:

NONFICTION

People of the Deer, Little, Brown, 1952, revised edition, McClelland & Stewart, 1975.
The Regiment, McClelland & Stewart, 1955, revised edition, 1973.

The Dog Who Wouldn't Be, Little, Brown, 1957.

(Editor) Samuel Hearne, *Coppermine Journey: An Account of a Great Adventure,* Little, Brown, 1958.

The Grey Seas Under, Little, Brown, 1958.

The Desperate People, Little, Brown, 1959, revised, McClelland & Stewart, 1976.

(Editor) *Ordeal by Ice* (first part of "The Top of the World" series; also see below), McClelland & Stewart, 1960, Little, Brown, 1961.

The Serpent's Coil, McClelland & Stewart, 1961, Little, Brown, 1962.

Never Cry Wolf, Little, Brown, 1963, revised edition, McClelland & Stewart, 1973.

Westviking: The Ancient Norse in Greenland and North America, Little, Brown, 1965.

(Editor) *The Polar Passion: The Quest for the North Pole, with Selections from Arctic Journals* (second part of "The Top of the World" series; also see below), McClelland & Stewart, 1967, Little, Brown, 1968, revised edition, 1973.

Canada North, Little, Brown, 1967.

This Rock within the Sea: A Heritage Lost, photographs by John de Visser, Little, Brown, 1969, new edition, McClelland & Stewart, 1976.

The Boat Who Wouldn't Float, McClelland & Stewart, 1969, Little, Brown, 1970.

Sibir: My Discovery of Siberia, McClelland & Stewart, 1970, revised edition, 1973, published as *The Siberians,* Little, Brown, 1971.

A Whale for the Killing, Little, Brown, 1972.

Wake of the Great Sealers, illustrated by David Blackwood, Little, Brown, 1973.

(Editor) *Tundra: Selections from the Great Accounts of Arctic Land Voyages* (third part of "The Top of the World" series; also see below), McClelland & Stewart, 1973, Peregrine Smith, 1990.

(Editor) *Top of the World Trilogy* (includes *Ordeal by Ice, The Polar Passion,* and *Tundra*), McClelland & Stewart, 1976.

The Great Betrayal: Arctic Canada Now, Little, Brown, 1976, published as *Canada North Now: The Great Betrayal,* McClelland & Stewart, 1976.

And No Birds Sang (memoir), McClelland & Stewart, 1979, Little, Brown, 1980.

The World of Farley Mowat: A Selection from His Works, edited by Peter Davison, Little, Brown, 1980.

Sea of Slaughter, Atlantic Monthly Press, 1984.

My Discovery of America, Little, Brown, 1985.

Woman in the Mists: The Story of Dian Fossey and the Mountain Gorillas of Africa, Warner Books, 1987, published as *Virunga: The Passion of Dian Fossey,* McClelland & Stewart, 1987.

The New Founde Land: A Personal Voyage of Discovery, McClelland & Stewart, 1989.

Rescue the Earth, McClelland & Stewart, 1990.

My Father's Son: Memories of War and Peace, Houghton, 1993.

Born Naked, Key Porter, 1993, Houghton, 1994.

FOR YOUNG ADULTS

Lost in the Barrens (novel), illustrated by Charles Geer, Little, Brown, 1956, published as *Two Against the North,* illustrated by Alan Daniel, Scholastic-TAB, 1977.

Owls in the Family, illustrated by Robert Frankenberg, Little, Brown, 1961.

The Black Joke (novel), illustrated by D. Johnson, McClelland & Stewart, 1962, illustrated by Victory Mays, Little, Brown, 1963.

The Curse of the Viking Grave (novel), illustrated by Geer, Little, Brown, 1966.

SHORT STORIES

The Snow Walker, McClelland & Stewart, 1975, Little, Brown, 1976.

OTHER

Also author of television screenplays *Sea Fare* and *Diary of a Boy on Vacation,* both 1964. Contributor to *Cricket's Choice,* Open Court, 1974; contributor to periodicals, including *Argosy, Maclean's,* and *Saturday Evening Post.* Mowat's books have been translated into more than thirty languages and anthologized in more than two hundred works.

A collection of Mowat's manuscripts is housed at McMaster University, Hamilton, Ontario.

WORK IN PROGRESS: Two feature films; an autobiography.

ADAPTATIONS:

A Whale for the Killing (television movie), American Broadcasting Companies, Inc. (ABC-TV), 1980.

Never Cry Wolf (feature film), Buena Vista, 1983.

The New North (documentary), Norwolf/Noralpha/CTV, 1989.

Sea of Slaughter (award-winning documentary; part of "The Nature of Things" series), Canadian Broadcasting Corporation (CBC-TV), 1990.

Lost in the Barrens (television movie), Atlantis Films, 1990.

Curse of the Viking Grave (television movie), Atlantis Films, 1992.

Several of Mowat's books have been recorded onto cassette, including *Grey Seas Under, Lost in the Barrens, People of the Deer, The Snow Walker,* and *And No Birds Sang.*

SIDELIGHTS: Farley Mowat is one of Canada's most internationally acclaimed writers. His many books for both young-adult and adult readers offer a reflective glimpse at the ill-fated future of wild species at the hand of mankind, and he presents a clear warning as to the consequences of our continued drain on the earth's limited natural resources. Although often categorized as a nature writer, Mowat considers himself a storyteller or "saga man" whose works derive from his concern about the preservation of all forms of life. An outspoken advocate for the Canadian North with an irreverent attitude toward bureaucracy, Mowat has repeatedly aroused the ire of Canadian officials through his harsh indictments of government policies concerning the treatment of endangered races of people as well as endangered animal species. With characteristic bluntness, Mowat once remarked in *Newsweek:* "Modern man is such an arrogant cement head to believe that he can take without paying."

Mowat first became aware of humanity's outrages against nature in the late 1940s when he accepted a position as a government biologist in the barren lands of northern Canada. He took the assignment in part because it offered him a respite from civilization—Mowat had recently returned from the battlefields of World War II where he served in the Canadian Army and witnessed brutal combat during the invasion of Italy. "I came back from the war rejecting my species," he told Cheryl McCall in *People* magazine. "I hated what had been done to me and what I had done and what man did to man."

Mowat's assignment in the Barrens was to study the area's wolf population and their behavior. The Canadian government suspected that the wolves were responsible for the dwindling caribou population and enlisted Mowat to get evidence to corroborate their suspicions. However, after months of observing a male wolf and his mate—whom he named George and Angeline—Mowat discovered wolves to be intelligent creatures who ate only what they needed for survival. Subsisting primarily on a diet of field mice, the wolves would only eat an occasional sickly caribou—by killing the weakest of the species, the wolves actually helped strengthen the caribou herd.

Although the results of his study were quickly dismissed by the government, as were any expectations he may have had of further employment, Mowat eventually fashioned his findings into a fictional work, *Never Cry Wolf,* which was published in 1963. A *Chicago Tribune Book World* critic calls Mowat's experience "a perfect example of the bureaucrats getting more than they bargained for." Much to Mowat's dismany, according to a reviewer for *Atlantic,* "the Canadian government . . . has never paid any discernible attention to the information it hired Mr. Mowat to assemble." Fortunately, through his book Mowat's message was heeded by both the reading public and the governments of other countries. Shortly after a translation of *Never Cry Wolf* appeared in Russia, officials in that country banned the slaughter of wolves, whom they had previously thought to be arbitrary killers. Noting the long-range repercussions of the book, David Graber comments in the *Los Angeles Time Book Review* that "by writing *Never Cry Wolf,* [Mowat] almost single-handedly reversed the public's image of the wolf, from feared vermin to romantic symbol of the wilderness."

Although not popular with officials of the Canadian government, *Never Cry Wolf* was welcomed by both readers and critics. Harry C. Kenney notes that the book "delightfully and instructively lifts one into a captivating animal kingdom" in his review for the *Christian Science Monitor.* "This is a fascinating and captivating book, and a tragic one, too," writes Gavin Maxwell in *Book Week,* "for it carries a bleak, dead-pan obituary of the wolf family that Mr. Mowat had learned to love and respect. It is an epilogue that will not endear the Canadian Wildlife Service to readers. . . . Once more it is man who displays the qualities with which he has tried to damn the wolf."

During the months spent studying wolves in the Barrens, Mowat also befriended an Eskimo tribe called the Ihalmiut, or "People of the Deer," because they depend almost solely on caribou for food, clothing, and shelter. After learning a simplified form of their native language, Mowat was able to learn that the Ihalmiut people had been dwindling in numbers for several years due to the decreasing availability of caribou. Mowat, enraged at the government's apathy toward preserving the tribe, immediately began to compose scathing letters that he distributed to government officials. When such letters only resulted in the loss of his job, he turned his pen to a more productive enterprise. In the book *People of the Deer,* published in 1952, Mowat put the plight of the Ihalmiut squarely before the Canadian people. As *Saturday Review* contributor Ivan T. Sanderson observes: "What [Mowat] learned by living with the pathetic remnants of this wonderful little race of Nature's most perfected gentlemen, learning their language and their history, and fighting the terrifying northern elements at their side, so enraged him that when he came to set down the record, he contrived the most damning indictment of his own government and country, the so-called white race and its Anglo-Saxon branch in particular, the Christian religion, and civilization as a whole, that had ever been written."

Other reviewers have expressed admiration for *People of the Deer.* A *Times Literary Supplement* reviewer writes: "The author traces with a beautiful clarity the material and spiritual bonds between land, deer and people, and the precarious ecological balance which had been struck between the forefathers of this handful of men and the antlered multitude." Albert Hubbell agrees: "It is not often that a writer finds himself the sole chronicler of a whole human society, even of a microcosmic one like the Ihalmiut, and Mowat has done marvelously well at the job, despite a stylistic looseness and a tendency to formlessness," he observes in the *New Yorker.* "Also, his justifiable anger at the Canadian government's neglect of the Ihalmiut, who are its wards, intrudes in places where it doesn't belong, but then, as I said, Mowat is something of a fanatic on this subject. His book, just the same, is a fine one." T. Morris Longstreth concludes in *Christian Science Monitor:* "Mr. Mowat says of his book, 'This is a labor of love, and a small repayment to a race that gave me renewed faith in myself and in all men.' It will widen the horizons of many who are at the same time thankful that this explorer did the widening for them."

Mowat has written several other books about man's mistreatment of wildlife. *A Whale for the Killing,* published in 1972, recounts the slow torture of a marooned whale in a pond in Newfoundland. But his most bitter account of man's abuse of nonhuman life has been *Sea of Slaughter,* published in 1984. "Built of the accumulated fury of a lifetime," according to Graber, *Sea of Slaughter* has been counted by critics as among the author's most important works. Tracy Kidder notes in the *Washington Post Book World* that compared to *Never Cry Wolf,* this book "is an out and out tirade." The book's title refers to the extinction and near-extinction of sea and land animals along the North Atlantic seaboard in the area extending from Cape Cod north to Labrador. Mowat traces the area's history back to the sixteenth century when the waters teemed with fish, whales, walruses, and seals, and the shores abounded with bison, white bears (now known as polar bears because of their gradual trek northward), and other fur-bearing mammals. Currently, many of these species have been either greatly diminished or extinguished because of "pollution, gross overhunting . . . , loss of habitat, destruction of food supplies, poachings and officially sanctioned 'cullings,' " writes Kidder.

Mowat depicts the stark contrast between past and present in a manner that is tremendously affecting, reviewers note. Although admitting that the book contains some inaccuracies and a lack of footnotes, *Detroit News* contributor Lewis Regenstein claims that these "shortcomings pale in comparison to the importance of its message: We are not only destroying our wildlife but also the earth's ability to support a variety of life forms, including humans. As Mowat bluntly puts it, 'The living world is dying in our time.' " Graber believes that "the grandest anguish comes from Mowat's unrelenting historical accounts of the sheer *numbers* of whales, bears, salmon, lynx, wolves, bison, sea birds; numbers that sear because they proclaim what we have lost, what we have thrown away." And Ian Darragh writes in *Quill & Quire:* "Mowat's description of the slaughter of millions of shorebirds for sport, for example, is appalling for what it implies about the aggression and violence apparently programmed into man's genetic code. There is little room for humour or Mowat's personal anecdotes in this epitaph for Atlantic Canada's once bountiful fish and wildlife." Concludes *Commonweal* critic Tom O'Brien: "*Sea of Slaughter* provides some heavier reading [than Mowat's other books]; the weight in the progression of chapters starts to build through the book like a dirge. Nevertheless, it may help to focus the burgeoning animal rights movement in this country and abroad. The cause has no more eloquent spokesperson."

Sea of Slaughter received some unintended but nevertheless welcome publicity in 1984 when Mowat was refused entrance into the United States, where he was planning to publicize the book. While boarding a plane at a Toronto airport, Mowat was detained by officials from the United States Immigration and Naturalization Service (INS) who acted on the information that Mowat's name appeared in the *Lookout Book,* a government document that lists the names of those individuals who represent a danger to the security of the United States. Mowat later speculated in the *Chicago Tribune* about some possible reasons for his exclusion: "At first, . . . the assumption was that I was excluded because of the two trips I made to the Soviet Union [in the late 1960s]. . . . Then some guy at the INS supposedly said I was being kept out because I'd threatened the U.S. Armed Forces by threatening to shoot down American aircraft with a .22 caliber rifle. The fact is the *Ottawa Citizen* [where the story supposedly appeared in 1968] can't find any record of it, but that doesn't matter. I admit it, happily." Mowat added that the suggestion was later put forth that the "gun lobby and anti-environmentalists" might have wanted to prevent efforts to promote *Sea of Slaughter.*

Mowat's works for children contain a gentler, more lighthearted echo of his message to adult readers—his nature books for young people have given him a reputation as one of the best known Canadian writers for children outside his homeland. *Lost in the Barrens* is a novel about a pair of teenaged boys who become lost and must face the winter alone in the tundra. *The Dog Who Wouldn't Be* and *Owls in the Family* are memoirs of eccentric family pets. "[Mowat] knows children and what they like and can open doors to adventures both credible and entertaining to his young readers," notes Joseph E. Carver in his essay in the *British Columbia Library Quarterly.* "His stories are credible because Mowat wanted to write them to give permanence to the places, loyalties and experiences of his youth, entertaining because the author enjoys the telling of them." Mowat continues to take his role as a children's author seriously, viewing it as "of vital importance if basic changes for the good are ever to be initiated in any human culture," he noted in *Canadian Library Journal.*

Mowat departs from his usual focus—the Canadian wilderness—in *And No Birds Sang,* a memoir describing his experiences in the Canadian Army Infantry during World War II. Written in 1979, thirty years after his return from the war, Mowat wrote the memoir in response to the growing popularity of the notion that there is honor in dying in the service of one's country. The book chronicles Mowat's initial enthusiasm and determination to fight, the gradual surrender to despair, and its culmination in a horrifying fear of warfare that Mowat calls "The Worm That Never Dies." Reviewers have expressed reservations about the familiar nature of Mowat's theme, but add that Mowat nevertheless manages to bring a fresh perspective to the adage, "War is hell." David Weinberger remarks in *Macleans:* "Everybody knows that war is hell; it is the author's task to transform that knowledge into understanding." While noting that the book occasionally "bogs down in adjectives and ellipsis," Weinberger praises the work: "It takes a writer of stature—both as an author and as a moral, sensitive person—to make the attempt as valiantly as Mowat has." A similar opinion is expressed by Jean Strouse in *Newsweek:* "That war is hell is not news, but a story told this well serves, particularly in these precarious, saber-rattling days, as a vivid reminder." *And No Birds Sang* has been called by some reviewers a valuable addition to the literature of World War II. *Washington Post Book World* contributor Robert W. Smith calls the book "a powerful chunk of autobiography and a valuable contribution to war literature." *Time* critic R. Z. Sheppard writes: "*And No Birds Sang* needs no rhetoric. It can fall in with the best memoirs of World War II, a classic example of how unexploded emotions can be artfully defused."

In 1985, shortly after the death of noted primatologist Dian Fossey, Mowat was approached by Warner Books to write her biography. Although he initially refused—because he had never written a commissioned book—after reading one of Fossey's *National Geographic* articles, he reconsidered. Mowat told Beverly Slopen of *Publishers Weekly* that while reading Fossey's letters and journals he "began to realize that the importance of the book was her message, not my message. . . . I really became her collaborator. It was the journals that did it. They weren't long, discursive accounts. They were short, raw cries from the heart."

Mowat's biography *Woman in the Mists: The Story of Dian Fossey and the Mountain Gorillas of Africa* was published in 1987. The work relies heavily on Fossey's journal entries and letters to tell the story of her life: Her invitation by anthropologist Louis Leakey to study primates in the African Congo in 1967, an invitation that culminated in an escape to Uganda in the wake of political uprisings, and ultimately in her establishment of a research center on the Rwandan side of the Virunga Mountains where Fossey remained until her death. Fossey's murder has not been solved, but the book "goes a long way toward revealing what it was about her that made a violent death seem inevitable," notes Eugene Linden in the *New York Times Book Review.* Fossey was known to stalk gorilla poachers and she lived by the biblical motto, "An eye for an eye." She also angered government officials by opposing "gorilla tourism" and the development of park land for agrarian purposes. But Mowat's biography also reveals a side of Fossey that was generous, kind, witty, and romantic. She had a succession of affairs throughout her lifetime, including one with Leakey, and longed for a stable, monogamous relationship. Mary Battiata, a *Washington Post Book World* contributor believes that Mowat "puts to rest—forever one hopes—the shopworn notion of Fossey as a misanthrope who preferred animals to her own species." But, she goes on to add, "Though Mowat offers an intriguing and credible solution to the mystery of Fossey's unsolved murder, there is little else that is genuinely new here." *Chicago Tribune* contributor Anita Susan Grossman similarly observes that Mowat "limits himself to presenting excerpts from Fossey's own writings, strung together with the barest of factual narration. As a result, the central drama of Fossey's life remains as murky as the circumstances of her death." Although Linden concurs that *Woman in the Mists* does have several problems, including a lack of footnotes, Mowat's "pedestrian" prose, and "interlocutory words [that] add little to our understanding of Fossey or her world," he adds: "Despite these problems, this is a rare, gripping look at the tragically mingled destinies of a heroic, flawed woman and her beloved mountain gorillas amid the high mists of the Parc des Volcans."

Critical appraisal aside, Mowat states that the writing of Fossey's biography had a profound, sobering effect on him and that he will not undertake another biography. "It was a disturbing experience," he told Slopen. "It's almost as though I were possessed. I wasn't the master. I fought for mastery and I didn't win. It really was a transcendental experience and I'm uncomfortable with it."

Although Mowat has spent nearly a lifetime trying to convince humanity that we cannot continue to abuse nature without serious and sometimes irreversible repercussions, he believes that "in the end, my crusades have accomplished nothing." Mowat continues in *People* magazine: "I haven't saved the wolf, the whales, the seals, primitive man or the outpost people. All I've done is to document the suicidal tendencies of modern man. I'm sure I haven't altered the course of human events one iota. Things will change inevitably, but it's strictly a matter of the lottery of fate. It has nothing to do with man's intentions."

BIOGRAPHICAL/CRITICAL SOURCES:

BOOKS

Authors and Artists for Young Adults, Volume 1, Gale, 1988, pp. 175-188.

Contemporary Literary Criticism, Volume 26, Gale, 1983.

Dictionary of Literary Biography, Volume 68: *Canadian Writers, 1920-1959, First Series,* Gale, 1988, pp. 253-258.

Egoff, Sheila, *The Republic of Childhood: A Critical Guide to Canadian Children's Literature in English,* Oxford University Press, 1975.

Lucas, Alex, *Farley Mowat,* McClelland & Stewart, 1976.

Twentieth Century Children's Writers, St. James Press, 1989, pp. 702-03.

PERIODICALS

Atlantic, November, 1963.

Audubon, January, 1973.

Best Sellers, February, 1986.

Books in Canada, March, 1985; November, 1985.

Books of the Times, April, 1980.

Book Week, November 24, 1963.

Book World, December 31, 1972.

Canadian Children's Literature, number 5, 1976; number 6, 1976.

Canadian Forum, July, 1974; March, 1976.

Canadian Geographical Journal, June, 1974.

Canadian Literature, spring, 1978.

Chicago Tribune, October 29, 1980; December 23, 1983; May 6, 1985; October 22, 1987.

Chicago Tribune Book World, November 13, 1983.

Christian Science Monitor, May 1, 1952; October 3, 1963; May 15, 1969; May 10, 1970; April 15, 1971; March 6, 1974.

Commonweal, September 6, 1985.

Contemporary Review, February, 1978.

Detroit News, April 21, 1985.

Economist, January 15, 1972.

Globe and Mail (Toronto), November 25, 1989.

Illustrated London News, September 20, 1952.

Los Angeles Times, December 13, 1985.

Los Angeles Times Book Review, March 16, 1980; April 28, 1985.

MacLeans, October 8, 1979.

Nation, June 10, 1968.

New Republic, March 8, 1980.

Newsweek, February 18, 1980; September 30, 1985.

New Yorker, April 26, 1952; May 11, 1968; March 17, 1980.

New York Times, December 13, 1965; February 19, 1980.

New York Times Book Review, February 11, 1968; June 14, 1970; February 22, 1976; November 6, 1977; February 24, 1980; December 22, 1985; October 25, 1987.

Observer, March 4, 1973.

People, March 31, 1980.

Publishers Weekly, October 2, 1987.

Quill & Quire, December, 1984.

Saturday Evening Post, July 29, 1950; April 13, 1957.

Saturday Night, October 18, 1952; October 25, 1952; November, 1975.

Saturday Review, June 28, 1952; April 26, 1969; October 21, 1972.

Scientific American, March, 1964.

Sierra, September, 1978.

Spectator, November 21, 1952.

Time, February 18, 1980; May 6, 1985; October 26, 1987.

Times Literary Supplement, September 12, 1952; March 19, 1971; February 16, 1973.

Washington Post, October 9, 1983; April 25, 1985; October 25, 1985.

Washington Post Book World, February 24, 1980; May 12, 1985; October 25, 1987.*

* * *

MUELLER, Gerhardt
See BICKERS, Richard (Leslie) Townshend

* * *

MYERS, Walter Dean 1937-
(Walter M. Myers)

PERSONAL: Given name Walter Milton Myers; born August 12, 1937, in Martinsburg, WV; son of George Ambrose and Mary (Green) Myers; raised from age three by Herbert Julius (a shipping clerk) and Florence (a factory worker) Dean; married second wife, Constance Brendel, June 19, 1973; children: (first marriage) Karen, Michael Dean; (second marriage) Christopher. *Education:* Attended State College of the City University of New York; Empire State College, B.A.

ADDRESSES: Home—2543 Kennedy Blvd., Jersey City, NJ 07304.

CAREER: New York State Department of Labor, Brooklyn, employment supervisor, 1966-69; Bobbs-Merrill Co., Inc. (publisher), New York City, senior trade book editor, 1970-77; writer, 1977—. Has also taught creative writing and black history on a part-time basis in New York City, 1974-75. *Military service:* U.S. Army, 1954-57.

MEMBER: PEN, Harlem Writers Guild.

AWARDS, HONORS: Council on Interracial Books for Children Award, 1968, for the manuscript of *Where Does the Day Go?;* Woodward Park School Annual Book Award, 1976, for *Fast Sam, Cool Clyde, and Stuff;* American Library Association "Best Books for Young Adults" citations, 1978, for *It Ain't All for Nothin',* 1979, for *The Young Landlords,* and 1982, for *Hoops;* Coretta Scott King Awards, 1980, for *The Young Landlords,* and 1984, for *Motown and Didi: A Love Story;* Notable Children's Trade Book in Social Studies citation, 1982, for *The Legend of Tarik; Scorpions* was named a Newbery Honor Book, 1989; Coretta Scott King Award, 1991, for *Now is Your Time!: The African-American Struggle for Freedom.*

WRITINGS:

FOR CHILDREN

(Under name Walter M. Myers) *Where Does the Day Go?,* illustrated by Leo Carty, Parents' Magazine Press, 1969.
The Dragon Takes a Wife, illustrated by Ann Grifalconi, Bobbs-Merrill, 1972.
The Dancers, illustrated by Anne Rockwell, Parents' Magazine Press, 1972.
Fly, Jimmy, Fly!, illustrated by Moneta Barnett, Putnam, 1974.
The World of Work: A Guide to Choosing a Career, Bobbs-Merrill, 1975.
Fast Sam, Cool Clyde, and Stuff, Viking, 1975.
Social Welfare, F. Watts, 1976.
Brainstorm, with photographs by Chuck Freedman, F. Watts, 1977.
Mojo and the Russians, Viking, 1977.
Victory for Jamie, Scholastic Book Services, 1977.
It Ain't All for Nothin', Viking, 1978.
The Young Landlords, Viking, 1979.
The Black Pearl and the Ghost; or, One Mystery after Another, illustrated by Robert Quackenbush, Viking, 1980.
The Golden Serpent, illustrated by Alice Provensen and Martin Provensen, Viking, 1980.
Hoops, Delacorte, 1981.
The Legend of Tarik, Viking, 1981.
Won't Know Till I Get There, Viking, 1982.
The Nicholas Factor, Viking, 1983.
Tales of a Dead King, Morrow, 1983.
Mr. Monkey and the Gotcha Bird, illustrated by Leslie Morrill, Delacorte, 1984.
Motown and Didi: A Love Story, Viking, 1984.
The Outside Shot, Delacorte, 1984.
Sweet Illusions, Teachers & Writers Collaborative, 1986.
Crystal, Viking, 1987.
Shadow of the Red Moon, Harper, 1987.
Fallen Angels, Scholastic, Inc., 1988.
Scorpions, Harper, 1988.
Me, Mop, and the Moondance Kid, Delacorte, 1988.
The Mouse Rap, Harper & Row, 1990.
Now Is Your Time!: The African American Struggle for Freedom, HarperCollins, 1991.
Somewhere in the Darkness, Scholastic, 1992.
A Place Called Heartbreak: A Story of Vietnam, illustrated by Frederick Porter, Raintree Steck-Vaughn, 1992.
The Righteous Revenge of Artemis Bonner, HarperCollins, 1992.
Mop, Moondance, and the Nagasaki Knights, Delacorte Press, 1992.
Young Martin's Promise, Raintree Steck-Vaughn, 1992.
Malcolm X: By Any Means Necessary, Scholastic, 1993.

"THE ARROW" SERIES; FOR CHILDREN

Adventure in Granada, Viking, 1985.
The Hidden Shrine, Viking, 1985.
Duel in the Desert, Viking, 1986.
Ambush in the Amazon, Viking, 1986.

CONTRIBUTOR TO ANTHOLOGIES

Orde Coombs, editor, *What We Must See: Young Black Storytellers,* Dodd, 1971.
Sonia Sanchez, editor, *We Be Word Sorcerers: Twenty-five Stories by Black Americans,* Bantam, 1973.

OTHER

Contributor of articles and fiction to periodicals, including *Black Creation, Black World, McCall's, Espionage, Alfred Hitchcock Mystery Magazine, Essence, Ebony Jr.!,* and *Boy's Life.*

ADAPTATIONS: The Young Landlords was filmed by Topol Productions.

SIDELIGHTS: Walter Dean Myers is commonly recognized as one of modern literature's premier authors of fiction for young black people. Two of his novels for teens, *The Young Landlords* and *Motown and Didi: A Love Story,* have won the prestigious Coretta Scott King Award, and his text for the picture book *Where Does the Day Go?* received the Council on Interracial Books for Children Award in 1969. As Carmen Subryan notes in the *Dictionary of Literary Biography,* "Whether he is writing about the ghettos of New York, the remote countries of Africa, or social institutions, Myers captures the essence of the developing experiences of youth."

While Myers is perhaps best known for his novels that explore the lives of young Harlem blacks, he is equally adept at producing modern fairy tales, ghost stories, and adventure sagas. Subryan finds a common theme throughout Myers's far-ranging works. "He is concerned with the development of youths," she writes, "and his message is always the same: young people must face the reality of growing up and must persevere, knowing that they can succeed despite any odds they face. . . . This positive message enables youths to discover what is important in life and to reject influences which could destroy them."

In the *Interracial Books for Children Bulletin,* Myers describes his priorities as an author. He tries, he says, to provide good literature for black children, "literature that includes them and the way they live" and that "celebrates their life and their person. It upholds and gives special place to their humanity." He elaborates on this point in an essay for *Something about the Author Autobiography Series:* "I realized how few resources are available for Black youngsters to open the world to them. I feel the need to show them the possibilities that exist for them that were never revealed to me as a youngster; possibilities that did not even exist for me then."

One possibility Myers never foresaw as a youth was that of supporting himself as a writer. He was born into an impoverished family in Martinsburg, West Virginia, and at age three was adopted by Herbert and Florence Dean, who settled in New York City's Harlem district. Although he wrote poems and stories from his early teens onward and won awards for them, his parents did not encourage his literary talents. "I was from a family of laborers," he remembers in his autobiographical essay, "and the idea of writing stories or essays was far removed from their experience. Writing had no practical value for a Black child. These minor victories [and prizes] did not bolster my ego. Instead, they convinced me that even though I was bright, even though I might have some talent, I was still defined by factors other than my ability." The dawning realization that his possibilities were limited by race and economic status embittered Myers as a teen. "A youngster is not trained to want to be a gasoline station attendant or a clerk in some obscure office," he states. "We are taught to want to be lawyers and doctors and accountants—these professions that are given value. When the compromise comes, as it does early in Harlem to many children, it comes hard."

Myers admits he was not ready to accept that compromise. Through high school and a three-year enlistment in the Army, he read avidly and wrote short stories. After his discharge from the service, he worked in a variety of positions, including mail clerk at the post office, interoffice messenger, and interviewer in a factory. None of these tasks pleased him, and when he began to publish poetry, stories and articles in magazines, he cautiously started to consider a writing profession. "When I entered a contest for picture book writers," he claims, "it was more because I wanted to write *anything* than because I wanted to write a picture book."

Myers won the contest, sponsored by the Council on Interracial Books for Children, for his text of *Where Does the Day Go?* In that story, a group of children from several ethnic backgrounds discuss their ideas about night and day with a sensitive and wise black father during a long walk. Inspired by the success of his first attempt to write for young people, Myers turned his attention to producing more picture books. Between 1972 and 1975, he published three: *The Dancers, The Dragon Takes a Wife,* and *Fly, Jimmy, Fly!* More recent releases include *The Golden Serpent,* a fable set in India, and an animal adventure, *Mr. Monkey and the Gotcha Bird.*

Myers accepted an editorial position with the Bobbs-Merrill publishing company in 1970 and worked there until 1977. His seven-year tenure taught him "the book business from another viewpoint," as he puts it in his autobiographical essay. "Publishing is a business," he writes. "It is not a cultural institution. . . . It is *talked* about as if it were a large cultural organization with several branches. One hears pronouncements like 'anything worthwhile will eventually be published.' Nonsense, of course. Books are published for many reasons, the chief of which is profit." In retrospect, however, Myers feels that he has benefitted from his experiences at Bobbs-Merrill, even though he was laid off during a restructuring program. "After the initial disillusionment about the artistic aspects of the job, I realized how foolish I had been in not learning, as a writer, more about the business aspects of my craft," he concludes. Armed with the pragmatic knowledge of how the publishing industry works, Myers has supported himself by his writing alone since 1977.

By the time he left Bobbs-Merrill, Myers had already established a reputation as an able author of fiction for black children, based largely upon his highly successful novels for teens such as *Fast Sam, Cool Clyde, and Stuff* and *Mojo and the Russians.* Both tales feature, in Subryan's words, adventures depicting "the learning experiences of most youths growing up in a big city where negative influences abound." Central to the stories is the concept of close friendships, portrayed as a positive, nurturing influence. Subryan states: "Because of the bonding which occurs among the members of the group, the reader realizes that each individual's potential for survival has increased." Myers followed the two upbeat novels with a serious one, *It Ain't All for Nothin',* that Subryan feels "reflects much of the pain and anguish of ghetto life." The account of a boy caught in a web of parental abuse, conflicting values, and solitary self-assessment, *It Ain't All for Nothin'* "pretties up nothing; not the language, not the circumstances, not the despair," according to Jane Pennington in the *Interracial Books for Children Bulletin.* The story has a positive resolution, however, based on the care and support the central character receives from fellow community members.

Myers strives to present characters for whom urban life is an uplifting experience despite the potentially dangerous influences. In his first Coretta Scott King Award-winner, *The Young Landlords,* several teens learn responsibility when they are given a ghetto apartment building to manage. Lonnie Jackson, the protagonist of *Hoops,* profits from the example of an older friend who has become involved with gamblers. Concerned with stereotyping of a sexual as well as a racial sort, Myers creates plausible female characters and features platonic friendships between the sexes in his works. "The love in *Fast Sam, Cool Clyde, and Stuff* is not between any one couple," writes Alleen Pace Nilsen in the *English Journal.* "Instead it is a sort of a general feeling of good will and concern that exists among a group of inner city kids." Nilsen, among others, also notes that Myers's fiction can appeal to readers of any race. She concludes that he "makes the reader feel so close to the characters that ethnic group identification is secondary." Subryan expresses a similar opinion: "By appealing to the consciousness of young adults, Myers is touching perhaps the most important element of our society. Myers's books demonstrate that writers can not only challenge the minds of black youths but also emphasize the black experience in a nonracist way that benefits all young readers."

With *Scorpions,* Myers tells the story of Jamal, a seventh grader whose life is forever changed when he accepts a gun from an older teen. For this provocative story Myers received the Newbery Honor Book award in 1989. In *Fallen Angels,* a Harlem teenager volunteers for service in the Vietnam War. Mel Watkins in the *New York Times Book Review* writes, "*Fallen Angels* is a candid young adult novel that engages the Vietnam experience squarely. It deals with violence and death as well as compassion and love, with deception and hypocrisy as well as honesty and virtue. It is a tale that is as thought-provoking as it is entertaining, touching and, on occasion, humorous." Jim Naughton, reviewing *Me, Mop, and the Moondance Kid* in the *Washington Post Book World,* calls Myers "one of the best writers of children's and young adult fiction in the country and *Me, Mop, and the Moondance Kid* shows why" in relating the schemes of two recently adopted orphans to find a home for their friend, left behind in the orphanage. In the Coretta Scott King Award-winning *Now Is Your Time! The African-American Struggle for Freedom,* a *Washington Post Book World* contributor finds that Myers "writes with the vividness of a novelist, the balance of an historian and the passion of an advocate. He tells a familiar story and shocks us with it all over again." Focusing on the black experience in America, Myers relates tales of Malcolm X, Coretta Scott King, Frederick Douglass, businessman James Forten, rebels Nat Turner and John Brown, journalist Ida B. Wells, inventor Lewis Latimer, and sculptor Meta Vaux Warrick, and even the Dandridges of Virginia, the "owners" of Myers's great-grandmother. The *Washington Post Book World* critic calls *Now Is Your Time!* a "thrilling portrait gallery, expertly delineated. . . . Quite a story, quite a book."

Myers writes in *Something About the Author Autobiography Series* that the reception of his novels gave him a new role as an author. "As my books for teenagers gained in popularity I sensed that my soul-searching for my place in the artistic world was taking on added dimension. As a Black writer I had not only the personal desire to find myself, but the obligation to use my abilities to fill a void." Children and adults, he suggests, "must have role models with which they can identify," and he feels he must "deliver images upon which [they] could build and expand their own worlds." Noting that in his own life he has "acquired the strengths to turn away from disaster," Myers concludes: "As a Black writer, I want to talk about my people. . . . The books come. They pour from me at a great rate. I can't see how any writer can ever stop. There is always one more story to tell, one more person whose life needs to be held up to the sun."

BIOGRAPHICAL/CRITICAL SOURCES:

BOOKS

Children's Literature Review, Volume 4, Gale, 1982.

Contemporary Literary Criticism, Volume 35, Gale, 1985.

Dictionary of Literary Biography, Volume 33: *Afro-American Fiction Writers after 1955,* Gale, 1984.

Rush, Theressa G., editor, *Black American Writers: Past and Present,* Scarecrow Press, 1975.

Something about the Author Autobiography Series, Volume 2, Gale, 1986.

PERIODICALS

Christian Science Monitor, May 1, 1992, p. 10.

Ebony, September, 1975.

Interracial Books for Children Bulletin, Volume 10, number 4, 1979; Volume 10, number 6, 1979.

New York Times Book Review, April 9, 1972; May 4, 1975; January 6, 1980; November 9, 1980; July 12, 1981; June 13, 1982; April 19, 1987, p. 21; September 13, 1987, p. 48; January 22, 1989, p. 29; May 20, 1990, p. 44; February 16, 1992, p. 26.

Tribune Books (Chicago), February 26, 1989, p. 8.

Washington Post Book World, July 9, 1989, p. 10; March 8, 1992, p. 11.*

* * *

MYERS, Walter M.
See MYERS, Walter Dean

N

NASH, Simon
See CHAPMAN, Raymond

* * *

NEWCOMBE, Eugene A. 1923-1990
(Jack Newcombe)

PERSONAL: Born July 25, 1923, in Burlington, VT; died following an accidental fall, February 14, 1990, in New York, NY. *Education:* Attended University of Missouri, University of California, Pomona College, and American University at Biarritz; Brown University, B.A.

CAREER: Editor, journalist, and author. Journalist with *Providence Journal,* late 1940s; managing editor of *Sport,* early 1950s; *Life,* New York City, began as text editor, London bureau chief, 1968-70, Washington bureau chief, 1970; executive editor of Book-of-the-Month Club, 1974-79. *Military service:* Served in U. S. Army.

WRITINGS:

UNDER NAME JACK NEWCOMBE

In Search of Billy Cole (adult novel), Arbor House, 1984.

Also author of *Northern California: A History and Guide.*

UNDER NAME JACK NEWCOMBE; CHILDREN'S NONFICTION

Floyd Patterson: Heavyweight King, Bartholomew House, 1961.
The Fireballers: Baseball's Fastest Pitchers, Putnam, 1964.
The Game of Football, illustrations by Paul Frame, Garrard, 1967.
Six Days to Saturday: Joe Paterno and Penn State, photographs by Dick Swanson, Farrar, Straus, 1974.
The Best of the Athletic Boys: The White Man's Impact on Jim Thorpe, Doubleday, 1975.

UNDER NAME JACK NEWCOMBE; EDITOR

The Fireside Book of Football, Simon & Schuster, 1964.
A Christmas Treasury, Viking, 1982, revised edition published as *A New Christmas Treasury,* 1991.
Travels in the Americas, Grove, 1989.

BIOGRAPHICAL/CRITICAL SOURCES:

PERIODICALS

Sport, July, 1980.

OBITUARIES:

PERIODICALS

New York Times, February 16, 1990.
Washington Post, February 19, 1990.*

* * *

NEWCOMBE, Jack
See NEWCOMBE, Eugene A.

* * *

NIMBLE, Jack B.
See BURGESS, Michael (Roy)

* * *

NORA, James Jackson 1928-

PERSONAL: Born June 26, 1928, in Chicago, IL; son of Joseph James (a physician) and Mae (a nurse; maiden name, Jackson) Nora; married Audrey Hart (a physician), April 9, 1966; children: Wendy, Penelope, Marianne,

James, Jr., Elizabeth. *Education:* Harvard University, A.B., 1950; Yale University, M.D., 1954; University of California, Berkeley, M.P.H., 1978. *Politics:* Democrat. *Religion:* Presbyterian.

ADDRESSES: Home—3110 Fairweather Ct., Olney, MD 20832.

CAREER: Detroit Receiving Hospital, Detroit, MI, rotating intern, 1954-55; private practice, Cambridge, WI, 1955-59; University of Wisconsin—Madison, pediatric resident, 1959-61, chief resident, 1961; private practice in pediatrics, Beloit, WI, 1961-62; University of Wisconsin—Madison, instructor, 1962-64, assistant professor of pediatrics, 1965; Baylor University, College of Medicine, Houston, TX, assistant professor, 1965-69, associate professor of pediatrics, 1969-71, head of section of human genetics and director of Birth Defects Center, 1967-71; University of Colorado, School of Medicine, Denver, CO, associate professor, 1971-74, professor of pediatrics, 1974-93, professor of preventive medicine, 1979-93, professor of biochemistry, biophysics, and genetics, 1979-93, emeritus professor, 1993—, director of Pediatric Cardiovascular-Pulmonary Training Center, 1972-78, director of Preventive Cardiology, 1978-93, director of genetics at Rose Medical Center, 1980-93.

Research fellow in cardiology at University of Wisconsin—Madison, 1962-64; special National Institutes of Health fellow in genetics at McGill University and at Montreal Children's Hospital, Montreal, Quebec. Texas Children's Hospital, Houston, associate director of cardiology, 1965-71, chief of genetics service, 1967-71; director of pediatric cardiology at Colorado General Hospital, 1971-77. Served on task force of National Heart, Blood Vessel, Lung, and Blood Program, 1973, in U.S.-U.S.S.R. Exchange Program on Congenital Heart Disease, 1975, and on Human Research Committee of Children's Hospital of Denver. Diplomate of National Board of Medical Examiners, of American Board of Pediatrics, of American Sub-board of Pediatric Cardiology, and of American Board of Medical Genetics. Served on institutional committees at University of Colorado, including faculty council, human research committee, computer committee, faculty risk committee, fourth year pediatric curriculum committee, 1972-74. Associated with National Foundation-March of Dimes, American Heart Association, Colorado Heart Association, American College of Cardiology. *Military service:* U.S. Army Air Corps, 13th Air Force, 1945-47; became second lieutenant; stationed in the Philippine Islands.

MEMBER: Transplantation Society, Genetics Society of America, Teratology Society, American Pediatric Society, American Society of Human Genetics, American Federation for Clinical Research, American Institute of Biological Sciences, American Heart Associations and Councils, American College of Cardiology (member of ad hoc committee on pediatric cardiology), American Academy of Pediatrics (fellow), American College of Medical Genetics, Society for Pediatric Research, Society for Experimental Biology and Medicine, Southern Society for Pediatric Research, Western Society for Pediatric Research.

AWARDS, HONORS: Received grants from National Foundation—March of Dimes, 1966-71, from National Heart and Lung Institute, 1972-78, from National Institute of Child Health and Human Development, 1974-77, from Johnson Foundation, 1978—, from American Heart Association, from Junior League of Denver, and from local heart associations; Virginia Apgar Memorial Award.

WRITINGS:

Introduction to Immunology, Kimtec, 1970.

(With F. C. Fraser) *Medical Genetics: Principles and Practice,* Lea & Febiger, 1974, 4th edition, 1993.

(With Fraser) *Genetics of Man,* Lea & Febiger, 1975, 2nd edition, 1986.

Genetics and Cardiology, ACCEL, 1976.

(With wife, Audrey Hart Nora) *Genetics and Counseling in Cardiovascular Diseases,* C. C. Thomas, 1978.

The Whole Heart Book, Holt, 1980.

The New Whole Heart Book, Mid-List, 1989.

(Editor with Atsuyoshi Takao) *Congenital Heart Disease: Causes and Processes,* Futura Publishing, 1984.

Genetics, Epidemiology and Preventive Cardiology, ACCEL, 1984.

The Upstart Spring (novel), Mid-List, 1989.

The Psi Delegation (novel), Mid-List, 1989.

CONTRIBUTOR

Hamish Watson, editor, *Pediatric Cardiology,* Lloyd-Luke, 1968.

Oscar Jaffe, editor, *Cardiac Development with Special Reference to Congenital Heart Disease: Proceedings of the 1968 International Symposium,* University of Dayton Press, 1970.

C. Henry Kempe, H. K. Silver, and D. O'Brien, editors, *Current Pediatric Diagnosis and Treatment,* Lange Medical Publications, 2nd edition, 1972, 3rd edition, 1974, 4th edition, 1976.

Birth Defects Compendium, National Foundation, 1973, 2nd edition, Alan R. Liss, 1979.

W. F. Friedman, M. Lisch, and E. H. Sonnenblick, editors, *Neonatal Heart Disease,* Grune, 1973.

B. S. Langford Kidd and Richard D. Rowe, editors, *The Child with Congenital Heart Disease after Surgery,* Futura Publishing, 1976.

A. J. Moss, F. Adams, and G. C. Emmanouilides, editors, *Heart Disease in Infants, Children and Adolescents,*

Williams & Wilkins, 2nd edition, 1977, 3rd edition, 1983.

H. A. Kaminetzky and L. Iffy, editors, *New Techniques and Concepts in Maternal and Fetal Medicine,* Van Nostrand, 1979.

R. Neil Schmike and Laird G. Jackson, editors, *Clinical Genetics: A Source Book for Physicians,* Wiley, 1979.

Richard Van Praagh and Takao, editors, *Etiology and Morphogenesis of Congenital Heart Disease,* Futura Publishing, 1980.

T. O. Cheng, editor, *The International Textbook of Cardiology,* Pergamon, 1986.

OTHER

Contributor of over 200 papers and articles and fifteen poems to journals. Member of editorial board of *Circulation* and of *Blakiston's New Gould Medical Dictionary,* 4th edition.

WORK IN PROGRESS: Two novels and a volume of poetry.

SIDELIGHTS: James Jackson Nora's major research fields include the etiology of cardiovascular diseases, congenital heart disease, atherosclerosis, hypertension, and rheumatic fever. He is also interested in general topics in the areas of cardiology, genetics, teratology, human development, maternal and child health, epidemiology, and preventive medicine.

Nora once told *CA:* "Since I first submitted a short story (which was rejected) to the Atlantic First Contest at the age of seventeen, I have been a frustrated fiction writer. I write scientific books because it is part of my job as an academician, but I would much rather write fiction and poetry." He more recently added, "My wish expressed in the previous edition has been fulfilled. I am now professor emeritus, which permits me more time for writing. Two of my novels have been published and two have been completed and are being revised. I hope to keep a semi-retired hand in medicine through a modest involvement in research and perhaps health care reform."

* * *

NORTH, Colin
See BINGLEY, David Ernest

* * *

NORWOOD, Frederick Abbott 1914-

PERSONAL: Born July 11, 1914, in San Diego, CA; son of Frederick Adolph (a pharmacist) and Florence (Abbott) Norwood; married Florence Corbett, June 13, 1943; children: Mary Beth, Pamela Zoe. *Education:* Ohio Wesleyan University, B.A., 1936; Yale University, B.D., 1939, Ph.D., 1941. *Religion:* Methodist.

ADDRESSES: Home—560 Executive Blvd., Delaware, OH 43015.

CAREER: Methodist minister in Mantua and Akron, OH, 1942-46; Baldwin-Wallace College, Berea, OH, professor of history, 1946-52; Garrett Theological Seminary, Evanston, IL, associate professor, 1952-58, professor of history of Christianity, 1958-78, research professor, 1978-80.

MEMBER: American Society of Church History, Phi Beta Kappa.

AWARDS, HONORS: Brewer Essay Prize, American Society of Church History, 1942; Guggenheim fellow, 1958; American Association of Theological Schools fellow, 1965; Huntington Library fellow, 1977.

WRITINGS:

The Reformation Refugees as an Economic Force, American Society of Church History, 1942.

The Development of Modern Christianity, Abingdon, 1956.

History of the North Indiana Conference, 1917-1956, Conference Historical Society, 1957.

Church Membership in the Methodist Tradition, Methodist Publishing House, 1958.

Great Moments in Church History, Abingdon, 1962.

(Co-author) *Reformation Studies,* John Knox, 1962.

Strangers and Exiles: A History of Religious Refugees, two volumes, Abingdon, 1969.

The Story of American Methodism, Abingdon, 1974.

From Dawn to Midday at Garrett, Garrett Theological Seminary, 1978.

Young Readers Book of Church History, Abingdon, 1982.

Source Book of American Methodism, Abingdon, 1982.

(Contributor) R. Greaves, editor, *Triumph over Silence,* Greenwood Press, 1984.

Also author of *Delaware High School, 1928-1932,* 1982, and *Contemporary Journey: United Methodists in Ohio,* 1984. Member of editorial board, *History of American Methodism,* three volumes, Abingdon, 1964, and *Encyclopedia of World Methodism,* two volumes, Abingdon, 1974. Contributor to *Encyclopaedia Britannica* and to history and religion journals. Co-editor, *Church History,* 1956-62.

WORK IN PROGRESS: Methodism and the American Indian; a work on Edward Thomson, president of Ohio Wesleyan University, 1846-60.

SIDELIGHTS: Frederick Abbott Norwood told *CA:* "I've been moving from large to small, broad coverage to specific, [from the] world to where I live."

BIOGRAPHICAL/CRITICAL SOURCES:

PERIODICALS

Christian Century, March 10, 1971.

* * *

NUNIS, Doyce B(lackman), Jr. 1924-

PERSONAL: Born May 30, 1924, in Cedartown, GA; son of Doyce Blackman and Winnie Ethel (Morris) Nunis. *Education:* University of California, Los Angeles, B.A., 1947; University of Southern California, M.S., 1950, M.Ed., 1952, M.A., 1953, Ph.D., 1958.

ADDRESSES: Home—4426 Cromwell Ave., Los Angeles, CA 90027. *Office*—Department of History, University of Southern California, Los Angeles, CA 90089-0034.

CAREER: Redondo Beach Elementary School District, Redondo Beach, CA, teacher, 1948-51; University of Southern California, Los Angeles, lecturer in American history and government, 1951-56; El Camino College, Torrance, CA, instructor, 1956-59; University of California, Los Angeles, associate professor of education and history and head of Office of Oral History, 1959-65; University of Southern California, associate professor, 1965-68, professor of history, 1968-89, professor emeritus, 1989—. Lecturer and speaker.

MEMBER: American Historical Association, American Association of University Professors, Organization of American Historians, California Historical Society, Southern California Historical Society, Westerners (Los Angeles Corral), Zamorano Club, Phi Alpha Theta, Pi Sigma Alpha.

AWARDS, HONORS: Grant for research abroad, Del Amo Foundation, 1956; grant-in-aid, Henry E. Huntington Library, 1960; joint winner of Louis Knoot Koontz Memorial Award, 1960, for best contribution to *Pacific Historical Review;* Guggenheim fellow, 1963-64; award of merit, American Association for State and Local History, 1965, 1974; fellowship, American Philosophical Society, 1969; award of merit, Los Angeles Corral of Westerners, 1971; Southern California Historical Society, certificate of merit, 1972, 1974, and fellow, 1990; award for teaching excellence, University of Southern California Associates, 1975, 1988; faculty fellow, University of Southern California, College of Letters, Arts, and Sciences, 1974-78; named Outstanding Professor, University of Southern California Mortar Board, 1981; California Historical Society, fellow, 1981, and Henry Raup Memorial Award, 1988; Rounce & Coffin Club Award, Western Americana, 1982, for *The Letters of Jacob Baegert, 1749-1761: Jesuit Missionary in Baja California* and *Men, Medicine and Water: The Building of the Los Angeles Aqueduct, 1908-1913; A Physician's Recollections by Raymond G. Taylor, M.D.;* University of Southern California, Raubenheimer Distinguished Faculty Award, 1983, for "outstanding contributions in the areas of teaching, research and service," and Distinguished Teaching Award—Social Science Division, 1986; citations from City and County of Los Angeles, and keepsake and certificate from Huntington Corral of Westerners, all 1983, all for twenty years of service as editor of *Southern California Quarterly;* Benemerenti Medal (Pontifical Honor) bestowed by Pope John Paul II, 1984, for exceptional accomplishment and service; award of distinction, California Committee for the Promotion of History, 1985; Award of Merit, Conference of California Historical Societies, 1986.

WRITINGS:

Andrew Sublette, 1808-1853: Rocky Mountain Prince, Dawson's Book Shop, 1960.

(Author of introduction) Francis J. Weber, *George Francis Montgomery,* Westernlore, 1966.

The Trials of Isaac Graham, Dawson's Book Shop, 1967.

The Past Is Prologue: A Centennial Profile of Pacific Mutual Life Insurance Company, Ritchie, 1968.

(Author of introduction) Weber, *A Bibliography of California Bibliographies,* Ritchie, 1968, revised edition, 1992.

History of American Political Thought, two volumes, Addison-Wesley, 1975.

The Mexican War in Baja California, Dawson's Book Shop, 1977.

(Author of introduction) Alfred Robinson, *Life in California,* Da Capo Press, 1979.

The Life of Tom Horn Revisited, Los Angeles Corral of Westerners, 1992.

(Author of introduction) Joseph S. O'Flaherty, *The South Coast and Los Angeles, 1850-1917,* Historical Society of Southern California, 1992.

EDITOR

The Golden Frontier: The Recollections of Herman Francis Rinehart, 1851-1869, University of Texas Press, 1962.

Josiah Belden, 1841 California Overland Pioneer: His Memoir and Early Letters, Talisman Press, 1962.

The California Diary of Faxon Dean Atherton, 1836-1839, California Historical Society, 1964.

Letters of a Young Miner, John Howell Books, 1964.

Journey of James H. Bull: Baja California, October 1843-January, 1844, Dawson's Book Shop, 1966.

P. Garnier, *A Medical Journey in California,* Zeitlin & VerBrugge, 1967.

Hudson's Bay Company's First Fur Brigade to the Sacramento Valley, Sacramento Book Collectors Club, 1968.

Sketches on a Journey on the Two Oceans, Dawson's Book Shop, 1971.

San Francisco Vigilante Committee of 1856, Los Angeles Corral of Westerners, 1971.

Drawings of Ignacio Tirsch, S.J., Dawson's Book Shop, 1972.

Los Angeles and Its Environs in the Twentieth Century: A Bibliography of a Metropolis, Ritchie, 1973.

Westerners Brand Book Number 14, Los Angeles Corral of Westerners, 1974.

(Co-editor) *A Guide to Historic Places in Los Angeles County,* Kendall/Hunt, 1978.

Henry F. Holt, *A Frontier Doctor,* R. R. Donnelley & Sons, 1979.

Saint Stanislaw, Bishop of Krakow, Saint Stanislaw Publications Committee, 1979.

W. W. Robinson, *Los Angeles from the Days of the Pueblo: A Brief History and Guide to the Plaza,* revised edition, California Historical Society, 1981.

Men, Medicine and Water: The Building of the Los Angeles Aqueduct, 1908-1913; A Physician's Recollections by Raymond G. Taylor, M.D., Friends of the LACMA Library with Department of Water and Power, 1982.

Elsbeth Schulz-Bischof, translator, *The Letters of Jacob Baegert, 1749-1761: Jesuit Missionary in Baja California,* Dawson's Book Shop, 1982.

James Donohue, Maynard J. Geiger, and Iris Wilson Engstrand, translators, *The 1769 Transit of Venus: The Baja California Observations of Jean-Baptiste Chappe d'Auteroche, Vicente de Doz, and Joaquin Velasquez Cardenas de Leon,* Natural History Museum of Los Angeles, 1982.

Francis J. Weber: The Monsignor of the Archives, Dawson's Book Shop, 1983.

Southern California Historical Anthology, Historical Society of Southern California, 1984.

George W. Coe, *Frontier Fighter,* R. R. Donnelley & Sons, 1984.

(Co-editor) *A Guide to the History of California,* Greenwood Press, 1989.

The Bidwell-Bartleson Party, 1841 California Emigrant Adventure, Western Tanager and Los Angeles Corral of Westerners, 1992.

Southern California's Spanish Heritage, Historical Society of Southern California, 1993.

Southern California Local History: A Gathering of the Writings of W. W. Robinson, Southern California Historical Society, 1993.

The Rush for California Gold, R. R. Donnelley & Sons, 1993.

OTHER

Contributor to books, including *The Mountain Men,* edited by LeRoy R. Hafen, Arthur H. Clark, 1966-71; *University of California Centennial History,* University of California Press, 1968; *Notable American Women, 1607-1950,* Harvard University Press, 1971; and *Historians of the American West,* edited by John R. Wunder, Greenwood Press, 1988. Contributor of articles to periodicals, including *Pacific Historical Review, Montana Magazine,* and *American West.* Editor, *Southern California Quarterly,* 1982—.

WORK IN PROGRESS: An economic history of the American West, 1800-40; a biography of Michel Laframboise, "Captain of the California Trail," which will include an historical overview of Hudson's Bay Company activities in California to 1848; editing a series of five memoirs of Californios which are dictations held by the Bancroft Library, Berkeley; *The California Diary of Henry Mellus.*

SIDELIGHTS: Doyce B. Nunis, Jr., told *CA:* "My interest in history was rooted in my childhood. On my maternal grandfather's grave marker, a handsome slab of white Tennessee granite, the following is chiseled: 'Here lies Robert Greenlee Morris, direct descendant of Robert Morris, signer of the Declaration of Independence, the Articles of Confederation, and the Constitution of the United States. Erected in loving memory by the Sons of the American Revolution." Although as a young lad I did not know this family connection, I am sure that that historic ancestry had some special role in motivating me toward history.

"It seems to me in retrospect that I was born with history in my blood. This explains why I read so furiously as a young growing boy. While my peers played, I read or was in the library getting new books to take home to devour. In the elementary school I attended, every Friday we had a two-hour library period. During the course of the year I completely read out the biography, history, and political science sections. Each student had to give an oral report to the teacher/librarian on each book read. I keep the poor woman so busy she finally said to me, 'Please write out your reports,' hoping no doubt this would slow me down. I outfoxed her. I kept up a steady stream of reports. All in all I devoured almost five hundred books that school year.

"When my family transplanted itself to Los Angeles in 1938, I entered the Los Angeles Unified School District. I took a battery of tests and was immediately promoted a full grade. But one of my new joys was that students in the school I attended could volunteer for various duties in the school. I chose the school library. That devotion to libraries has continued to be a force in my life and work.

"I revel in the fact that learning is a lifelong process, and I am convinced that adherence to that dictum has made me a better informed and knowledgeable professional, a more caring and concerned person. I always like to close my lectures each year with those wonderful lines, slightly modified editorially, from the play *The Tea House of the August Moon:* 'Learning not always easy / sometimes very painful / but pain makes man think / thought makes man wise / and wisdom makes life more endurable.' I would add—more enjoyable."

BIOGRAPHICAL/CRITICAL SOURCES:

BOOKS

Lamar, Howard R., *Reader's Encyclopedia of the American West,* Cromwell, 1977.

PERIODICALS

Historical Society of Southern California Newsletter, Volume 1, numbers 3 and 4.

* * *

NURENBERG, Thelma
See GREENHAUS, Thelma Nurenberg

O

O'FARRELL, Patrick (James) 1933-

PERSONAL: Born September 17, 1933, in Greymouth, New Zealand; son of Patrick Vincent (a tailor) and Mai Briget (a teacher; maiden name, O'Sullivan) O'Farrell; married Deirdre Genevieve MacShane, December 29, 1956; children: Clare, Gerard, Virginia, Richard, Justin. *Education:* University of Canterbury, B.A., 1954, M.A. (with honors), 1956; Australian National University, Ph.D., 1961. *Religion:* Roman Catholic.

ADDRESSES: *Office*—School of History, University of New South Wales, P.O. Box l, Kensington, New South Wales 2033, Australia.

CAREER: University of New South Wales, Kensington, New South Wales, Australia, lecturer, 1959-64, senior lecturer, 1964-68, associate professor, 1969-71, professor of history, 1972—. Visiting professor at University College, National University of Ireland, Dublin, 1965-66, and Trinity College, Dublin, 1972-73.

MEMBER: Australian Academy of the Humanities (fellow).

WRITINGS:

Harry Holland, Militant Socialist, Australian National University Press, 1964.

The Catholic Church in Australia: A Short History, 1788-1967, Thomas Nelson, 1968.

(Editor) *Documents in Australian Catholic History,* Volume 1: *1788-1884,* Volume 2: *1884-1968,* Geoffrey Chapman, 1969.

Ireland's English Question, Schocken, 1971.

England and Ireland since 1800, Oxford University Press, 1975.

The Catholic Church and Community in Australia: A History, Thomas Nelson, 1977, revised edition published as *The Catholic Church and Community: An Australian History,* New South Wales University Press, 1985, 3rd edition, 1992.

Letters from Irish Australia, 1825-1925, New South Wales University Press, 1984.

The Irish in Australia, New South Wales University Press, 1986, revised edition, 1992.

Vanished Kingdoms: Irish in Australia and New Zealand, New South Wales University Press, 1990.

SIDELIGHTS: Patrick O'Farrell told *CA:* "My recent books move in approach and style toward history as literature. While adhering strongly to the traditional orthodoxies of the discipline—chronology, argument based on evidence, the visual research procedures—*Vanished Kingdoms: Irish in Australia and New Zealand*—adopts a free-ranging style and various literary devices to evoke a mood and convey a message in regard to the emigration/immigration predicament. As genre, it is experimental, part history, part memoir, part autobiography, part meditation, with my Irish parents in New Zealand used, with their family and a variety of other similar and contrasting families, as case studies illustrative of the whole immigration process.

"My current work is on immigrant mentalities, focused on the Irish, and situated in Australia and New Zealand, as this is the group and these are the areas I know best, and thus are best able to offer the degree of detail and personal exploration which is the foundation of my historical approach. Although I write what is properly described as general history, I build this on individual insights and particular localities in an effort to place wider observation on a base of personal historical experience and events. The aim is to produce living history in a style which will approximate to a conversation with the past, and engage the readers in mental dialogue with a history in which he/she can find identity and meaning, can gain information, but also feel resonance."

OGILVIE, Elisabeth May 1917-

PERSONAL: Born May 20, 1917, in Boston, MA; daughter of Frank Everett (in insurance) and Maude (a teacher; maiden name, Coates) Ogilvie. *Education:* Attended public schools in Massachusetts. *Politics:* Republican. *Religion:* Baptist.

ADDRESSES: *Home*—Pleasant Point, ME 04563. *Agent*—Watkins Loomis Agency, Inc., 150 East 35th St., Ste. 530, New York, NY 10016.

CAREER: Writer.

MEMBER: Author's League of America, Authors Guild, Mystery Writers of America, American Crime Writers, Foster Parents' Plan, Nature Conservancy, Maine Publishers and Writers Alliance.

AWARDS, HONORS: Fiction awards, New England Press Association, 1945, and North-East Woman's Press Association, 1946, both for *Storm Tide.*

WRITINGS:

High Tide at Noon, Crowell, 1944, reprinted, Down East, 1970.
Storm Tide, Crowell, 1945, reprinted, Down East, 1972.
The Ebbing Tide, Crowell, 1947, reprinted, Down East, 1974.
Honeymoon (based on a story by Vicki Baum), Bartholomew House, 1947.
Rowan Head, Whittlesey House, 1949.
My World Is an Island (autobiographical), illustrated by Paul Galdone, Whittlesey House, 1950, reprinted, Down East, 1990.
Whistle for a Wind: Maine, 1820, illustrated by Charles H. Geer, Scribner, 1954.
The Dawning of the Day, McGraw, 1954.
Blueberry Summer (juvenile), illustrated by Algot Stenbery, Whittlesey House, 1956.
No Evil Angel, McGraw, 1956.
The Fabulous Year (juvenile), Whittlesey House, 1958.
How Wide the Heart (juvenile), Whittlesey House, 1959, published as *A Steady Kind of Love,* Scholastic Book Service, 1979.
The Witch Door, McGraw, 1959.
The Young Islanders (juvenile), illustrated by Robert Henneberger, Whittlesey House, 1960.
Becky's Island, Whittlesey House, 1961.
Turn Around Twice, Whittlesey House, 1962.
Call Home the Heart, McGraw, 1962.
Ceiling of Amber (juvenile), McGraw, 1964, published as *Until the End of Summer,* Scholastic Book Service, 1981.
There May Be Heaven, McGraw, 1964.
Masquerade at Sea House, McGraw, 1965.
The Seasons Hereafter, McGraw, 1966.
The Pigeon Pair (juvenile), McGraw, 1967.
Waters on a Starry Night, McGraw, 1968.
Bellwood, McGraw, 1969.
Come Aboard and Bring Your Dory (juvenile), McGraw, 1969.
The Face of Innocence, McGraw, 1970.
A Theme for Reason, McGraw, 1970.
Weep and Know Why, McGraw, 1972.
Strawberries in the Sea, McGraw, 1973.
Image of a Lover, McGraw, 1974.
Where the Lost Aprils Are, McGraw, 1975.
The Dreaming Swimmer, McGraw, 1976.
An Answer in the Tide, McGraw, 1978.
A Dancer in Yellow, McGraw, 1979.
Beautiful Girl, Scholastic Book Service, 1980.
The Devil in Tartan, McGraw, 1980.
The Silent Ones, McGraw, 1981.
Too Young to Know, Scholastic Book Service, 1982.
A Forgotten Girl, Scholastic Book Service, 1982.
Jennie Glenroy, McGraw, 1983.
The Road to Nowhere, McGraw, 1983.
Jennie about to Be, McGraw, 1984.
My Summer Love, Scholastic Book Service, 1985.
The World of Jennie G., McGraw, 1986.
The Summer of the Osprey, McGraw, 1987.
When the Music Stopped, McGraw, 1989.

OTHER

Contributor of short stories to periodicals, including *Woman's Day.*

WORK IN PROGRESS: A novel set on Bennett's Island; a suspense novel.

SIDELIGHTS: Elisabeth May Ogilvie began writing books after taking a college extension course about writing for publication. Her instructor, a literary agent, helped her with her first novel and was her agent for nineteen years afterward. Ogilvie's books are primarily concerned with life on the Maine coast and its nearby islands. *High Tide at Noon,* the author's first novel, introduces the Bennett family, who reside on a Maine island. Critics reacted favorably to the book. Sterling North of *Book Week* declared that "there can be no doubt that Miss Ogilvie has a brilliant future," while Margaret Wallace noted in the *New York Times* that Ogilvie "has a warm, and homespun quality which suits her story well." David Tilden observed in the *Weekly Book Review,* "You feel and delight in the distinctive zestful life of a particular place and a particularly engaging family," adding, "Beyond these, the book has a vigor and substance which would do credit to an author with a long string of titles to her credit." Ogilvie continued the saga of the Bennetts and especially Jo Bennett in her next two novels, *Storm Tide* and *The Ebbing Tide.*

Ogilvie once told *CA:* "I would rather write than do anything else. In fact, I can't imaging a day going by without my having put *something down,* if it's only notes or a paragraph of description. Along with being a compulsive writer who likes to type in the dark at four in the morning so as to have an extra-long morning, I'm an outdoor person, and life on the coast of Maine gives me plenty of opportunities for scraping and painting boats, fishing, beachcombing, digging clams, and just wandering around.

"I hope my writing has matured over the years. The Bennetts and Sorensens of my earliest books are still very much alive to me, and I return to them at intervals. Many things have changed with the times on Bennett's Island, and the six young Bennetts of *High Tide at Noon* have gray in their hair and grown-up kids. But they're still islanders in their own kingdom.

"I've branched out into suspense stories and to some settings away from the Maine coast such as Nova Scotia and Scotland, which is where *The Silent Ones* takes place. I know I'm far from being a *great* writer, but I think I'm a good storyteller."

BIOGRAPHICAL/CRITICAL SOURCES:

BOOKS

Marquardt, Dorothy A., and Martha E. Ward, *Authors of Books for Young People,* Scarecrow, 1967.

Ogilvie, Elisabeth May, *My World Is an Island* (autobiographical), illustrated by Paul Galdone, Whittlesey House, 1950, reprinted, Down East, 1990.

Warfel, Harry R., *American Novelists of Today,* American Book Co., 1951.

PERIODICALS

Book Week, April 9, 1944.

Christian Science Monitor, May 10, 1956.

New York Times, April 16, 1944.

New York Times Book Review, May 7, 1967.

Weekly Book Review, April 16, 1944.

Wilson Library Bulletin, September, 1951.

* * *

OLIVARES, Julian (Jr.) 1940-

PERSONAL: Born December 6, 1940, in San Antonio, TX; son of Julian (a theatre concession superintendent) and Benicia (a garment worker; maiden name, Carrillo) Olivares; married Kathleen M. Sayers (a university administrator), June 6, 1975. *Education:* California State College, Los Angeles (now California State University, Los Angeles), B.A., 1968; University of Texas at Austin, M.A., 1974, Ph.D., 1977.

ADDRESSES: Home—3510 Maroneal, Houston, TX 77025. *Office*—Hispanic and Classical Languages, University of Houston, University Park, Houston, TX 77004.

CAREER: Bridgewater State College, Bridgewater, MA, assistant professor of Spanish, 1978-81; University of Houston, Houston, TX, assistant professor, 1981-86, associate professor of Hispanic and classical languages, 1986-93, professor of Spanish and Mexican American studies, 1993—. Arte Publico Press, associate editor, 1982-86, senior editor, 1986—. Visiting scholar, University of Texas at Austin, 1985-86. Lecturer and speaker at national and international conferences. Member of board, Friends of Houston Public Library. *Military service:* U.S. Navy, 1959-62.

MEMBER: American Association of Teachers of Spanish and Portuguese, National Association of Chicano Studies, Modern Language Association of America.

AWARDS, HONORS: Ford Foundation fellowship, 1975-77; grant-in-aid from American Council of Learned Societies, 1979; distinguished service award from Bridgewater State College, 1981; grants from National Endowment for the Humanities, 1984, 1987, 1989, 1992; senior postdoctoral fellowship for minorities from National Research Council/Ford Foundation, 1985-86; certificate of achievement for editorial excellence and vision, Coordinating Council of Literary Magazines, 1986, 1987; grant, Directorate of Cultural Relations, Spanish Ministry of State, 1988, 1992; American Philosophical Society grant, 1992.

WRITINGS:

The Love Poetry of Francisco de Quevedo: An Aesthetic and Existential Study, Cambridge University Press, 1983.

(Contributor) J. A. Garcia, J. Garcia, and T. Cordova, editors, *The Chicano Struggle,* Bilingual Press/Editorial Bilingue, 1984.

EDITOR

International Studies in Honor of Tomas Rivera, Arte Publico Press, 1986.

The Harvest/La cosecha, Arte Publico Press, 1989.

Tomas Rivera, *The Searchers: Collected Poetry,* Arte Publico Press, 1990.

Tomas Rivera: The Complete Works, Arte Publico Press, 1992.

Cuentos Hispanos de las Estados Unidos, Arte Publico Press, 1993.

(With Elizabeth S. Boyce) *Tras el espejo la musa escribe: Lirica femenina de las Siglos de Oro,* Siglo Veintiumo Editores, 1993.

Also editor of numerous other books.

OTHER

General editor of "U.S. Hispanic Literary Heritage" series. Also contributor to numerous books, including *New Frontiers in American Literature: Chicana Creativity and Criticism,* edited by Maria Herrera-Sobek and Helena Maria Viramontes, Arte Publico Press, 1987. Contributor to periodicals, including *Neophilologus* (Amsterdam), *Hispanic Review, Confluencia, Hispanic Journal, Critica, Modern Language Studies, Revista de Estudios Hispanicos,* and *Hispania.* Senior editor of *American Review* (formerly *Revista Chicano-Riquena*), 1983—.

WORK IN PROGRESS: A critical study of Spanish women's poetry of the sixteenth and seventeenth centuries.

SIDELIGHTS: In *The Love Poetry of Francisco de Quevedo* Julian Olivares examines the love poems of the seventeenth-century Spanish writer, revealing Quevedo's vision of love. Olivares concentrates on three main motifs seen throughout the poems—Petrarchan chivalric love, Neoplatonism, and an acute awareness of death; "in his love poetry [Quevedo] became his own tormentor and victim," explained Alan Paterson in a *Times Literary Supplement* review, "conducting a remorseless inquisition into a mind and body racked by the expectations and limitations of desire." Calling *The Love Poetry of Francisco de Quevedo* a "close and erudite analysis," Paterson reflected that "it is not easy poetry; it is composed with unremitting intensity." He added: "It takes courage to confront this kind of poetry, and Julian Olivares emerges with great credit; certainly this is a major contribution to studies of seventeenth-century Spanish poetry."

Olivares told *CA* that his interests lie in the literature of sixteenth- and seventeenth-century Spain and in editing *American Review,* "the oldest and most respected review dedicated to the expression of U.S. Hispanic creativity." He added: "As senior editor of Arte Publico Press, I have edited books by such highly regarded Hispanic writers as Gary Soto (*Small Faces*), Tino Villanueva (*Shaking Off the Dark*), Pat Mora (*Chants*), Ana Castillo (*Women Are Not Roses*), Lorna Dee Cervantes (*The Cables of Genocide*), Luis Omar Salinas (*Sometimes Mysteriously*), and Denise Chavez (*The Last of the Menu Girls*). The *American Review* and Arte Publico Press are dedicated to bringing national recognition to the contributions to the national heritage by Hispanic American writers and to assuring their place in the tradition of American letters."

BIOGRAPHICAL/CRITICAL SOURCES:

PERIODICALS

Times Literary Supplement, April 13, 1984.

ONDAATJE, (Philip) Michael 1943-

PERSONAL: Born September 12, 1943, in Colombo, Ceylon (now Sri Lanka); son of Mervyn Ondaatje and Doris Gratiaen. *Education:* Attended St. Thomas' College, Colombo, and Dulwich College, London; attended Bishop's University, Lennoxville, Quebec, 1962-64; University of Toronto, B.A., 1965; Queen's University, Kingston, Ontario, M.A., 1967.

Avocational Interests: Hound breeding, hog breeding.

ADDRESSES: Agent—c/o Ellen Levine, 15 East 26th St., Suite 1801, New York, NY 10010. *Office*—Department of English, Glendon College, York University, 2275 Bayview Ave., Toronto, Ontario M4N 3M6, Canada.

CAREER: Taught at University of Western Ontario, London, 1967-71; member of Department of English, Glendon College, York University, Toronto, Ontario, 1971—. Visiting professor, University of Hawaii, Honolulu, summer, 1979; Brown University, 1990. Editor, *Mongrel Broadsides.* Director of films, including *Sons of Captain Poetry,* 1970; *Carry on Crime and Punishment,* 1972; *Royal Canadian Hounds,* 1973; and *The Clinton Special,* 1974. Inventor of Dragland Hog Feeder, 1975.

AWARDS, HONORS: Ralph Gustafson Award, 1965; Epstein Award, 1966; E. J. Pratt Medal, 1966; President's Medal, University of Western Ontario, 1967; Canadian Governor-General's Award for Literature, 1971, 1980; Canada-Australia prize, 1980; Booker McConnell Prize, British Book Council, 1992, for *The English Patient.*

WRITINGS:

POETRY

The Dainty Monsters, Coach House Press, 1967.

The Man with Seven Toes, Coach House Press, 1969.

The Collected Works of Billy the Kid: Left Handed Poems (also see below), Anansi, 1970, Norton, 1974.

Rat Jelly, Coach House Press, 1973.

Elimination Dance, Nairn Coldstream (Ontario), 1978, revised, Brick, 1980.

There's a Trick with a Knife I'm Learning To Do: Poems, 1963-1978, Norton, 1979, published as *Rat Jelly, and Other Poems, 1963-1978,* Boyars, 1980.

Secular Love, Coach House Press, 1984, Norton, 1985.

All along the Mazinaw: Two Poems (broadside), Woodland Pattern (Wisconsin), 1986.

The Cinnamon Peeler: Selected Poems, Pan, 1989, Knopf, 1991.

NOVELS

Coming Through Slaughter (biographical novel), Anansi, 1976, Norton, 1977.

In the Skin of a Lion (also see below), Knopf, 1987.

The English Patient, Knopf, 1992.

PLAYS

The Collected Works of Billy the Kid (based on his poetry), produced in Stratford, Ontario, 1973, New York City, 1974, and London, 1984.

In the Skin of A Lion (based on his novel), Knopf, 1987.

EDITOR

The Broken Ark (animal verse), Oberon Press, 1971, revised as *A Book of Beasts,* 1979.

Personal Fictions: Stories by Munro, Wiebe, Thomas, and Blaise, Oxford University Press, 1977.

The Long Poem Anthology, Coach House Press, 1979.

(With Russell Banks and David Young) *Brushes with Greatness: An Anthology of Chance Encounters with Greatness,* Coach House Press, 1989.

(With Linda Spalding) *The Brick Anthology,* Coach House Press, 1989.

From Ink Lake: An Anthology of Canadian Short Stories, Viking, 1990.

The Faber Book of Contemporary Canadian Short Stories, Faber, 1990.

OTHER

Leonard Cohen (literary criticism), McClelland & Stewart, 1970.

Claude Glass (literary criticism), Coach House Press, 1979.

Tin Roof, Island (British Columbia), 1982.

Running in the Family (memoir), Norton, 1982.

Author's manuscripts are included in the National Archives, Ottawa, Canada, and the Metropolitan Toronto Library.

SIDELIGHTS: Canadian writer Michael Ondaatje dissolves the lines between prose and poetry through the breadth of his works in both genres. "Moving in and out of imagined landscape, portrait and documentary, anecdote or legend, Ondaatje writes for the eye and the ear simultaneously," notes Diane Wakoski in *Contemporary Poets.* Whether reshaping recollections of friends and family from his childhood in old Ceylon in *Running in the Family,* or retelling an American myth in *The Collected Works of Billy the Kid,* the experiences of many individuals are made vivid, heard, and almost real for his readers. In addition to writing novels, plays, and poetry collections, Ondaatje has edited several books, including *The Faber Book of Contemporary Canadian Short Stories,* praised as a "landmark" by reviewer Christine Bold in the *Times Literary Supplement* for its representation of "Canadian voices accented by native, black, French, Caribbean, Indian, Japanese and Anglo-Saxon origins."

Ondaatje's poetry is seen by critics as continually changing, evolving as the author experiments with the shape and sound of words. Although his poetic forms may differ, his works focus on the myths that root deep in common cultural experience. As a poet, he recreates their intellectual expression in depicting the affinity between the art of legend and the world at large. "He cares more about the relationship between art and nature than any other poet since the Romantics," exclaims Liz Rosenberg in the *New York Times Book Review,* "and more than most contemporary poets care about any ideas at all." Some of Ondaatje's verse has approached the fragmentary, as in *Secular Love,* a collection of poems he published in 1985. In contrast, his most widely-known work, *The Collected Works of Billy the Kid* verges on a prose format while retaining a strong poetic lyricism.

"Concerned always to focus on the human, the private, and the 'real' over the theoretical and the ideological, Ondaatje examines the internal workings of characters who struggle against and burst through that which renders people passive," notes Diane Watson in *Contemporary Novelists,* "and which renders human experience programmatic and static." *In the Skin of a Lion,* the author's 1987 novel, focuses on a man raised in rural Canada who, at the age of twenty-one, comes to the growing city of Toronto and lives among the immigrants that inhabit its working-class neighborhoods. Physical actions and inner challenges define Ondaatje's characters as individuals, creators within their own lives, and give both purpose to their existence and redemption to their inner reality. In this work, a historical epoch is seen as the struggle of the individual to break free of the confines of his culture rather than simply a collection of social and political goals. As Michael Hulse describes *In the Skin of a Lion* in the *Times Literary Supplement,* it "maps high society and the sub culture of the underprivileged in Toronto in the 1920s and 1930s. . . . But it is also . . . about communication, about men 'utterly alone' who are waiting (in Ondaatje's terms) to break through a chrysalis."

In *Coming Through Slaughter,* a novel well-grounded in the history of early twentieth-century New Orleans, Ondaatje creates a possible life of the late jazz musician Buddy Bolden, remembered as a brilliant coronetist whose performances were never recorded due to a tragic mental collapse at an early age. Mixing interviews with those who remember Bolden, historical fact, and his richly-imagined conception of the musician's inner thoughts on his way to madness, Ondaatje fashions what Wilson terms a "fractured narrative . . . [tracing] the personal anarchy of . . . Bolden and the perspectives on him of those who knew him best."

The English Patient, published in 1992 as Ondaatje's fifth novel, tells the story of a Canadian nurse who stays behind in the bombed remains of a villa near the World War II battlefields of northern Italy to tend to an English soldier who has been severely burned. Joined by two other solders, relationships form between these four characters that parallel, as Cressida Connolly notes in the *Spectator,* "those of a small and faded Eden." Ranking the author among such contemporary novelists as Ian McEwan and Martin Amis, Connolly praises the poetic quality of Ondaatje's fiction. "The writing is so heady that you have to keep putting the book down between passages so as not to reel from the sheer force and beauty of it," the reviewer exclaims, adding that "when I finished the book I felt as dazed as if I'd just awoken from a powerful dream."

Running in the Family, a memoir, was published in 1992. In it, Ondaatje blends together family stories—some which attain the stature of myth—with poems, photographs, personal anecdotes, and the like to create a novel that reads more like a poem. As his family history follows a path leading from the genteel innocence of the Ceylonese privileged class as the sun set on the British Empire to the harsh glare of the modern age, so Ondaatje's narrative seeks the inner character of his father, a man of whom the author writes, "my loss was that I never spoke to him as an adult." "In reality, this is a mythology exaggerated and edited by the survivors," writes Anton Mueller in the *Washington Post Book World.* "Seduced by the wealth and luxury of its imaginative reality, Ondaatje enters the myth without disturbing it. With a prose style equal to the voluptuousness of his subject and a sense of humor never too far away, *Running in the Family* is sheer reading pleasure."

BIOGRAPHICAL/CRITICAL SOURCES:

BOOKS

The Annotated Bibliography of Canada's Major Authors 6, ECW Press, 1985.

Contemporary Novelists, fifth edition, St. James Press, 1991, pp. 710-11.

Contemporary Poets, fifth edition, St. James Press, 1991, pp. 724-25.

Solecki, Sam, editor, *Spider Blues: Essays on Michael Ondaatje,* Vehicule Press, 1985.

PERIODICALS

Fiddlehead, spring, 1968.

New York Times Book Review, April 24, 1977; December 22, 1985, pp. 22-23.

Saturday Night, July, 1968.

Spectator, September 5, 1992, p. 32.

Times Literary Supplement, September 4, 1987, p. 948; November 3, 1989, p. 1217; October 19, 1990, p. 1130: September 22, 1992, p. 23.

Washington Post Book World, January 2, 1983, pp. 9, 13; November 1, 1987, p. 4.*

—Sketch by Pamela L. Shelton

* * *

ORBACH, Susie 1946-

PERSONAL: Born November 6, 1946, in London, England; daughter of Maurice (a member of Parliament) and Ruth (a teacher; maiden name, Huebsch) Orbach. *Education:* Attended University of London; School of Slavonic and East European Studies, B.A., (Russian and East European history), 1968; Richmond College of the City University of New York, B.A., (women's studies), 1972; State University of New York at Stony Brook, MSW, 1975. *Politics:* "Socialist/Feminist." *Religion:* Jewish.

ADDRESSES: Home and office—Women's Therapy Centre Institute, 80 East 11th St., #101, New York, NY 10003; and 2 Lancaster Drive, London NW3 4HA, England.

CAREER: New York Law Commune, New York City, in city planning, 1969-71; group psychotherapist, 1971-78; Richmond College of the City University of New York, New York City, faculty member, 1972-74; Greenwich House, New York City, psychotherapist, 1973-75; Women's Therapy Centre, London, England, cofounder and director, 1976-81; Women's Therapy Centre Institute, New York City, cofounder and codirector, 1981-84, supervising psychotherapist, 1982—. Lecturer on women's psychology, eating disorders, and women's self image at colleges and universities in the United States and Europe, including Leeds University, Vassar College, and Harvard University.

WRITINGS:

Fat Is a Feminist Issue: The Anti-Diet Guide to Permanent Weight Loss, Paddington, 1978.

Fat Is a Feminist Issue II: A Program to Conquer Compulsive Eating, Berkley Publishing, 1982.

(With Luise Eichenbaum) *Outside In Inside Out: A Feminist and Psychoanalytic Approach to Women's Psychology,* Penguin Books (London), 1982, revised edition published as *Understanding Women: A Feminist and Psychoanalytic Approach,* Basic Books, 1983.

(With Eichenbaum) *What Do Women Want?,* Coward McCann, 1983.

Hunger Strike: The Anorectic's Struggle as a Metaphor for Our Time, Norton, 1986.

(With Eichenbaum) *Bittersweet: Love, Competition, & Envy in Women's Friendships,* Century, 1987, published in the United States as *Between Women: Love, Envy and Competition in Women's Relationships,* Viking, 1988.

Also author of introductions to various books. Contributor to books, including *A Handbook of Psychotherapy for Anorexia Nervosa and Bulimia,* edited by D. M. Garner and P. Garfinkel, Guilford, 1984, and *Women Therapists Working with Women,* edited by C. Brody, Springer Publishing, 1984. Also contributor of articles to journals, including *Issues in Radical Therapy, British Journal of Sexual Medicine, Feminism & Psychology, Journal of Social Work Practice,* and *Science for the People.* Columnist for the *Guardian Weekend* (London).

SIDELIGHTS: Susie Orbach once told CA: "I do not see myself as a writer. In fact I find it excruciating work, but I think it is important to share ideas that are nurtured in the women's liberation movement to a mass audience. I think it is important to give a different view of ways to see and change the world than we learn through conventional channels. Hence I write from the perspective of one who is attempting to change our ways of doing and seeing."

In *Fat Is a Feminist Issue: The Anti-Diet Guide to Permanent Weight Loss,* Orbach endeavors to modify the way compulsive eaters approach dieting. One difference between Orbach's book and other diet books is that it emphasizes permanent reduction. This is an important distinction, for Orbach estimates that of all the weight that is lost, ninety-five percent is gained back. Devoid of diet gimmicks, the book proposes that the key to losing weight is to understand the various reasons for compulsive eating. *Listener* critic Gill Pyrah describes Orbach's method this way: "Each woman must undermine her fantasy of perfection and her fat's role of barrier or protest movement incarnate, and learn to live as her whole self, flab and all. Then, gradually, as she learns to react accurately to her hunger pangs, her extra pounds may disappear, almost incidentally." Orbach suggests that *Fat Is a Feminist Issue* be used in selfhelp groups, and while Pyrah cautions against the use of the book by inexperienced groups, he concludes: "Even so, no argument should dissuade a woman who thinks herself as little as five pounds overweight from reading this startling book."

BIOGRAPHICAL/CRITICAL SOURCES:

PERIODICALS

Listener, May 4, 1978.
New York Times Book Review, March 16, 1980.
Times Literary Supplement, April 25, 1986.

* * *

ORTNER, Toni 1941-
(Toni Ortner-Zimmerman)

PERSONAL: Born March 11, 1941, in Brooklyn, NY; daughter of Melvin (a lawyer and owner of a machine corporation) and Sylvia (a teacher) Ortner; married Stephen Michael Zimmerman (a college professor), May 27, 1962 (divorced, 1988); children: Lisa Michelle. *Education:* Hofstra University, B.A., 1962; Western Connecticut State College, M.A., 1979.

ADDRESSES: Home—Bell Hollow Rd., Putnam Valley, NY.

CAREER: Bronx Community College of the City University of New York, Bronx, NY; adjunct lecturer in English, 1971-80; staff member of writing department at School of New Resources, College of New Rochelle, New Rochelle, NY; currently member of English and social science department, Monroe College, Bronx. Adjunct lecturer in English, Mercy College. Has given readings, lectured, and conducted workshops for numerous organizations, including Greater Middletown Arts Council, Putnam Valley Free Library, Hofstra University, State University of New York, and City College of the City of New York Noon Poetry Series.

MEMBER: Poets and Writers, Inc.

WRITINGS:

POETRY

Requiem, Black Tie Press, 1991.

UNDER NAME TONI ORTNER-ZIMMERMAN

Woman in Search of Herself, Know, Inc., 1974.
To an Imaginary Lover, Morgan Press, 1975.
Entering Another Country, Basilisk Press, 1976.
I Dream Now of the Sun, Konglomerati, 1976.
Never Stop Dancing, Greenfield Press, 1976.
Stones, hand-set limited edition with woodcut engravings, Huffman, 1976.
As If Anything Could Grow Back Perfect, Mayapple Press, 1979.
Dream in Pienza, Timberline Press of Texas, 1979.
Life/Generations/Dancing, privately printed, 1980.

OTHER

Work has appeared in anthologies, including *True to Life Adventure Stories,* Volume 2, Crossing Press, 1981; *Hyperion Black Sun, New Moon,* Carolina Wren, 1980; *American Poetry Confronts the 1990s,* Black Tie Press, 1990; and *Above Underground Poets,* Merging Media, 1990. Contributor to over one hundred literary periodicals, including *Canadian Forum, Minnesota Review, Maryland Review, Kansas Quarterly, New England Review, Mudfish,* and *Literary Review.*

WORK IN PROGRESS: Giving Myself over to J. S. Bach; Ides of March; The House in the Woods and Other Poems.

ORTNER-ZIMMERMAN, Toni
See ORTNER, Toni

* * *

OVESEN, Ellis
See SMITH, Shirley M(ae)

* * *

OXNARD, Charles (Ernest) 1933-

PERSONAL: Born September 9, 1933, in Durham, England; son of Charles (an engineer) and Frances Anne (maiden name, Golightly) Oxnard; married Eleanor Arthur, February 2, 1959; children: Hugh, David. *Education:* University of Birmingham, B.Sc. (first class honors), 1955, M.B. and Ch.B., 1958, Ph.D., 1962.

ADDRESSES: Home—44 Langham Street, Nedlands, Western Australia, 6009. *Office*—Center for Human Biology, Nedlands, University of Western Australia, 6009.

CAREER: Queen Elizabeth Hospital, Birmingham, England, house physician, 1958-59, house surgeon, 1959; University of Birmingham, Birmingham, research fellow, 1959-62, lecturer, 1962-65, senior lecturer in anatomy, 1965-66; University of Chicago, Chicago, IL, associate professor, 1966-70, professor of anatomy, anthropology, and evolutionary biology, 1970-78, faculty associate of Center for Graduate Studies, 1969-78, master of Biology Collegiate Division and associate dean of Biological Sciences Graduate Division and Pritzker School of Medicine, 1972-73, dean of the College of Letters, Arts and Sciences, 1973-78; University of Southern California, Los Angeles, CA, professor and dean of Graduate School, 1978-83, University Professor of anatomy and biology, 1983-87; University of Western Australia, Perth, professor of anatomy and human biology, 1987—, director, Center for Human Biology, 1989—, director, Division of Science, 1990—. Overseas associate, University of Birmingham, 1970—; research associate, Field Museum, 1984—; board member, Pasteur Institute of America, 1987—.

MEMBER: Society for Study of Human Biology (treasurer, 1962-66), Anatomical Society of Great Britain and Ireland (councillor, 1972-73), Australasian Society for Human Biology (president, 1987-90), Anatomical Society of Australia and New Zealand (president, 1989—), American Society of Biomechanics (president, 1979-80), American Society of Zoologists, American Association for the Advancement of Science, New York Academy of Sciences (fellow), American Association for the Advancement of Science (fellow), Phi Beta Kappa, Sigma Xi.

AWARDS, HONORS: Research grants from U.S. Department of Health, Education, and Welfare, 1963-66 and 1967-70, U.S. Public Health Service, 1967-70, National Science Foundation, 1971, 1974, and 1977, Rane Foundation for Medical Research, 1986-91, Australian National Health and Medical Research Council, 1988-91, and Australian Research Council, 1988-91; D.Sc., University of Birmingham, 1975; named honorary professor, University of Hong Kong, 1977; Chan Memorial Medal, 1982; Phi Kappa Phi Book Award, 1984; Hong Kong Council Book Award, 1984.

WRITINGS:

Form and Pattern in Human Evolution, University of Chicago Press, 1973.

(With J.T. Stern, Jr.) *Primate Locomotion: Some Links with Evolution and Morphology,* Albert J. Phiebig, 1973.

Uniqueness and Diversity in Human Evolution: Morphometric Studies of Australopithecines, University of Chicago Press, 1975.

Human Fossils: The New Revolution, Encyclopaedia Britannica, 1977.

Beyond Biometrics: Holistic Views of Biological Structure, University of Hong Kong Press, 1981.

The Order of Man: A Biomathematical Anatomy of the Primates, Yale University Press, 1984.

Humans, Apes and Chinese Fossils, Hong Kong University Press, 1985.

Fossils, Teeth and Sex, University of Washington Press, 1987.

Animal Lifestyles and Anatomies, University of Washington Press, 1990.

WORK IN PROGRESS: Bone, Bones and Biomechanics, The Physicians Apprentice, and *Evolution: The Human Enigma;* other studies in primate and human evolution.

SIDELIGHTS: Charles Oxnard told *CA:* "My business is research. My books are a plea to do science. My subject, human evolution, long accepted in Europe, is almost violently controversial in the United States. And the controversies are not only those engendered by the religious fundamentalists, but also those inherent among evolutionary biologists themselves. (Indeed, the latter have been the fiercer!)

"One set of controversies has concerned the methods used in untangling the fossil part of the human evolutionary story. Three decades ago, the study of fossils encompassed mainly visual assessments of old bones; quantification and analysis were not only generally ignored, but actually denigrated. Ten years later, though still controversial to some, measurement and analysis were generally regarded as unexceptional. Two decades ago, the developing discipline of biomechanics as applied to fossils was new and rarely applied. Ten years later, biomechanical inferences about fossils had arrived. One decade ago, image analysis of fossil form and pattern was merely show and tell. Today, image analysis provides new insights about old bones. I am happy to have been in the vanguard in each of these additions to our investigatory armamentarium (though it has to be acknowledged that the most recent of these is still to be generally accepted).

"A second group of controversies has concerned the results of human evolutionary investigations. Again, as recently as three decades ago, the australopithecines were believed undoubted human ancestors. Ten years later, and even today, many workers draw evolutionary trees that place one or other of these fossil groups away from the human lineage. Two decades ago the australopithecines were believed to be undoubted human-like striding bipeds. Ten years later (and even today), many workers suggested that, to the australopithecines' bipedality—itself rather different from that of modern humans—must be added degrees of arboreal activity. One decade ago it was believed that the sexual difference in the great apes of today (e.g. the male double the size of the female, two or three adult females to each male, and major behavioral differences between the sexes) is the way humans were. Ten years later, it seems likely that small sexual differences, one-to-one sex ratios, and sexual cooperation as a human characteristic are far older (at least two to three million years) than ever before believed. It is, indeed, even possible that the old saw "The way the great apes are is the way we were" should be revised. The way we are may well have been the way the great apes were.

"Again, I am happy to have been in the forefront of each of these changes of mind, though, again, it has to be acknowledged that the third of these is yet to be substantially accepted. Whence Man? Whence Woman? And Whither Humanity? We still do not know. But the fun (and the angst) has been in being ahead of the game."

* * *

OXORN, Harry 1920-

PERSONAL: Born December 31, 1920, in Romania; son of Milan (a lawyer) and Karla (Mallek) Oxorn; married Pearl Futterman, June 15, 1947 (divorced, 1982). *Education:* McGill University, B.A., 1941; Dalhousie University, M.D., C.M., 1945. *Religion:* Jewish.

ADDRESSES: *Home*—17 Algonquin Dr., Aylmer, Quebec, Canada J9J 1A8.

CAREER: Private practice of obstetrics and gynecology in Montreal. Civic Hospital, Ottawa, Ontario, obstetrician and gynecologist in chief, 1972-86. University of Ottawa, professor, 1972-82, department of obstetrics and gynecology, professor and chair, 1982-86. *Military service:* Royal Canadian Army, Medical Corps, 1943-46; became captain.

MEMBER: Canadian Medical Association, Royal College of Physicians and Surgeons of Canada, Society of Obstetricians and Gynecologists of Canada.

WRITINGS:

(With W. R. Foote) *Human Labor and Birth,* Appleton, 1964, 5th edition, 1986.

(With Peter A. Fried) *Smoking for Two,* Free Press, 1980.

H. B. Atlee, M.D.: A Biography, Lancelot, 1983.

P

PAINTER, Daniel
See BURGESS, Michael (Roy)

* * *

PALMER, Peter John 1932-

PERSONAL: Born September 20, 1932, in Melbourne, Australia; son of Roy Tasman (a clerk) and Marjorie (a tailor; maiden name, Evans) Palmer; married Elizabeth Fischer, December 22, 1955 (divorced March, 1974); children: David, Ellen. *Education:* University of Melbourne, B.A., 1953, B.Ed., 1967. *Religion:* None.

Avocational Interests: Painting, war games.

ADDRESSES: Home—34 Ardgower Court, Lower Templestowe, Victoria 3107, Australia.

CAREER: High school teacher of history and geography in Ouyen, Australia, 1954-57, in Alexandra, Australia, 1958-60, 1962-63, in Luton, England, 1961, in Burwood, Australia, 1964-68, in Ashwood, Australia, 1969, and in Waverley, Australia, 1970-76; Koonung High School, Box Hill North, Australia, deputy principal, 1977-80; Preston East High School, Victoria, Australia, principal, 1981-88. Part-time tutor at University of Melbourne, 1965-67; part-time lecturer at Monash University, 1968.

WRITINGS:

The Past and Us (textbook; self-illustrated), F. W. Cheshire, 1957.

The Twentieth Century (textbook; self-illustrated), F. W. Cheshire, 1964.

(Executive editor) *Macmillan Australian Atlas,* Macmillan, 1983, 4th edition, 1993.

Geography 10 (textbook; self-illustrated), Macmillan, 1992.

EDITOR, CONTRIBUTOR, AND ILLUSTRATOR

Confrontations, Macmillan, 1971.
Interaction, Macmillan, 1973.
Expansion, Macmillan, 1974.
Survival, Macmillan, 1975.
Three Worlds, Macmillan, 1977.
Earth and Man, Macmillan, 1980.
Man on the Land, Macmillan, 1981.
Man and Machines, Macmillan, 1983.
Challenge, Macmillan, 1985.

SIDELIGHTS: Peter John Palmer commented to *CA:* "In Australia, at least, I believe that during the past decade the methodologists have led school geography into a dreary wasteland of jargon and statistics; whereas the subject should be one of interest, enjoyment, and enlightenment. I have tried to produce books which will help ordinary kids, who will never be teachers or professional geographers, gain an understanding of the world around them and an awareness of the physical, economic, and political agents which have shaped and continue to change that world."

* * *

PARKER, Pat 1944-1989

PERSONAL: Born January 20, 1944, in Houston, TX; died of cancer, June 4, 1989; daughter of Ernest Nathaniel (a tire retreader) and Marie Louise (a domestic; maiden name, Anderson) Cooks; married Ed Bullins, June 20, 1962 (divorced, January 17, 1966); married Robert F. Parker, January 20, 1966 (divorced); children: Cassidy Brown, Anastasia Dunham-Parker. *Education:* Attended Los Angeles City College and San Francisco State College (now University). *Politics:* "Black Feminist Lesbian."

ADDRESSES: Home—Oakland, CA. *Office*—Aya Enterprises, 1547 Palos Verdes Mall, Walnut Creek, CA 94569.

CAREER: Worked variously as a proofreader, proof operator, waitress, maid, clerk, and creative writing instructor. Director, Feminist Women's Health Center, Oakland, California, 1978-89; founder, Black Women's Revolutionary Council, Oakland, 1980.

AWARDS, HONORS: WIM Publications Memorial Poetry Award established in her name.

MEMBER: Gente.

WRITINGS:

VERSE

Child of Myself, Women's Press Collective, 1972.
Pit Stop: Words, Women's Press Collective, 1974.
Movement in Black: The Collected Poetry of Pat Parker, 1961-1978 (includes work from *Child of Myself* and *Pit Stop*), foreword by Audre Lorde, introduction by Judy Grahn, Diana Press, 1978.
WomanSlaughter, Diana Press, 1978.
Jonestown and Other Madness, Firebrand Books, 1985.

OTHER

Where Would I Be without You: The Poetry of Pat Parker and Judy Grahn (audio recording), Olivia Records, c. 1976.
Contributor, *This Bridge Called My Back: Writings by Radical Women of Color,* edited by Cherrie Moraga and Gloria Anzaldua, Women of Color Press, 1981.

Contributor to *Plexus, Amazon Poetry, I Never Told Anyone, Home Girls,* other anthologies, magazines and newspapers.

SIDELIGHTS: "This loud and rich-mouthed poet," Lyndie Brimstone writes of Pat Parker in *Feminist Review,* "who planted her feet firmly on platforms all over America and demanded that her audiences, whoever they may be, pay attention, was not only working class, she was Black and lesbian: the very first to refuse to compromise and speak openly from all her undiluted experience." Until her death from cancer in 1989, Parker was not only a highly visible black Lesbian poet—Adrian Oktenberg, writing in the *Women's Review of Books,* calls her "the poet laureate of the Black and Lesbian peoples"—but a committed activist in radical politics and community issues. In addition to urgent, angry poems against racism, sexism, and homophobia, Parker wrote "exquisitely sensual love poems," Brimstone reports.

In a *Callaloo* review of the 1978 collection *Movement in Black,* which includes poems from her earlier books, Gerald Barrax commends Parker's qualities of "wit, humor, and irony" but suggests that her work often falls into "rhetoric, sentimentality and didacticism." He particularly praises the autobiographical poem "Goat Child" for its "ease, speed and charm." Brimstone terms the same poem "a courageous, sinewy work" and "a fine example of Pat Parker's skill." In her review of Parker's final book, *Jonestown and Other Madness,* Oktenberg suggests that if Parker's poetry is "simple," it is "deceptively so." "She gets down on paper complicated states of feeling, lightning-quick changes of thought, and she deals with complex issues in language and imagery that any bar dyke can understand," Oktenberg says, adding, "You don't have to have an education in poetry to read [Parker's work], though the more you have, the better the work becomes." Parker's "standpoint as a black lesbian mother," Rochelle Ratner comments in *Library Journal,* "imbues her poetry with a highly political consciousness." The feeling and vision behind Pat Parker's poetry may perhaps be summed up in the closing lines of the first poem in *Jonestown and Other Madness:* " I care for you/ I care for our world/ if I stop/ caring about one/ it would be only/ a matter of time/ before I stop/ loving/ the other."

BIOGRAPHICAL/CRITICAL SOURCES:

BOOKS

McEwen, Christian, editor, *Naming the Waves: Contemporary Lesbian Poetry,* Virago, 1988.
Moraga, Cherrie, and Gloria Anzaldua, *This Bridge Called My Back: Writings by Radical Women of Color,* Women of Color Press, 1981.
Parker, Pat, *Jonestown and Other Madness,* Firebrand Books, 1985.

PERIODICALS

Callaloo, winter, 1986, pp. 259-62.
Colby Library Quarterly (Waterville, Maine), March 1982, pp. 9-25.
Conditions: Six, 1980, p. 217.
Feminist Review, No. 34, spring 1990, pp. 4-7.
Library Journal, July 1985, p. 77.
Margins, Vol. 23, 1987, pp. 60-61.
Women's Review of Books, April 1986, pp. 17-19.*

* * *

PAXTON, Robert O(wen) 1932-

PERSONAL: Born June 15, 1932, in Lexington, VA; son of Matthew W. (a lawyer) and Nell B. (Owen) Paxton; married Sarah Plimpton, December 9, 1983. *Education:* Washington & Lee University, B.A., 1954; Oxford University, B.A., 1956, M.A., 1961; Harvard University, Ph.D., 1963.

ADDRESSES: Home: 460 Riverside Dr., #72, New York, NY 10027. *Office:* Department of History, Columbia University, New York, NY 10027.

CAREER: University of California, Berkeley, instructor, 1961-63, assistant professor of history, 1963-67; State University of New York at Stony Brook, associate professor of history, 1967-69; Columbia University, New York City, professor of history, 1969—, department chairman, 1980-82, director, Institute on Western Europe, 1991—. *Military service:* U.S. Navy, 1956-58. U.S. Naval Reserve, 1951-66; became lieutenant commander.

MEMBER: American Academy of Arts and Letters (fellow), American Historical Association, Society for French Historical Studies, Societe d'histoire moderne (Paris), Linnaean Society of New York (president, 1978-80).

AWARDS, HONORS: Rhodes scholar, 1954-56; D.Letters from Washington & Lee University, 1974; American Council of Learned Societies fellow, 1974-75; Rockefeller Foundation fellow, 1978-79; with Michael R. Marrus, History Prize and Book Prize nominations, both from the *Los Angeles Times,* and National Jewish Book Award, all 1982, all for *Vichy France and the Jews;* German Marshall Fund fellow, 1986; decorated *chevalier,* Ordre National des Arts et des Lettres and *officier,* Ordre National du Merite (France).

WRITINGS:

Parades and Politics at Vichy: The French Officer Corps under Marshall Petain, Princeton University Press, 1966.

Vichy France: Old Guard and New Order, 1940-44, Knopf, 1972.

Europe in the Twentieth Century, Harcourt, 1975, second edition, 1985.

(With Michael R. Marrus) *Vichy France and the Jews,* Basic Books, 1981 (first published in France as *Vichy et les juifs,* 1981).

Several of Robert O. Paxton's books have been published in French.

SIDELIGHTS: Historian Robert O. Paxton has published several studies of Vichy France, that portion of France that escaped direct German occupation for most of World War II but was governed by a regime that cooperated with Nazi Germany. His best known and most critically acclaimed book, published in 1981, is *Vichy France and the Jews,* co-authored with Canadian historian Michael R. Marrus. Based on newly accessible French archives as well as German and American records, it examines the Vichy government's treatment of French and non-French Jews under its jurisdiction during World War II. Defenders of the Vichy government, Roger Kaplan points out in *Commentary,* long claimed that Vichy's anti-Jewish policies were "all due to the presence of a brutal occupying power [Nazi Germany]; for all their sins, the Vichy collaborators had at least shielded the French, including the Jews, from the worst." Paxton and Marrus refute this claim, arguing that the Vichy government acted on its own initiative in taking action against its Jewish population and passed up numerous opportunities to protect Jews from the depredations of the Third Reich.

Exploring the reasons for the Vichy government's anti-Jewish policies, Paxton and Marrus point in particular to the xenophobia of the French political Right and to a French attachment to cultural assimilation, both exacerbated by a chronic economic recession and a massive influx of Jewish and other refugees from German-occupied countries. Their book examines the anti-Semitic legislation adopted by the Vichy government, including confiscation of Jewish property, denaturalization of Jewish immigrants, and restrictions on where Jews could live, their freedom of movement, and their participation in various professions. It also documents extensive French administrative collaboration in the deportation of Jews to Germany following the Nazis' adoption in 1942 of the wholesale annihilation of the Jews known as the Final Solution. By placing the French police at the disposition of the Germans, the book argues, the Vichy government provided records and personnel without which the German authorities could not have carried out the massive deportations of Jews from France to the death camps that took place in the final years of the war.

In *Vichy France and the Jews,* Paxton and Marrus "provide a graphic and often heartrending account of official cruelty, administrative callousness, public prejudices and popular indifference," writes Stanley Hoffmann in the *New York Times Book Review.* "Their exhaustive research and the sobriety of their prose makes this indictment far more powerful than previous works on the subject."

BIOGRAPHICAL/CRITICAL SOURCES:

PERIODICALS

Commentary, January, 1982, p. 72-75.

Los Angeles Times Book Review, November 29, 1981, p. 7.

New Republic, November 18, 1981, p. 33-35.

New York Review of Books, December 3, 1981, p. 15.

New York Times Book Review, November 1, 1981, p. 1.

Times Literary Supplement, March 23, 1967, p. 241; July 23, 1982, p. 804.

PEARCE, Brian Louis 1933-

PERSONAL: Born June 4, 1933, in Acton, England; son of Louis Alfred James (a carpenter) and Marjorie Alison (a civil servant; maiden name, Longhurst) Pearce; married Margaret Wood (a teacher), August 2, 1969; children: Ann Gillian. *Education:* Attended Acton County School; University College, London, M.A., 1976. *Politics:* "Liberal/Moderate." *Religion:* Protestant.

Avocational Interests: Walking, chess, turn-of-the-century English and European painting.

ADDRESSES: Home—The Marish, 72 Heathfield S., Twickenham, Middlesex TW2 7SS, England.

CAREER: Chiswick Public Library, Chiswick, England, librarian, 1949; Acton Public Library, Acton, England, librarian, 1950-51; Buckinghamshire County Library, Buckinghamshire, England, librarian, 1954-57; Twickenham Public Library, Twickenham, England, reference librarian, 1958-61; Acton Technical College, Acton, librarian, 1962-66; Twickenham College of Technology, Twickenham, tutor and librarian, 1966-77; Richmond-upon-Thames College, Richmond, England, college librarian, 1977-88. Library Association examiner in English literature from 1750 to present, 1964-70; tutor in creative writing, 1981—; occasional lecturer, National Portrait Gallery, 1990—. Chairman of Twickenham United Christian Council, 1974-75, 1980-81, 1984-85. Adjudicator, Sussex Poet of the Year competition, 1981 and 1985, and Richmond Arts Council Young Writers competition, 1984, 1985, 1986. Member, Greater London Arts Writers in Schools. *Military service:* Royal Air Force, 1951-53.

MEMBER: International PEN, Browning Society, Royal Society of Arts (fellow), Library Association (fellow), Richmond Poetry Group (founding member, 1961; chairman, 1970-84).

WRITINGS:

POETRY

Poems, Poet's Press, 1956.
The Americas and Other Poems, Outposts Publications, 1962.
A Sense of Wonder, Scrip, 1963.
Saga, Guild Press, 1963.
Thames Music: A Poem, privately printed, 1968.
Coombe Hill: A Poem, Ore Publications, 1969.
The Argonauts and Other Poems, Quarto Press, 1970.
Requiem for the Sixties: Verse Sequence, privately printed, 1971.
Selected Poems, 1951-1973, Outposts Publications, 1977.
The Vision of Piers Librarian, Woodruff Press, 1981.
Off Cape Oil, Stride Publications, 1982.
Leaves for Palinurus, Downlander Publications, 1982.
Office Hours: Stages in an Obsession, Woodruff Press, 1983.
Ave Acton Vale, Stride Publications, 1983.
Browne Study, Lomond Press, 1984.
Dutch Comfort: Poetry, Prose, Translations, Stride Publications, 1985.
Gwen John Talking, Tallis Press, 1985.
Jack o' Lent: Headpieces, Stride Publications, 1991.
Leaving the Corner: Selected Poems 2: 1973-1985, Stride Publications, 1992.
Coeli et terra, Cornerstone Press, 1993.
Thames Listener: Poems, 1949-89, Institute of English and American Studies, University of Salzburg, in press.

EDITOR

Old Ascot: Diaries of George and G. A. Longhurst, 1833-1881, privately printed, 1964.
Twickenham Eyot: An Anthology (poetry), Quarto Press, 1973.
(And compiler and author of introduction) *Palgrave (F. T.): Selected Poems,* Brentham Press, 1985.

Editor of "Quarto Poets Series," Quarto Press, 1973-76.

NONFICTION

My Grandfather's Uncle: A Memoir of the Reverend Caleb Mark Longhurst (Baptist), 1840-1928, privately printed, 1964.
The Ascot of Gilbert Longhurst: A Memoir, privately printed, 1967.
The Art of Eric Ratcliffe: An Appreciation, privately printed, 1970.
Twickenham College of Technology: A History, the First Thirty-Five Years, 1937-1972, Twickenham College of Technology, 1974.
Free for All: The Public Library Movement in Twickenham, Twickenham Local Historical Society, 1985.
Thomas Twining of Twickenham (1806-1895), Twickenham Local Historical Society, 1988.
The Fashioned Reed: Poets of Twickenham from 1500, Twickenham Local Historical Society, 1992.

PLAYS

Conchubar: A Play in Verse (one-act; first produced in Twickenham at Richmond Poetry Group, 1964), privately printed, 1963.
The Blind Man at the Gate of Lethe: A Lyric Play (one-act; first produced in Twickenham at Richmond Poetry Group, 1965), privately printed, 1964.
Paolo and Francesca, privately printed, 1965.
The Frozen Forest: A Contemporary Play (one-act; first produced in Twickenham at Richmond Poetry Group, 1966), privately printed, 1965.

The Eagle and the Swan (three-act; first produced in Twickenham at Richmond Poetry Group, 1966), Mitre Press, 1966.

Holman, Mitre Press, 1969.

Shrine Rites (first produced in Twickenham at Richmond Shakespeare Society, 1990), Envoi, 1990.

FICTION

Bond Street Snatches, Stride Publications, 1984.

Victoria Hammersmith: A Novel, Stride Publications, 1987.

London Clay: Stories and Novellas, Stride Publications, 1991.

A Man in His Room, Stride Publications, 1992.

The Bust of Minerva, Oasis Books, 1992.

CONTRIBUTOR TO ANTHOLOGIES

New Poetry 3, Arts Council of Great Britain, 1977.

New Poetry 6, Hutchinson, 1980.

Finn, editor, *Voices of Today,* J. Murray, 1980.

Gordon Bailey, editor, *One Hundred Contemporary Christian Poets,* Lion, 1983.

New Poetry 9, Hutchinson, 1983.

A. Topping, editor, *The Least Thing,* Stride Publications, 1989.

Also contributor to *New Poems, 1976-77,* and *New Poems, 1977-78.*

OTHER

Contributor to journals and newspapers, including *Acumen, Dutch Crossing, Green Book, Oasis, PEN Broadsheet, New Welsh Review, South Coast Poetry Journal, Outposts, Word and Image, Green River Review, Guardian, Poetry Review,* and *Message.* Editor of *Expression One,* 1965-67; former associate editor of *Envoi;* former advisory editor of *Ore.*

WORK IN PROGRESS: "*Battersea Pete* (a short novel) and *The Tufnell Triptych* (three pieces on 'loners,' illustrating the Nonconformist experience) are things I've recently completed. Over 1990-92 I've drafted four novel-length fictions, along with some shorter pieces that are taking shape, too. Some of this fiction is straightforward in narrative; some experimental, montaged, and full of wordplay. There are a couple of novels written in the 70s, too—based on my Baptist background. I'd like to take another look at those. There are two new collections of poetry: *The Proper Fuse,* and *City Whiskers,* a sequence. Then there's *The Unready,* a play I want to get right."

SIDELIGHTS: Brian Louis Pearce once wrote *CA:* "I would summarize myself as a poet, author, and lecturer. Sometimes the three intermingle, sometimes they don't. My current interest is fiction, though poetry has been my abiding concern since the age of sixteen. I am grateful for my nonconformist background, initially at Acton as a Baptist. Among my literary heroes are Yeats, Eliot, Pound, Rilke, Ted Hughes, George Barker, and Arthur Waley, as well as Joyce, Woolf, Forster, Isherwood, Proust, Cyril Connolly, and Mark Rutherford, but such lists change with the years.

"I see the poem as an emotionally charged, intellectually ordered, carefully made thing, with meaning and value inherent in its structure, just like music or a landscaped garden, a conscientious piece of carpentry or a painting. It will have its roots in one's own time and place but may sometimes have historical or nostalgic, overt subject matter while keeping one's contemporary problems and anxieties at heart. I like it to have the sound energy of a tightly ordered pattern of sounds. It should have 'bounce' and be on its own terms 'fun.' Lately, I have been exploring the poetry on the borders of prose and inherent in prose. This trend may take me over, may represent a parallel development on a wider canvas, or may be only a phase. One accepts the present, the past, and the need for growth and experiment."

Pearce later told CA: "My publisher has remarked that the cultural past often seems to be the real 'hero' of my work, and I think that's very well observed. An anxiety to see it preserved and appreciated could be seen as the focus of apparently diverse activities. I relate to actual or imagined figures in many different ways, poetic (*Gwen John Talking*), fictional (*Victoria Hammersmith,* or Tessa Black-Friars in *London Clay*), or non-fictional, as in local history (*Thomas Twining*) and my preaching and lecturing, the latter often on late nineteenth-century literary figures. It is the less successful characters (in history as in my fiction) that often interest me most. I write (or speak) to give them a new lease on life. The past gives a point of reference, in art as in life. It provides the undergirding strata and a sense of continuity. Its characters and their legacies often provide the spark I need—just as music and the visual arts also do. I want to hand on what I've received and valued—I feel that's what we're here for to some extent—just as I want to record the here and now, that I and my generation have experienced. Art can delay or soften our 'heroes' (or 'heroines') fall into oblivion.

My interest in the visual arts can be seen in many guises (*Gwen John* again, and most of the published fiction), while my response to place and history has often been noted. One sometimes feels a very poignant affinity with particular places or people of long ago, whose deepest experiences were very similar to our own so far as we can judge from their literature or our own feelings when we visit their sites. It comes out again in the *Leagrave MS* sequence on Saxon and National Service themes in *Leaving the Corner: Selected Poems II.* There are some prose poems in that sequence as a change from the traditional poetry that I have written throughout my career, and the experimental 'thin' short-lined rhymed syllabic structures that I developed in *Office Hours* and *Jack o' Lent* (a sequence on Easter, the death of an acquaintance, the heads of Francis Bacon and folk myth) partly as a way of expressing (and ordering) emotional and religious questionings, echoing in language what Francis Bacon did in paint.

"*Shrine Rites* (one-act, 1990) is a sequel to Eliot's *Murder in the Cathedral* in which one actor plays both Henry and Becket."

BIOGRAPHICAL/CRITICAL SOURCES:

PERIODICALS

Cut, winter, 1991-92.

Green River Review, Volume 10, number 2, 1979, pp. 230-233; Volume 12, number 2, 1981, pp. 60-63.

Oasis, November, 1991, pp. 24-25.

Orbis, spring, 1982, pp. 58-60; autumn 1983, pp. 115-117.

Ore, June, 1983.

Strait, Volume 22, 1985.

Stride, May, 1983; July, 1984; Volume 31, 1988; June, 1993.

Tenth Decade, Volume 13, 1990, pp. 35-37.

Third Way, October, 1991, pp. 29-30.

* * *

PEPPIATT, Michael 1941-

PERSONAL: Born October 9, 1941, in High Wycombe, Buckinghamshire, England; son of Edward George (a company director) and Elsa Eugenie (a housewife) Peppiatt; married Jill Lloyd (an art historian), 1989; children: Clio Patricia. *Education:* Cambridge University, M.A. (with honors), 1964.

Avocational Interests: Squash and court tennis.

ADDRESSES: Home—77, rue des Archives, 75003 Paris, France. *Agent*—Kim Witherspoon, Witherspoon & Chernoff, 130 West 57th St., Ste. 14C, New York, NY 10019.

CAREER: Realites, Paris, France, literary and arts editor, 1966-68; *Le Monde,* Paris, literary and arts editor, 1969-71; *Art International,* Paris (formerly Lugano, Switzerland), correspondent, 1968-73, senior editor, 1983-87, owner and editor, 1987—. Arts correspondent for *Financial Times* (London), 1972-76, and *Art News,* 1973-80. Founder, Archive Press, 1987. Organizer of art exhibitions; art film consultant and commentator.

MEMBER: International Art Critics Association, Jeu de Paume Club (Paris), Oxford and Cambridge Club (London).

WRITINGS:

(With Alice Bellony-Rewald) *Imagination's Chamber: Artists and Their Studios,* New York Graphic Society, 1982.

A School of London: Six Figurative Painters, British Council, 1987.

Francis Bacon: A Vision Fulfilled (exhibition catalogue), Electa, 1993.

Contributor of essays to numerous exhibition catalogues. Contributor to periodicals, including *Architectural Digest, Connaissance des Arts, New York Times Book Review,* and *Times* (London).

WORK IN PROGRESS: A biography of the painter Francis Bacon (1909-1992), for Farrar, Straus.

SIDELIGHTS: In *Imagination's Chamber: Artists and Their Studios,* Michael Peppiatt and co-author Alice Bellony-Rewald explore the world of the artist's studio throughout history. It is the authors' contention that "art history can be told through the studio," and their work attempts to support this thesis. However, as Tom Phillips of the *Times Literary Supplement* asserts, "this entertaining book" cannot be considered a "serious and scholarly attempt" to cover "the whole of the history of art." In addition to noting numerous "obvious gaps," Phillips believes the work suffers from sketchiness—the authors "have leapt from the caveman to eighteenth-century France by page 27." *New York Times Book Review* critic Janet Hobhouse comments on the absence of a sound historical and sociological framework in *Imagination's Chamber* and argues that Peppiatt and co-author Bellony-Rewald "take little account" of the actual factors determining an artist's choice of studio. The book, maintains Hobhouse, "deals inflatedly with the trivia of artistic life and its fortuitous and haphazard settings."

Conversely, the *Times Literary Supplement*'s Phillips observes that some periods—Renaissance Italy, for instance—are richly documented. He further acknowledges the authors' depiction of nineteenth-century Paris as a "fascinating and well-illustrated tale of change and continuity, enlivened by rich anecdote, of the famous, and even of the obscure."

Phillips remarks that, thanks to Peppiatt's and Bellony-Rewald's sense of detail, the reader experiences "many glimpses of painters and sculptors in their working quarters." Specifically, the critic applauds the authors for introducing the reader to a wide variety of studios. "We see clinical studios ('Like a laboratory,' said [artist Pablo] Picasso after a visit to [artist Paul] Klee's studio)," Phillips writes, "heroic studios, studios encrusted, domestic, opulent, and even (like [Hans] Bellmer's) fetishistic."

Listener reviewer Stephen Gardiner describes one of the book's fascinations as "the discovery of how little comfort and appearance in general mattered to great artists." *Imagination's Chamber* shows, according to Gardiner, that indifference to comfort can range from the simplicity of Jacob Epstein's studio to the "excessively crude" simplicity of La Ruche, "a warren of studios founded in 1902 on the outskirts of Paris where [Chaim] Soutine, [Amedeo] Modigliani, [Fernan] Leger, [Berthold] Lubetkin and others worked." Concurring with Peppiatt's and Bellony-Rewald's premise that a studio "can tell us a great deal about an artist," Gardiner characterizes *Imagination's Chamber* as "an extraordinarily interesting book, where the illustrations are as illuminating as the commentary."

Peppiatt once told *CA:* "Writing *Imagination's Chamber* helped me to get closer to the actual processes by which painting and sculpture are made. The art criticism I had written before was based mainly on an aesthetic (and occasionally biographical or historical) appreciation. This applies to many critics, most of whom have not held a paintbrush since their schooldays and know little of the technical problems that artists encounter constantly. Understanding how a work of art takes form, not only in the artist's mind but in its physical substance, now seems to me essential to serious criticism, and the only way to find out how a work evolves is by spending time in the studio. My co-author, Alice Bellony-Rewald, had a privileged knowledge of studios since she had visited Picasso at 'La Californie' near Cannes and had her portrait drawn by Giacometti, Balthus, and Kokoschka.

"Together we assembled a large number of paintings, engravings, and photographs of artists' studios, many of which had never been published before. This entailed visiting artists, contacting the specialist photographers, and doing research in libraries in Paris, London, and New York. At the same time, we culled information about every aspect of studios and the way artists live and work in them from as many sources as we could find. Since no authoritative book existed on the subject, we had to do a great deal of reading in quite different areas in order to piece together a 'history' of the studio. Little enough is known about pre-Renaissance studios, but the closer one gets to our own period the more abundant the information becomes. As far as contemporary studios were concerned, my co-author and I were often able to draw on first-hand experience.

"Studios can be 'read' in terms of their light, space, and, above all, their contents—from tools and materials to the books, objects, and illustrations the artist keeps and consults there. Thus the studio provides an invaluable guide to the work produced within its walls—a point quite lost on the *New York Times Book Review* critic quoted above, who approached the subject as a problem in real estate! Since *Imagination's Chamber* appeared, I have been asked by *Connaissance des Arts* and *Art International* to write a series of long essays on twentieth-century artists from Pollock to Bacon and Kitaj. And nowadays, before writing about living artists, I try to spend as much time as possible in their studios because they are as eloquent—and at least as telling—about the work as the artists themselves."

BIOGRAPHICAL/CRITICAL SOURCES:

PERIODICALS

Listener, February 10, 1983.
New Statesman, March 18, 1983.
New York Times Book Review, January 23, 1983.
Times Literary Supplement, April 29, 1983.

* * *

PEREIRA, W(ilfred) D(ennis) 1921-

PERSONAL: Born November 16, 1921, in London, England; son of Ernani Horace (an export agent) and Helen Elizabeth (Gonsalves) Pereira; married Irene Elizabeth Crawford, June 12, 1948; children: Helen Elizabeth. *Education:* Attended Wimbledon College, 1930-1939, and College of Aeronautical Engineering, London, England, 1939-41.

ADDRESSES: Home—Woodfold Cottage, Down Hatherley, Gloucester GL2 9QB, England.

CAREER: Technical writer for De Havilland Aircraft Co., Hatfield, England, 1947-48, and for Rotol, Gloucester, England, 1948-58; Dowty, Cheltenham, England, press officer, 1958-61; Daniels/Unochrome International, Stroud, England, publicity manager, 1961-73; business consultant, 1973-78; performed marketing and public relations services for Dowty Rotol, Gloucester, 1978-86; business consultant, 1986—.

WRITINGS:

FICTION

Time of Departure, R. Hale, 1956.
Serene Retreat, R. Hale, 1957.
Johnson's Journey, R. Hale, 1958.
The Lion and the Lambs, R. Hale, 1959.
North Flight, R. Hale, 1959.
Lark Ascending, R. Hale, 1960.
The Cauldrons of the Storm, R. Hale, 1961.
Arrow in the Air, Jarrolds, 1963.
The Wheat from the Chaff (short stories), Dent, 1967.
An Uncertainty of Marriages (short stories), Dent, 1969.
Funny Business (short stories), R. Hale, 1980.
More Funny Business (short stories), R. Hale, 1981.

SCIENCE FICTION

Aftermath Fifteen, R. Hale, 1973.
The Charon Tapes, R. Hale, 1975.
Another Eden, R. Hale, 1976.
Contact, R. Hale, 1977.
The King of Hell, R. Hale, 1978.
Celeste, R. Hale, 1979.

OTHER

The Siege of Gloucester, Line One, 1983.
The Battle of Tewkesbury, Line One, 1983.
Boat in the Blue, Line One, 1985.
RAF Lyneham, Haynes, 1990.
RAF Brize Norton, Patrick Stephens, 1993.

Also author of three plays produced on television and ghost-writer of four books. Contributor of articles and stories to magazines.

SIDELIGHTS: W. D. Pereira told *CA:* "Primarily I write to communicate. It has never been my intention to convey a message but rather to introduce and share areas of interest. I try to capture my readers from the opening sentence and then lead them on paragraph by paragraph, chapter by chapter. If the story line has not progressed in half a page, I scrap that sheet and start again. It is my belief that any subject can be made readable, though this depends on the art of the writer. Authors have a part to play in every age, promoting awareness and compassion rather than force and greed. They represent a facet of creativity, and, if they have the gift, they also have the responsibility. This keeps me writing in my quiet way. I can write anywhere—on trains, planes, in hotel foyers, and in airport lounges. I have never suffered from writer's block. My talent, though small, has remained constant for over forty years."

* * *

PERL, Teri (Hoch) 1926-

PERSONAL: Born November 19, 1926, in New York, NY; daughter of Nathan (a furrier) and Rose (Gross) Hoch; married Martin Lewis Perl (a physicist), June 18, 1948 (divorced, 1988); children: Jed, Anne, Matthew, Joseph. *Education:* Brooklyn College (now Brooklyn College of the City University of New York), B.A., 1947; San Jose State University, teaching credential, 1969; attended San Jose State University, 1973; Stanford University, Ph.D., 1979.

ADDRESSES: Home and office—525 Lincoln Ave., Palo Alto, CA 94301.

CAREER: Ventura Elementary School, Palo Alto, CA, mathematics consultant and resource teacher, 1971-77; San Jose State University, San Jose, CA, instructor in mathematics, 1977; San Francisco State University, San Francisco, CA, lecturer in mathematics, 1977-79; University of Wisconsin—Madison, project specialist, 1979-80; The Learning Co., Menlo Park, CA, co-founder, director of educational marketing, and developer of educational software, 1980-87; Teri Perl Associates, Palo Alto, educational consultant and software designer, 1987—. Instructor at San Jose State University and University of California, Santa Cruz, 1973; instructor at University of California, Berkeley, Extension and lecturer at San Francisco State University, 1987-93. Member of California Mathematics Council. Co-director of evaluation, Math Science Conferences for Girls, 1978. Has given workshops and presentations at professional meetings for educators at national, state, and local levels in the U.S., Canada, and Europe.

MEMBER: International Society for Technology in Education, National Council of Teachers of Mathematics, Association for Women in Mathematics, Mathematical Association of America, Association for Computing Machinery, Women and Mathematics Education, Santa Clara Valley Mathematics Association.

AWARDS, HONORS: Citation for outstanding contribution to mathematics from *Choice* magazine, American Library Association, 1982, for *Math Equals.*

WRITINGS:

(With M. K. Freedman) *A Sourcebook for Substitutes,* Addison-Wesley, 1974.
Patches (teacher activity book; also see below), Cuisenaire Co., 1975.
Math Equals: Biographies of Women Mathematicians Plus Related Activities, Addison-Wesley, 1978.
Alphagrams (also see below), Cuisenaire Co., 1979.
Rocky's Boots School Edition, Addison-Wesley/Learning Co., 1985.
Gertrude's Secrets School Edition (also see below), Learning Co., 1985.
Gertrude's Puzzles School Edition (also see below), Addison-Wesley/Learning Co., 1985.
Bumble Games School Edition, Learning Co., 1985.
Bumble Plot School Edition, Learning Co., 1985.
MetroGnomes Music (also see below), Learning Co., 1992.
Women and Numbers, Wide World Publishing/Tetra Tech, 1993.

Also contributor, with R. C. Cronkite, to *Women and Minorities in Science: Strategies for Increasing Participation,* edited by Sheila M. Humphreys, American Academy for the Advancement of Science. Contributor to periodicals, including *Classroom Computer Learning, Historia Mathematica, Mathematics Teacher,* and *Journal for Research in Mathematics Education.* Designed curriculum for RE-

LATIONSHAPES, a math manipulative product developed by Cuisenaire Co., including *Patches* and *Alphagrams* as well as a teacher guide and activity cards. Produced *MetroGnomes Music,* computer software, Teri Perl Associates, 1992. Designed computer software *Gertrude's Secrets,* 1982, *Gertrude's Puzzles,* 1982, and *Math Rabbit,* 1986.

WORK IN PROGRESS: A book for older children on women in mathematics.

SIDELIGHTS: Teri Perl once told *CA:* "My career has taken an interesting turn. In 1980 I became the co-founder of an educational software company. The Learning Company has emerged as one of the top developers and publishers of educational software in the country. I have had many roles in this startup company. One of my major contributions has been defining the need to develop teacher materials to help teachers incorporate software into their regular classroom activities. To this end, I have been the major author of a nine-volume series of books for teachers and students that has been published and is presently being distributed to the education market by Addison-Wesley.

"Currently, another book of mine, similar to *Math Equals* and developed under a Women's Educational Equity Grant, is being published by World Wide Publishing/Tetra, in San Carlos, California. This book contains biographies of contemporary as well as non-contemporary women who have worked with mathematics and is generally written for a . . . ten- to fourteen-year-old age group."

* * *

PIRSIG, Robert M(aynard) 1928-

PERSONAL: Born September 6, 1928, in Minneapolis, MN; son of Maynard Ernest (a professor) and Harriet Marie (Sjobeck) Pirsig; married Nancy Ann James (an administrator), May 10, 1954 (divorced August, 1978); married Wendy L. Kimball, December 28, 1978; children: (first marriage) Christopher (deceased November 17, 1979), Theodore; (second marriage) Nell. *Education:* University of Minnesota, B.A., 1950, M.A., 1958.

ADDRESSES: Office—c/o Bantam Books, 1540 Broadway, New York, NY 10036.

CAREER: Montana State College (now University), Bozeman, instructor in English composition, 1959-61; University of Illinois, Chicago, instructor in rhetoric, 1961-62; technical writer at several Minneapolis, MN, electronic firms, 1963-67; Century Publications, Minneapolis, contract technical writer, 1967-73; writer. Minnesota Zen Meditation Center, member of board of directors, 1973—, vice-president, 1973-75. *Military service:* U.S. Army, 1946-48.

MEMBER: Society of Technical Communicators (secretary, 1970-71; treasurer, 1971-72).

AWARDS, HONORS: Guggenheim fellowship, 1974; Friends of Literature Award, 1975; outstanding achievement award, University of Minnesota, 1975; American Academy and Institute of Arts and Letters Award, 1979.

WRITINGS:

Zen and the Art of Motorcycle Maintenance: An Inquiry into Values, Morrow, 1974.

Lila: An Inquiry into Morals, Bantam, 1991.

Author of introduction, *Writing down the Bones: Freeing the Writer Within,* by Natalie Goldberg, Shambhala, 1986. Contributor to periodicals, including *New York Times Book Review.*

WORK IN PROGRESS: Anthropological research, intended to relate metaphysics of quality, as defined in first book, to cultural problems of today.

SIDELIGHTS: Novelist and metaphysician Robert Pirsig explores the underlying values and morals of modern American society in his works. His *Zen and the Art of Motorcycle Maintenance* is "a bold book," judges Richard Todd in the *Atlantic Monthly.* "High intelligence, high intention, and deeply flawed self-knowledge: ingredients of tragedy, and so they have been in the life this book recounts, but they have also produced a self-sacrificial document of a strength that is not commonly found in works of more deliberate art." Written as an autobiography, Pirsig's book tells the story of his motorcycle journey across America in the company of his eleven-year-old son, from Minneapolis west through the Dakotas, the Rockies, and on to the Pacific Coast. As the miles speed by, Pirsig contemplates life, technology, and himself. "*Zen and the Art of Motorcycle Maintenance* is trying to initiate a philosophical change, and simultaneously a change of imagination and sensibility, in its readers. It's an ambitious and exciting aim," notes Herbert Lomas in *London Magazine,* who calls Pirsig's story "deeply moving" at points. *New Yorker* contributor George Steiner sums up his reaction: "A detailed technical treatise on the tools, on the routines, on the metaphysics of a specialized skill; the legend of a great hunt after identity, after the salvation of mind and soul out of obsession, the hunter being hunted; a fiction repeatedly interrupted by, enmeshed with, a lengthy meditation on the ironic and tragic singularities of American man—the analogies with *Moby Dick* are patent. Robert Pirsig invites the prodigious comparison."

In *Lila: An Inquiry into Morals,* Pirsig again uses the imagery of a journey, this time by boat and in the company of a middle-aged woman named Lila. "She is guinea pig, puzzle piece and plot device rolled into one," describes Chris Goodrich in the *Los Angeles Times Book Review.* Lila is an unstable, morally loose person, in whom the narrator sees a little bit of himself, and who serves as inspiration for his writing. "*Lila* is a marvelous improvisation on a most improbable quartet: sailing, philosophy, sex and madness," concludes *New York Times Book Review* contributor Richard Restak. Robert Coles comments in the *Washington Post Book World:* "*Lila,* as was its predecessor, is an intellectual rebel's book, a loner's book—the writing of a thoughtful, sensitive social and cultural observer who has had his fill of academic pretentiousness and phoniness, not to mention the arrogance of our various secular experts."

BIOGRAPHICAL/CRITICAL SOURCES:

BOOKS

Contemporary Literary Criticism, Gale, Volume 4, 1975, Volume 6, 1976.

PERIODICALS

Atlantic Monthly, September, 1974, pp. 92-94.
Economist, November 30, 1974.
Harvard Economic Review, February, 1975.
London Magazine, December, 1974.
Los Angeles Times Book Review, October 27, 1991, pp. 2, 8.
New Statesman, November 15, 1974.
Newsweek, June 3, 1974.
New Yorker, April 15, 1974, pp. 147-50.
New York Times Book Review, March 30, 1975; March 4, 1984; October 13, 1991, pp. 15-16.
Science, January 24, 1975.
Time, April 15, 1974.
Times Literary Supplement, October 18, 1991, p. 21.
Washington Post Book World, October 13, 1991, pp. 3, 11.

* * *

PLUMMER, Ben
See BINGLEY, David Ernest

* * *

POMFRET, Richard 1948-

PERSONAL: Born May 21, 1948, in Manchester, England. *Education:* University of Reading, B.A. (with honors) 1969; University of East Anglia, M.A., 1970; Simon Fraser University, Ph.D., 1974.

ADDRESSES: *Office*—Bologna Center, Johns Hopkins University, via Belmeloro 11, 40126 Bologna, Italy.

CAREER: University of Kiel, Kiel, West Germany, research fellow at Institut fuer Weltwirtschaft, 1974-76; Concordia University, Montreal, Quebec, assistant professor of economics, 1976-79; Johns Hopkins University, Baltimore, MD, associate professor of economics at Bologna Center, 1979-88, professor of international economics, 1988—. Research assistant at University of Reading, 1968; visiting fellow at La Trobe University, 1979; visiting professor at University of Florence, 1982. Consultant to World Bank, the EC, the Arab Monetary Fund, and Instituto Bancario San Paolo di Torino.

WRITINGS:

Trade Policies and Industrialization in a Small Country: The Case of Israel, J.C.B. Mohr, 1976.
(Contributor) Herbert Gierseh, editor, *On the Economics of Intra-Industry Trade,* J.C.B. Mohr, 1979.
(With Benjamin Toren) *Israel and the European Common Market: An Appraisal of the 1975 Free Trade Agreement,* J.C.B. Mohr, 1980.
(Contributor) H. Gierseh, editor, *Economic Integration of Israel in the EEC,* J.C.B. Mohr, 1980.
The Economic Development of Canada, Methuen, 1981.
Mediterranean Policy of the European Community: A Study of Discrimination in International Trade: An Introduction to Theory and Policy, Macmillan, 1986.
Unequal Trade, Blackwell, 1988.
Joint Ventures in Jiangen Province, Longman, 1989.
Investing in China: Ten Years of the "Open Door" Policy, Harvester Wheatsheaf, 1991.
Diverse Paths of Economic Development, Harvester Wheatsheaf, 1992.

Contributor to economics, history, and international studies journals.

WORK IN PROGRESS: Research on the theory of preferential trading arrangements; foreign investments in China.

SIDELIGHTS: Richard Pomfret once told *CA:* "The connecting thread of my work is a desire to understand the process of economic development, either from a historical perspective (Canada, for example) or as a more contemporary issue (Israel, for example). My more specialized research has focused on the relationships between trade policies and development. Currently, I am concerned about the drift in international trade policies away from the principle of nondiscrimination, which is both a threat to economic prosperity and full of undesirable political possibilities."

PORTER, Eliot (Furness) 1901-1990

PERSONAL: Born December 6, 1901, in Winnetka, IL; died of cardiac arrest while suffering from amyotrophic lateral sclerosis (Lou Gehrig's disease), November 2, 1990; son of James Foster and Ruth (Furness) Porter; married Marian Brown, 1927 (divorced, 1934); married Aline Kilham (a painter), May 8, 1936; children: (first marriage) Eliot F., Jr., Charles Anthony; (second marriage) Jonathan, Stephen, Patrick. *Education:* Harvard University, B.S., 1924, M.D., 1929. *Politics:* Democratic Party.

CAREER: Writer and photographer. Harvard University and Radcliffe College, Cambridge, MA, instructor and tutor in biochemistry, 1929-39; worked on the development of radar at the radiation laboratory of the Massachusetts Institute of Technology, Cambridge, 1943-44; Yale University, Morse College, New Haven, CT, associate fellow, 1967. Photographs included in exhibitions at the Metropolitan Museum of Modern Art, Chicago Art Institute, George Eastman House, and other institutions.

MEMBER: American Academy of Arts and Sciences (fellow), American Civil Liberties Union, American Ornithologists' Union, Wilson Society, Cooper Ornithological Club, Audubon Society, Sierra Club (former member of board of directors).

AWARDS, HONORS: Guggenheim fellow, 1941, 1946; silver medal, *Country Life* international exhibition of wildlife photography, 1950; U. S. Department of the Interior Conservation Service Award, 1967; Maine Commission on Arts and Humanities award, 1968; Distinguished Son of Maine Award, 1969; Newhouse Citation, Syracuse University, 1973; Governor's Award, New Mexico Arts Commission, 1976; honorary doctorates from Colby College and the University of Albuquerque.

WRITINGS:

(Editor) Henry David Thoreau, *In Wilderness Is the Preservation of the World,* Sierra Club, 1962.
The Place No One Knew: Glen Canyon on the Colorado, Sierra Club, 1963, revised edition, 1966, abridged edition, 1968.
Forever Wild: The Adirondacks, Harper, 1966.
Summer Island: Penobscot Country, Sierra Club, 1966.
Galapagos: The Flow of Wildness, Sierra Club, 1968.
Baja California: The Geography of Hope, Ballantine, 1969.
Appalachian Wilderness: The Great Smoky Mountains, Dutton, 1970.
Birds of North America: A Personal Selection, Dutton, 1972.
The African Experience, Dutton, 1972.
Moments of Discovery: Adventures with American Birds, Dutton, 1977.
Antarctica, Hutchinson, 1978.
Intimate Landscapes, Metropolitan Museum of Art, 1979.
The Greek World, Dutton, 1980.
All Under Heaven: The Chinese World, Gollancz, 1980.
Eliot Porter Calendar, Dutton, 1981.
(With others) *American Places,* Dutton, 1981.
Eliot Porter's Southwest, Holt, 1985.
Maine, New York Graphic Society, 1986.
Mexican Churches, University of New Mexico Press, 1987.
Eliot Porter, New York Graphic Society, 1987.

ILLUSTRATOR

Land Birds of America, McGraw, 1953.
American Water and Game Birds, Dutton, 1956.
Living Birds of the World, Doubleday, 1958.
Living Insects of the World, Doubleday, 1959.
The Lower Animals, Doubleday, 1960.
The Birds of Arizona, University of Arizona Press, 1964.
Gleick, James, *Nature's Chaos,* edited by Janet Russek, Viking, 1991.

OTHER

Contributor of articles to *U. S. Camera, New England Naturalist,* and other publications.

SIDELIGHTS: A photographer of nature subjects, Eliot Porter was a longtime advocate of conservation of wildlife areas as well. He was also one of the first to use color photography in his work. His many books of photographs, often concerned with birds and wild animals, set new standards in the field. As a critic for the *Christian Science Monitor* noted in his review of *Summer Island:* "Technically [Porter's] photographs are unusually fine. . . . As works of art they are exceptional." Speaking of the book *Galapagos: The Flow of Wildness,* R. C. Murphy of *Natural History* found that "the artistry of Eliot Porter is not restricted to magic with his camera. . . . His narrative [is] the most informing general scientific record ever made at the archipelago."

BIOGRAPHICAL/CRITICAL SOURCES:

PERIODICALS

Atlantic, February, 1984, p. 104.
Backpacker, summer, 1973.
Chicago Tribune Book World, December 7, 1980, section 7, p. 2; December 1, 1985, p. 6.
Christian Century, December 16, 1970, p. 1518.
Christian Science Monitor, December 3, 1979, p. B10; December 8, 1980, p. 86.
Economist, February 3, 1979, p. 98.
Life, December 18, 1970, p. 12.
Los Angeles Times Book Review, November 1, 1981, p. 8; November 13, 1983.

Modern Photography, October, 1969, p. 92; July, 1981, p. 32; February, 1984, p. 40.
National Review, August 18, 1972, p. 907.
Natural History, February, 1967, p. 68; January, 1969; December, 1972, p. 92; November, 1983, p. 100.
New Age Journal, October, 1983, p. 64.
New Republic, December 8, 1979, p. 30.
Newsweek, October 30, 1972, p. 103; December 11, 1978, p. 95; January 7, 1980, p. 60.
New York Review of Books, January 25, 1973, p. 19; October 8, 1981, p. 35.
New York Times, November 16, 1969, p. 70; October 17, 1972, p. 39.
New York Times Book Review, December 4, 1966, p. 3; December 6, 1970, p. 70; January 15, 1978, p. 23; November 25, 1979, p. 92; November 30, 1980, p. 64; December 8, 1985, p. 22; December 20, 1987, p. 3.
Saturday Review, December 3, 1966, p. 37; December 2, 1972, p. 84; November 26, 1977, p. 32; November 25, 1978, p. 38.
Spectator, May 30, 1981, p. 24.
Time, December 4, 1972, p. 73.
Times Literary Supplement, October 26, 1980, p. 1206.
Virginia Quarterly Review, winter, 1978, p. 30.
Wall Street Journal, December 11, 1978, p. 28.
Washington Post Book World, December 7, 1986, p. 12; December 6, 1987, p. 16.

OBITUARIES:

PERIODICALS

Chicago Tribune, November 4, 1990.
Washington Post, November 5, 1990.*

* * *

POTTKER, Janice Marie 1948-

PERSONAL: Born October 22, 1948, in Lake Forest, IL; daughter of Ralph Eugene (a small business owner) and Olga Norma (a journalist; maiden name, Somenzi) Pottker; married Andrew Stuart Fishel (a financial manager), August 17, 1969; children: Tracy Lynn, Carrie Gene. *Education:* American University, B.A., 1969; University of Maryland at College Park, M.A., 1971; Columbia University, Ph.D., 1978.

ADDRESSES: Home—10104 Lloyd Rd., Potomac, MD 20854.

CAREER: Brooklyn College of the City of New York, Brooklyn, NY, instructor in sociology, 1972-73; New York State Department of Mental Hygiene, research scientist in biometric research, 1973-74; Human Sciences Research, McLean, VA, research associate, 1974-75; Center for the Study of Sex Differences in Education, Bethesda, MD, director, 1974-79; chief of research and evaluation branch of U.S. Department of Education Office of Civil Rights, 1979—. Member of board of directors of International Institute of Women's Studies, 1970-73; president of Writer's Camp, Inc., 1986—.

MEMBER: Washington Independent Writers, Authors Guild.

WRITINGS:

(With husband, Andrew Fishel) *National Politics and Eliminating Sex Discrimination in Education,* Lexington Books, 1977.
(Editor with Fishel) *Sex Bias in the Schools: The Research Evidence,* Fairleigh Dickinson University Press, 1983.
(With Bob Speziale) *Dear Ann, Dear Abby: An Unauthorized Biography of Ann Landers and Abigail Van Buren,* Dodd, 1987.
Born to Power: Heirs to America's Leading Businesses, Barron's, 1992.

WORK IN PROGRESS: Women heirs who are socially and politically progressive; America's most prominent families.

SIDELIGHTS: Janice Marie Pottker told *CA:* "America's only royalty are the very rich. Yet we democratic citizens have a love-hate relationship with these families. We discount all they have given to this country—their industrial, business and financial contributions as well as their political contributions. As a writer, I want to re-examine America's great families and acknowledge their representation of the eras in which they've thrived."

In 1987, Pottker took a break from sociological research to co-author *Dear Ann, Dear Abby: The Unauthorized Biography of Ann Landers and Abigail Van Buren* with political speechwriter Bob Speziale. Their book describes the lives of twin sisters Esther Pauline (Eppie) and Pauline Esther (Popo) Friedman, from their childhood in Sioux City, Iowa, to their prominence as America's most popular advice columnists. Though they did not receive permission or cooperation from either sister (in fact, both tried various methods to block the book's publication), Pottker and Speziale did interview more than 150 of the columnists' friends, co-workers, and relatives. Those who knew the Friedman twins recount the stories of their early sibling rivalries, culminating with their double wedding—Eppie to a salesman, Popo to a millionaire. When Eppie was hired to write for the syndicated "Ann Landers" column in 1955, Popo quickly garnered her own advice column, calling herself "Dear Abby"; thus began a bitter feud that has continued almost uninterrupted for nearly 40 years. "Readers of Pottker and Speziale's biography may find themselves wondering how Ann and Abby dare to offer advice (about sibling relationships, anyway) considering their own stormy past," writes a *Booklist* reviewer. Marcia Froelke Coburn of *Tribune Books* called *Dear Ann, Dear Abby* "an incredibly juicy story," enjoying the way the authors "spin out the delicious details of the rift, showing how and why [Eppie and Popo] have spent years trying to outdo each other. In the end, the book proves that sisterhood may indeed be powerful, but it can also be plenty catty."

BIOGRAPHICAL/CRITICAL SOURCES:

PERIODICALS

Booklist, October 1, 1987, p. 187.
Tribune Books (Chicago), November 8, 1987, p. 3.

* * *

PRESCOTT, Caleb
See BINGLEY, David Ernest

* * *

PURDY, A(lfred Wellington) 1918-

PERSONAL: Born December 30, 1918, in Wooler, Ontario, Canada; son of Alfred Wellington (a farmer) and Eleanor Louisa (Ross) Purdy; married Eurithe Mary Jane Parkhurst, November 1, 1941; children: Alfred Alexander. *Education:* Attended Trenton Collegiate Institute and Albert College. *Politics:* New Democratic Party, "i.e., labour or socialist." *Religion:* "Nil."

ADDRESSES: Home and office: R. R. 1, Ameliasburgh, Ontario K0K 1A0, Canada.

CAREER: Writer. Worked in factories until about 1960. Visiting associate professor at Simon Fraser University, Burnaby, British Columbia, 1971; writer-in-residence at Loyola University, Montreal, Quebec, 1973-74, University of Manitoba, Winnipeg, 1975-76, and University of Western Ontario, London, 1977-78. Conducted creative writing classes at Banff Center School of Fine Arts, summers, 1972-74. Has served on the Judging Committee of the Canada Council for junior and senior arts grants and the awards committee for the Governor General's literary awards. *Military service:* Royal Canadian Air Force, six years service during World War II.

MEMBER: League of Canadian Poets.

AWARDS, HONORS: President's Medal, University of Western Ontario, 1964, for "The Country North of Belleville"; Canada Council fellowships, 1965, 1968-69, 1971; Governor General's Literary award, 1966, for *The Cariboo Horses,* and 1986, for *The Collected Poems of Al Purdy;* Centennial Medal, Canadian Federal Government, 1967, for outstanding service; Senior Literary award, Canada Council, 1973; A. J. M. Smith Award, 1974, for *Sex and Death;* elected to Academy of Canadian Writers, 1977; Jubilee Medal, 1978; Order of Canada, 1987.

WRITINGS:

POETRY

The Enchanted Echo, Clarke & Stuart, 1944.
Pressed on Sand, Ryerson, 1955.
Emu, Remember!, University of New Brunswick Press, 1956.
The Crafte So Longe to Lerne, Ryerson, 1959.
The Old Woman and the Mayflowers, Blue R, 1962.
Poems for All the Annettes, Contact Press, 1962, enlarged edition, Anansi, 1968, enlarged edition, 1973.
The Blur in Between: Poems, 1960-61, Emblem Books, 1962.
The Cariboo Horses, McClelland & Stewart, 1965.
North of Summer: Poems from Baffin Island, McClelland & Stewart, 1967.
The Winemakers Beat: Etude, Fiddlehead Press, 1968.
Wild Grape Wine, McClelland & Stewart, 1968.
Spring Song, Fiddlehead Press, 1968.
Interruption, Fiddlehead Press, 1968.
Love in a Burning Building, McClelland & Stewart, 1970.
(With others) *Five Modern Canadian Poets,* edited by Eli Mandel, Holt Rinehart, 1970.
The Quest for Ouzo, M. Kerrigan Almey, 1971.
Selected Poems, McClelland & Stewart, 1972.
Hiroshima Poems, Crossing Press, 1972.
On the Bearpaw Sea, Blackfish Press, 1973.
Sex and Death, McClelland & Stewart, 1973.
Scott Hutcheson's Boat, Bailey and McKinnon, 1973.
In Search of Owen Roblin, McClelland & Stewart, 1974.
Sundance at Dusk, McClelland & Stewart, 1976.
The Poems of Al Purdy: A New Canadian Library Selection, McClelland & Stewart, 1976.
A Handful of Earth, Black Moss Press, 1977.
At Marsport Drugstore, Paget Press, 1977.
No Second Spring, Black Moss Press, 1977.
Moths in the Iron Curtain, Black Rabbit Press, 1977.
Being Alive: Poems 1958-78, McClelland & Stewart, 1978.
The Stone Bird, McClelland & Stewart, 1981.
Bursting into Song: An Al Purdy Omnibus, Fiddlehead Press, 1982.
Birdwatching at the Equator: The Galapagos Islands Poems, illustrated by Eurithe Purdy, Paget Press, 1982.
Piling Blood, McClelland & Stewart, 1984.
The Collected Poems of Al Purdy, edited by Russell Brown, McClelland & Stewart, 1986.
Two/Al Purdy, Colophon, 1990.

A Woman on the Shore, McClelland & Stewart, 1990.

EDITOR

The New Romans: Candid Canadian Opinions of the United States, St. Martin's, 1968.

Fifteen Winds: A Selection of Modern Canadian Poems, Ryerson, 1969.

Milton Acorn, *I've Tasted My Blood: Poems 1956-1968,* Ryerson, 1969.

Storm Warning: The New Canadian Poets, McClelland & Stewart, 1971.

Storm Warning II: The New Canadian Poets, McClelland & Stewart, 1976.

Andrew Suknaski, *Wood Mountain Poems,* Macmillan, 1976.

C. H. Gervais, *Into a Blue Morning: Poems Selected and New 1968-1981,* Hounslow Press, 1982.

OTHER

No Other Country (articles and essays), McClelland & Stewart, 1977.

Morning and It's Summer: A Memoir, Quadrant, 1983.

(With Charles Bukowski) *The Bukowski/Purdy Letters: A Decade of Dialogue 1964-1974,* edited by Seamus Cooney, Paget Press, 1983.

(Author of introduction) R. G. Everson, *Everson at Eighty,* Oberon, 1983.

The George Woodcock-Al Purdy Letters: Selected Correspondence 1964-1984, edited by George Galt, ECW Press, 1988.

A Splinter in the Heart (novel), McClelland & Stewart, 1990.

Cougar Hunter (essay), Phoenix Press, 1993.

The Margaret Laurence-Al Purdy Letters, McClelland & Stewart, 1993.

Work also represented in anthologies, including *Five Modern Canadian Poets,* edited by Eli Mandel, Holt, 1970; *The Norton Anthology of Modern Poetry,* edited by Richard Ellman and Robert O'Clair, Norton, 1973; *Twentieth Century Poetry and Poetics,* edited by Gary Geddes, Oxford University Press, 1973; *Canadian Poetry: The Modern Era,* edited by John Newlove, McClelland & Stewart, 1977. Contributor of original and adapted material to Canadian Broadcasting Corporation, both radio and television, 1956—, including *A Gathering of Days,* produced by CBC-Radio, 1954; *Point of Transfer,* produced on CBC-TV's "Shoestring Theatre"; and "Poems for Voices," 1970. Contributor of poems, reviews, articles, and essays to numerous publications, including *Canadian Literature, Fiddlehead, Saturday Night, Maclean's Magazine,* and *Canadian Forum.*

Selected poems have been translated into Russian.

Collections of Purdy's papers are housed at the Douglas Library, Queen's University, Kingston, Ontario, and the University of Saskatchewan Library, Saskatoon. The University of British Columbia Library, Vancouver, the Lakehead University Library, Thunder Bay, Ontario, and the Thomas Fisher Rare Book Library, University of Toronto, hold some manuscripts and drafts of Purdy's works.

SIDELIGHTS: Al Purdy is one of Canada's most prolific and respected poets. Purdy's use of an informal colloquial voice, a variety of geographic and historic settings, and unconventional verse forms has commanded the attention of readers and critics alike, and his work brims with wit and energy. In his roles as author, editor, and teacher, Purdy has exerted a tremendous influence on younger Canadian poets through his own accomplishments as well as his support and promotion of their literary efforts.

Largely self-educated, Purdy began writing poetry in the late 1930s but developed his craft slowly, finding it necessary to take a number of factory jobs to support himself. He didn't emerge as a major figure on the Canadian literary scene until the 1960s, when he reached middle age. Dennis Lee, in his afterword to *The Collected Poems of Al Purdy,* wrote of Purdy's career: "A less likely bard-in-the-making would be hard to imagine. And the fact is, Purdy would turn out to be among the slowest developers in the history of poetry. To trace the process by which he became one of the fine poets in the language is an intriguing experience . . . only in retrospect can we discern the sureness of instinct and the tenacity of purpose which were propelling him."

An important stage in Purdy's development as a poet came after he left the urban centers of Vancouver and Montreal where he had been living and moved to rural Ontario. Ronald B. Hatch, discussing Purdy's career in the *University of Toronto Quarterly,* noted that his early work was often derivative of the Victorian poets that he had read and studied. "Only in the late 1950s," Hatch observed, "when [Purdy] and his wife built a house on Roblin Lake in southern Ontario and Purdy began writing about this region in the speech rhythms of everyday life, did he find an expression adequate to his needs." Some of Purdy's best known works, including *The Crafte So Longe to Lerne, Poems for All the Annettes,* and *The Cariboo Horses,* were written shortly after he settled at Roblin Lake. In fact, many critics consider *The Cariboo Horses* to be Purdy's breakthrough work. Lee found the book to be a great improvement over Purdy's earlier efforts, stating, "There is now a wonderful sure-footedness in the rangy, loping gait which had become his signature—with its ability to open out into vast perspectives of space and time, then narrow down to focus on a single image or moment." While Purdy agrees that *The Cariboo Horses* represents his finest achievement to that point, he once told *CA* that *Poems for All the Annettes* is, in his opinion, "the most important book of mine from a personal development viewpoint. It might be called a 'watershed' in some sense, in that the poems were very different from what went before."

Perhaps the definitive volume of Purdy's work is the award-winning *The Collected Poems of Al Purdy.* For this book, Purdy selected only those poems that he felt merited inclusion. Arranged according to the decade in which they were written, the poems are taken almost exclusively from Purdy's works of the late 1960s, the 1970s, and the early 1980s, including *The Cariboo Horses, Being Alive,* and *The Stone Bird.* In a review of *The Collected Poems* in *Books in Canada,* George Galt stated that the volume "is a rare accomplishment, because Purdy's poetry is unique, but also because few poets approaching old age exhibit his fresh imagination and still expanding insights." Galt concluded, "Certainly long after most books from our little slice of the eternal now have been forgotten, the best poems of Al Purdy will continue to give light."

Critical acclaim such as that from Galt led Mike Doyle in *Canadian Literature* to ask why Purdy is "so significant a poet for Canada today." In answering his question, Doyle discovered certain parallels between country and poet. "To an outsider Canada must present a somewhat puzzling international image: innocent yet canny, straightforward yet oblique, open and yet shut in, eclectic and yet groping for a single image of itself," wrote Doyle, who continued, "Purdy . . . seems as much as anyone writing today to sense what it is, the Canadian thing."

BIOGRAPHICAL/CRITICAL SOURCES:

BOOKS

Contemporary Authors Autobiography Series, volume 17, Gale, 1993.

Contemporary Literary Criticism, Gale, Volume 3, 1975, Volume 6, 1976, Volume 14, 1980, Volume 50, 1988.

Contemporary Poets, St. James Press, 1991.

Dictionary of Literary Biography, Volume 88: *Canadian Writers, 1920-1959,* Gale, 1989.

Purdy, Al, *The Collected Poems of Al Purdy,* edited by Russell Brown, McClelland & Stewart, 1986.

PERIODICALS

Books in Canada, January-February, 1987, pp. 16-17.

Canadian Literature, spring, 1966; summer, 1969; winter, 1970; winter, 1972; spring, 1973; winter, 1973; summer, 1974.

Canadian Forum, September, 1965, p. 139; November, 1968; June, 1972, p. 42; January, 1975, p. 47; November, 1984, p. 38; August, 1985, p. 34; April, 1991, p. 30.

Journal of Canadian Studies, May, 1971.

Maclean's Magazine, January, 1971.

Modern Age, summer, 1969.

Poetry, June, 1969, p. 202.

Queen's Quarterly, winter, 1969; summer, 1987, p. 475.

Quill and Quire, May, 1981, p. 31; February, 1985, p. 39; May, 1987, p. 24; November 1990, p. 20.

Saturday Night, August, 1971; July, 1972; September, 1972; December, 1973.

University of Toronto Quarterly, fall, 1987, pp. 33-34.*

* * *

PURDY, Al

See PURDY, A(lfred Wellington)

* * *

PUZO, Mario 1920-

PERSONAL: Born October 15, 1920, in New York, NY; son of Antonio (a railroad trackman) and Maria (Le Conti) Puzo; married Erika Lina Broske, 1946; children: Anthony, Joey, Dorothy, Virginia, Eugene. *Education:* Attended New School for Social Research and Columbia University.

Avocational Interests: Gambling, tennis, Italian cuisine, dieting.

ADDRESSES: Home—Long Island, NY. *Office*—c/o Random House Inc., 201 East 50th St., New York, NY 10022.

CAREER: Novelist. Variously employed as messenger with New York Central Railroad, New York City, public relations administrator with U.S. Air Force in Europe, administrative assistant with U.S. Civil Service, New York City, and editor-writer with Magazine Management. *Military service:* U.S. Army Air Forces, during World War II; served in Germany; became corporal.

AWARDS, HONORS: Academy Award, American Academy of Motion Picture Arts and Sciences, and Screen Award, Writers Guild of America, West, Inc., for best screenplay adapted from another medium, 1972, for *The Godfather,* and 1974, for *The Godfather: Part II;* Golden Globe Award for best screenplay, Hollywood Foreign Press Association, 1973, for *The Godfather,* and 1990, for *The Godfather: Part III.*

WRITINGS:

The Dark Arena, Random House, 1955, revised edition, Bantam, 1985.

The Fortunate Pilgrim, Atheneum, 1964.

The Godfather (also see below), Putnam, 1969.

Fools Die, Putnam, 1978.

The Sicilian, Linden Press/Simon & Schuster, 1984.

The Fourth K, Random House, 1991.

SCREENPLAYS

(With Francis Ford Coppola) *The Godfather* (based on Puzo's novel of same title), Paramount, 1972.

(With Coppola) *The Godfather: Part II,* Paramount, 1974.

(With George Fox) *Earthquake,* Universal, 1974.

(With David Newman, Leslie Newman, and Robert Benton) *Superman* (based on the comic strip created by Jerry Siegel and Joel Shuster), Warner Bros., 1978.

(With D. Newman and L. Newman) *Superman II,* Warner Bros., 1981.

(With Coppola) *The Godfather: Part III,* Paramount, 1990.

(With John Briley and Cary Bates) *Christopher Columbus: The Discovery,* Warner Bros., 1992.

OTHER

The Runaway Summer of Davie Shaw (juvenile), illustrated by Stewart Sherwood, Platt & Munk, 1966.

(Contributor) Thomas C. Wheeler, editor, *The Immigrant Experience: The Anguish of Becoming an American,* Dial, 1971.

"The Godfather" Papers and Other Confessions, Putnam, 1972.

Inside Las Vegas (nonfiction), photographs by Michael Abramson, Susan Fowler-Gallagher, and John Launois, Grosset, 1977.

Contributor of articles, reviews, and stories to *American Vanguard, New York, Redbook, Holiday, New York Times Magazine,* and other publications.

Manuscript collection is held at Boston University, Boston, MA. *The Godfather* has been translated into Russian.

ADAPTATIONS: A Time to Die, based on a story by Puzo, was adapted for the screen by John Goff, Matt Cimbert, and William Russel, and released by Almi, 1983. *The Cotton Club,* based on a story by Puzo, Coppola, and William Kennedy, was adapted for the screen by Kennedy and directed by Coppola for Orion Pictures, 1984; *The Fortunate Pilgrim* was adapted for television and broadcast as *Mario Puzo's The Fortunate Pilgrim* by the National Broadcasting Co., April 3, 1988; *The Sicilian* was adapted for the screen by Steve Shagan and directed by Michael Cimino for Twentieth Century-Fox, 1989.

SIDELIGHTS: "Late in 1965 a Putnam editor stopped in at Magazine Management's offices, overheard [Mario] Puzo telling Mafia yarns and offered a $5,000 advance for a book about the Italian underworld," a writer for *Time* reports. The result was *The Godfather,* and "the rest," that writer notes, "is publishing history." *The Godfather* has been phenomenally successful; it has sold over thirteen million copies, spawned three award-winning movies, and made Puzo a wealthy, famous, and sought-after novelist and screenwriter.

The fame and the money are particularly important to Puzo. Prior to *The Godfather* he had written two critically well-received but commercially unsuccessful novels. In *Time,* Puzo relates an incident that occurred in 1955, shortly after the publication of his first novel, *The Dark Arena:* "It was Christmas Eve and I had a severe gall-bladder attack. I had to take a cab to the Veterans Administration Hospital on 23rd Street, got out and fell into the gutter. There I was lying there thinking, here I am, a published writer, and I am dying like a dog. That's when I decided I would be rich and famous." *The Godfather,* he states in *"The Godfather" Papers and Other Confessions,* was written "to make money. . . . I was 45 years old and tired of being an artist." Nevertheless, as Robert Lasson of the *Washington Post Book World* contends, "Puzo sat down and produced . . . a novel which still had enormous force and kept you turning the pages." Others agree. *The Godfather* became the best-selling novel of the 1970s, outselling that decade's other blockbusters—*The Exorcist, Love Story,* and *Jaws*—by millions.

Puzo's story details the rise of Don Vito Corleone, the fall of his sons Sonny and, especially, Michael, the Mafia's peculiar behavior code and honor system, and the violent power struggle among rival "families." To some reviewers, Puzo's tale is a symbolic treatment of the corruption of the American dream. Although not all critics view the novel so seriously, most agree with Polly Anderson in the *Library Journal* that "the book is well written, suspenseful and explodes in a series of dramatic climaxes." *Newsweek*'s Pete Axthelm calls Puzo "an extremely talented storyteller" and states that *The Godfather* "moves at breakneck speed without ever losing its balance." And a critic for the *Saturday Review* contends that "Mario Puzo has achieved the definitive novel about a sinister fraternity of crime."

Several reviewers have noted the realism and believability of the book's settings and characters. "He makes his frightening cast of characters seem human and possible," according to the *Saturday Review* critic. And in another *Saturday Review* article, "A Mafioso Cases the Mafia Craze," Vincent Teresa, who apparently knows his subject, praises the author for portraying the Godfather as a fair and compassionate administrator of justice: "Puzo also showed the compassion of a don, the fair way Corleone ruled. That's the way most dons are. . . . If you go to a don . . . and you've got a legitimate beef . . . and it proves to be the truth, you'll get justice. That's what makes the dons so important in the mob. They rule fair and square."

Such remarks have given rise to the suspicion that Puzo's knowledge of the Mafia and its people is firsthand. The author disclaims this rumor in *"The Godfather" Papers and Other Confessions* by explaining that the book is based on research and anecdotes he had heard from his mother, an Italian immigrant, and on the streets. Still, the doubts persisted. Real-life underworld figures began approaching Puzo, convinced that he had some sort of link to organized crime. "After the book became famous, I was introduced to a few gentlemen related to the material," the author states in *Time.* "They were flattering. They refused to believe that I had never had the confidence of a don."

While most critics praise *The Godfather*'s realism, others have chastised Puzo for presenting his subjects in too favorable a light. These critics contend that because Puzo consistently justifies Don Vito's violent actions and solutions, certain readers have found the character and his family worthy of compassion and esteem. "The author has chosen to portray all Godfather's victims as vermin and his henchmen as fairly sympathetic," *Esquire*'s Barton Midwood asserts, "and in this way the book manages to glamorize both the murderer himself and the [imbalanced] economy in which he operates." In *Critical Inquiry,* John G. Cawelti voices a similar complaint. "Throughout the story," the reviewer writes, "the Corleone family is presented to us in a morally sympathetic light, as basically good and decent people who have had to turn to crime in order to survive and prosper in a corrupt and unjust society." Puzo addresses this issue in a *Publishers Weekly* interview with Thomas Weyr. He expresses surprise at the positive response accorded the Corleones, particularly Vito: "I was awfully surprised when people loved the Godfather so much. I thought I showed him as a murderer, a thief, a villain, a man who threw babies in the oven. . . . So I was astounded when I was attacked for glorifying the Mafia. It's a little tricky. I think it is a novelist's job not to be a moralist but to make you care about the people in the book."

After *The Godfather* and *"The Godfather" Papers and Other Confessions* Puzo focused his attention on screenwriting, first as co-author of *The Godfather* and *The Godfather: Part II,* then as co-author of *Earthquake, Superman,* and *Superman II.* Special effects, rather than story or plot, highlight the last three films. Pauline Kael of the *New Yorker* comments: "You go to *Earthquake* to see [Los Angeles] get it, and it really does. . . . *Earthquake* is a marathon of destruction effects, with stock characters spinning through it." A *Time* movie reviewer finds that *Superman,* for which Puzo wrote the first draft, is "two hours and fifteen minutes of pure fun, fancy and adventure." Garnering far more serious attention are *The Godfather* movie and its sequels.

The first film covers the period from the mid-1940s to the mid-1950s, when Michael takes command of the "family"; the second film charts the youth and early manhood of the original Godfather, Vito, and contrasts his coming-of-age with Michael's. Vincent Canby of the *New York Times* remarks that "the novel is a kind of first draft—an outline of characters and an inventory of happenings—that has only now been finished as a film." In another *New Yorker* review, Kael deems *The Godfather* "the greatest gangster picture ever made" and praises the "metaphorical overtones that took it far beyond the gangster genre." Part II, according to Kael, is even more "daring" in "that it enlarges the scope and deepens the meaning of the first film." The critic maintains that "the second film shows the consequences of the actions of the first; it's all one movie, in two great big pieces, and it comes together in your head while you watch."

Although Puzo is given co-author status for both screenplays, Francis Ford Coppola's direction and interpretation are credited with giving the films their "epic" quality. "[Coppola] turns *The Godfather: Part II* into a statement, both highly personal and with an epic resonance, on the corruption of the American dream and on the private cost of power," Paul D. Zimmerman writes in *Newsweek.* Puzo is the first to agree. "Coppola fought the battle for the integrity of the movies; if it weren't for him, they would have been 30's gangster pictures," he tells Herbert Mitgang in a *New York Times Book Review* interview. "*Godfather* is really his movie." Yet, Kael notes, "There was a Promethean spark" in Puzo's novel that afforded Coppola "an epic vision of the corruption of America." Kael adds, "Much of the material about Don Vito's early life which appears in Part II was in the Mario Puzo book and was left out in the first movie, but the real fecundity of Puzo's mind shows in the way this new film can take his characters further along and can expand . . . the implications of the book."

In October of 1978 Puzo's long-awaited fourth novel, *Fools Die,* was published. The headlines and cover stories surrounding its publication began in June—four months before the first hardcover edition went on sale—when New American Library paid an unprecedented \$2.2 million for the paperback rights, plus \$350,000 for the reprint rights to *The Godfather.* In spite of the hoopla concerning this record-setting price, or perhaps because of it, critical reaction to *Fools Die* has been mixed. "It seems a publishing event rather than a novel," Roger Sale opines in the *New York Review of Books.* In a *New Republic* review, Barbara Grizzuti Harrison offers a similar appraisal, claiming that "it is a publishing event (though hardly a literary one)." And the *Village Voice*'s James Wolcott asks: "In all this commotion, a fundamental question has gone unasked. . . . Has anyone at Putnam actually *read* this book?"

The action of *Fools Die* moves from Las Vegas to New York to Hollywood, purporting to "give us the inside skinny" on gambling, publishing, and movie-making, according to *Washington Post Book World*'s William McPherson. Harrison adds that "the events loosely strung together in this . . . book are meant to dramatize ambition, power, and corruption. I say *meant* to," she explains, "because Puzo, through the offices of his narrator John Merlyn, keeps reminding the reader that these are his themes, as if we might otherwise forget." Geoffrey Wolff of *New Times* airs a corresponding complaint: "Because he won't trust a reader to remember the climaxes of a few pages earlier, he recapitulates the plot, as though *Fools Die* were a serial, or a television series." Wolff suggests that "perhaps Puzo doesn't trust a reader to remember what he has just written because he himself has such trouble remembering what he has just written." The critic goes on to detail several contradictory descriptions given throughout the novel concerning characters' appearances, habits, and lifestyles. Wolcott also notes that "there are discrepancies in Puzo's *narrative* as gaping as crevasses."

Wolcott further criticizes the novel's structure and syntax: "The novel seems to have evolved from manuscript to book without anyone daring . . . to make sorely needed corrections. . . . Tenses are jumbled, punctuation is eccentric . . . , and the author never quite masters the use of the participle phrase." Wolff attacks the book's "slipshod craftsmanship," and *Newsweek*'s Peter S. Prescott states, "Structurally, *Fools Die* is a mess."

Despite such less-than-favorable reviews, the novel has been a popular success (it was the third highest selling hardcover novel of 1978), and Prescott and others admit that *Fools Die* can be entertaining, humorous, and, in some instances, inspired. "I had a fine time reading it," Prescott writes. "Its many stories, developed at varying lengths, are slickly entertaining." A *Time* reviewer comments: "*Fools Die* contains the sort of mini-dramas and surprises that keep paperback readers flipping pages; a man wins a small fortune at baccarat and blows his brains out; a straightforward love affair turns baroque with kinky sex; an extremely cautious character makes a stupid and fatal error." Moreover, Prescott finds: "Puzo here reveals an unsuspected talent for gross comedy. . . . In [the character] Osano, the most famous living American novelist, he has written an inspired caricature of our own dear Norman Mailer."

"I wrote *Fools Die* for myself," the author tells Mitgang. "I wanted to say certain things about gambling, Las Vegas and the country." According to David Robinson of the *Times Literary Supplement,* Puzo is quite successful at capturing the flavor and feel of Las Vegas: "The first and best section of *Fools Die* is set in Las Vegas. Puzo's forte is the neo-documentary background; and . . . his portrayal of [that city] has the appearance of authenticity." The *Time* critic agrees: "Puzo's description of Las Vegas, its Strip, showgirls, characters, and the variety of ways one can lose money swiftly and painlessly, are carried off with brio. The green baize world of casino management has never seemed more professional, entertaining and lethal."

In 1984 Puzo returned to the safer ground of Sicily, the Mafia, and the Corleone family with his novel *The Sicilian,* which Christopher Lehmann-Haupt of the *New York Times* claims "might more aptly be designated *The Godfather, Part I I/II.*" Based upon actual events in the 1950s, it is the story of Salvatore Giuliano, a Robin Hood-style outlaw who, with the support of the church and the Mafia, terrorized the Sicilian aristocracy. *The Sicilian* begins as Michael Corleone is preparing to return to America after a two year self-imposed exile in Sicily. Shortly before departure, Michael is ordered by his father to find Giuliano and bring him to America before the authorities catch up with him. It is during Michael's search that Giuliano's history is revealed, along with the history of the Mafia itself. "[*The Sicilian*] gives Mr. Puzo another chance to do what he seems to do best, which is to spin a yarn of treachery, violence, sex, sadism, revenge and bloody justice," writes Lehmann-Haupt. "But it's also a little sad that [Puzo] has felt it necessary to return to his Italian gangsters. . . . Though *The Sicilian* is fun and compelling, it seems like an admission of defeat in a way."

Author Gay Talese was impressed by the detailed and accurate account of Giuliano's life and the events that made him into a hero. Writing in the *New York Times,* Talese calls *The Sicilian* "a fine, fast-paced novel about Sicily in the mid-1940s that is historically useful and, given events there in the mid-1980s, hardly out of date." Lehmann-Haupt, too, praised Puzo's well-researched look at the birth and evolution of the Sicilian Mafia. However, he found the characters "a little undernourished" in comparison to those strong personalities that were immortalized in the Godfather movies. "Even the familiar characters seem pale compared with their movie counterparts," he continues. "Not that we will have to wait too long, I would imagine, before we see [*The Sicilian*] . . . up there on the screen."

Three years, to be exact: *The Sicilian* was released by 20th Century-Fox in 1987, having been delayed by production problems and a handful of lawsuits. Though Puzo's novel showed tremendous cinematic potential, the film (adapted by Steve Shagan) was panned by reviewers: Sheila Benson of the *Los Angeles Times* described it as "fuzzy and inert," while the *Washington Post*'s Hal Hinson called the film "unambiguously atrocious. . . . [*The Sicilian*] isn't just bad, it's bad in a uniquely emblematic, Hollywood way." Not long after the release of *The Sicilian* another Puzo novel, *The Fortunate Pilgrim,* was adapted, this time as a television miniseries. "Never has so much tedium been crammed into so little time," laments a reviewer in *People.* "At only five hours, *The Fortunate Pilgrim* is far from the longest miniseries ever made. It just seems like it."

In 1988, Puzo was once again approached by Coppola, who had come upon an idea for continuing the Godfather saga, and less than a year later the screenplay for *The Godfather: Part III* was completed. Picking up twenty years after Part II left off, Part III shows Michael as the head of the tremendously rich and influential Corleone family. However, their influence extends in different directions now, for Michael has taken the Corleone fortune out of gambling and used it for more legitimate investments. In addition, he has donated hundreds of millions of dollars to the Catholic church in an attempt to purchase his redemption. Michael, though, is losing control of the family: frail, stricken with diabetes, and reluctant to act against his enemies, he does not command the respect he once did. Eager to replace him as don is Vincent, the illegitimate son of Michael's dead brother, Sonny. Michael struggles to regain his hold on the Corleone family, simultaneously seeking to gain influence within the Vatican; all the while, rival families plot to destroy both him and his investments. The novel culminates with an international banking scandal and the assassination of Pope John Paul I.

When *The Godfather: Part III* was released on Christmas Day, 1990, sixteen years had passed since the last *Godfather* movie—enough time for critics and moviegoers to build almost insurmountable expectations for this newest installment. The *Los Angeles Times*' Michael Wilmington finds Part III to be "not quite a fitting climax to a series that ranks among the American cinema's most remarkable sustained achievements." Stuart Klawans writes in *Nation:* "*The Godfather: Part III* turns out to be as good as a post-sequel can be. . . . [It] is less gripping than the first *Godfather* and less interesting as a narrative structure than the second." Yet these flaws become apparent only when Part III is compared to the previous Godfather films; when judged on its own, Klawans observes, "it gives and keeps giving and doesn't give out until you're sated with the hero's doom." Wilmington, too, ultimately describes *The Godfather: Part III* as "one of the best American movies of the year—a work of high ensemble talent and intelligence, gorgeously mounted and crafted, artistically audacious in ways that most American movies don't even attempt."

Less than a month after the release of *The Godfather: Part III,* Puzo used the increased media attention to promote his political thriller entitled *The Fourth K.* Set in the first decade of the twenty-first century, it details the events occurring during the presidency of Francis Xavier Kennedy, a distant cousin of John, Robert, and Edward (and the fourth "K" of the novel's title). At the time of FXK's administration, terrorism is out of control: the Pope is assassinated on Easter Sunday by a group of Middle Eastern radicals; when the gunman is captured in New York, the terrorist leader, a man named Yabril, kidnaps and murders the president's daughter. Intended to demonstrate the ineffectuality of the United States as a world power, these actions instead drive Kennedy to near-madness, prompting him to bomb the capital of Sherhaben, Yabril's oil-rich native land. This evokes the wrath of the Socrates Club, a California-based group of billionaire investors with significant interests in Sherhaben. Meanwhile, a group of ultra left-wing intellectuals detonate a small atomic bomb in Manhattan in an attempt to illustrate the danger of nuclear proliferation. R. Z. Sheppard of *Time* writes: "The aggressive ways in which FXK handles foreign and domestic threats to his presidency and his life allow Puzo to pull out all the stops." A reviewer in the *West Coast Review of Books* concurs, saying: "Action and intrigue infuse the narrative, and the reader is captivated as the story lines converge in an explosive finale."

Because *The Fourth K* attempts to juggle a number of intricate storylines, it has been accused by several critics of being improbable and unwieldy. "Yes, this is your classic page turner," admits E. J. Dionne, Jr., in the *Washington Post Book World.* "But it's a page-turner not only for the right reasons but also for the wrong ones. Part of why you want to get to the end is to see how Puzo's Rube Goldberg machine of a plot resolves itself." Frederick Busch, however, defends the author in Chicago's *Tribune Books:* "Puzo is a veteran novelist and screenwriter, so he knows how to make his improbable plot and story-board characters mesh and move." Ross Thomas concludes his *Los Angeles Times* review by proclaiming *The Fourth K* "a witty, sometimes wise, often mordant tale about the American politics of tomorrow. And if [Puzo's] intricately plotted tale offers more insight than hope, it is still fine entertainment, which is more than can be said of today's politics."

In general, critics contend that the jury is still out regarding Puzo's status in American literature. They agree that his first two novels display great promise (Frederic Morton of the *New York Herald Tribune Book Review,* for example, finds that *The Dark Arena* "reveals Mr. Puzo to be a writer of power and precision," and the *New York Times Book Review*'s David Borloff judges *The Fortunate Pilgrim* "a small classic"), but suggest that his later works are too commercial. Nevertheless, a *Time* writer concludes: "If Mario Puzo never writes another word he will already have earned the title of Godfather of the Paperbacks. . . . Puzo's *The Godfather* and 'an offer you can't refuse' have already become part of the language. This may find him a niche in American letters. He is already assured a place in American numbers."

BIOGRAPHICAL/CRITICAL SOURCES:

BOOKS

Contemporary Literary Criticism, Gale, Volume 1, 1973, Volume 2, 1974, Volume 6, 1976, Volume 36, 1986.

Dictionary of Literary Biography, Volume 6, *American Novelists since World War II,* Second Series, 1980.

Green, Rose B., *The Italian-American Novel,* Fairleigh Dickinson University Press, 1974.

Madden, David, editor, *Rediscoveries,* Crown, 1972.

Puzo, Mario, *"The Godfather Papers" and Other Confessions,* Putnam, 1972.

Wheeler, Thomas C., editor, *The Immigrant Experience: The Anguish of Becoming An American,* Dial, 1971.

PERIODICALS

Chicago Tribune, June 19, 1981.

Commonweal, May 6, 1955; June 4, 1965.

Critical Inquiry, March, 1975.

Esquire, February, 1971.

Library Journal, April 1, 1969.

Life, July 10, 1970.

Los Angeles Times, February 14, 1987; October 23, 1987.

Los Angeles Times Book Review, January 13, 1991, p. 2.

Maclean's, March 18, 1991, p. 62.

McCall's, May, 1971.

Nation, June 16, 1969.

New Republic, November 18, 1978.

Newsweek, March 10, 1969; December 23, 1974; September 18, 1978; January 1, 1979.

New Times, October 2, 1978.

New York, March 31, 1969.

New Yorker, December 12, 1974; December 23, 1974; February 11, 1991, p. 95.

New York Herald Tribune Book Review, March 6, 1955.

New York Review of Books, July 20, 1972; October 26, 1978.

New York Times, February 27, 1955; March 12, 1972; March 16, 1972; June 19, 1981; November 22, 1984; June 5, 1986; May 22, 1987; January 10, 1991, p. C23.

New York Times Book Review, January 31, 1965; February 18, 1979; January 13, 1991, p. 7.

People, July 3, 1978.

Publishers Weekly, May 12, 1978.

Saturday Review, February 26, 1955; January 23, 1965; March 15, 1969; January 20, 1973.

Time, March 13, 1971; December 16, 1974; August 28, 1978; November 27, 1978; January 14, 1991, p. 62.

Times (London), May 3, 1985.

Times Literary Supplement, December 1, 1978.

Tribune Books (Chicago), January 20, 1991, p. 10.

Village Voice, September 4, 1978.

Wall Street Journal, January 11, 1991, p. A8.

Washington Post, March 12, 1970; October 23, 1987; October 24, 1987.

Washington Post Book World, March 9, 1969; April 9, 1972; September 24, 1978; January 20, 1991, p. 9.

World & I, March, 1991, p. 363.*

—Sketch by Brandon Trenz

R

R. R.
See BURGESS, Michael (Roy)

* * *

RALE, Nero
See BURGESS, Michael (Roy)

* * *

RAPPOPORT, Ken 1935-

PERSONAL: Born February 14, 1935, in Brooklyn, NY; son of Jacob (a marine engineer) and Margie (a bookkeeper; maiden name, Geller) Rappoport; married Bernice Goodman (a teacher), March 26, 1961; children: Felicia, Sharon, Lawrence. *Education:* Rider College, B.S., 1956.

Avocational Interests: Travel, photography.

ADDRESSES: *Home*—29 Owens Rd., Old Bridge, NJ 08857. *Office*—Associated Press, 50 Rockefeller Plaza, New York, NY 10020.

CAREER: Dorf Feature Service, Newark, NJ, feature writer and reporter, 1960-61; *Doylestown Intelligencer,* Doylestown, PA, reporter, 1961-63; Associated Press, reporter in Philadelphia, PA, 1963-69, sports writer in New York, NY, 1969—. *Military service:* U.S. Army, 1958-60.

MEMBER: Baseball Writers Association of America, Professional Hockey Writers Association.

AWARDS, HONORS: *Sports Digest* Best Story of the Month, November, 1973; second place award, *Writer's Digest* National Writing Competition, 1991.

WRITINGS:

(Contributor) Will Grimsley, editor, *A Century of Sports,* Associated Press, 1971.
(Contributor) Grimsley, editor, *The Sports Immortals,* Prentice-Hall, 1972.
The Nittany Lions: A Story of Penn State Football, Strode, 1973, revised edition, 1979.
The Trojans: A Story of Southern California Football, Strode, 1974.
The Syracuse Football Story, Strode, 1975.
Wake Up the Echoes: Notre Dame Football, Strode, 1975, revised edition, 1979.
Tar Heel: North Carolina Football, Strode, 1976.
Tar Heel: North Carolina Basketball, Strode, 1976, revised edition, 1979.
(Contributor) Ben Olan, editor, *A Century of Champions,* Associated Press, 1976.
Great College Football Rivalries, Grosset, 1978.
The Classic: The History of the NCAA Basketball Playoffs, National Collegiate Athletic Association-Lowell Press, 1979.
Diamonds in the Rough, Grosset, 1979.
Super Sundays, Grosset, 1980.
Pigskin Power, Grosset, 1981.
Doubleheader: Yankees and Dodgers, Grosset, 1982.
Football's Special Teams: Cowboys and Raiders, Grosset, 1982.
(Contributor) *Football's Fifty Greatest Games,* Bobbs-Merrill, 1983.
(Contributor) *101 Greatest Athletes of the Century,* Bonanza Books, 1987.
Nolan Ryan, Dillon, 1992.
Bobby Bonilla, Walker & Co., 1993.

Also contributor to *The World in 1974,* edited by Tom Hoge, Associated Press. Contributor to national sports journals, and to *Saturday Evening Post.*

WORK IN PROGRESS: Shaquille O'Neal, for Walker & Co., spring 1994.

SIDELIGHTS: Ken Rappoport once offered *CA* these thoughts on writing: "I write because I have a need, a hunger. It is almost like breathing and eating, really. And although I have written ten books, I am not completely happy with any of my work. Which is all to the good, I suppose, because I would never improve as a writer otherwise. And that, particularly, is my main motivation now, to reach my potential. If I do that, I will be happy with my work."

* * *

RAUF, Abdur 1924-

PERSONAL: Born May 10, 1924, in Amritsar, India; son of Allama Hussain (a journalist) and Hajirah Mir; married Naseem Chughtai (a medical educator), February 2, 1958; children: Asad, Amer, Asim. *Education:* Punjab University, M.A. (philosophy), 1945, M.A. (psychology), 1949; University of London, Ph.D., 1955. *Religion:* Islam.

ADDRESSES: Home—47 Empress Rd., Lahore, Pakistan.

CAREER: Bureau of Education, Lahore, Pakistan, director, 1958-73; Text-Book Board, Lahore, chairman, 1973-74; Curriculum Research and Development Centre, Lahore, director, 1974; Government College of Education, Lahore, chairman of department of psychology, 1974, principal, 1975-76; Punjab Government, Lahore, additional education secretary, 1977-78, director of public instruction, 1979-82; Punjab Public Service Commission, Lahore, member, 1982-84; *The Nation,* Lahore, editor, 1987; Ferozsons Ltd. (publishing house) Lahore, editor, 1987—. President of education and social sciences section of Pakistan Science Conference, 1964. Resident Asian senior specialist in education at University of Hawaii's East-West Center, 1966-67.

MEMBER: Pakistan Association for the Advancement of Science, Institute for the Study and Treatment of Delinquency (London, England), Lions International.

AWARDS, HONORS: United Nations social defense fellow in Great Britain, 1952-53; NBCP Award for children's literature, 1989.

WRITINGS:

Dynamic Educational Psychology, Ferozsons Ltd., 1958, revised edition, 1962.
(Editor) *Baccon ke li'e Qu'ran,* [Pakistan], 1963.
Religious Education in West Pakistan, Bureau of Education (Lahore), 1964.
Renaissance of Islamic Culture and Civilization in Pakistan, Ashraf Publications, 1965.
West Pakistan: Rural Education and Development, East-West Center Press, 1970.
Badunwani aur Rishwatstani (title means "Corruption and Bribery"), Shaikh Ghulam Ali & Sons, 1977.
Islamic Culture in Pakistan, Ferozsons, Ltd., 1988.
Illustrated History of Islam, Ferozsons, Ltd, 1992.
Dictionary and Encyclopaedia of Islam, Jang, 1993.

FOR CHILDREN

Qu'ran for Children, Ferozsons Ltd., 1976.
Prophet Muhammad's Guidance for Children, Ferozsons Ltd., 1977.
Islam for Children, ISESCO (Morocco), 1989.
Stories from Prophet's Life: Illustrated Biography of the Holy Prophet for Children, Ferozsons Ltd., 1990.

Also author of ten books in Urdu. Editor of *Sanvi Taaleem* and *Taaleem-o-Tadrees,* both 1967-74.

WORK IN PROGRESS: Human Capital Formation in the Third World; Educational Crises in Pakistan.

SIDELIGHTS: Abdur Rauf once remarked to *CA:* "Human capital formation is a great motivational force in my writing and field operations. I strongly believe that in the ultimate analysis technological advancement and economic prosperity are dependent upon human creativity rather than sheer material resources. This belief is reflected in my books as well as policy decision as Pakistan's educational planner. I play an active role in promoting mass awakening on the dignity of human rights, which is also appropriately reflected in my contributions to the Human Rights Days and my community development pursuits as a social work missionary."

Rauf has traveled in England, the United States, Canada, Mexico, Puerto Rico, Japan, Hong Kong, Vietnam, Australia, Bangladesh, India, Saudi Arabia, Abu Dhabi, and Egypt. He speaks Urdu, English, Arabic, French, and Spanish.

* * *

REANEY, James 1926-

PERSONAL: Born September 1, 1926, in South Easthope, Ontario, Canada; son of James Nesbitt and Elizabeth (Crerar) Reaney; married Colleen Thibaudeau (a poet), December 29, 1951; children: James Stewart, Susan Alice. *Education:* University of Toronto, B.A., 1948, M.A., 1949, Ph.D., 1958.

ADDRESSES: Office—Department of English, University of Western Ontario, London, Ontario, Canada N6A

2J9. *Agent*—John Miller, Cultural Support Services 206, Gerrard St. East, Toronto, Ontario, Canada M5A 2E6.

CAREER: Playwright, poet, and novelist. University of Manitoba, Winnipeg, Canada, faculty member, 1949-57, assistant professor of English, 1957-60; University of Western Ontario, London, Canada, associate professor, 1960-63, professor of English, 1964—. Founder and editor of *Alphabet,* 1960-1971; founder of Listener's Workshop, London, 1966.

MEMBER: Association of Canadian University Teachers of English, Canadian Association of University Teachers, Canadian Theatre Co-op, League of Canadian Poets, Royal Society of Canada (fellow).

AWARDS, HONORS: Governor General's Award, 1949, for *The Red Heart,* 1958, for *The Suit of Nettles,* 1969, for *The Killdeer and Other Plays,* and for *Twelve Letters to a Small Town;* Massey Award, and Governor General's Award, both 1960, both for *The Killdeer;* Chalmers Outstanding Play Award finalist, 1973, for *The Donnellys: Sticks and Stones,* and 1975, for *The Donnellys: Handcuffs;* Chalmers Outstanding Play Award, 1974, for *The Donnellys: St. Nicholas Hotel;* Officer of the Order of Canada, 1975; Honorary D.Litt., Carleton University, 1975.

WRITINGS:

POETRY

The Red Heart (also see below), McClelland & Stewart, 1949.

A Suit of Nettles, Macmillan, 1958, 2nd edition, 1975.

Twelve Letters to a Small Town (also see below), Ryerson, 1962.

The Dance of Death at London, Ontario, Alphabet Press, 1963.

Poems (includes *The Red Heart* and *Twelve Letters to a Small Town*), edited by Germaine Warkentin, New Press, 1972.

Selected Longer Poems, edited by Warkentin, Porcepic, 1976.

Selected Shorter Poems, edited by Warkentin, Porcepic, 1976.

Performance Poems, Moonstone Press, 1990.

PLAYS

Night-Blooming Cereus (one-act libretto; broadcast as radio play, 1959; also see below), produced in Toronto, Canada, 1960.

The Killdeer (three-act; also see below), produced in Toronto, 1960, revised version, (two-act; also see below), produced in Vancouver, Canada, 1970.

(And director) *One-Man Masque* (one-act; also see below), produced in Toronto, 1960.

The Easter Egg (three-act; also see below), produced in Hamilton, Ontario, Canada, 1962.

Names and Nicknames (children's; produced in Winnipeg, Canada, 1963; also see below), published in *Nobody in the Cast,* edited by Robert Barton and others, Longmans, 1969, published alone, Talonbooks, 1978.

(With Alfred Kunz) *Let's Make a Carol: A Play with Music for Children,* Waterloo Music Co., 1965.

(And director) *Aladdin and the Magic Lamp* (children's with marionettes), produced in London, Ontario, 1965.

(And director) *Apple Butter* (children's with marionettes; produced in London, 1965; also see below), Talonbooks, 1978.

(And director) *Little Red Riding Hood* (children's with marionettes), produced in London, 1965.

The Sun and the Moon (three-act; also see below), produced in London, 1965.

(And director) *Listen to the Wind* (three-act; produced in London, 1966), Talonbooks, 1972.

Ignoramus (children's; produced in London, 1966; also see below), Talonbooks, 1978.

Three Desks (two-act; also see below), produced in London, 1967.

The Canada Tree, produced in Morrison Island, Ontario, 1967.

(And director) *Geography Match* (children's; produced in London, 1967; also see below), Talonbooks, 1978.

Colours in the Dark (produced in Stratford, Ontario, 1967), Talonbooks-Macmillan (Canada), 1970, revised edition, 1971.

(And director) *Genesis,* produced in London, 1968.

Don't Sell Mr. Aesop, produced in London, 1968.

Sticks and Stones (part one of "The Donnellys" trilogy; produced in Toronto, 1973; also see below), published in *Canadian Theatre Review,* spring, 1974.

The Saint Nicholas Hotel (part two of "The Donnellys" trilogy; also see below), produced in Toronto, 1974.

Handcuffs (part three of "The Donnellys" trilogy; also see below), produced in Toronto, 1975.

(With John Beckwith) *All the Bees and All the Keys,* Porcepic, 1976.

(With Marty Gervais) *Baldoon* (two-act; produced in Toronto, 1976), Porcupine's Quill, 1977.

The Dismissal (produced in Toronto, 1977), Porcepic, 1978.

Wacousta, produced in Toronto, 1977.

At the Big Carwash (puppet play), produced on tour with Caravan Stage Company, 1979.

King Whistle!, produced in Stratford, 1980.

Antler River, produced at the Grand Theatre, London, 1983.

Gyroscope, produced in Toronto, 1983.

I, the Parade, produced at the University of Waterloo, 1983.

The Canadian Brothers, produced at the University of Calgary, 1984.

Imprecations—The Art of Swearing, produced in London, 1984.

Traps, produced in London, 1984.

Also author of the play *Cloud Shadows.* Author of unpublished and unproduced plays, including *The Rules of Joy, The Bacchae,* and *The Shivaree.*

PLAY COLLECTIONS

The Killdeer and Other Plays (contains *Night-Blooming Cereus, The Killdeer, One-Man Masque,* and *The Sun and the Moon,*), Macmillan (Canada), 1962.

Masks of Childhood (contains *The Killdeer* [revised version], *The Easter Egg,* and *Three Desks,*), edited by Brian Parker, New Press, 1972.

Apple Butter and Other Plays for Children (contains *Names and Nicknames, Apple Butter, Ignoramus,* and *Geography Match*), Talonbooks, 1973.

The Donnellys: A Trilogy, Porcepic, Part 1: *Sticks and Stones,* 1975, Part 2: *The Saint Nicholas Hotel,* 1976, Part 3: *Handcuffs,* 1976.

RADIO PLAYS

Poet and City—Winnipeg (broadcast on *Wednesday Night,* Canadian Broadcasting Corporation [CBC], 1960), edited by Eli Mandel and Jean-Guy Pilon, Ryerson Press, 1962.

The Journals and Letters of William Blake, broadcast on *Wednesday Night,* CBC, 1961.

Wednesday's Child, broadcast on *Wednesday Night,* CBC, 1962.

Canada Dash, Canada Dot: Across (Part 1), broadcast on CBC, 1965.

Canada Dash, Canada Dot: The Line Up and Down (Part 2), broadcast on CBC, 1966.

Canada Dot (Part 3), broadcast on CBC, 1967.

LIBRETTO

(With Beckwith) *Crazy to Kill* (opera), Guelph Spring Festival, 1990.

(With Harry Sanes) *Serinette* (opera), Music at Sharon, 1991.

OTHER

The Boy with an "R" in his Hand (juvenile novel), illustrated by Leo Rampen, Macmillan (Canada), 1965.

Aspects of Nineteenth Century Ontario, edited by F. H. Armstrong, University of Toronto Press, 1974.

Fourteen Barrels from Sea to Sea (travel diary), Porcepic, 1977.

Take the Big Picture (juvenile fiction), illustrated by Barbara Di Lella, Porcupine's Quill, 1986.

Also author of the novel *Afternoon Moon.* Adaptor of *The Revenger's Tragedy.* Collaborator with composer John Beckwith on operas and other musical settings of text. Also contributor of poems, stories, and critical articles to various periodicals, including *Atlantic Monthly, Canadian Forum, Canadian Short Stories, Canadian Theatre Review, Canadian Art, Globe, Contemporary Verse, Black Moss, Canadian Poetry, Queen's Quarterly,* and *Canadian Literature.*

ADAPTATIONS: Reaney's play, *One-Man Masque,* was adapted by Ron Cameron and published as *Masque* by Simon & Pierre, 1975.

WORK IN PROGRESS: Plays on Emily Bronte and Chatterton; a book on the founding of national theatre; a Donnellys sourcebook; an anthology of material from *Alphabet; Alice Through the Looking Glass,* for Stratford Festival; *Taptoo,* an opera for Toronto Historical Board at Old Fort York.

SIDELIGHTS: English professor James Reaney's long and varied writing career encompasses everything from poetry and plays to children's books. Initially Reaney concentrated on writing poetry, producing four collections of poems between 1949 and 1963. Then, in the early 1960s, he began focussing on playwriting, composing over thirty plays since first beginning. Eventually Reaney expanded his writing oeuvre to children's books. "The length of Reaney's career, and the breadth and variety of his achievement mark him as a leading figure in the Canadian theatre," claims John H. Astington in the *Oxford Companion to Canadian Theatre.*

Reaney's interest in theatre began when he was in high school. This interest was fostered by the establishment of the Stratford Festival in his area in 1953. He has written over twenty-five diverse plays, including plays for children, which "liberated Reaney's instinct for fun and energy in the theatre," relates Astington. In 1978 Talonbooks reissued a revised edition of a collection of Reaney's children plays, *Apple Butter, Geography Match, Ignoramus, and Names and Nicknames,* along with a teacher's guide, to promote the teaching of drama as literature. "As theatre, these plays have been enjoyed by both child and adult audiences. The scope for creativity and imagination on the part of the actors, the emphasis on rhythm, chorus, movement and mime, and the fast-paced, zany action all add up to a lively theatrical experience. . . . It is guaranteed that everyone will enjoy them," comments Anne Bradin in *In Review.*

In addition to writing plays for children, Reaney has also written books for children. His first novel, *The Boy with an "R" in His Hand,* illustrates the divided loyalties and conflicts during the Mackenzie Rebellion of 1837 and the effect of this division on two brothers who align with opposing sides. Commenting on its 1980 reprint, Terence Scully writes in *Canadian Children's Literature* that *The Boy with an "R" in His Hand* "has already served a generation well with its spirited fantasy, and could very effectively be read aloud to a third generation."

In the fall of 1976, Reaney took a sabbatical from the University of Western Ontario and accompanied a professional Canadian drama group as they toured Canada with his play, *The Donnellys: A Trilogy.* The subsequent record of his impressions and of the experiences of the NDWT Company players while on this tour are chronicled in his book *Fourteen Barrels from Sea to Sea.* Dubbing it a "travel book" for lack of a better term, Reaney once told *CA* that it is actually a commentary on the state of drama in Canada today.

Reaney told *CA:* "Interviewers often ask me if I'm postmodern or do I deconstruct. I'm afraid I'm too naive for that. What I've ended up doing is shamelessly celebrating my love for my portion of the province of Ontario, the same bailiwick as Alice Munro's—Southwestern Ontario. She has all that lies north of Exeter, I've got everything south of that dear prosperous town.

"I'm particularly proud of the opera libretti because our music theatre tradition was incredibly thin when I started in 1944 to write a libretto for my favorite composer, John Beckwith. I've been called the Father of Community Theatre in Canada; I don't know if I want to be a father, but it has been fun going into towns and, at their invitation, livening things up with a play they help me write. In my hometown, Stratford, my proudest achievement along these lines was being asked to write a play—a musical comedy—for the centenary of my high school; *King Whistle.* My other obsession is the Brontes, and Beckwith and I want to do a grand opera on Branwell Bronte and his visionary kingdom of Angria—sort of Tales of Hoffman only it's the Bronte children. Of course, the Brontes lived for years on the moors of Southwestern Ontario."

BIOGRAPHICAL/CRITICAL SOURCES:

BOOKS

Benson, Eugene, and L. W. Conolly, editors, *Oxford Companion to Canadian Theatre,* Oxford University Press, 1989.

Lee, Alvin, *James Reaney,* Twayne, 1969.

Reaney, James Stewart, *James Reaney,* Gage 1976.

Rubin, Don, and Alison Crammer-Byng, editors, *Canada's Playwrights: A Biographical Guide,* Canadian Theatre Review Publications, 1980.

Woodman, Ross, *James Reaney,* McClelland & Stewart (Toronto), 1972.

PERIODICALS

Books for Young People, April 1988, p. 7.

Canadian Children's Literature, Number 23/24, 1981, p. 98.

Canadian Literature, autumn/winter, 1989, pp. 251-53.

In Review, February, 1980, pp. 54-55.

* * *

REED, H(erbert) Owen 1910-

PERSONAL: Born June 17, 1910, in Odessa, MO; son of Joseph M. and Della (Fine) Reed; married Esther Richard Morris (an assistant professor emeritus at Michigan State University), August 18, 1931 (died, 1981); married Mary L. Arwood, 1982; children: (first marriage) Sara Jo Reed Ferrar, Carol Ann Reed Wetters. *Education:* Attended University of Missouri, 1929-33; Louisiana State University, B.M. (with distinction), 1934, M.M., 1936, B.A., 1937; University of Rochester, Ph.D., 1939; studied folk music in Mexico, 1948-49, and Norway, 1977; studied composition and orchestration with Howard Hanson and Bernard Rogers; also studied with Bohuslav Martinu at Berkshire Music Center and privately with Roy Harris. *Religion:* United Presbyterian.

ADDRESSES: Home—(summer) 7805 West Lake Dr., Canadian Lakes Club, Stanwood, MI 49346; (winter) 1391 Calle Mendoza, Green Valley, AZ 85614.

CAREER: Michigan State University, East Lansing, instructor, 1939-41, assistant professor, 1941-45, associate professor, 1945-53, professor of music, 1953-76, professor emeritus, 1976—, chairman of theory and composition, 1958-67, chairman of composition, 1967-76. Visiting professor at Montana State University, summer, 1950, and Gettysburg College, spring, 1969. Pianist and trumpet player; composer of works for band, stage, orchestra, chorus, and of chamber music; commissions include compositions for Michigan State University Centennial, for dedication of University of Illinois Band Building, for Detroit Symphony Orchestra's 50th anniversary, for Ohio Music Education Association, and for the International Trumpet Guild. Assistant conductor and arranger for Louisiana Kings (30-piece brass ensemble), on tour, 1936; guest conductor with symphony orchestras and wind ensembles until 1976.

MEMBER: American Society of Composers, Authors and Publishers, American Society of University Composers, American Music Center (associate member), National Association of Composers, Michigan Orchestra Association,

Michigan School Band and Orchestra Association (honorary member), Phi Mu Alpha, Sinfonia, Kappa Sigma, Kappa Kappa Psi (honorary member), Tau Beta Sigma (honorary member), Michigan State University Club (president, 1966).

AWARDS, HONORS: Guggenheim fellowship for composition, 1948-49; Symphonic Award of Composers Press, 1949, for *Concerto for Violincello and Orchestra;* Huntington Hartford Foundation resident fellowship, 1960; Michigan State University Distinguished Faculty Award, 1962; Greater Michigan Foundation Citation for distinguished contributions in the arts, 1963; Helene Wurlitzer Foundation resident fellowship, 1967; Neil A. Kjos Memorial Award for best hand composition in 1974, for *For the Unfortunate;* first place in Brooklyn College Chamber Opera competition, 1985; various grants from American Society of Composers, Authors, and Publishers.

WRITINGS:

A Workbook in the Fundamentals of Music, Belwin-Mills, 1947.

Basic Music (college theory text with workbook), Belwin-Mills, 1954.

(With Paul Harder) *Basic Contrapuntal Technique* (with workbook), Belwin-Mills, 1964.

(With Joel T. Leach) *Scoring for Percussion and the Instruments of the Percussion Section,* Prentice-Hall, 1969, revised edition, Belwin-Mills, 1978.

(With Robert E. Sidnell) *The Materials of Music Composition,* Addison-Wesley, Book I: *Fundamentals,* 1978, Book II: *Exploring the Parameters,* 1980.

ORCHESTRAL WORKS

Symphony Number 1, Belwin-Mills, 1939.

Overture, Belwin-Mills, 1940.

Concerto for Violincello and Orchestra, Seesaw Music Corp., 1951.

Overture for Strings, Belwin-Mills, 1961.

The Turning Mind, Belwin-Mills, 1968.

Ut Re Mi, Belwin-Mills, 1979, transcribed for band, 1980.

STAGE WORKS

Peter Homan's Dream (two-act folk opera; first performed at Michigan State University Centennial celebration, 1955), Belwin-Mills, 1955, revised version, 1959, musical version, 1971.

Earth Trapped (Indian spirit legend based on story by Hartley Alexander), Belwin-Mills, 1960.

Living Solid Face (Indian spirit legend based on story by Alexander), libretto by Forest Coggan, Belwin-Mills, 1974.

Butterfly Girl and Mirage Boy (Indian spirit legend based on story by Alexander), Belwin-Mills, 1980.

BAND WORKS

Spiritual, Associated Music Publishers, 1948.

Missouri Shindig, Belwin-Mills, 1952.

Theme and Variations, Belwin-Mills, 1954.

La Fiesta Mexicana, Belwin-Mills, 1956, transcription for orchestra, 1964 (first performed by Detroit Symphony Orchestra, 1965).

Renascence, Belwin-Mills, 1959.

Che-ba-kun-ah (for band and string quartet), Belwin-Mills, 1959.

Fanfares, Belwin-Mills, 1962.

The Touch of the Earth (for concert band, chorus, and soloists), Belwin-Mills, 1972.

For the Unfortunate (for concert band and chorus on tape), Neil A. Kjos Music Co., 1975.

The Awakening of the Ents, Ludwig Music Publishing, 1986.

Of Lothlorien (for wind ensemble), Manuscript Press, 1987.

CHAMBER MUSIC

Three Nationalities, Belwin-Mills, 1951.

Michigan Morn (from *Peter Homan's Dream*), Belwin-Mills, 1955.

The Ox-Driving Song, Belwin-Mills, 1955.

Scherzo for Clarinet and Piano, Belwin-Mills, 1959.

The Passing of John Blackfeather, lyrics by Merrick F. McCarthy, Belwin-Mills, 1959.

Mountain Meditation, lyrics by Marian Cuthbertson, Belwin-Mills, 1960.

Symphonic Dance, Belwin-Mills, 1963.

El Muchacho, Belwin-Mills, 1963.

Fanfare for Remembrance, Triplo Press, 1992.

CHORAL WORKS

Two Tongue Twisters, Belwin-Mills, 1951.

Ripley Ferry, text by Merrick F. McCarthy, Belwin-Mills, 1958.

A Psalm of Praise, Sam Fox, 1959.

Rejoice! Rejoice!, Boosey & Hawkes, 1979.

Also author of *A Tabernacle for the Sun,* libretto by McCarthy.

OTHER

Works included in *Panorama,* American Music Publishers, 1953, and *Music for the High School Chorus,* Allyn & Bacon, 1967. Composer of other performed but unpublished orchestral, band, choral, and chamber music.

SIDELIGHTS: H. Owen Reed spent six months in Mexico composing and studying folk music, 1948-49, and studied folk music there again in the summer of 1960. Many of his works, including *La Fiesta Mexicana* and selections from *Peter Homan's Dream,* have been recorded by such bands as the Eastman Symphonic Wind Ensemble, U.S. Air Force Band, University of Illinois Concert Band, Michigan State University Symphonic Band, Dallas Wind Orchestra, and Tokyo Kosei Wind Orchestra.

* * *

REEVES, Marjorie E(thel) 1905-

PERSONAL: Born July 17, 1905, in Bratton, Westbury, Wiltshire, England; daughter of Robert J. (an agricultural engineer) and Edith S. (Whitaker) Reeves. *Education:* St. Hugh's College, Oxford, B.A. (with first class honors), 1926; Westfield College, London, Ph.D., 1931.

ADDRESSES: Home—38 Norham Rd., Oxford, England.

CAREER: Roan School for Girls, London, England, assistant mistress of history, 1927-29; St. Gabriel's College, London, lecturer in history, 1931-38; Oxford University, St. Anne's College, Oxford, England, beginning 1938, started as tutor, became fellow in history, vice-principal, honorary fellow, 1972—. Member of Central Advisory Council, British Ministry of Education, 1947-59, and academic planning boards of University of Kent, University of Surrey, School Broadcasting Council, British Broadcasting Corp., and Education Council of Independent Television Authority. Lecturer on four U.S. tours.

MEMBER: British Academy (fellow), Royal Historical Society (fellow), Medieval Academy of America (corresponding fellow), Historical Association, Christian Frontier Council, University Teachers Group (chairman).

AWARDS, HONORS: D.Litt., Oxford University, 1972, and University of Bath, 1992; Medlicott Medal, 1993, "for services to history."

WRITINGS:

(With John Drewett) *What is Christian Education?,* Macmillan, 1942.

Growing up in a Modern Society, University of London Press, 1946, 4th edition, 1956.

(With Leone Tondelli and Beatrice Hirsch-Reich) *Il Libro delle Figure dell'abate Gioachino da Fiore,* Societa Editrice Internazionale, 1953.

(Editor) *Eighteen Plus: Unity and Diversity in Higher Education,* Faber, 1965.

The Influence of Prophecy in the Later Middle Ages: A Study in Joachimism, Clarendon Press, 1969.

(With Hirsch-Reich) *The Figurae of Joachim of Fiore,* Clarendon Press, 1972.

Joachim of Fiore and the Prophetic Future, S.P.C.K., 1976, Harper, 1978.

Sheepbell and Ploughshare, Moonraker Press, 1978.

Why History?, Longman, 1980.

(With Warwick Gould) *Joachim of Fiore and the Myth of the Eternal Evangel in the Nineteenth Century,* Oxford University Press, 1986.

The Crisis in Higher Education: Competence, Delight, and the Common Good, Open University Press, 1988.

(Editor, with Jean Morrison) *The Diaries of Jeffery Whitaker, 1739-1741,* Wiltshire Record Society, 1989.

(Editor) *Prophetic Rome in the High Renaissance Period,* Clarendon Press, 1992.

"THEN AND THERE" SERIES

Elizabethan Court, Longmans, Green, 1956.

The Mediaeval Town, Longmans, Green, 1958.

The Mediaeval Monastery, Longmans, Green, 1958.

The Mediaeval Village, Longmans, Green, 1959.

The Norman Conquest, Longmans, Green, 1959.

Alfred and the Danes, Longmans, Green, 1960.

(With Paule Hodgson) *Elizabethan Citizen,* Longmans, Green, 1961.

The Mediaeval Castle, Longmans, Green, 1963.

A Mediaeval King Governs, Longman, 1971.

Explorers in the Elizabethan Age, Longman, 1978.

Elizabethan Country House, Longman, 1983.

The Spanish Armada, Longman, 1987.

OTHER

Editor of "Then and There" series, Longmans, Green, beginning c. 1956. Contributor to books, including *Moral Education in a Changing Society,* edited by William Roy Niblett, Faber, 1963; and *Studies in Church History: Popular Belief and Practice,* edited by G. J. Cuming and Derek Baker, Cambridge University Press, 1971. Contributor of articles on historical topics to *Times Educational Supplement, New Era, Speculum, Medieval and Renaissance Studies, Traditio, Recherches de Theologie, Medievalia et Humanistica,* and other journals.

WORK IN PROGRESS: Vaticinia de Summis Pontificibus, an edition of a medieval text; and further work on family papers.

SIDELIGHTS: Marjorie E. Reeves once told *CA* that as a writer she wears "three hats: 1) as a professional historian, researching on Joachim of Fiore; 2) as an educationalist, writing on the philosophy of education and working, as editor and author, on a well-known series of history books for schools (which has been redesigned); 3) as a local historian on family history in the Wiltshire village to which I belong."

Reeves is competent in Latin, French, and Italian; she knows some German.

REGINALD
See BURGESS, Michael (Roy)

* * *

REGINALD, R.
See BURGESS, Michael (Roy)

* * *

REGINALD, Robert
See BURGESS, Michael (Roy)

* * *

REMINGTON, Mark
See BINGLEY, David Ernest

* * *

RENTSCHLER, Eric 1949-

PERSONAL: Born April 8, 1949, in Portland, OR; son of Robert Earl (an engineer) and Bonnie Jean (an administrative assistant) Rentschler. *Education:* Attended University of Stuttgart, 1968-70, University of Bonn, 1972-74, and Charles University, summers, 1973-74; Oregon State University, B.A., 1970; University of Washington, Seattle, M.A., 1971, Ph.D., 1977.

ADDRESSES: Home—2014-E Los Trancos Dr., Irvine, CA 92715. *Office*—Program in Film Studies, University of California, Irvine, CA 92717.

CAREER: Ohio State University, Columbus, assistant professor of German, 1978-82; University of California, Irvine, associate professor, 1982-86, professor of German, 1986-91, professor of film studies and director of Program in Film Studies, 1991—.

MEMBER: Modern Language Association of America, American Association of Teachers of German, American Film Institute, Society for Cinema Studies, German Studies Association, University Film and Video Association.

AWARDS, HONORS: Fulbright fellow, 1972-74; grants from American Council of Learned Societies, 1978, and German Academic Exchange Service; Alexander von Humboldt fellow, 1983-84 and 1986-87; Guggenheim fellow, 1990-91.

WRITINGS:

(Editor) *West German Film in the 1970's,* Redgrave, 1980.
West German Film in the Course of Time, Redgrave, 1984.
(Editor) *German Film and Literature: Adaptations and Transformations,* Methuen, 1986.
(Editor) *Visions and Voices: Writings of New German Filmmakers,* Holmes & Meier, 1988.
(Co-editor) *Augenzeugen,* Verlag der Autoren, 1988.
(Editor) *The Films of G. W. Pabst,* Rutgers University Press, 1990.

Contributor to film and German studies journals.

WORK IN PROGRESS: The Ministry of Emotion; Films and Their Afterlife; German Film after Fassbinder and Beyond the Wall.

* * *

RICHARDS, David
See BICKERS, Richard (Leslie) Townshend

* * *

RICHARDS, Larry
See RICHARDS, Lawrence O.

* * *

RICHARDS, Lawrence O. 1931-
(Larry Richards)

PERSONAL: Born September 25, 1931, in Milan, MI; son of Vivian S. and Charlotte M. (Zeluff) Richards; children: Paul, Joy, Timothy. *Education:* University of Michigan, B.A., 1958; Dallas Theological Seminary, Th.M., 1962; Northwestern University, Ph.D., 1972. *Politics:* Independent. *Religion:* Protestant.

ADDRESSES: Home—13209 Sumpter Cr., Hudson, FL 33567.

CAREER: Scripture Press Publications, Wheaton, IL, editor, 1962-65; Wheaton College, Graduate School, Wheaton, IL, assistant professor of Christian education, 1965-72; writer, 1972—. *Military service:* U.S. Navy, 1951-55.

MEMBER: Phi Beta Kappa.

WRITINGS:

(Editor) *The Key to Sunday School Achievement,* Moody, 1965.
Creative Bible Teaching, Moody, 1970.
A New Face for the Church, Zondervan, 1970.
Teaching Youth Asks Books, Moody, 1971.
Creative Bible Study, Zondervan, 1971.

You, the Teacher, Moody, 1972.
Youth Ministry: Its Renewal in the Local Church, Zondervan, 1972.
(With Marvin Keene Mayers) *Reshaping Evangelical Higher Education,* Zondervan, 1972.
(With Elsiebeth McDaniel) *You and Children,* Moody, 1973.
You and Youth, Moody, 1973.
Sixty-nine Ways to Start a Study Group and Keep It Growing, Zondervan, 1973.
You, the Parent, Moody, 1974.
You and Adults, Moody, 1974.
(With McDaniel) *You and Preschoolers,* Moody, 1975.
You and Teaching: Leader's Guide, Moody, 1975.
Three Churches in Renewal, Zondervan, 1975.
A Theology of Christian Education, Zondervan, 1975.
Helping My Child Know Jesus, edited by Marian Bennett, Standard Publishing, 1975.
Helping My Child Love, edited by Bennett, Standard Publishing, 1975.
Helping My Child Memorize Scripture, edited by Bennett, Standard Publishing, 1975.
Helping My Child Obey, edited by Bennett, Standard Publishing, 1975.
Helping My Child Overcome Fears, edited by Bennett, Standard Publishing, 1975.
Helping My Child Pray, edited by Bennett, Standard Publishing, 1975.
Helping My Child Share, edited by Bennett, Standard Publishing, 1975.
Helping My Family Worship, edited by Bennett, Standard Publishing, 1975.
How Far I Can Go, Zondervan, 1980.
How I Can Be Real, Zondervan, 1980.
How I Can Experience God, Zondervan, 1980.
How I Can Fit In, Zondervan, 1980.
How I Can Make Decisions, Zondervan, 1980.
(With Clyde A. Hoeldtke) *A Theology of Church Leadership,* Zondervan, 1980.
Our Life Together: A Woman's Workshop on Fellowship, Zondervan, 1981.
The Word Bible Handbook, Word, Inc., 1982.
The Word Parents Handbook, Word, Inc., 1983.
The Believer's Guidebook from Aspirin to Zoos, Zondervan, 1983.
Believer's Promise Book: Seven Hundred Prayers and Promises from the NIV, Zondervan, 1984.
Expository Dictionary of Bible Words, Zondervan, 1985.
The Teacher's Commentary, Victor, 1987.
The Zondervan Dictionary of Christian Literacy, Zondervan, 1987.
A Practical Theology of Spirituality, Zondervan, 1988.
(General editor) *The Revell Bible Dictionary,* Revell, 1989.
The 365-Day Devotional Commentary, Victor, 1990.
The Bible Reader's Companion, Victor, 1991.
The Small Group Members Commentary, Victor, 1992.
The Bible Background Commentary, New Testament, Victor, 1993.

UNDER NAME LARRY RICHARDS

Are You for Real?, Moody, 1968.
How Far Can I Go?, Moody, 1969.
Is God Necessary?, Moody, 1969.
How Do I Fit In?, Moody, 1970.
What's in It for Me?, Moody, 1970.
Youth Asks: A Leader's Guide, Moody, 1971.
One Way, Victor Books, 1972.
Science and the Bible . . . Can We Believe Both?, Victor Books, 1973.
Becoming One in the Spirit, Victor Books, 1973.
You Can Be Transformed!, Victor Books, 1973.
Born to Grow: For New and Used Christians, Victor Books, 1974.
How to Understand the Old Testament without Being a Seminary Student, Victor Books, 1974.
What You Should Know about the Bible, Victor Books, 1974.
The Complete Christian: Insights for Life from the Book of Hebrews, Victor Books, 1975.
Christ's Mission on Earth, Victor Books, 1975.
Freedom Road, edited by Timothy E. Udd, David Cook, 1976.
Let Day Begin, David Cook, 1976.
The Servant King, David Cook, 1976.
Years of Darkness: Days of Glory, David Cook, 1977.
Edge of Judgment, David Cook, 1977.
The Great Adventure, David Cook, 1977.
Regions Beyond, David Cook, 1977.
Springtime Coming, David Cook, 1978.
Pass It On, David Cook, 1978.
(With Gib Martin) *Theology of Personal Ministry,* Zondervan, 1981.
Basic Christian Values, Zondervan, 1981.
First Steps for New and Used Christians, Zondervan, 1981.
Fruit of the Spirit, Zondervan, 1981.
The Good Life, Zondervan, 1981.
Teaching Youth, Beacon Hill, 1982.
(With Paul Johnson) *Death and Caring Community,* Multnomah, 1982.
When It Hurts Too Much to Wait: Understanding God's Timing, Word, Inc., 1985.
Love Your Neighbor: A Woman's Workshop on Fellowship, Zondervan, 1986.
Tomorrow Today, Victor Books, 1986.
Personal Ministry Handbook, Baker Book, 1986.
The Children's Bible Handbook, Sweet, 1986.
When People You Trust Let You Down, Word, Inc., 1988.
It Couldn't Just Happen, Sweet, 1989.

When Life Is Unfair, Word, Inc., 1990.
Remarriage, a Healing Gift from God, Word, Inc., 1991.
Talkable Bible Stories, Baker, 1992.
Promises for the Graduate, Zondervan, 1993.
Wisdom for the Graduate, Zondervan, 1993.

SIDELIGHTS: Lawrence O. Richards's books have been translated into twenty-two languages and his textbooks are used worldwide in teaching religion.

* * *

RINPOCHE
See CHOGYAM TRUNGPA

* * *

ROBARDS, Karen 1954-

PERSONAL: Born August 24, 1954, in Louisville, KY; daughter of Walter L. (an orthodontist) and Sally (Skaggs) Johnson; married Douglas J. Robards (a marketing executive), January 21, 1977; children: Peter Douglas. *Education:* University of Kentucky, B.A., 1976, graduate study, 1976-79.

ADDRESSES: Home—Columbus, OH. *Agent*—Shirley Burke, 370 East 76th St., Suite B-704, New York, NY 10021.

CAREER: Writer.

MEMBER: Authors League of America, Romance Writers of America, Mensa.

AWARDS, HONORS: Named best new contemporary writer of 1985, *Romantic Times,* and Silver Certificate Award, *Affaire de Coeur,* 1986, for *To Love a Man;* Reviewers Choice Award, *Romantic Times,* 1986, for *Wild Orchids;* Silver Pen Award, *Affaire de Coeur,* 1986; Gold Certificate Award, *Affaire de Coeur,* 1986, for *Dark Torment,* and 1987, for *Loving Julia.*

WRITINGS:

ROMANCE NOVELS

Island Flame, Leisure Books, 1981.
Sea Fire, Leisure Books, 1982.
Forbidden Love, Leisure Books, 1983.
Amanda Rose, Warner Books, 1984.
To Love a Man, Warner Books, 1985.
Dark Torment, Warner Books, 1985.
Wild Orchids, Warner Books, 1986.
Loving Julia, Warner Books, 1986.
Some Kind of Hero, Warner Books, 1987.
Night Magic, Warner Books, 1988.
Dark of the Moon, Avon, 1988.
Desire in the Sun, Avon, 1988.
Tiger's Eye, Avon, 1989.
Morning Song, Avon, 1990.
Green Eyes, Avon, 1991.
This Side of Heaven, Dell, 1991.
Nobody's Angel, Delacorte, 1992.
One Summer, Delacorte, 1993.

Also author of *Once a Lady,* Avon.

SIDELIGHTS: Karen Robards once told *CA:* "I have always been a writer. My first 'book,' written and illustrated at age five, was a present to my grandmother. During elementary school, I was editor and chief reporter for our school paper. I worked on newspapers and yearbooks throughout high school and college. My first 'big' sale, at age eighteen, was to *Reader's Digest* for 'Life in These United States,' and it showed me that what I did as automatically as breathing might also be a way to earn a living. But I don't write for money. (Eating is a fringe benefit, not the primary purpose of what I do.) I write because, through some strange quirk of nature, I cannot help myself."

BIOGRAPHICAL/CRITICAL SOURCES:

PERIODICALS

Inside Books, November, 1988, p. 51; May, 1989, p. 67.*

* * *

ROBERTS, John
See BINGLEY, David Ernest

* * *

ROBINET, Harriette Gillem 1931-

PERSONAL: Surname is pronounced "ro-bi-*nay*"; born July 14, 1931, in Washington, DC; daughter of Richard Avitus (a teacher) and Martha (a teacher; maiden name, Gray) Gillem; married McLouis Joseph Robinet (a health physicist), August 6, 1960; children: Stephen, Philip, Rita, Jonathan, Marsha, Linda. *Education:* College of New Rochelle, B.S., 1953; Catholic University of America, M.S., 1957, Ph.D., 1963. *Politics:* Democrat. *Religion:* Roman Catholic.

Avocational Interests: Pets, bird watching, growing plants (especially orchids), knitting, crocheting, sketching.

ADDRESSES: Home and office—214 South Elmwood, Oak Park, IL 60302.

CAREER: Children's Hospital, Washington, DC, bacteriologist, 1953-1954; Walter Reed Army Medical Center,

Washington, DC, medical bacteriologist, 1954-1957, research bacteriologist, 1958-1960; Xavier University, New Orleans, LA, instructor in biology, 1957-58. *Military service*—U.S. Army, Quartermaster Corps, civilian food bacteriologist, 1960-1961.

MEMBER: American Orchid Society.

WRITINGS:

Jay and the Marigold (juvenile), illustrated by Trudy Scott, Children's Press, 1976.
Ride the Red Cycle (juvenile), illustrated by David Brown, Houghton, 1980.
Children of the Fire (juvenile), Maxwell Macmillan International, 1991.

Contributor to magazines.

SIDELIGHTS: Influenced by observations of her disabled son as well as by her black slavery roots, Harriette Robinet provides insight in her juvenile works into children's struggles and victories over physical and emotional obstacles. As a *Kirkus Reviews* commentator asserts, Robinet depicts "the sheer concentration conveyed, and the self faith" of her young protagonists.

Robinet's first book, 1976's *Jay and the Marigold,* portrays an eight-year-old boy who, like Robinet's own son, is handicapped by cerebral palsy. His inability to communicate clearly or control his physical movements make him an outsider, until he is befriended by a new student. According to Karen Harris in *School Library Journal,* "the story likens Jay to a marigold which manages to bloom under the most unfavorable conditions."

The author's associations with handicapped children are drawn upon in *Ride the Red Cycle,* her 1980 work. An illness which resulted in brain damage has confined Jerome Johnson, an eleven-year-old boy, to a wheelchair. Jerome's dream is to ride a tricycle, even though he cannot walk, and after a summer of trying, he finally succeeds on Labor Day. "Simply written," declares a *Horn Book* reviewer, the "story conveys not only Jerome's physical struggle but his emotional one to achieve individuality and self-respect."

Robinet's 1991 *Children of the Fire* describes the changing reactions of a young orphan to the Chicago fire of 1871. The protagonist, Hallelujah, is a black orphan whose mother was a runaway slave. At first, Hallelujah is enthusiastic about the fire, thinking it a spectacle. Her perspective changes drastically, however, after she sees the once-stately courthouse destroyed and after she assists a young, lost white child. "No reader will doubt," proclaims Joanne Schott in *Quill and Quire,* "that Hallelujah's experiences in the Chicago fire are great enough to work changes in her."

A contributor to *Bulletin of the Center for Children's Books* believes that Robinet "has clearly done a great deal of research, and many of the historical details are of interest" in *Children of the Fire.* The comment affirms the author's ability to provide a moving story based on both historical fact and personal experience. Robinet's books reflect the many handicapped children and adults who, as cited in *Something about the Author,* "have shared some of their anger, dreams, and victories" with her.

BIOGRAPHICAL/CRITICAL SOURCES:

BOOKS

Something about the Author, Gale, Volume 27, 1982, p. 173.

PERIODICALS

Bulletin of the Center for Children's Books, September, 1991, p. 20.
Horn Book Magazine, June, 1980, p. 303.
Kirkus Reviews, July 15, 1980, pp. 911-12.
Quill and Quire, January, 1992, p. 34.
School Library Journal, January, 1977, p. 84.*

* * *

ROBINS, Patricia
See LORRIMER, Claire

* * *

RODWIN, Lloyd 1919-

PERSONAL: Born September 14, 1919, in New York, NY; son of Abraham and Nettie (Small) Rodwin; married Nadine Posniak, December 26, 1943; children: Victor George, Marc Andre, Julie Ann. *Education:* City College (now City College of the City University of New York), B.S.S., 1939; New School for Social Research, certificate in housing, 1940; University of Wisconsin, M.A., 1945; Harvard University, M.P.A., 1946, Ph.D., 1949.

ADDRESSES: Home—15 Arlington Street, Cambridge, MA 02140. *Office*—Department of Urban Studies and Planning, Massachusetts Institute of Technology, Massachusetts Ave., Cambridge, MA 02139.

CAREER: Massachusetts Institute of Technology (MIT), Cambridge, research associate, 1946-58, professor of land economics, 1959-74, Ford International Professor, 1974—, chairman of department of urban studies and planning, 1970-74, director of special programs for urban and regional studies of developing areas (SPURS), 1967—. Visiting lecturer, professor, or fellow at colleges, universities, and institutes in the U.S., Canada, Great Britain, Europe, the Middle East, and South America, including New School for Social Research, 1951, University of Liverpool, 1951-52, University of California, summers, 1952 and 1969, Yale University, 1971, Battelle Seattle Research Center, summer, 1974, Churchill College, Cambridge, 1974—, and Sir Leslie Martin Center of Land Use and Built Form, Cambridge, 1974. Co-founder and chairman of faculty committee, Joint Center of Urban Studies, MIT—Harvard University, 1959-69; member of review committee of metrocenter, Nation Institute of Mental Health, 1976—. Consultant to numerous private and government organizations worldwide.

MEMBER: International Federation for Housing and Town Planning, American Institute of Planners, Regional Science Association (president-elect, 1985-86), American Economic Association.

AWARDS, HONORS: Littauer fellow, 1945-46; Guggenheim fellow, 1965-66.

WRITINGS:

The British New Towns Policy, Harvard University Press, 1956.
Housing and Economic Progress, Harvard University Press/MIT Press, 1961.
Nations and Cities: A Comparison of Strategies for Urban Growth, Houghton, 1970.
Cities and City Planning, Plenum, 1981.

EDITOR

The Future Metropolis, Braziller, 1961.
Planning Urban Growth and Regional Development, MIT Press, 1968,
(With Robert M. Hollister) *Cities of the Mind,* Plenum, 1984.
Shelter, Settlement and Development, United Nations, 1986.
(With Hidehiko Sazanami) *Deindustrialization and Regional Economic Transformation,* Unwin Hyman, 1989.
(With Sazanami) *Industrial Change and Regional Economic Transformation,* HarperCollins, 1991.

Editor of "Community and Regional Development" series, Plenum, 1980—. Associate editor, *Daedalus,* 1961-66; member of board of advisors, *New Atlantis,* 1969-72; member of editorial board, *International Regional Science Review,* 1979—.

SIDELIGHTS: Lloyd Rodwin once told *CA:* "Writing helps me dig deeper into what I do professionally. I teach, consult, and, on occasion, manage enterprises; and I often, not always, write about these experiences. There are at least two interrelated themes in most of what I have written. One involves the different ways of thinking about new and existing problems of the city and regional transformation; the other concerns unsuspected things that people working with cities, regions and development have to know or do to cope more effectively."

*   *   *

ROGOFF, Barbara 1950-

PERSONAL: Born January 5, 1950, in Brookings, SD; daughter of William M. (an entomologist) and Esther J. (an artist; maiden name, Petersen) Rogoff; married Salem Magarian (a pediatrician), October 12, 1975; children: Luisa, Valerie, David. *Education:* Pomona College, B.A. (cum laude), 1971; attended University of Geneva, 1971-72; Harvard University, Ph.D., 1977.

ADDRESSES: Office—Department of Psychology, Kerr Hall, University of California, Santa Cruz, CA 95064.

CAREER: Institute of Nutrition of Central America and Panama, Guatemala City, Guatemala, field psychologist and ethnographer, 1974-75; University of Utah, Salt Lake City, assistant professor, 1977-82, associate professor, 1982-85, professor of psychology, 1985-92, coordinator of Cross-Cultural Psychology Program.

MEMBER: International Association for Cross-Cultural Psychology, International Society for the Study of Behavioral Development, American Psychological Association, American Psychological Society, American Anthropological Association, American Educational Research Association, Society for Research in Child Development, Society for Cross-Cultural Research, Society for Psychological Anthropology.

AWARDS, HONORS: Fellow of Foundation for Child Development, 1978, Kellogg Foundation, 1983-86, Center for Advanced Study in the Behavioral Sciences (Stanford), 1988-89, and Spencer Foundation, 1988-89. Grants from National Institutes of Health, 1979, Society for Research in Child Development, 1980, National Institute of Education, 1980-82, National Institute of Child Health and Human Development, 1983—, and National Institute of Mental Health, 1986-87.

WRITINGS:

(Editor with Jean Lave, and contributor) *Everyday Cognition: Its Development in Social Context,* Harvard University Press, 1984.
(Editor with J.V. Wertsch, and contributor) *Children's Learning in the "Zone of Proximal Development,"* Jossey-Bass, 1984.
(Editor with M. E. Lamb and A. L. Brown) *Advances in Developmental Psychology,* Volume III, Lawrence Erlbaum, 1984.

Apprenticeship in Thinking: Cognitive Development in Social Context, Oxford University Press, 1990.

(With J. Mistry, A. Goencue, and C. Mosier), *Guided Participation in Cultural Activity by Toddlers and Caregivers* (monograph), Society for Research in Child Development, 1993.

ILLUSTRATOR

S. Cole, *The Hen That Crowed,* Lothrop, 1983.

OTHER

Contributor of about 100 articles and reviews to psychology journals and chapters to edited volumes; editor of newsletter of the Society for Research in Child Development, 1985-91; member of editorial advisory boards of *Journal of Cross-Cultural Psychology, Child Development, Developmental Psychology, Social Development,* and *Cognitive Development.*

* * *

ROMNEY, Steve
See BINGLEY, David Ernest

* * *

ROSE, Gerald (Hembdon Seymour) 1935-

PERSONAL: Born July 27, 1935, in British Crown Colony of Hong Kong; son of Henley Hembdon and Rachel Grace (Law) Rose; married Elizabeth Jane Pretty (an author of children's books), July 27, 1955; children: Martin, Richard, Louise. *Education:* Attended Lowestoft School of Art; Royal Academy, national diploma in design (with honors), 1955.

Avocational Interests: Trips to the seaside, fishing, swimming, and lazing in the garden.

CAREER: Author and illustrator of children's books. Teacher of drawing and painting at Blackpool College of Art, Blackpool, England, 1960-64; teacher of graphic art, Maidstone College of Art, Maidstone, England, beginning 1965.

AWARDS, HONORS: New York Herald Tribune's Children's Spring Book Festival Honor Book, 1959, for *How Saint Francis Tamed the Wolf;* Kate Greenaway Medal commendation, British Library Association, 1959, for *Wuffles Goes to Town,* 1960, for *Old Winkle and the Seagulls;* Premio Critici in Erba (Bologna), 1979, for *"Ahhh!" Said Stork.*

WRITINGS:

SELF-ILLUSTRATED JUVENILES

Ironhead, Merrimack Book Service, 1973.

Trouble in the Ark, Puffin Books, 1975, Penguin, 1976, new edition with new illustrations, Bodley Head, 1985, Morehouse, 1989.

"Ahhh!" Said Stork, Merrimack Book Service, 1977.

Watch Out!, Penguin, 1978.

The Tiger-Skin Rug, Prentice-Hall, 1979.

Rabbit Pie, Merrimack Book Service, 1980.

PB Takes a Holiday, Merrimack Book Service, 1980.

How George Lost His Voice, Bodley Head, 1981, Merrimack Book Service, 1983.

PB on Ice, Bodley Head, 1982, Merrimack Book Service, 1983.

The Bag of Wind, Bodley Head, 1983, Merrimack Book Service, 1984.

Scruff, Bodley Head, 1984, Merrimack Book Service, 1985.

(Adapter) *The Hare and the Tortoise,* Aladdin, 1988.

(Adapter) *The Raven and the Fox,* Aladdin, 1988.

(Adapter) *The Lion and the Mouse,* Aladdin, 1988.

The Fisherman and the Cormorants, Bodley Head, 1987.

The Bird Garden, Magnet Books, 1988.

Can Hippo Jump?, Macmillan, 1991.

WITH WIFE, ELIZABETH ROSE; SELF-ILLUSTRATED JUVENILES

Old Winkle and the Seagulls, A. S. Barnes, 1960.

Punch and Judy Carry On, Faber, 1962.

Saint George and the Fiery Dragon, Faber, 1963, Norton, 1964.

Alexander's Flycycle, Faber, 1967, Walker & Co., 1969.

The Great Oak, Merrimack Book Service, 1970.

Androcles and the Lion, Merrimack Book Service, 1971.

Albert and the Green Bottle, Merrimack Book Service, 1972.

Wolf! Wolf!, Merrimack Book Service, 1974.

Lucky Hans, Merrimack Book Service, 1976.

OTHER

Illustrator of over forty-five books, including Barbara Ireson, *Seven Thieves and Seven Stars,* Faber, 1960, A. S. Barnes, 1961; Irmengarde Eberle, *Pete and the Mouse,* Abelard, 1964; Jeremy Kingston, *The Dustbin Who Wanted to Be a General,* Merrimack Book Service, 1970; Janet McNeill, *Look Who's Here,* Macmillan, 1976; N. Hunter, *Professor Branestawm's Building Bust-Up,* Merrimack Book Service, 1982; and *Laugh out Loud: More Funny Stories for Children,* edited by Corrin and Corrin, Faber, 1991. Also illustrator of more than ten books by wife, Elizabeth Rose, including *How Saint Francis Tamed the Wolf,* Faber, 1958, Harcourt, 1959, new edition, Merrimack Book Service, 1983; *Wuffles Goes to Town,* Faber, 1959,

A. S. Barnes, 1960; *Good King Wenceslas,* Faber, 1964, Transatlantic, 1966; and *Mick Keeps a Secret,* Benn, 1974. Also illustrator of books in the "Breakthrough Books" series of learning-to-read volumes and in the Language Project "Language in Action" series.

SIDELIGHTS: Gerald Rose is one of the most original illustrators working in children's book publishing today. He was awarded the British Library Association's Kate Greenaway Medal in 1960 for *Old Winkle and the Seagulls,* the story of a fisherman whose association with seabirds brings him success. "His work," states Frank Eyre in *British Children's Books in the Twentieth Century,* "is especially attractive to children because although it has nearly all the infectious gaiety of colour . . . it is also still recognisably representational," and it combines, writes Bettina Huerlimann in *Picture-Book World,* "a boldly original approach to form and colour" with "a rich sense of the comic and the grotesque particularly appealing to small children."

Rose was born in Hong Kong shortly before the Second World War began, of an English father and Chinese mother. He, his mother, and his sister were interned by the Japanese after they seized Hong Kong in 1941. He spent the next four years in Stanley Camp. In 1945, he traveled to England and settled in Lowestoft, where he later attended the School of Art and trained as a professional painter and artist. "It was there that I met him," writes Elizabeth Rose in the *Third Book of Junior Authors,* "as I was a student there, too." They were married several years later, in London.

"I started illustrating children's books when I met my wife," Gerald Rose writes in *Illustrators of Children's Books: 1957-1966,* "who was then teaching in a primary school. At that time she was frustrated by the lack of reasonable picture books so we were stimulated into producing something ourselves. *How St. Francis Tamed the Wolf* was the first." *How Saint Francis Tamed the Wolf* was followed by many other successful collaborations, ranging from *Wuffles Goes to Town,* a Greenaway Medal nominee, and *Old Winkle and the Seagulls* to *Saint George and the Fiery Dragon, Good King Wenceslas,* and *Lucky Hans,* an adaptation of a Grimm fairy tale about stupid peasants.

Rose later began writing and illustrating his own books, often basing his stories on folk tales or using characters from the Bible or classic fables. *Trouble in the Ark,* for instance, tells how a fly buzzing at a mouse begins a ruckus that ends only when Noah sights land. *The Hare and the Tortoise, The Raven and the Fox,* and *The Lion and the Mouse* are all based on the fables of Aesop, while *The Fisherman and the Cormorants* explains how fishermen in China came to use cormorants to help them fish. *The Bird Garden* explains how the myna bird got all the other exotic birds kicked out of the Sultan's magnificent garden by teaching them to insult their royal host. And *Can Hippo Jump?* tells how all the animals of the jungle tease Hippo because he cannot jump like them—and of the catastrophe that happens when Hippo tries to do so.

Rose's success, suggests Eyre, lies in the fact that he, along with many other successful artists, concentrates on artwork that appeals to the children themselves. "The first task," he writes, "is to *illustrate,* to bring the characters and incidents in the book a little more alive, to illumine and enlarge the text." And Rose himself adds, "Given a fine-art training, illustration is not a case of coming from the lofty heights of art with a capital 'A,' but rather a problem of adjusting oneself to a new set of values and some tricky customers."

BIOGRAPHICAL/CRITICAL SOURCES:

BOOKS

Eyre, Frank, *British Children's Books in the Twentieth Century,* Longman, 1971, pp. 51-52, 57.

Huerlimann, Bettina, *Picture-Book World,* translated and edited by Brian W. Alderson, World Publishing, 1969, p. 29.

Kingman, Lee, and others, compilers, *Illustrators of Children's Books: 1957-1966,* Horn Book, 1968, p. 166.

Montreville, Doris D., and Donna Hill, editors, *Third Book of Junior Authors,* H. W. Wilson, 1972, pp. 242-43.

Peppin, Brigid, and Lucy Micklethwait, *Book Illustrators of the Twentieth Century,* Arco, 1984, p. 261.

Ward, Martha E., and Dorothy A. Marquardt, *Illustrators of Books for Young People,* Scarecrow, 1975.

PERIODICALS

Books for Keeps, January, 1987, p. 6; November, 1987, p. 4; July, 1988, p. 7.

British Book News Children's Supplement, December, 1987, p. 16.

Growing Point, July, 1988, p. 5017.

Junior Bookshelf, February, 1983; October, 1987, p. 219; June, 1990, p. 131.

Library Association Record, May, 1961.

* * *

ROSE, Reginald 1920-

PERSONAL: Born December 10, 1920, in New York, NY; son of William (a lawyer) and Alice (Obendorfer) Rose; married Barbara Langbart, September 5, 1943 (marriage ended); married Ellen McLaughlin, July 6, 1963; children: (first marriage) Jonathan, Richard, Andrew and Steven (twins); (second marriage) Thomas, Christopher. *Education:* Attended City College (now of the City University of New York), 1937-38.

ADDRESSES: *Home*—20 Wedgewood Rd., Westport, CT 06880. *Office*—Defender Productions, c/o Philip Plumer, 105-58 Flatlands 5th St., Brooklyn, NY 11236. *Agent*—Sy Fischer, 10590 Wilshire Blvd., Los Angeles, CA 90024.

CAREER: Worked as a clerk, publicity writer, and advertising copywriter in the late 1940s and early 1950s; writer of plays for stage and screen, 1951—. Producer with Henry Fonda of film *Twelve Angry Men,* 1957. President, Defender Productions, Inc., 1961—, and Reginald Rose Foundation, 1963—. *Military service:* U.S. Army, 1942-46; became first lieutenant.

AWARDS, HONORS: Emmy Award for best-written dramatic material, National Academy of Television Arts & Sciences, and Writer's Guild of America Award, both 1954, both for "Twelve Angry Men" (teleplay); Emmy Award nomination for best teleplay writing of one hour or more, 1956, for "Tragedy in a Temporary Town" (teleplay); Academy Award nominations for best picture (with Henry Fonda) and best screenplay based on material from another medium, and Edgar Allan Poe Award for best motion picture screenplay, Mystery Writers of America, all 1957, all for *Twelve Angry Men* (film); Golden Berlin Bear, Berlin Film Festival, 1957, for *Twelve Angry Men;* Laurel Award, Writer's Guild of America, 1958; Emmy Award nomination for outstanding writing achievement in a drama special, 1960, for "The Sacco-Vanzetti Story" (teleplay); Writer's Guild of America Award, and Emmy Award for outstanding writing achievement in a drama series, both 1962, both for *The Defenders* series; Emmy Award for outstanding writing achievement in a drama series (with Robert Thom), 1963, for "The Madman" episode of *The Defenders;* Emmy Award nomination for outstanding writing achievement in a drama special, 1968, for "Dear Friends" (teleplay); Laurel Award, Writer's Guild of America, and Emmy Award nomination for outstanding writing in a mini-series, both 1987, both for *Escape from Sobibor.*

WRITINGS:

Six Television Plays, Simon & Schuster, 1957.

(Contributor) R. G. Harrison and H. D. Gutteridge, editors, *Two Plays for Study,* McClelland & Stewart, 1967.

The Thomas Book, Harcourt, 1972.

FOR TELEVISION

"The Bus to Nowhere," *Out There,* Columbia Broadcasting System, Inc. (CBS), 1951.

"Dino," *Studio One,* CBS, 1954.

"The Death and Life of Larry Benson," *Studio One,* CBS, 1954.

"The Remarkable Incident at Carson Corners," *Studio One,* CBS, 1954.

"Thunder on Sycamore Street," *Studio One,* CBS, 1954.

"Twelve Angry Men" (also see below), *Studio One,* CBS, 1954.

"Crime in the Streets," *Elgin Hour,* American Broadcasting Co., Inc. (ABC), 1955.

"The Expendable House," *Philco Television Playhouse-Goodyear Playhouse,* National Broadcasting Company (NBC), 1955.

"The Incredible World of Horace Ford," *Studio One,* CBS, 1955.

"Tragedy in a Temporary Town," *Alcoa Hour-Goodyear Playhouse,* NBC, 1956.

"The Defender" (pilot for series *The Defenders;* also see below), *Studio One,* CBS, 1957.

"The Cruel Day," *Playhouse 90,* CBS, 1959.

"A Marriage of Strangers," *Playhouse 90,* CBS, 1959.

"A Quiet Game of Cards," *Playhouse 90,* CBS, 1959.

"The Sacco-Vanzetti Story" (also see below), *Sunday Showcase,* NBC, 1960.

(With others, and creator) *The Defenders* (series), CBS, 1961-65.

"Dear Friends" (also see below), *CBS Playhouse,* CBS, 1967.

(And creator) *The Zoo Gang* (series), NBC, 1975.

The Four of Us (pilot), ABC, 1977.

Studs Lonigan (mini-series), NBC, 1979.

The Rules of Marriage (movie), CBS, 1982.

(With Rita Mae Brown) *My Two Loves* (movie), ABC, 1986.

Escape from Sobibor (mini-series), CBS, 1987.

PLAYS

Black Monday, first produced off-Broadway at Vandam Theater, New York City, 1962.

Twelve Angry Men, first produced at Queen's Playhouse, London, England, 1964.

The Porcelain Year, produced at Locust Street Theatre, Philadelphia, PA, then Shubert Theatre, New Haven CT, both 1965.

Dear Friends (first produced in Edinburgh, Scotland, 1968; produced at Lakewood Little Theatre, Cleveland, OH, 1969), Dramatists Play Service, 1990.

This Agony, This Triumph (based on "The Sacco-Vanzetti Story"), first produced in California, 1972.

SCREENPLAYS

Crime in the Streets, Allied Artists, 1956.

Dino, Allied Artists, 1957.

(Also producer with Henry Fonda) *Twelve Angry Men,* United Artists (UA), 1957, published as *Twelve Angry*

Men: A Screen Adaptation, Directed by Sidney Lumet, Irvington, 1989.

Man of the West (based on the novel *The Border Jumpers* by Will C. Brown), UA, 1958.

The Man in the Net (based on the novel *Man in the Net* by Patrick Quentin), UA, 1958.

Baxter! (based on the novel *The Boy Who Could Make Himself Disappear* by Kin Platt), National General, 1972.

Somebody Killed Her Husband, Columbia, 1978.

The Wild Geese (based on the novel of the same title by Daniel Carney), Allied Artists, 1978.

The Sea Wolves (based on the novel *The Boarding Party* by James Leasor), Paramount, 1981.

(With Brian Clark) *Whose Life Is It Anyway?* Metro-Goldwyn-Mayer (MGM)/UA, 1981.

The Final Option (based on the novel *The Tiptoe Boys* by George Markstein; also known as *Who Dares Wins*), MGM/UA, 1983.

Wild Geese II (based on the novel *The Square Circle* by Carney), Universal, 1985.

Also author of television play *Black Monday.*

WORK IN PROGRESS: Undelivered Mail, a memoir.

SIDELIGHTS: Reginald Rose has had a lengthy career as a playwright, television writer, and screenwriter. In the *Dictionary of Literary Biography,* Carola Kaplan writes, "Rose's main subjects are crime; juvenile delinquency; the problems of children and adolescents; and contemporary social issues, including bigotry, poverty, and urban blight. He has treated these problems in a variety of forms—Westerns, war movies, urban and courtroom dramas—but however exotic or prosaic the setting and whatever the form, at its best Rose's work is powerful, committed, intense; at worst it is didactic or descends from drama into sociology."

Twelve Angry Men, Rose's most acclaimed and best-known work, deals with themes of social injustice, Kaplan says, and gives a "thoughtful examination of the jury system," according to *Commonweal* reviewer Philip T. Hartung. Starring Hollywood heavyweight Henry Fonda, who was also the co-producer with Rose, the story focuses on a jury deciding the fate of a young man charged with killing his father. Charlotte Bilkey Speicher in the *Library Journal* praises the film's "brilliant script" and the *Saturday Review*'s Hollis Alpert calls the film "a tight, absorbing drama."

Rose is also renowned for his Emmy-winning television series about a father-and-son lawyer team, *The Defenders,* which attracted controversy because it featured sensitive issues such as euthanasia, blacklisting, and abortion. Rose has continued to receive recognition for his television writings, including an Emmy nomination for the 1987 miniseries *Escape from Sobibor.* In addition to his extensive resume of teleplays, Rose has proceeded with his screenwriting career as well. In a review of his 1978 film *Wild Geese,* Janet Maslin of the *New York Times* called Rose "an old-fashioned scenarist mindful of such old-fashioned niceties as pacing, clarity and economy," and stated that his 1981 drama written with Brian Clark, *Whose Life Is It Anyway?,* was a "thoughtful, warm, touching film."

Kaplan notes, "As Rose himself describes it, 'In all my work, . . . my main purpose has always been to project my own view of good and evil—and this is the essence of controversy.' "

BIOGRAPHICAL/CRITICAL SOURCES:

BOOKS

Dictionary of Literary Biography, Volume 26: *American Screenwriters,* Gale, 1984.

PERIODICALS

AB Bookman's Weekly, October 17, 1977.
America, April 27, 1957, p. 150.
Chicago Tribune, November 14, 1978.
Christian Science Monitor, December 4, 1967.
Library Journal, April 15, 1957, p. 1047.
Los Angeles Times, September 19, 1983.
Nation, April 27, 1957, p. 379.
Newsweek, April 15, 1957, p. 113.
New York, April 13, 1987, p. 92.
New Yorker, April 27, 1957, pp. 66, 68.
New York Herald Tribune, June 1, 1960.
New York Times, July 16, 1975; August 6, 1977; November 11, 1978; December 2, 1981; May 10, 1982; September 23, 1983.
New York Times Magazine, March 31, 1957, pp. 64-65.
Saturday Review, April 20, 1957, pp. 29, 30.
Time, April 29, 1957, p. 94.
Washington Post, November 14, 1978, p. B11.
Variety, January 19, 1972; April 23, 1986, p. 86.

* * *

ROSENTHAL, Robert 1933-

PERSONAL: Born March 2, 1933, in Giessen, Germany; came to United States in 1940, naturalized citizen in 1946; son of Julius (a merchant) and Hermine (Kahn) Rosenthal; married Mary Lu Clayton, April 20, 1951; children: Roberta, David C., Virginia. *Education:* University of California, Los Angeles, A.B., 1953, Ph.D., 1956; postdoctoral clinical training in psychology at Wadsworth Veterans Administration Hospital, 1956-57, and Los Angeles Veterans Administration Mental Hygiene Clinic,

1957; diplomate, American Board of Examiners in Professional Psychology. *Politics:* Liberal. *Religion:* Jewish.

ADDRESSES: Home—12 Phinney Rd., Lexington, MA 02173. *Office*—Harvard University, 33 Kirkland St., Cambridge, MA 02138.

CAREER: University of California, Los Angeles, Los Angeles, CA, instructor, 1957; University of North Dakota, Grand Forks, ND, assistant professor, 1957-58, associate professor, 1958-62, coordinator of clinical training, 1958-62; Harvard University, Cambridge, MA, lecturer, 1962-67, professor of social psychology, 1967—, department chair, 1992—. Certified clinical psychologist in North Dakota. Lecturer at University of Southern California, 1956-57, and Boston University, 1965-66; visiting associate professor, Ohio State University, 1960-61.

MEMBER: American Psychological Society (fellow), American Association for the Advancement of Science (fellow), Society for Projective Techniques (past treasurer), Society of Experimental Social Psychology, Society for Social Studies of Science, Eastern Psychological Association, Midwestern Psychological Association, North Dakota Psychological Association (past president), Massachusetts Psychological Association (fellow), Phi Beta Kappa, Sigma Xi.

AWARDS, HONORS: American Association for the Advancement of Science socio-psychological prize, 1960; Cattell Fund Award, American Psychological Association, 1967; senior Fulbright scholar, Australian-American Educational Foundation, 1972; Guggenheim fellow, 1973-74; Distinguished Career Contribution Award, Massachusetts Psychological Association, 1979; Wiener Award, University of Manitoba, 1979; Distinguished Lecture award, American Psychological Association, 1982; Landsdowne Visitor, University of Victoria, 1982; fellow, Center for Advanced Study in the Behavioral Sciences, 1988-89; Donald Campbell award, Society for Personality and Social Psychology, 1988; distinguished lecturer, Eastern Psychological Association, 1989.

WRITINGS:

(Author of introduction) Oskar Pfungst, *Clever Hans,* Holt, 1965.

Experimenter Effects in Behavioral Research, Appleton-Century-Crofts, 1966, enlarged edition, Halsted, 1976.

(With Lenore Jacobson) *Pygmalion in the Classroom: Teacher Expectation and Pupils' Intellectual Development,* Holt, 1968, expanded edition, Irvington, 1992.

(Editor with Ralph L. Rosnow, and contributor) *Artifact in Behavioral Research,* Academic Press, 1969.

(With Rosnow, J. A. Cheyne, K. H. Craik, Benjamin Kleinmuntz, and R. H. Walters) *New Directions in Psychology,* Holt, 1970.

(With Rosnow) *The Volunteer Subject,* Wiley, 1975.

(With Rosnow) *A Primer of Methods for the Behavioral Sciences,* Wiley, 1975.

(With J. A. Hall, M. R. DiMatteo, P. L. Rogers, and D. Archer) *Sensitivity to Nonverbal Communication: The PONS Test,* Johns Hopkins University Press, 1979.

(With Hall, Archer, DiMatteo, and Rogers) *Profile of Nonverbal Sensitivity (PONS): The Test Manual,* Irvington, 1979.

(Editor, and contributor with B. M. DePaulo) *Skill in Nonverbal Communication,* Oelgeschlager, 1979.

(Editor, and contributor with D. B. Rubin) *New Directions for Methodology of Social and Behavioral Science: Quantitative Assessment of Research Domains,* Jossey-Bass, 1980.

(Editor with T. A. Sebeok, and contributor) *The Clever Hans Phenomenon: Communication with Horses, Whales, Apes, and People,* Annals of the New York Academy of Sciences, 1981.

(With Rosnow) *Essentials of Behavioral Research: Methods and Data Analysis,* McGraw-Hill, 1984.

(With Rosnow) *Understanding Behavioral Science,* McGraw, 1984.

Meta-analytic Procedures for Social Research, Sage Publications, 1984, revised, 1991.

(With Rosnow) *Contrast Analysis: Focused Comparisons in the Analysis of Variance,* Cambridge University Press, 1985.

(With B. Mullen) *BASIC Meta-analysis Programs for Micro-computers,* Lawrence Erlbaum, 1985.

(Editor with P. D. Blanck and R. W. Buck) *Nonverbal Communication in Clinical Context: Brain, Behavior, and Treatment,* Pennsylvania State University Press, 1986.

Judgement Studies: Design, Analysis, and Meta-analysis, Cambridge University Press, 1987.

(With V. Gheoghiu, P. Netter, and H. J. Eysenck, editors) *Suggestibility: Theory and Research,* Springer, 1989.

(With Ralph L. Rosnow) *Essentials of Behavioral Research: Methods and Data Analysis,* McGraw-Hill, 1991.

(With Ralph L. Rosnow) *Beginning Behavioral Research: A Conceptual Primer,* Macmillan, 1993.

Contributor to psychological works including *Research in Organizations: Issues and Controversies,* edited by R. T. Mowday and R. M. Steers, Goodyear, 1979; *Nonverbal Communication,* edited by S. Weitz, revised edition, 1979; *Communication and Parapsychology,* edited by B. Shapin and L. Coly, Parapsychology Foundation, 1980; *Handbook of Methods in Nonverbal Behavior Research,* edited by K. R. Scherer and P. Ekman, Cambridge University Press, 1982; *Measuring Emotions in Infants and Children,* with B. M. DePaulo, Cambridge University Press, 1982;

Development of Nonverbal Behavior in Children, edited by R. S. Feldman, Springer-Verlag, 1982; *Bias in Psychotherapy,* edited by J. Murray and P. R. Abramson, Praeger, 1983; *Placebo: Clinical Phenomena and New Insights,* edited by L. White, B. Tursky, and G. Schwartz Guilford. Author of more than 300 studies and reports for scholarly journals. Advisory editor for academic journals including *Journal of Consulting and Clinical Psychology, Journal of Experimental Social Psychology, Journal of Educational Psychology, Current Psychological Reviews, Journal of Nonverbal Behavior,* and *Journal of Personality.*

* * *

ROTH, Geneen 1951-

PERSONAL: Given name is pronounced like "Janine"; born August 30, 1951, in New York, NY; daughter of Bernard S. (a lawyer) and Ruth (Penn) Roth. *Education:* Tulane University, B.A. (magna cum laude), 1973.

ADDRESSES: Home and office—Breaking Free, P.O. Box 2852, Santa Cruz, CA 95062.

CAREER: Suicide Prevention and Crisis Center, Buffalo, NY, outreach counselor, 1974-75; Breaking Free, Santa Cruz, CA, founder and leader of eating disorder workshops, 1979—. Also worked as astrologer. Active in nuclear freeze movement.

MEMBER: Phi Beta Kappa.

WRITINGS:

(Editor and contributor) *Feeding the Hungry Heart: The Experience of Compulsive Eating,* Bobbs-Merrill, 1982.

Breaking Free from Compulsive Eating, Bobbs-Merrill, 1984.

Why Wait?: A Guide to Ending Compulsive Eating, New American Library, 1989.

When Food Is Love: Exploring the Relationship between Eating and Intimacy, Dutton, 1991.

Also contributor to *Ariadne's Thread,* edited by Margaret B. Parkinson and Barbara Lagowski, Harper, 1982.

WORK IN PROGRESS: A collection of short stories.

SIDELIGHTS: Author Geneen Roth writes about the unhealthy relationships some people form between food and behavior, basing her work on the seminars she holds and her own childhood. Raised by an abusive mother, Roth turned to the comfort of food instead of human contact, eventually becoming an anorexic. Through her work, she tries to help others overcome their psychological and emotional dependence on food. In *Breaking Free from Compulsive Eating* Roth presents a handbook for overcoming the eating disorder, relating her personal experiences and describing exercises that have helped her. A reviewer in *Publishers Weekly* labels the book "a wise, practical guide" providing support and encouragement to those who seek it. And "her advice is practical and realistic," judges Anne H. Ross in the *Library Journal.* A reviewer in *Kirkus Review* notes that Roth's chief strength in *Breaking Free from Compulsive Eating* is "reassurance," and concludes: "Turn to others for specifics, look to Roth for peer support."

Roth continues to examine eating disorders in *When Food Is Love: Exploring the Relationship between Eating and Intimacy.* In this book Roth looks at food as a substitute for a loving relationship, delving into issues such as overcoming "comfortable" suffering and learning how not to play the victim. Roth emphasizes that being thin does not equate with happiness, making it clear that "losing weight doesn't automatically gain one success, respect and love," notes a reviewer in *Publishers Weekly.* Barbara Jacobs, writing in *Booklist,* concludes that "by caring, and with warmth, Roth conveys sympathy, reassurance, and hope" in *When Food Is Love.*

Roth once commented: "I had always thought writers sat down at their desks and wrote for eight hours a day. It has been difficult for me to call myself a writer because I don't do that, except for the long stretches of weeks or months that I spend on a particular project.

"I see the world in words. Sentences take root in my chest, they bloom, and I write about their colors. Writing a book in this way is not very practical. I'm good at the blooming part, not so good at the discipline, but I love creating with words, so I do it.

"Recently I have been traveling around the country—to Alaska, Los Angeles, New Orleans, and New York—lecturing and giving workshops on compulsive eating. It's as if I have two distinct parts of me that must be allowed expression. There is the solitary being who writes and the other one, connected intensely to human beings and their pain, who gets fed by watching the light explode in someone's eyes. Both of them are very different and equally important to me. Integrating them into one's life requires patience and self-confidence, both of which I am slow to learn."

BIOGRAPHICAL/CRITICAL SOURCES:

PERIODICALS

Booklist, February 15, 1991, p. 1169.

Kirkus Review, December 1, 1984, p. 1144.

Library Journal, February 15, 1985, p. 172.

New Age, May, 1983.

Publishers Weekly, December 21, 1984, p. 76; January 25, 1991, p. 44.*

ROWAT, Donald C(ameron) 1921-

PERSONAL: Born January 21, 1921, in Somerset, Manitoba, Canada; son of William Andrew and Bertha Elizabeth (Moore) Rowat; married Frances Louise Coleman, 1948; children: Linda, Steven. *Education:* University of Toronto, B.A., 1943; Columbia University, M.A., 1946, Ph.D., 1950.

ADDRESSES: *Office*—Department of Political Science, Carleton University, Ottawa, Ontario, Canada K1S 5B6.

CAREER: Canadian Department of Finance, Ottawa, Ontario, research assistant, 1943-44; Canadian Department of National Health and Welfare, Ottawa, administrative officer, 1944-45; North Texas State College (now North Texas State University), Denton, lecturer in political science, 1947; Dalhousie University, Halifax, Nova Scotia, director of research, Institute of Public Affairs, and lecturer in political science, 1947-49; University of British Columbia, Vancouver, lecturer in political science, 1949-50; Carleton University, Ottawa, Ontario, assistant professor, 1950-53, associate professor, 1953-58, professor of political science, 1958-92, adjunct research professor, 1992—, acting director of School of Public Administration, 1957-58, department chairman, 1962-65, supervisor of graduate studies in political science, 1965-66. Visiting professor, University of California, Berkeley, 1972; exchange fellow, University of Leningrad, 1974; Canada Council Leave fellow, 1974-75; North Atlantic Treaty Organization (NATO) fellow, 1977; Social Science Research Council of Canada fellow and lecturer, 1981-82. Researcher and lecturer in Australia and New Zealand, 1990. Expert in public administration in Ethiopia, Technical Assistance Administration, United Nations, 1956-57. Member of Commission on Relations between Universities and Governments, 1968-69, Ontario Council on Graduate Studies, 1977-80, 1983, National Archives Advisory Council on Public Records, 1977-87, and Carleton Senate, 1979-81.

MEMBER: International Bar Association (chairman of academic advisory board of Ombudsman Forum, 1984—), Canadian Political Science Association (member of board, 1974-78; president, 1975-76), Canadian Association of University Teachers (member of executive committee, 1965-67), Social Science Research Council of Canada (member of council and executive committee, 1974-77; vice-president, 1978-79), Canadian Civil Liberties Association (member of board of directors, 1981-84).

AWARDS, HONORS: Canada Council senior research fellowships, 1960-61, and 1967-68; award from International Ombudsman Institute.

WRITINGS:

The Reorganization of Provincial-Municipal Relations in Nova Scotia, Department of Municipal Affairs (Halifax), 1949.

The Public Service of Canada, Queen's Printer, 1953.

Your Local Government: A Sketch of the Municipal System in Canada, Macmillan, 1955, revised edition, 1975.

Comparison of Governing Bodies of Canadian Universities, School of Public Administration, Carleton College, 1955.

Ottawa's Future Development and Needs, City Corporation (Ottawa), 1956.

Administrative Directory of the Imperial Ethiopian Government, Imperial Ethiopian Institute of Public Administration, 1957.

Cases on Administration, School of Public Administration, Carleton University, 1959, 2nd edition, 1960.

The Proposal of a Federation Territory for Canada's Capital, Advisory Committee on Confederation, 1967.

The Canadian Municipal System: Essays on the Improvement of Local Government, McClelland & Stewart, 1969.

(With Rene Hurtubise) *The University, Society, and Government,* University of Ottawa Press, 1970.

Public Access to Government Documents, Ontario Commission on Freedom of Information, 1978.

EDITOR

Basic Issues in Public Administration, Macmillan, 1961.

The Ombudsman: Citizen's Defender, Allen & Unwin, 1965, 2nd edition, 1968.

(With Hurtubise) *Studies on the University, Society, and Government,* two volumes, Commission on the Relations between Universities and Governments, 1970.

The Government of Federal Capitals, University of Toronto Press, 1972.

Provincial Government and Politics: Comparative Essays, Department of Political Science, Carleton University, 1972, 2nd edition, 1973.

The Ombudsman Plan: Essays on the Worldwide Spread of an Idea, McClelland & Stewart, 1973.

(And author of introduction) *The Finnish Parliamentary Ombudsman,* Institute of Governmental Studies, University of California, 1973.

Urban Politics in Ottawa—Carleton, Carleton University, 1974, 2nd edition, 1983.

(Co-editor) *The Provincial Political Systems,* Methuen, 1976.

(Co-editor) *Political Corruption in Canada,* McClelland & Stewart, 1976.

The Referendum and Separation Elsewhere: Implications for Quebec, Carleton University, 1978.

Administrative Secrecy in Developed Countries, Macmillan, 1979.

The Right to Know: Essays on Governmental Publicity and Public Access to Information, Carleton University,1980, 3rd edition, 1981.

International Handbook on Local Government Reorganization, Greenwood Press, 1980.

Provincial Policy-Making, Carleton University, 1981.

Canada's New Access Laws, Carleton University, 1983.

Global Comparisons in Public Administration, Carleton University, 2nd edition, 1984.

Recent Urban Politics in Ottawa—Carleton, Carleton University, 1985.

The Making of the Federal Access Act: A Case Study of Policy-Making in Canada, Carleton University, 1985.

Public Administration in Developed Democracies, Dekker, 1988.

OTHER

Also contributor to numerous books, including *Ombudsmen for America, Government?,* edited by Stanley V. Anderson, Prentice-Hall, 1968; *Urban Studies: A Canadian Perspective,* edited by N. H. Lithwick and Gilles Paquet, Methuen (Toronto), 1968; and *Le Systeme politique du Canada,* edited by L. Sabourin, Editions de l'Universite d'Ottawa, 1968. Contributor to numerous periodicals. Member of board, *International Review of Administrative Sciences,* 1983-92.

S

SANSOM, William 1912-1976

PERSONAL: Born January 18, 1912, in London, England; died April 20, 1976; son of Ernest Brooks and Mabel (Clark) Sansom; married Ruth Grundy (an actress), 1954; children: Sean, Nicholas. *Education:* Attended Uppingham School; also studied in Europe.

CAREER: Novelist and short story writer. Worked in a bank, for an advertising agency, as a fireman in London during World War II, and as a script writer for motion pictures.

MEMBER: Royal Society of Literature (fellow).

AWARDS, HONORS: Society of Authors travel scholarship, 1946, literary bursary, 1947.

WRITINGS:

(With James Gordon and Stephen Spender) *Jim Braidy: The Story of Britain's Firemen,* Drummond, 1943.

Fireman Flower, and Other Stories, Hogarth, 1944, Vanguard, 1945, 3rd edition published as *Fireman Flower,* Hogarth, 1966.

Three Stories by William Sansom, Hogarth, 1946, Reynal & Hitchcock, 1947.

(Editor) *Choice: Some New Stories and Prose,* Progress Publishing (London), 1946.

Westminster in War, Faber, 1947.

Something Terrible, Something Lovely (stories), Hogarth, 1948, Harcourt, 1954.

South: Aspects and Images from Corsica, Italy, and Southern France (travel stories), Hodder & Stoughton, 1948, Harcourt, 1950.

The Equilibriad, Hogarth, 1948.

(Editor) Edgar Allan Poe, *The Tell-Tale Heart, and Other Stories,* Lehmann, 1948.

The Body (novel), Harcourt, 1949.

The Passionate North (stories), Hogarth, 1950, Harcourt, 1953.

The Face of Innocence (novel), Harcourt, 1951.

A Touch of the Sun (stories), Hogarth, 1952, Reynal & Hitchcock, 1958.

Pleasures Strange and Simple (essays), Hogarth, 1953.

It Was Really Charlie's Castle (juvenile), Hogarth, 1953.

The Light That Went Out (juvenile), Hogarth, 1953.

A Bed of Roses (novel), Harcourt, 1954.

Lord Love Us (ballads), Hogarth, 1954.

The Loving Eye (novel), Reynal & Hitchcock, 1956.

A Contest of Ladies (stories), Reynal & Hitchcock, 1956.

Among the Dahlias, and Other Stories, Hogarth, 1957.

The Icicle and the Sun (travel), Hogarth, 1958, Reynal & Hitchcock, 1959.

The Cautious Heart (novel), Reynal & Hitchcock, 1958.

(Translator) Astrid Bergman, *Chendru: The Boy and the Tiger,* Harcourt, 1960.

Selected Short Stories, Chosen by the Author, Penguin, in association with Hogarth, 1960.

(Editor) Kurt Otto-Wasow, *The Bay of Naples,* Viking, 1960.

The Last Hours of Sandra Lee (novel), Little, 1961, reprinted as *The Wild Affair,* Popular Library, 1964.

Blue Skies, Brown Studies (travel), Little, 1961.

(Editor) Hjalmar Soderberg, *Doctor Glas,* Chatto & Windus, 1963.

The Stories of William Sansom, introduction by Elizabeth Bowen, Little, 1963.

Away to It All (travel), Hogarth, 1964, New American Library, 1966.

The Ulcerated Milkman (stories), Hogarth, 1966, Merrimack Book Service, 1979.

Goodbye (novel), Hogarth, 1966, New American Library, 1967.

Grand Tour Today, Hogarth, 1968.

A Book of Christmas (Book-of-the-Month Club selection), McGraw, 1968, published in England as *Christmas,* Weidenfeld and Nicolson, 1968.

The Vertical Ladder and Other Stories, Chatto & Windus, 1969.

Hans Feet in Love (novel), Hogarth, 1971.

The Birth of a Story, Chatto & Windus/Hogarth, 1972.

Proust and His World, Scribner, 1973, published in England as *Proust,* Thames & Hudson, 1986.

The Marmalade Bird (short stories), Hogarth, 1973.

Skimpy (juvenile), pictures by Hilary Abrahams, Deutsch, 1974.

(Author of introduction) *Victorian Life in Photographs,* photographic research by Harold Chapman, Thames & Hudson, 1974.

A Young Wife's Tale (novel), Hogarth, 1974, Merrimack Book Service, 1979.

Contributor to magazines. Also author of song lyrics and composer of music.

William Sansom's manuscript collection is kept in the New York Public Library Berg Collection.

SIDELIGHTS: William Sansom's stories and novels were continually praised for their precision of vision, language, and craftsmanship. Reviewers have described his works as technically flawless. On the other hand, many critics remarked that Sansom's writings were often deprecated for weakness in plot and, most often, for a lack of three-dimensional characters. Walter Allen noted in his book *The Modern Novel: In Britain and the United States* that Sansom was a writer "for whom the sensual surface of things seems to offer the greater part of experience. . . . His first novel, *The Body* . . . is still perhaps his best. It is, as it were, a comedy of exacerbation in which the distorted vision of the hero-narrator is expressed mainly through a minute rendering of the objects that make up the external world. They are seen in an unnatural clarity, magnified as though through an eye that is not a human eye. . . .. The result suggests the literary equivalent of paintings Rousseau might have made had he been turned loose in London immediately after the war." Richard Sullivan added: "In William Sansom's astonishingly productive career he has written few things to which the adjective 'brilliant' does not apply. . . . [However,] even the extraordinary brilliance of the prose does not offer adequate compensation for the coolness, the aloofness, the detachment of the characterization."

"Sansom is not a writer to whom one can be indifferent," wrote James Dean Young. "The praise is, as far as one can judge, real praise; the damning almost always condescension—as if the stories needed putting down. And so they do." Young primarily objected to Sansom's explicitness and added that "Sansom's stories are written, but they are not made." Other critics contended that he was in perfect control of what he was doing. Max Cosman noted that "Sansom's is a noticeable temperament. It is antiromantic, chance-ridden, smotheredly violent." He missed nothing that interested him. "The flesh of William Sansom's stories is their uninterrupted contour of sensory impressions," Eudora Welty wrote. "The bone is reflective contemplation. There is an odd contrast, and its pull is felt in the stories between the unhurriedness of their actual events and their racing intensity. . . . Sansom has never been anything less than a good writer. I think as time passes his writing becomes more flexible without losing its tightness of control. . . . And what is perhaps more unusual among writers so good, his work with time seems to have gained, not lost, spontaneity."

Among his novels, *The Body,* as Allen noted, is generally his most highly regarded. As a study in jealousy, according to Harvey Breit, "it has no contemporary peer. . . . [It is] a serious, psychological novel, with sociological overtones and thriller undertones, by a man with superb control of his material and with a language and style that is simplicity itself." Herbert Barrows commented in the *Times Literary Supplement* that he believed that this novel could "disappoint only those who respond to the slick." Barrows had only praise for this first novel: "The whole book is written at a high pitch of sensibility often achieved in a compressed form but seldom sustained throughout a longer work. Mr. Sansom adds to this rare power of concentration a sense of humour, acute observation, sound psychological insight and a distinguished descriptive prose style." With the publication of his second novel, *The Face of Innocence,* he was hailed as "an accomplished virtuoso." The novel's "great virtues," wrote Ernest Jones, "like the virtues of the books which preceded it, lie somewhere outside fiction, with the essay, with the best travel writing, sometimes with poetry." Breit concurred: "Sansom, I believe, writes as ably as anyone writing in English today. His language is quietly distinctive, effortless, and exact. . . . He doesn't try what he can't do. Maybe that is the reason he hasn't written a great novel. So far his works have been minor ones. But this modest phenomenon is pleasing within the current context of ego-mania."

After receiving mediocre reviews for *A Bed of Roses* Sansom published *The Loving Eye,* of which R. C. Butz wrote: "All of Mr. Sansom's virtues are here—the freshness of vision, the sensuousness, and the melancholy gaiety similar to the acrid smell of woodsmoke." *The Cautious Heart* was also well received, though Sandra Lee, the protagonist of his *The Last Hours of Sandra Lee,* was considered by some a women's magazine heroine, and the novel was only partly saved from disaster by Sansom's virtuosity. His penultimate novel, *Hans Feet in Love,* was met with little enthusiasm from the critics, who found the main character "unattractive," to use *Books and Bookmen* contributor Diane LeClercq's word, and one *Times Literary Supplement* reviewer remarked that Hans's adventures had already been done by Sansom "with more wit, invention and care in other places." Estimations of *A Young Wife's Tale,* however, were more generous. In a *New Statesman* article, for example, Valerie Cunningham found the novel "fetchingly jokey," though *Listener* critic Neil Hepburn did complain that the book's narration was "too elegant to believe in." Of the mixed reactions to the author's works, C. J. Rolo once offered this summary: "Sansom is a writer whose novels have at once impressed and disappointed me. He is an artist to his fingertips, and one is tempted to expect great things of him, but egregious flaws appear in his fiction." Rolo noted that a Sansom novel may hinge on an improbable situation and end with a neat resolution, but he added that, "if these things are accepted, the rewards are large."

Although he was primarily a fiction writer, Sansom once admitted that travel writing provided a respectable second income for him. David Depledge said: "He didn't have to seek his first commissions for travel work. 'It was about 14 years ago. An American editor saw some stories of mine which were set in Naples. I had set them there deliberately, I now realize, because I wanted to write about Naples. This American recognized something in them, and invited me to write travel pieces for him.' He has been writing for a few of the top American magazines ever since." Elizabeth Bowen praised his travel books as anti-provocative and non-egotistical. Most of these books read like collections of stories, "fresh, instant, exact, inhumanly brilliant," wrote Welty, and suggested that Sansom was a "wizard twice over." Elizabeth Young noted that Sansom "is not precious, meretricious, burning, or sticky." He "writes like an angel," said Jones, "and his joy in the performance communicates itself directly to the reader." Reversing the theology, J. J. Maloney added: "It is all too seldom . . . that one comes across a man who can tell a rattling good story and write like the devil."

BIOGRAPHICAL/CRITICAL SOURCES:

BOOKS

Allen, Walter, *The Modern Novel: In Britain and the United States,* Dutton, 1965, p. 269.

Allsop, Kenneth, *The Angry Decade,* P. Owen, 1958.

Contemporary Fiction in America and England, 1950-1970, Gale, 1976.

Contemporary Literary Criticism, Gale, Volume 2, 1974, p. 383, Volume 6, 1976, pp. 482-485.

PERIODICALS

Atlantic, September, 1949; September, 1951; February, 1957.

Books and Bookmen, September, 1968; July, 1971, pp. 30-32; November, 1971, p. 44; December, 1973, p. 90.

Chicago Sunday Tribune, January 19, 1958.

Commonweal, September 9, 1949.

Critique, spring, 1964.

Listener, September 9, 1971, p. 343; February 6, 1975, p. 190.

London Magazine, December, 1974/January, 1975, pp. 128-132.

Manchester Guardian, May 5, 1961.

Nation, October 14, 1950; August 18, 1951.

National Review, August 27, 1963.

New Statesman, November 3, 1961; September 3, 1971, p. 308; December 13, 1974, p. 871.

New Yorker, March 24, 1956; April 1, 1967.

New York Herald Tribune Book Review, April 20, 1947; October 15, 1950; August 12, 1951; October 7, 1954; January 12, 1958.

New York Review of Books, August 24, 1967.

New York Times Book Review, August 7, 1949; September 10, 1950; October 10, 1954; March 25, 1956; February 10, 1957; January 12, 1958; June 17, 1961; June 30, 1963; December 1, 1968.

Observer, June 16, 1968.

San Francisco Chronicle, August 9, 1951; February 24, 1957.

Saturday Review of Literature, August 27, 1949; September 23, 1950; April 7, 1956; September 20, 1958.

Time, September 29, 1958.

Times Literary Supplement, April 30, 1949; April 13, 1956; November 16, 1956; January 24, 1958; October 27, 1966; September 24, 1971, p. 1138; September 14, 1973, p. 1045.

OBITUARIES:

PERIODICALS

AB Bookman's Weekly, June 14, 1976.

New York Times, April 21, 1976.

Washington Post, April 24, 1976.*

* * *

SCHALL, James V(incent) 1928-

PERSONAL: Born January 20, 1928, in Pocahontas, IA; son of Lawrence Nicholas and Mary (Johnson) Schall. *Education:* Gonzaga University, B.A., 1954, M.A., 1955; Georgetown University, Ph.D., 1960; University of Santa Clara, M.S.T., 1964; Oude Abdij, Drongen, Belgium, Jesuit studies, 1964-65. *Politics:* Democrat.

ADDRESSES: *Office*—Department of Government, Georgetown University, 37th and 0 Sts. N.W., Washington, DC 20057.

CAREER: University of San Francisco, San Francisco, CA, instructor in political science, 1955-56; ordained Roman Catholic priest, Society of Jesus (Jesuits), 1963; Gregorian University, Istituto Sociale, Rome, Italy, lecturer, 1965-77; Georgetown University, Washington, DC, associate professor in department of government, 1978—. Associate professor in department of government, University of San Francisco, springs, 1968-77. Member of Pontifical Commission on Justice and Peace in Rome, 1977-82, and National Council of the Humanities of the National Endowment for the Humanities, 1984-90.

WRITINGS:

(With Donald J. Wolf) *American Society and Politics,* Allyn & Bacon, 1964.

(Editor with Wolf) *Current Trends in Theology,* Doubleday, 1965.

Redeeming the Time, Sheed, 1968.

Human Dignity and Human Numbers, Alba, 1971.

Play On: From Games to Celebrations, Fortress Press, 1971.

Far Too Easily Pleased: A Theology of Contemplation, Play, and Festivity, Benziger/Macmillan, 1976.

Welcome, Number 4,000,000,000!, Alba, 1977.

The Sixth Paul, Alba, 1977.

The Praise of "Sons of Bitches": On the Worship of God by Fallen Men, St. Paul Publications, 1978.

Christianity and Life, Ignatius Press, 1981.

Christianity and Politics, St. Paul Editions, 1981.

Church, State and Society in the Thought of John Paul II, Franciscan Herald Press, 1982.

The Social Teaching of John Paul II, Franciscan Herald, 1982.

Liberation Theology, Ignatius Press, 1982.

The Distinctiveness of Christianity, Ignatius, 1982.

The Politics of Heaven and Hell: Christian Themes from Classical, Medieval, and Modern Political Philosophy, University Press of America, 1984.

Unexpected Meditations Late in the Twentieth Century, Franciscan Herald Press, 1985.

Reason, Revelation, and the Foundations of Political Philosophy, Louisiana State University Press, 1987.

Another Sort of Learning, Ignatius Press, 1988.

Religion, Wealth and Poverty, Fraser Institute, 1990.

What Is God Like?, Michael Glazer/Liturgical Press, 1992.

EDITOR AND AUTHOR OF INTRODUCTION

The Whole Truth about Man: John Paul II to University Students and Faculties, St. Paul Editions, 1981.

Sacred in All Its Forms, St. Paul Editions, 1984.

Out of Justice, Peace: Pastorals of the German and French Bishops, Ignatius Press, 1984.

(With George Carey) *Essays in Christianity and Political Philosophy,* University Press of America, 1984.

G. K. Chesterton, *Collected Poems,* Volume 4, *What's Wrong with the World,* Ignatius Press, 1986.

On the Intelligibility of Political Philosophy: Essays of Charles N. R. McCoy, edited with John J. Schrems, Catholic University of America Press, 1989.

Contributor of articles to *Commonweal, World Justice, New Scholasticism, Catholic World, America, Social Order, Modern Age, Worship, Thomist,* and to political science journals. Columnist for *Crisis.*

SIDELIGHTS: James V. Schall once told *CA:* "A number of my titles are distinctly odd. The word 'meditations' in [*Unexpected Meditations Late in the Twentieth Century*] comes directly from the classic [*Meditations*] of Emperor Marcus Aurelius, and is intended to be a Christian reconsideration, as well as something of an autobiography, of the classic Stoic's own reflections. The irreverent 'sons of bitches' [in *The Praise of 'Sons of Bitches': On the Worship of God by Fallen Men*] comes from the playwright Arthur Miller's comment that we are all either 'sons of God or sons of bitches, as God and the prophets have always held.' The point of this book is that we are all both sons of God and sons of bitches at the same time; we are 'not pure spirits.' "

BIOGRAPHICAL/CRITICAL SOURCES:

PERIODICALS

Encounter, autumn, 1968.

* * *

SCHAUER, Frederick Franklin 1946-

PERSONAL: Born January 15, 1946, in Newark, NJ; son of John Adolph (a credit executive) and Clara (Balayti) Schauer; married Margery Clare Stone (a writer), August 25, 1968 (divorced June, 1982); married Virginia Jo Wise (a law librarian and library educator), May 25, 1985. *Education:* Dartmouth College, A.B., 1967, M.B.A., 1968; Harvard University, J.D., 1972.

Avocational Interests: Cooking, eating, travel, ship model building, skiing, bicycling, woodworking.

ADDRESSES: Office—Kennedy School of Government, Harvard University, Cambridge, MA 02138.

CAREER: Admitted to the Bar of the Commonwealth of Massachusetts, 1972, and the Bar of the U.S. Supreme Court, 1976; Fine & Ambrogne, Boston, MA, attorney, 1972-74; West Virginia University, Morgantown, assistant professor, 1974-76, associate professor of law, 1976-78; College of William and Mary, Williamsburg,

VA, associate professor, 1978-80, Cutler Professor of Law, 1980-84, Cutler Lecturer, 1989; University of Michigan, Ann Arbor, professor of law, 1984-90; Harvard University, Kennedy School of Government, Cambridge, MA, Frank Stanton Professor, 1990—. Visiting scholar at Wolfson College, Cambridge, and member of the faculty of law at Cambridge University, 1977-78; Legacy of George Mason Lecturer, George Mason University, 1984; Bush Foundation Lecturer, Hamline University, 1987; visiting professor of law, University of Michigan, 1983-84; visiting professor of law, University of Chicago, 1990; William Morton distinguished senior fellow in humanities, Dartmouth College, 1991. Guest lecturer at various universities in the United States and abroad. Commissioner, Attorney General's Commission on Pornography, 1985-86. *Military service:* U.S. National Guard, 1970-71.

MEMBER: American Academy of Arts and Sciences (fellow); American Philosophical Association, American Society for Political and Legal Philosophy, Association of American Law Schools (vice-chairperson of section on law and the arts, 1975-76; member of executive committee of section on constitutional law, 1982-84; chairperson of section on constitutional law, 1985-87).

AWARDS, HONORS: National Endowment for the Humanities summer fellowship, 1980, for research on constitutional language; American Bar Association Certificate of Merit, 1983, for *Free Speech: A Philosophical Enquiry.*

WRITINGS:

The Law of Obscenity, BNA Books, 1976.

Free Speech: A Philosophical Enquiry, Cambridge University Press, 1982.

Playing By the Rules: A Philosophical Examination of Rule-Based Decision Making in Law and in Life, Oxford University Press, 1991.

(Editor) *Law and Language,* New York University Press, 1992.

Also author of supplements to Gunther's *Constitutional Law,* 11th and 12th editions, Gunther's *Individual Rights in Constitutional Law,* 4th edition, and Foundation Press University Casebook Series, 1983— (Schauer was not associated with earlier editions or supplements).

CONTRIBUTOR

Burton Leiser, editor, *Values in Conflict,* Macmillan, 1981.

Richard Rutyna, editor, *Conceived in Conscience,* Donning, 1983.

Leonard Levy, editor, *Encyclopedia of the American Constitution,* Macmillan, 1987.

Judith Lichtenberg, editor, *Democracy and the Mass Media,* Cambridge University Press, 1990.

John H. Garvey, editor, *The First Amendment: A Reader,* West Publishing, 1992.

Michael Meyer, editor, *The Constitution of Rights,* Cornell University Press, 1992.

Dennis Patterson, editor, *Wittgenstein and Legal Theory,* Westview, 1992.

Contributor to law and philosophy journals, including *Harvard Law Review, Yale Law Journal, Supreme Court Review, Philosophical Quarterly, Northwestern University Law Review, Georgetown Law Journal, Virginia Law Review, William and Mary Law Review, Stanford Law Review, Columbia Law Review, Southern California Law Review, American Bar Foundation Research Journal,* and *Nomos.* Member of editorial board, *Ethics.*

WORK IN PROGRESS: Research and writing on the relationship between legal and ordinary language, the nature of legal positivism, obligations to the law, and freedom of speech.

SIDELIGHTS: In his 1982 book *Free Speech: A Philosophical Enquiry,* Frederick Franklin Schauer reexamines the theoretical justifications for freedom of speech. In doing so, the author criticizes some of the arguments for freedom of speech put forward by such philosophers as John Stuart Mill, Thomas Scanlon, and Aristotle. These criticisms are so effective that, as J. N. Gray explained in the *Times Literary Supplement,* "paradoxically, and from his point of view no doubt regrettably, Schauer's book does more to strengthen skepticism about the importance of free speech than it does to establish the credentials of a branch of political philosophy concerned with free speech theory."

Schauer's 1991 book *Playing by the Rules: A Philosophical Examination of Rule-Based Decision Making in Law and in Life* continues to challenge basic moral and philosophical assumptions, exploring the origins and importance of rules, as well as society's motivation to obey them. Walter Sinnott-Armstrong, writing in *Philosophical Books,* calls *Playing by the Rules* "a very useful framework for analyzing the degree to which rule-based decision making is justified in any particular area." While Sinnott-Armstrong admits that the author "sometimes seems to confuse explanation with justification," he concludes: "Despite these limitations, the instrumental rules that Schauer does discuss are both fascinating and important, and Schauer provides the most comprehensive and profound analysis of these rules to date."

Schauer told *CA:* "I suppose that much of my writing has been devoted to questioning the unquestionable or thinking the unthinkable. Academic discourse, ideally unencumbered by many of the ordinary pressures and biases of other forums, is the place where one can ask questions such as 'What is so special about freedom of speech?' or

'Why should the Constitution be interpreted according to the intentions of those who drafted it?' or 'What can be said for formal or literal legal decision making?' If the answers to questions like these turn out to be consistent with the received wisdom, then understanding has been substituted for blind acceptance and analysis substituted for platitudes. And if the answers turn out to reject the received wisdom, then something has been added to the existing knowledge. But most important is to get people thinking about fundamental questions and to get them to examine carefully their traditional and often unthinking assumptions. That is what academic thought and academic institutions are all about. If the goals of academic discourse are aimed at provoking serious thought about fundamental questions, then it is much better to be importantly wrong than trivially right. Ideally, of course, it is best to be importantly right, but we will rarely achieve that goal if we become preoccupied with avoiding any risk of error. In thinking, as in anything else, the greatest rewards go to those who are willing to take the greatest risks."

BIOGRAPHICAL/CRITICAL SOURCES:

PERIODICALS

American Journal of Jurisprudence, 1984.
Dartmouth Alumni Magazine, June, 1983.
Law and Philosophy, April, 1985.
Listener, January 13, 1983.
Northwestern University Law Review, December, 1983.
Philosophical Books, October, 1983; April, 1992, pp. 116-118.
Texas Law Review, October, 1985.
Times Literary Supplement, March 11, 1983.
Wisconsin Law Review, January, 1985.

* * *

SCHMANDT-BESSERAT, Denise 1933-

PERSONAL: Born August 10, 1933, in Ay, France; U.S. citizen; daughter of Victor (a champagne producer) and Jeanne (Crabit) Besserat; married Jurgen Schmandt (a professor), December 27, 1956; children: Alexander, Christopher, Phillip. *Education:* Paris University, Baccalaureat, 1953; attended Ecole du Louvre, 1965.

ADDRESSES: Home—11 Hull Cir., Austin, TX 78746. *Office*—Department of Art, University of Texas, Austin, TX 78712.

CAREER: Harvard University, Peabody Museum, Cambridge, MA, research fellow, 1969-71; University of Texas, Austin, assistant professor, 1972-81, associate professor, 1981-88, professor of Middle Eastern Studies, 1988—, assistant director of the Center for Middle Eastern Studies, 1976-79, acting chief curator of the University of Texas Art Museum, 1978-79. Fellow at Radcliffe Institute, 1969-71. Guest curator at University Art Museum, University of Texas, 1975. University of California, Berkeley, visiting associate professor, 1987, Una Lecturer in the Humanities, 1989. Guest scholar, German Archaeologic Institute, 1987. Lecturer, exhibition consultant, and symposium coordinator.

MEMBER: Archaeological Institute of America (secretary of Austin, TX Society, 1973-74; president of Austin Society, 1974-76; member of governing board, 1983-89), American Anthropological Association (fellow), American Oriental Society, Bunting Institute (fellow).

AWARDS, HONORS: National Endowment for the Arts grant, 1974-75, 1977-78, fellowship for independent study and research, 1979-80, grant, 1990; University of Texas Research grants, 1974, 1977, 1980, 1991; Jean Holloway teaching award from the University of Texas at Austin, 1978; named Outstanding Woman in Humanities by the American Association of University Women, 1979; American Council of Learned Societies grant, 1984; Institute for Research in the Humanities fellowship, University of Wisconsin—Madison, 1984-85; German Academic Exchange Service study visit grant, 1986; book award, Kayden National University Press, 1993.

WRITINGS:

JUVENILES

Archaeology, Steck, 1974.
(With S. Mayer) *The Story of Sumer: The First Civilization* (exhibit catalog), University of Texas Press, 1975.
(With M. Timko) *Egypt in the Days of the Pharaohs* (exhibit catalog), University of Texas Press, 1975.
(With S. Otto-Diniz) *Open Sesame: The Story of Persian Locks* (exhibit catalog), University of Texas Press, 1976.
(With S. Otto-Diniz and Jacqueline Pinsker McCaffrey) *At the Court of the Great King: The Art of the Persian Empire* (exhibit catalogue), University of Texas Art Museum, 1977.
Origins and Development of Western Writing (video), Alarion Press, 1987.
The Origin and Development of Writing (sound film strip), Alarion Press, 1980.

FOR ADULTS

The Legacy of Sumer: The First Civilization (exhibit catalog), University of Texas Press, 1975.
(Editor) *The Legacy of Sumer,* Undena, 1976.
Ancient Persia—The Art of an Empire (exhibit catalogue), University of Texas Art Museum, 1977.
(Editor) *Immortal Egypt,* Undena, 1978.

(Editor and contributor) *Early Technologies,* Undena, 1979.

(Editor) *Ancient Persia,* Undena, 1980.

Before Writing, Volume 1: *From Counting to Cuneiform,* Volume 2: *A Catalog of Near Eastern Tokens,* University of Texas Press, 1992.

OTHER

Contributor to numerous books, including *Mountains and Lowlands: Essays in the Archeology of Greater Mesopotamia,* edited by T. C. Young, Jr. and L. D. Levine, Undena, 1977; *Popular Culture Before Printing,* edited by F. E. H. Schroeder, Bowling Green University Press, 1980; *Prehistoric Times,* edited by Brian M. Fagan, W. H. Freeman, 1983; *Language, Writing, and the Computer,* edited by William S. Y. Wang, W. H. Freeman, 1986; *The Emergence of Language,* edited by Wang, W. H. Freeman, 1990; and *Language Origin: A Multidisciplinary Approach,* edited by Brunetto Chiarelli and Bernard Bichakjian, 1992. Contributor to professional journals, including *Biblical Archaeologist, Society for Near Eastern Studies, Das Altertum, Written Communication, Archaeology, Vicino Oriente,* and *Acheomaterials.* Advisory editor of *Technology and Culture,* 1978-92; member of advisory board, *Visible Language,* 1985—.

WORK IN PROGRESS: Uruk, Where Civilization Began; The History of Counting.

SIDELIGHTS: Denise Schmandt-Besserat told *CA:* "When my children were three to twelve years old, reading together was part of our everyday lives, and it may not be exaggerated to say that often it was the best part of the day. We would read after dinner when the five of us, already tired from our busy days spent in our different ways, would at last be together in the living room. The feeling was always warm and peaceful, and I looked forward to reading time as much as the children. I realized the true importance of this sharing when Phillip was asked in class to define the word 'security.' The answer he wrote was 'security is when I am reading with my mother.' All of which leads me to say that I wrote my first book, *Archaeology,* for my children.

"I am an archaeologist and on several occasions had to leave for a whole summer to join excavations in the Middle East, especially in Iran. My children did not really know what I was doing over there, so I looked for books on archaeology which we could read together and which would help explain my work. As I could not find any which fulfilled this purpose, I decided to write one myself.

"Through my work at the University of Texas, I have been able to bring to Austin a series of exhibits on the ancient Middle East. Remembering the joy and interest my children have had in learning, I have been concerned that the children visitors appreciate and enjoy these exhibits. Thus, I have initiated a series of children's catalogues which make the information attractive and understandable to elementary school children. Many teachers have indicated to me that the books are effective teaching aids, and I have seen proof of this when one day I saw a group of third graders enter the gallery of the Egyptian exhibit proudly wearing the large paper Egyptian necklace which they had made following the catalogue instruction. They were so anxious to see the real Egyptian necklaces.

"I enjoy my work as an archaeologist immensely. My main contribution may be to have detected an early recording system consisting of small clay objects in geometric and odd shapes which are the direct precursor of Sumerian Cuneiform writing. I came across these little objects, as it so often happens, totally by chance, when studying man's earliest uses of clay in the Middle East. The publication of my findings should lead to a whole new area of research on communication and counting and to a better understanding of the organization of archaic societies."

* * *

SCHUDSON, Michael 1946-

PERSONAL: Born November 3, 1946, in Milwaukee, WI; son of Howard M. (a small business proprietor) and Lorraine (Spira) Schudson. *Education:* Swarthmore College, B.A., 1969; Harvard University, M.A., 1970, Ph.D., 1976.

ADDRESSES: Home—San Diego, CA. *Office*—Department of Communication, University of California, San Diego, La Jolla, CA 92093.

CAREER: University of Chicago, Chicago, IL, assistant professor of sociology, 1976-80; University of California, San Diego, La Jolla, associate professor, 1980-85, professor of sociology and communication, 1985—.

MEMBER: International Communication Association, American Sociological Association, Association for Education in Journalism, Organization of American Historians.

AWARDS, HONORS: Guggenheim fellowship, 1990; MacArthur Prize fellowship, 1990-94; Center for Advanced Study in the Behavioral Sciences fellowship, 1992-93.

WRITINGS:

Discovering the News: A Social History of American Newspapers, Basic Books, 1978.

Advertising, the Uneasy Persuasion: Its Dubious Impact on American Society, Basic Books, 1984.

(With Robert Manoff) *Reading the Newspaper,* Pantheon, 1986.

(With Chandra Mukerji) *Rethinking Popular Culture,* University of California Press, 1991.

Watergate in American Memory: How We Remember, Forget, and Reconstruct the Past, Basic Books, 1992.

WORK IN PROGRESS: A book on the history of media, politics, and the public sphere in the United States.

SIDELIGHTS: Michael Schudson reports in *Discovering the News: A Social History of American Newspapers* that while the concept of "news" originated in the 1830s, it was not until nearly a decade later that " 'objectivity' . . . became the law of the news pages," writes James Aronson in the *Nation.* This same ideal was challenged in the 1960s when "the press began asking itself if objectivity was possible at all," comments *New Leader* contributor Seth Cropsey, who also observes that "by tracing how objectivity came to be the press' goal, Schudson shows that it has not been the only one. In the process, he prompts the reader to wonder whether it is a practicable, or even a worthy goal."

While Cropsey describes *Discovering the News* as "a worthwhile book because it raises important issues," he suggests that if the book were "a full account of the evolution of American journalism [it] would tell us not only how society has affected our newspapers but how our newspapers have affected society." Aronson, however, maintains: "Schudson has managed to trace the development of the American newspaper and its interplay with public and government thoughtfully and intelligently, and provocatively enough to raise legitimate doubts about the usefulness of most published histories of the American press."

BIOGRAPHICAL/CRITICAL SOURCES:

PERIODICALS

Harper's, January, 1985.
Los Angeles Times Book Review, December 2, 1984.
Nation, October 7, 1978.
New Leader, February 12, 1979.
New Republic, November 11, 1978.
New York Times Book Review, December 23, 1984.

* * *

SCHUYLER, George Samuel 1895-1977

PERSONAL: Born February 25, 1895, in Providence, RI; died August 31, 1977, in New York, NY; son of George (a chef) and Eliza Jane (Fischer) Schuyler; married Josephine E. Lewis (a painter), January 6, 1928 (died, 1969); children: Philippa (deceased). *Education:* Educated in Syracuse, NY.

CAREER: U.S. Civil Service, clerk, 1919-20; *Messenger* (magazine), cofounder and associate editor, 1923-28; *Pittsburgh Courier,* Pittsburgh, PA, columnist, chief editorial writer, and associate editor, 1924-66, special correspondent to South America and West Indies, 1948-49, to French West Africa and Dominican Republic, 1958; *Review of the News,* analysis editor, 1967-77. *New York Evening Post,* special correspondent to Liberia, 1931; *National News,* editor, 1932; *Crisis* (magazine), business manager, 1937-44; *Manchester Union Leader,* literary editor. National Association for the Advancement of Colored People (NAACP), special publicity assistant, 1934-35. Member of international committee of Congress for Cultural Freedom, and U.S. delegation to Berlin and Brussels meetings, 1950. President of Philippa Schuyler Memorial Foundation. *Military service:* U.S. Army, 1912-18; became first lieutenant.

MEMBER: American Writers Association (served as vice president), American Asian Educational Exchange, American African Affairs Association, Authors Guild.

AWARDS, HONORS: Citation of Merit award from Lincoln University School of Journalism, 1952; American Legion Award, 1968; Catholic War Veterans Citation, 1969; Freedoms Foundation at Valley Forge Award, 1972.

WRITINGS:

Racial Intermarriage in the United States, Haldeman-Julius, 1929.

Black No More: Being an Account of the Strange and Wonderful Workings of Science in the Land of the Free, A.D. 1933-1940 (novel), Macaulay, 1931, reprinted, with introduction by Charles R. Larson, Collier Books, 1971. *Slaves Today: A Story of Liberia,* Brewer, Warren & Putnam, 1931, reprinted, McGrath, 1969.

The Communist Conspiracy against the Negroes, Catholic Information Society, 1947.

The Red Drive in the Colonies, Catholic Information Society, 1947.

Black and Conservative: The Autobiography of George S. Schuyler, Arlington House, 1966.

Black Empire (novel; part of the Northeastern Library of Black Literature series) Northeastern University Press, 1991.

Also author of *A Negro Looks Ahead,* 1930; *Fifty Years of Progress in Negro Journalism,* 1950; *The Van Vechten Revolution,* 1951; and *The Negro-Art Hokum,* published by Bobbs-Merrill with Langston Hughes's *The Negro Artist and the Racial Mountain.* Contributor to Spadeau Columns, Inc., 1953-62, and to North American Newspaper Alliance, 1965-77. Contributor to the annals of the American Academy of Political Science and to periodicals, including *Nation, Negro Digest, Reader's Digest, American*

Mercury, Common Ground, Freeman, Americans, and *Christian Herald American.* Contributing editor to *American Opinion* and *Review of the News.*

SIDELIGHTS: George S. Schuyler was a satirist on race relations and was known for upholding the opposite stance from what was popularly held on the subject. His shifting views attacked Marcus Garvey's back-to-Africa movement and civil rights leader Martin Luther King, Jr.'s practice of nonviolence. Black historian John Henrik Clarke was quoted in Schuyler's *New York Times* obituary as saying: "I used to tell people that George got up in the morning, waited to see which way the world was turning then struck out in the opposite direction."

"He was a rebel who enjoyed playing that role," continued Clarke. Schuyler put his wit and sarcasm to work with the publication of *Black No More,* a satirical novel that gave a fictitious solution to the race problem. Through glandular treatments, blacks could take a cream that would eventually turn them white and they would disappear into white society.

This novel and other works by Schuyler were initially highly rated by various black leaders, despite the ridicule present in his works that was directed toward some of these spokesmen. Rayford W. Logan, chairman of the department of history at Howard University, stated that "he could cut deeply and sometimes unfairly, but he was interesting to read."

In the early 1960s, however, when the civil rights movement began to gain momentum, civil rights leaders became less enthusiastic about Schuyler, whose positions moved farther right and seemed reactionary compared with those of most blacks. This era of civil rights proved to be too powerful for Schuyler, and he was soon overtaken completely. "His outlets became more and more limited," remarked George Goodman, Jr., in the *New York Times,* though "he nonetheless continued to champion conservative issues such as the presence of U.S. troops in Southeast Asia."

BIOGRAPHICAL/CRITICAL SOURCES:

BOOKS

Dictionary of Literary Biography, Gale, Volume 29: *American Newspaper Journalists, 1926-1950,* 1984, Volume 51: *Afro-American Writers from the Harlem Renaissance to 1940,* 1987.

Peplow, Michael W., *George S. Schuyler,* Twayne, 1980.

Schuyler, George Samuel, *Black and Conservative: The Autobiography of George S. Schuyler,* Arlington House, 1966.

PERIODICALS

Black American Literature Forum, Volume 12, 1978.

Black World, Volume 21, 1971.

Books and Bookmen, Volume 16, 1971.

Journal of the School of Languages, Volume 8, 1981-82.

Library Journal, December, 1991.

New York Times Book Review, Sept 20, 1992.

OBITUARIES:

PERIODICALS

AB Bookman's Weekly, November 21, 1977.

New York Times, September 7, 1977.

Washington Post, September 9, 1977.*

* * *

SCHUYLER, Judy
See ESHBACH, Lloyd Arthur

* * *

SEUPHOR, Michel
See ARP, Jean

* * *

SHANNON, Thomas A(nthony) 1940-

PERSONAL: Born September 28, 1940, in Indianapolis, IN; son of John E. (an industrial engineer) and Clara (an artist; maiden name, Schmalz) Shannon; married Catherine Haenn (a reading teacher), August 12, 1972; children: Ashley Elizabeth, Courtney Marie. *Education:* Quincy College, B.A., 1964; St. Joseph Seminary, Teutopolis, IL, S.T.B., 1968; Boston University, S.T.M., 1970, Ph.D., 1973. *Politics:* Independent. *Religion:* Roman Catholic.

ADDRESSES: Home—132 Coolidge Rd., Worcester, MA 01602. *Office*—Department of Humanities, Worcester Polytechnic Institute, Worcester, MA 01609.

CAREER: Quincy College, Quincy, IL, instructor in theology, 1968-69; Massachusetts Bay Community College, Watertown, MA, instructor in humanities, part-time, 1971-72; Worcester Polytechnic Institute, Worcester, MA, assistant professor, 1973-76, associate professor of social ethics, 1977—. Visiting instructor at Wellesley College, 1976, and Mercy College (New York), 1977; University of Massachusetts Medical School, visiting assistant professor of bioethics, 1976, associate professor of medical ethics, half-time, 1978-82, visiting associate professor, 1982-88. Lecturer and discussion leader of seminars at churches in the eastern United States, and at colleges and universities, including Vassar College, St. Louis University School of Medicine, University of Massachusetts Medical School, University of Kentucky, and Assumption College. Chairman of human rights committee, First Few Steps, Inc.; member of institutional review board, University of Massachusetts Medical Center, 1979-93. Consultant to Cooper Union School of Engineering, 1976-77. Member of Ethics Committee, the Medical Center, Memorial Hospital, Worcester.

MEMBER: American Society of Christian Ethics, American Academy of Religion, Catholic Theology Society of America, Institute of Society, Ethics, and the Life Sciences.

AWARDS, HONORS: Institute of Society, Ethics, and the Life Sciences fellowship, 1976-77.

WRITINGS:

Render unto God: A Theology of Selective Obedience, Paulist/Newman, 1974.
(Editor) *Readings in Bioethics,* Paulist/Newman, 1976, revised edition published as *Bioethics,* 1980.
(Editor with David J. O'Brien) *Renewing the Earth: Documents on Peace, Justice and Liberation,* Image Books, 1977.
(With James DiGiacomo) *An Introduction to Bioethics,* Paulist/Newman, 1979, revised edition, 1986.
(Editor) *War or Peace? The Search for New Answers,* Orbis, 1980.
(With JoAnn Manfra) *Law and Bioethics,* Paulist Press, 1982.
What Are They Saying about Peace and War?, Paulist Press, 1983.
Twelve Essays in Health Care Ethics, Edwin Mellen, 1984.
What Are They Saying about Genetic Engineering?, Paulist Press, 1985.
(With Charles N. Faso) *Let Them Go Free,* Sheed & Ward, 1985.
(With Lisa S. Cahill) *Religion and Artificial Reproduction,* Crossroad, 1988.
Surrogate Motherhood: The Ethics of Using Human Beings, Crossroad, 1988.
(Editor with Patricia B. Jung) *Abortion and Catholicism: The American Debate,* Crossroad, 1988.
(Editor with James J. Walter) *Quality of Life: The New Medical Dilemma,* Paulist Press, 1990.
(Editor with O'Brien) *Catholic Social Thought: The Documentary History,* Orbis Books, 1992.

Contributor of articles and reviews to periodicals, including *Commonweal, Journal of College Science Teaching, U.S. Catholic, Bioethics Digest, National Catholic Reporter,* and *Theological Studies.* Associate editor of *IRB: A Review of Human Studies Research.*

WORK IN PROGRESS: Book on the ethics of genetic engineering; co-editing a book on the history of the moral theory of casuistry; a book on the ethical theory of John Duns Scotus.

SIDELIGHTS: Thomas A. Shannon once told *CA:* "I am continually impressed with both the complexity of contemporary medicine—as it is practiced and developed within an ever-increasing, sophisticated, technological context—[and] the continued manifestation of the human face of medicine through the variety of health care providers with whom I have come in contact, whether these be physicians, nurses, attorneys, or patient advocates. I have tried to capture the sense of that complexity in many of my writings and in books that I have edited. I have also tried to attend to the many dimensions of the drama that occurs when significant value questions are raised in the delivery of health care, whether this be in the extreme tragedies of trying to determine when a person will benefit from an extremely sophisticated, technological intervention or the routine kind of decisions that need to be made with respect to modifications of lifestyle in terms of accepting a medical therapy that promises benefits but also has risks associated with it. [In] my own writings and the works that I have edited, [I] have tried to give a flavor of the constant ambiguities present in the situations by providing access to a variety of viewpoints, as well as [by] trying to articulate many of the inherent dilemmas that are present . . . in contemporary medicine."

* * *

SHARPE, Lucretia
See BURGESS, Michael (Roy)

* * *

SHIVPURI, Gopi Krishna 1903-1984
(Gopi Krishna)

PERSONAL: Born June 3, 1903, in Gairoo, Kashmir, India; died of pneumonia, July 31, 1984, in Srinigar, Kashmir, India; son of Ganga (an accountant) and Kulwanti Rama; married Roopwanti (Mughlani Devi), 1926; children: Ragina Kaul, Jagdish Chander Shivpuri, Nirmal Chander Shivpuri. *Education:* Attended secondary school in Srinagar, Kashmir, and Lahore, Punjab.

CAREER: Government of India, 1923-50, worked as clerk in Irrigation Division in Srinagar, Kashmir, Office of the Chief Engineer, Irrigation Department in Jammu, and Office of the Director of Education, in Jammu and Srinagar; writer, 1950-75; Central Institute for Kundalini Research, Nishat, India, founder and president, 1975-84. President of Samaj Sudhar Samiti, 1946-84; member of Bharat Sevak Samaj, 1958-70.

WRITINGS:

UNDER NAME GOPI KRISHNA

From the Unseen, privately printed, 1952.

Kundalini, Ramadhar & Hopman, 1967, published as *Kundalini: The Evolutionary Energy in Man,* Shambhala, 1971.

The Shape of Events to Come, privately printed, 1968, revised edition, Kundalini Research & Development Trust, 1979.

The Biological Basis of Religion and Genius, Harper, 1972.

The Secret of Yoga, Harper, 1972.

Higher Consciousness, Julian Press, 1974.

The Awakening of Kundalini, Dutton, 1975.

Panchastavi (in English; title means "The Hymn with Five Chants"), Central Insitute for Kundalini Research, 1975.

The Riddle of Consciousness, Kundalini Research Foundation, 1976.

The Dawn of a New Science, Kundalini Research & Publication Trust, 1978.

Secrets of Kundalini in Panchastavi, Kundalini Research & Publication Trust, 1978.

Yoga: A Vision of Its Future, Kundalini Research & Publication Trust, 1978.

The Real Nature of Mystical Experience, New Concepts Publishing, 1978.

Kundalini in Time and Space, Kundalini Research & Publication Trust, 1979.

Reason and Revelation, New Age Publishing, 1979.

Biblical Prophecy for the Twentieth Century, New Age Publishing, 1979.

The Present Crisis: A Critical Analysis of the Human Mind, Life Science Institute, 1981.

Also author of *The Story of My Life.*

Shivpuri's books have been translated into French, German, Spanish, Italian, Dutch, Gujarati, Portuguese, Hindi, Marathi, Malayan, and Japanese.

SIDELIGHTS: The late Gopi Krishna Shivpuri wrote of kundalini, an energy inherent in human beings which is capable of awakening a higher consciousness when it is activated through certain yogic practices. It is sometimes called the Serpent Power because of its manifestation through the body's spinal column and central nervous system. An ancient belief among India's practitioners of yoga, kundalini energy has not been scientifically proven to exist. Shivpuri worked in India's civil service until the age of 37 when he experienced a spiritual awakening while practicing yoga. Thereafter he devoted himself to the study and teaching of kundalini.

Shivpuri's secretary, Paul Beattie, once told *CA:* "The main thrust of Gopi Krishna Shivpuri's writings is to prove that there is a dormant center in the human brain and a reserve store of bio-energy in the human body which, when activated, leads to the illuminated state of consciousness peculiar to prophets and mystics, conferring the extraordinary intellectual or artistic talents that characterize genius, or bestowing the miraculous or psychic gifts as exhibited by saints and mediums. In those cases where there is a malfunctioning of these mechanisms, their activity can result in intractable forms of mental or nervous disorder.

"Based on the strength of the ancient tradition relating to the Serpent Power in India and his own experience, Gopi Krishna Shivpuri believes that a still unrecognized psychic activity in the cerebro-spinal system is at the root of many still inexplicable paranormal and abnormal phenomena of the human mind."

Shivpuri's Samaj Sudhar Samiti organization worked for social reforms in India, including the abolition of the dowry system, reduction in expenditure on marriages and other social functions, remarriage of widows, rehabilitation of widows, orphans, and destitutes, as well as the improvement and beautification of shrines and holy places.

BIOGRAPHICAL/CRITICAL SOURCES:

PERIODICALS

Psychic Dimensions, November, 1978.

OBITUARIES:

PERIODICALS

New York Times, August 3, 1984.*

* * *

SHORT, Michael 1937-

PERSONAL: Born February 27, 1937, in Paget, Bermuda; son of Reginald and Bella (McLean) Short; married Elaine Braithwaite (a weaver). *Education:* University of Bristol, B.Sc., 1958; attended Morley College and University of London.

ADDRESSES: *Home*—73 Trowbridge Rd., Bradford-on-Avon, Wiltshire BA15 1EG, England. *Office*—Royal Military School of Music, Kneller Hall, Twickenham, England. *Agent*—Mark Paterson, 10 Brook St., Wivenhoe, Essex CO7 9DS, England.

CAREER: Musical composer. Bath College of Higher Education, Bath, England, principal lecturer in music, 1981-87; Royal Military School of Music, professor of music history, 1989—. Worked as a music librarian; has taught music for Open University and at Cambridge University; composer in residence at Dolmetsch Summer School of Music.

MEMBER: Composers Guild of Great Britain.

AWARDS, HONORS: Mendelssohn Scholarship recipient, 1966.

WRITINGS:

(Editor) *Gustav Holst: Letters to W. G. Whittaker,* University of Glasgow, 1974.
Gustav Holst: A Centenary Documentation, White Lion, 1974.
Your Book of Music, Faber, 1982.
Gustav Holst: The Man and His Music, Oxford University Press, 1990.

Also composer of musical pieces commissioned for and performed by professional musical ensembles, including the London Sinfonietta, the Scottish Baroque Ensemble, the Alberni String Quartet, the Philip Jones Brass Ensemble, and the British Broadcasting Corporation (BBC) Singers. Contributor to music journals.

WORK IN PROGRESS: Musical commissions.

SIDELIGHTS: Michael Short told *CA:* "My music ranges widely in scope, ranging from works especially commissioned for professional ensembles to pieces for amateurs, educational music, jazz arrangements, and radio commercials. Recently I have tended to specialize in music for wind ensemble and wind band.

"My interest in the music of Gustav Holst began when I collaborated with the composer's daughter, Miss Imogen Holst, in research into her father's music. Although my book on Holst is substantial, it was not intended to be definitive, and I am always interested in acquiring new information on Holst for inclusion in a possible future revision."

* * *

SILLIPHANT, Stirling (Dale) 1918-

PERSONAL: Born January 16, 1918, in Detroit, MI; son of Leigh Lemuel (a sales director) and Ethel May (Noaker) Silliphant; married Tiana Du Long (an actress; professional name Tiana Alexandra), July 4, 1974; children: Stirling, Dayle, Loren (deceased). *Education:* University of Southern California, B.A. (magna cum laude), 1938.

Avocational Interests: Ocean sailing, karate, traveling.

CAREER: Walt Disney Studios, Burbank, CA, publicist, 1938-41; Twentieth Century-Fox Film Corp., New York City, publicist, 1942, publicity director, 1946-53; screenwriter and independent producer in Hollywood, CA, 1953. President, Pingree Productions. *Military service:* U.S. Navy, 1942-46.

MEMBER: California Yacht Club, Writers Guild of America West, Mystery Writers of America, Authors League, Foreign Correspondents' Club (Thailand), Phi Beta Kappa.

AWARDS, HONORS: Academy Award ("Oscar"), Academy of Motion Picture Arts and Sciences, Edgar Award, Mystery Writers of America, and Golden Globe Award, Hollywood Foreign Press Association, all 1968, all for screenplay *In the Heat of the Night;* Golden Globe Award, 1969, for screenplay *Charly;* Image Award, National Association for the Advancement of Colored People (NAACP), 1972, for production of *Shaft;* box office writer of year awards, National Association of Theater Owners, 1972 and 1974.

WRITINGS:

Maracaibo (also see below), Farrar, Straus, 1955, Ballantine, 1985.
The Slender Thread (also see below), Signet, 1966.
(With Neil D. Isaacs) *Fiction into Film: A Walk in the Spring Rain* (includes the screenplay for *A Walk in the Spring Rain;* also see below), University of Tennessee Press, 1970.
Pearl (also see below), Dell, 1978, Mutual Publishing, 1991.
Steel Tiger, Ballantine, 1983.
Bronze Bell, Ballantine, 1985.
Silver Star, Ballantine, 1986.

SCREENPLAYS

(With William Bowers and John Barnwell) *Five against the House* (adapted from a story by Jack Finney), Columbia, 1955.
Huk! (adapted from a novel by Silliphant), United Artists, 1956.
Nightfall (adapted from the novel *The Dark Chase* by David Goodis), Columbia, 1957.
Damn Citizen, Universal, 1958.
The Lineup (adapted from the television series of the same title), Columbia, 1958.
(With Wolf Rilla and George Barclay) *Village of the Damned* (adapted from the novel *The Midwich Cuckoos* by John Wyndham), Metro-Goldwyn-Mayer, 1960.
The Slender Thread (adapted from the novel by Silliphant), Paramount, 1965.
In the Heat of the Night (adapted from the novel by John Ball), United Artists, 1967.
Charly (adapted from the short story "Flowers for Algernon" by Daniel Keyes), Cinerama, 1968.

Marlowe (adapted from the novel *The Little Sister* by Raymond Chandler), Metro-Goldwyn-Mayer, 1969.
(With Jesse Hill Ford) *The Liberation of Lord Byron Jones* (adapted from the novel by Ford), Columbia, 1970.
A Walk in the Spring Rain (adapted from the novel by Rachel Maddux), Columbia, 1970.
Murphy's War (adapted from the novel by Max Catto), Paramount, 1971.
The New Centurians (adapted from the novel by Joseph Wambaugh), Columbia, 1972.
(With Wendell Mayes) *The Poseidon Adventure* (adapted from the novel by Paul Gallico), Twentieth Century-Fox, 1972.
Shaft in Africa, Metro-Goldwyn-Mayer, 1973.
The Towering Inferno (based upon the novels *The Tower,* by Richard Martin Stern, and *The Glass Inferno,* by Thomas N. Scortia and Frank M. Robinson), Twentieth Century-Fox, 1974.
Killer Elite (adapted from the novel by Robert Rostand), United Artists, 1974.
(With Dean Reisner) *The Enforcer,* Warner Bros., 1976.
(With Peter Hyams) *Telefon,* Metro-Goldwyn-Mayer, 1977.
The Swarm (adapted from a novel by Arthur Herzog), Warner Bros., 1978.
(With Stanley Mann) *Circle of Iron* (also released as *The Silent Flute;* adapted from a story by Silliphant, Bruce Lee and James Coburn), Avco Embassy, 1979.
(With Carl Foreman) *When Time Ran Out* (adapted from the novel *The Day the World Ended* by Gordon Thomas), Warner Bros., 1980.
(With Sylvester Stallone) *Over the Top,* Cannon, 1987.
Catch the Heat (also released as *Feel the Heat*), Trans World, 1987.

TELEVISION SCRIPTS

(With others) *Mickey Mouse Club* (series), American Broadcasting Co. (ABC), 1955-59.
Brock Callahan (also broadcast as *The Silent Kill*), Columbia Broadcasting System, Inc. (CBS), August 11, 1959.
(With others) *Tightrope* (series; also known as *The Unnamed Agent* and *The Undercover Agent*), CBS, 1959-60.
(And creator) *Naked City* (series), ABC, 1960-63.
(And creator) *Route 66* (series), CBS, 1960-64.
(And producer) *New Healers,* ABC, March 27, 1972.
(And creator) *Movin' On,* National Broadcasting Co., Inc. (NBC), July 24, 1972.
(And creator) *Longstreet* (series), ABC, 1972-74.
(And executive producer) *Pearl* (mini-series; adapted from the novel by Silliphant), ABC, 1978.
(And producer) *Fly Away Home,* ABC, September 18, 1981.
Golden Gate, ABC, September 25, 1981.
Hardcase, NBC, December 6, 1981.
Travis McGee (based upon the stories by John D. MacDonald), ABC, May 18, 1982.
(And executive producer) *Welcome to Paradise,* CBS, June 12, 1984.
(And producer) *Mussolini: The Untold Story* (mini-series), NBC, 1985.
(With Dick Berg) *Space* (mini-series; adapted from the novel by James A. Michener), CBS, 1985.
(And producer, with Mel Damski) *The Three Kings* (mini-series), ABC, 1987.

Also author of mini-series *The Sands of Time,* and of television scripts for *Chrysler Theatre, Schlitz Play-House, Suspicion, Alfred Hitchcock Presents, G. E. Theatre, Alcoa-Goodyear Theater,* and *CBS Playhouse.*

Silliphant's novel *Pearl* was translated into Spanish.

ADAPTATIONS: Maracaibo was adapted for film by Ted Sherdeman and released by Paramount in 1958.

WORK IN PROGRESS: Pizzaro, an original screenplay.

SIDELIGHTS: Stirling Silliphant was working as the Eastern publicity manager for Twentieth Century-Fox in 1950 when he heard that a rival studio was looking for a script for Joan Crawford. Hoping to supply that script, he wrote *Maracaibo.* It was flatly rejected by the studio, but Silliphant reworked it into a novel, and, when published, his first book received excellent reviews. "Characterized by both taut and poignant writing, *Maracaibo* is off-beat adventure handled in a gripping off-beat way," wrote Rex Lardner in the *New York Times.* Ironically, film rights to the book were later purchased by Paramount, but when Silliphant applied for the job of screenwriter for that project, he was turned down.

Silliphant's next taste of screenwriting came while producing *The Joe Louis Story* in 1953. Unhappy with the script, he rewrote several sections of it. He told Catherine A. Peters in the *Chicago Tribune:* "When I saw the film, the only scenes I liked in it were the ones I had written. I said, 'Hey, maybe I'm a scriptwriter.' " Encouraged by his work on *The Joe Louis Story,* he bought the rights to a story by Jack Finney, *Five against the House,* wrote a screenplay based on that story, and produced the film. *Five against the House* was praised by A. H. Weiler in the *New York Times* as a "suspenseful diversion" with "crisp, idiomatic and truly comic dialogue and a story line that suffers only from surface characterizations." Silliphant followed this success by writing and producing what Peters terms a trio of film-noir classics: *Nightfall, Damn Citizen,* and *The Lineup.*

In 1959 Silliphant turned to television, creating and writing most of the scripts for two classic series, *Route 66* and

Naked City. Route 66 chronicled the adventures of two American drifters driving a Corvette; *Naked City* was a documentary-style police show set in New York. "Those were probably the most exciting, absorbing four years of my life," Silliphant told Peters. "I lived on the road, traveled all over the U.S. looking for ideas. Then I'd go to New York to work on *Naked City.* That's how I learned to meet deadlines. We'd have crews waiting for pages from my typewriter. Never missed a deadline." The high productivity demanded by television gave Silliphant an increased feeling of autonomy as a writer. He told Jay Stuller in *Writer's Digest:* "There's not as much time or money to waste [as in films] and so the writer's vision comes through stronger. I'm a defender of television and what can be done on it."

When the programs were cancelled, Silliphant returned to screenwriting. His 1967 film *In the Heat of the Night* won an Academy Award for best screenplay. Later work included a string of disaster films for producer Irwin Allen: *The Poseidon Adventure, The Towering Inferno, When Time Ran Out,* and *The Swarm.* Though generally dismissed by critics, these films were successes at the box office, and Silliphant was much in demand. "When producers call and want you to write a script from an idea, or write a screenplay from a novel, then you tend to feel satisfied, successful, wanted and admired. More than money, writing films was an ego thing. I could have been secure, at the top of my field, and gone on writing movies until the day I died. But I was not growing and developing," Silliphant told Stuller. Therefore, the writer returned to fiction with the 1983 publication of *Steel Tiger,* the first in a planned series of twelve novels detailing the adventures of John Locke, soldier of fortune. "The characters in this novel are lively and eccentric, . . . and the plot's complex action is fast paced," a *Publishers Weekly* reviewer wrote of *Steel Tiger.*

"Once you leave [Hollywood], the studios often won't let you back in," Silliphant told Stuller. Despite this and the fact that writing the novels "has represented a major financial change," it is something the author says he "had to do . . . I have some freedom and am finally released from committee- and group-thinking. . . . Most writing is pretty automatic for me. I like the emotional preparation of research; that's perhaps the best part. But in all 85,000 to 90,000 words of *Steel Tiger,* there are only about 5,000 words that are to me a mystery. Where I read back and feel a kind of magic, that third wind where you're in another place. . . . Those passages are what make you want to keep writing."

In 1987 Silliphant moved his family to Bangkok, where he is presently researching a long novel about American exports in Thailand and concentrating on original screenplays.

BIOGRAPHICAL/CRITICAL SOURCES:

BOOKS

Dictionary of Literary Biography, Volume 26: *American Screenwriters,* Gale, 1984.

PERIODICALS

American Film, March, 1988, pp. 13-15.
Chicago Tribune, April 3, 1980; August 23, 1983; February 15, 1987.
Christian Science Monitor, July 9, 1969.
Los Angeles Times, February 13, 1987.
Newsweek, January 31, 1972.
New Yorker, December 20, 1974.
New York Post, January 6, 1975.
New York Times, March 13, 1955; June 22, 1955; January 24, 1957; September 24, 1968; October 23, 1969; January 18, 1970; July 2, 1971; August 4, 1972; December 13, 1972; January 14, 1973; June 21, 1973; December 20, 1974; December 18, 1975; April 12, 1976; December 23, 1976; December 17, 1977; July 23, 1978; January 19, 1979; March 29, 1980; February 12, 1987.
Publishers Weekly, April 29, 1983.
Time, January 6, 1975.
Women's Wear Daily, December 18, 1974.
Writer's Digest, March, 1984.

* * *

SILVESTER, Frank
See BINGLEY, David Ernest

* * *

SINICROPI, Giovanni Andrea 1924-

PERSONAL: Born December 6, 1924, in Reggio Calabria, Italy; son of Domenico and Filomena (Catalano) Sinicropi; married; children: Cynthia, Philip, Adriana, Patricia, Sandra. *Education:* Universita di Messina, Dottore in Lettere e Filosofia, 1949; University of Toronto, M.A., Ph.D., 1963.

ADDRESSES: Home—63 Blue Ridge Dr., Manchester, CT 06040. *Office*—Department of Romance and Classical Languages, University of Connecticut, Storrs, CT 06268.

CAREER: University of Toronto, Toronto, Ontario, instructor, 1957-60, lecturer in Romance languages, 1960-62; Rutgers University, New Brunswick, NJ, assistant professor, 1964-66, associate professor of Romance and classical languages, 1966-70; University of Connecticut, Storrs, professor of Romance and classical languages, 1970—.

MEMBER: Modern Language Association of America, American Association of Teachers of Italian, Dante Society of America.

AWARDS, HONORS: Canada Council fellowship, 1961; American Philosophical Society grants, 1966, 1971, and 1976.

WRITINGS:

(Critical editor) *La natura nelle opere di Giovanni Verga,* Italica, 1960.

El arte nuevo y la tecnica dramatica de Lope de Vega, Mapocho (Chile), 1963.

(Contributor) *Pirandello,* Prentice-Hall, 1967.

Novelle di Giovanni Sercambi, Laterza, 1972.

Saggio sulle Soledades di Gongora, Cappelli, 1976.

Il Segno linguistico del Decamecon, Studi Sul Boccaccio, 1977.

The Metaphysical Dimension and Pirandello's Theater, Modern Drama, 1977.

Also contributor to periodicals, including *Studi Sul Boccaccio* and *Modern Drama.*

BIOGRAPHICAL/CRITICAL SOURCES:

PERIODICALS

Modern Language Review, July, 1978, p. 671.*

* * *

SKINNER, B(urrhus) F(rederic) 1904-1990

PERSONAL: Born March 20, 1904, in Susquehanna, PA; died of leukemia, August 18, 1990, in Cambridge, MA; son of William Arthur (an attorney) and Grace (Burrhus) Skinner; married Yvonne Blue, November 1, 1936; children: Julie Skinner Vargas, Deborah Skinner Buzan. *Education:* Hamilton College, A.B., 1929; Harvard University, M.A., 1930, Ph.D., 1931.

ADDRESSES: Home—11 Old Dee Rd., Cambridge, MA 02138. *Office*—William James Hall, Harvard University, Cambridge, MA 02138.

CAREER: Harvard University, Cambridge, MA, research fellow with National Research Council, 1931-32, junior fellow in Harvard Society of Fellows, 1933-36; University of Minnesota, Minneapolis, instructor, 1936-37, assistant professor, 1937-39, associate professor of psychology, 1939-45; Indiana University, Bloomington, professor of psychology and department chairman, 1945-48; Harvard University, Cambridge, William James Lecturer, 1947, professor of psychology, 1948-57, Edgar Pierce Professor of Psychology, 1958-74, professor emeritus, 1974-90. Lecturer. Conducted war research for the Office of Scientific Research and Development, 1942-43.

MEMBER: American Psychological Association, American Association for the Advancement of Science, Society of Experimental Psychologists, National Academy of Sciences, American Philosophical Society, American Academy of Arts and Sciences, Royal Society of Arts (fellow), Swedish Psychological Society, Phi Beta Kappa, Sigma Xi.

AWARDS, HONORS: Howard Crosby Warren Medal, 1942; Guggenheim fellow, 1944-45; National Institute of Mental Health career grant; American Psychological Association award, 1958; National Medal of Science, 1968; American Psychological Association gold medal, 1971; Joseph P. Kennedy, Jr., Foundation award, 1971; Humanist of the Year award, American Humanist Society, 1972; Creative Leadership in Education Award, New York University, 1972; American Educational Research Association award, 1978; National Association for Retarded Citizens first annual award, 1978; life-time achievement award, American Psychology Association, 1990. Honorary degrees from many universities and colleges, including Sc.D., University of Chicago, 1967, University of Exeter, 1969, and McGill University, 1970; Litt.D., Ripon College, 1961; LH.D., Rockford College, 1971; L.L.D., Ohio Wesleyan University, 1971.

WRITINGS:

(Editor with father, William A. Skinner) *A Digest of Decisions of the Anthracite Board of Conciliation,* [Scranton, PA], 1928.

Behavior of Organisms: An Experimental Analysis, Appleton-Century-Croft, 1938, reprinted, Prentice-Hall, 1966.

(With others) *Current Trends in Psychology* (lectures), University of Pittsburgh Press, 1947, reprinted, Arden Library, 1982.

Walden Two (novel), Macmillan, 1948, revised edition, Macmillan (London), 1969, published with introduction by Skinner, Macmillan, 1976.

Science and Human Behavior, Macmillan, 1953, reprinted, Irvington, 1979.

(Editor with Peter B. Dews) *Techniques for the Study of Behavioral Effects of Drugs,* Annals of the New York Academy of Sciences, 1956.

(With C.B. Ferster) *Schedules of Reinforcement,* Prentice-Hall, 1957.

Verbal Behavior, Prentice-Hall, 1957.

(Editor) *Cumulative Record: A Selection of Papers,* Prentice-Hall, 1959, 3rd edition, 1972.

(With James G. Holland) *The Analysis of Behavior: A Program for Self-Instruction,* McGraw, 1961.

Teaching Machines, Freeman, 1961.

(With others) *Understanding Maps: A Programmed Text,* Allyn, 1964.

(With Sue-Ann Krakower) *Handwriting with Write and See* (patented method of teaching writing), Lyons & Carnahan, 1968.

The Technology of Teaching, Prentice-Hall, 1968.

Earth Resources (textbook), Prentice-Hall, 1969, 2nd edition, 1976.

Contingencies of Reinforcement: A Theoretical Analysis, Prentice-Hall, 1969.

(With Arnold J. Toynbee and others) *On the Future of Art* (lectures), Viking, 1970.

Beyond Freedom and Dignity, Knopf, 1971.

About Behaviorism, Knopf, 1974.

Particulars of My Life (also see below; autobiography), Knopf, 1976.

Reflections on Behaviorism and Society, Prentice-Hall, 1978.

The Shaping of a Behaviorist: Part Two of an Autobiography (also see below), Knopf, 1979.

Notebooks, Prentice-Hall, 1981.

Skinner for the Classroom: Selected Papers, edited by Robert Epstein, Research Press (Champaign, IL), 1982.

A Matter of Consequences: Part Three of an Autobiography (also see below), Knopf, 1983.

(With Margaret E. Vaughn) *Enjoy Old Age: A Program of Self Management,* Norton, 1983, published in England as *How to Enjoy Your Old Age,* Sheldon Press, 1985.

Particulars of My Life [and] *The Shaping of a Behaviorist* [and] *A Matter of Consequences* (three-book set), New York University Press, 1984.

Upon Further Reflection, Prentice-Hall, 1987.

The Selection of Behavior: The Operant Behaviorism of B. F. Skinner: Comments and Consequences, edited by A. Charles Catania and Steven Harnad, Cambridge University Press, 1988.

Recent Issues in the Analysis of Behavior, Merrill, 1989.

RECORDINGS

(With Carl Rogers) *A Dialogue on Education and the Control of Human Behavior,* Jeffrey Norton, 1976.

(With Rogers) *Sound Seminars,* Jeffrey Norton, 1976.

Also recorded on three albums from the Center for the Study of Democratic Institutions.

SIDELIGHTS: An influential and controversial figure in modern psychology, B. F. Skinner was "the most famous of behaviorist psychologists," Harold Kaplan once stated in *Commentary.* Writing in *Behavioral and Brain Sciences,* Joseph M. Scandura called Skinner "contemporary behaviorism personified." His belief that people are controlled solely by external factors in the environment—specifically, that rewarded behavior is encouraged and unrewarded behavior is extinguished—and his rejection of the human individual as an autonomous being capable of independent, self-willed action made Skinner notorious among many of his colleagues. His supporters maintained, however, that Skinner made an important contribution to behaviorism and that his insights could be used to improve society radically.

Behaviorism, Daniel Goleman explained in the *New York Times,* "holds that people act as they do because of the rewards and punishments—positive and negative reinforcements—they have received. The mind and such things as memory and perception cannot be directly observed, and so . . . are unworthy of scientific study." "From the 1930s to the 1960s," Goleman reported, "behaviorism dominated academic psychology." The ideas and findings of behaviorism had a tremendous impact on such areas as drug and alcohol rehabilitation where the chief concern is behavior modification. Skinner stood out from most other behaviorists in that he not only dismissed the scientific analysis of human consciousness but also believed that "feelings and mental processes are just the meaningless byproducts of [the] endless cycle of stimulus and response," John Leo wrote in *Time.* As Skinner explained in *A Matter of Consequences,* the third volume of his autobiography, "I . . . do not think feelings are important. Freud is probably responsible for the current extent to which they are taken seriously." Skinner also advocated the use of "behavioral technology" to restructure society. He suggested that the same techniques that successfully train laboratory animals could be used to control man's negative behavior and thereby eliminate such social ills as crime, poverty, and war. Because his critics saw a totalitarian danger in his suggestions for social change, they called Skinner "politely, a social engineer; less politely, a neo-fascist," Elizabeth Mehren wrote in the *Los Angeles Times.* Despite such criticism, "Skinner . . . influenced everything from crib toys for babies to inventory management systems in industry," Webster Schott wrote in the *Washington Post Book World.*

Skinner's interest in psychology began in the 1920s. A college English major who for a time nurtured literary aspirations, he eventually shifted his focus to the scientific exploration of human behavior. Skinner's behaviorist beliefs were derived from a series of laboratory experiments he conducted using rats and pigeons during the 1930s and 1940s. By rewarding his test animals whenever they performed desired behavior—a process he called positive reinforcement—Skinner succeeded in training them to do a number of difficult tasks. His pigeons could play Ping-Pong, dance, walk in figure eights, and distinguish between colors. He taught rats to push buttons, pull strings, and push levers to receive food and drink. These experiments convinced Skinner that behavior control could be achieved through the manipulation of environmental stimuli. The special environment in which Skinner's animals were trained—an enclosed, soundproof box equipped with buttons, levers, and other training devices—was "a marvelous tool for conditioning animals," John Langone pointed out in *Discover.* Widely used by other researchers, this training environment became known as the Skinner Box.

Convinced that the techniques used on his pigeons and rats could work on human beings as well, Skinner built a training box for children in 1943. Called the Air-Crib by Skinner, but popularly dubbed the "baby box" by the media, the device was "nothing more than an elaborate, insulated, glassed-in crib with the temperature carefully controlled," Langone reported. It was designed to provide a child with "a very comfortable, stimulating environment," Skinner told Lawrence Meyer in the *Washington Post.* Skinner used the box for two and a half years while raising his daughter Deborah. When his account of the child-rearing experiment was published in the *Ladies' Home Journal,* it sparked a national controversy. Skinner was accused of carrying out monstrous experiments on his own children. He was attacked in newspaper editorials and featured on radio shows and in newsreels. His daughter suffered no ill effects from the experiment, grew up normally, and had a good relationship with her father. Nonetheless, Skinner's attempt to market the "baby box" under the name "Heir Conditioner" was a failure.

In 1948, Skinner speculated on how the findings from his laboratory work and his experiment with his daughter's upbringing could be applied to the structuring of society. In his novel *Walden Two,* he portrayed a behaviorist society in which positive and negative reinforcements were built into the social structure. The novel's plot revolved around a tour of the community taken by two college professors. As T. Morris Longstreth reported in the *Christian Science Monitor,* the community was conceived as "a sort of managed democracy." Children, raised in communal nurseries, were taught to think and learn instead of called upon to memorize specific facts. Theology and history were suppressed. All members of the society encouraged social harmony by practicing positive reinforcement for approved behavior. "One can admire much of this and only marvel that such large adjustments in human nature are to be bought at such a cheap price," Longstreth commented. Tabitha M. Powledge pointed out in *Nation* that in *Walden Two* "ideal social behavior is shaped by gentle means for good ends; the fascist dystopia which is equally possible from such techniques seems not to trouble [Skinner]." In his review of the novel for the *New York Times Book Review,* Charles Poore wondered "why anyone should want to spend his days in this antiseptic elysium," but allowed that the book was "a brisk and thoughtful foray in search of peace of mind, security, and a certain amount of balm for burnt-fingered moderns." Mehren described *Walden Two* as "a kind of behavioristic book of the Bible: a road map to a future in which free will would recede to the positive and negative reinforcements of culture and the environment." Speaking to *Psychology Today,* Skinner expressed some reservations about the book. "If I were to rewrite *Walden Two,*" he explained, "I would have more in it about the nitty-gritty conditions of our incentive systems. I was counting on everybody being willing to give four hours a day in exchange for the privilege of living in the community. That's Marx, and I don't think it really works. I would change *Walden Two*'s education. . . . I dealt too timidly with sex. . . . Also, *Walden Two* has no criminals, no psychotics, no retardates—I would do something about them now."

Where Skinner spoke fictionally about a new society in *Walden Two,* in *Beyond Freedom and Dignity,* described by Kaplan as "the culminating book of [Skinner's] career," he openly argued for radical social change based on behaviorist findings. "Almost all our major problems involve human behavior, and they cannot be solved by physical and biological technology alone. What is needed is a technology of behavior," Skinner asserted in the book. This proposed technology of behavior would utilize our knowledge about "the interaction between organism and environment" to design a society capable of altering man's destructive behavior through a system of positive and negative reinforcements. But before this could come about, Skinner maintained, the belief in an autonomous, self-directed individual and the related concepts of freedom and dignity must be discarded. Freedom and dignity, Skinner wrote, "are the possessions of the autonomous man of traditional theory, and they are essential to practices in which a person is held responsible for his conduct and given credit for his achievements. A scientific analysis shifts both the responsibility and the achievement to the environment."

Reaction to *Beyond Freedom and Dignity* was divided. Those critics opposed to Skinner's ideas thought his denial of human autonomy and his plans for social manipulation were incorrect and possibly dangerous. Writing in the *National Review,* Michael S. Gazzinaga stated: "No one denies reinforcement is an important controlling influence on our behavior. Skinner is correct to say we could order our society a little more logically than we do. But to extend the limited benefits of the obvious to a new worldview that eliminates concepts such as free will is both pretentious and incredibly naive." Kaplan called Skinner's proposals "nothing less than a bid for power by a new leader class, called, in [Skinner's] words, the 'technologists of behavior.' " Skinner "knows almost nothing about human beings," Robert Claiborne charged in a review of the volume for *Book World,* an opinion echoed by Richard Sennett, who claimed in the *New York Times Book Review* that Skinner "appears to understand so little, indeed to care so little, about society itself that the reader comes totally to distrust him."

But those who found value in *Beyond Freedom and Dignity* pointed to its basic insight that man's behavior is shaped by his environment, although some critics disagreed with Skinner's conclusions based on that insight. As Michael Novak wrote in *Beyond the Punitive Society: Operant Conditioning, Social and Political Aspects,* "few question the technical validity of his laboratory work, or even the technically expressed theory interpreting it. Many do question Professor Skinner's extrapolation therefrom." In another article in *Beyond the Punitive Society,* Karl H. Pribram argued that because of information omitted from the book, such as evidence that the human brain is modified by experience, Skinner's conclusions were not entirely correct. "Designs of cultures, therefore, cannot, in and of themselves, completely specify behavior," Pribram wrote. But there was "much good in the book," Pribram maintained, including "a good case for . . . behavioral technology." Pribram also admired "Skinner's contributions to our knowledge of the environmental contingencies that lead to reinforcement." W. F. Day, writing in *Contemporary Psychology,* stated that Skinner's "frontal attack on what he calls the concept of autonomous man" was essentially correct. We do "incalculable damage . . . to ourselves, to those we love, and to those others for whom we want to assume some responsibility when we base our social decisions on the model of autonomous man," Day declared. Gerald Marwell countered critics who saw Skinner's suggestions as totalitarian. In a *Contemporary Sociology* article, Marwell contended that what Skinner proposed was a society in which those who were controlled would have power over society's control mechanisms. Skinner "asserts that social control over populations will be exercised by someone. The choice which remains is only *who* shall control and by what means," Marwell explained.

The questions raised in *Beyond Freedom and Dignity* continued to be addressed in Skinner's three volumes of autobiography—*Particulars of My Life, The Shaping of a Behaviorist,* and *A Matter of Consequences.* Each of these books covered a particular period in Skinner's career. The first traced his childhood and education; the second addressed his years of research during the 1930s and 1940s; the third chronicled his later life as one of the leading psychologists in the country. Skinner's approach to autobiography reflected his beliefs about behavior and motivation. As he explained in *A Matter of Consequences:* "I have tried to report my life *as it was lived.* . . . I have seldom mentioned later significances. When I first bent a wire in the shape of a lever to be pressed by a rat, I was making the prototype of many thousands of levers, but did not know it then, and mentioning it would have been a mistake." This approach led Christopher Lehmann-Haupt in the *New York Times* to complain that "instead of reflecting on or trying to pick out and organize whatever shaped him as a behaviorist, Mr. Skinner simply slogs his way chronologically through the years." But Eugene Kennedy wrote in the *Chicago Tribune Book World* that *The Shaping of a Behaviorist* "opens to us the life of a genius."

The publication of the autobiographies gave critics the opportunity to appraise Skinner's contributions to his field. Schott suggested that "Skinner has been working at what scientists everywhere work at: meaning. Except he has devoted his life to the refinement of what precedes meaning—observation and description." In the Toronto *Globe and Mail,* Andrew Nikiforuk held that Skinner had "long argued that a scientific analysis of human behavior need not slight the dignity of mankind. Behaviorism, he says, examines what people do and why they do it, points to conditions that can be changed and shows the inadequacies of other views."

In the 1960s, by Goleman's account, the dominance behaviorist ideas had enjoyed began to wane in favor of "the so-called cognitive revolution" that "would go on to sweep psychology." "The vast majority of psychologists," according to Langone, "disagree strongly with [Skinner's] basic theories." Nonetheless, Harvey Mindess in the *Los Angeles Times Book Review* called Skinner "the undisputed leader of modern behaviorism" and possibly "the most influential American psychologist who ever lived." While he was, Kennedy pointed out, "the favorite villain of a wide range of supposedly intellectual Americans," he also "served as a model for scientists of all kinds, since his hypotheses flowed from the work he was doing, rather than from the fashion of the day." Skinner "made enormous contributions to [psychology] and demonstrated the awesome control the experimenter can have over the behavior of an animal under specified conditions," George W. Barlow wrote in *Behavioral and Brain Sciences.* Characterizing Skinner as "a man of many talents," Gazzinaga described him as "a superb writer, a brilliant polemicist, a clever inventor and a trained scientist," as well as "a philosopher manque and an incredible egoist."

The controversy Skinner's life and writings caused continued throughout his life, with most attention focusing on the validity of applying his laboratory findings about animal behavior and control to the structuring of modern society. Rosemary Dinnage stated her objections to Skinner's ideas in the *New York Times Book Review:* "The control it is possible to exercise over the behavior of small caged animals . . . has led Professor Skinner into the almost appealingly naive view that there is a science of behavior that can be used to control wars and all the other social problems that beset us. He has still to give practical proof of how this could be done." But within the field of psychology Skinner had many supporters for his theories. In *Behavioral and Brain Sciences,* H. J. Eysenck compared Skinner to Sigmund Freud: "It is no wonder that both men have formed a tightly knit group of supporters, founded their own journals, and have, in their attempt to inaugurate a new psychology, separated themselves from the broad basis of general psychology." Even in the final years of his life, outside criticism never diminished the intensity of Skinner's belief in the correctness of his theories. "Despite decades of controversy," Leo reported, "Skinner remains convinced that his principles of fifty years are correct." As Skinner wrote in *A Matter of Consequences:* "I am sometimes asked, 'Do you think of yourself as you think of the organisms you study?' The answer is yes."

BIOGRAPHICAL/CRITICAL SOURCES:

BOOKS

Chomsky, Noam, *For Reasons of State,* Pantheon, 1973.
Contemporary Issues Criticism, Volume 2, Gale, 1984.
Koestler, Arthur, *The Ghost in the Machine,* Hutchinson, 1967.
Skinner, B. F., *Beyond Freedom and Dignity,* Knopf, 1971.
Skinner, B .F., *Particulars of My Life,* Knopf, 1976.
Skinner, B. F., *The Shaping of a Behaviorist: Part Two of an Autobiography,* Knopf, 1979.
Skinner, B. F., *A Matter of Consequences: Part Three of an Autobiography,* Knopf, 1983.
Wheeler, Harvey, editor, *Beyond the Punitive Society: Operant Conditioning, Social and Political Aspects,* W. H. Freeman, 1973.

PERIODICALS

American Journal of Sociology, September, 1980.
Behavioral and Brain Sciences, December, 1984.
Book World, October 10, 1971.
Chicago Tribune Book World, May 20, 1979.
Christian Science Monitor, June 24, 1948.
Commentary, February, 1972.
Contemporary Psychology, September, 1972; September, 1979.
Contemporary Sociology, January, 1972.
Discover, September, 1983.
Globe and Mail (Toronto), March 10, 1984.
Journal of Individual Psychology, Volume 26, 1970.
Journal of the Experimental Analysis of Behavior, May, 1969; March, 1971.
Los Angeles Times, September 22, 1982.
Los Angeles Times Book Review, October 9, 1983.
Nation, July 28-August 4, 1979.
National Review, November 5, 1971; November 22, 1974.
New Republic, October 16, 1971; June 1, 1974; August 4, 1979.
New Yorker, October 9, 1971.
New York Review of Books, December 30, 1971.
New York Times, June 6, 1979; August 25, 1987; September 13, 1987.
New York Times Book Review, June 13, 1948; October 24, 1971; July 14, 1974; May 20, 1979; January 1, 1984.
Psychology Today, September, 1983.
Saturday Review, October 9, 1971.
Science, June 8, 1979.
Time, October 10, 1983.
Times Literary Supplement, February 29, 1975; December 4, 1981.
Washington Post, August 24, 1982.
Washington Post Book World, July 8, 1979.

OBITUARIES:

PERIODICALS

Chicago Tribune, August 20, 1990.
Detroit Free Press, August 20, 1990; August 21, 1990.
New York Times, August 20, 1990.
People, September 3, 1990.
Time, September 3, 1990.
Times (London), August 20, 1990.*

* * *

SMITH, D(wight) Moody, Jr. 1931-

PERSONAL: Born November 20, 1931, in Murfreesboro, TN; son of Dwight Moody and Nellie (Beckwith) Smith; married Jane Allen, November 26, 1954; children: Cynthia Beckwith, Catherine Mitchell, David Burton, John Allen. *Education:* Davidson College, A.B., 1954; Duke University, B.D., 1957; Yale University, M.A., 1958, Ph.D., 1961.

ADDRESSES: Home—2728 Spencer St., Durham, NC 27705. *Office*—Box 33, Divinity School, Duke University, Durham, NC 27706.

CAREER: Ordained minister of United Methodist Church, 1959; Methodist Theological School in Ohio, Delaware, instructor, 1960-61, assistant professor of New Testament, 1961-65; Duke University, Divinity School, Durham, NC, associate professor, 1965-70, professor of New Testament, 1970-87, George Washington Ivey Professor of New Testament, 1987—, director of graduate studies in religion, 1974-80. Visiting instructor at Ohio Wesleyan University, 1960-61. Center of Theological Inquiry fellow, 1990-91.

MEMBER: American Theological Society, Society for Values in Higher Education, Society of Biblical Literature, Studiorum Novi Testamenti Societas, Phi Beta Kappa.

AWARDS, HONORS: Lilly postdoctoral fellowship in religion, 1963-64; Guggenheim fellowship, 1970-71; Association of Theological Schools research grant, 1977-78.

WRITINGS:

The Composition and Order of the Fourth Gospel, Yale University Press, 1965.

(With Robert A. Spivey) *Anatomy of the New Testament,* Macmillan, 1969, 5th edition, 1994.

John (gospel commentary), Fortress, 1976, revised edition, 1986.

Interpreting the Gospels for Preaching, Fortress, 1980.

First, Second, and Third John, John Knox, 1991.

John among the Gospels: The Relationship in Twentieth-Century Research, Fortress, 1992.

The Theology of the Gospel of John, Cambridge University Press, in press.

Also contributor to numerous books, including *Interpreter's Dictionary of the Bible,* edited by George A. Buttrick and Keith R. Crim, Abingdon, 1976; *Harper's Bible Dictionary,* edited by Paul J. Achtemeier, Harper, 1985; *Encyclopedia of Religion,* Macmillan, 1987. Contributor to *Journal of Biblical Literature, New Testament Studies, Journal of Religion, Interpretation, Catholic Biblical Quarterly, Biblica, Perspectives in Religious Studies, Religious Studies Review,* and *Journal of American Academy of Religion.*

WORK IN PROGRESS: Research on the relationship of the Gospel of John to other Gospels; commentaries on the Gospel of John and the Epistles of John.

* * *

SMITH, Murphy D(e Witt) 1920-

PERSONAL: Born October 16, 1920, in Birmingham, AL; son of Murphy De Witt (a mechanic) and Damie Emmaline (Hogan) Smith. *Education:* University of Tennessee, B.A., 1949, M.A., 1950; additional study at University of Pennsylvania.

ADDRESSES: Office—American Philosophical Society Library, 105 South Fifth St., Philadelphia, PA 19106.

CAREER: American Philosophical Society Library, Philadelphia, PA, manuscripts librarian, 1952-70, associate librarian, 1971-84.

MEMBER: American Historical Association, Manuscripts Society.

WRITINGS:

A Guide to Manuscripts Relating to the American Indian in the Library of the American Philosophical Society, American Philosophical Society, 1966.

Guide to the Archives and Manuscript Collections of the American Philosophical Society, American Philosophical Society, 1966.

Oak from an Acorn: A History of the American Philosophical Society Library, 1770-1803, Scholarly Resources, 1976.

Sherman Day: Artist, Forty-Niner, Engineer, Michael Glazier, 1980.

Historical American Sketches: An Illustrated Guide to Sketches in the Manuscript Collections of the American Philosophical Society, G. K. Hall, 1984.

Realms of Gold: A Catalogue of the Map Collection in the Library of the American Philosophical Society, American Philosophical Society, 1991.

Due Reverence: Antiques in the Possession of the American Philosophical Society, American Philosophical Society, 1993.

A Museum: The History of the Cabinet of Curiosities of the American Philosophical Society, American Philosophical Society, 1994.

Contributor to professional journals.

WORK IN PROGRESS: Travel through North America to view Indian remains, with a book expected to result; "wide-ranging travel which I hope to utilize for a personal history of travel in my lifetime."

SIDELIGHTS: Murphy D. Smith told *CA:* "My work has been done to make the riches of the collections of the American Philosophical Library more generally known and available for all researchers."

* * *

SMITH, Richard Joseph 1944-

PERSONAL: Born October 30, 1944, in Sacramento, CA; son of Joseph B. (a teacher) and Margaret E. (a teacher; maiden name, Stoddard) Smith; married Alice E. Weisenberger (a teacher), July 1, 1967; children: Tyler. *Education:* University of California, Davis, A.B., 1966, M.A., 1968, Ph.D., 1972. *Politics:* Independent. *Religion:* None.

ADDRESSES: Office—Department of History, Rice University, Houston, TX 77251.

CAREER: Sacramento State College (now University), Sacramento, CA, lecturer in history, 1969; Chinese University of Hong Kong, Hong Kong, China, lecturer in history, 1971-72; University of California, Davis, lecturer in history, 1972-73; Rice University, Houston, TX, assistant professor, 1973-78, associate professor, 1979-82, professor of history, 1983—. Adjunct professor at University of Texas at Austin, 1977—. Member of National Committee on U.S.-China Relations and Texas China Council; president of Texas Foundation for China Studies, 1989-92.

MEMBER: Society for Ch'ing Studies, Society for the Study of Chinese Religions, Association for Asian Studies, Asia Society (member of local advisory committee), Southwest Conference on Asian Studies (member of board of directors, 1979-81, 1989-92; president, 1990-91).

AWARDS, HONORS: Nine teaching awards, including the Minnie Stevens Piper Professorship, 1987, and the George R. Brown Certificate of Highest Merit, 1992.

WRITINGS:

Mercenaries and Mandarins: The Ever-Victorious Army in Nineteenth-Century China, Kraus-Thomson, 1978.
Traditional Chinese Culture: An Interpretive Introduction, Rice University Press, 1978.
(Editor with B. E. Wallacker, R. G. Knapp, and A. J. Van Alstyne) *Chinese Walled Cities: A Collection of Maps from Shina Jokaku no Gaiyo,* Chinese University Press, 1979.
China's Cultural Heritage: The Ch'ing Dynasty 1644-1912, Westview, 1983, second revised and expanded edition, 1994.
(Editor with J. K. Fairbank and Katherine Bruner) *Entering China's Service: The Early Career of Robert Hart 1853-1863,* Harvard University Press, 1985.
Fortune-tellers and Philosophers: Divination in Traditional Chinese Society, Westview, 1991.
(Editor with Fairbank and Bruner) *Robert Hart and China's Early Modernization,* Harvard University Press, 1991.
Chinese Almanac, Oxford University Press, 1992.
(Editor with D. W. Y. Kwok) *Cosmology, Ontology, and Human Efficacy: Essays in Chinese Thought,* University of Hawaii Press, 1993.

Author of photographic slide programs on China, with commentary. Contributor to history and Asian studies journals.

SIDELIGHTS: Richard Joseph Smith once told *CA:* "The present scholarly fashion in the study of premodern China is to emphasize the particularism of local and 'popular' culture rather than the 'holism' of elite culture. This trend toward 'disaggregation' (most recently advocated in Paul Cohen's historiographical critique of American scholarship on China) has much to commend it. But the dialectic between holistic and particularistic studies of China must not be abandoned. How, after all, can we discuss dissidence, diversity, and change without a better understanding of consensus, conformity, and continuity? Surely China is more than the sum of its parts. The purpose of my book *China's Cultural Heritage,* as well as my books on divination and Chinese almanacs, is to explore the relationship between the perceptions, attitudes, and practices of different social groups in China, as well as to understand that relationship in terms of space (i.e., regional variations) and time (history)."

BIOGRAPHICAL/CRITICAL SOURCES:

PERIODICALS

American Historical Review, December, 1979.
Canadian Journal of History, December, 1979.
Chinese Culture, December, 1984.
Focus on Asian Studies, winter, 1984.
Journal of Asian Studies, November, 1979; February, 1985.
Military Affairs, December, 1979.
Ming Studies, spring, 1985.

* * *

SMITH, Robert G(illen) 1913-

PERSONAL: Born October 16, 1913, in Dover, NJ; son of John W. (a publisher) and Elizabeth (Gillen) Smith; married Lois Squier, December 23, 1942; children: Robert L., Donald P. *Education:* Drew University, A.B. (summa cum laude), 1936; Columbia University, M.A., 1939, Ph.D., 1950, postdoctoral study, 1953-55; New York University, postdoctoral study, 1962.

ADDRESSES: Home and office—250 Rugby Rd., Arnold, MD 21012.

CAREER: Drew University, Madison, NJ, instructor in history, 1940-44, assistant professor, 1944-54, professor of political science, 1954-71, Pfeiffer Professor of Political Science, 1971-77, emeritus professor, 1977—, founder and chair of department, 1946-71, founder and director of off-campus programs in London, Washington, DC, and United Nations, 1962-71, founder and director of Institute for Research on Government, 1964-77. Adjunct professor of political science, Hunter College of the City University of New York, 1965-67; visiting professor of public administration, New York University, 1966-67; lecturer on educational television series, Center for New York City Affairs, New School for Social Research, 1967; chairman of board of directors of university fellowship program, College-Federal Agency Council (of U.S. Civil Service Commission), 1969—. Political commentator, WDHA-FM radio, 1963-65. Pioneer consultant on special purpose government, 1950—; consultant, New York City commission on city-state relations, 1972—; consultant, Transportation Research Board, National Research Council, 1979—.

Military service: U.S. Army, editor of medical publications from Office of the Surgeon General, 1943-45, chief medical historian, China theater, 1945-46; received Bronze Star.

MEMBER: Morris-Somerset United Nations Association (member of board of directors, 1963-70), International Political Science Association, American Association of University Professors, American Political Science Association, American Public Transit Association, American Society for Public Administration (senior member; member of New Jersey executive council, 1965-67), Conference of University Bureaus of Government Research, National Municipal League, New Jersey Social Science Academy (president, 1965-67), New Jersey Association of High School Political Science Clubs, Policy Studies Organization.

AWARDS, HONORS: Alumni Achievement award, Drew University, 1960; Federal Agency Council plaque, 1965; Danforth Foundation grant, 1967; Eagleton Foundation grant, 1967; Ford Foundation grant, 1967; Twentieth Century Fund grant, 1967; National Science Foundation grant, 1971; LL.D., Drew University, 1977; Robert G. Smith Scholarships established, Drew University, 1979, 1983; campus political science building dedicated as the Robert G. Smith House, Drew University, 1983.

WRITINGS:

(Editor with George Ainlay, and contributor) *Military Medical Manual,* Medical Service Publishing, 1945.

Public Authorities, Special Districts, and Local Government, Research Foundation, National Association of Counties, 1964.

(Editor and contributor) *Metropolitan Problems as Presented by Eight of America's Recognized Experts,* Drew University, 1966.

Public Authorities, Special Districts, and Local Government: A Digest of Excerpts, Research Foundation, National Association of Counties, 1969.

Public Authorities in Urban Areas, Research Foundation, National Association of Counties, 1969.

Ad Hoc Governments: Special Public Transportation Authorities in Britain and the United States, Sage Publications, 1974.

Contributor to *Perspectives in Pragmatism,* edited by William Kroeger and J. George Longworth, Center for New York City Affairs, 1967; *Guide to County Organization and Management,* National Association of Counties, 1968; *The Municipal Governing Body in New Jersey,* Bureau of Government Research and University Extension Division, Rutgers University, 1970; and *Public Authorities and Public Policy,* edited by Jerry Mitchell, Greenwood Press, 1992. Also contributor to *Dictionary of Political Science* and to periodicals, including *New Jersey Municipalities, Drew University Magazine, Bulletin of the Metropolitan Regional Council, Airport Operators Council Management Handbook, Public Management* and *Policy Studies Journal.*

WORK IN PROGRESS: A study of the role of public authorities as implementers of public policy on all levels.

BIOGRAPHICAL/CRITICAL SOURCES:

BOOKS

Cunningham, John T., *University in the Forest,* Afton Publishing, 1972.

* * *

SMITH, Robert Kimmel 1930-
(Peter Marks)

PERSONAL: Born July 31, 1930, in Brooklyn, NY; son of Theodore (in civil service) and Sally (Kimmel) Smith; married Claire Medney (a literary agent), September 4, 1954; children: Heidi Medney, Roger Kimmel. *Education:* Attended Brooklyn College (now Brooklyn College of the City University of New York), 1947-48.

ADDRESSES: Home—210 Rugby Rd., Brooklyn, NY 11226. *Agent*—(Literary) Harold Ober Associates, 40 East 49th St., New York, NY 10017; (television/plays) Lois Berman, WB Agency, 156 East 52nd St., New York, NY 10022.

CAREER: Writer. Doyle, Dane, Bernback (advertising agency), New York City, copywriter, 1957-61; Grey Advertising, New York City, copy chief, 1963-65; Smith & Toback (advertising agency), New York City, partner and writer, 1967-70, full-time writer, 1970—. *Military service:* U.S. Army, 1951-53.

MEMBER: Authors Guild, Writers Guild, Dramatists Guild, Eugene O'Neill Theatre Center, Eugene O'Neill Playwrights (co-chairman, 1974-75), Kayoodle Club (president, 1969).

AWARDS, HONORS: ANDY Award, Advertising Club of New York, 1967; CLIO Award for creative excellence in advertising, 1968; named Eugene O'Neill Playwright, 1971, for *A Little Singing;* OPIE Award for best comic novel, 1973, for *Sadie Shapiro's Knitting Book;* Massachusetts Children's Book Award, 1980, for *Chocolate Fever; Jane's House* was named one of the best books of 1982 by the American Library Association; Young Hoosier Award, 1984, Carolina Children's Book Award, 1984, and Nene Award, 1986, all for *Jelly Belly;* Dorothy Canfield Fisher Award, 1986, South Carolina Childrens Book Award, 1986, William Allen White Award, 1987, Mark Twain Award, 1987, and Pacific Northwest Young Readers Choice Award, 1987, all for *The War with Grandpa.*

WRITINGS:

Ransom (novel), McKay, 1971.
A Little Singing (play), first produced at O'Neill Memorial Theatre, CT, July, 1971.
Up in Smoke (play), first produced at Berkshire Theater Festival, MA, winter, 1972.
Sadie Shapiro's Knitting Book, Simon & Schuster, 1973.
A Little Dancing (play), published in *Best Short Plays of 1975,* edited by Stanley Richards, Chilton, 1975.
Sadie Shapiro in Miami, Simon & Schuster, 1977.
Sadie Shapiro, Matchmaker, Simon & Schuster, 1979.
Jane's House (novel), Morrow, 1982.

Also author of teleplays. Contributor of short fiction to periodicals, writing under pseudonym Peter Marks prior to 1970.

JUVENILE

Chocolate Fever, Coward, 1972.
Jelly Belly, Delacorte, 1981.
The War with Grandpa, Delacorte, 1984.
Mostly Michael, Delacorte, 1987.
Bobby Baseball, Delacorte, 1989.
The Squeaky Wheel, Dell, 1992.

OTHER

Sadie Shapiro's Knitting Book has been translated into ten languages.

SIDELIGHTS: Robert Kimmel Smith told *CA:* "In 1970, at the age of forty, I decided to give full-time writing a shot and haven't looked back since. I published four novels and a juvenile within the next decade, wrote three plays and a number of television scripts. Most of my work turned out to be on the humorous side."

Smith's first commercial success came with the publication of his 1973 novel *Sadie Shapiro's Knitting Book.* In it we meet Sadie Shapiro, a slightly eccentric septuagenarian who, while out jogging, meets Marian Wall, an editor with a failing publishing company. Inspired, Sadie composes a how-to book on knitting and submits it to Marian for publication. The book becomes something of a phenomenon, revitalizing Marian's career and launching Sadie onto the celebrity circuit. "Robert Kimmel Smith translates the banality of book promotion into broad, old-fashioned farce," says a reviewer for the *New York Times Book Review.* The novel garnered Smith an OPIE award in 1973, and earned a large enough audience to warrant two more books, *Sadie Shapiro in Miami* and *Sadie Shapiro, Matchmaker.*

By 1980, Smith said in a *Publishers Weekly* interview, "I had a liking for trying to write something bigger in scope than just Sadie Shapiro. I think I know how to tell a story and create real characters. I wanted to prove I could write a serious book, too." The result of this determination was *Jane's House,* published in 1982. Inspired by a serious injury suffered by Smith's wife, Claire, *Jane's House* is the story of a woman's abrupt death, and the efforts of her husband and children to live on without her. The house, which the late Jane had kept running smoothly, becomes the standard by which the widower and, later, his new bride, are judged, both by the children and themselves. While a reviewer in the *West Coast Review of Books* admits that the story of *Jane's House* is not original, it is told with "a calm, wry humor that makes virtually every page a joy to read. It makes you cry without being sentimental; it makes you laugh without being silly. It contains some of the most superbly funny scenes since the Marx Brothers." The novel did not fare so well with some British critics, however; *Times Literary Supplement* reviewer Claire Duchen calls *Jane's House* "a morass of American schmaltz" that "takes the highly sensitive issue of the reconstituted family and steamrollers all over it."

In recent years, Smith has concentrated almost exclusively on children's books. This type of writing is not new to him: in 1972 he wrote the award-winning *Chocolate Fever,* a book based upon one of his daughter's favorite bedtime stories. He has since received numerous other awards for children's literature, including the 1987 Mark Twain Award for *The War with Grandpa.* "Writing juveniles has been very rewarding," Smith told *CA.* "Kids are a responsive audience. I'll continue to be funny for them."

BIOGRAPHICAL/CRITICAL SOURCES:

PERIODICALS

Los Angeles Times Book Review, July 25, 1982, p. 9.
New York Times Book Review, October 10, 1971, p. 46; July 16, 1972, p. 8; May 13, 1973, p. 39; April 26, 1981, p. 68; May 13, 1984, p. 21.
Observer, August 6, 1972, p. 25.
Times Literary Supplement, November 16, 1973, p. 1407; December 17, 1982, p. 1398.
Washington Post Book World, June 10, 1973, p. 15.
West Coast Review of Books, November, 1977, p. 27; November, 1982, p. 32.

* * *

SMITH, Shirley M(ae) 1923- (Ellis Ovesen)

PERSONAL: Born July 18, 1923, in New Effington, SD; daughter of Einar W. and Augustine (Ovesen) Johnson; married Thor Lowe Smith (a chemist), August 28, 1949; children: Theodore Lowe, Glen Everett. *Education:* University of Wisconsin, M.A. (cum laude), 1948; San Jose

State Collge (now University), California teachers credential, 1962. *Religion:* Christian.

Avocational Interests: Art, prophecy, travel, golf, bowling, gardening, bird watching, collecting rocks, singing and religious dancing.

ADDRESSES: Home—Box 482, Los Altos, CA 94023.

CAREER: Poet. English instructor at University of Wisconsin—Milwaukee, 1946-48 and San Jose State College, 1963; Poetry instructor, Terman Junior High School, 1970. Advertising copywriter at E. I. duPont Co., 1948-49.

MEMBER: American Association of University Women (publicity chair, 1949-53), National League of American Pen Women, National Writers Club, National Poetry Society, Poetry Society of America, Women's Museum of Art, California State Poetry Society (president), California Federation of Chaparral Poets (founder and president of Toyon branch, 1969-70), California Writers Club, San Francisco Poetry Society, Pacific Art League, Peninsula Poets (charter member and president), South Dakota Music Composers, Palo Alto Art Club.

AWARDS, HONORS: Second place award for beauty of content and design, Printing Industries of America, 1974, for *Lives Touch;* Los Altos Hills Poet, 1976-90; honorable mention, National League of American Pen Women Biennial, 1977, for *A Time for Singing;* Honorary Ph.D., World Academy of Arts and Culture, 1986; Dame of Merit, Knights of Malta, 1988; Golden Poet award, 1988, 1989; World Poet, 1989.

WRITINGS:

POETRY; UNDER PSEUDONYM ELLIS OVESEN

Gloried Grass, West Coast Lithographers, 1970.
Haloed Paths, American Poetry Fellowships, 1972.
Lives Touch, St. Mary's Press, 1973.
(With Helen Carter King) *To Those Who Love,* Harlo, 1974.
The Last Hour, American Poetry Fellowships, 1975.
A Book of Praises, Golden Quill, 1977.
A Time for Singing (self-illustrated haiku), American Poetry Fellowships, 1977.
Beloved I, American Poetry Fellowships, 1980.
The Green Madonna, Golden Quill Press, 1984.
The Wing Brush, Golden Quill, 1986.
The Year of the Horse: A Book of Poems and Prophecies, Golden Quill Press, 1991.

Also author of *The Keeper of the Word,* 1985; *The Flowers of God,* 1985; *The Year of the Snake,* 1989; *Beloved II,* 1990; *Another Man's Moccasins.*

SMITH, T(homas) Lynn 1903-1977

PERSONAL: Born November 11, 1903, in Sanford, CO; died 1977; son of Nephi Nathaniel (a farmer and stockman) and Emma (Holyoak) Smith; married Louvina Jackson, May 29, 1928; children: Jackson Lynn, Richard Lisle. *Education:* Brigham Young University, B.S., 1928; University of Minnesota, M.A., 1929, Ph.D., 1932; Harvard University, graduate study, 1930-31. *Politics:* Democrat.

ADDRESSES: Home—Gainesville, FL

CAREER: Louisiana State University, Baton Rouge, became professor and department head, 1931-47; Vanderbilt University, Nashville, TN, professor and head of sociology department, director of Institute for Brazilian studies, 1947-49; University of Florida, Gainsville, professor of sociology, 1949-59, graduate research professor, 1959-74, head of sociology department, 1961-64, professor emeritus of sociology, 1974—. Senior agricultural analyst with assignments to Brazil, Colombia, and El Salvador, U.S. Department of State, 1942-1945.

MEMBER: International Population Union, Institut International de Sociologie, Asociacion de Sociologos de Lengua Espanola y Portuguesa, Inter-American Statistical Institute, American Philosophical Society (fellow, 1970), Population Association of America (first vice-president, 1963-64), American Sociological Association, Rural Sociological Society (president, 1941), Southern Sociological Society (president, 1947), Omicron Delta Kappa.

AWARDS, HONORS: Doctor honoris causa, Universidade de Brasil, 1946, Universidade de Sao Paulo, (1949), and Order of Southern Cross, Brazilian Government, 1953, all for *Brazil: People and Institutions*; outstanding achievement award, University of Minnesota, 1959.

WRITINGS:

The Sociology of Rural Life, Harper, 1940.
Brazil: People and Institutions, Louisiana State University Press, 1946.
Population Analysis, McGraw, 1948.
(With C. A. McMahan) *The Sociology of Urban Life,* Dryden, 1950.
(With Alexander Marchant) *Brazil: Portrait of Half a Continent,* Dryden, 1951.
(Editor) *The Problems of America's Aging Population,* University of Florida Press, 1951.
(With H. L. Hitt) *The People of Louisiana,* Louisiana State University Press, 1952.
(Editor) *Living in the Later Years,* University of Florida Press, 1952.
Analise de Populacao, Universidade do Brasil, 1954.

(Contributor) *Social Problems,* Crowell, 1955.

Fundamentals of Population Study, Lippincott, 1960.

Sociologia Rural, Universidad del Zulia, 1963.

(Editor) *Agrarian Reform in Latin America,* Knopf, 1965.

Colombia: Studies of Social Structures and the Process of Development, University of Florida Press, 1967.

The Process of Rural Development in Latin America, University of Florida Press, 1967.

Studies of Latin American Societies, Doubleday, 1970.

(With Paul E. Zopf) *Demography: Principles and Methods,* F. A. Davis, 1970.

(With Zopf) *Principles of Inductive Rural Sociology,* F. A. Davis, 1970.

Organizacao Rural: Problemas e Solucoes, edited by Jose Arthur Rios, Biblioteca Pioneira de Ciencias Socias, 1971.

The Sociology of Agricultural Development, E. J. Brill, 1972.

Brazilian Society, University of New Mexico Press, 1974.

Studies of the Great Rural Tap Roots of Urban Poverty in the United States, Carlton, 1974.

The Race between Population and Food Supply in Latin America, University of New Mexico Press, 1976.

A Legacy of Knowledge: Sociological Contributions of T. Lynn Smith, edited by Thomas R. Ford, Joseph S. Vandiver, and Man Singh Das, [India], 1980.

Managing editor of periodical *Rural Sociology,* 1936-41; contributor of articles to professional journals.

SIDELIGHTS: T. Lynn Smith told *CA* that his principle motivation was "to help develop a genuine pragmatic science of society. To this end I have done my best to become acquainted personally with all sections of the United States, have learned Spanish and Portuguese (in addition to the French and German I learned as a student), and have devoted many years of my time to research, travel, and teaching in Brazil, Colombia, Mexico, Chile, and the other Latin American countries, and to research in Spain and Portugal."*

* * *

SOLOMON, Barbara H. 1936-

PERSONAL: Born September 25, 1936, in Brooklyn, NY; daughter of Lothar and Rose (maiden name, Gruber) Hochster; married Stanley J. Solomon (a professor of communication arts and writer of film books), January 26, 1958; children: Nancy Jane, Jennifer Ann. *Education:* Brooklyn College (now Brooklyn College of the City University of New York), B.A., 1958; University of Kansas, M.A., 1960; University of Pittsburgh, Ph.D., 1968.

ADDRESSES: Residence—New Rochelle, NY. *Office*—Department of English, Iona College, New Rochelle, NY 10801.

CAREER: Doane College, Crete, NE, instructor in English, 1960-62; Temple University, Philadelphia, PA, instructor in English, 1965-67; Iona College, New Rochelle, NY, assistant professor, 1969-70, associate professor, 1976-80, professor of English, 1980—.

MEMBER: Modern Language Association of America.

WRITINGS:

EDITOR

The Awakening and Selected Stories of Kate Chopin, New American Library, 1976.

The Experience of the American Woman: Thirty Stories, New American Library, 1978.

Short Fiction of Sarah Orne Jewett and Mary Witkins Freeman, New American Library, 1979.

Ain't We Got Fun?: Essays, Lyrics, and Stories of the Twenties, New American Library, 1980.

(With Paula S. Berggren) *A Mary Wollstonecraft Reader,* New American Library, 1983.

American Wives: Thirty Short Stories by Women, New American Library, 1986.

American Families: Twenty-Eight Short Stories, New American Library, 1989.

OTHER

Contributor to *The Classic Cinema: Essays in Criticism,* edited by Stanley J. Solomon, Harcourt, 1973. Also contributor to *Conradiana.*

WORK IN PROGRESS: Editing *Modern Women Writers: Essays in Feminist Criticism* (tentative title), with Constance Ayers Denne.

SIDELIGHTS: Barbara Solomon once told *CA:* "As a writer and teacher, my major area of special interest is feminist literary criticism—particularly of American literature. I teach courses on the image of women in modern American fiction on both undergraduate and graduate levels."

* * *

SPARTACUS, Tertius
See BURGESS, Michael (Roy)

* * *

STANTON, Edward F(eagler) 1942-

PERSONAL: Born October 29, 1942, in Colorado Springs, CO; son of Edward F. (self-employed) and Rose

(Sunseri) Stanton; married Raquel Diaz, June 16, 1970 (divorced); children: Daniel E., Carlos A. *Education:* University of California, Los Angeles, B.A., 1964, M.A., 1969, Ph.D., 1972.

ADDRESSES: Office—Department of Spanish and Italian, University of Kentucky, Lexington, KY 40506.

CAREER: University of Kentucky, Lexington, assistant professor, 1972-78, associate professor, 1978-88, professor of Spanish and Italian, 1989—.

MEMBER: Modern Language Association of America, Hemingway Society, Phi Beta Kappa.

WRITINGS:

The Tragic Myth: Federico Garcia Lorca and Cante Jondo, University Press of Kentucky, 1978.
(Editor with Frederick C. H. Garcia) *The Uruguay,* University of California Press, 1982.
Hemingway and Spain: A Pursuit, University of Washington Press, 1989.
Road of Stars to Santiago, University Press of Kentucky, in press.

Contributor of articles, poems, translations, and reviews to literary journals in the United States and abroad, including *Antioch Review, Epoch, Hemingway Review, New River Review,* and *Symposium.*

Hemingway and Spain: A Pursuit has been translated into Spanish and published by Castalia (Madrid), 1989.

WORK IN PROGRESS: Rages and Ennuis, poems; *Vida: A Life,* an autobiography.

* * *

STARR, Henry
See BINGLEY, David Ernest

* * *

STEWART, Frank 1946-

PERSONAL: Born May 3, 1946, in Grand Island, NE; son of Emmett and Frances (Swann) Stewart; married in 1968 (divorced, 1974); children: Chloe. *Education:* Attended University of New Mexico, 1964-65, and American University, 1965-66; University of Hawaii, B.A., 1968, M.A., 1972; attended Harvard University, summer, 1972.

ADDRESSES: Office—Department of English, University of Hawaii, Honolulu, HI 96822.

CAREER: Barre Publishers and Imprint Society, Barre, MA, production manager and editor, 1972-73; free-lance technical editor and compositor in Honolulu, HI, 1973-74; University of Hawaii, Honolulu, instructor, 1974-80, assistant professor, 1980-85, associate professor, 1985-92, professor of English 1992—. Director of Petronium Press, 1975—.

MEMBER: Hawaii Literary Arts Council (founding president, 1974).

AWARDS, HONORS: Whiting Writer's Award, 1986.

WRITINGS:

(Editor with Eric Chock and others) *Talk Story: An Anthology of Hawaii's Local Writers,* Petronium Press, 1978.
(Editor with John Unterecker) *Poetry Hawaii: A Contemporary Anthology,* University of Hawaii Press, 1979.
(Editor with Linda Spalding) *InterChange: A Symposium on Regionalism, Internationalism, and Ethnicity in Literature,* InterArts Hawaii, 1980.
The Open Water (poetry), Floating Island, 1981.
Reunion (poetry), Paper Press, 1986.
Flying the Red Eye (poetry), Floating Island, 1986.
(Editor) *Passages to the Dream Shore: Short Stories of Contemporary Hawaii,* University of Hawaii Press, 1987.
(Editor) *A World between Waves: Essays on Hawaii's Natural History,* Island Press/Shearwater Books, 1992.

Also author of script for television documentary, *Ka Na'i Pono: Striving for Excellence,* broadcast in 1983 by Hawaii Public Television. Contributor of poetry and essays to anthologies, including *Peace Is Our Profession,* East River, 1981; *Carrying the Darkness: The Poetry of the Vietnam War,* Avon, 1985; *Editor's Choice II,* The Spirit That Moves Us Press, 1987; *Crossing the River: An Anthology of Poets of the Western U.S.,* Permanent Press, 1987; *Men of Our Time,* University of Georgia Press, 1992; *Nature's New Voices,* Fulcrum, 1992. Contributor of poetry, translations, essays, and book reviews to periodicals, including *Southwest Review, Ploughshares, Indiana Review, Ironwood, Ohio Review, American Book Review, Los Angeles Times Book Review, Brick,* and *Modern Poetry Studies.* Co-editor with Robert Shapard of *Manoa: A Pacific Journal of International Writing,* University of Hawaii Press, 1989—.

* * *

STEWART, Fred Mustard 1936-

PERSONAL: Born September 17, 1936, in Anderson, IN; son of Simeon (a banker) and Janet (Mustard) Stewart; married Joan Richardson (a theatrical agent), March 18, 1968. *Education:* Princeton University, A.B., 1954.

ADDRESSES: Home—P.O. Box 632, Sharon, CT 06069.

CAREER: Novelist. *Military Service:* U.S. Coast Guard, 1955-58; became lieutenant junior grade.

MEMBER: PEN.

WRITINGS:

The Mephisto Waltz, Coward, 1969.
The Methuselah Enzyme, Arbor House, 1970.
Lady Darlington, Arbor House, 1971.
The Mannings, Arbor House, 1973.
Star Child, Arbor House, 1974.
Six Weeks, Arbor House, 1976.
A Rage against Heaven, Viking, 1978.
Century, Morrow, 1981.
Ellis Island (also see below), Morrow, 1982.
(With Christopher Newman) *Ellis Island* (television miniseries; based on the novel by Stewart), Columbia Broadcasting System, 1984.
The Titan, Simon & Schuster, 1985.
Glitter and the Gold, New American Library, 1989.
Pomp and Circumstance, Dutton, 1992.

Also author of *The Debutante* (screenplay).

ADAPTATIONS: The Mephisto Waltz was adapted for film and released by Twentieth Century-Fox in 1971; *The Norliss Tapes,* based on a story by Stewart, was broadcast by NBC-TV on February 21, 1973; *Six Weeks* was adapted for film and released by Universal in 1982.

SIDELIGHTS: Fred Mustard Stewart received widespread recognition as a talented writer with his first novel, *The Mephisto Waltz.* It is the story of a young writer, Myles Clarkson, whose life becomes intertwined with that of an elderly concert pianist, Duncan Ely, and his beautiful daughter. As the story unfolds, the friendly father and daughter become more and more sinister—particularly after the old man's death. Allen J. Hubin, reviewing *The Mephisto Waltz* for the *New York Times Book Review,* calls the novel "a must for every addict of the Satanic and the supernatural," with an "eerie plot, which [Stewart] weaves, with diabolical skill, to the last page."

Though he produced two more horror novels (*The Methuselah Enzyme* and *Star Child*), Stewart has since concentrated on writing family sagas—historical novels which tell of the trials and triumphs of a family through several generations. His most successful novels to date, *Century* and *Ellis Island,* belong to this genre. Because of the tremendous breadth—and length—necessitated by this type of writing, certain pitfalls inevitably accompany family sagas. Stewart, however, has consistently negotiated these pitfalls, as James K. Glassman states in the *Washington Post:* "Stewart has a talent for writing sparely, for jamming in facts and feelings without giving readers the impression that he's skipping along from one melodrama to another—which, of course, is exactly what he's doing." A reviewer for the *West Coast Review of Books,* though, is less tolerant of such shortcomings; in a review of the 1985 novel *The Titan,* he proclaims: "The problem with Stewart's novel is its clumsy writing, shallow characters, and inept contrivances. . . . For a potboiler, *The Titan* barely simmers." *New York Times Book Review* writer Jodi Daynard defends Stewart, saying, "in the course of any 500-page saga . . . there are bound to be snags, and the best thing to be said about *The Titan* is that it has just enough momentum to surmount them." Glassman concludes: "Stewart . . . is a craftsman. He has the family saga down pat."

BIOGRAPHICAL/CRITICAL SOURCES:

PERIODICALS

America, May 3, 1969, p. 539.
Book World, March 29, 1970, p. 13.
Los Angeles Times, March 7, 1985.
Los Angeles Times Book Review, April 26, 1981, p. 21; March 13, 1983, p. 8; October 15, 1989, p. 14; September 23, 1990, p. 14.
New York Times, March 14, 1969, p. 39; December 1, 1973, p. 31.
New York Times Book Review, April 6, 1969, p. 27; June 8, 1969, p. 28; August 30, 1970, p. 34; January 9, 1972, p. 32; October 28, 1973, p. 48; October 3, 1976, p. 39; March 6, 1983, p. 28; January 29, 1984, p. 30; April 7, 1985, p. 14; November 5, 1989, p. 24.
Saturday Review, April 19, 1969, p. 42.
Tribune Books (Chicago), November 19, 1989, p. 9.
Wall Street Journal, October 30, 1973, p. 18; September 11, 1978, p. 24; April 9, 1985, p. 28.
Washington Post, April 3, 1981, p. C8.
Washington Post Book World, July 2, 1972, p. 13; February 6, 1983, p. 6.
West Coast Review of Books, March, 1983, p. 34; May, 1985, p. 33; Volume 15, number 2, 1989, p. 42.

* * *

STOKES, William Lee 1915-

PERSONAL: Born March 27, 1915, in Hiawatha, Utah; son of William Peace (a rancher) and Grace Elizabeth (Cox) Stokes; married Betty Asenath Curtis (a teacher), September 7, 1939; children: Betty Lee Stokes Huff, Mary Susan Stokes Griffith, William Michael, Patricia Jane Stokes Naughton, Jennifer Joy. *Education:* Brigham Young University, B.S., 1937, M.S., 1938; Princeton University, Ph.D., 1941. *Religion:* Church of Jesus Christ of Latter-day Saints (Mormon).

ADDRESSES: Home—1283 East S. Temple, No. 504, Salt Lake City, UT 84102. *Office*—Department of Geological and Geophysical Sciences, University of Utah, Salt Lake City, UT 84112.

CAREER: U.S. Geological Survey, junior geologist, 1942-43, geologist, 1943-47; University of Utah, Salt Lake City, assistant professor, 1947-49, associate professor, 1949-54, professor of geology, 1954-81, head of department, 1954-68, director of Cooperative Dinosaur Project, 1960-68, director of Earth Science Museum, 1961-68. Geological consultant, Standard Oil Co., summers, 1950-52, and Atomic Energy Commission, summers, 1953-55.

MEMBER: Geological Society of America, American Association of Petroleum Geologists, Society of Vertebrate Paleontologists, Society of Economic Paleontologists and Mineralogists, American Geophysical Union, American Association for the Advancement of Science, Utah Geological Association (president, 1951), Sigma Xi, Phi Kappa Phi, Explorers Club.

WRITINGS:

(With D. J. Varnes) *Glossary of Selected Geologic Terms,* Colorado Scientific Society, 1955.
Essentials of Earth History: An Introduction to Historical Geology, Prentice-Hall, 1960, 4th edition, 1982.
The Great Salt Lake, Utah Geological Society, 1966.
(With M. D. Picard and Sheldon Judson) *Introduction to Geology: Physical and Historical,* Prentice-Hall, 1968, 2nd edition, 1978.
Scenes of the Plateau Lands and How They Came to Be, illustrations by Stokes, privately printed, 1969, 2nd edition, Publishers' Press, 1971, 10th edition, 1986.
(With Albert Ervin Thompson) *Stratigraphy of the San Rafael Group,* Utah Geological and Mineralogical Survey, 1970.
(With son, W. M. Stokes) *Messages on Stone,* Publishers' Press, 1980.
The Genesis Answer: A Scientist's Testament of Divine Creation, Prentice-Hall, 1984.
The Cleveland-Lloyd Dinosaur Quarry, U.S. Department of the Interior, Bureau of Land Management, 1985.
The Geology of Utah, Utah Geological and Mineral Survey, 1986.
Dinosaur Tour Book, Starstone Publishing, 1988.
Evolution? The Scriptures Say Yes!, Vantage, 1988.
Scriptures for the Age of Science, Starstone Publishing, 1992.

Author and editor of guidebooks for geological excursions. Contributor of annual reviews of geology to *Americana Annual/Encyclopedia Yearbook.* Contributor of over 130 articles to scientific journals. Associate editor, *Bulletin of American Association of Petroleum Geologists,* 1954-66.

WORK IN PROGRESS: A book on dinosaurs; a book on time; a book on the meaning and origin of fossils; a book on the possibility of extraterrestrial intelligent life; a book on scripture, science and atheism; a high-school text that "may satisfy both scriptural and scientific constraints"; an autobiography.

SIDELIGHTS: Born in central Utah, a region known for its beautiful geologic scenery, William Stokes told *CA* that he has "built a teaching and writing career on an obsession to explain the earth in its details as well as its cosmic setting." He added, "So far this has resulted in a number of successful college-level textbooks and many tourist-oriented pamphlets that sell in large quantities throughout the Southwest." Hoping to produce a book or two that will sell in Christian bookstores as well as in regular trade book outlets, he said he is "looking for co-authors who can help him finish a high school level textbook on natural science that would be acceptable to both creationists and evolutionists." Now retired, he remarked that he spends most of his time "reading in the many subjects that will help [me] finish these ambitious projects."

BIOGRAPHICAL/CRITICAL SOURCES:

PERIODICALS

Utah Natural History, Volume 3, number 3, 1971.

* * *

STONEHOUSE, Bernard 1926-

PERSONAL: Born May 1, 1926, in Hull, England; married Sally Clacey, September 17, 1954; children: Caroline, Ann Felicity, Paul. *Education:* Attended University College, Hull, 1943-44; University College, London, B.Sc., 1953; Merton College, Oxford, D.Phil., 1957, M.A., 1959.

ADDRESSES: Home—Old Thatch, 43 Commercial End, Swaffham Bulbeck, Cambridge CB5 0ND, England. *Office*—Scott Polar Research Institute, Cambridge University, Lensfield Rd., Cambridge CB2 1ER, England.

CAREER: University of Canterbury, Christchurch, New Zealand, senior lecturer, 1960-64, reader in zoology, 1964-69; University of British Columbia, Vancouver, Commonwealth research fellow in zoology, 1969-70; University of Bradford, Bradford, Yorkshire, England, senior lecturer in ecology and chairman of Postgraduate School of Environmental Science, 1972-82; Cambridge University, Scott Polar Research Institute, Cambridge, England, editor of *Polar Record,* 1982-92. Yale University, visiting associate professor of biology, 1969. Teacher and freelance writer, 1970-72. *Military service:* Royal Navy, 1944-45; Royal Air Force Volunteer Reserve, 1950-53.

AWARDS, HONORS: Polar Medal for services in Antarctica, 1953; Union Medal from British Ornithologists Union, 1971; New Zealand Antarctic Society Voicey Conservation Trophy, 1979.

WRITINGS:

The Emperor Penguin: Aptenodytes forsteri Gray, H.M.S.O., 1953.
The Brown Skua: Catharacta skua loennbergi (Mathews), of South Georgia (illustrated), H.M.S.O., 1956.
Het Bevroren Continent (title means "The Frozen Continent"), C. de Boer, Jr., 1958.
The King Penguin: Aptenodytes patagonica, of South Georgia, H.M.S.O., 1960.
Wideawake Island: The Story of the B.O.U. Centenary Expedition to Ascension, Hutchinson, 1960.
Penguins, Golden Press, 1968.
Birds of the New Zealand Shore, A. H. & A. W. Reed, 1968.
Animals of the Arctic: The Ecology of the Far North, Holt, 1971.
Animals of the Antarctic: The Ecology of the Far South, Holt, 1972.
The Way Your Body Works, Mitchell Beazley, 1974.
Young Animals: The Search for Independent Life, Viking, 1974.
Mountain Life, Aldus, 1976.
(Editor) *The Biology of Penguins,* University Park Press, 1977.
(Editor with D. P. Gilmore) *Biology of Marsupials,* University Park Press, 1977.
(Editor with C. M. Perrins) *Evolutionary Ecology,* University Park Press, 1977.
Kangaroos, Raintree Publishers, 1977.
Penguins, Bodley Head, 1978.
Shark!, Scimitar, 1978.
(Editor) *Animal Marking,* University Park Press, 1978.
Living World of the Sea, Hamlyn, 1979.
(With M. Borner) *Orangutan: Orphans of the Forest,* W. H. Allen, 1979.
Bears, Wayland, 1980.
(Editor) *Philips' Illustrated Atlas of the World,* Philips, 1980.
Saving the Animals: The World Wildlife Fund Book of Conservation, Macmillan, 1981.
(Editor) *Biological Husbandry: A Scientific Approach to Organic Farming,* Butterworth, 1981.
(Editor with L. Rey) *The Arctic Ocean,* Macmillan, 1982.
Britain from the Air, Crown, 1982.
(Editor) *Pocket Guide to the World,* Philips, 1985.
Sea Mammals of the World, Penguin, 1985.
(With M.P. Casarini) *Unternehmen Polarstern* (title means "Operation Polarstern"), Econ verlag, 1988.
Polar Ecology, Chapman and Hall, 1989.
North Pole, South Pole: A Guide to the Ecology and Resources of the Arctic and Antarctic, McGraw-Hill Ryerson, 1990.
(Editor with C. Harris) *Antarctica and Global Climate Change,* Bellhaven, 1991.
Snow, Ice, and Cold, Evans, 1992.

JUVENILE

Whales, A. H. & A. W. Reed, 1964.
Gulls and Terns, A. H. & A. W. Reed, 1965.
Charles Darwin and Evolution, Wayland, 1981.
Venomous Snakes, Wayland, 1981.
Buffaloes, Wayland, 1981.
Parrots, Wayland, 1981.
Just Look at . . . Life in the Sea, Macdonald, 1984.
Just Look at . . . Living at the Poles, Macdonald, 1986.

"A CLOSER LOOK AT" SERIES

A Closer Look at Whales and Dolphins, F. Watts, 1978.
A Closer Look at Plant Life, F. Watts, 1978.
A Closer Look at Reptiles, F. Watts, 1979.

OTHER

Contributor of about seventy articles to scientific journals worldwide.

SIDELIGHTS: Bernard Stonehouse once commented: "Part of my job is writing about my research for scientists and students, and teaching students at university level. But I enjoy writing and talking about my work to others as well—to anyone who shares my interests, or who would share them if they had the chance. People who, as taxpayers, have subsidized my research and travels have a right to know what I have been up to if they want to know, and I am glad to tell them in my nonacademic books. And I am happy to tell young people about the plants and animals that fill their world, and for which they will be responsible once my generation has moved over. Many enter biology classes with a live interest in plants and animals, and are told all about cells and biochemistry or whatever is the scientific fad of the moment. I think they are being short-changed, and I am glad of any opportunity to foster their natural interests in whole animals, whole plants, and the whole living world that they can feel, touch, and respond to. People who start by liking plants and animals, and are encouraged to do so, usually end up liking other people—and I'm all for that."

* * *

STRAITON, E(dward) C(ornock) 1917- (Eddie Straiton; pseudonym: T. V. Vet)

PERSONAL: Born March 27, 1917, in Clydebank, Scotland; son of George Ramsay (a farmer) and May

(Cornock) Straiton; married Loraine Harrison, March 2, 1943 (died, 1981); married Penny Stanier, 1982; remarried; children: (first marriage) Loraine Mary; (second marriage) Edward James. *Education:* Glasgow University, M.R.C.V.S., 1940. *Politics:* Conservative. *Religion:* Christian.

ADDRESSES: Home—Darlaston Hall, Darlaston Park, Stone Staffs ST15 0ND, England. *Office*—Veterinary Hospital, Penkridge, Staffordshire ST19 5RY, England.

CAREER: Veterinarian in private practice, Penkridge, Staffordshire, England, 1943-93; writer and specialist in embryo transfer, 1958-89. Television veterinarian for British Broadcasting Corporation, 1956-91; veterinarian for the *Jimmy Young Radio Programme.* Advisor to *All Creatures Great and Small* television series.

MEMBER: Royal Society of Medicine (fellow), Royal College of Veterinary Surgery, British Veterinary Association, British Small Animal Veterinary Association, Institute of Advanced Motorists.

WRITINGS:

UNDER NAME EDDIE STRAITON

The T. V. Vet Book for Stock Farmers, Farming Press, Volume 1: *Cattle Ailments: Recognition and Treatment,* 1964, 6th edition, 1993, Volume 2: *Calving the Cow and Care of the Calf,* 1965, 5th edition, 1993.

Junior Book of Pet Care, Farming Press, 1978.

Animals Are My Life (autobiography), J. A. Allen, 1979.

Vet at Large! (autobiography), Arrow Books, 1981, hardbound edition, Severn House, 1982.

Positively Vetted! (autobiography), Severn House, 1983.

Vet on the Set! (autobiography), Arrow Books, 1985.

Also author of *Vet in Charge,* Hutchinson.

UNDER PSEUDONYM T. V. VET

The T. V. Vet Book for Pig Farmers: How to Recognize and Treat Common Pig Ailments, Farming Press, 1967, 6th edition, 1988.

The T. V. Vet Horse Book: Recognition and Treatment of Common Horse and Pony Ailments, Farming Press, 1971, 9th edition, 1984, published under real name as *The Horse Owner's Vet Book: Recognition and Treatment of Common Horse and Pony Ailments,* Lippincott, 1973, revised edition, 1979, 9th edition published as *T. V. Vet Horse Book,* 1992.

The T. V. Vet Sheep Book: Recognition and Treatment of Common Sheep Ailments, Farming Press, 1972, 6th edition, 1992.

The T. V. Vet Dog Book: Recognition and Treatment of Common Dog Ailments, Farming Press, 1974, 4th edition, 1989.

Cats, Their Health and Care: Owner's Guide to Cat Ailments and Conditions, Farming Press, 1977, 2nd edition, 1991.

OTHER

Contributor to professional journals, including *British Farmer and Stockbreeder* and *Horse and Pony.*

WORK IN PROGRESS: Vetting through the Ages, a history of vetting during the last 250 years.

SIDELIGHTS: E. C. Straiton's "T. V. Vet" books have been published in twelve languages, including Portuguese, Hebrew, and Tarsi.

* * *

STRAITON, Eddie
See STRAITON, E(dward) C(ornock)

* * *

STRANGE, James F(rancis) 1938-

PERSONAL: Born February 2, 1938, in Pampa, TX; son of Jerry Donald and Buena (Frost) Strange; married Carolyn Midkiff, August 19, 1960; children: Mary, James, Katherine, Joanna. *Education:* William M. Rice Institute (now Rice University), B.A., 1959; Yale University, M.Div., 1964; Drew University, Ph.D., 1970. *Religion:* Baptist.

ADDRESSES: Home—9712 Woodland Ridge Dr., Tampa, FL 33617. *Office*—Department of Religious Studies, University of South Florida, Tampa, FL 33620.

CAREER: Ordained Southern Baptist minister, 1964; Shreiner Institute, Kerrville, TX, instructor in French and German, 1961-63; Bridgeport Engineering Institute, Bridgeport, CT, lecturer in philosophy, 1963-64; Upsala College, East Orange, NJ, lecturer in religion, 1965-66; Union College, Cranfield, NJ, lecturer in history, 1970; University of South Florida (USF), Tampa, assistant professor, 1972-75, associate professor, 1975-79, professor of religious studies, 1980—, dean of College of Arts and Letters, 1981-91, chairperson of religious studies, 1992—. Area supervisor of Expedition to Tell Gezer, Israel, 1969, Expedition to Tell er-Ras, Jordan, 1970, and Expedition to Caesarea Maritima, Israel, 1971; Joint Expedition to Khirbet Shema', Israel, area supervisor, 1970, associate director, 1971-73; director of Salvage Excavations at French Hill, Jerusalem, Israel, 1970-71, Survey in Lower Galilee, Israel, 1982 and 1984, and Excavations at Sephoris, Israel, 1983—; field supervisor of Salvage Excavations at Khirbet elKom in Jordan's West Bank, 1971; associate director of Meiron Excavation Project, 1974-81; co-director (field director) of Expedition to En Gedi, Israel, 1979.

Also Norton Lecturer for Archaeological Institute of America, 1973; visiting lecturer at University of the Orange Free State, 1979. Curator and director of Living Center for Biblical and Archaeological Studies, 1980—; chairman of executive committee of Florida Institute for Knowledge and Policy, 1981-84; founder and chairman of executive committee of Florida Institute for the Liberal Arts and Sciences, 1984—. Chairman of Committee for Computer Archaeology, American Schools of Oriental Research, 1974-90; member of advisory committee, Heritage Commission of World Jewish Congress, 1979; member of board of directors, Florida Endowment for the Humanities, 1983-87, local Hillel Foundation, 1983—, USF Foundation, 1991—, USF Language Center, 1991—, and Madeira Beach Holocaust Memorial Museum and Education Center, 1992—.

MEMBER: Society for Biblical Literature, American Academy of Religion and Psychical Research, Israel Exploration Society, Phi Kappa Phi, National Association for Baptist Professors of Religion, World Congress of Jewish Studies.

AWARDS, HONORS: Montgomery fellow at W. F. Albright Institute for Archaeological Research, Jerusalem, Israel, 1970-71; fellow of Office of Judeo-Christian Studies at Duke University, 1971-72; grant from International Business Machines (IBM) Corp., 1974; National Endowment for the Humanities fellow at W. F. Albright Institute for Archaeological Research, 1980.

WRITINGS:

(With E. M. Meyers and A. T. Kraabel) *Ancient Synagogue Excavations at Khirbet Shema', Upper Galilee, Israel, 1970-1972,* Duke University Press, 1976.

(With E. M. Meyers and C. L. Meyers) *Excavations at Ancient Meiron, Upper Galilee, Israel, 1971-1972, 1974-1975,* American Schools of Oriental Research, 1981.

(With E. M. Meyers) *Archaeology, the Rabbis, and Early Christianity,* Abingdon, 1981.

(Contributor) Henry O. Thompson, editor, *The Answers Lie Below: Essays in Honor of Lawrence Edmund Toombs,* University Press of America, 1984.

(With E. M. Meyers and C. L. Meyers) *The Excavations at the Ancient Synagogue of Gush Halav, Israel,* Eisenbrauns, 1990.

Also writer for television series *Your Open University,* for WUSF-TV, 1975-76. Art and archaeology editor for *Macmillan Dictionary of Judaism.* Contributor to *Interpreter's Dictionary of the Bible, Anchor Bible Dictionary, Harper's Bible Dictionary, Mercer Dictionary of the Bible,* and *International Standard Bible Encyclopedia.* Contributor of articles and reviews to scholarly journals. Member of editorial board of annual series published by American Schools of Oriental Research.

WORK IN PROGRESS: Interpretation in Archaeology; The Excavations of Ancient Sepphons, and articles for *Macmillan Dictionary of Judaism.*

SIDELIGHTS: James F. Strange told *CA:* "I am particularly interested in how both archaeology and the Bible illuminate a single people, those of ancient Israel, and their religious beliefs and practices. I want to show how they are utterly different from us, yet the same—one of the paradoxes of history. I am very interested in 'unofficial religion,' or those beliefs that people hold—like reincarnation—even when they are not normally sanctioned by church or synagogue.

"I got into archaeology as a result of studying ancient society and the Bible, particularly the New Testament. It seemed natural to move from excavating in the library stacks to excavating in ancient debris. It still seems to me that the two activities form a kind of natural liaison. They also form a drama with two actors, one who has lines, and the other building something. We locate and read what one ancient actor wrote, then we locate and 'read' what the other built. These non-verbal leavings are sometimes as eloquent as any ancient orator.

"It is true that I generally write for an academic audience, which means that for some I am a 'scientific writer.' Yet I shudder to think that I should write lifeless prose for such readers. I agree with an old friend who once observed that academic writing should be good writing and that popular writing is good academic writing without footnotes.

"In this vein I must admit that some of my contemporaries seem bent on boring us all to death when they are relating what surely is one of the most fascinating stories to emerge from the earth and from the physical traces of our ancestors. Here were real, living, breathing, and loving human beings reluctantly leaving behind their signatures in the earth. Why, then, should we write it up like a grocery list of finds? Are not faith, religion, and history more than information?

"Unfortunately for archaeologists, we now all live with a little of the aura of movie hero Indiana Jones. I say 'unfortunately' because most people have no idea how much unremitting labor must go into an excavation. Furthermore, no one is out there looking for the gold statue. We are mostly happy to be able to infer an ancient value or a pattern of life from the bits and pieces we do recover.

"It has always seemed to me since my boyhood in East Texas that people acted out and talked about religion on two levels. On the one hand is what people are supposed to do and believe. That I call 'official religion.' The other side is in fact what people are up to and how they talk when the priest is away. I call that 'unofficial religion' and find it very fascinating. I am not talking about hypocrisy, though that has its own interest. I am talking about real people acting upon and believing in their personal religion what they please. My own view is that a society acts on unofficial religion far more than on the official. In other words, the values of a society about religion may have shifted dramatically away from whatever the priests have said. Therefore, they act on their own convictions. . . . I found in my classes that nearly a quarter believed in reincarnation, even though that doctrine has no place in traditional (official) Judaism or Christianity. By the way, I also find the reverse phenomenon. Even though I hear that modern people don't believe in angels, I find that about twelve percent of my students admit to such a belief. Our average student is age twenty-seven, so we are not talking about kids."

* * *

SULEIMAN, Michael W(adie) 1934-

PERSONAL: Born February 26, 1934, in Tiberias, Palestine (now Israel); son of Wadie Michael and Jameeleh (Ailabouny) Suleiman; became a U.S. citizen; married Penelope Ann Powers (a bacteriologist), August 31, 1963; children: Suad Michelle, Gibran Michael. *Education:* Bradley University, B.A., 1960; University of Wisconsin, M.S., 1962, Ph.D., 1965.

ADDRESSES: Home—427 Wickham Rd., Manhattan, KS 66502. *Office*—Department of Political Science, Kansas State University, Manhattan, KS 66506.

CAREER: Kansas State University, Manhattan, assistant professor, 1965-68, associate professor, 1968-72, professor, 1972-90, university distinguished professor of political science, 1990—, head of department, 1975-82. Bishop's School, Amman, Jordan, teacher, 1953-55; Abbotsholme School, England, teacher, 1955-56. Guest lecturer at many universities in the United States and Canada as well as Uppsala University, Sweden; University of Juba, Sudan; University of London, England; and Hankuk University, Korea. Has participated in numerous conferences and seminars sponsored by organizations in the United States and abroad, including League of Arab States, International Congress of Human Sciences in Asia and North Africa, Middle East Studies Association of North America, Rockefeller Foundation Bellagio Study and Conference Center, Italy, Istituto Affari Internazionali, Italy, Middle East Institute of Japan, Chinese Academy of Social Sciences, Thai Social Science Association, Korean Political Science Association, Center for Maghribi Studies in Tunis (CEMAT), Federation of Arab Entities (FEARAB) in Santiago, Chile and United Arab Emirates Ministry of Information and Culture. Has reviewed grant proposals for such institutions as League of Arab States, Institute of International Education, Department of Health, Education and Welfare, Department of Education, American Research Center in Egypt, Radcliffe Institute of Independent Study, National Endowment for the Humanities, and National Science Foundation. Has reviewed manuscripts for a number of university presses and scholarly journals.

MEMBER: International Association for Mass Communication Research, American Political Science Association, Middle East Institute, Middle East Studies Association of North America (member of Committee on Middle East Images in Secondary School Texts, 1972-75; chair of Committee on Pre-Collegiate Education, 1975-78; member of board of directors, 1980-82), American Institute of Maghribi Studies (member of board of directors, 1985-88), Association of Arab-American University Graduates (president, 1977), Midwest Political Science Association, American Research Center in Egypt (Cairo and New York; member of board of governors, 1991-94).

AWARDS, HONORS: University of Wisconsin Vilas traveling fellowship, 1963-64; Kansas State University faculty research fellowship, summer, 1966 and 1986; University of Denver-Social Science Foundation research associate, summer, 1968; Ford Foundation fellowship, 1969-70; American Research Center in Egypt fellowship, 1972-73; American Philosophical Society traveling fellowship, 1974; Fulbright-Hayes Faculty Research Abroad Program fellowship, 1983-84 and 1993-94; Center for International Exchange of Scholars (CIES) Islamic Civilization Grant, 1984; University of Minnesota Immigration History Research Center Grant, 1985; Mid-America State Universities Association Honor Lecturer, 1986-87; Kansas State University Distinguished Graduate Faculty Member Award, 1987.

WRITINGS:

Political Parties in Lebanon: The Challenge of a Fragmented Political Culture, Cornell University Press, 1967.

American Images of Middle East Peoples: Impact of the High School, Middle East Studies Association, 1977.

The Arabs in the Mind of America, Amana Books, 1987.

(Editor with Baha Abu-Laban) *Arab-Americans: Continuity and Change,* Association of Arab-American University Graduates, 1989.

Also author of *Guide to a Correspondence Course in International Relations,* 1966. Contributor to books, including

The American Mass Media and the Arabs, edited by Michael C. Hudson and Ronald G. Wolfe, Georgetown University, 1980; *Split Vision,* edited by Edmund Ghareeb, American-Arab Affairs Council, 1983; *Political Behavior in the Arab States,* edited by Tawfic E. Farah, Westview Press, 1983; *Palestine: Continuing Dispossession,* edited by Glenn E. Perry, Association of Arab-American University Graduates, 1985; *Political Socialization in the Arab States,* edited by Tawfic Farah and Yasumasa Kuroda, Lynne Rienner, 1987; *Crossing the Waters: Arabic-Speaking Immigrants to the United States before 1940,* edited by Eric J. Hooglund, Smithsonian Institution Press, 1987; *The Political Economy of Morocco,* edited by I. William Zartman, Westview Press, 1987; *The Politics of Arab Integration,* edited by Giacomo Luciani and Ghassan Salame, Croom Helm, 1988.

Also co-editor with John Entelis of Westview Press series on "State, Culture and Society in Arab North Africa," 1989—. Editor of *The Intifada,* a special issue of the *Journal of Arab Affairs* (spring 1989), and *America and the Palestinians,* a special issue of *Arab Studies Quarterly* (winter/spring 1990). Has published over forty articles and numerous book reviews in scholarly journals, including *American Political Science Review, American Journal of Sociology, American Politics Quarterly, Journal of Cross-Cultural Psychology, International Journal of Middle East Studies, Arab Studies Quarterly,* and *Western Political Quarterly.* Member of editorial boards of *Arab Studies Quarterly,* 1979—; *Journal of Arab Affairs,* 1980—; *Arab Journal of International Studies* (Arabic), 1987—; and *Maghreb Review,* 1988—; member of editorial board and book review editor, social sciences, *International Journal of Middle East Studies,* 1982-88.

A number of Michael W. Suleiman's books and articles have been published in Arabic and in several European languages.

SIDELIGHTS: Michael W. Suleiman, who speaks Arabic and has reading knowledge of French, has conducted field research in several countries of the Middle East and North Africa. His publications include writings on the Arab-American community, education in the United States and the Arab countries, Arab politics, the Palestine question, and U.S. policy and public attitudes with regard to the Middle East. He has appeared as a guest commentator or panelist on National Public Radio, the Cable News Network, CBS television, PBS (with Bill Moyers), C-Span, and local and regional radio and television stations in North America and the Middle East. He has also published numerous articles in the American and Arab popular press.

SUMMERTREE, Katonah
See WINDSOR, Patricia

* * *

SUPPES, Patrick 1922-

PERSONAL: Born March 17, 1922, in Tulsa, OK; son of George Biddle and Ann (Costello) Suppes; married Joan Farmer, 1946 (divorced, 1970); married Joan Sieber, 1970 (divorced, 1973); married Christine Johnson, 1979; children: (first marriage) Patricia, Deborah, John; (third marriage) Alexandra Christine, Michael Patrick. *Education:* University of Chicago, B.S., 1943; Columbia University, Ph.D., 1950.

ADDRESSES: Home—678 Mirada Ave., Stanford, CA 94305. *Office*—Center for the Study of Language and Information, Ventura Hall, Stanford University, Stanford, CA 94305-4115.

CAREER: Stanford University, Stanford, CA, instructor, 1950-52, assistant professor, 1952-55, associate professor, 1955-59, professor of philosophy, 1959—, professor of statistics, education, and psychology, 1961—, associate dean of School of Humanities and Sciences, 1958-61, director of Institute for Mathematical Studies in the Social Sciences, 1959-92. Visiting professor, College de France, 1979. John Smyth Memorial Lecturer, Victorian Institute of Educational Research, 1968; Haegerstroem Lecturer, Uppsala University, 1974; Howison Lecturer in Philosophy, University of California, Berkeley, 1979; S. Richard Silverman Lecturer in Hearing and Deafness, Central Institute for the Deaf, Washington University, 1979; Messenger Lecturer, Cornell University, 1981. *Military service:* U.S. Army Air Forces, 1942-46; became captain.

MEMBER: International Institute of Philosophy, International Union of History and Philosophy of Science (president of Division of Logic, Methodology, and Philosophy of Science, 1975-79; president of organization, 1976 and 1978), American Philosophical Association (president of Pacific Division, 1972-73), American Philosophical Society, Mathematical Association of America, American Mathematical Society, American Association for the Advancement of Science (fellow), American Psychological Association (fellow), American Psychological Society (fellow), National Academy of Education (president, 1973-77), National Academy of Sciences, American Association of University Professors, American Federation of Information Processing Societies, American Academy of Arts and Sciences (fellow), American Education Research Association (president, 1973-74), Society of Experimental Psychologists, Society for Mathematical Psychology, Philosophy of Science Association, Psychonomic Society,

Econometric Society, Association for Computing Machinery, Association for Symbolic Logic, Societe Francaise de Psychologie (associe etranger), Academie Internationale de Philosophie des Sciences (membre titulaire), Finnish Academy of Science and Letters (foreign member), Sigma Xi.

AWARDS, HONORS: Fellow, Center for Advanced Study in Behavioral Sciences, 1955; fellow, National Science Foundation, 1957; research award from Social Science Research Council, 1959; Nicholas Murray Butler Silver Medal, Columbia University, 1965; Palmer O. Johnson Memorial Award, 1967, and Phi Delta Kappa Meritorious Researcher award, 1971, from American Educational Research Association; Guggenheim Foundation fellowship, 1971-72; Distinguished Scientific Contribution Award, 1972, and E. L. Thorndike Award for Distinguished Psychological Contribution to Education, 1979, from American Psychological Association; Columbia University Teachers College Medal for Distinguished Service, 1978; honorary doctor's degree, University of Nijmegen, The Netherlands, 1979; docteur honoris causa, Academie de Paris, Universite Rene Descartes, 1982; National Medal of Science, 1990.

WRITINGS:

(With D. Davidson and S. Siegel) *Decision Making: An Experimental Approach,* Stanford University Press, 1957.

Introduction to Logic, Van Nostrand, 1957.

Axiomatic Set Theory, Van Nostrand, 1960, revised edition, Dover, 1972.

(With R. C. Atkinson) *Markov Learning Models for Multiperson Interactions,* Stanford University Press, 1960.

(With Shirley Hill) *First Course in Mathematical Logic,* Blaisdell, 1964, 2nd edition, Ginn, 1965.

(With E. Crothers) *Experiments in Second-Language Learning,* Academic Press, 1967.

(With M. Jerman and D. Brian) *Computer-Assisted Instruction: Stanford's 1965-66 Arithmetic Program,* Academic Press, 1968.

Studies in the Methodology and Foundations of Science: Selected Papers from 1951 to 1969, Reidel, 1969.

A Probabilistic Theory of Causality, North-Holland, 1970.

(With D. H. Krantz, R. D. Luce, and A. Tversky) *Foundations of Measurement,* Academic Press, Volume 1, 1971, Volume 2, 1989, Volume 3, 1990.

(With M. Morningstar) *Computer-Assisted Instruction at Stanford, 1966-68,* Academic Press, 1972.

Probabilistic Metaphysics, two volumes, Philosophical Society and Department of Philosophy, University of Uppsala, 1974; revised edition, Blackwell, 1984.

(With B. Searle and J. Friend) *The Radio Mathematics Project: Nicaragua 1974-75,* Institute for Mathematical Studies in the Social Sciences, Stanford University, 1976.

Logique du Probable, Flammarion, 1981.

Estudios de filosofia y metodologia de la ciencia, Alianza Universidad, 1988.

Language for Humans and Robots, Blackwell, 1991.

Models and Methods in the Philosophy of Science, Kluwer, 1993.

ELEMENTARY SCHOOL BOOKS

Sets and Numbers (with teacher's manual), preliminary edition, Singer, 1959, Books 1A-1B and 2A-2B, [Stanford], 1961, Book 3, Singer, 1966.

(With Hawley) *Geometry for Primary Grades,* Books 1-2, Holden-Day, 1960.

EDITOR AND CONTRIBUTOR

(With L. Henkin and A. Tarski) *The Axiomatic Method,* North-Holland, 1959.

(With K. J. Arrow and S. Karlin) *Mathematical Methods in the Social Sciences,* Stanford University Press, 1960.

(With E. Nagel and Tarski) *Logic, Methodology and Philosophy of Science,* Stanford University Press, 1962.

(With J. H. Criswell and H. Solomon) *Mathematical Methods in Small Group Processes,* Stanford University Press, 1962.

(With J. Hintikka) *Aspects of Inductive Logic,* North-Holland, 1966.

(With L. J. Cronbach) *Research for Tomorrow's Schools: Disciplined Inquiry for Education,* Macmillan, 1969.

(With S. Morgenbesser and M. White) *Philosophy, Science, and Method: Essays in Honor of Ernest Nagel,* St. Martin's, 1969.

(With J. Hintikka) *Information and Inference,* Reidel, 1970.

(With Hintikka and J. M. E. Moravcsik) *Approaches to Natural Language,* Reidel, 1973.

Space, Time and Geometry, Reidel, 1973.

(With Henkin, A. Joja, and G. C. Moisil) *Logic, Methodology and Philosophy of Science IV,* North-Holland, 1973.

(With D. H. Krantz, R. C. Atkinson, and R. D. Luce) *Contemporary Developments in Mathematical Psychology,* W. H. Freeman, 1974, Volume I: *Learning, Memory, and Thinking,* Volume II: *Measurement, Psychophysics, and Neural Information Processing: Logic and Probability in Quantum Mechanics,* Reidel, 1976.

Impact of Research on Education: Some Case Studies, National Academy of Education, 1978.

(With Searle and Friend) *The Radio Mathematics Project: Nicaragua 1976-77,* Institute for Mathematical

Studies in the Social Sciences, Stanford University, 1978.

Studies in the Foundations of Quantum Mechanics, Philosophy of Science Association, 1980.

(With Friend and Searle) *Radio Mathematics in Nicaragua,* Institute for Mathematical Studies in the Social Sciences, Stanford University, 1980.

University-Level Computer-Assisted Instruction at Stanford, 1968-1980, Institute for Mathematical Studies in the Social Sciences, Stanford University, 1981.

OTHER

Also author with Hill of *Mathematical Logic for the Schools,* Book 1, revised edition, 1962. Contributor of more than 300 articles to professional journals.

BIOGRAPHICAL/CRITICAL SOURCES:

BOOKS

Bogdan, R. J., editor, *Patrick Suppes,* Reidel, 1979.

Humphreys, P. W., editor, *Patrick Suppes: Scientific Philosopher,* Kluwer, in press.

* * *

SVIRSKY, Grigori (Tsezarevich) 1921-

PERSONAL: Born September 29, 1921, in Ufa, U.S.S.R. (now Commonwealth of Independent States); immigrated to Israel, 1972; son of Cezar Rozenbert (a fitter) and Goda Svirsky (a bookkeeper); married Polina Zabejenskaia (a chemist), January 25, 1949; children: Efim. *Education:* Attended Moscow Law School, 1939; State University of Moscow, M.A., 1951. *Politics:* Democrat.

ADDRESSES: Home—15 Tangreen Court, Apt. 604, Willowdale, Ontario M2M 3Z2, Canada.

CAREER: Author of novels, short stories, and film scenarios in Russia, 1947-64; work removed from publication or destroyed due to outspoken criticism of Soviet censorship, beginning 1965; expelled from Communist party, 1968; editorial assistant for Russian journal *Novyi mir,* 1956-70. Lecturer at higher education institutions in Soviet Union and occasional teacher of creative writing at State University in Moscow, 1948-56; visiting professor of modern Russian literature, University of Toronto, 1975, and University of Maryland, 1977-78. *Military service:* Soviet Air Force, 1939-46; received nine decorations.

MEMBER: Authors League of America, Authors Guild, PEN, Canadian Authors Association.

AWARDS, HONORS: Grant from Union of Soviet Writers, 1970, to gather materials for never-published novel about Russian arctic.

WRITINGS:

NOVELS

Zapoved' druzhby (title means "The Command of Friendship"), Voengis (Moscow), 1947.

Zdravstvuy, universitet! (title means "Greetings, University!"), Volume I, [Moscow], 1952, Volume 2, [Moscow], 1968.

Leninsky prospekt (title means "Lenin Prospect"), [Moscow], 1962, 2nd edition, 1964.

Tikhiye mesta, [Moscow], 1967.

Proriv, (title means "Breakthrough"), Ermitazh, 1983.

Proshchanie s Rossiei: povest' (title means "Farewell to Russia"), Ermitazh, 1986.

OTHER FICTION

Polyarnaya tragediya (collection of short stories; title means "The Polar Tragedy"), Possev-Verlag (Frankfort, West Germany), 1976.

Also author of as yet unpublished novel, *Gosudarstvennyi ekzamen,* 1964.

NONFICTION

Zslozhniki (autobiography), YMCA Press (Paris), 1974, translation by Gordon Clough published as *Hostages: The Personal Testimony of a Soviet Jew,* Knopf, 1976.

Na lobnom meste, Overseas Publications (London), 1979, translation by Robert Dessaix and Michael Ulman published as *A History of Post-War Soviet Writing: The Literature of Moral Opposition,* Ardis, 1981.

Mother and Stepmother, Erudite Books, 1990.

Also author of critical study, *Zhanr, Stil e Kompositsia "Dela Artamonovikh" M. Gorkogo,* forbidden publication in U.S.S.R., 1952.

FILMSCRIPTS

Tichiye mesta (title means "The Quiet Place"), produced in Moscow, 1966.

Korol pamira (adapted from author's short story; title means "King of the Pamirs"), [Moscow], 1967.

Evrei nalevo (title means "Jews to the Left!"), [Jerusalem], 1972.

Contributor of short stories, essays, critical articles, and sociological studies to journals. Author's work has been translated into other languages, including French.

SIDELIGHTS: Grigori Svirsky told *CA* that he forfeited his position as a successful Russian novelist because of his public statements "attacking the role of censorship in Soviet literature and the 'Great Russian' nationalist chauvinism of such figures as Vasilii Smirnov, chief editor of *Druzhba norodov.*" These speeches and statements led to his expulsion from the Party and to a ban on the publication of his writings. With the loss of his income from royalty fees, he took a job offered by his friends on the journal *Novyi mir.*

In 1970 he was given a chance to "reinstate himself." The Union of Soviet Writers, through the influence of his friends, gave Svirsky a grant to write an "optimistic and 'life-asserting' novel" of the Russian far north. In the north Svirsky found that "the setting and background hardly correspond to the official picture of the Soviet north as a flourishing region, tamed and civilized by human effort despite its remoteness and arctic climate." Svirsky told *CA* he saw "a land whose terrain and population were permanently scarred by the marks and memories of the Stalinist labor camps." He found "former prisoners still continue to settle scores with former camp guards, state law still contrives to make criminals of the innocent, protest is suppressed, and there is a general sense of misrule by authority and grievance and demoralization among the ordinary citizens." He returned to Moscow and, unable to write the book, he decided to emigrate to Israel.

A reviewer for the *Economist* described Svirsky's book *Hostages* as a "*Bildungsroman* of a young couple painfully learning what it means to be Jewish in the Soviet Union . . . . This story movingly illustrates how persecution makes nationalists and why would-be emigrants to Israel increased from a trickle to a flood. It is sometimes asked: 'Why make so much fuss about Soviet persecution of the Jews, when so many others are oppressed in that "prison of nations"?' This book gives the answer."

In the *Times Literary Supplement,* Geoffrey Hosking wrote that in *A History of Post-War Soviet Writing* Svirsky equates real literature in totalitarian conditions to "partisan warfare." Hosking continued, "The whole book is permeated by the idealism . . . of the men who had won a great victory over evil on the battlefield, and had now returned home to achieve the same on the campaign trails of the spirit . . . . The result was moral warfare, between literary bureaucrats anxious to suppress the truth and writers fighting to reveal it."

When asked about the difficulty of getting his manuscripts published in the original Russian, Svirsky replied: "I thought I was going to write all my life in Russian. I knew contemporary colloquial Russian, its nuances and its dialects as well as its professional jargon. I believe I will never know English as well as Russian."

BIOGRAPHICAL/CRITICAL SOURCES:

PERIODICALS

Economist, October 30, 1976, p. 127.

Times Literary Supplement, October 29, 1976, p. 1366; April 2, 1982, pp. 367-68.*

T

TALBOTT, Strobe 1946-

PERSONAL: Born April 25, 1946, in Dayton, OH; son of Nelson S. (a businessman) and Helen Josephine (Large) Talbott; married Brooke Lloyd Shearer (a journalist), November 17, 1971; children: Devin Lloyd. *Education:* Yale University, B.A. (summa cum laude), 1968; Oxford University, B.Litt. (now M.Litt.), 1971.

ADDRESSES: Home—Washington, DC.

CAREER: Time magazine, Washington, DC, Eastern European correspondent, 1971-73, State Department correspondent, 1974-76, White House correspondent, 1976-77, diplomatic correspondent, 1977-1984, Washington Bureau Chief, 1985—. Notable assignments include coverage of the Iranian revolution, visits by Henry Kissinger and James Schlesinger to the People's Republic of China, the Presidential mission to Hanoi and Vientiane in search of Americans missing-in-action, and the Non-Aligned Movement Summit in Havana in 1979. Appointed "Ambassador-at-large for Russia and other former Soviet republics" by President Bill Clinton, 1993.

MEMBER: Council on Foreign Relations, Phi Beta Kappa.

AWARDS, HONORS: Rhodes scholar at Oxford University; fellow, Yale Corp, 1976—; honorary M.A. from Yale University, 1976; Edward Weintal Prize for Distinguished Diplomatic Reporting, 1981; Overseas Press Club Award, 1983; Sidney Hillman Foundation Prize Award, 1984, for *Deadly Gambits.*

WRITINGS:

Endgame: The Inside Story of SALT II, Harper, 1979.

The Russians and Reagan, foreword by Cyrus Vance, Vintage Books, 1984.

Deadly Gambits: The Reagan Administration and the Stalemate in Nuclear Arms Control, Knopf, 1984.

(With Michael Mandelbaum) *Reagan and Gorbachev,* Vintage, 1987.

The Master of the Game: Paul Nitze and the Nuclear Peace, Knopf, 1989.

Also author of *Mikhail S. Gorbachev: An Intimate Biography,* 1988; and, with Michael Beschloss, *Bush and Gorbachev,* 1991.

EDITOR AND TRANSLATOR

Nikita Khrushchev, *Khrushchev Remembers,* introduction and notes by Edward Crankshaw, Little, Brown, 1970.

Khrushchev, *Khrushchev Remembers: The Last Testament,* introduction by Jerrold L. Schecter and foreword by Crankshaw, Little, Brown, 1974.

Also author of foreign affairs column for Time International, 1977-78. Contributor to *Foreign Affairs.*

SIDELIGHTS: "I decided on a career in journalism early in my college years at Yale," noted journalist Strobe Talbott once told *CA.* "Russian language and literature was my academic major, and it has been a continuing interest of mine; but I always saw that study primarily as a way of developing a tool that would be useful to me as a journalist." His journalistic career began while he was still a student of Russian literature at Oxford. Talbott worked as a stringer for *Time* magazine; between his second and third years at Oxford he was fortunate to be able to substitute for the Moscow bureau chief of *Time,* who was then on leave, gaining some valuable experience in translation.

The following year, when *Time* acquired some tapes containing the reminiscences of former Soviet premier Nikita Khrushchev, the editors asked then twenty-four-year-old Talbott to undertake the task of translating and editing

Khrushchev's memoirs. The first volume of these memoirs, published in 1970 as *Khrushchev Remembers,* generated considerable publicity. Because no outside authority had been permitted to examine the tapes on which the text was based (a condition imposed by the Khrushchev family as long as the retired leader was alive), there was some question as to the book's authenticity. By and large, however, critics concluded that the majority of the material in the book originated with Khrushchev. By the time that the second volume came out in 1974, Khrushchev's death had caused the conditions imposed by family members to be lifted; there was no longer any doubt that the memoirs were genuine. An independent voice printing company verified that the voice on the tapes was indeed Khrushchev's.

Describing his work on this massive project, Talbott told an interviewer for the *Cleveland Press* that he had worked from a direct Russian transcript of Khrushchev's tapes. "Much of it was rambling and sometimes confusing, so I had to do quite a bit of editing to make it into a readable book," he explained. "Some of the dates [Khrushchev] refers to are faulty and should be checked against other sources. But although he was in his late 70s, I was amazed at how he remembers events of 50 and 60 years ago. He was by no means senile."

Talbott's background in Russian studies proved useful once again when he took on another major project for *Time,* the reconstruction of the two-and-a-half years of the Strategic Arms Limitations Treaty (SALT) negotiations. Originally run as a *Time* cover story on May 21, 1979, the article was expanded into a book, *Endgame: The Inside Story of SALT II.* "My purpose in writing both the article and the book was to give people a coherent, narrative explanation of what SALT II is and how it came about," Talbott once pointed out. "I have decided not to editorialize but to concentrate on trying to make an extremely complex, technical, and secrecy-shrouded subject comprehensible to the layman."

Most critics felt that Talbott accomplished the aforementioned purpose. A reviewer for *Foreign Affairs* declared: "Talbott seems to have had unusual access to the principal Washington policymakers and he describes their deliberation and struggles over two and a half years with skill, apparent accuracy and considerable detail." Robert W. Sellen was equally admiring. "[*Endgame*] is not light reading; the subject prevents that," he noted. "But Talbott explains complex matters clearly and has written a model of explanation of how international agreements are made—the process inside the U.S. government and the problem of dealing with Russians so wary as to be almost intractable."

On the other hand, *Washington Post* reviewer Deborah Shapley had some reservations about *Endgame.* While praising it as "a remarkably detailed and readable history of the horse-trading within the administration and with the Soviets," she faulted the book for not being sufficiently analytical. She also complained that the story of SALT II was written largely from the perspective of then-Secretary of State Cyrus Vance, and that other viewpoints received short shrift. In contrast, Leslie H. Gelb, one of the key figures in the actual SALT II negotiations, felt that the strength of *Endgame* was that it gave "full play to different versions of reality rather than insisting on finding a single truth to each event." Like Shapley, Gelb wished that *Endgame* had been more analytical, but he praised Talbott for cutting through to the heart of the negotiations: "In the SALT II negotiations—and here Mr. Talbott unravels their very essence—'the object of the game is a draw.' If either side attempted to checkmate the other's king, to threaten vital interests, the whole board would be overthrown. This is a very subtle and central insight into nuclear diplomacy."

In *Deadly Gambits: The Reagan Administration and the Stalemate in Nuclear Arms Control,* Talbott once again turns to the politics of arms control, this time recounting the tale of the making and unmaking of arms control policy under the Reagan Administration. McGeorge Bundy, writing in the *New York Times Book Review,* called *Deadly Gambits* "a masterly account of the Reagan record" on arms control, and predicted that "historians will be using [this book] for years to come." Talbott demonstrates how the Reagan Administration's proposal to the Soviet Government in the Strategic Arms Reduction Talks (START) was so unbalanced that it stood no chance of being accepted. "Mr. Talbott," according to Bundy, "shows us just what happens to nuclear arms control when the interest and attention of the President are concentrated not on the substance of the matter but on what will sound good to Americans."

While Bundy observed that Talbott's "heroes and antiheroes live and breathe," the *Washington Post Book World*'s Solly Zuckerman reached a similar conclusion. "Talbott's book is unique because of the vivid human detail with which he clothes the story," Zuckerman noted, later adding: "If [Richard] Perle seems a devious, shortsighted and unimaginative creature, it is because that is the way he emerges in Talbott's story, in which all the characters, including the Russian negotiators, obdurate but consistent, come to life as real people."

Talbott documents his work with a number of high-level sources. In *Newsweek* Jim Miller wrote: "Talbott seems to have had access to virtually every key actor on the American side. The result is a fascinating glimpse at the intrigues, petty power struggles and recondite debates that have shaped American policy." Although Bernard Gwertzman, reviewing *Deadly Gambits* in the *New York Times,* agreed that Talbott seems to offer material from all sides, he complained that some dialogue from top-secret meetings is not attributed. "One problem with this book," contended Gwertzman, "is the lack of sources for some of its most interesting material . . . Mr. Talbott says he had to use the material confidentially because of its sensitive nature. Sometimes, one wonders if grudges are being settled through information given to him." Similarly, Richard Owen in the London *Times* asked: "Yet there nags at the mind the uncomfortable question: what exactly is an *Inside Story,* and how does Mr. Talbott know so much about the internal workings of the Administration?"

A sequel to *Endgame* and *Deadly Gambits,* Talbott's *The Master of the Game: Paul Nitze and the Nuclear Peace* is constructed around one man's persistent efforts to reach a diplomatic resolution of the arms race, a mission that Nitze carried out for over forty years—from his participation in the official survey of strategic bombing at Hiroshima and Nagasaki to his eventual position as Reagan's special advisor for arms control. According to *Washington Post Book World* reviewer John Lewis Gaddis, "this volume reflects the careful blending of journalism with history for which Talbott has deservedly won wide-spread respect." Gaddis called Talbott's account, "contemporary history at its best."

"Talbott admires Nitze," observed Gregory F. Treverton in the *Los Angeles Times Book Review,* "but his portrait is not altogether admiring. At one level, Nitze seems principled and determined, devoting his adult life to the service of his country. At another, though, he comes across as vain and ambitious." In the *New Republic* Stanley Hoffmann called the biographical account "rather sketchy," and elaborated: "The problem with Talbott's biography of Nitze is that it is neither a full-fledged psychological life history nor a thorough study of a career. Talbott provides us with clues to Nitze's character and personality, but no more." Lord Zuckerman, writing in the *New York Review of Books,* addressed the same point, but reached a different conclusion. "In his preface, Mr. Talbott warns that his new book should be treated neither as biography nor as history, insofar as his journalistic 'literary devices' provide only a first or second draft of history. If the book is not definitive history, it nonetheless is a storehouse of instant information . . . by the many people who flit through his pages."

"In general," Talbott once remarked, "I find journalism an almost sinfully satisfying profession. One of my heroes in that profession, I. F. Stone, once said that he has so much fun in it, there probably ought to be a law against it. (If some of the politicians and judges we cover had their way, there would be.) What attracted me to journalism in college was that it seemed like a good way to see the world, meet interesting people, have adventures, continue one's education—and get paid for it. That's what attracts me to the job today, too."

BIOGRAPHICAL/CRITICAL SOURCES:

BOOKS

Authors in the News, Volume 1, Gale, 1976.

PERIODICALS

Atlantic Monthly, December, 1984.
Christian Science Monitor, January 7, 1971; July 31, 1974.
Cleveland Press, March 7, 1974.
Commentary, June, 1971.
Commonweal, November 30, 1984.
Foreign Affairs, winter, 1980; June, 1984; December, 1984.
Globe and Mail (Toronto), October 27, 1984.
Guardian Weekly, October 14, 1984, p. 18; January 20, 1985, p. 21; December 11, 1988, p. 20.
Listener, January 31, 1985.
Los Angeles Times Book Review, October 14, 1984, p. 10; September 29, 1985, p. 14; January 25, 1987; October 23, 1988, p. 2.
New Republic, June 29, 1974; October 15, 1984, p. 32; January 30, 1989, p. 31.
Newsweek, January 11, 1971; June 24, 1974; November 5, 1984, p. 91.
New Yorker, July 22, 1974; November 5, 1984, p. 171; December 5, 1988, p. 157.
New York Review of Books, February 25, 1971, p. 3; August 8, 1974; June 28, 1984, p. 38; November 8, 1984, p. 5; January 19, 1989, p. 21.
New York Times, September 29, 1984, p. 13; November 3, 1988.
New York Times Book Review, January 3, 1971; June 30, 1974; November 4, 1979, p. 3; November 25, 1979, p. 30; May 20, 1984, p. 17; October 7, 1984, p. 1; January 25, 1987, p. 7; November 6, 1988, p. 1; December 17, 1989, p. 32.
Observer Review, January 24, 1971.
Saturday Review, December 26, 1970.
Times (London), January 24, 1985.
Times Educational Supplement, January 18, 1985, p. 26.
Times Literary Supplement, January 22, 1971; May 17, 1985, p. 557.
Tribune Books (Chicago), May 6, 1984; November 6, 1988, p. 3.
Village Voice, September 17, 1979, p. 48; March 5, 1985, p. 47.
Virginia Quarterly Review, winter, 1986.
Washington Post, December 23, 1970; January 13, 1987.
Washington Post Book World, March 14, 1971; October 28, 1979, p. 8; September 9, 1984, p. 14; September

23, 1984, p. 1; September 29, 1985, p. 12; February 22, 1987, p. 7; September 15, 1988, p. 100; October 23, 1988, p. 5.*

* * *

TETEL, Julie 1950-
(Julie Tetel Andresen; Julia Joyce, a pseudonym)

PERSONAL: Surname is accented on second syllable; born October 16, 1950, in Glenview, IL; daughter of Herman John (a businessman) and Joyce (Hicks) Andresen; married Marcel Tetel (a professor), August 28, 1976; children: Francis, John Gerard. *Education:* Duke University, B.A., 1972; University of Illinois at Urbana-Champaign, M.A., 1975; University of North Carolina at Chapel Hill, Ph.D., 1980.

ADDRESSES: Home—Durham, NC. *Agent*—Maria Carvainis, Maria Carvainis Agency, 235 West End Ave., New York, NY 10023.

CAREER: Writer, 1980—. Duke University, Durham, NC, assistant professor of English, 1986—, director of graduate studies, 1992—.

MEMBER: Henry Sweet Society for the History of Linguistic Thought (London), Societe d'Historie et d'Epistemologie des Sciences du Langage (Paris), Studienkreis Geschichte der Sprachwissenschaft (Munster), Modern Language Association, North American Association for the History of the Language Sciences, Linguistics Society of America, Romance Writers of America, Novelists, Inc., Southeastern Conference on Linguistics.

AWARDS, HONORS: Reviewer's Choice Award, Best Exotic Romance, *Romantic Times,* and Best Historical Romance nomination by the Romance Writers of America, both for *Swept Away,* 1990; Trinity College Distinguished Teaching Award, Duke University, 1992.

WRITINGS:

FICTION

(Under pseudonym Julia Joyce) *Lord Laxton's Will,* Fawcett, 1985.
For Love of Lord Roland, Warner Books, 1985.
The Viking's Bride, Warner Books, 1987.
Tangled Dreams, Warner Books, 1989.
Swept Away, Warner Books, 1989.
And Heaven Too, Warner Books, 1990.
Sweet Suspicions, Harlequin, 1992.
Sweet Seduction, Harlequin, 1993.
Sweet Sensations, Harlequin, 1993.
The Temporary Bride, Harlequin, 1993.
Simon's Lady, Harlequin, 1994.

NONFICTION

(Under name Julie Tetel Andresen) *Linguistics in America 1769-1924: A Critical History,* Routledge, 1990.

Contributor of numerous articles to linguistic journals, under name Julie Tetel Andresen.

WORK IN PROGRESS: The Kissing Gate, a romance novel set in the eighteenth century; *Twentieth-Century Linguistic Discourses and the Social and Biological Sciences,* a scholarly book.

SIDELIGHTS: Julie Tetel told *CA:* "For the past ten to fifteen years, I have been engaged in a variety of writing activities and written across a variety of forms, from historical romance novels set anywhere between the twelfth and the nineteenth centuries, to academic scholarship in the field of linguistic historiography. I view writing as an aerobic activity, a kind of mental breathing, and believe that there is such a condition as 'being in writing shape.' Getting in shape took me about ten to twelve years. Staying in shape requires daily exercise. For me, writing is a passion and as necessary as breathing.

"I particularly love writing romance because the conventions of the genre provide me with a gentle embrace within which my imagination flourishes. I write always with the intention of respecting the conventions of the genre while at the same time pushing at its possibilities. Even after a decade of writing romances, I still find the topic of romantic love and desire to be fresh and inexhaustible. All of my romances are studies of the effects of some aspect of a particular romantic chemistry on the development of a love relationship. For me, romantic love and desire function something like the Mont Sainte-Victoire made famous by the French postimpressionist painter, Cezanne, who painted his beloved mountain from one angle and another angle and then another, capturing various plays of light and texture, depending on the time of day. So it is with me and the topic of romantic love, and each of my stories represents one complex combination of shades and textures out of the many and richly varied possibilities of intimate relationships.

"I am sometimes asked how it is that I write in such disparate genres as the mass-market romance and academic linguistics. My answer is that I love both language and the language of love. Romance is highly linguistically informed, most importantly at the level of the verbal interactions between the two main characters. My academic field of linguistic historiography engages with the study of language at a similarly 'conversational' level. That is, I am greatly interested in the development of the study of language as a discipline in the last several hundred years, and view the discipline as an elaborate, multi-voiced dialogue engaged among linguists, philosophers, psychologists, and neurolinguists, among others, as they repeatedly and variously attempt to describe the elusive object 'language.' I have taken great delight in entering that noisy and fractious conversation."

* * *

THURLEY, Jon (Mark)

PERSONAL: Born in Murree, Pakistan; son of Sidney Thomas (a headmaster) and Doreen Gertrude (a teacher; maiden name, Game) Thurley; married Diana Cynthia Bennett (a costume designer's agent), March 31, 1967. *Education:* Cambridge University, M.A. (with honors), 1964.

ADDRESSES: Home—30 Cambridge Rd., Teddington, Middlesex TW11 8DR, England. *Office*—213 Linen Hall, 162-8 Regent Street, London WIR 5TA, England.

CAREER: Jon Thurley (literary agency), London, England, owner, 1969—.

WRITINGS:

The Burning Lake, Bodley Head, 1985.
Household Gods, Hamish Hamilton, 1987, Morrow, 1988.
The Enigma Variations, Viking, 1988.
Tenements of Clay, Hamish Hamilton, 1989.
Unnatural Practices, Hamish Hamilton, 1992.

SIDELIGHTS: Jon Thurley was born in Pakistan and raised in India during the time of the Indian/Pakistani Partition riots. He described his early years in India to *CA:* "In some senses my childhood in India (as India was then) was idyllic. Until 1947 we lived in a mountain girt valley with a clear view of the Himalayan range. Life was completely rural, and we children had to make our own amusements."

Thurley recalled many of these experiences in his first novel, *The Burning Lake.* When the narrator, David, is introduced, he is living in England, and is attempting to cope with the dissolution of his marriage and the death of his older brother, Jonathan. Like Thurley, David was raised in British-ruled India, and as he pieces together his life he reflects on his childhood there. "British India transmuted through the eyes of childhood gives both power and poise to an intesely discursive novel," writes Maria Couto in the *Times Literary Supplement.* "Its best sections are . . . those that attempt a total recall of relationships with people and nature—fields, streams, sunsets and cloud—in India." Thurley again used the India of his childhood as the setting for his novels *Household Gods* and *Unnatural Practices.*

Thurley told *CA* about the India he remembers and his writings that take place there: "Historical accounts of British rule and the partition of India tend to ignore the patronizing, paternalistic, and separatists nature of the British who were there 'officially' that is to say, as opposed to those who had entered trade or ran plantations and who were by virtue of their working lives more acceptable to the Indian community than to the British. It was rare, in retrospect, to find anybody British who didn't talk of England as 'home' with nostalgia, even those whose families had lived there for generations. Above all, the official histories gloss over the absurd simplifications of the process of division as presided over by the British leader Louis Mountbatten—a division which treated the entire simmering partition dispute as merely a Holy War between Muslim and Hindu and ignored the enormous variety of parochial factors that contributed to the war. Many of these factors pertained to the ownership of property, with people moved from fertile and arable land where their families had lived for generations to somewhere entirely new. To rural Indians who had lived as farmers for generations, this was a terrible, life-wrecking experience.

"I believe strongly that people are motivated by unconscious forces which are often at variance with what they purport to believe or wish for. David, the narrator of *The Burning Lake,* is just such a man, seeking some coherent meaning and continuity to his life in external symbols and only half aware of the inner life that truly governs his actions and his feelings.

"I believe, too, that people invest the things or the people they desire with idealistic qualities. In *The Burning Lake,* David invests Rachel with the idealized qualities so imbued in him from his childhood, but the couple's true relationship can only become possible when David has seen her, and himself, as they really are. It was meant to be a novel about a man who recognizes, finally, that what he does is not a rehearsal for some future rerun or for an afterlife. Like many people, he prevents himself from taking action by hedging with society's rules."

In 1989 Thurley wrote the spy thriller *The Enigma Variations,* a tale of espionage and political intrigue behind the scenes of a disarmament summit. Though found wanting by *New York Times Book Review* writer Newgate Callendar ("it is as hazy as those Monet paintings of the Thames in a fog," he says. "The author is going somewhere, but where?"), *The Enigma Variations* received a favorable review from Phil Vettel of Chicago's *Tribune Books:* he describes the novel as "a thoroughly modern tale" that "has as much to do with personal integrity as it does the unraveling of a complex mystery. Spy novels don't come written much better than this one."

BIOGRAPHICAL/CRITICAL SOURCES:

PERIODICALS

New York Times Book Review, April 23, 1989, p. 33.
Observer, October 25, 1987, p. 26.
Times Literary Supplement, July 12, 1985, p. 777; September 4, 1992, p. 20.
Tribune Books (Chicago), February 26, 1989, p. 7.

* * *

TIGER, Madeline 1934-

PERSONAL: Born November 17, 1934, in New York, NY; daughter of Howard Lang (a chemical engineer) and Elinor (a bacteriologist; maiden name, Hamburg) Tiger; married, November 3, 1956 (divorced July, 1975); children: Randall, Barbara Joan, Joseph, Timothy, Homer. *Education:* Wellesley College, B.A. (with honors), 1956; Harvard University, M.A.T., 1957; Columbia University, M.F.A., 1986. *Politics:* Democrat. *Religion:* Jewish.

ADDRESSES: Home—15 Victoria Ter., Upper Montclair, NJ 07043. *Office*—New Jersey State Council on the Arts, 4 North Broad St., Trenton, NJ 08625.

CAREER: High school English teacher in Watchung Hills, NJ, 1957-58, and Maplewood, NJ, 1959-60; staff development teacher-trainer in Montclair, NJ, 1971-74; Seton Hall University, South Orange, NJ, writing teacher in Upward Bound program, 1974-78; poet-in-residence and current master poet/trainer for the Arts in Education program of the New Jersey State Council on the Arts, 1973—. Adjunct instructor, Upsala College, 1988-91. Has given poetry readings at libraries, universities, and museums, for New Jersey public television and New York and New Jersey radio programs, and at local cafes. Past member of Democrat County Committee; past chairman of Montclair Fair Housing Committee.

MEMBER: International PEN, Poetry Society of America, Phi Beta Kappa, Pi Lambda Theta.

AWARDS, HONORS: Fellow in creative writing, New Jersey State Council on the Arts, 1977-78, 1979-80, and 1987-88; fellowships from Columbia University School of the Arts, 1985-86, Virginia Center for the Creative Arts, 1987, 1988, 1990, and Blue Mountain Center, 1988; manuscript prize, *Journal of New Jersey Poets,* 1977, for *Keeping House in This Forest,* and 1987-88; Arts for Peace Prize, Colorado State University, 1983, for "Ceremonies for July," and 1984, for "The Fist" and "Your Hand"; first prize, *Crazy Quilt Literary Quarterly,* 1988, 1990; poetry prize, Womanspace, 1990.

WRITINGS:

Keeping House in This Forest (poetry chapbook), Department of Creative Writing, Fairleigh Dickinson University, 1977.
Toward Spring Bank (poems), Damascus Road, 1981.
The Chinese Handcuff (poems), privately printed, 1984.
(With Toi Derricotte) *Creative Writing Manual for Teachers,* New Jersey State Council on the Arts, 1985.
Mary of Migdal (poems), Still Waters Press, 1991.
My Father's Harmonica (poems), edited by Roy Zarucchi and Carolyn Page, Nightshade Press, 1991.

Work represented in numerous anthologies, including *We Become New,* Bantam, 1975; *I Sing the Song of Myself,* Morrow, 1978; *Women: Portraits,* McGraw, 1978; *Mother-Poet Anthology,* Mothering Publications, 1983; *State of Peace,* Gull Books, 1987; *Blue Stones and Salt Hay,* Rutgers University Press, 1990; and *The Unmade Bed: Sensual Writing of Married Love,* HarperCollins, 1992. Contributor of poems, articles, and reviews to magazines, including *Andover Review, American Poetry Review, Berkeley Poets Cooperative, Greenfield Review, Judaism, Negative Capabilities, Literary Review, National Forum, Sinister Wisdom, Poets On, Worcester Review, Stone Country, New Directions for Women,* and *Home Planet News.*

SIDELIGHTS: Madeline Tiger told *CA:* "I have to write. Life itself is, revision. To teach my students is to educate myself. I am also involved in teaching others to teach. I am always talking to somebody—on paper, on the phone, around tables, in my dreams—trying to heal, to render significance, to get at meaning. Thing of the world, of generations, of cruelties, of love, of what to write. Sorting, editing, *revising.*"

* * *

TINDALL, Kenneth (Thomas) 1937-

PERSONAL: Born January 26, 1937, in Los Angeles, CA; son of Kenneth Verlin and Ferdeythyl (Leemans) Tindall; married Tove Skjerning; married second wife, Marianne Dohm; children: (first marriage) Seth. *Education:* Attended public school in Newark, NJ. *Religion:* Danish Lutheran.

ADDRESSES: Home—c/o Schwarck Dalgas, Boulevard 48, 2000 Copenhagen F., Denmark; and Kirkebakken 47, 3390 Hundested, Denmark.

CAREER: Writer; translator and letter-carrier in Copenhagen, Denmark. Earlier employment includes positions as advertising clerk in Detroit, MI; factory worker in Jersey City, NJ, Copenhagen, and Long Island, NY; handyman in Galway, Ireland; magazine salesman in Paris,

France; farm worker in Jutland; caretaker and folk musician in Copenhagen; and street-peddler and postal clerk in New York City. *Military service:* U.S. Navy, 1954-56.

WRITINGS:

Vindharpen, Hans Reitzel (Copenhagen), 1967, translation published as *Great Heads,* Grove, 1969.

(Translator) Bodil Kaalund, *The Art of Greenland,* University of California Press, 1983.

The Banks of the Sea, Dalkey Archive Press, 1987.

(Translator from Danish) Poul Vad, *Vilhelm Hammershoi: And Danish Painting at the Turn of the Century,* Yale University Press, 1992.

Also author of *Sea Urchins* (short stories), *The Boonkeeper* (poetry), and *The Head Wars* (novel).

WORK IN PROGRESS: A new novel; poetry; another book of short stories; an essay on "love in the sight of God, from the Danish word Asyn."

SIDELIGHTS: Kenneth Tindall once told *CA:* "Never do anything you don't believe in or that you really don't want to do, or that you know is wrong. My dad always said that if you build a better mousetrap the world will beat a path to your door, and so I live where I want to live and write what I want to write, avoiding professionalism and literary scenes. I am most inspired and write best when with a woman and working at a regular job, and in everyday contact with ordinary people. I write from fullness of feeling, because my cup runneth over, the giving that is the desiring of one's beloved. My writing is lyrical and strong."

* * *

TOLSTOY, Alexandra L(vovna) 1884-1979

PERSONAL: Born July 1, 1884, in Yasnaya Polyana, Russia; died September 26, 1979, in Valley Cottage, NY; came to United States in 1931, became U.S. citizen, 1941; daughter of Leo N. (a writer) and Sophya (Bers) Tolstoy. *Education:* Educated privately. *Religion:* Eastern Orthodox.

Avocational Interests: Fishing.

CAREER: Secretary to father Leo N. Tolstoy at Yasnaya Polyana, Russia, 1901-1910; served as literary executor of her father's will, and edited manuscripts for posthumous publication, 1910-14; worked as nurse in Moscow, East Prussia, and Turkish Armenia, 1914-15; represented Zemsky Unity on Western war front, with rank equivalent to colonel, co-founded schools and relief food centers for 10,000 children, and founded four military medical field detachments, 1916-17; returned to Russia, 1918, and founded the Society for the Dissemination and Study of Tolstoy's Works, for the purpose of completing a 91-volume edition of Tolstoy's writing; imprisoned by Soviets for political activities, 1920; after her release in 1921, was appointed curator of Leo Tolstoy Museum and Educational Center at Yasnaya Polyana, and founded schools and medical facilities, 1921-29; left Russia, 1929, for lecture tour in Japan; came to United States, 1931, as lecturer and farmer in New Square, PA, 1931-33, and Haddan, CT, 1933-39; founder and president of Tolstoy Foundation Inc., New York City, and Resettlement Center, Valley Cottage, NY, 1939-79. Vice-president of CARE, 1946-79; lecturer at colleges and universities, including University of Michigan, University of Illinois, Smith College, Michigan State University, Ohio State University, and Vassar College; also appeared on many radio and television programs.

AWARDS, HONORS: St. Georges medals (Russia), 1915 and 1916, for World War I relief work; Presidential citation, 1946, for World War II relief work; Russian Red Cross in Exile citation, 1946; Kalmuk Society awards, 1952 and 1955; Chicago Civic Committee for World Refugees award, 1960; Order of Lafayette Freedom award, 1961; L.H.D. from Hobart and William Smith Colleges, 1962; U.S. Committee for Refugees award, 1966.

WRITINGS:

The Tragedy of Tolstoy, Yale University Press, 1933.

I Worked for the Soviets, Yale University Press, 1934.

Tolstoy: A Life of My Father, translation by Elizabeth Reynolds Hapgood, Harper, 1953, reprinted, Octagon, 1973.

The Real Tolstoy: A Critique and Commentary, H. S. Evans, 1968.

Out of the Past, Columbia University Press, 1982.

Contributed to periodicals, including *Pictorial Review* and *Russian Review.*

SIDELIGHTS: The youngest daughter among the thirteen children of Count Leo N. Tolstoy, Alexandra Tolstoy remained devoted to her father during his last years and throughout her own long life. The great writer's favorite child, she refused several offers of marriage in order to remain by his side. She took his part during quarrels between Leo and Sophya Tolstoy, and abetted his abortive escape from his estate to the railway station of Astapovo, where he died on November 7, 1910. At the age of seventeen, she became her father's secretary; on his death in 1910, she was named literary executor in his will.

In order to fulfill the terms of Tolstoy's will, Alexandra Tolstoy edited and prepared his previously unpublished manuscripts. Also in accordance with Tolstoy's instructions, she used the proceeds of the publication (approximately $200,000) to buy back approximately 2,500 acres of land from the estate at Yasnaya Polyana, and distributed it among the peasants from neighboring villages.

Because Alexandra Tolstoy shared her father's belief in nonviolence, she devoted much of her life to welfare work. Shortly after completing the land redistribution project, she was licensed as a practical nurse. During World War I she served as a nurse behind the front lines. Afterwards, she devoted her life to the care of refugees. Forced to leave her native Russia in 1929 because she objected to Communist antireligious propaganda, she traveled east, spending two years in Japan. She crossed the Pacific to San Francisco, then went to Chicago, where the social worker Jane Addams, of Hull House, befriended her. Often feeling displaced and sometimes impoverished and hungry, her aristocratic training saw her through difficulties. In 1939 she founded the Tolstoy Foundation, a New York-based organization that assists refugees from former Communist-bloc nations. For the rest of her life she was deeply involved in spreading the Tolstoyan message of peace and nonviolence.

Three of the books she wrote concern her father: *The Tragedy of Tolstoy, Tolstoy: A Life of My Father* and *The Real Tolstoy: A Critique and Commentary.* At various times during her life she also wrote autobiographical sketches, and these were collected posthumously in 1982 as *Out of the Past.* Although Leo Tolstoy's presence is impossible to overlook in the memoir, "Alexandra's own forceful personality was never eclipsed by her father's memory," according to W. Gareth Jones in the *Times Literary Supplement.* Commenting on Alexandra Tolstoy's literary technique, Jones wrote, "She engages our attention with vivid, snapshot-like memories" as opposed to prolonged analysis. A *New Yorker* reviewer called *Out of the Past* "a fascinating record" and termed the author's anecdotes about her father "as amusing as they are enlightening." The *Atlantic's* reviewer summarized *Out of the Past* as a chronicle of "a brave woman with a sharply observant eye, immense energy, and a nice dry humor."

BIOGRAPHICAL/CRITICAL SOURCES:

BOOKS

Tolstoy, Alexandra L. *The Tragedy of Tolstoy,* Yale University Press, 1933.

Tolstoy, Alexandra L. *I Worked for the Soviets,* Yale University Press, 1934.

PERIODICALS

Atlantic, January, 1982, p. 87.

New Yorker, March 15, 1952, pp. 34-47; March 22, 1952; January 18, 1982, p. 130.

New York Times, July 2, 1974.

Times Literary Supplement, June 4, 1982.

OBITUARIES:

PERIODICALS

Chicago Tribune, September 28, 1979, Sec. 1, p. 11.

Newsweek, October 8, 1979, p. 57.

New York Times, September 28, 1979.

Time, October 8, 1979, p. 106.

Washington Post, September 27, 1979, p. B4.*

* * *

TOMA, David 1933-

PERSONAL: Born March 7, 1933, in Newark, NJ; son of Vincent (a tailor) and Jenny (a housewife; maiden name, Fressola) Toma; married Patricia D'Amore, November 26, 1955; children David, Jr. (died, 1961), James, Patty, Donna, Janice. *Religion:* Catholic.

Avocational Interests: Playing the piano and other musical instruments; music from the 1940s and 1950s.

ADDRESSES: Home—37 Conger Way, Clark, NJ 07066. *Agent*—Al Zuckerman, 21 West 26th St., New York, NY 10010.

CAREER: Played baseball in Canada on a minor league team in Philadelphia Phillies' farm system; Newark Police Department, Newark, NJ, began as patrol officer, became detective in the Bureau of Investigations; youth counselor and lecturer, 1976—; writer. Occasional actor on the American Broadcasting Companies, Inc. (ABC-TV) series, *Toma,* 1973-74; host of *The Dave Toma Show,* broadcast by WOR-TV in Secaucus, NJ; portrayed himself in "The Drug Knot," a *CBS Schoolbreak Special,* Columbia Broadcasting System, Inc. (CBS-TV), 1986; actor, guest appearing in numerous movies produced by various broadcasting companies. Speaker in seminars on numerous social issues, including suicide prevention, AIDS, gangs, and substance abuse, c. 1951—. Founder, David Toma Center (a drug treatment facility), Tecate, Mexico. *Military service:* U.S. Marine Corps, 1952-55; served as drill instructor; received Outstanding Special Marine Award, 1953.

AWARDS, HONORS: Olympic Gold Medal for work with youth in Canada, awarded from Canadian government, 1976; award from The 100 Club, for outstanding service to humanity; story of the year honoree, International Reader's Digest; numerous honorary degrees and awards for anti-drug crusade.

WRITINGS:

(With Michael Brett) *Toma, the Compassionate Cop,* Putnam, 1974.

(With Jack Pearl) *The Airport Affair,* Dell, 1975.

(With Pearl) *The Affair of the Unhappy Hooker,* Dell, 1976.

(With Irv Levey) *Toma Tells It Straight—With Love,* Books in Focus, 1981.

(With David Villaire) "The Drug Knot," *CBS Schoolbreak Special,* CBS-TV, 1986.

(With C. Biffle) Turning Your Life Around: David Toma's Guide for Teenagers, HarperCollins, 1992.

Scriptwriter for *Toma,* ABC-TV. Toma's books have been translated into several languages.

WORK IN PROGRESS: A sequel to "The Drug Knot."

SIDELIGHTS: An undercover detective on the Newark, New Jersey, vice and narcotics squad, David Toma gained national attention for his innovative use of disguises and daring strategems to penetrate and break up illegal gambling operations and prostitution rings. His exploits inspired two network television series, *Baretta* and *Toma,* aired by the American Broadcasting Company in the 1970s. (Over the course of the series, Toma both wrote several episodes and acted in bit parts.) Since retiring from police work in 1976, Toma has devoted himself to counselling people in trouble, offering advice and practical help on how to overcome the drug habit. Toma has subsequently written several books focusing on the subject of drugs and drug abuse, including *Toma, the Compassionate Cop, Toma Tells It Straight—With Love,* and *Turning Your Life Around: David Toma's Guide for Teenagers.* "Maybe it sounds naive," he wrote in *Toma,* "but I believe that most addicts in the country can be cured with rehabilitation programs and, even more important, love and understanding."

The youngest of twelve children of an Italian immigrant father, Toma grew up poor on the tough streets of Newark, New Jersey. As a slightly built boy, he was often bullied by his peers but later developed into an outstanding high school athlete in baseball and track. He declined a baseball scholarship to Duke University and instead opted to play semi-professional baseball for two years in Canada in the Philadelphia Phillies' farm system. Toma later served a stint in the U.S. Marine Corps and became middleweight boxing champion at his training camp on Parris Island.

After his discharge, Toma joined the Newark police force and worked three years as a uniformed officer on a beat. He was promoted to the Bureau of Investigations as a detective charged with enforcing narcotics, gambling, and prostitution statutes. Toma's operating style and his manner of dealing with suspects and offenders soon marked him as a maverick. Disdaining the standard practice of deploying large police teams on stakeouts, Toma preferred to work alone, using trusted informants in the criminal underworld and an abundant array of disguises to infiltrate targets and gather evidence. He took a compassionate approach toward young prostitutes and drug addicts, sometimes talking for hours with arrested suspects to convince them to change their lives. "I can't lock someone up in jail and then just walk away and forget him," Toma declared. "That's when [an offender] needs help the most." Being sensitive to the problem addicts faced, he eventually began to volunteer his time as a drug counselor, speaking at jails, schools, and churches.

Both Toma's life as a detective and his counseling career have been the basis for television shows. The ABC-TV police drama series *Toma,* starring Tony Musante, premiered in October, 1973. Like the actual Toma, the television protagonist was a disguise expert who worked alone using unorthodox methods. The series was discontinued after one season, but reappeared in January, 1975, under the name *Baretta,* with minor format changes and a new star, Robert Blake. Toma later hosted a weekly anti-drug forum called *The Dave Toma Show,* on WOR-TV. The program, which lasted for two years, provided a chance for ordinary teenagers to voice their views on such topics as drug and alcohol abuse and suicide.

Toma published his first book *Toma, the Compassionate Cop,* in 1974. In the autobiography, the detective whom the local press once dubbed "the Man With a Thousand Faces" recounts some of his more harrowing adventures working undercover in the 1960s and 1970s. Assuming such disguises as a priest, derelict, and female prostitute, he broke several Mafia-controlled lottery operations, including one that generated revenues of $200 million per year. "I don't like to bang in doors," Toma told *Reader's Digest.* "I'd rather slip in by wearing a disguise. That way I can arrest someone before he can get rid of the evidence." The detective's use of disguises was extraordinarily successful, allowing him to make a record seven thousand arrests with an unparalleled 98 percent conviction rate—a feat made more remarkable by the fact that Toma never fired his gun.

Upon his 1976 retirement from the Newark police force, Toma began to concentrate more and more on preventing drug abuse through counseling. His decision to devote himself full time to youth guidance grew not only out of his professional experience but also out of his personal experiences with drug dependency. Toma's own drug abuse began after his four-year-old son, David, Jr., died while choking during a family dinner. Suffering a prolonged bout of depression, Toma began taking tranquilizers—sometimes up to one hundred pills a day—to numb his grief. Within a short period of time, he realized he was addicted. Toma also watched four of his nephews become victimized by drugs, and over a period of time arrested one of them, a heroin addict, more than twenty-five times. Once Toma was able to overcome his own dependence, he was determined to help others escape, too. "My addiction was what really made me aware of the drug scene," he wrote in *Toma, the Compassionate Cop.* "I began to see . . . what was happening in society, with my nephews and with other young people. They were all running away from problems they couldn't face. . . . I used drugs to forestall unpleasantness and depression before they got to me. When you can't beat a problem without [drugs], you're hooked."

Toma discusses overcoming his own addiction and his work as a drug counselor in *Toma Tells It Straight—With Love.* In the book, he cites evidence that the drug culture is growing in the United States, especially among preteens; he also offers suggestions on how to cope with personal drug problems. Toma's most recent book, *Turning Your Life Around: David Toma's Guide for Teenagers,* outlines a step-by-step guide to the resolution of such crises as depression, suicide, conflicts with parents, and the temptations of substance abuse, as well as offering advice on how to overcome these concerns and "start living a new life." In reviewing the work, a *Publishers Weekly* critic stated that "the philosophy is sound and encouraging" adding that *Turning Your Life Around* is "a useful, informative self-help manual."

In addition to his writing, Toma is a motivational speaker. He has traveled extensively, speaking to groups of young people at schools, churches, prisons, and hospitals, to reveal "how and why drugs are destroying this world." In 1986, Toma's work as an anti-drug messenger was the basis of a *CBS Schoolbreak Special* entitled "The Drug Knot." In the film, Toma, acting as himself, delivers a speech on drugs in a fictionalized high school setting, a speech that affects the lives of two young students, Lori and Doug. "The power of the program," writes a *Variety* critic, "comes from the talks delivered in the school auditorium and in the conferences with youngsters as he tries helping them." The reviewer concluded that "The Drug Knot" "delivers a powerful message."

Toma has found the experience of helping others overcome their addictions intensely rewarding. "Talk to someone who is in the living hell of drugs, lend a helping hand, give him a kind word and the assurance he needs to last out his agony, and you're doing God's work," he wrote in *Toma.* "There's no other way for me to describe the satisfaction, gratification, and the plain down-to-earth feeling of riches I experience when I see someone who has fought his way back."

BIOGRAPHICAL/CRITICAL SOURCES:

BOOKS

Toma, the Compassionate Cop, Putnam, 1974.

Toma Tells It Straight—With Love, Books in Focus, 1981.

Turning Your Life Around: David Toma's Guide for Teenagers, HarperCollins, 1992.

PERIODICALS

Kliatt Young Adult Paperback Book Guide, April, 1988, p. 37.

Newsweek, July 19, 1971; September 28, 1981; July 17, 1991, p. 40.

Publishers Weekly, January 1, 1992, p. 57.

Reader's Digest, November, 1973, pp. 229-32, 234-36.

Variety, October 1, 1986, p. 62.

*   *   *

TOWNSHEND, Richard
See BICKERS, Richard (Leslie) Townshend

*   *   *

TRAVER, Robert
See VOELKER, John D(onaldson)

*   *   *

TRESILIAN, Liz
See GREEN, Elizabeth Sara

*   *   *

TREZZA, Alphonse F(iore) 1920-

PERSONAL: Born December 27, 1920, in Philadelphia, PA; son of Vincent (a waiter) and Amalia (a homemaker; maiden name, Ferrara) Trezza; married Mildred Di Pietro (a teacher), May 19, 1945; children: Carol Johnston, Alphonse, Jr. *Education:* University of Pennsylvania, B.S., 1948, M.S., 1950; Drexel Institute of Technology (now Drexel University), certificate in library science, 1949.

ADDRESSES: Home—2205 Napoleon Bonaparte Dr., Tallahassee, FL 32308. *Office*—School of Information Studies, Florida State University, Tallahassee, FL 32306.

CAREER: Villanova University, Villanova, PA, cataloger/reference librarian, 1949-50; University of Pennsylvania, Philadelphia, head of library's circulation department, 1950-56; Catholic Library Association, Villanova, executive secretary of Library Administration Division, 1956-60; American Library Association, Chicago, IL, associate director of association and executive secretary of Library Administration Division, 1960-69; Illinois State Library, Springfield, director, 1969-74; National Commission on Libraries and Information Science, Washington, DC, executive director, 1974-80; Intergovernmental Library Cooperation Project, Library of Congress, Washington, DC, director, 1980-82; Florida State University, Tallahassee, associate professor, 1982-87, professor of library and information studies, 1987-93, professor emeritus, 1993—. Lecturer at Drexel University, 1951-60, University of Illinois, 1973, Catholic University of America, 1975-82, and Texas Women's University, 1978. Consultant to various libraries, government agencies, associations, and private companies; member and past president of Joliet, Illinois, Diocesan Board of Education.

MEMBER: International Federation of Library Associations, American Library Association (member of council, 1972-82, 1989-92; member of executive board, 1974-78), Association for Library and Information Science Education, Association of Specialized and Cooperative Library Agencies, Catholic Library Association (member of advisory council), Southeastern Library Association, Illinois Library Association (chairman of library development committee, 1963-70), Pennsylvania Library Association, Virginia Library Association, Florida Library Association (member of board of directors, 1987-89; vice-president and president-elect, 1990-91; president, 1991-92), Beta Phi Mu, Kappa Phi Kappa.

AWARDS, HONORS: Illinois Library Association, special librarian's citation, 1965, librarian's citation, 1974; commendation from White House Conference of Library and Information Science, 1979; tribute from Council of the American Library Association, 1980; exceptional achievement award from Association of Specialized and Cooperative Library Agencies, 1981; grant from National Commission on Libraries and Information Science, 1982; Joseph W. Lippincott Award, American Library Association, 1989.

WRITINGS:

EDITOR

Standards and Guidelines for Florida Public Library Services, Florida Library Association, 1985.

Public Libraries and the Challenges of the Next Two Decades, Libraries Unlimited, 1985.

Not Alone . . . But Together, Florida State University, 1987.

Effective Access to Information: Today's Challenge, Tomorrow's Opportunity, G. K. Hall, 1989.

Changing Technology Opportunity and Challenge, G. K. Hall, 1989.

Commitment to Service: The Library's Mission, G. K. Hall, 1990.

Issues for the New Decade: Today's Challenge, Tomorrow's Opportunity, G. K. Hall, 1991.

The Funding of Public and Academic Libraries: The Critical Issue for the '90s, G. K. Hall, 1992.

OTHER

Contributor to numerous books, including *ALA Yearbook of Library and Information Services,* edited by Robert Parent, American Library Association, 1976-91; *The Special Role in Networks,* edited by Robert W. Gibson, Jr., Special Libraries Association, 1980; *Strategies for Meeting the Information Needs of Society in the Year 2000,* edited by Martha Boaz, Libraries Unlimited, 1981; and *ALA World Encyclopedia of Library and Information Services,* 2nd edition, American Library Association, 1986. Also contributor to many journals, including *Journal of Library Administration, Government Publications Review,* and *Special Libraries.* Editor of *Catholic Library World,* 1956-60, *FLASH,* 1990, and *Florida Libraries,* 1991—.

SIDELIGHTS: Alphonse F. Trezza told *CA:* "As a professional librarian for over three decades I have strived in both my writings and my career opportunities to implement my philosophy of librarianship—equal opportunity of access to information for all. A democracy depends on an informed and educated electorate. Public libraries are one of the few institutions that are open to all, regardless of age, education, economic status, race, or creed. The only requirement is desire, need, or curiosity. To achieve this goal of equal opportunity of access for all, a challenge well within our grasp before the year 2000, all types of libraries—academic, public, school, and special—must come together. Libraries must be willing to share their resources, books, and other types of materials, as well as human resources, ideas, creativity, and dreams. Each type of library brings a special role and expertise to a cooperative relationship. The lessons all librarians must remember are that life is never equal or fair, and that it is in the giving that we receive. This philosophy works not only in our private lives but in our professional work and lives.

"One of the greatest challenges for libraries and librarians is to reduce and overcome the many barriers to access. One that is difficult to cope with is fear—the fear that by cooperating and sharing we somehow will lose our autonomy and independence; that our primary clientele will somehow have less, rather than more, service; that we haven't the time or the funds to develop, through meetings and planning, our cooperative relationships. Funding is obviously never enough, and redirecting our priorities is not easy, but the real problem is fear: fear of change, of the unknown, of being wrong, or of making a mistake.

"In all of my opportunities in my many career positions, I have tried to not only espouse my philosophy, but to implement it through action, both legislative and administrative. In my writings I strive to describe, explain, and exclaim the need for access to information for all as a basic right in a democracy. Information and library services are not a commodity but a public good supported, traditionally, indirectly through taxes rather than directly through user fees. Ability to pay ought not be the criteria for access to information. I am optimistic about the future of libraries and librarians in our complex technological and information-oriented society. Libraries are dynamic, and change, albeit slowly sometimes, to meet the needs of their constituencies. Libraries will always be among the basic providers of information and educational opportunities, and places for relaxation and recreation for the child as well as the senior citizen. All are welcome."

* * *

TRIMMER, Joseph F(rancis) 1941-

PERSONAL: Born August 4, 1941, in Cortland, NY; son of Francis W. (a clergyman) and Margaret (maiden name, Sieber) Trimmer; married Carol L. Straley (a congressional aide), June 12, 1966; children: Robert Gorden. *Education:* Colgate University, B.A., 1963; Purdue University, M.A., 1966, Ph.D., 1968.

Avocational Interests: Photography.

ADDRESSES: Home—409 Tyrone Dr., Muncie, IN 47304. *Office*—Department of English, Ball State University, Muncie, IN 47306.

CAREER: Ball State University, Muncie, IN, 1968—, began as assistant professor, became full professor of English. Instructor, Martha's Vineyard Summer Writing Workshop, 1985—; Westminster Exchange fellow, Oxford, 1989.

WRITINGS:

A Casebook on Ralph Ellison's "Invisible Man," Crowell, 1972.
Black American Literature: Notes on the Problems of Definition, Ball State University, 1972.
Writing with a Purpose, Houghton, 1984, revised edition, 1987.
A Guide to MLA Documentation, Houghton, 1988.
(With Tilly Warnock) *Understanding Others: Cultural and Cross-Cultural Studies and the Teaching of Literature,* National Council of Teachers of English, 1992.

EDITOR

(With others) *American Oblique: Writing about the American Experience,* Houghton, 1976.
The National Book Award for Fiction: An Index to the First Twenty-Five Years, G.K. Hall, 1978.
(With Maxine Hairston) *The Riverside Reader,* Houghton, Volume 1, 1981, Volume 2, 1983.
Fictions, Harcourt, 1985, revised edition, 1989.

TUCKER, Link
See BINGLEY, David Ernest

* * *

TUNSTALL, (C.) Jeremy 1934-

PERSONAL: Born October 14, 1934, in London, England; son of Brian (a historian) and Elizabeth (Corbett) Tunstall; married Sylvia Korte; children: Rebecca, Helena, Paul. *Education:* Cambridge University, B.A., M.A., 1958.

ADDRESSES: Home—19 South Villas, Camden Sq., London NW1 9BS, England. *Office*—Communications Policy Centre, Department of Sociology, City University, London EC1V OHB, England.

CAREER: University of London, London School of Economics and Political Science, London, England, research officer, 1962-64; University of Essex, Essex, England, Leverhulme fellow, 1965-69; Open University, Buckinghamshire, England, senior lecturer, 1969-74; City University, London, professor of sociology, 1974—, director of Communications Policy Centre. Sabbatical at George Washington University, 1983-84; visiting professor at University of California, San Diego.

MEMBER: British Sociological Association.

WRITINGS:

The Fishermen, MacGibbon & Kee, 1962.
The Advertising Man in London Advertising Agencies, Chapman & Hall, 1964.
Old and Alone: A Sociological Study of Old People, Routledge & Kegan Paul, 1966.
(Editor) *Media Sociology: A Reader,* University of Illinois Press, 1970.
The Westminster Lobby Correspondents: A Sociological Study of National Political Journalism, Routledge & Kegan Paul, 1970.
(Editor with Kenneth Thompson and Francis G. Castles) *Sociological Perspectives: Selected Readings,* Penguin, 1971.
Journalists at Work: Special Correspondents; Their News Organizations, News Sources, and Competitor-Colleagues, Sage Publications, 1971.
(With Frederick Spencer Brooman) *Economy and Society,* Open University Press, 1971.
(With Brooman) *Money, Wealth and Class,* Open University Press, 1971.
Stability, Change and Conflict, Open University Press, 1971.
The Sociological Perspective, Open University Press, 1972.
(Editor) *The Open University Opens,* University of Massachusetts Press, 1974.

The Media Are American, Columbia University Press, 1977 (published in England as *The Media Are American: Anglo-American Media in the World,* Constable, 1977).
(With Oliver Boyd-Barrett) *Studies on the Press,* H.M.S.O., 1977.
(With David Walker) *Media Made in California: News, Politics, the New Hollywood,* Oxford University Press, 1981.
The Media in Britain, Columbia University Press, 1983.
Communications Deregulation, Basil Blackwell, 1986.
(With Michael Palmer) *Liberating Communications: Policy-Making in France and Britain,* Blackwell, 1990.
(With Palmer) *Media Moguls,* Routledge, 1991.
Television Producers, Routledge, 1993.

Also author with Peter George James Jenkins of recording "The Mass Media," Holt Information Systems, 1972.

WORK IN PROGRESS: Newspaper Power, based on interviews with British newspaper editors.

SIDELIGHTS: C. Jeremy Tunstall once told *CA* that *Media Made in California: News, Politics, the New Hollywood* "seeks to fill a gap in the existing literature by looking at the links between Hollywood, state politics, and state media. California is the great cross-over land, and it takes a cross-over book to explain it. In Hollywood we look not only at film and TV but also at the popular music industry. We also discuss the major inadequacies of the California news media in covering politics at the state level, in presenting the enormous Hispanic minority, and . . . in covering the grubbier aspects of Hollywood. The book covers a very broad sweep, but also has more detailed discussions about certain groups, such as the editors of the major newspapers in the state, television series producers, [and] record executives. Other topics discussed include the Screen Actors Guild, the Sacramento press corps, Ronald Reagan, Richard Nixon, Jerry Brown, the way in which the owned and operated TV stations slant their news coverage in Los Angeles towards the affluent North West, the *Los Angeles Times,* the inadequacies of the Bay Area press, California's weirdest newspaper, Hollywood agents, the ties between popular music and politics, the polling principle in state politics, [and] the future 'new media' prospects."

Tunstall more recently commented, "In the 1990s I have published two books with a co-author, Michael Palmer; despite his English name he is Professor of Communications Theory at the University of Paris 3, Sorbonne Nouvelle. These two books involved many flights between London and Paris. My latest book, *Television Producers,* is . . . based on interviews with 254 British television producers; it is the first comprehensive account of BBC, ITV, and Channel Four producers. As such I hope that it will help to make the mysteries of British 'Public Service TV' more understandable. I am working on a new book based on interviews with senior editors on British national newspapers; it will be called *Newspaper Power.* After that I will return to the theme of world mass media. Following my 1977 book, it might be called *The Media Are No Longer American.*"

BIOGRAPHICAL/CRITICAL SOURCES:

PERIODICALS

Times Literary Supplement, December 23, 1983.

* * *

TURNER, Gwenda 1947-

PERSONAL: Born May 11, 1947, in Kyogle, Australia; daughter of Walter David and Mary (a housewife; maiden name, Bugden) Williams; married John Turner (an advertising executive), July 31, 1974. *Education:* Wellington Polytechnic School of Design, Diploma in Graphic Design, 1970.

ADDRESSES: Home and office—18 Greenwood Close, Christchurch, Canterbury 1, New Zealand. *Agent*—Anne Bower Ingram, 4/6 Boronia St., Wollstonecraft, Sydney, New South Wales 2065, Australia.

CAREER: Secretary in Brisbane, Australia, 1964-66; graphic design consultant, 1970-74; full-time artist, 1974-76; full-time writer and illustrator, 1976—.

MEMBER: Australian Society of Authors, Canterbury Society of Arts.

AWARDS, HONORS: Russell Clark Award, New Zealand Library Association, 1984, for illustrations in *The Tree Witches; The Tree Witches* was shortlisted for the Australian Children's Book of the Year Award for best picture book, 1985.

WRITINGS:

ALL SELF-ILLUSTRATED

Akaroa: Banks Peninsula, New Zealand, John McIndoe, 1977.
Buildings and Bridges of Christchurch, John McIndoe, 1981.
Daydream Journey, Collins, 1982.
The Tree Witches, Kestrel, 1983.
Creepy Cottage, Omnibus Books, 1983.
Catnip Mice and Tussie Mussies, Omnibus Books, 1983.
New Zealand ABC, Whitcoulls, 1985.
Gwenda Turner's Playbook, Viking Kestrel, 1985.
Snow Play, Collins, 1986.
New Zealand 123, Whitcoulls, 1986.
New Zealand Colours, Penguin, 1989.

Colors, Viking Kestrel, 1989.
Once upon a Time, Viking Penguin, 1990.
Shapes, Viking Penguin, 1991.
Gwenda Turner's Australian ABC, Penguin, 1992.
Opposites, Viking Penguin, 1992.
Over on the Farm, Viking Penguin, 1993.

SIDELIGHTS: Gwenda Turner once told *CA:* "From the age of about eight, I had an idea that I would like to write and illustrate books. Openings in this field in the 1960s, during high school, were rare, and I subsequently ended up as a shorthand typist. After three years of this work fate led me to New Zealand, where I immediately took up study in graphic design.

"I feel that it was an advantage having been out in the work force for three years before I took up tertiary education. I knew what I wanted and was prepared to go through the financial difficulties to see myself through the course. Subsequently—after working at magazine and advertising art and design for several years—I began drawing old houses and buildings. Many of these buildings had a story behind them and this led me to write and illustrate my first book.

"It seemed a natural progression to lead into children's books. One of the appealing aspects of children's books is that one can work in full color. In the case of the children's picture book, which I specialize in, there are very few restrictions. Design, layout, shape of book, and choice of typeface are just as important to me as the storyline and illustrations. I enjoy producing books because I can bring together all aspects of my creativity and express them in the form of 'a book.'

"I had a very happy and secure childhood. I didn't read a great deal—I was always making up games and playing. Enid Blyton's books were wonderful, especially the series 'The Mystery of. . . .' My ideas for stories come from my childhood experiences. I think what is exciting is what sparks off a particular idea for a story. I remember when I heard the words 'partners in foolishness' in a play on television. I wrote down those words and within a week had written the first draft of *The Tree Witches.* A foreign language edition of this book was published in Germany.

"I have been influenced by author/illustrators such as Beatrix Potter, N. C. Wyeth, Howard Pyle, Andrew Wyeth, Carl Larsson, Arthur Rackham, Maurice Sendak, John Burningham, and Norman Lindsay. Potter's work appeals because one feels that she sincerely loved what she wrote and painted. Somehow this comes across in an intangible way. I admire Sendak's work because with each book he has developed and improved his craft.

"After writing my story and planning the illustrations, I then go looking for animals, people, and so forth, because my style of illustrating is true-to-life and I research everything I draw. I enjoy starting work at 8:00 A.M. each day. Very few days pass by when I haven't nibbled away with a pen or brush. I like working to deadlines. Being an author/illustrator is a way of life. There are not enough hours in a day!

"Emerson was correct when he wrote: 'Success is constitutional; depends on a PLUS condition of mind and body, on power of work, on courage.' "

U-V

UNGER-HAMILTON, Clive (Wolfgang) 1942-

PERSONAL: Born June 2, 1942, in Preston, England; son of Wolfgang (a physician) and Mori (Boursnell) Unger; married Romana Blacher (an archaeologist), December 8, 1968 (divorced); married Cordelia Chitty, December 21, 1982; children: (first marriage) Felix, Ferdinand; (second marriage) Augustus, Prosper. *Education:* Attended National University of Ireland, 1961-62, and Trinity College of Music, London, 1963-66.

ADDRESSES: *Home*—La Roussiere, 61240 Godisson, France.

CAREER: Fellow of Trinity College of Music, London, England, 1966; concert harpsichordist, 1966-70; free-lance journalist, 1970-73; writer and editor, 1977—.

WRITINGS:

(Compiler) *Royal Collection,* Novello, 1977.
The Music Makers, Abrams, 1979.
Encyclopedia of Theatre: The Entertainers, Pitman, 1980.
Keyboard Music, Phaidon, 1981.
The Great Symphonies, Facts on File, 1982.
The Children's Guide to Paris, Blackie & Sons, 1983.
Domenico Scalatti, Uniepers, 1985.
The Great Concertos, Uniepers, 1986.
(With Irma Kurtz) *The Children's Guide to . . . Rome,* Bedrick Blackie, 1986.

Also compiler of the *Victorian Christmas Song Book,* 1980.

van der PLOEG, Johannes P(etrus) M(aria) 1909-

PERSONAL: Born July 4, 1909, in Nijmegen, Netherlands; son of Harke Antonius and Petronella Anna (Snijers) van der Ploeg. *Education:* Attended Dominicans, Zwolle, Netherlands, 1927-30, and Paris Dominicans "Le Saulchoir," 1931-32; Collegio Angelico, Rome, Italy, D.Theol., 1936, Doctor S. Scripturae, 1946; additional study at Ecole Biblique Francaise Jerusalem.

ADDRESSES: *Home*—Sterreschansweg 57E, 6522 GK Nijmegen, Netherlands. *Office*—Catholic University, Institutes for Theology and Semitics, Nijmegen University, 6522 GL Nijmegen, Netherlands.

CAREER: Ordained Roman Catholic priest of Dominican order, 1932; lecturer on Old Testament introduction and Hebrew, Dominican Monastery, Zwolle, Netherlands, 1934-37, and Dominican Monastery "Albertinum," Nijmegen, Netherlands, 1938-51; Catholic University of Nijmegen, Nijmegen, Netherlands, professor of Old Testament exegesis and Hebrew, 1951-79, professor emeritus, 1979—.

MEMBER: Royal Dutch Academy of Sciences.

AWARDS, HONORS: Named Knight of the Dutch Lion, 1979.

WRITINGS:

Les Chants du Serviteur de Jahve, Gabalda, 1936.
Oud-Syrisch monniksleven, E. J. Brill, 1942.
(Translator and editor) *Spreuken vit de grondtekst vertaald en vitgelegd,* Romen & Zonen, 1952.
(Translator and editor) *Prediker,* Romen & Zonen, 1953.
De Kerk en Israel, Gooi & Sticht, 1954, translation published as *The Church and Israel,* Blackfriars Publications, 1956.

Vondsten in de woestijn van Juda, Het Spectrum, 1957, 4th edition, 1970, translation by Kevin Smyth published as *The Excavations at Qumran: A Survey of the Judaean Brotherhood and Its Ideas,* Longmans, Green, 1958.

(Translator and author of introduction and notes) *Le Rouleau de la guerre,* E. J. Brill, 1959.

La Sectre de Qumran et les origines du Christianisme, Desclee, De Brouwer, 1959.

Mens tegenover mens in het Oude Testament, Dekker & Van de Vegt, 1960.

Bij-belverklaring te Qumran, Noord-Hollandsche, 1960.

(Editor) *Le Targum de Job de la grotte XI de Qumran,* Noord-Hollandsche, 1962.

Une Theologie de l'Ancien Testament: Est-elle possible?, Publications Universitaires de Louvain, 1962.

(Translator and editor) *De Psalmen,* Romen & Zonen, Volume 1, 1963, Volume 2, 1973-79.

(Translator and editor) *De Boeken van het Oude Testament,* Volume 1, Romen, 1970.

Sacrifice and Priesthood in the Catholic Church, Augustine, 1977.

Veertig Preken, over Geloof en Evangelie, [Tilburg], 1978.

Aspecten van het Godbegrip in het Oude Testament, Noord-Hollandsche, 1981.

Il Geloof, [Tilburg], 1983, translation published as *I Believe,* Long Prairy, 1986.

In Beeld en Gelijkenis, Venlo, 1989.

Also author of *Schrift en Overlevering,* 1928, *Voorspellingen over den Verlesser in het Oude Testament,* 1941, and *The Christmas of St. Thomas in South India and Their Syriac Manuscripts,* 1983. Editor, "Series on the Texts of the Desert of Judah," E. J. Brill, 1957. Contributor to journals. Editor, *Katholieke Stemmen.*

WORK IN PROGRESS: Research on the Dead Sea Scrolls.

SIDELIGHTS: Johannes P. M. van der Ploeg has traveled extensively; his first journey was to Palestine in 1947. Since then he has traveled to the countries of the Near East and to Kerala, India, to study Christian problems.

* * *

Van SERTIMA, Ivan 1935-

PERSONAL: Born January 26, 1935, in Kitty Village, Guyana; son of Frank Obermuller (an administrator and trade union leader) and Clara (Smith) Van Sertima; married Maria Nagy, October 24, 1964; children: Lawrence Josef. *Education:* London School of Oriental and African Studies, London, B.A. (with honors), 1969; Rutgers University, M.A., 1977.

ADDRESSES: Home—59 South Adelaide Ave., Highland Park, NJ 08904. *Office*—Department of African Studies, Douglass College, Rutgers University, New Brunswick, NJ 08094.

CAREER: Government Information Services (Guyana Civil Service), Georgetown, Guyana, press and broadcasting officer, 1956-59; Central Office of Information, London, England, broadcaster, 1969-70; Rutgers University, Douglass College, New Brunswick, NJ, instructor, 1970-72, assistant professor, 1972-79, associate professor of African studies, 1978—. Nominator for Nobel Prize in Literature, 1976-80. President of *Journal of African Civilizations* Ltd. Inc.

MEMBER: African Heritage Association, American Association of University Professors, Caribbean Artists Movement.

AWARDS, HONORS: Clarence L. Holte Prize, Twenty-first Century Foundation, 1981, for *They Came before Columbus: The African Presence in Ancient America.*

WRITINGS:

River and the Wall (poems), Miniature Poets, 1958.

Caribbean Writers: Critical Essays, New Beacon Books, 1968, Panther House, 1971.

Swahili Dictionary of Legal Terms, [Tanzania], 1968.

They Came before Columbus: The African Presence in Ancient America, Random House, 1977.

(Editor) *Blacks in Science: Ancient and Modern,* Transaction Books, 1983.

(Editor) *Black Women in Antiquity,* Transaction Books, 1984.

(Editor) *African Presence in Early Europe,* Transaction Books, 1985.

(Editor with Runoko Rashidi) *African Presence in Early Asia,* Transaction Books, 1985.

(Editor) *Great African Thinkers, Volume I: Cheikh Anta Diop,* Transaction Publishers, 1986.

(Editor) *African Presence in Early America,* Transaction Books, 1987.

(Editor) *Great Black Leaders: Ancient and Modern,* Transaction Publishers, 1988.

(Editor) *Egypt Revisited,* Transaction Publishers, 1985, revised edition, 1991.

(Editor) *The Golden Age of the Moor,* Transaction Publishers, 1991.

Editor of *Nile Valley Civilizations: Proceedings of the Nile Valley Conference, Atlanta, September 26-30,* 1985. Contributor to books, including *Black Life and Culture in the United States,* edited by Rhoda Goldstein, Crowell, 1971; *Enigma of Values,* edited by Anna Rutherford, Dangaroo Press, 1975; *Seminar in Black English,* edited by Tom Trebasso, Lawrence Erbaum Associates, 1976. Contributor to periodicals, including *Inter-American Review.* Editor of *Journal of African Civilizations.*

WORK IN PROGRESS: Research on African presence in the art of the Americas.

SIDELIGHTS: Ivan Van Sertima is a prolific writer who has published numerous books dealing with African history and influence in the histories of the United States and other countries. He is also a poet and has published a collection of poems titled *River and the Wall. They Came before Columbus* is one of his first publications about African history. In this book Van Sertima argues that African people had a significant impact on the Precolumbian civilizations of the New World. He also claims that black Africans came to the Americas long before they were discovered by Christopher Columbus. He presents as evidence a negroid skeleton found in the Virgin Islands dating back to 1250 A.D., as well as the discovery by archeologists of pyramids in Central America. Other books by Van Sertima include *African Presence in Early Europe* and *Egypt Revisited.*

BIOGRAPHICAL/CRITICAL SOURCES:

BOOKS

Contemporary Poets, St. James Press, 1970, p. 1119.

PERIODICALS

New York Times Book Review, March 13, 1977, p. 8.*

* * *

VARGAS LLOSA, (Jorge) Mario (Pedro) 1936-

PERSONAL: Born March 28, 1936, in Arequipa, Peru; son of Ernesto Vargas Maldonaldo and Dora Llosa Ureta; married Julia Urquidi, 1955 (divorced); married Patricia Llosa, 1965; children: (second marriage) Alvaro, Gonzalo, Morgana. *Education:* Attended University of San Marcos; University of Madrid, Ph.D., 1959. *Politics:* Liberal.

Avocational Interests: Movies, jogging, football.

CAREER: Writer. Journalist with *La Industria,* Piura, Peru, and with Radio Panamericana and *La Cronica,* both in Lima, Peru, during 1950s; worked in Paris, France, as a journalist with the radio-television network ORTF, and as a language teacher; University of London, Queen Mary College and Kings College, London, England, faculty member, 1966-68; Washington State University, Seattle, writer in residence, 1968; University of Puerto Rico, Rio Piedras, Puerto Rico, visiting professor, 1969; *Libre,* Paris, co-founder, 1971; Columbia University, New York City, Edward Laroque Tinker Visiting Professor, 1975; host of Peruvian television program "The Tower of Babel", 1981; Peruvian presidential candidate, Liberty Movement, 1990; Harvard University, visiting professor, 1992; Princeton University, visiting professor, 1993; former fellow, Woodrow Wilson Center, Washington, DC.

MEMBER: Liberty Movement (Peru).

AWARDS, HONORS: Premio Leopoldo Alas, 1959, for *Los jefes;* Premio Biblioteca Breve, 1962, and Premio de la Critica Espanola, 1963, both for *La ciudad y los perros;* Premio de la Critica Espanola, Premio Nacional de la Novela, and Premio Internacional Literatura Romulo Gallegos, all 1967, all for *La casa verde;* Ritz Paris Hemingway Award, 1985, for *The War of the End of the World.*

WRITINGS:

Los jefes (story collection; title means "The Leaders"), Editorial Rocas, 1959.

Los cachorros (novella), Editorial Lumen, 1967, translation by Ronald Christ and Gregory Kolovakos published with six short stories as *The Cubs and Other Stories,* Harper, 1979.

Carta de batalla por "Tirant lo Blanc," Seix Barral, 1969.

Antologia minima de M. Vargas Llosa, Editorial Tiempo Contemporaneo, 1969.

(With Julio Cortazar and Oscar Collazos) *La litteratura en la revolucion y la revolucion en la litteratura,* Siglo Vientiuno Editores, 1970.

Garcia Marquez: Historia de un deicidio, Seix Barral, 1971.

La historia secreta de una novela, Tusquets, 1971.

Obras escogidas, Aguilar, 1973.

La orgia perpetua: Flaubert y "Madame Bovary," Seix Barral, 1975, translation by Helen R. Lane published as *The Perpetual Orgy: Flaubert and "Madame Bovary,"* Farrar, Straus, 1986.

Art, Authenticity and Latin American Culture: A Dialogue with Mario Vargas Llosa and Ariel Dorfman, Wilson Center (Washington, DC), 1981.

La senorita de Tacna, Seix Barral, 1982, first produced under title *Senorita from Tacna* in New York at INTAR Hispanic American Arts Center, 1983; produced under title *The Young Lady from Tacna* in Los Angeles at the Bilingual Foundation of the Arts, May, 1985.

Kathie y el hipopotamo: Comedia en dos actos, Seix Barral, 1983, translation by Kerry McKenny and Anthony Oliver-Smith produced as *Kathie and the Hippopotamus* in Edinburgh, Scotland, at the Traverse Theatre, August, 1986.

Contra viento y marea, Seix Barral, 1983.

La cultura de la libertad, la libertad de la cultura, Fundacion Eduardo Frei, 1985.

La chunga, Seix Barral, 1986, translation by Joanne Pottlitzer first produced in New York at INTAR Hispanic American Arts Center, February 9, 1986.

(With Garcia Marquez) *Dialogo sobre la novela Latinoamericana,* Peru Andino, 1988.

(Translator and author of prologue) *Un coeur sous une soutagne,* J. Campodonico, 1989.

(With Publio Lopez Mondejar) *Martin Chambi, 1920-1950,* Circulo de Bellas Artes, 1990.

La verdad de las mentiras: ensayos sobre literatura, Seix Barral, 1990.

Contra viento y marea, III (1964-1988), Seix Barral, 1990.

A Writer's Reality, edited and with introduction by Myron I. Lichtblau, Syracuse University Press, 1991.

El pez en el agua: Memorias del inca, Seix Barral, 1993.

Also author of play *La huida* produced in Piura, Peru. Contributor to *The Eye of the Heart,* 1973.

NOVELS

La ciudad y los perros, Seix Barral, 1963, translation by Lysander Kemp published as *The Time of the Hero,* Grove, 1966.

La casa verde, Seix Barral, 1966, translation by Gregory Rabassa published as *The Green House,* Harper, 1968.

Conversacion en la catedral, Seix Barral, 1969, translation by Rabassa published as *Conversation in the Cathedral,* Harper, 1975.

Pantaleon y las visitadoras, Seix Barral, 1973, translation by Christ and Kolovakos published as *Captain Pantoja and the Special Service,* Harper, 1978.

La guerra del fin del mundo, Plaza & Janes (Barcelona), 1981, translation by Lane published as *The War of the End of the World,* Farrar, Straus, 1984.

Aunt Julia and the Scriptwriter, Farrar, Straus, 1982 (published in the original Spanish as *La tia Julia y el escribidor,* 1977).

Historia de Mayta, Seix Barral, 1985, translation by Alfred MacAdam published as *The Real Life of Alejandro Mayta,* Farrar, Straus, 1986.

Quien mato a Palomino Molero?, Seix Barral, 1986, translation by MacAdam published as *Who Killed Palomino Molero?,* Farrar, Straus, 1987.

El hablador, Seix Barral, 1987, translation by Lane published as *The Storyteller,* Farrar, Straus, 1989.

Elogio de la madrastra, Tusquets, 1988, translation by Lane published as *In Praise of the Stepmother,* Farrar, Straus, 1990.

ADAPTATIONS: "The Cubs" was filmed in 1971; *Captain Pantoja and the Special Service* was filmed in 1976, directed by the author, and banned in Peru; *Aunt Julia and the Scriptwriter* was adapted as a television series in Colombia and as the film *Tune in Tomorrow,* released by Cinecom Entertainment in 1990.

SIDELIGHTS: Peruvian writer Mario Vargas Llosa often draws from his personal experiences to write of the injustices and corruption of contemporary Latin America. Once an admirer of communist Cuba, since the early 1970s Vargas Llosa has been opposed to tyrannies of both the political left and right. He now advocates democracy, a free market, and individual liberty, and he cautions against extreme or violent political action, instead calling for peaceful democratic reforms. In 1989 he was chosen as the presidential candidate of Frente Democratico, a political coalition in Peru, for the elections of 1990, which he did not win. Through his novels, marked by complex structures and an innovative merging of dialogue and description that add to their real-life feeling, Vargas Llosa has established himself as one of the most important of contemporary writers in the Spanish language. His novels, a London *Times* writer commented, "are among the finest coming out of Latin America."

Vargas Llosa's first novel, *The Time of the Hero* (originally published in Spanish as *La ciudad y los perros*), was inspired by the two years he spent at the Leoncio Prado Military Academy. Sent there by his father, who felt the boy's poetry writing endangered his masculinity, Vargas Llosa found the school, with its "restrictions, the military discipline and the brutal, bullying atmosphere, unbearable," he recalled in an article for the *New York Times Magazine.* The book struck a nerve with the school's officials. "One thousand copies were ceremoniously burned in the patio of the school and several generals attacked it bitterly," he noted. "One of them said that the book was the work of a 'degenerate mind,' and another, who was more imaginative, claimed that I had undoubtedly been paid by Ecuador to undermine the prestige of the Peruvian Army." *Time* reviewer R. Z. Sheppard described *The Time of the Hero* as "a brutal slab of naturalism about life and violent death."

The Green House (*La casa verde*) also began with a childhood memory, of a brothel known as the Green House in the Peruvian coastal town of Piura where Vargas Llosa lived with his family for several years. The book's several stories explore the brothel and the family that owns it, the military that runs a town in the jungle, a dealer in stolen rubber in the nearly jungle, and a prostitute who was raised in a convent. "Scenes overlap, different times and places overrun each other . . . echoes precede voices, and disembodied consciences dissolve almost before they can be identified," Luis Harss and Barbara Dohmann wrote in *Into the Mainstream: Conversations with Latin-American Writers.* Gregory Rabassa, writing in *World Literature Today,* noted that the novel's title "is the connective theme that links the primitive world of the jungle to the primal lusts of 'civilization' which are enclosed by the green walls of the whorehouse." Rabassa also found that

Vargas Llosa's narrative style "has not reduced time to a device of measurement or location, a practical tool, but has conjoined it with space, so that the characters carry their space with them too . . . inseparable from their time." *The Green House* "is probably the most accomplished work of fiction ever to come out of Latin America," Harss and Dohmann declared. "It has sweep, beauty, imaginative scope, and a sustained eruptive power that carries the reader from first page to last like a fish in a bloodstream."

Whereas in previous novels Vargas Llosa had sought to recreate the repression and corruption of a particular place, in *Conversation in the Cathedral* (*Conversacion en la catedral*), he attempted to provide a panoramic view of his native country. The novel "presents a wider, more encompassing view of Peruvian society," John M. Kirk stated in *International Fiction Review.* "[Vargas Llosa's] gaze extends further afield in a determined effort to incorporate as many representative regions of Peru as possible." Set during the dictatorship of Manuel Odria in the late 1940s and 1950s, the society depicted in the novel "is one of corruption in virtually all the shapes and spheres you can imagine," Wolfgang A. Luchting wrote in the *Review of the Center for Inter-American Relations.* Penny Leroux, in a *Nation* review, calls it "one of the most scathing denunciations ever written on the corruption and immorality of Latin America's ruling classes."

The nonlinear writing of *Conversation in the Cathedral* is seen by several critics to be the culmination of Vargas Llosa's narrative experimentation. Writing in the *Review of the Center for Inter-American Relations,* Ronald Christ called the novel "a masterpiece of montage" and "a massive assault on simultaneity." Christ argued that the author achieves a montage effect that "promotes a linking of actions and words, speech and description, image and image, point of view and point of view." Kirk explained that in *Conversation in the Cathedral,* Vargas Llosa attempted "the ambitious and obviously impossible plan of conveying to the reader all aspects of the reality of [Peruvian] society, of writing the 'total' novel." By interweaving five different narratives, Vargas Llosa forces the reader to study the text closely, making the reader an "accomplice of the writer [which] undoubtedly helps the reader to a more profound understanding of the work." Kirk concluded that the novel is "both a perfect showcase for all the structural techniques and thematic obsessions found in [Vargas Llosa's] other work, as well as being the true culmination of his personal anguish for Peru."

D. P. Gallagher argued in *Modern Latin American Literature* that one intention of the complex nonlinear structures of Vargas Llosa's early novels was to "re-enact the complexity of the situations described in them." By juxtaposing unrelated elements, cutting off dialogue at critical moments, and breaking the narration, Vargas Llosa suggests the disparate geological conditions of Peru, recreates the difficulties involved in living in that country, and re-enacts "the very nature of conversation and of communication in general, particularly in a society devoted to the concealment of truth and to the flaunting of deceptive images." Ronald de Feo pointed out in the *New Republic* that these early novels all explore "with a near-savage seriousness and single-mindedness themes of social and political corruption." But in *Captain Pantoja and the Special Service* (*Pantaleon y las visitadoras*), "a new unexpected element entered Vargas Llosa's work: an unrestrained sense of humor." A farcical novel involving a military officer's assignment to provide prostitutes for troops in the Peruvian jungle, *Captain Pantoja* is "told through an artful combination of dry military dispatches, juicy personal letters, verbose radio rhetoric, and lurid sensationalist news reports," Gene Bell-Villada wrote in *Commonweal.* Vargas Llosa also mixes conversations from different places and times, as he has in previous novels. And like these earlier works, Captain Pantoja "sniffs out corruption in high places, but it also presents something of a break, Vargas Llosa here shedding his high seriousness and adopting a humorous ribald tone," Bell-Villada concluded. The novel's satirical attack is aimed not at the military, a *Times Literary Supplement* reviewer noted, but at "any institution which channels instincts into a socially acceptable ritual. The humor of the narrative derives less from this serious underlying motive, however, than from the various linguistic codes into which people channel the darker forces."

The humorous tone of *Captain Pantoja and the Special Service* is also found in *Aunt Julia and the Scriptwriter* (*La tia Julia y el escribidor*). The novel concerns two characters based on people in Vargas Llosa's own life: his first wife, Julia, who was his aunt by marriage, and a writer of radio soap opera who Vargas Llosa named Pedro Camacho in the novel. The eighteen-year-old narrator, Mario, has a love affair with the thirty-two-year-old Julia. Their story is interrupted in alternate chapters by Camacho's wildly complicated soap opera scripts. As Camacho goes mad, his daily scripts for ten different soap operas become more and more entangled, with characters from one serial appearing in others and all of his plots converging into a single unlikely story. The script displays "fissures through which are revealed secret obsessions, aversions and perversions that allow us to view his soap operas as the story of his disturbed mind," Jose Miguel Oviedo remarked in *World Literature Today.* "The result," Nicholas Shakespeare explained in the *Times Literary Supplement,* "is that Camacho ends up in an asylum, while Mario concludes his real-life soap opera by running off to marry Aunt Julia." Although *Aunt Julia and the Scriptwriter* is as humorous as *Captain Pantoja,* "it has a thematic richness and density the other book lacked," de Feo observed. This richness is found in the novel's exploration of the writer's life and of the relationship between a creative work and its inspiration. In the contrasting of soap opera plots with the real-life romance of Mario and Julia, the novel raises questions about the distinctions between fiction and fact. In a review for *New York,* Carolyn Clay called Aunt Julia "a treatise on the art of writing, on the relationship of stimuli to imagination." It is, de Feo observed, "a multilayered, high-spirited, and in the end terribly affecting text about the interplay of fiction and reality, the transformation of life into art, and life seen and sometimes even lived as fiction."

Vargas Llosa chose a setting other than Peru for the first time in *The War of the End of the World* (*La guerra del fin del mundo*), turning instead to nineteenth-century Brazil and the documenting of an apocalyptic religious movement which gained momentum towards the end of the century. Convinced that the year 1900 marked the end of the world, these zealots, led by a man named the Counselor, set up the community of Canudos. The Brazilian government sent in troops to break up the religious community because of the Counselor's continued denunciations of it. The first, second, and third military assaults were repulsed, but the fourth expedition of 4000 soldiers laid waste to the area and killed nearly 40,000 people. Vargas Llosa told Wendy Smith in *Publishers Weekly* that he was drawn to write of this bloody episode because he felt the fanaticism of both sides was exemplary of modern-day Latin America. "Fanaticism is the root of violence in Latin America," he said. In a *Washington Post* article, Vargas Llosa told Curt Suplee that "in the history of the Canudos war you could really see something that has been happening in Latin American history over the 19th and 20th centuries—the total lack of communication between two sections of a society which kill each other fighting *ghosts,* no? Fighting fictional enemies who are invented out of fanaticism. This kind of reciprocal incapacity of understanding is probably the main problem we have to overcome in Latin America."

Vargas Llosa returned to Peru in *The Real Life of Alejandro Mayta* (*Historia de Mayta*), in which a novelist prepares to write about a small rebellion led by Alejandro Mayta against the Peruvian government in the 1950s. "Everything in the book conspires initially to establish 'Alejandro Mayta' as a real figure of Peruvian history," John Butt wrote in *Times Literary Supplement.* In the end when the novelist finds Mayta, the reader discovers the fictionalization. "What seemed like a straightforward dramatization of an event of rather obvious political meaning is deftly turned on itself and shown up as problematically imaginary," Butt continued. *Choice* contributor J. J. Hassett noted that the novel "presents an unforgettable image of the violent and chaotic society that is, for Vargas Llosa, contemporary Peru."

In *Who Killed Palomino Molero?* (*Quien mato a Palomino Molero?*) Vargas Llosa presents life in 1950s Peru as "meagre, furtive, and faintly menacing," *New Yorker* contributor John Updike remarked. Two investigators search for clues to the brutal torture and murder of Palomino Molero in a story in which "the ruling oligarchy of 'the big guys' figures as a presiding apathy, an ominous airlessness in which the two policemen gasp for truth," Updike continued. The detectives persist in their investigation despite obstacles within their department as well as their government because, as Updike concluded, "Just as no society is ideal enough to erase our darker impulses, so our more noble and altruistic tendencies persist, it would seem, even in the worst-managed system." *New York Times Book Review*'s Richard Lourie noted that with *Palomino Molero* Vargas Llosa explored a new genre—detective fiction—and succeeded. "Evoking landscape and mores in writing that is spare, rich and cruelly beautiful, he both satisfies the requirements of the genre and demonstrates that it too can resonate like any other form of fiction," Lourie commented. "Moving at a slow pace that only heightens the tension, the novel manages to meditate on evil, art, love and race while going about its business of solving a crime, all in the span of 150 pages." *Chicago Tribune Book World* contributor Bruce Allen found *Palomino Molero* "a modest addition to the accumulating proof that Mario Vargas Llosa continues to develop into one of the world's finest writers."

A novelist is once again the central character in *The Storyteller* (*El hablador*), which addresses the infiltration of modern life into primitive cultures and societies. The narrator travels to Florence where he encounters a photograph featuring a silhouetted Peruvian Amazon storyteller. "The narrator recognizes in that silhouette his old college friend Saul Zuratas," Ursula K. Le Guin remarked in *New York Times Book Review.* "And so he begins to tell the story of the storyteller, for this is a book of and about stories, the stories that history silences, the stories of the obscure, the private, the prehistoric; and it all centers on that point, the person at the heart of a circle of people, speaking." Le Guin continued, "Certainly the concerns of *The Storyteller* are intellectual, ethical and artistic, all at once and brilliantly so. To me this is Mr. Vargas Llosa's most engaging and accessible book, for the urgency of its subject purifies and illuminates the writing." *Los Angeles Times Book Review*'s Richard Eder acknowledged the book's social significance. "In the most daring, difficult and in some ways the most moving of his books, [Vargas Llosa] brings together the voices of a primeval culture and that of his sophisticated, Europeanized narrator," Eder commented. "It is a wide gap to bridge. It takes Latin

America's irreconcilable distances and suggests, for a moment, that beginning of commonality that consists of recognizing the wound that distance makes."

"Oedipus walks tall in Lima," *New York Times Book Review* contributor Anthony Burgess remarked of *In Praise of the Stepmother* (*Elogio de la madrastra*). When prepubescent Alfonsito's widowed father, Don Rigoberto, remarries, the boy sets out to drive his stepmother away. "Beautiful as a cherub, amoral as the tiny love-god, malevolent as a vengeful Puck, he seduces his stepmother," a *Los Angeles Times Book Review* critic remarked. "More exactly, he helps her to seduce herself." Alfonsito then arranges for his father to discover the affair, after which "the totally appalled Don Rigoberto expels his wife from the polluted household, which is precisely what Alfonsito, the little hypocrite, wanted," Burgess noted. *In Praise of the Stepmother* marked the addition of another form of writing to Vargas Llosa's repertoire. "Latin America is not known for its artistic contributions to erotic literature," George R. McMurray wrote in *World Literature Today,* "but [*In Praise of the Stepmother*] moves Vargas Llosa to the forefront of contemporary practitioners of this genre."

Vargas Llosa's appreciation of craftsmanship in fiction writing led to several nonfiction projects, including a study of Gustave Flaubert's *Madame Bovary* entitled *The Perpetual Orgy: Flaubert and "Madame Bovary."* "This work of love and conviction belongs to a small class of studies by one great novelist on another. . . . *The Perpetual Orgy* is the most spirited and helpful introduction to *Madame Bovary* we now have," Roger Shattuck commented in *New York Review of Books.* Julian Barnes remarked in *New York Times Book Review,* "Students of literature who want to know how a novel works could not be better advised that to listen to Mr. Vargas Llosa hunched over this masterpiece like some vintage car freak over the engine of a Lagonda. Yet it's more, of course, than a question of valves and pumps and tubes—of engineering. Mr. Vargas Llosa rightly and keenly stresses the irrational factor in writing, the organic element, the part that may even hide itself from as scrupulous and self-conscious a creator as Flaubert."

Vargas Llosa's unsuccessful bid for the presidency of Peru was viewed as a fortuitous occurrence by many critics, who felt that his work as a writer is of greater value than what he could accomplish as a politician. Vargas Llosa told Suplee that, as a Latin American writer, he feels obligated to speak out on political issues. "If you're a writer in a country like Peru, you're a privileged person because you know how to read and write, you have an audience, you are respected. It is a moral obligation of a writer in Latin America to be involved in civic activities." In an article for the *New York Times Book Review,* Suzanne Jill Levine remarked, "Very deliberately, Vargas Llosa has chosen to be his country's conscience." *Los Angeles Times Book Review*'s Eder concluded, "Vargas Llosa is the artist of a nation; a thing we no longer know, though we did once, and called them Melville, Whitman and Thoreau."

BIOGRAPHICAL/CRITICAL SOURCES:

BOOKS

Contemporary Literary Criticism, Gale, Volume 3, 1975, Volume 6, 1976, Volume 9, 1978, Volume 10, 1979, Volume 15, 1980, Volume 31, 1985, Volume 42, 1987.

Feal, Rosemary Geisdorfer, *Novel Lives: The Fictional Autobiographies of Guillermo Cabrera Infante and Mario Vargas Llosa,* University of North Carolina Press, 1986.

Gallagher, D. P., *Modern Latin American Literature,* Oxford University Press, 1973.

Harss, Luis, and Barbara Dohmann, *Into the Mainstream: Conversations with Latin-American Writers,* Harper, 1967.

Rossmann, Charles, and Alan Warren Friedman, editors, *Mario Vargas Llosa: A Collection of Critical Essays,* University of Texas Press, 1978.

Williams, Raymond Leslie, *Mario Vargas Llosa,* Ungar, 1986.

PERIODICALS

Bookletter, April 28, 1975.

Bulletin of Bibliography, December, 1986.

Chicago Tribune, January 3, 1989; June 23, 1989; August 3, 1989.

Chicago Tribune Book World, October 7, 1979; January 12, 1986.

Choice, September, 1987, p. 134.

Commonweal, June 8, 1979.

Hispania, March, 1976.

Hudson Review, winter, 1976.

International Fiction Review, January, 1977.

Los Angeles Times, May 20, 1985; December 18, 1988.

Los Angeles Times Book Review, February 2, 1986; November 26, 1989, p. 3; October 14, 1990, p. 3.

Nation, November 22, 1975.

National Review, December 10, 1982.

New Leader, March 17, 1975; November 15, 1982.

New Republic, August 16, 1982; October 8, 1984.

Newsweek, February 10, 1986.

New York, August 23, 1982.

New Yorker, August 24, 1987, p. 83.

New York Review of Books, March 20, 1975; January 24, 1980; July 16, 1987, p. 35.

New York Times, March 30, 1985; January 8, 1986; February 9, 1986; February 12, 1986; September 10, 1989.

New York Times Book Review, March 23, 1975; April 9, 1978; September 23, 1979; August 1, 1982; December 2, 1984; February 2, 1986; December 21, 1986, p. 10;

May 31, 1987, p. 13; October 29, 1989, p. 1, 49-50; October 14, 1990, p. 11.

New York Times Magazine, November 20, 1983.

Partisan Review, Volume 46, number 4, 1979.

Publishers Weekly, October 5, 1984.

Review of the Center for Inter-American Relations, spring, 1975.

Saturday Review, January 11, 1975.

Spectator, May 14, 1983.

Time, February 17, 1975; August 9, 1982; January 27, 1986; March 10, 1986; September 7, 1987.

Times (London), May 13, 1985; August 5, 1986.

Times Literary Supplement, October 12, 1973; May 20, 1983; March 8, 1985; May 17, 1985; November 14, 1986, p. 1290; July 1, 1988.

Tribune Books (Chicago), October 29, 1989.

Washington Post, August 29, 1983; October 1, 1984; March 26, 1989.

Washington Post Book World, August 26, 1984; February 9, 1986.

World Literature Today, winter, 1978; spring, 1978; winter, 1990, p. 80.

—Sketch by Deborah A. Stanley

* * *

VENTURI, Marcello 1925-

PERSONAL: Born April 21, 1925, in Lucca, Italy; son of Ugolino and Adelina (Della Nina) Venturi; married Camilla Salvago Raggi (a writer), February 10, 1960. *Education:* Studied foreign languages at University of Milan. *Religion:* Roman Catholic.

ADDRESSES: Home—Villa Campale, 15074 Molare, Italy 15074.

CAREER: Journalist in Italy, 1948-56; Giangiacomo Feltrinelli, (publishers), Milan, Italy, literary adviser, 1956-64.

AWARDS, HONORS: Premio Viareggio, 1952, for *Dalla Sirte a casa mia;* Premio Saint Vincent, 1957, for journalism; Premio Puccini-Senigallia, 1965, for *Gli anni e gli inganni;* Premio Chianciano, 1967, for *L'appuntamento;* Premio Bancarellino, 1967, for *L'ultimo veliero;* Premio Civinini, 1970, for *Piu lontane stazioni;* Premio Napoli, 1979, for *Il padrone dell'agricola;* Premio Nazionale letteratura per l'infanzia, 1980, for *Collefiorito;* Premio Stresa, 1982, for *Sconfitti sul campo;* Premio Internazionale Firenze, 1985, per la narrativa; Premio Oplonti d'oro, 1985; Premio citta della Magna Grecia, 1986, for *Dalla parte sbagliata.*

WRITINGS:

Dalla Sirte a casa mia, Macchia, 1952.

Il treno degli Appennini (title means "The Train of the Apennines"), Einaudi, 1956.

Vacanza tedesca (title means "German Vacation"), Feltrinelli, 1959.

L'ultimo veliero (title means "The Last Sailboat"), Einaudi, 1961, 1993.

Bandiera bianca a Cefalonia (title means "The White Flag"), Feltrinelli, 1963, translation by William Clowes published as *The White Flag,* Anthony Blond, 1966, Vanguard, 1969.

Gli anni e gli inganni (title means "Years and Deception"), Feltrinelli, 1965.

L'appuntamento (title means "The Appointment"), Rizzoli, 1967.

Piu lontane stazioni (title means "The Farthest Stations"), Rizzoli, 1970.

Terra di nessuno (title means "Land of Nobody"), Rizzoli, 1975.

Il padrone dell'agricola (title means "Head of the Farm"), Rizzoli, 1979.

Collefiorito, Stampatori, 1980, Eizioni E. Elle, 1993.

Sconfitti sul campo (title means "Defeat at Camp"), Rizzoli, 1982.

Dalla parte sbagliata (title means "The Wrong Parts"), De Agostini, 1985.

Il giorno e l'ora (title means "Day and Hour"), De Agostini, 1987.

Sdraiati sulla linea (title means "Lying on the Line"), Mondadori, 1991.

Un uomo di successo (title means "A Successful Man"), Guida Editore, 1991.

SIDELIGHTS: Marcello Venturi left the Communist Party "after the Hungarian facts and the revelations on Stalinism." The recurrent theme of many of his novels is war. "I dare say this is the fact which most appeals to me," he told *CA,* "especially in regard [to] man as victim of violence." This is also the theme of his novel, *Terra di nessuno* ("Land of Nobody"), in which, he continues, "there is a young man, born during the last world-war, who does not know whether his father is a German or an American soldier, and in his quest for an identity ends up . . . committing an absurd crime."

Of his novel *Sdraiati sulla linea* ("Lying on the Line"), he told *CA:* "[it] is an autobiographical characterization, but it contains a story of a whole generation. It is the story of those young people who, after participating in the resistance during World War II, accepted communism. The narrator reveals the behind-the-scenes politics at *L' Unita* of Milano (the Italian Communist Party newspaper) where he serves as the cultural writer, until he leaves the communist party after the Hungarian Facts."

VET, T. V.
See STRAITON, E(dward) C(ornock)

* * *

VOELKER, John D(onaldson) 1903-1991
(Robert Traver)

PERSONAL: Born June 29, 1903, in Ishpeming, MI; died of a heart attack, March 19, 1991, in Marquette, MI; son of George Oliver (a saloon keeper) and Annie (Traver) Voelker; married Grace Taylor, August 2, 1930; children: Elizabeth (Mrs. Victor N. Tsaloff), Julie (Mrs. H. Jordan Overturf), Grace (Mrs. Ernest Wood). *Education:* Attended Northern Michigan Normal School (now Northern Michigan University), 1922-24; University of Michigan, L.L.B., 1928.

Avocational Interests: Trout fishing.

CAREER: Admitted to Michigan bar, 1928; attorney in private practice; Marquette County, MI, prosecuting attorney, 1934-52; State of Michigan, supreme court justice, 1957-60; author, 1960-91.

AWARDS, HONORS: L.L.D., Northern Michigan University, 1958.

WRITINGS:

UNDER PSEUDONYM ROBERT TRAVER

Troubleshooter: The Story of a Northwoods Prosecutor, Viking, 1943.
Danny and the Boys: Being Some Legends of Hungry Hollow, World Publishing, 1951.
Small Town D.A., Dutton, 1954.
Anatomy of a Murder (novel), St. Martin's, 1957.
Trout Madness, St. Martin's, 1960.
Hornstein's Boy (novel), St. Martin's, 1962.
Anatomy of a Fisherman, McGraw, 1964.
Laughing Whitefish (novel), McGraw, 1965.
The Jealous Mistress, Little, Brown, 1968.
Trout Magic, Crown, 1974.
People versus Kirk (novel), St. Martin's, 1981.

Also author of short stories, articles, essays, and book reviews. Author of weekly column for *Detroit News,* 1967-69.

ADAPTATIONS: *Anatomy of a Murder* was adapted by Wendell Mayes for a Columbia Pictures film released in 1959; *Trout Madness* was filmed in 1964, with Voelker appearing in it.

SIDELIGHTS: During his career as a private attorney, a county prosecutor, and a Michigan Supreme Court justice, John Voelker amassed a love for and a knowledge of the law. Drawing on this experience, he achieved success as an author under his pen name, Robert Traver, with his 1957 novel, *Anatomy of a Murder.*

The best-selling courtroom drama/mystery was based on a real-life murder case in Big Bay, Michigan, for which Voelker served as the defense attorney. In 1959, Columbia Pictures filmed the story on location at the Lumberjack Tavern, where the murder occurred. Directed by Otto Preminger and starring Jimmy Stewart, Lee Remick, and George C. Scott, *Anatomy of a Murder* is considered a Hollywood classic, and the book remained Voelker's most important, popular, and best-remembered work throughout his writing career. Upon the release of the novel, critic and author James Cain asserted in the *New York Times Book Review,* "It held me as few books have, I couldn't put it down," although he also maintained that the work was "jackleg in its organization" and "much, much too long" at 437 pages. Voelker "lavishes much care on the architecture of his trial, but stays away from its subtler human material," comments Joseph Hitrec in the *Saturday Review,* and he praises the author for keeping the trial reconstruction "mobile and interesting."

Subsequent efforts by Voelker centered on his much-loved pastime, trout fishing, including *Trout Madness* and *Trout Magic.* He also continued to write books dealing with court cases, including *Laughing Whitefish, The Jealous Mistress,* and *People versus Kirk.*

In 1989, Voelker told the *Detroit Free Press,* "Spinning yarns is a protection against the nuttiness, the bull----, the greed, the hate, all around us. I'm a fisherman who likes to observe and tell yarns and so I told stories about the things that I knew about." Voelker lived, wrote, and fished in Ishpeming, Michigan, until his death in 1991.

BIOGRAPHICAL/CRITICAL SOURCES:

PERIODICALS

Booklist, October 15, 1981, p. 289.
Book World, December 19, 1982, p. 12; May 26, 1968.
Chicago Tribune, October 24, 1989; March 19, 1991.
Detroit Free Press, September 18, 1989, pp. 1B-2B.
Kirkus Reviews, August 15, 1974, p. 932; August 15, 1981, p. 1035.
Kliatt Paperback Book Guide, winter, 1984, p. 20.
Library Journal, September 1, 1974, p. 2086; November 1, 1981, p. 2155.
New York Times Book Review, February 5, 1958, p. 4, 29; January 18, 1959; November 1, 1981, p. 15; October 30, 1983, p. 14.
Progressive, January, 1975, p. 55.
Publishers Weekly, January 11, 1960; August 12, 1974, p. 55; August 21, 1981, p. 43; June 10, 1983, p. 58; March 7, 1986, p. 92.

Saturday Review, January 4, 1958, p. 14.
Virginia Quarterly Review, summer, 1983, p. 523.
West Coast Review of Books, February, 1982, p. 39.
Wilson Library Bulletin, January, 1982, p. 372; April, 1983, p. 695.

OBITUARIES:

PERIODICALS

Chicago Tribune, March 19, 1991.
Los Angeles Times, March 20, 1991.
New York Times, March 20, 1991.
Time, April 1, 1991, p. 61.
Times (London), March 29, 1991.
Washington Post, March 20, 1991.*

* * *

von FRISCH, Karl (Ritter)
See FRISCH, Karl (Ritter) von

W-Z

WAGNER, Anthony Richard 1908-

PERSONAL: Born September 6, 1908, in London, England; son of Orlando Henry and Monica (Bell) Wagner; married Gillian Mary Millicent Graham, February 26, 1953; children: Lucy Elizabeth Millicent (Mrs. Robert Anthony Page), Roger Henry Melchior, Mark Anthony. *Education:* Attended Eton College, 1921-27; Balliol College, Oxford, M.A., 1931, D.Litt.

ADDRESSES: *Home*—10, Physic Place, Royal Hospital Rd, London SW3 4HQ, England. *Office*—College of Arms, Queen Victoria St., London EC4V 4BT, England.

CAREER: British official serving as Porticullis Pursuivant, 1931-43, Richmond Herald, 1943-61, Garter Principal King of Arms, 1961-78, and Clarenceux King of Arms, 1978—. Served in British War Office, 1939-43; Ministry of Town and Country Planning, beginning 1943, private secretary to minister, 1944-45, advisory committee on buildings of special architectural or historic interest, secretary, 1945-46, member, 1947-66; secretary, Order of the Garter, 1952-61; registrar, College of Arms (London), 1953-60; genealogist, Order of the Bath, 1961-72, and Order of St. John, 1961-75; inspector of Regimental Colours, 1961-77. President, Chelsea Society, 1967-73, and Aldeburgh Society, 1970—; chairman of trustees, Marc Fitch Fund, 1971-77; trustee, National Portrait Gallery, 1973-80. Member of council, National Trust, 1953-74; master, Vintners Co., 1973-74.

MEMBER: Society of Antiquaries of London (fellow), Royal Historical Society (fellow), Society of Genealogists (fellow), American Society of Genealogists, Heraldry Society of Canada (honorary fellow), Georgian Group (former vice-chairman), Athenaeum Club, Beefsteak Club, Roxburghe Club, Society of Dilettanti, Garrick Club.

AWARDS, HONORS: Commander, Royal Victorian Order, 1953; Knight Commander, Royal Victorian Order, 1961, and Most Honourable Order of the Bath, 1978; honorary fellow, Balliol College, Oxford.

WRITINGS:

(Compiler) *Catalogue of the Heralds' Commemorative Exhibition, 1934,* [London], 1936.

Historic Heraldry of Britain: An Illustrated Series of British Historical Arms, Oxford University Press, 1939.

Heralds and Heraldry in the Middle Ages, Oxford University Press, 1939.

Heraldry in England, Penguin, 1946.

Catalogue of English Mediaeval Rolls of Arms, Harleian Society, 1950.

The Records and Collections of the College of Arms, Burke's Peerage, 1952.

English Genealogy, Oxford University Press, 1960, 3rd edition, Phillimore & Co., 1983.

English Ancestry, Oxford University Press, 1961.

Drake in England: Genealogical Researches with Particular Reference to the Drakes in Essex from Medieval Times, New Hampshire Historical Society, 1963, revised edition, 1970.

The Family of Bowser: Genealogical Researches with Particular Reference to Bowser of Yorkshire from Medieval Times, MacLehose, 1966.

Heralds of England: A History of the Office and College of Arms, H.M.S.O., 1967.

(Contributor) Hugh Stanford London, *The Life of William Bruges, the First Garter King of Arms,* [London], 1970.

Pedigree and Progress: Essays in the Genealogical Interpretation of History, Phillimore & Co., 1975.

Heralds and Ancestors, British Museum Publications, 1978.

Heraldo-Memoriale, Roxburghe Club, 1982.

Wagners of Brighton, Phillimore & Co., 1984.
How Lord Birkenhead Saved the Heralds, H.M.S.O., 1986.
Herald's World, privately printed, 1988.
(With A. L. Rowse) *John Dustis: Garter King of Arms,* H.M.S.O., 1992.

Also contributor to *Chamber's Encyclopaedia.* Contributor to professional journals.

BIOGRAPHICAL/CRITICAL SOURCES:

BOOKS

Wagner, Anthony Richard, *Wagners of Brighton,* Phillimore & Co., 1984.

* * *

WAGNER, Jane 1935-

PERSONAL: Born February 22, 1935, in Morristown, TN. *Education:* Attended School of Visual Arts, New York City.

ADDRESSES: Office—P.O. Box 27700, Los Angeles, CA 90027.

CAREER: Writer, actress, and director and producer of motion pictures. Worked as designer with Kimberly-Clark and Fieldcrest; cowriter and producer for comedian Lily Tomlin in various recording, television, and stage performances; composer and lyricist. Textile designs have been exhibited at Brooklyn Museum of Art.

AWARDS, HONORS: Peabody Award, 1969, for television screenplay *J. T.;* Child Study Association selection for Children's Books of the Year, and Georgia Children's Book Award, both 1972, both for *J. T.;* Emmy Award, best writing in a comedy-variety or music special, 1974, and Writer's Guild award, 1975, both for *Lily;* Emmy Award, outstanding writing in a comedy-variety or music special, 1975, for *Lily Tomlin;* Emmy Award, outstanding writing in a comedy-variety or music special, 1982, for *Lily: Sold Out;* Tony Award, a special production award, and New York Drama Critics Circle special citation, both 1986, both for *The Search for Signs of Intelligent Life in the Universe.*

WRITINGS:

TELEPLAYS

J. T. (Columbia Broadcasting System, Inc. [CBS-TV], 1969), photographs by Gordan Parks, Van Nostrand, 1969.
(With others) *Rowan and Martin's Laugh-In,* National Broadcasting Company, Inc. (NBC-TV), 1970-73.
(With Lily Tomlin, Richard Pryor, and others) *The Lily Tomlin Show* (special), CBS-TV, 1973.
(With Tomlin, Pryor, and others; and producer) *Lily* (special), CBS-TV, 1973.
Earthwatch (special), Public Broadcasting Service, 1975.
(With Tomlin and others; and produced) *Lily* (special), American Broadcasting Companies, Inc. (ABC-TV), 1975.
(With Tomlin and others; and producer) *Lily Tomlin* (special), ABC-TV, 1975.
People (special), NBC-TV, 1975.
(With others; and executive producer) *Lily: Sold Out,* CBS-TV, 1981.
(With Tomlin and others; and executive producer) *Lily for President,* CBS-TV, 1982.

PLAYS

(With Tomlin; and director) *Appearing Nitely* (revue), produced on Broadway, 1977.
(And director) *The Search for Signs of Intelligent Life in the Universe* (produced on Broadway, 1985; also see below), illustrated by Annie Liebowitz, Harper, 1986.

SCREENPLAYS

(And director) *Moment by Moment,* Universal, 1978.
(And executive producer) *The Incredible Shrinking Woman,* Universal, 1980.
(And executive producer with Tomlin) *The Search for Signs of Intelligent Life in the Universe,* Orion, 1991.

RECORDINGS WITH TOMLIN

And That's the Truth, Polydor, 1972.
Lily Tomlin on Stage, Arista, 1977.

OTHER

Also author of material for the recording *Modern Scream;* contributor to periodicals with Tomlin.

ADAPTATIONS: The Incredible Shrinking Woman was adapted into a book by Jody Sibert, Jove, 1981.

WORK IN PROGRESS: A screenplay for Metro-Goldwyn-Mayer.

SIDELIGHTS: Best known as the writer behind comedic talent Lily Tomlin, Jane Wagner is renowned for her skillful penning of one-liners. The author of plays, movies, children's books, and comedy albums, Wagner has received numerous awards for her work. Initially unsure of her career direction, Wagner knew from the beginning that she would not be a novelist. As she reports to *New York Times* contributor Esther B. Fein, southern writers such as Carson McCullers and Eudora Welty had already "said all I ever wanted to say about the South." Instead she decided to use her humor in playwrighting: "I loved the way plays look on paper. It's so poetic looking, the way the stage directions are in italics and separated off in parenthesis. I wanted to write things that would look like that."

At first Wagner supported herself as a designer and wrote on the side because she did not feel competent enough as a writer. At one time she even thought about becoming a lyricist. Her career changed focus, however, when her song "J. T." was turned down by a record company for being too long. Wagner revised the song into a teleplay which subsequently won a Peabody Award; she eventually published *J. T.* as a children's book. The story is about a little boy, J. T., who steals a radio because his mother cannot afford to buy him anything but practical gifts for Christmas. Two older children who observe his theft pursue J. T. because they want the radio for themselves. Hiding in an abandoned building, J. T. befriends a stray cat and is devastated when the cat is later killed by a car. J. T.'s grandmother assists him in dealing with his grief and eventually rectifying his crime.

The teleplay caught comedienne Lily Tomlin's attention. Tomlin was working on a new comedy album but was dissatisfied with the results; she was looking for ways to add depth to her character. Attracted by the humor, insight, and gentleness of Wagner's story, Tomlin wrote to Wagner, soliciting her help for the album. Wagner reports to Fein that at this point in her career she "was in a rut," so she sent Tomlin some of her material. Tomlin was impressed and the two began their first collaborative project: the comedy album *And That's the Truth* featuring Tomlin's character Edith Ann. Since then Wagner has written solely for Tomlin. Together they have created many successful albums, television specials, and plays, including the Emmy Award-winning television special *Lily Tomlin,* and the Tony Award-winning comedy revue *Appearing Nitely.* Along with the award winners, however, were the less successful movie ventures *The Incredible Shrinking Woman* and *Moment by Moment.*

Moment by Moment was a project initiated by actor John Travolta. After seeing the theatre production *Appearing Nitely,* Travolta approached Wagner and Tomlin about collaborating with him on a project; he wanted Wagner to write the screenplay and direct the film. The story illustrates the developing romantic relationship between a divorced, sophisticated, older woman played by Tomlin and an aimless, younger, less-educated man played by Travolta. Throughout the relationship, Tomlin's character fosters and promotes Travolta's character to grow and become whatever he wants. While offering him support and encouragement, though, Tomlin's character sadly realizes that she herself has never desired to be anything. In general, critics were not impressed with the film. "It's very difficult to understand what . . . [Tomlin and Wagner] wanted to do in *Moment by Moment.* As romantic drama it's pretty tepid. . . . The script doesn't seem to have been thought through to a finish," writes Vincent Canby in a *New York Times* review. *Chicago Tribune*'s Cheryl Lavin notes in her review that the critics were particularly hard on Wagner. "The hostility was all out of proportion to the film," asserts Wagner to Lavin. "If it's a bad movie, so it's a bad movie. There are a great many talented people who make bad movies. It's funny how ill-prepared we were for that." Wagner continues, "In some ways you never recover from that. You think you'll never work again; you think no one will ever want you to work again. I said to Lily, 'The terrible thing about the bad reviews we got is that all those doubts that you have about yourself, suddenly everyone has them. . . . I didn't work for awhile. I didn't want to."

When Wagner did begin working again, she created a very successful enterprise: the 1985 one-woman play featuring Tomlin, *The Search for Signs of Intelligent Life in the Universe.* In contrast to the previous experience, Wagner comments to Lavin that this project "has been affirming and validating." The play became "one of the real theatrical phenomena of the '80s," according to the *Chicago Tribune*'s Sid Smith. Coproduced, written and directed by Wagner, the play was awarded a special citation from the New York Drama Critics Circle and was later released as a book and a movie. *The Search,* Wagner reports to Fein, is a product of her desire to achieve comedy that balances "black humor and sentimentality." "It's so easy to be shrewd and mean. I thought we needed something else. We needed something loving. . . . We wanted a reflection, a balance of the absurdity and the realism, and we decided that after all, what is more absurd than real life?" The *New York Times*' Frank Rich describes the play as Wagner's attempt "to sum up a generation of social history in a tightly compressed saga of a few representative lives." *The Search* is "a kind of Gulliver's travelogue of the latter half of the 20th century," relates David Richards of the *Washington Post*, adding that it revolves around a bag lady named Trudy played by Tomlin. Trudy, "whose insanity is actually a higher form of wisdom," is a character who has been selected as a "tour guide to 'a planet still in its puberty' " for a group of invisible aliens, writes Richards. In act one Trudy points out a variety of materialistic characters suffering from their own self-made neurosis and anxieties, and searching for self-fulfillment, including aerobics freak Chrissy, punk teen Angus, and a "new age Ward Cleaver." Act two focusses on Lynn, a feminist housewife from California who finds it difficult "to be politically conscious and upwardly mobile at the same time." The aliens conclude the play by explaining to Trudy why, despite a myriad of flaws, humans are such special creatures. The play is "not just a daisy chain of monologues, but a tapestry made up of interlocking destinies," reports Richards, with the "unmistakable theme . . . that we're all in this cosmic soup together—mad punker, bored matron, hip hooker, radical feminist and chauvinist pig."

The Search was a huge success and ran in theatres for over two years. This success is in part due to the Wagner-Tomlin team's "savvy ability to change," asserts Smith, and their ability to create entirely new characters "from the Tomlin-Wagner bottomless catalog of human personalities." "The stage presentation, directed by Ms. Wagner, looked like a model of simplicity," praises Canby in his review of the film version. "In fact, it was a masterly blend of split-second sound and lighting cues, a shrewdly wise and witty text, and the grand display of Ms. Tomlin's talents, with which nothing was allowed to interfere." In addition to the success of the play, the book version, published in 1986, sold over 100,000 copies in hard bound, a record for a script. Ryan Murphy writes in the *Chicago Tribune* that Wagner's book is "filled with slick Annie Liebowitz montages and additional Wagner sketches," and according to Harper and Row, it is the "first play in 20 years to become a national best seller." The 1991 release of the movie also drew wide acclaim. *Newsweek*'s Jack Kroll hails the movie version, stating that it is "written brilliantly." Noting the "ingenious construction and compassionate wit of the material that Wagner has written," Terrence Rafferty in a *New Yorker* review maintains that "[The] film version . . . mostly does justice to the extraordinary talents of these women."

The success of these collaborative projects is dependent on both the writer and the performer. Wagner elaborates to Fein: "We have nothing to hide behind but each other. When you deal with an expository form like this you have nothing to shield you. There's just Lily and the material. . . . Every word becomes a delicate choice because every word is so obvious. You want to be very clear, while maintaining the complexity. Basically, when there is one person up there performing, what else do you have to go on but words? Sometimes I think there's more of an insecurity for her, she's up there all alone. But then I think it's harder on me. She at least gets endorphines from performing." Fortunately the two enjoy a mutual respect for their differing work and skills. Tomlin "reveres Wagner's script, and sometimes when she feels she hasn't lived up to it emotionally, she hates to go out for her curtain call," explains Richards. And Wagner imparts to Fein, "As a writer, I'm so lucky, particularly with this form, with the monologue, to work so intimately with Lily. It's really rare to have someone like her who can bring a soul to your work." Wagner realizes that writing exclusively for Tomlin has its advantages and disadvantages. "It would be a good career move for me if the next thing I do is not for Lily," confesses Wagner to Lavin. "A lot of people have put that idea out. From a practical standpoint it's a wise thing, but I'm spoiled. To work with Lily is very safe for me. It's secure. Maybe I lack courage. It's safe for her, too, though. Maybe that's at the heart of any collaboration."

BIOGRAPHICAL/CRITICAL SOURCES:

BOOKS

Wagner, Jane, *The Search for Signs of Intelligent Life in the Universe,* illustrated by Annie Liebowitz, Harper, 1986.

PERIODICALS

Chicago Tribune, November 30, 1986; April 27, 1988; August 28, 1988.
Library Journal, September 15, 1970, p. 3055; December 1986, p. 130.
Los Angeles Times, October 11, 1991, p. F10.
New Republic, October 7, 1991, pp. 28-29.
Newsweek, October 7, 1991, p. 65.
New Yorker, October 7, 1991, p. 102.
New York Times, December 22, 1978, p. C18; September 22, 1985; September 27, 1985; May 13, 1986; September 27, 1991, p. C8.
Washington Post, October 1, 1985, pp. E1-E4; March 27, 1988; April 4, 1988, pp. B1-B9.*

—Sketch by Pamela S. Dear

* * *

WALKER, Walter (Herbert III) 1949-

PERSONAL: Born September 12, 1949, in Quincy, MA; son of Walter H. Jr. (a railroad employee) and Irene (a painter; maiden name, Horn) Walker; married Anne DiSciullo (a freelance producer), June 17, 1972; children: Brett Daniel. *Education:* University of Pennsylvania, B.A., 1971; University of California, San Francisco, J.D., 1974. *Politics:* Democrat. *Religion:* Protestant.

ADDRESSES: *Home*—211 Meda Lane, Mill Valley, CA 94941. *Office*—Walker & Durham, 50 Francisco St., San Francisco, CA 94133. *Agent*—Al Hart, Fox Chase Agency, Inc., Public Ledger Building, Independence Square, Philadelphia, PA 19106.

CAREER: U.S. Government, Washington, DC, appellate attorney, 1975-77; Gerald Sterns (now Sterns, Smith & Walker; law firm), San Francisco, CA, attorney, specializing in plaintiff's personal injury litigation, 1977-88; Walker & Durham (law firm), attorney, San Francisco, 1988—.

MEMBER: Association of Trial Lawyers of America, California Trial Lawyers Association, San Francisco Trial Lawyers Association, Mystery Writers of America.

AWARDS, HONORS: Silver medal for Best First Novel by a California Writer, Commonwealth Club of California, 1983, for *A Dime to Dance By.*

WRITINGS:

NOVELS

A Dime to Dance By, Harper, 1983.
The Two-Dude Defense, Harper, 1985.
Rules of the Knife Fight, Harper, 1986.
The Immediate Prospect of Being Hanged, Viking, 1989.
The Appearance of Impropriety, Pocket Books, 1993.
Dickie Dolan's Darling Daughter, Pocket Books, 1994.

SIDELIGHTS: Walter Walker told *CA:* "As a trial lawyer, I draw from my interest and experience in litigation. I have had some experience in congressional politics, both in California and Washington, DC, and I draw from that as well. My characters are generally drawn from conversations I have heard. Often, once I have heard the conversation, I have the character. My themes include compromised ambitions, moral ambiguity, and the need to 'get out of town.'

"*A Dime to Dance By* grew out of an actual cemetery scandal in Quincy, Massachusetts, where I spent a good part of my youth. As a result of the fact that a cemetery superintendent was discovered re-selling old graves, a political machine was thrown out of office by suddenly irate voters. I saw the situation as a good vehicle to write about small-city New England politics, but the people about whom I was writing soon overwhelmed both the mystery and the political aspects of the story. Most of the events and many of the people involved were amalgamations of real events and real people.

"In *The Two-Dude Defense,* a book I wrote while living in San Francisco, I was trying my hand at a Chandler-Ross McDonald private eye, with the idea that the private eye himself was more interesting and more important than the case in which he was involved. I did not care as much about who shot whom as I did about what made my protagonist the type of man who would be involved in such a case. Here, characters and events were wholly fictionalized.

Rules of the Knife Fight, Walker's third book, is a law/crime mixture, where investigator Owen Carr traces the death of a local boy to a rich San Francisco lawyer and his wife. The last part of the book deals with the ensuing murder trial. *Kirkus Reviews* evaluates *Rules of the Knife Fight* as "strong . . . sharply detailed storytelling . . . often mesmerizing." Walker said about the book that, "*Rules of the Knife Fight* involves a courtroom battle and the events leading up to it. The legal tactics are ones I have experienced myself. Here the suburban characters are decidedly upscale in comparison with the working-class people of *Dime* and the urban lowlife of *Two-Dude.* Perhaps that has something to do with my own move to the suburbs of Marin County."

"*The Immediate Prospect of Being Hanged* was set among the gentry of my father's hometown of Weston, Massachusetts. The issue of moral dilemma is seen through the eyes of a bright but disaffected investigator working for a young, politically motivated district attorney, who is prosecuting the murder of a socialite." In a *New York Times Book Review* article, Marilyn Stasio calls *Prospect* a "scandalously entertaining legal thriller" written in an "exceptionally fluid style." In a *Washington Post Book World* review, Frank McConnell says the book evolves on two planes. The first is the typical murder mystery being investigated and narrated by detective Patterson Starbuck, the main character. The second plane is Patt's own story, which unfolds along with the narrative. The reader discovers that Patt himself belongs to the "black-sheep side" of one of the families implicated in the crime he is investigating. McConnell feels that in the end, the two planes "collide . . . with chilling efficiency"; he calls Walker's variation on the typical mystery novel "brilliant." A reviewer writing in the *West Coast Review of Books* praises Walker's realistic handling of the story, and says that the book is "a very well-written mystery that will keep the reader guessing all the way."

Discussing his book *The Appearance of Impropriety,* Walker said, "This is the story of a professional basketball team and the sportswriter who, in his effort to prove that one of the players is fixing games, digs up dirt on each player until someone retaliates. The book's themes and scenes are taken from today's sport headlines."

BIOGRAPHICAL/CRITICAL SOURCES:

PERIODICALS

Armchair Detective, fall, 1990, p. 424.
Christian Science Monitor, December 17, 1990, p. 13.
Kirkus Reviews, August 15, 1986, p. 1246.
New York Times Book Review, May 28, 1989, p. 27.
Washington Post Book World, June 18, 1989, p. 9.
West Coast Review of Books, May, 1989. p. 34.

* * *

WALLACE, Ronald (William) 1945-

PERSONAL: Born February 18, 1945, in Cedar Rapids, IA; son of William Edward (a professor of law) and Loretta (Kamprath) Wallace; married Margaret McCreight, August 3, 1968; children: Molly Elizabeth, Emily Katherine. *Education:* College of Wooster, B.A., 1967; University of Michigan, M.A., 1968, Ph.D., 1971.

Avocational Interests: Gardening, bicycling, piano, fishing, volleyball, softball, travel, novelties.

ADDRESSES: Home—2220 Chamberlain Ave., Madison, WI 53705. *Office*—Department of English, University of Wisconsin—Madison, 600 North Park St., Madison, WI 53706.

CAREER: University of Wisconsin—Madison, assistant professor, 1972-75, associate professor, 1975-82, professor of English and director of creative writing, 1982—.

MEMBER: Associated Writing Programs.

AWARDS, HONORS: Avery Hopwood Award, 1970, for poetry; American Council of Learned Societies fellowship, 1975-76, 1981; Poetry Book Award, Council for Wisconsin Writers, 1977, for *Installing the Bees,* 1983, for *Tunes for Bears to Dance To,* 1985, for *The Owl in the Kitchen,* 1988, for *People and Dog in the Sun,* and 1992, for *The Makings of Happiness;* Wisconsin Arts Board fellowship, 1979, 1980; Scholarly Book Award, Council for Wisconsin Writers, 1979, for *The Last Laugh: Form and Affirmation in the Contemporary American Comic Novel,* and 1984, for *God Be with the Clown: Humor in American Poetry;* Distinguished Teaching Award, 1984; Helen Bullis Prize, *Poetry Northwest,* 1985.

WRITINGS:

Henry James and the Comic Form (nonfiction), University of Michigan Press, 1975.
Cucumbers (poetry chapbook), Pendle Hill, 1977.
Installing the Bees (poems), Chowder Chapbooks, 1977.
The Facts of Life (poetry chapbook), Mary Phillips, 1979.
The Last Laugh: Form and Affirmation in the Contemporary American Comic Novel (nonfiction), University of Missouri Press, 1979.
Plums, Stones, Kisses and Hooks (poems), University of Missouri Press, 1981.
Tunes for Bears to Dance To (poems), University of Pittsburgh Press, 1983.
God Be with the Clown: Humor in American Poetry (nonfiction), University of Missouri Press, 1984.
The Owl in the Kitchen (poetry chapbook), Heatherstone Press, 1985.
People and Dog in the Sun (poems), University of Pittsburgh Press, 1987.
Vital Signs: Contemporary American Poetry from the University Presses, University of Wisconsin Press, 1989.
The Makings of Happiness (poems), University of Pittsburgh Press, 1991.

Contributor of poems, articles, and reviews to periodicals, including *Atlantic Monthly, New Yorker, Poetry, Nation, Poetry Northwest, Prairie Schooner, American Poetry Review, Paris Review, North American Review, Iowa Review, Nineteenth-Century Fiction, Essays in Literature,* and *Genre.* Series editor for the University of Wisconsin Press poetry series, 1984—.

WORK IN PROGRESS: Time's Fancy; Quick Bright Things, a short story collection; a book of poetry.

* * *

WALLIN, Amos
See KUNICZAK, W(ieslaw) S(tanislaw)

* * *

WAMBAUGH, Joseph (Aloysius, Jr.) 1937-

PERSONAL: Born January 22, 1937, in East Pittsburgh, PA; son of Joseph A. (a police officer) and Anne (Malloy) Wambaugh; married Dee Allsup, November 26, 1955; children: Mark (deceased), David, Jeannette. *Education:* Chaffey College, A.A., 1958; California State College (now University), Los Angeles, B.A., 1960, M.A., 1968. *Religion:* Roman Catholic.

ADDRESSES: Home—70-555 Thunderbird Mesa, Rancho Mirage, CA 92270.

CAREER: Los Angeles Police Department, Los Angeles, CA, 1960-74, began as patrolman, became detective sergeant; writer, 1971—. Creator and consultant, *The Blue Knight,* Columbia Broadcasting Company (CBS-TV), and *Police Story,* National Broadcasting Company (NBC-TV). *Military service:* U.S. Marine Corps, 1954-57.

AWARDS, HONORS: Edgar Allan Poe Award, special award for nonfiction, Mystery Writers of America, 1974, for *The Onion Field;* Edgar Allan Poe Award, best motion picture, 1981, for *The Black Marble;* Rodolfo Walsh Prize for investigative journalism, International Association of Crime Writers, 1989, for *Lines and Shadows.*

WRITINGS:

NOVELS

The New Centurions, Atlantic-Little Brown, 1971.
The Blue Knight, Atlantic-Little Brown, 1972.
The Choirboys, Delacorte, 1975.
The Black Marble (also see below), Delacorte, 1978.
The Glitter Dome (also see below), Morrow, 1981.
The Delta Star, Morrow, 1983.
The Secrets of Harry Bright, Morrow, 1985.
The Golden Orange, Morrow, 1990.
Fugitive Nights (also see below), Morrow, 1992.
Finnegan's Week, Morrow, 1993.

NONFICTION

The Onion Field (also see below), Delacorte, 1973.

Lines and Shadows, Morrow, 1984.
Echoes in the Darkness (also see below), edited by Jeanne Bernkopf, Morrow, 1987.
The Blooding, edited by Bernkopf, Morrow, 1989.

OTHER

The Onion Field (screenplay), Avco Embassy, 1979.
The Black Marble (screenplay), Avco Embassy, 1980.
The Glitter Dome (teleplay), Home Box Office, 1984.
Echoes in the Darkness (miniseries teleplay), CBS-TV, 1987.
Fugitive Knights (teleplay; based on the novel *Fugtitive Nights*), NBC-TV, 1993.

Creator and consultant for *Police Story* television series, NBC-TV, 1973-77.

ADAPTATIONS: The New Centurions was directed by Richard Fleischer and released by Columbia Pictures, 1972; *The Choirboys,* was directed by Robert Aldrich and released by Universal Studios, 1977; *The Blue Knight* was produced by NBC-TV as a television miniseries starring William Holden, and then by CBS-TV as a regular series with George Kennedy in the title role, both 1973.

SIDELIGHTS: Though Joseph Wambaugh spent ten years with the Los Angeles Police Department before publishing his first novel, *The New Centurions,* he is more than just a cop-turned-writer, and his novels are much more than just "cop stories": they have effectively redefined the genre of police drama and the way police officers are depicted therein. Wambaugh's cops are frightened, profane, violent, and fallible, forced to protect citizens who resent them. His writing—both fiction and nonfiction—"takes us into the minds and hearts, into the nerves and (sometimes literally) into the guts of other human beings," claims Thomas Fleming in the *New York Times Book Review.* "It achieves a mixture of empathy and objectivity that creates genuine understanding." His ability to evoke sympathy for crude and often distasteful characters has made Wambaugh popular with both readers and critics. "Let us dispel forever the notion that Mr. Wambaugh is only a former cop who happens to write books," comments Evan Hunter in the *New York Times Book Review.* "This would be tantamount to saying that Jack London was first and foremost a sailor. Mr. Wambaugh is, in fact, a writer of genuine power, style, wit and originality, who has chosen to write about the police in particular as a means of expressing his views on society in general."

Wambaugh's reputation as a powerful writer was established with his first four books: *The New Centurions, The Blue Knight, The Onion Field,* and *The Choirboys.* The first two were penned while Wambaugh was still a full-time police officer, and while in retrospect he often dismisses them as his "moonlighting" novels, they instantly shattered the preconceptions many readers had of cops. Published in 1971, *The New Centurions* follows four young men through the Police Academy, onto the streets of Los Angeles, and ultimately to the battlefield of the 1965 riots in Watts. Along the way, the reader witnesses how idealistic cadets become callous and distant, feeling that they have been cast—against their wills—in the role of civilization's front line. John Greenway, writing in the *National Review,* hails Wambaugh's first novel as "incomparably the best revelation of the lives and souls of policemen ever written."

Whereas *The New Centurions* depicts the beginnings of a police officer's career, 1972's *The Blue Knight* depicts the end. It's protagonist, Officer Bumper Morgan, spends his last three days on the force in much the same way he had spent the previous twenty years: accepting free meals, leaning on "stoolies," taking liberties with certain obliging females, and occasionally making an arrest. David K. Jeffrey, writing in the *Dictionary of Literary Biography,* describes Morgan as "a fallible human being, fat, crude, and stubborn, [who] has been a cop for so long he now believes he *is* the law. He believes, too, that the legal system often corrupts and thwarts justice; he therefore 'bends the law' to ensure that criminals do not go unpunished." In the end, Morgan perjures himself during a trial to obtain a conviction. *The Blue Knight* "is an effective study of the ways in which police work can corrupt and change policemen," Jeffrey continues. The *New York Times*'s Eric Pace writes that, despite some flaws, "*The Blue Knight* abounds in vivid vignettes of police life and the Los Angeles streets. It effectively conveys the loneliness of an aging man who puts too much of himself into his work." Pace goes on to predict: "Its warty portrayal of the police will make it controversial in some quarters."

Wambaugh's "moonlighting" novels did, in fact, create something of a stir, particularly in the offices of the Los Angeles Police Department (L.A.P.D.). Wambaugh's superiors were not pleased that the young officer had written an inside view of their department, let alone one that featured officers who accepted gratuities and committed perjury. Wambaugh recalls in a *Publishers Weekly* interview the reaction of his superior officers: "The problem arose because [my novels] depicted cops as human beings, complete with rotten moods and frailties, and not as the robots people are accustomed to seeing on television shows about policemen. . . . I could see the administration being mad if I were giving away secrets, but I'm not: there are no secrets to reveal." Still, pressure from superiors and his increasing celebrity forced Wambaugh to take an extended leave from the L.A.P.D., during which time he researched and wrote what would become his most important work.

In 1963 two young Los Angeles policemen, officers Ian Campbell and Karl Hettinger, pulled over a suspicious-looking car; the men inside, a pair of small-time criminals who had spent the evening robbing liquor stores, overpowered the policemen and drove them, at gunpoint, to a remote onion field, where Campbell was executed. Hettinger escaped, and the two men were apprehended the next day. Though they were soon brought to trial and convicted of murder, the introduction of the Escobedo and Miranda laws (designed to protect the rights of criminals) delayed their executions; the ensuing appeals and retrials dragged on for seven years, making theirs the longest criminal proceeding in California history. In the meantime, Hettinger suffered a nervous breakdown, became suicidal, and was thrown off the force for shoplifting. He finally became a farmer, working just a few miles from that same onion field.

Wambaugh transformed the story of officers Campbell and Hettinger into his 1974 book *The Onion Field.* It was his first work of nonfiction, based entirely upon interviews, case records, and some 45,000 pages of court transcriptions. An officer during the time of the murder, Wambaugh often cites the Hettinger case as his motivation for becoming a writer. He explains in *Playboy:* "I feel I was put on earth to write this story, and I've never had that feeling before or since. Nothing could ever stop me from writing *The Onion Field.* I felt it was my sole reason for living, and that no one else understood or knew the ramifications of the onion-field murder."

James Lardner of the *New York Times Book Review* calls *The Onion Field* "a perfect double helix of a narrative in which the harrowing stories of two policemen and two criminals wound around each other, replicating what is laughably called the criminal justice system." The novel's principle theme is guilt and punishment: for the murderers, who feel no guilt at all, punishment is slow in coming; however, for Hettinger, who has assumed the blame for his partner's death, punishment in the form of ostracization is swift. Jeffrey, quoting Wambaugh, explains: "Policemen believe that 'no man-caused calamity happens by chance, that there is always a step that should have been taken, would have been taken if the [officer] had been alert, cautious, brave, aggressive—in short, if he'd been like a prototype policeman. . . .' By this measure, Hettinger was a failure who shared responsibility for the murder of Campbell just as surely as did [the murderers]."

Critics praised *The Onion Field.* Christopher Lehmann-Haupt, writing in the *New York Times,* comments: "Before he is finished, Mr. Wambaugh tries to explore all the ambiguities of the case, and even to see the hopeful side of what he could easily have dismissed as a thoroughly destructive series of incidents. In fact, *The Onion Field* is finally quite an impressive book." Reviewer James Conaway compares the work to another chilling non-fiction work, Truman Capote's *In Cold Blood,* praising the author's ability to adapt his skill as a novelist in writing non-fiction narrative history. "Wambaugh takes greater liberties with his characters and he lacks Capote's neatness," Conaway admits in the *New York Times Book Review.* "But in terms of scope, revealed depth of character, and dramatic coherence, this is the more ambitious book." He concludes: "With his third book, Wambaugh convincingly demonstrates that he belongs to the tradition of Dreiser and Farrell—constructing, from a glut of well-observed detail, unspectacular and often squalid lives lived among the concrete freeways, the bright, tawdry strips, the transience, brutality and beleaguered decency of a society set on the edge of America."

It was after the publication of *The Onion Field* that Wambaugh resigned from the police force, citing as reasons the constant phone calls and visitations to the station by interviewers and fans. "Yet, if his resignation saddened him personally, it also seems to have had a liberating effect on his writing," observes Jeffrey. Beyond the reach of superior officers, Wambaugh set out, in 1975, to write his "truest" police novel yet.

"Very little in Wambaugh's first two novels prepares one for the scabrous humor and ferocity of *The Choirboys,*" notes John Leonard of Wambaugh's third novel in the *New York Times Book Review.* According to a reviewer for *Atlantic Monthly,* "Mr. Wambaugh appears to have thrown into this novel everything that loyalty and discretion deleted from his work while he remained a member of the Los Angeles Police Department. The action is constant and the dialogue is tough. The writing has a careless barbarity that may be deliberate, for Mr. Wambaugh is explaining that police work is a one-way ticket to hell."

The Choirboys is the story of ten Los Angeles cops who alleviate the pain and stress of their job through a ritual called "choir practice"—debaucherous after-hours meetings in MacArthur Park, filled with aimless violence and alcoholic howling. Jeffrey explains: "The manic hilarity and drunkenness at their meetings serve the choirboys as defense mechanism against full consciousness of the fact that the ordinary people they protect are, by and large, barbaric savages, capable of any horror." The tone of *The Choirboys* is dark and satiric, told in a series of comic, yet ominous, vignettes. In this way, Wambaugh's novel has been compared to Joseph Heller's *Catch-22*—a work Wambaugh cites as a major influence. He recalls in the *Chicago Tribune:* "After [*The Onion Field*] I decided to try something very different, to use black comedy to deal with serious themes. And Heller enabled me to find my voice."

In retrospect, Wambaugh often describes the writing of *The Choirboys* as the turning point in his career, the place where he "found his voice." The novels that followed—among them *The Black Marble, The Glitter Dome,* and *The Golden Orange*—have maintained the gallows humor established in *The Choirboys.* Richard Eder observes in the *Los Angeles Times Book Review:* "Wambaugh's cops, like the soldiers in *Catch-22,* are men and women in a frenzy, zany grotesques made that way by the outrageous nature of the things they deal with," while the *New York Times*'s John Leonard proclaims: "There is more absurd action in a chapter of Wambaugh than there is in the entire collected works of George V. Higgins." Digby Diehl, looking back on Wambaugh's career in the *Detroit News,* calls the ex-cop "a good writer who becomes better with each successive book."

Reviewers also continue to praise Wambaugh's nonfiction works, which include *Lines and Shadows, Echoes in the Darkness,* and *The Blooding.* Whether examining the chaotic relations between the police and illegal aliens along the California-Mexico border, as he does in *Lines and Shadows,* or tracing the search for a brutal English killer, as in *The Blooding,* Wambaugh has proven his ability to create suspense and drama with accounts of actual events. While some critics suggest that Wambaugh excels in writing fiction rather than nonfiction, most agree that Wambaugh's books make for absorbing reading. Writing in the *New York Times Book Review,* Walter Walker called *The Blooding* "a well-written, meticulously researched, nontechnical tour de force," and the *Washington Post Book World*'s Douglas E. Winter hails it as "a blessed respite from the lubricious leers of the tabloid school of crime journalism."

Before *The New Centurions, The Blue Knight* and the highly praised television series *Police Story* (for which Wambaugh wrote and consulted), law enforcement officers were usually presented as cool and cerebral, like *Dragnet*'s Joe Friday, or as fearless superhero-detectives, like *The Untouchables*'s Elliot Ness, who crash into a villain's hideout with both guns blaring. "Generally the cops in my books don't perform heroic acts the likes of which will earn them a Medal of Valor," Wambaugh explains in the *Los Angeles Times.* "No, the heroic acts they perform are just coping with their character disorders or neuroses or whatever, and continuing to do the job with the worst of people. They don't all make it. . . . But while they cope, they're heroic to me."

Wambaugh's willingness and ability to display police as human has earned his work a special place in American literature. "What he writes is important because there are few really knowledgeable men who try to tell the public what a cop's life is like," claims Pace, and Greenway concurs: "Joseph Wambaugh's narrative revelations of that most misunderstood of all professions are absolutely required reading for anyone hoping to know humanity in its naked reality." Wambaugh himself expresses the purpose of his novels more simply: "The cops in my books have been called brutal, racist, cheating, fornicating bastards [but] all they are, in the end, is people. What the hell does anybody expect?"

BIOGRAPHICAL/CRITICAL SOURCES:

BOOKS

Authors in the News, Volume 1, Gale, 1976.
Bestsellers 89, Issue 3, Gale, 1989.
Contemporary Literary Criticism, Gale, Volume 3, 1975, Volume 18, 1981.
Dictionary of Literary Biography, Volume 6: *American Novelists Since World War II, Second Series,* Gale, 1980.
Dictionary of Literary Biography Yearbook: 1983, Gale, 1984.

PERIODICALS

America, January 19, 1974, p. 38; May 22, 1981, p. 549; May 19, 1984, p. 386.
Atlantic Monthly, October, 1973, p. 129; November, 1975, p. 124; August, 1981, p. 88; April, 1984, p. 149.
Best Sellers, January 15, 1971, p. 438; February 15, 1972, p. 518; October 15, 1973, p. 323; February, 1976, p. 334.
Bookviews, January, 1978.
Chicago Tribune, September 28, 1979, p. 15; March 10, 1980; June 17, 1981; February 8, 1987, p. 3; February 5, 1989, p. 3.
Detroit Free Press, March 29, 1989.
Detroit News, July 12, 1981, p. E2; October 20, 1985.
Globe and Mail (Toronto), March 10, 1984; February 14, 1987; March 4, 1989.
Inside Books, February, 1989, pp. 52-53.
Insight, June 4, 1990, p. 63.
Los Angeles Times, March 9, 1983, p. 12; August 5, 1987; May 4, 1990, p. E1.
Los Angeles Times Book Review, March 6, 1983; February 19, 1984, p. 3; November 10, 1985, p. 2; March 1, 1987, p. 3; February 5, 1989, p. 2; April 29, 1990, p. 4; June 9, 1991, p. 14; January 5, 1992, p. 1.
Los Angeles Times Magazine, February 26, 1989, pp. 8-42.
Midwest Quarterly, summer, 1980, pp. 470-483.
National Review, March 9, 1971, p. 271; April 2, 1976, pp. 343-344.
New Republic, March 13, 1971, p. 29; April 4, 1983, p. 36.
Newsweek, May 2, 1983, p. 78; February 6, 1984, p. 80; March 2, 1987, p. 76; January 20, 1992, p. 61.
New Yorker, April 1, 1972, p. 105; August 31, 1981, p. 108; May 9, 1983, p. 136; November 18, 1985, p. 177.

New York Times, January 22, 1971, p. 37; September 7, 1973, p. 33; January 8, 1978; January 12, 1978, p. 25; September 19, 1979; September 24, 1979, p. C14; October 9, 1979; March 7, 1980; June 22, 1981; February 23, 1987, p. 15.

New York Times Book Review, January 31, 1971, p. 34; February 13, 1972, p. 4; September 2, 1973, p. 5; December 2, 1973, p. 74; November 2, 1975, p. 6; January 8, 1978, p. 11; June 28, 1981, p. 3; March 20, 1983, p. 12; January 8, 1984, p. 34; February 5, 1984, p. 12; October 6, 1985, p. 11; March 1, 1987, p. 12; February 19, 1989; May 6, 1990, pp. 7-9; May 19, 1991, p. 42. February 2, 1992, p. 12.

Playboy, July, 1979, p. 69.

Publishers Weekly, August 23, 1971, pp. 33-35; January 3, 1972; July 23, 1973; September 1, 1975; July 12, 1976.

Rapport, May 5, 1992, p. 29.

Saturday Review, March 13, 1971, p. 12; September 11, 1973, p. 47; July, 1981, p. 78.

Time, February 15, 1971, p. 82; February 28, 1972, p. 83; September 24, 1973, p. 126; June 8, 1981, p. 76; March 5, 1984, p. 84; October 28, 1985, p. 96; February 23, 1987, p. 75.

Times (London), June 6, 1987; February 18, 1989.

Times Literary Supplement, March 16, 1973, p. 303; November 1, 1974, p. 1220; April 9, 1976, p. 413.

Tribune Books (Chicago), June 13, 1982; March 27, 1983, p. 2; October 6, 1985; February 8, 1987, p. 3; February 5, 1989, p. 3; May 15, 1990, p. 6; May 26, 1991, p. 8; December 29, 1991, p. 6.

Wall Street Journal, February 16, 1984, p. 32; November 22, 1985, p. 28; March 19, 1987, p. 32; January 24, 1992, p. A12.

Washington Post, February 19, 1979; October 19, 1979, p. B1, B3, 31; June 30, 1981; April 1, 1983; March 6, 1984; September 30, 1985; February 12, 1987; April 17, 1990; December 31, 1991, p. C3.

Washington Post Book World, March 5, 1972, p. 6; September 2, 1973, p. 15; October 20, 1974, p. 4; October 3, 1976, p. F4; January 24, 1978; March 22, 1987, p. 8; March 19, 1989; December 29, 1991, p. 12.

West Coast Review of Books, March, 1978, p. 31; March, 1983, p. 41; March, 1984, p. 34; November, 1985, p. 23; number 2, 1987, p. 31.

—*Sketch by Brandon Trenz*

* * *

WATSON, George (Grimes) 1927-

PERSONAL: Born October 13, 1927, in Brisbane, Queensland, Australia; son of Richard Grimes (a farmer) and Mary Lindsay (Dowrie) Watson. *Education:* University of Queensland, B.A., 1948; Trinity College, Oxford, B.A., 1950, M.A., 1954; Cambridge University, M.A., 1959. *Politics:* Liberal.

ADDRESSES: Home—St. John's College, Cambridge University, Cambridge, England.

CAREER: Council of Europe, Strasbourg, France, member of information staff, 1952-57; Cambridge University, Cambridge, England, lecturer in English, 1959—, fellow of St. John's College. Lecturer at universities in the United States. Editor, Unservile State Group.

WRITINGS:

(Editor) Samuel Taylor Coleridge, *Biographia Literaria*, Dent, 1956, new edition, 1976.

(Editor) *Cambridge Bibliography of English Literature*, Volume V, Cambridge University Press, 1957.

(Editor) *The Unservile State: Essays in Liberty and Welfare*, Allen & Unwin, 1957, Macmillan (New York), 1958.

The British Constitution and Europe, Sijthoff, 1958.

(Editor) *Concise Cambridge Bibliography of English Literature, 600-1950*, Cambridge University Press, 1958, revised edition, 1965.

(Editor) *Radical Alternative: Studies in Liberalism*, Eyre & Spottiswoode, 1962.

(Editor) John Dryden, *Of Dramatic Poesy*, two volumes, Dent, 1962.

The Literary Critics: A Study of English Descriptive Criticism, Penguin, 1962, enlarged edition, Chatto & Windus, 1986.

(Editor) Maria Edgeworth, *Castle Rackrent*, Oxford University Press, 1964.

(Editor) *The English Mind*, Cambridge University Press, 1964.

Coleridge the Poet, Barnes & Noble, 1966.

The English Petrarchans: A Critical Bibliography of the "Canzoniere," Warburg Institute, 1967.

The Study of Literature, Allen Lane, 1969, Scribner, 1970.

(General editor) *The New Cambridge Bibliography of English Literature*, Cambridge University Press, five volumes, 1969-77.

The Literary Thesis: A Guide to Research, Longmans, Green, 1970.

(Editor) *Literary English since Shakespeare*, Oxford University Press, 1970.

The English Ideology: Studies in the Language of Victorian Politics, Allen Lane, 1973.

Politics and Literature in Modern Britain, Macmillan, 1977.

The Discipline of English: A Guide to Critical Theory and Practice, Macmillan (London), 1978, Barnes & Noble, 1979.

The Story of the Novel, Barnes & Noble, 1979.

(Editor) *The Shorter Neiv Cambridge Bibliography of English Literature,* Cambridge University Press, 1981.
The Idea of Liberalism, Macmillan, 1985.
Writing a Thesis, Longmans, Green, 1987.
The Certainty of Literature, Harvester, 1989.
British Literature since 1945, Macmillan, 1991.
Lord Acton's History of Liberty, Scolar Press, 1993.

Also author of *Modern Literary Thought,* 1978.

SIDELIGHTS: "George Watson is a historian, literary critic, and a regular practising Liberal," comments Kenneth Minogue in the *Times Literary Supplement.* As such, Watson has written on a wide range of subjects, often focusing on the areas where history, literature, and politics intersect. His book *The Study of Literature* deals not only "with such elements of the literary act as judgment, value, the language of verse and prose, the theory of kinds, [and] the editorial art" points out a contributor to the *Times Literary Supplement,* but also with "the influences upon literary study of such related disciplines as linguistics, psychoanalysis, sociology, [and] the history of ideas."

For the subject matter of *The English Ideology: Studies in the Language of Victorian Politics,* Watson turned to the nineteenth century, because as he explains in the book, "Victorian England offers the supreme example of a civilization where the political and the literary are richly linked; and it is the nature of these links that is my theme." Observes a *Times Literary Supplement* reviewer: "Mr Watson's chapters on rank and class, democracy and equality, the terms of party politics, and socialism make *The English Ideology* . . . stimulating." The reviewer adds that "his pages on the evolution of such descriptions as Tory, Conservative, Whig, Liberal, Radical contain the essence of political history. So does his chapter on social status." W. W. Robson concludes in the *Times Literary Supplement* that "in [this] examination of British nineteenth-century intellectual history he has shown himself a vigorous defender of the achievements of Victorian Liberalism."

Watson probes twentieth-century developments in the relations between the political and the literary in *Politics and Literature in Modern Britain.* This collection of essays, which includes examinations of members of the New Left of the 1960s, and such figures as George Orwell, Matthew Arnold, W. H. Auden, and D. H. Lawrence, is arranged in reverse chronological order "to guide the reader from the more familiar to the less," notes Robson. "It certainly gives the book a sharp opening and establishes at once the controversial and polemical tone which persists throughout." Robert Jack Van Dellen, a contributor to *Modern Fiction Studies,* is critical of the book. Van Dellen maintains that Watson's "historical perspective only outlines the very broadest of political and literary developments." He concludes, "Watson does not risk enough. As a result, he stereotypes the stereotypes." Robson, on the other hand, finds that "the writing throughout is spirited and lively." "And," he writes, "George Watson makes some telling points against the intellectual community, and intellectual fashions, of our time; at the very least, he presents a case that requires answering."

As a Cambridge lecturer in English, Watson believes that like the study of history and politics, the study of English has practical value. "I visit schools as well as teach in universities, and am often struck by the fact that those who study English do not know that it is useful, . . . " he writes in a *Times Literary Supplement* essay, "and, more astonishingly, that they do not want to be told. . . . The literary theorist is not merely ignorant of the world he lives in: he does not even want to know about it. . . . Modern theory . . . glories in its uselessness. " Watson, on the other hand, speaks for the practitioners of English and calls for a recognition of their contribution to civilization. "We who profess literature are teaching some of the arts by which, in a post-industrial age, Britain may hope to survive. We are teaching the skill of using the world's first language . . . [and] are showing how to advance English among those whose first language is something else." "Theory, by contrast, is the recent past" he continues, ". . . and a last-ditch stand in favour of the gentility of being useless. It was a discourse by which professionals talked self-indulgently to one another, indifferent to a world beyond themselves."

BIOGRAPHICAL/CRITICAL SOURCES:

PERIODICALS

Books and Bookmen, October, 1977.
Modern Fiction Studies, winter, 1979.
Modern Language Review, October, 1980.
New Statesman, September 16, 1977.
Times Literary Supplement, October 2, 1969; March 16, 1973; July 21, 1978; December 10, 1982; January 17, 1986.

* * *

WAYNE, Jane Ellen 1936-

PERSONAL: Born April 6, 1936, in Philadelphia, PA; daughter of Jesse Allen and Eleanor Mae (Brundle) Stump; married Ronald Wayne, May 26, 1957 (divorced May 26, 1967); children: Elizabeth Jo. *Education:* Attended Grove City College, 1955-57, American Academy of Dramatic Arts, 1957, and New York University, 1957. *Politics:* Republican. *Religion:* Protestant.

Avocational Interests: Travel; Wayne has been all over the world, and found Egypt "the most fascinating."

ADDRESSES: Home—17-85 215 St., Apt. 14M, Bayside, NY 11360.

CAREER: National Broadcasting Co., New York City, member of promotional staff, 1957-65; New York World's Fair, Prestige Club, New York City, manager, 1965-66; Abbott & Abbott Corp. (wood manufacturers), Long Island City, NY, vice-president, 1974—. Free-lance writer. Creator of Beauty and Poise private classes for businesswomen, 1963-66.

MEMBER: Sigma Delta Phi.

WRITINGS:

The Life of Robert Taylor, Warner Paperback, 1973.
Kings of Tragedy, Manor, 1976.
Stanwyck, Arbor House, 1986.
Gable's Women, Simon & Schuster, 1987.
Cooper's Women, Simon & Schuster, 1988.
Crawford's Men, Simon & Schuster, 1988.
Robert Taylor: The Man with the Perfect Face, St. Martin's, 1989.
Ava's Men, St. Martin's, 1990.
Grace Kelly's Men, St. Martin's, 1991.
Marilyn's Men, St. Martin's, 1992.
Clark Gable: Portrait of a Misfit, St. Martin's, 1993.
The Life and Loves of Lana Turner, St. Martin's, 1994.

Also author of *Tiffany Belle,* 1978, *Lividia,* 1978, and *The Love Gap,* 1978.

* * *

WEBB, Lucas
See BURGESS, Michael (Roy)

* * *

WECHSLER, Judith Glatzer 1940-

PERSONAL: Born December 28, 1940, in Chicago, IL; daughter of Nahum Norbert (a professor) and Anne (a teacher; maiden name Stiebel) Glatzer; married Richard Wechsler, September 15, 1963 (divorced, 1969); married Benson R. Snyder, 1976; children: (from first marriage) Johanna. *Education:* Brandeis University, B.A., 1962; Columbia University, M.A., 1967; University of California, Los Angeles, Ph.D., 1972. *Politics:* Democrat. *Religion:* Jewish.

ADDRESSES: Home—68 Fuller St., Brookline, MA 02146. *Office*—Tufts University, Department of Art History, Medford, MA 02155.

CAREER: Shocken Books, New York City, assistant editor, 1963-65; Brown University, Providence, RI, lecturer, 1970; Massachusetts Institute of Technology, Cambridge, MA, assistant professor, 1970-74, associate professor, 1974-79, fellow, Center for Advanced Visual Studies, 1977-79; Tufts University, Medford, MA, associate professor, 1979-81, professor of art history and department chairperson, 1989—; Rhode Island School of Design, Providence, RI, associate professor of art, 1981-89. Visiting professor, Harvard University, 1989. Producer and director, Judith Wechsler, Inc., 1985—.

MEMBER: College Art Association (board of advisors, 1988, 1989), Swann Foundation for Study of Caricature (board of directors, 1985-93).

AWARDS, HONORS: National Endowment for the Humanities grants, 1973, 1975, 1983, 1984, 1985-86, 1988-89; National Endowment for the Arts grants, 1980, 1987-89; Cine Golden Eagle awards, 1983, 1985, 1988, 1989, 1992; red ribbon, American Film Festival, 1989, 1992; juror, Montreal International Art Film Festival, 1989; gold plaque, Chicago International Film Festival, 1991.

WRITINGS:

(Editor and author of introduction) *Cezanne in Perspective,* Prentice-Hall, 1975.
(Contributor) Fishbane and Flohr, editors, *Texts and Responses,* Leider, 1975.
(Editor and author of introduction) *On Aesthetics in Science,* MIT Press, 1978.
The Interpretation of Cezanne, UMI Research Press, 1981.
A Human Comedy: Physiognomy and Caricature in Nineteenth Century Paris, University of Chicago Press, 1982.
(With William H. Helfand) *The Picture of Health,* Philadelphia Museum of Art, 1991.
(Contributor) *The Face of Physiognomy,* Camden House, 1993.

OTHER

Screenwriter and director of films, including (with Charles Eames) *Daumier: Paris and the Spectator,* 1977; (with Eames) *Cezanne: The Late Work,* 1978; *Pissaro: At the Heart of Impressionism,* 1981; (script with Jehane Burns) *Manet: At the Heart of Impressionism,* 1982; *The Artist and the Nude,* 1985; *The Training of Painters,* 1987; (script with Henri Zerner) *Abstraction,* 1989; *The Arrested Moment,* 1988; (script with Linda Nochlin) *Portraits,* 1988; *Painting and the Public,* 1988; (with Hans Namuth) *Jasper Johns: Take an Object,* 1990; *Aaron Siskin: Making Pictures,* 1991; *Harry Callahan,* 1993.

Contributor to periodicals, including *Artforum, Art News, Aperture, Daedalus, Gazette des Beaux Arts, Studies in Vi-*

sual Communication, Stanford French and Italian studies, and *Technology Review.*

SIDELIGHTS: Judith Wechsler has lived in Jerusalem, Paris, and Oxford.

* * *

WELCH, James 1940-

PERSONAL: Born in 1940, in Browning, MT; married, wife's name, Lois (a professor). *Education:* University of Montana, B.A.; attended Northern Montana College.

ADDRESSES: Home—Roseacres Farm, Rt. 6, Missoula, MT 59801. *Office*—c/o W. W. Norton and Co., 500 Fifth Ave., New York, NY 10110. *Agent*—Ellen Levine.

CAREER: Poet and novelist. Visiting professor at University of Washington and Cornell University; served on Montana State Board of Pardons; served on literature panel of National Endowment for the Arts.

AWARDS, HONORS: National Endowment for the Arts grant, 1969; *Los Angeles Times* Book Prize, and Pacific Northwest Booksellers Association Book award, both 1987, both for *Fools Crow.*

WRITINGS:

Riding the Earthboy 40: Poems, World Publishing, 1971.
Winter in the Blood, Harper, 1974.
The Death of Jim Loney, Harper, 1979.
Fool's Crow, Viking, 1986.
(Editor with Ripley S. Hugo and Lois M. Welch) Richard Hugo, *The Real West Marginal Way: A Poet's Autobiography,* 1986.
James Welch, Confluence Press, 1986.
The Indian Lawyer, Norton, 1990.

Also author of introduction, *Death and the Good Life,* by Richard Hugo, Clark City Press, 1991; contributor of poetry to periodicals, including *New American Review.*

SIDELIGHTS: A *Saturday Review* critic made this prediction in a review of James Welch's first book of poetry, *Riding the Earthboy 40:* "His poems are alert, sorrowful, and true. For a young man he is very strong. . . . If Welch stays put in his own life, I think his strengths should develop; his voice is clear, laconic, and it projects a depth in experience of landscape, people, and history that conveys a rich complexity. You realize his is not looking at a thing, but seeing into it—which is vision."

Welch's promise was realized in his first novel, *Winter in the Blood,* the story of a young Indian living on a reservation in Montana. The unnamed narrator is, like Welch, part Blackfoot and part Gros Ventre Indian. He describes himself as a "servant to a memory of death." Both his father and brother are dead; in the course of the novel, his beloved grandmother dies as well. In the *New York Times Book Review,* Reynolds Price described the narrator's life as a "black sack tied firmly shut." But just as the story "threatens to die in its crowded sack," Price wrote, "it opens onto light—and through natural, carefully prepared, but beautifully surprising narrative means; a recovery of the past; a venerable, maybe lovable, maybe usable past. . . ."

Welch's next work, *The Death of Jim Loney,* about an alienated, alcoholic half-breed of both white and Indian parentage, continues the themes of identity and purpose set down in *Winter in the Blood. Fools Crow,* Welch's acclaimed third novel, marks a change in direction for the author, telling the story of a band of Blackfoot Indians in Montana Territory in the 1870s. The book follows the life of Fools Crow, who grows from a reckless young warrior to become the tribe's medicine man. A vision Fools Crow has of his tribe's bleak future foreshadows the end of the entire Indian prairie culture—a culture already threatened by disease, the extinction of the buffalo herds, and the encroachment of white settlers.

Welch's ability to recapture the Blackfoot way of life, especially its spiritual aspects, was a strength of the novel. Reviewing *Fools Crow* in the *Washington Post Book World,* Dennis Drabelle declared: "If *Fools Crow* succeeds . . . it does so because Welch, himself part Blackfoot, manages to convey a sense of his people's world view." Peter Wild of the *New York Times Book Review* agreed, noting that "the book becomes a series of dreams acted out, a chronicle of the Indians' visions as applied to daily life." And Lewis D. Owens, writing in the *Los Angeles Times Book Review,* stated: "In this novel, Welch is remembering the world of his ancestors, putting that world together again in a way that will tell both author and reader what has been lost and what saved."

Owens argued that Welch's work was significant for other reasons as well. "Perhaps the most profound implication of this novel," Owens suggested, "is that the culture, the world-view brought so completely to life in *Fools Crow,* is alive and accessible in the self-imagining of contemporary Blackfeet and other American Indians. In recovering the world found in this novel, Welch serves as storyteller, bearer of oral tradition and definer of what it means to be Indian today."

After the success of *Fools Crow,* Welch returned to a contemporary setting for his next novel, *The Indian Lawyer,* a tale of corruption involving prominent Indian attorney Sylvester Yellow Calf. Yellow Calf, a leading congressional candidate who also serves on the Montana prison parole board, falls victim to a blackmail scheme after he is seduced by the wife of a prison inmate whose case is under study by the parole board. Afraid that he has compromised his personal ethics as well as his political standing, Yellow Calf drops out of the congressional race and begins a law practice on the reservation where he was born.

Critics determined that *The Indian Lawyer* accurately reflects the conflicts that exist between white and Indian cultures. In the *Washington Post Book World,* Walter Walker remarked: "The concept of a man caught between two worlds is fresh and alive when it comes to American Indians, and Welch handles that beautifully, as he does his physical descriptions of virtually every location in the book." Walker also believed, however, that the novel's weak storyline undermined the author's message, stating: "Like many a human being, *The Indian Lawyer* starts off with great promise and ends marred by the scars of what might have been." He continued: "James Welch clearly had a very serious idea in mind that is all but lost in the banality of his plot."

Welch acknowledges that his work as a novelist places him in a small, select group of Indian writers. He told Will Nixon of *Publishers Weekly* that finding good fiction by Indian authors is difficult, adding, "I think Indians tend toward poetry instead. A lot of people have said that poetry more approximates the rhythms of their own traditions, such as songs. And Indians prefer to write poetry because they have something to say about their culture and society and it's harder to be political and polemical in fiction." Welch, though, seems committed to using the novel as a showcase for what Nixon called the author's "real subject . . . the American Indian's search for identity in his native land."

BIOGRAPHICAL/CRITICAL SOURCES:

PERIODICALS

Globe and Mail (Toronto), January 30, 1988.

Los Angeles Times, March 30, 1983, pp. 6-7.

Los Angeles Times Book Review, September 21, 1986, p. 13; December 14, 1986, pp. 1-2, 6; October 14, 1990, p. 3.

New York Times, November 28, 1979.

New York Times Book Review, April 12, 1981, p. 43; November 2, 1986, p. 14; November 25, 1990, p. 7.

Publishers Weekly, October 5, 1990, pp. 81-82.

Times Literary Supplement, May 2, 1980, p. 500.

Tribune Books (Chicago), December 21, 1986, p. 6; September 23, 1990, p. 3.

Washington Post Book World, March 5, 1981, p. 12; December 24, 1986; January 25, 1987, p. 10; December 12, 1990, p. 9.

WEST, D(onald) J(ames) 1924-

PERSONAL: Born June 9, 1924, in Liverpool, England. *Education:* University of Liverpool, M.B. and Ch.B., 1947, M.D., 1958; University of London, Diploma in Psychological Medicine, 1952.

ADDRESSES: *Home*—Cambridge, England. *Office*—Institute of Criminology, Cambridge University, 7 West Rd., Cambridge CB3 9DT, England.

CAREER: Cambridge University, Institute of Criminology, Cambridge, England, 1960—, began as professor, currently professor emeritus. Former honorary consultant psychiatrist, Cambridge Psychiatric Service. Member, Mental Health Act Commissioners, 1989—.

MEMBER: Royal College of Psychiatrists (fellow), Society for Psychical Research (president, 1964-65, 1985-86), British Society of Criminology (vice-president).

AWARDS, HONORS: Litt.D., Cambridge University, 1978.

WRITINGS:

Eleven Lourdes Miracles, Duckworth, 1957.

Homosexuality, Penguin, 1960.

Psychical Research Today, Penguin, 1962.

The Habitual Prisoner, Macmillan, 1963.

Murder Followed by Suicide, Heinemann, 1965.

The Young Offender, Penguin, 1967.

Present Conduct and Future Delinquency, Heinemann, 1969.

Who Becomes Delinquent, Heinemann, 1973.

The Delinquent Way of Life, Heinemann, 1977.

Homosexuality Re-examined, University of Minnesota Press, 1977.

Understanding Sexual Attacks, Heinemann, 1978.

Delinquency: Its Roots, Careers, and Prospects, Harvard University Press, 1982.

(Editor) *Unlawful Sex: Offences, Victims, and Offenders in the Criminal Justice System of England and Wales,* Waterlow, 1985.

Sexual Victimisation: Two Recent Researches into Sex Problems and Their Social Effects, Gower, 1985.

Sexual Crimes and Confrontations, Gower, 1987.

(With C. K. Li and T. P. Woodhouse) *Children's Sexual Encounters with Adults,* Duckworth, 1990.

Male Prostitution, Duckworth, 1992, Haworth Press, 1993.

SIDELIGHTS: D. J. West once wrote *CA:* "I write about subjects that are of general interest, trying to present the results of research in a readable manner."

West recently told *CA* that he has had a "lifelong interest in psychical research. Trained as a psychiatrist, [I] specialised in criminological work and sex offending based at Cambridge University Institute of Criminology."

* * *

WHEAT, (Marcus) Ed(ward, Jr.) 1926-

PERSONAL: Born September 3, 1926, in Nashville, AR; son of Marcus Edward (a county superintendent of schools) and Gladys (a teacher; maiden name, Gibson) Wheat; married D. Gaye Eagle (an author and housewife), September 24, 1948; children: Melinda Wheat Mason, Joy Wheat Shoemaker, Merry Ann Wheat Peoples. *Education:* Hendrix College, B.A., 1947; University of Arkansas School of Medicine (now University of Arkansas for Medical Sciences), M.D., 1951. *Religion:* Undenominational—attends Fellowship Bible Church.

ADDRESSES: *Office*—Scriptural Counsel, Inc., 130 North Spring St., Springdale, AR 72764.

CAREER: Private practice of family medicine, 1952-88; Wheat Clinic, Springdale, AR, owner, 1956-88. President, Scriptural Counsel, Inc., 1975—; founder and chairman of board, Bible Believers Cassettes, Inc. Guest lecturer at University of Arkansas School of Medicine, 1962-63. Vice chairman, Arkansas Commission on Alcoholism; member of National Council on Alcoholism. Past chief of staff of Springdale Memorial Hospital. *Military service:* U.S. Navy, 1944-46; became ensign.

MEMBER: American Academy of Family Physicians, American Medical Society, American Association of Sex Educators, Counselors, and Therapists, Arkansas Academy of Family Physicians, Arkansas Medical Society, Washington County Medical Society (past president), Springdale Lions Club (past president).

AWARDS, HONORS: Jaycee Distinguished Service Award, 1958.

WRITINGS:

Intended for Pleasure, Fleming Revell, 1977, revised edition, 1981.
Love Life for Every Married Couple, Zondervan, 1980, revised edition, Harper Collins, 1991.
How to Save Your Marriage Alone, Zondervan, 1983.
The First Years of Forever, Zondervan, 1988.
Secret Choices: Personal Decisions That Affect Your Marriage, Zondervan, 1989.

Author of counseling cassette series "Sex Technique and Sex Problems in Marriage," "Love-Life," and "Before the Wedding Night."

Wheat's works have been translated into Spanish.

SIDELIGHTS: Ed Wheat told *CA:* "My objective in writing is to bring permanent quality improvement into the lives of those who read and heed the counsel given in the pages of my books."

* * *

WHITE, James P(atrick) 1940-

PERSONAL: Born September 28, 1940, in Wichita Falls, TX; son of Joseph and Minnie (Mann) White; married Janice Lou Turner, September 11, 1961; children: Christopher Jules. *Education:* University of Texas, B.A. (with honors), 1961; Vanderbilt University, M.A. (history), 1967; graduate study at Texas Christian University, 1969-71; Brown University, M.A. (creative writing), 1973.

ADDRESSES: *Home*—P.O. Box 428, Montrose, AL 36559. *Office*—Department of Creative Writing, University of South Alabama, Mobile, AL 36688. *Agent*—Eric Ashworth, Candida Donadio, Inc., New York, NY 10017.

CAREER: Blue Mountain College, Blue Mountain, MS, associate professor of history, 1964-66; free-lance writer in Europe and the United States, 1967-70; University of Texas of the Permian Basin, Odessa, assistant professor, 1973-74, associate professor of creative writing and chairman of department, 1974-76; Texas Center for Writers, Dallas, TX, founder and director, 1976-77; University of Texas at Dallas, visiting university professor, 1977-78; University of Southern California, Los Angeles, director of master of arts program in professional writing, 1979-83; University of South Alabama, Mobile, professor and director of creative writing, 1983—. Member of state executive committee, Texas Joint English Committee for Schools and Colleges, 1973-74; chairman of advisory board, Down Center Stage, Dallas Theater Center, 1978-79.

MEMBER: American Literary Translators Association (member of international editorial board, 1978—), Associated Writing Programs (member of national editorial board, 1973-75), Conference of College Teachers of English (state chairman of creative writing section, 1975-76), Modern Language Association of America (South Central section), Texas Association of Creative Writers (founding president, 1973-74), Gulf Coast Association of Creative Writing Teachers (founding president, 1993), Theta Xi, Phi Delta Phi, Phi Alpha Theta, Phi Eta Sigma.

AWARDS, HONORS: Marston fellow, 1971; Guggenheim fellow, 1988-89; Fulbright fellow, 1991.

WRITINGS:

(Editor) *Bicentennial Collection of Texas Short Stories,* Texas Center for Writers Press, 1974.

(Editor) *New and Experimental Literature,* Texas Center for Writers Press, 1975.

Birdsong (novel), Copper Beech Press, 1977, third edition, Methuen, 1990.

Poems, Calliope Press, 1978.

(With Anne Reed Rooth) *The Ninth Car* (novel), Putnam, 1978.

(With wife, Janice L. White) *Clarity: A Text on Writing,* Paul Hanson, 1981.

The Persian Oven (novella; also see below), Imperial Press, 1983.

The Persian Oven [and] California Exit (novellas), Methuen, 1987.

(Editor with Don Bachardy) *Where Joy Resides: A Christopher Isherwood Reader,* Farrar, Straus, 1989.

PLAYS

Broadside (three-act), first produced in Cleveland, OH, at Muse Theater, 1969.

Family Circle (three-act), first produced in Providence, RI, at Brown University, 1973.

Also author of *Clara's Call,* in *Two Short Novels* (with R. V. Cassill), Texas Center for Writers Press; editor of *King's S.W.,* 1975, and *Gulf Coast Collection of Stories and Poems,* Texas Center for Writers Press; co-editor with W. McDonald of *Texas Stories and Poems,* 1978, and with J. White of *Poetry Dallas,* 1978. Contributor of articles, poems, and short stories to over forty periodicals, including *Kansas Quarterly, Quartet, Texas Quarterly, Arizona Quarterly, Arts and Letters, Mundus Artium, Contemporary Literary Scene, Journal of African History, Markham Review,* and *New Writers.* Editor, *Texas Writer's Newsletter,* 1973-76, and *Sand,* 1976—; co-editor and publisher, *Texas Books in Review,* 1975-78.

SIDELIGHTS: "I think that the most important thing about writing," James P. White once told *CA,* "is obviously the work itself—enjoying, developing, and caring about it and the writing of others. I've been involved in a lot of literary activities and have run several writing programs. What matters is a person's work. I particularly admire Christopher Isherwood and Thomas Williams and Susan Fromberg Schaeffer. Building a literary career is difficult; much of it adds up to nothing. But what really matters is continuing to learn about writing and caring about writing well."

* * *

WHITE, John Hoxland, Jr. 1933-

PERSONAL: Born November 10, 1933, in Cincinnati, OH; son of John Hoxland (an accountant) and Christine (Seebaun) White. *Education:* Miami University, Oxford, OH, B.A., 1958.

ADDRESSES: *Office*—Division of Transportation, Smithsonian Institution, Washington, DC 20560.

CAREER: Smithsonian Institution, National Museum of American History, Washington, DC, associate curator, 1958-67, curator of transportation, 1967–90. Lecturer, University of Pennsylvania, 1966, University of California, 1970, and University of Moscow, 1973. Consultant, Pennsylvania State Railroad Museum, 1968-90, and California State Railroad Museum, 1970-90.

MEMBER: Railway and Locomotive Historical Society, Society for the History of Technology, Cincinnati Historical Society.

AWARDS, HONORS: National Book Award nominee, 1979, for *The American Railroad Passenger Car;* railway history award, Railroad & Locomotive Historical Society, 1982.

WRITINGS:

Cincinnati Locomotive Builders, 1845-1868, Smithsonian Institution Press, 1965.

American Locomotives: An Engineering History, 1830-1880, Johns Hopkins University Press, 1968, reprinted as *A History of the American Locomotive: Its Development, 1830-1880,* Dover, 1979.

(Editor) *Development of the Locomotive Engine,* MIT Press, 1970.

Early American Locomotives, Dover, 1972.

Horsecars, Cable Cars and Omnibuses, Dover, 1974.

American Railroad Passenger Car, Johns Hopkins University Press, 1978.

The John Bull: 150 Years a Locomotive, Smithsonian Institution Press, 1981.

A Short History of American Locomotive Builders in the Steam Era, Bass, 1982.

The Great Yellow Fleet, Golden West Books, 1986.

American Railroad Freight Cars, Johns Hopkins University Press, 1993.

Contributor of articles on railroad subjects to museum bulletins and transportation journals. Editor, *Railroad History,* 1970-79.

BIOGRAPHICAL/CRITICAL SOURCES:

PERIODICALS

New Republic, December 9, 1978.

New York Times Book Review, June 4, 1978; April 13, 1980.

Village Voice, December 3, 1980.

WHITTINGTON, Geoffrey 1938-

PERSONAL: Born September 21, 1938, in Warsop, England; son of Bruce and Dorothy Gwendoline (Gent) Whittington; married Joyce Enid Smith (a mathematician and psychologist), September 7, 1963; children: Alan Geoffrey, Richard John. *Education:* London School of Economics and Political Science, B.Sc., 1959; Fitzwilliam College, Cambridge, Ph.D., 1971.

ADDRESSES: Office—Faculty of Economics and Politics, University of Cambridge, Austin Robinson Building, Sidgwick Ave., Cambridge CB3 9DD, England.

CAREER: Cambridge University, Fitzwilliam College, Cambridge, England, research officer in applied economics, 1962- 72, fellow, 1966-72; University of Edinburgh, Edinburgh, Scotland, professor of accountancy and finance, 1972-75; University of Bristol, Bristol, England, professor of accounting and finance, 1975-88, dean of the faculty of social sciences, 1985-87; Cambridge University, Cambridge, Price Waterhouse Professor of Financial Accounting and professorial fellow of Fitzwilliam College, 1988—. Member of Meade Committee on the Structure of Direct Taxation in the United Kingdom, 1975-77, and Monopolies and Mergers Commission, 1987—. Academic adviser, Accounting Standards Board, 1990—.

MEMBER: Institute of Chartered Accountants in England and Wales (fellow).

WRITINGS:

(With Ajit Singh) *Growth, Profitability, and Valuation,* Cambridge University Press, 1968.

Prediction of Profitability and Other Studies of Company Behaviour, Cambridge University Press, 1971.

(With Geoffrey Meeks) *The Financing of Quoted Companies in the United Kingdom,* H.M.S.O., 1974.

Inflation Accounting: An Introduction to the Debate, Cambridge University Press, 1983.

(With David Tweedie) *The Debate on Inflation Accounting,* Cambridge University Press, 1984.

(Editor with R. H. Parker and G. C. Harcourt) *Readings in the Concept and Measurement of Income,* Philip Allan, 1986.

The Elements of Accounting: An Introduction, Cambridge University Press, 1992.

OTHER

Contributor to numerous books, including *Current Issues in Accounting,* edited by Bryan Carsberg and Tony Hope, Philip Allan, 1978; *Taxation and Social Policy,* edited by Cedric Sandford and Chris Pond, Heinemann, 1980; *External Financial Reporting,* edited by Carsberg and Susan Dev, Prentice-Hall, 1984; *Accounts, Accounting, and Accountability,* edited by G. Macdonald and B. A. Rutherford, Van Nostrand, 1989; *Foundations of Economic Thought,* Basil Blackwell, 1990; and *Financial Reporting: The Way Forward,* edited by J. A. Arnold, M. J. D. Cooper, and J. C. Shaw, Institute of Chartered Accountants in England and Wales and Institute of Chartered Accountants of Scotland, 1991. Also contributor to economic and business journals.

* * *

WHITTINGTON-EGAN, Richard 1924-

PERSONAL: Born October 22, 1924, in Liverpool, England; son of Cyril and Helen Margaret (Barrington) Whittington-Egan. *Education:* Studied under private tutors; read medicine.

ADDRESSES: Home—Bravo House, Foley Terr., Malvern, Worcester, England.

CAREER: Liverpolitan, Liverpool, England, assistant editor, 1950-52; *Liverpool Daily Post and Echo,* Liverpool, free-lance writer and columnist, 1953-56; Associated Newspapers, London, England, 1958—. Director of *Contemporary Review.* Broadcaster. *Military service:* British Army, 1943-46.

MEMBER: National Union of Journalists, Instituto Palaeontologia Umana (Florence), Medico-Legal Society, Our Society, Organon Club.

WRITINGS:

Liverpool Colonnade, Philip, Son & Nephew, 1955.

Liverpool Roundabout, Philip, Son & Nephew, 1957.

(With G. T. Smerdon) *A Life of Richard Le Gallienne,* Secker & Warburg, 1960, published as *The Life and Letters of Richard Le Gallienne,* Dufour, 1961.

The Quest of the Golden Boy, Unicorn Press, 1960, Barre, 1962.

Tales of Liverpool: Murder, Mayhem, Mystery, Gallery Press, 1967.

(Contributor) *Treasures of Britain and Ireland,* Drive Publications for Automobile Association, 1968.

Liverpool Characters and Eccentrics, Gallery Press, 1968.

Liverpool Soundings, Gallery Press, 1969.

The Ordeal of Philip Yale Drew: A Real Life Murder Melodrama in Three Acts, Harrap, 1972.

Liverpool: This Is My City, Gallery Press, 1973.

Casebook on Jack the Ripper, Wildy, 1975.

Weekend Book of Ghosts, Harmsworth, 1975.

Second Weekend Book of Ghosts, Harmsworth, 1978.

Third Weekend Book of Ghosts and Horror, Harmsworth, 1981.

Fourth Weekend Book of Ghosts and Horror, Harmsworth, 1982.

Fifth Weekend Book of Ghosts and Horror, Harmsworth, 1985.

(With Molly Tibbs) *The Strange Case of Mr. George Edalji,* Grey House Books, 1986.

(With Molly Tibbs) *The Bedside Book of Murder,* David & Charles, 1987.

William Roughead's Chronicles of Murder, Lochar, 1991.

(With Molly Tibbs) *The Murder Almanac,* Neil Wilson, 1992.

Contributor of articles to *Times, Guardian, Chambers's Journal, Contemporary Review,* and other periodicals, and of book reviews to *Books and Bookmen, New York Times,* and *Tomorrow.*

WORK IN PROGRESS: Stephen Phillips: A Critical Biography; The Oscar Slater Case.

* * *

WIDEMAN, John Edgar 1941-

PERSONAL: Born June 14, 1941, in Washington, DC; son of Edgar and Betty (French) Wideman; married Judith Ann Goldman, 1965; children: Daniel Jerome, Jacob Edgar, Jamila Ann. *Education:* University of Pennsylvania, B.A., 1963; New College, Oxford, B.Phil., 1966.

ADDRESSES: Office—Department of English, University of Massachusetts—Amherst, Amherst, MA 01002.

CAREER: Howard University, Washington, DC, teacher of American literature, summer, 1965; University of Pennsylvania, Philadelphia, 1966-74, began as instructor, professor of English, 1974, director of Afro-American studies program, 1971-73; University of Wyoming, Laramie, professor of English, 1975-1986; affiliated with department of English, University of Massachusetts—Amherst, MA. Made U.S. Department of State lecture tour of Europe and the Near East, 1976; Phi Beta Kappa lecturer, 1976; visiting writer and lecturer at numerous colleges and universities; has also served as administrator/teacher in a curriculum planning, teacher-training institute sponsored by National Defense Education Act. Assistant basketball coach, University of Pennsylvania, 1968-72. National Humanities Faculty consultant in numerous states; consultant to secondary schools across the country, 1968—.

MEMBER: National Humanities Faculty, Association of American Rhodes Scholars (member of board of directors and of state and national selection committees), Phi Beta Kappa.

AWARDS, HONORS: Received creative writing prize, University of Pennsylvania; Rhodes Scholar, Oxford University, 1963; Thouron fellow, Oxford University, 1963-66; Kent fellow, University of Iowa, 1966, to attend creative writing workshop; named member of Philadelphia Big Five Basketball Hall of Fame, 1974; Young Humanist fellow, 1975—; PEN/Faulkner Award for fiction, 1984, for *Sent for You Yesterday;* National Book Award nomination, 1984, for *Brothers and Keepers;* John Dos Passos Prize for Literature from Longwood College, 1986; honorary doctorate, University of Pennsylvania.

WRITINGS:

A Glance Away (novel), Harcourt, 1967.

Hurry Home (novel), Harcourt, 1970.

The Lynchers (novel), Harcourt, 1973.

Damballah (short stories), Avon, 1981.

Hiding Place (novel), Avon, 1981.

Sent for You Yesterday (novel), Avon, 1983.

Brothers and Keepers (memoirs), H. Holt, 1984.

The Homewood Trilogy (includes *Damballah, Hiding Place,* and *Sent For You Yesterday*), Avon, 1985.

Reuben (novel), H. Holt, 1987.

Fever (short stories), H. Holt, 1989.

Philadelphia Fire (novel), H. Holt, 1990.

All Stories Are True, Vintage Books, 1992.

The Stories of John Edgar Wideman, Pantheon Books, 1992.

Contributor of articles, short stories, book reviews, and poetry to periodicals, including *American Poetry Review, Negro Digest, Black American Literature Forum, Black World, American Scholar, Gentleman's Quarterly, New York Times Book Review, North American Review,* and *Washington Post Book World.*

SIDELIGHTS: John Edgar Wideman has been hailed by Don Strachen in the *Los Angeles Times Book Review* as "the black Faulkner, the softcover Shakespeare." Such praise is not uncommon for this author, whose novel *Sent for You Yesterday* was selected as the 1984 PEN/Faulkner Award winner over works by Bernard Malamud, Cynthia Ozick, and William Kennedy. Wideman attended Oxford University in 1963 on a Rhodes scholarship, earned a degree in eighteenth-century literature, and later accepted a fellowship at the prestigious University of Iowa Writers' Workshop. Yet this "artist with whom any reader who admires ambitious fiction must sooner or later reckon," as the *New York Times* calls him, began his college career not as a writer, but as a basketball star. "I always wanted to play pro basketball—ever since I saw a ball and learned you could make money at it," he told Curt Suplee in the *Washington Post.* Recruited by the University of Pennsylvania, Wideman first studied psychology, attracted by the "mystical insight" he told Suplee that he thought this major would yield. When his subjects of study instead "turned out to be rats" and clinical experiments, Wideman changed his major to English, while continuing to be mainly concerned with basketball. He played well enough to earn a place in the Philadelphia Big Five Basketball Hall of Fame, but, he told Suplee, as his time at the university drew to a close, "I knew I wasn't going to be able to get into the NBA [National Basketball Association]. What was left?" The Rhodes scholarship answered that question. Wideman began to concentrate on his writing rather than sports and did so with such success that his first novel, *A Glance Away,* was published just a year after he earned his degree from Oxford.

The story of a day in the life of a drug addict, *A Glance Away* reflects the harsh realities that Wideman saw and experienced during his youth in Pittsburgh's ghetto, Homewood. And, though the author later resided in other locales, including Wyoming, his novels continued to describe black urban experiences. He explained to Suplee, "My particular imagination has always worked well in a kind of exile. It fits the insider-outside view I've always had. It helps to write away from the center of the action."

Wideman's highly literate style is in sharp contrast to his gritty subject matter, and while reviews of his books have been generally favorable from the start of his writing career, some critics initially expressed the opinion that such a formal style was not appropriate for his stories of street life. For example, Anatole Broyard praised *The Lynchers* in his *New York Times* review, stating: "Though we have heard the themes and variations of violence before in black writing, *The Lynchers* touches us in a more personal way, for John Edgar Wideman has a weapon more powerful than any knife or gun. His weapon is art. Eloquence is his arsenal, his arms cache. His prose, at its best, is a black panther, coiled to spring." But Broyard goes on to say that the book is not flawless: "Far from it. Mr. Wideman ripples too many muscles in his writing, often cannot seem to decide whether to show or snow us. . . . [He] is wordy, and *The Lynchers* is as shaky in its structure as some of the buildings his characters inhabit. But he can *write,* and you come away from his book with the feeling that he is, as they say, very close to getting it all together." In the *New York Times,* John Leonard commented on the extensive use of literary devices in *The Lynchers:* "Flashback, flashforward, first person, third person, journals, identity exchange, interior monologue, dreams (historical and personal), puns, epiphanies. At times the devices seem a thicket through which one must hack one's weary way toward meanings arbitrarily obscure, a vegetable indulgence. But John Edgar Wideman is up to much more than storytelling. . . . He is capable of moving from ghetto language to [Irish writer James] Joyce with a flip of the page."

Saturday Review critic David Littlejohn agreed that Wideman's novels are very complex, and in his review of *Hurry Home* he criticized those who would judge this author as a storyteller: "Reviewers . . . are probably more responsible than anyone else for the common delusion that a novel is somehow contained in its discernible, realistic plot. . . . *Hurry Home* is primarily an experience, not a plot: an experience of words, dense, private, exploratory, and non-progressive." Littlejohn described *Hurry Home* as a retelling of an American myth, that of "the lonely search through the Old World" for a sense of cultural heritage, which "has been the pattern of a hundred thousand young Americans' lives and novels." According to Littlejohn, Wideman's version is "spare and eccentric, highly stylized, circling, allusive, antichronological, far more consciously symbolic than most versions, than the usual self-indulgent and romantic works of this genre—and hence both more rewarding and more difficult of access." Reviewing the same book in the *New York Times Book Review,* Joseph Goodman stated: "Many of its pages are packed with psychological insight, and nearly all reveal Mr. Wideman's formidable command of the techniques of fiction. Moreover, the theme is a profound one—the quest for a substantive sense of self. . . . The prose, paratactic and rich with puns, flows as freely as thought itself, giving us . . . Joycean echoes. . . . It is a dazzling display. . . . We can have nothing but admiration for Mr. Wideman's talent."

Enthusiastic reviews such as these established Wideman's reputation in the literary world as a major talent. When his fourth and fifth books—*Damballah,* a collection of short stories, and *Hiding Place,* a novel—were issued originally as paperbacks, some critics, such as John Leonard and Mel Watkins, reacted with indignation. Leonard's *New York Times* review used extensive quotes from the books to demonstrate Wideman's virtuosity, and stated, "That [these] two new books will fall apart after a second reading is a scandal." Watkins's *New York Times Book Review* article on the two books, which were published simultaneously, had special praise for the short-story volume, and ends with a sentiment much like Leonard's on the books' binding. "In freeing his voice from the confines of the novel form," Watkins wrote, "[Wideman] has written what is possibly his most impressive work. . . . Each story moves far beyond the primary event on which it is focused. . . . Like [Jean] Toomer, Mr. Wideman has used a narrative laced with myth, superstition and dream sequences to create an elaborate poetic portrait of the lives of ordinary black people. . . . These books once again demonstrate that John Wideman is one of America's premier writers of fiction. That they were published originally in paperback perhaps suggests that he is also one of our most underrated writers." Actually, it was the author himself who had decided to bring the books out as original paperbacks. His reasons were philosophical and pragmatic. "I spend an enormous amount of time and energy writing and I want to write good books, but I also want people to read them," he explained to Edwin McDowell in the *New York Times.* Wideman's first three novels had been slow sellers "in spite of enormously positive reviews," he told Suplee, and it was his hope that the affordability of paperbacks would help give him a wider readership, particularly among "the people and the world I was writing about. A $15.95 novel had nothing to do with that world."

Damballah and *Hiding Place* had both been set in Homewood, Wideman's early home, and in 1983 he published a third book with the same setting, *Sent for You Yesterday.* Critics were enthusiastic. "In this hypnotic and deeply lyrical novel, Mr. Wideman again returns to the ghetto where he was raised and transforms it into a magical location infused with poetry and pathos," wrote Alan Cheuse in the *New York Times Book Review.* "The narration here makes it clear that both as a molder of language and a builder of plots, Mr. Wideman has come into his full powers. He has the gift of making 'ordinary' folks memorable." States Garett Epps in the *Washington Post Book World,* "Wideman has a fluent command of the American language, written and spoken, and a fierce, loving vision of the people he writes about. Like the writing of William Faulkner, Wideman's prose fiction is vivid and demanding—shuttling unpredictably between places, narrators and times, dwelling for a paragraph on the surface of things, then sneaking a key event into a clause that springs on the reader like a booby trap. . . . *Sent for You Yesterday* is a book to be savored, read slowly again and again."

When he ventured into nonfiction for the first time with his book *Brothers and Keepers,* Wideman continued to draw inspiration from the same source, Homewood. In this book, Wideman comes to terms with his brother Robby, younger by ten years, whose life was influenced by the street, its drugs, and its crime. The author writes, "Even as I manufactured fiction from the events of my brother's life, from the history of the family that had nurtured us both, I knew something of a different order remained to be extricated. The fiction writer was a man with a real brother behind real bars [serving a life sentence in a Pennsylvania penitentiary]." In his review in the *Washington Post Book World,* Jonathan Yardley called *Brothers and Keepers* "the elder Wideman's effort to understand what happened, to confess and examine his own sense of guilt about his brother's fate (and his own)." The result, according to the reviewer, is "a depiction of the inexorably widening chasm that divides middle-class black Americans from the black underclass." Wideman's personal experience, added Yardley, also reveals that for the black person "moving out of the ghetto into the white world is a process that requires excruciating compromises, sacrifices and denials, that leaves the person who makes the journey truly at home in neither the world he has entered nor the world he has left."

Wideman has, however, made a home for himself in literary circles, and at the same time has learned from his experience how to handle his success. When *Sent for You Yesterday* won the PEN/Faulkner Award—the only major literary award in the United States to be judged, administered, and largely funded by writers—Wideman told Suplee he felt "warmth. That's what I felt. Starting at the toes and filling up. A gradual recognition that it could be real." Still, the author maintained that if such an honor "doesn't happen again for a long time—or never happens again—it really doesn't matter," because he "learned more and more that the process itself was important, learned to take my satisfaction from the writing" during the years of comparative obscurity. "I'm an old jock," he explained. "So I've kind of trained myself to be low-key. Sometimes the crowd screams, sometimes the crowd doesn't scream."

The narrator of Wideman's 1987 novel, *Reuben,* provides inexpensive legal aid to residents of Homewood. One of his clients is Kwansa, a young black prostitute whose husband, a recovering drug addict, kidnaps and seeks legal custody of their illegitimate child as revenge against her. Another customer is Wally, an assistant basketball coach at a local white university who seeks Reuben's counsel for two reasons, one being the killing of a white man in Chicago and the other being his fear that he will be blamed for the illegal recruiting practices of his department. Reviewing the book in *Washington Post Book World,* Noel Perrin characterized Wideman's novels as myths. "In the end," Perrin writes, "one sees that all the shocks—the murders, the fantasies, burnings, strong words—all of them amount to a kind of metaphor for the psychic damage that human beings do to each other and that is no less hurtful than spread-eagled beating, just less visible to the outer eye."

In *Philadelphia Fire,* Wideman brings together two stories, combining fact in fiction. In the first, he describes the events in Philadelphia when the police, under the direction of black mayor Wilson Goode, bombed the headquarters of an organization known as Move, a group that had defied city eviction notices and was armed with weapons. The police bombing killed six adults and five children, destroyed fifty three homes, and left 262 people homeless. Wideman's novel begins with a quote by William Penn, the founder of Pennsylvania, stating his dream that the town would "never be burnt, and always be wholesome." As Chicago *Tribune Books* reviewer Paul Skenazy points out, *Philadelphia Fire* tries to make sense of the changes that have occurred since Penn's statement, changes that include poverty and racism and that result in the burning of the Philadelphia neighborhood. The other story being told in the book is that of Wideman's relationship with his son who has received a life sentence for murder. "Few pages of prose," Skenazy says "carry as much pain as do Wideman's thoughts on his son, his words to him in prison, his feelings of confusion as a father." Skenazy concludes that *Philadelphia Fire* is "about a person, and a nation, losing its grip, destroying the very differences and dissonance that provide spirit, beauty, life." Rosemary L. Bray in the *New York Times Book Review* concurred; "the author takes his readers on a tour of urban America perched on the precipice of hell," Bray wrote, "a tour in which even his own personal tragedy is part of the view."

In 1992, Wideman published *The Stories of John Edgar Wideman,* a volume that combined several earlier story collections, including *Damballah,* originally published in 1981, 1989's *Fever,* and *All Stories Are True* from 1992. Michael Harris wrote in the *Los Angeles Times Book Review* that a comparison between Wideman and Faulkner makes sense "because of the scope of Wideman's project, his ear for voices, . . . and the way he shows the present as perpetually haunted by the past." *New York Times Book Review* contributor Michael Gorra also believes the Faulkner comparison is apt. "It is appropriate," Gorra wrote, "because both are concerned with the life of a community over time. It is appropriate because they both have a feel for the anecdotal folklore through which a community defines itself, because they both often choose to present their characters in the act of telling stories, and because in drawing on oral tradition they both write as their characters speak, in a language whose pith and vigor has not yet been worn into cliche." It is Gorra's conclusion that "the more you read John Edgar Wideman, the more impressive he seems."

BIOGRAPHICAL/CRITICAL SOURCES:

BOOKS

Contemporary Literary Criticism, Volume 5, Gale, 1976.

Dictionary of Literary Biography, Volume 33: *Afro-American Fiction Writers after 1955,* Gale, 1984.

O'Brien, John, editor, *Interviews with Black Writers,* Liveright, 1973.

Wideman, John Edgar, *Brothers and Keepers,* H. Holt, 1984.

Wideman, John Edgar, *Philadelphia Fire,* H. Holt, 1990.

PERIODICALS

American Scholar, autumn, 1967.

Christian Science Monitor, July 10, 1992.

Journal of Negro History, January, 1963.

Los Angeles Times, November 11, 1987.

Los Angeles Times Book Review, April 17, 1983; December 23, 1984; December 29, 1985; September 30, 1990; September 13, 1992.

Michigan Quarterly Review, winter, 1975.

Negro Digest, May, 1963.

New Republic, July 13, 1992.

Newsweek, May 7, 1970.

New York Magazine, October 1, 1990.

New York Times, April 2, 1970; May 15, 1973; November 27, 1981; May 16, 1984; October 29, 1984; September 4, 1986; July 21, 1992.

New York Times Book Review, September 10, 1967; April 19, 1970; April 29, 1973; April 11, 1982; May 15, 1983; November 4, 1984; January 13, 1985; December 15, 1985; May 11, 1986; November 30, 1986; November 8, 1987; October 16, 1988; December 10, 1989; September 30, 1990; October 14, 1990; November 17, 1991; June 14, 1992.

Saturday Review, October 21, 1967; May 2, 1970.

Shenandoah, winter, 1974.

Time, October 1, 1990.

Times (London), December 6, 1984.

Times Literary Supplement, December 21, 1984; January 16, 1987; August 5, 1988; August 23, 1991.

Tribune Books (Chicago), December 23, 1984; November 29, 1987; October 28, 1990; November 24, 1991.

Washington Post, May 10, 1984; May 12, 1984.

Washington Post Book World, July 3, 1983; October 21, 1984; November 15, 1987; October 16, 1988; October 21, 1990.*

* * *

WIEBE, Rudy (Henry) 1934-

PERSONAL: Born October 4, 1934, in Fairholme, Saskatchewan, Canada; son of Abram J. (a farmer) and Tena (Knelsen) Wiebe; married Tena F. Isaak, March, 1958; children: Adrienne, Michael, Christopher. *Education:* University of Alberta, B.A., 1956, M.A., 1960; Mennonite Brethren Bible College, B.Th., 1961; additional study at University of Tuebingen, 1957-58; University of Manitoba, 1961, and University of Iowa, 1964. *Religion:* Mennonite.

Avocational Interests: Photography, watching people, travel.

ADDRESSES: Home—5315 143rd St., Edmonton, Alberta, Canada. *Office*—Department of English, University of Alberta, Edmonton, Alberta, Canada T6G 2E5.

CAREER: Glenbow Foundation, Calgary, Alberta, research writer, 1956; Government of Canada, Ottawa, Ontario, foreign service officer, 1960; high school English teacher, Selkirk, Manitoba, 1961; *Mennonite Brethren Herald,* Winnipeg, Manitoba, editor, 1962-63; Goshen College, Goshen, IN, assistant professor of English,

1963-67; University of Alberta, Edmonton, assistant professor, 1967-70, associate professor, 1970-76, then professor of English, 1976—; University of Kiel, Germany, chair of Canadian studies, 1984.

MEMBER: Writers Union of Canada (president, 1985-86), Writers Guild of Alberta (founding president, 1980-81).

AWARDS, HONORS: Rotary International fellow, 1957-58; Canada council bursary, 1964; senior arts award, 1972; Governor General's Award for Fiction, 1973, for *The Temptations of Big Bear;* honorary D.Litt., University of Winnipeg, 1986; Lorne Pierce Medal, Royal Society of Canada, 1987.

WRITINGS:

NOVELS

Peace Shall Destroy Many, McClelland & Stewart, 1962, Eerdmans, 1964.
First and Vital Candle, Eerdmans, 1966.
The Blue Mountains of China, Eerdmans, 1970.
The Temptations of Big Bear, McClelland & Stewart, 1973.
Riel and Gabriel, McClelland & Stewart, 1973.
The Scorched-Wood People, McClelland & Stewart, 1977.
The Mad Trapper, McClelland & Stewart, 1980.
My Lovely Enemy, McClelland & Stewart, 1983.

SHORT STORIES

Where is the Voice Coming From?, McClelland & Stewart, 1974.
Alberta: A Celebration, photographs by Harry Savage, edited by Tom Radford, Hurtig, 1979.
The Angel of the Tar Sands, and Other Stories, McClelland & Stewart, 1982.

EDITOR

The Story Makers: A Selection of Modern Short Stories, Macmillan, 1970.
Stories from Western Canada, Macmillan (Canada), 1972.
(With Andreas Schroeder) *Stories from Pacific and Arctic Canada,* Macmillan (Canada), 1974.
Double Vision, McClelland & Stewart, 1976.
Getting Here, NeWest Press, 1977.
(With Aritha van Herk) *More Stories from Western Canada,* Macmillan (Canada), 1980.
(With van Herk and Leah Flater) *West of Fiction,* NeWest Press, 1983.

OTHER

(With Theatre Passe Muraille) *As Far as the Eye Can See* (play), NeWest Press, 1977.
(And compiler, with Bob Beal) *War in the West: Voices of the 1885 Rebellion* (history), McClelland & Stewart, 1985.
Playing Dead (essays), McClelland & Stewart, 1989.

Work represented in anthologies, including *Fourteen Stories High,* edited by David Helwig, Oberon Press, 1971; *The Narrative Voice,* edited by John Metcalf, McGraw, 1972; *Modern Stories in English,* edited by W. H. New and H. J. Rosengarten, Crowell, 1975; *Personal Fictions,* edited by Michael Ondaatje, Oxford University Press, 1977; and *Wild Rose Country: Stories from Alberta,* edited by David Carpenter, Oberon Press, 1977.

Contributor of articles and short stories to periodicals, including *Fiddlehead, Tamarack Review, Camrose Review, Canadian Literature, Maclean's, Saturday Night,* and *The Bote.*

ADAPTATIONS: "Someday Soon" was adapted for television by the Canadian Broadcast Corp., January, 1977.

SIDELIGHTS: Canadian novelist Rudy Wiebe explores his personal religious beliefs, modern society, and the traditional values and character of western Canada in his many novels and short stories. His direct and forceful style has earned him the respect of critics and readers alike, and he has been called one of the "most visionary" of Canada's contemporary novelists. In addition, Wiebe has earned two of his country's most prestigious literary awards, the Governor General's Award and the Lorne Pierce Medal, for his portrayal of the people who inhabit the prairie lands of western Canada.

Wiebe's first novel, *Peace Shall Destroy Many,* was published in 1962 to mixed critical review. While perceived as a promising first effort, the work caused a great deal of controversy in the Mennonite community due to its exploration of how man's quest for independence conflicts with his relationship with his god. As with his second novel, 1966's *First and Vital Candle,* reviewers found Wiebe's work to be heavily dogmatic. It was not until his third novel, *The Blue Mountains of China,* was published four years later that Wiebe's characters assumed a fully fleshed-out form and evolved from mere symbols used to illustrate a point into complex human beings.

"Rudy Wiebe's first three novels were good, but *Big Bear* represents a quantum jump beyond their achievement," writes Douglas Barbour in a review of *The Temptations of Big Bear* for *Canadian Literature.* "Wiebe's achievement here is to convince us that the white man's view of things is strange and somehow wrong, and that the Indian's perception is the truer one. . . . This is an exciting and arresting narrative, gripping in its violence and passion. . . . I don't think we can ask much more of a novel than that it create for us a world which is so achingly real it becomes our world while we read." Wiebe's sensitive portrayal of the Cree Indians caused Myrna Kostash to note in *Saturday Night:* "I began to understand how it *felt* to grow homeless, to face the buffalo across the border . . . and know they were dying along with you, . . . to live cramped and immobile, told to be a farmer on one, small, designated piece of land."

In his later works, Wiebe has stretched the confines of his religious perspective, dealing with other controversial issues. *The Scorched-Wood People* is a history of the nineteenth-century rebellions led by Louis Riel to aid native Canadian indians in preserving their land. *My Lovely Enemy,* which proved to be confusing in focus to some reviewers, is an exploration of the conflict between physical lust and man's love for his god. While peopled with interesting characters, Lawrence Mathews notes in the *Dictionary of Literary Biography* that the main character "seems to escape his author's control. . . . *My Lovely Enemy* does demonstrate Wiebe's willingness to take risks, to break new ground. . . . but [it] seems destined to represent a false step in an otherwise impressive development."

Through his body of work, Wiebe has filled a gap in the body of Canadian literature. As he wrote in *Canada Writes:* "In my fiction I try to explore the world that I know; the land and people of western Canada, from my particular world view: a radical Jesus-oriented Christianity." Mathews praises Wiebe's effort, noting that Wiebe "has developed from a chronicler of an obscure minority group to a forger of the conscience of the Canadian West and one of the few writers in the country to articulate a Christian vision in literature."

BIOGRAPHICAL/CRITICAL SOURCES:

BOOKS

Cameron, Donald, *Conversations with Canadian Novelists,* Macmillan, 1973.

Contemporary Literary Criticism, Gale, Volume 6, 1976, Volume 11, 1979, Volume 14, 1980.

Dictionary of Literary Biography, Volume 60: *Canadian Writers since 1960,* Gale, 1987, pp. 387-394.

Harrison, Dick, *Untamed Country,* University of Alberta Press, 1977.

Morley, Patricia, *The Comedians, Hugh Hood, and Rudy Wiebe,* Clarke, Irwin, 1976.

Moss, John, *Sex and Violence in the Canadian Novel,* McClelland & Stewart, 1977.

PERIODICALS

Canadian Forum, January, 1968; December, 1977; December, 1980, p. 42; May, 1983; p. 29; January, 1990, p. 30.

Canadian Literature, summer, 1974; winter, 1975; spring, 1990, p. 320.

Saturday Night, April, 1971, p. 26; February, 1974, p. 33.

* * *

WIGAN, Christopher
See BINGLEY, David Ernest

* * *

WILKES, Paul 1938-

PERSONAL: Born September 12, 1938, in Cleveland, OH; son of Paul Thomas (a carpenter) and Margaret (Salansky) Wilkes; married Tracy Gochberg; children: Paul Noah, Daniel Thomas. *Education:* Marquette University, B.A., 1960; Columbia University, M.A., 1967.

ADDRESSES: Home and office—Star Route, Gilbertville, MA 01031. *Agent*—Alison Bond, 171 West 79th St., New York, NY 10024.

CAREER: Free-lance writer. *Boulder Daily Camera,* Boulder, CO, staff member, 1964-66; *Baltimore Sun,* Baltimore, MD, writer, 1967-68; Harper & Row, New York City, editor, 1969; Harper's Magazine Press, New York City, editor, 1970. Lecturer in feature writing, Brooklyn College, 1973-75; visiting writer, University of Pittsburgh, 1979-89; lecturer in documentary filmmaking, Boston University, 1981; visiting writer, College of the Holy Cross, 1986; visiting writer, Clark University, 1989—. Cofounder of Christian Help in Park Slope (CHIPS), 1973-75. *Military service:* U.S. Navy, communications officer, 1961-64; became lieutenant junior grade.

MEMBER: Slovak Studies Association (president, 1985-87).

AWARDS, HONORS: Julius Ochs Adler fellow, 1966; best nonfiction awards from Society of Midland Authors and Friends of American Writers, both 1974, both for *Fitzgo: The Wild Dog of Central Park;* By-Line Award from Marquette University, 1977, for distinguished service in journalism; alumni award from Columbia University Graduate School of Journalism, 1978, for distinguished service in journalism; Alfred I. DuPont-Columbia Survey and Award in Broadcast Journalism, 1978, for *Six American Families;* Matica Slovenska fellow, 1979; Christopher Award, 1991.

WRITINGS:

Fitzgo: The Wild Dog of Central Park (nonfiction), Lippincott, 1973.

These Priests Stay (biography), Simon & Schuster, 1973.

Trying Out the Dream: A Year in the Life of an American Family (nonfiction), Lippincott, 1975.

Six American Families (based on his television documentary series of the same title; also see below), Seabury, 1977.

Merton: By Those Who Knew Him Best (biography), Harper, 1984.

In Mysterious Ways: The Death and Life of a Parish Priest (biography), Random House, 1990.

Companions along the Way (essays), Thomas More Press, 1990.

My Book of Bedtime Prayers (illustrated by Sandra S. Shields), Augsburg, 1992.

The Education of an Archbishop: Travels with Rembert Weakland (biography), Orbis, 1992.

Temptations, Random House, 1993.

TELEPLAYS

Six American Families (documentary), Public Broadcasting Service (PBS), 1977.

Men of Iron (drama), PBS, 1978.

(Co-author) *The Molders of Troy* (drama), PBS, 1980.

Merton (documentary), PBS, 1984.

Contributor to numerous periodicals, including *New York, New Yorker, New York Times Magazine, Atlantic, America,* and *Commonweal.*

BIOGRAPHICAL/CRITICAL SOURCES:

PERIODICALS

Best Sellers, August 1, 1973; March 1, 1974.
Chicago Tribune Book World, January 27, 1984, p. 24.
Christian Science Monitor, June 13, 1973; April 2, 1975.
Los Angeles Times Book Review, March 17, 1985, p. 10.
New Republic, April 26, 1975.
Newsweek, March 24, 1975.
New York Times Book Review, December 23, 1984, p. 1.

* * *

WILKINSON, John (Donald) 1929-

PERSONAL: Born March 28, 1929, in Wimbledon, England; son of Donald Frederick (a priest, Church of England) and Hilda Mary (Smyth) Wilkinson. *Education:* Attended Haileybury and Imperial Service College, 1944-48; Merton College, Oxford, B.A., 1953, M.A., 1956; also attended Cuddesdon College, 1954-56, and Catholic University of Louvain, 1959-60.

ADDRESSES: Office—1703 32nd St. N.W., Washington, DC 20007.

CAREER: Ordained priest, Church of England, 1956; Parish of St. Dunstan and All Saints', Stepney, London, England, assistant priest, 1956-59; Theological College, Ely, England, tutor, 1960; St. Augustine's College, Canterbury, England, assistant lecturer, 1961; St. George's College, Jerusalem, tutor, 1961-63, dean of studies, 1969; United Society for the Propagation of the Gospel, London, England, general editor, 1963-69; Bishops' Director of Clergy Training, London Diocese, 1975-79; British School of Archaeology, Jerusalem, director, 1979-85; Dumbarton Oaks Center for Byzantine Studies, Washington, DC, fellow, 1985—. *Military service:* British Army, 1948-49; became second lieutenant.

WRITINGS:

No Apology, Darton, Longman & Todd, 1961.

Jerusalem Prayers, St. George's College, 1962.

Interpretation and Community, St. Martin's, 1963.

The Stations of the Cross in Jerusalem, St. George's College, 1963, published as *Jerusalem Stations of the Cross,* Society for Promoting Christian Knowledge (S.P.C.K.), 1967.

(Editor) *Mutual Responsibility: Questions and Answers,* S.P.C.K., 1964.

The Supper and the Eucharist: A Layman's Guide to Anglican Revision, Macmillan (London), 1965, St. Martin's, 1966.

Together to Work—The USPG Review of 1965, United Society for the Propagation of the Gospel, 1966.

Family and Evangelistic Services: An Outline, Church Information Office, 1967.

Louder than Words—The USPG Review of 1966, United Society for the Propagation of the Gospel, 1967.

(Editor) *Catholic Anglicans Today,* Darton, Longman & Todd, 1968.

(Translator) *Egeria's Travels,* S.P.C.K., 1971, revised edition published as *Egeria's Travels to the Holy Land,* Aris & Phillips, 1981.

(Translator) *Jerusalem Pilgrims before the Crusades,* Aris & Phillips, 1977.

Jerusalem as Jesus Knew It: Archaeology as Evidence, Thames & Hudson, 1978, published as *The Jerusalem Jesus Knew: An Archaeological Guide to the Gospels,* Thomas Nelson, 1983.

Health and Healing: Studies in New Testament Principles and Practice, Handsel Press, 1980.

Column Capitals in al Haram al Sharif (from 138 A.D. to 1118 A.D.), Administration of Wakfs and Islamic Affairs, Islamic Museum, al-Haram al-Sharif, 1987.

(Editor with Joyce Hill and W. F. Ryan) *Jerusalem Pilgrimage, 1099-1185,* Hakluyt Society, 1988.

BIOGRAPHICAL/CRITICAL SOURCES:

PERIODICALS

Choice, November, 1966, p. 806; October, 1978, p. 1111; May, 1981, p. 1284.
Library Journal, July, 1978, p. 1407.

Times Literary Supplement, March 20, 1969, p. 310; November 10, 1978, p. 1319.*

* * *

WILKINSON, Rosemary C(halloner) 1924-

PERSONAL: Born February 21, 1924, in New Orleans, LA; daughter of William Lindsay (in wholesale jewelry materials) and Julia (Sellen) Challoner; married Henry Bertram Wilkinson, 1949; children: Denis, Marian, Paul, Richard. *Education:* Attended College of San Mateo, 1964-66; University of Minnesota, student by correspondence, 1967; attended Canada College for training in television communications; San Francisco State University, lifetime credential to teach poetry, 1978. *Politics:* Democrat. *Religion:* Catholic.

ADDRESSES: Home—3146 Buckeye Ct., Placerville, CA 95667.

CAREER: Bookkeeper at hospitals in Lafayette and New Albany, IN, 1939-44; St. James Hospital, Chicago Heights, IL, administrative supervisor, 1944-47; St. Joseph Hospital, Phoenix, AZ, administrative supervisor, 1947-48; West Disinfecting Co., San Francisco, CA, bookkeeper, 1948-51; Peninsula Hospital, Burlingame, CA, billing officer, 1961-62; full-time writer, 1963—. World Congress of Poets, advisor of Third World Congress of Poets, 1976, member of board of Fourth World Congress of Poets, 1979, chairman of organizing committee and president of Fifth World Congress of Poets, 1981, president, 1981—. Vice-president, Poetry in Media, charter 1981; founder, San Mateo County Fair Poetry Competition. Coordinator of California's second chapter of Hospital Audiences, Inc., 1972. Has given poetry readings to school and hospitals and has been interviewed on radio and television about poetry.

MEMBER: International Poets Academy, World Poetry Society Intercontinental, Soroptomist International, World Academy of Arts and Culture (secretary-general, 1985—), World Congress of Poets (president, 1981), United Writers Association, World Literary Academy, National League of American PEN Women (president of Berkeley branch, 1988-90), Authors Guild, PEN (New York branch), Centro Cultural Literario E Artistico (honorary life member), Poetry Society of Japan, Poetry Society of London, Gwynedd Family History Society, Avalon Library Association.

AWARDS, HONORS: Plaque and medal, Second World Congress of Poets (Republic of China), 1973; certificate of merit, American Poets Fellowship Society, 1973; named International Woman of 1975 with laureate honors (Philippines); Danae Award, Clover International, 1976; Knight Grand Dame of Merit (Grace), Knights of Malta, Europe, 1981; order of Imperial Constantine, Knights of St. George (Greece), 1987; order of Polonia Restituta, Commanders Cross, 1989; dame commander, St. Sepulchre (Australia), 1990; Yunus Emre Award (Istanbul, Turkey), 1991; honorary special mention for an essay on Waka/Tanka, Poetry Society of Japan; also received numerous awards from International Order of Volunteers for Peace, T. S. Eliot Society, Accademia Italia delle Arti, Academia Universelle de Lausanne, World Jnana Sadhak Society, International Poets Academy, United Writers Association, and many others. Honorary diplomas from Universita Delle Arti, Accademia International Leonardo da Vinci, and Accademia Internazionale di Lettere, Scienze, Arti, all in Italy; honorary doctorates from L'Universita Libre (Pakistan), 1975, and World Academy of Arts and Culture (Republic of China), 1982.

WRITINGS:

POETRY

A Girl's Will, Prairie Press, 1973.
An Historical Epic, New Literature (Republic of China), 1975.
California Poet, Burlingame Press, 1976.
Earth's Compromise, Burlingame Press, 1977.
It Happened to Me, Burlingame Press, 1978.
I Am Earth Woman, Burlingame Press, 1979.
The Poet and the Painter, Burlingame Press, 1981.
Poetry and Arte, Farris Press, 1982.
Gems Within, Farris Press, 1982.
Nature's Guest, Farris Press, 1984.
In the Pines, Sayeeda-India, 1985.
Longing for You, Annamalai University, 1988.
Sacred in Nature, Pul-Star, 1988.
Purify the Earth, Pul-Star, 1988.
Earth's Children, Pul-Star, 1990.
New Seed, Pul-Star, 1991.

Also author of *Epic of the Ship's Captain/Artist* (biographical poem), 1992, and *Poet: Uplift Mankind* (autobiographical poem), 1993.

OTHER

Author of music and lyrics to songs "Alabama March of 1965," "200 Years U.S.A.," 1976, "Something's Happening," 1977, "Birthday Sonnet to Dr. Yuzon," 1981, "When Did I?," 1986, "This Is the Man," 1986, and "Walk the Streets," 1991. Contributor to numerous poetry anthologies, including *Toyon Poems, Anthology of New American Verse, Poetic Village,* and *Crow's Nest* (all in the United States), *Album of International Poets* (India), *Anthology of World Brotherhood and Peace* (Philippines), 1982, and *World Poetry* (Korea), 1983. Contributor of articles, poems, and reviews to numerous periodicals, including *Transnational Perspectives* (Switzerland), *Pen Woman,* and *New Hye Armenian Weekly* (Spain).

WORK IN PROGRESS: Poetry and Photography; a major collection of poems.

SIDELIGHTS: Rosemary C. Wilkinson once told *CA:* "I wrote my first poem at age fourteen and my second at age forty, when President Kennedy was shot. From then on I could not stop the poetry from erupting. I study from seven in the morning until noon, writing three of those hours. My poems just come at any time, but I work at my prose. I have had the first epic published in the Republic of China, about World War II here in the United States. The epic-biography of the artist/ship's captain is the life of an unknown nineteenth-century painter, and the third epic is my own autobiography, having served as a hospital administrator, a mother of four, and a writer and internationally known poet since 1963.

"I read the classical poets and teach classical forms. I would like to see more historical documentaries on television, for they enhance our culture. Poetry is my soul's sustenance. The work of the poet serves to uplift all mankind."

Wilkinson recently wrote *CA:* "I am the secretary-general for the World Academy of Arts and Culture here in the United States and Republic of China since 1985. I contact the Ministers of Culture and Education to host World Congress of Poets and so far you can see that I was responsible for bringing about the World Congress of Poets in India, Thailand, Egypt, Turkey, and Israel."

Wilkinson's work has been translated into thirty-one foreign languages, including Chinese, Korean, Romanian, Armenian, Hindi, Russian, Sanskrit, Greek, German, and French. She has traced her ancestry to an ancient Welsh tribe of poets and clerics. As president of the Fifth World Congress of Poets, she gathered representatives of forty-two nations for meetings in San Francisco, CA.

* * *

WILSON, August 1945-

PERSONAL: Born in 1945 in Pittsburgh, PA.

ADDRESSES: Home—St. Paul, MN. *Agent*—c/o Dutton, 375 Hudson St., New York, NY 10014.

CAREER: Writer. Black Horizons Theater Company, St. Paul, MN, founder and director, beginning in 1968; scriptwriter for Science Museum of Minnesota.

AWARDS, HONORS: Award for best play of 1984-85 from New York Drama Critics Circle and Antoinette Perry ("Tony") Award nomination from League of New York Theatres and Producers, both 1985, and Whiting Writers' Award from the Whiting Foundation, 1986, all for *Ma Rainey's Black Bottom;* Outstanding Play Award from American Theatre Critics, 1986, Pulitzer Prize for drama, Tony Award for best play, and award for best Broadway play from Outer Critics Circle, all 1987, all for *Fences;* John Gassner Award for best American playwright from Outer Critics Circle, 1987; named Artist of the Year by *Chicago Tribune,* 1987; award for best play from New York Drama Critics Circle and Tony Award nomination, both 1988, for *Joe Turner's Come and Gone;* Pulitzer Prize for drama, 1990, for *The Piano Lesson;* award from Black Filmmakers Hall of Fame, 1991.

WRITINGS:

Jitney (two-act play), first produced in Pittsburgh, PA, at Allegheny Repertory Theatre, 1982.

Ma Rainey's Black Bottom (play; first produced in New Haven, CT, at Yale Repertory Theatre, 1984; produced on Broadway at Cort Theatre, October, 1984), New American Library, 1985.

Fences (play; first produced at Yale Repertory Theatre, 1985; produced on Broadway at 46th Street Theatre, March, 1987), New American Library, 1986.

Joe Turner's Come and Gone (play; first produced at Yale Repertory Theatre, 1986; produced on Broadway at Barrymore Theatre, March, 1988), New American Library, 1988.

The Piano Lesson (play; first produced at Yale Repertory Theatre, 1987; produced on Broadway at Walter Kerr Theatre, 1990), Dutton, 1990.

Three Plays (contains *Ma Rainey's Black Bottom, Fences,* and *Joe Turner's Come and Gone*), University of Pittsburgh Press, 1991.

Two Trains Running (play; first produced at Yale Repertory Theatre, 1991; produced at Walter Kerr Theatre, 1992), Dutton, 1992.

Also author of play *Fullerton Street* and the book for a stage musical about jazz musician Jelly Roll Morton. Poetry represented in anthologies, including *The Poetry of Blackamerica.* Contributor to periodicals, including *Black Lines* and *Connection.*

WORK IN PROGRESS: A screenplay adaptation of *Fences.*

SIDELIGHTS: August Wilson has been hailed since the mid-1980s as an important talent in the American theatre. He spent his childhood in poverty in Pittsburgh, Pennsylvania, where he lived with his parents and five siblings. Though he grew up in a poor family, Wilson felt that his parents withheld knowledge of even greater hardships they had endured. "My generation of blacks knew very little about the past of our parents," he told the *New York*

Times in 1984. "They shielded us from the indignities they suffered."

Wilson encountered a few hardships of his own during his schooling. He was harassed as a "nigger" by white students at a Roman Catholic academy, even though his own father was white, and in public high school a teacher accused him of turning in his sister's work as his own. That was Wilson's last day in school. "The next day," he said in a 1988 *Time* article, "I went and played basketball outside the principal's window, obviously in the unconscious hope someone would ask why I wasn't in class. No one did, and that was that." His subsequent education was largely gained in a local library.

At age sixteen Wilson began working at menial jobs. But he also pursued a literary career and successfully submitted poems to black publications at the University of Pittsburgh. In 1968 he became active in the theatre by founding—despite lacking prior experience—the Black Horizons Theatre Company in St. Paul, Minnesota. Recalling his early theatre involvement, Wilson described himself to the *New York Times* as "a cultural nationalist . . . trying to raise consciousness through theater."

In St. Paul Wilson wrote his first play, *Jitney,* a realistic drama set in a Pittsburgh taxi station. *Jitney* was accepted for workshop production at the O'Neill Theatre Center's National Playwrights Conference in 1982. This brought Wilson into contact with other playwrights. Inspired, he wrote another play, *Fullerton Street,* but this work failed to strengthen his reputation.

Wilson then resumed work on an earlier unfinished project, *Ma Rainey's Black Bottom,* a play about a black blues singer's exploitation of her fellow musicians. This work, whose title role is named after an actual blues singer from the 1920s, is set in a recording studio in 1927. In the studio, temperamental Ma Rainey verbally abuses the other musicians and presents herself—without justification—as an important musical figure. But much of the play is also set in a rehearsal room, where Ma Rainey's musicians discuss their abusive employer and the hardships of life in racist America.

Eventually, the musicians are all revealed to have experienced, in varying degrees, racist treatment. The most resigned member is the group's leader, a trombonist who has learned to accept racial discrimination and merely negotiates around it. The bassist's response is to wallow in hedonism and ignore his nation's treatment of blacks, while the pianist takes an intellectual approach to solving racial problems. The group's trumpeter, however, is bitter and cynical. He is haunted by the memory of his mother's rape by four white men. Tensions mount in the play when the sullen trumpeter clashes with Ma Rainey and is fired. The manager of the recording studio then swindles him in a recording rights agreement, and a subsequent and seemingly insignificant incident precipitates violence from the trumpeter, who has simply endured too much abuse. The London *Times*'s Holly Hill called the play's climactic moment "a melodramatically violent act."

Ma Rainey's Black Bottom earned Wilson a return to the O'Neill Center's play writing conference in 1983. There Wilson's play impressed director Lloyd Richards from the Yale Repertory Theatre. Richards worked with Wilson to refine the play, and when it was presented at Yale in 1984 it was hailed as the work of an important new playwright. Frank Rich, who reviewed the Yale production in the *New York Times,* acclaimed Wilson as "a major find for the American theater" and cited his ability to write "with compassion, raucous humor and penetrating wisdom."

Wilson enjoyed further success with *Ma Rainey's Black Bottom* after the play came to Broadway later in 1984. The *Chicago Tribune*'s Richard Christiansen reviewed the Broadway production as "a work of intermittent but immense power" and commended the "striking beauty" of the play's "literary and theatrical poetry." Christiansen added that "Wilson's power of language is sensational" and that *Ma Rainey's Black Bottom* was "the work of an impressive writer." The London *Times*'s Hill agreed, calling Wilson "a promising new playwright" and hailing his work as "a remarkable first play."

Wilson's subsequent plays include the Pulitzer Prize-winning *Fences,* which is about a former athlete who forbids his son to accept an athletic scholarship, and *Joe Turner's Come and Gone,* which concerns an ex-convict's efforts to find his wife. Like *Ma Rainey's Black Bottom,* these plays underwent extensive rewriting. Guiding Wilson in this process was Lloyd Richards, dean of Yale's drama school and director of the school's productions of Wilson's plays. "August is a wonderful poet," Richards told the *New York Times* in 1986. "A wonderful poet turning into a playwright." Richards added that his work with Wilson involved "clarifying" each work's main theme and "arranging the material in a dynamic way."

Both *Fences* and *Joe Turner's Come and Gone* were praised when they played on American stages. The *New York Times*'s Frank Rich, in his review of *Fences,* wrote that the play "leaves no doubt that Mr. Wilson is a major writer, combining a poet's ear for vernacular with a robust sense of humor (political and sexual), a sure instinct for cracking dramatic incident and passionate commitment to a great subject." And in his critique of *Joe Turner's Come and Gone,* Rich speculated that the play "will give a lasting voice to a generation of uprooted black Americans." Rich contended that the work was "potentially its author's finest achievement yet" and described it as "a teeming canvas of black America . . . and a spiritual allegory."

Wilson's next play, *The Piano Lesson,* added to his stature with another Pulitzer Prize, won before the play ever reached Broadway. A largely realistic play, it focuses on a family conflict over an heirloom piano. Berniece Charles's slave ancestors were traded for it, and another family member carved African-style portraits of them on it. Later Berniece's father died reclaiming it. Now Berniece's brother Boy Willie wants to sell it to buy farmland, and the issue threatens to tear the family apart. Reviewing a pre-Broadway production of *The Piano Lesson* in a 1989 *Time* article, Henry judged it Wilson's "richest" play yet. Some were less enthusiastic, specifically questioning Wilson's use of the supernatural at the end of the drama. Opining that *The Piano Lesson* did not measure up to Wilson's earlier work, Robert Brustein of *New Republic* suggested that the playwright should "develop the radical poetic strain that now lies dormant in his art." Despite perceived weaknesses, however, critics applauded Wilson's strengths in humor and language. And Henry, who also admitted flaws in the play's ending, nonetheless maintained that "already the musical instrument of the title is the most potent symbol in American drama since Laura Wingfield's glass menagerie" in a classic play by Tennessee Williams.

In 1992 a new Wilson play, *Two Trains Running,* came to Broadway, depicting the lives of patrons of a run-down diner in the late 1960s. With a quiet central plot involving the pending sale of the diner, the play seemed more a "slice of life" to critic Henry than the kind of explosive conflict of some of Wilson's previous plays. In contrast, Henry wrote, *Two Trains Running* is a "delicate and mature work" that shows Wilson "at his lyrical best." The play touches on troubled black urban youths, the low self-esteem of some black women, injustices perpetrated by whites, and problems in the ways blacks treat each other, among other subjects. Reviewing the play for the *New Yorker,* Mimi Kramer found "something awe-inspiring" about a play so focused on race and black character. "All the same," she added, "I like my August Wilson a little subtler." Victor Dwyer, on the other hand, called *Two Trains Running* "a dramatic glimpse into the life of black America" in his *Maclean's* review. Praising the language of the play, which he felt sometimes achieves "musical eloquence," David Ansen of *Newsweek* characterized it as "thematically rich."

Throughout his career Wilson has stressed that his first objective is in getting his work produced. "All I want is for the most people to get to see this play," he told the *New York Times* while discussing *Joe Turner's Come and Gone.* Wilson added, however, that he was not opposed to having his works performed on Broadway. He told the *New York Times* that Broadway "still has the connotation of Mecca" and asked, "Who doesn't want to go to Mecca?"

In his 1988 *Time* article, Henry noted how Wilson's attitude differs from that of some of his predecessors. "Wilson is not a 'black' playwright in the sense the term was applied in the confrontational 1960s and '70s," Henry wrote. "He movingly evokes the evolving psychic burden of slavery but without laying on guilt or political harangues." By 1992 Wilson's lyrical approach had made him, according to Henry, "the foremost American stage voice of his generation."

BIOGRAPHICAL/CRITICAL SOURCES:

BOOKS

Black Literature Criticism, Gale, 1992.

Contemporary Literary Criticism, Gale, Volume 39, 1986, Volume 50, 1988, Volume 63, 1991.

Drama Criticism, Volume 2, Gale, 1992.

PERIODICALS

Chicago Tribune, October 15, 1984; June 8, 1987; December 17, 1987; December 27, 1987.

Chicago Tribune Book World, February 9, 1986.

Ebony, January, 1985.

Los Angeles Times, November 24, 1984; November 7, 1986; April 17, 1987; June 7, 1987; June 8, 1987; June 9, 1987; February 6, 1988.

Maclean's, May 28, 1990, p. 62; May 18, 1992, pp. 56-57.

Nation, April 18, 1987, p. 518; June 11, 1990, pp. 832-33; June 8, 1992, p. 799-800.

New Republic, May 21, 1990, pp. 28-30.

Newsweek, April 6, 1987; April 11, 1988, p. 82; April 27, 1992, p. 70.

New York, April 6, 1987, pp. 92, 94.

New Yorker, April 6, 1987, p. 81; April 11, 1988, p. 107; April 30, 1990; April 27, 1992, p. 85.

New York Times, April 11, 1984; April 13, 1984; October 12, 1984; October 22, 1984; May 6, 1986; May 14, 1986; June 20, 1986; March 27, 1987; April 5, 1987; April 9, 1987; April 17, 1987; May 7, 1987; December 10, 1987; December 11, 1987.

Saturday Review, January/February, 1985.

Theater, fall-winter, 1984, pp. 50-55.

Time, April 6, 1987, p. 81; April 27, 1987; April 11, 1988, pp. 77-78; January 30, 1989, p. 69; April 27, 1992, pp. 65-66.

Times (London), November 6, 1984; April 18, 1987; April 24, 1987.

Washington Post, May 20, 1986; April 15, 1987; June 9, 1987; October 4, 1987; October 9, 1987.*

WINDSOR, Patricia 1938-
(Colin Daniel, Katonah Summertree)

PERSONAL: Born September 21,1938, in New York, NY; daughter of Bernhard Edward and Antoinette (Gaus) Seelinger; married Laurence Charles Windsor, Jr., April 3, 1959 (divorced, 1978); married Steve Altman, 1986 (divorced, 1987); children: Patience Wells, Laurence Edward. *Education:* Attended Bennington College and Westchester Community College; New York University, associate degree.

ADDRESSES: *Office*—Summertree Studios, 208 West Bay St., Savannah, GA 31401. *Agent*—Patricia White, 20 Popwis Mews, London, England.

CAREER: Windsor-Morehead Associates (advertising agency), New York, NY, vice-president, 1960-63; novelist. Teacher of creative writing, Westchester, NY, 1975-78; member of faculty, Institute of Children's Literature, Redding Ridge, CT, 1976—; director, Wordspring Literary Consultants, 1982—; director, Summertree Studios, 1992—. Instructor, University of Maryland Writers Institute, 1981-83, and OPEN University, Washington, DC; editor-in-chief of *Easterner* for American Telephone and Telegraph, Washington, DC, 1979-81. Member, Citizens' Committee on Employment, Chicago, 1963-64; Family Planning Associations, London, England, assistant director of central inquiries, 1972-73, counselor, 1974-75; correspondent, National Council of Social Science, London, 1974—; active in YWCA and North Westchester Association for Retarded Children.

MEMBER: PEN American Centre, Children's Book Guild.

AWARDS, HONORS: Honor book award, *Chicago Tribune Book World,* 1973, Best Books for Young Adults Award, American Library Association, 1973, Austrian State Award for Books for Children and Youth, 1981, all for *The Summer Before*; *Diving for Roses* was named a notable book of 1976 by the *New York Times*; Mystery Writers of America, Edgar Allan Poe Award, 1985, for *The Sandman's Eyes*, nomination, 1992, for *The Christmas Killer.*

WRITINGS:

The Summer Before (novel), Harper, 1973.
Something's Waiting for You, Baker D (novel), Harper, 1974.
Home Is Where Your Feet Are Standing (novel), Harper, 1975.
Diving for Roses (novel), Harper, 1976.
Mad Martin (novel), Harper, 1976.
Killing Time (novel), Harper, 1980.
The Sandman's Eyes, Delacorte, 1985.
How a Weirdo and a Ghost Can Change Your Entire Life, Delacorte, 1986.
The Hero, Delacorte, 1988.
Two Weirdos and a Ghost, Dell, 1991.
A Very Weird and Moogly Christmas, Dell, 1991.
The Christmas Killer, Scholastic Inc., 1992.

SHORT STORIES

Old Coat's Cat, Macmillan, 1974.
Rain, Macmillan, 1976.
The Girl with the Click Click Eyes, Heinemann, 1977.

Also author of short stories *A Little Taste of Death,* 1992, *The Proof of the Pudding,* 1992, and *Teeth,* 1993.

UNDER THE PSEUDONYM COLIN DANIEL

Demon Tree, Dell, 1983.

OTHER

Also lyricist for popular songs composed by Yseult Freilicher. Contributor of short stories to periodicals in Sweden, Denmark, South Africa, Australia, England, and the United States.

WORK IN PROGRESS: A novel, *The House of Death.*

SIDELIGHTS: Patricia Windsor told *CA:* "I've been writing stories ever since I was ten and my parents gave me a battered old typewriter to bang on. I planned out hundreds of novels and made long lists of titles. By the time I was sixteen, I'd collected thirty-five rejection slips. I got this early start because I grew up in the Bronx where, as everyone knows, all great writers come from!

"I hope that my writing for young people helps them see they are not alone . . . that their heartaches, problems, pains and joys are shared by us all, adults included!

"I love to read books, and I'm pleased there are people who may right now be taking one of my books off a library shelf and getting ready to enjoy it as much as I enjoy the books of other writers. But if people don't like what I write, or hate the characters or the plot, that's all right with me [as] long as I made them think and react a little."

* * *

WISE, David 1930-

PERSONAL: Born May 10, 1930, in New York, NY; son of Raymond L. (an attorney) and Karena (Post) Wise; married Joan Sylvester, December 16, 1962; children: Christopher James, Jonathan William. *Education:* Columbia College, A.B., 1951.

ADDRESSES: *Agent*—Sterling Lord Literistic, 1 Madison Ave, New York, NY 10010.

CAREER: *New York Herald Tribune,* New York City, reporter, 1951-53, New York city hall bureau chief, 1953-57, Albany, NY, bureau chief, 1956-57, Washington, DC, bureau staff member, 1958-60, White House correspondent, 1960-62, Washington, DC, bureau chief, 1963-66. Woodrow Wilson International Center for Scholars, fellow, 1970-71; University of California, Santa Barbara, lecturer in political science, 1977-79.

MEMBER: Washington Independent Writers, American Political Science Association.

AWARDS, HONORS: Page One Award, Newspaper Guild of New York, 1969, for *New York Times* article, "The Twilight of a President"; George Polk Memorial Award, 1974, for *The Politics of Lying.*

WRITINGS:

NONFICTION

(With Thomas B. Ross) *The U-2 Affair,* Random House, 1962.
(With Ross) *The Invisible Government,* Random House, 1964.
(With Ross) *The Espionage Establishment,* Random House, 1967.
(With Milton C. Cummings, Jr.) *Democracy under Pressure: An Introduction to the American Political System,* Harcourt, 1971, 7th edition, 1993.
The Politics of Lying: Government Deception, Secrecy, and Power, Random House, 1973.
The American Police State: The Government against the People, Random House, 1976.
The Spy Who Got Away: The Inside Story of Edward Lee Howard, the CIA Agent Who Betrayed His Country's Secrets and Escaped to Moscow, Random House, 1988.
Molehunt: The Secret Search for Traitors that Shattered the CIA, Random House, 1992.

NOVELS

Spectrum, Viking, 1981.
The Children's Game, St. Martin's/Marek, 1983.
The Samarkand Dimension, Doubleday, 1987.

CONTRIBUTOR

The Kennedy Circle, Luce, 1961.
None of Your Business: Government Secrecy in America, Viking, 1974.
The CIA File, Grossman, 1976.

Also contributor of articles to national magazines.

SIDELIGHTS: Although he was never employed as an operator for the Central Intelligence Agency, writer David Wise, in the words of author Seymour M. Hersh, "knows more about the CIA than many of the people who have spent a lifetime working there." In addition to the many articles he has written for the *New York Herald Tribune,* Wise has teamed with Thomas B. Ross to write several books that demonstrate the two men's comprehensive knowledge of both U.S. national security and the intelligence industry. *The Invisible Government,* a critical study of intelligence activity overseas that Wise and Ross published in 1964, was followed nine years later by Wise's *The Politics of Lying,* wherein the author sets forth the argument that deception and cover-ups on the part of the U.S. Government have been responsible for massive distrust on the part of the American public, a condition that ominously prefigured the Watergate Era that was shortly to follow.

Wise is also the author of several other books on domestic intelligence operations. *The Spy Who Got Away,* an account of the first CIA defector to the U.S.S.R. published in 1988, grew out of an article Wise had written for the *New York Times* two years earlier. With an increasing U.S.-Soviet openness born of *glasnost,* Wise was afforded the opportunity of interviewing ex-CIA agent Edward Lee Howard in Budapest in 1987, two years after Howard's defection to the East. Combining this interview with a wealth of other information, Wise has been able to piece together what had been a confusing chain of events: how Howard's career with the CIA's Soviet/East European division ended after questions surfaced about his past and current emotional stability; how he was dismissed and then escaped to Moscow despite surveillance by the FBI, and how he betrayed the CIA's secrets to the Soviet KGB. "The result is," writes Steven Luxenberg in the *Washington Post Book World,* "a compelling yarn that is part detective story, part biography, part expose. . . . *The Spy Who Got Away* is a revealing and, it must be said, damning account of how the CIA mishandled Edward Lee Howard from the day he was hired until the day he fled."

In *Molehunt: The Secret Search for Traitors that Shattered the CIA,* published in 1992, Wise examines how the CIA searched its own closets for Soviet double agents during the 1960s, a hunt that preoccupied the agency to the detriment of its own security. Reviewer David Ingatius comments in the *Washington Post Book World* that "what Wise has done is to focus on the chase itself, and its victims. That is what makes his account so readable, and so devastating." *Molehunt* is "rich in the human detail and disclosures about intelligence tradecraft that are so characteristic of Mr. Wise's earlier books," states Michael R. Beschloss in the *New York Times Book Review,* adding praise for the book as a "well-researched volume [that] will serve as a vital source for both intelligence buffs and scholars seeking to weigh the danger of Soviet subversion of American society against the cost that the internal security investigations of the cold war enacted upon American lives and institutions."

Wise has brought his thorough understanding of the world of spies to the arena of fiction as the author of several popular novels of espionage, including *Spectrum, The Children's Game,* and *The Samarkand Dimension.* As he told Christian Williams of the *Washington Post,* "When *The American Police State* came out, *Newsweek* said it read like an espionage thriller. So I said, why not?" *Spectrum,* published in 1981, takes the reader on a tour of the London office of the CIA as the director goes bad and plots the theft of weapons-grade uranium to fuel his private nuclear arsenal. *The Children's Game,* involving the search for a spy in the ranks of the CIA, and *The Samarkand Dimension,* dealing with Soviet research into the paranormal, were also commended for their detailed descriptions of the inner workings of the CIA. As Jonathan Yardley notes in the *Washington Post Book World:* "Like *Spectrum, The Children's Game* is a serious commentary on the role of the Central Intelligence Agency masquerading as a mere piece of escapist entertainment."

BIOGRAPHICAL/CRITICAL SOURCES:

PERIODICALS

Book World, November 5, 1967.
Los Angeles Times Book Review, May 22, 1988, p. 14.
New Republic, May 9, 1981, p. 36.
Newsweek, June 22, 1964; May 21, 1973.
New York Review of Books, September 10, 1964; December 7, 1967; July 19, 1973.
New York Times, April 24, 1981; May 16, 1988.
New York Times Book Review, June 28, 1964; November 26, 1967; June 17, 1973; March 22, 1981, p. 14; January 8, 1984; June 12, 1988, pp. 1, 33; October 15, 1989, p. 56; March 15, 1992, p. 11.
Times Literary Supplement, May 29, 1981, p. 595.
Wall Street Journal, March 19, 1981, p. 26.
Washington Post, March 4, 1981; June 3, 1988.
Washington Post Book World, February 25, 1981; October 12, 1983, pp. B1, B17; December 16, 1984, p. 12; April 26, 1987, p. 11; June 12, 1988, pp. 1, 17; October 1, 1989, p. 16; March 8, 1992, pp. 1-2.
West Coast Review of Books, Number 1, 1988, p. 45.

* * *

WOOD, Margaret (Lucy Elizabeth) 1910-

PERSONAL: Born March 4, 1910, in Great Yarmouth, Norfolk, England; daughter of Ernest Charles (a company director) and Ethelmary (Child) Bellamy; married Edward Rudolf Wood (a school teacher), April 27, 1927; children: Margaret Helen, Caroline. *Education:* University of London, B.A. (second class honours); *Religion:* Church of England.

ADDRESSES: Home—White House, Much Birch, Hereford, England.

CAREER: Playwright. Scriptwriter, British Broadcasting Corporation Radio Schools. Justice of the Peace, Hereford, England.

AWARDS, HONORS: First place, Amateur Stage Playwriting Competition, 1956, for *Road to Damascus;* British Drama League One-Act Play Award, and Geoffrey Whitworth Cup, both 1962, both for *The Day of Atonement.*

WRITINGS:

ONE-ACT PLAYS

Instruments of Darkness, Samuel French, 1955.
Women's Ward, Samuel French, 1955.
The Road to Damascus, Samuel French, 1956.
The Copper Kettle, Samuel French, 1956.
Home Is the Sailor, Samuel French, 1957.
(With E. C. Bellamy) *Withington Warrior,* Samuel French, 1958.
The Guilty Generation, Samuel French, 1958.
Cato's Daughter, Samuel French, 1958.
Dark Horses, Samuel French, 1959.
Fools' Errand, Samuel French, 1960.
Atalanta, Samuel French, 1961.
Out-patients, Samuel French, 1961.
A Dog's Life, Samuel French, 1962.
Day of Atonement, Samuel French, 1962.
The Primrose Path, Samuel French, 1964.
Crying in the Wilderness, Samuel French, 1964.
The Witches, Evans, 1964.
(Contributor) *The Third Windmill Book of One-act Plays,* Heinemann, 1965, ninth edition, 1977.
A Kind of Justice, Samuel French, 1966.
Plays for Christmas and Easter (contains *Fit for a King, The Safety of the State, A Christmas Musical, The Substitute, Week-end in Bethany,* and *The Interrogation*), Heinemann, 1966.
The King and the Quaker, Samuel French, 1968.
The Double Dealers, Samuel French, 1968.
Covenant with Death, Evans, 1970.
Robert of Sicily, Samuel French, 1970.
A Fishy Business, Evans, 1973.
Top Table: A Satirical Comedy, Samuel French, 1973.
Susanna and the Welsh Elders (from the Apocrypha), Samuel French, 1974.
Donatus and the Devil, Samuel French, 1975.
"Peace Hath Her Victories," Samuel French, 1975.
A Person of No Consequence, Samuel French, 1976.
My Dear Evans, Evans, 1976.
A Person of No Consequence, Samuel French, 1976.

Pilgrims' Way, Evans, 1976.
A Moving Story, Samuel French, 1977.
Parochial Problems, Samuel French, 1977.

OTHER

The Sun over the High Mountain, Chivers, 1980.

WORK IN PROGRESS: Educational scripts for television.*

* * *

WOOD, William P(reston) 1951-

PERSONAL: Born April 23, 1951, in Bronxville, NY; son of W. Preston (a writer) and Eleanor Catherine (Auby) Wood. *Education:* Middlebury College, B.A. (cum laude), 1973; University of the Pacific, J.D., 1976.

ADDRESSES: *Home*—Sacramento, CA. *Agent*—Jane Dystel, Acton and Dystel, 928 Broadway, New York, NY 10010.

CAREER: Deputy district attorney of Sacramento County, CA, 1977-82; director of publications of California District Attorneys Association, 1984-85; writer.

MEMBER: Writers Guild of America (West), Federalist Society of Sacramento.

WRITINGS:

NOVELS

Rampage, St. Martin's, 1985.
Gangland, St. Martin's, 1988.
Fugitive City, St. Martin's, 1990.
Court of Honor, Pocket Books, 1991.

Writer for television series *Kaz,* Columbia Broadcasting System, Inc., 1979. Contributor to law journals and popular magazines, including *America, Christian Century,* and *Commonweal.*

Wood's works have been translated into many languages, including French, German, Japanese, Greek, and Polish.

ADAPTATIONS: *Rampage* was directed by William Friedkin and released by Miramax, 1992; *Fugitive City* was adapted as a screenplay by Dave Lewis; and *Court of Honor* was also adapted as a screenplay, by Joan Didion and John Gregory Dunne.

WORK IN PROGRESS: "A non-fiction book on the trial of serial killer Dorothea Puente as her former prosecutor."

SIDELIGHTS: William P. Wood drew heavily on his own experiences as deputy district attorney of Sacramento County, California, in writing his successful first novel, *Rampage.* As critic Newgate Callendar of the *New York Times Book Review* observed, *Rampage* "is a portrait of justice as practiced in the courtrooms of America, with all-too-fallible humans trying to interpret the law and sometimes bending it in the process. . . . A feeling of truth permeates this book." In addition to Wood's first-hand knowledge of the American legal system, critics cited his vivid writing style and his ability to create morally complex, believable characters as important factors in the success of *Rampage.*

A federal sting to weed out corruption among California judges is the subject of the novel *Court of Honor.* Superior Court justice Tim Nash is enlisted by Neil Roemer, an aggressive investigator for the U.S. Justice Department, to offer payments to the local judiciary in exchange for certain rulings. Nash becomes disillusioned when colleagues he would never suspect greedily accept his bribes; and he eventually has second thoughts about entrapping normally honest people. Wood's "writing is straightforward and sticks to the subject, making this an entertaining story that also turns out to be chillingly informative," commented Paul Craig in the *Sacramento Bee.*

Wood told *CA:* "Growing up with the sound of a typewriter set me on the course to become a writer myself. My father wrote for many years, largely for television, and I heard him typing so often that it came to seem the only natural way to spend your productive moments.

"In all of my novels I have tried to find a moral dilemma and force the characters to meet it or seek shelter from it. My four years as a prosecutor undoubtedly pointed me toward this sort of fiction."

BIOGRAPHICAL/CRITICAL SOURCES:

PERIODICALS

Cleveland Plain Dealer, June 19, 1985.
Newsday, April 19, 1985.
New York Times, October 30, 1992.
New York Times Book Review, July 21, 1985.
Sacramento Bee, October 10, 1991.

* * *

WOOLRYCH, Austin (Herbert) 1918-

PERSONAL: Born May 18, 1918, in London, England; son of Stanley Herbert Cunliffe and May Gertrude (Wood) Woolrych; married Muriel Edith Rolfe, 1941 (died, 1991); children: Jane Caroline, Richard Humphrey. *Education:* attended Westminster School, 1931-35; Pembroke College, University of Oxford, B.A., 1949, B.Litt., 1952, M.A., 1952.

Avocational Interests: Opera, walking, travel.

ADDRESSES: Home—9 Hollowrayne, Burton-in-Kendal, Carnforth, Lancaster LA6 1NS, England.

CAREER: University of Leeds, Leeds, England, lecturer, senior lecturer, 1949-64; University of Lancaster, Lancaster, England, professor, 1964-85, professor emeritus of modern history, 1985—, pro-vice-chancellor, 1972-75. Visiting fellow, All Souls College, Oxford, 1981-82; Commonwealth Visiting Fellow to universities in Australia and New Zealand, 1983. *Military service:* British Army, Royal Tank Regiment, 1939-46, attained rank of captain.

MEMBER: British Academy (fellow), Royal Historical Society (fellow), Historical Association, Association of University Teachers.

AWARDS, HONORS: D.Litt., University of Lancaster, 1986.

WRITINGS:

Battles of the English Civil War, Batsford, 1961, revised edition, Pimlico, 1991.
Oliver Cromwell, Oxford University Press, 1964.
(Author of historical introduction) *Complete Prose Works of John Milton,* Volume 7: *1659-60,* edited by Robert W. Ayers, Yale University Press, 1974, revised edition, 1980.
Commonwealth to Protectorate, Clarendon, 1982.
England Without a King, 1649-1660, Methuen, 1983.
Soldiers and Statesmen: The General Council of the Army and Its Debates, 1647-48, Clarendon, 1987.

Contributor of articles and reviews to historical journals.

WORK IN PROGRESS: Britain in Revolution, 1637-1660.

SIDELIGHTS: Austin Woolrych once commented to *CA* that he had "entered academic life comparatively late, after four years in commerce and six and a half years in the army." He has done several programs on historical subjects for the British Broadcasting Corporation.

* * *

WORSTER, Donald E(ugene) 1941-

PERSONAL: Born November 14, 1941, in Needles, CA; son of Winfred Delbert (a railroad worker) and Bonnie Pauline (Ball) Worster; married Beverly Marshall, August 23, 1964; children: William Thomas, Catherine Anne. *Education:* University of Kansas, B.A., 1963, M.A., 1964; Yale University, M.Phil., 1970, Ph.D., 1971.

ADDRESSES: Office—Department of History, University of Kansas, Lawrence, KS 66045.

CAREER: Brandeis University, Waltham, MA, assistant professor of American studies, 1971-74; University of Hawaii at Manoa, Honolulu, associate professor, 1975-80, professor of American studies, 1980-83; Brandeis University, professor of history and American studies, 1984-89; University of Kansas, Lawrence, Hall Distinguished Professor of American History, 1989—. Mellon fellow at Aspen Institute for Humanistic Studies, summer, 1974; fellow, Humanities Research Centre, Australian National University, 1984.

MEMBER: Organization of American Historians, Forest History Society, Wilderness Society, Sierra Club, American Society for Enviromental History (president).

AWARDS, HONORS: National Endowment for the Humanities fellowship, 1974-75; American Council of Learned Societies fellow, 1977-78; Bancroft Prize, Columbia University, 1980, for *Dust Bowl: The Southern Plains in the 1930s;* Guggenheim fellow, 1981-82; Pulitzer Prize nomination for *Rivers of Empire: Water, Aridity, and the Growth of the American West.*

WRITINGS:

(Editor) *American Environmentalism: The Formative Period, 1860-1915,* Wiley, 1973.
Nature's Economy: The Roots of Ecology, Sierra Books, 1977, 2nd edition, Cambridge University Press, 1984.
Dust Bowl: The Southern Plains in the 1930s, Oxford University Press, 1979.
Rivers of Empire: Water, Aridity, and the Growth of the American West, Oxford University, 1985.
(Editor and contributor) *The Ends of the Earth: Perspectives on Modern Environmental History* (essays), Cambridge University Press, 1988.
Under Western Skies: Nature and History in the American West, Oxford University Press, 1992.
The Wealth of Nature: Environmental History and the Ecological Imagination, Oxford University Press, 1993.

SIDELIGHTS: Reflecting on the scope of his research, Donald E. Worster once told *CA:* "I am interested in finding ways for myself, [my] family, and others to live on this fragile planet with the least impact, the fullest humanity, and the greatest amount of personal freedom compatible with ecological integrity." Worster's concern for environmental issues, evident in this statement, is central to his Bancroft Prize-winning book, *Dust Bowl: The Southern Plains in the 1930s,* as well as his Pulitzer Prize-nominated work, *Rivers of Empire: Water, Aridity and the Growth of the American West.*

James W. Ware in the *Journal of American History* explains the thesis of *Dust Bowl:* "Worster argues that more than prolonged drought and high winds created the Dust Bowl. He maintains that the aggressive greed inherent in capitalism was responsible for the problems of southern plains farmers during the 1930s." Although Ware does not agree completely with Worster's theory, he praises the book, declaring, "Worster has contributed a major work to the historiography of the United States in the twentieth century." Historian Gilbert C. Fite in *American Historical Review* expresses a similar position, remarking, "While I disagree with many of the positions taken in this book, I found it an exciting, provocative, and stimulating study."

Rivers of Empire explores the issue of irrigation in the arid lands of the United States and the politics involved in it. In the *New York Times Book Review,* critic David M. Kennedy calls the book "impassioned and lyrical" and observes Worster's opinion that "the West has evolved a 'hydraulic society' that is 'increasingly a coercive, monolithic, and hierarchical system, ruled by a power elite based on the ownership of capital and expertise.' " Dean E. Mann, in the *Los Angeles Times Book Review,* proclaims, "This is a brilliant book, clear in its argument, exceptional in its literary qualities. Worster is capable of making the most prosaic facts come alive through his mastery of the language, his imagery, and his ability to weave his ideas with events and personalities into a fascinating historical record."

BIOGRAPHICAL/CRITICAL SOURCES:

PERIODICALS

American Historical Review, June, 1980.
Journal of American History, June, 1980.
Los Angeles Times Book Review, August 10, 1986, pp. 1, 9.
New York Times Book Review, February 23, 1986, pp. 7, 9.
Pacific Historical Review, May, 1981.
Reviews in American History, December, 1980.
Times Literary Supplement, September 12, 1980.
Washington Post Book World, January 24, 1986; July 5, 1987, p. 13.

* * *

WORTIS, Avi 1937-
(Avi)

PERSONAL: Given name is pronounced "Ah-vee"; born December 23, 1937, in New York, NY; son of Joseph (a psychiatrist) and Helen (a social worker; maiden name Zunser) Wortis; married Joan Gabriner (a weaver) November 1, 1963 (divorced); married Coppelia Kahn (a professor of English); children: Shaun Wortis, Kevin Wortis; Gabriel Kahn (stepson). *Education:* University of Wisconsin—Madison, B.A., 1959, M.A., 1962; Columbia University, M.S.L.S., 1964.

ADDRESSES: Home—15 Sheldon St., Providence, RI 02906. *Agent*—Dorothy Markinko, McIntosh & Otis, Inc., 475 Fifth Ave., New York, NY 10017.

CAREER: Writer, 1960—. New York Public Library, New York City, librarian in Performing Arts Research Center, 1962-70; Lambeth Public Library, London, England, exchange program librarian, 1968; Trenton State College, Trenton, NJ, assistant professor and humanities librarian, 1970-86. Visiting writer in schools across the United States.

MEMBER: PEN, Authors Guild, Authors League of America.

AWARDS, HONORS: Best Book of the Year citation, British Book Council, 1973, for *Snail Tale: The Adventures of a Rather Small Snail;* Grants from New Jersey State Council on the Arts, 1974, 1976, and 1978, and from Trenton State College, 1978; Mystery Writers of America Special Award, 1975, for *No More Magic,* 1979, for *Emily Upham's Revenge,* and 1983, for *Shadrach's Crossing;* Christopher Book Award, 1980, for *Encounter at Easton;* Children's Choice Award, International Reading Association, 1980, for *Man from the Sky,* and 1988, for *Romeo and Juliet—Together (& Alive) at Last;* Best Books of the Year citations, *School Library Journal,* 1980, for *Night Journeys,* 1987, for *Wolf Rider,* and 1990, for *The True Confessions of Charlotte Doyle;* New Jersey Authors Award, New Jersey Institute of Technology, 1983, for *Shadrach's Crossing;* Scott O'Dell Award for historical fiction, *Bulletin of the Center for Children's Books,* 1984, for *The Fighting Ground;* Best Books for Young Adults citations, American Library Association, 1984, for *The Fighting Ground,* and 1986, for *Wolf Rider;* Best Books of the Year citations, *Library of Congress,* 1989, for *Something Upstairs,* and 1990, for *The Man Who Was Poe;* Best Book of the Year citation, Society of Children's Book Authors, 1990, for *The True Confessions of Charlotte Doyle;* Virginia Young Readers' Award, 1990, for *Wolf Rider;* Newbery honor award, American Library Association, *Horn Book-Boston Globe* Award, and Golden Kite Award, Society of Children's Book Authors, all 1991, for *The True Confessions of Charlotte Doyle;* Newbery honor award, American Library Association, 1992, for *Nothing but the Truth.*

WRITINGS:

Things That Sometimes Happen (picture book), illustrated by Jodi Robbin, Doubleday, 1970.
Snail Tale: The Adventures of a Rather Small Snail (picture book), illustrated by Tom Kindron, Pantheon, 1972.
No More Magic, Pantheon, 1975.
Captain Grey, Pantheon, 1977.

Emily Upham's Revenge; or, How Deadwood Dick Saved the Banker's Niece: A Massachusetts Adventure, Pantheon, 1978.
Night Journeys, Pantheon, 1979.
Encounter at Easton (sequel to *Night Journeys),* Pantheon, 1980.
The Man from the Sky, Knopf, 1980.
History of Helpless Harry: To Which Is Added a Variety of Amusing and Entertaining Adventures, Pantheon, 1980.
A Place Called Ugly, Pantheon, 1981.
Who Stole the Wizard of Oz?, Knopf, 1981.
Sometimes I Think I Hear My Name, Pantheon, 1982.
Shadrach's Crossing, Pantheon, 1983.
The Fighting Ground, Lippincott, 1984.
S.O.R. Losers, Bradbury, 1984.
Devil's Race, Lippincott, 1984.
Bright Shadow, Bradbury, 1985.
Wolf Rider: A Tale of Terror, Bradbury, 1986.
Devil's Race, Avon, 1987.
Romeo & Juliet—Together (& Alive) at Last (sequel to *S. O. R. Losers)* Avon, 1988.
Something Upstairs: A Tale of Ghosts, Orchard Books, 1988.
The Man Who Was Poe, Orchard Books, 1989.
The True Confessions of Charlotte Doyle, Orchard Books, 1990.
Windcatcher, Bradbury, 1991.
Nothing but the Truth, Orchard Books, 1991.
Who Was That Masked Man, Anyway?, Orchard Books, 1992.
Blue Heron, Bradbury, 1992.
Judy with Punch, Bradbury, 1993.
The Shortest Day, Orchard Books, in press.

Also author of numerous plays. Contributor to books, including *Performing Arts Resources, 1974,* edited by Ted Perry, Drama Book Publishers, 1975. Contributor to periodicals, including *New York Public Library Bulletin, Top of the News, Children's Literature in Education, Horn Book,* and *Writer.* Book reviewer for *Library Journal, School Library Journal,* and *Previews,* 1965-73.

Translations of Avi's books have been published in Germany, Austria, Denmark, Norway, Spain, and Japan.

ADAPTATIONS: A recording of *The Fighting Ground* was produced by Listening Library. *Emily Upham's Revenge, Shadrach's Crossing, Something Upstairs, The Fighting Ground,* and *The True Confessions of Charlotte Doyle,* were produced on the radio programs *Read to Me,* Maine Public Radio, and *Books Aloud,* WWON-Rhode Island.

SIDELIGHTS: Avi Wortis is known to critics, teachers, parents, and young readers for a body of work highlighted by colorful characters and intricate plots. Encompassing a wide variety of genres, Avi's books typically offer complex, thought-provoking, and sometimes disturbingly realistic reflections on American history and culture. A longtime champion of literary issues involving young readers, the author summed up his writing goals for *Twentieth-Century Children's Writers* by saying: "I try to write about complex issues—young people in an adult world—full of irony and contradiction, in a narrative style that relies heavily on suspense with a texture rich in emotion and imagery. I take a great deal of satisfaction in using popular forms—the adventure, the mystery, the thriller—so as to hold my reader with the sheer pleasure of a good story. At the same time I try to resolve my books with an ambiguity that compels engagement. In short, I want my readers to feel, to think, sometimes to laugh. But most of all I want them to enjoy a good read."

Avi once noted that the first step on his course to writing professionally was reading. He learned more from reading—everything from comic books and science magazines to histories, plays, and novels—than he learned in school. Despite the skepticism of many of his teachers, Avi was determined to make a career of writing. Eventually, he enrolled in some playwriting classes at the University of Wisconsin. "That's where I really started to write seriously," he once commented. "The first playwriting instructor that I had would say, 'this is the way you do it.' You didn't have much choice in it, you had to do it in a very specific way. He even had charts for you to fill out. And I think I learned how to organize a story according to this man's precepts. It didn't even matter what [his system] was except that I absorbed it."

After obtaining two master's degrees and working at a variety of jobs, Avi began a twenty-five year career as a librarian when he found employment in the theater collection of the New York Public library. Despite his new career responsibilities, Avi's determination to be a writer never flagged; in fact, the author had written nearly 800 pages of his "great American novel" before turning his attention to children's literature. This change in focus came about largely because Avi found that he had such fun telling stories to his two sons. "My oldest would tell me what the story should be about—he would invent stuff, a story about a glass of water and so forth. It became a game, and here I had a writing background so I was telling some fairly sophisticated stories," Avi remarked.

Avi's first children's book, *Things That Sometimes Happen,* appeared in 1970. Since this first publication, Avi has produced a number of works whose structure defies genre classification. He is perhaps best known for his experimentation with the format of the historical novel. Several of his early books—including *Captain Grey, Night Journeys,* and *Encounter at Easton*—place fictional characters against the backdrop of actual historical events. In other books, such as *Something Upstairs* and *The Man Who Was Poe,* Avi combines elements from history, traditional ghost stories, mythology, and science fiction to create a unique mix of fantasy and reality. Although an enthusiastic reader of history, the author is by no means tied to the historical novel—in fact, his contemporary tales about young people, such as *S.O.R. Losers,* have proven as popular with readers as his historically-based stories.

Avi maintains regular interaction with his young audience by traveling around the country and talking in schools about his work. In his travels, he has noticed that his readers are increasingly hungry for well-told stories that they can relate to. With this in mind, Avi strives to keep his books both timely and lively. "More than anything else," he asserted in an interview for *Horn Book,* "children's literature is about the place and role of the child in society. . . . If we—in the world of children's literature—can help the young stand straight for a moment longer than they have done in the past, help them maintain their ideals and values, those with which you and I identify ourselves, help them demand—and win—justice, we've added something good to the world."

BIOGRAPHICAL/CRITICAL SOURCES:

BOOKS

Behind the Covers: Interviews with Authors and Illustrators of Books for Children and Young Adults, Libraries Unlimited, 1985, pp. 33-41.

Twentieth-Century Children's Writers, St. Martin's, 1989, pp. 45-46.

PERIODICALS

Bulletin of the Center for Children's Books, June, 1984, p. 180; October, 1989, p. 27.

Horn Book, August, 1979, p. 410; April, 1980, pp. 169-70; October, 1980, pp. 517-18; April, 1981, p. 136; June, 1981, pp. 297-98; August, 1983, p. 439; June, 1984, p. 325; January-February, 1985, p. 49; September-October, 1987, pp. 569-576; January-February, 1992, p. 24-27.

New York Times Book Review, September 11, 1977; March 1, 1981, p. 24.

Publishers Weekly, January 30, 1981, p. 75; November 16, 1984, p. 65; December 26, 1986, p. 61; August 28, 1987, p. 81; September 14, 1990, p. 128; September 6, 1991, p. 105.

School Library Journal, March, 1978, p. 124; May, 1980, p. 64; November, 1980, p. 68; September, 1984, p. 125; October, 1984, p. 164; December, 1986, pp. 111-12; January, 1987, p. 21.

Voice of Youth Advocates, August, 1981, pp. 23-24; August, 1982, p. 27; December, 1984, pp. 261-62; February, 1985, p. 321; February, 1989, p. 293.

* * *

WULFFSON, Don L. 1943-

PERSONAL: Born August 21, 1943, in Los Angeles, CA; son of Charles Robin (an engineer) and Corinne (a real estate broker; maiden name, Lockwood) Wulffson; married June 29, 1969; wife's name, Pamela (a teacher); children: Jennifer, Gwendolyn. *Education:* University of California, Los Angeles, B.A., 1965, Teaching Credential, 1967. *Politics:* "Indifferent." *Religion:* "Confused."

ADDRESSES: *Home*—18718 Kirkcolm Lane, Northridge, CA 91326. *Office*—11133 O'Melveny, San Fernando, CA.

CAREER: San Fernando High School, Los Angeles, CA, teacher of English, creative writing, and reading, 1967—. Free-lance writer. Sun Pictures, story consultant, 1992.

MEMBER: United Teachers of Los Angeles.

AWARDS, HONORS: Leather Medal from New Directions Publishing Corp., 1971, for "You Too Can Be a Floorwax That Even Your Husband Could Apply"; distinguished achievement award from Educational Press Association of America, 1978, for *Writing You'll Enjoy.*

WRITINGS:

JUVENILE BOOKS

(Co-author) *Themes and Writers* (literature series, 4 volumes), McGraw, 1973.

Eyebrowse (stories and essays), Economy Co., 1976.

Building Vocabulary (workbook), Xerox Education Publications, 1976.

Writing You'll Enjoy (workbook), Xerox Education Publications, 1977.

The Touchstone Series (workbooks), three volumes, Steck, 1977.

Punctuation Errors You Hate to Make (and How to Avoid Them) (workbook), Xerox Education Publications, 1978.

The Wonderful Word Book (workbook), Xerox Education Publications, 1978.

Strange, Extraordinary Stories behind How Sports Came to Be, Lothrop, 1980.

True Stories You Won't Believe, Xerox Education Publications, 1980.

Supergrammar (workbook), Pruett, 1980.

Mindgame: Experiences in Creative Writing (workbook), Xerox Education Publications, 1980.

Visions (stories and essays), Globe Book Co., 1980, reprinted as *Facts and Fantasies,* 1982.
Extraordinary Stories behind the Invention of Ordinary Things, Lothrop, 1981.
The Basics of Writing, three volumes, Globe Book Co., 1985.
Incredible True Adventures (non-fiction), Dodd, Mead, 1986.
The Upside-down Ship (novel), Whitman, 1986.
Terror at Sea (non-fiction), Field Publications, 1988.
More Incredible True Adventures (non-fiction), Cobblehill Books, 1989.
Ordinary Things (non-fiction), Avon, 1990.
Amazing True Stories, Cobblehill Books, 1991.

Also author of "Skillmaster Series," Xerox Education Publications.

JUVENILE PLAYS

Heartbreak on the Beach (one act), published in *Read Magazine,* November 29, 1978.
Herbie's Comeuppance (one act), published in *Read Magazine,* April 11, 1979.
Revelations, published in *Read Magazine,* 1985.

OTHER

Point Blank (novel for adults), Signet, 1987.

Contributor of articles, poems, and children's plays to journals, including *Hyperion, Tangent Poetry Quarterly, Journal of Reading, Read Magazine, Boys' Life, Cricket,* and *Child Life,* and anthologies, including *New Directions Twenty-Three,* New Directions, 1971; *Words and Beyond,* Ginn, 1973; *National Poetry Anthology,* National Poetry Press, 1975; and *Isaac Asimov's Book of Facts,* Volume 2, Grosset & Dunlap, 1982. Consultant for *Above and Beyond* (non-fiction), Time-Life, 1992.

WORK IN PROGRESS: War Stories You Won't Believe (young adult non-fiction), for Random House; *Time-Fix and Other Tales of Terror* (young adult fiction), for Dutton; *Journey of Fear* (young adult fiction); *The Hills of Amara* (adult novel).

SIDELIGHTS: Don L. Wulffson told *CA:* "For me, writing is an expression of my dissatisfaction with reality and my need to render it into a form that is more interesting to me personally. Not a noble goal. Perhaps not a goal at all. It's simply how I pass the time."

* * *

WYNNE, Ronald D(avid) 1934-

PERSONAL: Born October 19, 1934, in New Haven, CT; son of William Harris (an economist) and Evelyn (an artist and teacher; maiden name, Burman) Wynne; married Suzan Fischer (a social worker, genealogist, and writer), August 27, 1967; children: Michael, Melanie. *Education:* University of Maryland, B.A., 1955; Catholic University of America, M.A., 1958, Ph.D., 1961. *Religion:* Jewish.

ADDRESSES: Office—3801 Connecticut Ave. N.W., Suite 203, Washington, D.C. 20008; and West Office Bldg., Suite 203, Landover Mall, Landover, MD 20785.

CAREER: Research psychologist, National Institute of Mental Health, 1956-57, 1958-59; Institute of the Pennsylvania Hospital, Philadelphia, research psychologist, 1961-62; New Jersey Bureau of Research in Neurology and Psychiatry, Princeton, research psychologist, 1962-64; Queens College of the City University of New York, Flushing, NY, assistant professor of psychology, 1964-65; Office of Economic Opportunity, Washington, D.C., director of center assessment branch of Job Corps, 1965-67; private social science consultant, 1967-72; Wynne Associates (social science consultants), Washington, D.C., director, 1972-78; private practice in clinical and community psychology in Washington, D.C., 1978—. Director, Washington Assessment and Therapy Services, 1982—. Diplomate in family psychology, American Board of Professional Psychology, 1992. Conducts workshops and seminars on drug abuse, career planning, geriatrics, psychological assessment, adolescence, family therapy, psychology and the law; guest on television and radio programs. Active in civic and professional groups, including Maryland Governor's Advisory Board on Homelessness, 1988-93.

MEMBER: American Psychological Association, District of Columbia Psychological Association (president, 1992).

WRITINGS:

(With wife, Suzan Wynne, and others) *Effective Coordination of Drug Abuse Programs: A Guide to Community Action,* U.S. Government Printing Office, 1973.
(With Joel L. Phillips) *Cocaine: The Mystique and Reality,* Avon, 1980.
(With S. Wynne, Shoshana Churgin, and James Kendrick) *Community Organization of Alcoholism Services: A Technical Assistance Guide,* National Institute on Alcohol Abuse and Alcoholism, 1980.
(With Margaret Blasinsky and Paddy Cook) *Community Action and Legal Responses to Drug Paraphernalia* (monograph), National Institute on Drug Abuse, 1980.
(With Stephen Martinez and John Blanton) *Prevention of Foster Care Placement via In-home Crisis Intervention with Troubled Families* (monograph), U.S. Department of Human Services, 1985.
Insurance Reimbursement and Practice Management Issues: A Manual for Psychologists and Other Mental

Health Professionals (monograph), D.C. Psychological Association, 1990.

Contributor to numerous books, including *Developments in the Field of Drug Abuse: National Drug Abuse Conference, 1974*, edited by Edward Senay, Vernon Shorty, and Harold Alksne, Schenkman, 1975; and *Cocaine: Chemical, Biological, Clinical, Social, and Treatment Aspect*, CRC Press, 1976.

WORK IN PROGRESS: Research on the impact of government bureaucracy on the practice of psychotherapy; monograph on dealing with your aging parents; research on home-based mental health services.

SIDELIGHTS: Ronald D. Wynne told *CA:* "For me, writing is about making the technical more accessible, about detoxifying the mysterious, especially in mental health, a quagmire of mumbo-jumbo if ever there was one."

* * *

YORKE, Roger
See BINGLEY, David Ernest

* * *

ZACK, Arnold M(arshall) 1931-

PERSONAL: Born October 7, 1931, in Lynn, MA; son of Samuel George (an attorney) and Bess (Freedman) Zack; married Norma Wilner, August 10, 1969; children: Jonathan, Rachel. *Education:* Tufts University, A.B., 1953; Yale University, LL.B., 1956; Harvard University, M.P.A., 1961.

ADDRESSES: *Home and office*—170 West Canton St., Boston, MA 02118.

CAREER: Attorney, arbitrator, and mediator in Boston, MA, 1956—. Lecturer in labor economics, Northeastern University; Haile Selassie I University, Ethiopia, Fulbright professor, 1963-64. Director, Labor Management Institute, 1966-68. Member of foreign service labor relations board, Government of Greece, 1981-83. Consultant to agencies, including International Labor Organization, United Nations Development Program, United Nations Congo Operation, U.S. Peace Corps, Department of Labor, and Ethiopian Ministry of National Community Development.

MEMBER: National Academy of Arbitrators (member of board of governors, 1976-79; vice-president, 1980-83; president-elect, 1993-94), African Studies Association (fellow), Industrial Relations Research Association (chapter officer and program chairman at 1959 national meeting), American Arbitration Association (chairman of Labor Management Education Advisory Committee, 1985-88), Society for Professionals in Dispute Resolution (chairman of International Relations Committee, 1985-92).

AWARDS, HONORS: Whitney North Seymour Medal, American Arbitration Association, 1980; Distinguished Service Award for Arbitration of Labor Management Disputes, 1989; Mildred Spaulding Award, 1984; Cushing Gavin Award, Archdiocese of Boston, 1986.

WRITINGS:

The New Labor Relations in Ethiopia, Department of Economics, Haile Selassie I University, 1964.
Labor Training in Developing Countries: A Challenge in Responsible Democracy, Praeger, 1964.
Understanding Fact-Finding in the Public Sector, U.S. Government Printing Office, 1974.
Understanding Grievance Arbitration in the Public Sector, U.S. Government Printing Office, 1974.
Grievance Arbitration: A Practical Guide, International Labor Office, 1977.
(With R. Bloch) *Arbitration of Discipline and Discharge Cases*, American Arbitration Association, 1979.
(With Bloch) *The Agreement in Negotiation and Arbitration*, BNA, 1982.
Arbitration in Practice, Cornell University Press, 1983.
Public Sector Mediation, BNA, 1985.
Grievance Arbitration: Issues on the Merits in Discipline, Discharge and Contract Interpretation, Lexington Books, 1989.
A Handbook for Grievance Arbitration: Procedural and Ethical Issues, Lexington Books, 1992.

Contributor to books, including *Africa: A Handbook to the Continent*, edited by Colin Legum, Praeger, 1962; and *Public Workers and Public Unions*, edited by Sam Zageria, Prentice-Hall, 1972. Contributor to reports. Contributor to periodicals.

Contemporary Authors®

NEW REVISION SERIES

OUTSTANDING ALA RASD REFERENCE SOURCE

Contemporary Authors
was named an
"Outstanding Reference Source" *by the American Library Association Reference and Adult Services Division after its 1962 inception.*
In 1985 it was listed by the same organization as one of the twenty-five most distinguished reference titles published in the past twenty-five years.